ENCYCLOPEDIA OF WORLD DRESS AND FASHION

Volume 5

Central and Southwest Asia

ENCYCLOPEDIA
WORLD

OF
DRESS
AND FASHION

Volume 5

Central and Southwest Asia

Edited by Gillian Vogelsang-Eastwood

OXFORD
UNIVERSITY PRESS
2010

OXFORD
UNIVERSITY PRESS

Oxford University Press, Inc., publishes works that further
Oxford University's objective of excellence
in research, scholarship, and education.

Oxford   New York
Auckland   Cape Town   Dar es Salaam   Hong Kong   Karachi
Kuala Lumpur   Madrid   Melbourne   Mexico City   Nairobi
New Delhi   Shanghai   Taipei   Toronto

With offices in
Argentina   Austria   Brazil   Chile   Czech Republic   France   Greece
Guatemala   Hungary   Italy   Japan   Poland   Portugal   Singapore
South Korea   Switzerland   Thailand   Turkey   Ukraine   Vietnam

© Berg Publishers 2010

Published by Oxford University Press, Inc.
198 Madison Avenue, New York, NY 10016
http://www.oup.com/us/

Oxford is a registered trademark of Oxford University Press

Published simultaneously outside North America by Berg Publishers.

The Library of Congress Cataloging-in-Publication Data

Encyclopedia of world dress and fashion.
v. cm.

"Published simultaneously outside North America by Berg Publishers"–V. 1, t.p. verso.

"Available online as part of the Berg Fashion Library"–V. 1, t.p. verso.

Includes bibliographical references.

Contents: v. 1. Africa / editors, Joanne B. Eicher, Doran H. Ross – v. 2. Latin America and the Caribbean /
editor, Margot Blum Schevill ; consulting editor, Blenda Femenías – v. 3. The United States and Canada /
editor, Phyllis Tortora ; consultant, Joseph D. Horse Capture – v. 4. South Asia and Southeast Asia /
editor, Jasleen Dhamija – v. 5. Central and Southwest Asia / editor, Gillian Vogelsang-Eastwood –
v. 6. East Asia / editor, John Vollmer – v. 7. Australia, New Zealand, and the Pacific Islands /
editor, Margaret Maynard – v. 8. West Europe / editor, Lise Skov ; consulting editor, Valerie Cumming –
v. 9. East Europe, Russia, and the Caucasus / editor, Djurdja Bartlett ; assistant editor, Pamela Smith –
v. 10. Global perspectives / editor, Joanne B. Eicher ; assistant editor, Phyllis Tortora.

ISBN 978-0-19-537733-0 (hbk.)

1. Clothing and dress–Encyclopedias.   I. Eicher, Joanne Bubolz.   II. Oxford University Press.

GT507.E54   2010
391.003—dc22   2010008843

ISBN 978-0-19-975728-2 (vol. 1)
ISBN 978-0-19-975729-9 (vol. 2)
ISBN 978-0-19-975730-5 (vol. 3)
ISBN 978-0-19-975731-2 (vol. 4)
ISBN 978-0-19-975732-9 (vol. 5)
ISBN 978-0-19-975733-6 (vol. 6)
ISBN 978-0-19-975734-3 (vol. 7)
ISBN 978-0-19-975735-0 (vol. 8)
ISBN 978-0-19-975736-7 (vol. 9)
ISBN 978-0-19-975737-4 (vol. 10)

1 3 5 7 9 8 6 4 2

This Encyclopedia is available online as part of the Berg Fashion Library.
For further information see www.bergfashionlibrary.com.

Typeset by Apex CoVantage, Madison, WI.
Printed in the USA by Courier Companies Inc., Westford, MA.

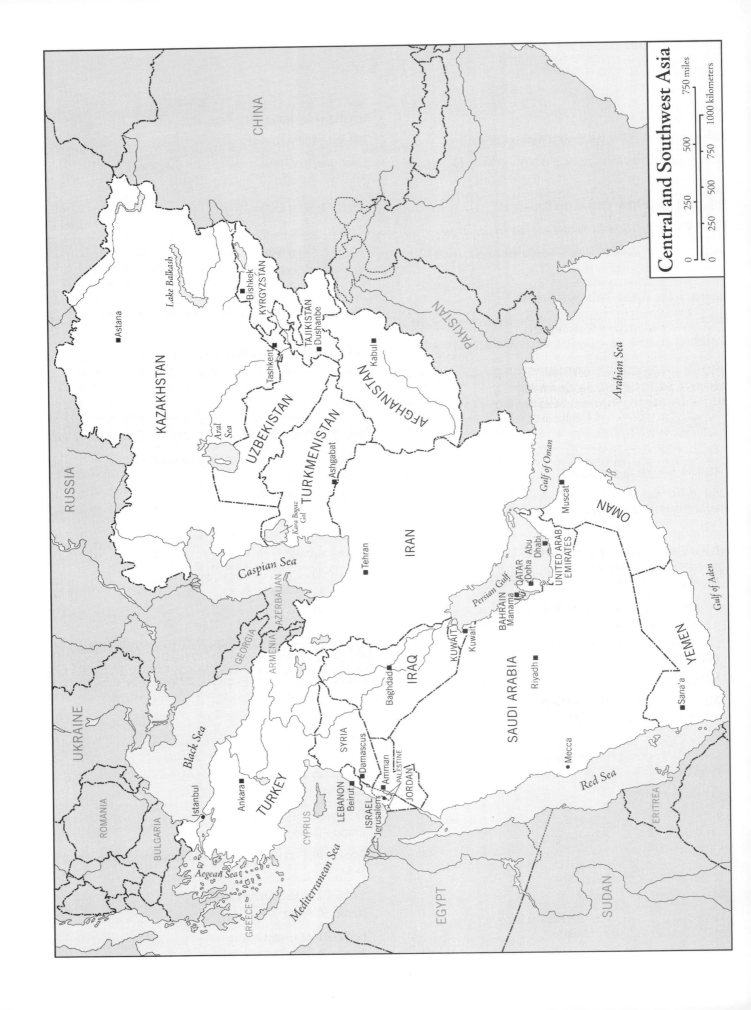

Central and Southwest Asia

RUSSIA

CHINA

KAZAKHSTAN

■ Astana

Lake Balkash

■ Bishkek
KYRGYZSTAN

TAJIKISTAN
■ Dushanbe

Tashkent ■

UZBEKISTAN

Aral Sea

TURKMENISTAN

AFGHANISTAN

■ Kabul

PAKISTAN

Ashgabat ■

Kara Bogaz Gol

Caspian Sea

Tehran ■

IRAN

UKRAINE

Black Sea

GEORGIA

ARMENIA
AZERBAIJAN

Gulf of Oman

Muscat ■

OMAN

Abu Dhabi ■
UNITED ARAB
EMIRATES

QATAR
■ Doha

BAHRAIN
Manama ■

Persian Gulf

Arabian Sea

KUWAIT
Kuwait ■

SAUDI ARABIA

Riyadh ■

Gulf of Aden

YEMEN

Sana'a ■

Baghdad ■

IRAQ

ROMANIA

BULGARIA

Istanbul ●

Ankara ■

TURKEY

CYPRUS

SYRIA

Damascus ■

LEBANON
Beirut ■

Amman ■
ISRAEL
Jerusalem ■
JORDAN

PALESTINE

● Mecca

Red Sea

ERITREA

GREECE

Aegean Sea

Mediterranean Sea

EGYPT

SUDAN

250   500   750   1000 kilometers

0   250   500   750 miles

Contents

PART 4: Arabian Desert and Peninsula

PART 5: Iranian Plateau

PART 6: Central Asia

Contributors

Ulrike Al-Khamis, *Sharjah Museum of Islamic Civilization,
    United Arab Emirates*
Wesam al-Othman, *Qatar University, Qatar*
Julia M. AlZadjali, *Centre for Omani Dress, Sultanate of Oman*
Derek Bryce, *University of Strathclyde, United Kingdom*
Beverly Chico, *Regis University, United States*
M. Catherine Daly, *University of Minnesota, United States*
Margaret Anne Deppe, *Universty of Minnesota, United States*
Sibba Einarsdóttir, *Moesgaard Museum, Denmark*
Fadwa El Guindi, *University of Southern California, United States*
Irene Good, *Harvard University, United States*
Stewart Gordon, *University of Michigan, United States*
Nour Majdalany Hakim, *Independent Scholar, Lebanon*
Saad Lafta Hami, *Independent Researcher, Iraq*
Mary Harlow, *University of Birmingham, United Kingdom*
Karel C. Innemée, *Leiden University, the Netherlands*
Charlotte Jirousek, *Cornell University, United States*
Esther Juhasz, *The Hebrew University, and The Israel Museum, Israel*
Widad Kawar, *Independent Researcher, Jordan*
Sumru Belger Krody, *The Textile Museum, Washington DC,
    United States*

Abby Lillethun, *Montclair State University, United States*
Christina Lindholm, *Virginia Commonwealth University, United States*
Lloyd Llewellyn-Jones, *University of Edinburgh, United Kingdom*
Carter Malik, *Yunnan Mountain Heritage Foundation, China*
Fatma Mete, *Cornell University, United States*
Nancy Micklewright, *The Getty Foundation, United States*
Layla Pio, *Independent Scholar, Jordan*
Bradley Quinn, *Independent Scholar, United Kingdom*
Ayala Raz, *Shenkar College of Engineering and Design, Israel*
Tineke Rooijakkers, *Textile Research Centre and Leiden University,
    the Netherlands*
Jennifer M. Scarce, *University of Dundee, United Kingdom*
Irvin Cemil Schick, *Sabanci University, Turkey*
Ashgar Seyed-Gohrab, *Leiden University, the Netherlands*
Christina Sumner, *Powerhouse Museum, Australia*
Hülya Tezcan, *Independent Scholar (formerly Topkapi Saray Museum),
    Turkey*
Willem Vogelsang, *National Museum of Ethnology, the Netherlands*
Gillian Vogelsang-Eastwood, *Textile Research Centre,
    and the National Museum of Ethnology, the Netherlands*
Heike Weber, *ANAT, Syria*

Encyclopedia Preface

The *Encyclopedia of World Dress and Fashion* covers a fundamental and universal human activity relating to personal and social identity—the vast topic of how more than six billion people dress across the globe. To accomplish this, the first nine volumes are organized geographically, and the tenth addresses global issues. The approach throughout is both cross-cultural and multidisciplinary and allows readers to appreciate the richness and complexity of dress in all its manifestations. However, even a ten-volume encyclopedia must limit itself in either time or geography in order to provide in-depth scholarship. The focus is therefore on the nineteenth to the early twenty-first centuries, although overview materials covering the long history of dress have been included to provide essential context, as is appropriate in so ambitious a scholarly undertaking.

Many disciplines have developed an interest in dress studies, underscoring the need for a major reference work with a broad scope. The range of interpretations will help readers develop a critical understanding of cultural practices. The intended audience for the *Encyclopedia* is broad and encompasses general and curious readers as well as students and teachers in the humanities and social sciences, in short, anyone interested in the full spectrum of issues relating to dress in a given time and place. More specialized researchers in anthropology, apparel design, art and cultural history, cinema, cultural studies, dance and drama, fashion, folklore, history, and sociology will also find the *Encyclopedia* an invaluable reference.

Dress, *costume*, and *fashion* are often used interchangeably in common parlance, but this work makes crucial distinctions between them because terminology is important. The aim of this preface is to clarify for readers the distinctions that have been drawn throughout this particular project by the editors and contributors, in order to achieve scholarly consistency across the work. Contributors were asked to define *dress* as any supplement or modification to the body, the purpose of which is either to cover or to adorn. Dress is a broad category that includes costume and fashion, with the term *costume* defined as a specific type of dress that is worn for theatrical, dance, or masquerade performances. *Costume* is frequently used by many distinguished museum curators and scholars in connection with both the historical study and the display of clothing in a general way. In contrast to dress, which ordinarily expresses a wearer's identity, costume hides or conceals it in various degrees. *Fashion* is defined as changes relating to body modifications and supplements, usually easily perceived and tracked, often within short periods of time.

While fashions may have permanent consequences with respect to an individual (as in the case of tattooing, for example), most are characterized by impermanence within the larger socioeconomic or fashion system (a complex process by which changing fashions in dress spread through formal and/or informal channels of design, manufacture, merchandising, and communication).

Supplements to the body include conventional attire such as clothing, jewelry, and items typically called *accessories*, such as hats, shoes, handbags, and canes. Modifications include cosmetics, hair care (cutting, combing, and styling), scarification, tattooing, tooth filing, piercings, and gentle molding of the human skull or binding of feet (the latter two usually done during infancy). Thus, in many cultures where people display these modifications alone, a person can be unclothed but still dressed. In addition to visually oriented practices, the definition of *dress* acknowledges that all senses may be incorporated, not just the visual. Therefore, sound (for example, rustling or jingling), odor (perfumes or incense), touch (such as tight or loose, silky or rough), and even taste when applicable (some cosmetics, breath fresheners, and tobacco products) frequently feature in discussions.

Being dressed is a normative act because human beings are taught what is right and wrong in concealing and revealing the body and keeping it clean and attractive. Contributors to this encyclopedia primarily describe dress and explain how it is worn within specific cultural contexts, although, where it is likely to be helpful, they have been encouraged to embrace and explain theoretical approaches to the interpretation of dress (for example, postmodernism, psychoanalytic theory, semiotics, and queer theory). The geographic organization provides overviews by country. An attempt has been made to focus on all countries, but in some cases, qualified authors could not be found and an entry was regrettably omitted. Readers may, however, find references to a country in the volume and section introductions and in the index. Supplementing country essays are articles on types or categories of dress along with select articles on influential or particularly well-known ethnic groups. Shorter "snapshots" on specific topics serve as sidebars to longer articles. Volume 10 addresses issues of global interest relating to the first nine volumes and is divided into five main sections: Overview of Global Perspectives; Forms of Dress Worldwide; Dress and the Arts Worldwide; Fashion Worldwide; and Dress and Fashion Resources Worldwide. Inclusion of a timeline on the development of dress and related technologies is a special feature.

At the end of each article, a list of references and suggestions for further reading has been included. Where possible, cross-references to other relevant articles in the *Encyclopedia* have also been inserted. Each volume has its own index, and readers will find a cumulative index to the entire set in volume 10. Volumes 1 to 9 also each feature a regional map.

While it is tempting when writing on the body and dress to focus on the most spectacular or visually engaging examples of dress from a given culture, authors have been asked to balance their discussions between the ordinary dress of daily life and the extraordinary dress of special occasions. In both instances this includes protective clothing of various sorts as well as general distinctions between genders, among age groups and various vocations, and within other realms of social status, as defined by religion, wealth, and political position. Along with prehistoric and historical traditions of dress, authors have been charged with addressing contemporary fashions in their own areas of interest, as well as traditional dress forms. An important aim of the *Encyclopedia* is to show the full range and transformative power of dress in cultural exchanges that occur all over the world, of which the influence of Western fashion on other parts of the world is only one example.

The editor in chief recruited scholars with particular expertise in dress, textiles, and fashion in their geographic areas and a scholarly network to edit specific volumes, develop tables of contents, draft a descriptive scope for articles requested, and contact and commission contributors. (Some experts were not available to participate in contributing articles.) The ten volumes include 854 articles written by 585 authors residing in over 60 different countries. Authors had freedom to develop their articles but always with a general reader in mind. Scholarship around the world and in different disciplines has many approaches; this presents daunting challenges for authors, who were asked to employ a relatively broad but consistent definition of dress. As a result of a rigorous review and revision process, their work has resulted in a comprehensive compilation of material not found before in a reference work of this type. Their efforts allow readers to find the excitement, variety, sensuality, and complexity of dress presented in clear descriptions, reinforced by historical and cultural context. As much as possible, entries have been written by experts from within the culture being discussed. Each was assigned a certain number of words, determined by the volume editor and editor in chief in the context of the desired depth and balance of the *Encyclopedia* as a whole, and each followed instructions and guidelines developed by the editorial board and publisher. The structure of each volume also varies according to the editor's perspective, the constraints of the historical, political, and social configuration of the geographic area, and the research known to be available.

A variety of images have been included, from museum photographs that show detail, to anthropological photographs that show dress in action and context, to fashion and artistic images that help to convey attitudes and ideals. Many of these have come from the contributors' own fieldwork. The goal is that the variety of approaches and interpretations presented within the *Encyclopedia*'s architecture combine to create a worldwide presentation of dress that is more varied, less biased, and more complete than any heretofore published. Articles are extensively illustrated with 2,300 images—many seen here for the first time.

The process of conceiving of and completing the *Encyclopedia* took place over a number of years and involved much scholarly consultation among editors, contributors, and staff. The common goal demanded a flexible approach within a set framework, and such a balancing act presented a range of challenges. Doubtless some decisions could be argued at further length, but hopefully readers will find most were sensible, bearing in mind the daunting ambitions of the work. Specific terms for items of dress vary throughout the world, and such variation often also reflects regional differences in the item of dress itself. Where possible, the editors have worked with contributors and translators to preserve the closest regional spelling of the indigenous term for the area under discussion, bearing in mind also the necessity to translate or transliterate such terms into English, the language of publication. While the *Encyclopedia* cannot be perfectly complete and consistent, the goal has been to produce a landmark achievement for its scholarly standards and impressive scope. The editorial team has endeavored to present authoritative treatments of the subject, with the particular hope that readers will find in the *Encyclopedia*'s pages a measure of the excitement, fun, and fascination that characterize dress across time and cultures. Browsing or reading in depth, volume to volume, will provide readers with many examples of what people wear, whether mundane or marvelous, uniform or unique, commonplace or rare. The encyclopedia will continue to grow as articles on recent developments, new information, and research add to knowledge on dress and fashion in the online Berg Fashion Library.

The volume editors and contributors are gratefully acknowledged and thanked for their enthusiasm for and dedication to the enormous task that has culminated in this encyclopedia. Many thanks also go to the publisher and project management team, who have valiantly seen the project to its successful completion.

Joanne B. Eicher

Preface to Central and Southwest Asia

This volume of the *Encyclopedia of World Dress and Fashion* looks at dress and fashion from the huge expanse of land that links Central Asia to the eastern Mediterranean. It is a vast area of wide-reaching historical, and current, importance. It has been torn apart and reassembled numerous times by politics, wars, and economic and social upheavals, as well as by religion and modern requirements such as oil. At the same time, it has created some of the most spectacular and long-lasting art and architectural themes and forms, and it is the birthplace of three world religions. Three important cultural and ethnic groups dominate the region, namely, the Arabs, the Iranians, and the Turks. All of this has had an influence on the range and appearance of dress and fashion worn in this part of the world.

The term *Southwest Asia* may be unfamiliar to some, but it was chosen to describe the region from Iran to the eastern Mediterranean for two reasons. First, more well-known terms such as the *Middle East* and *Near East* are regarded as Eurocentric—there is Europe, the Middle East, and eventually the Far East. In contrast, the term *Southwest Asia* is seen as neutral. Second, the terms *Middle East* and *Near East* are not generally understood to include the Arabian Peninsula or Iran, regions that are very important for the history and development of dress and fashion. Instead, *Middle East* and *Near East* tend to be taken to mean the lands bordering the Mediterranean as well as Syria. To avoid potential problems, it was decided to describe this vast area using the term *Southwest Asia*.

Despite the historical, and indeed modern, importance of Central and Southwest Asia, information about dress in this region still tends to be patchy. In the recent past, certain imperial or colonial powers were very interested in particular regions and groups; the Ottomans, with their capital in Istanbul, for example, collected information about their subjects, including their dress, throughout their vast empire for centuries. The Russians have been collecting ethnographic material from Central Asia for over a hundred years. In recent decades, with the growing importance of Islam and oil, more and more attention has been directed toward Arab culture, including dress. Thus, some specific regions and groups have been studied for many years, while others have been sadly neglected. The production of the *Encyclopedia of World Dress and Fashion*, and in particular this volume on Central and Southwest Asia, is a major step forward in changing this situation. Many of the articles included in this volume cover subjects that have rarely been discussed in depth before, such as Kurdish dress, Iraqi clothing, hajj clothing, and the role of the hajj market.

This volume has been divided into three sections. Parts 1 and 2 include general and introductory articles on various historical and geographic subjects, including pre-Islamic and early Islamic dress forms, that have had a long-term influence on the region. Parts 3, 4, 5 and 6 include the greatest number of articles; these describe the regional dress and fashion of Central and Southwest Asia. These articles have been arranged in a roughly west-to-east order, starting with Turkey and Ottoman subjects, then moving on to the Arab world, followed by Iran, Afghanistan, and Central Asia. Part 7 includes articles of a more specific nature includes articles of a more specific nature and covers subjects that have played an important role in the history of dress in the region, such as the influence of Islam, laws of differentiation, Orientalism, tourism, and so forth. There are also several shorter snapshots that present more personal insights or ideas, such as one on the tenth-century writer and fashion guru al-Washsha, demonstrating that some people's profound interest in what they wear, and the presence of fashion critics, are nothing new, nor confined to the West.

Wherever possible, scholars from or directly involved with the relevant cultural and religious groups were commissioned to write articles. Authors therefore come from a wide range of backgrounds, with sometimes very diverse approaches to the subject of dress. The articles are not intended to be the last word on the subject but should instead be read as an introduction to the various themes. Readers who wish to delve deeper into this fascinating world should follow the cross-references to related articles in this volume and other volumes and consult the bibliographic references at the end of each article.

In some areas of the world, such as North America, *dress* and *fashion* have become nearly synonymous. But this is not the case in Central and Southwest Asia. The concept of fashion, especially Western fashion, exists and is growing in importance, but there are many groups who prefer, for various reasons, to continue wearing their traditional, regional, and ethnic forms of clothing and accessories. For this reason, this volume of the *Encyclopedia* focuses on the concept of dress rather than fashion. But this does not mean that fashion and fashion designers are excluded. Various articles look at designers from the region, some of whom work with a combination of local and Western forms and others of whom deliberately focus on their own regional dress but with a modern, fashionable touch.

The terminology used to refer to the dress of Central and Southwest Asia is problematic. Names are often variably spelled and pronounced. Moreover, the same name may be used to describe different items produced and used in a number of regions. It was, therefore, decided to try to use a consistent spelling for most indigenous dress terms. The transliteration of the words follows normal, international standards. It was also decided not to include diacritical marks, thus making it easier for readers to gain a sense of the word.

Thanks to the publishing team for their patience and help during the production of this volume. They were supportive throughout, especially in the difficult moments. Special thanks in particular to the editor in chief, Joanne B. Eicher, for her encouragement and advice.

On the home front, no doubt Willem Vogelsang learned more about dress than he really wanted to know, but, hopefully, it has served him well.

Gillian Vogelsang-Eastwood

PART 1

Overview of Dress and Fashion in Central and Southwest Asia

Introduction to Dress and Fashion in Central and Southwest Asia

- The Main Cultural and Religious Divisions
- Central and Southwest Asian Dress
- Hair and Hairstyles
- Dress and Accessories
- Dress, Islam, Family, and Society
- Dress and Governmental Groups
- Dress, Oil, and Fashion
- Dress and Global Trade
- Inside/Outside and Survival of Regional Dress Forms

Dress is what people wear and do to their bodies in order to indicate who they are, to provide information about their identity. Dress includes permanent changes or modifications to the body such as tattoos and piercings as well as temporary variations like the wearing of perfume or a new hairstyle. Dress also includes the garments people wear and the accessories they carry—jewelry, bags, walking sticks, weapons, and so forth. It is not surprising, therefore, that in a geographic area as vast and complex as Central and Southwest Asia, a wide range of dress forms is found. They have been influenced by factors such as geography, climate, availability of materials, technology, ethnic and social bonds, economics and trade, as well as religion.

Central and Southwest Asia is immense: It stretches from Turkey in the west through to Kazakhstan and Kyrgyzstan in the east and includes areas that are covered by mountains, forests, subtropical plants, and agricultural lands as well as desert sands. The climate ranges from very cold to extremely hot; there is high rainfall in some areas—as much as 67 inches (170 centimeters) per year in northern Iran around the Caspian Sea—but in the deserts, drought conditions prevail.

THE MAIN CULTURAL AND RELIGIOUS DIVISIONS

Although many different cultural and ethnic groups live in the region, they can be divided into three main groups: Turks, Iranians, and Arabs. Numerous minority groups such as Armenians, Kurds, and Russians have moved, either voluntarily or not, to various parts of the region over the centuries. The first of the main groups is the Iranian peoples, who originated in Central Asia and then settled all across the Iranian Plateau. Iranian ethnic groups and cultures can be found in the Iran of the early twenty-first century and in the surrounding regions of eastern Turkey, Afghanistan, and Tajikistan.

The Turkic peoples are a Eurasian people living in northern, central, and western Eurasia. They originated in Central Asia

and, over the millennia, moved westward to the area that includes Turkey in the twenty-first century. These include a large number of subgroups such as the Azerbaijani, Kazakhs, Ottomans, Seljuks, Turkmen, and Uzbeks.

The third group, the Arabs, migrated from the Arabian Peninsula into the northern Arabian Desert and the Levant. Arab culture and the Arabic language spread with the Islamic religion to Morocco, Egypt, the Levant, Syria, Iraq, and beyond. It is not surprising, therefore, to find many links between the dress of Southwest Asia and that of North Africa and of Egypt in particular.

Southwest Asia is also the birthplace of three world religions: Judaism, Christianity, and Islam. The oldest of these is Judaism, which is believed to have developed in the second millennium B.C.E. and became established in the first millennium B.C.E. Christianity developed in the first century C.E. and spread throughout the Roman and Byzantine empires and beyond in the first millennium C.E. The third religion, Islam, came into existence in the seventh century C.E. in the Arabian city of Mecca. It quickly spread throughout Southwest Asia and northern Africa and then to many countries and groups throughout the world.

Over the centuries, the interrelationship between these Abrahamic religions has seen everything from peaceful coexistence to bloody warfare. Religion is a strong force in the lives of people throughout Central and Southwest Asia. Not surprisingly, therefore, religion had, and still has, a profound influence on dress in the region, not only with respect to the outward appearance of individual items but also in the choice of colors, materials, combinations of garments, differences between indoor and outdoor dress, and what people may or may not legally wear.

CENTRAL AND SOUTHWEST ASIAN DRESS

The size and complexity of Central and Southwest Asia mean that defining what is characteristic of the dress of this region is challenging, yet certain elements have influenced the appearance of garments throughout this area. One of the most important is the position of Central and Southwest Asia along the ancient and vast trading system often called the Silk Road, which stretched from Asia, notably China, via Central Asia and northern India to the Mediterranean region and the rest of Europe. This trading route thrived for about three thousand years, from the second millennium B.C.E. to the first millennium C.E., and then it gradually died out because of political, social, and religious instability such as the Crusades and the collapse of the Mongol Empire and, from the seventeenth century on, European mercantile expansion and the development of new sea routes. This area has seen and been influenced by many different cultures and ethnic and religious groups over the millennia and has provided a wide range of material products, notably in the form of wood, pottery, glass, precious and semiprecious stones, textiles, furs, and clothing.

A later influence on Central and Southwest Asian dress was the role of the annual pilgrimage, or hajj, to the holy cities of Mecca and Medina. Although the hajj has pre-Islamic origins, the development of Islam in the seventh century C.E. caused this annual pilgrimage to take on a greater importance. The importance of the hajj continues in the twenty-first century. Over the centuries, millions of Muslims have carried out the hajj. Many died en route, some stayed in Mecca and Medina, and others returned home. This vast yearly movement of people has encouraged the movement of ideas, goods, and wealth from countries as far away as Indonesia and Morocco and, since the advent of trains and air travel, the relatively easy movement of Muslims throughout the world. All of this has influenced the textiles and dress within the area.

One way of looking at dress in Central and Southwest Asia is to define how it is actually worn. In general, garments can be divided into four basic forms: (a) draped garments made from a piece of cloth laid over the body in some manner, such as shawls draped over the head or shoulders; (b) wrapped garments for which a length of material is wrapped around the body, such as the sari from India; (c) sewn garments consisting of two or more pieces of cloth of varying sizes stitched to create a simple clothing item; and (d) tailored garments made from one or more pieces of material, deliberately shaped by cutting or sewing gathers, pleats, darts, or tucks to fit a garment more closely to the human shape than the other three types.

Some draped or wrapped garments are worn in Central and Southwest Asia. These include men's headgear in the form of head cloths and turbans, hip wraps used as underwear, or (more commonly) women's outer garments, such as the chador, which is a simple, sewn garment draped over the head and body to disguise the wearer's shape, appearance, and identity. In general, however, sewn and tailored garments are preferred in Central and Southwest Asia. A further division can be made, because historically Arabs have tended to wear loose-fitting, sewn garments, which

A young Adwan-Louzi Bedouin with plaited hair, Jordan, ca. 1934. The family or group to which a Bedouin belongs can be discerned by the way the hair is plaited. Library of Congress Prints and Photographs Division LC-DIG-ppmsca-18429-00042.

are more suitable for living in hot and dry desert conditions. Turkic groups generally tailor garments, a choice of garment type perhaps related to their origins in Central Asia, where horseback riding was the dominant form of transportation, and fitted garments were regarded as more practical. The Iranians used a mixture of minimally and closely tailored garments.

Many other influences contribute to the appearance of garments. Social conventions and politics have all played an important role in everyone's economic and daily life for millennia. But perhaps one of the greatest influences on dress was religion. At the beginning of the first millennium C.E., many different religious groups spread throughout Central and Southwest Asia, including Buddhists, Christians (Orthodox, Catholic, Nestorians), Hindus, Jews, and Zoroastrians. The advent and rapid spread of Islam in the seventh century C.E. further complicated the situation. Within a relatively short period, the religious and cultural demographics of the region changed dramatically. Islam and Arab culture became the dominant force, with the other religions forming minority groups, a situation remaining into the twenty-first century.

Outsiders to this area often presume that dress in Central and Southwest Asia is static and has changed little over the centuries, but this is not the case. Change may have been slow in some areas, but it did take place, whether for social, economic, religious, or political reasons, or indeed because of some other factor.

HAIR AND HAIRSTYLES

Head and facial hair are important throughout the region for both men and women and, in particular, for both Jewish and Muslim communities. The locks worn by some Orthodox male Jews, for instance, were and remain an important sign of their religious beliefs. Within the Muslim world, hair fashions for both men and women vary considerably both geographically and chronologically. In general, however, it is normal for women's hair to be long, well groomed, perfumed, and, in some groups, decorated with jewelry and other items. Within some Iranian groups, for example, if a woman is perceived as misbehaving, she might have her hair cut off as punishment.

There seem to be more variations for male hair—for example, males may have long hair in some areas of Central and Southwest Asia but not in others. Bedouin in Arabia, for instance, have traditionally had long hair that is often plaited, with different styles of plaiting indicating their family or group. In other areas of this vast region, a Muslim man's head hair was shaved off except for a lock of hair, so, according to various traditional accounts, he could be pulled to heaven by the angels with this lock. At the beginning of the twenty-first century, however, it is more common for men to have short hair similar in cut to styles worn in the West.

Similarly, there are variations in male facial hair in Central Asia because many groups—notably those of Chinese or Mongolian descent—genetically cannot grow facial hair, so luxurious beards and mustaches are virtually impossible. In contrast, countries such as Afghanistan encourage the growth of long and thick beards to show a man's social and religious status. In other areas—in Turkey and among the various Kurdish groups—a mustache is more important than a beard. A man's social status is based on his mustache, but the style of mustache—such as upward- or downward-pointing—can be and is used to state his political and religious affiliations.

DRESS AND ACCESSORIES

Accessories in Central and Southwest Asia can range from small finger rings to elaborate daggers. In particular, jewelry is important for women, and weapons, together with tack for horses or camels, are important for men.

Some accessories, such as perfumes, are used by both men and women. These are regarded as important because many cultures require that people are properly dressed in public and are not offensive in their behavior or appearance; in particular, they should not smell unpleasant—something that is important in countries where the climate is hot and humid and people sweat copiously. In addition, women's personal presentation often includes the use of makeup. If a woman appears before her family or friends without her hair in order and suitable makeup, she may be asked if all is well, because a poor presentation may be taken to signify distress or illness.

DRESS, ISLAM, FAMILY, AND SOCIETY

The Islamic religion is a powerful influence on all aspects of the daily lives of its followers. The Qur'an and the hadiths contain some important statements on dress. It is made clear in these texts that both men and women should dress modestly, which meant covering the area of the body between the waist and the knees and also, in the case of women, the breasts. It was further deemed appropriate for men and especially women to cover their heads, a woman's hair and neck being considered erogenous zones in many cultures in this part of the world. Over time these ideas were transformed into sometimes strictly enforced sumptuary laws specifying the types of materials and garments that could be worn (especially in public places) and outlining the basic elements of the concept of *fitrah* as applied to the human body, namely how people should look after their bodies. For example, guidance was given on such subjects as the removal of body hair, the length of fingernails, and the use of perfumes. Another body of rules, known as the laws of differentiation, also evolved; these prescribed how Muslims and non-Muslims were to dress in order that they could be distinguished from each other. In Islamic countries such as Iran and Saudi Arabia, both types of law are still applied.

Another way of looking at the dress of the region is to see how it is used in various social situations—for example, to display various aspects of gender, family life, occupation, and status. Society plays a role at an individual level, as well as in larger groups, to control, strengthen, and guide a community. Social control can take the form of not accepting spitting on the streets or saying that a skirt length is too short or too long. It can also be used to state what a person's role and position are within a particular group.

Within Central and Southwest Asian communities, for example, there has long been a strong dividing line between male and female roles. Men's lives used to be centered on the public and open society, where transportation, ideas, and coming into contact with a wide range of people were the norm. In contrast, a woman's domain was seen as the private world of the home, where she was surrounded by family and female friends, looking after domestic issues such as the household, food, clothing, and child rearing. In the twentieth century, the dividing lines between these two worlds collapsed in many cultures. The need for women to work outside the home for economic reasons and greater knowledge of the world via television, the Internet, and so forth have meant a shift in what women are prepared to accept and to want. These changes have also had an effect on what women and men wear in public.

It is sometimes said that Central and Southwest Asian family life, and thus life in general, is based around marriages: who is ready for marriage, who is getting married, the ceremonies and rituals around marriage, and, most important, the children who come after marriage. And then the cycle begins again.

The role of the family also brings into focus another important factor that has influenced the form of women's clothing: the bearing and feeding of babies. Clothing often was very loose so that special maternity clothing was not needed; similarly, dresses or blouses tended to have long front openings to provide easy access for breast-feeding. A development of this concept is that within some groups, such as in nineteenth-century Iran, an unmarried girl has a short central slit on the bodice at the neckline so that her breasts are not visible, while a married woman with children has a much longer slit or two slits.

On a larger and more public scale, Central and Southwest Asian society is divided into three groups: city or town dwellers (urban), village people, and nomadic groups. The reality is much more complicated because some nomadic groups, for example, include members who live permanently in villages, others who travel to cities and towns to earn money to send back to their families, and nomads who follow their herds to different grazing areas in the summer and winter months.

Historically, in some areas of Central and Southwest Asia, rigid social hierarchies meant that people could move horizontally but very rarely vertically; the son of a merchant became a merchant, as did his son; a farmer's daughter married a farmer

and so on, but people did not often marry across social strata. People were expected to wear garments appropriate to their social role, so there were special outfits for merchants, scribes, mullahs (Islamic clergy in Persia), water carriers, and so on. Such a situation existed in the social structure of both Iran and Turkey for centuries and could still be felt up to the mid-twentieth century. At the beginning of the twenty-first century, mullahs still wear turbans and gowns, but this attire is no longer worn on a daily basis by the other groups. Some special outfits linger on, such as those worn by water carriers in Turkey and Egypt, which are based on late-nineteenth-century outfits.

DRESS AND GOVERNMENTAL GROUPS

Western influence and direct colonial rule in some cases added a new factor to the sartorial developments in Central and Southwest Asia, especially in the late nineteenth and early twentieth centuries. Groups wanting to appear modern wore Western clothing; non-Muslim groups also tended to wear Western clothing to show their religious affiliations. For example, in 1918, Russian and Communist revolutionaries took over various Central Asian regions and over the next two decades created five Soviet republics—Kazakhstan, Kyrgyzstan, Tajikistan, Turkmenistan, and Uzbekistan. It was not long before the wearing of regional dress, for example kaftans and turbans, was discouraged and then officially forbidden. People were told to wear Soviet versions of Western-style shirts, trousers, and dresses. Some local garments survived in a slightly different form, such as the ikat dresses and trousers worn by women in Tajikistan and Uzbekistan (ikat is a form of cloth in which the warp and/or weft threads are tied before dyeing to resist the dye, thus allowing a pattern to be

An Afghan woman wearing a *chadari* (a head and body covering composed of a cap, face veil, and mantle) passes by mannequins wearing Western-style clothes at a shopping center in Herat, Afghanistan, 2005. Since the early twentieth century, many regional outfits have disappeared, replaced by "modern" Western-style garments. Behrouz Mehri/AFP/Getty Images.

produced when woven), but the vast array of ikat garments and colors formerly seen in historic cities such as Bukhara and Samarkand is no longer to be found. It is worth noting that, since the fall of the Soviet regime in 1991, these countries have attempted to reintroduce ikat garments for men and women in an effort to rebuild national pride.

The example of Soviet influence in Central Asia refers to changes that originated with outside powers. However, in the first half of the twentieth century, in various countries—notably Turkey, Iran, and Afghanistan—the ruling authorities tried to force both men and women to wear Western-style clothing as a sign of the country's "modern" status. For example, Mustafa Kemal Atatürk (1881–1938), founder and first president of the Turkish republic, enacted a number of laws in the 1920s and 1930s, as part of his Westernization and secularization project, that laid down what men and women were allowed to wear in public. In Iran, Shah Reza Pahlavi (r. 1925–1941) also forced through a series of changes beginning in the late 1920s, including the reorganization of the Iranian legal system along West European lines. It became an official requirement for judges, lawyers, and other court officials to wear secular dress, as opposed to the traditional dress of the 'ulama, or Islamic clergy. In a further attempt to modernize and unite Iran, in 1936 Reza Shah banned the wearing of veils of any kind, provoking considerable controversy and unrest that persisted until the ban was lifted ten years later. Following the lead of Turkey and Iran, King Amanullah (r. 1919–1929) of Afghanistan urged women in 1928 to abandon purdah (seclusion; literally, "curtain") and the veil and become more prominent members of society. However, when conservative forces overthrew Amanullah later that year, it was officially announced that women had to return to purdah and the wearing of the chadari (an all-enveloping head, face, and body cover used by women in Afghanistan). The effects of these and other measures still reverberate throughout Southwest Asia in the twenty-first century.

DRESS, OIL, AND FASHION

The role of oil in changing the appearance of dress in the region should not be underestimated. The discovery of oil in the region, especially the Arabian Peninsula, before the mid-twentieth century created vast wealth in a relatively short period of time. At a local level, the range of material used to decorate clothing changed, and at the same time more and more Bedouin women in the Negev Desert region started to embroider their clothing like village women in nearby Palestine. On a wider scale, urban men and women started to wear imported Western garments as a sign of their urban sophistication and wealth. The number of European and U.S. fashion houses, such as Dior, Yves Saint-Laurent, Calvin Klein, Ralph Lauren, and many others, who have branches in oil-producing countries is testament to the importance of oil in the study of Southwest Asian dress.

One result of this interest in Western fashions is the development of some fashion designers who adapt Western forms to local needs and others who are determined to express their cultural identity by using regional dress as the basis for their creations. An example of the latter trend is the work of Nawal bint Hamed bin Hamid AlHooti in Oman, who uses traditional cuts but with modern textiles and colors. Her work is sold throughout the Gulf region. In addition, a growing number of fashion designers on

the world fashion scene are mixing regional and Western styles to create new forms. Two such designers are Rıfat Özbek and Hussein Chalayan, both of whom are of Turkish origin.

DRESS AND GLOBAL TRADE

Although much has been written in the early twenty-first century about increases in global trade and how regional differences in dress are being eroded, it is important to note that trade routes have been helping to spread particular forms and styles of dress for hundreds of years. Central Asia has long been regarded as a crossroads for trade, with goods traveling from China westward and European goods going eastward. The Eastern Roman Empire in the early centuries of the Common Era, for example, saw both men and women wearing a mixture of Roman-, Syrian-, and Sassanian-style clothing.

During the medieval period and up to the beginning of the twentieth century, the great hajj market and the movement of pilgrims to the holy cities of Mecca and Medina from throughout the Islamic world meant that vast quantities of goods were transported across the world. Pilgrims and merchants brought goods with them to barter and sell and in turn bought goods from other areas in an annual frenzy that lasted one to two months. What is different in the early twenty-first century, however, from these historical examples is (a) the speed at which objects can travel as a result of modern transportation technology; (b) the development of manmade materials that are much cheaper and colorful and technology to produce a wider range of cloth forms and sizes than ever before possible; and (c) global telecommunication links such as telephones, television, and the Internet, giving people far more knowledge about other cultures than ever before. Nomadic people from remote regions of the Arabian Peninsula or in Central Asia in the twenty-first century have easy access to the global market.

INSIDE/OUTSIDE AND SURVIVAL OF REGIONAL DRESS FORMS

An intriguing aspect of dress which is prominent in the region is that of inside/outside. There is sometimes a significant difference between how local people regard their traditional dress and how others—for instance, migrants or refugees—view the dress that is worn in their homeland. As a result of a diaspora, some people have an "outside" view of the land of their ancestors and try to recapture or re-create a feeling of national or ethnic identity and affiliation via their clothing. A comparable development can be seen with political leaders who want to create a national dress to promote nation building, in this case working from "inside" the country.

Throughout the twentieth century, many regional forms have vanished, to be replaced by modern Western-style garments. There are areas, however, where this has not taken place; for example, Omani men are required to wear loose gowns called dishdashas at work, and the Omani government thus deliberately encourages the garment's survival. In another example, in the Kingdom of Saudi Arabia, regional dress for men is being changed by government policy. In this case, however, this is occurring not by banning Western clothing but by the royal family wearing an outfit consisting of a long gown (thob), head cloth (keffiyeh), and head rope ('aqal), an outfit that is being copied by more and more men throughout the kingdom. This, in turn, has caused a decline in the use of traditional men's regional dress in areas such as Asir in the southwestern corner of the country.

In contrast, one manner in which regional dress survives in the twenty-first century is through people deliberately wearing it as a public proclamation against what they regard as interference from central government. In Iran, for example, both Kurdish men and women often choose Kurdish dress to state their ethnic and cultural origins despite efforts by the Iranian government to ban Kurdish dress or at least encourage the wearing of pan-Iranian dress, basically a form of Western-style clothing. Nevertheless, as a generalization, men's regional dress had more or less died out in Central and Southwest Asia by the mid-twentieth century, and women's regional dress was heavily under threat by the century's end.

References and Further Reading

Harvey, Janet. *Traditional Textiles of Central Asia*. London: Thames & Hudson, 1997.

Stillman, Yedida. *Arab Dress: A Short History from the Dawn of Islam to Modern Times*. Leiden: Brill, 2000.

Stillman, Yedida, and Norman Stillman. "Libas." In *Encyclopaedia of Islam*, edited by P. J. Bearman, Th. Bianquis, C. E. Bosworth, E. van Donzel, W. P. Heinrichs, et al., vol. 5. 2nd ed. Leiden: Brill, 1960–2005.

Wilber, Donald. *Riza Shah Pahlavi: The Resurrection and Reconstruction of Iran*. Hicksville, NY: Exposition Press, 1975.

Gillian Vogelsang-Eastwood

Climate, Geography, and Dress

- The Arab Lands
- The Turkish-Iranian Highlands
- Central Asia

Central and Southwest Asia are geographic terms that together refer to an immense extent of land that stretches over a distance of some three thousand miles (five thousand kilometers), from the Bosporus in the northwest to the Indus Valley in the southeast. It is nearly four thousand miles (six thousand kilometers) from Yemen in the southwest to Kazakhstan in the northeast. Southwest Asia is the extreme southwestern part of this expanse. It is also often called West or Western Asia. The names overlap with two older and more traditional appellations: the Middle East and the Near East. These terms often include the northeastern parts of the African subcontinent (Libya, Egypt). In the twenty-first century, both names, the Middle East and the Near East, are regarded as Eurocentric, and, except for their use in a historical or cultural context, these terms have become somewhat obsolete.

The precise extent of Southwest Asia is still a moot point. Afghanistan, for instance, is often regarded as part of Central Asia. Whether the island of Cyprus and the modern State of Israel should be included is not clear. For present purposes, the term is defined as referring to the lands that stretch from the Bosporus and Istanbul in the west to the Afghanistan/Pakistan borderlands in the east, and from the Indian Ocean in the south to the Caspian Sea in the north.

Central Asia is an equally poorly defined area. The term as used here describes the lands that stretch north from Iran (ancient Persia) and Afghanistan—thus including the new Central Asian republics that arose out of the collapse of the former Soviet Union in 1991—as far as the steppes of modern Kazakhstan. This part of the world used to be called West Turkistan, named after the primarily Turkish population of the area.

The history of all these lands is closely interlocked: Islam is the dominant religion, and many customs are age-old and common to the whole area. This also applies to the clothing traditions throughout the ages. The spread of Islam from the mid-seventh century c.e., the Turkish invasions from the late first millennium c.e., the continuous Central Asian influence from the north, and the European influence from the west and south are all factors that have affected, in varying degrees, local sartorial traditions all over Central and Southwest Asia.

In general, all of the lands of Central and Southwest Asia may be divided into three main geographic zones: the plains and deserts of the eastern Mediterranean and the Arabian Peninsula and adjoining lands; the mountainous lands and highlands of the Turkish-Iranian belt; and the mountains and deserts of Central Asia. In the broadest of terms, the people from Central Asia and from the Turkish-Iranian belt of lands traditionally wear trousers and tailored garments made from wool, silk, and cotton, while the people from the Arab lands prefer loose gowns.

Likewise, the people from the Arab lands prefer to cover their heads with a head cloth (which protects the head from the sun and keeps it relatively cool), while those from the Turkish-Iranian lands have tended to wear, at least until recently, turbans that can sometimes be very elaborate (again to protect the head but somewhat warmer than a single head cloth). The people from Central Asia in general prefer a warm headdress such as a *bashlyq* (a men's head covering for the hair, mouth, and nose) or a fur hat. The need for warmth in the winter is also reflected in the use of numerous layers of silk and woolen garments and felt footwear, which has been a feature of Central Asian clothing for millennia.

The introduction of modern artificial and synthetic fibers created many changes in the range of materials, colors, and designs worn by both men and women, but it is noticeable that the basic trends of Turkish-Iranian and Central Asian clothing, essentially consisting of trousers and tailored garments, and those of Arab clothing and its loose-fitting garments, have remained the same.

THE ARAB LANDS

The Arab lands include the modern states of Saudi Arabia, Yemen, Oman, the United Arab Emirates, Qatar, Bahrain, Kuwait, Israel and the Palestinian lands, Jordan, Lebanon, Syria, and Iraq. These are the lands that are mostly occupied by Arabic-speaking groups. Climatically, this part of the world is characterized by little annual rainfall (less than twelve inches, or thirty centimeters). The average temperature in these lands can be extremely hot, especially in the summer. In the Saudi Arabian desert, daytime temperatures may rise above 122 degrees Fahrenheit (50 degrees Celsius). During the winter, the temperature in the Saudi capital of Riyadh fluctuates between 46 and 68 degrees Fahrenheit (8–20 degrees Celsius). Along the coast of the Mediterranean Sea, the weather is more moderate.

The Arab lands include not only the barren deserts of the Arabian Peninsula—such as the Rub' al-Khali ("the Empty Quarter") in the southeast, the Nejd Desert in the center, and the Nafud Desert in the north—but also the relatively fertile and productive area that abuts the Turkish-Iranian mountains further to the north and east. This belt is often known as the Fertile Crescent. It stretches from the coastal plains of Palestine, via Syria, to what is, in the early twenty-first century, the modern state of Iraq. In this area are the major cities of Amman, the capital of Jordan; Damascus, the capital of Syria, and Aleppo, an ancient and modern city in the northwest of Syria; Mosul in northern Iraq, and Baghdad further to the south, the capital of Iraq. Iraq is known in history as Mesopotamia, the "Land between the Rivers," indicating its location along two major rivers—the Euphrates and the Tigris—that descend from the mountains in the far north. These two rivers created the fertile lands that gave rise, some five thousand years ago, to the earliest civilizations in this part of the world. They also led to the emergence of the city of Babylon, not far from modern Baghdad, which for millennia was one of the largest and most famous cities of the ancient world. Both cities were important trading centers that moved goods, including textiles, furs, and garments, as well as sartorial ideas, between East and West.

Along the coast of the Mediterranean, the modern states of Lebanon, Israel, and the Palestinian lands, together with the coastal lands of Syria and Turkey, mark a transition zone between the inland mountains and deserts and the wide expanse of the sea. Here there is often more rainfall, small rivulets descend from the mountains, and the sea offers fishing and trade opportunities. This area is traditionally called the Levant. Here, European influence often first reached the Islamic lands of Southwest Asia; here also, the establishment of the State of Israel in 1947 led to a conflict that remains unresolved and has led to enormous misery among all parties involved.

The geographic location of the Arab lands of Southwest Asia has also influenced their sartorial traditions. Along the Mediterranean coast, the people have always felt the effect of other peoples living along the sea—for instance, the Greeks in the centuries B.C.E., the Romans in the early centuries C.E., and

European nations during the last centuries. In particular, the use of wool as a clothing material is a feature of European and Mediterranean cultures. Anyone who has ever been to Lebanon will understand the extent of Western influence on the clothing of the local people. Yet outside influence was also felt along the coast of the Arabian Peninsula, as for instance in Yemen, where East African and Indian elements have been incorporated into local dress traditions, notably in the Tihamah region of western Yemen.

The same applies to neighboring Oman, the people of which maintained many connections with East Africa, especially Tanzania and Zanzibar. Historical links have led to some groups of women living in eastern and coastal Oman wearing a type of cloth called a *kanga*, which is also worn by women of Arab descent in East Africa. Kangas are made out of thin cotton, which

A young Pashtun woman wearing decorative clothing that features beaded panels and jewelry, Afghanistan, 1980. Some Pashtun nomads still roam the region, moving their flocks into the mountains by springtime and returning in the autumn. AFP/Getty Images.

is printed with bold, brightly colored designs. Kangas are cool to wear in the summer months. Expensive versions of these cloths are printed in Tanzania, and cheaper forms are printed in India, especially for the Omani and East African market.

Oman and the adjoining Gulf states (the United Arab Emirates, Qatar, and Bahrain) have also always maintained strong contacts with the Iranian lands on the other side of the Persian Gulf: The famous *batullah*, or masklike face veil worn by some women in Oman and the Gulf states, is also worn by many women in the Bandar region of Iran. Iraq has always been influenced by its powerful eastern neighbor, Iran, in the development of dress. In the ninth century C.E., the courtiers of the Abbasid capital in Baghdad (a place-name derived from Persian *baga-data*, "given by God") were known for their Iranian-style clothing.

At the same time, the Arabs' rise to power in the seventh century C.E. and the spread of Islam meant that sartorial traditions linked to Islam (Islamically "correct" clothing) were widely distributed and that, consequently, clothing that was originally "Arab" became firmly established within the dress traditions of much of Southwest Asia. In public, it became important for women to cover the shape of their entire bodies. Correct clothing included undertrousers as well as tunics and gowns that covered the body from the neck to the ankles. In some cultures, face veils were required, but not everywhere, and certainly the parts of the face that needed to be covered and the form of face veil varied considerably in Central and Southwest Asia.

Men were also expected to cover the shape of their bodies, especially the region from the waist to the knee, and it was regarded as preferable to cover the whole region between the neck and ankles. Because of the differences in temperature between summer and winter and between early morning and midday, Arab dress for men tends to be made up of numerous layers, which can be taken off easily. In general, men from the desert prefer long, loose-fitting garments in two main layers in the summer, including a long, wide gown, called a *dishdasha* or *thob*, and a cloak, such as the *aba* (a sleeveless, cloaklike garment open down the front) or *bisht* (a cloaklike garment with or without sleeves, also open down the front). Historically, these garments were made of silk or cotton, which were cool to wear in the heat of the summer months. During the cooler weather of winter, three or more layers were worn, including thobs, jackets, and the aba or bisht, but the garments were made out of warm wool or camel hair. In the early twenty-first century, synthetic materials are widely used, which makes keeping warm or cool much more difficult.

At first, it was normal but not essential for men to cover their heads, but for climatic reasons, it was preferable. Later, however, it became a quintessential Muslim deed for a man to cover his head in specific ways out of respect to Allah and as a sign of being a Muslim. Because of the warmth associated with desert conditions, it is normal to wear a small skullcap (*'araqiyeh* or *taqiyeh*) under the head cloth. The names derive from the Arabic word meaning "to sweat." This small cap was intended to catch any sweat that might damage or stain the head cloth; it is a small but very practical garment given the climate.

The general footwear in the Arab lands has always been sandals or loosely fitting shoes, often of the mule type. Both types can easily be taken off, which is extremely useful since, whenever a man or woman enters a house or mosque, footwear is supposed to be removed.

THE TURKISH-IRANIAN HIGHLANDS

The Turkish-Iranian highlands border the Arab lands to the north and east. They include the modern states of Turkey, Georgia, Armenia, Azerbaijan, Iran, Afghanistan, and the western parts of Pakistan. Modern Turkey also includes part of Europe; the Asian part of Turkey is generally known as Anatolia.

These lands all lie at a relatively high altitude, and they are all dominated by large mountain ranges, including the Caucasus, the Zagros, the Elburz, and the Hindu Kush. Precipitation in some of these highlands during the winter is almost double that in the Arab lands to the south. The Zagros and much of the Caucasus were originally covered with forests of coniferous and deciduous trees. The temperatures in this region are decidedly harsh; it can be very hot in the summer and very cold in the winter.

In the past, the people from the Arab lands were often scared of the inhospitable mountainous lands that formed such a threatening barrier to further expansion: The people from ancient Mesopotamia often complained in their texts of the warriors who swooped down from the mountains to overrun the settled lands in the plains. A vague echo of these feelings can still be found in the general tension between the Arabs of Iraq and elsewhere and the people from Anatolia and the Iranian Plateau. One of the main reasons for this antagonism has a religious context: Most of the people in Iran belong to the Shia branch of Islam, and many people in modern Turkey also follow a Shia interpretation, while most of the Arab population follows the Sunni line.

The main countries of this part of the world—Turkey and Iran—are separated by the southern spurs of the Caucasus Mountains. However, each country is individually bounded by a ring of mountains that surrounds the central highlands; modern Turkey is formed by the Caucasus in the east, the Pontic Mountains to the north (bordering the Black Sea), and the Taurus Mountains to the south (separating the country from the Mediterranean). The modern Islamic Republic of Iran is formed by a ring of mountains including the Zagros and Caucasus to the east, the Elburz and the Kopet Dagh to the north, and the Hindu Kush to the east.

In Turkey and in Iran, and in the neighboring Islamic Republic of Afghanistan, inland settlements sprang up at places with a plentiful supply of water. The main towns, both ancient and modern, can be found in the small strip of land between the central deserts and the surrounding ring of mountains, along the various caravan tracks that lead across the continent. Small rivers descend from the mountains and create small oases before emptying their water into the nearby inhospitable desert. The modern capital of Turkey, Ankara, lies just north of the Turkish highlands and south of the Pontic Mountains. Tehran, the capital of Iran, lies between the Elburz Mountains to the north and the Central Iranian Desert (the Dasht-i Kabir) to the south. Kandahar, the former capital of Afghanistan, lies between the spurs of the Hindu Kush Mountains to the north and the impenetrable Registan Desert to the south.

Unlike the Arab lands to the south, the Turkish-Iranian highlands are mainly populated and dominated by ethnic groups that derive from Central Asia. The Iranian-speaking groups first arrived in what are, in the twenty-first century, Iran and Afghanistan from the early second millennium B.C.E. on. They ultimately gave their name to Iran (from *arya*, the name used by the people to indicate themselves). They introduced many of the Iranian languages to the area, including Persian, Kurdish, Baluchi, and

Pashto. These Iranian languages are completely different from the Semitic languages, including Arabic, that are spoken in the Arab lands to the west and south. The Iranian languages, it should be noted, belong to the Indo-European family of languages, which also includes the Germanic tongues (English, German, Dutch) and most other languages spoken in Europe.

The Turkish languages, which are different from the Semitic and Iranian tongues, were also introduced by groups deriving from the northern parts of Central Asia and Siberia, but this development occurred only from the second half of the first millennium C.E. on. It was a slow process, and Turkish-speaking groups arriving from Central Asia first traversed the area that, in the early twenty-first century, forms northern Iran and subsequently settled in the area that is northwestern Iran and Azerbaijan (where, in fact, Turkish is still the dominant language). It was not until the end of the eleventh century C.E. that Turkish-speaking groups infiltrated en masse the land that used to be called Anatolia and later was renamed after them.

The mountainous nature of the Turkish-Iranian highlands has made this part of the world eminently suitable for extensive animal husbandry and, especially, nomadism. Until the 1970s, nomads in Iran and eastern Turkey moved annually from their semipermanent winter camps to summer pastures high in the mountains and back again. In Afghanistan, the *kuchis* (the everyday name for the mainly Pashtun nomads in Afghanistan) still roam the lands, moving their flocks into the mountains by springtime and returning in the autumn. They still constitute a conspicuous feature, with their black goat-hair tents, the women going around without face veiling and proudly showing their colorful dresses (mostly in greens and reds), decorative beaded panels, and dangling jewelry.

The history of the long belt of Turkish-Iranian lands also determined the sartorial traditions of the area. The Iranian-speaking Scythians who invaded this part of the world, beginning in the early first millennium B.C.E., introduced trousers, riding coats, and special cavalry weaponry. These items have been worn since then by almost all of the people in the Turkish-Iranian world and beyond, and they distinguish that mountainous belt from the Arab lands further south and west, where long gowns are still generally worn by the men. The introduction of the Scythians' sartorial traditions was, in succeeding centuries, supported by the advent of the similarly dressed Turks and Mongols. The empty-sleeved riding coat of the early Scythians developed into the kaftan of the Turks. This garment was again open in front and often had long sleeves, which were sometimes left empty. The kaftan was the garment par excellence of the Ottoman Turks. In Iran, this open-fronted gown, which is often kept in place by a sash around the waist, is known as the *qaba*, and it is still worn by Islamic clerics.

Another sartorial dividing line, though less obvious, is the face veil as worn by Muslim women from Central and Southwest Asia. Turkish women, especially from among the Turkmen in modern Turkmenistan but also among the Turkish groups in northwestern Iran (Azerbaijan), prefer a face veil that is wound around the head, covering the mouth and nose (called a *lisam* or *litham*). The same type was also worn in medieval—and, later, Ottoman—Turkey. In Arab lands, however, and also in settled Iran, women tend to wear a face veil that hangs down the forehead, covering the eyes, nose, and mouth. These face veils are generally made of cloth and are sometimes elaborately embroidered and decorated, a feature not found in Turkic face veils.

CENTRAL ASIA

Central Asia includes a number of modern states that arose from the ashes of the former Soviet Union, including Turkmenistan, Uzbekistan, Tajikistan, Kyrgyzstan, and Kazakhstan. The area includes a number of huge deserts in the west toward the Caspian Sea (for instance, the Kara-Kum and the Kyzyl Kum deserts) and also immense mountain ranges that separate the area from modern China (the Karakorum, Pamir, and Tien Shan).

Two main rivers traverse these lands: the Amu Dar'ya (known to the ancients as the Oxus) and the Syr Dar'ya (also known to the Greeks as the Iaxartes). The Amu Dar'ya springs in the Karakorum Mountains along the Afghanistan-China-Pakistan borders. It is one of the longest rivers in Asia, being some fifteen hundred miles (twenty-four hundred kilometers) long. The Syr Dar'ya arises somewhat further north and is about fourteen hundred miles (twenty-two hundred kilometers) long. Both rivers flow in a general northwestern direction and drain into the Aral Sea, which used to be very large but, due to large-scale irrigation projects along the rivers, has shrunk to what may best be described as a large pond, causing an enormous ecological disaster in the area.

The climate in most parts of Central Asia is harsh. It is an extreme continental climate, with hot summers and cold winters. In Ashkhabad, the capital of Turkmenistan, the mean temperature varies between 23 degrees Fahrenheit (minus 5 degrees Celsius) during the winter and 115 degrees Fahrenheit (46 degrees Celsius) in the summer.

Most of the lands are occupied by Turkish-speaking groups such as the Turkmen, the Uzbeks, and the Kyrgyz, but these peoples are relatively new to the area, arriving here from the first millennium C.E. on. The Uzbeks, for instance, arrived in what is, in the early twenty-first century, Uzbekistan only in the early sixteenth century C.E. Before that, all of these lands were occupied by Iranian-speaking groups. In fact, there are still large numbers of people who speak an Iranian language, such as the Tajiks, who speak Tajiki (a dialect of Persian).

The traditional clothing of Central Asia is similar to the clothing introduced by the Scythians to the Iranian Plateau and Anatolia beginning in the early first millennium B.C.E.—trousers, boots, and riding coats. The striped *chapan* (a long coat, usually open down the front, often with empty sleeves), widely worn by the Uzbeks in Uzbekistan and northern Afghanistan in the early twenty-first century and popularized by President Hamid Karzai of Afghanistan after 2001, belongs to the same tradition as the *kandys* (also a long coat with empty sleeves), which was worn by the Scythians depicted at the Persian Achaemenid capital of Persepolis, dating to the late sixth century B.C.E.

In general, Central Asian clothing is based on the use of numerous layers of different types of clothing for insulation purposes, including undertrousers, long shirts, overtrousers, gowns, kaftans, and coats such as the chapan. There was also a marked difference between winter and summer clothing. Summer chapans, for example, were made out of silk or cotton, while winter versions were padded, using raw silk or cotton, and then quilted to keep the padding in place. Those of richer, higher-status families were lined with fur; the type of fur reflected their social position. Much of the fur was imported from Siberia, Russia, and, in some periods, East Europe.

The different types of footwear in Central Asia also reflect the extremes in climate. Summer sandals and shoes of thin leather, sometimes decorated with metal-thread embroidery, contrast with the thick woolen socks and thick leather or felt boots worn in the freezing winter months. The love of decoration remains, however, with rich embroidery carried out on the boots, especially those worn by women.

References and Further Reading

Barber, Elizabeth Wayland. *The Mummies of Urumchi.* New York: W. W. Norton, 1999.

Bier, Carol, ed. *Woven from the Soul. Spun from the Heart. Textile Arts of Safavid and Qajar Iran, 16th–19th Centuries.* Washington, DC: Textile Museum, 1987.

Faroqhi, Suraiya, and Christoph Neumann, eds. *Ottoman Costumes: From Textile to Identity.* Istanbul: Eren, 2004.

Gervers, Veronika. *The Influence of Turkish Textiles and Costume in Eastern Europe.* History of Art Monograph Series, no. 4. Toronto: Royal Ontario Museum, 1982.

Harvey, Janet. *Traditional Textiles of Central Asia.* London: Thames & Hudson, 1997.

Kalter, Johannes. *The Arts and Crafts of Turkestan.* London: Thames & Hudson, 1984.

Scarce, Jennifer. *Women's Costume of the Near and Middle East.* London: Unwin Hyman, 1987.

Stillman, Yedida K. *Arab Dress: A Short History from the Dawn of Islam to Modern Times.* Leiden: Brill, 2000.

Willem Vogelsang

See also Trade, Textiles, and Dress in Central and Southwest Asia; Historical Survey of Textiles and Dress in Turkey; Introduction to the History of Dress on the Iranian Plateau; History of West Turkistan and Its Influence on the Dress of South Central Asia; Trouser Wearing by Horse-Riding Nomads in Central Asia; Face Veils.

History of Dress and Fashion

People have been living in Central and Southwest Asia for many thousands of years. Some groups developed complex social communities based on farming, cooperation, and international trade; other groups relied on hunting and following animals to support their way of life. Throughout the vast area that stretches from the eastern Mediterranean to the deserts of Central Asia, many civilizations have grown, flourished, and then vanished. Some have left many traces, while others are known just from a handful of pottery shards.

Almost since the first people came out of Africa and started to move across the deserts, plains, mountains, and steppes, humans have been using dress not only for warmth and protection but also as a form of communication. A feature of all groups—nomadic, village, or urban—is their use of clothing and accessories to express themselves, their way of life, and their beliefs.

From these thousands of years, considerable information in the form of textiles, items of clothing, and accessories has come down to the early twenty-first century, providing firsthand information about ancient dress. This information is supported by secondary evidence in the form of visual records: paintings, reliefs, mosaics, depictions on walls and pottery, and written descriptions. The more advanced or bureaucratic groups left records about the cost of flax and wool, the different types, how much could be bought, taxes due, and what was left to various heirs following someone's death.

By using all of these sources, plus others, it is possible to recreate features of dress from past civilizations in Central and Southwest Asia. But it should be stressed that the information is patchy in some areas where surviving evidence is poor, to say the least. What is certain, however, is that, throughout all of this time, dress never stopped developing and changing to meet current demands and needs. It depends on what is currently available, but

it is also capable of diversifying as new ethnic groups, ideas, and inventions come along. In an area as vast as Central and Southwest Asia, therefore, it is not surprising that the history of dress is complex—and made even more so by the added factors of language, economics, religion, and politics.

THE MAIN ETHNIC GROUPS

Central and Southwest Asia covers a huge area of land, from Turkey in the west to Kazakhstan and Kyrgyzstan in the east. It includes mountains, valleys, deserts, and oases. The climate and weather can range from very cold at night to extremely hot in the day, with heavy snowfall in winter, subtropical rainstorms and sandstorms in the warmer months, plus many variations in between. Although the rainfall is high in some areas—notably in northern Iran around the Caspian Sea—most of the region receives water only via various major rivers and lakes; other parts have virtually no water at all.

Many different cultural and ethnic groups live in the region. Many of these can be broadly grouped into three major entities—Turks, Iranians, and the Semitic groups (Arabs)—but this distinction is mainly based on linguistic and historical criteria. There are numerous minority groups that do not belong to any of the three, such as the Armenians in the southern Caucasus.

The Iranian peoples originated in Central Asia, and they settled all across the Iranian Plateau (named after the newcomers) from the second millennium B.C.E. on. Iranian ethnic groups and cultures can be found in what is, in the early twenty-first century, Iran, as well as surrounding regions, such as the areas that are part of eastern Turkey, Afghanistan, and Tajikistan in the early twenty-first century. They include, for instance, the Kurds along the Iran-Iraq-Turkey borders; the Baluchi in southeastern Iran; and the Pashtun in Afghanistan/Pakistan.

Evidence for the dress of these early Iranian groups comes from various sources, including metal objects such as pins, belts, and weaponry, notably those from Luristan (Iran, second and first millennia B.C.E.); the gold treasure from the Oxus (Amu Dar'ya), which dates from the Achaemenid period (550–330 B.C.E.); and from Tillya Tepe (Afghanistan). Monumental reliefs such as those at Behistun and Naqsh-i-Rustam and the palace complex at Persepolis (from around 515 until around 340 B.C.E.) in southern Iran also provide information about men's dress. Further details come from wall paintings, statues, and depictions on metal plaques and plates, coins, and pottery.

By the early first millennium C.E., there are written records from both Persian and Western sources, as well as occasional Chinese references, regarding the trade in textiles and clothing along the Silk Road. It is from the Sassanian period (226–651 C.E.) and later that textiles and fragments of clothing survive. These come from various sites both in Iran and outside, notably in Egypt, where the dry conditions have preserved thousands of textiles. These Sassanian textiles have added invaluable information about the nature of Iranian textile technology as well as the dress forms used.

The second group is the Turkic peoples, who are also of Central Asian origin. From their homelands they moved west and southwest, and some of them, by the early second millennium C.E., reached what subsequently came to be called Turkey. The Turks

Patterned woven polychrome silk, possibly from Bukhara, Uzbekistan, 800–1000. The face-to-face lions in circles and running animals below show the influence of Sassanian art and designs of textiles from Southwest Asia. © Victoria and Albert Museum, London. www.vam.ac.uk

include many subgroups, such as the Azerbaijani in northwestern Iran, the Kazakhs in Central Asia, the Turkmen in and around modern Turkmenistan, and the Uzbeks.

Before the advent of the Turks in what is, in the early twenty-first century, called Turkey, and what used to be called Anatolia, there were already some flourishing civilizations in the area. Some of the earliest known textiles come from this part of the world, notably those from Çatal Hüyük (fifth millennium B.C.E.) and Alishar (late fourth millennium B.C.E.). Although these fragments provide data about the textile technology of the period, they are mostly very small and give few details about contemporary dress.

Because of the dry conditions in Central Asia—the homeland of the Turks and, before that, the Iranians—considerably more evidence in the form of textiles and dress has survived from this region. These may belong to ancient Turks but more likely to Iranian-speaking groups that lived in the region before being pushed out by the Turkic-speaking groups, toward the area that makes up Iran in the early twenty-first century. Some of the clearest evidence comes from Urumchi, in northwestern China, which dates to about 1000 B.C.E. These finds belong to a rich conglomerate of finds from northwestern China and neighboring Kazakhstan, which relate to the mainly nomadic cultures of Central Asia. The textiles include silks, woolens, and hemp garments.

Although of a later date, there also have been finds at Pazyryk in the Altai Mountains in Siberian Russia, near the border with Kazakhstan. The burials from this site date to about 500 B.C.E. and include a wide range of textiles from China, Central Asia, and Persia. The men's garments from Pazyryk are similar to those worn at Urumchi: trousers and tunics; this resemblance provides insight into the extent of the ancient trade in textiles and how similar some of these nomadic cultures were.

The third main group is the Arabs, who for millennia have occupied the Arabian Peninsula and later, from the early first millennium C.E., spread across the northern Arabian Desert and the Levant. Following the advent and diffusion of Islam in the seventh century C.E., Arab culture spread as far as Morocco, Egypt, the Levant, Syria, and Iraq. As the official language of Islam, Arabic was disseminated along with the new religion. The Arabic language belongs to the Semitic language family, which includes Hebrew and Aramaic, indicating the close historical association between Arab and Jewish groups within the region; this is an important point given the political and religious disputes and wars that have plagued the region over the centuries and that continue into the early twenty-first century.

There is very little evidence about the dress of the early Semitic groups. One of the best sources with respect to Jewish dress comes from biblical references and finds from sites relating to biblical events. There are finds of early textiles from various excavations, such as Nahal Hemar (around 6500 B.C.E.), the Cave of Treasures at Nahal Mishmar (fourth millennium B.C.E.), and the slightly later site of Jericho. But these finds are few and far between; although details about textile technology can be gained from them, they provide little information about dress. This situation is further complicated by the Jewish tradition of not depicting humans, which means that there are very few illustrations of ancient Jewish dress. The finds from Massada, dating to the first century C.E., are a major exception and provide fascinating insight into the textiles, textures, and colors worn by Jewish men and women during this period.

There is even less information about the early dress of the Arabs. In general, because of the climatic and soil conditions in many Arab lands, few ancient textiles or clothing items have survived, and these tend to be small fragments. Some of the main finds come from the site of Terqa, on the west bank of the Euphrates River, which date to around 1600 B.C.E.

Numerous written references to textiles exist, notably from old Assyrian records that have survived in the form of clay tablets. Many of these refer to the raising of sheep and the production of woolen cloth and garments. However, relating the written texts to actual textiles or garments—or even depictions of garments—has proven very difficult. Classical Western literature contains brief references to ancient Arab dress, notably in the work of the Greek historian Herodotus (fifth century B.C.E.), and there are a few depictions of Arabs on reliefs. The best examples depict the siege of the ancient city of Lachish in the kingdom of Judah (Israel in the twenty-first century); these date to around 701 B.C.E. and are held in the British Museum in London.

By the early first millennium C.E., there are written records from both Arab and Western sources, but references to textiles and dress tend to be incidental. It is only with the advent of Arab historians and travelers from the ninth century on that more detailed information becomes available. Evidence concerning the appearance of medieval Arab textiles and dress comes from Egyptian archaeological sites, where the dry conditions have preserved thousands of examples. Some of the most important sites for textiles are Fustat (Cairo), Gebel Adda (southern Egypt), and Quseir al-Qadim (Red Sea coast).

THE ROLE OF ISLAM

Religious life in Central and Southwest Asia in the early first millennium C.E. was highly diverse. There were Buddhists, Christians (Orthodox, Catholic, Nestorians), Hindus, Jews, Zoroastrians, and adherents of other faiths. This situation changed dramatically in the early seventh century, when a new religion was preached by the Prophet Mohammed. Starting from the Arabian Peninsula and the towns of Mecca and Medina, the new religion of Islam quickly spread across many parts of Central and Southwest Asia. Islam and Arab culture became the dominant forces in the region, and other religions and their followers were soon in the minority.

Whereas in modern Western society state and religion are officially separated, they are often regarded as one and the same in the Islamic world. Consequently, religion tends to play a far greater role in daily life, including in the dress of men and women. The main religious text of Islam is the Qur'an (literally, "the recitation"). It is regarded as presenting divine guidance and the final revelation of God's intentions for humankind. It was revealed to the Prophet Mohammed by the angel Jibril (Gabriel) over a period of some twenty-three years. Of great importance furthermore are the hadiths ("narratives"), which include the oral traditions that describe the words and deeds of the Prophet and his immediate successors. The hadiths are accepted by all the traditional schools of Islamic jurisprudence as providing the basic prescription for the Muslim way of life.

The Qur'an and the hadiths contain many references to daily life and, in particular, dress. Men, for example, should avoid wearing or using any of seven materials or objects: silver vessels, gold rings, garments of *harir* (silk), *dibaj* (brocade), *qassi* (a striped fabric from Egypt containing silk), *istabraq* (satin), and *mayathir humr* (tanned hides). However, exceptions are made for some people with skin diseases. Over time, however, other traditions emerged that allowed men to wear silk and other costly materials. But the general feeling that men should not wear golden ornaments remains, and many men still prefer to wear silver rings. Women, on the contrary, were allowed to wear whatever material they wanted.

The Qur'an states that modesty in dress applies to both men and women. Sura 24 (Light), verses 30–33, first describes what men should wear and then women:

> Say to the believers, that they cast down their eyes and guard their private parts; that is purer for them. God is aware of the things they work. And say to the believing women, that they cast down their eyes and guard their private parts, and reveal not their adornment save such as is outward, and let them cast their veils over their bosoms, and not reveal their adornment save to their husbands, or their fathers … , nor let them stamp their feet, so that their hidden ornament may be known.

The "private parts" mentioned in these verses refer to the genitalia, but the term was soon used to indicate the area from the waist to the knees. It was also regarded as suitable for both men and women to cover their heads. The concept of female modesty was also applied to the hair and neck, since these areas of the female body are seen as erogenous zones throughout this part of the world.

A number of the Islamic dress codes are placed under the general heading of *fitrah*. This essentially tells how a Muslim should care for his or her body with regard to appearance, grooming, and modesty. Over time, official laws were developed, called sumptuary laws, which further prescribe the range of materials and garments to be worn (especially in public places) and present the

A fragment of carpet depicting a mounted warrior wearing trousers and a tunic, from the Pazyryk Burial Mounds, Altai Mountains, Russia, fifth to fourth century B.C.E. Items excavated from the burial mounds include a wide range of textiles from China, Central Asia, and Persia and give an insight into the extent of the ancient trade in textiles. Hermitage, St. Petersburg, Russia/The Bridgeman Art Library.

basic elements of the fitrah, such as removal of body hair, length of fingernails, and the use of perfumes. There are also laws of differentiation, which specify who is a Muslim and who is not and what they should wear to indicate their difference. Both of these types of laws are still applied in various Islamic countries, as can be seen in Iran and Saudi Arabia.

THE OTTOMAN EMPIRE

After Turkish settlers from Central Asia arrived in what used to be called Anatolia, they opposed the Eastern Roman, or Byzantine, Empire, leading in 1453 C.E. to the capture of the city of Constantinople, which was soon renamed Istanbul. At that time, the Turks were led by a new dynasty, that of the Ottomans. The Ottoman Empire would soon dominate most of Southwest Asia, and it twice laid siege to the mid-European town of Vienna. The Ottoman Empire would last to the early twentieth century, and its culture and customs—including dress traditions—deeply influenced the lands under Ottoman control.

Images of early, pre-Muslim Turks from Central Asia show elaborate dress that included coats and trousers and also very elaborate headgear, a feature of Ottoman court dress in the years to come. Dress played an important role in the complex bureaucracy of the Ottomans. The Ottomans, however, also adopted many aspects of Byzantine court dress that had been popular in the vanquished empire of Constantinople. They continued the production and use of silk textiles, and their dresses included many forms of Byzantine decoration in addition to Turkish motifs. They also used elaborate embroidery to ornament their court dress, including their veils, sashes, napkins, and garments. Jewelry included necklaces, earrings, and bracelets and also complicated pieces that were designed to be worn in headdresses by both men and women. For men, these pieces included plumed crests (sorguç) with precious gems. The sorguç in the dress of the sultan was basically the equivalent of a royal crown, which was worn with a large and elaborate turban reserved for this office.

Many Turks from the Ottoman Empire spent most of their lives in an urban environment. Their dress and other aspects of their culture were, however, based on their nomadic heritage. At the same time, they borrowed from the previous rulers of the country and from the specific place where they were living. Urban Ottoman dress thus developed in a different way than rural clothing, mainly because of the wide availability of more costly materials. Dress prescribed for local officials and the military also affected the appearance of urban dress. All this applied not only to the Turkish ruling class but also to others, including non-Muslim subjects.

There were official distinctions between the various communities of the empire. These regulations applied to specific materials and colors of footwear, garments, and headgear. Dress identified the wearer as the holder of specific rights, privileges, and responsibilities. These distinctions continued to be honored for many centuries. However, by the eighteenth and nineteenth centuries, these sumptuary regulations became less effective, as the decline of the Ottoman economy led to a breakdown of regulated society. Some urban minorities adopted forms of dress that officially were reserved for other groups, and some adopted European features. Nonetheless, modern Turkish society still harbors the belief that society can be regulated by managing dress, a belief that led to some serious conflicts over dress regulations in the late twentieth century.

THE ROLE OF INTERNATIONAL TRADE IN CENTRAL AND SOUTHWEST ASIAN DRESS

The vast region from Central Asia to the eastern Mediterranean has seen many changes. For thousands of years, vast empires stretched across the region: The Romans, the Persians (notably the Sassanian dynasty), the early Islamic empires, the vast Mongolian realm conquered by Genghis Khan and his successors, the Ottomans, and many others brought with them new ideas of what could and could not be worn by various groups in society. The eastern Mediterranean was a crossroads not only for trade but also for religious ideas. Jerusalem, the holiest city for Jews and Christians, also became a holy city within Islam in the seventh century C.E. Travelers from the West were moving around the eastern Mediterranean from the tenth century on, especially pilgrims going to Jerusalem. Many wrote about their experiences and what they saw.

The eastern Mediterranean was the focus of considerable international interest from the eleventh century on as a result of the religious Crusades. One consequence of these wars was that ideas moved from the East to the West and vice versa. The changes in women's clothing—especially in northern Europe, with its increased use of head veils in the later medieval period—can be seen as one example.

Throughout all these centuries, Central and Southwest Asia was located along an ancient trading system known as the Silk Road. It stretched from China westward, via Central Asia, to the Mediterranean region and the rest of Europe. The contacts established along this route led to the spread of many different groups and cultural features. The Silk Road also facilitated the transport of a wide range of material products, notably in the form of wood, pottery, glass, precious and semiprecious stones, textiles, furs, and clothing. However, the Silk Road not only made it possible for people to travel across wide distances and transport precious products but also helped the diffusion of various skills and technologies. This led to the further development of a rich and varied textile industry throughout Central and Southwest Asia.

Information about the range of textiles and garments traded along the Silk Road and other trade channels can be found in a variety of historical sources, including the *Periplus of the Erythrean Sea*, a sea manual from the first century C.E. It describes, for example, how cotton cloth of the best "broad sort" and coarser cotton were produced in Gujarat and exported to East Africa from Barygaza (near modern Vadodara, Gujarat), together with muslins and girdles and a third kind of coarse "mallow-colored" cotton cloth. Similar textiles were sent to Arabia from Barygaza and then on to Egypt. Examples of Indian cottons from the Roman period have been found at various excavations in Egypt, notably Berenica and Quseir al-Qadim, which testifies to the extent of this ancient trade in textiles.

During the medieval period, information about the Silk Road can be found in various travelogues, such as Marco Polo's *Travels* from the thirteenth century and the accounts of the Maghrebi (Moroccan) Arab, Ibn Battuta (1304–1368/1369), who traveled throughout the Arab world and India. Information can also be found in the record books of various medieval European courts, in which different types of cloth from Central Asia and further east are noted, including a form of gold cloth that was a prestige item, especially for the English. Clearly, the concept of globalization is not new.

Woven Ottoman silk textile, Bursa, Turkey, 1550–1600. The cloth is faced "from end to end" with wefts of expensive silver thread, indicating that it is a *seraser* textile, and it has a pattern of roundels worked in red and green. The Silk Road helped to disseminate various cloth-making skills, resulting in the development of a rich and varied textile industry throughout Central and Southwest Asia. © Victoria and Albert Museum, London. www.vam.ac.uk

Similarly, the so-called process of Westernization, a west-to-east movement of ideas usually associated with the twentieth century, has far earlier antecedents. A motivating factor in the early movement was not religion but trade. European merchants were moving eastward in search of trade goods and trading partners, first into the eastern Mediterranean and the Ottoman world and then on to the areas that, in the twenty-first century, make up Iraq and Iran. Depictions of northern Europeans in their strange, exotic clothing can be found from the late sixteenth century in manuscripts from Iran. In the seventeenth century, elements of European dress, especially large men's hats, became popular accessories for members of the Persian Safavid court. These were exotic items that could show off one's knowledge of the world—exactly the same process that was taking place in Europe with the increase in Orientalism, with wealthy Europeans wearing exotic Turkish and Persian dress.

The trade in textiles and items of dress became an increasingly important element in international trade from the seventeenth century on. Vast quantities of Southwest Asian textiles were imported into Europe by the British East India Company and the Dutch East India Company. Similarly, northern European textiles, especially wool, were sold to the Ottomans. A similar attempt to sell woolens to India was not as successful for climatic reasons.

It was the advent of mass transportation in the nineteenth century, however, that brought significant changes. During the previous centuries, foot, animal, and sail power had been the dominant forms of transportation, and there was a natural limit to the amount of goods that could be transported and where. However, the technological changes in the nineteenth century—notably the advent of steam trains, then steam-powered ships, and, in the twentieth century, airplanes—meant that reaching what had been remote areas of the world became much easier. The speed and scale of change upset long-standing trading patterns and, as a result, changed the kinds of textiles and related items that could or could not be obtained locally. This had

consequences with respect to what was worn and the appearance of dress.

It should also be remembered that the development of mass transportation in the form of buses, cars, and motorbikes has also had a great effect on dress throughout the world, not just in Central and Southwest Asia. Multilayered garments, such as the voluminous skirts worn by Qashqa'i nomadic women in Iran as an expression of their wealth, are suitable for displaying on the back of horses and camels, but they are not easy to manipulate in a small car. Dress forms that can adapt to modern life survive; those that cannot disappear or remain only for high days and holidays.

THE INDUSTRIAL REVOLUTION AND LATER

Another significant change came in the eighteenth and nineteenth centuries with the move from hand looms to steam-powered machine looms: the process of industrialization. The increase in cheap cotton and woolen textiles being produced in Europe, especially Britain, meant that long-established trading patterns were interrupted and in many places destroyed.

Another major change in the nature of dress throughout Central and Southwest Asia was the advent of artificial and, later, synthetic fibers from the mid-nineteenth century on. These were developed in Europe and the United States and were to replace much of the natural-fiber industry—sheep wool, camel hair, linen, cotton, silk, and so forth. Although natural fibers are regarded as sustainable and authentic, they are often much more difficult to spin, dye, weave, and keep clean. They are also usually much more expensive. It is not surprising, therefore, that many people prefer cloth made from synthetic yarns.

Commercialization has always been present, but it is the scale of global business that has changed dramatically from the nineteenth to the early twenty-first century. In the nineteenth century, goods made in Britain, France, and Russia caused considerable commercial problems in Central and Southwest Asia, because machine-produced items were much cheaper and quicker to produce than handmade pieces. In the twentieth century, the role of European countries was taken over by Asian countries such as China, Korea, Japan, and Taiwan. In many countries, local production had to be stimulated by governments and special groups in order to survive. In some cases, this gave an artificial appearance of survival, which was suitable for the tourist trade.

TOURISM AND THE MEDIA

An effect of the increase in transportation was the growth of international tourism. The role of tourism in preserving, creating, and destroying dress forms in Central and Southwest Asia in the late nineteenth and twentieth centuries should not be underestimated. Nor should it be thought, however, that tourism is a question of Westerners visiting places; it was a two-way process, and there are many records of Arabs, Persians, and Turks traveling to Europe and later the United States not just for trade reasons but also for pleasure. In doing so, they created an exchange in dress ideas.

Another aspect of tourism that should be considered is that it does not have to be international. There have always been local tourists, such as pilgrims going from one shrine to another and those people who became wealthier due to trade and oil and were curious about their own culture, country, or history and wanted to see more. One result of tourism was that souvenirs were made and bought by various groups as typical products until some people were no longer sure what was authentic and what had been locally assimilated to please the tourists.

The communication revolution of the twentieth century has also had a profound effect, not only on the appearance of dress in Central and Southwest Asia but also on the rate of change. The development of radio for the masses meant that people were more aware of what was happening, especially in the world of politics; but the arrival of photographs, illustrated journals, and, later, cinema and films meant they were visually aware of the wider world, and people started to emulate the dress of the wealthy and powerful. This process increased with the advent of mass television in the second half of the twentieth century, when visual images of what people were wearing in different parts of the world became more readily available. Television also led to strange misunderstandings. There were women in Yemen who veiled themselves when confronted with a man on the television. At first, they did not distinguish between a real man and the image of a man. Men were men, and a woman had to be veiled in their presence.

The advent of the World Wide Web and satellite communication has also led to profound changes in many remote regions, where it is becoming more and more common to find satellite dishes attached to roofs. Seclusion, separation, and distance are no longer important factors when people can react to events on the other side of the world literally in seconds. It also means that many people want what they see on the screen; they want to be modern, which, in many cases, means to be dressed in Western-style clothing.

The other side of the communication coin is that many governments have banned certain television programs, and even the owning of satellite dishes, to prevent people from seeing unsuitable images and copying dress forms. When the film *Titanic* appeared in 1997, for example, many young men in Afghanistan started to copy the hairstyle of the hero, Jack Dawson (played by Leonardo DiCaprio). Soon afterward, the Afghan (Taliban) government banned the watching of the film and punished men who wore *Titanic*-inspired hairstyles as being un-Islamic.

POLITICS, WESTERNIZATION, AND DRESS

In the early twentieth century, some leaders in Turkey, Iran, and Afghanistan tried to enforce the wearing of Western-style dress. In Turkey, for example, Mustafa Kemal Atatürk (1881–1938), one of the main leaders of the Turkish Revolution and later president of Turkey, introduced new laws concerning what men and, to a lesser extent, women had to wear when in public during the 1920s and 1930s. The Iranian king, Reza Shah Pahlavi (r. 1925–1941), also imposed a series of social changes. In 1928, he passed new laws that related to commercial, civil, family, and penal matters. In doing so, he moved away from the traditional sharia (Islamic law) and introduced legislation that was more in line with the European legal system. It included the prescription that state officials, including judges, should wear secular dress, differentiating them from the outfit of the 'ulama (Islamic clergy). In general, and officially, Reza Shah wanted to unite all the people of Iran and to create a feeling among all his subjects that they belonged to one state, whether they were Kurds, Qashqa'i, Baluchi, Turkmen, or members of another group. As noted by U.S. writer Donald Wilber, the shah was "determined to have all Iranians wearing the same clothes, since when the Shirazis, Tabrizis, and all others no longer wear different costumes there will be no reason for difference among them."

Another of the shah's objectives was to modernize the country and bring it up to the perceived level of the West. There was some sense of inferiority in his measures, as he wanted to make the Iranians "as good" as the Europeans. In 1936, he abolished the wearing of veils of any kind. This led to great unrest in the country. The official ban did not last long, because there was too much opposition.

There was a comparable development in Afghanistan. King Amanullah (r. 1919–1929) in 1928 wanted the women of Afghanistan to abandon purdah (seclusion; literally, "curtain"), including the veil, and to take a more prominent position in society. However, when Amanullah was removed in 1929, it was officially proclaimed that women were to return to purdah and the wearing of the *chadari* (an all-enveloping outer covering for women, better known in the West as the burqa).

The effects of all the attempts at modernization are still felt in the early twenty-first century. In Turkey, there is a continuing struggle concerning whether women should be allowed to wear head scarves in public buildings. In revolutionary Iran after 1979, women were again forced to wear "Islamic" clothing. In Afghanistan under the Taliban, men and women had to wear what the leaders regarded as Islamically correct clothing, including the chadari for women.

At the end of the twentieth century, there was a question about whether politicians attending high-profile international conferences—especially meetings of the Organization of Petroleum Exporting Countries (OPEC) and those relating to peace in the region—should dress in Western-style suits or whether they should stress their regional and cultural origins by wearing local clothing. Some Arab groups from the eastern Mediterranean chose to wear Western-style garments because this was what was

ETIQUETTE DEPOSÉE-A. VOLPINI & FILS.

Made in Czechoslovakia

Two fez box labels for the red cloth section of a fez, early twentieth century. Made in Czechoslovakia and Hungary, fez boxes included labels with images that corresponded to their intended destinations. Those sent to Istanbul often had stylized and Orientalized images of Turks on them, while those for Arab lands featured European interpretations of Arab dress. Based on actual garments, the label on the right depicts an Ottoman, while the label on the left depicts an "Arab" wearing a fantastical mixture of Ottoman, Indian, and Arab dress. Textile Research Centre, Leiden.

normal for their communities. Others, including Arabs from Saudi Arabia and the Gulf states, deliberately came in flowing gowns and distinctive headdresses to emphasize their Arab identity.

In some Gulf states, notably Oman, it became law, rather than a choice, that a male Omani citizen had to wear Omani dress when at work or on government business. This was done to stress men's shared Omani identity. One consequence, however, was that it soon became clear who was a native Omani and who was an expatriate, especially those from the Philippines, India,

and Pakistan, working in Oman. This law was seen by some as a form of clothing discrimination, while others saw it as a means of preserving Omani culture and identity.

POLITICAL DRESS: A CHANGE OF MEANINGS

There is a tendency to think that the symbolic meaning of garments remains static or is very slow to change. Yet some garments have changed their symbolic meaning several times over a relatively short period of time. A good example is the checked head covering worn by Arab men, called a *keffiyeh*. Keffiyehs are woven from cotton (cheap), cotton and wool (medium price), or silk (expensive) in black-and-white or red-and-white checks. It is believed that they originated in the winter head coverings worn by farmers in Syria and Jordan in the early twentieth century, as a very practical garment that protected the wearer from heat and dust. This type of headgear was used as part of the uniform of various military and police groups in the region, such as the Trans Jordan Frontier Force, later the Jordanian army.

During the twentieth century, the keffiyeh, in various forms, became generally accepted as suitable for Arab men to wear and could be found throughout the Arab world. A change in how it was perceived came after 1948, when Palestinian groups adopted it as a symbol of their revolt and rebellion against the Israelis. Yasir Arafat (1929–2004), the Palestinian leader, wore the keffiyeh on a regular basis, both as a head covering and around his neck. At some point, he started to fold the keffiyeh into an elongated triangular shape that was said to represent the country of Palestine. He is also known to have given people gifts of keffiyehs: woven silk versions for important guests and woven cotton versions for others.

Another Palestinian figure who became associated with the keffiyeh is Leila Khaled, a member of the militant Popular Front for the Liberation of Palestine (PFLP), who wore the keffiyeh in the style of a Muslim woman's head scarf—wrapped around the neck and head, thus giving a man's garment a female twist but at the same time stressing her equal position within a predominantly male organization.

The color of the keffiyeh became loosely associated with various Palestinian factions and parties, so that black-and-white keffiyehs were associated with Fatah, while red-and-white ones were linked to Hamas, who were connected with the PFLP and were more left-wing and militant in nature. In the 1970s, the keffiyeh became associated with Western left-wing politics. In the 1980s and 1990s, however, the political role of the keffiyeh became less prominent in the West, especially after it was adopted by British troops fighting in the Gulf Wars; here it was called a *shamagh*. In the early twenty-first century, tan-colored shamaghs are issued to British soldiers deployed in desert conditions overseas.

In the early twenty-first century, the keffiyeh, much to the disgust of some, was adapted by various Western fashion designers as a retro design item. It was worn by fashion icons such as David Beckham and Justin Timberlake and featured in the 2007 autumn and winter collection of the Balenciaga Fashion House. Keffiyehs became widely available but this time as a fashion statement. It would appear, however, that few of the younger wearers, both men and women, understood or were even interested in the political history of the garment.

THE CONCEPT OF NATIONAL DRESS

In 1936, a competition for the design of an Israeli national dress took place at the Orient Fair in Tel Aviv. The winning design, by Pennina Riva, an Israeli fashion designer, combined Oriental and Western clothing with biblical elements. There was a heated discussion in the press at the time about whether such attempts to create a dress suitable for the Jewish nation's way of life were appropriate or whether such a design would indicate a contrived

culture and nation. This period also saw the adaptation of simple utilitarian khaki work clothes, which became very popular after World War II (1939–1945). The addition of sandals, plus the *tembel* ("dummy") hat, created the trademark of the typical Israeli figure, a form of national dress that had developed naturally.

Another example of the creation of a form of national dress can be seen in the Palestinian six-branch dress, which is widely viewed as one of the traditional dresses of Palestinian women, when in fact it dates to the 1960s. It is named after the six vertical bands of embroidery that run from the waist to the hem of the dress. Many of the designs on this type of dress are derived from European pattern books, especially those produced by the French firm Dollfus, Mieg et Cie. This company also manufactured the embroidery threads used to decorate the dress. These garments were originally intended for sale to Western markets, but they became popular with local and international Arab communities. In the early 1980s, another form of dress developed called a *shawal*. It was made from pre-embroidered linen that was sewn onto the dress. It was often sold with a fringed shawl with similar embroidery,

Leila Khaled, member of the militant Popular Front for the Liberation of Palestine (PFLP), Palestine, 1970. Khaled gave the male *keffiyeh* a female twist by wearing it in the style of a Muslim woman's head scarf, which indicated her equal position within the predominantly male organization. AFP/Getty Images.

thus creating a set. They were originally designed for the Western market but again became popular with Arab women in the whole region. They have become a Palestinian fashion statement.

A different example, but based on economic reasons, can be found in the Central Asian state of Uzbekistan. During the nineteenth and early twentieth centuries, Uzbekistan was famous for the production of ikat textiles (in which the warp or weft threads are resist dyed—in a manner similar to tie-dye—and then woven to create a pattern) for dresses and coats. During the early Communist period, beginning in the 1920s, people were forbidden to wear ikats. However, in the 1970s, as part of developing a national identity and to boost the economy, women were encouraged to wear dresses made of factory-produced ikats in synthetic silks. This was done both to stimulate the local production of these textiles and to make a statement that the people of the region were still using an ancient form—it was felt that by continuing to use such a well-known type of cloth for clothing, they could confirm and strengthen their historical existence and position in the region.

Ironically, following the fall of Communism in the 1990s, ikat production and sales have increased dramatically. This seems to have occurred because many ikats are for sale via the Internet as traditional forms from this region. Some of these ikats are sold at considerable prices, even though many are factory made, of synthetic yarns, rather than made in weaving ateliers, out of silk (and therefore are not "genuine").

THE ROLE OF COMMUNISM, CAPITALISM, AND ISLAMIC FUNDAMENTALISM

Around 1920, Russian and Communist revolutionaries took over various Central Asian regions. During the next two decades, they created five Soviet republics: Kazakhstan, Kyrgyzstan, Tajikistan, Turkmenistan, and Uzbekistan. The new rulers soon started to discourage the wearing of regional dress, including kaftans, turbans, face veils, and other related garments. Soon they were banned altogether. Instead, people had to wear "Soviet-style" Western clothing. Some versions of local dress, however, survived, such as the ikat dresses of Uzbek women. Nonetheless, most of the ikat clothes that used to decorate the ancient cities of Samarkand and Bukhara vanished.

Since the fall of the Soviet regime in 1991, these countries have been trying to reintroduce ikat garments for men and women as part of a policy of rebuilding national pride and culture; but this movement is also motivated by economics and the possibility of selling these garments, especially via the Internet, on the international markets.

When the Soviet empire collapsed in the early 1990s, Islamic groups soon tried to fill the vacuum, and many women were forced to wear Islamically correct clothing. But this process of Islamification is not limited to Central Asia. It can be seen throughout the Islamic world. Some groups choose more modesty in dress, especially among women. The most extreme of these is the Taliban in Afghanistan and its ideas of correct Islamic dress. Other groups have taken to wearing Saudi-style clothing, white for men and black for women. Based on the prestige of the country and its wealth, this can be seen in virtually every country of the world where there are Muslim communities.

An interesting side effect of this movement can be seen in Turkey, where a new mass-fashion style has emerged. In the 1980s,

religious women dressed the same as their neighbors but with the addition of a scarf and more modest garments. By the 1990s, a new fashion industry aimed at religious women began to emerge. This included garments—from pantsuits to wedding dresses and swimwear—that were specifically designed for religious modesty but also for fashionable flair. It also included new forms of hijab headgear, designed to match the fashionable garments. Pan-Islamic dress for women has also developed, which includes the use of a wimple-like garment called a *khimar*—sometimes called a chador if it is very long—with a tight head cloth (*mandil*) that covers the hair.

THE RISE OF CENTRAL AND SOUTHWEST ASIAN FASHION DESIGNERS

Some fashion designers have opted to follow purely Western styles of garments and create new designs based on such trends. Other designers with cultural connections to this vast region have decided to create contemporary looks based on traditional and regional textiles and fashion styles. Some, such as Rıfat Özbek, Dice Kayek, and Hussein Chalayan, use a mixture of Turkish and Western cuts and textiles. The Omani fashion designer Nawal bint Hamed bin Hamid AlHooti, however, chooses to keep the traditional cut of Omani dress, but she changes the range of materials, the textures, and the color combinations. In general, clothing in Oman has gone from being based on two or more colors to being monochrome, with a dress, trousers, and head covering in one color, a change influenced by AlHooti. But it is still regarded by Omani women as traditional.

Some of these fashion designers have experienced problems with regard to whether their creations are acceptable in an Islamic world. It has been argued that the garments are for indoor wear and, therefore, it does not matter; it has also been argued that this region is not occupied only by Muslims, so Islamic values should not be forced on Christian, Druze, Jewish, and other groups. There is also the question of what is Islamically correct, because cultural groups may differ in their ideas of what is and is not acceptable: What is worn by Muslim women in Lebanon is totally different from what is worn by women in Yemen or in Afghanistan. Who is correct? It is all a question of personal interpretation.

References and Further Reading

Atabaki, Touraj, and Erik J. Zürcher, eds. *Men of Order: Authoritarian Modernization under Atatürk and Reza Shah.* London: I.B. Tauris, 2004.

Barber, E.J.W. *The Mummies of Ürümchi.* New York: W.W. Norton, 1999.

Barber, Elisabeth. *Prehistoric Textiles: The Development of Cloth in the Neolithic and Bronze Ages.* Princeton, NJ: Princeton University Press, 1991.

Barker, Patricia L. *Islamic Textiles.* London: British Museum Press, 1995.

British Library. *Database of the International Dunhuang Project: The Silk Road Online.* http://idp.bl.uk/ (accessed 7 January 2009).

Coleridge, Nicholas. "The Islamic Factor." In *The Fashion Reader*, edited by Linda Welters and Abby Lillethun, 364–368. New York: Berg, 2007.

Eicher, Joanne B., and Barbara Sumberg. "World Fashion, Ethnic, and National Dress." In *Dress and Ethnicity*, edited by Joanne B. Eicher, 295–306. Oxford: Berg, 1995.

Fitz Gibbon, Katherine, and Andrew Hale. *Ikat: Splendid Silks of Central Asia*. London: Laurence King Publishing with Alan Marcuson, 1999.

Good, Irene. "Bronze Age Cloth and Clothing of the Tarim Basin: The Chärchän Evidence." In *The Bronze Age and Early Iron Age Peoples of Eastern Central Asia*, edited by V. H. Mair, 656–658. Philadelphia: University of Pennsylvania Museum of Archaeology, 1998.

Gordon, Stewart. *Robes of Honour. Khil'at in Pre-Colonial and Colonial India*. New Delhi: Oxford University Press, 2003.

Harvey, Janet. *Traditional Textiles of Central Asia*. London: Thames & Hudson, 1997.

Jacoby, David. "Silk Economies and Cross-Cultural Interaction: Byzantium, the Muslim World, and the Christina West." *Dumbarton Oaks Papers* 58 (2004): 197–240.

Keddy, Nikki R. *Modern Iran: Roots and Results of Revolution*. New Haven, CT: Yale University Press, 2003.

Quataert, Donald. *The Ottoman Empire: 1700–1922*. Cambridge, UK: Cambridge University Press, 2005.

Rubinson, Karen S. "The Textiles from Pazyryk: A Study in the Transfer and Transformation of Artistic Motifs." *Expedition* 32, no. 1 (1990): 49–61.

Stillman, Yedida Kalfon. *Arab Dress: A Short History from the Dawn of Islam to Modern Times*. Leiden: Brill, 2000.

Swedenburg, Ted. "Seeing Double: Palestinian/American Histories of the Kufiya." *Michigan Quarterly Review* 31, no. 4 (1992): 557–577.

Warmington, E. H. *The Commerce between the Roman Empire and India*. London: Curzon Press, 1974.

Wilber, Donald Newton. *Riza Shah Pahlavi: The Resurrection and Reconstruction of Iran*. Hicksville, NY: Exposition-University Book, 1975.

Wood, Frances. *The Silk Road: Two Thousand Years in the Heart of Asia*. Berkeley: University of California Press, 2002.

Willem Vogelsang

Pre-Islamic Dress Codes in the Eastern Mediterranean and Southwest Asia

- Assyrian Dress
- Persian Dress
- Post-Hellenistic, Parthian, and Sassanian Dress
- Pre-Islamic Dress in the Eastern Mediterranean

In pre-Islamic Southwest Asia, dress was an important indicator of status, providing a portable method for expressing wealth, skill, and rank, as well as affiliations and individuality, all factors that contribute to social status. Ancient Southwest Asian dress was complex and loaded with symbolism, such as color codification. Decoration, such as a border, expressed information about different types of status through its width and position on a garment. Many garments, for example, were decorated with tasseled hems or borders that could have a symbolic or religious function. Tassels, commonly found on the hems of Mesopotamian dress, were worn as decorations or amulets to keep away evil spirits. Tassels also symbolized the wearer's authority. Cutting off the hem of a king's robe symbolically demonstrated that the monarch's authority could be cut off too (1 Sam. 24:10).

ASSYRIAN DRESS

The Assyrian Empire (ca. 2400–612 B.C.E.) was centered on Mesopotamia—the land between the Tigris and Euphrates rivers. At the height of the Assyrians' power, they controlled the areas that equate to parts of modern Syria, Iraq, Iran, and as far as Egypt to the west and the Caspian Sea to the north. The empire finally came to an end with the arrival of the Persians. The Persians were the people of the Iranian Plateau, and the Persian ruler Achaemenes established a dynasty and empire that lasted from 558 B.C.E. until the arrival of Alexander the Great in 330 B.C.E.

The Assyrians and Persians were both highly organized and cultured societies, and their social divisions are evident in the material they left behind. Status among women is difficult to define by dress terms alone, although a series of law texts from the Middle Assyrian period (ca. 1076 B.C.E.) shows that the veiling of women was a thorny problem. The laws state that only the wives of elite men were permitted to veil themselves out of doors, although a man's concubine could veil herself when she accompanied a higher-ranking wife in public. Slave girls and prostitutes were not permitted to use veils, and the laws stipulate severe physical punishments for any slave or prostitute who dared to violate the social order. Far from being an instrument of control, the veil is here regarded as a high-status garment, worn with pride by women who see it as a privilege of their rank.

The study of Babylonian, Assyrian, and Israelite (and related) dress is severely hampered by a lack of textual evidence and an incomplete understanding of the technical terminology of clothing found in the cuneiform and related corpus. In the late eighth century B.C.E., the Old Testament prophet Isaiah, for example, criticized the women of Jerusalem for indulging themselves in fashion (Isa. 3:16–24); he provides a long list of fashionable items worn by Zion's elite women, but the passage continues to baffle translators. The terminology of dress he employs is so specific to his time and place that the text can barely be decoded. The technical terms for Southwest Asian dress, dressmaking, and textiles remain, by and large, elusive.

Nevertheless, the visual evidence is substantial and often detailed, although it mostly focuses on the clothing of the elite classes or on ethnic variations in dress. The stone reliefs and frescoes of neo-Assyrian palaces, particularly those of King Ashurbanipal (r. 669–624 B.C.E.), are important sources for study and reveal that the Assyrian artist was keen to depict the nuances of fashion and dressmaking. Monarchs depicted in these reliefs are shown in different outfits for different occasions, although it is hard to distinguish exactly why one style of dress is preferred to another. The basic garment is an ankle-length T-shaped tunic, embroidered and fringed around the hems; over this is worn a voluminous shawl or shawls, also heavily worked with fringed borders. This style of dress is worn in ceremonial, religious, and court scenes and was perhaps an official court dress. When hunting or at war, kings and nobles wore simpler outfits: knee-length, short-sleeved tunics and high-laced boots. The introduction of appliquéd ornaments and embroidered geometric, rosette, and asterisk patterns added variety and texture to the garments. These may have acted as talismans, but it is difficult to decode the symbolism.

PERSIAN DRESS

More information is available about dress in Achaemenid Iran (558–330 B.C.E.). As in Mesopotamia, dress was loaded with symbolic displays of status. Nothing is known about the dress of ordinary Persians, because the Persian iconography concentrates on representations of royal scenes of audiences, warfare, hunting, and worship rather than daily life. Similarly, evidence for the dress of the common folk is not found in local written sources. Nevertheless, there are three types of rich primary source materials that help one understand Persian dress and its social functions: classical authors writing in Greek and Latin (for example, Herodotus' *Histories* 7.61–80 and Xenophon's *Cyropaedia* 7.3.13–14), Greek and Persian art, and rare finds of Achaemenid textiles.

The artwork, including official palace art from Persepolis and Susa; seal-stone depictions from central Iran, Anatolia, and the Levant; as well as precious metal finds from Afghanistan, reveals that the Achaemenids essentially had two basic types of garment: a court gown, known to modern scholarship as the Persian robe, and a two-piece tunic-and-trouser suit, conventionally called Median dress. The latter name is somewhat misleading, because this style of dress cannot be used as a criterion for identifying nationality. In fact, it is clear that Persian kings and nobles frequently wore this style of dress, and it is perhaps more appropriate to term this outfit a riding ensemble, although its frequent depiction in court scenes makes it clear that the outfit was not worn

Stone relief at Persepolis, Iran, ca. 515 B.C.E. The man on the left is wearing "Median dress" consisting of a pair of *anaxyrides* (leather trousers) under an *ependytēs*, a tunic long enough to be secured around the waist with a belt. Getty Images.

only while hunting or on the battlefield. The riding outfit as court dress might be explained by the Achaemenids' origins: They were originally a nomadic tribe of central Iran, and the clothes once routinely worn on horseback as the tribe moved from place to place became part of an imperial court ensemble that resonated with nostalgia for an itinerant past.

Essentially, the riding outfit consisted of a pair of *anaxyrides* (leather trousers) under an *ependytēs*, a tunic long enough to be secured around the waist with a belt. Reliefs at the palace of Persepolis show that the ependytēs had straight side seams and was not fitted. The ensemble could be augmented with a coat with long, hanging sleeves, known to the Greeks as the *kandys* (Old Persian *gaunaka*), which was often draped over the shoulders like a cape or sometimes fastened over the chest with ties. The Greeks were fascinated by this outfit, calling it "the most beautiful of garments" (Xenophon, *Cyropaedia* 8.3.3), which fueled Greek artistic visualizations of Amazons and was associated by the Greeks with

hunting dress and military dress: Alexander the Great wore a version following his victory over Darius III.

Xenophon makes some important observations about the nature of the kandys, stating that its ultralong sleeve, known as a *korē*, was not actually used except in the presence of the Persian king, when a supplicant placed his arm into the sleeve, allowing the excess fabric to fall over his hand. The ends of the *korai* were sewn together at the cuff, preventing the wearer, says Xenophon, from holding any weapons; the long sleeves thus safeguarded the monarch. For Xenophon, security and the correct posture for court ceremony were invariably linked, although he might have misinterpreted a long-standing Iranian custom whereby the concealment of the hand was a mark of respect for a figure of authority.

Persian art implies that the kandys could be lined or trimmed with fur, suggesting a garment with connotations of wealth. It certainly indicated a high social rank and was worn in public by the king as he traveled throughout the empire and participated in religious ceremonies. The importance of the kandys as a symbol of royalty was stressed by its incorporation into the coronation ritual and by its color: purple. The king's status was further enhanced by his wearing of the *kidaris*, a soft, pointed felt hat with a cowl that was commonly worn with the riding dress, although only the king wore the top of the kidaris standing upright.

It was probably a kandys that, according to Herodotus (9.109), was woven by Xerxes' wife, Amastris, and presented to her husband as an official gift. The Achaemenids may have inaugurated the practice of giving robes of honor to high-ranking dignitaries or fellow royals; the practice was later codified into a court ceremony known as *khil'at* and is well attested in India and Southwest Asia. The same robe was requested from Xerxes as a gift by a woman of a rival branch of the royal family (that of Intaphernes, Xerxes' brother), and it is possible that the king's kandys was regarded as such a symbol of power that the acquisition of the coat was understood as a bid for royal status.

The kandys appears in Greek and especially Athenian art worn by foreign, Oriental women such as Medea. However, surviving written records suggest that the kandys was a popular garment with Athenian women, which they remodeled in linen and often embellished with bright embroidery or woven designs. The popular trend of effeminizing Persia in the Greek imagination transformed a Persian garment denoting high male social status within Persian society into an Athenian luxury item for women's use.

The Persian robe, meanwhile, was a huge and voluminous *kalasiris*: a tunic sewn up the sides from hem to waist, placed over the head, and fastened at the waist with a sash, through which the excess fabric was pulled into hanging waterfall folds. All of this could be created without cutting, shaping, or intricate stitching. Traces of paint and incised decoration on the Persepolis reliefs demonstrate that these robes were brightly dyed and elaborately worked with colorful embroidery and woven patterns (glazed tiles from Susa depict imperial guards wearing tunics with geometric patterns and schematic fortress designs). Such robes were often decorated with appliquéd gold or metallic studs; these were clearly costly and striking outfits. The kalasiris was worn with a high (often fluted) crown made from metal or leather. This ensemble was certainly worn at court and might be termed the official court dress since it is the garment worn exclusively by the king and the prince in audience scenes depicted at Persepolis. In contrast, the *chiliarch* (a military commander) in these scenes wears the riding outfit while performing obeisance to the king.

The informal relief scenes at Persepolis show courtiers mingling together in an animated and friendly manner; they wear both riding dress and the court dress. But in the formal procession scenes of tribute bearers from all parts of the empire, Persian dignitaries are depicted only wearing court dress, which probably reflects the preeminence of this style as the highest rank of court dress. Reliefs of the king at Persepolis show the long garment girded for more robust action: The front of the robe is hitched up and tucked into the sash, and the sleeves (or overfall of cloth at the shoulders) are also hitched up and possibly pinned at the shoulder line. Whether this means that the court dress could be used as an alternative form of hunting dress is open to debate.

Women's dress followed men's court dress, augmented with a turret crown and a veil of varying lengths. High-ranking women on seal stones are depicted in floor-length veils; those of lesser status are shown in shorter veils. Images on seals and gems from

Detail of a funeral relief from Palmyra, second century C.E. The woman on the left wears a Greek chiton-like garment in a light fabric and armbands and cuffs. Her head is partly covered by the mantle being pulled up and over it. Over time, Palmyrene women were depicted with increasing amounts of jewelry, especially layers of necklaces and pendants, brooches, earrings, and heavy bracelets. Damascus, National Museum. © 1990. Photo Scala, Florence.

western Anatolia depict Persian women wearing these robes of pleated linen and sometimes veiled, although a coiffure of a long plait decorated with tassels was very fashionable. As the empire grew, increasing wealth encouraged more luxurious fabrics, such as linen, with richer decoration and rare dyes. Persians of rank, men and women, wore rich jewelry.

Following his conquest of the Persian Empire, Alexander of Macedon (Alexander the Great) adopted many Persian court customs, including aspects of Achaemenid royal dress, although this met with some hostility from his Macedonian and Greek followers. When the empire split after Alexander's death in June 323 B.C.E., his general Seleucus inherited the lands of the east, and the period to the late first century B.C.E. saw the steady incursion of Hellenism into the area. Although the monarchs of the Seleucid dynasty undoubtedly wore elements of Persian court dress in imitation of Alexander's practice, it is difficult to know how much, or how often, Oriental dress was utilized at the Seleucid court. It was probably used very little on a daily basis, although it is possible that, when officiating in cult ritual at the ancient centers of Southwest Asian life, particularly at Babylon, Seleucid rulers donned antique outfits loaded with the symbolism of the Babylonian monarchy.

Practically nothing is known of the dress styles of Southwest Asia in the Hellenistic world, and it is likely that indigenous dress was worn alongside (or in combination with) Greek styles throughout the period. By the second century B.C.E., Roman modes of dress were also becoming part of the mix of fashionable dress in Southwest Asia, blurring the distinction of ethnicity and social structure that is a feature of the later Hellenistic age generally.

POST-HELLENISTIC, PARTHIAN, AND SASSANIAN DRESS

As the Hellenistic kingdoms collapsed, western Asia became dominated first by the Parthians (247 B.C.E.–224 C.E.) and then the Sassanians (224–642 C.E.). Both peoples came into close contact, and sometimes conflict occurred with the expanding Roman Empire. The Romans at this time were the dominant power in the western Mediterranean, with ambitions to control more of the eastern Mediterranean and western Asia. The mix of Hellenistic, Roman, and Persian cultures is evident in both the written and visual sources of the period. It appears that, in areas to the west, dress styles signifying very different identities coexisted.

As in the earlier period, the visual sources are relatively few—rock carvings, silverware, and so forth. These sources tend to portray particular scenes, usually kings and queens or gods and goddesses, and so reveal little about the everyday clothing of the majority of the population. In terms of literary evidence, the material is skewed by the abundance of information from Greek and Latin authors and the lack of surviving evidence from the East until the later Arab period. Greek and Latin authors tend to reflect Western prejudices about the East. In Western literature, for instance, there existed a long-standing tradition of stereotyping that makes these sources impossible to use as a reflection of social reality. Dress was often used as shorthand method to describe character: The inability of an individual to dress correctly for a particular occasion suggested an inability to behave correctly and so unsuitability for a particular office. For example, Herodian's description of the Syrian emperor, Heliogabalus, who caused great scandal by appearing in public at Rome wearing patterned trousers (Herodian 5.3.6), is intended to symbolize his ineffectiveness as a ruler, because the toga, not trousers, was regarded as the correct public dress for an emperor.

Descriptions of particular types of textiles, especially silk, and the overuse of gold or richly decorated material assumed luxury, which in turn was associated with decadence and immorality. Furthermore, the Eastern origin of silk and richly decorated textiles meant that authors could use them as stereotypes of the East, which were in turn seen to be foreign and decidedly non-Roman. A Western author could assume that his or her audience would immediately connect the idea of "Eastern" with notions of excess, softness, effeminacy, decadence, and the barbarian. These ideas were given currency by the way Eastern foreigners chose to clothe themselves. Romans were suspicious of both long sleeves and trousers—essential aspects of Southwest Asian dress—and thus many contemporary written descriptions carry both prejudice and moral overtones.

In contrast, and despite a literature that might suggest the opposite, cultural and commercial interaction between West and East continued and thrived throughout this period. One of the reasons Rome was so interested in western Asia was the trade routes across to India and China and the Arabian Peninsula. The

A statue of a Parthian prince, Tehran, second century B.C.E. to second century C.E. He wears a round-necked tunic and a jacket with long sleeves and bands on the front and bottom edges, perhaps representing fur. His overtrousers seem to be made of lighter material, implied by the suggestion of voluminous folds. Photograph by Gillian Vogelsang-Eastwood.

West actively sought the luxuries that the East could provide, and, even if some parties chose to label them as exotic and decadent, they were markers of status for the rich and powerful. Silk, in particular, was increasingly used by the upper classes as a mark of wealth. Its expense and quality made it a luxury item that was much sought after.

The essential difference between the garments worn by those who identified themselves with the Greco-Roman world and those who were Persian is the contrast between the draped, pinned, belted, and relatively plain dress of the Greeks and Romans in the West—the Greek chiton (tunic) and himation (mantle or cloak) or the Roman tunic and toga—and the decorated trousers, short tunics, and cut and sewn jackets of the Persians. Up to the late twentieth century, scholars spent a lot of time trying to track Greco-Roman influences in Eastern dress, but this approach has been seriously questioned by Gillian Vogelsang-Eastwood and others. It will suffice to say that, clearly, where the two cultures were closest, exchanges and integration of fashion ideas occurred, and in some areas there is clear evidence of both types appearing together. Common sense would suggest that individuals dressed to suit their social situation, official role, and own comfort for particular occasions: What was worn when meeting the ruler was different from dress in a private house, and perhaps different again from a portrayal on a tomb sculpture.

PRE-ISLAMIC DRESS IN THE EASTERN MEDITERRANEAN

Palmyra, an oasis city in Syria on the caravan route from east to west, is a city that demonstrates this cultural mix in its monuments. Here, statues survive that show both men and women dressed in stereotypical Roman style, recognizable from thousands of similar models throughout the western Mediterranean. Men are usually shown wearing full-length tunics and carefully draped togas, while women are depicted in long tunics and mantles (palla) that are wrapped around the body and clasped across the chest. The bodies of both men and women are normally hidden beneath layers of heavy drapery. However, far more typical of Palmyrene depictions are funerary monuments that demonstrate a very different style of dress following Eastern traditions. This style has echoes of the riding dress from Persepolis.

Men are shown wearing knee-length, long-sleeved tunics and loose trousers. The tunic is decorated with bands down the front and on the cuffs, is belted at the waist, and has slits at the sides. Over this is worn a short cloak fastened on the right shoulder. The trousers are also decorated with a band running down the center of the leg and are tucked into short boots tied with thongs. This outfit is seen both on funerary images and on figures on horseback, suggesting that it had both functional and formal attributes. Women's dress shows more of a mix of styles in a single outfit. From the second century C.E., a female figure wears a garment like a Greek chiton in what looks like a light fabric, full length and bloused over at the waist, but worn over a highly decorated undertunic with long sleeves and decorated armbands and cuffs. The head is partly covered by the mantle being pulled up and over it. Anklets are visible. This figure may have some remnants of Greek style in its drapery carving, but the overall image would look "Eastern" to any Greek or Roman of the period. Over time, Palmyrene women are depicted with increasing amounts of jewelry, especially layers of necklaces and pendants, brooches, earrings, and heavy bracelets.

A version of the trousers, tunic, and cloak ensemble worn by men is repeated in various forms across Southwest Asia. Evidence is scarce, but one of the finest and most detailed examples of Parthian dress is the Shami Prince in the National Museum of Archaeology in Tehran (dating from between the second century B.C.E. and the second century C.E.). The figure wears a round-necked tunic reaching to the upper thigh, just below the jacket. The jacket has long sleeves and crosses over at the front. It also reaches to the upper thigh. It has bands on the front and bottom

edges, perhaps made of fur. The jacket is pulled across the body and fastened at the waist by a belt, giving a V-shaped opening at the front over the chest. The belt is decorated with plaques, a type that has been found at many sites across Iran. Two pairs of leg coverings are apparent. The narrower underpair seem to fit from the waist to the ankle and would perhaps be made of linen or wool. The overtrousers seem to be made of lighter material, implied by the suggestion of voluminous folds. They are not full trousers but separate legs suspended from a waistband with a separate section of cloth to cover the buttocks.

This is one detailed example, but other types of Parthian dress are variations on this theme. Loose-legged trousers of fine textiles were common, topped with either a loose, long-sleeved tunic, patterned or with decorated bands and cuffs, or a fitted, front-opening jacket, both worn belted. The fitted jacket style appears as early as the first century C.E. and is shown worn by kings on monuments and coins as well as in depictions of nonroyals. Long-sleeved, knee-length coats are also known in a royal context, worn over a tunic.

The evolution of this basic ensemble into the Sassanian period (224–651 C.E.) is evidenced by the rock reliefs found in Iran, most notably those at Naqsh-i-Rustam, Bishapur, and Taq-i-Bustan, and on silverware. As with the Persepolis reliefs, these often depict kings, courtiers, and gods and are therefore unlikely to be representative of everyday wear. Servants are shown in the hunting scenes from Taq-i-Bustan, and their garments may represent the dress of ordinary folk; however, they must still be read with caution. In these images, the basic dress is again that of trousers and overtrousers, tunic and overtunic or jacket with long sleeves, shoes or short boots, and belts. Cloaks and front-fastening coats are also evident and, by the later period at Taq-i-Bustan, the heavily decorated kaftan, a long, outer robe that is open down the front and fastened at one side.

These reliefs show the changing shape of the basic tunic, although the long sleeves remain a constant. At Naqsh-i-Rustam, Shapur I (r. 241–272 C.E.) is shown wearing a full-skirted tunic with slits at the sides, as are the figures in the scene showing the investiture of Naresh (r. 293–302 C.E.). At Taq-i-Bustan, in the scene showing the investiture of Shapur II (r. 309–379 C.E.), the full-skirted tunic is worn by the gods on either side of king, while Shapur himself wears a round-edged version. The full-skirted tunic appears to be out of fashion by the end of the fourth century, replaced by a straighter, narrower version with a straight or flat edge. Yet another style, known as indented, is visible on silverware and rock reliefs by the fourth century. This appears as a concave front edge with points at the sides, all edged with decorated borders. This garment appears to have been worn by courtiers by the late Sassanian period.

At Naqsh-i-Rustam, both kings and queens are shown with lightweight cloaks fastened on the shoulder and fluttering out behind them. Some figures appear to have cloaks fastened at the front. Later images from Taq-i-Bustan show a longer cloak on the front of the body. Versions of the jacket worn by the Shami Prince are also evident in the Sassanian rock carvings, as are other types of coats. There are some examples at Bishapur that show a long, calf- or knee-length, full-skirted, round-edged coat with long sleeves that is fastened at the front by either ribbons or a clasp. These appear to have antecedents from earlier reliefs, notably one of Antiochus I (r. 281–261 B.C.E.) from Nimrud Dag, but, like the full-skirted tunic, it does not appear after the fourth

Relief of Shapur I, commemorating the victory of the Sassanian Persian king Shapur I over the Roman emperor Valerian, Naqsh-i-Rustam, Persepolis, Iran, ca. 1000 B.C.E. Shapur I wears a full-skirted tunic with slits at the sides. Photograph by Mary Harlow.

century. The latest version is the coat with extra-long sleeves. This is different from the kandys of the Achaemenids, because in this later form the sleeves appear to be worn, and the extra length is used to cover the hand as a sign of respect—a custom still adhered to in some Southwest Asian countries in the early twenty-first century. This coat may also be of the same type as garments found during excavations at the Egyptian city of Antinoopolis, but direct comparisons are difficult due to the lack of surviving Sassanian examples.

Images from Taq-i-Bustan depicting hunting and court scenes from the reign of Khosrow II (r. 591–628 C.E.) suggest the use of heavily brocaded and decorated silks as well as metal threads, semiprecious stones, and pearls as part of the decoration of dress (from a distance, they would have looked similarly lavish to contemporary Byzantine court dress, although up close it would have been clear that the cut of the garments was different). Moreover, these images provide evidence of the kaftan worn by the Sassanian king and some of his courtiers. This appears to be full skirted with side slits, decorated, and fastened on the left side.

If there is little evidence for men's dress in this period, there is even less for women's apparel. Parthian women, when they do appear in reliefs, seem to have worn a long, full garment, belted at the waist. They also wore a veil that covered the back of the head. There is slightly more evidence for the dress of Sassanian women, but it is still difficult to be exactly sure of what they wore. Long-sleeved, ankle-length dresses seem to be worn both belted (under the bust or at the waist) and loose, made from plain or patterned material. The dresses may have decorated cuffs and necklines. Tunics were usually worn with some form of mantle, sometimes

worn partly as a veil on the back of the head but often draped around the body in a number of ways. Presumably, this was a rectangular length of cloth, like the Roman palla, that could be draped to suit the occasion and climate. Depictions of hairstyles imply that the head covering was not essential for women appearing in public. More recently, Vogelsang-Eastwood has suggested that an ensemble consisting of a long-sleeved blouse and skirt was a common mode of attire for some Sassanian women. As with men's dress, the lack of actual finds will continue to hinder interpretation.

References and Further Reading

Briant, Pierre. *From Cyrus to Alexander: A History of the Persian Empire.* Winona Lake, IN: Eisenbrauns, 2002.

Fluck, Cäcilia, and Gillian Vogelsang-Eastwood, eds. *Riding Costume in Egypt: Origin and Appearance.* Brill Studies in Textile and Costume History, vol. 3. Leiden: Brill, 2004.

Goldman, Bernard. "Graeco-Roman Dress in Syro-Mesopotamia." In *The World of Roman Costume,* edited by Judith L. Sebesta and Larissa Bonfante, 163–181. Madison: University of Wisconsin Press, 1994.

Goldman, Bernard. "Women's Robing in the Sasanian Period." *Iranica Antiqua* 32 (1997): 233–300.

Gordon, Stewart. *Robes of Honour: Khil'at in Pre-Colonial and Colonial India.* New Delhi: Oxford University Press, 2003.

Kawami, Trudy S. "Clothing III: In the Arsacid Period." In *Encyclopedia Iranica,* edited by E. Yarshater, vol. 5, 737–739. London: Routledge and Kegan Paul, 1992.

Koch, Heidemarie. *Persepolis: Glänzende Hauptstadt des Perserreichs.* Mainz am Rhein, Germany: Philipp von Zabern, 2001.

Peck, Elsie H. "The Representation of Costumes in the Reliefs of Taq-i-Bustan." *Artibus Asiae* 31, no. 2/3 (1969): 101–146.

Peck, Elsie H. "Clothing III: In the Sasanian Period." In *Encyclopedia Iranica*, edited by E. Yarshater, vol. 5, 739–752. London: Routledge and Kegan Paul, 1992.

Salman, Isa. *Assyrian Costumes*. Baghdad: Directorate General of Antiquities Publication, 1971.

Vogelsang-Eastwood, Gillian M. "Was There Greek or Roman Influence on Sasanian Women's Clothing?" In *The Roman Textile Industry and Its Influence: A Birthday Tribute to John Peter Wild*, edited by Penelope Walton Rogers, Lise Bender Jørgensen, and Antoinette Rast-Eicher, 65–76. Oxford: Oxbow Books, 2001.

Vogelsang-Eastwood, Gillian M. "Sasanian 'Riding-Coats': The Iranian Evidence." In *Riding Costume in Egypt: Origin and Appearance*, edited by Cäcilia Fluck and Gillian Vogelsang-Eastwood, 209–230. Brill Studies in Textile and Costume History, vol. 3. Leiden: Brill, 2004.

Watson, Philip J. *Costume of Old Testament Peoples*. London: B. T. Batsford, 1987.

Mary Harlow and Lloyd Llewellyn-Jones

See also Trouser Wearing by Horse-Riding Nomads in Central Asia.

The Coming of Islam and Its Influence on Dress

- Pre-Islamic or *Jahili* Dress
- Early Islamic Clothing
- Medieval Islamic Dress
- Islamic Clergy and Dress

The advent of Islam in the seventh century C.E. had a profound effect not only on the religious and philosophical aspects of life but also on the social and economic structures of Central and Southwest Asia. The new religion brought with it concepts about what was and was not acceptable in all aspects of life, including dress, with reverberations into the twenty-first century.

When looking at dress in Southwest Asia, it is important to note that the two Abrahamic religions of the region, Judaism and Christianity, fundamentally differed from Islam in the way that the body and clothing were perceived. This difference can be seen by looking at the creation story of Adam and Eve. In the Jewish and Christian versions, Adam and Eve are created naked: "And the man and his wife were both naked, and were not ashamed" (Gen. 3:1). After eating the apple from the Tree of Knowledge, they realize that they are naked and make clothing from fig leaves to cover their genitalia: "Then the eyes of both were opened, and they knew they were naked; and they sewed fig leaves together and made themselves aprons" (Gen. 3:7). In the Qur'anic version, Adam and Eve are created fully clothed and were later stripped of their garments by Satan so that they became aware of their nakedness, the "shamefulness" of human genitalia, and the need for modesty:

> O Children of Adam! We have sent down on you a garment to cover your shameful parts. ... Let not Satan tempt you as he brought your parents out of the Garden, stripping them of their garments to show them their shameful parts. (Sura 7:25–26)

This moralistic view on the purpose of clothing and dress in general has played an important role in the history of the Islamic world from the moment Islam came into being.

Islam, one of the major monotheistic religions of the world, was founded in the early seventh century in the region that comprises western Saudi Arabia in the early twenty-first century. It is based on the concept that Allah revealed a message to the Prophet Mohammed (ca. 570–632 C.E.) through the angel Jibril (Gabriel). Followers of Islam believe that their holy book, the Qur'an, is flawless, immutable, and the final revelation of God to humanity and that its teachings will be valid until the Day of Resurrection (Day of Judgment). Islam is centered on the holy cities of Mecca and Medina in Saudi Arabia. In the first decade of the twenty-first century, Islam is estimated to have nearly one and a half billion adherents throughout the world.

PRE-ISLAMIC OR *JAHILI* DRESS

The period before the arrival of Islam is called *Jahiliyya*, generally meaning "days of ignorance" or "ignorance of divine guidance,"

an important period because many garments worn in the later Islamic period, and into the twenty-first century, originated then. Although no garments have survived from this period, various written descriptions exist, both from the Greco-Roman world and in Arabic, particularly in Jahili poetry. The latter is a rich source of information in which clothing imagery features prominently; the range of garments described includes many terms that are still in use, such as the *burda, izar, mirt, rida,* and so forth. Care has to be taken with these words because they can be misleading; although the terms sound familiar and some are still used, it does not follow that the words applied to the same type of garment or even a comparable garment.

Basic outfits for men and women prior to Islam consisted of three layers and included an undergarment such as a chemise or undershirt of some kind; a long dress or gown; and an overgarment such as a mantle, coat, or wrap; plus some form of headgear. Footwear, if worn, generally consisted of sandals or shoes.

One point common to these various sources is that in the Jahiliyya there was less concern about covering the body than became the norm in later centuries. The covering of women's bodies, however, did exist and apparently applied more to urban women than to villagers or Bedouin. There are, for example, various oblique references in classical literature from this period to Arab women wearing some kind of mantle when in public. One of the clearest references to a type of enveloping mantle worn by Arab women can be found in the work *De Virginibus Velandis* by the early Christian writer Tertullian (third century C.E.), who remarked that Arabian women appeared in public with only one eye visible:

> The women of Arabic origin, who cover not only their heads, but also their faces, would condemn us, because they prefer to enjoy the light with one eye, rather than show their whole faces. It is better for a woman to see, than be seen.

These women likely wore their mantles in a similar manner to that depicted in a relief of a group of Nabatean women found at the Syrian site of Palmyra. The women in this stylized depiction are shown with their faces and bodies covered.

In addition to covering their bodies, some women also covered their faces in public, in front of strangers, with a separate garment. Used for this purpose were the burqa, a face veil fastened around the upper forehead and used to cover the face but not the eyes; the qina, a face veil that was draped over the head and used to cover the complete face; and the *lithmah,* a face veil that wrapped around the lower face. This type of veiling appears to be culturally dictated rather than being regarded as a religious essential.

EARLY ISLAMIC CLOTHING

Not surprisingly, the dress of the earliest Muslim community was based on the garments worn in the preceding period. Certain modifications were made, however, for the new, moral sensibilities developed by Islam. These forms continued for centuries and constituted the basic clothing of men and women throughout Southwest Asia and further afield.

According to the dress historian Yedida Stillman, the austere nature of the early Muslim community reflected the conviction that the Last Judgment was not far away; as a result, many traditions recommended modesty and austerity in dress and the avoidance, if not condemnation, of extravagance. As part of this desire for austerity, the Prophet noted that various clothes were inappropriate in this life for men but not, apparently, for women. Men were forbidden various items, including silver vessels, gold rings, garments of *harir* (silk), *dibaj* (brocade), *qassi* (a striped cloth from Egypt containing silk), *istabraq* (satin), and *mayathir humr* (tanned hides). Nevertheless, various exceptions were made in the case of individuals who had skin conditions that made it impossible for them to wear fibers such as wool or camel hair. Inevitably, over the centuries, there have been many instances when these forbidden items have been used or worn by men. But, in general, the concept of men not wearing gold jewelry still plays an important role in the dress of many Muslim men.

The three layers worn by men and women at the time of the Prophet were undergarments (underpants, chemises, and so forth); middle garments (gowns, robes, and dresses), which could be worn indoors or outdoors depending on the occasion; and outer garments (wraps, mantles, cloaks, and coats). A basic outfit would have consisted of an undergarment such as a chemise, a dress or gown, an overgarment, and headwear of some kind. For going out in public, an outer garment would be added. Footwear generally consisted of sandals or shoes; very poor people went barefoot.

As in later periods, a person might wear one garment or many, depending on the temperature, his or her social and economic position, his or her occupation, and the time of year. Many items of clothing worn by men and women were identical and in many cases were probably based on a simple, large piece of fabric that the wearers wrapped themselves in, similar to the haik worn in the Maghreb well into the twentieth century. Probably women's fashion and identity were indicated by the choice of fabric, colors, and decoration as well as the manner of wrapping and draping the garments, the accessories worn (especially silver jewelry), and, finally, the style of headdress.

During the pre-Islamic period, attitudes toward nudism appeared easygoing, but the arrival of Islam brought with it a new modesty code to cover the private parts, defined as from the navel to the knees, and more specifically the shape of the male and female genitalia or "shameful parts." The basic undergarment was the *izar*, which was a hip wrap made out of a length of cloth wrapped around the waist or hips—a garment still commonly worn in parts of southwestern Saudi Arabia and Yemen, similar to the *lungi* worn by men in India.

A floor fresco showing musicians (upper section) and a rider and horse (lower section), from Qasr al-Hayr al-Gharbi, Syria, ca. 730 c.e. Female musicians are wearing long, belted gowns with trousers, slippers, and mantles and have elaborate hairdos. The hunter is wearing a long gown with side slits and a belt, together with trousers and boots. Damascus, National Museum. © 1990. Photo Scala, Florence.

Pants (*sirwal*) or underdrawers appear to have come from Persia by, at the latest, the sixth century C.E. and were adopted by many urban Arab communities. In contrast, the Bedouin did not accept them, and many Bedouin in the twenty-first century still refuse to wear underpants as something urban, unnatural, and unhygienic. There are hadiths that both state and deny that the Prophet wore sirwal, so this remains a controversial issue. But seemingly many women in this period did wear drawers of some kind, but exactly how they were constructed is unknown. By the medieval period, many types existed: knee-, calf-, and ankle-length ones; narrow or baggy ones; ones with a high or low crotch; and so forth, each type with its own name and group of people that liked to wear it. By this period, it was normal for both urban and village men and women to wear them at all times, a tradition that survives into the early twenty-first century in many Islamic countries.

On top of the hip wrap or undertrousers was an undergarment or chemise of some kind, generally known in Arabic as *qamis*, deriving from the Latin term *camisia*, which in turn developed into the French and English term *chemise*. This garment was originally worn by both men and women. It had short or long sleeves and ranged in length from midthigh to the feet.

One of the most important garments was the robe or dress, with a wide variation of types in this period, including the *thob*, which is a sleeved gown or dress worn by both men and women. It is still a staple in the Southwest Asian wardrobe. Another form of gown was the *jubba*, similar in appearance and cut to the T-shaped tunics worn in the later Roman and Byzantine empires and Syria, likely adapted from these countries. Like the thob, the jubba could be worn by men or women.

A popular men's garment was the *qaba*, a long-sleeved robe open down the front and fastened with a row of buttons or with a single button at the waist if the opening was diagonal. The qaba could be made from a variety of materials depending on the wearer's economic and social status. Wool ones padded with raw cotton were often worn in the winter, and thinner cotton or silk versions were worn in the hotter summer months. The qaba was often worn with a cummerbund or waist sash of some kind. The *farruji*, a less common form of gown similar in appearance to the qaba, had an opening at the back. It is said that this garment was not widely used because the Prophet Mohammed was given a silk one and threw it off, saying it was not fit for a God-fearing community. Whether the Prophet was referring to the cut of the garment or the fact it was made of silk, or indeed both, is not clear.

Of the wide range of outer garments worn during this period, the most popular was the wrap or mantle made from large pieces of cloth wrapped around the head and body in various ways. Although numerous written references to different types of wraps and mantles exist, their actual appearance and construction during this period is unknown. Many types were worn by both men and women, and others were gender specific. The well-known *rida*, for example, is usually associated with men, while the *mirt* was regarded as a woman's wrap, but the *izar*, a large sheet that was wrapped around the body, was worn by both men and women.

Many wraps and mantles were also known by the material they were made from; a *namira*, for instance, was a man's wrap with stripes of varying colors like a tiger's skin, while a *burda* was made of striped woolen cloth produced in Yemen. A *siyara* was a mantle of Seres or Chinese silk, worn by men and women, but according to one hadith, as Stillman has pointed out, the Prophet said "only those who have no chance for the world to come" would wear a mantle made from such silk. The other main group of outer garments are cloaklike forms, such as the *aba* (also known as a *bisht*), a sleeveless, square garment with a front opening, worn draped over the shoulders and still used throughout the Arab world.

A wide range of head coverings was worn by both men and women in this period; covering the head was regarded as a sign of modesty and respect. As in the Jewish tradition, Muslim men pray with their head covered, unlike Christian men who are said to stand in humility and bareheaded before God. The turban is the headwear most associated with Islam, but it is pre-Islamic in origin and can be traced back for hundreds of years in Southwest Asia. The word *turban*, commonly used in the West, derives from the Persian term *dulband* via the Turkish word *tulbant*, but, within the Arab world, the preferred term is *imamah*.

At first, the turban did not have direct Islamic significance, but, over the centuries, it developed into the badge of Islam (*sima al-Islam*), and various caliphs made wearing it a way to differentiate between Muslim and non-Muslim men (the latter were not allowed to wear it). Various types of turbans have developed, from small, neat, compact ones to the elaborate headdress of the Mamluks and Ottomans, made from tens of yards of material.

Written evidence suggests that, during the early Islamic period, both men and women practiced the veiling of their faces in some manner, but, in general, men covered themselves only occasionally, whereas women were more often encouraged, and finally required, to dress modestly, including covering the head, hair, and parts of the face when in public. Three types of face veils used by the early Muslim community—the qina, burqa, and lithmah—all derive from the earlier Jahili period and can be considered a continuation of a long-standing usage rather than an innovation brought by the coming of Islam. In fact, the requirement that women wear face veils does not appear in either the Qur'an or the hadiths; instead, the use of face veils may be regarded as a cultural addition to Muslim views on women's modesty. As a result, over the centuries, a wide range of face veils has developed, from very small ones that cover just part of the face to garments that cover most of the body. These garments reflect the social and cultural mores of the various communities, and it should be stressed that not all Muslim communities require women to wear face veils.

In addition to the garments worn by Muslim men and women, new Islamic regulations developed about the body and its presentation, which come under the general title of *fitrah*, referring to what people can and cannot do with their bodies, and which are related to various hadiths. For example, the Prophet Mohammed said, "Five practices are characteristic of the fitrah: circumcision, shaving the pubic hair, trimming the mustache, clipping the nails, and depilating the hair of the armpits." It was intended that men and women would regularly remove body hair from the face (other than the eyebrows), underarms, arms and hands, pubic region, legs, and feet. Washing was encouraged at all times so that the body would smell fresh. In addition, the use of perfumes among men and women was encouraged, so that others would not be distressed by unpleasant bodily smells.

Some things were not encouraged; in theory, for example, tattoos and piercings were regarded as unacceptable because the Qur'an states that God was also described as he "Who has created you, and properly formed you, and justly proportioned you; into whatever form He willed, He cast you" (Infitār 82:7–8).

Therefore, to change anything that God had created was potentially punishable. However, many Muslims, especially women, have pierced their ears and nose to wear jewelry and have tattoos to indicate ethnic affiliations. Thus, cultural norms sometimes take precedence, especially for women, over religious requirements. All of these dress requirements are in existence at the beginning of the twenty-first century, and they are important for understanding discussions and controversies surrounding the fashions of tattoos and body piercings.

MEDIEVAL ISLAMIC DRESS

Following the rapid spread of Islam throughout Southwest Asia and northern Africa, notably in Egypt and the Maghreb, Arabs first tried to keep apart as an ethnic and religious elite distinct from the "others." However, over time, an effort was made to Arabize groups by letting all groups wear Arab-style dress if they wished. Later, laws were passed to define Muslim and non-Muslim dress (the laws of differentiation) in order to make a clear distinction between those who were and those who were not Muslim, rather than stressing who was or was not an Arab.

At the same time, the vastness of the Islamic world (*Dar al-Islam*) meant that various types of clothing systems could be combined. In general, in Southwest Asia, three types of dress prevailed: (1) loose, flowing, and untailored Arab garments, suitable for living in very hot and dry conditions; (2) Greco-Roman tunics and wraps of various kinds that included cut and sewn garments; and (3) cut and shaped Irano-Turkic garments, with tailored forms emphasizing the shape of the human body. The foundation and expansion of Islam meant that, over time, these three forms came together and over the centuries created what the French linguist and philosopher Roland Barthes has described as the vestimentary system and what Stillman has described as the Islamic vestimentary system or style of dress. It should be stressed, however, that numerous variations in this system exist over time and place. Combinations of different styles of dress can still be seen in Southwest Asia, for example, in the wearing of a loose-fitting gown such as a thob with a fitted waistcoat derived from Turkish clothing traditions.

But the question remains, what made Islamic dress Islamic during the medieval period? Basically, garments were worn in three or more layers: under-, middle, and outer garments, covering and concealing the shape of the wearer's body. The number of layers and garments, however, depended on the wearer's financial resources. Women's outdoor garments were meant to hide the body further and to emphasize modesty and restraint. Similarly, men's clothing was designed to be modest and unostentatious, but dress could emphasize a man's social position and occupation publicly so that people would recognize his status.

During the later medieval period, the sayyids (descendants of the Prophet Mohammed) started to distinguish themselves with clothing to emphasize their special social position. Primarily, this meant a man wearing a cap, scarf, turban, or cummerbund made of green material, a tradition that continues in the twenty-first century.

ISLAMIC CLERGY AND DRESS

Islam does not have a complex system of clergy like that found within Christian churches; however, over the centuries, a system has developed that includes men learned in Islamic theology who have studied the Qur'an, hadiths, and Islamic law (*fiqh*). The terms *imam* (Arabic) or *mullah* (Persian) are used to describe the leader of a mosque or community. These men are regarded as spiritual leaders, and they prayers during Islamic gatherings, guide various religious ceremonies such as birth rites and funeral services, and answer questions about daily life based on Islamic precepts.

The garments worn by both imams and mullahs appear as conservative, traditional clothing that is medieval or at least nineteenth century in style. The general outfit consists of a pair of underdrawers (sirwal), an undergarment (qamis), a gown (qaba) that fastens down the middle or to one side, and a sleeveless mantle of some kind, such as an aba or bisht, worn from the shoulders.

The most important element is the headgear. In general, learned religious leaders wear smoothly wrapped, flat, white turbans, but the style varies depending on where the imam lives and his personal choice. In the eastern Mediterranean and Egypt, for example, he is normally called a sheikh and would wear a *tarbush* (a red cap shaped like an up turned flower pot, usually made of felted material; also called a fez) with a white cloth (*laffeh*) wrapped around it to signify his position. In other countries, imams wear skullcaps, again covered by a large cloth wrapped to create a much larger turban. In Shiite lands, the turbans of mullahs are distinct, normally white to indicate an ordinary mullah or black to indicate that the wearer is a sayyid or descendant of the Prophet Mohammed. The outfit worn by Turkish imams while leading prayers generally consists of a long coat (*cübbe*) fastened down the front, which is worn over Western-style clothing, because these and other traditional garments were banned in the 1920s and 1930s by the Turkish state. The headgear, however, remains a tall fez wrapped tightly with a long white cloth, which allows the top few inches of the fez to be visible. The combination of fez and cloth is called a *laffeh sarık*.

Wrapping techniques used in Turkey, the eastern Mediterranean, Egypt, and Iran differ, and, from a distance, it is possible to identify an imam's or mullah's origin. A similar situation must have existed in the medieval period, when the vast majority of people wore regional clothing of some kind.

References and Further Reading

Barthes, Roland. "Histoire et sociologie du vêtement: quelques observations méthodologiques." *Annales: Economies, Sociétiés, Civilsations* 3 (1957): 430–441.

Dozy, R.P.A. *Dictionnaire détaillé des noms des vêtements chez les Arabes.* Amsterdam: Jean Müller, 1845.

Stillman, Yedida. *Arab Dress: A Short History from the Dawn of Islam to Modern Times.* Leiden: Brill, 2000.

Stillman, Yedida, and Norman Stillman. "Libas." In *Encyclopaedia of Islam,* edited by P. J. Bearman, Th. Bianquis, C. E. Bosworth, E. van Donzel, W. P. Heinrichs, et al., vol. 5, 2nd ed. Leiden: Brill, 1960–2005.

Yusofi, Gh-H. "Clothing, XXVII. Historical Lexicon of Persian Clothing." In *Encyclopaedia Iranica,* edited by Ehsan Yarshater. http://www.iranica.com/newsite/. Accessed on 24 July 2008.

Gillian Vogelsang-Eastwood

See also Ottoman Dress; Saudi Arabian Dress; Fitrah: Temporary and Permanent Body Modifications for Muslims; Laws of Differentiation; Sumptuary Laws; Face Veils.

Jewish Dress in Central and Southwest Asia and the Diaspora

The variety of Jewish dress that evolved from postbiblical times to the early twenty-first century was shaped by a combination of internal and external factors. The major internal factor is the Jewish code of law, halacha; the external factors are various types of contacts with other religions and cultures.

The halacha is the whole legal system of Judaism, which embraces all laws and observances. It is based on the Bible and is considered the primary and most authoritative source, and hence is the authority on all interpretations, codes of conduct, and customs practiced and regulated by Jewish communities. The halacha deals in detail with the desired conduct of a Jew in everyday life, including dress—sometimes as explicit rulings and, on other occasions, as recommended attitudes.

Even though Jewish codes of law refer specifically to aspects of external appearance, no specific dress was ever mandated by Jewish law, and, as a result, no universal Jewish dress evolved. Therefore, each section of Jewish dress studied in its respective local and temporal contexts constitutes a segment of a wider entity that has some common underlying principles but that displays a variety of styles and modes of dress.

Two presumptions regarding Jewish dress direct halachic rulings on dress. The first is the requirement to differ from the Gentile environment, as is stated generally in the Bible, "nor shall you follow their laws" (Lev. 18:3). More specifically, Maimonides, the renowned medieval Jewish scholar, stated as relating to dress, "One must not follow in the ways of those who worship the stars nor imitate them either in dress or hairstyle" (*Mishneh Thorah, Hilkhot Avodat Kokhavim* 11:1). A second major concern of halachic rulings are issues of modesty in dress. These two directives

can fluctuate according to time and place in relation to prevailing norms and fashions and historical circumstances.

The external factors that imprint on Jewish dress and its variations are extensive. Since postbiblical times, most of the Jews have dispersed to many regions and, as a result, have come in contact with various cultures. It might safely be said that a Jew from Bukhara resembles in outer appearance more closely a Muslim from the region than a Jew from Poland. These contacts were manifested on a formal legislative level through rulings, mainly restrictive decrees and edicts, by non-Jewish authorities in countries where Jews lived.

On a less formal level, the encounter with prevailing local sartorial styles, textile techniques, and dress codes in varying geographic and historical settings generated an ongoing dynamic dialogue between the dress of the wider population and that of the Jews. This encounter revolves around the tension between tendencies toward integration and tendencies toward segregation that are present simultaneously within the Jewish communities and the outer society.

In some places, Jews played an active role in the production of dress for themselves and others, such as in Kurdistan or Yemen; in many places—such as Italy, England, Turkey, Iraq, Iran, and Bukhara—they were involved in trading clothes and textiles, new and old. Since the early nineteenth century, Jews have been highly active in manual and industrial textile manufacture and the production of clothes, especially in East Europe and then later in the United States, to which they emigrated in large numbers around the turn of the twentieth century. Their occupations range from small tailors and sweatshop workers to rich entrepreneurs, from street peddlers to wealthy merchants.

One of the recurring features encountered in the evolution of Jewish dress in places as diverse as East Europe and Iraq is conservatism, anachronism, or so-called fossilized dress. Jews had a tendency to retain dress styles or certain items of dress long after these had been abandoned by their non-Jewish neighbors. These anachronistic clothes came to be considered as exclusive to the Jews, and even an identifying trait. They were identified by both the Jews themselves and the non-Jewish population as an identity symbol, and the Jews sometimes clung to them as if they were a religious tradition.

The most well-known example of this phenomenon is the male Hasidic, or ultra-Orthodox, dress comprised of a kaftan and fur-trimmed hat, which is said to be derived from the dress of eighteenth-century Polish noblemen. This dress, which has been appropriated and preserved by Hasidic Jews all over the world up through the early twenty-first century, has thus become their distinctive attire, a kind of uniform exclusive to them, with variations designating each specific Hasidic group.

ASPECTS OF JEWISH DRESS SHAPED BY INTERNAL AND EXTERNAL FACTORS: TRADITION AND MODERNITY

The majority of Jewish communities who developed distinctive dress habits do not exist anymore in situ, as they did in the

An Ashkenazi Jew wrapped in a prayer shawl, East Europe, early twentieth century. The prayer shawl has black and white stripes with a typical East European narrow decorated neckband (*atarah*) made with *shpanyer* lace work. Isidore and Anne Falk Information Center for Judaica and Jewish Ethnography, The Israel Museum, Jerusalem.

nineteenth or early twentieth centuries, or only very small communities remain. Large waves of immigration around the beginning of the twentieth century and after World War I (1914–1918) and later caused major demographic changes and created sizable communities of Jews from East and West in the United States, South America, Canada, and Australia. The largest centers of East Europe—Poland, Russia, Hungary, and other communities in Greece and North Africa—perished in the holocaust of World War II (1939–1945).

Migrations of particular significance were the ideological Zionist immigration of Jews to Palestine before the foundation of the State of Israel in 1948 and the so-called mass immigration, mainly from Islamic countries, into Israel shortly after its

foundation. These massive migrations—whether forced; imposed by expulsion, war, or economic necessity; or even ideologically initiated—affected Jewish dress and sometimes transformed it entirely, even within the confines of the religious code of law. Prior to modernization and mass immigration, Jewish dress was more geographically and culturally bound; during the twentieth century, the distinctions were less geographic and attested more to the wearers' religious, ideological group affiliation and degree of religiosity.

Material pertaining to premodern/traditional dress during the nineteenth and twentieth centuries and the process of modernization derives from a variety of textual and visual sources, including Jewish rabbinical texts, travelogues, dress albums, photographs, memoirs, and historical documents such as marriage contracts, trousseau lists, and others. But, first and foremost, it is based on fieldwork research studies initiated in the Israel Museum by Aviva Muller-Lancet, the pioneer of the ethnographic study of Jewish dress. This work was carried out among Jews originating from diverse communities. It took place mostly in Israel and, when possible, in the countries of origin, and was based on the collection of the Israel Museum in Jerusalem. A large part of the Israel Museum's collection was accumulated at the same time through these studies and related fieldwork. Not all communities were researched to the same extent, and, as a result, the data might not be balanced.

Another reservation is that many of the premodern clothing items preserved by families or in museum collections do not mirror everyday simple attire. They are, in many cases, festive items that belonged to the wealthier classes who could afford and preserve them but were by no means typical of the majority of the Jewish communities.

RELIGIOUS RULINGS REGARDING DRESS COMMON TO ALL JEWS AND LOCAL CUSTOM

Biblical precepts regarding dress are extremely few. The most significant, and indeed the sole, explicit biblical dictate concerning dress is the wearing of fringes (tzitzit) on the corners of one's main garment:

> You shall make yourself tassels [fringes] on the four corners of the garment with which you cover yourself. (Deut. 22:12)

> That shall be your fringes: look at it and recall all the commandments of the Lord and observe them. (Num. 15:39)

These dictates are traditionally interpreted in Judaism as directed to men only, but this viewpoint is contested in the early twenty-first century by women of Reform Judaism. The principal function of the fringes is to serve as constant bodily reminders of faith and of the religious precepts a Jew has to observe.

In biblical times, fringes were attached to one's outer garments, which were probably sheetlike wraps with four corners. In time, when dress styles changed, two separate ritual garments evolved to fulfill this precept. The tallith is a rectangular fringed shawl worn for prayer and important events in the Jewish life cycle. The tzitzit, which literally means "fringe," or *tallith katan* (literally, "small tallith") is a poncholike undershirt with fringes that is worn at all times by Orthodox Jewish men. The fringes consist of four cords folded to produce eight ends, which are knotted in different numerical combinations equivalent to the numerical value of the letters of the names of God. The religious, mystic-symbolic meaning attributed to these garments imbued them with protective and magical powers as well. Undoubtedly, the magical protective properties attributed to the Jewish fringes or tassels are probably related to similar powers attributed to tassels in ancient Southwest Asian dress. According to Numbers 15:18, one tassel should be blue, but, because the production process of extracting the blue dye from the *Murex purpura* (a snail used for dyeing blue and purple in the Mediterranean) was lost, the fringes are usually white.

The Jews of Yemen are the only community that preserved most closely, until modern times, the biblical precept of attaching fringes to one's outer garment. The typical prayer shawl worn in

Sana'a is the black goat-hair outer shawl worn at all times by all Jewish men, to the four corners of which the Jews attach the ritual fringes. In other places, prayer shawls are separate ritual garments made of various materials and decorated in styles according to local customs. It is recommended that a prayer shawl be made of fine wool, but in the early twenty-first century, some are made of silk and a variety of synthetic fabrics.

In Sephardi (descendants of the Jews expelled from Spain in 1492) and Oriental communities, the four corners are the locus of decoration. In silk-producing centers such as Iran, Afghanistan, Turkey, the former emirate of Bukhara (in Uzbekistan in the early twenty-first century), and also in Italy and the Netherlands, prayer shawls were made of silk; to these embroidered square or round pieces accentuating the corners around the holes for the fringes were appended.

Traditional prayer shawls from Italy are made of ivory-colored silk with light blue stripes and exquisitely embroidered with white silk. Among the upper-class Sephardim in the Netherlands, sumptuous silk prayer shawls were used that had rich embroidered squares with silk threads, golden-thread couched embroidery, or fine lace incorporating family symbols and monograms of the owners. In Turkey, fine, blue-striped silk prayer shawls were made in the town of Bursa, a famous center for silk weaving, in the twentieth century. These were at times adorned with four velvet squares embroidered with metal thread that were attached to the corners. Another variation of the prayer shawl was a cashmere shawl to which fringes were added.

The corners of some prayer shawls from Kurdistan were densely embroidered with biblical verses or blessings in colorful Kurdish embroidery. In Iraq and Iran, they were adorned with amuletic motifs such as hands in typical local tinsel embroidery. In early-twenty-first-century Uzbekistan, in Bukhara or Samarkand, some prayer shawls are still made of silk with attached decorated corners made of local ikat dyed silk.

Among Ashkenazi Jews (Jews from Germany and East Europe), since the sixteenth century, it has become customary to sew a band of decorative cloth onto the prayer shawl on one of its long sides. This marks one edge of the prayer shawl as the upper part, identifying which part of the shawl is draped over the head. The decorative band remains visible when worn. In Germany, since the fifteenth century, a square of woven, patterned cloth has been appliquéd onto a silk damask shawl to mark its top part. In East Europe, it was a narrow decorated neck band (*atarah* in Hebrew) on top of a striped woolen shawl. Since the nineteenth century, the most prevalent neck band has been made of a typical metal-thread lace called *shpanyer arbet*, denoting in Yiddish "Spanish work" or "spinning work." The principal place of manufacture until the early twentieth century was the Galician Polish town of Sasów, but it was and is still made by hand in Israel and the United States. In the early twenty-first century, machine-made imitations of this technique are produced in China and sold globally. This technique was practiced by observant Jews and transmitted secretly from one artisan to another during the second half of the nineteenth century and early twentieth century; it was even believed to be exclusive to Jews. It was used to embellish only specifically Jewish dress items—mainly *atarot* (skullcaps), *brusttuch* (women's bodices), and caps. These prestigious neck bands are worn in the early twenty-first century by ultra-Orthodox Jews, mainly Hasidim, where they feature as one of the precious presents given to the groom and a status symbol.

Festive headwear worn by a married woman, Poland, nineteenth century. This forehead kerchief (*shterntikhl*) is a coronet sewn onto a cap studded with pearls and precious stones. It would have been worn by an aristocratic Polish woman. The *brusttuch* (bodice covering the chest opening of the dress from the neck to the waist), *shterntikhl*, and apron are typical of Jewish women's wear in Poland. The Israel Museum, Jerusalem.

Since at least the second half of the twentieth century, black-and-white-striped woolen prayer shawls made in Israel and Europe have reached the remotest communities and replaced much of the local variation. In the early twenty-first century, one can find an array of workshops weaving new types of prayer shawls from a variety of fabrics, some related to former traditions and some inventing new traditions incorporating biblical verses, the blessing for the tallith, and explicit Jewish symbols such as the Magen David (Star of David).

The tzitzit is worn daily, usually under the shirt with the fringes showing; some (especially small children) wear it on top of the shirt. Modern ones are mainly white and are made of cotton or synthetic fiber. In the past, they were made in many ways: crocheted, embroidered, and of various fabrics. In Iraq, for example, the tzitzit was occasionally made from striped atlas satin weave and had the shape of a vest, worn as the top part of the local dress to match the *umbaz* (a coatlike robe fastened diagonally and held by a sash) worn by men, or in Afghanistan it was used as a top part of a child's shirt.

Another explicit biblical ruling is *sha'atnez*, the prohibition on wearing a garment made of a mixture of wool and linen (Deut. 22:11). Because it is not outwardly apparent, sha'atnez, though kept into the early twenty-first century by observant Jews, is not a visible sign of Jewish dress. In the past, partly to obey this prohibition, tailoring became a prevalent Jewish occupation in many communities so that the combination of fibers and textiles in their clothes could be controlled.

Some rabbinic authorities deduce the *peoth orside* side locks (Lev. 19:27) worn by Jewish men, which remain distinctive features of Jewish ultra-Orthodox men's external appearance in the early twenty-first century, also as biblical precepts. In Yemen, they were called *simonim* (literally, "signs"), because they demarcated the Jews' appearance.

The tefillin—or phylacteries—are small leather boxes containing sacred and protective texts that are tied to the forehead and the left arm of Jewish men during morning prayer (based on Exod. 13:9, 16 and Deut. 6:8; 11:18). In the early twenty-first century, these are ritual accessories to which utmost importance is attributed, but in Talmudic times (third to fifth centuries C.E.), some scholars wore them throughout the day.

HEAD COVERING FOR MEN

The two designators of Jewish religious dress that are most conspicuous are men's and women's head coverings. The man's head covering has become obligatory only in the last few centuries. In the Talmud, it is a custom practiced only by certain people such as Torah scholars and at certain times such as during prayers and benedictions. This practice was conceived as a sign of submission before God and respect for authorities. In the *Shulhan Aruch*, the code of Jewish law written in the sixteenth century and accepted by all Jewish communities, covering the head is considered halachically normative, but it has not yet become mandatory.

In Christian countries, the Jewish practice of covering the head in the synagogue evolved in order to distance Jews from the male Christian practice of uncovering one's head as a sign of reverence. In the Muslim world, Jews were no exception to the general practice of covering the head, more as part of the surrounding culture's etiquette and norm, which coincided with their recommended habit.

In both Christian and Muslim lands, Jews were required to wear hats, the shape and color of which would identify them as Jews. In medieval Europe, it was the *judenhut* (literally, "Jewish hat"), a pointed hat by which the Jews were recognized and which has become a symbol of Jewish identity; it appears abundantly in Jewish and non-Jewish visual sources of the period. In the thirteenth century, it was mandatory in the regions that, in the early twenty-first century, form Germany, Austria, and Poland and was imposed by the authorities, but it seems that the Jews wore it willingly and even proudly, in contrast to their dislike of the yellow Jewish badge they were required to wear somewhat later.

In Turkey, the Jewish distinctive headgear was the *boneta*; this was a dark, cylindrical hat widening slightly at the top; around its lower part was a small turban crossed above the forehead. In the early nineteenth century, the boneta was replaced by the fez. In Morocco, Jews were distinguished by their black caps. In Iran, Jews wore tight woolen skullcaps called *araqchin*, tall conical hats, or, later, short cylindrical hats. In Uzbekistan and Afghanistan, especially on festive occasions, Jews wore different types of skullcaps of the local variety. These came in a wide variety of materials and forms, from simple ones of quilted cotton, to elaborate colorful cotton ones with Uzbek or Turkmen embroidery, to the most sumptuous couched metal-thread embroidery on velvet. In the 1920s, Jews began to wear karakul hats made of astrakhan (the skin of new born lambs).

But perhaps the hat most identified as a Jewish form of headgear is the Sabbath and festive fur-trimmed hat called a *shtrayml*. It was probably adopted in the eighteenth century from Polish dress and in the early twenty-first century continues to be preserved by various Hasidic groups in several shapes and under

several names. It consists of a velvet cap with a fur brim, preferably of sable or fox, but in the early twenty-first century synthetic fur is also used. It is worn over a small cap called a yarmulke. The everyday hat, especially for working-class Jews in East Europe, was the black-brimmed and black-visored hat called a *kashket*.

The wearing of a small skullcap as a head covering by religious Jews evolved only in the nineteenth century in Europe and was part of the controversy between Reformists and traditionalist groups. Reformist Jews, who discarded covering the head for most of the time, sometimes while at certain rabbinical schools, wore small caps when studying religious texts or at prayer. To counter this perceived laxity or liberal attitude, men in some Orthodox circles began to wear a double head covering consisting of a small skullcap under a larger hat so as not to remain bareheaded. This custom has since persisted as a norm among all Orthodox Jewish groups.

Since the early twentieth century, especially in Israeli society, the presence or absence of a head covering is used to distinguish secular and observant Jewish men. The type of covering used indicates socioreligious, ideological, and political affiliation; for instance, the *kippah sruga*, a crocheted skullcap, has become an identity mark of the national religious community and political party.

HEAD COVERING FOR WOMEN

In contrast to the headgear worn by men, the covering of married women's hair is the most basic halachic requirement of modesty for women. The rabbis of the Mishnah and Talmud (between the second and fifth centuries C.E.) considered the covering of a married woman's hair so vital that they allowed the husband to divorce his wife unconditionally if she exposed her hair immodestly (Mishnah Ketubbot 7:6). Since that period, the practice has become mandatory, pervasive, and universal throughout the Jewish world.

Both the manner and style of the head covering have taken many forms and differ immensely from place to place, from simple kerchiefs to composite constructions. The fashion of covering the hair is one of the most varied and charged condensed symbols in Jewish attire. Prior to modernization, women's head covering attested to marital status, socioeconomic status, place of residence, and communal affiliation. In the twenty-first century, the distinction is less geographic and attests to religious group affiliation, degree of religiosity, local fashions, and a certain degree of individual creativity and taste.

The extent of covering the hair also varies; in some places, it became customary to cut the hair or shave it shortly before or after the wedding. Shaving women's hair is practiced among some of the Ashkenazi ultra-Orthodox groups. This was considered by some to be the ultimate understanding of concealing women's hair but was met with rabbinical opposition on the grounds that, by doing so, the women disfigure themselves and resemble men. In some places, it was the norm to cover the hair entirely, while in other areas women would allow some parts to be seen.

In Sana'a, Yemen, Jewish women from childhood on wore the distinctive *gargush*, a hoodlike headgear that concealed the hair, the forehead, and the neck. It distinguished Jewish women from Muslim women and Jewish women of Sana'a from women of other localities. Women had several hoods; the most sumptuous was the *gargush mezahhar merassaf* (the full golden hood), which

A Jewish family from Sana'a, Yemen, twentieth century. The men wear the Jewish cap and tunic-dresses with black goat-hair prayer shawls (*shamlah*) wrapped around their shoulders. They are recognized by their side locks, called *simonim* ("signs"). The women wear black antari dresses with black head coverings (*gargush*). These garments are decorated with embroidery and silver work made by the Jewish jewelers in Sana'a. Isidore and Anne Falk Information Center for Judaica and Jewish Ethnography, The Israel Museum, Jerusalem. Photograph by Yihye Haybi.

was decorated with gilt silver filigree pieces and with several coins. All these riches formed part of the woman's dowry, which she received from her father, and were used as her cash reserve. Jewish women of rural Yemen wore a variety of head coifs that distinguished them from Muslim women.

In Istanbul, the capital of the Ottoman Empire, both Jewish and Muslim women wore the Turkish egg-shaped *hotoz*; however, Jewish women concealed their hair, while Turkish women let part of their hair show. Jewish women of Kurdistan left two side locks flanking their face, as did Kurdish Muslim women, and allowed their plaits to show under their turbans.

The wearing of wigs was more prevalent among Ashkenazi Jewish women, but in several places, such as in Morocco and Georgia, Jewish women's coifs incorporated false hair that served as a partial wig. Rural and urban Moroccan Jewish women's headgear was especially varied and complex. According to local halachic rulings, it was forbidden to use human hair in the wigs, so horse and cattle hair, woolen threads, and feathers were used. A fine example of Jewish Moroccan headgear is the elaborate *mehdor* of the Jewish women of the Sousse region on the southern coast of Morocco. This is an intricate work of silver wire interwoven

with the hair of a horse's tail, two locks of which frame the woman's forehead; it is topped with parallel silver cylinders decorated with colorful cloisonné typical of the region's jewelry. In Tunis and Algeria, Jewish women wore various versions of small, conical caps (*duka*) on top of the head. The cap was held in place by several scarves; some of their hair locks were allowed to show at the forehead.

In Bukhara, married Jewish women wore a combination of several kerchiefs that framed the face. This headdress consisted of a forehead band of folded stiff brocaded fabric (*rūmoli peshona-band*) and, either over it or under it, according to local variation, a folded triangular scarf that was tied at the back of the head. Sometimes, older women added another piece of cloth that covered the chin and neck, thus framing the face all around. Underneath these, Jewish women wore the local prevalent *kulta peshak*, a cap with a snood attached to its back, into which the women put their hair. Although these caps were richly embroidered with colorful silks or metal threads, they were totally concealed by the other covers. These caps fell out of fashion among non-Jewish women in the early twentieth century, but Jewish women held on to them much later. In Iran, Jewish women wore a large folded triangular kerchief called a *maghneh*, joined with a pin under the chin and falling over the shoulders. In photographs, one can see that some women conceal their hair with a tighter scarf underneath, and some show their hair.

In nineteenth-century East Europe, Jewish women wore small caps and bonnets, while, on a daily basis, lower-class Jewish women wore kerchiefs tied under the chin or at the nape. A more elaborate headgear consisted of a cap and a strip of dark-colored fabric covering the front part of the head over the forehead, imitating combed hair or arranged as lace curls. Above these curls and on the crown of the head were arranged ornaments made from ribbons, lace tulle, and feathers, as well as fabric flowers in the form of a small basket. The most sumptuous headgear was the *shterntikhl* ("forehead kerchief" in Yiddish), which was a coronet sewn onto a cap, with scalloped edges encircling the face; it was normally studded with pearls and precious stones. It stemmed from Polish aristocratic urban women's dress and was a desired part of an upper-class bride's trousseau and a family heirloom.

In the early twenty-first century, the wearing of wigs remains a highly controversial issue among the different Orthodox groups. Some claim that the display of hair, even false hair, does not conform to the prohibition to conceal it, since the showing of any hair is considered erotic and therefore immodest. Whereas in Russia and Poland in the mid-nineteenth century, the wearing of a wig (*sheitel*) was considered a fashionable innovation replacing the former types of headgear, it soon became a symbol of obsolete Jewish otherness. It persisted despite being banned by the Russian authorities in the mid-nineteenth century. When religious East European Jewish women arrived in the United States, it turned into the symbol of the old country, and its use put it outside fashion.

In the early twenty-first century, there are a variety of hair coverings among religious Jewish women. They range from knotted scarves to knitted snoods, elegant hats, and many others denoting religious and sometimes political affiliation. Hasidic Jews are divided into two courts, one of which originated in Szatmar, Hungary, and the other in Belz, Poland, and this division is reflected in head coverings: Szatmar Hasidic women in New York and Jerusalem wear similar head coverings—a scarf covering their hair entirely, sometimes with padding under it or a small piece of synthetic wig in front, or a whole wig worn under the scarf. Belz Hasidic women wear a wig and a small cap on top of it. The women of the Neturei Karta, one of the most extreme ultra-Orthodox groups, cover their shaven head with a tight black scarf. Sephardi Oriental women in Israel in the early twenty-first century tend to wear fashionable hats and scarves following the ruling of the influential Rabbi Obadiah Joseph, which prohibits the wearing of wigs. Some Jewish women who belong to the Reform movement, who believe in equality between men and women in their religious duties, cover their head with skullcaps similar to those used by men.

MODESTY

Jewish halachic rulings and ethical literature deal extensively with questions of modesty in dress. Modesty is addressed with regard to norms of revealing or concealing the body, and modesty in dress (as opposed to luxuriousness) is preached. A basic requirement is to be decently dressed and covered during prayer (Tosefta Brachot 2:14, second century C.E.). This attitude was later interpreted as the separation between the upper part of the body, considered spiritual and pure, and the lower part, considered mundane and impure. Among the Hasidim of East Europe (from the eighteenth century on), this division of the body acquired a rich symbolic meaning and is fulfilled by the *gartl*, a belt donned ritually before prayer.

The equivalent item among women was the apron, the purpose of which was to cover and protect the reproductive organs. These aprons, worn under or over the skirt or both, were a symbol of modesty and were considered magically protective. The wearing of aprons persisted among East European Jewish women and in the early twenty-first century, after having almost vanished, is making a comeback among some ultra-Orthodox women, who wear them while lighting Shabbat candles and during festive occasions. They regard them as charms that will bring them well-mannered children.

Jewish women's outdoor dress in Muslim countries demonstrates an appropriation of external dress habits that conform to and coincide with internal modesty norms and requirements. In Muslim societies, there was and remains a marked distinction between indoor clothes and streetwear in women's dress. When going out, mainly in urban surroundings, all respectable women had to cover their body entirely with a wrap or cloak and veil their faces as a protective measure to secure their virtue from strange men. Low-status women such as servants, prostitutes, and non-Muslim women were not required to veil themselves. Veiling was considered the prerogative of Muslim women, and others were not considered worthy of its protection. Yet it has become the accepted norm for women in some Jewish communities. Jewish women veiled themselves when going out of their houses or out of the Jewish quarters, sometimes so as not to place themselves in danger. In some places, Jewish women wore wraps and coats covering their bodies and did not veil their faces. In cities under Ottoman rule, Jewish women, for example, wore the *ferace*, the customary coat with a long, rectangular collar. The ferace worn by Jewish women was dark colored, mainly brown, as required by the sultanic edicts. They covered their indoor headgear with a long scarf called a *marama*, which they only occasionally lifted up to their eyes.

In Herat, Afghanistan, Jewish women wore a black chador (a large rectangular cloth used to cover the head and body of a woman) and hid their faces behind a netted embroidered white veil called a *ru-band*, whereas Muslim women wore a colored, one-piece *chadari*, a garment that covered the head and most of the body (also known as an Afghan burqa). In Iran, the evidence concerning Jewish women and veiling is scarce. Under Shah 'Abbās II (1642–1666), Jewish women were obliged to don a two-colored chador to distinguish them from Muslims, and they were not allowed to veil their faces. In the nineteenth and early twentieth centuries, there are contradictory data, perhaps due to local variations. Some maintain that Jewish women were forbidden to veil their faces and to wear the black chador worn by Muslim women, and, as a result, they wore a dark blue chador; others say that Jewish women wore the black chador as did Muslim women but differed in their white face veil from the Muslims, who wore a black veil.

In Baghdad, Jewish women veiled their bodies and faces well into the 1930s under the British mandate, when they were wearing modern European dresses beneath the coverings. They wore the *izar*, a sheetlike wrap made from two attached rectangular pieces of fabric, which was wrapped around the body and covered the head. The face was covered by a square black veil called a *khiliya*

Jewish bridal attire from Sana'a, Yemen, early twentieth century. This elaborate outfit was worn by Jewish San'ani brides for the *Kidushin* (benediction) ceremony of the wedding. It was known as *tishbuk lu'lu* ("pearl ornament"), stemming from the triangular head ornament decorated with pearls. Some of the jewelry belonged to the bride, but most of the chest necklaces were loaned to her. As part of ethnic revivals in prenuptial ceremonies, this outfit was repeatedly reconstructed in late-twentieth-century Israel. Reconstruction by Rabbanit Bracha Qafih and the Zadok Family, The Israel Museum, Jerusalem.

that was woven from horsehair; this was replaced in the 1920s by a more transparent black scarf. In the early twentieth century, the izar worn by Jewish women was made of pastel-colored patterned silk interwoven with metal threads. At that period, Muslim women had replaced their izars with plain black wraps, and the colored izars were considered a distinctly Jewish outfit. They were sumptuous items, status symbols, brought by Jewish brides in their trousseaus, laid on their coffins before burial, and donated to synagogues as Torah ark curtains. In the 1930s, there was a conflict within the Jewish community between traditionalists and modernists that was termed "the veil war"; while modern Jewish women refused to wear the veil, conservative families tried to force them to continue wearing it.

With modernization, but particularly with the secularization of Muslim states such as Turkey and Iran in the early twentieth century, veiling for all women was abandoned or prohibited.

In the late twentieth century, with the rise of Muslim religiosity and the advent of religious Muslim states, the veil has become the expression of Muslim religious identity and political affiliation for women and an encompassing rule for many women living in these states.

JEWISH SYMBOLS AND INNER MEANINGS

Explicit Jewish symbols are quite scarce in Jewish dress. They appear on some prayer shawls and amulets; for example, embroidered head scarves worn by women during childbirth in Turkey were inscribed with protective Hebrew inscriptions. One of these few items is the sequin-embroidered tulle scarf (called a *pulaki* or *pulakce*) worn by Jewish women from eastern Iran, Bukhara, and Afghanistan, which was considered to be exclusively Jewish. These scarves abound with Jewish symbols and inscriptions, such as the Magen David, a seven-branched lamp (the Temple lamp), a pair of hands (symbols of the priestly blessing and the *hamsa*, or the hand of Fatima), biblical verses and blessings in Hebrew, the names of the bride and groom, and other amuletic motifs. They were given to the bride by the groom's family at the engagement ceremony and were worn at the wedding and afterward on family festive occasions.

However, Jewish dress communicates also on a less overt level, as does any sartorial system. There are hidden signs and inner meanings attributed to aspects of dress by Jews, which, in many cases, are expressed in code and directed at the closer circles, nuanced in a way not noticed by outsiders. The Jewish woman's dress at the time of her menses conveys a message to her husband and informs those in her immediate surroundings. Jewish married couples are forbidden to have sexual intercourse or even touch one another at the time of the woman's menses and for seven days afterward. During that time, the woman is considered impure until she purifies herself in the ritual bath. It was customary among Jewish women of some communities to wear different clothing during that time. Some brides in Afghanistan, for example, had clothes for this purpose in their trousseaus. In many cases, there were no specific clothes, but women wore older, shabby clothes.

An interesting example of an entire code system of nonverbal communication was that transmitted through women's leggings from Yemen. In Yemen, women (both Jews and non-Jews) wore trousers with decorated embroidered leggings that showed from under their dress. The leggings, embroidered in many cases by Jewish women for themselves and in different designs for Muslim women, conveyed a whole array of messages—geographic and ethnoreligious affiliation, social and marital status, age group, and the periodic ritual impurity of the woman during her menses.

Other layers of meanings attributed to dress are mystical interpretations of dress aspects. For example, the wearing of four white garments representing the four-letter name of God on the Sabbath is recommended for men in the teachings of the sixteenth-century Rabbi Isaac Luria Ha'ari, who was one of the most influential kabbalists and whose teachings introduced the kabbalah into everyday ritual. Wearing white on the Sabbath is said to help the person sanctify himself toward the Sabbath and to intercede for him in the world to come. Similarly, the Hasidic men's kaftan is imbued with mystical meanings; for example, it is closed right over left to symbolize the victory of good (right) over evil (left) forces. The community also assigned its own symbolic meanings to aspects of dress imposed by governmental edicts.

Customs regarding dress are numerous, sometimes encompassing, and even mandatory, such as the wearing of special dress for the Sabbath or the wearing of white or light colors on the Day of Atonement. Some customs are practiced by Sephardi or Ashkenazi Jews in general, and some are strictly local or group customs; for example, it is customary among Ashkenazi East European Jewish men to don a white robe called a *kittl* on their wedding day, on the Day of Atonement (the day of divine judgment), and on the eve of Passover, all of which are critical moments in life. The kittl is principally associated with the clothes of the dead, the shroud. Its whiteness carries notions of purity and sacredness, possibly associated with the white clothes of the high priest at the Temple in Jerusalem during biblical times on the Day of Atonement. The kittl serves as a memento mori, a reminder of the wearer's mortality. A man clad in it is confronted with his inevitable death and with his deeds on earth, which should induce the wearer to be more humble, remember his sins, and amend his ways.

DECREES AND REGULATIONS

Since they dispersed from the land of Israel after the destruction of the first Temple, and then of the second Temple in 70 C.E., and later, Jews have lived as a religious minority. During the Middle Ages and until the nineteenth and twentieth centuries, Jews lived under various Christian and Muslim authorities, and their legal status was inferior. One of the implications of this status was that they had to be distinguished by their external appearance and apparel. Restrictive decrees issued by the authorities, often called laws of differentiation, imposed various forms of dress distinction on the population. They required Jews, for example, to wear special garment items, prohibited them from wearing particular fabrics and colors, and obliged them to mark their dress with badges but did not dictate entire outfits.

Up to the nineteenth century, governmental edicts and laws sought mostly to differentiate the Jews from the majority population, but during the nineteenth century, some restrictions were eliminated, and, as part of modernization reforms, there were also opposite tendencies seeking to integrate Jews into society by prohibiting distinctive dress. Within Jewish societies, tendencies shifted also for some segments of the Jewish communities from segregation to assimilation and integration.

Under Muslim rule, Jews' official status as nonbelievers reflected their low legal and social status and determined aspects of their external appearance. After the eighth-century Pact of 'Umar and its derivative edicts in Muslim countries, "people of the book"—Jews, Christians, and Zoroastrians (*dhimmi*)—had to differentiate themselves from the Muslim population. Such edicts guaranteed the dhimmi security and protection, and they in turn promised the Muslim ruler, among other things, not to resemble the Muslims with regard to elements of their dress.

These restrictions were by no means uniform in all Islamic countries, and they were imposed differently depending on local circumstances and on the minority community's relationship with the local ruler. It is difficult to assess the extent to which these restrictions were obeyed and what influence they had on practically shaping dress modes. The issuing of many repetitive decrees, despite the threat of punishment, suggests that infringements were frequent.

In the regions under Ottoman rule, the decrees dealt mainly with colors, quality, and sometimes particular components of dress such as headgear or shoes. Nonbelievers, for example, were supposed to wear black or dark-colored outer garments, while green was reserved for Muslims because it is the holy color of Islam. Jews had to wear black shoes and were prohibited from wearing the yellow leather shoes worn by Muslims.

There were also restrictions on the quality of fabrics Jews were permitted to use. They were not allowed to use fabrics such as *kemha* (a classic sumptuous Ottoman compound weave) or *atlas* (satin) or ermine and sable furs, although they could use less expensive textiles and furs. In addition, there were restrictions pertaining to the size and cut of garments; the gowns and especially turbans, for example, had to be less ample than those of Muslims. In Turkey, the size of the turban was of great significance; the larger and grander the turban, the higher the rank of its wearer. Thus, the sultanic edicts included restrictions regarding the length of the turban fabric and the width of the cloak.

In Yemen, especially in Sana'a, Jewish men and women were to wear only dark-colored clothes on a daily basis. Only on the Sabbath, when they stayed within the Jewish quarter, were they permitted to wear white clothes. Men wore a type of gown over which they were not allowed to don belts as did the Muslims, because these belts were used to carry daggers, which Jews were not permitted to wear. Daggers were important symbols of social and economic status, so not being allowed to wear them clearly indicated someone's lack of social status.

In the former emirate of Bukhara, Jews were subject to restrictions that continued even after the Russian conquest in the mid-nineteenth century, as the emirate remained independent but under Russian protection. Jewish men, for instance, could only come to the market wearing dark outer gowns that did not have silk trimmings, and they had to put on a coarse horsehair rope belt. Jews were not allowed to wear turbans at all and were supposed to wear a certain type of fur hat called a *telpek*, which is a black square cap made of luster or glued calico trimmed with lambskin. These restrictions were in sharp contrast to the colorful and sumptuous dress of Muslim men. It is recounted that some Jews replaced the coarse rope with a silk cord, and some bought permission to wear leather belts.

In Shiite Iran, beginning in the Safavid period, the Jews were considered *najes*, meaning "impure," and the edicts were particularly extreme. A male Jew had to mark himself with a red or yellow badge, wear mismatching shoes, refrain from wearing a turban, and don a rope belt. In the late nineteenth century, new local restrictive orders were issued in some cities, such as the prohibition to wear jewelry and eyeglasses in Yazd; in Tehran in 1897, Jews were obliged to wear a badge on their chest. These discriminating signs were abolished only under the rule of Reza Shah Pahlavi (r. 1925–1941) and, in particular, by the clothing regulations of 1936.

Similar restrictions were imposed in medieval Europe by the church councils. In 1215, the Lateran Council issued its well-known dress restriction as a reaction to the forbidden mingling of Christians with Jews and Muslims:

> That they may not, under such pretext resort to excusing themselves in the future for the excesses of such accursed intercourse, we decree that such (Jews and Saracens) of both sexes in every Christian province and at all times shall be distinguished in the eyes of the public from other peoples by the character of their dress. (Quoted from Rubens 1973)

These decrees also included the wearing of a badge. The badge differed in shape and color as well as in the place where it was supposed to be displayed—either on the right shoulder or on the hat. In the duchies of Italy, a yellow patch was worn. In England, its shape was that of the Tablets of the Law, and in Germany, the badge was a ring-shaped sign. The Jews were also obliged to purchase these badges from the government. Although this distinction disappeared in the early modern era, it was revived by Nazi Germany, which imposed the yellow star badge as a race discriminator.

The Jews' attitude toward these restrictions differed. In many cases, the edicts were resented and regarded as discriminating and humiliating. For example, the rope belt imposed on the Jews of Bukhara was called by them *nakhi-i la'nat*, "the curse rope." But sometimes Jews regarded the regulations as a positive factor that helped them distinguish themselves from non-Jews as required by the Jewish codes of law. In some instances, restrictions were interpreted by the Jews as self-imposed and having an inner Jewish

A Jewish family from Bukhara, Uzbekistan, early twentieth century. In this wedding photograph, men and women wear a mix of rich, local, wide gowns and European clothing. The married women wear a forehead kerchief known as *rūmoli peshonaband*. Isidore and Anne Falk Information Center for Judaica and Jewish Ethnography, Israel Museum, Jerusalem.

significance. For example, in Morocco and in Sana'a, Yemen, the Jews interpreted the black dress imposed on them as a sign of mourning for the destruction of the Temple; similarly, on the island of Jerba in Tunisia, Jews wound a black turban around a red fez to commemorate the destruction of the Temple. Symbols of the commemoration of the Temple in Jerusalem and mourning over its destruction abound in Jewish tradition; in a Jewish home, for instance, there is supposed to be an unpainted square on the wall, and, at a Jewish wedding, a glass is broken or ashes are put on the head of the groom.

The segregationist aspects of the governmental decrees were, at times, met by Jewish communal regulations. In addition to the sumptuary aspects of governmental decrees, there were also corresponding Jewish communal regulations and sumptuary laws referring especially to women's ostentatious dress, excessive finery, and opulent jewelry. Women were prohibited from wearing luxurious dress, especially in public. The purposes of these regulations were twofold: first, to avoid arousing jealousy among non-Jews, because it was feared that excess finery in Jewish dress might bring about additional edicts by the authorities; and, second, to avoid provoking internal tensions between rich and poor within the Jewish communities. In Jewish ethical literature, ostentatious dress is often blamed for calamities and harsh decrees. The book *Orhot Yosher*, for example, from the eighteenth century, blamed the Jews' expulsion from Spain (in 1492) on women's love of excessive clothes and jewelry.

The detailed rules and regulations of each community provide important historical sources for the study of dress customs in each community. The rabbis of the community of Fez, Morocco, pronounced in 1613 (quoted from Bar Asher 1991):

> We have unanimously decided that from this day forward … no woman, young or old, shall wear arm bracelets, or chains, or gold bracelets, or gold hoops, or gold rings, or any gold ornament … or pearl necklaces, or nose rings. … [A woman] cannot wear any garment made of wool or silk, and [she] certainly [cannot wear] gold or silver embroidery, even if the lining is inside out, except for a head covering, which is all she is allowed to wear … and as for children and infants, neither boys nor girls may [dress] themselves [in articles made] either of gold or of silver or of silk.

Jewish regulations for clothing and weddings in Hamburg, Germany, in 1715 stated (quoted by Rubens):

> Velvet for dresses, even for linings, is forbidden to women and girls, with the exception of black velvet. The bride may wear any kind of velvet under the canopy during her wedding … any type of skirt which is stiffened with a hoop of wire or … other devices is forbidden to married and single women … even small children. … From today until further notice, no silk dresses of two colours should be made for women, with the exception of dark grey and brown (Fine: 20 thalers). Whoever offends openly or in secret will be excommunicated and treated as someone who has sinned against God.

THE MODERN ERA: MODERNIZATION IN DRESS

In the late eighteenth century and during the nineteenth century, many Jewish communities went through radical changes brought about from without and within. A principal course of change revolved around the process of modernization and secularization. Regarding dress, it was the transition from traditional attire to modern dress. In this complex process, modes of dress were at times crucial and debated issues, and, in many cases, they were the symbolic markers of change. Jewish traditional attire went through a complex and nonhomogenized process of modernization, from dress dictated by traditional religious societies to modern European fashionable dress, with transitional stages and retractions.

Jews greeted modernization in dress with ambivalence, because it was not simply a change in style but involved a change in attitude toward religion, modesty, and conduct; boundaries between groups; aesthetic norms; and body image. Some segments of the Jewish communities welcomed the changes, and some fought against them. Jews made selective changes in dress, in some cases attesting to deeper changes in values and norms and in other cases imitating expected manners and forms. In many Jewish communities, the changes in dress were tied up with the degree of religiosity and attitude to secularism and therefore met with rabbinical opposition.

In West Europe, especially Germany and France, the Enlightenment and the beginning of the emancipation of the Jews included the advent of equal citizenship. This changed the legal status of the Jews and had implications for their dress and appearance. Changes within Jewish society toward reform and secularization and the Jewish enlightenment movement Haskala contributed to the will of some sectors of the Jewish communities to assimilate into the general society, especially as part of the rising bourgeoisie. Indeed, German Jews were the pioneers in adapting fashionable civil dress.

In East Europe—notably in Poland and Russia—the Jewish enlightenment caused a schism within Jewish society between "enlightened" *maskilim*, who were open to Western culture and secular education, and traditionalists. The opening to secular nonreligious studies attracted some and instigated strong resistance among others, actually creating the new ultra-Orthodox Jewry, who rejected strongly any novelty and clung vigorously to what they believed to be true Judaism. This nascent ultra-Orthodox group, called Hareidi Jewry, saw attachment to tradition as a central pillar of Judaism and considered Jewish dress as one of the essential traits of its identity. One of the leading rabbis of this movement was the Hungarian Rabbi Moses Schreiber (also known as the Hatam Sofer), who conferred on dress the status of a religious obligation and regarded it as a safeguard against assimilation and secularization. The maskilim, who had not necessarily become secular, did not consider dress a religious essential but a local custom that could be changed depending on circumstances and fashion. Disputes over dress were a central issue in the conflict between these two groups.

The traditional clothes in question were those that, at that time, were recognized by all as Jewish, though some of them were former fashionable styles worn by the Polish urban population and preserved by the Jews. These included, for men, long kaftans, dark coats, Jewish hats (the shtrayml), and skullcaps and, for women, the head covering.

In Russia and later in Poland, cultural, administrative, and educational reforms were administered as part of a wider "civilizing process," by which the tzars Alexander I (r. 1801–1825) and Nicholas I (r. 1825–1855) aimed to unify the Russian state and

Dress for a Jewish woman (*daria kassa*), Baghdad, Iraq. The *daria kassa* was the hallmark of the traditional clothing of married Jewish women from Baghdad in the late nineteenth century. It displays a unique local blend of European fashion and Ottoman style. The Israel Museum, Jerusalem. Photograph by Noam Bar'am BenYosef.

minimize, actually and symbolically, differences between sectors of the population. Governmental edicts were issued (in 1804, 1835, 1839, 1845, and 1851) prohibiting the display of any ethnoreligious marks of dress; these edicts ordered Jews to shed all their distinctive dress items so that they would not be different from the general population. The edicts, for example, forbade Jewish men to grow side locks and wear long coats, fur hats, yarmulkes, short trousers, and belts, and women were forbidden to shave their heads and wear wigs. Ritual clothes such as prayer shawls were permitted only in the synagogue.

These reforms, which were intended to "amend" the Jews and their culture, society, and organization and integrate them into the state, were welcomed and supported by some Jewish maskilim, who criticized and ridiculed traditional Jewish dress in their writings. The edicts, however, were differential. They applied first to the large towns and only later in the smaller villages; people over sixty years of age could be exempt from them and continue wearing traditional clothes. Different measures were used to enforce the regulations. High fines and taxes were inflicted on people who sewed traditional clothes or insisted on wearing them. The police

were sent to the streets to enforce the rules physically, and there are surviving accounts of police officers cutting coats and side locks and tearing wigs off women's heads.

Nonetheless, the efficacy of the implementation of these decrees was questionable, and the provincial authorities were unable or unwilling to enforce them. At the same time, the decrees met with strong reactions and resistance among religious Jews, especially Hasidim, who were most identified by their attire. The decrees were perceived as a catastrophic attack on Jewish religion and identity. The identification of these clothes as Jewish attire grew stronger in some circles and has been maintained into the early twenty-first century among the ultra-Orthodox. Others changed their clothes gradually with Westernization and modernization in other domains of life.

In Islamic countries in North Africa and Central and Southwest Asia, modernization took a somewhat different course and was bound up with Westernization and with colonial rule. As a result, modernization differed in pace and manner; in some communities, it was part of the process of the entire society, whereas, in others, Jews were catalysts of modernization. Many factors converged to bring about this transition, and it occurred through several channels.

Throughout the Ottoman Empire, for instance, the government instigated modernization through the Tanzimat reforms of the nineteenth century. The reforms of 1856 eliminated theoretically the need to distinguish between Muslims and others, although opinions differ as to the degree of compliance with these decrees throughout the empire. These reforms had explicit orders as well, such as the abolishment of the variety of turbans in favor of the fez. The fez was introduced in 1825 as the official Ottoman headgear, but it was only in 1856 that the obligation for non-Muslims to wear different clothes was abolished.

In some places, the need to mark Jewish dress was eliminated or diminished with the advent of European colonial rule, but it did not disappear altogether straightaway. Jews in many communities identified with the colonial rulers and served as translators and intermediaries as well as emulating their modes of dress. Trade with West Europe, in which Jews were highly involved, brought to urban centers an increased flow of goods and fashions, textiles, ready-made clothing, sewing machines, fashion journals, and more.

Educational systems also contributed to the dissemination of modern European dress among Jews. The Alliance Israélite Universelle, which was founded by French Jews in 1860, propagated modernization and Europeanization among the Jewish communities of the Mediterranean and Southwest Asia. It opened a network of schools for boys and girls all over the eastern Mediterranean and Southwest Asia, from Egypt to Syria, as well as in Iraq and Iran. These schools spread European fashions and dress ideologically as well as by imitation, as the students regarded their teachers' European clothing as a desired style.

Some rabbis objected to modern dress and its influence but not quite as fiercely as in East Europe. They believed that changing a person's mode of dress was an act of apostasy and feared that it would unsettle Jewish life and that following European fashion would lead to breaking the rules of modesty. Such reservations were expressed, for example, by the influential Rabbi Yoseph Hayyim of Baghdad (1832–1909), who warned the Jewish women of his town to cling to their traditional dress because it fulfilled the required rules of modesty.

In central urban communities such as Istanbul, modernization was well under way in the second half of the nineteenth century or somewhat earlier. However, in remote and rural communities such as in Kurdistan or Afghanistan, Jews adhered to traditional attire well into the twentieth century. Some of the communities underwent the transition from their traditional attire to modern Western dress while residing in their places of origin, and others changed their attire only upon migration.

The casting off of traditional dress took many forms, and in every community or locale a variant of modern dress emerged. In the intermediary phases, one could see traditional dress side by side with the latest European fashions as well as different degrees of transition and local combinations of the two modes of dress. Men replaced their robes with European suits, sometimes retaining the local hat such as the fez or *sidara* (an elongated cap worn folded like a military hat). In some places, Jews wore modern dress to work on weekdays and traditional attire on the Sabbath, on Jewish holidays, or for life events such as weddings. Changes in women's clothes were gradual, infiltrating through imported fabrics; alterations in cut such as the addition of cuffs, set-in sleeves, and darts; and the use of accessories such as gloves and umbrellas. In intermediary stages, women wore old-fashioned European attire with hair coverings.

The process of modernization yielded some unusual combinations of modern and traditional dress and did not always present clear dichotomies between traditional and modern. For example, the *daria kassa* dress worn by Jewish women in Baghdad displayed a unique local mélange of Ottoman style and European fashion. It was cut in European style with a long, gathered skirt sewn to a long-sleeved top, of which the most prominent feature was the décolleté trimmed with a flounce. These dresses were made of local or imported fabrics and decorated with European laces and local tinsel (*tel*) embroidery. This dress, introduced as a novelty, became the hallmark of the traditional attire of married Jewish women in Baghdad in the late nineteenth century; somewhat later, it became elderly women's dress and eventually was abandoned altogether in favor of modern fashionable dress.

JEWISH DRESS IN THE OTTOMAN EMPIRE

On the whole, Jewish Ottoman traditional dress tended to follow prevailing Ottoman urban dress styles, with certain distinctive details or signs. But a closer examination of the dress and the attitude of the people toward their dress discloses several layered identities. Many of the Jews in these communities were Sephardim, descendants of the Jews who were expelled from Spain in 1492 and arrived in the Ottoman Empire shortly afterward. They kept a close attachment to their Spanish heritage through language and other aspects of culture even five hundred years after the expulsion, and they also believed it to be manifested in their dress. This is apparent mainly in the Spanish nomenclature of their clothing items and maybe in some aspects of the dress of the Jewish women in Salonika, which was renowned for its distinctiveness. Nevertheless, attachment to past historical identities through dress, even if quasimythical, was an important facet in the constitution of their collective identity. In general, men's dress was uniform with other men's dress in the region, and women's dress displayed a number of local variations.

The most important part of men's dress was the headgear, which, along with the color of the dress and the shoes, were the distinctive signs of Jewish dress. A whole outfit consisted of a wide-sleeved felted-wool cloak in a dark color or black worn over an inner robe with a diagonally cut overlapping front part commonly made of plain or striped satin weave, held by a sash (*umbaz*) that was folded and wrapped around the waist; there were local variations in how the umbaz was wrapped. Wide *şalvar* (trousers) were worn under the robes. The ensemble was finished with black shoes.

From the early nineteenth century on, with the introduction of the fez, Jews stopped wearing the boneta. With the advent of modernization, by dictates of law or fashion, men started to wear European dress when at work, but many of them still wore the traditional robes at home, and these Turkish clothes have become identified as their traditional Jewish clothing. The appropriation of traditional Ottoman attire by the Jews as expressing their Jewish identity at the beginning of modernization was articulated in the writings of the most prominent rabbi of Izmir in the nineteenth century, Rabbi Hayyim Pallaggi (1788–1868). He objected to the wearing of modern clothes on the grounds that they were different from the "Jewish costume," which consisted of, as he enumerated, the *entari* and *cubbe*, stating that "by this the Jew transgresses the injunction 'Nor shall you follow their laws'" (Lev. 18:3).

Women's indoor garb featured local distinctive variations, especially in headgear. Women's attire consisted of the basic item of Ottoman dress—the *entari*, which was a long-sleeved, fitted coatdress with different shapes of décolleté and sometimes slits down the sides—which was worn over a shift or chemise. This basic dress was made of a variety of fabrics, from patterned or embroidered silks to cashmere-weave wool for festive occasions to simple printed cotton for everyday. The dresses were worn in layers and sometimes with a belt with jeweled buckles, as in Izmir. Over the dress were worn short jackets or longer coats, which were sometimes lined with fur, as was the Ottoman fashion.

The hair covering worn by married women in early-nineteenth-century Istanbul was called the *halebi* and was an enormous ball-like headgear; it was abandoned and replaced by a simple scarf until all forms of hair covering were discarded altogether by the late nineteenth century. In Izmir in the early twentieth century, women wore a small black velvet cap called a *tokado* over a black scarf that covered the hair. It was decorated by a diamond brooch (*rozeta*), which was taken off if the woman became a widow. This type of small black cap was already a transitional headgear, the last remaining token of traditional attire in Izmir, and was worn with European frocks.

JEWISH DRESS IN BUKHARA

Bukharan Jews are, in fact, all Jews from the towns of the former emirate of Bukhara in Central Asia, including the cities of Samarkand and Shakhrisabz. In the nineteenth and twentieth centuries, they were largely involved in the textile trade; in former generations, Jews specialized in indigo dyeing.

Their dress was rich and opulent and differed very slightly from that of the urban Muslim population. Men's and women's dress consisted of ample colorful gowns, such as men's kaftan-type robe (*djoma*) and two types of women's gowns: The older form was a wide, open coat (*kaltacha*), and the second, the *kamzol*, was considered a more recent dress with European innovations in cut such as a narrow waist. These were worn over the *kurta*,

Two Jewish women from the region of Tafilalet, Morocco. The woman on the left wears the typical red, embroidered tunic together with the distinctive hornlike multilayered married woman's hair covering called *grun* ("horns"). Isidore and Anne Falk Information Center for Judaica and Jewish Ethnography, The Israel Museum, Jerusalem. Photograph by Jean Besancenot.

a very wide, closed shirtdress. All these were made largely from local silks using renowned and intricate dyeing techniques such as tie-dye, block printing, and especially ikat (*abrbandi*) and were trimmed with the typical local trimming called *zeh*, a band with patterned stripes that looks as if it is woven in card weaving but is, in fact, a kind of finger weave with a needle. The dresses were lined with a variety of fabrics, notably Russian printed cottons and other imported textiles.

For festive occasions, the Jews of Bukhara prefer velvet robes decorated with metal-thread embroidery. In the early twenty-first century in Israel, families of Bukharan descent, when celebrating life events or Jewish holidays, don opulent robes, some of which are family heirlooms and some newly made and brought from Bukhara. For this purpose, and probably for touristic reasons as well, the metal-thread embroidery workshop in the town of Bukhara introduced Jewish motifs into the robes, such as the seven-branched lamp and the Magen David.

It seems that, in the late nineteenth century, the choice of certain textiles was identified with Jews. A certain striped silk called *alochai karatagi* was used by Jews for women's dresses. Jewish women brought in their trousseaus special grayish-green-striped *kaltacha* gowns to be worn on the seven days of mourning. The custom of wearing mourning clothes in gray hues was probably appropriated from the surrounding Tajik and Uzbek population, among whom it is clearly seen in the early twenty-first century, but the use of these specific textiles is described as one of the distinctive features of Jewish dress. It is also noteworthy that on the Day of Atonement (the most sacred Jewish holiday), Jews (both men and women) changed their colorful dress to white robes especially made for the day.

Jewish dress in Bukhara provides one example of the complexity and contradictory tendencies in the move toward modernization. On the one hand, Jews imported textiles and shawls and were among the first to adopt tailored alterations to their traditional dress; on the other hand, Jews preserved items of dress considered obsolete by the surrounding population.

JEWISH DRESS IN KURDISTAN

The dress of Kurdish Jews was indistinguishable from that of the Kurds. The cut of dress was quite uniform in all Kurdistan, whereas the fabrics and embellishments differed locally. Men and women cooperated in the production of clothes: The women spun the threads, sewed, and embroidered men's and women's garments, and the men specialized in weaving.

Men's typical suit consisted of wide, straight-cut trousers gathered at the waist by a drawn narrow sash and a short, straight jacket (sal-sepik) worn with a wide sash girdle made of patterned cotton or a local cashmere-weave shawl. Simpler suits were made of undyed sheep wool, and more luxurious ones were made from fine goat wool called mar'az. These were woven by Jewish weavers; the most sumptuous suits were brocaded with colorful designs and were made and worn by local Armenians, who also specialized in this weaving.

Women's dress consisted of three parts: a long, straight dress with long, pointed sleeves; a short, tight bodice worn over the dress; and a long coat worn on top. Everyday clothes were made of handwoven cotton, and festive dresses were made of silk. When machine-made fabrics were imported into the region, the festive dresses began to be made of patterned multicolored fabrics. In some locales, such as Aqra and Sandor, festive clothes were embellished by embroidery; in Zakho, men's dress was embroidered.

The dress of both men and women was topped by the typical Kurdish turbans, the more festive of which were made from either black silk patterned with silver threads or block-printed scarves adorned by a row of silver-thread tassels with amuletic turquoise beads.

JEWISH DRESS IN MOROCCO

Jewish dress in Morocco was particularly varied between urban and rural Sephardi and local styles. It has also been relatively extensively documented and researched, but the foundation work is no doubt the invaluable studies by French ethnographer Jeanne Jouin, who documented dress in situ in the 1930s.

Restrictions on men's dress were severe; they were obliged to wear black or dark-colored robes called djellaba made of coarse fabric and to walk barefoot in front of a mosque. In rural Morocco, both Jewish and non-Jewish men wore a hooded cloak called a burnoose; a particular type of burnoose was the akhnif, a richly decorated gown with a large eye-shaped motif on its back, worn in the Atlas Mountains, where Jews were obliged to don this gown inside out.

In the rural areas, Jewish women wore draped dresses held by fibulae, as was common practice in the area. In some places, the color of the dress was different for Jews and non-Jews, as in the region of Tafilalet, where Jewish women wore a red wrap (haik), and Muslim women wore white. Jewish women in that region wore white for mourning.

In the urban communities of Morocco in the twentieth century, especially in communities of Spanish origins, Jewish women wore variations of the "great dress" (el kiswa el kebira) as a bridal and festive dress. This outfit consisted of a wraparound skirt (jelteta or faltita); a short jacket or bolero (gumbayz qasot) with a low-cut front, mostly with short sleeves; separate wide sleeves attached under the jacket sleeves and joined at the back; and a front piece (uzha ktef or punta) covering the chest and held in place by two strings. A belt or sash of stiff brocade folded up several times joined the jacket and skirt and made the outfit look like a dress.

The names of the parts of the dress have parallels in Arabic Spanish words, and research has shown the Spanish sources and prototypes of this outfit to lie in sixteenth-century Hispanic urban dress, which was not necessarily Jewish. Its materials (velvet and metal threads), the cut of the wraparound skirt and jacket, and the style of decoration (the gold-thread or cord-couched embroidery) all point distinctly to Spanish origins. Although it is probable that in Spain this outfit was also worn by Jews, in Morocco, it was exclusive to them, as was abundantly described and depicted by Europeans visiting Morocco.

This dress was known both by its Arab name, el kiswa el kebira, and, curiously enough, by its Spanish name, traje de berberisca, denoting the opposite identification of this dress as the dress of the Berbers (rural Moroccan tribes). In the early stages after the Jews who were expelled from Spain arrived in Morocco, this festive, even majestic, dress was identified as Jewish, belonging to the Jewish immigrants coming from Spain, known as megorashim ("expelled" in Hebrew) and forasteros ("strangers" in Spanish), distinguishing them from the local Muslim and Jewish population. In time, the use of el kiswa el kebira spread with the Sephardic Jews to other urban centers of Morocco, and it became an outfit that distinguished urban Jewish dress from the garb of Jewish women from rural areas in the Atlas and Anti-Atlas, who wore variations of local dress based on draped, uncut outfits.

El kiswa el kebira become a symbol, an identity mark of urban Jewish families in Morocco, representing different local, urban, and regional styles. Probably in the nineteenth century, different styles of the dress evolved, varying in color and motifs but mainly recognizable by the headgear—not an integral part of this outfit—which identified the various urban localities such as Rabat and Meknes, Marrakesh, and others.

El kiswa el kebira was still worn as a wedding dress even after Jewish women changed their everyday clothes to modern dress. When they started wearing European white wedding gowns, el kiswa el kebira was moved to the prenuptial ceremonies, especially the henna ceremonies, which were parties in which henna paste was put on the hands and feet, leaving a red hue. This is practiced in many Islamic countries; the color is believed to be protective, and these parties have become a symbol of tradition. In the early twenty-first century, in places where Moroccan Jews who have emigrated from Morocco to other countries reside, there is a revival of henna ceremonies in Moroccan style. In these henna parties, el kiswa el kebira, in conjunction with other Moroccan-style dresses such as kaftans, features as a central symbol.

AFTERLIVES OF TRADITIONAL DRESS

In some Jewish communities, it was customary to donate precious articles of dress to the synagogue to serve as furnishings, Torah ark curtains, Torah mantles, and reader's desk covers. This was regarded as a great honor, as the Torah scroll is the most sacred in the synagogue, and its covers are considered holy. These garments were dedicated to the memory of departed members of the family. In Iraq, the izar wraps were donated to the synagogue.

The "great dress" (*el kiswa el kebira*), Tetuan, Morocco, twentieth century. Dresses like this one were brought by Jews expelled from Spain in 1492 and came to be identified with twentieth-century urban Jews in Morocco. It consists of a wraparound skirt *jelteta* or *faltita*) and a short jacket or bolero (*gumbayz qasot*) with a low-cut front. The Zeyde Schulman Collection, Israel Museum, Jerusalem. Photograph by Avshalom Avital.

In Turkey, around the turn of the twentieth century, many families donated sumptuous wedding dresses, particularly those made of velvet and satin with couched metal-thread embroidery known as *bindallis*. These dresses at one time were fashionable among the urban bourgeoisie of all religions, but when they went out of fashion and were replaced by white wedding dresses, the bindallis were given to the synagogues, where they survive as tokens of memory. In synagogues in Iran, Bukhara, Iraq, Afghanistan, and Kurdistan, Torah cases are abundantly adorned with women's scarves tied to their finials. These scarves create a bond between the women who donated the scarves and the Torah scroll, of which the women did not take part in the ritual, because they are seated in a separate women's section far from the ark.

The foundation of the State of Israel in 1948 was followed by mass immigration of Jews, mainly from Islamic countries to Israel. To integrate the immigrants from diverse cultures and traditions, a policy was implemented that suppressed and eliminated diversity in favor of uniformity to create a homogenized modern state and culture. In this process, external appearance was the most obvious marker. People were expected to replace their traditional attire, or sometimes their elegant European dress, with simple modern dress in line with the dominant Socialist ideology. In the 1970s, some twenty years after the mass immigration, there was a growing awareness in Israeli society of the damage the "melting pot" policy had caused. This instigated several reactions: civil demonstrations by Oriental Jews, the Black Panther movement, roots-seeking movements, ethnic revivals, and a whole series of salvage projects aimed at retrieving what could still be captured of the cultural diversity. Traditional attire—either preserved items brought from the countries of origin or ones newly made with inventive creativity—played a central role in the ethnic revival, folk-dance groups, henna parties before weddings, and others. These outfits have become a focus of nostalgia and an ethnic identity symbol in a multicultural, postmodern society.

References and Further Reading

Bar'am-Ben Yossef, Noam, ed. *Brides and Betrothals: Jewish Wedding Rituals in Afghanistan.* Jerusalem: Israel Museum, 1998.

Bar'am-Ben Yossef, Noam, and Esther Juhasz. "Traditional and Transitional Bridal Costumes in Middle Eastern Jewish Communities." In *Romance and Ritual: Celebrating the Jewish Wedding*, edited by Grace Cohen Grossman, 47–56. Los Angeles: Skirball Cultural Center, 2001.

Berg, Hetty, ed. *Facing West: Oriental Jews of Central Asia and the Caucasus.* Amsterdam: Waanders Publishers Zwolle, 1997.

Bronner, Leila Leah. "From Veil to Wig: Jewish Women's Hair Covering." *Judaism* 42, no. 4 (1993): 465–477.

Frankel, Giza. "Notes on the Costume of Jewish Women in Eastern Europe." *Journal of Jewish Art* 7 (1980): 50–57.

Goldberg-Mulkiewicz, Olga. "Dress." In *The YIVO Encyclopedia of Jews in Eastern Europe*, edited by Gershon Hundert, vol. 1, 421–427. New Haven, CT: Yale University Press, 2008.

Goldman, Carrel Barbara. "Women's Head—Coverings: A Feminized System of Hasidic Distinction." In *Religion, Dress, and Body*, edited by Linda Arthur, 163–180. Oxford: Berg, 1999.

Jouin, Jeanne. "Le costume de la femme israelite au Maroc." *Journal de la Societe des Africanistes* 6 (1936): 167–185.

Juhasz, Esther. "Costume." In *Sephardi Jews in the Ottoman Empire: Aspects of Material Culture*, edited by Esther Juhasz, 120–171. Jerusalem: Israel Museum, 1990.

Juhasz, Esther. "Marriage." In *Sephardi Jews in the Ottoman Empire: Aspects of Material Culture*, edited by Esther Juhasz, 196–217. Jerusalem: Israel Museum, 1990.

Lichtenstadter, Ilse. "The Distinctive Dress of Non-Muslims in Islamic Countries." *Historia Judaica* 5 (1943): 35–52.

Muchawsky-Schnapper, Ester. "Costume." In *The Yemenites: 2000 Years of Jewish Culture*, edited by Ester Muchawsky-Schnapper, 60–76. Jerusalem: Israel Museum, 2000.

Muller-Lancet, Aviva. *Bokhara.* Jerusalem: Israel Museum, 1967.

Muller-Lancet, Aviva. "On Jewish Women's Costume in Baghdad." In *Studies in the History and Culture of Iraqi Jewry*, edited by Shmuel Moreh, vol. 1, 203–227. Tel Aviv: Center for the Heritage of Iraqi Jewry, Tcherikover, 1981.

Nilsson Ben-Zvi, Avi. "The Caftan of the 'Jerusalem Costume.'" *Israel Museum Journal* 1 (1982): 55–62.

Rubens, Alfred. *A History of Jewish Costume.* London: Weidenfeld and Nicolson, 1973.

Sahim, Haideh. "Clothing and Makeup." In *Esther's Children: A Portrait of Iranian Jews,* edited by Houman Sarshar, 175–196. Philadelphia: Jewish Publication Society, 2002.

Shwartz-Be'eri, Ora. "Clothing." In *The Jews of Kurdistan: Daily Life, Customs, Arts and Crafts,* edited by Ora Shwartz-Be'eri. Jerusalem: Israel Museum, 2000.

Shwartz-Be'eri, Ora. "Embroidery and Ornamentation." In *The Jews of Kurdistan: Daily Life, Customs, Arts and Crafts,* edited by Ora Shwartz-Be'eri. Jerusalem: Israel Museum, 2000.

Shwartz-Be'eri, Ora. "Weaving." In *The Jews of Kurdistan: Daily Life, Customs, Arts and Crafts,* edited by Ora Shwartz-Be'eri. Jerusalem: Israel Museum, 2000.

Slapak, Orpah, and Esther Juhasz. "Jewish Dress." In *Encyclopedia of Clothing and Fashion,* edited by Valerie Steele. Detroit, MI: Charles Scribner's Sons, 2005.

Stillman, Yedida K. "The Costume of the Moroccan Jewish Woman." In *Studies in Jewish Folklore,* edited by F. Talmage. Cambridge, MA: Magnes Press, 1981.

Stillman, Yedida K., and Nancy Micklewright. "Costume in the Middle East." *Middle East Studies Association Bulletin* 26 (1992): 13–38.

Wertheim, Aaron. *Law and Custom in Hasidism.* Hoboken, NJ: Ktav, 1992.

Zimmer, Eric. "Men's Head Covering: The Metamorphosis of This Practice." In *Reverence, Righteousness and Rahamanut: Essays in Memory of Rabbi Dr. Leo Jung,* edited by Jacob J. Schacter, 325–352. Northvale, NJ: J. Aronson, 1992.

Esther Juhasz

See also Dress in Modern Israel.

Dress Reforms of the Early Twentieth Century in Turkey, Iran, and Afghanistan

During the 1920s and 1930s, three states—Turkey, Iran, and Afghanistan—embarked on a series of wide-ranging programmatic reforms designed to transform their respective societies fundamentally. Often called "modernization from above" because of their association with authoritarian elites, these reforms attempted to impose changes in state, economic, and sociocultural spheres that favored broadly Western models and to replace or restrict the practice of corresponding traditional, indigenous, or Islamic forms. The success of the implementation of these reform schemes varied among the three states, with their permanent adoption most evident in Turkey and their interruption and reversal occurring in Iran and Afghanistan.

Because of its obvious visible immediacy, the adoption of Western styles of dress was vitally important in these reform programs as symbolic evidence of a break with what was considered to be a discredited past and the embracing of modernity and progress (the criteria for all three were defined by each country's respective new ruler). Western dress, despite being the product of a specific cultural milieu, was imagined by the rulers of Turkey, Iran, and Afghanistan to be a potent signifier of universal standards of civilization and modernity.

HISTORICAL ANTECEDENTS: SUMPTUARY LAWS AND OTTOMAN TANZIMAT REFORMS

The early-twentieth-century reforms did not represent the first time laws prescribing particular forms of dress had been implemented. This is especially evident in the Ottoman Empire, a state founded in Anatolia during the fourteenth century by the Turkic Osmanlı dynasty, which was the predecessor of the Republic of Turkey. There, sumptuary laws designed to visibly indicate differences between and status within religious communities had been in place for several centuries. Until the mid-nineteenth century, the Ottoman state had been organized using a system called the *millet*, which assigned subjects to specific semiautonomous communal or religious groups. In this system, Islam, in both religious and judicial terms, was supreme. So, for example, certain colors and garments were reserved for Muslims, Christians, and Jews, respectively, and indeed assigned to specific trades, professions, and ranks within the administrative class.

Sumptuary laws were also in place in the predecessors of Iran and Afghanistan, including the Safavid Empire in Iran from the late fifteenth to early eighteenth centuries. Their importance in the Ottoman context, however, was perhaps most pronounced given that empire's majority non-Muslim population for much of its history. These laws were intended to reinforce *distinctions* within the population, where political emphasis was on subjects' intracommunal identification, which, in turn, acknowledged the supremacy of the person and ruling house of the sultan.

What makes the clothing laws of the early twentieth century quite different from the old sumptuary laws is that they were intended to enforce *uniformity* among the population as a visible manifestation of adherence to the ideologies and priorities of the state. Yet even in this respect, the twentieth-century dress reforms were not unprecedented, at least in the Ottoman context. From the late eighteenth century, partly as a response to the declining Ottoman military and economic position in relation to the empire's European neighbors, "modernizing" reform programs were initiated by several sultans. These at first sought to reinforce the observance of the existing sumptuary laws, but those implemented from the 1820s by Sultan Mahmud II rescinded the sumptuary laws that had mandated physical markers among communal groups and introduced the headgear called a fez—a flat-topped, conical, brimless hat often accessorized on top with a tassel—and a men's frock coat known as the *stambouline*, replacing the turban and kaftan as the standard official and professional attire.

In both the Ottoman Empire and Iran under the Qajars (a Turco-Persian royal family that ruled Persia from 1794 to 1925), changes in dress during the nineteenth century were often initiated in the military, with the adoption of elements of Western-style uniforms (an irony, given that European armies had been influenced by items of dress, drill practices, and indeed the marching band of the Ottomans' elite Janissary infantry corps). Court society also played an important role, as both the Ottoman Sultan Mahmud II (r. 1808–1839) and Mohammed Shah of Iran (r. 1834–1848) adopted European-style suits in preference to traditional attire. This was followed to a certain extent, as in many court cultures, by the men and, to a lesser degree, the women of both empires' elites. Increasing numbers of Ottoman and Iranian subjects not only followed the court example but also traveled to and within the West on trade and diplomatic business, often finding it agreeable and convenient to adopt elements of Western dress. Dress became a visual signifier of the struggle for legitimacy between traditionalists and modernizers in both empires.

Headgear was particularly significant, with şapkalı (hat wearer) being a Turkish euphemism for modernizers. Because the turban was held to be the traditional head covering of the Prophet Mohammed and to be bareheaded in public, indoors or out, was an indication of poor etiquette among Muslim men, changes in this particular item of men's dress were emotive and controversial. During the Ottoman period, it was important that religious and social proprieties be taken into account and reconciled with modernizing reform programs. During prayer, it is necessary for a Muslim man's forehead to touch the ground; therefore, hats with brims were out of the question at a time when men were still accustomed to covering their heads indoors. Therefore, the fez in the Ottoman Empire and the Iranian *kolah* (a rimless cap of lambskin or felt)—introduced in the nineteenth century as modernizing, standardizing elements of dress reform—were actually quite distinct from headgear worn in the West and so themselves became new visually distinctive signifiers for both empires. The twentieth-century reforms that followed, and that did away with both styles of headgear, were, in fact, opposed to the results of the previous century's reform programs.

TWENTIETH-CENTURY REFORMS

Turkey, Iran, and Afghanistan found themselves in analogous circumstances in the 1920s. All three had avoided coming under the direct colonial rule of European powers, although the Ottoman Empire and Qajar Iran had become increasingly dependent on a nexus of Western commercial and financial interests. Afghanistan had managed to resist British military incursions and had reached a settlement whereby it maintained domestic sovereignty while its foreign affairs were run from British India. In all three cases, new governments—whether republican, as in Turkey's case, or monarchical, as in Iran and Afghanistan—had replaced established regimes.

The Ottoman Empire had allied itself with Germany and Austria-Hungary during World War I (1914–1918); under the terms of the 1918 armistice ending the conflict, the Ottoman Empire lost its Arab provinces, and Istanbul was occupied by the Allies. The cooperation of the sultan and his government with the Allies in the proposed partition of Anatolia led the army officer Mustafa Kemal Pasha (later known as Atatürk) to declare a national convention in 1919 to assert the existence of the Turkish nation and its corresponding right to independence. The Greek invasion of 1920, launched with Allied consent to subdue the Turkish nationalists, was successfully resisted. The victorious nationalists abolished the sultanate, and the Turkish republic, its capital moved from the old imperial center to Anatolian Ankara, was proclaimed in 1923. In 1924, the caliphate, the status as titular head of Sunni Islam retained by the Ottoman imperial family, was also abolished.

Iran, ruled by the Qajar dynasty since 1796, had remained neutral during World War I, but its strategic location meant that it was used as a battlefield by that conflict's various belligerents. There was direct intervention by the Ottomans, Russians, and British, while Germany engaged in a proxy war by encouraging Iranian resistance to the Russo-British presence in the country. Immediately following the war, the authority of the central government in Tehran was greatly diminished in favor of regional and tribal centers of power. British troops occupied much of the country, spending money freely to ensure influence over tribal, regional, and central sites of power. By 1923, an army officer, Reza Khan, had acquired sufficient political power and became Iran's prime minister. In 1924, inspired by the example of Atatürk in neighboring Turkey, he campaigned for the replacement of the Qajar monarchy with a republic. Clerical and conservative interests opposed this, and, instead, Reza Khan moved in 1925 to assume the throne himself. He adopted the name of a heroic

ancient dynasty, the Pahlavi, deposed the Qajars, and emerged as Iran's new monarch, Reza Shah.

Afghanistan had, during the nineteenth century, been the principal focus of the "Great Game"—the struggle for geopolitical supremacy in Central Asia between Britain and tsarist Russia. By the latter part of the century, Britain had established the supremacy of its interests with the implementation of a treaty allowing it to control and supervise Afghan foreign affairs via an association with neighboring British India. The ruling emirs Abdur Rahman Khan and Habibullah Khan had maintained this arrangement while initiating modest domestic modernizing and administrative reform programs. However, Afghan subordination to the British and residual Russian influence were increasingly resented, particularly by the Young Afghan nationalists (modeled on the Young Turk reform movement in the Ottoman Empire) as well as Habibullah's son, Amanullah, and so, with the outbreak of World War I, Afghanistan declared its neutrality. Immediately following the war, negotiations opened with the British pursuant to Afghanistan gaining its full independence. The Young Afghans advocated an immediate settlement of this question, while Emir Habibullah favored a gradualist route. In 1919, Habibullah was assassinated, it is supposed by one of his own ministers, and the throne was seized by Amanullah, who imprisoned all rival claimants and elevated supporters of outright Afghan independence to key government positions.

This was the situation of all three states by the early 1920s. Established monarchical regimes had been overthrown and replaced by governments that wished to implement reform programs that would adopt aspects of Western sociocultural and administrative practice.

TURKEY

In many respects, Turkey acted as, and was perceived to be, an exemplar for the other two states in terms of programmatic modernizing reforms. The fez, itself the result of an earlier Ottoman modernizing program in the nineteenth century, had, by the early twentieth century, come to represent reaction and pan-Islamism to modernizing groups like the Young Turks, who had begun to conceive of and construct something quite new during the Ottoman Empire's final decades: the idea of a Turkish nation (hitherto the emphasis had been on the empire as a cosmopolitan milieu united around the legitimacy of the sultan).

When the empire was dissolved after World War I and was replaced by the Turkish republic, the fez, as distinctive Ottoman headgear, was earmarked for removal. Mustafa Kemal himself had resented wearing the fez during his travels in West Europe as a young man, perceiving it as a visible marker of his inferiority and status as an outsider with respect to supposedly universal norms of civilization. Even before the Ottoman Empire's dissolution, Turkish modernists had disdained the fez in favor of a fur cap called the *kalpak* derived from Central Asian and Caucasian examples. The kalpak was similar to the Iranian kolah, but, whereas the latter narrowed toward the top, the Turkish cap widened. This had the symbolic utility of directing the idea of "Turkishness" away from Southwest Asian and pan-Islamic milieus and toward cultural and ethnic origins in Central Asia (from where Turkic peoples had indeed migrated westward and southward from at least the early Middle Ages). The kalpak's associations with Asia, however, did not fit well with Mustafa

Mustafa Kemal Atatürk with his wife, Latife Hanm, Turkey, 1923. Atatürk is wearing a Western suit under his large coat and a *kalpak* hat, while his wife wears Western-style garments. Atatürk preferred the *kalpak* to the more traditional fez because it represented his desire to move away from Islamic influences and emphasize ethnic origins in Central Asia. Later, as the first president of Turkey, he would mandate the wearing of completely Western clothes. Time & Life Pictures/Getty Images.

Kemal's vision for a Turkey that would orient itself toward certain Western norms in terms of sociocultural practice, and so it is best seen as a provisional step away from the fez rather than a replacement.

At any rate, as in the nineteenth century, the introduction of European styles of headgear was first evident within the military and the governing elite of the new Turkish republic. The Turkish navy, for example, was instructed in 1925 to switch from the fez to a peaked cap, ostensibly to shield the eyes from the glare of the sun. The peak was so small, however, that the cap's stated utility was minimal. In fact, the switch was symbolic. Thereafter, European-style hats began to appear among elements of the male civilian population in Istanbul.

The increasingly authoritarian ideology of the Turkish state, named Kemalism after its founder (the appellation *Atatürk*, meaning "father of the Turks," was voted for Mustafa Kemal by the Turkish parliament in 1934), united nationalism with a form of secularism that did not separate religion from, but rather subordinated it to, the state. In real terms, Islam was still the state religion of Turkey, but severe restrictions were placed on the forms,

scope, and contexts of its practice. For example, the Islamic religious shrines (*türbes*) as well as the convents (*tekkes*) of the dervish orders—devotees of Sufism (the mystical forms of Islam)—which had been such important features of religious life during Ottoman times, were closed. In addition, the distinctive raiment of the dervish orders was banned. Religious affairs had come within the purview of the new Turkish state, and so its associated directorate accordingly reflected the wishes of the government by issuing a declaration to the effect that there was no Qur'anic verse nor hadith (traditions relating to the Prophet's life) that proscribed the wearing of hats and other elements of Western attire.

Mustafa Kemal decided to introduce, and indeed mandated, the wearing of Western headgear and general attire in the civilian population of the republic at large. He did so by dramatic example, with a staged appearance in the northern coastal province of Kastamonou, known for its citizenry's religious conservatism as well as nationalist sympathies and personal loyalty to Kemal. The president arrived in the city dressed in a white, European-style summer suit, an open-necked sports shirt, and a Panama hat. In his speech to the local populace, he declared that the Turkish people were indeed civilized but needed to prove this partly via their outer aspect—their forms of dress. He went on to maintain that Turkish dress was not national and neither was it civilized nor international. Civilized, international forms of dress were appropriate to the Turkish nation, and Kemal listed them in explicit terms: boots and shoes; trousers, shirts, and ties; and, vitally, a *brimmed* covering for the head, which he made clear was called a hat (*şapka*).

This speech was followed by a number of decrees, including a prohibition of the wearing of religious vestments by anyone other than those holding state-sanctioned clerical office. All civil servants were instructed to wear Western-style suits and hats, and a supplementary decree was added to the effect that hats should be removed indoors and that salutes performed outdoors should involve the doffing of the hat and bowing of the head. By November 1925, these new modernizing dress and dress-related laws were extended to the general male populace. Turkey's Law no. 671 (the Law Concerning the Wearing of the Hat) made the wearing of the fez a criminal offense and mandated the wearing of brimmed hats for all male citizens.

The elites quickly complied with the new laws, but among the general populace the reaction was mixed, ranging from acceptance to reluctance and outright resistance. There was the immediate practical obstacle of an insufficient supply of hats to meet the new demand, and so many men had to improvise by adding ad hoc brims to existing headgear. However, existing prejudice against hats as symbolic of the ways of "Franks" (Westerners), and therefore undermining Islam, persisted. Rumors that the hat law would soon be followed by prohibitions on wearing the veil and possessing the Qur'an led to widespread unrest in conservative regions of Turkey, during which many demonstrators were shot by the gendarmerie, with martial law being declared in some areas. Resistance persisted into the 1930s, and by 1947 there had been as many as 579 arrests for infringements of the republic's dress laws.

Along with the hat law came specific encouragement from the state for men to tolerate the changing dress habits of their wives and daughters. The new state was committed to overcoming Western Orientalist stereotypes that conceptualized Turkey in terms of images of veiled women and their confinement behind harem walls. Therefore, it was important that some Turkish women had begun to adopt Western styles of dress in support of the state's institutionalized disciplinary policies with regard to modernization, which did indeed open professional, public, and then, in 1934, political life to them.

Dress reforms for women were not prescriptive in the same sense as men's in that the emphasis was not on prohibiting specific items of clothing and replacing them with others but on encouraging the adoption of modern forms of women's dress. Kemalist ideology discouraged the veiling of Muslim women, yet no statewide laws were passed to ban the practice (although in some areas local government regulations were used to ban the veil). Instead, Western dress was promoted and encouraged under the auspices of organizations such as the state-backed "Girls' Institutes," whose students produced European-style garments accessorized with Turkish motifs and embroidery but never with a head scarf. The students would then exhibit the items for their family members (male and female) as well as for the approving eyes of the Kemalist republican elites of the 1920s and 1930s. Yet laws prohibiting the wearing of the veil were not enacted until after this period, when laws were passed such as those prohibiting the wearing of the head scarf by women parliamentarians in the legislature and, in the 1980s, by students attending Turkish universities.

IRAN

In Iran, in 1927, as part of a reform package including conscription for the army and the secularization of the judiciary, an analogous hat law was passed. In this case, a particular tall, peaked style known as the Pahlavi hat, similar to the kepi (associated principally with the French army and gendarmerie), was introduced. Resistance, as in Turkey, stemmed from religious concerns, since the peak of the Pahlavi hat impeded the forehead's touching the floor during prayer. After initial unrest, the government was able to stabilize the situation and extend the reforms to other items of men's dress. At the same time, women's dress became a political issue for perhaps the first time in Iran; when female relatives of Reza Shah celebrated the Iranian New Year, Nauruz, at the holy shrine in Qom, they donned chadors, the outer robe and head covering for women that is typical in the country, but these were semitransparent, which mullahs regarded as equivalent to the women being naked.

State-sanctioned slogans were printed in the Iranian press linking the uniformity of modernized dress with notions of patriotism, and, in December 1928, an official dress code was passed into law. Similar to the corresponding Turkish law, uniform dress in the form of European suits was required for all male subjects, with exceptions made only for those engaged in state-recognized civil, military, and religious roles that required deviations from the new norm. Resistance continued, particularly among the clergy and Kurdish and Arab minorities, and indeed the pace of reform was slowed temporarily by the example of the deposition of King Amanullah of Afghanistan in 1929, which was prompted by conservative resistance to the modernizing reforms in that country.

By 1934, however, the Turkish example had been reasserted over the Afghan one. Reza Shah undertook the only state visit of his reign by traveling to Ankara to meet Atatürk and to witness for himself the reform programs in Turkey. Indeed, the Turkish president's acceptance of a reciprocal invitation to Tehran perhaps accelerated the pace of change in Iran so as not to appear backward compared to its western neighbor and (in this regard) exemplar. Reza Shah's regime had become increasingly autocratic, and, in a 1935 decree, the Pahlavi hat was replaced by the new requirement that all Iranian men must henceforth wear Western-style brimmed hats. As in Turkey, the manufacturing capacity could not initially keep pace with the suddenness of the change, leading to absurdities like men in small rural communities sharing a communal hat for excursions into larger centers where the eye of the state was more likely to fall on them. Again, following the Turkish precedent, rules were enforced mandating the type of hat to be worn in given situations and associated forms of etiquette, such as tipping it in greeting.

In terms of women's dress, this time going beyond Atatürk's example in Turkey, Reza Shah went so far as to ban the veil in Iran. Resistance was met with state brutality when, for example, demonstrations centered on Mashad's Gowharshad mosque were put down by the security forces, leading to the death and burial in mass graves of large numbers of protestors and the exile of their clerical leaders. This atrocity was not forgotten, and, during the 1979 revolution, General Iraj Matbu'i, the officer in charge of the government forces at Gowharshad, by then in his eighties, was arrested and executed.

AFGHANISTAN

In Afghanistan, under the rule of King Amanullah, an ambitious series of modernizing reforms was undertaken as a means to reinforce the country's independence from British involvement in its affairs. The main objectives were structural: the formation of a system of constructional monarchical government, the development of professional armed forces, the forging of Afghanistan's microsocieties into a cohesive nation-state, and the fostering of sociocultural changes that were liberal in spirit and purpose and reconcilable with Islamic proprieties.

Parallels with the Turkish and Iranian examples were apparent. Amanullah undertook a series of foreign state visits, including to Ankara, where Atatürk warmly welcomed him and praised the Afghan reform program. On his return from Turkey, as did Reza Shah when he returned from Ankara, the king speeded up the pace of reform, imposing Western styles of dress on the male populace, restricting the wearing of clerical raiment, and encouraging unveiling among women. The latter was initially mandated only among the women of the royal household; it was seen as a first step toward full female emancipation. Thereafter, Western dress was required for attendees at all court functions and in certain parts of the capital. Amanullah's reforms, however, remained confined to Kabul and other major cities and did not achieve the wide-ranging success of dress reforms in Turkey and Iran.

CONCLUSION

Turkey had acted, with respect to particular forms of programmatic dress reforms, as an exemplar to Iran and Afghanistan. It had undertaken them as a specific means to break away from what the leaders of the Kemalist republic saw as a backward Ottoman past, wedded too closely to Islam and premodern ways. Indeed, precedents already existed within the Ottoman context in the form of the nineteenth-century Tanzimat reforms. Among the three states, the reforms also proved to be the most durable (in terms of adhering to their original ideological spirit and function) in Turkey, where the Kemalist secularist state maintains its essential form and authority into the twenty-first century. Although the practice of multiparty democracy has been extended in Turkey, and Islam and appeals to the Ottoman past have demanded and achieved a more prominent place in the Turkish public and political spheres (the center-right Islamist Justice and Development Party was returned to power in the 2007 elections), this has been accompanied by assurances that the fundamental boundaries between secular and religious life enshrined in the republic's constitution will remain sacrosanct.

In Iran, the reforms were essentially maintained until the veil was reintroduced as compulsory for women after the Islamic Revolution of 1979, while men's attire generally retained its existing form minus the necktie (which was deemed emblematic of Western cultural imperialism). In Afghanistan, after the overthrow of Amanullah in 1929, many of his government's reforms were revoked. However, in 1959, under the premiership of Mohammed Daoud and again under the Communist government from 1978 on, specific dress reforms regarding the veiling of women were reasserted. After the fall of the Soviet-backed regime in 1992, and particularly after the rise to national power of the Taliban from 1997 to 2001, strict codes of Islamic dress for men and women were reinforced.

References and Further Reading

Akşin, Sina. *Turkey: From Empire to Revolutionary Republic*. London: Hurst and Company, 2007.

Atabaki, Touraj, and Erik J. Zürcher, eds. *Men of Order: Authoritarian Modernization under Atatürk and Reza Shah*. London: I. B. Tauris, 2004.

Çınar, Alev. *Modernity, Islam and Secularism in Turkey: Bodies, Places and Time*. Minneapolis: University of Minnesota Press, 2005.

Faroqhi, Suraiya. *Subjects of the Sultan: Culture and Daily Life in the Ottoman Empire*. London: I. B. Tauris, 2005.

Keddy, Nikki R. *Modern Iran: Roots and Results of Revolution*. New Haven, CT: Yale University Press, 2003.

Navaro-Yashin, Yael. *Faces of the State: Secularism and Public Life in Turkey*. Princeton, NJ: Princeton University Press, 2002.

Quataert, Donald. *The Ottoman Empire: 1700–1922*. Cambridge, UK: Cambridge University Press, 2005.

Saikal, Amin. *Modern Afghanistan: A History of Struggle and Survival*. London: I. B. Tauris, 2006.

Zürcher, Erik J. *Turkey: A Modern History*. London: I. B. Tauris, 2005.

Derek Bryce

See also Laws of Differentiation.

Snapshot: Turkish Fashion Designers

The Ottoman Empire was at the center of interactions between the Eastern and Western worlds for six centuries and was, in many respects, an Islamic successor to earlier Mediterranean empires, especially the Roman Empire and the Byzantine Empire. Throughout its history, the Ottoman Empire was constantly interacting with other countries, cultures, and regions; its unique Turkish culture therefore evolved by absorbing the cultures of conquered lands and their peoples. At the same time, it was influenced to a great extent by the traditions and languages of Islamic cultures, notably those of the Arabic and Persian worlds. By adding new dimensions to Turkish culture and also affecting the others, these cross-cultural influences and the full diversity of the Ottoman Empire's people and ways of dressing impacted on the richness of Turkish culture and dress as well as global fashion. Following the establishment of the Turkish republic, Turkey moved toward a Western mode of fashion in the belief that this would bring the benefits of industrial and social reform. The unique aesthetics of Turkish culture and its Ottoman past became an inevitable casualty of this change.

The characteristic traditional Turkish dress can be summarized as semifitted garments, including coats, loose trousers, turbans, veils, and plumes. These garments are arranged by layering or asymmetrically draping them. Front openings and easy removal are important features, and all garments are worn with various accessories and feature design details such as Turkish hanging sleeves or layered sleeves. Intercultural marriages played their part in altering Turkish fashion by introducing elements of Western style, but, at the same time, Western fashion borrowed from the essential forms of Turkish dress.

In the early twenty-first century, contemporary fashion is apparent in both its social and economic dimensions in Turkey, as it is in the whole world. Fashion designers everywhere borrow from every culture, since the world is becoming increasingly a shared source of inspiration and common vocabulary for designers. The visual language of fashion has become a world language, although still with numerous local dialects.

Turkish fashion designers are divided into two categories: designers who have been working abroad for years and have absorbed international input and culture and designers working in Turkey who are committed to ensuring that Turkish design obtains the recognition it deserves. These designers and their global counterparts are able to explore the cultural and artistic riches of Turkey, from Inner Asia to Anatolia, the Bosporus, and far beyond: the wealth of textiles, traditional arts, miniatures, calligraphy, woodwork, metalwork, and ceramics.

Over the last two decades, a few expatriate Turkish designers have joined the ranks of international fashion designers: Hussein Chalayan, Dice Kayek, and Rıfat Özbek. They have gained attention for the universal appeal of their work and have started blending their understanding of modern fashion with their own culture. They have become participants in the aesthetic dialogue, creating designs that participate in world fashion, often with a certain Turkish flavor. Important fashion designers working in Turkey include Vural Gökçaylı, Cemil İpekçi, Yıldırım Mayruk, and Zuhal Yorgancıoğlu. A new generation of rising designers includes Bora Aksu, Arzu Kaprol, Bahar Korçan, Atıl Kutoğlu, Ozlem Suer, and Ümit Ünal. Many other creative personalities have been contributing to the global language of fashion.

Rıfat Özbek, a Turkish-born designer who made a name for himself in the 1980s, established himself internationally. He moved to the United Kingdom in 1970 and graduated from Central Saint Martins in London in 1976. In the 1980s, his collections included design elements drawn from traditional Turkish culture and art, which included the use of long, lightweight coats or sleeveless vests worn over trousers, dresses, or skirts. In his recent collections, his opulent clothing is often inspired by different ethnic groups and cultures. He melds ethnic influences into contemporary shapes but mainly plays with combinations of patterns, prints, and surface design elements in contemporary styles. For example, his autumn/winter 2006 collection featured motifs and decorations from Ottoman kaftans (long, outer robes), such as tulips and Ottoman tile designs, on ultrashort and lean modern silhouettes and cuts. In addition to the Ottoman motifs and patterns, fur-trimmed collars and cuffs, embroideries, sashes, and kaftan-type coats reinterpreted in short and lean modern silhouettes are the main characteristics of this collection.

The Turkish designer Dice Kayek has also established herself in Paris with the essential simplicity of short and lean little dresses. Playing with forms, the dominant shape of her collections is the structured shift dress. The most important designer of Turkish origin, however, is Hussein Chalayan, who graduated from Central Saint Martins in London in 1993. His designs bridge the gap between countries, cultures, regions, religions, and beliefs; he explores everyday experiences in the light of change and expresses them in human terms reflected in a concrete image. For example, he produced a show with a series of models wearing face veils but less and less clothing, thus making the "normal" unusual and triggering the audience to think about what they had seen. But, implicitly, his work reflects his Turkish/Cypriot roots. The main theme of the designer's collections is change. He searches for his own identity and his cultural identity in his garments. Since the launch of his own label in 1994, Chalayan has developed a reputation for designing "difficult" clothes that are seen as challenging due to his intellectual approach to fashion. For example, in one of his shows, he began with a traditional Turkish dress, deconstructing the elements of this dress gradually into modern

A model wearing a dress with a tesselated tile pattern on the skirt, designed by Rıfat Özbek for the spring/summer 2008 collection, Milan, Italy, 2007. Some of Özbek's creations are inspired by elements from traditional Turkish culture and art. Damien Meyer/AFP/Getty Images.

and high-tech dresses, and then started reconstructing the same traditional dress again. The show started and ended with the same traditional dress, questioning the evolution of global fashion and change.

Since the beginning of the 1990s, a new generation of young contemporary Turkish designers has contributed a new dimension and individual vision to global fashion. These Turkish designers tend to be truer to their roots, managing to transform their uniquely Turkish sources of inspiration into modern designs, acting as change agents in global fashion. Typically showing at alternative shows both in Turkey and abroad, they approach the international fashion market with an open mind, determined to bring their intellect and local flavor to the global fashion scene.

REFERENCES AND FURTHER READING

Evans, Caroline, Suzy Menkes, Bradley Quinn, and Ted Pol-
hemus. *Hussein Chalayan*. Rotterdam, the Netherlands:
NAI Publishers–Groninger Museum, 2005.
Gocek, Fatma Muge. *East Encounters West*. New York:
Oxford University Press, 1987.
Jirousek, Charlotte. "Ottoman Influences in Western Dress."
In *Ottoman Costumes: From Textile to Identity*, edited by
S. Faroqhi and C. Neumann. Istanbul: Eren Publishing,
2005.

Fatma Mete

See also Hussein Chalayan: Controversial Fashion Designer or
Bridge between East and West?; Snapshot: Turkish Costume
Albums.

Snapshot: ANAT, Syria

ANAT is a textile and clothing design firm that was founded in 1988 in Damascus, Syria. It was an initiative of a group of women who wanted to work and provide their families with extra income. The embroidery projects in Syria at the time were all connected to Palestinian political organizations. Disorganization and unprofessionalism led to the failure of similar enterprises as economically independent projects, and all of them needed to be sponsored by political organizations. ANAT's challenge, therefore, was to create a self-reliant organization.

The company's aims, according to its 1988 mission statement, were to provide employment for women, cultivate traditional textile arts, and promote cultural exchange. Employment for women is often a first step to greater independence and improved self-esteem. ANAT supports this objective and tries to help women by teaching them traditional techniques of sewing, macramé, and tassel making. A short, personally tailored education is very important, especially for mothers, because it leads to financial benefits very quickly. The company researches the meaning of patterns and colors and the history of embroidery. At the same time, ANAT integrates the old embroidery arts into everyday life by using traditional knowledge in new and fashionable designs. ANAT's last aim, to promote cultural exchange, is rooted in a hope that displaying Arab traditions and fine handicrafts to the world might win some friends for the Arab people, who have created a cultural treasure and influenced European development in many ways.

These aims were quite ambitious considering that, in 1988, it was not possible to register as a nongovernmental organization in Syria, and therefore it was necessary to finance all programs without any outside help. To reduce the marketing costs, which are normally very high for handicraft products, ANAT engaged its customers by offering services such as lectures about embroidery and social subjects and trips to the villages of the traditional embroiderers. In return, ANAT received a lot of help from customers in marketing the products. ANAT was also able to develop a program of "learning by doing" to minimize the costs for teaching and to integrate the teaching program into the production. This meant that the designs had to be adapted to the teaching process.

In the beginning, there was an intensive discussion about the meaning of tradition and whether it is appropriate to modernize traditional designs. ANAT took the view that traditions always change when new techniques are introduced and when economic, social, or political circumstances change; it proved this point by researching the history of embroidery in Palestine. For a long time, social conditions were quite stable in the area of Greater Syria, and it appeared that the traditions were unchanging. But social and cultural changes in the twentieth century were so large and overwhelming that traditions were not able to keep up with the developments, resulting in a gap between tradition and modern life—a gap that ANAT sought to bridge.

Such an undertaking often requires conscious action and the support of an institution of the state, a political organization, or a civic organization. The Palestinian political organizations, which recognized the traditions' importance in supporting national identity, argued that the traditions must be protected and repeated as they were practiced in Palestine before the expulsions of 1948 and afterward. ANAT argued that Palestinian life had changed, and, if Palestinian embroidery traditions did not keep up with these changes, they would become romantic, sentimental memories without relevance to modern life. One result would be that these traditions would find a final resting place in a museum, which is seen by many as the graveyard of culture.

Therefore, ANAT decided to create modern clothes and lifestyle items. To do so, it was necessary to define the relationship of fashion to tradition, which is a complex matter in an increasingly globalized society. Fashion is no longer determined solely by traditions and has become accessible to greater numbers of people. There is, in some contexts, a stark and problematic juxtaposition between rapidly changing fashions and traditions that have developed slowly from generation to generation. ANAT is trying to highlight these historical cultural values instead of producing new collections every year.

ANAT emphasizes using traditional embroidery stitches, embroidery patterns, cutting patterns, materials, colors, and finishing techniques in new ways. This alone does not make the products part of the Palestinian tradition. Only if the proposals are accepted by consumers and become an integral part of the Arab lifestyle can they be seen as a development of Arab tradition. In the early twenty-first century, ANAT's customers are Arabs as well as foreigners who are interested in Arab culture. ANAT is not trying to connect to the fashion industry but to stay independent. Nevertheless, ANAT has been able to enlarge its production volume every year, to employ more and more women, and to increase the quality of its products. Since its establishment in 1988, ANAT has become a sustainable and independent organization that is established in and integrated into the international market.

Heike Weber

See also Palestinian Women's Dress.

Snapshot: An Omani Fashion Designer

In December 2003, the Omani Women's Association sponsored a special Omani fashion show that unlike other fashion shows that have been held in Oman, was comprised entirely of Omani fashion and showcased the work of three Omani nationals. The fashion show took place at the Al-Bustan Palace and Hotel just outside of Muscat and was attended by many dignitaries. The special guest of honor was His Highness Sayyid Haithem bin Tariq AlSaid, minister of heritage and culture.

Three designers were featured in the fashion show. Zakia bint Hamed bin Saud Al-Busaidi, president of the Omani Women's Association, which sponsored the event, was responsible for five of the outfits showcased. Khadija bint Abdullah Al-Kunji designed the *abayehs* on display (long-sleeved, full-length outer coverings or overcoats made from black crepe). The third designer, Nawal bint Hamed bin Hamid AlHooti, made her official debut that evening as a fashion designer.

Nawal is an Omani national, mother of six, wife, and ex-banker. Throughout her youth, Nawal had a love for fashion and frequently visited the tailor's shop near her home. With the support of her family, and in particular her father and her husband, she decided to make fashion her career. Entirely self-taught, she developed many of her early ideas in private, at a time when the Omani people were not as open to international fashions as they are in the early twenty-first century.

Traditional Omani designs have never achieved international acclaim the way the Indian sari and the Japanese kimono have. Among the many reasons for this is perhaps the fact that Oman is situated in a far corner of Arabia. This obscurity has lessened in the last thirty years, following the ascension to the throne in 1970 of Sultan Qaboos bin Said Al-Said, who has introduced many social and economic changes. In that time, Nawal has created garments that are based on traditional designs but belong in the modern era. She uses less fabric than was conventional, creating a sleeker and tidier look but without revealing the shape of a woman's body or exposing too much of it.

An example of these changes to the basic Omani style can be seen in Nawal's *Dhofar*-style wedding dresses. The traditional knee-length dress (*thob*) is made of velvet, has a long train at the back, and is normally worn with a pair of pants in a contrasting color, for example, a black dress with white trousers (*sirwal*). The outfit is normally completed with a large head covering (*shaylah*) of some kind. Omani wedding dresses have traditionally combined many bright colors to create a vibrant look. However, the use of no more than two different colors has become increasingly common.

Nawal introduced a new idea to the Gulf: white Omani wedding dresses. The white wedding dress commonly seen in the West made its appearance in the Gulf in the late twentieth century and came to be regarded as highly desirable by modern Omani women. When conceptualizing the future of an Omani wedding dress, Nawal saw no reason why white,

A model wearing a design by Nawal bint Hamed bin Hamid AlHooti, Beirut, Lebanon, 2006. The Omani designer has specialized in re-creating specific regional designs in order to present them to wider audiences. Ramzi Haidar/AFP/Getty Images.

with its connotations of purity, could not be combined with an Omani design. Nawal's version of the Dhofar bridal dress was made from a combination of fabrics and heavily adorned with thousands of iridescent sequins and an array of pastel-colored beadwork, primarily pink. Worn with white netting for the shaylah and white satin sirwal, this sequined wedding thob had a coordinated beaded choker for the bride's neck, which was the perfect accessory for such a design and again something new for the Omani market.

The thob's long train provided Nawal with a blank canvas for her artwork. A distinguishing characteristic of a traditional Dhofari thob is the hand embroidery in multiple colors along all the edges, which can be very ornate and is often done by machine in the early twenty-first century. Nawal modified this traditional embroidery and drew attention to the edges of the train by creating curvy scallops and terraced corners.

Nawal once said that she would like Omani dresses to be worn by women all over the world. This ambition is beginning to be realized, as her designs gain more and more international recognition. Most of her buyers are from the Gulf states (Oman, the United Arab Emirates, Saudi Arabia, Kuwait, Bahrain, and Qatar), but she has presented her designs in fashion shows in Rome, twice in Lebanon, and also in Paris.

In a testament to her reputation and accomplishments, Nawal was recruited by the Ministry of Manpower to support local women in setting up their own tailoring businesses. This is one of the ways Nawal has been able to use her success to benefit others.

Julia M. Al-Zadjali

A version of this article appeared in *Khil'a*, Volume 1 (2005).

See also Omani Dress.

Snapshot: An Afghan Fashion Show

For nearly forty years, it was not possible to hold a fashion show in Afghanistan because of the Russian invasion of the country, civil wars, and the strict rule of the Taliban, who did not permit women to be seen in public. When it was announced that a fashion show would be held in Kabul in 2006, great excitement arose in some quarters, since this was regarded as potentially heralding a return to "normal" life. This fashion show, however, also caused controversy, thanks to the inclusion of one particular garment—a white silk *chadari* (head and body covering composed of a cap, face veil, and mantle sewn together, often known in the West as an Afghan burqa). The controversy raged not in Afghanistan or Kabul but outside the country and among various feminist groups in particular.

The motivation behind the fashion show was to present a different face of Afghanistan. With many Western people viewing Afghanistan in negative terms, presenting a fashion show, often thought of as relating to "modernity," could demonstrate to the outside world that, as everyday life once again became more normal, investing in the country would also become worthwhile again.

Plans for the fashion show were originally proposed in April 2006; it was organized by Gabriella Ghidoni, an Italian fashion designer, and her company, Royah, which was working in Afghanistan to help establish textile and fashion workshops run by and for Afghan women. The name *Royah* means "vision" in the local language (Dari). Royah produces fashionable but traditionally inspired Afghan garments. Sponsorship and help for the fashion show came from various sources, particularly Zolaykha Sherzad from Zarif, another company based in Kabul.

The idea behind the garments shown was to use locally produced, traditional textiles embellished with regional embroidery, because many ethnic groups have their own embroidery patterns. According to an e-mail from Ghidoni, "Afghan materials, Afghan patterns, Afghan embroidery, all revised in fashionable, contemporary designs" was the main theme of the fashion show and the outfits on display. The line was called Abresium (based on the Dari word for silk).

For the fashion show at the Serena Hotel, Kabul, on 8 July 2006, women from the international expatriate community in Kabul modeled twenty-six outfits. The women were deliberately chosen so as not to raise concerns in the local community, as might have occurred if Afghan women had been asked to act as models. But the use of non-Afghans as models also made some Muslim women outside Afghanistan angry because they felt it belittled Afghan cultural heritage.

The apparel presented included a woman's coat in the green-and-purple-striped cloth normally used for making men's coats (*chapans*). This type of cloth, originally from Mazar-e Sharif, has become famous by being chosen for the coats worn by Afghan president Hamid Karzai. Other materials included cottons, woolens, and silks from Herat and Mazar-e Sharif. Some silks were those used for making men's turbans, along with ikat textiles (in which the warp or weft threads are resist dyed—in a manner similar to tie-dye—and then woven to create a pattern) from northern Afghanistan.

Nonfigurative Islamic art and local designs inspired the embroidery for the garments. In particular, designs from the Lakai (an Uzbek group in the north of the country) were a source of inspiration, with their animistic tradition of valuing natural elements such as the sun and the moon. In keeping with local dress codes, the garments and ensembles on display were described as being body skimming rather than skimpy. They covered the models' chests, legs, and arms. Some, but not all, of the models also wore head coverings of some kind.

The white silk chadari decorated with lines of black hand embroidery attracted particular attention and created the most controversy outside of Afghanistan. According to Ghidoni, the white chadari was conceived and designed as a metaphor for Afghanistan's passage from its past to its future. The chadari has been worn in Afghanistan for over two hundred years and much longer in the region that makes up Pakistan in the early twenty-first century. The model wearing the chadari was walking toward another woman dressed in the Afghan flag, thus expressing the concept of the past, in the form of the white chadari, meeting the future, in the form of the Afghan flag.

The use of silk for the white chadari was intended to bring attention to the fact that chadaris in modern synthetic materials are not suitable in the heat and can be uncomfortable. The designers wanted to encourage a return to natural materials such as cotton and silk. Another aim of the designers was to inform people that the chadari was not simply a garment intended to conceal (oppress) women but also represents a complex history with great social significance. The chadari, for example, is used to protect the body from dust as well as from being seen. It can be regarded as an aid to personal freedom because the wearer does not have to worry about what people will say.

One of the ironies is that the white silk chadari has caused more controversy outside of Afghanistan than within the country, being featured in various media from Canada to China and condemned by a number of feminist groups as encouraging the repression of Afghan women. The international media virtually ignored the other garments in the event.

Was the fashion show a success? That depends. It attracted considerable press attention throughout the world and made people aware that something new was happening in Afghanistan. Did many orders for garments come in? Not as many as the organizers had hoped for, but orders did come in. However, the fact that such an event could take place at all indicated a gradual change in Afghanistan with regard to the position and role of women. The fact that Royah continues to operate and employs many Afghan women is also seen as positive.

REFERENCES AND FURTHER READINGS

"Afghans Get a Taste of the Catwalk." BBC News. 9 July 2006. http://news.bbc.co.uk/2/hi/south_asia/5163282.stm. Accessed on 22 June 2008.

"Kabul's First Night of Fashion." *The Sydney Morning Herald*, 10 March 2006, based on a Reuters new release, 9 July 2006.

"Afghan Women Witness the First Fashion Show in Decades." The Muslim Woman. 10 July 2006. www.themuslimwoman.org/entry/afghan-women-witness-the-first-fashion-show-in-decades/. Accessed on 8 December 2009.

Gillian Vogelsang-Eastwood

See also Snapshot: Textiles of Central Asia; The Chadari/Burqa of Afghanistan and Pakistan.

Hussein Chalayan: Controversial Fashion Designer or Bridge between East and West?

- Collection Highlights
- Commercial Collaborations
- The Architect of Fashion
- Material Innovation

Artist, filmmaker, architect, designer: descriptions like these are often attached to Hussein Chalayan, a fashion designer and self-styled "ideas person" who forges unexpected alliances between garments, environments, imagery, and technology. Chalayan frequently brokers significant connections between fashion and other creative disciplines. As Chalayan builds bridges between the visual, the ideological, the invisible, and the tangible, his designs challenge preconceived notions of what clothing can mean. Chalayan is not alone in forging bonds between fashion, architecture, art, and design; this interdisciplinary rapport is also shared by product designers, architects, artists, and academics.

As he engages with other disciplines, Chalayan produces a wide range of fresh looks, silhouettes, and body aesthetics. His garments provide room for self-fashioning and eschew the conformity of trend-based clothing. Yet he is still a designer of real clothes. "I do produce clothes that create a new space for the body, but I am still making a garment," Chalayan explained in an interview with Bradley Quinn in 2004. "There is a duality in my work because a few of my designs are made as showpieces purely to express an idea, while around 95 percent of the collection is designed with wearability in mind. It would be too contrived to expect people to buy the clothes just for the ideas behind them, and I don't expect everyone to want to absorb their meanings. The showpieces inspire the wearable clothes, so the architectonics, the ideas and the issues they deal with are still present."

Numbering among Chalayan's unique expressions are candid references to his Southwest Asian heritage, which he often aligns with elements of Western culture. Chalayan was born in the Turkish Republic of Northern Cyprus in 1970 and describes his early years in Cyprus as a childhood spent on the "fault line" between the Muslim and Christian worlds. Following his parents' separation, Chalayan joined his father in London in 1982, when the Turkish spelling of his given name (Hüseyin Çağlayan) was anglicized. Chalayan obtained British citizenship and later studied at Central Saint Martins University of the Arts in London, graduating in 1993.

In a 2005 interview with *International Herald Tribune* fashion editor Suzy Menkes, Chalayan described how he was shocked when he was described as a Muslim designer—but delighted that there is a fashion designer called Hussein. Chalayan acknowledges how his work is influenced by his nonreligious Turkish roots and tempered by his later education at Central Saint Martins. Chalayan's British upbringing has given him "Anglo-Saxon tolerance where anyone has a chance," according to his interview

with Menkes, and an insatiable thirst for London living. He earned the British Designer of the Year award in 1998 and 2000 and was awarded the Most Excellent Order of the British Empire in 2006. Yet Chalayan is still true to his Turkish roots, teaching part-time in Istanbul and collaborating with Turquality, an organization promoting Turkish brands.

Some of Chalayan's collections, such as Ambimorphous in (autumn/winter) 2003, have showcased the beauty of Anatolian embroidery and the craft traditions associated with Turkish textiles. The collection featured dresses, jackets, and coats pieced together in a patchwork of Turkish cloth and fragments of embroideries derived from Turkish folk dress.

Collections such as the groundbreaking After Words (autumn/winter 2000) heightened awareness of the tensions that have resulted from conflicts between Muslims and Christians. After Words referenced the 1974 Turkish military intervention that displaced both Turkish and Greek Cypriots from their homes. The collection was intended to express displacement and expatriation. A group of furniture belonged to the collection, with slipcovers designed to transform into dresses and skirts; the furniture frames could become suitcases. According to Chalayan, there were stories of people sneaking back home to gather their possessions, and this is what he intended to re-create in the collection. "A part of the idea was camouflage, so that things could be left in an obvious place and still be there when people came home again. That was part of the concept behind the dresses, that they were something valuable disguised as chair covers that no one would take" (interview by Quinn, 2004).

Chalayan's Between collection (spring/summer 1998) brought traditional Islamic dress to his London Fashion Week catwalk. Chalayan sent six models onto the catwalk wearing black chadors of varying lengths and nothing else underneath, exploring the capacity of traditional dress to define and de-individuate the body as it concealed the wearer's identity. The shortest chador exposed the model's body from the navel downward, while another model roamed the catwalk in only a yashmak. The veils enabled the wearers to gauge the audience's reactions while remaining anonymous to the onlookers. "That part of the collection was about defining your cultural environment with your clothes," Chalayan explained (interview by Quinn, 2004).

An expert on the social significance of veiling, Fadwa El Guindi, supports Chalayan's claim: "Dress form and behavior," she has written, "are not accompanied by withdrawal, seclusion, or segregation." Vision and mobility are among the essential concerns of Islamic dress, and the sense of privacy afforded by veiling is comparable to the refuge of a building. Yet even as veiling allows the wearer to wander freely, it regulates her behavior in line with the codes followed by other Muslim women. Chalayan's inversion of revealing and concealing juxtaposed veiling with contemporary modes of visuality, demonstrating the power that masking can provide for a wearer who wishes to see and yet remain unseen.

In Chalayan's work, veiling is interpreted as an architectural device, and the veil itself is in many ways emblematic of the themes featuring in his work. The veil separates, conceals, defines space, and demarcates cultural boundaries but also evokes dualities and duplicitous meanings. Veils are uncodified, intractable, and forbidding while, at the same time, dramatic, exotic, and even enchanted. To Chalayan, a veil can function as both a boundary and a border and symbolize isolation and dislocation, too.

These sentiments came into play in Chalayan's 2004 film *Anaesthetics*, in which a character is veiled to indicate removal, detachment, and disembodiment. Although the film was produced in Istanbul, the veil was not chosen to symbolize Islam but refers to a contemporary geisha, selected by Chalayan to represent the restrained codes of behavior he observed in Japan and not Turkey. "In Japan I was fascinated by how important aesthetics are and how unimportant emotional expression is," he recalled. "I was told that it is considered inhuman to express certain thoughts. I was surprised by how violent processes are completely hidden behind aesthetics—it's as if confrontations or things that rouse angry feelings or disgust are proscribed completely" (interview by Quinn, 2004).

In the first of the film's eleven scenes, the geisha struggles to see her reflection in a mirror through the veil covering her face. The camera cuts from the grisly image of a chef preparing sashimi from live fish to the passive gaze of the geisha. "This scene created an abstract situation where the geisha could not see reality," Chalayan explained in an interview with Quinn in 2004. "She only removed the veil when she was served the finished sashimi, which looked very aesthetic. The veil could represent a built object like a screen or a wall, but here it created a coping mechanism that enabled her to accept the meal without being disgusted by the brutality of the chef on the other side of the screen." Chalayan considers this scene representative of processes that exist in the West, especially in media reports. He explained, "The media give us a disembodied experience of looking at events through a screen. It removes us from brutality by censoring and prefabricating the reports that we are supposed to interpret as reality. We participate in something we are not a part of without really thinking about what really goes on." Chalayan's reflections on the media spectacle reveal an insidious ideological force, which he is keen to expose: "We should look, and think, to really see life itself. Part of my work is about revealing the veiled processes that humanity chooses to ignore" (interview by Quinn, 2004).

The *Anaesthetics* film, the After Words collection, and the Between collection were represented at Chalayan's ten-year retrospective exhibition held at the Groninger Museum in the Netherlands in 2005. At the time, in the context of troubled multiethnic relations in the Netherlands, Chalayan's exploration of the chador and the female body took on a particular resonance that briefly bridged East and West, at least artistically.

COLLECTION HIGHLIGHTS

Chalayan's graduate collection, The Tangent Flows, received media acclaim and was later displayed in the shop windows of the influential Browns fashion boutique in London. His collection was made with fabric that he had buried in the garden with steel filings to create random patterns of rust on the garments. Magnets positioned on the catwalk were intended to draw out steel rods inserted in the garments' seams, but they failed to do so. Even though the collection was radically cutting edge, it included commercial pieces that sold immediately.

Although his followers quickly saw him as the proud father of conceptual fashion, ironically, clothing per se has always been Chalayan's unwanted child. Chalayan had considered studying architecture before deciding on fashion, and he determined to use clothing as a site of exploration rather than creating garments made with only functionality in mind. As a result, Chalayan's collections have always been characterized by a heightened sense of meaning, an allusion to a more intense experience somewhere else, or the promise of a richer, wider horizon to be found. "He's in his own world," said fellow designer Tristan Webber of Chalayan, "and you have to get into his world to understand his work" (according to Chalayan in an interview by Quinn, 2004).

But Chalayan's world, in comparison to the vast stranglehold of mainstream fashion, could be a parallel universe. Certain collections took clothing to a place where they morphed the body into alien silhouettes, such as Panoramic (autumn/winter 1998), which featured conical headdresses that distorted the model's body shape. Designs such as the "Remote Control" dress (Before Minus Now collection, spring/summer 2000) used digital signals to relay messages by a remote-control device, highlighting the role that technology can play in transforming the fashioned body. Chalayan made garments that became metaphors of flight, such as the lightweight "Airmail" clothing (1999) that could be written on, folded into an envelope, sealed, and mailed. The Echoform collection (autumn/winter 1999) included aerodynamic dresses with architectonic components that mimicked aircraft interiors, intended to amplify the body's inherent capacity for speed.

Chalayan's drive to innovate has enabled him to find inspiration in a range of unexpected forms and technologies. His fascination with aerodynamic surfaces, for example, inspired his synthetic resin "Dwell Neck" and "Aeroplane" dresses, which introduced a range of streamlined forms and hard materials that were atypical of fashion. The molded seams of the "Dwell Neck" dress were fastened with hardware clasps, and the "Aeroplane" dress featured sliding panels that operated electronically. He stated, "I realized that the hard shell of the Dwell Neck dress and metal fastenings were new to fashion, but introducing those materials to fashion was not my intention. Because it wasn't possible to achieve that aerodynamic shape in conventional fabric, I was forced to look around and find other materials to work with" (interview by Quinn, 2004).

Chalayan cited the "Dwell Neck" dress as a typical example of how he encounters new materials in his work. "The idea usually comes first and then I start looking around for materials," he said. "The search for materials doesn't always result in being able to use something that would be right for the project. Often the most visionary materials out there aren't ready to be sold commercially or available in a form that can be handled easily, which means you have to look for something more conventional to use. So even if I knew that there were materials out there that could execute an idea perfectly, it was sometimes a case of finding out they weren't ready for use" (interview by Quinn, 2004).

As Chalayan's work engaged with technological systems, he also pioneered garments that feature wireless technology, electrical circuitry, and automated commands. His "Remote Control" dress was a high-tech triumph that married fashion to technology and technology to the body, establishing a dialogue between the body and the environment. "The dress expressed the body's

Models wearing creations from Cyprus-born Hussein Chalayan's Ambimorphous collection, Paris, 2002. In this collection Chalayan used craft traditions associated with Turkish textiles: Dresses, jackets, and coats were pieced together with embroidered cloth and fragments based on folk clothing from the Anatolian region. Jean-Pierre Muller/AFP/Getty Images.

relationship to a lot of invisible and intangible things—gravity, weather, flight, radio waves, speed, etc.," Chalayan said. "Part of it is to make the invisible tangible, showing that the invisible can transform something and say something about the relationship of the object—the dress in this case—between the person wearing it and the environment around it" (interview by Quinn, 2004).

The dress was designed by means of the composite technology used by aircraft engineers, mirroring the systems that enable remote-control airplanes to fly. It was made from glass fiber and resin, molded into two smooth, glossy, pink-colored front and back panels. Each panel was encased within grooves less than a tenth of an inch (two millimeters) wide that run throughout the length of the dress. These seams create the only textural differences in the dress, revealing interior panels made in translucent

white plastic, accentuated by lighting concealed within the solar plexus panel and the left side elevating panel.

The "Remote Control" dress was not designed specifically to explore the relationship of technology to the body but to examine how the form of the garment could evolve around the body in a spatial relationship to its environment. "The dress can also be transformed invisibly by the environment," explained Chalayan. "The idea was a technological force between the environment and the person" (interview by Quinn, 2004). Extending the function of a dress beyond clothing is central to Chalayan's work, and the "Remote Control" dress demonstrates that garments are capable of interaction with other humans and computerized systems distant in time and space.

The structural architecture of the "Remote Control" dress echoes the attributes of a fashioned body rather than an organic body. The structure of the dress forms an exoskeleton around the body, incorporating elements of body consciousness; its contours mimic the curves of the fashioned female body, arcing dramatically inward at the waist and outward at the hip, echoing the silhouette of the corset and the crinoline. This gives the dress a defined hourglass shape that incorporates principles of corsetry in its design, emphasizing a conventionally feminine shape while creating a solid structure that simultaneously masks undesirable body proportions.

Chalayan's fascination with air travel culminated in his interactive menswear collection, Place/non-place. The collection was partially inspired by Marc Augé's 1995 claim that airports are examples of transitional spaces dubbed "non-place"—areas built to facilitate the movement of people and information in and around urban space. Chalayan used Place/non-place as a catalyst for creating a temporary event space, attaching texts to the garments that invited the wearers to gather at London's Heathrow Airport in May 2002, some eighteen months after the collection was launched. Chalayan's aim was to create an event that would designate a sense of space for those present. "My idea was that the clothes would become a means of creating an experience," he explained. "I was questioning whether holding an event in a particular space could turn a non-place into a place" (interview by Quinn, 2004).

As well as uniting wearers, Chalayan wanted to see how the Place/non-place garments had been transformed through use. "I designed the collection with loads of inner compartments," he explained. "I wanted the clothes to have loads of pockets in them so that you could collect your memories and take them with you. Have you ever noticed how a cab driver has pictures of his kids in the car to remind him of his other life, as if he's recreating his home environment around him? I wanted the wearers to turn up at Heathrow and talk about the lives that the objects in their pockets represent. Garments acquire meaning through use and the more memories they contain the richer life they have" (interview by Quinn, 2004). Chalayan intended such discussions to create a heightened sense of place and give more meaning to the surroundings, even if it would exist only as a memory afterward.

COMMERCIAL COLLABORATIONS

Chalayan's career moved forward in 1995, when he won a fashion award organized by the Absolut Vodka brand and received £28,000 (about U.S. $45,000 in 2010 dollars) in financial support to produce an autumn/winter collection for London Fashion Week in October 1995. Inspired by flight, the collection featured illuminated airport traffic control flight-path patterns on the garments.

New York–based knitwear label TSE commissioned designs from Chalayan for three years, and he later produced designs for British retailer Top Shop—all while presenting his own collections during Fashion Week. In 2000, the British luxury label Asprey appointed Chalayan to create and direct a new ready-to-wear label. Asprey had not tackled women's wear since the 1920s, and the collaboration with Chalayan gave the brand a contemporary update. Chalayan's career moved in a new direction when, due to financial losses, he temporarily closed his company in 2001. Chalayan resumed business after he entered into partnership with Italian manufacturers Gibo, who obtained a worldwide license to distribute his ready-to-wear label.

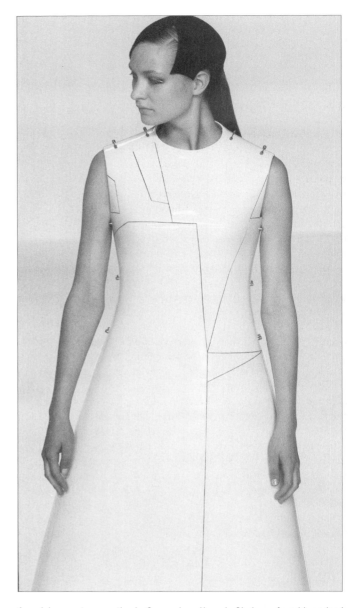

A model presents a creation by Cyprus-born Hussein Chalayan from his spring/summer 2000 Before Minus Now collection, London Fashion Week, 1999. Sinead Lynch/AFP/Getty Images.

Over the years, Chalayan was approached by agents and entrepreneurs proposing to open a Chalayan boutique in capital cities around the world. The first of these opened in Tokyo in 2004, then closed at the end of 2005. Chalayan retained creative control of the venture and designed an interior he described as "a meeting between architecture and fashion, as well as a meeting of worlds" (interview by Quinn, 2004). Chalayan commissioned London-based Block Architecture to explore the theme of omnipresence in the interior architecture and briefed the team to reflect on being in two places simultaneously. As a result, the interior contrasted the Mediterranean gardens of rural Cyprus with the high-tech sensibilities of urban Japan. "I wanted to recreate the Cypriot landscape to give the space the flavors of a foreign land," Chalayan explained, "but also to bring the outside in. So I planted olive trees in the shop's floor and hung clothes from a washing line just as they would outside a Cypriot home. The upper floor was inspired by the open-air cinemas in Cyprus where I watched films as a kid" (interview by Quinn, 2004).

THE ARCHITECT OF FASHION

Many of Chalayan's garments are characterized by graphic elements that echo architectural lines or have been constructed in shapes that bring built structures to mind. Although this creates an aesthetic that is often described as architectural, Chalayan has never intended to mimic the structure and silhouettes of architecture in his clothing. "Describing my clothes as 'architectural' is too simplistic, because there is a big difference between designing buildings and doing what I do, and I have never looked specifically at architecture for inspiration," he said. "One thing to keep in mind is that when fashion looks modular and structured people automatically call it architectural when it isn't" (interview by Quinn, 2004).

Leading architects generally draw more inspiration from theories of space than they do from existing buildings, and Chalayan's process is analogous to this approach. "My thinking is on a parallel with architects; sometimes I borrow concepts from architectural theory and apply them to something else," he said. "Of course, looking at those ideas as an outsider means that they become looser, so I would describe these influences as architectonic rather than strictly architectural" (interview by Quinn, 2004).

Chalayan's process mirrors the approach of the award-winning architect Zaha Hadid, also based in London. "When we designed the scenography for Charleroi Danses' Metapolis ballet production we saw how fashion and architecture can communicate in response to the body," said Patrik Schumacher, spokesperson for Zaha Hadid Architects. "The way that Chalayan interlinks them in his work is genius. You can identify a similar process in both Zaha and Chalayan's work. For example, one technique we use is called 'making strange' whereby we rotate, invert, and distort traditional building proportions to create something more visionary. Chalayan seems to be 'making strange' with clothing by restructuring proportions of garments to create something completely new and nontraditional" (quoted in Quinn 2003).

Like architecture, fashion is moving beyond traditional platforms, and, in Chalayan's hands, it radiates to new ideological territories and a range of uncertain destinations. In *The Fashionable Mind*, Kennedy Fraser located the spaces of fashion where "movies [are] made, books published, art exhibits mounted, critical columns turned out, dances danced, editorial policies formulated, academic theses germinated, wherever people think, speak or create shared forms of expression." Chalayan's quest for new platforms has enabled him to augment the meaning of his clothes by creating event spaces for them in the form of films, installations, and exhibitions. These provide the garments with a visual framework that can be interpreted as a text and decoded cinematically.

MATERIAL INNOVATION

Some of Chalayan's most groundbreaking uses of materials and processes were presented in his spring/summer 2007 collection, titled One Hundred and Eleven. Chalayan designed dresses powered by machine-driven levers that opened and closed to reconfigure the shape and silhouette of the garment. Hemlines rose autonomously, a bustier opened of its own accord, and a jacket unfastened itself and pulled away from the model's torso. These designs were made possible through collaboration with the team behind the special effects for the film *Harry Potter and the Prisoner of Azkaban*, who microchipped fabric panels so that they would move according to the sequences Chalayan programmed.

The mechanical dresses were made by hand and carefully fitted with electronic machinery. The garment's surfaces were painstakingly embroidered with thousands of Swarovski crystals, giving them the dual appeal of opulent elegance and high-tech savvy. Although the garments were powered by batteries, research into the capacity crystals have for harnessing solar power indicates that they may one day provide a viable power source for techno fashions.

Chalayan's use of shape-shifting fabrics enabled his garments to morph into entirely new designs, and his hats were able to radically change shape. Shape-memory fabrics, such as those woven from fibers of the shape-memory alloy Nitinol and interspersed with nylon, make these innovations possible. Nitinol is highly elastic and capable of changing shape when temperatures rise and fall, then returning to its original shape when temperatures stabilize. This shape-memory property enables the fabric to shorten and lengthen, which is how the dress will perform when temperatures fluctuate. Nitinol, an acronym for Nickel Titanium Naval Ordnance Laboratory, is a family of intermetallic materials that contain a mixture of nickel and titanium. Other materials can be added to enhance or adjust the material's properties. Because the fabric's weave has five nylon fibers to every Nitinol fiber, the clothing made from it will be high performance, washable, and comfortable.

Chalayan was one of the first big-name designers to use this kind of technology in fashion, and his success seems to anticipate a day when the integration of technology and garment design will be seamless and efficient. This moment marked a radical departure from a world where distinctions between body and technology, body and dress, natural and artificial once seemed clear. This illustrates how, as the French philosopher Michel Foucault has described, social and cultural discourses construct human bodies in a way that makes them as analogous to machines as possible. The design of the dress is imbued with technologies that make interaction efficient, productive, and empowered, akin to the machinelike principles of controlled automation. The presence of high-tech systems in fashion fuses the latter's body-conscious ideals with a belief in automation, speed, and accuracy as the means to achieve it.

Chalayan's expression of contemporary narratives reveals one of his essential qualities: He thinks in visual terms. The distinctive oeuvre he pioneers and his uniquely interdisciplinary approach make him a visionary designer, and the impact of his work will never be taken lightly. As he embraces theories of architecture and forges fresh directions for fashion, Chalayan's work continues to grow in appeal—especially to an audience with the confidence to wear clothing still heavy with the thought processes behind it.

Parts of this article are based on Quinn, Bradley: "An Architect of Ideas." In *Hussein Chalayan*. Rotterdam/Groningen, Netherlands: NAI Publishers/Groninger Museum, 2005.

References and Further Reading

Augé, Marc. *Non-Places*. London: Verso, 1995.

El Guindi, Fadwa. "Veiling Resistance." *Fashion Theory* 3, no. 1 (1999): 51–80.

Evans, Caroline, Suzy Menkes, Bradley Quinn, and Ted Polhemus. *Hussein Chalayan, 10 Years' Work*. Exhibition monograph, Groninger Museum, Groningen, the Netherlands. Rotterdam: NAI Publishers–Groninger Museum, 2005.

Fraser, Kennedy. *The Fashionable Mind*. Boston: David R. Godine, 1984.

Menkes, Suzy. "Hussein Chalayan: Cultural Dialogues." *International Herald Tribune*, 19 April 2005.

Nealon, Jeffrey. *Foucault beyond Foucault: Power and Its Intensifications since 1984*. Stanford, CA: Stanford University Press, 2007.

Quinn, Bradley. *Techno Fashion*. Oxford: Berg, 2002.

Quinn, Bradley. *The Fashion of Architecture*. Oxford: Berg, 2003.

Quinn, Bradley, ed. *UltraMaterials*. London: Thames & Hudson, 2007.

Sidlauskas, S. *Intimate Architecture: Contemporary Clothing Design*. Cambridge, MA: MIT Committee on the Visual Arts, 1982.

Bradley Quinn

See also Historical Survey of Textiles and Dress in Turkey.

Sources of Information about Dress in Southwest Asia

- Prehistory (until ca. 3000 B.C.E.)
- The First States (ca. 3300–334 B.C.E.)
- The Greco-Roman Period (334 B.C.E.–ca. 330 C.E.)
- The Byzantine Period (ca. 330–641 C.E.)
- Early Islam (641–1453 C.E.)
- The Ottoman Period (1453–1922 C.E.)
- The Twentieth Century

Information on dress in Southwest Asia (also referred to as the Middle East or the Near East) is derived from both primary evidence, such as actual textiles and garments or tools for textile production, and secondary evidence, which includes textual and pictographic sources. Textual sources incorporate not only written references to dress in prose or poetry but also laws, trade accounts, inventories, wedding contracts, travelogues, and so on. Depictions of dress can be found in paintings, frescoes, mosaics, and illustrations in books and on items such as pottery and jewelry. Although secondary sources can be misleading because they represent interpretations of reality, they are necessary to understand the primary sources.

PREHISTORY (UNTIL CA. 3000 B.C.E.)

Relatively little primary evidence exists from prehistoric times but even less secondary evidence exists. Depictions are relatively rare and are usually too stylized to allow one to distinguish exactly what type of dress was worn. The earliest evidence for woven textiles dates to the Neolithic period, although it is possible that textiles were made and used before this time. Impressions of textiles in clay balls have been found at Jarmo (Iraq) and date to around 7000 B.C.E. Actual textiles date slightly later and have been found at Nahal Hemar (Israel), Çayönü, and Çatal Hüyük (Turkey). These textiles are generally made from plant fibers such as flax, which grew wild in this region. There is no evidence of the use of wool at this time. Sheep were domesticated around 7000 B.C.E., but they seem to have been kept mainly for their meat and hides. Only later were products such as milk, wool, and traction power exploited. This is not surprising, because the fleece of these early sheep resembled the hairy pelt of their goat cousins and would therefore have been difficult to spin.

Tools for textile production dating to this period are found regularly in archaeological excavations. From around the end of the seventh millennium B.C.E. on, for example, spindle whorls were used throughout Southwest Asia. They came in various shapes and sizes, such as disks, bells, and stars but most often balls or (double) cones, and were made out of clay, potsherds, stone, and occasionally bone or antler. They were fastened onto a stick to form the complete spindle, which was used for spinning raw fibers into thread.

Although there are other ways of making textiles, such as felting or knotting, most textiles are woven on a loom. Weaving involves the interlacing at a right angle of two sets of threads, one of which is relatively fixed (the warp), while the other is not (the weft). Looms can differ greatly in appearance, but they are essentially the construct onto which the warp is fixed and which facilitates the interweaving of the weft. Unlike spindle whorls, wooden weaving equipment usually has not survived in the archaeological record, because plant-based organic materials decompose more easily. One exception is the cave site of Nahal Mishmar (Israel), dating to the fourth millennium B.C.E., where both textiles and the wooden remains of a loom have been found.

THE FIRST STATES (CA. 3300–334 B.C.E.)

Around 3300 B.C.E., the first alphabet was developed in Mesopotamia (a region roughly equivalent to Iraq in the early twenty-first century), marking the beginning of the historical era. During this time, the first city-states and kings emerged. These were the predecessors of the empires that ruled Southwest Asia in the Bronze Age (ca. 3300–1200 B.C.E.) and the Iron Age (ca. 1200–334 B.C.E.), such as those of the Babylonians, Assyrians, Hittites, Medes, and Persians.

Few textiles dating to this period have been excavated. At a few dozen sites, for example, in Ur (Iraq); Terqa (Syria); Alishar, Acemhöyük, Troy, and Gordion (Turkey); Nahal Mishmar and Timna (Israel); Jericho and Bab ed-Dhra (Palestine); and Hasanlu and Haftavan Tepe (Iran), scraps of cloth have been found. However, no site has yielded large enough textiles to permit reconstruction of an entire garment. In other cases, only the beads or (golden) ornaments that were sewn onto the fabric have survived, as in Troy, Acemhöyük, and Dendra in Turkey, showing only the outlines of former garments.

Flax continued to be an important textile fiber, but the earliest texts also include references to wool. The first clear evidence for the use of wool is a piece of cloth made from animal fiber that was wrapped around a Proto-Elamite figurine (ca. 3000 B.C.E.). Texts dating to the same period found in Uruk (Iraq) also designate flocks specifically as wool sheep. Wool production had become an important part of the Mesopotamian economy.

The manufacture and trade of textiles are often mentioned on clay tablets. From palace and temple administrations, such as the ones found at Uruk (Iraq), Ebla, and Mari (Syria), it appears that temples and palaces functioned as textile-production centers, employing large numbers of textile workers to process the flax and wool obtained from the palace and temple grounds. Raw wool, textiles, and garments were redistributed among the employees of the temple, but these products were also traded. However, because the texts derive from temple or palace archives, they probably do not reflect the complete extent of textile production in Mesopotamia; it is likely that textiles were also produced at home or in small workshops.

From 3300 B.C.E. on, women are depicted in the act of spinning on seals, ivories, and reliefs from, for example, Choga Mish and Susa (Iran), Mari (Syria), and Maraş (Turkey). Spindle whorls continue to be found at Bronze Age and Iron Age sites. However, from the Bronze Age on, complete metal spindles have also been excavated, and ivory and bone spindles or spindle rods seem to have become popular. Objects that resemble distaffs (sticks that are used to hold the raw fibers while spinning) have been found with copper spindles at Kish and Abu Salabikh (Iraq).

The main type of loom used in this period was the horizontal ground loom. A seal from Susa (Iran), for example, shows two women working on such a loom. In this case, the warp is strung between two beams, which are attached to pegs beaten into the ground. However, other types of loom were also used in this region, such as the warp-weighted loom. This loom is vertical (it was usually leaned against a wall) and is characterized by loom weights, which are tied to the warp threads to keep them taut. From the fourth millennium B.C.E. on, loom weights are found in western Anatolia. These come in various shapes (for example, ball, pyramid, crescent, tear-shaped) and materials, although they are mostly made from clay, and have a hole in them to tie the warp onto. It is likely that the warp-weighted loom originated on the European mainland and spread through the west of Turkey farther south along the coastal area of Southwest Asia, because, after 2000 B.C.E., loom weights were also used at Jericho (Palestine) and Megiddo (Israel). A third type of loom, the vertical two-beam loom, might have been introduced in the Bronze Age, but very little evidence for this loom has survived. Depictions

from Egypt show that it worked along the same principles as the horizontal ground loom, but the two beams were set into a vertical wooden frame.

Based on depictions of people in statues, wall paintings, reliefs, and ivories, it seems that the main types of outfits in the early Bronze Age consisted of wraparound skirts or kilts, sometimes with a draped mantle that could be pinned or tucked. In addition, women seem to have worn a large veil over their heads. The garments are often depicted with large fringes either on the hem or over the entire surface. These fringes are usually interpreted as tufts of wool; this effect could, for example, be achieved by loops woven into the textile or by brushing to make the surface more hairy. In general, the garments seem to have had very little tailoring. Toward the middle Bronze Age (ca. second millennium B.C.E.), clothing styles became more elaborate. Fringed hems were still used, but surface color effects—including embroidery, tapestry techniques, and pattern dyeing—were taking over. Also, tailored items such as short- and long-sleeved shirts and tunics appear.

Textiles often feature in texts relating to contracts and exchange records. These refer not only to trade but also to other methods of exchange, such as gift exchanges between kings, tribute, and dowries given to princesses being married off to foreign dignitaries. Good examples of this can be found in the Amarna letters, a diplomatic correspondence between various rulers of Southwest Asia and Egypt. Archaeological evidence has shown

The "Fresco of Conon" from Dura Europos, Syria, 70 c.e. The men wear long tunics, and the chief priest, Conon, wears the tall, conical white hat of a Persian magus. The woman in the center wears a large veil or mantle over the head. Both outfits show the influence of the East. Werner Forman Archive/ National Museum, Damascus.

that in the Uruk period (ca. the fourth millennium B.C.E.), a long-distance exchange route existed between Sumer (Iraq) and Elam (Iran). By the late Bronze Age, trade networks extended over all of Southwest Asia and overseas to Egypt, the eastern Arabian coast, and through to India.

Mesopotamia and Syria were famed for their high-quality woolen textiles and garments. An especially coveted export product of the coastal region was the Phoenician purple-colored cloth called Tyrian purple. The dye was obtained from a sea snail of the *Murex* genus. The archaeological excavation at Tyre (Lebanon) has shown that this natural secretion was probably obtained by crushing the shell and leaving the snails to decompose in large vats. Linen textiles were produced locally and sometimes imported from Egypt. Cotton was allegedly introduced in the seventh century B.C.E. by the Assyrian king Sennacherib, who mentions having trees bearing wool in his botanical garden. Cotton has been attested in the Indus region at this time and might have traveled to Southwest Asia with other goods, although no physical evidence of cotton has yet been found dating to this period.

THE GRECO-ROMAN PERIOD (334 B.C.E.–CA. 330 C.E.)

In 334 B.C.E., the Macedonian Alexander the Great and his army marched into Turkey and on to Iran and Egypt, eventually conquering most of Southwest Asia. After his death in 323 B.C.E., Alexander's massive empire was divided between his generals: The Seleucid dynasty came to rule Syria, Iraq, and Iran; the Antigonid kingdom consisted mainly of western Turkey and parts of Greece; and the Ptolemies held Egypt. However, the power of Rome was growing, and, by 31 B.C.E., these empires had all become part of the Roman Empire. Parthia had, by this time, already taken advantage of the weakness of the Seleucids, conquering the eastern half of the Seleucid Empire (consisting mainly of Iran and, roughly speaking, the eastern half of Southwest Asia).

Several sites dating to this period have yielded significant amounts of textiles: for example, At-Tar (Iraq); Dura Europos and Palmyra (Syria); Qumran Cave I and Murabba'at (Palestine); Masada, Cave of Letters, and Wadi ed-Daliyeh (Israel); and Qaryat-al-Fau (Arabia). From these archaeological textiles, it appears that wool and flax were still the most common textile fibers, although cotton has been found, for example, at Khirbet Qazone (Israel), and imported silks have been found at Dura Europos and Palmyra (Syria).

Relatively few texts have been preserved in this region due to the use of papyrus, which deteriorates easily. One important text dating to this period is the *Edict of Diocletian*, issued in 301; this is essentially a list of maximum prices for materials, products, and services in the Roman Empire. It provides a wealth of information on the availability and prices of fibers, thread, garments (from different centers of textile manufacture in the Mediterranean), spinning, weaving, sewing, embroidering, and fulling. It is fragmentary, however, and certain prices are missing. Remarkably, the highest sum mentioned is 150,000 denarii, the price for one pound of purple-dyed silk (three times the amount charged for refined gold).

Because of the rarity of textual finds in Southwest Asia, most of the sources used to interpret the character of the Greco-Roman textile industry in this region come from Egypt. Spinning was largely a household practice, while most commercial weaving was by this time in the hands of independent craftsmen. They were often specialized in a particular technique or product and organized in guilds. The ground loom and vertical two-beam loom continued to be used in this period. Also, the construction of some textiles suggests that they had been made on a warp-weighted loom, but this device was slowly losing ground to the vertical two-beam loom. The presence of intricate textiles such as twills and simple damasks suggests that a horizontal draw loom might have been in use, but these fabrics could also have been made on, for example, a warp-weighted loom.

Most pictographic sources from this period depict rulers and gods, who were usually dressed in traditional Greek or Roman garb. There are a few exceptions, such as the stelae from Palmyra and the wall paintings of Dura Europos, in what is Syria in the early twenty-first century. These show an interesting adaptation of Greek and Roman styles to local tastes. Both men's and women's dress varied regionally. Dress for women seems to have consisted of a very wide ankle-length tunic with or without sleeves. An overgarment that could be pinned at the shoulder was worn on top, belted either at the waist or underneath the bosom. Usually, a large veil or mantle was worn over the head. A more Eastern type of dress consisted of a blouse with a skirt and a veil. The men often wore a short tunic with a mantle wrapped around the body or pinned at the shoulder. Another possibility was the Parthian-influenced outfit, consisting of pants or chaps combined with a short, long-sleeved tunic, sometimes with a coat on top that was belted at the waist, and a mantle. Decorative bands and decorated textiles occur frequently, as also becomes clear from the textile evidence. The typical Roman *clavi* (two plain stripes running down the length of the garment from the shoulders) were often used but were transformed into elaborately decorated stripes.

Trade in Southwest Asia continued relatively along the same lines as in the previous period. Woolen fabrics and dyestuffs from Syria were widely exported, and trade in textiles between the various states still occurred. From the first century B.C.E. on, there was also regular trade between Southwest Asia and the Mediterranean. This trade was mainly centered on silk, a fiber coveted throughout the West and at times worth more than its weight in gold. Goods were transported on land by camel caravans along what would later be known as the Silk Road. These caravans led to the flourishing of towns such as Samarkand, Palmyra, and Petra, which controlled their passage into the West, growing rich on customs. The mastery of sericulture was at this time still in Chinese hands. Silk floss, yarn, and textiles were all imported from China and sometimes India. Often only small pieces or bands of silk cloth were used to decorate clothing. Another way of making a small piece of silk go a long way was to unravel it and reweave it in combination with a cheaper fiber. Both Chinese woven silk damasks and Syrian (rewoven) silk textiles have been excavated, for example, at Palmyra.

THE BYZANTINE PERIOD (CA. 330–641 C.E.)

The Byzantine Empire was essentially a continuation of the Roman Empire, although there were some changes, such as Christianity becoming the state religion. *Byzantine* is a modern term used to describe the eastern part of what was left of the Roman Empire in the third century; the people still considered themselves Romans. The Byzantine Empire lasted from about 330 to 1453, but, from the onslaught of the Arab armies in 641 on, the Byzantines controlled only part of Turkey and some areas outside Southwest Asia. Until the rise of Islam, the main other occupants of Southwest Asia were the Sassanians, the successors of the Parthians.

Some Byzantine and Sassanian silks have survived (for example, at Halabiyah in Syria, En Boqeq and Nessana in Israel, and Pella in Jordan), but, remarkably, most were preserved in the West. Silk not only was an important trade good but was also used by the government as a diplomatic gift, and many silks have therefore ended up in European (cathedral) treasuries. These precious silks often show large motifs with lions, mythical beasts, animals, riders, hunting scenes, and Christian imagery. Intricate patterns were produced using a draw loom with multiple heddles. The earlier looms had had only one heddle bar (a stick to which either the even or uneven warp threads were tied so that they could be raised as one, facilitating the insertion of the weft), and patterns were created by the manual manipulation of the warp threads or the insertion of different-colored warp threads. A draw loom, in contrast, has several heddles, so different groups of warp threads can be raised, and patterns can be woven into the cloth more easily.

Silk was still an extremely valuable trade good. Not surprisingly, the secrets of sericulture were jealously guarded by the Chinese. However, the story goes that silkworms were eventually smuggled into the Byzantine Empire by traveling monks. By the sixth century, silk was also manufactured in Southwest Asia. Textile production at the time continued largely along the lines of the previous Roman period. However, the *Code of Theodosian* (438 C.E.) describes large, state-run textile workshops (or factories) called *gynaecea*. This system was not restricted to the Byzantine Empire, as the Sassanians also had a large state-controlled weaving industry. This imperial control seems to have been directed at luxury textiles, especially silk. Legislative codes dating between the fourth and sixth centuries, such as the *Code of Theodosian* and *Justiniac Codes*, and later texts, such as the *Basilics' Law Code* and the *Book of the Prefect*, state the particular types of purple silks and specific garments that were reserved for the imperial court. The Byzantine scholar Procopius describes how the emperor Justinian established an imperial monopoly on silk manufacture.

Images of Byzantine dress can be found in textiles, mosaics, and wall paintings, usually in churches or tombs. Dress, until the seventh century, still consisted of a tunic, often with an overtunic. Men usually wore tight pants or shorter underpants underneath their tunic and seem to have preferred a pinned or sewn cloak over a wrapped mantle. In general, there was an increase in the use of tailoring, color, and decoration. An often-mentioned source on dress in this period are the mosaics of Ravenna (Italy), which depict the coronation of Justinian surrounded by his wife and court. It shows what the Byzantine court was famed for: elaborate hierarchy and ceremonial etiquette. The dress codes connected to the court have been meticulously recorded in the *Book of Ceremonies*, dating to the tenth century. It states exactly what type of dress in what color was to be worn on each occasion by the associated officials.

EARLY ISLAM (641–1453 C.E.)

By 641, Arab forces had largely conquered Southwest Asia, with the exception of Turkey, which was still in the hands of the Byzantines. In the beginning, these forces were led by a caliph who was elected by the elders, but struggles for leadership soon

A literary meeting from the *Maqâmât of al-Harîrî* (Assemblies), painted by Yahyâ ibn Mahmûd al-Wâsitî, Baghdad, Iraq, 1237. Illustrative illuminated manuscripts dating from the twelfth to the fourteenth centuries C.E. offer insight into the clothing that was worn in the past. Getty Images.

ensued, eventually causing the division of the Islamic world into the Shiites and the Sunnis. The following centuries were marked by the struggles of the various dynasties (in Southwest Asia, in relative chronological order, the Umayyads, Abbasids, Fatimids, Seljuks, Ayyubids, and Mamluks) among one another as well as against foreign enemies, such as the Byzantines, Mongols, and Crusaders. Turkey was eventually taken over by the Seljuks, but the Byzantine Empire was fully conquered only in 1453 with the capture of Constantinople (Istanbul) by the Ottomans.

Relatively few textiles dating to this period have been excavated in Southwest Asia (most have been found in Egypt). This lack of textiles is partly due to the fact that, for Muslims, it was customary to be buried in a simple shroud. Some textiles in European treasuries have, however, been identified as being Southwest Asian in origin; these are usually silks with large patterns on them, resembling Byzantine silks. Wool and linen were also still used, and the use of cotton seems to have been on the rise. When the Arabs established themselves in Southwest Asia, they left the existing textile-production systems intact, and most textiles (and other craft products) were therefore fabricated by local non-Muslims, who incorporated new Arab preferences into their existing repertoire. Household weaving occurred rarely, and most textiles were produced by men in workshops.

An important institution in the early Islamic era was *tiraz*, which were bands of texts embroidered onto textiles (although the word was also used to designate the garment or the factory). These texts contained references to Islam, the ruler, or the workshop in which the fabric was made. Tiraz garments were made in special workshops overseen by government officials, a continuation of the imperial factories in the Byzantine and the Sassanian empires. They were used to bestow honor or status on favored subjects, a practice called *khil'a*.

Depictions of people occur less frequently in the decorative arts, mainly because Sunni Muslims interpreted the hadiths (traditions of the Prophet Mohammed) as prohibiting the representation of human figures. There are some illuminated manuscripts dating from the twelfth to fourteenth centuries C.E., such as the *Maqâmât of al-Hârîrî*, for example, but the main sources on dress are texts. Textual sources in the Islamic era are bountiful, and many refer to garments; these include religious texts, such as the Qur'an and the hadiths, as well as laws, inventories, poetry, and the works of Arab geographers (such as Ibn Hawqal and al-Muqadassi).

The original ideas in Islamic dress were based on the existing Arabic dress conventions, such as covering the head when out in public. Arab dress was characterized by wraps and long, flowing garments. Like most outfits in the rest of Southwest Asia, it consisted of some type of undergarment, such as a loincloth or underdrawers; a body shirt; a tunic, dress, gown, or coat; a mantle, coat, or wrap when going out in public; some type of head covering; and shoes or sandals. Often, multiple layers of under- and overgarments were worn. However, there were certain dress codes specific to Islam. The hadiths recommend modest and austere clothing; silk and jewelry were considered inappropriate for men, for example.

Although initially the Arabic forces were deliberately kept isolated from the local people in Southwest Asia to ensure a cultural distinction, textiles soon made their way into the Arabic sphere as booty and tribute. Converted natives also brought their own modes of dress with them. The existing systems of Greco-Roman or Byzantine dress (consisting of tunics and wraps or mantles), Irano-Turkic dress (characterized by tailored garments, including pants and coats), and Arabic dress merged to form the Islamic vestimentary system. Later on, the Turkic military dynasties also introduced a more Central Asian style, with an emphasis on coats.

Already under the Umayyads, the restraint in dress preached in the hadiths was taken rather less strictly. The Umayyad court was modeled more along the lines of the Byzantine court's pomp and ceremony, and luxury silk garments became the norm. This continued into the later centuries as testified by, for example, court writer and fashion guru Abu l-Tayyib Muhammed al-Washsha's manuscript *On Elegance and Elegant People*, which described the fashions for cultured men and women in around 936, and the eleventh-century court manual written by Abu'l-Husayn Hilal b. Muhassin b. Ibrahīm al-Ṣābi' (969–1056), a historian, bureaucrat, and writer of Arabic prose and letters. Only a pious few continued to dress along the lines described in the hadiths. Fashions changed with each dynasty; not only did their geographic origins play a role but also opinions on what was considered appropriate (the Shiite dynasties, for example, used figured textiles while the Sunnis did not), and most regimes used a signature color to indicate allegiance.

Although the clothing traditions of the different regions had merged, there were attempts to distinguish the Muslim population from the nonbelievers or *dhimmis*. According to the Pact of [ayin] Umar (the initial treaty outlining the conditions of subjugation in the newly conquered lands), Christians and Jews were free to live, own property, and practice their religion within Muslim countries as long as they paid tribute, acted according to their status as a subject population, and did not try to resemble their overlords. This is rather vague, and later laws (for example, by Caliph al-Mutawakkil in 850) often made clearer statements, forbidding the use of certain colors or types of garments or prescribing the use of certain badges (such as tattoos, patches on clothing, or different-colored outer garments). However, it seems that these regulations usually did not last very long.

THE OTTOMAN PERIOD (1453–1922 C.E.)

The Ottoman period started with the establishment of a Turkic dynasty at the Byzantine city of Bursa in 1338 and lasted until 1922. In 1453, the Ottomans captured Constantinople, the last stronghold of the Byzantines, and renamed the city Istanbul. At its largest, the empire included the Balkans, Turkey, the Levant, Iraq, northwestern Iran, Egypt, northern Africa, and parts of western Arabia. The Ottomans' march into Europe was turned back at Vienna in 1683. Around the same time, the Safavid (1499–1722) and Qajar (1794–1925) dynasties ruled in Iran.

There are a number of good sources on Ottoman dress. Large quantities of textiles have been preserved, many of which have survived in European treasuries, museums, and private collections. These textiles include imported goods or gifts and elaborately decorated tents seized at the siege of Vienna. In addition, numerous examples of garments have been preserved in the collection of the Topkapi Palace, the former residence of the court in Istanbul. This collection still exists in the early twenty-first century because of the Ottoman tradition of carefully labeling and storing the wardrobe of deceased sultans. This is in contrast to the Persian Safavid court wardrobes, which were burned every seven years to retrieve the precious metals for bullion.

Ottoman textiles are characterized by large floral designs as well as bold geometric patterns. Safavid textiles from Iran, in contrast, show complete narratives with human and animal figures. Silk was still especially popular, and other coveted fabrics included brocades, especially with silver or gold thread, velvets, elaborately embroidered textiles, and moiré mohair textiles.

Many surviving texts, such as court archives, guild registers, wills, inventories, and dowries, give information on dress. These also include a number of memoirs by Ottoman court women—such as Muzbah Haidar, Emine Foat Tugay, and Ayşe Sultan—recounting the clothing worn for many receptions, visits, and ceremonies during the nineteenth century. Pictographic sources include texts with miniatures, which became popular from the fifteenth to sixteenth centuries (in Iran from the thirteenth century) on, and single-figure albums by artists such as Abdulcelil Levni and Abdullah Bukhari, as well as by photographer Osman Hamdi Bey. The albums meticulously illustrate indoor and outdoor dress in the court, in Istanbul, and throughout the different regions of the Ottoman Empire.

From the sixteenth century on, trade and diplomatic relations between the West and Southwest Asia increased, and many travel accounts have recorded the splendor encountered. From the eighteenth and nineteenth centuries, more objective accounts by Europeans living in the Ottoman Empire are also available, such as the letters by Lady Mary Wortley Montagu, wife of the English ambassador in Istanbul. There are also a number of studies on (parts of) the Ottoman Empire, such as *La Turquie d'Asie* (Turkish Asia) by the geographer Vital Cuinet, who also describes textile production, and accounts of travel in the Holy Land by British traveler James Silk Buckingham (in the nineteenth century), Swiss Orientalist John Lewis Burckhardt (early nineteenth century), and Czech Orientalist Alois Musil (early twentieth century), who often mention dress details.

Several European artists have recorded Eastern fashions, such as the sixteenth-century engravers Pieter Coecke van Aelst, Nicolas de Nicolay, and Melchior Lorch. There had always been a certain amount of European curiosity about the East, but, in the eighteenth century, a true "Turkomania" had taken hold of Europe, and artists such as the Belgian Jean-Baptiste Vanmour and the French Jean-Etiene Liotard, who lived in Turkey for a few years, were more than happy to satisfy the demand for exotic drawings and paintings of the Ottomans. In the nineteenth century, several artists, such as Remo Brindisi, Thomas Allom, and Amadeo Preziosi, found inspiration for their Orientalist paintings in the cosmopolitan city of Istanbul. By this time, photography had been introduced as a new medium for capturing images, and both Europeans and the local elite started to use it for portraits, illustrations, and postcards. A particularly good example is the collection of photographs of regional Turkish dress made for the Vienna exhibition of 1873 by Marie de Launay and Osman Hamdi Bey. Like paintings, however, photographs should be considered with care, because they were often staged and outfits were changed to make the picture more attractive.

Ottoman dress was very much a continuation of earlier Turkish styles, with its emphasis on coats and sleeves. Dress combinations usually consisted of a pair of underpants, a tunic or shirt, several layers of coats, and some type of head covering. There was an emphasis on layering, with the garments arranged in such a way that the lining and layers underneath were revealed, and the garments seem to have become increasingly more tailored. Khil'a—or *hil'at*, as it was called by the Ottomans—was still an important way of bestowing honor, status, and rank, although the practice of tiraz had largely disappeared. Imperial-governed silk weaving was located in both Bursa and Istanbul.

Silk was traded with Europe through Turkey and directly with Iran through the East India Company. The manufacture of silk was now also securely established in Europe, particularly in Italy. Already in the fifteenth century, large quantities of silks were imported by the Ottoman court from Italy, but also the other way around, and the designs clearly influenced one another.

European influence grew dramatically in the eighteenth and nineteenth centuries. The empire was weakened through several outbreaks of plagues, which also killed many skilled textile workers. Pattern weaving was in decline, although embroidery and printing seem to have flourished to compensate. European fashions became more popular among the rich, and, more important, because of the Industrial Revolution and the mechanization of weaving, large amounts of very cheap cloth were being introduced from Europe and India. This effect was strengthened by the dress-reform program of 1826, whereby first the army but later all government officials were subjected to new laws on dress, encouraging a more European dress style (including the frock coat and the fez). Although women were exempt from the dress reforms, they also started to follow European, and in particular Parisian, fashions.

THE TWENTIETH CENTURY

After World War I and the fall of the Ottoman Empire, much of Southwest Asia was divided between the French, English, and Russians. Southwest Asia was heavily influenced by the presence of these foreign powers, speeding up the process of Westernization. Another important event was the discovery of oil, a new source of money and power. In the 1940s, most current states gained independence. However, the region remains an area of conflict into the early twenty-first century, partly because of disputes over the State of Israel.

Dress was rapidly Westernized through the influence of various courts, government officials, Christian missionaries, and European businesses. In particular, the religious minorities of the Christians and Jews seem to have been eager to adopt European types of dress, copying the Judeo-Christian West. The rulers of Turkey and Iran, Mustafa Kemal Atatürk and Reza Shah, introduced dress reforms in the 1920s and 1930s, banning signs of religious affiliation outside the religious sphere and encouraging European dress in an attempt to modernize. Production of textiles became mechanized, and synthetic materials became very popular, further changing existing traditions.

For this period, many sources are available, including photographs and films made by locals, tourists, anthropologists, and commercial film producers. Several Western and Southwest Asian museums house collections of nineteenth- and twentieth-century dress. From the beginning of the twentieth century, ethnographic studies have tried to record Southwest Asian cultures, initially focusing on the Holy Land in particular. A good example of early ethnographic studies is Gustaf Herman Dalman's *Arbeit und Sitte in Palästina* (Work and customs in Palestine). There are also a number of late-twentieth-century studies focusing on dress, for example, those by Yedida Kalfon Stillman, Jehan Rajab, Shelagh Weir, and Heather Colyer Ross.

This Westernization, or globalization, of dress has not been the same in all areas of Southwest Asia. In the region of the Arabian Peninsula, for example, modern versions of traditional garments are still the norm. Moreover, there is a clear difference between town and countryside; in small villages and among the Bedouin, new fashions were adopted much more slowly. Also, within the privacy of the home or on festive occasions, Arabic-style clothing is still preferred. The tourism industry has further stimulated the persistence of certain folkloric costumes. This does not mean that these outfits are exactly the same as one hundred years before, because other types of fabrics and slight differences in cut and decoration can often be noted. Certain elements of clothing, such as headgear for men and the veil or enveloping wrap or coat for women, have changed over time but remain distinctly Arabian garments. In general, Southwest Asian dress is caught up in the current of globalization that is visible in most of the world at the moment. Some items of clothing have, however, gained a nationalistic or folkloric—and therefore a symbolic—meaning. Especially from the end of the twentieth century on, a movement toward a more pan-Islamic, Arabic style of dress can be noted, as part of the rise of Islamist and nationalistic movements, using neotraditionalist dress as a symbol.

Nautical festival before Sultan Ahmed III (1673–1736) from the *Surname-i Vehbi* (Book of festival) by Abdulcelil Levni, ca. 1720. Albums from this period meticulously illustrate indoor and outdoor dress in the court at Istanbul and throughout the Ottoman Empire, providing a rich pictographic source of information about clothing styles. The Bridgeman Art Library/Getty Images.

References and Further Reading

Barber, E.J.W. *Prehistoric Textiles: The Development of Cloth in the Neolithic and Bronze Ages, with Special Reference to the Aegean.* Princeton, NJ: Princeton University Press, 1991.

Barker, Patricia L. *Islamic Textiles.* London: British Museum Press, 1995.

Colyer Ross, Heather. *The Art of Arabian Costume: A Saudi Arabian Profile.* Clarens, Switzerland: Arabesque Commercial SA, 1994. (Originally published in 1981.)

Croom, Alexandra T. *Roman Clothing and Fashion.* Stroud and Charleston, UK: Tempus, 2000.

Cuinet, Vital. *La Turquie d'Asie: géographie administrative, statistique descriptive et raisonnée de chaque province de l'Asie-mineure.* Paris: Leroux, 1890.

Dalman, Gustaf Herman. *Arbeit und Sitte in Palästina.* Vol. 5, *Webstoff, Spinnen, Weben, Kleidung.* Gütersloh, Germany: Bertelsmann, 1935.

Harris, Jennifer, ed. *5000 Years of Textiles.* London: British Museum Press, 2004.

Jenkins, David, ed. *The Cambridge History of Western Textiles.* Cambridge, UK: Cambridge University Press, 2003.

Jones, A.H.M. "The Cloth Industry under the Roman Empire." *Economic History Review* 13, no. 2 (1960): 183–192.

Rajab, Jehan S. *Palestinian Costume.* London and New York: Kegan Paul International, 1989.

Stillman, Yedida Kalfon. *Arab Dress: A Short History from the Dawn of Islam to Modern Times.* Leiden: Brill, 2000.

Scarce, Jennifer M. *Women's Costume of the Near and Middle East.* London and Sydney: Unwin Hyman, 1987.

Vollmer, John E., E.J. Keall, and E. Nagai-Berthrong. *Silk Roads, China Ships.* Toronto: Royal Ontario Museum, 1983.

Weir, Shelagh. *Palestinian Costume.* London: British Museum Publications, 1989.

Tineke Rooijakkers

See also Tiraz: Textiles and Dress with Inscriptions in Central and Southwest Asia; Ottoman Dress; Saudi Arabian Dress; Laws of Differentiation; Sumptuary Laws; Khil'a: Clothing to Honor a Person or Situation.

Central and Southwest Asian Dress Studies

As with many areas of academia, the study of dress is not homogeneous. Many individuals and groups throughout the world are working (and often working in isolation) in the field of Central and Southwest Asian dress. In particular, there are scholars in Iran, Turkey, and parts of the Arab world who have a vast knowledge of their regional forms of dress, but this knowledge, for various reasons, is not widely available. Ironically, although dress is one of the easiest ways to gain access to another culture while learning more about one's own, Western traditional academia in general does not value the study of dress. Even with the widespread acceptance of anthropology and material culture studies in the second half of the twentieth century, this dismissive attitude toward textiles and dress is only slowly changing.

It has to be admitted, however, that some significant problems face Western scholars studying textiles and dress from Central and Southwest Asia, not least of which is the sheer size of the region involved and its wide range of geographic conditions (mountains and deserts), difficult terrain, and climatic variations. In addition, there are vast numbers of cultural, ethnic, political, and religious groups, many with their own languages and dialects and dress forms. As a result of these and other factors, the study of dress in Central and Southwest Asia is patchy, with some regions and groups studied in depth by the academic world and others, at best, committed to footnotes. This situation is changing, but it will be many years before Central and Southwest Asian dress has a literature list comparable to that of European or North American dress studies.

APPROACHES AND RANGE OF INFORMATION AVAILABLE

At the beginning of the twenty-first century, the approaches to the study of Central and Southwest Asian dress in Western academia range from anthropological, archaeological, art-historical, sociological, costume, and dress to economic, trade, and religious studies. However, in general, books and articles on dress can be divided into two main types: (1) those that are concerned with the theory of dress and fashion and illustrate very few actual garments and (2) publications that are more object oriented and include a variety of depictions of people, clothing, and accessories.

Nancy Lindisfarne-Tapper and Bruce Ingham's 1997 article, "Approaches to the Study of Dress in the Middle East," exemplifies this divide. It advocates the view that only a theoretical approach to the subject is valid: "The most compelling entry point for any critical discussion of the clothing of the Middle East is through particular, fine-grained ethnographic and sociolinguistic studies." Not every author, however, takes this view of the subject.

A considerable range of information is available in Central and Southwest Asian and Western sources concerning the history and development of textiles and dress in this vast region. The most important sources of information are the actual textiles, garments, and accessories, examples of which are preserved in various museums and private collections throughout the world. These objects are supported by secondary sources including a wide range of visual sources such as manuscript illustrations, wall and canvas paintings, cartoons (tapestries as well as "funny" drawings), metalwork, and so forth. Written accounts, such as official records, travelogues, gazetteers, newspapers, and magazines, provide many further details.

At the beginning of the twenty-first century, some notable collections of Central and Southwest Asian textiles and dress and related material can be found in the Museum of Anthropology and Ethnography, Saint Petersburg (Russia); the Topkapi Palace Museum, Istanbul (Turkey); the Israel Museum, Jerusalem; the Musée du Quai Branly, Paris; the Musée des Tissus et des Arts Décoratifs, Lyon (France); the Victoria and Albert Museum, London; the British Museum, London; the Textile Museum, Washington, D.C.; the Boston Museum of Fine Arts; the Chicago Institute of Art; and the Los Angeles County Museum of Art. Many of these collections include medieval and later textiles and dress and are particularly strong in nineteenth- and early-twentieth-century examples. The Textile Research Centre, Leiden (the Netherlands), has a diverse collection of mid- to late-twentieth-century dress from Central and Southwest Asia, notably from Afghanistan, Iran, and the Arabian Peninsula. The most comprehensive collection of Arab dress anywhere in the world belongs to a private collector, Widad Kawar, in Jordan. Another notable source in the region is the Rajab collection in Kuwait.

MEDIEVAL TRAVELERS AND PILGRIMS

Historical comments and commentaries on the various types of Central and Southwest Asian dress can be traced back hundreds of years. Arab and Persian scholars and travelers, for example, provide many of the early descriptions. Perhaps one of the most intriguing is that penned by the Moroccan-born writer Ibn Battuta (1304–1369), who traveled throughout the Maghreb (North Africa), Southwest Asia, India, and China during the early to mid-fourteenth century C.E. and left many incidental references about medieval dress. His book has been translated on various

Detail from a series of engravings showing Ottoman men's, women's, and children's clothing by Pieter Coecke van Aelst (1502–1550) from *Les Moeurs et Fachons de Faire des Turz* (The manners and customs of the Turks), Brussels, 1553. The Flemish tapestry designer van Aelst traveled from Belgium to the Ottoman court in the mid-sixteenth century to acquire orders for Flemish tapestries, and this book, a vivid source regarding Ottoman (Istanbul) dress from this period, reproduces his tapestry cartoons. Courtesy of Leiden University Library.

occasions since 1900, including one from the early twenty-first century: *The Travels of Ibn Battutah*.

Early Arab writings by pilgrims going to the holy cities of Mecca and Medina (Saudi Arabia) also provide various accounts of what they saw, wore, and took with them. The latter was important, because goods of all types were traded along the great hajj routes from Cairo, Istanbul, Damascus, and Baghdad in order to recuperate part of the high costs involved in going on a pilgrimage.

Various medieval European books that refer to dress in Southwest Asia were also written by pilgrims, both Christian and Jewish. Normally, they were traveling to Jerusalem either via areas that make up Turkey in the early twenty-first century or, more usually, by foot or boat in the eastern Mediterranean. Two useful sources of information in this genre are by Arnold von Harff and Salomon Schweigger. Von Harff was a fifteenth-century pilgrim from Germany who traveled throughout Turkey and the eastern Mediterranean. He includes numerous woodcuts with descriptions of dress in this region to show the exotic nature of the clothing and people. The second example is an account of Schweigger's travels in the Levant in the 1580s. A Jewish pilgrim from Germany, Schweigger uses various woodcuts to illustrate the people and the garments worn in the various countries he traveled through.

GEOGRAPHERS AND MERCHANTS

Incidental information about the trade in textiles and clothing can be found in a variety of sources, including items relating to the production and trade in these commodities. Numerous accounts by medieval Arab, Persian, and Turkish merchants and geographers, for example, concern the products they had seen in various cities and countries and what was popular where. Such geographers included Ibn al-Faqih (tenth century), ibn Hawqal (tenth century), and Yakut (1179–1229), who left numerous details about textiles and dress from Southwest Asia, especially Syria and Persia. These and other early Arab and Persian texts about textiles and dress were compiled and annotated by R.B. Serjeant in his 1972 study *Islamic Textiles: Material for a History up to the Mongol Conquest*.

For centuries, Turkish dress has been of interest to various Western merchants, especially those from Italy who were seeking textiles and furs. One such early merchant was the Flemish tapestry designer Pieter Coecke van Aelst (1502–1550), who traveled from Brussels (Belgium) to the Ottoman court in the mid-sixteenth century to acquire orders for Flemish tapestries. Although this trip proved to be financially disastrous, following the death of van Aelst in 1550, his wife published a series of illustrations by him called *Les Moeurs et Fachons de Faire des Turz*

(The manners and customs of the Turks). These representations provide a vivid and useful visual source regarding Ottoman (Istanbul) dress from this period.

Another form of information about commercial activities can be found in mercantile shipping registers. In particular, the British East India Company is very important; it was founded in 1600 C.E. A similar trading company was the Dutch East India Company (Vereenigde Oost-Indische Compagnie, or VOC), which was established in 1602. It was the first multinational corporation and, according to some, a megacorporation with semigovernmental powers. Textiles and garments such as cummerbunds, shawls, and a wide range of cottons were important trading items for both companies, as can be seen from official documents, such as the custom office receipts dating from the seventeenth century between the toll house in Al-Mukha, Yemen, and various VOC ships.

The increase in shipping during the nineteenth century meant an increase in the trade of textiles and items of dress throughout Southwest Asia. Many of these textiles were produced in India for export throughout the world. Egypt and Syria were also important textile producers and exported textiles throughout the Arab world. Significant European producers sending textiles to Central Asia were England and Russia, and, with respect to Southwest Asia, France, England, and, to a lesser extent, Switzerland. The role of Manchester firms in this extensive trade can be seen in the textile records housed in the Museum of Science and Technology, Manchester (England). Of particular interest are the textile sample albums, which sometimes list for which Central and Southwest Asian market the designs were intended.

By the mid-twentieth century, European and Southwest Asian textiles were declining in importance due to the rise of mass-produced Asian textiles, notably items from Japan and China and later from Korea. These gave rise to another form of this international trade—globalization of textiles and dress on a grand scale.

CORRESPONDENCE FROM DIPLOMATS

The letters and memoirs of Western diplomats and their wives also provide useful information concerning the dress of various courts throughout Central and Southwest Asia. One of the most famous examples of a diplomat's wife providing data can be found in the memoirs of Lady Mary Wortley Montagu (1690–1762), who came to Istanbul with her husband, the English ambassador. Montagu recounts in various letters to family and friends between 1717 and 1718 the details of her life in Istanbul. In particular, she describes the Turkish women's dress she had worn herself. Her written information is also supported by visual forms, as she had her portrait painted several times dressed in Ottoman dress. In one painting by Charles Jervas, from around 1716, she is shown standing alone in an indoor outfit (National Gallery of Ireland, Dublin). In another portrait by Jean-Baptiste Vanmour (National Portrait Gallery, London), Montagu is portrayed wearing an inner robe with a deep décolletage, a jeweled belt, and a fur kaftan, holding the hand of Edward, her small son. Both of these portraits provide invaluable information about textiles, cut, colors, and patterns of early-eighteenth-century Istanbul dress for women.

Sometimes the diplomats' memoirs include detailed information about the garments worn at various other courts. For example, the memoirs of the English diplomat James Morier, who first went to Iran in 1808–1809, are a valuable source of information about the outfits worn by men at the Persian court at the beginning of the nineteenth century. One of the developments that Morier notes is the increased role of European textiles, as in the following quotation taken from a conversation between Morier and an envoy of the shah:

> We talked of female dress. I asked the Envoy what effect the visit of a European woman dressed in her own way would produce in Persia. He replied that "if the King were to see her, He would probably order all his *Harem* to adopt the costume, and that every other man would follow his example, and enforce a fashion, which is not only so much more beautiful, but so much less expensive than their own." Their women are clothed in brocade and gold cloth, which is soon spoilt, or at least which is always cast off, whenever they hear that a new cargo arrives from Russia.

A studio portrait of a woman wearing a *badla* dress, Cairo, Egypt, 1920s–1930s. *Badla* is a form of metal-thread embroidery that originated in India. Its use had spread throughout Southwest Asia by the nineteenth century, due to trade in the region. *Badla* remains popular in the Gulf region of the Arabian Peninsula, Syria, and parts of Egypt. Textile Research Centre, Leiden.

EXPLORERS AND ACADEMICS

Information about dress and textiles from Southwest Asia can also be gleaned from the development of Western-style academic curiosity. From the seventeenth century on, for example, knowledge was collected for knowledge's sake, albeit sometimes with an emphasis on the curious and strange rather than the academic. This, in turn, led to the Age of Reason and later, in the nineteenth century, a desire to define and catalog everything in the natural and material worlds. The work of the naturalist Charles Darwin is often seen as one of classic results of this changing attitude toward the world.

European academic explorers also started to travel more regularly to Southwest Asia, and, during this period, one of the first serious Western studies on Arabic dress was produced: a dictionary of Arab dress by the Dutch Orientalist Reinhart Dozy. He compiled details about a small number of different types of Arab garments and published these in an 1845 book titled *Dictionnaire Detaillé des Noms des Vêtements chez les Arabes* (Detailed dictionary of the names of Arab garments). This remains a standard work on classical Arab dress for the era it covers.

But there was also an element of adventure and adventurism in this type of work, which led to some scholars becoming more explorers and adventurers than objective observers. Information about eighteenth-century Yemeni textiles and dress, for example, can be found in the accounts of the ill-fated Danish expedition to Yemen in 1761–1767. The only survivor of the expedition, Carsten Niebuhr, published *Beschreibung von Arabien* (Description of Arabia) in 1772, followed by two more volumes, *Reisebeschreibung von Arabien und anderen umliegenden Ländern* (Travel description of Arabia and other surrounding countries) in 1774–1778. These books were soon translated into French, Dutch, and English. At the time, there was a fascination with this expedition because it came to a bad end rather than because of what was recorded. All of these volumes are copiously illustrated and include a series of portraits depicting regional dress for both men and women.

Similarly, information about early-nineteenth-century Arab urban and Bedouin dress from this region is included in the 1830 work of the Swiss Orientalist John Lewis Burckhardt, *Notes on the Bedouins and Wahabys, Collected during His Travels in the East*. He traveled in the western parts of the Arabian Peninsula in what much later became Saudi Arabia.

The lure of Mecca, the holy city of Islam, which was officially off-limits to non-Muslims, was a real challenge to some Western travelers and Orientalists. One of the earliest known accounts of a non-Muslim going to Mecca dressed as a pilgrim is by the Italian Ludovico di Varthema (ca. 1470–1517), who went via Damascus to Mecca in 1503. He described what he saw and experienced, including some details on textiles and dress, in *The Travels of Ludovico di Varthema in Egypt, Syria, Arabia Deserta and Arabia Felix, in Persia, India, and Ethiopia, A.D. 1503 to 1508*. There are more examples, especially from the second half of the nineteenth century, when the British Orientalist Sir Richard Burton traveled in disguise to Mecca and Medina and recorded his observations and adventures in *Personal Narrative of a Pilgrimage to Al-Madinah and Meccah* (1855). Burton was interested in dress and made various references throughout this study to different forms of regional dress that he had seen and used.

Some European academics also became Muslims so that they could legally stay in Mecca. A notable example is the Dutch scholar C. Snouck Hurgronje, who lived in Mecca in 1885 under the name of Abd-el Ghaffar. During his year in Mecca, Snouck Hurgronje purchased a large collection of daily-life objects from the city, including men's and women's clothing and accessories and some jewelry and footwear, which are held in the collection of the National Museum of Ethnology, Leiden, the Netherlands, in the early twenty-first century. These garments illustrate the cosmopolitan nature of Mecca, because they are made out of textiles from France, India, Syria, and Yemen, as well as being made up by local tailors and embroidered with local decorative forms. In addition, Snouck Hurgronje published an album of photographs (1888) of mainly male Meccan officials and pilgrims coming to Mecca, which provide further details about dress at this time.

NINETEENTH-CENTURY PROFESSIONALS AND TOURISTS

During the nineteenth century, many Europeans and North Americans acquired jobs in Central and Southwest Asia. These included military advisers, such as Sir Henry Rawlinson (1810–1895), who, in the 1830s, was employed by the shah of Iran to modernize the Iranian army on European lines, which included the creation of uniforms and uniform-style outfits for court officials. Other professionals who were attracted to the region and worked there included the doctor Charles James Wills (in Iran) and the Russian photographer Anton Sevruguin (in Tehran, Iran). These men and others left behind information in the form of written and visual accounts, including many photographs.

The development of transportation links, notably trains and steamships, meant that more people could travel to Southwest Asia. Some of these people stayed a short time, while others traveled for several years. Many left memoirs and impressions of what they had seen, such as Isabella Bishop, who lived and traveled around Iran in the late nineteenth century. Similarly, travelogues about Turkish domestic life, including details about dress and accessories, are typified by the accounts of Julia Pardoe, who wrote *The City of the Sultan and Domestic Manners of the Turks in 1836* (1837); Lucy Garnett, author of *The Women of Turkey and Their Folk-Lore* (1890); and W. M. Ramsay, author of *Every-Day Life in Turkey* (1897).

POLITICS, THE MILITARY, AND NINETEENTH-CENTURY CHRISTIAN MISSIONARIES

During the nineteenth and early twentieth centuries, there was a massive expansion of various colonial powers—notably Britain, France, and Russia—in Central and Southwest Asia. At the same time, governments and official bodies became more active in learning about local groups and the locations of cities, towns, and villages. Some of this information was for military use, and sometimes it was gathered for political and economic ends. Various guides and gazettes, for example, were organized, which provided data on regions throughout this vast area. One such example is by William George Elphinstone (1782–1842), entitled *An Account of the Kingdom of Caubul and Its Dependencies in Persia, Tartary and India* (1815). This is an account of Afghanistan and its many

An Uzbek woman from Tashkent, Uzbekistan, 1900. In the photo on the left, her *chasmband* (face veil) covers her face, but on the right the *chasmband* is thrown back over her head, revealing her indoor garments and jewelry. From *A travers le Turkestan russe* (Journey through Russian Turkestan), Paris, 1902, by Hugues Krafft. Krafft (1853–1935) inherited a small fortune, which gave him the opportunity to travel extensively throughout the world for over twenty years. He documented his journeys with detailed accounts and was among the first to use instant photography in 1880, leaving behind a rich resource of over four hundred photos. Courtesy of Leiden University Library.

groups and includes details about garments and textiles used there. Another very detailed account (virtually house by house) was provided by the Finnish Orientalist Georg August Wallin, who kept meticulously detailed notes concerning his trips to the Arabian Peninsula in the 1840s. Many of these gazettes are still used for historical, archaeological, and cultural reasons.

Information about dress, albeit sometimes indirect, can also be found in the accounts of battles and conquests and adventurers' and explorers' notes that were published in popular newspapers, magazines, and journals of the late nineteenth and early twentieth centuries. In particular, magazines such as the *Illustrated London News* (founded 1842) provide considerable data in the form of both written accounts and illustrations. Some of these illustrations were based on firsthand observations and later on photographs that were used for engravings. On other occasions, however, it would appear that considerable artistic license was used to create something that was exotic and eye-catching for a European or U.S. market.

Details about textiles and dress have also come from the accounts, sometimes fanciful, left by men and women who had been spying in other countries. This is not confined to one country;

virtually every country in the world has been involved in spying at one time or another. One of the features of *Kim*, a fictional book by the British author Rudyard Kipling (1865–1936), was how, as a boy, Kim learned the appearance and dress of various tribal, religious, and urban groups living in northern India so that he would recognize where they came from. This book is basically about the tensions between the English and Russians during the nineteenth century and the desire to control Afghanistan and Central Asia in order to prevent Russian expansion into what the British felt was theirs—India.

The various wars and conflicts of the twentieth and early twenty-first centuries in Southwest Asia made this region sometimes difficult to visit and hindered seeing or studying dress. In addition, the closing off of much of Central Asia to the West following its incorporation into the Soviet Russian empire meant that travel in the region was at times very difficult and hazardous, even for Russian scholars. However, Russian academics were interested in ethnographic and anthropological studies and in dress studies in particular. But sometimes it seems that this work was designed to Russianize the locals and prove that they, too, were Russians rather than to stress differences in cultural traditions. This situation is similar to how the Ottoman Turks used dress albums to show the extent and diversity of the Ottoman Empire, while at the same time indicating that these people were Ottoman.

Much more information is available on Palestinian and Jordanian dress than other areas of Southwest Asian dress studies. One reason for this is the considerable increase in Christian missionary activity that occurred during the nineteenth and early twentieth centuries in many parts of Southwest Asia. In particular, attention was paid to Palestine, mainly because of historical and biblical connections to the region. Nineteenth- and early-twentieth-century missionaries frequently gave lectures in Europe and the United States about the situation in "modern" Palestine and often had collections of dress to show members of the public what clothing looked like in the time of Jesus and to make them more enthusiastic and generous in their donations. Many of these garments are held in museum collections throughout Europe and the United States.

Palestinian dress, especially that worn by women, was the subject of numerous books, articles, and exhibitions throughout the twentieth century. The artistic elements of the embroidered and woven dresses have a particular appeal throughout the world. In particular, the famous collection of Arab dress owned by Widad Kawar of Jordan has been the subject of various exhibitions, the most notable being Pracht und Geheimnis: Kleidung und Schmuck aus Palästina und Jordanien (Beauty and mystery: Dress and decoration from Palestine and Jordan), a traveling exhibition that started in Cologne, Germany, in 1987. Shelagh Weir used the Widad Kawar collection and the garments in what was the Museum of Mankind, London (part of the British Museum), in her 1989 book on the subject of Palestinian dress.

TWENTIETH-CENTURY STUDIES

Throughout the twentieth century, there was a slow increase in the number of exhibitions, articles, and books on the theme of Central and Southwest Asian dress. Many of these concentrated on the visually attractive items, such as Palestinian embroideries. The publication of Kate Fitz Gibbon and Andrew Hale's 2007 book, *Uzbek Embroidery in the Nomadic Tradition: The Jack A. and Aviva Robinson Collection at the Minneapolis Institute of Arts*, reflects the increased interest in Central Asian textiles and dress in the twentieth and early twenty-first centuries.

Since the fall of the Soviet Russian empire in the 1990s, various books on Central Asian dress have been published and made available in the West. Most of these books were published in Russian, but some have English summaries. A beautifully illustrated book on Uzbek caps and embroidery by Irina Bogoslovskaya and Larisa Levteeva, *Skullcaps of Uzbekistan, 19th–20th Centuries* was published in Russian in 2006.

From the 1970s on, there have been more sociological and anthropological studies on dress. Considerable attention has been paid to the subject of hijab (Islamically correct clothing) and the role of women within Central and Southwest Asian society. The subject is often discussed from the point of view of "why" rather than "what is," and the topic has become controversial in many Southwest Asian and Western societies. In contrast, Central and Southwest Asian fashion studies—both in the practical sense of fashion designers producing relevant designs and theoretical studies based on their works—are scarce. Attention is paid to this subject more in fashion magazines and newspaper articles than in serious publications.

Engraving of an Afghan family from the *Illustrated London News*, 27 December 1879. Many of the late-nineteenth-century illustrations in this newspaper were based on drawings and photographs by explorers, reporters, and military personnel. Such illustrations provide many details concerning dress, such as the amulet necklace around the woman's neck, the form of her spindle and the decoration on the man's turban and sandals and the "lifestyle" of various ethnic groups in this period. Courtesy of Willem Vogelsang.

CONCLUSION

In conclusion, there are no particular centers of excellence for the study of Central and Southwest Asian dress at the beginning of the twenty-first century. The study of dress in this vast region is scattered. There are scholars working in countries such as the Gulf region (notably Qatar and Oman), Jordan, Iran, and Turkey, as well as individuals and small groups working in relative isolation at various Western universities and related institutes. But because of various problems, such as the diversity of languages, there tend to be no strong, official links among the various groups.

The general situation with regard to Central and Southwest Asian dress studies, however, is changing because of developments in communication technology, particularly the Internet, e-mail, and satellites (telephones and televisions). All of these technologies have increased the opportunity for local and outside scholars to carry out research into the role of dress in various societies. If all goes well, then the work carried out on dress in the twenty-first century will have a different and more diverse nature than that during the previous centuries.

References and Further Reading

Aussen, A. *Coutumes des Arabes au pays de Moab*. Paris: Adrien-Maisonneuve, 1948.

Bishop, Isabella. *Journeys in Persia and Kurdistan*. 2 vols. London: MacMillan, 1891.

Bodman, Herbert L., and Nayereh Tohidi, eds. *Women in Muslim Societies: Diversity within Unity*. Boulder, CO: Lynn Rienner, 1998.

Brouwer, C.G. "White, Silk, Striped Commerbands with Silver Heads: Textiles in the Tollhouse of Seventeenth-Century Al-Mukha, Listed by Dutch Traders." *Khil'a* 1 (2005): 15–68.

Brouwer, C.G. "Cottons for Coins: Textile Transactions in Ottom-Kasimid al-Mukha: Observations by Dutch Participants." *Khil'a* 2 (2006): 23–82.

Burckhardt, John Lewis. *Notes on the Bedouins and Wahabys, Collected during His Travels in the East*. London: Henry Colburn and Richard Bentley, 1830.

Burton, Sir Richard. *Personal Narrative of a Pilgrimage to Al-Madinah and Meccah*. 2 vols. London: Tylson and Edwards, 1893.

Dozy, Reinhart. *Dictionnaire Detaillé des Noms des Vêtements chez les Arabes*. Amsterdam: Müller, 1845.

El Guindi, Fadwa. *Veil: Modesty, Privacy and Resistance*. Oxford: Berg, 1999.

Elphinstone, William George. *An Account of the Kingdom of Caubul and Its Dependencies in Persia, Tartary and India*. London: Smith, Elder and Co., 1815.

Fitz Gibbon, Kate, and Andrew Hale. *Uzbek Embroidery in the Nomadic Tradition: The Jack A. and Aviva Robinson Collection at the Minneapolis Institute of Arts*. Minneapolis, MN: Minneapolis Institute of Arts, 2007.

Garnett, Lucy. *The Women of Turkey and Their Folk-Lore*. 2 vols. London: David Nutt, 1890.

Gole, Nilufer. *The Forbidden Modern: Civilization and Veiling*. Ann Arbor: University of Michigan Press, 1996.

Halsband, Robert, ed. *The Complete Letters of Lady Mary Wortley Montagu*. 3 vols. Oxford: Clarendon Press, 1965–1967.

Lindisfarne-Tapper, Nancy, and Bruce Ingham, eds. *Languages of Dress in the Middle East*. London: SOAS, Curzon Press, 1997.

Mabro, Judy. *Veiled Half-Truths: Western Travellers' Perceptions of Middle Eastern Women*. London: I. B. Tauris, 1991.

Mackintosh-Smith, Timothy. *The Travels of Ibn Battutah*. New York: Picador, 2003.

Mernissi, Fatima. *The Veil and the Male Elite: A Feminist Interpretation of Women's Rights in Islam*. New York: Addison Wesley, 1991.

Morier, James. *A Journey through Persia, Armenia and Asia Minor to Constantinople in the Years 1808 and 1809*. London: Longman, 1812.

Niebuhr, Carsten. *Reisebeschreibung von Arabien und anderen umliegenden Ländern*. 2 vols. Copenhagen: Möller, 1774–1778.

Northrop, Douglas. *Veiled Empire: Gender and Power in Stalinist Central Asia*. Ithaca, NY: Cornell University Press, 2004.

Pardoe, Julia. *The City of the Sultan and Domestic Manners of the Turks in 1836*. 2 vols. London: Routledge, 1837.

Ramsay, W.M. *Every-Day Life in Turkey*. London: Hodder and Stoughton, 1897.

Schweigger, Salomon. *Eine newe Reyssbeschreibung auss Teutschland nach Constantinopel und Jerusalem*. Introduction by Rudolf Neck. Graz, Austria: Akademische Druck- und Verlagsanstalt, 1964.

Serjeant, R.B. *Islamic Textiles: Material for a History up to the Mongol Conquest*. Beirut: Librairie du Liban, 1972.

Snouck Hurgronje, C. *Mekka*. The Hague, the Netherlands: Martinus Nijhoff, 1888.

Varthema, Lodovico di. *The Travels of Ludovico di Varthema in Egypt, Syria, Arabia Deserta and Arabia Felix, in Persia, India, and Ethiopia, A.D. 1503 to 1508*. London: Hakluyt Society, 1863.

Vögler, Gisela, Karin van Welck, and Katharina Hackstein, eds. *Pracht und Geheimnis: Kleidung und Schmuck aus Palästina und Jordanien*. Ethnologica 13. Cologne: Gesellschaft für Völkerkunde, 1987.

von Harff, Arnold. *The Pilgrimage of Arnold von Harff, Knight: From Cologne through Italy, Syria, Egypt, Arabia, Ethiopia, Nubia, Palestine, Turkey, France, and Spain, Which He Accomplished in the Years 1496 to 1499*. Translated and edited by Malcolm Letts. London: Hakluyt Society, 1946.

Wallin, Georg August. *Travels in Arabia (1845 and 1848)*. Cambridge, UK: Oleander Press, 1979.

Weir, Shelagh. *Palestinian Costume*. London: British Museum Publications, 1989.

Wills, C.J. *In the Land of the Lion and Sun or Modern Persia, Being Experiences of Life in Persia from 1866 to 1881*. London: MacMillan, 1883.

Gillian Vogelsang-Eastwood

See also Sources of Information about Dress in Southwest Asia.

PART 2

Textiles of Central and Southwest Asia

Trade, Textiles, and Dress in Central and Southwest Asia

- Geography, Climate, and Religion
- Textiles and Dress in Prehistory
- The Silk Road
- The Modern Era

Textiles and dress provide invaluable opportunities for insight into the encounters of lifestyles with infrastructures of trade and exchange. Textiles and dress in Central and Southwest Asia cover a long historical arc, from the earliest known archaeological textile finds to the twenty-first century.

The cultures of Central and Southwest Asia reflect a variety of ethnicities, belief systems, and ways of life. Tribal nomadism, pastoral herding, agricultural settlement, and urban (oasis) dwelling can occur in a single country. The trade patterns of Central and Southwest Asia have ancient roots, but over time they have shifted along with the economic and sociopolitical relationships to the rest of the world. In the macro context, textiles have figured as trade commodities and as cultural prestige symbols. In micro contexts, textiles play important roles in expressing and sustaining ethnic identity, family continuity, and spiritual beliefs of the various groups. Thus, two major elements—the complex trade patterns and the various cultures across the regions that developed over a long historical arc dating back at least ten thousand years—feed the reservoir of techniques, motifs, and designs used to create the textiles and dress of Central and Southwest Asia.

GEOGRAPHY, CLIMATE, AND RELIGION

Central and Southwest Asia diverge in their geographic profiles, importantly configuring resources and trade patterns. Southwest Asia, although very dry, enjoys numerous coasts, and therefore sea routes handily connect it to an array of near and far ports. Central Asia has no major ports, but at its center, it served as a historical trade hub until the fifteenth century C.E. Production of textile goods for internal and export trade took place in the oases and port settlements. In the twenty-first century, air, road, and rail transportation link with the global trade system; however, some localities remain remote due to difficult terrain.

Southwest Asia includes many coastal areas, vast deserts, high plateaus, and mountains. Arid and semiarid climates predominate, with a Mediterranean climate present in the eastern Mediterranean, parts of Anatolia, and the Iranian Plateau. Most of the Arabian Peninsula is desert. Therefore, in the past, camels were used to traverse the large desert. On the southwestern coast, the Red Sea divides the Arabian Peninsula from Africa. On the eastern coast is the Persian Gulf. The eastern Mediterranean (also known as the Levant) is a semicircular region south of Anatolia and at the northwestern end of the Arabian Peninsula, just beyond the Syrian Desert. Holy sites of Judaism, Christianity, and Islam are located here, with many concentrated in historical Palestine (in Israel and the Palestinian territories). The Mediterranean Sea, which forms the western edge of the region, connects eastern Mediterranean ports to Anatolia, North Africa, and Europe. Bordering Israel, the southernmost nation in the eastern Mediterranean, is the Sinai Peninsula, part of Egypt that forms a land bridge between Africa and Southwest Asia.

Anatolia is comprised of the region to the west of the Caspian Sea, including the peninsula at the western edge of Asia; this is where the Republic of Turkey straddles the Bosporus Strait and extends into Europe. The Caucasus Mountains lie to the northeast.

Two mountain ranges edge the Iranian Plateau. The Zagros range is on the west toward the Arabian Peninsula, and the Hindu Kush is to the east. The Persian Gulf lies over the Zagros, dividing the Iranian Plateau from the Arabian Peninsula. The Caspian Sea is to the northwest of the Iranian Plateau, and the Kara-Kum Desert in Central Asia sits at the northeastern edge. The region called the Fertile Crescent, also known as the cradle of civilization, extends into the Iranian Plateau in Iraq and western Iran. Critical developments in agriculture and animal domestication fostered human settlement in the Neolithic era in this region.

The climate of Central Asia, although generally characterized as dry and thus a region where water is valuable, has more climatic variation than Southwest Asia. Large swaths of semiarid steppe and continental climate cover the region, yet the polar climate in the high altitudes of the Tien Shan Mountains, the subtropical climate in the Fergana Valley, and the arid Taklimakan Desert demonstrate the wide climatic range. In contrast to Southwest Asia's numerous coastal areas and sea routes, Central Asia borders only one large body of water, the Caspian Sea. The large Kazakh Steppe begins north of the Kyzyl Kum and east of the Ural Mountains and covers the northern section of Central Asia eastward to the Altai Mountains. Here, nomadic cultures developed based on moving seasonally to find fresh pastures for their grass-fed herd animals. This was possible, in part, due to the domestication of horses. Horses have served for centuries as a major trade good for Central Asia's nomads. Herd animals provide many nomadic necessities, including sheep wool, a material necessary to make the felt used in yurts (a circular tent using felt in its construction), furnishings, and some clothing.

On the eastern side of Central Asia is the Tarim Basin; the Kunlun Mountains on the south edge of the basin create a rain shadow, while the dry and salty Taklimakan Desert, an inhospitable gray terrain of pulverized rock, sits in the center of the basin. In contrast to this stark setting, the foothills of the Tien Shan Mountains rimming the north edge of the desert include areas more hospitable for settlement, where fruits, nuts, and other crops thrive. In the twenty-first century, most of the Tarim Basin is located in China's Xinjiang Uygur Autonomous Region. At the western end, the Tarim Basin edges into Uzbekistan, Kyrgyzstan, and Tajikistan. It is along the valleys of the Tien Shan or on the northern slope of the Kunlun that land travelers pushing east or west in Central Asia are forced to pass. The Tien Shan, Kunlun, Karakoram, and Hindu Kush ranges merge in the center of Central Asia, forming the Pamir mountain range, one of the highest in the world. Nestled in this area is the fertile Fergana Valley, a midpoint in the ancient Silk Road, where oasis settlements benefited from commerce brought by traders, who also traded in textiles, rugs, and leather goods.

In the early twenty-first century, the Islamic faith predominates across Central and Southwest Asia. Ardent followers arose from the Arabian Peninsula, the Prophet Mohammed's home, in the early eighth century. They spread along trade routes, taking their religion throughout Southwest and Central Asia and beyond to Africa and South and Southeast Asia. Many peoples converted to Islam or integrated it with their preexisting beliefs. In Israel, in the eastern Mediterranean, the majority practice Judaism, which originated there around 2000 B.C.E. For centuries, a significant Jewish population lived in Central Asia; however, most immigrated to Israel before the twenty-first century.

Other religions continue, particularly those belief systems that were widely practiced in the past. Zoroastrianism, based on the ancient teachings of Zoroaster of Iran, was brought by Iranian migrations eastward into Central Asia. Buddhism, based on the teachings of Siddhartha Buddha (ca. 563–483 B.C.E.), was transmitted along trade routes from South Asia (India) into Central and East Asia. Christianity, based on belief in Jesus Christ as the Savior, spread along trade routes during the Roman Empire (27 B.C.E.–476 C.E.) from the eastern Mediterranean. Other ancient beliefs, including animism and shamanism, infuse spiritual practices of some cultures.

TEXTILES AND DRESS IN PREHISTORY

Textile history reaches far into prehistory in Southwest Asia. The oldest textile artifacts date to the seventh millennium B.C.E. The arid conditions at Nahal Hemar in the Judean Desert in Israel and at Çatal Hüyük on the Anatolian Plateau allowed textile remains dating to the Neolithic era to survive. The evidence shows that humans manipulated bast fibers (stem fibers found in specific plants such as flax, hemp, and ramie) into textiles using weft twining, weft wrapping, and plain weave, including narrow warp-faced tapes. Archaeological evidence also suggests that the heddle, a technological advance in the loom, emerged in this region. The development of the heddle—individual holders for warp yarns attached to a heddle bar, allowing control of certain threads—permitted weavers to increase textile-production speed and pattern complexity. Moreover, the earliest documented felt, dating to the early Bronze Age (ca. 2600 B.C.E.), was found in Anatolia.

As U.S. anthropologist Elizabeth Barber has pointed out, "Making cloth and clothing soaked up more than half the human labor hours in most pre-industrial societies, even more than food

A nomadic Kyrgyz family carrying and wearing printed cottons, Golodnaya Steppe, Uzbekistan, between 1905 and 1915. Photograph by Sergei Mikhailovich Prokudin-Gorskii. Library of Congress, Prints & Photographs Division, Prokudin-Gorskii Collection, LC-DIG-prokc-21854.

production." Simply by noting the investment of time and labor, the importance placed on textiles in prehistory, and indeed well into the modern era, is easily understood. However, textiles were esteemed for dimensions beyond the labor involved in them (just as some are in the twenty-first century). Additional value can derive from skillful workmanship and rare materials. Textiles' important roles in extending human capacity for work and thus contributing to survival and enhancement of daily life through comfort also added to their significance. Based on these dimensions, textiles served as important elements in trade. Textiles also served as material repositories of cultural meaning connected to these and other attributes. Such dimensions of value can be assessed in part through analysis of the specific materials, techniques, motifs, and functions of textiles within a particular group of people. Archaeological textiles are rare and are not accompanied by descriptions of their value. Instead, scholars interpret exchange and cultural value through such elements as context and various dimensions of value.

In the twentieth century, several grave sites spanning approximately fifteen hundred years were discovered in and near the Tarim Basin in eastern Central Asia and provided new archaeological textiles for study. In particular, textiles from Qäwrighul at Loulan dating to 2000–1800 B.C.E.; those from Cherchen and Hami, stops on the Silk Road's northern route, dating to 1000 B.C.E.; and those from Turfan that date to the mid- to late first millennium B.C.E. should be noted. Most of the Tarim Basin artifacts are housed at the Urumchi Museum, located in the Xinjiang Uygur Autonomous Region in China. Textiles survived here due to the arid conditions of the forbidding Taklimakan Desert. The artifacts have proven rich sources to extend understanding of human migration and the transfer of wool eastward. The most striking aspects of the Tarim Basin finds are the physical characteristics of the mummified human remains. They possess physical attributes of people from the west. Barber has presented the evidence developed by scholars with respect to deciphering the mummies' origins. Analysis of the Tarim mummies' language, wheat agriculture, and, importantly, their sheep-wool textiles and weaving technology combine to suggest their origin was in Southwest Asia.

The mummies were dressed in ensembles made from skins and textiles, and, in some burials, textile grave gifts survived. The inclusion of textile grave gifts points to the cultural importance of textiles, perhaps for use in the afterlife. Garments worn or buried at Cherchen in the first millennium B.C.E. included woven wool coats, shirts, trousers, dresses, skirts, and shawls. Other textiles and dress accessories included wall hangings, body wrappings, leather boots and slippers, a mitten, hats, bags, and cords and sashes. Techniques for making and decorating textiles found at Cherchen include several weaving patterns as well as felting, oblique plaiting, and band weaving. Other techniques found there are *kumihimo* (multistrand plaiting of cord using bobbins on an upright frame); *naalbinding* (looping with a threaded needle); dyeing in blues, reds, yellows, and oranges; embroidery; and painting fabric.

Loulan, located toward the east end of the Tarim Basin and the oldest of the sites, dating to the early second millennium B.C.E., yielded the earliest wool textiles documented in Central Asia. These woolens—woven in solids, simple plaids, and checks—are in natural wool colors such as cream and shades of tan and brown. Barber has explained that the type of sheep needed for

producing wool suitable for making textiles emerged as a result of inbreeding in Mesopotamia in Southwest Asia about 4000 B.C.E. Thus, the presence of woolen textiles at Loulan suggests that the people had brought the woolly sheep from the west.

Not only does the presence of wool suggest eastward migration, but other attributes of the textiles point in that direction as well. Woven fabrics found in the Tarim Basin, for example, do not exceed twenty-four inches (sixty centimeters) in width, which suggests the loom type used. Producing narrow cloth requires only one weaver on the horizontal ground loom and the two-beam vertical loom. The two-beam vertical loom is also well suited to tapestry weave. In addition, these two loom types are easily set up and broken down, an attribute useful to nomadic migration. These loom types are attested in Southwest Asia before 2010 B.C.E. The textiles from the Tarim Basin demonstrate the spread of these weaving technologies into Central Asia via the migration of people from the west who were familiar with them.

Just as the loom dictates the potential width of fabric, the width of fabric can affect garment structure. Rectangles of woven cloth formed the garments in order to utilize the valuable woven cloth economically. For example, a Cherchen wears a shirt and trousers made of fabric rectangles of a plain-weave brown wool that has been overdyed with red. Two narrow loom-width panels form his shirt's body, with one panel over each shoulder. Tubes made of smaller rectangles form the sleeves, which are stitched to the body sections. Similarly, the skirt worn by a woman from Qäwrighul at Loulan and the dress worn by a Cherchen woman were made by sewing long, rectangular panels in arrangements to form garments without unnecessary cutting. A coat for a Cherchen man shows the garment maker's imperative for fabric economy. At first glance, the coat's sleeves implied tailoring through cutting; however, examination revealed that fabric was turned to the inside of the sleeve, thus shaping the outside without cutting the woven rectangle.

Historians concur that trousers, or bifurcated lower-body garments, developed among nomadic Eurasian horsemen and -women in the second millennium B.C.E. The close fit of pants added to comfort and efficiency while riding horseback. Elizabeth Barber and Irene Good's examination of a pair of trousers from a Cherchen grave showed they were fashioned of several woolen rectangles with a gusset (a square of cloth folded on the bias, inserted at the intersection of other garment segments to provide give or stretch) in the crotch to allow for leg movement. The finding of trousers at Cherchen fits with the discovery of horse bones there: These people rode horses.

Although woolly sheep, particular loom types, and twill and tapestry weaves can be traced to Southwest Asia, several textile techniques practiced in Central Asia between 2000 B.C.E. and about 500 B.C.E. have not been traced to origins. They may demonstrate transfer of techniques (for example, sprang—a form of fabric made by twisting together the warp threads in a set order to create a pattern, with no weft threads—and kumihimo) through trade from other sources; for example, cashmere fibers, found only in small amounts at Cherchen, suggest the availability of cashmere goats from India in the south or fibers acquired through trade.

The spiral motif used for decoration at Cherchen suggests possible pathways of contact and trade. The Cherchen man and woman wear spiraling yellow face paint. Large cloths, one with

A fabric merchant, Samarkand, Uzbekistan, between 1905 and 1915. His display includes silk, cotton, and wool fabrics in stripes, plaids, solids, and floral prints. The bold floral and striped printed fabric of his own coat was probably Russian roller-printed cotton. The framed page of the Qur'an hanging at the top of his stall indicates he follows Islam. Samarkand was one of the central cities on the Silk Road and attracted traders from many different countries. Photograph by Sergei Mikhailovich Prokudin-Gorskii. Library of Congress, Prints & Photographs Division, Prokudin-Gorskii Collection, LC-DIG-prokc-21725.

red and white spirals and one with red and blue spirals painted on a yellow ground, were found. A textile scrap and a shirt in tapestry weave have spiral motifs. Spirals are documented on carved objects as well. The spirals of Cherchen may relate to the decorative felt designs of the regional nomads of the modern era. Barber has explained that felt, a fabric central to the lifestyles of Eurasian steppe nomads, is well suited to curvilinear designs made through cutting. To the north of Central Asia, in the narrow band of steppe by the Altai Mountains in Russia, is the archaeological site Pazyryk (480–430 B.C.E.). Burials preserved by permafrost contained large textiles with spiral motifs, including a felt made using a counter-change mosaic or inlaid technique and a tapestry- and twill-weave wall hanging. Small felts with spirals

were also present. The Pazyryk spirals resemble the spirals seen at Cherchen. Central Asian felts with spiral decoration, made by nomads into the twenty-first century, suggest the possibility of sustained affinity for the motif across time in the region.

THE SILK ROAD

Long before permanent settlements dotted the lower altitudes of Central Asia, horse-riding nomadic tribes dominated the expansive Eurasian steppe. By 1800 B.C.E., people with western roots had settled early trade paths around the Tarim Basin. In approximately the first century B.C.E., parallel with expansion efforts of the Chinese Han dynasty (206 B.C.E.–220 C.E.), the ancient trade paths coalesced into a series of transcontinental routes. These intensified in use until the fifteenth century, when they became less important than sea routes. Later, archaeological discoveries of the late nineteenth and early twentieth centuries stimulated modern interest in the old Eurasian trade paths, and they became widely known as the Silk Road. Sometimes the sea routes connecting Europe and Asia are included when referring to the Silk Road in order to address premodern Eurasian trade patterns comprehensively.

The Silk Road was the pathway for transformative cultural exchange of beliefs, innovations, and goods. Religions moved across the continent, aided by the trade routes: In the third century b.c.e., Buddhism emerged from India, and in the eighth century c.e., Islam from Arabia. Printing, first developed in China, spread slowly, eventually revolutionizing human communication. In addition, paper came from China, then woodblock printing (seventh century c.e.), and later typesetting (late thirteenth century). Ideas like these led to other print innovations such as printed-paper currency and printed textiles. Central Asian archaeological discoveries from near Dunhuang attest to the westward movement of Chinese innovations and the migration of belief systems. The finds include artworks and textiles such as printed and painted silks; a felt and leather embroidered shoe (eighth to ninth century c.e.); and an undated woolen, hemp, and silk shoe. The chair, globally ubiquitous in the twenty-first century, transformed the dress, architecture, and lifestyle of the Chinese after it appeared in China in the second century c.e., long after it was in use in Southwest Asia. Another example of transcultural migration aided by the Silk Road was the adoption of trousers. Trousers originated among horse-riding nomads. Their use spread westward to the Romans in the first century b.c.e., who copied them for their horse-riding military. By the end of the seventeenth century, trousers, in the form of breeches, were common across Europe.

Loads carried on the Silk Road were not limited to silk. Wool, especially rugs from Iran and Anatolia, went both east and west. Cotton from India traveled north to the Central Asian markets, where it was both consumed locally and sold for eastern and western destinations. Astrakhan (karakul lamb pelt with a distinctive curly texture) from Central Asia was carried eastward. Caravan traders from all directions also procured Central Asian silks, gold embroideries, and leather products to carry in their loads. Glass, brass, gold, gems, and semiprecious stones were in the packs of traders traversing the continent. Even with all these prized items and more, the primary composition of the caravan loads was iron and other raw materials.

Seldom did a caravan travel the entire length of the Eurasian routes, although explorers, emissaries, pilgrims, missionaries, and some traders made the complete trip. Instead, caravans primarily traveled sections of the routes. For protection from bandits and to avoid navigation errors, caravan leaders hired local nomads familiar with the terrain. Even without traveling across the whole continent, the trek to and from the heart of Central Asia was arduous, as mountains, deserts, or vast grasslands had to be encountered. Thus, many traders paused to unload and sell one cache of goods and restock with another for their return trip. Among the prospering Central Asian oasis settlements were Bukhara, Samarkand, Tashkent (in Uzbekistan), and others in the Fergana Valley (in Uzbekistan, Kyrgyzstan, and Tajikistan). Commercial opportunities drew people from far away to the region. Thus,

the region hosted a mixture of ethnicities from across the continent and beyond. Taxes extracted from caravan traders as they entered the market settlements added to the coffers of the local magistrates.

Silk, the chief luxury good of the Silk Road, originated in China by at least 3000 b.c.e. Chinese legend credits Empress Xi-Ling (ca. 2640 b.c.e.) with discovering that a cocoon of the moth species Bombyx mori could be unwound to produce a filament. However, silk textiles dating to 3600 b.c.e. were found at Hemudu. Combining multiple silk filaments produces lustrous, soft, strong, and easily dyed yarns suitable for weaving. The processes of cultivation and production, called sericulture, and the looms for making prized patterned silk textiles were secret for centuries. However, once others saw silks, they desired them, and silk cultivation and pattern weaving spread.

Although silk from China appeared in Bactria (Afghanistan) in Southwest Asia as early as 1500 b.c.e., it was not seen widely in Central and Southwest Asia until after 200 b.c.e. At this time, the Han imperial court began to exchange silk for horses with the Huns to acquire mounts for their military. The Huns moved their excess silk—yarn, unfinished cloth, cloths with woven and embroidered Chinese motifs, and completed clothes made from silk—westward in trade. The damask weaves made possible by the Chinese treadle loom (from about 300–200 b.c.e.) were highly desired. The Hallstadt silks (Austria) date from around 500 b.c.e., giving an indication of the history of long-distance trade in textiles, especially silks, at an early date.

Increased availability of silk led to silk industries outside China. For example, Syria had long been a wool-weaving and textile-trade center, including the dye trade. Syrian weavers mastered intricate silk weaving and may have developed the draw loom (ca. sixth to seventh century c.e.), creating more complex weaves such as brocade. The Sassanid Empire, an Iranian culture, dominated much of the western end of the Silk Road in Central and Southwest Asia, including part of Syria, from 224 to 642 c.e. Their silk industry, which had started by the second to third century c.e., is renowned in the historical record for its excellence. Across Central Asia, in Islamic Spain, and as far as China, their intricate silken brocades and other compound weaves were imported and copied. The richly colored design repertoire of Persian motifs was abundant with animals in large repeats and pictorial hunt and battle scenes. The most noted motif is the senmerv, a munificent half-bird and half-dog of the Zoroastrian religion, enclosed in a roundel with a pearl border. In the carvings at Taq-i-Bustan in Iran (fifth to seventh century c.e.), an allover pattern, perhaps depicting these textiles, appears on men's tunics and coats worn over trousers.

The silk industry of the Byzantine Empire (330–1453 c.e.) commenced during the reign of Justinian I (483–565 c.e.), attaining a high level of refinement in Constantinople (Istanbul, Turkey), influenced by the Sassanian style. The exquisite textile production was important in the Orthodox and Catholic Christian textile traditions. The Muslim Ottoman Empire displaced Byzantium, and its imperial workshops, including those in Bursa, produced colorful, intricate textiles used in furnishings and kaftans worn by the nobility. During the Mongol Empire, trade along the Silk Road was well established. Silks imported from Central and Southwest Asia, especially the gold-embroidered ones, were admired in Europe and by the Mongol courts. Yet silk trade and production were not meeting the demand in Europe, and, in Italy, home to Marco Polo and many other traders, a silk-production industry blossomed using silk yarns obtained from China.

Marco Polo (1256–1323) is the most widely remembered European trader and traveler of the Silk Road. He traveled to China with his father and uncle and remained in China for seventeen years under the direction of Kublai Khan (1215–1294) of the Mongol Empire (1206–1368 C.E.). Long after his travels, Marco Polo recounted them in a book. Embellished by romance author Rustichello da Pisa, his writing assistant, it became medieval Europe's most widely known treatise about the Silk Road. He wrote of seeing silks in the markets in Georgia, Baghdad, and Yazd, Persia, where silk was made for export. The influence of the Silk Road is seen in reverberations from his book: Fifteenth-century European seafarers, including Christopher Columbus (1451–1506), inspired in part by Marco Polo's narrative, sought westward routes from Europe to Asia, leading to European settlement of the Americas.

The Mongol Empire, which had controlled most of the Eurasian continent, fractured after Kublai Khan's death in 1294. Eventually, land routes in eastern China lost protection from bandits in the early fourteenth century as the Ming dynasty (1368–1644 C.E.) turned inward. In addition, sea routes carried larger loads more quickly, and consequently traders increased their use of sea routes between Europe and South and East Asia. The decline of the land routes led to Central Asian isolation from eastern trade. However, the shift in trade patterns did not completely disrupt the Central Asian economy. Although the east-west overland caravan routes diminished, Central Asian north-south trade continued with India, Southwest Asia, Iran, and Russia.

THE MODERN ERA

Continued European demand kept the silk centers in Central and Southwest Asia thriving. During the Ottoman Empire's control, Central Asia was divided into smaller khanates. The sultan in Constantinople and regional khans maintained workshops to create silk textiles, hand-knotted carpets, and gold embroideries. They lavishly decorated their courts and garments with local goods, yet imported French silk fabrics held the highest status as prestige markers, and officials wore Chinese embroideries.

From the 1600s on, Central Asia and Iran relied on Indian textile production for linen, silk brocade, and chintz (glazed plain-weave cotton fabric with floral or striped printed patterns) for their own consumption. Russian trade with Central Asia also increased, with Central Asia playing the role of intermediary to Russia's demand for Indian goods into the eighteenth century. Again, horses proved critical for Central Asian trade; in exchange for printed cottons, Central Asia supplied horses for India's military cavalry well into the nineteenth century. The once-vast Ottoman Empire was shrinking, and this contributed to a stagnant economy.

Eventually, the depressed textile sector reemerged in the nineteenth century, despite the unstable political environment. Vibrant, colorful fabrics called ikats (textiles decorated using a resist-dye technique), made of silk and cotton, executed with masterful craftsmanship, were the zenith of this textile renaissance. To participate directly in the increasing market for cotton, the Khoqand Khanate (1709–1876 C.E.) in the Fergana Valley developed irrigation and increased cotton farming. Russia pressed its interests in direct access to Central Asian trade lines and cotton. Britain sought to ensure that its colonial territory India was not vulnerable to Russia. Eventually, Russia gained official control of much of Central Asia in 1907.

In the early twenty-first century, cotton remains important in the Central Asian economy. Uzbekistan is the second-largest exporter of cotton in the world (after the United States); however, Uzbekistan's irrigation system is failing. In the twentieth century, the Union of Soviet Socialist Republics (1922–1991), which controlled the entire Turkic region, instituted irrigation dependent on river flow that would have fed the Aral Sea. Constant cotton farming and the irrigation system have led to poor yields due to depleted soil or salty fields.

It is impossible to capture the variety of textiles and dress worn in twenty-first-century Central and Southwest Asia. Dress linked to long-held practices and beliefs, or ethnic dress, is seen in urban centers as well as in rural and remote locales. World dress, or world fashion, consisting of the array of globally common garments and styles, is ubiquitous, except in the most remote locales or in areas where religious preferences outline dress requirements. Fashion, in the classic sense of the fashion system and seasonal change cycles, is worn by elites, particularly those from oil-rich nations.

The textile arts were, and continue to be, central to the lives of the people of Central Asia. However, since the early nineteenth century, many traditions of the past have been lost. For example, the exquisite ikats of Central Asia are no longer made or worn in the same way they were in the past. The long, unisex ikat coats of the nineteenth century have been transformed: The "national gown" of Uzbekistan in the early twenty-first century is made from machine-made satin ikat, and, in Tajikistan and Uzbekistan, women wear handwoven ikat dresses and trousers in modern colorations and scales. Most women in Central Asia wear dress suited to modest Muslim taste. In Uzbekistan, urban and rural women often wear head scarves with long print dresses or skirts. In Kyrgyzstan, Islamic influence since 1996 has influenced some women to wear full body-enclosing outer garments. Others wear long-sleeved and floor-length garments with a head wrap, covering only some of their hair. In the nomadic regions, the basic elements of Turkic dress of the past few millennia maintain their place, although world-fashion items are also used. Layers of padded coats with split skirts for riding, trousers, and boots are still useful for nomads.

In the eastern Mediterranean and Anatolia, world fashion predominates. In Israel, a cosmopolitan population mixes with those observing the Jewish faith with conservative practices. Some Orthodox Jewish men wear black coats and homburg-style hats, as well as the tallith (prayer shawl) and *kippah* (skullcap), which are also commonly worn by observant Jews. Conservative and observant Jewish women dress modestly. The cosmopolitan sector wears fashionable Western styles and may dress in body-revealing athletic wear, beachwear, and evening wear. Palestine's heritage of the finely embroidered women's *thob* (a T-shaped garment worn in Southwest Asia) continues to be seen, although many women wear simple floor-length dresses. Most Palestinian men wear world dress. Military garb in khaki, black, and green is common, as the eastern Mediterranean has experienced conflagrations for several decades.

Dress in the Arabian Peninsula and in Iran responds to their dominant Islamic faith. In Iran, most men wear world fashion

A Bukhara bureaucrat in Uzbekistan, between 1905 and 1915. He wears a typical Central Asian wrapped coat with sleeves longer than his fingertips. It is made of locally dyed and woven silk fabric called ikat. The matched design from panel to panel suggests that he was able to pay for sufficient fabric to enable the tailor to align the pattern. Photograph by Sergei Mikhailovich Prokudin-Gorskii. Library of Congress, Prints & Photographs Division, Prokudin-Gorskii Collection, LC-DIG-prokc-21884.

while practicing modest dress. Women in the Islamic Republic of Iran (established 1979) are directed to cover their heads and bodies, and the women carry out the directives in a variety of ways. Some urban women dress in enveloping black chadors and head coverings, while others wear a colorful head scarf and a coat over a blouse, trousers, and boots. Dress in various Arab countries also responds to the desert climate, as the loose, flowing, body-covering clothes offer protection from the sun and provide cooling layers. Women in Saudi Arabia, for example, are required to wear a black *abayeh*, a full body–covering robe, and to conceal their hair in public. Women in urban locales wear world fashion, including Western-made clothing, under the abayeh. Saudi men wear a three-part head covering (a skullcap, a folded cotton cloth, and a circlet holding the cloth in place), and on their bodies they wear a long, gownlike thob. A *bisht*, a long-sleeved, floor-length coat of camel hair or wool, completes the ensemble. Thus, Arab men dress similarly, reflecting their belief that all men are equal before God.

Fashions from the West, both Parisian haute couture and U.S. luxury brands, are popular among wealthy Arabs. This is despite the cultural convention among conservative Muslims to cover the body, and sometimes the hair and face of observant Arab Muslim women. The divergent ways Western fashion magazines were distributed in private and public demonstrate the disjuncture between the taste for these fashions and the social controls on women's dress. In the 1980s, in Riyadh, publicly sold fashion magazines were shorn of fashion shots considered too revealing; yet in private among the elites, intact fashion magazines circulated. The magazine *Venus* used paste-up images to montage modest looks, such as head scarves, onto Western fashions.

Wealthy Arab women in the late 1980s appreciated couture-quality materials and techniques and the social prestige of branded luxury goods. Parisian haute couture, the pinnacle of fashionable dress, was preferred. Because Western-style fashions do not comply with the cultural standard of covering the body in public, when wealthy conservative Arab women dress fashionably, they do it privately for each other, away from the gaze of unrelated men.

The first surge in haute couture consumption among Arabs followed the rise in global oil consumption in the mid-twentieth century. The monetary influx to oil-rich nations transformed the consumption habits of tribal-based Muslim cultures of the Arabian Peninsula. Thus, in the early 1970s, French haute couture made with European fabrics benefited from the patronage of Kuwaiti clients, followed closely by clients from the United Arab Emirates, Saudi Arabia, and others. Because few people can afford haute couture's handmade products, the couture houses pursued Arab clients, seeking reliable sales. Arab interest in high-end fashion has increased in the twenty-first century. By 2006, 40 percent of haute couture sales were to Southwest Asians.

Central and Southwest Asia are producers and consumers of world fashion in the twenty-first century. Dubai in the United Arab Emirates emerged as the luxury retail destination of Southwest Asia. Retailers at the emirate's new malls—Mall of the Emirates, Dubai Mall, and Mall of Arabia—include French haute couture brands and luxury brands from the United States and Europe, as well as fast-fashion retailers. Dubai Fashion Week premiered in spring 2007 to display regional design talent, a promotional step that parallels the global trend of developing regional fashion identities in the globalized market. Turkey and Jordan are important manufacturing centers for apparel sold in the United States and Europe. Jordan, located in the northern Arabian Desert, entered beneficial agreements with the United States. In the 1990s, U.S. tariff-free production zones were established in Jordan. The program has been controversial, because the workers are mostly guest workers from Bangladesh, China, India, and Sri Lanka, and cases of overwork have been reported. The 2001 Jordan–U.S. Free Trade Agreement provided duty-free apparel imports to the United States. In 2005, Jordan exported 1.2 billion dollars of apparel to the United States.

References and Further Reading

Barber, E.J.W. *Prehistoric Textiles: The Development of Cloth in the Neolithic and Bronze Ages with Special Reference to the Aegean.* Princeton, NJ: Princeton University Press, 1991.

Barber, E.J.W. *The Mummies of Ürümchi.* New York: W.W. Norton, 1999.

Berg, Hetty, ed. *Facing West: Oriental Jews of Central Asia and the Caucasus.* Zwolle, the Netherlands: Waanders, 1997.

British Library. *Database of the International Dunhuang Project: The Silk Routes Online.* http://idp.bl.uk/ (accessed 24 August 2008).

Coleridge, Nicholas. "The Islamic Factor." In *The Fashion Conspiracy* (1988), edited by Linda Welters and Abby Lillethun, 364–368. New York and London: Berg, 2007.

Dymshits, Valery. "The Eastern Jewish Communities of the Former USSR." In *Facing West: Oriental Jews of Central Asia and the Caucasus,* edited by Hetty Berg, 7–32. Zwolle, The Netherlands: Waanders, 1997.

Eicher, Joanne B., and Barbara Sumberg. "World Fashion, Ethnic, and National Dress." In *Dress and Ethnicity,* edited by Joanne B. Eicher, 295–306. Oxford: Berg, 1995.

Fitz Gibbon, Katherine, and Andrew Hale. *Ikat: Splendid Silks of Central Asia.* London: Laurence King Publishing with Alan Marcuson, 1999.

Good, Irene. "Bronze Age Cloth and Clothing of the Tarim Basin: The Chärchän Evidence." In *The Bronze Age and Early Iron Age Peoples of Eastern Central Asia,* edited by V.H. Mair, 656–658. Philadelphia: University of Pennsylvania Museum of Archaeology, 1998.

Harvey, Janet. *Traditional Textiles of Central Asia.* London: Thames & Hudson, 1997.

Jacoby, David. "Silk Economies and Cross-Cultural Interaction: Byzantium, the Muslim World, and the Christina West." *Dumbarton Oaks Papers* 58 (2004): 197–240.

Levi, Scott. "India, Russia and the Eighteenth-Century Transformation of the Central Asian Caravan Trade." *Journal of the Economic and Social History of the Orient* 42, no. 4 (1999): 519–548.

McDowell, Joan Allgrove. "Sassanian Textiles." In *5,000 Years of Textiles,* edited by Jennifer Harris, 68–70. Washington, DC: Smithsonian Books, 1995.

Rubinson, Karen S. "The Textiles from Pazyryk: A Study in the Transfer and Transformation of Artistic Motifs." *Expedition* 32, no. 1 (1990): 49–61.

Wood, Frances. *The Silk Routes: Two Thousand Years in the Heart of Asia.* Berkeley: University of California Press, 2002.

Abby Lillethun

See also Climate, Geography, and Dress; Ottoman Dress; The Kaftan and Its Origins; Dress from the Gulf States: Bahrain, Kuwait, Qatar, United Arab Emirates; History of West Turkistan and Its Influence on the Dress of South Central Asia; Trouser Wearing by Horse-Riding Nomads in Central Asia; Khil'a: Clothing to Honor a Person or Situation.

Snapshot: Textiles of Central Asia

Textiles play important roles expressing and sustaining ethnic identity in Central Asia, in part by signifying continuity of family and spiritual beliefs. In addition, textiles have been crucial in transcultural exchange processes as trade commodities in economic systems and as prestige symbols in sociopolitical contexts. Further, Central Asian textiles reflect historical influences of internal groups on each other, as well as influences resulting from contact brought by invasions and trading cohorts. Thus, transcultural contact can be observed in textile materials, techniques, and motifs.

TEXTILE MOTIFS

The populations of Central Asia are predominantly Muslim. Islamic cultures generally adhere to decorative schemes that omit human figures, and some avoid illustrating animals. This practice is based on interpretations of the Qur'an's condemnation of idolatry, which resulted in plant and geometric motifs predominating in Islamic art. A common design element

portrayed in various forms is the tree of life. Borders around a central field or area, medallions, and arches are also common in the textile designs.

In Southwest Asia, where the Islamic faith originated, precise geometry forms the foundation of decoration. Stripes and bands of geometric motifs are common. Lattice structures underlie arabesque designs of stylized foliage and floral motifs unfolding in continuously recurring forms. This design genre invokes the Islamic belief in unity through the possibility of infinite repetition. Persian decorative arts diverge from the Islamic norm as they include human and animal representations. The flowering of the Safavid Empire (1501–1722 C.E.), which spanned the areas of twenty-first-century Iran and parts of Turkey, Iraq, and Afghanistan, brought forth imagery depicting Persian romances and epics showing people in domestic settings, at court, in gardens, and in hunting scenes. Thus, Persian decorative arts show geometry-based styles such as arabesques as well as naturalism in rendering people, fauna such as birds and leopards, and floral designs.

A Tajik wedding ritual, Tajikistan (formerly Turkistan), between 1865 and 1872. The groom in the center is wearing a striped coat and turban, and next to him is his bride, wearing a veil. She is attended by seven other females, all wearing ikat silk coats layered over other garments, including trousers and boots. The woman to the left of the groom, whose printed undersleeves hang well beyond her coat's sleeve hems, offers him a libation. Above the group two large *suzanis* (decorative embroidered cloths made by the bride and her family) drape over a pole. Library of Congress, Prints and Photographs Division, LC-DIG-ppmsca-14445.

Many Central Asian motifs are simplified, abstracted, and distorted forms based on nature. Despite the adoption of Islam by the majority in Central Asia by the twenty-first century, the aesthetic has remained distinct from the geometric style of decoration found in Southwest Asia. Motifs such as the sun, moon, the tree of life (a symbol of regeneration), and zoomorphic forms such as ram's horns (a symbol of union) denote the unity of humans, nature, and the spirit. Belief persists in the magical or healing power of these forms, particularly among Central Asian nomadic tribes. Through the particular decorative motifs used and because of the labor and skill of female family members employed to apply them, domestic textiles are treasured as meaningful to family life. Thus, domestic textiles were rarely traded or sold in the past.

WOOL TEXTILES OF CENTRAL ASIAN KYRGYZ NOMADS

The ancient nomadic lifestyle of the Central Asian steppes, although declining, continues to be practiced by some, such as Kyrgyz nomads, in the early twenty-first century. Nomads, whose lives are directly intertwined with nature, move periodically as dictated by needs for fresh grazing areas for their herds and seasonal changes. Thus, they require material goods that can be easily packed and transported using their animals.

Central Asian nomads herd camels, cattle, horses, sheep, and yaks, which provide leather, furs, food, and wool for textiles. Wild animals also provide fur pelts useful to nomads for trade as well as their own needs. Among the nomadic Kyrgyz clans in the twentieth century, wool was prepared and made into felt or spun into yarns and woven at home. Wool provided most of the Kyrgyz nomads' textile needs, thus contributing to their self-sufficiency far from commercial centers. The physical properties of wool—it is water repellent and insulates—combine with fabric's portability to make wool textiles ideal for the Central Asian nomadic lifestyle.

Until the mid-twentieth century, when there was increased access to other woven textiles, Kyrgyz women wove narrow lengths of wool (eleven to fourteen inches, or twenty-eight to thirty-five centimeters, wide) to use for making clothing. Because it is easily set up and broken down for transport, the ground loom suits the nomadic lifestyle. For coats and simple trousers, multiple lengths of narrow fabric arranged lengthwise side by side were sewn together. This technique allowed for minimal cutting and fabric waste. Everyday clothes used sheep wool, and, when fulled (thickened and compressed after weaving in a manner similar to felt), they were durable and very warm. The superior cloth *piazy* (fine camel-hair cloth) was reserved for ceremonial overcoats.

Longer lengths of narrow fabric accommodated several other clothing needs. Strips of white sheep wool about five feet (one and a half meters) long were wrapped to form the traditional men's *selde* (turban). Both genders used strips of woven cloth about two yards (two meters) long to wrap around the waist as belts to securely close their coats. Before putting on boots, women wrapped their legs with narrow strips woven of soft lamb and goat fibers. Gradually during the late nineteenth century, the Kyrgyz began buying cotton cloth in the markets, and eventually they wove cotton cloth from natural brown cotton fibers grown in the region. By the early twenty-first century, much of the wool-weaving tradition disappeared as Western dress styles encroached and garments and fabrics from outside the region became increasingly available for purchase.

IKAT TEXTILES

Vibrant, colorful fabrics called ikats, executed with masterful craftsmanship, were the zenith of a textile renaissance in nineteenth-century Central Asian urban centers. *Ikat*, an Indonesian word, refers to a textile-patterning technique involving binding yarns to resist dye before weaving and the textiles made using this tied-yarn dye-resist technique. The technique is found in several locations in the world and may involve binding both warp (lengthwise) and weft (crosswise) yarns, but, in Central Asia, only warp yarns are bound.

Central Asian cultural preference for pattern distortion and abstraction in surface decoration played out in ikats as bright, multihued designs in the shapes of roundels, buds, vases, triangles, and *çintemani* (a design motif of three dots in a triangle, underscored by two parallel wavy lines). Ikat textiles evoked a garden and in this way linked the home environment to Paradise, a potent image in both Jewish and Islamic beliefs. Ikat wall hangings, made of several narrow panels sewn together lengthwise (or vertically) in seemingly arbitrary pattern alignments, decorated urban homes and nomad yurts. They were also used to wrap religious items such as texts and relics.

Muslims and Jews alike used these textiles and worked in the complex production process required to create them. Both men and women wore ikat fabrics made into voluminous coats that allowed display of the colorful textile surface. Muslim women lived in seclusion away from the gaze of strangers, and therefore there are few records of their dress. Multiple coats, of ikat and other fabrics, were worn layered. Cotton fabrics lined both ikat robes and wall hangings. Linings ranged from locally made cottons in stripes and block prints, to *chit* (a type of mordant-dyed block-printed cotton), to imported Russian and Persian block prints and Russian roller prints. Thus, both the outer and the inner surfaces (or backs of flat pieces) bloomed with color and pattern. This aesthetic preference for multiple patterns combined in one item or ensemble continues into the twenty-first century among many Central Asians.

To achieve the multicolored designs found in intricate Central Asian ikats, a carefully planned progression of basic steps had to occur repeatedly. Silk or cotton yarns were prepared to form the warp, which was then set up on a tying frame. The *nishan-zan* (master designer), who planned designs, then drew the pattern in charcoal on the taut warp. Next, appropriate sections of the warp were tightly bound to resist dye absorption, and then wax, or another sealant, was applied to the bound areas to ensure resistance to the dye. Bundles for dyeing were formed after removing the warp yarns from the tying frame. Finally, dyeing of a color took place. Repetition of the entire process followed for each color of the design before any weaving could begin.

An Uzbek family in their domestic surroundings, which include colorful textiles in geometric designs, Uzbekistan, between 1905 and 1915. The women wear ikat silk coats and elaborate tribal jewelry and headdresses. Photograph by Sergei Mikhailovich Prokudin-Gorskii. Library of Congress, Prints & Photographs Division, Prokudin-Gorskii Collection, LC-DIG-prokc-20090.

As practiced in Central Asia, ikat production used specialists for each task. Tasks, practiced by specific ethnicities, were parceled out to workshops. Guilds formed for the various skills, and each had a holy patron, as told in oral histories. In general, Jews ran the dye trade, while women reeled and spun silk from homegrown cocoons. Framing, motif designing, and binding were done at an *abr-bandi* (ikat binding workshop) by Tajik workers. Applying hot dyes, also the domain of ethnic Tajik men, occurred before the cold-dye indigo process was executed by Jewish dyers. After dyeing, the warp yarns went to a weaving workshop. Weavers of ikat fabrics in silk and cotton were usually ethnic Uzbeks and Iranis (people of Persian ethnicity). To finish the ikats, Uzbeki glazers achieved a glossy surface with egg white, and Tajiks rubbed and polished the cloths with hammers and glass for a glazed effect.

Usually woven on a treadle loom using a cotton or silk weft, Central Asian ikats are warp-faced. The fine, dense, colorful warp yarns literally cover or obscure the less dense, solid-colored, usually white or red, weft yarns. Often about twenty-three feet (seven meters) long, ikats are commonly narrow, ranging from nine to twenty-four inches (twenty-four to sixty centimeters) in width, although wider widths for specific uses occur. During weaving, the characteristic soft or blurred-edge ikat patterns emerge. *Abr*, the Persian name for all-silk plain-weave ikat, means "cloud," a metaphor for the soft-edged designs.

The thickness and density of the warp yarns and the weaving pattern characterize the various types of ikat fabric. *Adras* (plain-weave ikat with a silk warp and cotton weft), *atlas* (satin-weave ikat), *baghmal* (velvet ikat), and, less commonly, twill weave are different types of ikat. The extremely difficult and costly production of baghmal occurred from approximately 1860 to the 1910s and was limited to Bukhara, an urban center in Uzbekistan with a thriving textile sector. Opulent baghmal and garments made from it signified precious luxury and epitomized prestige. They were worn at the Ottoman imperial court, by dignitaries in the Central Asian region and their family members, and by other affluent people. They were also given as gifts or tribute to important figures from outside the region.

Ikat production centered in Bukhara, with some production in Samarkand and eastward through the Fergana Valley (a geographic region in Kyrgyzstan, Tajikistan, and Uzbekistan) as well. Central Asian ikats attained their peak of virtuosity in the nineteenth century. As the twentieth century approached, the rise of industrialization encroached on intensive handcraft practices such as ikat, and their quantity and quality diminished. In the twentieth century, Russian controls, first from the Russian empire and later from the Union of Soviet Socialist Republics, altered the political, economic, and social structures. Individual workshops for ikat production ended around 1941.

Later in the twentieth century, interest in traditional crafts surged, generating a renewed production of ikat. The Yodgorlik Silk Factory in Margilan in the Fergana Valley was established in 1973 to produce ikat by traditional methods and still operates in the early twenty-first century. When freed from Soviet domination in 1991, many Central Asian states burgeoned with expressions of ethnic pride, including textile products. In Afghanistan, attempts to produce ikat south of the primary region of production in the Fergana Valley sputtered and then ended under the constraints of the wars of the late twentieth and early twenty-first centuries.

Revival and reinterpretation of culturally specific expressions included ikat and other textiles. In the late twentieth century, women in Kyrgyzstan wore simple, loose dresses of fabric printed with ikatlike patterns. In Uzbekistan in the early twenty-first century, women's national dress was a long-sleeved gown made of atlas, or satin-faced ikat, worn with trousers. Woven on mechanical looms, the designs are simpler than in the past, and the colors reflect contemporary tastes.

REFERENCES AND FURTHER READING

Antipina, Klavdiya. "Traditional Kyrgyz Costume." In *Kyrgyzstan*, by Roland Paiva, 21–179. Translated by Stephanie Bunn. Milan, Italy: Skira, 2006.

Balfour-Paul, Jenny. *Indigo in the Arab World*. Richmond, Surrey: Curzon Press, 1997.

Bunn, Stephanie, and Damira Sartbaeva. "Introduction." In *Kyrgyzstan*, by Roland Paiva, 15–20. Translated by Stephanie Bunn. Milan, Italy: Skira, 2006.

Clark, Ruby. *Central Asian Ikats from the Rau Collection*. London: V & A Publications, 2007.

Fitz Gibbon, Katherine, and Andrew Hale. *Ikat: Splendid Silks of Central Asia*. London: Laurence King Publishing with Alan Marcuson, 1999.

Gillow, John, and Bryan Sentence. *World Textiles: A Visual Guide to Traditional Techniques*. London: Thames & Hudson, 1999.

Harvey, Janet. *Traditional Textiles of Central Asia*. London: Thames & Hudson, 1996.

Mis, Zaira, and Marcel Mis. *Asian Costumes and Textiles from the Bosphorus to Fujiyama: The Zaira and Marcel Mis Collection*. Milan, Italy: Skira, 2001.

Abby Lillethun

See also Trade, Textiles, and Dress in Central and Southwest Asia.

Snapshot: Trade, Textiles, Dress, and the Hajj

For thousands of years, vast arrays of objects, including textiles and garments, have been used as trade items throughout Southwest Asia. There are, for example, references to textiles and clothing in the sea manual *The Periplus of the Erythrean Sea (Periplus Maris Erythraei)*. This is a Greek navigation and trading manual, written in about the mid-first century C.E., that describes the trade goods and ports along various coastal routes from Egypt, eastern Africa, via the Arabian countries to India. More famously, other trade routes, commonly known as the Silk Road, stretched from China, via Central Asia, India, Persia, and on to the eastern Mediterranean. Until the early twentieth century, another important international trade route existed that ended at Mecca and the great hajj marketplace in what is western Saudi Arabia in the early twenty-first century.

An essential element of the Muslim faith is the Five Pillars of Islam, which are regarded as the foundation of Muslim life. The fifth and last pillar of Islam is the hajj. This requires that any adult Muslim who is physically and financially able should try to make a pilgrimage to the holy city of Mecca once in his or her lifetime. Over the last fifteen hundred years, millions of pilgrims have traveled annually to Mecca. Until the twentieth century, it was normal for pilgrims to travel either via one of the giant pilgrim caravans from cities such as Cairo, Damascus, or Istanbul or, if they lived in Africa or Asia, by boat.

Many of the pilgrims carried local goods with them to trade along the way and fund their pilgrimage. Towns and villages along the routes also made a living from selling locally made products to the pilgrims. Sometimes these were sold directly to those traveling in the caravans; on other occasions, goods were sent with the caravans to Mecca for sale to pilgrims there. All this created a massive, annual trade in a wide variety of goods, including textiles, clothing, and jewelry, along a route that extended from Indonesia, via India and Central Asia, to the eastern Mediterranean and the Arabian Peninsula. The international nature of this link can be further highlighted by the fact that, until the mid-eighteenth century, pilgrims and goods were carried from India to Jidda on Turkish ships. But then the British East India Company, which by then was firmly established in India, tried to take over the transportation of the pilgrims and the merchandise in British ships. As a result, there was a small war as to who would control the Indian end of the hajj. All of this took place not for religious purposes but purely for the potential of vast commercial gains.

The link between textiles and the hajj is an ancient one and probably has pre-Islamic origins. References, for example, indicate that Yemeni textiles called *wasila* (probably cotton ikats) were sent to Arabia for covering the Kaaba, the building in Mecca that is the final destination of pilgrims. The Arabic writer Abu al-Walid Muhammad al-Azraqi (d. 843) wrote about how the Tubba' kings of Yemen "long before Islam" sent cotton cloth to cover this sacred building. It was also said that the Prophet Mohammed covered the Kaaba with Yemeni cloth.

One of the earliest descriptions of the markets associated with the hajj also comes from al-Azraqi, in his account of the history of Mecca:

> They stayed there twenty nights during which they set up Ikaz their market of all colors and all goods in small houses. … The "day of tawarih" is the last day of their markets. The people who were present at the markets of Ijaz and Majanna and Dhu al-Majaz are merchants, and those who wanted to trade, and even those who had nothing to sell and buy [go].

During the medieval period, the pilgrimage routes were controlled by various governments that offered to travelers (for a fee) reliable guides as well as protection from thieves, bandits, tax collectors, and Bedouin. The main routes started at Cairo (Egypt), Damascus (Syria), and Istanbul (Turkey). In addition, important caravans started from Kufa and Basra in Iraq. The trips were arduous and long. The Egyptian caravan, for example, took roughly three months for the round trip, about forty days each way.

A description by an anonymous pilgrim who traveled to Mecca in 1575 gives more details about the relationship between the caravan routes and trade:

> The Caravan carries with it six pieces of ordnance drawn by twelve camels, which serve to terrify the Arabians [Bedouin raiders], as also to make triumph at Mecca and other places. The merchants who follow the Caravan, some carry for merchandise cloth of silk, some coral, some tin, others wheat, rye and all sorts of grain. Some sell by the way, some at Mecca, so that everyone brings something to gain by.

In addition to this relatively small-scale trade, merchants over the centuries started sending vast quantities of goods—including textiles, clothing, jewelry, and carpets—to the holy cities of Mecca and Medina, and the neighboring port of Jidda, using the protection provided by the various governments for their own pilgrims. As a result, goods from all over the world arrived and turned the region for about one month into a vast, international marketplace. The early-nineteenth-century Swiss scholar John Lewis Burckhardt wrote:

> Few pilgrims, except the mendicants, arrive without bringing some production of their respective countries for sale. … The Maghribis, for example, bring red bonnets and woolen cloaks; the European turks shoes and slippers, hardware, embroidered stuffs, sweetmeats, amber, trinkets of European manufacture, knit silk purses etc.; The Turks of Anatolia bring carpets, silks and Angora shawls; the Persians cashmere shawls and large silk handkerchiefs; the Afghans tooth-brushes … made of the spongy boughs of a tree growing in Bukhara, beads of yellow soap-stone, and plain coarse shawls manufactured in their own country; the Indians, the numerous productions of their rich and extensive region;

A pilgrim caravan from the *Maqâmât of al-Hârîrî*, painted by Yahyâ ibn Mahmûd al-Wâsitî, Baghdad, Iraq, 1237. The costs incurred when going on a pilgrimage meant that people carried expensive goods and items with them to pay for everything. Clothing typical of the period was a turban, a long gown fastened at the waist, trousers, slippers, and boots. Once they reached the outskirts of Mecca, the pilgrims would change into white garments. Bridgeman Art Library/Getty Images.

the people of Yemen snakes for the Persian pipes, sandals and various other works in leather; and the Africans bring various articles adapted to the slave trade.

The foreign merchants at these fairs were divided into two basic groups: the "small" merchants and the "great" merchants. The small merchants were people or groups who brought with them a selection of goods to sell from their own countries. Often these were ordinary people who brought items to sell in order to pay for all or part of the costs incurred by going to Mecca. In contrast, the great merchants were the buyers who took large quantities of objects from literally all over the Islamic world back to their home cities—notably Cairo, Damascus, and Istanbul—for resale.

Not surprisingly, the hajj and its annual fair also had an influence on the traditional clothing in the area around Mecca and Medina. One of the earliest detailed descriptions of men's urban dress from this region, for instance, comes from Burckhardt's account of Medina and Mecca in about 1813. He notes that the clothing of the higher and middle classes consisted of a cloth outer cloak (*banish*) and undercoat (*djubbe*) from Turkey or a summer version in lighter Indian silk. A Syrian gown was fastened with a cashmere cummerbund, while the headgear consisted of a turban made of white Indian muslin; shirts were made of Indian silk (expensive) or Egyptian or Anatolian linen (cheaper). Lower classes wore hip wraps of Indian cotton or cheap striped Egyptian linen. Burckhardt's comments about Meccan clothing reflect the region's long history and role as a religious, economic, and political melting pot. It should also be noted that, at this time, the sultan in Istanbul was the official ruler of the Hijaz; as a result, Turkish-style dress was worn by some officials and their families. A similar international situation existed for women's clothing. So instead of being regarded as something typical to the region, the dress of Mecca and Medina should be seen as showing the international links between Arabia and the whole of the Islamic world, thanks to the area's religious, economic, and political history and, last but by no means least, the great annual hajj and its historical fair.

But where is this historical fair now? It ceased in the twentieth century as a result of various political and economic factors. Ironically, these factors were partly due to the greater ease and safety of transportation systems in the late nineteenth and twentieth centuries. The improvements in road and sea transportation, for example, and the introduction of air travel and affordable airfares meant that more and more pilgrims could come to Mecca. By the end of the twentieth century, an annual quota of about two million pilgrims was established by the Saudi government. That meant two million people coming to Saudi Arabia, staying for two to three weeks, and then leaving.

There were many accidents, and sometimes stampedes leading to deaths, during this period due to the sheer pressure of people. If the fair were also to take place, there would be considerably more logistical problems.

But air travel also meant that it was no longer necessary to take goods to trade in order to pay for the costs incurred while on the pilgrimage; these costs had to be paid in advance to the airline companies. In addition, these companies controlled the amount of luggage an individual could bring. So not only was it unnecessary to take trade items, it was actively discouraged. The Saudi government was not unhappy with this situation, because it meant that its own merchants were in a stronger position to sell merchandise (which had been taxed by the government) to the pilgrims, rather than allowing the ancient system of small and great merchants over whom the authorities had considerably less control with respect to taxation, dealing in goods. As a result of these factors—transportation, economics, and poitics—the historical great hajj fair vanished.

REFERENCES AND FURTHER READING

al-Azraqi, Abu al-Walid Muhammad. *Die Chroniken der Stadt Mekka*. Edited by F. Wüstenfeld. Leipzig: Brockhaus, 1858.

Burckhardt, John Lewis. *Travels in Arabia*. New York: Frank Cass, 1968. (Originally published in 1829.)

Burton, Sir Richard. *A Personal Narrative of a Pilgrimage to al-Madina and Meccah*. New York: Dover, 1964. (Originally published in 1855.)

"A Description of the Yarely Voyage or Pilgrimage of the Mahumetans, Turkes and Moores to Mecca in Arabia." In *The Principal Navigations, Voyages, Traffiques and Discoveries of the English Nation Made by Sea or Overland to the Remote and Farthest Distant Quarters of the Earth at Any Time within the Compass of Theses 1600 Years*, by Richard Hakluyt, vol. 3, 167–197. London and Toronto: J. M. Dent, 1927.

Peters, F. E. *The Hajj: The Muslim Pilgrimage to Mecca and the Holy Places*. Princeton, NJ: Princeton University Press, 1994.

Serjeant, R. B. *Islamic Textiles: Material for a History up to the Mongol Conquest*. Beirut: Librairie du Liban, 1972.

Wallin, Georg August. *Travels in Arabia (1845 and 1848)*. New York and London: Falcon-Oleander, 1979.

Gillian Vogelsang-Eastwood

See also Snapshot: Islamic Pilgrimage Dress (Ihram).

Tiraz: Textiles and Dress with Inscriptions in Central and Southwest Asia

- Arabic Script as Ornament
- Materials and Methods
- Social Context
- Private Tiraz
- Public or Commercial Tiraz
- Ornamental Tiraz
- Nonscript Tiraz
- Surviving Artifacts
- Modern Tiraz

The term *tiraz* comes from the Farsi word for "embroider." In Arabic, the word *tiraz* means "embellishment" and, by extension, "fashion." Tiraz describes the ornate Arabic script and associated designs on garments and other textile goods, as well as items adorned with them. Although inscribing the ruler's name on textiles dates back thousands of years to pharaonic Egypt, tiraz is a distinctly Islamic form of decoration. Beautiful lettering was considered to be among the highest art forms in many cultures, but, in the early Islamic world, fine calligraphy honored verses of the Qur'an and served as the principal vehicle for the dissemination of both the political and artistic ideals that shaped the early Muslim dynasties.

Tiraz designs may be woven into a textile as it is made, or they may be embroidered, appliquéd, painted, or printed onto a length of fabric or garment after its construction. Historically, the term *tiraz* also refers to state-run workshops where tiraz textiles were made and to the social and political circumstances under which inscribed textiles were commissioned and the ways they were distributed as royal patronage.

ARABIC SCRIPT AS ORNAMENT

Arabic is the most common language used for tiraz textiles, because Qur'anic verses and Sunni religious text are typically written in the Arabic language. In countries under Muslim rule, both Muslims and non-Muslims also used textiles with nonreligious inscriptions such as tributes, poetry, or blessings. These kinds of sayings are sometimes written in Arabic, Turkish, or Farsi, all of which were historically written using Arabic letter forms.

Early in the Islamic period, the height and shapes of letters varied from factory to factory, which makes it easier for scholars to determine where and when pieces were made, and who ordered the work done. The materials used are also a clue to where a tiraz textile was made. Later, styles of calligraphy were standardized so that letters within a certain style were drawn to specific proportions with less variation from factory to factory, and increased trade made a variety of materials available throughout the region.

Simple inscriptions were made on textiles during the period when Islamic lands were under the rule of dynasties led by successors to Mohammed known as caliphs. The earliest tiraz fragments in museums date from the mid-eighth century C.E., though literature from the period reports that inscribed textiles and garments were gifted at court much earlier. The practice of inscribing tiraz with the name of the caliph fell out of favor during the twelfth century, when a series of short-lived rulers in Egypt signaled the end of a unified dynasty. Although the name of the ruler was no longer used, textiles were still inscribed with tiraz ornamentation.

Inscriptions with plain lettering, such as the inscriptions on official tiraz, were usually legible, though highly stylized genuine lettering may not be readable. Fake lettering and abbreviated script motifs using real letter forms were also used on unofficial tiraz. Tiraz with nonsense inscriptions imitated the script seen on genuine tiraz made by order of the ruling caliph and bearing his name. Counterfeit inscriptions using the caliph's name were probably made during those periods as well, because the style of lettering and methods of embroidery on at least one surviving fragment are not consistent with the methods used in the royal factory at the time. Errors are also present in both genuine and fake tiraz inscriptions. Unlike calligraphers, who were carefully trained, weavers or embroiderers were often unfamiliar with script forms and occasionally were illiterate. They worked the script designs by copying prototypes or drawn samples.

Three classic forms of Arabic calligraphy are common to tiraz embellishment: *kufic*, *naskh*, and *thuluth*. In its basic form, kufic consists of simple letter forms, well suited for counted-thread embroidery, because angular or block-style letters can be easily rendered in linear motifs. Stylized kufic letters with foliate appendages were favored by Yemeni tiraz painters. Naskh is a gently rounded calligraphy style that lends itself to legibility, with moderate proportions. Thuluth is a flowing, curvilinear style with tall, vertical letters. Both naskh and thuluth lettering can be appliquéd, embroidered, or drawn using a variety of techniques. These beautiful scripts are commonly used for illuminated religious texts, and many ornamental variants of script evolved. One of the most elaborate script forms is the *calligram*, in which words and letter forms are guided into the shapes of animals and objects.

Weavers in al Andalus, as Muslim Spain was known, also produced beautiful inscribed textiles, many of which were purchased by non-Muslims and exported to northern Europe as luxury goods. Tiraz textiles brought to Europe following the Crusades were highly prized, and many were used in the construction of church vestments and reliquaries. The Shroud of St. Josse from the tenth century C.E., inscribed with kufic lettering and figures of elephants, is believed to be from Iran and to have been taken to France during the first Crusade. A Christian relic was discovered swathed inside the Veil of Hisham, a tiraz textile from early-eleventh-century Spain, with tapestry-woven script bearing

Abayeh with script ornament, ca. 2007. This Islamic woman's modesty dress ensemble consists of an overgarment and head covering ornamented with machine-embroidered Arabic letter forms. *Abayeh* courtesy of Sandra Shore. Photograph by Margaret Anne Deppe.

the name of the Umayyad ruler Hisham II of Cordoba. Italian weavers soon copied and modified the ornate Arabic borders into stylized Latin and imitation Arabic lettering. This influence on fashion endured, as demonstrated in medieval and Renaissance Christian religious art. Arabic-style lettering is depicted on the garments and the halos of holy figures in Gentile da Fabriano's painting *Adoration of the Magi* in the fifteenth century c.e.

MATERIALS AND METHODS

In the early years of tiraz manufacture, natural-colored flax, cotton, and wool were the main fibers used for weaving yarns, with the addition of dyed wool or silk for colored embellishment via

weaving or embroidery. Fine linen was imported from Egypt, and cotton was imported from India. Cotton takes dye better than flax and could be made into strong, less-expensive weaving yarn, and it was thus frequently used as a stable ground fabric to which ornament was applied. A type of cloth called *mulham*—a half-silk fabric with silk warp yarns and cotton weft yarns—was often used for tiraz textiles. Precious materials, such as silk or gold thread, were applied as the weft in tapestry-woven designs, or they were worked onto the cloth as embroidery.

Tapestry weaving was the prominent technique used to produce early tiraz from the Umayyad and early Abbasid and Fatimid periods, during the eighth to tenth centuries c.e. Tapestry is a method for weaving colored patterns into cloth by using different-colored weft yarns and weaving them into place to make a design during the weaving process. The tiraz factories of Egypt were especially well known for this technique. Using the tapestry weaving method, which is time consuming and requires a great deal of skill, dedicates the work from its inception and does not allow for a change to the design midway through the process. The use of simpler techniques, such as applied calligraphy or embroidery, speeds the production time and allows for modification of the inscription during its creation.

Colors found in early woven tiraz include red, blue, and black. Such textiles often feature white lettering on a dark-colored ground. Tiraz textiles from ninth- and tenth-century Yemen were fine cotton fabrics dyed using a tied-resist technique known as ikat. Yemeni tiraz from that period were embroidered in simple kufic letters and geometric patterns with natural-colored cotton yarn, or they bore lavish kufic lettering applied to the surface. Inscriptions were inked onto the fabric and outlined with gold, or lettering and designs were traced onto the fabric in black with gold leaf applied over the body of the lettering.

Embroidered tiraz made use of silk yarns dyed in many colors, including red, yellow, green, blue, and black. Counted chain stitch and double running stitch were used for early embroidered script, as well as variations of tent stitch, backstitch, and surface couching. Gilt yarns, created by applying gold, silver, or metal alloys to cording, thread, or sinew, were couched to the cloth because they are less flexible, and surface couching exposes all of the beautiful—and expensive—gold work. Embroidery techniques such as double running stitch, close-worked herringbone, and chain stitch worked in silk yarn were favored for later Abbasid tiraz, which bore a finely wrought line of text worked weftwise, from selvage to selvage. Inscribed textiles from the Ottoman period often bore the stylized signature of the sultan, known as the *tughra*. As with Abbasid tiraz, the display of the sultan's insignia implied that the owner was in good favor with the ruling class, and stylized motifs imitating the official tughra were popular.

SOCIAL CONTEXT

The use of religious inscriptions as medicinal or protective devices is ancient, and the giving of honorific garments or textiles inscribed with the name of a ruler was a well-established practice prior to the advent of Islam. Furthermore, textiles played a significant role in accounts of the earliest days of Islam; Mohammed gifted his own garments to individuals for their benefit, as shelter for the living or to be used as shrouds for the dead. In this way, the recipient was enveloped in the protection of God, by the cloth's association with the Prophet, bringing the individual closer to divine grace.

In the medieval Islamic world, as elsewhere, individuals also displayed wealth and social status through fine clothing and textiles. The color, style, and ornamentation of an individual's garments were dictated by fiscal standing, social convention, and, at times, sumptuary law. Individuals possessing fine textiles, especially tiraz, earned a great deal of prestige through their display, worn as clothing, exhibited on special occasions, or in evidence as livery or parade-ground standards.

Tiraz made a strong impact on fashion due to the high status conferred on those wearing inscribed garments or textiles granted as gifts by the ruling elite. The inherent value of the materials, including yarns of silk and gold leaf, intricately dyed or woven patterns, as well as inscriptions sanctioned by the royal court, marked an individual as socially well connected or having earned the respect of a military or administrative official of higher rank.

In addition to the private tiraz produced at the directive of the caliph or his representatives, state-run public factories also produced tiraz textiles for sale to members of the population who could afford them. These were luxury goods and also served as investments, because they could later be sold or used to pay debts or taxes. If not made into garments, tiraz textiles were stored away to be used as burial shrouds. Other textiles bearing ornamental writing include flags, standards, and tent panels. Remnants of this type from the Mamluk period in Egypt occasionally bear script in conjunction with heraldic devices indicating the owner's office or rank.

Unsanctioned factories produced a number of tiraz textiles, and inscribed garments and textiles were undoubtedly produced at home by those with the skills and means to purchase the materials. The distinction between these textiles lies mainly in their origins and the context surrounding their acquisition.

PRIVATE TIRAZ

Continuing a tradition already practiced in the region east of the Mediterranean by Byzantine emperors, state-run tiraz workshops were established under the Umayyad caliphs during the eighth century C.E. to produce fine woven textiles with Arabic inscriptions. Early tiraz often situated script within design elements such as floral motifs and geometric patterns or between stylized animal figures, drawing on the textile traditions of Sassanian Persia. With the ascendance of the Abbasid caliphate, tiraz styles changed and formulaic inscriptions embroidered onto fine plain-woven ground fabric became the standard. Inscriptions began with the *bismillah*—"In the name of God, the Merciful, the Compassionate"—or a similar devotional phrase and went on to name the ruler or patron who commissioned the piece. The name of the supervising official, artist, and place and date of manufacture are also sometimes included. A cotton tiraz fragment from the tenth century C.E., held in the Boston Museum of Fine Arts, is inscribed using kufic letters worked in silk split-stitch embroidery: "In the name of God the Compassionate the Merciful. My support is in God alone, and in Him I trust. ... The permanent ... Blessing from God and peace and beatitude and glory to the caliph, the Servant of God, Hamd el Muqtadir billah, Commander of the Faithful. May God strengthen him. Made in the royal workshop in Medinat as-Salam by the hands of Abu ... (the freedman of) the Commander of the Faithful. In the year 320" (932 C.E.).

Factories produced official tiraz across the Islamic Empire, from Persia westward, across the Mediterranean and North Africa to Andalusian Spain. When the Fatimids wrested governance of Egypt away from the Abbasid capital at Baghdad, tiraz styles again changed. While Sunni practice proscribed the depiction of living beings in the context of religious art, Shiite artisans in Egypt included animals in tiraz compositions. Ottoman-inscribed textiles follow a variety of traditions, ranging from bands of script to stylized tughra forms to more elaborate calligrams of both inanimate objects and animals.

In the sixteenth and seventeenth centuries C.E., special undergarments covered in Qur'anic verses, astrological tables, and numerological formulas were prepared for Turkish and Persian

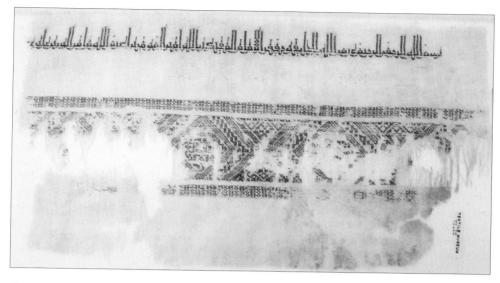

Tiraz textile fragment from the Abbasid caliphate, Iraq, tenth century. It has an embroidered formulaic inscription and geometric ornament in silk on a linen ground. The Textile Museum, Washington, D.C., 73.15. Acquired by George Hewitt Myers in 1931. Photograph by Margaret Anne Deppe.

rulers. Court astrologers painstakingly inscribed the garments with protective invocations to guard the wearer in battle.

PUBLIC OR COMMERCIAL TIRAZ

Much like the tiraz produced in private factories, public tiraz were often inscribed with the name of the caliph, usually the name of the official in charge of the workshop in which the garment or textile was made, and sometimes the place and date of its manufacture in a state-run public factory. A linen fragment embroidered in couched silk with kufic lettering in the Textile Museum, Washington, D.C., names the local governor of Egypt as well: "Abu'l-'Abbas, the Imam al-Mu'tadid billah, Commander of the Faithful, may God strengthen him, and the Amir Abu Musa bin Khumarawayh, client of the Commander of the Faithful. To be made in the public factory at Tinnis, under the direction of 'Umar bin Muhammad bin Shahin. Year 284" (897 C.E.). Other public tiraz, not labeled as such, substituted portions of religious text, poetry, mottoes, and blessings for the official inscriptions. Auspicious words such as *health, glory,* and *prosperity* were repeated in rows. Classical poetry indicates that personal items such as handkerchiefs and drawstrings for trousers may have been inscribed with erotic verses and love poems, especially as part of a woman's wedding trousseau.

Tiraz workshops depended on the support of the rulers who founded them, because imported silk, gold, and other expensive materials were purchased using funds allocated from royal treasuries. Officials who supervised the manufacture of tiraz enjoyed great prestige, and tiraz inscriptions often contained the supervisory official's name along with the name of the commissioning ruler.

During the height of royal tiraz production, whole cities were employed, working thousands of looms or embroidering lengths of plain fabric. Tapestry and brocade weaves and satin, twill, and tabby or plain weave were used to create tiraz textiles. Tablet weaving was used to make inscribed bands, often commemorative

straps for bags or canteens carried by pilgrims to Mecca. Script and other designs could be woven into a length of fabric during its manufacture. Tiraz ornamentation could also be made separately, either as a self-contained finished band, as in tablet weaving; as part of a larger textile, woven in rows that could be cut apart later; or added to a textile after its manufacture, as in embroidery or surface calligraphy.

Early decorated garments were woven as a single piece and sewn down the sides to finish the garment. Later garments and larger tiraz items were pieced, and surviving fragments show that at least some embroidery was worked before the garment was assembled, because the embroidery is sewn into the seam instead of over it. Embroidery sewn into the seam also occurs in the economical practice of reusing fabric, as when the good parts of an adult's garment are salvaged to make clothing for a child.

ORNAMENTAL TIRAZ

Long after the decline of the caliphal tiraz factories, tiraz ornamentation remained popular. Religious inscriptions and Qur'anic verses, such as the opening chapter or *fatiha,* were often repeated over and over in a border or in rows. These kinds of tiraz were often displayed on armor and garments, both outer and under, to protect the wearer. A shirt from Lombok, Indonesia, probably from the nineteenth century C.E., is inscribed all over with the Muslim profession of faith, the *shahada,* embroidered in vertical stripes. Other inscriptions, not specifically religious in nature, praised a benefactor, such as a patron or administrator. Frequently, these pieces were a gift from that person or given at his request. Some tiraz textiles bore contracted forms of a standardized wording of the tribute or acknowledgment or a stylized representation of a well-known inscription, such as the bismillah, instead of the intact phrase. Likewise, sometimes only the names of religious figures such as Mohammed, Abu Bakr, Fatima, and Ali were inscribed on garments. A remarkable example of this type is not cloth but rather a chain-mail armor shirt housed at the

Metropolitan Museum of Art in New York, in which the names of martyrs were worked in contrasting brass rings to provide protection for a warrior in battle.

Block-printed cotton textiles made in India were exported to the West and form a large portion of tiraz textiles with nonreligious texts such as "Blessing and success to its owner" and other generic inscriptions. These were most likely used as curtains, tablecloths, and bed linens. Stockings knitted from dyed cotton, found in Egypt but possibly made in India, are also decorated with strips of ornamental lettering.

NONSCRIPT TIRAZ

Other nonscript decorative elements included floral patterns, arabesque work, geometric patterns, and fantastic animals. Arabesque work is a highly stylized interwoven floral motif that

may have originally represented palm leaves. Animals commonly found on tiraz include birds, considered to be traditional messengers to heaven; rabbits, which represent virility and fertility; and fish, representative of great wealth and prosperity. Simple and ornate geometric patterns were also common; images of living things have at times been proscribed by Sunni religious authorities. At other times, human or zoomorphic images were allowed if they were highly stylized or headless. Calligrams are a notable exception, as birds are a very popular motif for religious inscriptions. Lamps are popular shapes for calligrams of the Sura of Light, and the Sura of Purity is often worked as a calligram of a water vessel, alluding to the practice of making ablutions before prayer. Mosques and *mihrabs*, the prayer niches located in the direction of Mecca, are also common calligram motifs.

In the earliest days of Islam, it was customary to avoid placing decorative lettering anywhere it might be sat on or stepped on,

Palestinian flag dress, to be worn as a political protest, Gaza, Palestine, ca. 1970. The dress is embroidered with Palestinian flag motifs and inscribed with the words *Palestine* and *Gaza* in English and Arabic as a symbol of nationalism and ethnic identity. Goldstein Museum of Design, University of Minnesota. Photograph by Margaret Anne Deppe.

lest one inadvertently tread on the word or name of God. Later, ornamental script was used on many kinds of textiles, including reed mats and rugs for prayer, as well as on hemlines and as all-over patterns on talismanic undergarments worn for protection. Illuminated manuscripts show that tiraz ornamentation was typically placed on hemlines, across the sleeve on the upper arm, and on the ends of belts, veils, and turbans. Small square motifs are also depicted in a fold of the turban; these were probably maker's marks bearing the date and name of the place the tiraz was produced and the name of the patron who commissioned the work. Some may also be blessing squares, small blocks that repeat fortuitous words such as *health* or *blessing*, again in fashionable imitation of genuine tiraz. Later Persian manuscripts show script ornamentation on the shoulder yoke of garments, around the back, along the neckline, and across the chest of the wearer—not unlike the placement of Syrian embroidery in the early twentieth century. Household textiles, curtains, and serving linens also carried inscriptions.

SURVIVING ARTIFACTS

Age, unfortunate events, and poor conservation by early collectors have left most medieval tiraz fragments in fragile condition, and a very small number of whole garments have survived. Although dry conditions preserved a number of tiraz fragments in good condition, textiles containing wool and silk were often damaged by insects that ate the fibers for their protein. Tiraz textiles used as burial shrouds were often folded around the deceased with the band of script over the face, presumably for symbolic protection, so the central portion of the inscription was damaged during the decomposition of the eyes. The corrosive effects of metals used in some dye processes as well as metal-alloy threads later oxidized and disintegrated the supporting fabric. Textiles bearing gold leaf as a surface design or in gilt yarns are rare because gilded fabrics were sometimes burned to reclaim the precious metal. Deliberate damage to tiraz items, cut away from funerary garments or shrouds by collectors, makes the original placement of tiraz ornamentation difficult to verify, although a few surviving garments or identifiable portions of clothing have tiraz embellishment. For example, the clothing of Bishop Timotheos, whose tomb from the fourteenth century C.E. was discovered in the cathedral at Qasr Ibrim, Egypt, includes a traveling cloak with tiraz fabric appliquéd to the back. A tenth-century shirt in the Textile Museum in Washington, D.C., made from a length of linen fabric with an embroidered silk inscription, has the line of script running along the sleeve in the same location indicated in contemporary illustrated texts.

MODERN TIRAZ

The most remarkable example of modern tiraz is the *Kiswa*, the textile covering for the Kaaba in Mecca. Since medieval times, a new Kiswa has been sent to Mecca each year from the rulers of the Islamic provinces, including Yemen, Iraq, and Egypt. During the earliest centuries of Islam, the Kiswa was made of fine cloth, such as white flax linen from Egypt or dyed cotton from Yemen. Green was a favored color for many years, although in the early twenty-first century, white or green are used only for the lining cloth. Eventually, black silk became the traditional fabric for the Kiswa. The Kiswa was not inscribed until 1340 C.E., when the ruler of Egypt had Qur'anic verses embroidered onto the cloth. In the early twenty-first century, a band of embroidery thirty-seven inches (ninety-five centimeters) high is worked across the panels on each side of the Kaaba, running approximately fifty-one yards (forty-seven meters) around the structure.

The installation of the new Kiswa each year is very important. World War I delayed delivery of the Kiswa from Egypt, and, in the following years, political tension developed between Egypt and the Kingdom of Saudi Arabia. The king of Saudi Arabia decided to build a factory in 1926 to produce the Kiswa locally. This reduced the risk to the Kiswa as it was transported to Mecca. As relations improved and peace was restored in the region following World War II, Egypt resumed production. In 1961, the king of Saudi Arabia reestablished the Umm al-Joud factory in Mecca to prepare the new Kiswa. In 1977, the factory was updated, and in the early twenty-first century approximately two hundred workers use both traditional methods and the latest computer technology to design and manufacture the Kiswa.

Following the investiture of the new Kiswa, by tradition the old one is cut into segments, which are in turn given as gifts. Small pieces of the Kiswa were originally distributed to pilgrims as a keepsake of the hajj, and many believe they bring good luck. In the early twenty-first century, large portions, especially the *sitara* or door covering, are gifted to foreign dignitaries, international organizations, and museums of Islamic art from around the world.

The tradition of embellishing textiles with religious text continues in the early twenty-first century. In Iran, Sufi masters create felt hats embroidered with poetry and devotional verses for their disciples. The inscription depends on the order to which the Sufi belongs. Qur'anic verses and calligrams are hand embroidered onto silk velvet with gold and silver or are embossed on leather in Turkey and Muslim countries in North Africa, and they are sold over the Internet, to be framed and displayed in private homes worldwide. In Egypt, as in Mamluk times, appliqué is painstakingly worked to produce tent panels and wall hangings, again with Qur'anic verses and calligrams, for weddings and household display. The availability of electronic embroidery machines and digital patterns means that inscriptions stitched in precise calligraphic lettering can be produced by home sewers as well.

The use of clothing and domestic textiles as a vehicle for political statements has led to another example of modern tiraz among Palestinian refugees. Dresses and household items embroidered using red, white, black, and green, the Palestinian flag, or the word *Palestine* and other political slogans are displayed as a symbol of nationalism and ethnic identity. Thus, modern tiraz also serve as a form of nonverbal and nonviolent protest.

References and Further Reading

Allenby, Jeni. *Portraits without Names: Palestinian Costume.* Canberra, Australia: Palestinian Costume Archive, 1995.

Atil, Esin. *Renaissance of Islam: Art of the Mameluks.* Washington, DC: Smithsonian Institution Press, 1981.

Bier, Carol, ed. *Woven from the Soul, Spun from the Heart.* Washington, DC: Textile Museum, 1987.

Blair, Sheila. "Inscriptions on Medieval Islamic Textiles." *Riggisberger Berichte 5: Islamische Textilkunst des Mittelalters: Aktuelle Probleme,* edited by Carol Bier. Riggisberg: Abegg-Stiftung, 1997.

Britton, Nancy. *A Study of Some Early Islamic Textiles in the Museum of Fine Arts, Boston.* Boston: Museum of Fine Arts, 1938.

Golombek, Lisa, and Veronica Gervers. "Tiraz Fabrics in the Royal Ontario Museum." In *Studies in Textile History*, edited by V. Gervers, 82–125. Toronto: Royal Ontario Museum, 1977.

Kühnel, Ernst, and Louisa Bellinger. *Catalogue of Dated Tiraz Fabrics.* Washington, DC: National Publishing Company, 1952.

Mackie, Louise. "Increase the Prestige: Islamic Textiles." *Arts of Asia* 26, no. 1 (1996): 82–93.

Thomas, Thelma. *Textiles from Medieval Egypt,* A.D. 300–1300. Pittsburgh, PA: Carnegie Museum of Natural History, 1990.

Welch, Anthony. *Calligraphy in the Arts of the Muslim World.* Austin: University of Texas Press, 1979.

Margaret Anne Deppe

PART 3

Anatolia and the Eastern Mediterranean

Historical Survey of Textiles and Dress in Turkey

- Geography and Climate
- Textiles and Textile Production
- Hemp, Silk, Wool, and Mohair
- From Traditional Dress to a Mass-Fashion System

The Turkic people have a long and far-reaching history that originates in Central Asia, where ethnic Turks are still found. Turkic people in the early twenty-first century reside across the length of Asia, from northwestern China to the Balkans. The term *Turkic* refers to the general ethnolinguistic group that includes existing societies such as the Kazakhs, Uzbeks, Kyrgyz, Tatar, Uighurs, Azerbaijani, Turkmen, and Turkish people. It also includes past civilizations such as the Xiongnu, Cumans, Avars, Bulgars, Huns, Seljuks, Khazars, Timurids, and Ottomans. Certain Turkish tribes gradually migrated to the region known as Turkey in the early twenty-first century but in classical times as Asia Minor and to the Turks as Anatolia. They came as nomadic, horse-riding herdsmen and as conquerors. They established a series of large and small empires along the path along which they had migrated since the beginning of the second millennium C.E. Their dress was the characteristic clothing ensemble worn by all Central Asian horse-riding peoples. This was an ensemble of trousers and layers of front-opening shirts and coats, all bound in place by sashes. Headgear was also an essential feature. This layered ensemble added bulk to the body image, and formality in dress involved great numbers of layers.

The Turkish tribes reached Anatolia more than a thousand years ago and established the Great Seljuk Empire, which encompassed not only the Anatolian lands they had taken from the Byzantine Empire but also most of Persia and the northern regions of what are known as Iraq and Syria in the early twenty-first century. Throughout the history of this region, the subject populations of these territories consisted of many ethnic groups, each maintaining its own language, religion, and culture as well as, for the most part, dress.

This empire ended with the Mongol invasion in the thirteenth century, but after the collapse of the Mongol Empire, Turkish rule returned to much of its former territory in the form of smaller independent kingdoms and emirates. By the fourteenth century, Turkish tribes had established rule over virtually all of Anatolia. The house of Osman, in northwestern Anatolia, was confronting the remains of the Byzantine Empire and came to dominate all other Turkish clans of Anatolia. They crossed into the Balkans by the end of the fourteenth century, establishing Turkish rule there. In 1452, the descendant of Osman, Sultan Mehmet II, captured Constantinople, bringing the Byzantine Empire to an end. The house of Osman came to be known to the West as the Ottoman Empire. By the end of the sixteenth century, it encompassed virtually all of the lands surrounding the eastern Mediterranean and North Africa, as well as most of the lands surrounding the Black Sea. Several times in the sixteenth and seventeenth centuries, Ottoman armies reached the gates of Vienna. During this period, and even to the end of the Ottoman era, Ottoman culture was very much in the awareness of European societies. Ottoman culture and dress therefore had an ongoing influence on Western culture and dress.

By the eighteenth century, it became apparent that the Ottoman Empire was in decline. Following a prolonged period of increasing chaos and violence in the later nineteenth century, the Ottoman Empire ended following World War I (1914–1918) in a war of independence from which a new Turkish leadership emerged. A treaty signed by both Turkish leaders and European powers partitioned the Ottoman Empire into a new set of countries, most of which had never previously existed as independent states: Iraq, Syria, Lebanon, Palestine, Saudi Arabia, Egypt, and Turkey.

The Republic of Turkey was founded on secularist principles derived from Euro-American ideas of social order. The new leaders of this republic believed that Westernization and secularization of this Muslim society were essential to modernization, and so Turkey was established with a secular constitution; this would have some interesting, and conflicting, effects on dress as the twentieth century progressed.

GEOGRAPHY AND CLIMATE

Geography and climate have had a considerable impact on traditional Turkish dress. This culture evolved in a landscape that experienced great swings in temperature and weather, both seasonally and daily. The great grasslands of Central Asia were ideal for grazing animals and were also the homeland of the horse. Therefore, Turkish culture evolved on horseback. The clothing ensemble of the early Turk included the loose trousers necessary to prevent chafing on horseback (as opposed to the tunics or wrapped garments worn by settled farmers) and a set of front-opening garments—coats and shirts—that could be layered as required by weather conditions and donned and doffed while on horseback (in contrast to tunics that had to be pulled over the head). These fundamental forms are common to all traditional Turkish dress, both men's and women's, wherever Turks are found.

The climate of the Anatolian Plateau is, like that of Central Asia, quite varied. Most of the plateau has been treeless since Roman times, and so it is semiarid with sparse grass in most areas. However, there are also high mountain pastures where nomads would take their flocks during the hot summers. Winters could be quite harsh, and many nomads either migrated to warmer coastal regions for the winter or established settled villages in which to pass the winter. Over time, many nomads came to live in settled villages on a permanent basis; there they could maintain gardens and fields as well as flocks. They kept the same essential ensemble of trousers, shirts, and layered jackets (*cepken* or *yelek*) or coats (dolman, kaftan, *entari*, or *üç etek*) that they had worn in their original homeland a thousand years before.

There were also rural farming populations in Anatolia before the Turks came. In the early twenty-first century, most of these

"Costume of the Province of Hudavendigar (NW Turkey)," photograph by Sebah Pascal, 1873. From Osman Hamdi Bey and Marie de Launay, *Les costumes populaires de la Turquie en 1873* (Traditional dress from Turkey in 1873). The man on the left wears wedding garments, and the man on the right wears similar clothing, with the same elaborate couched silk embroidery but with fewer layers. The woman also wears wedding garments. The dress of both men and women from Bursa is composed of the same components: a shirt and loose trousers (*şalvar*), over which short jackets and/or vests are layered. For the woman, the trousers are cut loose to the ankles, whereas the men's trousers are loose from the waist to the knee but more closely fitted on the lower leg. The woman also wears a long coat (*üç etek*) under the short jacket. Library of Congress Prints and Photographs Division LC-USZC4-11736.

ancient inhabitants are blended with the Turkish population, having adopted both their language and religion. However, the countless civilizations that have inhabited Anatolia since the Paleolithic period certainly have contributed to the culture that has evolved there and to the regional differences in traditional dress that have emerged.

The Anatolian Plateau is ringed by mountains that separate it from the more well-watered coastal regions along the Black Sea, Aegean, and Mediterranean coasts on three sides. These coastal regions have milder climates that permit the growing of tea on the Black Sea coast to the north and olives, oranges, and bananas on the southern and western coasts. These more forgiving

climates permitted a wide range of other crops including cotton, hemp, and silk. Most coastal villages in the past raised silkworms if they did not raise cotton or hemp. The availability of these fibers would have a considerable effect on dress.

The herding of sheep and goats also defined the dress as well as the shelter of the Turks, because these animals provided not only food but also wool and leather that could be used to make clothing, furnishings, and tents. Settled communities could also raise other crops, both for subsistence and for sale.

The essential forms of all Turkish dress derive from the basic forms of nomadic dress, but Turkish culture also included urban society from an early date. Turks appear in Chinese chronicles as rulers of their own kingdom with settled urban centers northwest of China as early as the sixth century c.e. Turkic empires arose across Asia in the course of history. The first Turkish empire in the region known in the early twenty-first century as Turkey was founded more than a thousand years ago as the Seljuk Empire (1037–1194 c.e.). Images of early, pre-Islamic Turks show elaborate dress that included coats and trousers but also elaborate headgear, a feature of Ottoman court dress in later centuries.

The Ottoman government was a complex bureaucracy in which dress played an important role as a mark of status. Ottoman court dress had even had an impact on Byzantine court dress in the last century of the Byzantine Empire, but Ottoman rulers and their courts also adopted many Byzantine forms, not only in government and social organization, but also in dress. The sophisticated silk-textile production of the Byzantine era was taken over by the Ottomans, who adapted Byzantine forms of decoration and added new motifs that were uniquely Turkish. Elaborate embroidery was also employed to embellish court dress and personal furnishings, including veils, sashes, napkins, and garments. Ornate jewelry was incorporated in court dress. In addition to necklaces, earrings, and bracelets, jewelry included complex pieces designed to be worn in headdresses by both men and women. For men, this would include elaborate plumed crests (*sorguç*) featuring precious gems. The sorguç in the dress of the sultan was essentially the equivalent of a royal crown and was worn with the large complex turban reserved for this office.

Many Turks lived their entire lives in cities. The dress and culture of these cities were marked by specifically Turkish features that were rooted in their nomadic heritage but also borrowed elements from the regional and cultural styles of the particular community. In the cities, Ottoman dress became somewhat different from rural Turkish dress, due mainly to the wider availability of fine materials. Bureaucratic mandates for the dress of court officials and the military also affected civilian dress in the cities. This was true not only for Muslim Turkish city dwellers but also for the non-Muslim subjects of the sultan.

Distinctions were maintained between the various religious and ethnic communities (*millet*) of the empire. Specific materials and colors of footwear, garments, and headgear were assigned to each ethnic community. As long as the empire remained stable and prosperous, these distinctions were honored. Dress identified everyone as the holder of specific rights and privileges as well as responsibilities. However, by the eighteenth and nineteenth centuries, these sumptuary regulations became less effective, as the decline of the Ottoman economy led to a breakdown of the millet system. Some members of urban minorities began to adopt features of dress reserved for other classes and also became early adopters of Western dress forms. Nonetheless, there remains into the early twenty-first century an ingrained belief in Turkish society that social behavior can be regulated by managing dress, a belief that led to some serious conflicts over dress regulations in the late twentieth century.

TEXTILES AND TEXTILE PRODUCTION

From classical times, Asia Minor was an important center of textile production and trade. In the Ottoman era, this continued to be a strong and varied industry. The Ottoman ports controlled trade between East and West, and textiles were among the most important goods traded there. The Silk Road, not a single route but rather a network of routes across Asia, terminated at the ports of the eastern Mediterranean, all part of the Ottoman Empire. These important trade routes carried not only goods but also skills and technologies from one end of Asia to the other. This continual cross-fertilization resulted in a vigorous and varied textile industry throughout this region.

Textile manufacturing in the Ottoman period was typically conducted in a putting-out system, in which the various steps of production (spinning, dyeing, weaving) were carried out in home workshops. The production was managed by an entrepreneur who provided materials, coordinated work, and marketed the finished product. In many towns and villages, virtually every household was engaged in this process. The presence of this activity in a community and its surrounding region also contributed to the choice of materials available for local dress. Some of the production was intended for regional use. For example, the outer veil worn by most women in public varied in color, pattern, and material from one region to another, and the veils were woven in the region where they were worn. In the past, these might have been made of silk or cotton, usually woven in stripes or checks and, in some cases, with ikat stripes (ikat is decoration produced using a resist-dye technique). Among the last of these weaving towns is Buldan, near Denizli, which still produces some of the traditional textiles that have been woven there for centuries. Most Buldan households had, until the mid- to late twentieth century, engaged in power-loom weaving, producing yardage on consignment for factories that printed and finished the cloth in the nearby city of Denizli. Buldan, Denizli, Rize, Kastamonu, and Carsibasi in Trabzon survived into the twenty-first century as places where traditional cloth for regional dress was produced, particularly the cotton textiles worn by women as head scarves and by men as turbans, or other textiles worn as sashes. Production of particular patterns or colors once woven in other communities for local use was picked up by these weaving communities to meet the remaining demand for these regional textiles. However, this production is supported mainly by the domestic and foreign tourist market in the early twenty-first century, and use of these textiles in local dress has dwindled.

Although there were local textiles that distinguished regional dress, there were also textiles common to many parts of Turkey that were essential to local ensembles. Among the most popular fabrics for traditional dress were a variety of textiles woven with a striped silk warp and a cotton weft. There were two types: *alaca* and *kutnu*. *Alaca* is a plain-weave, warp-faced cloth, usually with alternating narrow and wide stripes in various color combinations. *Kutnu* is a warp-faced satin weave, also usually striped but often with geometric patterns woven into the stripes. Some kutnu also has ikat stripes. The cotton weft dominates on the back of this satin weave, and this feature made this cloth important throughout the Muslim world. The hadiths, in a widely accepted passage, forbid men to wear luxurious silk against the skin. Kutnu is considered acceptable because of the predominance of cotton on the back of the fabric. This cloth is woven in Muslim (or formerly Muslim) regions from Turkey to Egypt and India, where it is known as *mashru* (meaning "approved").

In Turkey, both men's and women's traditional dress used either alaca or kutnu for jackets and coats, with the choice of color and pattern being specific to each community or region. These textiles are almost as fundamental to Turkish traditional dress as tartan plaids are to Scottish dress. This production was always part of a complex putting-out system, so, for most people, it was a textile that had to be bought. However, in the past, there were production centers all over Anatolia, as well as in other parts of the Ottoman Empire. In the early twenty-first century, the only production center for alaca and kutnu in Turkey is in Gaziantep.

In addition to the textiles produced for trade, many textiles were produced by villagers for their own use. Some of these textiles were for clothing. These textiles might be differentiated by their fiber content and the technique used to make them. Cotton was widely available in the Aegean coastal region of what is western Turkey in the early twenty-first century. It was also widely available along the southeastern Mediterranean coast, particularly on the Cukurova Plain around Adana, which had been an important cotton-growing region for centuries. It was also found further east along the Tigris and Euphrates river basins. Production of both madder dye and indigo plant dyes was important in this region as well. A typical cotton cloth would have been dyed indigo cotton with a fine white stripe or check. Red handwoven cottons were also common. These humble fabrics were widely used by the poor for basic garments, both in the regions where cotton was grown and also in cities and rural areas where cotton was not grown or woven.

Blue striped and checked plain-weave textiles have been found among the outer coats preserved by the Sufi orders because they were worn by saints, some of which are purported to date to the

"Costume of Istanbul, 1873." From Osman Hamdi Bey and Marie de Launay, *Les costumes populaires de la Turquie en 1873* (Traditional dress from Turkey in 1873). From left to right: Turkish woman of Constantinople (Istanbul) wearing indoor dress, Turkish schoolboy, married Turkish woman of Constantinople (Istanbul) wearing outdoor dress. The dress of women of the middle class is shown both as it would appear in the privacy of the home and also as it would be seen on the street. The street dress consists of a long, unshaped coat (*ferace*) and two veils, one pinned in place over the face and the other arranged to cover the hat, hair, and neck. At this date the face veil was frequently a very sheer silk that allowed the features of the face to be seen through the cloth. The young boy wears only a short jacket and vest, appropriate for his age. Library of Congress Prints and Photographs Division LC-USZC4-11731.

sixteenth century. These surviving older cotton coats were lined, filled, and quilted to provide warmth. Quilted cotton garments have been documented as part of the dress of villagers and the urban poor. They were adopted by members of the religious orders as part of a spiritual renunciation of material luxuries. Villagers who raised cotton as a cash crop would reserve some for domestic use. Women spun yarn and wove cloth for men's shirts and women's chemises (*gömlek* in either case) and the baggy trousers (*don* or *şalvar*) worn by everyone. In the Aegean region, this cloth might be embellished with brocading during weaving; it was usually also made of handspun cotton dyed blue or red. This cotton was also used to make sashes (*kuşak*), worn by men or women, and aprons (*önlük*), worn by married women. Embroidery was also used to embellish cotton garments.

Cotton gauze weaving was also widespread and can still be found in villages from the Aegean region to the Black Sea. In some instances, cotton may have replaced silk as the material for gauze weaving. The yarns are overspun so that, when washed, they form a sheer crepe-weave fabric. Inlay threads are also used to create patterns during weaving. In the south, these patterns are made with heavier, low-twist white cotton laid into the white crepe foundation. In the Black Sea region, the inlay threads are dyed a contrasting color, usually red and blue and occasionally yellow. The designs are specific to localities. These crepe gauze textiles are used for women's head coverings and have become one of the most identifiable features of dress from a village where this weaving is done. In the Black Sea region, *kilim* (discontinuous-weft) technique is also used to create borders on the gauze scarves or as decoration for napkins worn tucked into the sash as part of traditional dress.

HEMP, SILK, WOOL, AND MOHAIR

In some regions, particularly in the coastal and mountain regions around the Black Sea, hemp (*kenevir*) was raised and used for household goods and garments that might have been made of cotton in other regions, such as undergarments, shirts, and trousers. Hemp was also a cash crop, raised for sale. In the past, it was commonly found in southern Turkey. In the 1970s, the raising of hemp was officially banned, at the same time that opium was brought under government control. By the 1990s, however, hemp was again being raised under controlled conditions for the textile industry and discreetly in isolated rural locations for local production. The modern cloth is usually referred to as linen (*keten*), but there is no evidence that the flax plant has ever been raised in Turkey, so any textile, sash, shirt, or other garment that seems to be linen is most likely made of hemp.

Silk was once raised in villages all over the coastal regions of Turkey, where mulberry trees can be grown. Travelers as early as the sixteenth century described encounters with sericulture. This industry continued throughout the twentieth century, but, by the mid-1990s, government subsidies for sericulture were dropped. Consequently, village sericulture is rapidly disappearing. In the past, silk production was a cash crop, but, as with cotton, some silk was kept to be spun and woven for local use. The silk was used to make a heavy crepe used for women's head scarves and also for the bedsheets used to cover the locally made quilts. The crepe was also used to make a man's wedding shirt, which was usually made by his mother, to be worn on his wedding night.

Silk was also used to make the needlelace known as *oya*, which was used to decorate the borders of head scarves. This three-dimensional lace was usually done in color in the form of flowers, leaves, and fruit and is unique to Turkey and adjacent regions formerly part of the Ottoman Empire, in eastern Greece, the Balkans, and northern Syria. Urban forms of *oya* are often white or monochromatic and two-dimensional. This type is sometimes seen on the borders of special scarves reserved for prayer or attendance at a *mevlut*, a ceremonial reading of sacred texts.

The finest silk textiles used in the best clothing were the work of professional weavers, usually a set of craftsmen who each specialized in one stage of the production. The most elaborate silk textiles were reserved for imperial use. Bursa and Constantinople were the centers of this sophisticated production. However, there was a wide variety of simpler brocades in many styles made for ordinary citizens. In addition to the traditional alaca and kutnu, there were many floral, striped, and scattered small-pattern silks that could be produced at a moderate cost on less sophisticated looms. In addition, fine velvets in elaborate designs had been woven for court dress since the sixteenth century, but, by the nineteenth century, solid velvet was widely used for more formal dress. Velvet garments embellished with elaborate padded gold embroidery became fashionable for well-to-do urban women. These garments might be jackets or full-length chemise-style gowns. This form of dress became associated with urban wedding attire and eventually became wedding attire in small towns in many parts of the country.

Wool is by far the most widely available fiber and has been best known as the material of Turkish carpets and kilims. The wool of the fat-tailed Anatolian sheep is coarser than European wool but has a glossy finish very suitable to carpet weaving. However, traditional home weavers also produced textiles for clothing from this wool. Garment fabrics varied from one region to another and were most likely plain weave or twill. These textiles might be used for jackets, coats, or shawls. Twill-woven textiles were more likely to be used for shawls or sashes. In much of the northern region of Turkey, women wear a square shawl that is folded in a triangle so that the point, and the heavy fringe, fall over the hips in back. Originally, this was twill woven and might have small inlay patterns or other embellishment. Finer cloth was woven commercially in more elaborate patterns to be used for sashes and shawls. In eastern Turkey, women wore a full-length shawl as their veil in public. In the harsh climate of eastern Anatolia, this cloth was woven of overspun wool to make a wool crepe. Not unlike the cotton gauze crepe of southwestern Turkey, this textile was embellished with small inlay patterns.

The finest wool textile used in Ottoman Turkey was imported English woolen broadcloth. Although broadcloth was woven domestically, the finer imported cloth displaced local production by the seventeenth century and was used by the Ottoman government to clothe the imperial household. It was available in the marketplace, and so it was also used for the best clothing of ordinary citizens, either in simple coats and şalvar or embellished with couched silk or gold-thread embroidery.

Knitting was also an important use of wool for clothing. Colorfully patterned Turkish socks are well-known examples of Turkish knitting. The patterns were associated with regions and could carry other kinds of meaning as gifts from a girl to her fiancé or her new in-laws and as part of a dowry. Sweaters were knit in undyed handspun white wool, with openwork and

A family wearing Turkish traditional dress in the Milas region, southwestern Turkey, 1965. By the middle of the twentieth century, the traditional textiles used in this kind of dress had been largely supplanted by industrially produced textiles. Women in this region once wore layers of jackets and a long coat over a long chemise or shirt. By the 1960s, the long garments had merged into one cotton print garment, worn over traditional trousers. It is clear that the older woman is married, not only because she wears a head scarf, but also because she wears a second scarf bound around her forehead. Photograph by Charlotte Jirousek.

textured patterning. These sweaters were typically sleeveless button-front vests worn by both men and women. Pullover sweaters were worn by men under their shirts, as underwear, and long underwear has also been seen in regions with more severe winters.

Mohair is a fiber that was once unique to Turkey, and the cloth was a major commodity in world trade, where it was known as camlet. The mohair or Angora goat was unique to Anatolia, and the city of Ankara (known to Europeans as Angora in the Ottoman period) was the primary center of production for mohair cloth (*sof*). The fine, silky hair of the Angora goat made exceptionally fine cloth, considered a luxury fabric. Mohair was used for coats, cloaks, and sashes for court use and also was used in the communities that raised these goats. Finely woven patterned shawls, similar to shawls woven in Persia, were an important product of Sivas, east of Ankara. Village production included woven mohair that was used for sashes, purses, and clothing. In the Kurdish region of southeastern Turkey, mohair cloth is still woven and used for the entire men's ensemble.

FROM TRADITIONAL DRESS TO A MASS-FASHION SYSTEM

By the mid-nineteenth century, a combination of growing importation of cheap industrially woven textiles from Europe and domestic industrialization of textile manufacturing had begun to alter the traditional dress of Turkey. Even rural dress began to substitute inexpensive cotton prints for some traditional handwoven materials. However, the garment forms remained the same well into the twentieth century.

Urban dress went through a complex and dramatic change in the nineteenth century. As part of a dramatic restructuring of the imperial army in 1826, Sultan Mahmud II instituted a new dress code for his new army and also for all members of his government. This was part of a program of legal reforms that were based on European models of governance, law, and education. Since Westernization has been equated with reform and modernization, the new dress codes have moved official dress in the direction of European dress. The bureaucracy adopted a version of the frock coat and tailored trousers then fashionable in Europe. The one exception was headgear. Although the turban was abolished except for religious leaders, the Western-style brimmed hat was not acceptable for Muslims, because during prayers the Muslim must keep his head covered and touch his head to the ground. The fez was adopted for official dress of all kinds and became widely worn by the general populace. Initially, it was seen as the symbol of modernization; but, ironically, a century later in the closing years of the Ottoman Empire, before World War I, it became a symbol of old ways, corruption, and the failing sultanate.

The Western-style tailored suit was gradually adopted into the dress of urban men, although it would not appear in rural men's dress until after the founding of the republic in 1923. Meanwhile, the dress of urban women remained much the same during the first half of the nineteenth century, although a few travelers' accounts of the 1840s mention pieces of European fashionable dress being incorporated into the dress of well-to-do women. No doubt the transformation of official men's dress encouraged women to explore Western fashion as well. The first documentation of Western fashion being worn by a Muslim is a photograph of the young daughter of Sultan Abdulaziz. By the 1890s, upper-class urban Muslim women were frequently dressed in the latest Western styles.

Following the founding of the republic, its first prime minister, Mustafa Kemal Atatürk, set about modernizing his new country. A secular constitution was established that separated religion from the state. The reform program included many economic and educational projects and also included efforts at dress reform. The alteration of men's dress was encouraged directly, and all members of the new government appeared in Western suits, ties, and brimmed fedora hats. In 1925, the fez was banned, and men were encouraged to wear Western-style headgear.

Because the dress of women was a more controversial issue, there was no legal ban on the veil or any other aspect of women's dress. Instead, there was encouragement through example, in the form of the fashionable dress worn by the wives of government officials. For the most part, urban women adopted Western fashions, but more conservative women continued to wear a head scarf on the street. In rural areas, there was virtually no change in traditional dress, apart from the changes in materials that had already been occurring at the end of the Ottoman period.

Following World War II (1939–1945), Turkey became a member of the North Atlantic Treaty Organization and began to enjoy the benefits of economic aid from the West. At this time, a more rapid shift from traditional to modern or mass-fashion dress began. More accessible and prosperous regions, mainly in western Turkey, began to modify or abandon traditional dress as rural standards of living began to rise. However, in the more conservative regions of central and eastern Anatolia, traditional dress has been slower to disappear, although there have been modifications, as cheap mass-manufactured textiles have increasingly displaced the older handwoven textiles. There is a direct correlation between economic opportunity and the abandonment of traditional dress in favor of mass-fashion dress. This change occurs as a result of several factors: an increase in contact with the outside world made possible by new roads and access to information via media; the availability of surplus cash; and access to new goods, including new forms of dress. By the 1980s, Turkey was also generating fashion design of its own, and some of these new designers became figures in international fashion design—notably, Rıfat Özbek and Hussein Chalayan.

In the 1980s, a long period of warfare, insurgency, and terrorism decimated eastern Turkey, which had remained the most impoverished part of the country. One result of this was a massive migration of rural people to the urban centers of western Turkey. This in turn has generated a cultural conflict between the secularist culture of these cities and the more traditionalist populations that have generated enormous urban growth. There has, therefore, been a revival of the controversy over veiling. The Turkish constitution prohibits the wearing of any symbols of religious belief in government offices or institutions; this includes schools at all levels. This rule is particularly a problem for girls and women who wear hijab, a head scarf that is an expression of religious modesty. Since there is a long tradition in Turkey of managing dress as a way of managing social policy and behavior, there is a great deal of emotion around this issue. Secularist women fear that they will lose their hard-won rights and opportunities, whereas religious women feel that they are discriminated against and that their religious freedom is being curtailed. The rise of the religious right in Turkish politics has brought about a conservative government headed by leaders whose wives wear hijab. These contradictions between factions within the country, and with certain institutions such as the courts and the constitution

A woman wearing Turkish traditional dress in Azdavay, Kastamonu, 1994. Although by the 1990s almost all vestiges of traditional dress had disappeared in most of western Turkey, it survived in more isolated locations. In this remote community in the mountains of north-central Turkey, the traditional outfit is a mixture of industrially woven and printed cotton and textiles that are handwoven and embellished. Women who have reached marriageable age wear a flat hat, handmade and decorated with embroidery and beading, under their head scarves. In addition, a heavy handwoven wool shawl is worn around the waist (visible from the front as a checked sash). This shawl forms a triangle in the back with a deep fringe. A striped apron panel, also handwoven, is tied over the shawl. Photograph by Charlotte Jirousek.

itself, are continuing to keep these dress issues at the forefront of the Turkish struggle toward social equity.

An interesting side effect of this reemergence of Islamicism in Turkey is the emergence of a new mass-fashion style. In the 1980s, for the most part, religious women wore whatever their neighbors wore but with the addition of a scarf and more modest garments. By the 1990s, a new fashion industry aimed at religious women began to emerge. This included garments ranging from pantsuits to wedding dresses and swimwear that were specifically designed for religious modesty and also for fashionable flair. It also included new forms of hijab headgear designed to match the fashionable garments. This is a phenomenon that is occurring in Muslim countries all over the world.

In the first decade of the twenty-first century, one can see on the streets of Turkish cities young men and girls in tank tops and jeans; fashionable professionals alongside working-class people in shirts and modern trousers; and housewives in tailored skirts and head scarves. There are also women in total veiling and occasionally villagers who still wear traditional şalvar, sashes, and head coverings. There is an enormous diversity of dress styles reflecting the great variety of experience, belief, and identity expressed by Turkish people.

References and Further Reading

Atasoy, Nurhan, W. Denny, L. Mackie, and H. Tezcan. *Ipek: The Crescent and the Rose: Imperial Ottoman Silks and Velvets*. Edited by J. Raby. London: Azimuth Editions, 2002.

Atasoy, Nurhan, W. Denny, L. Mackie, and H. Tezcan. *Costume and Identity in the Ottoman Empire*. Istanbul: Bogazici University, Eren Publications, 2005.

Garnett, Lucy M.J. *The Women of Turkey and Their Folk-Lore: Jewish and Moslem Women*. Vol. 2. London: Macmillan, 1891.

Jirousek, Charlotte. "Dress and Social Policy: Change in Women's Dress in a Southwestern Turkish Village." *Dress* 23 (1997): 3–18.

Jirousek, Charlotte. "From 'Traditional' to 'Mass Fashion System' Dress among Men in a Rural Turkish Village." *Clothing and Textiles Research Journal* 15, no. 4 (1997): 203–215.

Marchese, R., ed. *The Fabric of Life: Cultural Transformations in Turkish Society*. Binghamton, NY: Global Publications, State University of New York, 2005.

Roxburgh, Donald J., ed. *Turks: Journey of a Thousand Years*. London: Royal Academy of Arts, 2005.

Scarce, Jennifer. *Women's Costume of the Near and Middle East*. Oxford: Oxford University Press, 1987.

Charlotte Jirousek

See also Jewish Dress in Central and Southwest Asia and the Diaspora; Dress Reforms of the Early Twentieth Century in Turkey, Iran, and Afghanistan; Snapshot: Turkish Fashion Designers; Hussein Chalayan: Controversial Fashion Designer or Bridge between East and West?; Turkish Embroidery; Ottoman Dress; The Kaftan and Its Origins; Royal Dress Preserved at the Topkapi Museum; Snapshot: Turkish Costume Albums; Regional Dress in Anatolia; Palestinian Women's Dress.

Turkish Embroidery

Embroidery and embroidered textiles offer a unique window into urban society in the Ottoman Empire. The history of the urban embroidery tradition from the sixteenth century on parallels that of the Ottoman Empire with its changing geography, economy, and social life. Embroidery was one of the art forms practiced both commercially and domestically by a large portion of the population in the empire. Both men and women embroidered textiles that were to be used personally or sold. Gender was the determining factor in where one would work, at least until the late nineteenth century. Men generally worked in workshops embroidering heavier materials that became tents, boots, saddles, quivers, and cuirasses. Female embroiderers, both professional and amateur, worked at home, producing smaller articles for domestic use.

The study of embroidery, one of the least-recognized resources for Ottoman studies, gives valuable insight into Ottoman art, the economy, and particularly the significant economic contributions of women through textile production. The role of women in textile production was considered to be subordinate to that of men. Women's duties included certain aspects of production that allowed them to finish their domestic tasks before they turned their attention to textile production. For an urban woman in the Ottoman Empire, embroidery was generally the most common means of contributing to her household's income. Although there have never been official statistics, embroiderers were probably the largest group of women textile workers in the empire.

OVERVIEW OF TECHNIQUES

Ottoman embroidery is unique. It is instantly recognizable and distinguishable from other embroideries around the world by its style. As in other Ottoman art forms, floral motifs predominate. Although a variety of flowers and trees are depicted in embroidered textiles, a few distinct motifs such as tulips, hyacinths, carnations, bouquets of roses, vases filled with many colorful flowers, as well as weeping willow and cypress trees are all considered typical Ottoman motifs.

Counted work, pattern darning, couching, pulled work, and tambour work were the most important techniques used. Ottoman embroidery was usually executed by counting the warp and weft yarns of a balanced plain-weave foundation fabric. This technique, called *hesap işi*, the Turkish term for "counted work," required very uniform stitching and minimized irregularities. Thus, the fineness of the embroidery depended on the fineness of the ground weave. Although the stitch repertoire was limited to a few stitches—such as running, double running, satin, and Turkish

stitches—Ottoman embroiderers were exceptional in their ability to create a great range of different effects by manipulating a single stitch in numerous ways. They were also distinguished by their masterly use of metallic threads to enhance their motifs. Hesap işi, for example, can be divided into two groups, termed for the sake of simplification as double-sided and single-sided hesap işi. Stitches such as the running stitch could be worked either to create a similar appearance on both sides of the foundation fabric, so a viewer could enjoy both sides of the textile, or to be viewed from one side of the fabric only, therefore conserving expensive silk embroidery thread.

Embroiderers used a *gergef*, a rectangular embroidery frame standing on four stubby legs that resembled a short, small table. Some were beautifully carved; others were decorated with inlaid mother-of-pearl. Each part of the frame could be easily detached, thus making it easy to carry and store. Before starting the work, the first task of the embroiderer was to stretch a foundation fabric on this frame with the help of string and another fabric called gergef cloth. The fabric to be embroidered was sewn onto the gergef cloth along its shorter ends. Strings attached to the gergef cloth were then threaded through holes in the frame and pulled so as to stretch the foundation fabric as tight as possible. The embroiderer sat cross-legged in front of the gergef, which was placed either on the floor or on a divan. She kept her right hand above and her left hand below the frame, passing the needle up and down very rapidly.

Simple needles made of bone, ivory, or metal were the basic tools for all types of embroidery. Designs were transferred onto the foundation fabric by way of several methods. In one of the methods, the pattern sample was an embroidered textile made previously; its motifs were copied by counting the warp and weft elements of the foundation fabric and inserting embroidery threads in corresponding places in the new fabric. This method of copying required a foundation fabric with a similar weave structure and similar warp and weft counts. This type of design transfer was most often practiced at home to copy older materials passed down through the generations. It offered a means of securing the continuity of the family's inherited design traditions.

Another method of design transfer, used primarily at home, was to use charcoal dust. A design was first drawn on paper, which was then pricked with a needle. Little holes were punched all along the outlines of the motif. The paper was then placed on the foundation fabric, and a bag of ground charcoal was pressed onto the paper. The charcoal dust slipped through the holes to transfer the motif to the fabric.

In workshops where there was a greater output, designs were frequently drawn on the foundation fabric by a professional design draftsman—either freehand with brushes or an inking pen or with the help of templates or print blocks. Templates and print blocks were also used to transfer outlines of motifs onto the foundation fabric. This method allowed the same motif to be used repeatedly on the same textile or on more than one textile. Some of the larger textiles were decorated with overall repeat patterning in ogival lattices (in which two pointed, curved surfaces are joined to create a curved oval shape) or ascending meanders using this method of design transfer. Because the templates or blocks generally carried a single motif, two or more of these were required to create the overall repeat patterns seen on many textiles. Sometimes a combination of freehand drawing and block patterns is observed on these textiles.

There are two distinct stylistic periods in the Ottoman urban embroidery tradition. The first period corresponded to the sixteenth and seventeenth centuries. This period can be referred to as the classical period. The earliest surviving Ottoman embroidered textiles date to this period. The second period started roughly in the middle of the eighteenth century and continued until the early twentieth century and might be termed the postclassical period.

THE CLASSICAL PERIOD

The embroidered textiles surviving from the sixteenth and early seventeenth centuries have foundation fabrics that are a balanced plain weave with no woven ornamental designs. They are made of loosely woven, undyed linen. The warp and weft yarn counts are low, generally thirty by twenty-six per square inch (per a 2.5-centimeter square). In the classical period, textiles composed of satin-weave and velvet foundation fabrics embroidered with gold and silver threads, pearls, and semiprecious stones were within reach of only the very wealthy elite, primarily the court in Istanbul. From very early on, silk threads were commonly used in Ottoman embroidered textiles. Their use continued through the centuries. Until the middle of the eighteenth century, untwisted and twisted silk threads or highly twisted and loosely twisted silk threads were often used side by side to give dimension to embroidered motifs.

Several nonreversible stitches, including running, *atma*, and Turkish stitches, were popular in classical-period embroidery. The running stitch used in Ottoman embroidery was always counted and placed in closely worked parallel rows in diagonal alignment. This stitch was favored until the middle of the eighteenth century, when it disappeared from the embroidery repertoire. Atma stitch, known sometimes as Oriental stitch, refers both to the technique of couching and to a specific composite stitch utilized in the couching technique. Turkish stitch, or triangular two-sided stitch, was also used frequently.

The designs on embroidered textiles from the classical period have well-balanced compositions, incorporating well-executed motifs and using a small number of bold colors like red, green, blue, yellow, and white. They show a close affinity with woven fabrics from the same period as well as other art forms. One or two motifs, sometimes combined with a lattice, usually form a large, flowing pattern covering the entire surface area of the fabric. These compositions have three important characteristics: They are often framed by a narrow or wide border; the overall design in the central field is an infinitely repeating pattern, which creates the illusion that the design continues beyond the border; and floral motifs and compositions are often stylistically harmonious creations that nonetheless are not found in the natural world. Flowers do appear realistic enough to be identifiable, but they are lifted from their environment, transformed, and combined to create compositions that do not exist outside of artistic expression.

Among these classical-period textiles, a staggered or diagonal layout for the overall design is the most common. Another favorite composition of this period is referred to as wavy vine, ascending leaves, or undulating vine. It is composed of three or four parallel meandering bands with different, alternating blossoms facing left or right at regular intervals. In a third composition, motifs are placed in straight alignment or a stacked layout. Although this composition may at first appear rigid, sinuous and curvilinear Ottoman floral motifs break the rigidity to create a playful and flowing composition.

Ottomans loved flowers, so floral forms and designs are common. Favored motifs included flower-filled medallions. The tulip was the most popular and was used as both a primary and secondary motif. The carnation fascinated designers with its many-layered petals. Portrayed in profile, it is always recognizable by its fanlike head. The hyacinth remained one of the most popular motifs until the turn of the twentieth century. Another motif called the arching flower branch gave a sense of movement even if the layout was rigid. Three other favored motifs were the crown, the pomegranate, and the *çintemani* (three balls and wavy lines).

Color was crucial to completing the work and achieving the desired bold but visually pleasing effects in early Ottoman embroidery. Very few colors were employed during this period. The limited palette relied on red, green, blue, white, and yellow for

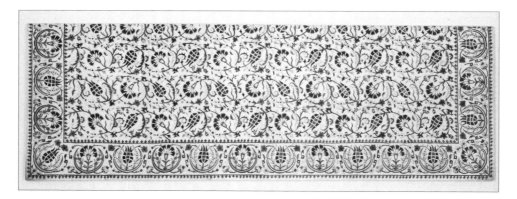

Detail of a cover, Ottoman, Turkey, seventeenth or early eighteenth century. Covers like this would have been used either as quilt covers or wall hangings. They ceased to be produced sometime in the second half of the eighteenth century, but the fine embroidery and detail show the skilled workmanship of Ottoman embroiderers. Textile Museum, Washington, D.C., 1.22. Acquired by George Hewitt Myers before 1940. http://www.textilemuseum.org/

motifs. Brown or black was used for outlining. Even with a limited palette, embroiderers were able to juxtapose colors to create vibrant and colorful compositions.

A traditional Ottoman home had little furniture and few rooms. The only large piece of furniture was a sofa or divan. Each room served many functions at different times of the day. Glazed tiles or wall hangings provided decoration on the walls in wealthy sixteenth- and seventeenth-century homes. Until the middle of the eighteenth century, large covers made of narrow embroidered strips of fabric were popular and might have been used as quilt covers as well as wall hangings either to decorate an empty wall or to cover existing niches. These covers ceased to be produced sometime in the second half of the eighteenth century.

Embroidered floor spreads were used as table settings in traditional Ottoman houses. A round cover was spread on the floor. This textile sometimes served alone as a table; at other times, a cylindrical stand was put on top of it to accommodate a food tray called a *tepsi*. This setup was used in the sultan's palace as well as in the homes of his humblest subjects until the nineteenth century. Similar floor spreads, although often not embroidered, continue to be used in Turkish villages in the early twenty-first century.

THE POSTCLASSICAL PERIOD

In the postclassical period of Ottoman urban embroidery, a greater variety of materials and weaves was used. Supplemental weft and warp yarns of cotton or silk were incorporated into the foundation fabrics. These supplemental yarns created bands and sets of repeating patterns in the linen or cotton foundation fabric. The weft and warp yarns seen on many late-eighteenth- and nineteenth-century foundation fabrics are also extremely fine and densely woven. In the finest examples, warp and weft yarn counts are approximately eighty by sixty per square inch (per 2.5-centimeter square). Textiles using expensive materials such as velvet, gold and silver threads, and semiprecious stones now became available to the increasingly prosperous middle class. As status symbols, these textiles represented a family's wealth and standing.

To give dimension to embroidered motifs, embroiderers began combining silk and metallic threads and different stitches on a single piece. At the beginning of the eighteenth century, metallic threads were widely used to enhance designs. Throughout that century and into the following century, the use of metallic threads continued to be fashionable and increased to the point that certain textiles were embroidered almost exclusively with metallic threads. The number of different kinds of stitches used in embroidery to achieve the desired or fashionable patterns and motifs increased. In the eighteenth century, the nonreversible running, atma, and Turkish stitches started being used less. These stitches were replaced by reversible stitches such as the double running, satin, and *muşabak* stitches. Reversible stitches created a similar appearance on each side of the foundation fabric. The double running stitch became the hallmark of embroidered textiles from the eighteenth century on. Another stitch frequently seen from this time on is the satin stitch. Satin and double running stitches were often used together. The double running stitch filled the flower heads, and satin stitch was used to create their stems.

Pulled work became popular in the early nineteenth century. The stitch most frequently used for Ottoman pulled work was called *muşabak* (or *müşebbek*). It was used to pull the warp and weft yarns of a foundation fabric out of alignment and to hold them in place under tension to create a netted effect.

In the nineteenth century, *kasnak işi* (tambour work) and *dival* embroidery also became popular. Kasnak işi derives its name from the large, round hoop called a *kasnak*. The embroidery fabric was stretched on it with the help of strings. To start embroidering, the embroiderer sat on a divan and held the kasnak between her or his chest and the backrest of the divan, with the hands left free. The embroiderer would hold the silk thread in the left hand underneath the kasnak and the *kasnak tığ* (kasnak needle) in the right hand above the kasnak.

Dival embroidery was done either in workshops or by professional embroiderers at home. It was sometimes referred to as *maraş işi* after the town of Maraş in southeastern Turkey, where embroiderers excelled at this type of embroidery. This embroidery required large equipment and strength. The stand used was called a *çülde*. A *çağ* (spool holder) and *biz* (sharp needle) to punch holes for the threaded needle to pass through were crucial to the process. The çülde resembled a large pair of tweezers and clasped the foundation fabric between its arms. The thick foundation fabric had to be secured and stationary to permit the embroiderer to push the needle through the thick fabric using force. Small çüldes were used in homes, and there were larger stands for workshops. Dival embroidery required an investment in both material and skill that not everyone was willing to make. Thus, textiles with dival embroidery were usually made by professionals and purchased in the bazaars. Household items or garments embroidered with dival embroidery were expensive, and special attention was given to their care. They were taken out rarely and passed on from one generation to the next.

All the changes in techniques and stitches used for embroidery were made to facilitate the application of new designs and motifs. After the mid-eighteenth century, compositions on embroidered textiles began to change. Infinitely repeating patterns lost favor. Most of these later textiles were embroidered around the edges or at the two narrow ends with the same motifs opposing one another. Individual motifs became smaller and were divided into small sections. The representation of individual motifs changed as well, becoming more and more natural in appearance but delicate in character. In simple scenes, embroiderers experimented with perspective and tried to achieve the appearance of depth by either the placement of motifs or shading.

In Ottoman embroidered textiles as well as in other decorative arts, flowers remained the most prominent thematic element after the middle of the eighteenth century. The rose replaced the tulip as the most popular flower. The carnation and hyacinth remained among the most favored motifs until the turn of the twentieth century. The floral sprigs of the eighteenth century represented by arching flower branches gradually became lavish floral sprays. Under the influence of what is often referred to as Turkish rococo, these floral sprays became large bouquets in the nineteenth century. They were basically images of abundance. Vases filled with large sprays of flowers joined the garden as the setting of these floral arrangements. New fruit motifs, including grapes and melons, appeared alongside pomegranates. Oriental plane trees, weeping willows, and palm trees began to accompany the cypress tree.

The postclassical period also marked the introduction of landscape designs depicting scenery and architectural features generally related to gardens. Arcades, arches, and columns were

Detail of an *uçkur* (sash), Ottoman Turkey, late eighteenth century. The *uçkur* was worn by both men and women to hold their *şalvar* (loose pants) tight around the waist. Both ends of the *uçkur* were embroidered so that when knotted at the front, the ends dangled down and the adornment could be seen. The Textile Museum, Washington, D.C., 1.88. Gift of Mrs. Philip Hoffman. http://www.textilemuseum.org/

employed as dividers for floral motifs. An expanding repertoire of motifs included shoreside villas, which lined both sides of the Bosporus in Istanbul; mosques; *mescids* (small prayer halls); *türbes* (mausoleums) with surrounding gardens; pleasure tents on hillsides; and ships sailing. Some embroiderers started to experiment with perspective by putting one motif behind another or by raising one motif above the others. These designs might have been copied from painted wall friezes, which became fashionable in Ottoman homes at the beginning of the eighteenth century.

Color was a key aspect of the postclassical period. Pastel tones were increasingly selected, and the number of colors used increased. Close to fifteen colors might be found in a single embroidered textile. Several shades of the same color were applied to create the effect of shading. By using two tones of the same color, embroiderers could create lighter and darker sections within a single motif, suggesting depth.

The most profound changes in the postclassical period occurred in the functions embroidered textiles served. This was especially true for embroidered textiles used for furnishings, for ceremonies, and as clothing. New types of textiles became widespread during the postclassical period, one of which was the coffee tray cover. Although coffee, when introduced in the sixteenth century, encountered considerable resistance, it became an indispensable part of etiquette and hospitality in Ottoman homes by the nineteenth century, and the instruments, including the embroidered textiles, used for this service became sumptuous.

Yağlıks (decorative pieces of cloth, either square or rectangular) had multiple functions. They appear to have been in use by the sixteenth century, if not earlier; but many examples surviving in collections date to the eighteenth, nineteenth, and twentieth centuries. It appears that, during the eighteenth century, the yağlık became a decorative or ceremonial object in addition to being a practical object. Yağlıks were used as towels to dry hands and napkins to be placed on a person's lap or chest to catch any spills during dining. Guests and household members were always presented with embroidered yağlıks to wipe their hands before and after they tasted food. Yağlıks were also used to wrap gifts, and the richer the wrapping, the greater the compliment. During ceremonies such as weddings and circumcisions, yağlıks were used as decorations.

In addition, some embroidered items continued to be used uninterrupted over many centuries. A *bohça*, or wrapping cloth, was a square piece of fabric that came in many sizes and was used for carrying or storage. It might be the oldest textile type used by the Turks. The first bohças likely functioned as carrying cloths in a nomadic environment. Similar to bohças, embroidered bath towels held undiminished importance for every household over many centuries. Going to the bathhouse was a frequent outing for otherwise secluded Ottoman women. At the bathhouse, women gathered socially and exhibited their exquisitely embroidered textiles.

The second-biggest change in the Ottoman way of life after the late eighteenth century was in clothing. Ottomans attached great importance and value to what they wore. Although the dress of both men and women changed slowly over the centuries, certain items retained their overall shape and function while losing and gaining minor characteristic features. Both men and women wore *şalvar* (loose pants), a *gömlek* (shirt), and robes—the *entari* for women and the *kaftan* for men. Men wore a *kavuk*, or a small turban, when they went out of the house. Women wore elaborate hairstyles, which changed frequently.

Differences in religion, rank, and class were immediately apparent from the turbans and robes men wore. In 1829, laws were passed to make "modern" dress compulsory for all men other than clerics. Accepting Western clothing with its frocks and trousers shook what was a highly structured Ottoman society. These new laws, besides obliterating visual distinctions of rank, class, and religion, caused some embroidered textiles, like turban covers, to disappear from the everyday lives of the Ottomans. To protect the kavuk from gathering dust when not in use, a textile made especially for that purpose had been placed over it. After 1829, the kavuk was replaced by the fez, and these turban covers lost their reason for being.

Among the clothing articles used by the Ottomans, the *uçkur* (sash) and the *çevre* (head scarf) were two important embroidered items. The uçkur was a narrow sash approximately eighty inches (two hundred centimeters) long and twelve inches (thirty centimeters) wide that was used by both men and women. It was drawn through the wide seam of the *şalvar* and knotted in front to hold the baggy pants tight around the waist. Both ends of the uçkur were embroidered so that, when tied, the ends dangled down the front as adornment. The çevre was a cloth approximately thirty-five inches (ninety centimeters) square and embroidered along all four sides. It was most often used as a head scarf. It was placed either folded or unfolded on the head and fastened beneath the chin. Sometimes it was wrapped around a cap or combined with other head scarves.

Women's clothing was free of government intervention, but fashionable Ottoman women were not willing to stay with their "old-fashioned" styles, and they very quickly accepted European-style garments as well. Initially, small features were added to their traditional dress of şalvar, uçkur, gömlek, embroidered entari (sometimes), and çevre. Eventually, European-style garments like full dresses, skirts, and tailored jackets appeared. The best example of this transformation in women's dress can be followed through changes that occurred in the *bindalli*, a type of dress for special occasions. Its distinguishing characteristics were the very fluid floral designs covering the entire surface and the style of gold dival embroidery applied on the velvet or satin-weave foundation fabric. The bindalli appears to have entered fashion with the introduction of dresses and skirts from Europe. It exhibited many variations through the nineteenth century and the early twentieth century, especially in its tailoring. Most bindallis were long dresses, sometimes with matching fitted jackets, skirts with long trains, and slippers.

CONCLUSION

The changes in the Ottoman urban embroidery tradition from the classical period to the postclassical period parallel changes in Ottoman art and society. These changes reflected Ottoman society's transformation into a new or different consumer culture whose people were demanding more luxury goods, preferably with aesthetics that combined traditional Ottoman Turkish art with artistic ideas originating from Europe.

Throughout the centuries, for Ottoman artists, European artistic ideas provided the means rather than the motivation to create new artistic traditions. At least by the middle of the eighteenth century, Ottoman artists found their clientele interested in and supportive of ideas originating in Europe; they shifted their attention farther to the West and began experimenting with artistic ideas from the West to satisfy the local interest.

The expanding influence of artistic ideas from Europe paralleled closely the sociopolitical changes taking place in the Ottoman Empire and the rest of the world, from the realignment of political power centers, to industrialization, to the expanding importation and availability of luxury goods, to new patterns in the distribution of wealth, to the rise of the middle class, to the expansion of educational opportunities nationally and internationally. Starting in the eighteenth century, improvements in the means of communication, the availability of foreign newspapers, and an increase in business and pleasure travel all contributed to the further diffusion of Western taste and products. These political, economic, and social changes were reflected in many art forms in the Ottoman Empire, including embroidered textiles.

References and Further Reading

Atasoy, Nurhan. *Splendors of the Ottoman Sultans*. Memphis, TN: Wonders, the Memphis International Cultural Series, 1992.

Atil, Esin. *The Age of Sultan Suleyman, the Magnificent*. Washington, DC: National Gallery of Art, 1987.

Delibas, Selma. "Embroidery." In *Arts of Weaving: Traditional Turkish Arts*, edited by Nazan Ölçen, 47–59. Ankara: Turkish Republic, Ministry of Culture and Tourism, General Directorate of Fine Arts, 1987.

Denny, Walter. "Textiles." In *Tulips, Arabesque and Turbans: Decorative Arts from the Ottoman Empire*, edited by Yanni Petsopoulos, 115–159. New York: Abbeville Press, 1982.

Faroqhi, Suraiya. *Subjects of the Sultan: Culture and Daily Life in the Ottoman Empire*. London: I. B. Tauris, 2000.

Faroqhi, Suraiya. *Ottoman Costumes: From Textile to Identity*. Istanbul: Eren, 2004.

Goodwin, Godfrey. *The Private World of Ottoman Women*. London: Saqi Books, 1997.

Helmecke, Gisela. "Embroideries." In *A Wealth of Silk and Velvet, Ottoman Fabrics and Embroideries*, edited by Christian Erber, 25–76. Bremen: Edition Temmen, 1995.

Inalcik, Halil. *The Ottoman Empire: The Classical Age 1300–1600*. Translated by Norman Itzkowitz and Colin Imber. London: Weidenfeld and Nicolson, 1975.

Johnstone, Pauline. *Turkish Embroidery*. London: Victoria and Albert Museum, 1985.

Krody, Sumru Belger. *Flowers of Silk and Gold: Four Centuries of Ottoman Embroidery*. Washington, DC: Textile Museum, 2000.

Micklewright, Nancy. "Late-Nineteenth-Century Ottoman Wedding Costumes as Indicators of Social Change." In *Muqarnas*, edited by Oleg Gabar, vol. 6, 162–173. Leiden: Brill, 1989.

Scarce, Jennifer. *Women's Costume of the Near and Middle East*. London: Unwin Hyman, 1987.

Scarce, Jennifer. *Domestic Culture in the Middle East: An Exploration of the Household Interior*. Edinburgh: National Museum of Scotland, 1996.

Taylor, Roderick R. *Ottoman Embroidery*. Yeovil and Ankara: Marston House, Marston Magna and the Ministry of Culture of the Republic of Turkey, 1993.

Ther, Ulla. *Floral Messages: From Ottoman Court Embroideries to Anatolian Trousseau Chests*. Translated by Michaela Nierhaus. Bremen: Edition Temmen, 1995.

Thomas, Mary. *Mary Thomas's Dictionary of Embroidery Stitches*. London: Hodder & Stoughton, 1954.

Wearden, Jennifer, and Marianne Ellis. *Ottoman Embroidery (Victoria & Albert Museum Studies)*. London: Victoria & Albert Museum, 2001.

Zilfi, Madeline, ed. *Women in the Ottoman Empire: Middle Eastern Women in the Early Modern Era*. Leiden: Brill, 1997.

Sumru Belger Krody

See also Historical Survey of Textiles and Dress in Turkey; Ottoman Dress; The Kaftan and Its Origins; Royal Dress Preserved at the Topkapi Museum; Snapshot: Turkish Costume Albums; Regional Dress in Anatolia.

Ottoman Dress

The Ottomans were a world power in the Mediterranean for several centuries, with their empire extending at its height from Tabriz in the east around the Arabian Peninsula, the Levant, Egypt, and across North Africa to Algiers. In Europe, they controlled much of Hungary, the Balkans, and Greece. Although it took nearly two hundred years to assemble this vast empire, their role as a world power was assured with their conquest of Constantinople in 1453. From that point until the defeat of the Ottomans (who sided with the Germans) in World War I in 1918, they were important players in the military, economic, and cultural arenas of the Mediterranean and the eastern Islamic world. Furthermore, their strategic location and control of important trade routes meant that matters within the empire were of great interest to European powers, even when the Ottoman military threat had waned.

From the point of view of dress history, there are a few characteristics of the Ottoman Empire that are important to note. First, the Ottoman court developed, over time, an extensive bureaucracy to administer its far-flung empire. High-ranking government officials and princes with their courts were sent to govern the Ottoman provinces, along with their families, providing a link for those living in remote areas with the news and customs of Istanbul. Second, the empire encompassed a disparate range of ethnic and religious groups, both in newly conquered areas and in the empire's Anatolian heartland. The Ottomans created taxation and legal structures to govern this diverse populace, which led to considerable autonomy for some of these communal groups. Each of these specific communities had its own traditions of dress, which added to the richness of Ottoman garments. Finally, the Ottoman Empire was always characterized by an awareness of and engagement with the cultures around it. This took different forms at specific periods of history, but there was continual military or diplomatic contact with important powers both to the east and to the west of its borders. Ottoman control of the eastern Mediterranean for much of its history, its location on the Silk Road, and the empire's large population meant that international and interregional trade was always a major component of the Ottoman economy, which obviously played an important role in dress history.

SOURCES FOR THE STUDY OF OTTOMAN DRESS

Although the garments of the Ottoman sultans were carefully preserved and remain in the collection of the Topkapi Palace Museum, relatively few examples of Ottoman dress have otherwise survived, especially from the earlier centuries of the empire. It is thus impossible to construct a history of Ottoman dress on the basis of surviving garments alone, but even if that could be done, the garments themselves do not provide all of the information necessary. Garments cannot explain, for example, who wore them, how they were acquired, on what occasions they were worn, or who made them. This sort of information must be found in sources external to the clothes, and since so few garments survive, these sources must also be relied on to provide information about clothing styles.

The Ottomans were inveterate record keepers, and their empire always attracted the close attention of numerous observers who documented what they saw in a variety of formats. Dress historians may consult a variety of materials: archival documents; illustrated manuscripts and paintings produced by Ottoman artists and by Europeans; local press directed at both Ottoman readers and resident foreigners; photographs; and the many books about Turkish customs and society written by visitors to the Ottoman Empire. Each of these kinds of sources yields a different sort of data, and each has specific limitations of accuracy and reliability; but used carefully, they yield a core of reliable information concerning Ottoman dress.

The archival documents of most interest to dress historians are generally the estate inventories that were assembled after an individual's death. Because clothing and textiles could comprise significant assets, these items were included in the inventories. Although these documents exist in many different areas of the empire and stem from different periods, their value is unfortunately limited by the fact that references to dress and textiles are often brief and without explanation, so it is difficult to know exactly what kinds of garments or textiles are being listed. Official court registers containing the edicts of the sultans also provide important information since they record laws regulating the dress of different social groups as well as responses to complaints concerning the materials and production of clothing. Finally, there are the rare but invaluable documents specifically related to an aspect of dress that have survived—for example, a late-nineteenth-century tailor's order book in the collection of the Sadberk Hanım Museum in Büyükdere.

Illustrated manuscripts fall into two general groups: those produced by Ottoman artists working within the court workshop system and those produced by independent, often European, artists for private patrons, both foreign and Ottoman. Illustrated Ottoman manuscripts provide detailed representations of dress and court customs over several centuries. Depictions of festivals and specific events such as guild parades are valuable evidence for the dress of numerous groups in Ottoman society. Unfortunately, few women are depicted in these paintings. The so-called costume manuscripts, which are handbooks of the types of people to be seen in the Ottoman context identified on the basis of their dress, are much more useful in terms of women's dress, and they also provide information about the dress of men. These manuscripts, dating from the sixteenth through the early nineteenth centuries, typically present a single figure on each page with a minimum of background and a short identifying caption. Little information is available concerning the artists responsible for the paintings or the patrons who purchased their work, but they are nonetheless important sources for Ottoman dress history. In the second half of the nineteenth century, Ottoman artists began experimenting with European-style easel paintings and subject matter, including portraiture. Their portraits provide crucial information concerning dress at a transitional period of Ottoman dress history.

In the late Ottoman period, there was an active press in Istanbul, with specific publications targeted at different groups within the city. During much of the nineteenth century, at least four newspapers were published in English and French, in addition to the Ottoman press. These provided a variety of information to readers: accounts of social events and the official functions of the diplomatic community, a regular column on fashion in one newspaper, and commercial advertisements offering the latest in ready-made clothing and fabric imported from Europe, as well as political news. These newspapers are crucial for the purpose of dress history because they describe the social context in which clothing operated and give details about the mechanics of clothing production. In the latter part of the nineteenth century, a number of women's periodicals began to be published in Ottoman Turkey; these provide evidence of a lively debate among readers concerning issues related to fashion and women's consumption of domestic and foreign goods.

Photographs are another important source of information concerning dress in the late Ottoman period. The first photographers reached Istanbul shortly after the invention of photography in 1839, opening studios that catered to both a foreign and domestic clientele. With the marketing of Kodak snapshot cameras in the 1880s and the incorporation of photography into the curriculum of the Imperial School of Engineers, Ottomans began taking their own pictures. While the majority of photographs from an Ottoman context that have been published were made for a tourist audience and are thus of limited value for dress history, some surviving images record Ottomans in their own homes or having their portraits taken in a commercial studio. These photographs are crucial for documenting what people were wearing and how dress was changing in the last decades of the Ottoman Empire. The thousands of photographs taken at the behest of the Ottoman government and organized into various albums are also of great interest for understanding aspects of Ottoman dress. Of particular importance for the study of Ottoman dress is the photograph album *Elbise-i 'Osmaniyye: Les costumes populaires de la Turquie* (Osmaniyye: Regional dress of the Turks), produced by the Ottoman government for the 1873 Vienna Exposition, which presents a meticulously arranged and carefully documented survey of the dress of the various ethnic and social groups of the empire.

Travel books describing the people and customs of the Ottoman Empire were popular among Europeans from the sixteenth century on and exist in great numbers. Many of these are illustrated with woodblock prints, engravings, or photographs (depending on the period) and are essential, if problematic, sources of information for dress history. Some of the most well known from the early centuries of the Ottoman Empire are *Quatre premiers livres des navigations et peregrinations orientales* (The four first books of navigation and Oriental peregrinations), by Nicolas de Nicolay, first published in Lyons in 1567 and then translated and republished several times; and the seventeenth-century

work by Jean de Thevenot, *The Travels of Monsieur de Thevenot into the Levant*. The letters of Lady Mary Wortley Montagu, the wife of a British ambassador to the Ottoman court who spent nearly two years in Istanbul, from 1716 to 1718, contain detailed descriptions of the dress worn by the Ottomans she encountered during her stay. Nineteenth-century travel accounts and other books written about the Ottoman Empire are much too numerous to mention individually; however, taken as a group, these provide a detailed and sequenced view of social customs and dress over the course of the century. Given the social and political agendas of some of the authors in this category, the information they provide must be assessed critically. As educated Ottomans began experimenting with Western forms of literature in the second half of the nineteenth century, the novels and memoirs they produced often contain crucial information concerning dress—for example, the autobiography of the Turkish composer, poet, and writer Leyla Saz Hanımefendi, which describes harem life in the last decades of the nineteenth century.

ELITE DRESS FOR MEN

It is far easier to document the clothing of the elite and, in the case of men's clothing, that worn by members of the court than the dress of ordinary men. The clothing of the sultan and his family was carefully saved, and particularly important garments belonging to the wealthy were passed down from one generation to the next, but the clothing of ordinary people was used until it disintegrated. Moreover, the ceremonies of the court and the military, as well as the person of the ruler, were of great interest to a wide audience of both Ottomans and foreigners and were thus relatively well documented visually and in various written sources. Much less attention was paid to what the average man was wearing, although there are fortunately a few important exceptions to that general tendency.

The diaries and official reports of foreign ambassadors to the Ottoman court, as well as the Ottoman archives, are full of references to the elaborate ceremonies of the Ottoman court and the central role of dress in this context. Dress, including fabric type and headdress style, was an important indicator of position. The presentation of gifts to the sultan, as well as gifts given by him, often involved textiles and robes of honor, or *hil'at*. Ottoman miniatures, which often depict court ceremonies in great detail, provide an excellent record of the precise gradations of rank visible in the dress of court officials as well as the various ceremonies in which clothing played a role.

The clothing of the Ottoman sultan resembled that of ordinary men, but the garment's fabric and decoration were much more lavish. Moreover, the sultan had access to specific kinds of fabric and fur that were completely unavailable to other people. Men's dress was layered, beginning with a *gömlek*, or loose undershirt, and *şalvar*, or baggy trousers. Depending on the season, a short- or long-sleeved *kaftan* (tunic or robe) belted with a sash would be worn over this, with additional garments if necessary for warmth. The sultan's dress varied according to the circumstances for which he was dressing. For special occasions, the gömlek and şalvar would be covered by a loose, long-sleeved robe, on top of which would be worn a short-sleeved kaftan of a luxurious, heavy silk fabric. Finally, the sultan would wear a *kapaniçe*, or long, lavishly ornamented cloak lined with fur. The sultan's wardrobe

A Dance for the Pleasure of Sultan Ahmet III (1673–1736), gouache on paper, from the *Surname* (Book of festivals), 1720. Paintings such as these provide detailed representations of dress and court customs over a range of several centuries. Depictions of festivals and specific events such as guild parades are valuable evidence for the dress of numerous groups within Ottoman society. Getty Images.

also included a range of other kinds of garments, variations of the kaftan that were distinguished by their cut, their length, or the kind of fabric from which they were constructed. The dress of court officials was also comprised of the şalvar and gömlek, along with a variety of kaftans, the kapaniçe, and other kinds of robes. Their dress would have served to indicate their status and, in some cases, their specific position at the court, but there were also opportunities for the expression of individual preferences in the selection of fabric type, color combination, and other aspects of the outfits of Ottoman officials.

Many occupational groups in Ottoman society were identified by their dress. First among these was perhaps the Ottoman military, for whom the hierarchy of rank and power was as clearly indicated by garb and headdress as it was among court officials. As the political institution most closely associated with the power of the sultan and, by extension, the entire empire, the Ottoman military was the public image of the empire at home and abroad. The distinctive headgear, for instance, of the Janissaries (an important corps of the Ottoman military, formally attached to the household of the sultan) would have been immediately recognizable to the inhabitants of Istanbul, and the colorful appearance of the Ottoman troops in battle was noted by foreign observers. The importance of Ottoman military dress as a visual symbol of the Ottoman Empire is underscored by the 1807 revolt of some auxiliary forces who rebelled when ordered by an officer to wear new Western-style uniforms. Although the

Woman with a Carnation, eighteenth-century painting by the Ottoman court artist Levni (ca. 1720–1735). The figure's dress displays the style of this period, with its soft, flowing fabric; long, loose trousers; and combination of colors and fabric designs. Topkapi Palace Museum.

new uniforms merely provided the spark that set off the revolt, which was carefully managed by antisultan palace officials (and did eventually lead to the deposition of Sultan Selim III), the incident demonstrates the significance of military clothing traditions as symbols of identity and power.

A second important group with distinctive clothing was the religious community. The Ottoman ulema, religious scholars who served as teachers and community leaders, generally wore the same range of garments as other men (şalvar and kaftan) but made with plainer fabrics and colors. Green was typically reserved for descendants of the Prophet. In addition to the ulema, numerous Sufi orders played a significant role in many arenas of Ottoman society. Each of these had its own traditions of clothing and headgear, which were regulated according to the status of the wearer and the specific occasion. In the Mevlevi order, for example, a dervish, or member, would wear a *tenure*, or sleeveless tunic with a wide skirt, a short jacket, and a mantle or *hırka*, a long, collarless coat with long sleeves. The Mevlevi wardrobe also included the garments worn in the mystical dance or *sema*, and a distinctive headdress, the *sikke*, a conical felt cap that could be ornamented with different kinds of fabric. Belts and other accessories specific to the order were also worn. Within the Mevlevi order, distinctions of rank and status were indicated by details of the headdress and by the color of specific garments. The clothing of other Sufi orders was similar, but each order had its own traditions in terms of the shape and fabric of the hırka; the specific kinds of accessories that made up the ensemble; and especially the headdress, which was the most distinctive aspect of Sufi dress.

ELITE DRESS FOR WOMEN

Ottoman dress in the sixteenth century is described in a 1545 book, *Costumi et i modi particolari della vita de'Turchi* (Turkish social life and costumes) by Luigi Bassano, and illustrated by Nicolay's *Quatre premiers livres des navigations et peregrinations orientales*, as well as by two manuscripts in British collections. According to the illustrations, which are consistent with one another, sixteenth-century women's dress consisted of a number of layers: şalvar; a gömlek (underdress); a *yelek* (sleeveless vest or tunic); an *entari* (dress or robe); a belt of some sort, either a *kuşak* or *kemer*; and a small pillbox hat made of velvet or felt called a *takke*. Shoes were either leather or velvet slippers called *sipsip* or high wooden clogs called *nalin*. For outside, boots, a long, full coat called a *ferace*, and a two-part head covering called a *yaşmak* were worn over the other layers. (Throughout the Ottoman period, traditions of modesty based in Islamic tradition, but also observed by Jewish and many Christian women, dictated that indoor dress be completely covered by an outer garment and that the hair and some part of the face be covered when women were exposed to the sight of men to whom they were not related.)

The Turkish clothing vocabulary used by dress scholars nowadays was recorded by travelers over several centuries, and many of the same words are still in use in the early twenty-first century, a fact that presents problems for dress historians. For example, in modern Turkish, the word *entari* means an inexpensive dress of a cotton or synthetic print purchased ready-made, worn only by a certain group of women. A sixteenth-century entari was a long robe, closing down the front, with full sleeves, and was a basic garment worn by all women. In the intervening four centuries, the word *entari* was used to describe garments of many shapes and fabrics. Given the challenges involved in understanding the clothing vocabulary that is found in the range of written sources, visual evidence is crucial to understanding what a particular clothing term meant in a specific context.

In any case, the şalvar and gömlek of the sixteenth century appear relatively standard. The şalvar are straight, loose-fitting trousers, extending to the ankle but exposing the feet, and made of plain, white fabric. The gömlek is an underdress with long, full sleeves and a skirt falling to within a few inches (about five centimeters) of the ankles. In most examples, it is made of thin white cloth, decorated with gold or another color along the length of the sleeves or around the sleeve edge, and down the center or two sides of the skirt. The yelek and entari are more confusing in their variety. The yelek is basically a sleeveless and collarless tunic, buttoned at the front with a series of small buttons, sometimes decorated with rows of gold braid at the buttons. It is usually hip length but may be longer, and is worn over the underdress, although occasionally it is worn over the entari. The entari is a long garment, buttoned down the front to the hips, with full, three-quarter-length sleeves and a round, collarless neck. The front of the entari was often decorated with rows of braid, similar to the decoration of the yelek.

Neither of the two manuscripts illustrating the dress of this period is detailed enough to provide an exact idea of the cloth used for the vests and robes, but Nicolay's illustrations depict elaborate fabric, brocades of many designs and colors. Women invariably wore sashes of some kind, wound around their waist or slightly lower. These were of fabric that contrasted with the entari and were draped and knotted in a variety of ways. The headdress in the sixteenth century consisted of a takke, decorated with jewels, plumes, or flowers and with an embroidered muslin scarf wound around it to keep it in place.

The basic elements of this dress continued to be worn well into the nineteenth century, with changes appearing along the way. Until the late twentieth century, it was a common misconception that traditional dress in societies outside Europe and North America was unchanging, unaffected by economic or social developments in the society in which its wearers were living. Although the rate of change was not as dramatic as it has become since the advent of a global economy (a development that began in earnest in the nineteenth century in terms of fashion), a close examination of the details of fabric, garment construction, and accessories reveals a constant, albeit slow, change in Ottoman dress.

In the seventeenth century, according to manuscript illustrations and the traveler Thevenot, the most important changes in women's dress involved the belt and the headdress. The belt, still worn around the hips over the entari, often appears to be of metal or of stiff cloth heavily decorated with metal studs or plates. Cloth sashes are also worn, either tied in an elaborate knot or fastened with a large metal buckle. The small pillbox hat and scarf of the sixteenth century have been replaced by a *tantura*, a tall, conical hat, often of a silver-brocade fabric with a scarf of a different color wound around the base, hanging either to the side of the face or down the back.

The basic elements of eighteenth-century dress remain much the same as earlier examples, but their shape and fabric have changed. The şalvar are voluminous, falling over the feet, and made of colored or printed fabric—orange, green, gold-and-white-striped, or pink brocade, or other light colors. The gömlek continues to be worn but at some point begins to be tucked into the trousers instead of worn over them. The yelek changes over the course of the century into a long, sometimes sleeveless garment worn over the entari. Both the entari and the outer robe appear to be more graceful, perhaps because of lighter or softer material. At the beginning of the century, the sash worn over the entari is a stiff belt of decorated fabric, but, by the end of the century, the sash is often an entire shawl of wool or silk draped elaborately around the hips, although the earlier style can still be seen. The conical tantura has disappeared, replaced by a small tasseled cap, sometimes decorated with jewels, around which one or more scarves would be wound.

Information about women's dress in the eighteenth century is provided by three illustrated manuscripts and two British women who described in detail the dress they saw (and, in the case of Lady Mary Wortley Montagu, also wore). However, there are also two surviving garments from this period, one in the Victoria and Albert Museum, London, and one in the Royal Scottish Museum, Edinburgh, generally considered to be the earliest Ottoman women's dress in museum collections. The Victoria and Albert entari is of particular interest because it is held by family tradition to have belonged to Lady Montagu, who also left a careful account of a woman's outfit of around 1717. The two entaris resemble those shown in manuscript illustrations, opening all the way down the front, with a narrow stand-up collar and long sleeves that could either be worn closed at the wrist or allowed to fall open. In both cases, the garments are decorated with trim, crocheted in a kind of floral design on one and gilt braid on the other. The trim is applied to the two edges of the center opening, the hem, and the sleeves. Each is made of a soft, pink-striped fabric—cotton and silk brocade in one case, French silk in the other. The outfits illustrated in the manuscripts appear to be made of a similar fabric—soft, light-colored cloth with small brocaded floral designs, very different from the stiff, brightly colored, large-patterned fabric of previous centuries.

During the first part of the nineteenth century, women's fashions continued to change, becoming softer and exaggerated in form. Şalvar are even wider; the fabric of the gömlek is even finer and more transparent; and the entari is longer, often trailing on the floor. When walking is necessary, the entari is tucked into the shawl that is wound around the hips. The sleeves of the entari extend below the fingertips and are always worn open from the elbow. A second robe, sometimes fur-trimmed, or a short, waist-length jacket with long, close-fitting sleeves called the cepken is worn on top of the entari. The fabrics used for these garments are delicate, light-colored silks and cottons with stripes or floral prints, decorated with ribbons, sequins, gold braid, and trim crocheted of silk. A rainbow of colors is commonly combined in a single ensemble.

The dress of Ottoman women in the nineteenth century is described in detail by numerous travelers and authors, appears in photographs and paintings, and has survived in museum collections in relatively good numbers. Some of the most important museum collections are those in the Topkapi Palace Museum and Sadberk Hanım Museum in Istanbul and the Victoria and Albert Museum. Of the numerous writers describing dress in the Ottoman context, the work of Charles White and Julia Pardoe in the early part of the century is particularly valuable, while Emine Fuat Tugay, Lucy Garnett, and Leyla Saz Hanımefendi are important for the last decades of the century.

CHANGES IN TRADITIONAL DRESS

The books, images, and garments themselves that remain as documents of the dress of the nineteenth century all demonstrate the dramatic changes that took place during that time in the dress of elite women and men in the Ottoman Empire. Although the exact circumstances of the transformation were quite different for men's and women's dress, by the end of the nineteenth century, many of the people living in Istanbul and other urban areas had adopted a version of European dress. Even among those who continued to wear more traditional garments, aspects of their dress such as the fabric used, changes in construction details, or specific accessories revealed the impact of increased exposure to European dress and manufactured goods.

Men in the military and of the court were the public face of the Ottoman Empire, as were, to a lesser extent, all of the men of the empire, regardless of their occupation. The issue of modernizing Ottoman military uniforms, which had set off the revolt leading to the deposition of the Ottoman sultan in 1807, was revisited by Sultan Mahmud II, who ruled from 1808 to 1839. Mahmud II set in motion the first steps of wide-ranging changes in the structure of the Ottoman government and the military. Following a Janissary revolt in 1826, the Janissaries were destroyed, the army

An Ottoman family, nineteenth century. The family is modestly dressed: The young boy wears trousers, a vest, a shirt, and a fez, and the woman wears her street attire. The girls wear a hybrid form of European dress and Ottoman *entari*, demonstrating the process of transition involved in the Ottoman population's adoption of European-style dress. Courtesy of Nancy Micklewright.

was completely reorganized, and foreign advisors were called in to assist with training. Military uniforms were redesigned along European models, and, in 1829, the dress of all Ottoman men was regulated by Mahmud II's proclamation ordering the şalvar, kaftan, and turban to be replaced by a European-style frock coat, trousers, and fez (a conical, flat-topped hat made of wool felt). Only members of the religious community were exempt from the new requirement. As with most examples of dress change, this dramatic shift did not take place overnight, despite the weight of the sultan's decree. Although men of the military and those who worked in the government bureaucracy were obliged to adopt the new clothing, men working in other places—and especially those living outside the main cities—continued to wear their old clothing for some time. However, the 1829 decree began a process of change in men's dress that was accelerated by other economic and social factors in the nineteenth-century Ottoman Empire.

While there had always been contact—whether military, diplomatic, economic, or cultural—between the Ottoman Empire and Europe, the extent of contact increased substantially in the nineteenth century. On the one hand, the Ottomans were interested in knowing more about European practices in a variety of arenas in order to make changes in their own government, military, education, and banking systems, to name a few examples. On the other hand, with the advent of a regular steamship service to Istanbul in the 1830s, more Europeans traveled to Istanbul and other parts of the Ottoman Empire. An expanded diplomatic presence, numerous military advisors, and increased numbers of travelers and European residents in the empire meant that the goods and services the Europeans required also began to be available, at least in Istanbul. Ottomans thus also had access to these same goods and services, some of which (tailors, milliners, and boot makers; fabrics, parasols, and other goods) were directly related to the issue of dress.

The changes in women's dress that took place over the course of the nineteenth century unfolded very differently from the changes in men's dress. In the Ottoman context, the concepts of public and private operated differently for men and women, and these differences affected how dress was regulated by the government. Men's dress, which was not covered in public, was open to government scrutiny and thus regulation. Women's dress on the street was covered by their overcoats and veils, so government regulation was confined to issues concerning these garments. There was no edict from the sultan regulating what women wore at home and thus no one moment at which an abrupt change can be pinpointed. Instead, there was a gradual change, a series of small adaptations or alterations that led eventually to a very different mode of dressing for women.

In the first two decades of the nineteenth century, European fabrics continued to be very popular for women's clothing, as they had been in the late eighteenth century. The basic components of women's dress remained the same, but the fashion silhouette changed, with an increase in the volume of fabric used and consequently in the length and drape of the garments. European accessories also began to be popular. Gloves, stockings, and parasols, among other things, were worn with traditional dress. Changes in the actual garments took place gradually, as first details of cut or decoration were modified to look more European and then garments of the new style replaced old ones. For example, the sleeves of the entari might be modified by the addition of cuffs,

or the sides of a robe altered to suggest a waistline. The shift from şalvar and entari to European dress did not take place until midcentury, and that too was a gradual change. At first, dresses were worn on certain occasions by some women, and, as time passed, more and more women wore dresses; but even at the end of the century, both styles of dress continued to be in use. The rate of dress change varied among different ethnic groups and according to the wearer's level of wealth. In each ethnic group, the wealthy were the fashion trendsetters and the first to adopt the new styles.

ETHNIC IDENTITY AND DRESS IN OTTOMAN TOWNS AND VILLAGES

The Ottoman Empire was socially, ethnically, and religiously complex. Dress was an important means of indicating membership in a particular group, and the regulation of dress was a tool by which the government attempted to achieve some measure of political, economic, and social control over its diverse population. Choices of dress indicated ethnic identity (Greek, Armenian, European, Turkish, Albanian, to name a few) as well as gender, class, occupation, and religion (Jewish, Muslim, Christian). Sumptuary laws regulated a wide variety of dress-related matters, from the use of specific furs and luxury fabrics to the color of shoe that could be worn by members of specific religious communities. At various times, sumptuary laws were intended to distinguish various religious groups and protect Muslims' access to certain goods, for example, by limiting the use of the color green to Muslims or limiting the size of turbans that could be worn by non-Muslims. In the nineteenth century, sumptuary regulations became a tool used by the state for different political purposes, as when Mahmud II sought to establish among his subjects an Ottoman identity that superseded ethnic or religious identity by requiring all men to wear the same kind of headdress, the fez.

Documenting the history of Ottoman dress in towns and villages is a challenging project. Nearly all of the surviving examples of actual garments date from the mid-nineteenth century or later, and the vast majority of examples are from the twentieth century. There are many collections of what is often called ethnographic dress or folk dress in provincial museums, private collections, and major museums, but accompanying information concerning provenance, date, original wearer, and use is often sparse. However, it is important to note that traditional dress from some areas of the Ottoman Empire, particularly the regions that are part of Greece, Hungary, and the Balkans in the early twenty-first century, is in general much better studied than the traditional dress of Anatolia.

The written and visual records concerning dress in towns and villages are also problematic. While nearly everyone who visited the region went to Istanbul, the same cannot be said for the town of Malatya, for example. The written record is incomplete and less consistent. Similar problems exist with the photographic record. Thus, dress historians working in this area must rely much more on ethnographic research for documentation of the garments themselves as well as for information concerning circumstances and techniques of production, use, and meaning.

Notwithstanding the difficulties involved in studying them, the dress traditions of the towns and villages of the Ottoman

Empire are rich and diverse. Although local dress was influenced to some extent by the dress worn by the Ottoman elite from Istanbul, via the elaborately organized Ottoman state bureaucracy that sent officials and their families to all corners of the empire, there were also very strong local customs concerning dress, with distinctive regional characteristics visible in nearly every aspect of what men and women wore. Moreover, even within a specific region, dress served to identify the wearer as a member of a specific ethnic or religious group.

In general, men's and women's dress in the towns and villages of Anatolia was composed of elements similar to what was worn by the elite in the capital. That is, both men and women generally wore a series of loose-fitting garments of various fabrics, layered on the body, and often held in place with a belt or sash. Differences from the dress of the urban elite are seen in the textiles used to make individual garments, which were often locally produced and regionally specific; in the decoration of particular pieces of the dress, especially for women; and in the way individual garments were put together to form a complete outfit. The headdress was also regionally distinctive and, along with other elements of dress, often served to indicate the wearer's marital status. This brief description does not do justice to the level of skill and creativity that went into the production of nearly every aspect of even everyday dress: the weaving, knitting, and embroidered decoration of socks, vests, trousers, aprons, sashes, robes, dresses, jackets, and innumerable varieties of headdress.

References and Further Reading

Atasoy, Nurhan. "Dervish Dress and Ritual: The Mevlevi Tradition." In *The Dervish Lodge: Architecture, Art, and Sufism in Ottoman Turkey*, edited by Raymond Lifchez, 253–268. Berkeley: University of California Press, 1992.

Çizgen, Engin. *Photographer/Fotoğrafcı Ali Sami, 1866–1936*. Istanbul: Haşet Kitabevi A.Ş., 1989.

Ersoy, Ahmet. "A Sartorial Tribute to Late Tanzimat Ottomanism: The Elbise-i ʿOsmaniyye Album." *Muqarnas* 20 (2003): 187–207.

Ertuğ, Ahmet. *Silks for the Sultans: Ottoman Imperial Garments from the Topkapı Palace*. Istanbul: Ertuğ and Kocabıyık, 1996.

Faroqhi, Suraiya, and Christopher K. Neumann, eds. *Ottoman Costumes: From Textile to Identity*. Istanbul: EREN, 2004.

Frierson, Elizabeth. "'Cheap and Easy': The Creation of Consumer Culture in Late-Ottoman Society." In *Consumption Studies and the History of the Ottoman Empire, 1550–1922; An Introduction*, edited by Donald Quataert, 243–260. Albany: State University of New York Press, 2000.

Garnett, Lucy. *The Women of Turkey and Their Folk-Lore*. London: David Nutt, 1891.

Hanımefendi, Leyla Saz. *The Imperial Harem of the Sultans; Daily Life at the Çırağan Palace during the 19th Century; Memoirs of Leyla (Saz) Hanımefendi*. Istanbul: Peva Publications, 1994.

Historical Costumes of Turkish Women. Istanbul: Middle East Video Corp. 1986.

Jirousek, Charlotte. "The Transition to Mass Fashion System Dress." In *Consumption Studies and the History of the Ottoman Empire, 1550–1922; An Introduction*, edited by Donald Quataert, 201–242. Albany: State University of New York Press, 2000.

Micklewright, Nancy. "Women's Dress in Nineteenth-Century Istanbul: Mirror of a Changing Society." Ph.D. dissertation, Philadelphia, University of Pennsylvania, 1986.

Micklewright, Nancy. "Tracing the Transformation in Women's Dress in Nineteenth-Century Istanbul." *Dress, The Annual Journal of the Costume Society of America* 13 (1987): 33–42.

Micklewright, Nancy. "Public and Private for Ottoman Women of the Nineteenth Century." In *Women, Patronage and Self-Representation in Islamic Societies*, edited by D. Fairchild Ruggles, 155–176. Albany: State University of New York Press, 2000.

Montagu, Lady Mary Wortley. *Letters from the Levant during the Embassy to Constantinople, 1716–1718*. New York: Arno Press, 1971. (Originally published in 1838.)

Nicolay, Nicolas de. *Quatre premiers livres des navigations et pérégrinations orientales*. [The navigations, peregrinations, and voyages made into Turkey by Nicholas Nicholay Daulphinois.] Translated from French by T. Washington. London: Thomas Dawson, 1585.

Pardoe, Julia. *The City of the Sultan and Domestic Manners of the Turks in 1836*. Philadelphia: Carey, Lea and Blanchard, 1837.

Quataert, Donald. "Clothing Laws, State, and Society in the Ottoman Empire, 1720–1829." *International Journal of Middle East Studies* 29 (1997): 403–425.

Scarce, Jennifer. *Women's Costume of the Near and Middle East*. London: Unwin Hyman, 1987.

Tezcan, Hulya. *19.yy Sonuna Ait Bir Terzi Defteri/A Late 19th Century Tailor's Order Book*. Istanbul: Sadberk Hanım Museum, 1992.

Thevenor, Jean de. *The Travels of Monsieur de Thevenot into the Levant*. London: H. Clark, 1687.

Tugay, Emine Fuat. *Three Centuries: Family Chronicles of Turkey and Egypt*. London: Oxford University Press, 1963.

White, Charles. *Three Years in Constantinople; or, Domestic Manners of the Turks in 1844*. London: Henry Colburn, 1845.

Nancy Micklewright

See also Historical Survey of Textiles and Dress in Turkey; The Kaftan and Its Origins; Royal Dress Preserved at the Topkapi Museum; Snapshot: Turkish Costume Albums; Regional Dress in Anatolia.

The Kaftan and Its Origins

The term *kaftan* (also spelled *caftan*) usually refers to a long, unfitted coat of Turkic, Persian, or Central Asian origin. It can also refer to the outermost layer of a series of coats and jackets, worn by either men or women. The word *kaftan* came into the English language in the late sixteenth century, when it was introduced as the Turkish term used to describe the long, formal coats worn by members of the Ottoman court. The word is also found in various forms in Turkish, Persian, Russian, and East European languages, as well as many Central Asian languages.

The coats differ somewhat in form in different regions, as does the local terminology used to describe the garments—for example, different terms indicated the shape of the garment, the class or ethnicity of the wearer, or its function. Some of the terms in the Turkish language include *dolman* (a long-sleeved outer coat worn by both men or women that may be belted shut or worn draped over the shoulders), *entari* (a long, unfitted coat typically made of less valuable materials), *ferace* (a loosely fitted outerwear coat, worn in different versions by men and women), and *hırka* (a loosely fitted coat of variable length worn by both men and women). *Chapan* (a man's or woman's long quilted coat), *chyrpy* (a woman's coat with long false sleeves), and *khalat* (a man's loose outer coat of thin silk or cotton) are some of the Turkmen or Uzbek terms. In general, these terms might be applied to garments worn by either men or women, although there are also gender-specific forms, particularly beginning in the eighteenth century. In English, the word *kaftan* is often, misleadingly, used to describe this entire class of garments.

EARLY HISTORY

Kaftan is the best-known term for the many front-opening coats that originated with Central Asian horse-riding nomads. These nomads were both Uro-Altaic and Indo-European in origin and were the ancestors of modern Turks, Persians, Mongols, and other Central Asians. Coats were worn by horse riders, in contrast to the tunics or wrapped garments typically worn by settled farmers. Seamed garments with a front opening could be more readily donned and doffed when on horseback. The coats were worn in layers over loose trousers that protected the legs from chafing. This basic system was worn by both men and women, with differences in embellishment, accessories, and sometimes cut and materials to distinguish gender and ethnic origins. Garments that could be layered were also needed in a climate that could undergo extreme changes of temperature during the course of a day.

The earliest examples of the wearing of kaftanlike coats are to be found in graves in the region of the Taklimakan Desert, in what is northwestern China in the early twenty-first century. This region was home to early nomadic herdsmen. Among the oldest physical examples are the coats found in burials dating to 1000 B.C.E. The coats found were quite heavy and woven of wool. The body of the garment was constructed from two lengths of cloth with straight side seams. There was a center front opening and long, tapered sleeves. One of the burials, identified as "Cherchen Man," was found wearing a shorter woolen front-opening garment identified as a shirt, as well as loose trousers that resemble those seen in Central Asian, Persian, and Turkish dress in the early to mid-twentieth century. The coat (or coats) would have been layered over these garments. These people were horse-riding nomads, and so, in this variable and frequently cold climate, this ensemble had the advantage of staying in place and protecting the body, while the coats could be easily taken off and put on as needed while on horseback.

Images of coat-wearing nomads were also depicted at the ancient city of Persepolis, which was built by Cyrus the Great in 550 B.C.E. and completed during the reigns of Darius and Xerxes I. The subjects of the Persian Empire were shown in procession on great friezes on the Gate of Victory and the stairways of the Apadana Palace. The friezes depict men wearing both short and long coats over loose-fitting trousers. Some figures wear the long coat draped over their shoulders, in the manner commonly seen in Ottoman and Central Asian usage of kaftans. Others, bearing gifts in procession, offer coats as gifts to the king, apparently an early version of the tradition of presenting coats of honor that would be practiced across Asia into the twenty-first century.

The kaftan came to western Asia with the waves of nomadic migrations and invasions from an early date. The Turkic invasions reached the eastern Mediterranean in the tenth century C.E., with the establishment of the Seljuk Empire. This empire stretched from what is, in the twenty-first century, western Afghanistan and northeastern Iran to Asia Minor (in the twenty-first century, Anatolia in Turkey). In the thirteenth century, the Seljuk Empire was broken up by the Mongol invasions; however, by the fourteenth century, Turkish emirates had reconquered most of the previous Seljuk emirates and expanded into the remaining Byzantine lands. One clan in particular established itself in northwestern Asia Minor under the leadership of the house of Osman (the Ottomans). By the end of the fourteenth century, the Byzantine Empire was reduced to a patch of land surrounding the city of Constantinople. The Ottoman Turks, who essentially surrounded them and even married into the Byzantine royal family, influenced late Byzantine dress in a number of ways. In particular, the Turkish kaftan became part of Byzantine court dress under the name *scaramagnon*. By the fifteenth century, the kaftan would also become part of fashionable dress in Italy, the main European trading partner with Constantinople and other eastern Mediterranean ports now in Turkish hands. After the fall of Constantinople in 1453, all trade access to the luxuries of the East was obtained only through ports controlled by the Ottoman Turks. The kaftan was by this time best known to the West as the luxurious outermost garment worn by Ottoman elites.

Elderly Sart or Tajik man wearing a simple version of the kaftan, Samarkand, Uzbekistan, between 1905 and 1915. Although the beautiful silk kaftans of the Ottoman court or the Turkmen ikat weavers are the best known, the origins of the kaftan are exemplified here in a simpler woolen garment. The kaftan was practical for horse-riding cultures in a variable climate, since the coat, unlike a tunic, could be easily put on or removed while in the saddle. Photograph by Sergei Mikhailovich Prokudin-Gorskii. Library of Congress, Prints & Photographs Division, Prokudin-Gorskii Collection, LC-DIG-prokc-21848.

THE FORM AND MATERIALS OF THE KAFTAN

The cut and fit of the kaftan varies considerably from one place to another. Garments worn by a wide variety of ethnicities and variations in status have been described with this term; therefore, form and materials can vary greatly. However, the Ottoman court kaftan is usually being referred to when this term is used by English speakers.

The design of the classic Ottoman kaftan is related to the loom width, with narrow panels of cloth seamed in the center back, while the garment is open down the center front. Typically, long triangular panels are inserted below the waist in the side seams and along the front seams to add width in the lower part of the garment. The materials of the imperial kaftans were the finest silks, velvets, and cloth of gold. Buttons and loops typically close

the kaftan at the center front to the waist. Sleeve styles vary; they may be long and narrow, short and wide, or completely absent. Long, narrow sleeves would extend beyond the wrist, but they are designed to be worn pushed back, so that the fabric gathers in pleats on the lower arm. Such sleeves may be detachable, with buttons and loops as attachments. Depending on whether the kaftan will be worn as an outer or inner layer, the sleeves may be worn, removed, or partially detached and allowed to hang to the back.

Other garments designated as kaftans have short, wide sleeves. These kaftans would always be worn as an outer layer, so that the long sleeves of the underlayer(s) could be seen. Kaftans as worn in Persia and farther east in Central Asia might conform to this general description. One common difference is that, east of Turkey, coats were more likely to be constructed with overlapping front panels that wrapped from right to left to close with buttons and loops on the left side. A wide, flat neckband frequently finished the neckline. This asymmetrical closure is increasingly common as one travels eastward. However, some Ottoman portraits also show underlayer coats that are constructed in the Persian style. Similar asymmetrical coats are also seen in Mughal India.

In most of these regions, kaftans may vary greatly in terms of closeness of fit. Some fit quite snugly to the upper torso but are much fuller below the waist. The variations in fullness are achieved through various alterations in cut.

Because Islam (officially) forbids men to wear silk against the skin, there is usually a lining of a different material such as cotton, linen, mohair, or wool that acts as a barrier between the skin and the silk outer layer of such a coat. In the most sumptuous coats, the lining may be fur.

USE OF THE KAFTAN

In addition to the functional provision of warmth, layered coats came to signify formality of dress in Central and Southwest Asian dress. The kaftan, as the outermost layer, was the most formal garment in this traditional system of dress. This outer layer was usually worn open and loose to show the ensemble beneath. A sash might be worn either over the layer beneath or around the outer kaftan layer. The edges of outer coats might be tucked up into the sash. They were caught up not only for convenience during riding or other physical activity but also to display the sumptuous variety of colors and materials in the underlayers of clothing. For this reason, the sleeves varied in width and length, with tighter, long-sleeved coats worn under coats with wider and shorter sleeves. Alternatively, the long sleeves might be attached with buttons that could be released partially, so that the sleeve could be left hanging down in back with the arm emerging through the armhole. The hanging sleeve has been a feature of the kaftan that has been copied in Western fashion since the Crusades.

Some outermost coats (kaftan, entari, dolman) were commonly worn simply cast over the shoulders, with the sleeves left to hang down. Even in the twentieth century, certain Turkish and Central Asian coats could still be seen worn this way. Some have sleeves too long and narrow to actually wear that have been sewn shut and attached to one another in back. Some Turkmen women still wear such coats as veils pulled over their heads. The fit of the "neckline" and shoulders causes the garment to drape closely around the face. Some women from Turkmen villages in northwestern Turkey still wear simple versions of such coats, usually made of black cotton with sleeves atrophied into narrow strips.

Diplomatic missions to the Ottoman court brought back actual examples of Ottoman kaftans to Europe. Royal exchanges of gifts usually included fine clothing. More important, it was traditional for the Ottoman court to present formal kaftans as part of the reception of visiting dignitaries. An account of such a presentation is found in the memoirs of Ogier Ghiselin de Busbecq, who served as Austrian envoy to the court of Suleiman the Magnificent from 1554 to 1562. At his final audience with Suleiman, de Busbecq was greeted with great ceremony, despite the fact that his mission to obtain a peace treaty had failed:

Two ample embroidered robes reaching to my ankles were thrown about me, which were as much as I could carry.

My attendants were also presented with silken robes of various colours and, clad in these, accompanied me. I thus proceeded in a stately procession, as though I were going to play the part of Agamemnon or some similar hero in a tragedy, and bade farewell to the Sultan after receiving his despatch wrapped up in cloth of gold.

A foreign envoy to the Ottoman sultan would first be received by high officials of the court, who would entertain the envoy and his retinue with at least the offer of Turkish coffee and usually also a meal, unless the envoy was in disfavor or viewed as of slight importance. The officials would then present all of the guests with robes of honor known as *hil'at* in Turkish (*khil'a* in Arabic and *khilat* in Persian). These were kaftans of fine materials, with the quality of the materials carefully calibrated to reflect the esteem with which the visitor was received. All of the attending members of the court would be dressed in even greater splendor to impress the visitors with the grandeur and power of the Ottoman state. When the ambassador was at last introduced into the presence of the sultan, he and his retinue would all be wearing the hil'at robes they had received. The sultan would be wearing even more magnificent garments.

The hierarchy of quality in hil'at robes indicated the degree of favor with which the visitor was received, as did the corresponding hierarchy of materials and embellishment in the dress of the sultan and decoration of his reception chamber. For ambassadors deemed less important or viewed unfavorably, the hil'at kaftans

Kaftan worn by an Ottoman prince, thought to have come from the grave of one of the younger sons of Sultan Murad III, Turkey, ca. 1600. The designs on this handwoven kaftan made of silk and metal-wrapped thread include a meandering vine set with tulips. Imperial kaftans were of the finest silks, and this example shows that young Ottoman princes were dressed in the same lavish style as the sultan and his courtiers. © Victoria and Albert Museum, London. www.vam.ac.uk

might be simple patterned silks (serenk) or velvet (kadife). The best kaftans incorporated gold thread in the patterned cloth (kemha, çatma, or seraser) and would be lined with fur, which could also vary in quality. In all instances, the degree of sumptuousness in the dress of the sultan would outshine that of his guests and his courtiers, but the imperial dress would be less elaborate when receiving less-favored visitors. Foreign ambassadors were well aware of the significance of these variations and often noted in their writings with satisfaction or concern the nature of the kaftans and ceremonial reception with which they were honored.

The practice of presenting hi'lat was also observed within the Ottoman court. The sultan would present robes of honor to his officials on ceremonial occasions and in recognition of distinctive service. Again, the quality of the kaftan given was a measure of the favor of the sultan and of the recipient's status. Since all members of the court were dependents of the sultan, it was the responsibility of the state to provide not only food and shelter but also clothing for all of his household, in accordance with their rank and responsibilities. These hil'at robes would thus become the court dress of the recipient.

From the seventeenth century on, it became common for returning European travelers to have their portrait done in the exotic dress they had acquired in distant places. A well-known example is the 1622 portrait of Robert Sherley by Anthony Van Dyk, in which he is dressed in Persian garments acquired during his mission to the shah of Persia in 1599 to 1608. He is depicted in a magnificent gold-brocade kaftan of the Persian style, which has the double-breasted overlapping front panels, evident even though it is worn over the shoulders, as hil'at kaftans usually were during the reception of the ambassador.

The symbolism of the kaftan as a robe of honor continues into the early twenty-first century, with visiting heads of state and emissaries being honored with ceremonial kaftans during visits to Central Asian countries. The president of Afghanistan, Hamid Karzai, always wears a kaftan over his shoulders as a sign of his office when making public appearances. Hil'at robes of honor are still an essential marker of the dignity of high office in some Muslim countries.

Wherever Islam has spread, the kaftan is a garment that has tended to be associated with religious dress, even where popular dress might take other forms. In West Africa, dress does not usually involve coats, but imams typically wear long, loose coats as ceremonial attire. In the modern Republic of Turkey, dress generally follows Western fashion, and Ottoman forms of dress deemed Islamic are either banned or discouraged by the secular constitution. The one legal exception is for the dress of imams, who are allowed to wear both the turban and the long, loose coat known as the kaftan.

THE KAFTAN IN OTHER ISLAMIC REGIONS

Although the Central Asian–based Turco-Persian-Mongol tradition is the primary source of the kaftan form, the kaftan is part of most Muslim dress, although the form may vary. Persian kaftans are similar to the Ottoman Turkish forms and were also worn over layers of other coats and jackets. The similarity of Persian and Turkish dress may be due to the fact that dynasties of Turkic origin ruled most of Persia from the Seljuk Turkish Empire of the tenth century through the Safavid rule that began in the sixteenth century and continued until the end of the eighteenth century. Persian coats might have a center-front closing like that

of typical Ottoman kaftans but were more likely to have an asymmetrical cross-over closure that wrapped from right to left. A neckband finished the edge of this garment. However, the terminology for these Persian coats included terms other than kaftan (qaba, jubbah).

Although the Arab vestimentary system is quite different and is based on a tunic that is pulled on over the head, a very wide square-cut coat is most typically worn as an outer garment. It has straight side seams that leave an opening at the top for the arms. The garment is so wide that it can cover the arms. The terms for this coat vary depending on the region and details such as the addition of a hood (jallâba or abâ; hooded burnus). In Western usage, these coats are also sometimes referred to as kaftans. The term kaftan is found in Arab dress nomenclature, but it generally refers to sleeved coats that may be borrowings from Turkish or Persian coats.

The kaftan spread with Islam to other parts of the world, including northern India (in the twenty-first century, Pakistan), Southeast Asia, and sub-Saharan Africa. In Asia, Islam was generally brought to new regions by Turkmen or Mongol invaders. In the thirteenth century, the Ghaznevid Turkmen crossed the Himalayas into India, bringing both Islam and their style of clothing to parts of northern India. Both the religion and the forms of dress were reinforced by the subsequent invasion of the Mongols (Mughals) in the sixteenth century. Because there were close commercial and diplomatic connections with Persia, the dress of Mughal India resembled that of Persia but with the use of the exceptionally fine silk and cotton textiles unique to India. A loose or semifitted kaftan (called angharakha, sherwani, or choga) could be worn over the more closely fitted and lightweight jamal (long coat-gown with a full, pleated skirt) and shalwar (a pair of trousers worn by men and women under other garments). Although there were many variations of cut in vernacular dress, the coats worn by members of religious orders and imams tended to remain the simple, loose coat that had been known as the kaftan.

In West Africa, the loose pullover garment commonly worn throughout the region by both men and women resembles the thob or qamis worn by the Arab traders who brought Islam to West Africa. It may be wider than the Arab prototype and often without sleeves in the tropical heat of sub-Saharan Africa. In West Africa, this garment was sometimes referred to as a dashiki if it was hip length (worn by a man), but it might be known as a kaftan if it was ankle length (worn by a woman or a man), despite the lack of a front opening. This may be an acknowledgment of the Islamic origin of the garment, since modest dress was adopted where Islam was accepted, in a culture that had not previously covered the body in this way. However, the additional layer of the Arab coat (jallâba or abâ) was not practical in the humid heat of the tropics for ordinary daily use, so loose outer coats might be worn for more formal dress.

INFLUENCE OF KAFTANS IN THE WEST

Kaftanlike garments first began to appear in Western dress among clerics during the later Crusades. Adoption of this convenient Eastern garment may have occurred first as a sign of having made the pilgrimage to the Holy Land. The association of this garment with scholars led to its widespread use as an academic robe worn in university contexts. It came into secular use in the fifteenth century in Italy, where a long, open coat was referred to as a turcha.

Turkmen girl wearing a kaftan in front of a felt yurt, Uzbekistan, between 1905 and 1915. She wears at least two layers of coats for warmth, and her fine silk ikat outer kaftan (also known as a *chapan* in this region) is characteristic of the Turkmen of Central Asia. Photograph by Sergei Mikhailovich Prokudin-Gorskii. Library of Congress, Prints & Photographs Division, Prokudin-Gorskii Collection, LC-DIG-prokc-20006.

The kaftan also became an accepted part of local dress throughout the regions of Europe where Ottoman rule or influence occurred, particularly in East Europe. The Balkans, Greece, and Hungary were under Ottoman rule for several centuries, while Poland maintained strong ties for several centuries with the Ottomans, who supported them against their common enemies, Russia and Austria. Russian use of the kaftan, in contrast, was a result of the country's expansion of authority across Central Asia and its own nomadic origins in the great steppes of Central Asia.

The kaftan was introduced to Europeans more widely via their encounters with the Ottoman Turks following their final conquest of the Byzantine Empire in 1453. Merchants, diplomats, and other travelers to Ottoman lands wrote accounts of their experiences, including illustrations of dress and descriptions of local customs. The images recorded by Nicolas de Nicolay in the sixteenth century were particularly influential. His book was widely translated, and his images copied for centuries in other works.

The wearing of long coats became widespread in Europe in the sixteenth century and thereafter, with occasionally recurring fashionable references to Ottoman coats associated with them. The kaftan is essentially the form of what came to be known in Europe as the *banyan*, or dressing gown, which became a fashionable article of informal dress beginning in the seventeenth century. The kaftan was an element in the man's suit introduced in England in the 1660s as the *vest*.

Kaftans and kaftanlike garments have continued to appear in Western fashion, notably in the later twentieth century. In the 1960s and 1970s, the civil rights movement in the United States was reflected in dress through the widespread adoption of African forms of dress—especially in the African American community but also in Western fashion at large. In particular, the West African garments known as the dashiki and the dashiki kaftan were widely adopted. The dashiki kaftan came to be known in popular usage simply as the kaftan in the Euro-American context, where the fashionable kaftan became not a coat but a long, loosely fitted dress that was pulled on over the head. Some had the embroidery framing the neckline that was characteristic of the African prototype. Most were made up in brightly colored cottons that might be African fabrics but also might be more modern patterns typical of fashion in this period.

The sources of Western fashion have broadened to include non-Western designers as well as borrowed ideas from non-Western traditional dress. For example, later in the 1980s, Rıfat Özbek, a designer of Turkish origin trained and working in London, established himself internationally. His work included elements drawn from traditional Turkish dress. This included the use of long, lightweight coats or sleeveless vests worn over trousers, dresses, or skirts. These coats were often split up the sides, as was common in Ottoman kaftans. This design was widely copied in the fashion of the late 1980s and 1990s. Thus, as globalization has moved forward, the dress of the exotic East is not merely a resource to be mined by Western designers. Rather, these cultural ideas are being explored and reintroduced to the West by designers able to reinterpret their own culture in the modern context of global fashion.

References and Further Reading

Atasoy, Nurhan, Walter B. Denny, Louise Mackie, and Hülye Tezcan. *Ipek: The Crescent and the Rose: Imperial Ottoman Silks and Velvets.* Edited by Julian Raby. London: Azimuth Editions, 2001.

Barber, Elizabeth Wayland. *The Mummies of Urumchi.* New York: W. W. Norton, 1999.

de Busbecq, Ogier Ghiselin. *The Turkish Letters of Ogier Ghiselin de Busbecq, Imperial Ambassador at Constantinople, 1554–1562.* Elzevir edition, 1633. Oxford: Clarendon Press, 1968.

Faroqhi, Suraiya, and Christoph Neumann, eds. *Ottoman Costumes: From Textile to Identity.* Istanbul: Eren, 2004.

Gervers, Veronika. *The Influence of Turkish Textiles and Costume in Eastern Europe.* History of Art Monograph 4. Toronto: Royal Ontario Museum, 1982.

Hansen, Henny H. *Mongol Costumes.* London: Thames & Hudson, 1993.

Harvey, Janet. *Traditional Textiles of Central Asia.* London: Thames & Hudson, 1997.

Koçu, Reşat Ekrem. *Giyim Kuşam Sözlüğü* [Dictionary of dress and accessories]. Istanbul: Sümerbank Kültür Yayınevi, 1969.

Scarce, Jennifer. *Women's Costume of the Near and Middle East.* Oxford: Oxford University Press, 1987.

Stillman, Yedida Kalfon. *Arab Dress from the Dawn of Islam to Modern Times: A Short History.* Edited by Norman Stillman. Leiden: Brill, 2000.

Charlotte Jirousek

See also Ottoman Dress; Royal Dress Preserved at the Topkapi Museum; Snapshot: Turkish Costume Albums; Regional Dress in Anatolia; Snapshot: The Abayeh in Oman; Snapshot: Orientalism in Western Dress and Stage Costume; volume 9, East Europe, Russia, and the Caucasus; The Influences of Ottoman Culture.

Royal Dress Preserved at the Topkapi Museum

The Topkapi Palace is home to a collection of opulent historical Ottoman apparel. There are 1,550 garments in the collection, ranging from kaftans (an outer garment) to stockings. Most of the garments were worn by men; there are few women's items. The existence of this collection arises from a palace tradition whereby when a sultan or male member of the immediate court died his clothes and related items were removed from his rooms for safekeeping and placed in protective wrappers. Some garments were also described on a paper attached to the wrapper before it was stored in the treasury; these written descriptions provide valuable additional information about the garment, such as its name, the date, who wore it, and when it was worn. This tradition continued even after the Topkapi Palace was abandoned in 1844. Thus, the collection begins with kaftans belonging to Mehmed II (the Conqueror; r. 1444–1446, 1451–1481) and is completed with garments owned by the last sultan, Mehmed V (r. 1909–1918), from the beginning of the twentieth century.

From the sixteenth century on, it became standard practice to wrap, record, and store the garments of the sultans in the treasury. The most comprehensive information on this subject is from the treasury inventory register dated 1680, which specifies that these garments were stored in forty-five wrapped bundles. In later inventories, that of 1756, for instance, mention is made of various bejeweled items, emerald-studded cloaks, removable collars embellished with emeralds and pearls, the robes of deceased sultans, jeweled quilts, cushions, and wrappers.

According to the memoirs of Bobovi (in Fisher and Fisher), who was a teacher of music at the court during the seventeenth century, the stored garments were removed under the supervision of the chief of the white eunuchs in the imperial treasury, with the assistance of the pages, cleaned, and then replaced in the treasury.

FABRICS FOR SULTANS' GARMENTS

The Ottoman sultans placed great importance on their apparel and wore robes and kaftans sewn of the most expensive and luxurious fabrics. Their taste for luxury and superior-quality materials significantly influenced the development of Ottoman textile weaving. During the classical Ottoman period (in the sixteenth century), for example, the development of weaving reached a pinnacle with the addition of gold and silver threads (or gold- or silver-plated threads) to silk textiles. During this period, the fame of Ottoman silks began to spread abroad, and orders for textiles came to the Turkish workshops of Bursa and Istanbul from several other countries.

The designs for the fabrics used for court apparel and furnishings were created at special workshops in the palace by court designers known as *hassa nakkaşları*. Because the palace workshops were unable to meet the demand, orders were also given to workshops in Bursa and Istanbul. Both those fabrics that were woven for the palace and those for the general public—particularly the silk fabrics—were subject to stringent control by the state. Details about the number of warp threads, their weight, length, twist, and dye were established and communicated to the relevant artisans via municipal codes. After the fabric was woven, it was sent to a fabric-quality inspector (*arşıncı*), who examined the cloth; if the width, length, and weaving standards were approved, the cloth was stamped and released to the market.

The splendid garments of the sultans were made of various fabrics woven in these workshops, including heavy silks such as *kemha* (brocade), *kadife* (velvet), *çatma* (brocaded velvet), *seraser* (a precious silk fabric woven with threads of gold and silver), *diba* (a silk brocade), satin, and silk lampas; lighter silks such as taffeta, *canfes* (fine taffeta), and *valâ* (a gauzelike fabric); woolens (broadcloth), mohair, and cashmere; and a variety of cotton fabrics. Cloth was also ordered from the renowned weaving centers of the West—notably those in Italy, such as Venice, Genoa, and Florence. In addition, a great deal of fabric and many garments arrived as both commercial products and diplomatic gifts from countries such as Iran, India, and China, all of which were famous for their production of silk textiles.

FASHIONS OF THE OTTOMAN SULTANS

The Turks are a society devoted to their traditions, and this extends to their dress. The trousers (*şalvar*), inner robe, and outer kaftan they wore in Central Asia came to Anatolia with the Seljuks (1037–1157 C.E.) and continued to be worn by the Ottomans. The range of dress worn by the Anatolian Seljuks is revealed through the miniatures and ceramics of the period. The most striking aspects of Seljuk dress are the V shape of the neck opening and the decoration of the seam of the outer kaftan where the arm joins the body. This seam normally has a narrow, inscribed band on it known as a *tiraz*. As time passed, the Ottomans introduced changes to this style of dress that resulted in greater variety.

Among the earliest examples in the Topkapi Palace apparel collection are two fur-lined outer garments made of dark brownish-green and red broadcloth with V necklines; slightly longer than jacket length, one has long sleeves, and the other has short sleeves.

The fur linings have been turned to the exterior at the collar, front, and sleeve openings. These garments display a strong Seljuk influence. They are registered as *kazaki* in the palace's early registers. This term also appears in the work of the Italian traveler Luigi Bassano da Zara, who visited Istanbul in 1545 and presented the first Western information about Turkish dress. It appears that kazakis continued to be used throughout the early eras of the empire, but then both the term and the garment vanished. However, other garments, known as *kaba* and *cübbe* (long gowns, with a diagonal opening down the front; often kept in place with a sash or cummerbund), were used by the Seljuks, and these continued to be worn until the end of the Ottoman Empire.

Ottoman art was strongly influenced by the Timurids, who dominated much of eastern Southwest Asia, both politically and artistically, from the fourteenth century on. The richly embellished detachable collars that were fashionable during the Timurid era were also adopted by the Ottoman court. Called a "cloud collar" in the West, this diamond-shaped collar with fluted edges is worn over the head, with one end over the breast and the other extending toward the center of the back, covering the shoulders. This type of collar can be seen in a painting by Gentile Bellini, who was invited to Istanbul by Sultan Mehmed II in the second half of the fifteenth century. Bellini's painting, called *Seated Scribe* (1479–1481), depicts a man wearing a kaftan with a detachable collar.

It can be observed from the Topkapi Palace collection that the use of such detachable collars continued in an altered form during the sixteenth century. The collar was now made of wide embroidered bands (cloud bands) that decorated the entire front opening of the kaftan to the hem, extending from the front collar and the nape of the neck to the shoulders to form a back collar.

DESIGN MOTIFS OF NAKKAŞHANE

The term *nakkaşhane* derives from the Persian word *naqsha*; both mean "a pattern or design." One of the most famous of these designs is the *çintemani* motif composed of three balls and a wavy line. It is believed that the çintemani motif was widely used during the Timurid era and that it was adopted in Turkish art after the confrontation between the Ottomans and the Timurs at the Battle of Ankara in 1402. It was widely used in Ottoman art from the fifteenth century on. This motif can be found on shoes and garments such as kaftans, şalvar, and sleeves until the end of the seventeenth century.

Early Turkish fabrics also frequently display motifs employed in Chinese art, including floral motifs such as the *hatayi* (flowers in profile) and lotus, spiraling branches with tiny leaves, the Chinese cloud motif, and the endless-knot motif. Another motif often used for the sultans' kaftans was the crown, which was adopted from Western—and particularly Italian—weaving and interpreted according to Ottoman taste. The crown motif, an appropriate royal image, was very carefully worked, although it was generally used only as a connecting motif in the primary design scheme.

Celestial motifs such as the sun, moon, stars, and clouds, which were also well suited to the imperial image, can be found in court fabrics. The inclusion of Tabriz (western Iran) into the Ottoman Empire in 1514 resulted in the arrival at the Ottoman court of various renowned Tabrizi designers. They were responsible for a new wave in Ottoman book ornamentation characterized by the

A short-sleeved silk *kemha* (brocade) kaftan associated with the Ottoman sultan Bayezid II (1481–1512). Topkapi Palace Museum.

use of stylized composite blossoms of Far Eastern origin, known as the *saz* style. The new saz forms included flowers depicted at different angles and combined with twisting and turning serrated leaves with pointed tips. Saz designs soon began to appear on a wide range of textiles. Floral designs in the saz style became a feature of palace design workshops. Such designs have the appearance of thick reeds, with flowers surrounded by large, serrated, dagger-shaped leaves. The characteristic of this style is the naturalistic representation of the flowers of paradise, such as the blossoms of the rose, tulip, carnation, hyacinth, lily, and jonquil, as well as flowering spring branches. These flowers, identified with the garden of paradise, became the central motifs embellishing court kaftans of the classical period. They can be found, for example, among the kaftans of the two princes of Sultan Suleiman the Magnificent (1520–1566; also known as Suleiman the Lawgiver).

OUTER GARMENTS OF THE OTTOMAN SULTANS

The clothing made of the gold-threaded fabrics woven with these motifs was worn by the sultans in their daily life as short (jacket-like) or long kaftans over şalvar and a shirt or inner robe. On formal occasions, a long-sleeved inner robe with sleeves that buttoned from elbow to wrist with adjustable cuffs would first be donned; over this were worn a short-sleeved kaftan meticulously crafted of heavier silk, such as brocaded silk, velvet, or brocaded velvet, and then an outer, fur-lined, long-sleeved, full-length robe with buttons made of precious jewels. This sumptuous outer garment was known as a *kapaniçe*. There is mention of bands of bejeweled frogged bands used as fastenings among a large number of kapaniçe listed in the treasury register dated 1680. There is also mention of a buttonless kapaniçe of a prince, which in general is similar in appearance to those of the sultans as portrayed in miniatures.

Among other outer garments that are well known from various sources is the *dolama*, which can be one of three types depending on its cut. The first is a short, semifitted jacket, short-sleeved, collarless, and open in front. This description was given to a *sırt dolaması* in a note affixed to a jacket sent for adjustment to the tailor of Sultan Mahmud I (1730–1754). The other two types are known as *divan* and *sipahi dolamaları*, which have longer skirts, the first of which has a longer and wider skirt and sleeves.

The *ferace* is another well-known Ottoman outer garment that was worn by both men and women. Both local and foreign sources from the sixteenth century state that the ferace was a type of robe (*cübbe*), open in front with a wide body and sleeves (the body was more fitted on the women's garments). Its skirts were floor length, its neck opening was fitted around the throat (either rounded or in a slight V shape), and there were vertical slit pockets on either side of the front opening. The summer ferace were made of lightweight silk fabric, while the winter versions were of woolens (broadcloth) or mohair and lined with fur.

Kaftan is the general term for a type of outer garment worn over şalvar (trousers), whose length might cover the hips, reach to below the knees, or extend as far as the ankles. The examples in the Topkapi Palace collection are fitted to the neck, collarless, and open from the front; they widen from the waist downward, with the addition of triangular pieces at the sides and the front opening, cut with rounded protrusions at hip level. The side seams have vents to approximately ten inches (twenty-five centimeters) above the hem. As in other Ottoman garments, the sleeves are sewn to the body of the garment without a curved armhole. The pockets are pouches sewn to openings left in the side seams.

The şalvar that were worn on the lower body consisted of a wide variety of forms: They could be narrow or wide; they could vary from knee length to ankle length; the lower legs could be wide or narrow; and the legs could be adjusted at the ankles with buttons. Another form of trousers (*çakşır*) had legs with soft leather slippers stitched to the feet. Şalvar were normally secured at the waist with waistbands that were embroidered at either end and passed through a two- to four-inch (five- to ten-centimeter) seam stitched at the top of the trousers, gathering the top to fit. After the first half of the nineteenth century, during the process of Westernization, the şalvar underwent a period of transition in which they were belted like trousers, but the crotch was left wide as in the original şalvar and narrowed toward the lower leg.

Certain preferences of the sultans are reflected in palace sources. It is believed, for instance, that Bayezid I (1389–1403) wore garments woven of gold cloth ornamented with gold buttons. In contrast, Murad II (1421–1444, 1446–1451) was very unassuming and is said to have worn only garments made of mohair. Mehmed II apparently took great interest in his dress and dressed very elegantly and tastefully. Bayezid II (1481–1512), like his ancestors, wore gowns with collars and the *mücevveze* (a plaited and pointed headgear around which a turban was wound, which appeared like a finial above it), while Sultan Selim I (1512–1520) preferred local silks. Finally, Sultan Suleiman the Magnificent wore colorful and dazzling dress in his youth but simpler garments in his maturity.

The palace also witnessed short-lived fashions from time to time. Abaza Mehmed Pasha (d. 1634), one of the viziers of Murad IV (1623–1640), liked to dress like a wrestler and had his eunuchs dressed accordingly. According to the sources, whenever a sultan was on good terms with his vizier, they would wear jackets cut of the same cloth and wrap their turbans in the same manner. One of the innovative sultans was Mahmud II (1808–1839). The movement toward Westernization of dress began during his reign, and it is noticeable that half of his garments were traditional, and the other half were in Western style.

It was not permitted, however, either at court or outside it, for anyone to dress as they chose; dress was regulated according to a dress code prepared and enforced by the palace. At the beginning of winter, for example, sable furs would be worn first by the sultan, after which the courtiers were permitted to wear them. A dress code is discussed among the events recorded in the *Şemdanizade Tarihi* (palace records that regularly report what was happening, new regulations, and so on) between 1755 and 1759. According to this account, during the months of November and December, the wearing of lynx and ermine furs, flowered kaftans and robes, and *kemerbend* (cashmere sashes) by servants and tradesmen was prohibited by imperial proclamation. In Ottoman society, Muslims wore shoes and boots made of yellow leather or dark red morocco leather made from goatskin. To differentiate Muslims from non-Muslims, the latter were required to wear blue and black shoes and to abstain from wearing fur kalpaks and any other imported goods, such as fur or Indian cashmere, which would display extravagance in their clothing.

THE HEADGEAR OF THE OTTOMAN SULTANS

The earliest types of headgear to complete the dress of the Ottoman sultans were made of wool and consisted of *horasani* (conical headpieces). A tall version of this headgear had long been part of the dress worn by Turkic women as well. During the reign of Murad I (1359–1389), a style of horasani was instituted that was generally called a *börk*. It was made from a long, tubular piece of white felt, half of which was folded back and hung to the rear. When worn by the sultan and Janissaries, it was decorated with gold embroidery worked on the front of the headpiece and known as an *üsküf*. It is said to have been worn by Murad I during the conquests in Europe in the late fourteenth century. During the same period, the sultans wore the üsküf with a turban wrapped around it when they participated in meetings of the council of state. This style of headgear became known as the *tac-ı sultani*, or sultanic headgear.

During the reign of Mehmed II, the royal headgear took a cylindrical form, around which fine muslin was wrapped. This new type of headgear was known as the *mücevveze*. Sultan Selim I wore a headpiece that was named after him, *selimi*, which was somewhat longer than the mücevveze.

Another type of headgear that is considered to be the invention of Suleiman the Magnificent is known as the *yusufi*. It is the same height as the selimi; however, its crown was wider and fluted, and it was worn when the sultans were seated on the throne. The gold-trimmed börks made of felt, however, that were known as üsküf continued to be worn in battle.

DRESS WORN ON SPECIAL OCCASIONS

Sultans had different outfits for ceremonies during religious festivals, the events following the death and funeral of a sultan, the enthronement of a new sultan, the reception of ambassadors, and going to war. Witnesses to Sultan Mehmed IV's (1648–1687) attendance at the holiday prayers at the Selimiye Mosque in Edirne in 1672 described both the public procession and the variety of garments worn. Chevalier Laurent d'Arvieux, who witnessed a similar ceremony, wrote in 1735 that the sultan wore a garment of green brocade embroidered in gold, with beech marten fur and tassels in the front, with twelve gold buttons and buttonholes that were trimmed with diamonds and emeralds, and that his şalvar were made of Chinese white silk satin with tiny checks. The participation in the ceremony of all the functionaries wearing clothing and headgear made of precious fabrics, along with the bejeweled trappings of the horses, is an indication of the theatrical nature of this event. A similarly sumptuous display occurred during the reception of ambassadors. In this case, the bejeweled horses were replaced by the decorative, bejeweled covers on the thrones in the reception rooms.

The death of a sultan was announced throughout the realm, and a great state of mourning was proclaimed. The new sultan and the men of state wore black, navy blue, or dark purple kaftans and wrapped their heads in a black covering known as a şemle. The period of mourning continued for five days, after which the mourning robes would be exchanged for garments made of brilliant fabrics in light colors woven with gilded threads. In addition, the şemle were replaced with turbans. Later, the statesmen would be presented with light-colored ceremonial robes, and the enthronement (cülus) would be celebrated.

On the field of battle, the sultans wore both armor and armored clothing, as well as a type of outer garment called a *dır-i postiyni* that was made of fine steel chain and covered with fur. The sultan would also wear talismanic shirts that were believed to provide spiritual protection if worn directly against the skin; these were inscribed in colored ink and gilt with verses from the Qur'an and suitable prayers. The surface of the shirt was divided into squares and filled with letters and numbers, thus protecting the wearer from illness, the evil eye, and malediction, in addition to any dangers from battle.

THE WESTERNIZATION OF OTTOMAN COURT GARMENTS

From the seventeenth century on, the Ottoman Empire began to fall under the influence of the West. These influences were felt as much in technology as in the arts, and they coincided with the period of the Ottoman Empire's political and economic reverses. Economic pressure influenced weaving as well, and, by the end of the century, the quality of fabric had declined. The weight of the silk used for weaving diminished, and the quantity of gold and silver in the alloy used for metallic threads was reduced. The replacement of natural dyes with synthetic dyes in the nineteenth century resulted in a further reduction in the quality of Ottoman weaving.

At the same time, changes were also taking place in the designs used. The strong ground scheme of the surface degenerated, and only individual motifs from the patterns continued to be used, not the overall design. Toward the end of the seventeenth century, the most common pattern was scattered bouquets of flowers. It would appear that, during the eighteenth century, as Western influence increased, the flowers became larger and an attempt was made to create a sense of depth through the use of shades of colors. Flowing ribbons connecting bouquets of flowers and compositions that opened to either side like the curtains of a stage appeared in Turkish art. Lace, needlework, and gilded bands began to appear as decorations on court dress. Massive buttons and buttonholes the size of walnuts and rounded collars are among the notable characteristics of the dress of this period.

The principal changes that can be observed in the realm of clothing took place during the Tanzimat period, when Westernization was formally adopted as a policy of the state. This process began when Sultan Mahmud II abolished the Janissary Corps in 1826 and replaced it with a new military organization in which

A short-sleeved atlas kaftan associated with the Ottoman sultan Suleiman II (1687–1691). It has appliquéd crescents and stylized tulips in *seraser* (silk fabric woven with gold and silver threads). Topkapi Palace Museum.

everything from equipment to uniforms was based on Western models. Westernization of military uniforms required that the sultans, like Western commanders, wore uniforms as well. Suits that looked like uniforms started to appear. These were made from black or navy blue material, and the trousers had stripes down the sides of the legs. In addition, jackets were worn whose chests, cuffs, and collars were covered with heavy yellow or gold metallic embroidery. With the replacement of the turban by the fez in the 1820s, the four-hundred-year-old outward appearance of the Ottoman sultans was finally changed forever.

WOMEN'S GARMENTS

There was no tradition in the Ottoman palace of preserving the apparel of women, and consequently there are very few items of women's clothing in the Topkapi Palace collection. Nevertheless, visual documentation, such as manuscripts illustrated with miniatures as well as written sources such as legislation and judgments, illustrated travel diaries, and engravings, provides information on this subject. According to these sources, the palace garments were sewn in the workshops of the palace tailors based on prepared samples. This is supported by a note attached to an item of women's headgear (unknown owner) stating, "Sample, twenty five to be sewn." The primary components of women's dress consisted of şalvar, a shirt or robe, an inner kaftan, and an outer kaftan. The şalvar were generally very wide and lavishly gathered at the waist and ankle, draping over the feet. However, the şalvar could be cut in a variety of ways: with legs that narrowed and were fitted at the ankles, leaving the feet exposed; tied below the knees; short or long; full or tight.

A long-sleeved cream-colored shirt of a type of raw silk crepe known as bürümcük was worn over the şalvar. This extended over the hips or all the way to the heels. The neckline and cuffs of the shirt were often embroidered with colored thread and the edges embellished with needlelace. The bürümcük used for shirts could be transparent or patterned with designs such as stripes or checks of the same thread or with tiny, colored, woven flowers. The inner kaftan worn over the shirt was cut with a U-shaped neckline and long sleeves. In some images dating from the fifteenth to sixteenth centuries, the lace-trimmed sleeves of the shirt are visible emerging freely over the wrist from the openings in a full-length sleeve; in other inner kaftans whose sleeves can be adjusted at the wrist and pulled toward the elbow, creating generous folds, the shirt sleeves are visible under the shorter sleeves of the outer kaftan. Both inner and outer kaftans were sewn with the most prevalent fabrics of the era: heavy silks such as brocaded silk, velvet, brocaded silk with metallic threads in lampas structure, and cloth of gold and silver. The outer kaftan had short sleeves and a deep U décolletage; in winter, it would be lined with fur such as sable, marten, squirrel, or ermine.

It is apparent that the old Central Asian Turkic traditions prevailed in the dress and headgear of women from an early era. Diadems, whose uninterrupted use has been traced from Central Asia to the Anatolian Seljuks, are mentioned in the Divan-ı Lugat-it Türk, a dictionary of Turkish written in the twelfth century. The kaşbastı, a type of diadem that encircles the head and is embellished with an almond-shaped stone at the center of the forehead, was worn by the women of the palace and later throughout the Ottoman Empire. Kaşbastı were worn by the women of the sultan's family in their daily life as an indication of their rank. The most beautiful extant examples of this magnificent headgear are the kaşbastı that belonged to Hurrem and Safiye Sultan. It would appear that the popularity of the kaşbastı declined in the seventeenth century, because depictions of it are not often seen thereafter. During this period, high, blocked headgear with rounded crowns was in vogue, while garments maintained their previous lines.

Significant changes in the dress of Turkish women began to appear in the eighteenth century during the reign of Ahmed III (1703–1730). Lady Mary Montagu, who came to Istanbul with her husband, the English ambassador, recounts in her letters to family and friends between 1717 and 1718 the details of her life in Istanbul and describes in detail the Turkish women's garments she had sewn for herself. She also had her portrait painted in the clothes she loved so well. In one painting by Jean-Baptiste Vanmour (National Portrait Gallery, London), Montagu is portrayed wearing an inner robe with a deep décolletage, a jeweled belt, and a fur kaftan, holding the hand of her small child. During this period, some changes can be observed in the cut of the dress. The long sleeves of the inner kaftan are left open from wrist to elbow, allowing them to hang freely from the elbow and extend as far as the vents in the two side seams, as reflected in depictions by the renowned miniaturist Abdulcelil Levni in his album dated 1720–1725. However, it appears that the visibility of women's faces through the transparent veils and the colors of their ferace discomfited the male population, and in 1725–1726, a judgment was sent from the palace warning women about their clothing. It would appear, however, from the repetition of the same warning in 1734, that women did not always heed these restrictions.

The extremes in women's dress and headgear continued into the beginning of the nineteenth century, and women were constantly at odds with the palace. As the headgear increased in size, the judgments issued from the palace increased in severity. For instance, in a judgment sent to the kadı (the chief judge) of Eyüp in 1807, women were forbidden to appear in public in unseemly colors, ferace with long collars, or the headgear of a köçek (the dancing boys who impersonated women, a comparison intended to demean the wearers). Again, in 1811, it was announced that women were not to go about in unseemly colored, long-collared ferace in public and that those who ignored the judgment would have their headgear and collars cut off. At the same time, the interest of the women of the palace in Western goods was increasing, and every type of clothing fabric and accessory was being ordered from Europe. The import of these goods resulted in the issue of large sums of money from the treasury, causing depletion of its funds. A seven-page booklet of fashion plates from Paris, dating to 1873–1874, which is preserved in the Topkapi Palace archives, is interesting from the viewpoint of the passion of the women of the palace for Western goods.

THE USE OF FURS AND SKINS IN THE OTTOMAN COURT

The furs and skins of wild animals in the Topkapi Palace collection have a special significance. While the basic purpose of wearing furs and covering oneself with animal skins is to provide warmth, the roots of this tradition are related to a belief that extends as far back as shamanism in ancient Central Asian life. According to

A broadcloth kaftan associated with the Ottoman sultan Mehmed III (1595–1603). Topkapi Palace Museum.

this belief, shamans could transform themselves into animal form or be transported to the heavens by animals. This shamanistic belief continued even after the Turks in Central Asia accepted Buddhism. There, the tiger skin symbolized power and consequently came to personify the power of the ruler. The tradition of the tiger and similar savage animals symbolizing the sovereign continued after the Turks accepted Islam and is evidenced in the miniatures that illustrated manuscripts. It has been asserted that the leopard skins that were in widespread use in the Ottoman Palace, particularly spread out on either side of the throne, are related to contact with the protective spirit in Turkic mythology, thus representing the protective spirit of the sovereign.

Another valuable fur that is mentioned in Arab sources is ermine, known to the Ottomans as *kakum*. It is considered to have the finest fur of all the members of the squirrel family. The medieval Arab traveler Ibn Battuta (1304–1368/1369) describes ermine as having snow-white fur, with a very long tail that was highly esteemed and consequently left intact when the fur was sewn. Ibn Battuta also states that one of the qualities of this fur is that it does not harbor lice, and, for this reason, kings and Chinese noblemen would attach one of them to the collars of their furs—a custom practiced by Iranian and Iraqi merchants as well.

THE USE OF FUR IN THE OTTOMAN PALACE

The use of fur and skins was extensive in the Ottoman palace. The Turkic tradition of granting fur-lined robes of honor, *hil'at*,

to newly appointed government officials as well as their use as rewards went back to very early times. The type of fur that lined a garment and the fabric that covered it varied depending on the importance of the official's position and significance of the service he rendered. Before the end of the eighteenth century, fur was used only as a lining and never worn on the outside of garments. When the fashion for wearing fur as an outer covering began, the wearers became objects of ridicule and were satirized in poems.

The use of different types, qualities, and forms of fur also changed according to the season. It is clear from sultanic commands that furs were also worn in summer and that the type of fur worn changed seasonally. A command issued in 1754 ordered that summer and winter furs were to be acquired in a timely manner and that every type of fur delivered to the city was to be inspected by the official who was responsible for the imperial furs (*hassa kürkçübaşı*), who was to reserve the best examples for the sultan's use. The diary of Sultan Selim III (1789–1807), *Rüzname*, states for 2 May 1791 that the sultan declared that the temperature was rising and gave permission for lighter ermine fur to be worn (presumably in place of the sable worn during the winter).

From labels that have fallen off garments in the palace and from records in the treasury registers, it appears that, after the most highly prized sable, the furs most commonly used were ermine, lynx, pine marten, fox, lamb, foal, jackal, and the throats of wolves. The majority of these furs arrived from trading centers such as Russia, the Caucasus, and Bosnia. The first of the official traders to travel to Moscow to acquire furs on behalf of the Ottoman Empire were the *hassa tacirler*, who traveled there via Poland and the Grand Duchy of Lithuania.

Wild animal skins were also supplied to Istanbul from various areas in Anatolia. In fact, during the sixteenth century, animal skins hunted in Divriği were subject to income tax, collected for the skins of lynx and tiger. However, from a sultanic letter issued to the kadıs of Ankara, Kangırı, Kastamonu, and Bolu, it would appear that such taxes were not to be collected from the hunters who supplied furs to the state.

Both imported and domestic furs were transformed into garments by independent craftsmen who served customers in the city and also by a special group of imperial furriers employed at the palace. The 1526 register of an elite group of salaried craftsmen (*ehl-i hiref*) who worked exclusively for the court lists furriers (*postindüzan*). This group consisted of seven master craftsmen, six *şagird* (apprentices), and eleven names added later whose status is not mentioned. The size of this group is a good indication of the importance placed on this craft and the volume of work accomplished. While most of the furriers were Bosnian, among them were also Circassians, Georgians, Russians, and persons from Tabriz. The highest salary was paid to one Ismail Tabrizi, next to whose name is a note that he had been exiled from Tabriz.

It is noteworthy that, in an eighteenth-century register of the ehl-i hiref, a division of labor is evident among the postindüzans; five of the furriers worked exclusively with sable, while the remaining nineteen worked with other furs. This branch of specialization was in all likelihood due to the renowned fondness of Sultan İbrahim (1640–1648) for sable. The Turkish historian Ahmet Refik has recounted this series of events in a semidocumentary work and has given the appellation "sable period" to this time in Turkish history.

URBAN CONSUMPTION OF FUR

The use of fur for garments was as widespread among the general population as it was in the Ottoman palace. When writing about Turkish dress in the log of his travels in Anatolia between 1437 and 1439, the Spanish traveler Pedro Tafur (or Pero Tafur; ca. 1410–ca. 1487) noted that sable and ermine constituted the majority of the furs worn. The municipal codes, *ihtisap kanunları*, published for the cities of Istanbul, Bursa, and Edirne in 1502 contain certain admonitions to furriers. The Bursa *İhtisabı*, for example, states that, while formerly forty pieces of sable, pine marten, stone marten, and fox were used for a *beden* (a short, outer fur garment), a current inspection showed that a similar garment was made of only twenty-eight pieces. However, the furriers responded that they were hard pressed to find adequate supplies of fur. They complained that formerly no one but the furriers themselves had purchased whatever type of skin and fur was available, whereas now market sellers and perfume merchants, who were not at all involved in the manufacture of furs, had begun to purchase these items. This situation was duly recorded in the presence of all concerned, at which time it was also noted in the minutes that a *tahta* (a measure of regularly shaped pieces of fur that had been stitched together in the first stage of the manufacturing process) of lambskin (*post-ı bere*), which had just been measured, was found to be somewhat shorter than standard.

The preparation of the skins that arrived in the city required a great deal of expertise, and the Turks were masters of the subject. The skins were first tanned by master tanners, then separated into four categories—back, neck, stomach, and paw—by the furriers. The furriers then stitched the pieces together using a special fine cotton thread known as Istanbul thread. There were also furrier's needles that were apparently made specifically for the purpose. They were used, in particular, for the stitching of sable, delicately joining the furs to form pieces known as *tahta*. These tahtas were produced in different sizes: two narrow pieces for the front of a kaftan and a wider piece for the back. Furs prepared in this manner were covered with fabric by the craftsmen, *kürkçüyan*, and sold by the merchants identified in documents as *kürk fûrûşân*, whose shops faced one another along a long street in the covered bazaar in Istanbul.

During the seventeenth century, the lack of goods on the market, the shortage that resulted from the purchase of furs by unauthorized persons, and the consequent increase in cost caused prices to rise. Eventually, the state attempted to take control of the situation by establishing the *narh* system, in which official prices were fixed on commodities. A judgment written by the palace in 1694 states that it had been established that long furs were being produced in shorter dimensions and that used sable furs were being cut up again and resewn in the form of a tahta, resulting in injustice to the buyer.

The renowned seventeenth-century Ottoman traveler Evliya Çelebi (1611–1682), who is known to have sometimes relayed exaggerated numbers, speaks of the Istanbul furriers as consisting of five hundred shops and one thousand artisans. In 1754, the chief furrier of the palace was commanded to ensure the processing of sables and Moscow fox in eleven, Frank sable and lynx in nine, ermine in fifteen, and white fox in six chambers and under no circumstances in any other locations. When furs were acquired, the chief imperial furrier was to inspect them, and if the furriers had adhered to the regulations, they would be permitted to proceed with their work.

FURS OF THE SULTANS IN THE TOPKAPI PALACE COLLECTION

Among the wide variety of garments that belonged to the Ottoman sultans and were made of costly silk fabrics in the palace collection, nearly seventy of them consist of furs. Furs in the Ottoman palace were covered with the heaviest and most opulent silk fabrics, including cloth of gold and silver, brocaded velvet, velvet, brocaded silk, and satin. For winter and daily wear, they were covered with simpler fabric, such as mohair made from the spring fleece of the Angora goat and broadcloth made from the fleece of sheep. For ceremonial use, public appearances, and the reception of ambassadors, cloth of gold covered a lining of fox fur.

Furs were worn not only by the sultan but also by the women of the palace, as well as children and palace officials. The beden, which were lined with fur, covered the upper part of the body up to the neckline. Special beden for children's dress reached to the waist, covering the back as well as the front. There are no surviving examples of the furs worn by women in earlier periods. However, the clothes that Lady Mary Montagu, who lived in Istanbul during the first half of the eighteenth century, purchased before her return to England, along with the series of portraits she had painted of her wearing them, show that women's garments were generally lined with sable and squirrel fur.

Ignatius Mouradgeo d'Ohsson, who lived in Istanbul at the end of the eighteenth and the beginning of the nineteenth century, describes women's cloaks and states that wealthy women changed their furs several times a year. According to his account, women wore ermine in the late autumn, exchanging it for Siberian squirrel three weeks later, sable during the winter, and Siberian squirrel again in the spring. This information is confirmed by G. A. Olivier, who lived in Istanbul from 1792 to 1798; he states that the furs changed seasonally, that in summer women wore ferace made of mohair lined with Siberian squirrel, and that most women had ten to twelve furs in their closets.

Sable and ermine were the preferred furs for palace apparel. The well-prepared fur of these small animals could be cut as easily as fabric and, with the proper expertise, fashioned into the desired design. The designs often resembled the surface designs used on fabrics, and the furs were partially dyed blue, light yellow, and light pink. Noteworthy among the motifs used on fur-lined kaftans are the endless-repeat pattern of medallions opening onto one another, the seal of Solomon, knots, the Chinese cloud pattern, spots, and the star and crescent that are frequently seen on woven fabrics. Kaftans covered with squirrel and angora fleece are also preserved in the collection.

SKINS

The skin of the leopard, the most powerful of jungle animals, whose strength was identified with that of the empire, was widely used both within the palace and on the horse gear used by the sultan. The sultan's horses were covered with leopard skins for the ceremonial processions held when the sultan attended festival or Friday prayers or paraded before the public before

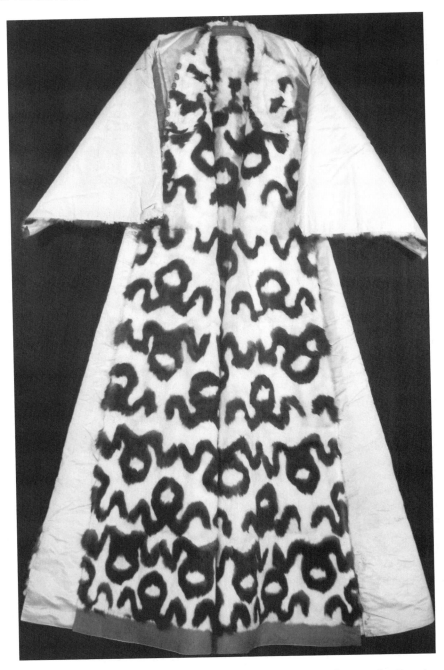

Ottoman *seraser* kaftan with ermine fur and a cloud-band design, sixteenth to seventeenth centuries. *Seraser* is a precious silk fabric woven with gold and silver threads. Ermine was considered a fine fur that did not harbor lice and therefore was often worn at the collar. Topkapi Palace Museum.

departing on a military campaign. The register of the inventory of the Raht hazinesi, or "Treasury of Horse Gear," taken in 1637 during the reign of Murad IV, lists ten tiger skins, four *bebr* (Indian wildcat) skins, and two sable skins, which must be the items used in such ceremonies. Antoine Galland, an employee of the French embassy during the 1670s who observed the procession of Sultan Mehmed IV to holiday prayers in Edirne, describes with admiration the sultan's nine spare horses bedecked with jeweled gear, the leopard skin on the rump of the horse he rode, and the cover that was visible beneath it, which was edged

in large diamonds and pearls. The most important source of images of a sultan's horses covered with the skins of animals like leopards and tigers is the *Surname-i Vehbi*, illustrated by Levni, prepared in commemoration of the circumcision of the sons of Sultan Ahmed III in 1720.

The sultans used the skins of wild animals to decorate not only their horses but sometimes also their persons. The literature mentions that Sultan Murad IV, known for his harsh personality and love of flamboyance, returned from the Baghdad campaign with a leopard skin worn over his shoulder. It is also interesting to note that the official attire of the palace *zağarcıbaşı* (the commander of the greyhound-keeper's company of the Janissaries) included a leopard skin thrown over the shoulder and that the musicians who accompanied the tradesmen in their procession wore leopard skins in a similar manner.

The skins of wild animals were used as symbols of imperial power in the Ottoman palace much as they were used for the same purpose by other rulers. In the early fifteenth century, the Spanish traveler and ambassador Ruy González de Clavijo (d. 1412) observed that when he visited the Blachernae Palace in the Byzantine capital of Istanbul on his way to Samarkand to meet with Timur (1336–1405; founder of the Timurid Empire and also known as Tamerlane), the reception room was decorated with the skins of lions.

The notes of Andrea Gritti (1455–1538), a doge of Venice who, together with his secretary, was received in the Arz Divanhanesi in the second courtyard of the Topkapi Palace next to the inner treasury in 1503, indicate that the throne was covered with black velvet embroidered in gold thread, leopard skins, and leather work.

Most of the thirty skins in the collection were the sultans' personal possessions and are registered with the names of their owners. Records indicate that two leopard skins lined with green woolen broadcloth belonging to Sultan Mehmed II have been present in the Ottoman palace since the fifteenth century, and they are known to have been spread across the throne. From this standpoint, it is not surprising that Suleiman the Magnificent, the longest ruling of all the sultans, would have owned eight leopard skins. The most important visual source displaying skins spread on the throne is a series of illuminated manuscripts dated 1584, the *Hünername* (the name refers to the Harem and Imperial Garden in the Topkapi Palace), in which the throne area is clearly portrayed. Animal skins were used as symbols of power well into the seventeenth century, after which they appear to have gradually lost their significance, a view that is supported by the fact that, of the six skins registered to Sultan Murad IV, two consist of skins of Angora goat (hardly a savage animal), one of them dyed yellow and the other blue. In an eighteenth-century register of the furnishings of the Arz Odası (the audience hall of the Topkapi Palace), the two leopard skins mentioned must be the last representatives of this tradition.

References and Further Reading

Baker, Patricia. *Silks for the Sultan: Ottoman Imperial Garments from the Topkapi Palace*. Istanbul: Ertug and Kocabiyik, 1996.

Bassano da Zara, Luigi. *I Costumi et I modi particolari de las vita de Turchi*. Rome, 1545. Repr. ed. Munich: H. Huber, 1963.

Çelebi, Evliya. *Evliya Çelebi's Book of Travels. Evliya Çelebi in Albania and Adjacent Regions (Kosovo, Montenegro). The Relevant Sections of the Seyahatname*. Translated and edited by Robert Dankoff. Leiden and Boston: Brill, 2000.

d'Arvieux, Laurent. *Mémoires du chevalier d'Arvieux*. 6 vols. Paris: C.J.B. Delespine, 1735.

d'Ohsson, Ignace de Mouradja. *Tableau général de l'empire othoman*. 7 vols. Paris: Firmin Didot, 1787.

de Clavijo, Ruy González. *Embassy to Tamerlane 1403–1406*. Translated by Guy LeStrange. London: Routledge, 1928.

Fisher, C.G., and A. Fisher "Topkapı Sarayı in the Mid-Seventeenth Century: Bobovi's Description." *Archivum Ottomanicum* 10 (1985/1987): 5–81.

Galland, Antoine. *Journal d'Antoine Galland pendant son séjour à Constantinople (1672–1673)*. Paris: E. Leroux, 1881.

Gibb, H.A.R., and C.F. Beckingham, trans. and eds. *The Travels of Ibn Battuta, A.D. 1325–1354*. London: Hakluyt Society, 2000.

Halsband, Robert, ed. *The Complete Letters of Lady Mary Wortley Montagu*. 3 vols. Oxford: Clarendon Press, 1965–1967.

Ibn Battuta. *The Travels of Ibn Battutah*. Edited by Timothy Mackintosh-Smith. London: Picador, 2003.

Necipoğlu, Gülrü. *Architecture, Ceremonial and Power, The Topkapı Palace in the Fifteenth and Sixteenth Centuries*. Cambridge, MA: MI Press, 1991.

Olivier, Guillaume Antoine. *Voyage dans l'Empire Othoman, l'Ègypte et la Perse I–III, Paris 1803* [Travels in the Ottoman Empire, Egypt and Persia]. Translated by O. Gökmen. Ankara: Türkiye Seyahatnamesi, 1977.

Raby, Julian, and Alison Effeny, eds. *Ipek, İmperial Ottoman Silks and Velvets*. Istanbul: Türk Ekonomi Bankası, 2001.

Ribeiro, Aileen. "Turkish Dress and English Fashion in the Eighteenth Century." *The Connoisseur*, May 1979, 16–23.

Scarce, Jennifer. *Women's Costume of the Near and Middle East*. London and Sydney: Unwin Hyman, 1987.

Tafur, Pero. *Travels and Adventures 1435–1439*. London: Routledge, 2004.

Taylor, Roderick. *Ottoman Embroidery*. Northampton, MA: Interlink Publishing Group, 1993.

Tezcan, Hülya. *Silks for the Sultans: Ottoman Imperial Garments from Topkapı Palace*. Milan: Ertuğ & Kocabıyık yayını, 1996.

Tezcan, Hülya. "Fashion at the Ottoman Court." *P Dergisi* 3 (Spring–Summer 2000): 2–49.

Tezcan, Hülya. "Ottoman Fabric Weaving and Women's Fashion in the Eighteenth Century." *P Dergisi* 3 (Spring–Summer 2000): 18–30.

Tezcan, Hülya. "Sixteenth and Seventeenth Century Women's Fashion at the Ottoman Palace." *P Dergisi* 3 (Spring–Summer 2000): 4–18.

Tezcan, Hülya. "The Sultanic Costumes in the Attire Collection at the Topkapı Palace Museum." *P Dergisi* 3 (Spring–Summer 2000): 30–50.

Tezcan, Hülya. "Furs and Skins Owned by the Sultans." In *Ottoman Costumes from Textile to Identity*, edited by Suraiya Faroqhi and Christoph K. Neumann, 63–79. Istanbul: Eren, 2004.

Tezcan, Hülya, and Selma Delibas. *Topkapi: Costumes, Embroideries and Other Textiles*. Translated, expanded, and edited by Michael Rogers. London: Thames & Hudson, 1986.

Woman in Anatolia, 9000 Years of the Anatolian Woman. Exhibition catalog (29 November 1993–28 February 1994). Istanbul: Topkapı Sarayı Museum.

Hülya Tezcan

See also Turkish Embroidery; Ottoman Dress: Snapshot: Turkish Costume Albums; Regional Dress in Anatolia; Laws of Differentiation.

Snapshot: Turkish Costume Albums

The expansion of the Ottoman Turkish Empire—from modest beginnings in Anatolia during the thirteenth century to control over territories spanning the Balkans, the east coast of the Mediterranean and Egypt, much of North Africa, Iraq, and Arabia by the late sixteenth to early seventeenth centuries—provoked much concern and curiosity among the European states who encountered its power. From the late fifteenth century on, Europeans visited the capital, Istanbul, and the rest of the Ottoman world in increasing numbers as diplomats, merchants, military and naval personnel, scholars, artists, and travelers. There was much to interest them in the extraordinarily varied environment of the multicultural empire—especially dress, which became one of the most popular and appealing subjects for pictorial representation. Many European residents adopted Turkish dress, which in turn encouraged the fashion for *Turquerie* in the early eighteenth century. *Turquerie* is a general term for Turkish influence on fashionable dress, ballet, theater, and interior design from the late seventeenth to late eighteenth century, mainly in France but also to a lesser extent in England. British and French aristocrats had their portraits painted wearing Turkish dress, while Turkish themes inspired drama, masques, and costume balls.

Two main sources illustrate Turkish dress from the sixteenth to nineteenth centuries: European drawings, engravings, and paintings and Turkish albums of single-figure studies of supposedly typical characters and nationalities. European topographical books of the sixteenth century contain sections on the dress and customs of many nationalities, including those of the Ottoman Empire. The most accurate and frequently consulted illustrations of sixteenth-century Turkish dress are the woodcut engravings in Nicolas de Nicolay's *Les Quatres Premiers Livres des Navigations et Peregrinations Orientales* (*The First Four Books of Navigation and Oriental Peregrinations*), published in 1567. Nicolay came to Istanbul in 1551 in the entourage of Gabriel d'Aramon, the French ambassador to the Ottoman court, and stayed there for fifteen years, which gave him time and opportunity for direct observation. Long residence in Istanbul through embassy service continued to be an advantage, both for personal advancement and the gathering of dress information.

Ignatius Mouradgeo d'Ohsson, the Armenian interpreter to the Swedish embassy from 1763 to 1782, wrote an encyclopedic survey in three volumes, based on research into government documents and interviews with important Ottomans. His *Tableau General de l'Empire Ottoman* (General view of the Ottoman Empire) was published in Paris between 1787 and 1820 and was also translated into English, German, and Russian. His text—accompanied by 233 illustrations—also discusses Turkish dress.

European artists attached to embassies produced albums of illustrations of Turkish daily life, occupations, and customs. One of the most important examples is the *Recueil de Cent Estampes Representant Differentes Nations du Levant* (Compilations of one hundred prints representing different nations of the Levant) commissioned by Count Charles de Ferriol,

the French ambassador in Istanbul from 1699 to 1707, from the artist Jean-Baptiste Vanmour and published in 1715. The paintings, which include officials and races in their local dress, were so popular that volumes of engravings made from them were widely copied as the main source of information about Turkish dress. The Swiss Jean-Etienne Liotard, who accompanied the British ambassador William Ponsonby, lived in Istanbul from 1738 to 1742; there he painted Europeans, Armenians, and Greeks in meticulously observed Ottoman fashions. Illustrations of Turkish dress survived into the nineteenth century through the paintings and engravings of independent artists such as the Maltese count Amadeo Preziosi, who visited Istanbul in the 1850s and recorded the changes from traditional to Western fashions.

Parallel with the illustrated books and albums by European authors and artists is a group of Turkish paintings that are more didactic in their treatment of dress. From the late fifteenth century on, a distinctive style of Ottoman Turkish court painting developed that illustrated in scrupulous detail the manuscripts of the histories of sultans' reigns, military expeditions, and important festivities such as the circumcision of

Detail from an early-nineteenth-century Turkish costume album depicting an Armenian (Christian) bride. Hundreds of illustrations were drawn for albums to be given to Ottoman and provincial officials, as well as for the general public and tourists (especially those from Europe). Such albums depict men and women in different dress from throughout the Ottoman Empire. Textile Research Centre, Leiden.

princes. By the seventeenth century, albums of single-figure studies, the enlarged format of which allows for close observation of dress and accessories, had become popular. They range from idealized portraits of Ottoman sultans to studies of the exquisitely dressed young women painted by the court artist Abdulcelil Levni between 1720 and 1730.

A modest version of this tradition are the albums of single-figure dress studies depicting typical characters and nationalities painted by mainly anonymous Turkish and Levantine artists to satisfy European curiosity about the Ottoman world. These are basically commercial productions of varying artistic merit for mass circulation. They were produced from the middle of the sixteenth to the early nineteenth century and have survived in quantity in public and private collections in Europe, the United States, and Turkey. As the artists aimed to inform, they chose to present each subject in a static frontal pose, giving as much detail as possible with regard to the layers and textures of garments.

Two albums from the early seventeenth and late eighteenth century in the British Museum are good examples of the format because they are relatively well documented and lavishly illustrated. The English merchant Peter Mundy, who visited Istanbul in 1618, left a manuscript account of his experiences dated and signed with his initials. Mundy illustrated his text with a series of Turkish paintings of officials, nationalities, and types of dress. Each figure is painted in bright mineral pigments—red, green, orange, blue, and black—on paper in a flat, precise style that clearly shows, for example, the many garments and fabrics required for the dress of court ladies. Later, one of the most comprehensive albums was reputedly commissioned by Sultan Abdul Hamit I (1774–1789) as a gift for Friedrich Heinrich von Diez, the Prussian ambassador to the Ottoman court from 1784 to 1791. The work is in two volumes, illustrated respectively with 112 and 110 watercolor paintings, and includes many studies of women's dress. These are painted in a style that emphasizes the garments' folds, pleats, and volume and the fabrics' light colors and delicate patterns, which are all characteristic of eighteenth-century Turkish fashions.

By about the mid-nineteenth century, the painting of dress was replaced by the technique of photography, which was adopted enthusiastically by Turks and Europeans. Photographs of dress filled albums of exhibitions, illustrated memoirs, and travel accounts, and picture postcards catered to the tourist market.

REFERENCES AND FURTHER READING

Germana, Semra, and Zeynep Inankur. *Constantinople and the Orientalists*. Istanbul: Isbank, 2002.

Mansel, Philip. *Constantinople: City of the World's Desire*. London: John Murray, 1995.

Scarce, Jennifer. *Women's Costume of the Near and Middle East*. London: Unwin Hyman, 1987.

Sint Nicolaas, Eveline, Duncan Bull, Gunsel Renda, and Gul Irepoglu. *Jean-Baptiste Vanmour: An Eyewitness of the Tulip Era*. Istanbul: Kocbank, 2003.

Jennifer M. Scarce

See also Regional Dress in Anatolia.

Regional Dress in Anatolia

The importance of dress as visible evidence of the wearer's roles and responsibilities in both public and private domains (such as rank, profession, religious and ethnic identity, wealth, age, and marital and familial status) and, to a certain extent, personal taste within the limits of acceptable codes of behavior is an eloquent statement of the multicultural diversity of the Ottoman Turkish Empire, whose territories extended from Southeast Europe to Arab lands. Anatolia, the empire's hinterland separating Europe from Asia, was a remarkable mosaic of different histories, populations, religions, urban and rural communities, and conditions of geography and climate. Geographically, Anatolia was self-contained within the natural boundaries of the Black Sea and the Mediterranean Sea to the north, west, and south. Its eastern frontiers with Iran and Syria were, however, less clearly defined and were vulnerable to invasion. Historically, Anatolia had experienced Hittite, Phrygian, Greek, and Roman settlements, conflict between the Byzantines and Seljuk Turks, and a sequence of independent principalities before the imposition of Ottoman control. Populations were inevitably mixed—Turks, Greeks, Armenians, Circassians, Georgians, Kurds, Arabs, and Jews practicing their religions of Islam, Christianity, and Judaism and speaking a bewildering range of languages and dialects. Standards of living varied from affluence in the cities and towns of the fertile regions of western Anatolia to the harshness of life in the villages of southeastern Anatolia.

Regional variation in dress in Anatolia was yet another contribution to the cultural mosaic, additionally enriched by the sartorial traditions of the dominant Ottoman elite. Regional variants for both sexes were based on the general principle of an elegant combination of layers of well-crafted garments—trousers, shirts, gowns, robes, jackets, scarves, and turbans—of silks, velvets, and fine wool, either plain or embellished with patterns using embroidery or complex weaving and brocade techniques. Accessories included belts, jewelry, shoes, and boots. This fashion was admired and imitated throughout the empire by subjects who aspired to emphasize their wealth, status, and taste through dress. In Anatolia, versions of metropolitan style, mainly worn in towns such as Smyrna (called Izmir in the early twenty-first century), Bursa, Ankara, and Kutahya, were complemented by the robust vitality and color of more specifically local dress in both urban and rural environments. The analysis and interpretation of this rich provincial tradition require a cautious approach, however, because they depend on primary and secondary sources, which vary in rates of survival, depth and quality of information, and ease of access.

SOURCES

Collections of garments are obviously the primary source, but these are far from providing a complete representation of dress. The textiles of dress are vulnerable to conditions of climate such as exposure to light and water damage, attacks by insects, and the owner's wish to discard them when they are torn and frayed beyond repair. The main collections of regional dress that have survived are principally from the nineteenth and twentieth centuries and are found in museums in Turkey, which usually have informative permanent displays and temporary exhibitions. Among the best are the Museum of Turkish and Islamic Art and the Sadberk Hanim Museum, both in Istanbul; the Museum of Ethnography in Ankara; the regional museums of Antalya and Gaziantep; and, in Bursa, the City Museum and the Uluumay Ottoman Turkish Folk Costume and Jewelry Museum, which is dedicated to the regional dress of both Anatolia and the Balkans. All these collections are occasionally supplemented by donations from families who are sometimes the descendants of the original wearers; in some cases, valuable documentation concerning the history of these garments has been provided. Private sources, however, are not readily accessible.

The secondary sources that supplement the collections of garments are both pictorial and written. Turkish manuscript illustrations and single-figure studies dating from the early sixteenth century on, while meticulous in their treatment of the conventions of dress and accessories, are limited because they concentrate on the styles of the Ottoman court and upper classes. Occasionally, depictions of regional dress are found in the pictorial cycles of the processions of guilds, trades, and spectators that accompanied major festivities such as the circumcisions of Ottoman princes. There are, however, so-called typical representations of regional dress in the very popular costume albums that were painted by local Turkish and Levantine artists to inform European residents and visitors about Ottoman life and customs; these include people and occupations in the European, Anatolian, and Arab provinces. European painters of the eighteenth and nineteenth centuries such as the Swiss Charles Gleyre (1806–1874) and Jean-Etienne Liotard (1702–1789), the English Thomas Allom (1804–1872), and the Maltese Count Amedeo Preziosi (1816–1882), while painting dress studies with sensitive observation and grace, concentrated on Istanbul and did not venture across the Bosporus to Anatolia.

The introduction of photography by the late nineteenth century meant that dress could be recorded more objectively, resulting in a more extensive survey. One of the most comprehensive sets of records is preserved in the large album of photographs of men and women in dress from all regions of the Ottoman Empire that was prepared for the Vienna Exhibition of 1873 by Osman Hamdi Bey (1842–1910) and Marie de Launay. Photography then became the accepted medium for recording dress in albums, as book illustrations, and as collections of postcards aimed at the tourist market.

Written sources are equally variable in range and accuracy. The most accessible are the official reports, memoirs, and travel accounts written by European visitors from the sixteenth century on. The most informative and detailed about dress are the works

A studio portrait of (from left to right) a peasant from Safranbolu, a Kurd from Viranşehir, and a laborer from Kastamonu. From Osman Hamdi Bey and Marie de Launay, *Les costumes populaires de la Turquie en 1873* (Traditional dress from Turkey in 1873). The peasant wears *şalvar* (a pair of voluminous trousers) and a *yelek* (waistcoat), while the Kurd wears a striped kaftan (long robe) under his cape. The laborer's clothing is very basic, consisting of a simple kaftan with a *sal kusak* (sash) tied around the waist and *corap* (wool stockings). They all wear a type of *sarik* (turban), but the quality and number of garments worn by each of them are indicative of their occupation and financial status. Library of Congress Prints and Photographs Division LC-USZC4-11833.

written in the nineteenth century, especially those by the increasing number of merchants, teachers, missionaries, scholars, and archaeologists, as well as women accompanying their fathers and husbands or traveling independently, who spent many years in the main cities and provinces. Especially valuable for descriptions of regional dress are, for example, Julia Pardoe, who came to Istanbul with her father in 1835 and subsequently published many books about Turkey; Lucy Garnett, who spent a lot of time during the 1890s collecting information about folklore and women's lives and customs; and Mrs. W.R. Ramsay, who traveled through Anatolia with her husband, the classical scholar W.R. Ramsay, both recording inscriptions and observing the customs and dress of Afyon-Karahissar, a town near Konya. The use of Ottoman Turkish sources is a continually evolving specialization. Apart

from the court documents of Istanbul, for the provinces there are guild registers, judicial returns, and, more specifically for dress, wills and household inventories, which all require expert archival and linguistic skills to catalog, transcribe, and interpret.

GENERAL FEATURES

A necessarily selective choice from both primary and secondary sources provides a general survey of the main features of the regional dress of men and women and allows for variables such as interaction between urban and rural environments, integration of external influences, and the availability of materials for garments and accessories. During the nineteenth century, it seems that there were still plenty of locally woven fabrics. Cotton production flourished in the Aegean and Black Sea regions, despite increasing imports of industrially spun yarn from Europe: Plain weaves from Denizli and crepe from Kastamonu were used for shirts and scarves. Silk continued to be woven in Bursa, traditionally the main supplier to the Ottoman court, and also in Smyrna, Gaziantep, and Diyarbakir. Other materials, which were plentiful in the pastoral hinterland of Anatolia, included leather (for belts, shoes, and boots) and wool, which was spun into yarns used for knitting the brightly patterned stockings and slippers of rural dress and woven into cloth for all garments. There were many techniques of decoration—complex supplementary weaves, embroidery in cotton and silk threads and gold, block printing, plaiting and braiding of cord, and lace-making.

MEN'S DRESS

Men's dress, at least in the nineteenth century, ranged between versions of the European-inspired combination of a frock coat and straight-legged trousers worn with a fez (a pillbox-shaped felt cap), which had been introduced by Sultan Mahmud II (1808–1839) in 1826 as part of his reform program for the Ottoman Empire, and variations on conservative traditional clothing. While the wearing of the sober formal uniform of coat and trousers was mandatory for Ottoman officials in Istanbul, it also would have been seen in the garments of both provincial administrators and among the elite of coastal cities such as Smyrna, whose cosmopolitan population and trading networks opened access to European fashions. Beyond these privileged circles, however, men's clothing basically consisted of a gömlek (a blouse with long sleeves) and şalvar (a pair of voluminous trousers), as well as a selection of yelek (waistcoats), cepken (jackets), and a kaftan (a heavy robe, usually of a rich silk brocade and frequently lined with fur for winter, which was worn by both men and women). The kaftan was optionally clasped with a kemer (belt) or sal kusak (sash or waist shawl). A sarik (turban), corap (wool stockings), and leather cedik (shoes) and cizme (boots) completed the outfit. The wearer's occupation and personal and financial status influenced both the quality and number of garments worn. Clothes were more elaborate for special ceremonies such as weddings, for which lavishly embroidered jackets and richly woven sashes and turbans were commissioned and then kept for future occasions.

Within this format, there was scope for colorful and spectacular interpretation using all the resources of fabric and decoration available. A few examples illustrate the richness of this variation. In western Anatolia, in the region of Aydin and Kutahya, the young men known as efes and zeybek (a dashing young man or dandy) wore a distinctive outfit based on a striped silk shirt, dizlik (short, draped, knee-length trousers), and a salta (a tight-fitting jacket with long, slashed sleeves). The dizlik and salta were both made of wool broadcloth and lavishly decorated with designs of foliage couched in plaited silk braid. Sashes and massive leather belts were accessorized with embroidered yağlıks (handkerchiefs), and the turban was draped with strands of flowers worked in colored oya (needle-woven and knotted cotton or silk lace). Black leather knee-length boots, often worn with embroidered felt gaiters, completed the efes's ensemble.

Versions of young men's dress from the region of Ankara in central Anatolia shared the striped shirt and embroidered jacket, but the trousers were long and tucked into knitted stockings worn with plain leather shoes. The swathed sashes and turbans

continued to be important accessories but were generally only of striped wool and silk. Clothing from other regions, however, was strongly influenced by the dress of close neighbors. Men from Bitlis in southern Anatolia traditionally wore close-fitting jackets and tuman (long, wide-legged trousers), both of wool fabric with gray or white stripes, and head coverings of tightly wound and knotted black fringed scarves, all characteristic of the styles of the Kurdish element of the local population. A contrast to these flowing garments was seen in men's dress from the Kars region of northeastern Anatolia, where the influence of Georgia was dominant. The shirt had a high neck and full sleeves gathered into cuffs and was worn with a rubashka (a tight-fitting coat with a full skirt that flared out over the knee). Gold-embroidered cartridge bands decorated the chest, the turban was replaced by a black lambskin papak (pillbox-shaped hat), and straight-legged trousers were tucked into long, soft, black leather boots.

WOMEN'S DRESS

Women's dress in Anatolia shows a comparable set of differences between town and regional styles. Precious archival evidence consisting of ten surviving inventories of the estates of wealthy women dated from 1486 to 1489 offers some insight into women's dress in Bursa during the late fifteenth century. A survey reveals that the most valuable garment was the kaftan of silk or velvet embroidered in gold. Lightweight versions in silk and cotton are also recorded. Open-fronted coats are mentioned, as are sashes and belts and a range of head scarves.

Until the nineteenth century, with the exception of cosmopolitan Smyrna, there was relatively little European influence on women's dress, because the women of the families of provincial Ottoman officials were not involved in a public role. In general, the main garments were an iclik (a long-sleeved blouse) and full, loose trousers gathered at the ankle. Over them, either a salta or an entari (the principal garment, specifically, a long dress with a wrapover front and a full skirt) was worn, wound with shawls and belts. Headdresses consisted of elaborate arrangements of colorful yemeni (cotton scarves block-printed with flower motifs and usually trimmed with edgings of oya and crochet lace). Footwear ranged from terlik (slippers) for indoor wear to soft leather cizme for outdoors. All was concealed by a peche (opaque face veil usually of woven black horsehair) and a carsaf (a wrap of cotton or silk extending from head to ankle), which were required for outdoor wear. This ensemble was standard in Bursa during the nineteenth century.

Little seems to have changed in this basic wardrobe during the following centuries. Variations, however, in the fabric and shape of garments could be seen in the towns of central and northeastern Anatolia. Women in Sivas, for example, wore matching sets of trousers, jackets, and ankle-length robes in kutnu cloth (satin-weave fabric made of a mixture of cotton and silk) patterned with narrow stripes in white and red. Their headdress consisted of numerous scarves of cotton block-printed with floral motifs and trimmed with edgings of oya (needle-woven lace), all wound into a turban. Kutnu was a popular choice of fabric for traditional urban and rural dress in Anatolia and was woven in Istanbul, Bursa, Diyarbakir, and Aleppo to supply this market.

Dress in the Kars region was strongly influenced by the styles of neighboring Georgia; it was based on long, full skirts and a tight jacket that flared over the hips. During the nineteenth

A studio portrait of two elaborately dressed men from Zeybek, Turkey (left and center), and an artisan from Aydin, Turkey (right). From Osman Hamdi Bey and Marie de Launay, *Les costumes populaires de la Turquie en 1873* (Traditional dress from Turkey in 1873). The men from Zeybek wear elements of clothing usually worn by the young men known as *efes* and *zeybek* (which translates roughly as a dandy). They both wear a striped silk shirt under their outerwear, a braided *salta* (tight-fitting jacket with long, slashed sleeves), *dizlik* (short, draped, knee-length trousers), extremely wide leather belts that hold their weapons, and knee-high black leather boots with felt gaiters. To finish the ostentatious ensemble, their turbans are mostly hidden by decorative tassels, which were often worked in colored oya (needle-woven and knotted lace). Library of Congress Prints and Photographs Division LC-USZC4-11712.

century, European garments were gradually introduced into provincial urban dress, reaching central Anatolia. Mrs. Ramsay, visiting a small market town near Afyon in the 1890s, noted that red dressing gowns were placed over Turkish dress and that black kid leather French boots with high heels were worn. All this finery was concealed under the traditional carsaf (wrap) and peche for outdoor wear. In Afyon, by the beginning of the twentieth century, women were wearing suits of long skirts and fitted coats in matching fabrics based on European tailored styles.

Regardless of the region, the most precious garment in a woman's wardrobe was her wedding dress, colloquially known as a *bindalli* (a dress of velvet or silk heavily embroidered with gold thread). It seems that a basic style was worn throughout Anatolia,

based on the evidence of surviving examples attributed to Bursa, Ankara, Kutahya, Safranbolu, and Maras. In its simplest form, the bindalli is a loose, straight dress that has long, tight sleeves and reaches to the ankles; it could be clasped at the waist with an ornate belt. The most popular fabric was deep crimson, purple, or black silk velvet, which provided an effective background for bold designs of sprays and scrolls of floral and foliage motifs that were worked all over the garment in gold- and silver-thread embroidery in the complex technique of *dival isi*. This garment required the skills of professional embroiderers, particularly those from the town of Maras in southeastern Anatolia, which claimed the best reputation for this ornate craft of decoration. The motifs of the design scheme were drawn on stiff cardboard, which was then cut into templates that were attached to the fabric of the bindalli. Gold or silver thread was then laid and couched over the template until it was completely covered, producing a design in which flower petals and leaves were in prominent raised relief; they were further embellished with outlines stitched using fine gold or silver twisted-wire thread and scattered beads and sequins. The preparation of a bindalli was clearly an expensive and laborious process requiring a commission well in advance of the wedding.

Gradually, fashionable changes were introduced, such as a tight blouse and bell-shaped skirt instead of the traditional loose gown and the use of satin-faced silk fabric in light colors of rose pink, mauve, yellow, and white instead of dark-colored velvet. A bride's ensemble was completed by plaiting gold and silver threads into her hair and applying sequins to her whitened and rouged face, before enveloping her in a red veil for the procession to her new home. A bindalli was valuable and kept as a best dress for special occasions such as family celebrations and religious festivities. As a treasured family heirloom, it was passed to daughters and granddaughters to be used as their wedding dress unless a fashionable bride preferred a new outfit. The bindalli is directly comparable to the kaftans listed in the inventories of Bursa from the fifteenth century, which had survived to be regarded as precious assets.

In contrast to urban provincial fashion, where tradition was increasingly mingled with external influences that gradually resulted in widespread standardization at the expense of local identity, a rich diversity of dress survived in rural areas. Again, the strength of individual regional styles depended on the degree of contact or isolation in communities, but it is possible to find dress traditions unique to specific villages in western Anatolia. An outstanding example is Kocakovacik, one of twenty-seven villages in the Keles district, south of the Uludag Mountains near Bursa. The villagers, who are all from the Karakecili tribe, form a close-knit community whose identity is symbolized visually by their handsome dress. Women wear layers of clothing following the general principle of all Turkish dress but make use of spectacularly decorated garments to indicate stages of the life cycle more visibly than in a town. A headdress, for example, can differentiate a young girl, an engaged girl, a bride, a newlywed woman, a mother, a recent widow still in mourning, and a widow available for remarriage.

At its most elaborate and complete, the outfit consists of as many as fourteen garments plus jewelry. This includes a gömlek and şalvar, usually made of white cotton, as the foundation garments; they are plain but can be decorated with bands and panels of embroidery. The next layer consists of the ucetek or isleme entari (coat with long sleeves), which is made of a patterned fabric such as the striped kutnu cloth of mixed cotton and silk. Several layers of garments are placed over the ucetek: up to two waistcoats (known as kapakli and siktirma) and the guduk (a short jacket with long, flaring sleeves), which is worn open to reveal and frame the adornment and jewelry beneath. The decoration of the guduk is an important symbol of the wearer's status. A young unmarried woman, for example, can wear a guduk lavishly embroidered with floral motifs in gold and silver thread on the back, front, and sleeves. After marriage, however, women wore a plain version of the guduk.

A series of wraps and belts were draped and tied around the waist and hips, beginning with the sal kusak. This consisted of two lengths of woolen fabric, which could be plain or woven with striped and checked designs, stitched together to form a simple rectangle whose ends are embroidered and finished with a deep fringe of wool tassels. The shawl is folded diagonally and wrapped around the body so that the fringes fall over the back. A long wool peskir (apron) is worn over the shawl at the front of the body and again is an opportunity for display because the fabric can be woven with panels of diamond-shaped motifs, tie-dyed with bold spots, and covered with sequins and tufts of colored thread. A dizge (belt), also of wool, is woven as a very long narrow strip; this is tied around the waist to hold the shawl and apron together. It may be plain or woven with colored stripes or checked patterns and has long fringes of knotted tassels of wool and goat hair at the ends, which fall down over the wearer's back and swing as she walks. Again, decoration is significant: A young woman's belt fringes are adorned with beads, shells, and colored yarns, which, together with the shawl and apron, show that she is attractive and would consider proposals of marriage.

The headdress also conveys messages of status. This is a layered construction that consists of a takke (close-fitting skullcap) over which a stiff fez trimmed with panels and fringes of beadwork is placed and covered with two head scarves—first, the cember, a head scarf that frames the face and is tied either at the back or on top of the head, and, second, the ikisibiryerde cember, a shawl that is kept loose and falls like a mantle over the shoulders and back. This second shawl is usually of a lightweight fabric such as cotton and may be decorated with block-printed floral designs. The complete headdress was traditionally worn by married women. Unmarried girls, however, usually began to wear only the cember around puberty, loosely tied as a pretty head scarf, and were able to add lavish embellishments such as sequins, braids, fringes, and borders of oya (needle-woven lace). Unmarried girls could also further adorn their dress with silver jewelry—necklaces with amulet boxes attached, chains fringed with drop pendants, and belts with large, curved clasps. All women completed their dress with wool stockings knitted in intricate colored patterns and either closed leather shoes or carik, a laced sandal.

THE SURVIVAL AND MODIFICATION OF REGIONAL DRESS

The rich mosaic of dress in both towns and villages, while respecting tradition, was receptive to degrees of change, a process that was to continue more rapidly beginning in the early twentieth century. Three main factors contributed to these changes: modernization of Turkish society, official dress reform, and the emergence of a Turkish national identity.

Modernization—through trade contacts, diplomatic exchange, the importation of technology and knowledge, and the establishment of the manufacturing industry—was already well established during the nineteenth century. The economic and social impact is seen in changing patterns of consumption. Factory-made fabrics competed with locally woven ones and influenced shopping, garment making, and employment, as mass production threatened the livelihoods of traditional craftspeople. Modernization in dress, in the form of a move toward more European-inspired styles, which had already begun in the nineteenth century with Mahmud II's decree of 1826, was sharply accelerated by the clothing reforms of Atatürk (the first president of the

A studio portrait of (from left to right) an Armenian woman from Burdur, a Turkmen woman from Konya, and a Kurdish woman from Sarikaya, Turkey. The Armenian woman wears a typical *entari* (a long dress with a wrapover front and a full skirt) and soft leather *cizme*. The Turkmen woman wears a *kaftan* (robe) over her striped *ucetek* or *isleme entari* (coat with long sleeves), which is likely to have been made from *kutnu* fabric. The Kurdish woman is wearing a long dress, very wide decorative sash or cumberband, and a long-sleeved jacket; on her head she wears a cap with tassel bound with a decorative cloth. Library of Congress Prints and Photographs Division LC-USZC4-11844.

Republic of Turkey; he served from 1925 to 1938). These began formally on 25 November 1925, when a law was passed prescribing that all men should exchange their fezzes, turbans, and robes for European hats, shirts, neckties, jackets, and trousers. Women were encouraged to substitute modern European dress for their mantles and veils. The reforms continued steadily until 1934, also transforming regional dress in different ways.

In the early twenty-first century, Turkey is a fashion leader manufacturing imaginatively designed and well-crafted clothing for both domestic and export markets, which affects towns and villages in Anatolia. Towns show the greatest variation; there, both sexes are smartly dressed in well-chosen and accessorized European styles—for example, in Izmir (former Smyrna) and Bursa, where there is a permanent class of officials, business leaders, and professionals such as university teachers, doctors, and lawyers whose choice of garments is supported by the textile-production and retail industry. Conservative townspeople adapt modern garments to suit their taste; men prefer soberly cut and styled suits and shirts open at the neck, while women wear long coats and head scarves. The availability of blue denim has drastically influenced the dress of young men and women, who wear jeans with a range of tops—T-shirts, blouses, long-sleeved tunics, and so forth.

Village dress is also affected by the standardization of the market economy. Men's appearance varies between a choice of black şalvar trousers, straight-legged European trousers, and jeans, worn with shirts, jackets, and a stiff, flat, black peaked cap depending on age, occupation, and taste. The handsome and distinctive dress of Kocakovacik, which was worn by all women until about 1970, has given way to simpler ready-made garments bought at the weekly market from traders who bring in truckloads of clothing, fabric, haberdashery, and accessories for sale.

Where traditional garments are still made and worn, they include commercially produced trimmings of braids, ribbons, and sequins. Women's village dress in the early twenty-first century mainly consists of loose şalvar or an ankle-length skirt worn with a long-sleeved blouse or dress and a waistcoat or jacket, which may be hand- or machine-knitted. A simple white head scarf is worn, which young unmarried women embroider to indicate their single status. Wedding dress is a compromise between tradition and modernity. A bride in either a town or a village chooses an elaborate white European-style dress but may still be wrapped in a red veil as she moves to her new home.

Paradoxically, the creation of the Republic of Turkey, which aimed to replace the old Ottoman structures with modern systems, has contributed to the survival of traditional dress. Territorially, early-twenty-first-century Turkey corresponds to the old province of Anatolia, which was the focus of a deliberate policy to forge a new identity. After the clothing reforms of 1925 to 1934, the practice of group dances to celebrate weddings, religious feasts, and public holidays continued. For these dances, the performers still chose to wear the colorful dresses of the past. This was seen as a means of promoting pride in the indigenous culture of Turkey, so that dances were recorded and performed by state groups. Teams of folklorists and ethnographers studied the outfits in depth, and their results were formalized into an identifiable regional dress. Great efforts were made to ensure that these costumes were accurate, which has led to a revival of traditional craftsmanship. This is seen, for example, in Kocakovacik, where women skilled in weaving and embroidery make garments on commission for folk dance groups and researchers and also for sale through dealers to collectors and tourists.

References and Further Reading

Breu, Marlene R. "Traditional Turkish Women's Dress: A Source of Common Understandings for Expected Behaviors." In *Folk Dress in Europe and Anatolia*, edited by Linda Welters, 33–52. Oxford: Berg, 1999.

Davis, Fanny. *The Ottoman Lady*. New York: Greenwood Press, 1986.

Faroqhi, Suraiya. *Towns and Townsmen of Ottoman Anatolia: Trade, Crafts and Food Production in an Urban Setting 1520–1650*. London: Cambridge University Press, 1984.

Faroqhi, Suraiya. *Subjects of the Sultan: Culture and Daily Life in the Ottoman Empire*. London: I. B. Tauris, 2000.

Faroqhi, Suraiya. "Female Costumes in Late Fifteenth-Century Bursa." In *Ottoman Costumes: From Textile to Identity*, edited by Suraiya Faroqhi and Christoph K. Neumann, 81–91. Istanbul: Eren, 2004.

Garnett, Lucy. *The Women of Turkey and Their Folk-Lore*. 2 vols. London: David Nutt, 1890.

Hamdi Bey, Osman, and Marie de Launay. *Les Costumes Populaires de la Turquie en 1873. Ouvrage Publiee sous le Patronat de la Commission Imperiale Ottomane pour L'Exposition Universelle de Vienne*. Constantinople: The Levant Times and Shipping Gazette Press, 1873.

Krody, Sumru Belger. *Flowers of Silk and Gold: Four Centuries of Ottoman Embroidery*. Washington, DC: Textile Museum, 2000.

Lewis, Raphaela. *Everyday Life in Ottoman Turkey*. London: Batsford, 1971.

Ozel, Mehmet. *Turkish Folkloric Costumes*. Ankara: Fine Arts Development Foundation of Turkey, 1992.

Pardoe, Julia. *The City of the Sultan and Domestic Manners of the Turks in 1836*. 2 vols. London: Henry Colburn, 1837.

Quataert, Donald, ed. *Manufacturing in the Ottoman Empire and Turkey 1500–1950*. Albany: State University of New York Press, 1994.

Quataert, Donald, ed. *Consumption Studies and the History of the Ottoman Empire 1550–1922: An Introduction*. Albany: State University of New York Press, 2000.

Ramsay, Mrs. W. M. *Every-Day Life in Turkey*. London: Hodder and Stoughton, 1897.

Renda, Gunsel, ed. *Woman in Anatolia: 9000 Years of the Anatolian Woman*. Istanbul: Ministry of Culture, 1993.

Scarce, Jennifer. *Women's Costume of the Near and Middle East*. London: Unwin Hyman, 1987.

Scarce, Jennifer. *Domestic Culture in the Middle East*. Edinburgh: National Museums of Scotland, 1996.

Scarce, Jennifer. "Gold Embroidery in the Ottoman World." In *Shimmering Gold: The Splendor of Gold Embroidered Textiles*, edited by Nitza Behroozi Baroz and Gania Dolev, 16–20. Tel Aviv: Eretz Israel Museum, 2007.

Jennifer M. Scarce

See also Snapshot: Turkish Costume Albums.

Dress in Modern Israel

Dress in Palestine at the end of the nineteenth century and up until the establishment of the independent State of Israel in 1948 reflected the many changes that took place in the area during that time. The most prominent change was the end of the Ottoman Empire, which had ruled for over one hundred years, and the takeover by the British Mandate (1922) following the occupation of Palestine by the British Army in World War I (1917).

At the beginning of the twentieth century, the population of Palestine was approximately 500,000, 10 percent of whom were Jews. Textile factories were nonexistent, most of the city streets were yet unpaved, and the progress that took place in the West at that time bypassed this area totally. Under the rule of the British Mandate, industry forged ahead furiously, however, with the Jewish inhabitants of Jerusalem, Haifa, and mainly Tel Aviv catching up and rapidly closing the gap with the West. The British influence is most marked in the establishment of numerous textile factories in cooperation with Jewish government agencies as well as in the changed style of dress in Jewish society, which began to break away from traditional Arab influences and adopt Western attire. World War II (1939–1945) was a powerful catalyst for the textile industry in Palestine for two main reasons: the need to supply the British Army, based in the area, with tents, underwear, and other textiles; and the immigration of Austrian and German Jews, experts in the various fields of textile production, who brought both modern equipment and professional know-how to the textile works.

To fully understand the changes that took place in the style of dress and in the fashion industry in Israel from the birth of the State of Israel in 1948 until the end of the 1990s, it is necessary to understand the origins of the Jewish settlers in Palestine from the start of the first Zionist immigration to Palestine in 1882 on, which is the point in time when the history of dress in modern Israel commences.

THE ORIENTAL STYLE (1882–1932)

During the initial period of Jewish settlement in Palestine, at the end of the nineteenth and the beginning of the twentieth century, the influence of Oriental culture was evident in the West. This influence found expression in the works of the German romantics Johann Wolfgang von Goethe and Friedrich von Schiller, who attributed to the Orient qualities of nobility stemming from the innate naïveté of its primitive tribes: the Greeks and the Hebrews. This influence was also fed by German philosopher Friedrich Wilhelm Nietzsche's idea of the Übermensch ("Superman"), the veritable superhuman that was expected to bring change and progress to all civilization. The ideal of "the new Jew" who came to the Holy Land at the beginning of the twentieth century, who was a worker and idealist, was based extensively on the image of the Übermensch and was the complete opposite of "the old Jew." While the old Jew was a pale, weak-bodied spiritual being occupied mainly by holy studies, the new Jew was tall and muscular and worked in manual labor.

This Oriental influence is apparent in the popular mode of dress among the Jews living in Palestine at the beginning of the twentieth century, who, in addition to the prevalent Western attire, adopted clothing of Oriental origin. The Bezalel Art Academy, established at that time, encouraged adoption of the Oriental style. According to the Bezalel concept, the Israeli woman had a typically Oriental look, was heavily adorned with jewelry, and looked like a biblical figure. The typical man was Oriental, dressed in a multicolored cloak with a turbaned head. Bezalel was an influential cultural institution, and the garments influenced by it at the time reflected the ideal in modern Jewish dress. This attire was basically Western with certain prominent Oriental influences, such as the *galabiyeh* (a loose, long-sleeved, ankle-length garment with a small collar)—popular apparel worn mainly by men in Arab society.

In older cities such as Jerusalem and Jaffa, and even in Tel Aviv, founded in 1909, there was a small population of wealthy Jews whose custom it was to wear fashionable Western clothes according to the latest fashion from Paris. In Tel Aviv, the Oriental fashion expressed itself mainly in dances choreographed by Baruch Agadati and Rina Nikova, whose costumes had an Eastern flavor, as well as in the dress of Queen Esther in the local Purim Carnival in Tel Aviv. The Oriental style reached its peak at the end of the 1920s and then from the 1930s began to disappear in favor of the Western style, which increased in popularity with the growing immigration from Central Europe in the 1930s.

Some of the agricultural settlements that were founded in Palestine at the end of the nineteenth century were Rishon-Le-Zion and Zichron Yaacov, which was founded by the French Rothschild family. This group adopted French fashion, which was either imported or sewn from imported cloth by local seamstresses. It is important to bear in mind that, in Palestine of those years, there was no fashion industry until the mid-1920s, and it was therefore impossible to purchase locally made fashion items. Women chose mainly dress patterns from French magazines and the local press, which provided current fashion updates.

The leading fashion trend in Tel Aviv of the 1920s was the flat, boyish silhouette emphasized by tubular-style dresses that flattened the bust, narrowed the hips, and made the waist unnoticeable. Inspiration for this look was derived from World War I (1914–1918), during which women replaced the recruited men in industry. When the war ended, women would not return to their former attire, which was uncomfortable and restricted their movement.

The second wave of Zionist immigration, which began in 1903 and continued until the outbreak of World War I in 1914, brought many of the Zionist movement leaders to Palestine. This was a Socialistic immigration whose ideology steered clear of luxury items, Western fashion, and a bourgeois lifestyle. The young pioneers who came with this immigration usually wore simple, unremarkable, shabby clothing to demonstrate their Socialistic ideology. The style of this simple clothing was a mixture of Eastern and Western influences: White Oriental garb was worn to blend into the Oriental environment, while Western men's clothes were worn by the young women pioneers to express their sexual equality. In the agricultural settlements, it was also customary for young men and women, both at work and leisure, to wear the *keffiyeh*, a traditional Arab men's headdress made of a square of woven cloth, usually cotton, with a black-and-white design, folded and wrapped in various styles around the head. This style of headgear was worn by the Arab *fallah* (laborers).

The third wave of Jewish immigration to Palestine (1919–1923) also brought a group of young East Europeans who believed in Socialism and came to put their theory into practice. They demanded total equality—both socioeconomic and gender—which was reflected in their clothing, which was even shabbier than their predecessors' in order to express their ideology that opposed any kind of luxury and comfort.

The mid-1920s saw yet another wave of immigration, the fourth Zionist immigration (1924–1929), the major part of which was from Poland, especially from Lodz, which was a textile city. Among them were the textile professionals who started the textile and clothing industry in Tel Aviv, which, at that time, was

becoming the most important Jewish city in Palestine. The city of Tel Aviv enjoyed a bustling, urban lifestyle, and the wealthy residents, who dressed in the latest Paris fashion, totally ignored the Oriental style and its influence, as did the inhabitants of other cities in Palestine, who followed suit, adopting a Western lifestyle and dressing accordingly.

ATTEMPTS TO CREATE A LOCAL STYLE (1933–1948)

The fifth wave of immigrants began arriving in Palestine in 1929 and increased greatly with the Nazis' rise to power in Germany. From 1929 to 1939, approximately 250,000 Jews, mainly of the middle class, immigrated to Palestine, swelling the population by a third. The first immigrants were wealthy Jews of German and Austrian descent who founded and established the fashion industry. The early textile plants, most of which were in Tel Aviv, enjoyed immediate success due to their high professional standards and ability to adapt their wares to the needs of the changing market. The peak of success was achieved at the beginning of World War II (1939–1945), when many of the buyers who had been accustomed to purchasing in Germany or Austria before the outbreak of war came to Tel Aviv to buy from the same manufacturers with whom they had been acquainted before the war. From the beginning of 1941 until the end of 1945, fashion weeks were held in Tel Aviv twice a year for the spring/summer and autumn/winter seasons. The garments shown at these events excelled in their high standards and wide range.

The Jewish community of the "Kfar Hasidi" Colony at Nachalat Yaakov in the Zebulun Valley, Palestine, 1926. In the photograph are Rabbi Yabloner, the leader of the colony, and Achad Ha'am, a Jewish philosopher. From the late nineteenth century on, some Jewish settlers in Palestine adopted Western dress, wearing the latest Paris fashions, while other Jewish immigrants wore unremarkable, shabby clothing to demonstrate their Socialistic ideology. Hulton Archive/Getty Images.

Given that, until the mid-1920s, there had been no fashion industry in Tel Aviv at all, the rapid development of this field in less than two decades is amazing, and this progress made Tel Aviv the fashion center of Southwest Asia. The Arab states that had ceased purchasing in Palestine at the beginning of the 1930s for political reasons once again began to buy fashion items in Tel Aviv during the war since there was no other available fashion source. Buyers from Cyprus, Iran, and Turkey did so as well. The British high commissioners in Palestine during the mandate supported the local garment industry and cooperated closely with the local Jewish authorities—among them, the Foreign Trade Institute, which was responsible for the initiation and organization of the fashion weeks in Tel Aviv. Other factors that contributed to the success of the garment industry in Palestine at the time were the convenient port of export through the Red Sea, available crude oil piped from Iraq directly to Haifa, and the high-quality cotton purchased in nearby Egypt. The major reason for this immediate success, however, was the presence of the large British Army bases in the country, which required tents, underwear, and socks—items that were supplied by the local Jewish textile industry. All these factors contributed to the unprecedented success of the local garment industry.

The vast numbers of immigrants from Austria and Germany made their mark on the way of life in Tel Aviv, where most of them had chosen to settle. They dressed in Tel Aviv exactly in the same manner they had in Vienna or Berlin, despite the nearly unbearable summer heat. The women insisted on wearing elegant Western-style tailored suits, fashionable high-heeled shoes with matching handbags, and gloves; the men wore suits and ties even in the height of summer. This immigration was also the driving force behind the establishment of fashionable clothing shops and salons in Tel Aviv as well as fashionable coffee shops and posh restaurants in the best European tradition. Tel Aviv nightlife of the 1930s included crowded parties and glamorous events at which the women were dressed in long, backless evening gowns and the men sported either tuxedos or elegant suits.

The absorption of large numbers of immigrants, the lack of raw materials, and soaring prices during World War II created a need for a utility program to provide basic clothing and footwear for the penniless immigrants who were streaming into the country. The utility program enabled the equal distribution of items among the population and was set in motion by the mandate government in collaboration with the fashion industry union from September 1942. In accordance with this plan, eleven textile plants were selected, each of which was required to manufacture a limited number of designs suited to the local climate. These garments, in the fashion of World War II, were far cheaper than those sold on the free market and were sold to the public by allocated quota. The utility plan in textiles and footwear reaped great success due to high-quality designs and low prices. This utility program, in force until 1946, was further followed by the Mad'Am program (meaning "nation's uniform"), which ended with the outbreak of the War of Independence and the subsequent establishment of the independent State of Israel.

Khaki clothes, a new style of fashion, became popular from the mid-1930s. This fashion appeared not only in the agricultural settlements but also in major cities such as Tel Aviv, which was considered the capital city of fashion in Israel. These clothes, mainly produced by Ata textile industries in Haifa—comprised of long trousers with long-sleeved masculine shirts for winter and short khaki pants with short-sleeved khaki shirts in summer—were generally worn by both youngsters and adult men. In some of the youth movements, it was customary for the members to wear khaki clothes year-round, and they were the mandatory uniform for any scout exercise and Gadna training (pre-army training for Israeli youth). Khaki clothes were worn not only to save money but also, mainly, to express the ideology and the dogged unity of the Jewish population in Palestine and their aspiration to establish an independent Jewish state. This was a kind of national religion that united the Jewish population, narrowing the socioeconomic differences among them. Khaki clothes—notably the khaki shorts and open-necked shirt—became the hallmark of the Sabra identity (sabra is a thorny cactus bearing sweet fruit), the symbol of the new young generation of Jews in the State of Israel: Jews, healthy in body and spirit, ready for the struggle to establish the independent State of Israel.

The aspiration to establish an Israeli culture in the land of Israel was expressed in the field of fashion as well. A fashion competition for the design of a national dress took place at the Orient Fair in Tel Aviv in 1936. The winning design by Pennina Riva combined Oriental and Western clothing with biblical elements. The press of the time repeatedly discussed the attempts to create the appropriate dress for the Jewish nation's way of life and highlighted the efforts to contrive a national dress. These attempts reflect the naive aspiration to create a national identity in all aspects of life. Nevertheless, none of these experiments was accepted or adopted. This period is characterized by a mixture of styles, from simple utilitarian khaki work clothes to formal evening gowns worn at the bourgeois Tel Aviv parties and interspersed with styles brought by immigrants who had fled Europe possessing only the clothes on their back.

THE ISRAELI STYLE AND FASHION DURING THE AUSTERITY PERIOD (1949–1959)

The trend of searching for ethnic roots in the ancient Orient expanded and gathered momentum in the mid-1940s. This trend stemmed from the need to disengage from the historical Jewish fate, which had led to the Holocaust, and to reestablish the connection with the pure and innocent ideals of the ancient Canaanite past. The establishment of the State of Israel in 1948 strengthened the bond with the ancient Orient and biblical times, which became part of the mainstream canon. In addition, the new symbols of Israeli culture were supported by symbols from the common past of Israel, such as the seven-branched candelabrum (menorah) and the reproduction of ancient coins, which became the official local currency. During the years 1948 to 1950, thousands of immigrants were absorbed into Israel, and the population doubled. The necessity to absorb so many immigrants in such a short time obliged the government to create jobs for everyone, which was difficult. One of the solutions to this demanding problem led to the founding of Maskit, headed by Ruth Dayan, in 1954. This project was geared toward the preservation of the ethnic handicrafts brought by the immigrants and their incorporation into commercial fashion products for sale on the local market. Maskit thus became the melting pot for Israeli fashion. It succeeded in combining the traditional handicrafts of Jews from Yemen, Bukhara, Iraq, Kurdistan, and Morocco with the modern, up-to-date designs of Finny Leitersdorf. The stylish Maskit garments were renowned on the local market and were later successfully exported overseas.

One of the most successful Maskit designs by Leitersdorf was the "Desert Coat." It was the ultimate Israeli fashion creation in which fashion and folklore were perfectly combined. The Desert Coat was a handwoven garment of roughly textured sheep wool cut from one piece of fabric that draped diagonally over the body. The immigrants who sewed these garments at home did not have sewing machines; therefore, the trimmings were hand-embroidered, which gave the garments the famed unique character that continued over the years to characterize later versions. The Desert Coat was considered the faithful representative of Israeli fashion for almost three decades.

Maskit's influence on Israeli fashion in the 1950s was also expressed in the many designs that incorporated Yemenite embroidery. The concept of embroidered folklore designs coupled with Western patterns led to a successful line of fashion exports characterized by ethnic elements of embroidery, handweaving, and local materials such as raffia. The 1950s also saw the development of modern fashion plants that created designs in the leading international fashion trends. The first to achieve international acclaim were Gottex (swimsuits) and Beged-Or (leather wear). The 1950s were characterized not only by the Israeli style but also by the style of the Austerity Regime (tzena), which was imposed on the public due to depleted reserves of foreign currency caused by the changeover from the British pound to the Israeli lira.

This plan provided each citizen with a book of coupons commonly known as points. Clothes, food, and household items could be purchased only with these points. The austerity plan for clothing came into force at the beginning of January 1949, when several basic textile products began to be sold at reduced prices, followed by the chosen brand name Lakol (meaning "suitable for all without discrimination"). The first Lakol clothing products included shirts; trousers and dresses were gradually added to the range of basic textile products. The first dresses manufactured under the Lakol brand name were old-fashioned, poorly sewn, and unattractive. Although these garments were 60 percent cheaper than their counterparts, they were not in great demand, and women who could afford it had clothes privately sewn or purchased them on the black market. By the end of 1949, the entire textile industry was under complete government supervision relative to the supply of raw materials and manufacturing. In February 1950, Lakol's production levels reached 2,600,000 knitted items and 1,400,000 sewn goods, which included trousers, dresses, shirts, and other garments for men and women. Shoes were also manufactured under the Lakol trademark.

Lakol shoes were 30 percent cheaper than other similar products; the quality was good and the design satisfactory. Unlike the Lakol clothing, which was not very successful, Lakol shoes were a great success and were preferred over similar products that were far more expensive. Lakol fashion attempted to provide reasonably priced products for all, and in that respect it achieved the declared goal. However, in so doing, it inadvertently damaged the textile industry in Israel. The vital competition between manufacturers to create up-to-date and attractive fashions was eradicated due to the government dictates over the design and quality of the garments, which were not always in keeping with the latest fashion call of the free market. The austerity plan for clothing and footwear gradually tapered off and finally ended in December 1952.

The austerity plan and the Lakol brand were responsible for the popularity of khaki clothes and "biblical" sandals (made of two parallel strips of leather across the instep, a strap around the ankle, and either with or without a buckle). Because these items were cheap, practical, and comfortable and could be purchased for a minimum of allocated points, they were widely used by everyone irrespective of gender and status, bringing to the streets a uniform, equal look, which in some ways narrowed the severe social and economic differences between the penniless immigrants from the diaspora and the veteran, economically well-established population of the time. The tembel (dummy) hat joined these Israeli symbols and became the trademark of the typical Israeli figure.

The 1950s are remembered in the collective Israeli ethos as the period of khaki and biblical sandals that marked the birth of the State of Israel—a time when the founders' Socialistic ideology bonded with the forced austerity and when the khaki clothes and sandals served as an ideological tool for the young regime struggling to build the new state.

THE ORIGINAL STYLE (1960–1973)

The 1960s began with great hopes. The austerity period had ended, and the economy had improved, awakening awareness of new fashion trends that were a far cry from the purposely drab, monotonous, and boring fashions of the 1950s. The improved economic climate enabled Israelis to travel abroad, and they returned with the latest fashions: miniskirts and jeans. Fashion in the 1960s gained great momentum in the wake of the Six Days' War (1967), when Israel's popularity attracted many volunteers from Europe and the United States who came to work on the kibbutzim. This was a time when the world belonged to the young. The young and dynamic Israeli society took note of the fashion innovations of the times and immediately embraced them. The very short miniskirt and the geometric hair designs of Vidal Sassoon took hold and were all the rage in the streets of Tel Aviv. Tiny, dark boutiques with the latest pop music playing in the background, like those of Carnaby Street in London, sprang up on Dizengoff Street (the main street of Tel Aviv). The clothes they stocked were mostly imported from Paris and London or were designed by young, local Israeli fashion designers taking their first steps into the world of fashion.

Israeli fashion in these times excelled in high quality and finishing standards and was characterized by creative and innovative designs containing ethnic elements. It was in great demand and achieved high prices. The original Israeli style that developed in the 1960s sought to draw inspiration from the clothing of the ancient Hebrews. Attempts to explore ancient Hebrew dress resulted in the "Ein Gedi" model, which was made of fabric woven according to an ancient motif copied from a piece of fabric from the second century B.C.E. that was discovered in the caves at Ein Gedi in the Judaean Desert. The garment was presented in two designs. The first was a sleeveless wool dress with fringed edges and a large fringed shawl. The second was similar to the first, with a coarser look and without fringes. The Israeli fashion houses spared no effort to create original designs that would keep up with international high-fashion innovations, and they succeeded for quite some time. The young designers who began establishing themselves in the local fashion industry also contributed to the growing prestige of Israeli fashion. A 1972

"Ein Gedi" woolen dress, designed by Finny Leitersdorf, Israel, ca. 1960. This garment was inspired by an ancient motif from a piece of fabric from the second century B.C.E. discovered in the caves at Ein Gedi in the Judaean Desert. Photograph by Gavra Mandil, Studio Gavra.

article in *Israel Fashion* magazine provides a glimpse of Israeli fashion's important role:

> Today [fashion's] spell has fallen upon Israel. Not for a whim, but because Israel has created something new and fresh, brimful of fun and joie de vivre—some original ideas and interesting designs, some dazzling new mediterranean colours, and also something cosmopolitan and international, as well as genuinely Israeli—all of which have won her a spotlight inside Fashion's magic circle. … Now that its status has been accepted as a trendsetter of Fashion, Israel looks to send out more ripples of the new waves and to create a wider sphere of influence in the fascinating field of dress.

The most prominent fashion areas were swimwear, leather goods, and jersey knits. Designs by Gottex, the leading producer of swimwear, were particularly outstanding and rapidly achieved the level of haute couture. The addition of accessories such as beachwear, shoulder capes, pants, and blouses by designer Leah Gottlieb branded Gottex swimwear as a lifestyle. The Gottex swimsuits excelled in their unique design, with the accent on stylish ethnic motifs, and they were made of high-quality materials using innovative technology. The Gottex swimsuits decorated with rich embroidery or multicolored artistic prints projected a look of uncompromising prestige. Gottex achieved international acclaim, and Gottlieb, the house designer, received many international awards for her work.

The leather goods industry achieved an international representation thanks to several factories producing leather wear, the most outstanding of these being Beged-Or. This factory, located in the periphery of Tel Aviv as part of the Ministry of Trade and Industry's ambitious plan to establish the fashion and textiles industries outside the cities, was originally intended to manufacture basic leather coats. In 1968, the factory was bought by Leslie Fulop, who decided to turn it into a modern factory for high fashion. For this purpose he established a research and development department that experimented with sophisticated processes combining natural and synthetic leather, furs, wool, and acrylic, thereby achieving interesting and unique textures never seen before. The Beged-Or collections, which presented a vast range in myriad colors, were an international hit. Beged-Or's products sold at very high prices and were worn by celebrities all over the world.

One of the noted Israeli designers of the time was Gideon Oberson, who studied in Paris, then returned to Israel in 1961 and immediately received the first prize at a fashion competition organized by the Israel Export Institute. This award paved his way to opening his own fashion house and participating in fashion shows for the Bonds in the company of other prominent Israeli designers such as Lola Behr and Finny Leitersdorf and French couturiers such as Nina Ricci and Pierre Cardin. Apart from the line he produced for his own fashion house, Oberson also designed collections for other Israeli fashion houses, earning himself a name as a very stylish and minimalistic designer in tune with international fashion trends.

Another designer who achieved great success was Penina Shalon, who started out in Maskit as a manual knitting machine instructor and proceeded to develop knits with unusual textures. Wool, silk, velvet, straw, and ribbons were made into thin threads, interwoven with the glittering effects of silver and gold

Lurex. These yarns were then knitted to create a range of fabrics. Her knits, characterized by a delicate, personal appearance, preserved a handworked look and ageless style. Shalon exhibited her designs at the Bonds shows and achieved great success both in Israel and abroad. Tamara Yuval-Jones, too, had a unique personal style. She was not influenced by Israeli sources but drew inspiration from the romantic style of the Victorian era. Her designs were most popular with designers, actors, and offbeat bohemians.

The Israeli designers responsible for leading the Israeli style to heights of international success were Leitersdorf, with her creations for Maskit, and Rozi Ben-Joseph, with her designs for Rikma. Leitersdorf based her designs on motifs of Israeli origin inspired by the landscape, heritage, and local materials, imbuing them with a timeless power, using haute couture techniques. Ben-Joseph employed the same sources of inspiration but created designs for mass production. Leitersdorf's garments were made of silk and pure wool, with silver accessories, while Ben-Joseph's were made of inexpensive cotton adorned with brilliant-colored stripes or with the addition of printed Oriental motifs and macramé knots. While Maskit items were very expensive and far beyond the reach of most people, the Rikma items were reasonably priced and affordable.

Riki Ben Ari was the first Israeli to have an international career as a fashion illustrator. She studied in Paris and, upon her return to Israel, began teaching fashion illustration in Tel Aviv and became a fashion consultant to Israeli manufacturers exporting abroad. Within a short time, she received an employment offer from the Israeli Wool Center in Tel Aviv, where she illustrated fashion forecasts side by side with famous designers such as Sonia Rykiel and Karl Lagerfeld. From there she progressed to Promostyl, which was the leading fashion forecaster in the world. During this time, she was also involved in creating designs for several Israeli fashion houses and, for a short time, she had her own factory. Her style was characterized by clean graphic lines and precise proportions.

The beginning of the 1970s heralded the appearance of the first maxi dresses, followed by hot pants. At this time, all the latest fashion innovations reached Tel Aviv. The romantic look was very popular in Israel, and the ethnic look, with the addition of a local interpretation, was very successful abroad.

THE GLOBAL STYLE (1973–1990)

The energy crisis that followed the Yom Kippur War (1973) resulted in a waning demand for Israeli fashion garments abroad. In an attempt to survive in the changing international fashion market, various experiments were made to create a new ultimate style that would revive the golden touch of the 1960s.

These experiments failed to bring back to Israeli fashion the prestige and high demand that had characterized it in the preceding decade. The textile factories that had once exported high-priced, top-quality fashion abroad now manufactured as subcontractors for cheap fashion chains or for catalogs. This period was characterized by many changing styles with no definite direction. Israeli fashion became global, and all attempts to bring to it a unique look failed. In addition, the new government policy regarding investments in textile factories, which had been very generous in the 1960s, became very strict, leaving the fashion industry to grapple on its own with the international market without being subsidized.

A 1974 article in *Israel Fashion* magazine indicates the new direction of Israeli fashion:

> Our collections for Spring/Summer 1975 reflect the new spirit of ready-to-wear, a return to ease, a soft romantic mood, and they reflect our manufacturers' awareness, our designers' talent for what is right, for what is fashion and for what is now. … What they have in common is the ability to interpret fashion trends, to create good contemporary marketable collections, and it is this shared trait that enables Israel to win a steadily-larger share of the buying programs of department and specialty stores, buying groups and chains in major cities across the globe.

In this period, Israeli fashion magazines bear no evidence of the former originality, use of local ethnic motifs, or historical inspiration and show no attempt to create an original Israeli fashion line. The aim was solely to manufacture standard, reasonably priced fashion goods based on international trends. Israeli fashion at this time surrendered any attempt to influence world fashion by

Modern Israeli dress designed by Sasson Kedem, 2006. The dress has a loose-fitted shape with dramatic stripes inspired by Eastern tradition. Kedem is one of several Israeli designers who create modern and original styles based on Israeli symbols. Photograph by Gadi Dagon.

becoming just another group of manufacturers of garments that followed the rules dictated by buyers from abroad.

Foreign buyers who came to the fashion week in Israel expressed disappointment because, instead of finding a unique Israeli style, they found an unremarkable international style that could be found elsewhere at cheaper prices. Starting in mid-1980s, Israeli fashion weeks were cancelled due to low buyers' interest.

In the late 1980s, the budding designers of Shenkar College of Engineering and Design (founded in 1970), imbued with creative talent, professionalism, and ambition to succeed, played an important role in Israeli fashion. Unfortunately, they too did not succeed in uplifting the sinking Israeli fashion industry, and most of them were forced into designing commercial styles according to the ruling trends, thereby giving up all attempts at originality.

In those years, trends became a crucial factor in international fashion. New trend centers sprouted rapidly in fashion capitals and manufactured their fashion predictions at a faster pace. The importance of the right colors, looks, and other seasonal characteristics was cardinal. Missing the right color or style could bring a factory to bankruptcy. In this atmosphere of indisputable dictated fashion dogma, young designers sank into mundane, mass-produced lines, losing their originality.

The 1980s introduced the "oversized look" for women into the international fashion arena. This style, with its accent on broad shoulders and wide clothes, steered clear of women's natural body lines, creating a powerful feminine look. This look, derived from the women who had succeeded in infiltrating the international work market (television programs such as *Dallas* also had a considerable role to play in this look), achieving authority in managerial positions that until then had traditionally been held by men. The oversized look damaged the Israeli fashion industry, hurting their sales and image, as they proceeded to manufacture one-size garments—a far cry from precise patterns and neat stitching. In addition, sportswear was rapidly becoming popular everywhere, which makes it possible to better understand the damage to manufacturers, who no longer invested effort to create elaborate styles in order to produce original designs but instead mass-manufactured tracksuits and sweatshirts, which were sold mainly to catalog companies abroad.

Despite the trendy style dominating the period, several attempts to create a unique look were made by Israeli designers such as Ivor Adler, who made romantic dresses from Indian crepe fabric. These were very successful at the beginning of the 1970s but lost their allure in the early 1980s, which led to the closing of the factory in 1983. Another designer who sought uniqueness in fashion was Dorin Frankfurt, who succeeded in combining the trends in fashion with a casual, informal look. Frankfurt has also designed stage outfits for Israeli singers abroad, among them the Eurovision singers, representing in their clothes the nonchalant directness that is characteristic of the Israeli way of life.

THE 1990s AND BEYOND

The international fashion of the 1990s is reflected in the fashion on the streets of Tel Aviv, bubbling with vitality, updated with the latest fashion novelties, and revealing a strong leaning toward the fashions of London and Japan. Young Israelis with fashion awareness and personal style designed for themselves eccentric outfits created from secondhand garments accessorized with a humoristic flair, bringing a gaiety, a joie de vivre, to the streets of Tel Aviv. Rumors of the novel street fashion rapidly attracted the attention of the hosts of popular television shows such as those produced by the Canadian Fashion Television or the popular music channel MTV, which, in the late 1990s, sent fashion reporters to Israel to cover its fashion scene. Exceptionally noted was Gottex, with its unique swimwear, which became an international trendsetter in the 1990s.

While street fashion flourished, local factories were finding it difficult to compete with the stream of inexpensive imports from Southeast Asia and East Europe that flooded the market. As a result, some of these factories were forced to shut down, and the rest barely survived. The global village syndrome was also evident in the trendy, international fashions of companies such as Zara and Mango, which opened prospering, highly successful branches in Tel Aviv, and the influence of top elite designers such as Christian Lacroix and Ralph Lauren to Kikar Hamedina, one of the most exclusive and prestigious shopping areas of Tel Aviv, on Israeli fashion designers in general.

Alongside the global trends dominating Israeli fashion, a wave of new and refreshing designs by young designers—mainly graduates of the Shenkar College—filtered into the market. Although influenced by international trends, these young designers sought to find a unique path of their own within the global complex. Some of them opened small studios, mostly in the northern end of Dizengoff and nearby streets in Tel Aviv. These designers stood out in international fashion competitions, where they were awarded first prizes and received high acclaim. Some of the talented young designers went abroad, where they acquired international reputations: Among them were Alber Elbaz, who became the chief designer for Lanvin in Paris, and Avshalom Gur, who was appointed head designer for Ossie Clark's in London.

The phenomenon of these up-and-coming young designers gathered momentum in 2000, when they suggested an interesting alternative to popular global fashion. Among the varying styles there emerged interesting attempts to create an original Israeli style based on legendary Israeli symbols such as the khaki clothes of Ata from the 1940s and 1950s, which appear in Ilana Efrati's collection, or the look-alike Desert Coat appearing in Sasson Kedem's collection. Another new development in fashion, in which Israel is playing a significant part, are "smart clothes." In this field, the Israeli textile company Polgat developed a fabric made of wool and outlast fibers for the National Aeronautics and Space Administration, or NASA; this new fabric was later used for making heat-regulating body suits. These developments join the wave of smart clothes already being manufactured by Delta Textiles, such as odor-repelling fabrics that retard bacterial growth resulting from perspiration as well as a range of clothes made from fabric impregnated with sunscreen protection to suit a variety of needs. Israel is also taking an active part in the development of computerized wearables, including, among others, clothing able to record physiological bodily functions as well as computer-based garments equipped with motion-identification sensors capable of utilizing solar energy aided by electronic control units.

The introduction of new methods of marketing and manufacturing, modern textile technology, and the concerted efforts to nurture creative and personal design provide a supportive environment for Israeli fashion.

References and Further Reading

Arbel, Rachel, ed. *Blue and White in Color: Visual Images of Zionism, 1897–1947*. Tel Aviv: Beth Hatefutsoth, 1997.

Bar-Am, Micha, ed. *Robert Capa: Photographs from Israel, 1948–1950*. Tel Aviv: Tel Aviv Museum of Art, 1988.

Bar-Am, Micha, and Orna Bar-Am. *Painting with Light: The Photographic Aspect in the Work of E. M. Lilien*. Tel Aviv: Tel Aviv Museum of Art, Dvir Publishing, 1991.

Donner, Batia, ed. *Shamir: Hebrew Graphics, Shamir Brothers Studio*. Tel Aviv: Tel Aviv Museum of Art, 1999.

Donner, Batia. "Israel Fashion (1965–1980)." In *Maskit: A Local Fabric*, edited by Batia Donner, 4–27. Tel Aviv: Eretz Israel Museum, 2003.

Donner, Batia, ed. *Maskit: A Local Fabric*. Tel Aviv: Eretz Israel Museum, 2003.

Jagendorf, Malka, and Vivianne Barsky, eds. *Faces, Facades, and More: The Photographs of Alfred Bernheim*. Jerusalem: Israel Museum, 1991.

Juhasz, Esther, ed. *Sephardi Jews in the Ottoman Empire: Aspects of Material Culture*. Jerusalem: Israel Museum, 1990.

Kofler, Hana, ed. *Tsalmania in Tel-Aviv: Rudi Weissenstein (1910–1992)*. Tel Aviv: Alpha Prints, 2002.

Raz, Ayala. "Fashion in Eretz-Israel." *Ariel—The Israel Review of Arts and Letters* 107 (1998): 161–182.

Shwartz-Be'eri, Ora. *The Jews of Kurdistan: Daily Life, Customs, Arts and Crafts*. Jerusalem: Israel Museum, 2000.

Tartakover, David, ed. *Finy Leitersdorf, Israeli Fashion Designer*. Tel Aviv: Tel Aviv Museum of Art, 1996.

Tevet-Klagsbald, Yael, ed. *Lola 1910–1997*. Ramat-Gan, Israel: Shenkar College of Textile Technology & Fashion, 1997.

Weir, Shelagh. *Palestinian Costume*. London: British Museum Publications, 1994.

Ayala Raz

See also Jewish Dress in Central and Southwest Asia and the Diaspora.

Christian Secular, Monastic, and Liturgical Dress in the Eastern Mediterranean

- Early Christian Liturgical Dress
- Byzantine Liturgical Dress
- Coptic and Syrian Liturgical Dress
- Coptic and Syrian Monastic Dress
- Byzantine Monastic Dress

The first Christian communities were established around the Mediterranean in the first century C.E. At that time, there was not yet a unifying structure in theological views, nor in organization, nor hierarchy. By the second century, however, in almost all communities, there were three ranks in the local hierarchy—an *episkopos* (bishop, literally "overseer") as the head, *presbyteroi* (priests), and *diakonoi* (deacons)—but they did not yet wear any kind of distinctive dress that indicated their rank.

The first Council of Nicaea (325 C.E.), a general meeting called by Constantine the Great, brought together representatives (bishops) from all over the Christian world, and a certain degree of unity was established. At the council a creed was formulated that contained the basic points of belief. The church was organized under the formal authority of the emperor, with three major cities or patriarchates (Rome, Alexandria, and Antioch) whose bishops had authority over the bishops in their hinterland. The bishops of Rome and Alexandria were endowed with the title *papa* (father) or pope. At subsequent councils, Constantinople and Jerusalem were added to the list of patriarchates.

Initially, the system of distinguishing clerics by their dress was more or less the same throughout the Christian world, but gradually differences started developing. Each patriarchate created its own traditions, and these separate developments became even more distinct after the schism between Rome and Constantinople and between Alexandria and Antioch (Council of Chalcedon, 451 C.E.) and the final separation between the Churches of Rome and Alexandria in 1054.

In the fourth century, monasticism became a factor of importance in Eastern Christianity. It started as an extra-ecclesiastical movement of men and women denying the world and retreating into the desert, individually or in groups. Some of these groups developed dress codes, and, by the time these communities had been incorporated into the Church in the course of the fifth century, monastic dress had gradually been formalized. When it became a custom, and later a rule, in Eastern churches that bishops should be recruited from monastic circles, monastic dress was intertwined with episcopal dress.

The term *religious dress* means the whole of vestments used to indicate the wearer's function or place within the ecclesiastical hierarchy. This applies not only to the dress of the clergy but also to monastic dress. Unlike the situation in some other religions, Christians have never (voluntarily) distinguished themselves from others in their civilian dress.

The origin of the most important religious vestments lies in the civil and aristocratic dress of late antiquity, especially of the fourth century C.E. Over time, the original (practical) function of many of these vestments was forgotten, and a symbolic religious meaning was given to them to explain their function as an insignia of the functionary wearing it. Thus, two important sources about early ecclesiastical dress—the Pseudo-Germanos of Constantinople in his *Historia Ekklesiastike* (Church history) and Symeon of Thessalonica (d. 1429) in his *Peri te tou theiou naou, Peri ton hieron teleton*, and *Peri tes hieras leitourgias*—explain the origin and meaning of liturgical vestments in a purely symbolic way. This symbolism is still evident in the Eastern churches in the early twenty-first century. A similar tendency to assign a symbolic meaning to vestments that once had a practical function is also apparent in monastic dress.

EARLY CHRISTIAN LITURGICAL DRESS

There is no evidence for the use of a special dress by the clergy during liturgy before the fourth century. Both the clergy and the congregation must have worn normal clothes during church services, perhaps reserving a special set for Sundays. It is likely that, during the fourth century, the development of a special dress for certain clerics had started. In this gradual process, lasting several centuries, certain civil garments slowly became associated with ecclesiastical offices until their use had become exclusively liturgical in character.

There is evidence that, in the late fourth century, certain bishops were endowed with the title *illustris*, a rank in the state hierarchy even higher than that of a Roman senator. This practice of granting clerics a place in the state hierarchy might have started during the reign of Constantine I (306–337 C.E.). Certain privileges were connected with a high rank as *illustris*, such as the use of special garments and insignia. Thus, the *pallium, mappa,* and *campagi*, at first social distinctives, must have become the forerunners of bishops' later liturgical vestment. The pallium in its civil form originally was an elongated strip of white fabric, measuring about four by two yards (about three and a half by two meters), which was draped around the body and worn over the tunic. In its liturgical version, it became narrower and was reduced to a shawl-like woolen strip, loosely worn around the neck and shoulders with one end hanging in front and the other hanging on the back. In the East, the pallium became known as the *omophorion*. It was made of white silk and was worn by all bishops. The mappa, a sort of kerchief, must have been the origin of the Eastern *enchirion* (hand cloth or handkerchief). The campagi were a special type of richly decorated shoes and the forerunners of the liturgical episcopal shoes. They were worn with luxury silk stockings called *udones*, the forerunners of the later episcopal socks called *caligae*. The campagi and udones, worn by both clerics and high secular officials, have been depicted in several fifth- and sixth-century mosaics—for instance, those in San Vitale in Ravenna, Italy. These aristocratic shoes and stockings did not continue to exist as episcopal attributes in the Eastern churches.

The first known prescription concerning a liturgical vestment is the forty-first canon of the Synod (official meeting of high clergy) of Carthage (ca. 400 C.E.), which states that the deacon should wear his alb (white tunic) only during the Eucharist and the reading. It is not until the canons of several sixth- and seventh-century synods that the use of special garments for the liturgy is attested to again.

Early Christian liturgical dress can be considered to be the basis for the liturgical dress in both Eastern and Western churches. Regional differences must have existed from the beginning but were probably small. After the ninth century, Western liturgical dress became more and more complicated, whereas the dress in Eastern churches underwent less change.

The vestments of the early Christian clergy comprised several components. The alb, its name deriving from *tunica alba*, the white tunic that was a common civil dress, was worn as an undergarment by all ranks. It was also referred to as the *tunica talaris*, the long tunic hanging down to the ankles. When, in the sixth century, it became the fashion to wear shorter tunics, the clergy kept the habit of wearing the tunica talaris both as liturgical and as civil dress. In this way, the alb became a distinctive garment for the clergy.

The *tunica dalmatica* was a long tunic with wide sleeves and was normally decorated with *clavi* (stripes running down the front and back of the garment in two parallel lines on either side of the neck opening). It was probably introduced from Dalmatia as early as the second century and was worn as an overgarment by both men and women. In the late fifth century, the tunica dalmatica must have gone out of fashion as a civil garment but remained in use by the Roman patriarch and his deacons. It was also worn outside Rome, as can be seen in the mosaic of Justinian and his train in San Vitale in Ravenna. The deacons appear in dalmatics, while Bishop Maximian wears a chasuble (the principal and most conspicuous mass vestment, covering all the rest, the chasuble consisted of a square or circular piece of cloth in the center of which there was a hole for the head) and pallium/omophorion as outer garments. By the ninth century, the dalmatic was generally accepted as a liturgical vestment for bishops and deacons.

Another Early Christian vestment is the *amice*, humeral, superhumeral, or *anaboladium*—a rectangular piece of linen worn around the neck. Its forerunner was the Roman *amictus*, worn to protect the tunic and other garments from sweat; it must have been worn especially on Sundays to keep clothes clean. It became part of ecclesiastical dress after the eighth century. In the civil dress of late antiquity, the tunic was worn with a simple textile *cingulum*, or girdle, to facilitate movement. The amice is still worn in the Eastern churches, where it is worn only by priests and bishops, but in the West it is common to all ranks. As a liturgical ornament, especially for bishops in Eastern churches, it has become an elaborately decorated garment.

The stole is a long, narrow strip of textile worn around the neck. It was used by deacons and priests and could, depending on the wearer's rank, be worn in different ways. The length depended on the way of wearing; the deacon's stole could be up to four yards (three and a half meters) long, while the priestly stole was generally two or two and a half yards (around two meters) long. Before the ninth century, it was called an *orarium*. Its origin and the etymology of the name are uncertain. According to one theory, *orarium* might be derived from *os*, meaning "mouth," presuming an original function as a napkin to wipe the mouth.

Mosaic of Emperor Justinian I (center) and his retinue, San Vitale, Ravenna, Italy, ca. 547. The deacons wear dalmatics, while Bishop Maximian (to the right of the emperor) wears a chasuble and *pallium* as outer garments. Early Christian liturgical dress such as this can be considered to be the basis for the liturgical garments used in both Eastern and Western churches. Getty Images.

It was worn on the left shoulder by deacons, with one end hanging in front, the other on the back. Priests wore it around the neck with both ends hanging in front. Until the ninth century, it must have been unusual for bishops to wear the orarium, because most of the representations from before that time (for instance, the mosaics of Ravenna) show bishops wearing the pallium over their chasuble as the insignia of their rank, while the orarium is absent in their dress.

The *casula*, or chasuble, is an ancient outer garment that is still being worn, generally by priests and bishops but originally also by deacons. Its original shape is an oval or circular piece of textile with a hole in the middle for the head. It had to be gathered up on the arms to allow the arms to be used freely. This garment, originally a traveling cloak, was also known as *planeta* and could have a hood. The fact that it covered almost the whole body explains the name *casula*, which is a diminutive of *casa* ("house").

Indicating the social status of a bishop at first, the pallium gradually became a liturgical vestment, reserved for the pope of Rome in the West, who could give it to metropolitan and other bishops as a personal distinction. In the East, it must have become a vestment for all bishops at a very early stage. It was worn around the neck, hanging in a loop over the breast, with one end flung over the left shoulder and the other end hanging down in front.

From an early time, bishops had the right to hold the mappa, a kerchief held in the hand, which was later known as the maniple in the West and as the enchirion in the East. Already in the sixth century, priests and deacons in the West had the right to use it, whereas in the East, it has remained reserved to bishops.

BYZANTINE LITURGICAL DRESS

Byzantine liturgical dress developed in the eastern Mediterranean on the basis of early Christian traditions. This was a gradual process, and, of course, no exact moment can be pinpointed for the transition from the early Christian to the Byzantine period. During the time of Justinian (527–565 C.E.), with whose reign the Byzantine era is generally considered to have begun, ecclesiastical dress in the East and West still had much in common. During the eighth and ninth centuries, a gradual divergence in the traditions of ecclesiastical dress occurred. Byzantine dress tended to be more conservative in its development than the dress of the Roman Church.

The sticharion is the basic undergarment for all ranks, comparable in function to the Western alb. In shape, it is, however, more comparable to the tunica dalmatica because of its wide sleeves and decoration with potamoi, the Greek term for clavi.

The epimanikia are separate cuffs or sleeves used to prevent the sleeves of the sticharion from hindering the wearer's movements. The first evidence for their existence is a letter from Patriarch Petros of Antiochia to Michael Kerullarios, which dates from the middle of the eleventh century. Until at least the late twelfth century, they were reserved for bishops; since then, they have been worn by priests as well.

The orarion corresponds to the Western stole. Until the eighth century, the term was used for both the priestly and deaconal stole; since then, the priestly stole has been called epitrachelion. In the course of the ninth century, the ends of the epitrachelion, which used to hang loose over the breast and knees of the priest, were buttoned and then eventually sewn together. Bishops continued to wear the epitrachelion after their consecration, during which they exchanged their priestly garments for episcopal ones. Byzantine deacons wore the orarion over their left shoulder until the beginning of the Eucharist. At that moment in the liturgy, they rearranged it and wore it around the waist, with both ends crossing diagonally over the back and flung over shoulders.

The zonarion is the girdle worn by priests and bishops, corresponding to the Western cingulum. The phelonion corresponds to the Western chasuble. Its name has been derived from the Latin paenula. Until the eleventh century, it was plain and undecorated. Then, a special variety called polystaurion was introduced. This is a phelonion decorated with a pattern of crosses, at first reserved for patriarchs. Metropolitans were also entitled to wear it beginning in the fourteenth century. The omophorion is the Eastern counterpart of the Western pallium. In the East, it has always been a vestment for bishops in general. The Byzantine omophorion is a strip of silk approximately three and a half yards (three meters) long and nine inches (twenty-three centimeters) wide. Its original color was white, but later several colors could be used. It is decorated with three crosses. In the eighteenth century, a small omophorion was introduced that was one and a half yards (one

and a half meters) long. Since then, the longer omophorion has been reserved for special occasions.

The epigonation is a vestment unique to the Eastern churches. Bishops and archimandrites (senior monks) have the right to wear it. It evolved from the enchirion. At first, this insignia must have been held in the hand, but in representations from the tenth century and later, it is seen hanging from the zonarion. In the fourteenth century, the shape of the enchirion changed from a kerchief into a stiff, lozenge-shaped piece of textile. It is likely that when it changed its shape, its name was changed into epigonation.

The sakkos is the Byzantine upper vestment that developed from the tunica dalmatica. In the mosaics of Ravenna, the dalmatica is shown to be still worn under the phelonion. It is not until the eleventh century that there is evidence for a wide tunic worn instead of the phelonion. As in the case of the polystaurion, it was a patriarchal vestment at first, but, from the thirteenth century, it was also worn by metropolitans. After the fall of Constantinople (1453), it became a vestment for all bishops. This can be explained from the fact that the sakkos was primarily an imperial garment and, as such, granted only to the highest clergy. A surviving example of a Greek patriarchal sakkos is the Dalmatic of Charlemagne (from the fourteenth century; held in Rome at the Vatican Museum) with a richly embroidered Calling of the Chosen (Christ on his throne in the Last Judgment, surrounded by the just) on the front and a Transfiguration (the appearance in glory of Christ to three of his apostles on Mount Tabor) on the back.

At the beginning of the eleventh century, the miter was introduced as headgear for Western bishops. At that time, it had the appearance of a round or slightly pointed bonnet. In the Byzantine Church, the miter lasted at least until the middle of the fifteenth century, after the fall of Constantinople, when a liturgical headgear with the name of mitra was introduced. Although the name for the Eastern and Western headgear is similar, these headdresses were of different origin. The Byzantine miter probably was an imitation of the imperial crown (kamelaukion), which bishops started to wear after the downfall of the Byzantine Empire. In Russia, the tsar could grant the mitra to priests and archpriests.

COPTIC AND SYRIAN LITURGICAL DRESS

The Egyptian or Coptic Church officially started its existence after the schism of the Council of Chalcedon (451), but it was not until the middle of the sixth century that it established its own hierarchy and continued to develop its own traditions in a state of isolation from the Byzantine Church and the other churches that followed the outcomes of the Council of Chalcedon (the so-called Chalcedonian churches).

Before 451, the Egyptian clergy had adhered to similar traditions in liturgical dress as elsewhere in the early Christian Mediterranean world. There were small local differences—for instance, the habit of wearing the omophorion tightly wound around the neck with both ends hanging in front. The most conspicuous difference from Byzantine dress, however, is the head cover for priests and bishops. It is uncertain when these heads covers were introduced into the Coptic vestimentary system. In Byzantine iconography, for example, the patriarchs of Alexandria, especially Athanasius and Cyril, are frequently depicted wearing a cap or hood. This cap may be a personal attribute, since it does not occur in any text, while other early patriarchs of Alexandria are depicted bare headed.

The sticharion (in Arabic called *tuniyah*) has always been the basic garment for all ranks. Originally a plain white tunic, it has been decorated with embroidery depicting the Virgin, archangels, and other figures since the eleventh century and up to the early twenty-first century. The orarion (Arabic *arariyya*), later called *epitrachelion* (Arabic *badrashil*), that was worn by priests developed in a similar way as in the Byzantine church: In its final shape, it was an elongated strip of embroidered fabric with a circular opening for the head at the end. This opening is called *sudra*. The orarion of the deacon is worn over the left shoulder, with a loop over the breast and under the right arm. The way it is worn by deacons during Communion in the Byzantine Church—around the waist, crossed on the back, with both ends hanging in front—became the accepted manner for subdeacons in the Coptic Church to wear the orarion.

On the basis of textual evidence (*The Book of the Consecration of the Sanctuary of Benjamin*, *The History of the Patriarchs*, and the *Canons of Athanasius*), it is known that there was also a shoulder veil worn by deacons. This item was called in Coptic an *apomis* and in Arabic *bumis*. No examples or representations of this vestment have survived.

The phelonion (Arabic *burnus*) originally had a shape similar to the casula: a circular or oval piece of fabric with an opening for the head in the center. At some point, possibly after the fourteenth century, its shape changed to a capelike garment, open in front and closed at the neck. For bishops, there has been a phelonion with a hood attached. This hood is referred to as *qasla* in Arabic, which is derived from the Latin *casula*. The qasla was apparently never or rarely worn on the head, and it was gradually reduced to a decorative border at the back of the phelonion.

The hood connected to the phelonion may be related to the *taylasan*. This is a separate pointed hood, which is worn only by priests in the early twenty-first century, but when it was introduced in the eleventh century, it was reserved for bishops. This hood as a distinctive form for bishops may have derived from monastic dress after it became a rule (probably in the tenth century) that all bishops should be recruited from the circles of monks. The hood thus symbolically expressed the monastic status of the bishop. A second kind of episcopal headdress is the *ballin*, which developed from the omophorion, which, according to local habit, had been worn around the head like a shawl since at least the fourteenth century. It gradually went out of fashion during the twentieth century.

Whereas the omophorion and the ballin were reserved for bishops, there was another priestly headdress, apparently closely related to the priestly taylasan, that was known as the *shamla*. It went out of fashion in the first half of the twentieth century and was replaced by the taylasan. The shamla was a long strip of white silk that could be worn either as a shawl, loosely draped over the head (the small version), or as a turban, with a long strip of fabric hanging on the back. Its origin is obscure, but it is possible that the hoodlike taylasan for priests is a conventionalized form of the shamla.

In general, it is possible to conclude that wearing liturgical headdresses in the Coptic Church started with bishops showing their monastic status, while priests continued celebrating the liturgy with uncovered heads. The priestly headgear seems to imitate the bishop's headgear, and probably in the thirteenth century it became normal for priests as well to wear a liturgical turban or hood.

Epimanikia (Arabic *kamam*) are loose sleeves or cuffs that are an important part of the dress of Coptic bishops. Several pairs of

A Palm Sunday procession at the Holy Sepulchre Church, Jerusalem, 2009. The man on the left wears the *hamnika* (or *epitrachelion*, the priestly stole). The archbishop (center) and priests wear the *eskema* as head coverings. Syrian liturgical garments are broadly based on earlier Byzantine dress. Gali Tibbon/AFP/Getty Images.

them can be found in the collections of monasteries and the Coptic Museum in Cairo, but it seems that they went out of fashion during the first half of the twentieth century. Surviving examples of these loose sleeves, which were often richly embroidered, all date from the eighteenth century and later. There is no evidence that the epimanikia were introduced into Coptic liturgical dress before the fifteenth century.

Syrian liturgical dress is also based on earlier Byzantine dress. As in the case of the Coptic Church, the Syrian Orthodox Church has its origin in the schism of the Council of Chalcedon. The close links between these two churches are reflected in a number of parallels within their liturgical dress. The sticharion is known as *kuttina* in Syria and seems not to differ in shape from the Byzantine sticharion. The *urrara* and the *hamnika* are the Syrian names for the orarion and the epitrachelion. In the development of their shape, they hardly differ from the Coptic orarion and epitrachelion. The *mindil* was the shoulder veil for the deacon. As in the Coptic Church, very little is known about this garment, which is no longer in use. The *payna* is the counterpart to the phelonion. It used to be a circular piece of fabric with an opening for the head. In the early twenty-first century, it has the shape of a cape, open in front.

Both priests and bishops wear head covers called *shaddaya* in the Syrian churches. The origins of the shaddaya are shrouded in mystery, but there seems to be a parallel with the Coptic taylasan. Originally, it was a white piece of fabric that was draped around the head and reserved for bishops; later it became a headdress for priests as well. In addition, a headdress called *mashnapta* is reserved to bishops. It is a wide, pointed hood, probably derived from the monastic hood. In the early twenty-first century, Syrian bishops wear a second monastic hood, the *eskema*, under the mashnapta. This duplication seems to be the result of the Syrian clergy forgetting the monastic origin of the mashnapta and its symbolic meaning.

The Syrian omophorion was called an *urrara rabba*, but despite this name, there is no reason to presume any connection with the orarion. As in the case of the Byzantine epimanikia, the Syrian counterparts (called *zende*) were introduced as attributes for bishops but became part of priestly dress as early as the thirteenth century.

COPTIC AND SYRIAN MONASTIC DRESS

The roots of monasticism and monastic dress are found in fourth-century Egypt and Syria. Two basic forms of monastic dress can be identified in Egypt. In Upper Egypt, monasticism was greatly influenced by the rule of St. Pachomius (290–346), in which prescriptions for dress were written down and adhered to. The founder of Lower Egyptian monasticism was regarded as St. Antony (251–356), and, in contrast to Pachomius, he never wrote down any rules, even about dress. The dress of his followers must have developed in the period following his death. Important sources for the knowledge of early Egyptian monastic dress are the rule of Pachomius (surviving in a Greek translation and titled *Patrologia Graeca*), the thirty-second chapter of Palladius's *Historia Lausiaca*, and Cassianus's *De Institutis Coenobiorum*.

The Pachomian dress consisted of the following parts (names are in Greek unless otherwise stated): a tunic or *lebiton*; a leather apron called in Coptic *rahtou*; a girdle of leather or textile (*zonarion*); a hood or *koukoullion*; a long linen scarf referred to in Latin as *balteolus* or *sabanum*; and a leather traveling coat called *melote*. The Pachomian monastic rule and its dress must have disappeared around the year 1000.

Lower Egyptian monks wore an ensemble consisting of the following parts: a tunic called *thorakeion* with a leather girdle (*zonarion*), which symbolized the monk's readiness to serve God and his chastity. Originally, the monks wore a scarf or *phakialion*, but this headdress was gradually replaced by a pointed hood called *koukoulla* or *kouklion*. At first, the hood was attached to a mantle called *phork* in Coptic or also *kouklion*; this mantle developed into a narrow scapular (a long length of cloth suspended from the shoulders of the wearer both in the front and the back, often reaching to the knees), sometimes with a hood attached, sometimes separated from each other.

The monks wore a system of thin leather straps called a *schema*; the straps are worn around the body in such a way that a diagonal cross is formed on the chest and back. Originally, it must have served to hold up the tunic during work, but around 600 c.e. it had the symbolic meaning of carrying Christ's cross on the monk's shoulder. It was probably a variation on a linen band that Cassianus called the *analabos*. Over this was outfit is worn an outer mantle called a *birros*.

The development of Syrian monastic dress largely corresponds to the dress of Lower Egypt, the only difference being that in Syria a schema or analabos does not occur.

BYZANTINE MONASTIC DRESS

Byzantine monastic dress follows the example of Lower Egypt. In the Greek and Russian tradition, the scapular (here often confusingly called *schema* or in Russian *analavon*) is often embroidered in red or white with images of the cross, Christ's instruments of torture, and different kinds of inscriptions. In the early twenty-first century, Greek monks often wear this scapular under instead of over their tunic. The Egyptian hood has been replaced with a cylindrical hat called *kamelaukion* (Russian *kamilávka*) over which a veil (*epirriptarion*, Russian *klobùk*) is worn.

References and Further Reading

Braun, Joseph. *Die liturgische Gewandung im Occident und Orient.* Freiburg im Breisgau, Germany: Herder, 1907.

Braun, Joseph. *Handbuch der Paramentik.* Freiburg im Breisgau, Germany: Herder, 1912.

Innemée, Karel C. *Ecclesiastical Dress in the Medieval Near East.* Leiden: Brill, 1992.

Oppenheim, Philip. *Das Mönchskleid im christlichen Altertum = Römische Quartalschrift für christliche Altertumskunde und für Kirchengeschichte,* 28. Supplementsheft, Freiburg im Breisgau, Germany: Herder, 1931.

Papas, Tano. *Studien zur Geschichte der Messgewänder im Byzantinischen Ritus.* Munich: Münchner Institut für Byzantinistik und Neugriechische Philologie der Universität, 1965.

Karel C. Innemée

Arab Men's Dress in the Eastern Mediterranean

- Basic Men's Garments
- Head Coverings
- The Keffiyeh and Palestinian Identity

Arab men's clothing, for village, seminomadic, and nomadic groups, was somewhat similar throughout the eastern Mediterranean from the medieval period through the end of the twentieth century; the basic men's wardrobe included long pants (*sirwal*), a long shirt (*thob*), a long coat (*qumbaz*), a sash (*hizam*), a cloak (*abayeh*), and some form of head covering.

BASIC MEN'S GARMENTS

During the nineteenth century, village men started to wear long pants; it is said that these sirwal were worn in imitation of those worn by Ottoman officials. The pants were normally made of white, black, or blue cotton; they were tight fitting on the lower leg and very wide at the waist. The excess material was gathered into folds at the waist with a drawstring (*tikka*). These baggy pants were worn by village men rather than Bedouin men. Narrow, Western-style pants were not popular until after World War II (1939–1945) and the end of the British Mandate period (1948), when men generally adopted Western garments throughout the eastern Mediterranean. In the early twenty-first century, it is rare to find a Palestinian man wearing the older-style baggy pants, but they are still worn by some elderly men in rural areas of Syria and Lebanon.

A basic garment worn by men was a long, plain shirt. Nineteenth-century examples were made of white or indigo-dyed material, either cotton or wool. The shirts covered the body from the shoulders to at least the knees, and in more expensive versions they came down to just above the ankles. Village men tended to wear thobs with long, narrow sleeves, while Bedouin had larger, triangular-shaped sleeves (*irdan*). These larger sleeves were seen as a sign of personal wealth. The thob was normally kept in place with a leather belt or sash, depending on where a man lived and his wealth.

During the late nineteenth century and in the early to mid-twentieth century, many men wore a leather belt (*sherihah*) for daily wear, to which various items such as powder horns, knives, and tobacco pouches were attached. Another form of sash (*kamr* or *ajami*) that was worn by urban and village men was made from lengths of tablet-woven bands exported from Syria to the whole region. These were usually made from red or brown wool and decorated with yellow stripes. In contrast, Bedouin men tended to wear a thick, practical leather belt, often with a bandolier for carrying bullets and with two pockets: one for a dagger and one for money.

Wealthier men would invest considerable sums of money in a cloth sash called a hizam. These were made of silk, wool, or cotton. Some of these sashes were plain, whereas others had intricately woven, multicolored designs. In general, urban men would buy a sash (ajami) made of handwoven wool with an intricate pattern. These sashes were usually about two and a half yards (two and a quarter meters) long and one yard (one meter) wide and were wrapped around the waist many times. The best examples came from Syria, Iran, and India; some of the most valuable sashes came from Kashmir and were used as very visible expressions of wealth.

For centuries, many village men went barefooted or wore locally made shoes (*wata*) of brown leather. Similarly, Bedouin also went barefooted or wore open-toed sandals (*ni'al*). Horsemen tended to wear red or yellow leather boots (*jezmeh*). This situation changed after the introduction of mass-produced European, and later Asian, footwear in the mid- and late twentieth century, respectively.

In the nineteenth century, the thob and abayeh were the main garments worn by village men, but by the beginning of the twentieth century, men were increasingly wearing a calf-length or ankle-length coat with long, narrow sleeves, which was usually called a qumbaz. The cut of the qumbaz was similar for all social classes; the differences between social groups were indicated by the type and quality of the fabric used to make the qumbaz. Wealthy urban men, for example, tended to have a qumbaz made of white silk (*rozah*), silk brocade made in Syria,

A man seated with two children, Ramallah, Palestine, ca. 1905. The man wears an undergown, a waistcoat, an overgown, a coat, and an *aba* (long cloak) on the shoulders. He also wears a *tarbush* (a felt cap with a tassel) with a turban, which indicates that he is a religious man. The boys wear elaborate tarbushes, which suggests that this is a special occasion such as a circumcision ceremony. Library of Congress Prints and Photographs Division, LC-USZ62-69092.

or *ghabani* (a white silk cloth often embroidered with designs in chain stitch), also from Syria. The more religious groups wore a *qumbaz* made of striped (*saya*) fabric from Syria or Egypt. Poorer village men tended to have qumbaz of cotton or linen, and the Bedouin usually wore plain white cotton qumbaz under their abayeh.

During the nineteenth and early twentieth centuries, a variety of jackets and waistcoats—first copied from the Syrian ruling elite and then from European visitors—were worn by Palestinian urban men and later by villagers. The Syrian-inspired garments were usually made of broadcloth and decorated with cord or braid trimmings; many of these were made in Damascus, Syria, for wear throughout the region. Ottoman-style waistcoats (*sidriyeh*) were made of satin and again decorated with braid. Western-style clothing included European coats, which were often worn over locally made shirts and coats. The availability of these different types of coats and jackets meant that some men wore various layers of Palestinian, Syrian, Turkish, and Western garments all together in one outfit.

Winter in the eastern Mediterranean can be very cold, so, not surprisingly, a range of coats were worn by men in the hill villages and by Bedouin in the desert. These overcoats included a sheepskin jacket (*farwah*), which had the wool turned inward for extra warmth; a broadcloth coat (*jibbeh*), which may have had a sheepskin lining; and a baggy, sleeveless cloak (*aba* or *abayeh*), which was worn draped over the shoulders.

Abayehs used to be made from handwoven goat hair, camel hair, or, in more expensive versions, silk. During the nineteenth century, these tended to be woven with stripes; the most common colors were indigo blue and white stripes or natural brown and white stripes. This type of abayeh can be seen in the paintings of the Scottish painter David Roberts (1796–1864). During the twentieth century, abayehs were usually in one color, such as black, brown, or white. Around Nablus, a coat similar to the abayeh was worn that had short sleeves; this was also called an abayeh or sometimes a *bisht*. It was made from thick, hand-spun and handwoven wool, with red-and-white or brown-and-white stripes. The abayeh was and remains the most famous and widely used of these garments and is still worn throughout the Arab world.

HEAD COVERINGS

Arab men normally cover their heads as a sign of respect for others. Unlike in the Western world, headgear is not taken off when entering a house or even when entering a mosque, because the head must be covered while saying prayers. Until the latter half of the twentieth century, not to wear something on the head when in public was regarded as being socially very low and uncouth. (The *'aqal*, or head rope, is taken off in religious places.)

Until the 1930s, headgear was used as a distinct and visually clear indicator of the wearer's religious, political, social, economic, and regional affiliations and connections. Headgear, for example, was used to show the difference between a boy and a man; boys may wear caps, but men wore more complicated forms of headgear. Urban men wore different headgear from villagers, from Bedouin, and so on. As Western styles were gradually adapted from the 1930s on, the subtle importance of headgear declined.

As a generalization, village men wore some form of cap and turban, while Bedouin wore head cloths and head ropes. Some half-nomadic groups might wear either form depending on the situation or who they were dealing with. During the nineteenth and early twentieth centuries, village men frequently wore a small cotton skullcap (*taqiyeh*), over which was placed a white or gray felt cap (*libbadeh*). A red felt cap (*tarbush*) was worn over both of these items. The tarbush had a floppy black or navy blue tassel, often made of silk, attached to the crown. The village tarbush was small, soft, and rounded at the crown. In contrast, the *tarbush istanbuli* worn by Ottoman officials and urban Palestinians was tall, stiff, and shaped like an upturned flowerpot.

A plain white cloth called *laffeh* was wrapped around the tarbush as a turban. The laffeh showed the wearer's social or religious position and gave him more prestige. The laffeh was often made from local cotton or silk fabrics from Syria. These cloths were usually striped or checked in various colors and had a fringe along the two transverse edges. The laffeh was wrapped around the tarbush in such a way as to leave the crown of the tarbush exposed.

The turban in the Islamic world is regarded as an important garment and the symbol of Arab and Islamic life (*tajan al-'arab*). Men often swore oaths on their turbans, and a poorly tied turban was regarded as a slovenly object reflecting the low character of the wearer. Turbans were also used to indicate the wearer's social position and religious identity through their size, shape, and color. Wide, bulky turbans with ornate decoration proclaimed a man's social importance; merchants, for example, often wore twisted and bulky forms. In contrast, learned, religious men tended to wear smoothly wrapped, flat, white turbans. Sayyids, descendants of the Prophet Mohammed, generally wore green turbans. However, at the beginning of the twentieth century, men who had been on the pilgrimage to Mecca (the hajj) started to wear green forms; so, in the 1920s, many sayyids started to wear large white turbans as a sign of their illustrious ancestry. In some villages, such as 'Aboud, where Christian and Muslim communities lived together, Muslim men tended to wear white turbans, and Christians wore red ones, reflecting a religious as well as a social difference. By the mid-twentieth century, these differences had all but vanished.

In contrast, the headgear of a Bedouin tended to be much simpler. The basic headgear consisted of a skullcap (*taqiyeh*), over which was worn a square head cloth (either a *hattah* or *keffiyeh*), which was folded diagonally and kept in place on the head with an '*aqal*. The hattah came in cotton, silk, or fine wool and various colors and patterns. The keffiyeh came in cotton, wool, or silk and had a black-and-white checked pattern. Like the hattah, it was folded diagonally in half and placed over the skullcap.

In the nineteenth century, 'aqal were relatively thick and later became thinner. They were made of black goat hair, brown camel hair, or brown sheep wool. High-status Bedouin wore special head ropes (*aqal maqasab*) of wool or camel hair bound at intervals with gold thread.

THE KEFFIYEH AND PALESTINIAN IDENTITY

In the late 1930s, many village men adopted the distinctive Bedouin-style headgear as an expression of their Arab/Palestinian

A Bedouin on the road to Petra, Jordan, 1938. He wears light-colored garments including an under-gown and overgown, a sash with tassels, braided hair, and a white head cloth kept in place with a head rope. The braided hair indicates his Bedouin status. Library of Congress Prints and Photographs Division, LC-DIG-ppmsca-17414-00111.

origins. The tarbush and turban, which were associated with Ottoman officialdom, went out of fashion except among old men. The use of a white head cloth and ʿaqal became widespread following the end of the British Mandate period, while the red-and-white keffiyeh was introduced by the British for the army in Jordan and is common all over Jordan and in the Persian Gulf in the early twenty-first century.

Following the war of 1967 and Israeli settlement of the West Bank and Gaza, the black-and-white checked keffiyeh was adopted by Yasir Arafat, chairman of the Palestine Liberation Organization, as a symbol of Palestinian national identity. Since then, this head cloth has been adopted as a global icon used by many groups as a symbol of defiance and perceived left-wing political affiliations.

References and Further Reading

Dalman, Gustaf. *Arbeit und Sitte in Palästina*. Vol. 5, *Webstoff, Spinnen, Weben, Kleidung*. Gütersloh: Georg Olms, 1937.

Vögler, Gisela, Karin V. Welck, and Katharina Hackstein, eds. *Pracht und Geheimnis: Kleidung und Schmuck aus Palästina und Jordanien*. Cologne: Rauntenstrauch-Joest-Museum der Stadt Köln, 1987.

Weir, Shelagh. *Palestinian Costume*. London: British Museum Publications, 1989.

Widad Kawar and Sibba Einarsdóttir

See also Snapshot: Trade, Textiles, Dress, and the Hajj; Ottoman Dress; Syria; Saudi Arabian Dress.

Palestinian Women's Dress

Palestine had a wide variety of traditional dress styles. Not only did every area have a different style, but often every village had its own distinctive dress, and sometimes the various large families living in one village would have a range of different styles. Occasionally, there were differences within the same family as women from different villages entered the family as wives and each brought her own embroidery traditions and clothing styles with her. All of this variety makes defining Palestinian dress difficult.

Palestine is a widely attested (and contested) Western and Southwest Asian term used to describe the geographic region between the Mediterranean Sea and the Jordan River and parts of Jordan, Lebanon, and Syria. For thousands of years, the region has been ruled by a variety of different empires and groups, including the Canaanites, ancient Egyptians, Romans, Byzantines, Arab caliphates, Mamluks, Ottomans, Egyptians, and British. From the medieval period on, Muslims formed the majority of the population, with Jewish and Christian minority groups.

During the twentieth century, the term *Palestine* was used for a loosely defined area that was included within the boundaries of British Mandate Palestine (1922–1948; often referred to as the Mandate period). This area covered a region that extended in a north-south direction from the Litani River (in Lebanon in the early twenty-first century) to Rafa (southeast of Gaza). The western boundary was the Mediterranean Sea, and the eastern boundary was approximately where the Syrian Desert began. The region excluded the Transjordan following the establishment of the independent Kingdom of Jordan in 1921.

To many Palestinians in the early twenty-first century, the boundaries of Palestine are those of the British Mandate excluding the Transjordan. Israel was established in three-quarters of this territory by the end of the Arab-Israeli War (1948), and the remaining quarter, comprising the Gaza Strip, the West Bank,

and East Jerusalem, was occupied by Egypt and Jordan until it was taken by Israel during the 1967 Arab-Israeli War (the so-called Six Days' War). The establishment of the State of Israel as well as the war in 1967 resulted in a mass flight from the towns and villages in the occupied areas, and refugee camps arose in the West Bank, Gaza, and the countries bordering on Israel/Palestine.

Given the many and various political and economic influences on the region, it is not surprising that Palestinian dress is one of the most varied in Southwest Asia. The situation is further complicated by the rapid changes that have occurred in the Arab world since the mid-twentieth century, all of which have impacted on traditional dress. The rich world of handwoven textiles and handmade dress has more or less been replaced by Western styles or what is called Islamic dress. The traditional village and Bedouin dress that once gave women in Palestine and Jordan an elegant look has become a rarity.

Historically, Arab society has been divided into three categories: urban dwellers (in towns and cities), village dwellers, and Bedouin. Each of these population groups had its own style of dress, and within these areas there are many variations.

MATERIALS AND EMBROIDERY

A feature of Palestinian dress is the wide variety of fabrics and materials that were used to create garments and accessories. There was a strong local weaving tradition throughout the country, and vast quantities of materials were imported into the region. Cotton, for example, was cultivated in the Galilee, dyed blue or black, and then used for everyday dresses. Although Bethlehem produced its own *malak* fabrics (flax and silk threads woven together), linen came from Egypt and East Europe, while a vast range of silk materials came from Syria and Lebanon. Many village women used these imported silks to decorate festive dress; in well-to-do towns and villages (like those around Jerusalem and Bethlehem), the whole ensemble for a woman was made from Syrian silk. In addition to these local and imported goods from neighboring countries, Iranian and Indian textiles were also imported into the Palestine region and were widely used. Machine-made textiles such as cheaper cotton fabrics and woolen broadcloths from England were also imported into the region; the cotton market was later taken over by manufacturers in Asia.

In the past, women in the Arab world devoted their creative skills to decorating their weaving, pottery, and dress. Even though they had little extra time or money, they created and applied beautiful embroidery (*tatriz*) to their garments, work that twenty-first-century machines cannot replicate. Dress in Palestine was distinguished by lavish embroidery with a great variety of patterns, stitches, and colors, and, as a result, the cut of a woman's dress and the type of embroidery used to decorate it signaled where she came from.

Although the Palestinian people are famous for their embroidery in the early twenty-first century, this is a relatively new development. Until the nineteenth century, woven decoration was the main source of texture, color, and patterning. It was not until the mid- to late nineteenth century that embroidery became more widespread and rapidly bloomed into a highly developed art. The main period of embroidery lasted from the late nineteenth century until the end of the Mandate period, when the various wars and movement of refugees meant that women no longer had the time or financial resources to carry out detailed and intricate embroidery. Various local and nongovernmental organizations have attempted to revive embroidery in the region; most of the work produced is sold to tourists, and the garments are made and worn by urban women throughout the Arab world.

In the nineteenth and twentieth centuries, girls in villages in Palestine would start to learn embroidery from their mothers around the age of ten. Each girl learned the special embroidery styles of her own village; she became proud of them, and they became part of her identity. Each village had its own pattern arrangement, which was copied from mother to daughter. In addition, new patterns were constantly being adapted to their specific needs and desires.

Although cross stitch is the stitch that is generally associated with Palestinian embroidery in the early twenty-first century, it is not common to all areas. Stem stitch, for example, was widely used in the north (Galilee), while couching was preferred in the Bethlehem and Jerusalem areas. A variety of other stitches were used for hems, yokes, and sleeve openings, as well as a range of connecting stitches that were used in the construction of the garments. The embroidery style of the area was also used to decorate women's garments such as head coverings, trousers, and jackets

A linen dress with silk patchwork in blue, green, and gold and cross-stitch embroidery at the back, Upper Galilee, Palestine, ca. 1890–1900. This elaborately decorated coatlike dress is known as a *jillayeh* and would be worn over pants and a shirt. Photograph by Myrtre Winters.

as well as household accessories such as cushions, curtains, and towels.

In general, specific areas of Palestinian garments were embroidered; with respect to dresses, for example, embroidered areas included the chest panel (*qabbeh*), the bands on the sleeves, the side skirt panels (*benayiq*), the hem of the dress (*diyal*), and a panel in the lower back of the skirt section (*shinyar*).

Appliqué with *heremzi* (taffeta) fabric is an embroidery technique whereby one or more pieces of material are sewn onto the surface of another piece of cloth; sometimes the term *patchwork* is incorrectly used to describe Palestinian appliqué. However, patchwork is where two or more pieces of cloth are sewn together to create a larger piece of material. Appliqué has the benefit of using up small pieces of material and creating a decorative effect relatively quickly. Appliqué was widely used in southern Palestine, especially in Gaza, Beersheba, Falujah, and Hebron. Here, dresses were decorated in a mixture of embroidery and color appliqué.

A wide variety of sources were used as inspiration for Palestinian embroidery. There was a strong local style of Arab art and symbolism using geometric, floral, and occasionally faunal sources as inspiration for designs. In addition, geographic (rivers, mountains) and climatic (rainbows) features, astrological symbols (sun, moon, stars), and household items such as carpets provided design motifs. Due to the political and economic influence of Turkey, Ottoman and East European motifs and designs influenced Palestinian embroidery, especially embroidery from Galilee and Bethlehem. During the nineteenth century, numerous European and U.S. Christian missionaries came to the Palestinian region, set up schools, and taught a wide variety of subjects including embroidery and lace-making. These missionaries brought with them their own embroidery styles, stitches, and designs, many of which were incorporated into the Palestinian repertoire. But perhaps one of the strongest influences, especially in the twentieth century, was the introduction of pattern books and a wide range of embroidery threads by the French company Dollfus, Mieg & Cie (DMC). Its influence on Palestinian, and indeed Southwest Asian, embroidery continues into the twenty-first century.

In the past, life in Arab society, whether urban or rural, revolved to a great extent around weddings. The garments prepared by the bride were very important, and they had to be prepared well in advance to serve as her dowry. Brides-to-be had to learn embroidery at an early age, and mothers and grandmothers passed their skills on to their daughters and granddaughters, making sure that they mastered the art. This was especially true among villagers, where a mother would seek the girl most skilled in embroidery as a suitable match for her son, on the assumption that if she was perfect in embroidery, she would be a perfect housekeeper as well.

VILLAGE AND NOMADIC DRESS

The basic outfit for Palestinian village and nomadic women from the late nineteenth to the mid-twentieth century consisted of a pair of pants (*sirwal* or *libas*) that were seldom seen, a chemise (*qamis*), a dress (*thob*), in some areas a coat, and a headdress of some kind. The thob was generally regarded as the most important element of the outfit.

Basically, a thob is a loose-fitting dress with sleeves. The fabrics from which the thob is made are usually narrow—no more than eight inches (twenty centimeters) wide—so the style of the dress is determined by the width of the fabric. A length of fabric is taken that matches the height of the woman and then doubled to form the front and back of the dress. To give the dress the desired width, two long triangles are cut and inserted in the sides (benayiq). The sleeves are set in a straight cut, and, for winged sleeves, a triangle is added. A square is cut separately and embroidered and sewn as a chest panel (qabbeh), which is often decorated with various embroidered patterns. A highly decorated qabbeh is regarded as a family heirloom, handed down from mother to daughter for use on several dresses. The cut of the Palestinian dress differs from one part of the region to another. In general, it ranges from a slim-fitting coatlike dress in the Galilee to a wider and wider version as one goes south, reaching its widest form in the Naqab Desert (Negev) among the Bedouin.

A similar form of headdress was worn by many women throughout Palestine, albeit with many variations. The basic elements were a simple cap (*qurs*) that was worn directly on the head. Over the cap every girl in Palestine prepared a special headdress to wear after she got married. Each area had a certain style of a headdress, from simple ones made of cotton to heavily embroidered examples from Ramallah and Hebron. All of these headdresses were decorated with coins, from the silver Ottoman *bara*, to gold Ottoman money, and, more commonly, the Austrian Maria Theresa dollar. These caps had embroidered bands (*laffayef*) attached to the back to go around the girl's braided hair. After the girl finished embroidering the cap according to the tradition of her area, she was allowed to get engaged. The girl would typically give between ninety and one hundred silver coins (*shakkeh*), given to her by her fiancé, to a specialist to put them on an embroidered band. This band was then attached to the cap in some manner. More elaborate examples had the coins attached to a broad band in a crescent shape (*saffeh*), which framed the woman's forehead. This money was the girl's personal account, and she was allowed to do with it as she pleased.

The most widespread form of headdress came from the Ramallah region. It was a rectangular piece of material with two flaps at the back and two long hair bands attached to the sides or back after marriage. The material was usually cotton and often embroidered, mainly with red silk or pieces of red satin. It was made into a bonnet by gathering the material at the back. Coins were often attached to a band that went around the forehead to just behind the ears. As one traveled to the Hebron hills, the style changed to a pointed cap where the coins were sewn onto a triangle flat at the back of the head or a flat-topped hat where the larger coins were sewn around the cap; this style of cap was called an 'araqiyeh.

Brides in the Hebron area wore a heavy ceremonial headdress known as "the hat of money" (*wuqayat al-darahem*) for the duration of the wedding and for the following week. The village would have one example kept with the head of the village, which a bride was allowed to borrow and then return after the ceremonies.

In Bethlehem, married woman wore a tall, narrow headdress (*shatweh*) decorated with couchwork embroidery. The front part of the cap was covered with gold or silver coins, rows of coral beads, and rows of *sabale* stitch (herringbone) in silk threads. During the Mandate period, the silver shakkeh coins were replaced by gold, and, as the economic condition declined, saffeh bands with coins ceased to be worn. However, the padded roll that was placed around the outer edge of the flat crown to give it extra height and covered with white lace was retained, and this

A Palestinian woman wearing festive Ramallah clothing from 1880. The dress is made from hand-woven linen, embroidered with vegetable-dyed silk threads using cross stitch and is worn with a traditional hat and linen shawl. Photograph by Myrtre Winters.

form of shatweh is still worn by some groups in the early twenty-first century.

Over the cap and coins an embroidered white shawl was worn, which was known as a *ghudfeh* in some areas (Hebron) or a *khirqah* in Ramallah. It was made from two or three pieces of handwoven linen, joined together by a connecting stitch (*'erq* or *manajel*). Some areas use special patterns for this work, such as "the tent of the pasha" in Hebron and rows of pine trees (*saru*), the *S* or leech design of Ramallah, and orange blossoms in the Jaffa area. In the early twenty-first century, the head cover is a white silk shawl.

Palestinian regional dress is usually divided into the Galilee area, central Palestine, coastal Palestine, and southern Palestine. Within each area there are significant differences.

GALILEE AREA

The outfits worn by Galilean women were different from those worn further south. The Galilean form was strongly influenced by Syrian styles. In general, a woman's outfit consisted of baggy pants; a thin, knee-length chemise with short sleeves; a longer dress with long sleeves; a coat; and an elaborate headdress.

The pants tended to be baggy with tight-fitting ankles. From the knees down, the pants were often made from decorative material, either woven or embroidered. The narrow ankle cuffs were also decorated, so the designs could be admired; these emphasized the economic status of the wearer. The part of the pants that was not seen, from the crotch to the waist, was often made of a plain cotton material with no decoration.

The inner dress was made of a loose weave, and the overdress was made of a white cotton material with some decoration on the long sleeves. These sleeves were intended to be seen; the nineteenth-century coats had shorter, elbow-length sleeves. Although the basic form of this outfit was Syrian, the materials and decoration were adapted to local needs, materials, and aesthetic tastes.

In contrast to other regions, until the mid-twentieth century, the most significant element of the Galilean dress for women was the short-sleeved, front-opening coat. In the late nineteenth and early twentieth centuries, these coats were usually made by Galilean women using locally woven cotton cloth dyed indigo blue. Sometimes, more expensive versions were made of pink or red silk. If the coat was relatively plain, it was called *dura'ah*; if it was elaborate, it was known as a *jillayeh*. The jillayeh were often richly decorated with geometric designs that were embroidered with mainly red silk yarns. The main stitches were cross stitch, hem stitch, running stitch, satin stitch, and stem stitch. These were also often decorated with applied red, yellow, and green taffeta (*heremzi*) or striped cloth. During the second half of the nineteenth century, the short-sleeved coat was replaced by another style of coat called a *qumbaz*, which was of a modern urban Turkish style; this style of coat was adopted first by urban Galilean women and later by village women. These new coats were made from brightly colored and striped Syrian atlas satins. This style of coat continued to be worn in the Nablus region until the 1960s. These various types of coat were kept in place with a long cloth sash (*zunnar tarabulsi*), which was made of checked red, white, black, and green silk. This sash was wound twice around the waist and knotted in front. In the lower Galilee around Nablus, Qalqilia, and Jenin, women wore similar outfits but replaced the embroidery with cord couching.

Galilean dresses (thobs) for nomadic and seminomadic Bedouin were very different from the village garments with respect to the choice of material, cut of the garments, and style of decoration. During the late nineteenth century, the Bedouin thobs were made from a locally dyed light blue cotton material; by the end of the twentieth century, they had changed to being made of imported black cotton. In the late twentieth century, black cotton was popular among older women, while younger women used a shinier black satin. In the 1980s, fashionable Bedouin women started to use black velvet. The dresses had long, tight sleeves and very long neck openings to facilitate breast-feeding. The thobs were decorated with embroidery along the sleeves and in four or five bands above the hem; they used a variety of stitches, including hem stitch, running stitch, satin stitch, and stem stitch, but, unlike the village embroidery, cross stitch was not used. These dresses were common in northern Jordan and southern Syria.

The basic Galilean headdress was a bonnet (*smadeh*) with coins attached, surmounted by a crescent-shaped band sewn with closely overlapping coins called a *saffeh*. A large cloth (*hattah*) was worn over the top. A simpler form of headdress consisted of a large white cotton or silk cloth with a fringe or tassels, which was folded diagonally in half and then wrapped around the head and neck. It was kept in place by a hattah that was folded into a wide band, wrapped around the head, and fastened in some manner at the back. The simpler forms were of black or dark blue material, but more elaborate and expensive examples were made of colorful silks decorated with woven bands of gold and silver metallic thread or dyed silks in contrasting colors. Sometimes bands of coins were added to the hattah. A square cloth (*asbeh*) was sometimes folded into a strip and used as a headband over the hattah. The asbeh was made of flowered muslin, brocades, or similar material and was used to show the wearer's economic status.

CENTRAL PALESTINE

The hill country of Judaea in the eastern half of central Palestine includes four important towns: Jerusalem, Hebron, Ramallah, and Bethlehem. Three distinct styles of Palestinian dress with embroidery as the major feature were produced here. Embroidery used couching and cross stitch.

The basic outfit in this region consisted of pants, a qamis, a thob, and a headdress of some kind. Coats were not generally worn in this area, except at weddings by the bride. A hybrid garment that was part coat and part dress was worn in the Ramallah and Jaffa areas up to the 1920s, but then it vanished. It had short sleeves and an opening in the front of the skirt extending from below the waist to the hem. Richly embroidered versions were called jillayeh.

The dresses in Isdud and the Gaza area had a neckline with no central yoke panel, although the neckline was often decorated with embroidered amuletic designs. A characteristic feature of thobs from this region was their narrow, tight, straight sleeves. Another feature of a woman's outfit of central Palestine was the use of a thob without a cloth sash. From 1948 on, dresses became less baggy and were typically made with long, tighter sleeves. After the 1980s, another change took place, and dresses tended to have bust darts following Western tailoring ideas and to have a long, narrow skirt (*shawal* or maxi) with short side slits at the bottom for ease of walking. Dresses in central Palestine can be divided into three groups depending on whether the main garments were white (*abiyad*), mid- to dark blue (known as black; *asmar*), or black. This division is sometimes used to define where a dress comes from.

A feature of central Palestinian dresses was the range of decoration, usually embroidered, that embellished them. There was an unwritten rule concerning the proper arrangement of the embroidery, however; it was never randomly carried out. It was symmetrically arranged, with the following main sections: a chest panel (*qabbeh*), a panel at the lower back of the skirt (*shinyar*), the front and back seams (*marwaris*), and the skirt sides (benayiq). This basic embroidery layout was common to all central Palestinian dresses, although the style of embroidery, patterns, colors, and textures could vary regionally.

RAMALLAH

The basic Ramallah thob was made from white linen (*rumi*) for summer and festive dresses and head coverings, while indigo-dyed ("black") linen was preferred by younger women in the winter and by older women year-round.

Embroidery was predominantly cross stitch worked in red silk thread, which contrasted with the white or black linen ground.

Embroidered Ramallah bonnet, Palestine, from ca. 1900. Worn by married women, this cap (*wuqa*) has a crescent-shaped padded roll (*saffeh*) with a row of silver coins attached. The *saffeh* slopes forward at the front and is joined at the back by a heavy pad that acts as a counterweight to the coins. Photograph by Kamal Kawar.

Ramallah was known for a great variety of distinguishable, very finely executed patterns. The qabbeh panel was often a separate piece of cloth that was stitched onto the dress. The sleeves were usually sparsely embroidered. A characteristic feature of a Ramallah thob was the two vertical bands on the front and back covering the seam lines; these could be narrow or wide with extra decorative motifs. There was normally an embroidered shinyar panel set between these two bands at the back of the garment near the hemline.

Popular Ramallah embroidery motifs included the date palm arranged in horizontal rows, a rainbow motif (*qos*), the leech or S design (*alaq*), stars (*nujum*), and the "moon feathers" motif (*qamar-ish*). Floral motifs tended to reflect Turkish, Greek, and European influences.

In Ramallah, thobs were often worn with a cloth sash or girdle. The main type of sash worn by young women was made from striped atlas, while those of older women and women in mourning were the so-called black girdles (*zunnar asmar*), which were made of black-and-red-striped satin.

A woman's headdress in Ramallah consisted of a cap (*wuqa*) over which was placed a saffeh with a row of silver coins attached. The saffeh sloped forward at the front and was joined at the back

by a heavy pad that acted as a counterweight to the coins. To secure the headdress in place, a ribbon was threaded through two small rings (*erweh*) behind the saffeh at each side and tied at the back of the head. A simple chin chain was usually suspended from each side to the headdress; this was sometimes decorated with ornamental bobbles or a large coin, which hung directly under the chin.

JERUSALEM AND BETHLEHEM

Jerusalem never really developed an indigenous style of dress, because urban women tended to borrow from local and international sources and sometimes wore urban dress with a Turkish influence. Major local influences in villages around Jerusalem largely came from Bethlehem.

During the nineteenth century, malak (linen and silk) and *ikhdary* (linen with silk stripes) fabrics needed for the Bethlehem dress were imported from Egypt; however, in the latter half of the century, the Naser family introduced the weaving of malak and ikhdary cloth to Bethlehem by opening a weaving factory. Flax yarns were imported from Egypt, and silk came from Lebanon. Other fabrics woven in Bethlehem included indigo-dyed cotton for dresses; white silk (*terbia*) for scarves; a black silk crepe for the large head coverings (*shambar*); pink and blue woolen belts; and plain wool or embroidered cotton and silk fabrics for the shawls used by women from Ramallah and Beit Dajan. The weavers also started to import all kinds of threads needed for embroidery from Egypt, Lebanon, and Syria. Thus, Bethlehem became the center of style in the Palestinian village fashion world. At the same time, Bethlehem businesses started to cater to brides in all areas of Palestine, preparing headdresses and shawls, embroidery panels and bands, jackets, and complete outfits (including jewelry). Not surprisingly, women from other regions started to copy and adapt Bethlehem designs and trends to their own needs.

So-called Bethlehem couching (*shughl talhami*) is a distinctive style of embroidery developed in the Bethlehem area and influenced by the Christian church. The main technique is couching with silver, gold, and silk cord that is twisted into elaborate floral and curvilinear patterns and attached to the ground fabric with tiny stitches and then framed and filled with herringbone and satin stitches.

Bethlehem was also an important center for embroidery, and women from around the region ordered embroideries from professional women embroiderers; these embroideries were later attached to their own garments. The Naser family, for example, in the 1930s had 360 Bethlehem women embroidering and making garments.

The basic outfit worn by Bethlehem women was similar to other central Palestinian dress but with the addition of either a sleeveless coat (*bisht*) or a short jacket (*taqsireh*). These jackets were made of velvet or broadcloth and were usually heavily embroidered with floral and geometric designs and techniques. These jackets were worn over the basic pants and dress, along with a headdress. Less formal Bethlehem thobs were generally made from indigo-dyed linen fabric and had relatively narrow sleeves. Thobs for special occasions were made of striped silk with winged sleeves. Bethlehem, however, was famous for the production of wedding dresses (called thob malak).

The early Bethlehem wedding dress did not have embroidery on the sleeves except at the cuff, it had less embroidery at the sides than later dresses did, and all seams were covered with multicolored chevron stitch. These wedding dresses were always trimmed on the sleeves and the side panels with bands of orange, red, and green heremzi or handloomed silks from Homs and Damascus. Over time, however, a new type of wedding dress developed, the so-called royal or elaborately embroidered wedding thob (*thob malak*). A feature of these dresses was the heavily embroidered chest panels; there was also couching on the sleeve and skirt panels, but these panels were not as elaborate as the chest panel, with crosses on the sleeves and sides.

The Bethlehem headdress (shatweh) consisted of an embroidered cap with bands of coins and coral beads at the front and a silver chin chain (*iznaq*) that often had numerous coins hanging from it. Over the shatweh was worn a large head covering, usually white with some embroidery, that was so large that often the shatweh itself was completely hidden.

HEBRON

The thobs worn in the Hebron region were similar in color and fabric to the Ramallah dresses and had the same patterns as well. They were usually made of indigo-dyed material (*qarawi*) made of linen, cotton, or silk that was woven in Hebron or the surrounding region.

There was generally much more embroidery on dresses in Hebron than in other regions, in terms of both quantity and density of work, although, in general, dresses for daily wear were less elaborately decorated than those for festive occasions. The sides and backs of the thobs were embroidered, usually with designs in vertical patterns. The qabbeh was similar to the Ramallah style and often included the rainbow (qos) motif, as well as stars, triangles, grapes, leeches, feathers, cypress trees, and floral designs. Patterns used on the qabbeh were frequently repeated on the shinyar of the skirt. Hebron embroidery was characterized by its use of cross stitch, with herringbone stitch used as a joining stitch. Dresses for special occasions were normally decorated with taffeta (heremzi) appliqué panels in the form of triangles and diamonds in a range of colors down the front skirt section of the garment called *jellayhe*.

The Hebron headgear ('araqiyeh) consisted of an embroidered cap decorated with coins, over which was often worn a white embroidered shawl.

JERICHO

In the vicinity of Jericho, some village women, especially those of Bedouin origin, wore an extremely long thob (*thob ibb*), which was usually two to three times the height of the woman wearing it. The excess fabric was gathered up and pulled through a handwoven belt, so that it fell over in a fold, forming three layers. The sleeves were large and triangular and were draped over the head as a form of head covering; the sleeves were kept in place with a silk headband. The amount of fabric used for this type of dress was a clear indication of the owner's social and economic status.

Similar dresses were worn by Bedouin women living in Salt in Jordan and the Jordan Valley in general, which is not surprising because there was considerable movement of Bedouin between the Jericho and Salt regions. It is unknown when women began to wear this type of dress, but it appears in photos from the 1920s, and it was still being worn by a few elderly women in the 1980s.

Younger women changed to wearing a one-length dress with vertical lines of embroidery on the entire front.

COASTAL PALESTINE

The central coastal regions stretch from the base of the Judaean Hills to the Mediterranean Sea. It was an agriculturally important region. The important areas were in and around the cities of Gaza, Jaffa, Majdal, and the village of Beit Dajan (depopulated in the 1948 war). Majdal was a major producer of textiles in the late nineteenth and early twentieth centuries. However, by the 1920s, textile production in Majdal was already beginning to decline in importance due to the importation of Western and later Asian textiles. Nevertheless, some handwoven textiles were still being made in Majdal until the late 1950s; their main market was the refugees living in the Gaza region. This handweaving industry was able to survive for so long because it was able to adapt to local needs and demands.

At the beginning of the twentieth century, the basic wardrobe of a woman from this region consisted of two types of dresses: a coat dress (jillayeh) in the Jaffa and Galilean area, with short sleeves and an opening in the front of the skirt, and the dress (thob) itself, with long, winged sleeves. Older jillayehs were always made from black (asmar) linen, and the festive thobs were

Festive dress (*malak*) worn in the Bethlehem and Jerusalem area, Palestine, ca. 1930. It is made of cotton velvet with couching embroidery using gold and silk cords. Photograph by Myrtre Winters.

of undyed white linen, never black; this tradition had, however, changed by the 1930s. These garments were often decorated with taffeta (heremzi) patches and a yoke panel of red-and-yellow-striped atlas satin. A white dress in the Beit Dajan style was an obligatory gift from the groom's family to the bride. The dress was normally made by one of the groom's female relatives. In addition, the bride would have items such as a white chemise with simple appliquéd decoration, two girdles of Syrian silk, a long-sleeved silk coat of narrow yellow- or wider red-striped atlas, a plain red crepe head veil, and a second head veil made of black crepe (shambar asmar) with a panel of red embroidery.

A wider range of decorative techniques was used for the thobs from this region. Festive dresses were decorated with applied fabrics as an important source of decoration. Many of these thobs were decorated with broad stripes of orange, red, magenta, and green fabrics. Much of this material was woven at the nearby city of Majdal. This city also produced black and blue cottons with pink, green, and white stripes on the selvage, which were used for another type of Gaza-region thob called abu hizz ahmar. The linen for this fabric came from Egypt, while the stripes were of locally produced silk.

A characteristic feature of a woman's outfit in the Isdod area and central and southern Palestine is the use of a thob without a cloth belt, which is still worn on special occasions in the twenty-first century. These dresses have a V neckline with no central yoke panel; the neckline is often decorated with embroidered amuletic designs. Another feature of thobs from the Isdod area is their narrow, tight, straight sleeves.

The most popular embroidery motifs for the thobs of this area included designs with diverse names such as the cypress tree, scissors (muqass), combs (musht), triangles (hijab), beads, feathers, cushions, pendants, flowers, keys of Hebron, pigeon's tears, and trays. These were often arranged in groups of three, five, and seven, which were regarded as auspicious numbers that are effective against the evil eye. A popular motif was the orange-flower pattern called nafnuf, a floral motif that may have been inspired by locally grown orange trees in the Jaffa area. In general, embroidery from this region mixes traditional geometric designs with softer lines and floral motifs.

SOUTHERN PALESTINE

The area known as southern Palestine is a roughly triangular area formed by the market towns of Gaza, Khan Yunis, and Beersheba. The most important market for southern Palestinians was at Beersheba, which was frequently used by the Bedouin population of the Negev Desert. As a result, there was considerable similarity between the garments worn by village women at Beersheba and the surrounding nomadic groups. The basic outfit for village women in this area consisted of pants (libas), a thob, and a shambar. In addition, many Bedouin women also wore a face veil (burqa). Historically, many of the dresses from this region were made from dubeit, a black sateen that was imported from England. More recent examples were often made out of a black synthetic material.

A common style of southern Palestinian thob was relatively narrow with tight, straight sleeves. The cloth for the Gaza thob was traditionally woven at nearby Majdal, either of black or indigo blue cotton or with stripes. The pink-and-green-striped fabrics of Majdal continued to be woven in the Gaza strip until the late

1960s by refugees from the coastal villages. In general, among the Bedouin population, the dress was cut very large, and the older dresses had long, pointed sleeves (irdan). These dresses were larger and fuller as part of their modification to suit desert conditions; they were cooler to wear due to the amount of air trapped inside.

Until the 1930s, village and Bedouin everyday dresses tended to be relatively plain with little or no embroidery. However, as cheaper perlé cotton threads became available, dresses began to include more cross-stitch embroidery in emulation of village women's thobs. These dresses were often decorated with a chest panel; bands of embroidery stretching from the shoulders to the sleeve hems; two narrow bands of embroidery over the seams in the skirt section and the side panels; and a panel of embroidery at the lower back. The layout of the embroidery elements reflected that used by central and southern Palestinian village dresses, except that, instead of the qabbeh (chest panel) being the focus of attention, it was the shinyar panel at the lower back of the dress.

Bedouin dresses also tend to have considerable geometric embroidery carried out in cross stitch. Each tribe has its own embroidery patterns, so the social affiliation of a woman is immediately apparent to those who understand the "dress code." In addition, the embroidery is carried out in either blue or red yarn; the color chosen for the embroidery is intended to reflect the marital status of the wearer. Young, unmarried girls and widows, for example, wear blue, while a married woman is allowed to wear red embroidery. These garments are often worn with a sash made from a heavy cotton or wool in reds, fuchsias, and blues. The woolen sashes are often made from plaited strips in black and white.

In general, unmarried girls do not wear face veils, although they might pull their head covering across their face as a sign of personal modesty. Face veils tend to be the preserve of married women. In addition to providing some protection from the sun and dust, burqas are also used by Bedouin women to display their personal and family wealth and status. The basic burqa consists of two pieces of cloth: the headband and veil section. These are sewn together at the sides and in the middle to create eye slits. The burqa varies in size quite considerably, but in general it is used to cover the forehead and nose and sometimes the mouth and neck regions. The headband and veil sections are often decorated with embroidery (cross stitch and herringbone stitch), while the part that covers the face is decorated with coins, beads, metal disks, metal and plastic chains, and so forth. The embroidery identifies the tribe the woman belongs to.

Over the head was worn a lightweight head scarf in black cotton and a heavier head covering made from cotton or silk, depending on the wealth of the wearer. These outer head coverings were often embroidered with designs that extended from the top of the head down the back.

JEWELRY

In addition to the elaborate headdress with coins, a variety of silver hair ornaments, earrings, necklaces, chokers, bracelets, and finger rings were worn by both village and Bedouin women. These items were made by silversmiths based in all the main towns as well as imported from Syria, Armenia, the Caucasus, western Saudi Arabia (Hijaz), and Yemen. Palestinian jewelry styles and techniques, therefore, are very diverse. Wealthier clients bought jewelry made from the highest grade of silver (often melted-down Maria Theresa coins mixed with some other metal), while poorer customers, especially the Bedouin, bought cheaper items made from lower-grade silver and brass.

Other materials used to make and decorate jewelry include cloves; pearls; coral; beads of glass, stone, or clay; and amulets of tortoiseshell and alum. Blue beads were often sewn onto children's dresses and caps as a form of protection against the evil eye. In addition to silver jewelry, some women wore a range of blue and brown glass bracelets, which were made in Hebron. Imitation pearl necklaces, again made of glass, were also made here.

From the late 1920s and 1930s, more and more women started to own gold jewelry, which was mass produced in Beirut and Damascus. Gradually, gold replaced traditional silver forms of jewelry and was also used for new forms such as earrings, hair slides, and brooches used to fasten dresses at the neck. In the early twenty-first century, few women wear silver jewelry on a regular basis.

POST-1948

Following the establishment of the State of Israel in 1948 in the northern, western, and southern parts of Palestine, there was a mass movement of people, and over half of the rural population became refugees in the Gaza and West Bank areas and surrounding countries. Following the 1967 war, there was another wave of refugees. As a result, very little remained of the dress and textile

traditions of the nineteenth and first half of the twentieth century. Traditional garments, especially dresses, experienced a resurgence after 1967 but in much plainer styles than before. Local weaving practices ceased, and, without access to imported textiles and embroidery threads, garments became less ornate and more practical. The elaborate headdress and shawls, for both daily and formal wear, were virtually lost.

Various new styles of dresses developed in the latter half of the twentieth century, including the "six-branch" form, the shawal style, and Intifada dresses. The six-branch style emerged in the 1960s and is named after the six vertical bands of embroidery that run from the waist to the hem of the dress, in a similar manner to the dresses from Ramallah. The six-branch dress usually also has a chest panel of the type found in central and southern Palestine. It is characterized by its curvilinear foliage and flower designs and various flower and bird designs; many of these designs are derived from European pattern books, especially those produced by the French firm DMC, a company that also manufactures embroidery threads. Perlé cotton thread is often used, with multi-shaded threads being popular in the late 1970s and early 1980s. These garments were originally intended for sale to Western markets, but they became popular with local and international Arab communities.

During the early 1980s, another new form of dress called *shawal* was developed; it was made from pre-embroidered linen, which was then sewn onto the main fabric of the dress. These

Detail of couching embroidery on the side panel of a dress worn in villages around Bethlehem and Jerusalem, ca. 1900. Photograph by Kamal Kawar.

were often sold with a fringed shawl with similarly worked embroidery, so creating a set. The main designs were geometric motifs. Although originally designed for the Western market, the shawal soon became popular among Arab women throughout the region and has developed into a kind of Palestinian fashion statement and even, some would claim, Palestinian haute couture.

During the Intifada period of the late 1980s, traditional dress was used as a silent, but effective, protest about the political situation and as a means of expressing national and cultural pride. A new style of shawal dress developed called the Intifada or flag dress. These dresses include motifs embroidered in the colors of the Palestinian flag and other nationalistic symbols such as the map of Palestine, the Dome of the Rock mosque, guns, grenades, and the pattern of the black-and-white checked *keffiyeh* (a head cloth worn by men). Many of the patterns are worked so that they resemble a floral border rather than a direct nationalistic symbol, but later the designs and messages became more visible. Although these dresses were made for a limited period only, the designs have been copied and adapted by various groups, including ANAT, a company that works with Palestinian refugees in Syria. These are popular among the Palestinian diaspora and the international Arab community.

Embroidery produced by refugees in the camps not only was used to send political messages but was also an important method of generating a stable income and creating an enduring symbol of Palestinian cultural heritage. The main people involved in these camp embroidery schemes were Samiha Khalil, who set up the Society of Ina'ash El-Usra in 1965 in the West Bank, and Serene Husseini Shahid of the Association of the Development of Palestinian Camps (founded 1969) in Lebanon. More recently, Palestinian designers such as Leila Jeryas of Amman, Jordan (starting in 2001), have been producing dresses with traditional designs and heremzi panels.

In the early twenty-first century, Palestinian dress no longer follows a traditional, regional pattern, and, as a result, some people have started to classify post-1970s dresses as refugee camp styles, Palestinian territories styles, or Bedouin dress. From the early 1970s, various groups, as in other parts of the Arab world, have sought to increase the use of *hijab*, or Islamically correct clothing, among Palestinian women. As a result, more and more women can be seen wearing a long, tailored overcoat (*shari'a dress*) with a head scarf of some kind. The garments worn underneath these plain outdoor garments are usually either international Islamic dress or some form of Western garments, but it is rare for a woman to wear Palestinian regional dress on a daily basis in the early twenty-first century, although it can frequently be seen on special occasions such as weddings and festival days because it has become a symbol of the lost homeland.

References and Further Reading

Allenby, Jeni. *Portraits without Names: Palestinian Costume*. Canberra, Australia: Palestine Costume Archive, 1995.

Baldensperger, Philip J. "The Immovable East: Clothes and Fashion." *Palestine Exploration Fund Quarterly* (1914–1915): 165–170.

Crowfoot, Grace, and Phyllis Sutton. "Ramallah Embroidery." *Embroidery* 3 (1935): 25–37.

Dalman, Gustaf. *Arbeit und Sitte in Palästina*. Vol. 5, *Webstoff, Spinnen, Weben, Kleidung*. Gütersloh, Germany C. Bertelsmann, 1937.

Kawar, Widad. *Costumes Dyed by the Sun*. Tokyo: Bunka Publishing House, 1982.

Kawar, Widad, and Tania Nasir. *Palestinian Embroidery, Traditional Fallahi Stitch*. Munich: National Ethnic Museum, 1992.

Rajab, Jehan S. *Costumes from the Arab World*. Kuwait: Tareq Rajab Museum, 2002.

Semple, Clara A. *Silver Legend: The Story of the Maria Theresa Thaler*. Manchester, UK: Barzan, 2005.

Skinner, Margarita, and Widad Kamel Kawar. *Palestinian Embroidery Motifs: A Treasury of Stitches 1850–1950*. London: Melisende, 2007.

Vögler, Gisela, Karin V. Welck, and Katharina Hackstein, eds. *Pracht und Geheimnis: Kleidung und Schmuck aus Palästina und Jordanien*. Cologne: Rauntenstrauch-Joest-Museum der Stadt Köln, 1987.

Weir, Shelagh. "A Bridal Headdress from Southern Palestine." *Palestine Exploration Fund Quarterly* 105 (January–June 1973): 101–109.

Weir, Shelagh. *Palestinian Costume*. London: British Museum Publications, 1989.

Weir, Shelagh. *Embroidery from Palestine*. London: British Museum Publications, 2006.

Widad Kawar and Sibba Einarsdóttir

See also Ottoman Dress; Palestinian Embroidery; Jordanian Women's Dress; Syria; Bedouin Jewelry; Birth, Marriage, and Death; Face Veils.

Palestinian Scarves and Flag Dresses

- The Palestinian Scarf in Western Culture
- The History of the Palestinian Flag Dress

The Palestinian scarf and the flag dress are powerful nationalistic and political icons. Their history is strongly connected to the disruptive occurrences of the twentieth century, such as the British Mandate period from 1922 to 1948, the foundation of the State of Israel in 1948, and the ensuing Arab-Israeli conflicts.

The Palestinian scarf is actually a rectangular head cloth worn mostly by men throughout the Arab world. Usually, it is folded diagonally and worn over the head with a head rope (*'aqal*) to keep it in place. It is a practical item of clothing that can be worn in several ways. Most often used to protect the head from the sun, wind, and sand, it can, on occasion, also function as a belt, corset, or purse. It is known in Arabic as a *keffiyeh* (plural *kuffiyaat*), *hattah*, *shamagh*, and *ghutra*. The use of these different terms depends on the regional context and the appearance of the cloth.

Both the terms *hattah* and *keffiyeh* were used by the Palestinian people, but *hattah* more often refers to the all-white version. In the early twenty-first century, the pattern associated with the keffiyeh resembles a knotted net or dog-tooth pattern, usually in red or black on a white background. Preferences for colors vary regionally. In Palestine, the black and red ones have a vague political association. Black is associated with the political party Fatah, and red is associated with the Socialist factions and, to a certain extent, with Hamas, a paramilitary organization and political party. However, there is no strict division between the two. The black-and-white version is most closely linked to the Palestinian struggle for independence.

Prior to the 1930s, only the Bedouin and some farmers wore the keffiyeh (or hattah) in Palestine. It came in various materials, colors, and patterns. Sometimes, a skullcap was worn underneath. The Palestinian villagers and townspeople usually wore a fez or *tarbush* (felted cap), which had been introduced by the Ottomans in the nineteenth century, with a skullcap underneath and sometimes a turban wrapped around it.

In 1936, the Palestinians rebelled against Jewish immigration into Palestine under the British Mandate. Although this revolt was officially led by the urban elite, the armed rebel groups mainly consisted of lower-class peasants. The keffiyeh was used by these guerrillas to wrap their faces, thereby avoiding identification. At the height of this rebellion in 1938, the rebel leaders commanded the Arab townspeople to don the keffiyeh, allowing the guerrilla forces to move undetected within the towns. This change, largely forced on the upper class and conservative townsmen, spread quickly. The tarbush became a clear sign of opposition to the rebel forces, and therefore few continued to wear it. This imposed dress code also had a more positive effect as a symbolic unification of the Palestinian people, obscuring class differences, and, as such, it was embraced by many. Most of the kuffiyaat were still white; only later did the checked version become more popular. However, after the rebellion, many of the elderly and more conservative Palestinians reverted back to the tarbush.

The keffiyeh once more gained political momentum in the 1960s. A new generation of Palestinian nationalist groups—for example, the Palestine Liberation Organization (PLO), the Popular Front for the Liberation of Palestine (PFLP), and the Democratic Front for the Liberation of Palestine—was founded and used the black-and-white patterned keffiyeh as a nationalistic symbol. This revival of the keffiyeh invoked the 1936–1939 rebellion and the sense of unity that had been created at that time. The change from white to black and white can probably be explained by the fact that, in the 1950s, Glubb Pasha, the English commander of the Jordanian forces, distinguished between the West Bank Palestinians and the East Bank Jordanians by equipping the Palestinians with black-patterned kuffiyaat and the Jordanians with red-patterned kuffiyaat. Up through the early twenty-first century, red kuffiyaat have been associated with Jordan.

Two important individuals in the keffiyeh's growth into a global symbol were Yasir Arafat and Leila Khaled. Arafat, as

Detail from a Palestinian-style flag dress, Syria, 1990s. This item was made by a pro-Palestinian group (ANAT) for the Southwest Asian market and is decorated with a cross-stitch design showing Palestinian boys with slings firing stones at Israel. It would have been worn as a silent protest against Israel. Textile Research Centre, Leiden.

chairman of the PLO and leader of Fatah, was, from the 1960s on, an international representative of the Palestinian cause. He wore a black-and-white keffiyeh in a very distinctive way, with one point draped into a triangle over the right shoulder, imitating the shape of Palestine. Khaled was a member of the PFLP and part of the 1969 and 1970 hijackings, both meant to gain international attention for the Palestinian cause. In 1970, pictures were published of her wearing a keffiyeh as a head covering. Up to this point, the keffiyeh had been a strongly male-associated item, but it now also became an item worn by women for political reasons. From the 1960s and 1970s on, the keffiyeh became internationally associated with the Palestinian people.

During the first Intifada (uprising) in 1987, kuffiyaat were worn as a sign of allegiance and to hide the face. They were worn by youngsters around the neck in a scarflike fashion. This shift from the head to the shoulders was influenced not only by Western fashions but also by the fact that a keffiyeh wrapped around the face was regarded as a possible target for Israeli soldiers. Around this time, thin, long neck scarves with crocheted ends in the colors of the Palestinian flag were made out of the keffiyeh. These could be worn as a scarf or headband. The black-and-white dog-tooth motif had by this time become such a prominent expression of Palestinian identity that it was used to represent the Palestinian nation in art.

THE PALESTINIAN SCARF IN WESTERN CULTURE

As a result of media images of keffiyeh-clad Palestinian stone throwers, suicide bombers, and hijackers, the keffiyeh has come to be associated with Islamic terrorism in the West. Both in spite of and because of this, the keffiyeh also plays a role within the Western language of dress. In the mid-1960s, the keffiyeh could be spotted at antiwar protests in the United States, at which it was worn as a sign of sympathy for the Palestinian cause. In the 1980s, kuffiyaat were also worn in apolitical daily life on the streets and became associated with the postpunk subculture, especially in big cities such as New York and London. This resurgence coincided with an international terrorism scare. According to U.S. anthropologist Ted Swedenburg, the wearing of a keffiyeh at the time was a small provocation, challenging the mass hysteria over all things Arab, Muslim, or Palestinian. However, through its inclusion in Western subculture, the keffiyeh also gradually lost its original meaning. It retained a hint of danger because it was not an item marketed by regular stores and had to be bought from street vendors. However, it was no longer a political statement. Only during the Gulf War of 1991 did it briefly become a sign of political allegiance again, worn by some opposing the war.

Remarkably, in the beginning of the twenty-first century, the keffiyeh once more became an item of discussion, through its appearance in the Western fashion world. It first appeared on the high-fashion catwalk and was soon adopted by celebrities. It was incorporated into mainstream fashion; the pattern was used for other items of clothing, its colors were changed, and the pattern on the scarf was replaced by a slightly different motif. This use of the keffiyeh is probably related to the military-chic fad, incorporating symbols of danger into fashion. This fashion has met with a wave of protest by both Zionists and those who support Palestine. Both felt the wearing of this item was an

affront to the history and meaning behind the keffiyeh, either as a symbol of opposition to the oppression of the Palestinians or as a symbol of anti-Israeli terrorism and the Intifada. However, the keffiyeh continued to be a popular fashion item (largely denuded of its original meaning) in both Europe and the United States. Even in Israel it was worn by certain youngsters, called the *keffiyeh-Kinderlach* as a provocation, or in a more Zionist-friendly version with the Magen David (star of David) instead of the Palestinian pattern. Although the keffiyeh has been incorporated further and further into the international fashion dialogue, it continues to be a controversial symbol.

THE HISTORY OF THE PALESTINIAN FLAG DRESS

Whereas the story of the keffiyeh is largely a tale of men, the Palestinian flag dress centers on Palestinian women. The histories of these two items are intertwined but nonetheless very different. Prior to 1948, Palestinian women's dress was a silent but very rich language. Urban dress was mostly a reflection of the occupiers of the time, but the village and Bedouin women had developed their own dress dialects, influenced only to a limited degree by urban fashions. The cut and decoration of the *thob* (loose-fitting dress) varied according to region, status, and religious affiliation. The embroidery of her garments showcased a woman's skills and wealth. Although traditional Palestinian dress is usually presented as consisting of several regional variations, it was by no means a static language, with elements changing over time and different regional types influencing one another. In the 1940s, the traditional thob was already slowly disappearing as European fashions brought in by the British and French began to take over in the towns and larger villages. The thob was worn on a daily basis only in the more isolated villages.

With the establishment of the State of Israel in 1948, more than half of the rural population was uprooted, and most of them ended up in refugee camps. The elaborate language of dress largely dissolved with the disappearance of regional affiliation and the loss of the time and the means to make these richly embroidered garments. Western-style dresses were easily available and relatively cheap, and they largely replaced the thob. However, the tradition of embroidering dresses did not entirely disappear; it survived in a modified form.

In the 1960s and 1970s, the so-called six- (or four-) branch dress first appeared. These dresses were of Western cut, usually made from sateen or acrylic fabrics. The name refers to the decoration, which consisted of a chest panel, a lower back panel, cuffs, and four or six embroidered bands running vertically from the hem to the waist. The embroidery was usually sparser than on traditional dresses, and sometimes it was replaced by machine embroidery. The motifs were heavily influenced by European embroidery patterns (such as floral motifs) introduced by British missionaries bringing along pattern books—notably, by the French company Dollfus, Mieg & Cie (DMC) in the 1930s.

An important factor in the development of this contemporary Palestinian dress was the emergence of women's projects and workshops in the refugee camps. These were realized by both foreign aid organizations and Palestinian women's organizations. The projects were a means of providing refugee women with a subsidiary source of income by selling handicrafts. The

Palestinian scarf, Syria, 2006. Printed cloth decorated with the design of the Palestinian flag, the checks of a keffiyeh, and a text in Arabic (upside down). The scarf is worn by Palestinian men and women, as well as people from overseas, to indicate their association with the Palestinian cause. Textile Research Centre, Leiden.

embroidery products were mainly aimed at the Western market, and, although some have consciously chosen to replicate traditional motifs or dress designs, others incorporate these features into more modern designs. The main product of these workshops was an embroidered cushion. However, dresses modified to appeal to Western tastes were also made. This type of dress is called the *shawal* dress; it was pre-embroidered and assembled later. The cut of the garment is slimmer than that of the thob, and bust darts were added. The embroidery consisted of a chest panel, cuff bands, and two vertical bands on the front and the back, joined by a horizontal band of embroidery at the hem.

Although this type of dress was originally developed for the foreign market, it also became popular among young Palestinian women. Like the keffiyeh, the embroidered dress used to be a sign of peasant backwardness but has become a signifier of national pride because of its association with Palestinian village life. This modern embroidered dress was no longer a garment to be worn daily but rather on special occasions, such as at demonstrations and political meetings but also parties and weddings; like the keffiyeh, it has become a political accessory. This simplified version of the thob has become part of the Palestinian tradition. Although some regional markers are still used on occasion,

the role of Palestinian dress has changed in this aspect; whereas before, the Palestinian thob was mainly a marker of regional difference, the modern traditional Palestinian dress is a symbol of unity.

Like the workshops and cooperatives that have kept embroidery traditions (and other handicrafts) alive, museums also play an important role by conserving Palestinian history. These do not include only local Palestinian museums; especially in the 1980s, interest in Palestinian heritage and dress grew internationally. Several museums, such as the British Museum's Museum of Mankind (London), the Museum of International Folk Art (Santa Fe, United States), the Israel Museum (Jerusalem), and the Tareq Rajab Museum (Hawelli, Kuwait), house comprehensive collections of Palestinian dress. This international recognition of Palestinian culture has undoubtedly contributed to a Palestinian sense of self.

With the wave of nationalism and resistance accompanying the Intifada in the 1980s, the embroidered dress, like the keffiyeh, gained political meaning. This change also gave rise to the type of dress known as the flag or Intifada dress. Most flag dresses date to the first Intifada, although there are earlier examples from the 1970s and later ones from the second Intifada. In fact, politically charged garments are still being made in the early twenty-first century—for example, by the ANAT workshop in Syria. They usually have the same features as other modern dresses of this period but distinguish themselves by the use of certain nationalistic embroidery motifs. During the first Intifada, when daily life had become saturated with political struggle and carrying the keffiyeh or the Palestinian flag in the Palestinian territories could lead to imprisonment, women embroidered the flag on their dresses as a kind of "symbolic defiance," according to Jeni Allenby, an Australian writer on Palestinian causes and dress. These symbols mostly include the Palestinian flag or its colors, maps of Palestine, and texts such as *Filasteen* (the Arabic word for Palestine) or *PLO*. However, far more subtle and complex symbols are also sometimes used.

The flag dresses are an expression of women's participation in the Palestinian uprising. These dresses were made and worn as symbolic defiance but generally do not make up the everyday wear of women in the refugee camps or the Palestinian territories. Most women do not own an embroidered dress, although smaller embroidered items can often be found in their households. Although embroidery has largely lost its function as an artistic expression of a woman's identity and skill, it is still a powerful expression of Palestinian culture.

References and Further Reading

Allenby, Jeni. "Symbolic Defiance: Palestinian Costume and Cultural Heritage since 1948." Palestinian Costume Archives. Unpublished.

KABOBfest. "Modern Chronology of the Keffiyah Craze." http://www.kabobfest.com/2007/07/modern-chronology-of-keffiyah-kraze.html (accessed 19 October 2009).

Seng, Yvonne J., and Betty Wass. "Traditional Palestinian Wedding Dress as a Symbol of Nationalism." In *Dress and Ethnicity: Change across Space and Time*, edited by Joanne B. Eicher, 227–254. Oxford: Berg, 1995.

Swedenburg, Ted. "The Palestinian Peasant as National Signifier." *Anthropological Quarterly* 63, no. 1 (1990): 18–30.

Swedenburg, Ted. "Seeing Double: Palestinian/American Histories of the Kufiya." *Michigan Quarterly Review* 31, no. 4 (1992): 557–577.

Weir, Shelagh. *Palestinian Costume*. London: British Museum Publications, 1989.

Tineke Rooijakkers

See also Ottoman Dress; Arab Men's Dress in the Eastern Mediterranean; Palestinian Women's Dress; Palestinian Embroidery.

Palestinian Embroidery

- The Embroiderers and the Uses of Embroidery
- Materials, Stitches, and Designs
- Variations in Regional Styles
- Bedouin Embroidery
- Post-1948 Dress and Embroidery Forms

Embroidery in the Palestinian region is perhaps best known for its cross-stitch patterns in various geometric or floral motifs. However, there is considerably more to Palestinian embroidery. It has its roots in personal and group identification (urban/nomad, rich/poor, northern/southern, married/unmarried, and so on) as well as being a simple, but very effective, manner of reflecting women's creative and artistic abilities. It has also been, on a more prosaic level, an important means by which women could and still can respectably earn money.

Unlike in many other regions in the world, embroidery and politics have become closely intertwined in the Palestinian region as a result of numerous political and economic events throughout the twentieth century. These include the fall of the Ottoman Empire in 1918, the British Mandate period (1922–1948), and the establishment of the State of Israel in 1948. At times, it has become impossible to separate the two subjects of embroidery and politics.

Due to historical reasons—notably, the extent of the Ottoman Empire—Turkish urban embroidery styles have had an influence on the embroidery in the region. In particular, the use of metal-thread embroidery is often related to regions where the Ottoman control was particularly felt.

THE EMBROIDERERS AND THE USES OF EMBROIDERY

Traditionally, there were two main groups of embroiderers: domestic and professional workers. In general, women worked at home producing items needed for household uses and, more important, embroidered garments needed for the dowry of the girls in the family. It was also quite common and acceptable for elderly women, widows, or the women of a poor family to take up embroidery to earn extra money for the family. The main exception was couched-thread embroidery, which used valuable gold and silver thread and was carried out by professional embroiderers working in villages and towns, notably in and around Bethlehem. Complete dresses (especially wedding dresses) and individual panels for dresses were ordered from these embroiderers. The panels were taken home and then sewn onto local dresses. This form of professional embroidery has virtually vanished and has been replaced by professional tailors (usually men) producing machine-made embroidery.

In the mid- to late twentieth century, considerable political and economic unrest in the region resulted in various mass migrations. Following World War II, there was an influx of Jewish communities from Russia and Europe into what was to become Israel. As a result of the arrival of these new groups, the emergence of Israel, and the Arab-Israeli War (1948), many Arab communities came under pressure, and there was a mass emigration

Detail of a chest panel from a woman's dress, Bethlehem, Palestine, ca. 1930s. The embroidery includes couching, which is a feature of Bethlehem work. Textile Research Centre, Leiden.

of mainly Palestinian Arabs to surrounding Arab countries (notably Jordan, Lebanon, and Syria) as well as to the West. One result of this unrest was that there was a generation of women who were either not taught to embroider or regarded embroidery as nonessential. It cost time and money, neither of which was readily available.

The situation changed somewhat by the late twentieth century, when various groups started to produce embroidery. Some elderly women had continued to work on embroideries as the women in their families had always done. But there was also a growing number of younger girls who were being deliberately introduced to embroidery. One reason is that the wearing of embroidered clothing was seen as a reflection of the wearer's cultural heritage and a statement of pride regarding that heritage. Wearing specific types of embroidery was regarded as having national rather than local or regional significance. This contrasts with the use of embroidery at the beginning of the twentieth century, when it was often used to identify a person as coming from a particular region and social group.

Another considerable difference that occurred during the twentieth century was the introduction of embroidery produced by nongovernmental organizations to support and supplement local women's groups, especially those of the Palestinian diaspora. Some of these groups went on to become commercial companies with the specific aim of encouraging local textile traditions and supporting various women's groups. ANAT, for example, is a commercial women's group that works from Syria. It is involved in making embroidered garments and objects to support Syrian women as well as the Palestinian diaspora in Syria. Their work is based on Syrian and Palestinian motifs and techniques but usually with a modern twist.

Before World War II, embroidery was used for a wide range of household objects, including curtains and cushions. But, in general, the most elaborate embroidery was used for women's clothing. As a generalization, embroidered garments were worn by town, village, and Bedouin women rather than elite women. Women's clothing—notably, dresses, jackets, and head coverings—was often heavily decorated with embroidery, and the dresses are the most impressive and memorable forms.

Women's dresses (thob), for example, include decoration in specific places. The most important area is the chest panel (qabbeh), which is usually made separately and then attached to the dress. The color and motifs used for this panel differ from village to village, and they are regarded as the most important indicator of the wearer's origin. There are two main types of sleeves for these dresses: narrow sleeves (kum), which are usually embroidered on the outer part of the sleeve in bands that start at the shoulder and end near the cuff. The cuffs are also sometimes heavily embroidered. The second form of sleeve (irdan) is long, pointed, and triangular. The pointed sections are usually left unembroidered, because they were tied behind the back while working.

The skirt of the dress can be divided into three sections: the side panels (benayiq), the front of the skirt (hiijer), and the lower back of the skirt (shinyar). The side panels are triangular pieces of fabric, which give ease of movement while walking. The amount of embroidery varies from region to region. The front section is the area that shows the most regional variations. Some dresses have very little embroidery here, and others have a considerable amount. Most dresses include two parallel bands of embroidery (mawaris) that start at the waist and end just above the hem. The

lower back panel is usually heavily embroidered. It is sometimes framed by two mawaris bands. This area of the dress is regarded as the most important and used to show off the embroiderer's skill. Sometimes, the skirt hem (diyal) is also embroidered, but this is mainly done to protect the lower edge of the dress from damage.

Embroidery is also used to decorate various types of coats (killayeh), short jackets (taqsireh), head coverings (such as the shaylah), and, in the more southern regions, women's face veils (burqa). In some areas, women wear elaborate headdresses that were embellished with gold and silver coins. In the Ramallah region, women wear an embroidered cap (smadeh) with a stiff, padded rim, which have a row of coins sewn around the top of the rim.

MATERIALS, STITCHES, AND DESIGNS

The ground materials for embroideries tend to be of cotton, linen, silk, or wool. Until the mid-twentieth century, these fabrics were generally woven in the Palestinian region at centers such as Bethlehem and Ramallah. The more expensive materials, such as silks, tended to be imported from Europe, India, and Syria. As a generalization, the silk forms were especially popular with the town and village markets, while cottons were associated with the Bedouin and poorer village women.

Until the 1930s, much of the embroidery was worked in floss silk (a soft, loosely twisted thread), which was twisted into harder threads of the required thickness by the embroiderer. In the 1930s, perlé cotton (also known as pearl or French perlé) thread became more popular. This is an S-twisted, two-ply thread with a high sheen. It is very strong and wears well. Much of the thread came from the French company Dollfus, Mieg & Cie (DMC), and this product is still highly valued in the region. Bedouin embroidery (especially from the south) also includes a range of other objects such as coins, beads, and shells. The coins used to be gold and silver, but in the early twenty-first century, gold-colored disks are more often used to symbolize the coins.

Two main types of stitches are associated with Palestinian embroidery: cross stitch and couching stitch. However, other stitches are also used in the region, including hem stitch, herringbone stitch, running stitch, satin stitch, stem stitch, zigzag stitch, and various forms of oversewing stitch for the edges.

In the older examples, the embroidery is normally worked over two warp and weft threads on an open-weave cotton or linen fabric. Examples from the mid-twentieth century and after tend to use machine-woven materials, which are much more closely woven. As a result, the size and style of embroidery had to be adapted. How this was done varied from region to region.

Although red is commonly associated with Palestinian embroidery, a range of other colors is also used. Red is regarded as the color of happiness and blood (fertility). It was used on white, dark blue, and black ground materials. Different colors such as yellow, green, pink, orange, and white were used to accentuate the red tones. After the 1930s, when cheaper cotton perlé was introduced into the region, the range of colors expanded. Multicolored shaded threads, in which the color changes over the length of thread, were popular in the 1970s and early 1980s.

The embroidery designs are not static and changed during the twentieth century due to the arrival of new materials, threads, designs, colors, and clothing fashions. The economic and political

Detail of an embroidered front panel from a woman's dress, Ramallah, Palestine, early 1970s. Ramallah dresses for daily wear are made from white linen fabric (*rumi*), and the fine embroidery can include motifs of date palms arranged in horizontal rows, rainbow or arch designs (*qos*), the S design also known as the horse's head or leech (*alaq*), the star, and "moon feathers." Textile Research Centre, Leiden.

situation has also dramatically affected the form of embroidery used in the region. At the end of the nineteenth century and in the early twentieth century, for example, the type of stitching, colors, designs, extra decoration (coins), and so forth all indicated where the woman came from, her social status, and whether she was married. In some cases, it also reflected whether she was a widow or was looking for a husband.

The designs at this time tended to be predominantly geometric and abstract patterns and included forms such as chevrons, eight-pointed stars (Bethlehem stars), lozenges, squares, and some more figurative motifs such as birds (for example, pigeons and cockerels), flowers (notably roses), grapes, and trees (especially orange and cypress trees). In the late nineteenth and early twentieth centuries, various Christian missionary groups opened various schools and introduced a range of bird and flower motifs into their sewing classes. In the 1930s, DMC introduced a range of pattern books, which considerably influenced and increased the range of embroidery motifs. Turkish influence in the north of the region is reflected in the use of stylized but flowing floral motifs, including tulips.

VARIATIONS IN REGIONAL STYLES

Northern Palestine (upper and lower Galilee) is famous for the use of cross stitch, drawn-thread work, hem stitch, satin stitch (straight and diagonal), stem stitch, and various types of joining stitches. The fronts of Galilee dresses and coats are often decorated with predominantly geometric designs, such as chevrons, diamonds, squares, and triangles. Sometimes, these are embroidered on, but on other occasions large appliqués of taffeta silk in bright red, yellow, and green geometric shapes are used, especially for women's coats.

Similarly, garments from Nablus use a wide range of colorful combinations of materials and fabrics, including silks from Damascus and Aleppo and cottons from Manchester. Bedouin women from the region use black dresses with decoration around the neck openings and on the sleeves. Normally, there are four or five wide bands of embroidery around the lower hems. Several embroidery stitches are used—notably, a zigzag stitch with gaps to create geometric black patterns where the dress material shows through the embroidery.

Central Palestine, the region around Judaea in the eastern half of the region, includes the important towns of Jerusalem, Hebron, Ramallah, and Bethlehem. This area is known for three distinct styles of embroidery from Bethlehem, Ramallah, and the Hebron region. Bethlehem embroidery is regarded as the most costly and desirable form of embroidery. It is characterized by the use of couching, normally the work of professional embroiderers (usually women). Gold or silver cord or a silk cord is sewn onto a silk, wool (broadcloth), felt, or velvet ground. This

Detail of a front panel from a woman's dress, Hebron, Palestine, ca. 1930s. The appliqué is made of silk taffeta pieces, with embroidered details. The area was known for producing some of the most elaborate forms of Palestinian embroidery. Textile Research Centre, Leiden.

technique is used for "royal" wedding dresses (*thob malak*, made from a silk material called *malak*), jackets, and the elaborate head covers (*shatweh*) worn by married women. The most important element of a Bethlehem dress is the chest panel, which is usually heavily decorated with couching, although couching can also be found on the sleeves and side panels. Velvet or broadcloth jackets are often embroidered using a gold-colored couching thread to create stylized floral motifs with free or rounded lines with details in red, blue, and yellow satin stitch. This style of embroidery is very similar to that being produced in Turkey.

Ramallah dresses are characterized by being made from white linen fabric (*rumi*, the classical Arabic word for *Rome*, meaning "Western") for daily wear and scarves, while indigo-dyed linen was used for special occasions and during the winter. The embroidery on these garments is mainly carried out in cross stitch using red silk thread. Ramallah is known for a wide variety of finely worked patterns. Popular Ramallah motifs include date palms arranged in horizontal rows, rainbow or arch designs (*qos*), the S design also known as the horse's head or leech (*alaq*), the star, and "moon feathers." Some of the designs in the Ramallah region derive from earlier Byzantine and Turkish influences, such as flowering plants, irises, and birds. In the late nineteenth century, more motifs were introduced by European missionaries, and, by the 1930s, DMC motifs had become widespread. Ramallah dresses are recognizable by the qabbeh panel that is often a separate piece of cloth sewn onto the garment; the sleeve embroidery; and two vertical bands on the front and the back of the skirt covering the seams. There is normally an embroidered back panel (*shinyar*) fitted between the vertical bands at the back lower hem.

The Hebron region also includes the villages of Beit Ummar, Bani Na'im, Beit Jibrin, and Samula. This area is known for producing some of the most elaborate and richest-looking forms of Palestinian embroidery. The ground materials used include handwoven linens, cottons, and indigo-dyed silks. As a generalization, the embroidered areas on the dress are much larger and denser than those of Ramallah, with the sides and back also embroidered in vertical patterns. The standard embroidery stitch is cross stitch, with herringbone stitch used to join two pieces of cloth. Dresses for special occasions are decorated with diamond- and triangular-shaped silk appliqué patches sewn onto the garments. The panel designs are similar to the Ramallah style in the use of arches (sometimes called rainbows). Popular motifs in the Hebron region include birds, cypress trees, grapes, stars, and triangles.

The central coastal plain extends from the base of the Judaean Hills to the Mediterranean Sea. The region includes the towns of Jaffa and Majdal. In general, this region produces very little embroidery. The reason for this may be reflected in the local saying that if embroidery is being carried out, then the women are not working, which gives an indication of the (male) attitude toward embroidery. Where embroidery occurs, it tends to be much less dense than the Hebron forms. Popular motifs from this area include scissors (*muqass*), combs (*musht*), and triangles (*hijab*). These designs are often arranged in clusters of five, seven, and three. In Arab folklore, odd numbers are regarded as masculine, auspicious, and helpful against the evil eye.

BEDOUIN EMBROIDERY

Prior to the 1930s, few items of Bedouin or nomadic dress were decorated with embroidery. This was not only because the materials and silk threads required were expensive but also because these groups lived in more remote areas. With the development of transportation links, notably the arrival of cars and trucks after

Detail of a Bedouin embroidered skirt panel from a woman's dress, North Sinai, Egypt, 1960s. The dress is predominantly blue with red embroidery, indicating that it was worn by a married woman (blue on its own is for unmarried girls). Textile Research Centre, Leiden.

World War I (1914–1918) and the introduction of perlé embroidery threads, embroidery began to be featured on Bedouin dress. By the 1950s, it had become widespread. Machine embroidery became popular in the 1950s and 1960s.

The Bedouin in the Sinai wear a form of clothing similar to the village forms but modified for the desert environment. It consists of a large and loose-fitting dress and a large head covering. The dresses are usually of heavy black cotton, poplin, or sateen. In some areas, face veils (burqa) are also worn.

Bedouin dresses are usually heavily embroidered with block-like geometric forms in dense cross stitch. The main areas of embroidery on a Bedouin dress are not on the front chest panel (qabbeh), as in many settled areas, but on the shinyar at the back of the dress. This is because the women would wear large embroidered shawls of black cotton or silk that extended from the top of the head to the embroidered back panel at the lower hem of the dress. As a generalization, early dresses were embroidered with simple patterns in vertical rows or zigzag patterns in white or white-and-green cotton. Later dresses have vertical rows of predominantly red cross-stitch motifs.

Sinai and Negev Bedouin women use the same brightly colored cross stitch as used throughout Palestinian villages. The color of the embroidery is important. Blue embroidery is worn by young, unmarried women and is regarded as a color that protected the young and vulnerable wearer from the evil eye, while married women wear red (for fertility). In some areas, widows wear blue again, and women who want to remarry wear dresses in a combination of red and blue embroidery.

Face veils come in various forms. In the north of the region, for example, they are made of a small band of cross-stitch embroidery to which two bands of cloth covered in coins are attached. In the northern Sinai, burqas are made from rectangles of red cloth with a forehead band with red and black cross-stitch embroidery. The veil sections are usually covered in coins, beads, tassels, chains, and so forth. These signify the wearer's wealth (especially the coins) and are also amulets and charms against the evil eye. In the southern part of the Sinai, the veils are orange or yellow, and, like those in the northern region, they are covered in a wide variety of objects.

POST-1948 DRESS AND EMBROIDERY FORMS

In the 1960s, a new form of urban dress decoration developed called the four-branch (arba' agruq) and six-branch (sit agruq) form. The former has four vertical bands of embroidery that run from the waist to the hem of the skirt, while the latter has six vertical lines. These styles emerged in the 1960s and are regarded as the first post-1948 style to evolve without being tied to one established regional style. It is characterized by its curvilinear foliage and flower designs and its various motifs of "branches with birds," which are based on European patterns (DMC influence again).

Refugees producing clothing for consumption by Western markets led to the development of the maris or shawal style of dress in the 1980s. This is a simple form of dress made from a heavy linen or cotton, in which the embroidery is worked prior to the garment being made up. The Western influence can be seen in the use of a slimmer cut and, in some cases, a zipper at the back. These garments were often sold as a set with a fringed shawl that had similar embroidery. Although originally developed for the foreign market, the maris has became popular among women in Jordan and other Arab countries and has developed into a form of what Iman Saca, a professor of anthropology, calls Palestinian haute couture.

From the late 1970s on, Palestinian embroidery was used for a far wider range of objects. For example, many Palestinian embroidery groups (both commercial and nongovernmental organizations) have been set up to make and sell "Palestinian" bellpulls, bookmarks, cushion covers, hanging pockets, shoulder purses and bags, sachets, eyeglass cases, table runners, wall hangings, and even Christmas cards and Christmas tree decorations. These are regarded as an important source of income for women, as well as reflecting Palestinian/Arab origins. They are frequently used and worn by urban Palestinian women all over the world to confirm and publicly announce their ethnic origins. These objects are also sold to tourists from all over the world, not just in the West. There is also a large market, for instance, for Palestinian work among wealthy Gulf and Saudi Arabs. The purchasing and wearing of Palestinian embroidery is regarded as showing solidarity with the Palestinians.

In the 1980s, some Israeli groups started to sell Palestinian handicrafts, including embroideries, that were described as Israeli handicrafts in English and Hebrew on the label attached to the objects. As a direct response, Palestinians incorporated Arabic calligraphy words and texts in the embroidery designs, such as "Palestine" and "PLO" and slogans such as "We shall return" as integral signs that these were Palestinian handicrafts and not Israeli or Jewish in origin. Care, however, should be taken with this situation, because, in the late 1940s and 1950s, many Jewish groups left Yemen and settled in what had become Israel. They brought with them Yemeni styles of embroidery, notably blue stitching on a white ground. Items made by this group were often sold as Israeli handicrafts; they are Yemeni Israeli, but they were made by Jewish embroiderers.

Embroidery was sometimes used in a very deliberate, overt, political manner to make nonverbal statements about the situation in the region. These embroideries were used for garments as well as for wall hangings, banners, and so forth. Another example of the political use of embroidery came in the late 1980s. The first Palestinian Intifada, a mass uprising against Israeli rule, took place between 1987 and 1993. It began in the Jabalia refugee camp and quickly spread throughout Gaza, the West Bank, and East Jerusalem. The Palestinian actions took many forms, including civil disobedience, general strikes, boycotts, graffiti, and barricades. Certain garments were banned by the Israelis: the so-called Arafat head covers for men (black-and-white checked head cloths called *keffiyeh*); garments in the colors of the Palestinian flag (black, white, green, and red); and *lahshe* (narrow scarves decorated with black-and-white checks and the colors of the Palestinian flag).

During this period, embroidery was used by various Palestinian groups as a silent symbol of protest and reaction to the situation. Some Palestinian women started to produce and wear the so-called Intifada or flag dresses (maris style). Garments with designs in the colors of the Palestinian flag became popular. Other motifs on the garments reflected the politics of the period—such as boys with slings throwing stones, representing Palestinian resistance to Israeli rule, and the phoenix, a symbol of death and renewal of life to reflect the future rebirth of Palestine. Other dresses included embroidered pictures of the Dome of the Rock or poetry about the Palestinian people and their position.

Palestinian embroidery is one of the most dramatic forms of embroidery in Southwest Asia. It not only looks attractive and is skillfully worked but also represents many different aspects and layers of life in the region: from gender, cultural, ethnic, and economic to political and religious differences. Few forms of decoration can claim so many meanings.

References and Further Reading

Abu, 'Umar, and 'Abd al-Sami. *Traditional Palestinian Embroidery and Jewelry*. Jerusalem: Al Shark Arab Press, 1986.

Allenby, Jeni. *Portraits without Names: Palestinian Costume*. Canberra, Australia: Palestine Costume Archive, 1996.

Grutz, Jane Waldron. "Woven Legacy, Woven Language." *Saudi Aramco World* (January/February 1991): 34–43.

Kawar, Widad. "Traditional Costumes of Jordan and Palestine." *Arts and the Islamic World* 2 (1984): 41–42.

Rajab, Jehan. *Palestinian Costume*. New York: Kegan Paul International, 1989.

Saca, Iman. *Embroidering Identities: A Century of Palestinian Clothing*. Chicago: Oriental Institute, 2006.

Weir, Shelagh. *Palestinian Embroidery: A Village Arab Craft*. London: British Museum Press, 1970.

Weir, Shelagh. *Palestinian Costume*. London: British Museum Publications, 1989.

Weir, Shelagh, and S. Shahid. *Palestinian Embroidery: Cross-Stitch Patterns from the Traditional Costumes of the Village Women of Palestine*. London: British Museum, 1988.

Tineke Rooijakkers and Gillian Vogelsang-Eastwood

See also Embroidery Workshops in Palestine; Jordanian Women's Dress; Palestinian Women's Dress; Syrian Dress.

Embroidery Workshops in Palestine

- Palestinian Embroidery after 1948
- Palestinian Embroidery at the End of the Twentieth Century

The first commercial embroidery workshops were founded in Palestine at the beginning of the twentieth century. The economic basis for this development was changes that had taken place in Palestinian society at the end of the nineteenth century. The Ottoman rulers, for example, passed a law about the registration of land ownership, which left many farming families without land. This law led to the creation of a new class of landlords and, in some areas, an increase in the number of agricultural workers for hire, as opposed to small-scale farmers working their own land.

These social changes also influenced the production and use of embroidery; groups of poorer women, instead of working for themselves or their families, organized embroidery workshops. The centers of this movement were Bethlehem, Ramallah, and Beit Dajan. Although the workshops were located in the cities, they employed women from the surrounding villages as embroiderers. The basic embroidery was carried out at home in the form of piecework, while the assembly of garments and special, more complicated embroideries were done by specialists in the workshops. The embroidery pieces—dresses, headwear, jackets, and coats—were ordered directly by the customers.

At the same time, a market for embroidery panels rather than complete dresses also developed. The couching technique used for Bethlehem dresses, for example, was used to produce panels in embroidery workshops in Bethlehem, and these spread as accessory parts for dresses all over Palestine. It became fashionable to adorn wedding and festive dresses with pieces of couching embroidery from Bethlehem; these pieces were integrated on the shoulders, in the middle of the sleeves, and on the front part of the skirt of the local dresses. A regional exchange took place, and the dresses became more and more elaborate, sometimes adorned with real gold and silver threads.

In addition to regional and local designs reflecting ancient pattern languages, foreign designs had been a part of the Palestinian repertoire since the end of the nineteenth century. In 1870, for example, Christian Quakers opened a school in Ramallah and taught the students European cross-stitch designs using embroidery pattern books (especially French and English versions) and pattern samplers. The Quakers supported and promoted the idea of embroidery as a source of income, especially for women. The pupils began to integrate the new patterns into their embroidery and created a new "Ramallah" style. Liberty patterns, mainly monochrome silhouettes, were combined with traditional patterns such as palm trees, feathers, and earthworms. The style that developed in Ramallah in the beginning of the twentieth century continues to be associated with the city at the beginning of the twenty-first century.

After World War I (1914–1918), perlé cotton thread produced by the French company Dollfus, Mieg & Cie (DMC) was sold on the Palestinian market and displaced the hand-dyed silk floss that had normally been used. To promote its yarns, DMC also sent pattern booklets. The embroidery workshops, searching for new patterns to satisfy the market and customers, welcomed the new ideas. The meaning of many of the old patterns had already been forgotten, which facilitated the integration and adoption of the new patterns. In general, the embroidery changed from locally inspired spiritual amulets to beautiful designs inspired by many cultures. These changes can be seen in the new names of the patterns. Previously, the names referred to mythological sources such as the sun, moon, and cow's eye (images of the ancient goddess), the cypress tree (symbolizing the tree of life), the ear of grain (a fertility symbol), and an amulet for personal and family protection. The new names, in contrast, referred to status symbols of the better-off: "two-story houses," "sofa," and "officer's pipe." Sometimes, the old patterns were renamed; the moon pattern became "pasha's tent," and in Syria the sun pattern was renamed "rails" after the railway network was extended in Syria.

PALESTINIAN EMBROIDERY AFTER 1948

Palestinian embroidery suffered a heavy setback in 1948, following the creation of the State of Israel, the diaspora of the Palestinian people, and the resulting poverty of the refugees. One result was that there was very little money to spend on clothes, especially on the decoration of clothing. For many, there was a developing sense of resignation about the situation, which led to a collective inferiority complex.

Many of the Palestinian refugees lived in camps on the outskirts of big cities in Egypt, Jordan, Lebanon, and Syria, where they felt ostracized. Many women stopped wearing traditional dress to conceal their status as refugees. Urban and younger women started to wear Western styles, and miniskirts became fashionable in the 1960s. In addition, women's hair was worn back-combed like that of Farah Diba, the Iranian queen. Many poorer women in the refugee camps started to wear long, wide dresses (dishdasha) made of colorful cotton material together with colorful pajama-style trousers, which did not require embroidery for decoration. It is not surprising, therefore, that under these circumstances embroidery workshops could not function as they used to. The exceptions were in the West Bank and in Jordan, where the Palestinian population was in the majority. Consequently, many women felt comfortable wearing traditional embroidered dresses there.

A revival of the embroidery tradition started with the Palestinian resistance in the mid-1960s. It was not possible to hoist a Palestinian flag anywhere in Bethlehem or Ramallah, so it was a form of silent protest when the women wore the traditional Palestinian dress (thob). It was no longer important for the dresses to show regional origins, but rather they emphasized the wearer's Palestinian affiliations. The decoration on the new Palestinian thob was a mixture of different local traditions and the new united Palestinian consciousness. It became equal to the keffiyeh, or checkered men's headwear, that became a national and global icon.

As part of this resistance, Palestinian women invented a number of new patterns, including one called "Aqsa mosque" after the famous mosque in Jerusalem; designs based on the colors of the Palestinian flag or the flag itself; embroidered slogans in Arabic and English; and a design called *fedayeen*, or Palestinian fighters. The developing resistance strengthened many women's self-confidence, and they wore these special dresses with consciousness and pride. This process shows how lively the Palestinian traditions still were. The Palestinian people were capable of developing their embroidery traditions as a collective effort and expression of their united cause, and they used their skills to propagate their cause and to secure an income. The new patterns are much simpler in form and color and lack the depth of meaning and complexity of traditional designs, but they can also be seen as true expressions of a collective aim and the unity of the Palestinian people at this period in their history.

At the same time, more embroidery workshops were set up to satisfy Palestinian women's demands for embroidery. Many of the embroidery workshops were founded or sponsored by Palestinian political organizations. The most important workshops were established in the West Bank, Jordan, and Lebanon. Some of the main customers were Palestinian women living in the Jordan, the Gulf states, and the United States. These women started to wear Palestinian dresses to emphasize their ethnic and cultural origins at official events and feasts. They also liked to adorn their reception rooms with embroidered cushions, tablecloths, and wall hangings in traditional and modern Palestinian patterns.

In addition to the workshops, there were always individual women who still earned their income by embroidering for neighbors or relatives. Many Palestinian women living abroad helped their relatives by commissioning pieces or individually selling their embroidered items. This kind of individual marketing became an important source of income for many women.

At this time, some Israelis started marketing Palestinian items as either being Israeli in origin or with a label that said "Made in the Holy Land." This angered many of the embroidery workshops and individual women embroiderers because it was seen as a form of cultural theft. Some embroiderers countered this by stitching "Palestine" or "Made in Palestine" into their embroideries themselves.

In 1970, the organization SAMED ("Resistance") was founded by Fatah, a major Palestinian political party and the largest faction within the Palestine Liberation Organization (PLO). The aim of the organization was to give work to poor Palestinians, especially those in the refugee camps in Egypt, Jordan, Lebanon, and Syria. SAMED ran workshops and factories for sewing, woodworking, and preparing foodstuffs (such as jams and special desserts), as well as embroideries. At one point, SAMED employed several thousand workers, which helped many families in the refugee camps to make a living. SAMED, however, is not regarded as having achieved a high quality of embroidered products. The same situation applies to the embroidery workshops set up by the General Union of Palestinian Women.

Other groups within the PLO founded their own embroidery workshops. Again, the primary aim of these workshops was to give work to refugee women, but they also used the products to promote the Palestinian cause. The embroideries produced in these workshops emphasized national symbols and presented nostalgic pictures of Palestinian life. Although of a slightly later date, a good example of a nostalgic embroidery design is the wedding panel that was designed by the ANAT workshop in Syria in 1988 depicting an idealized wedding scene with everyone happy and in their best clothing. Since then, this design has been embroidered by many other workshops and was printed as an embroidery chart with the name "Wedding Picture Panel."

One of the most important organizations involved with protecting and developing Palestinian embroidery traditions is the Society of Ina'ash El-usra, based in Al-Bira. This nongovernmental organization was founded in 1965 by Samiha Khalil and provides work to more than one thousand women. Ina'ash El-Usra also runs factories for the production of clothing and cookies and has founded an ethnological museum in Al-Bira in which clothes, household articles, and agricultural tools collected from Palestinian villages are displayed.

The main aim, however, of Ina'ash El-Usra was to encourage the production of embroideries at home. It cultivated the Ramallah style of embroidery using the colors red, black, and white and exported work mainly to the Gulf states and the United States, where many rich Palestinians live. The production and purchase of these embroideries performed a dual function: It supported poorer Palestinians, especially those in the refugee camps, and cultivated and supported the Palestinian identity and cause. Thus, a feeling of solidarity, social responsibility, and social partnership developed. Moreover, the embroidery became a vehicle to mobilize the entire people for a common cause. In the 1970s, Palestinian events in the diaspora often auctioned embroideries to support the resistance.

Another important local nongovernmental organization is Inaash Al Muchaiam, which was founded in 1969 in Lebanon. Inaash worked with refugees in Lebanon, who mainly came from northern Palestine and were used to embroidering in another style of embroidery based on the running stitch and cross stitch. Inaash cultivated this style in its embroideries and experimented with new color combinations. In the beginning, the organization mainly concentrated on producing cushions but later expanded the line to include a wider range of objects, such as clothing. The embroidery pieces from Ina'ash El-Muchaiam and Ina'ash El-Usra have value as collector pieces.

PALESTINIAN EMBROIDERY AT THE END OF THE TWENTIETH CENTURY

In the 1970s and 1980s, Palestinians who had made homes abroad began to view the Palestinians still living in Palestine as the real guardians of Palestinian heritage. This situation encouraged members of the younger generation to improve their knowledge of their history and traditions. Hundreds of young people started to visit old people in the villages to collect fairy tales, songs, dances, and embroidery patterns. The new embroiderers imitated Palestinian dresses and patterns from before World War II (1939–1945). They learned old techniques like appliqué, rare kinds of embroidery stitches, and tassel making. It became fashionable for a Palestinian bride to wear a thob on her wedding day, and younger women in Palestine started to wear traditional dresses for festive occasions. To satisfy the new demand for embroidery, workshops were founded in the West Bank and the Gaza Strip.

A Palestinian woman embroidering fabric with a traditional cross-stitch pattern at a workshop in the refugee camp of Ain el-Helweh on the outskirts of Sidon, Lebanon, 2007. Some workshops in Syria and Lebanon produce high-quality fashion and lifestyle items based on traditional designs, in the hope that they will be sold internationally. Marwan Naamani/AFP/Getty Images.

Since the end of the 1990s, however, production of embroideries has been stagnant. There are various reasons for this; for instance, the Southwest Asian and global markets have been saturated with Palestinian embroideries of varying degrees of quality. The organizations that used to produce high-quality embroideries, such as Ina'ash El-Usra, kept producing but were unable to sell because they were perceived as being too expensive.

Instead of high-quality embroideries, many workshops started to produce more small items intended for sale to the growing number of tourists. One effect, however, was that authenticity and quality were often no longer important factors. The cross stitch, for example, was no longer embroidered as a full cross with arms of an even length but as a long stitch overcrossed with smaller stitches. This kind of embroidery is called *med*. It requires less time to embroider, and therefore the production is cheaper. In addition, the expensive DMC embroidery thread was replaced with cheaper, poorer-quality thread from Turkey and China. Yet even these products are not really capable of competing in international markets with even cheaper embroidery-producing countries and embroidery machines.

At the end of the twentieth century, the main markets for Palestinian embroidery were local tourism and in the Gulf states. This shift to production for the tourist industry was seen in Jordan, where many workshops in the early twenty-first century produce not only for the local tourist market but also for the rising tourist market in the Gulf states. The five-star hotels in the Gulf have ordered embroidered outfits for their staff and embroidered bathrobes and towels for their customers. In Syria and Lebanon, another tendency can be seen. Workshops such as ANAT in Syria and Inaash Al Muchaiam in Lebanon try to find new local and international markets by producing high-quality fashion and lifestyle items based on the traditions of the area.

Politics, however, has never been far away from the history and development of Palestinian embroidery. Embroidery and embroidery workshops in the last thirty years of the twentieth century were very much linked with the Palestinian resistance and the Palestinian liberation organizations. Because of the political and economic crises associated with these groups, there was a dramatic weakening in the solidarity of the richer consumers, especially those living abroad, with these causes, at the expense of the embroidery workshops and individual embroiderers. Another important development has been the rise of fundamentalist Islamic organizations and their *hijab* (Islamically correct clothing) dress codes, which discourage the wearing in public of revealing traditional clothing, especially clothing with colorful embroidered patterns. These dress codes further reduce the range of embroidered garments being bought and worn.

As a result of these and other factors, such as the global recession at the beginning of the twenty-first century, there has been a dramatic reduction in the market for Palestinian embroideries and a further weakening of the embroidery workshops that were already in crisis. It is not certain how many will survive and in what form.

Reference and Further Reading

Weir, Shelagh. *Palestinian Costume.* London: British Museum Publications, 1989.

Heike Weber

See also Palestinian Women's Dress; Palestinian Scarves and Flag Dresses; Palestinian Embroidery.

Jordanian Women's Dress

Jordan, officially the Hashemite Kingdom of Jordan, lies in the southern part of the Syrian Desert on the Gulf of Aqaba. It shares borders with Syria, Iraq, Israel, the West Bank, and Saudi Arabia. Much of the country is desert; however, in the northwest, there is a fertile agricultural region. Jordan has a long history that can be traced back to the Sumerian period in the second millennium B.C.E. and earlier. During its long and rich history, Jordan has been part of the Babylonian, Persian, Egyptian, Roman, and Byzantine empires. Islam was introduced into the region during the seventh century C.E., and, since then, Jordan has been regarded as a Muslim Arab culture; it has 5 percent Christians. During the nineteenth and early twentieth centuries, the region was called Transjordan. It used to be part of a vast cultural and geographic region called the Balad Al Sham (Greater Syria), which was divided after World War I (1914–1918) into the states of Palestine, Syria, Jordan, and Lebanon. The official establishment of the Kingdom of Jordan took place in 1921. The capital city of Jordan is Amman, which lies in the northwest of the country. The other main cities are Irbid, Salt, and Ma'an. As in many countries in the region, the population is generally divided into urban, village, and nomadic (Bedouin) groups. Jordan's long and complex history has had an influence on the varied styles and forms of women's dress.

WOMEN'S DRESS IN NORTHERN JORDAN

Northern Jordan is bordered by southern Syria and the area of northern Palestine known as Huran. The style of dress worn in northern Jordan can be found throughout the Huran Plain. This area includes the city of Irbid, which was built on the ruins of the ancient city of Arbila, one of the ten Roman cities of the Decapolis. Irbid's market caters to all in the area, including villagers and Bedouin. The market has long had close trade connections with Damascus in Syria, especially with respect to textiles and jewelry. As in other areas of Arab Southwest Asia, notably Palestine, the basic outfits for women in the northern Jordan area consisted of pants (*sirwal*), a chemise (*qamis*), a dress (*thob*), and headgear of some kind.

The thob was usually made of blue or black cotton. It was ankle length and very wide; the neckline was low, and the opening was often covered by part of the head covering. The sleeves were normally long and narrow. This form of dress was worn without a sash. Various types of thobs used to be worn in northern Jordan, but the basic cut and style of the dress were the same; it was called *shirs*. *Thob Seani* means "Chinese dress" and refers to the origin of the cotton fabric used for this type of dress. This type of thob was of sky blue cotton with a little *raqma* (wave stitch) embroidery around the hem and yoke. *Thob margum abayad* means a dress with white embroidery. This dress was worn around the Irbid area. All the embroidery is done in white thread using a fine raqma stitch. The *thob Ajloun* comes from the town of Ajloun south of Irbid. This dress is smaller in cut and is also called *thob marduf*. A connecting stitch in multicolored threads runs around the hem, yoke, and sleeves. In the latter half of the twentieth century, this stitch was replaced by cross stitch. The *thob makena* is decorated with machine embroidery. The *thob shakhat* is a black festive dress that was worn on special occasions. It was trimmed with long panels of sky blue cotton on the sides and at the top of the sleeves. It was decorated around the hem, neck, and sleeves with raqma embroidery.

During the cold winters, a dark blue or white woolen jacket (*taqsireh*) was worn over the thob; these jackets were made by tailors in Damascus and were purchased there or sent to the Irbid market. They were decorated with black couching cords.

Women from this region used to cover their heads with a cotton shawl (*milfah*) or a silk crepe shawl (*shambar*), which was kept in place by a square of cloth folded into a band called an *asbeh*. These headbands were made of silk and metal threads and were handwoven in Homs in early-twenty-first-century Syria. They were expensive, and only married women would wear the asbeh.

CENTRAL JORDAN

The region of central Jordan covers an area roughly from the north of the capital city of Amman to the city of Al-Kerak. The two main styles of dress come from the cities of Salt and Al-Kerak. The city of Salt, also known as As-Sult, is an ancient agricultural town and administrative center. It lies on the old main highway between Amman and Jerusalem and is an important market center for the region.

The area is known for an unusual garment called a *khalaqa* or *thob ibb* (literally, "pocket dress"). This dress could be up to twelve feet (three and a half meters) in length and had very long, wide, triangular-shaped sleeves. The dress requires up to sixteen yards (fourteen and a half meters) of fabric, and the dresses are always made from a heavy black cotton sateen called locally *dubeit*, which was imported from Syria and Egypt and later England. The dress is gathered up at the waist and kept in place with a handwoven belt, which is sometimes made of goat hair. The extra length is doubled over the belt to form a fold that reaches to the wearer's ankles. This fold is sometimes used as a pocket where a woman could carry items needed for the day or hide valuables such as jewelry or money. Indigo blue bands run along the hem of the dress, down the sides, and around the sleeves. These bands are believed to protect the wearer because the color blue is thought to ward off the evil eye. The yoke doubles as a necklace and is decorated with colored silk embroidery. In addition, a silver or gold coin is sewn into the center of the neckline for good luck.

The large sleeves were either fastened together at the back of the neck or placed on top of the head to make an elaborate

A woman wearing a festive black cotton dress (*thob*) worn in northern Jordan, ca. 1940. The embroidery uses a stem stitch called "daughter of the needle." Photograph by Myrtre Winters.

headdress. If placed on top of the head, the excess fabric of the dress sleeves was kept in place by wrapping a folded silk scarf (asbeh) over and around the sleeve in the manner of a headband. An asbeh of red with gold dots was used by young women, and older women had a black version. To make the headband more prominent and so show the wearer's material wealth, the silk scarf would be folded around a newspaper. These asbeh were hand-woven from silk and normally had a simple geometric design made from gold-plated metallic thread. The metallic thread was manufactured in Aleppo, Syria, and the asbeh was woven in Homs.

This type of dress was generally replaced by a single-length dress with the same type of embroidery and a blue band on the hem, but a few elderly women were still wearing the thob ibb on

a regular basis in the 1980s. Similar very long thobs were also worn by Bedouin women in Al-Kerak as well as in the Jericho region of Palestine and in the Jordan Valley, which is not surprising because there were close social and economic links between these regions.

Women in Salt also wore a reversible felt jacket that was blue on one side and red on the other. They were often decorated with stylized floral motifs using cords couched onto the cloth. This type of jacket was made in Damascus and sold at the Salt market. For jewelry and amulets, women wore an amber necklace or a silver fish on a chain.

Like the women of Salt, women in Al-Kerak wore a long dress that was made of cotton dubeit. However, the Al-Kerak dress style worn by both townswomen and the Bedouin was

A headdress with silver chains, worn by married women in northern Jordan, ca. 1920. Photograph by Myrtre Winters.

somewhat shorter than the Salt version. The fold of the Salt dress ended at the ankles, while the fold of the Al-Kerak dress ended at the knees, and the sleeves were shorter. The women covered their head with a head cloth called a *tarhah*, which was made of a loosely woven black gauze cotton fabric. Sometimes women would also tie a headband of black silk around the forehead to keep the tarhah in place.

SOUTHERN JORDAN

The region of southern Jordan covers a large area south of Salt down to the Gulf of Aqaba. The most distinctive dress comes from the city of Ma'an in southern Jordan. There has been a city here for at least two thousand years. For centuries, Ma'an has been an important resting and market point along the caravan and

pilgrim routes between Damascus and the holy cities of Mecca and Medina in early-twenty-first-century Saudi Arabia. During the Ottoman period, pilgrims assembled in large groups in Damascus, and huge caravans would move southward. The pilgrims usually brought with them goods to sell or barter along the way in order to pay their traveling expenses. Merchants used these pilgrim caravans as opportunities to sell their wares and to travel safely with a well-protected group. Various groups of pilgrims passed through Ma'an on their way to Mecca and would stop for several days; not surprisingly, markets sprang up where temporary camps were made. The pilgrims and merchants, as well as the local townspeople and Bedouin, would come to these markets to buy and sell a wide range of goods.

Not only did Ma'an become quite wealthy as a result of this local and international trade, but a wide range of textiles became available for local women to make their clothing from. Ma'an women's festive dresses reflect this wealth and diversity by being made of various types of silk textiles. Ma'an festive attire was a long dress with large, triangular-shaped sleeves; it was made of colorful striped silk and satin (*atlas*) textiles. The dress was gathered at the waist with a woolen sash. The headgear consisted of a small embroidered cap (*taqiyeh*) that was fixed in place with a headband. The headband was usually decorated with silver coins and glass beads. One of the sleeves of the dress was made so that the right side of the cloth was on the inside of the sleeve. The sleeve was then folded back and draped over the head so that it covered the cap and headband. Finally, a coat (*qumbaz*) was draped over the cap, headband, and sleeve. (The coat was worn over the head with the shoulders hanging down along the side of the head and upper body.) These coats were made of patterned silk, a silk-cotton blend, or ikat cloth (in which either the warp or weft threads are resist-dyed, in a process similar to tie-dye, before the threads are woven, thereby creating a pattern or design), which was bought in Syria and made in Aleppo.

JORDANIAN EMBROIDERY

A variety of embroidery stitches are used for the decoration of a wide range of dress and household items in Jordan. The most important stitches are raqma and cross stitch. Raqma is a style of embroidery from the Huran region. It involves using an irregular long and short stitch as a filling stitch to create a solid surface while leaving areas of the ground fabric unworked, thus creating negative geometric designs. A variation of the raqma

A husband and wife from Salt City, Jordan, ca. 1940. The woman is wearing a heavy, black cotton "pocket dress" (*khalaqa* or *thob ibb*). The edges and yoke are decorated with red silk embroidery, and she wears a gold coin sewn into the center of the neckline for good luck. Photograph by Myrtre Winters.

style is worked in white thread on a white or plain-colored ground.

In the past, raqma was used to create complex geometric designs, but, by the end of the twentieth century, these designs tended to be simpler or they were replaced with cross-stitch designs or machine embroidery. At the end of the twentieth century, raqma embroidery was being preserved with the help of nongovernmental organizations that used this unusual style of embroidery to embellish modern shawls, vests, jackets, dresses, and cushions to be sold in the cities and to tourists.

Another widespread form of embroidery is cross stitch, which can be found throughout the western part of Southwest Asia. In Jordan, cross-stitch designs tend to be more floral than geometric. Cross stitch is replacing the raqma stitches on Jordanian dress. Satin stitch is often used for making bands in blocks of colors or for copying the effect of raqma embroidery by working small waves or triangle designs on narrow bands that are set slightly apart from each other; the area between these bands creates another negative design.

BEDOUIN DRESS IN JORDAN

The term *Bedouin* comes from the Arabic word *badia*, which means "desert"; these people move around within a limited area to feed their goats and sheep. Each group has its own style of dress and customs, which strictly belong to one particular tribe. The Bedouin and seminomadic tribes in Jordan—such as the Beni Hasan, Beni Sakha, Adwan, Abbadi, and Bedul—have long had their own forms of dress, which are used to emphasize their identity.

The Adwan, for instance, are a large tribe that lives in the southern part of the Jordan Valley, and their range extends to the mountains of Salt. The Adwan women's dress (thob) is made of black silk, and, like all dresses from southern Jordan, it is about three yards (three meters) long; the extra length is folded over a woven belt to form a pouch. The dress has narrow, pointed sleeves. Running-stitch embroidery decorates the front of the dress in vertical lines and geometric patterns. After 1940, these patterns were replaced with flower patterns in cross-stitch embroidery. The woman covers her head with a tubelike head scarf called a *milfah*, over which is tied a silk headband (asbeh), which is worn only by married women. The women wear particular forms of jewelry: For example, a long silver necklace with coins called a *jinod* is worn sideways on the neck and passes diagonally across the chest and under the armpit; they also wear glass bracelets in many colors.

The Bedul tribes of Petra provide another example of Bedouin dress. The city of Petra is the famous rose-red city carved into the rocks. This region became the home of a Bedouin tribe called Bedul, who used to live in the ancient caves; in the twentieth century, however, many were moved to a nearby settlement. The dress of Bedul women is made of dubeit cotton or velvet cotton with small, short sleeves. The women wear brightly colored blouses with long sleeves under the dress; because the dress has short sleeves, the blouse sleeves are visible and are a major feature of Bedul dress. The dress is decorated with cross-stitch embroidery (*nakish*), which is worked around the yoke and around the hem. The women also wore silver jewelry and silver and glass beads; these items were from the Ma'an and Kerabe. Finally, the women covered their heads with a black milfah and a colored scarf folded into a band and fastened on top of the milfah.

In general, Bedouin dress in Jordan is much simpler and less expensive than village dress. The Bedouin wear a lot of silver jewelry, but the silver is of a lower quality than that worn by villagers. Bedouin women wear a wide range of beads, from ancient beads to the latest glass beads from Damascus, all mixed with cowry shells and animal teeth and bones.

In Jordan, Bedouin women always cover their heads but never their faces. Jordanian Bedouin women do not wear face veils as do the Bedouin women living in the Sinai. Some tribes such as the Hweitat and Rwala live in Jordan, Saudi Arabia, and Syria and have access to these countries' customs and products; as a result, the basic line of, for example, a Hweitat outfit worn in Saudi Arabia differs very little from a Jordanian Hweitat outfit.

References and Further Reading

Abu Jaber, Kamel. *Jordanians and the Jordanian People.* Amman, Jordan: Royal Scientific Society Press, 1980.

Baldensperger, Philip J. "The Immovable East: Clothes and Fashion." *Palestine Exploration Fund Quarterly* (1914–1915): 165–170.

Dalman, Gustaf. *Arbeit und Sitte in Palästina.* Vol. 5, *Webstoff, Spinnen, Weben, Kleidung.* Gütersloh, Germany: C. Bertelsmann, 1937.

Kawar, Widad. *Research and Collection: Cultural Treasures of Jordan.* Amman, Jordan: Turab, 2000.

Patai, Raphael. *The Hashemite Kingdom of Jordan.* Princeton, NJ: Princeton University Press, 1958.

Rajab, Jehan S. *Costumes from the Arab World.* Kuwait: Tareq Rajab Museum, 2002.

Topham, John. *Traditional Crafts of Saudi Arabia.* London: Stacy International, 1981.

Vögler, Gisela, Karin V. Welck, and Katharina Hackstein, eds. *Pracht und Geheimnis: Kleidung und Schmuck aus Palästina und Jordanien.* Cologne, Germany: Rauntenstrauch-Joest-Museum der Stadt Köln, 1987.

Weir, Shelagh. *Palestinian Costume.* London: British Museum Publications, 1989.

Widad Kawar and Sibba Einarsdóttir

See also Snapshot: Trade, Textiles, Dress, and the Hajj; Arab Men's Dress in the Eastern Mediterranean; Palestinian Women's Dress; Palestinian Embroidery; Syria.

Syria

- Men's Outfits
- Women's Outfits

The Syrian Arab Republic, or Syria, lies in Southwest Asia and borders Lebanon and the Mediterranean Sea to the west, Israel to the southwest, Jordan to the south, Iraq to the east, and Turkey to the north. Its position between the eastern Mediterranean, the Iranian Plateau, and Central Asia has meant that, for centuries, Syria has been an important political and trading region that has influenced, and been influenced by, many cultures in the region. The capital of the country is the historical city of Damascus. The Syrian cities of Aleppo, Damascus, Hama, and Homs used to be famous for their woven and printed cloth throughout the Arab world and the eastern Mediterranean. The name *Damascus* has come into European languages as *damask*, a form of weave and textile.

For centuries, the woven textiles from Syria have included simple forms as well as damasks, brocades, striped satins (*atlas*), and striped ikats. (Ikat is a style of weaving in which a resist-dyeing process similar to tie-dye is used on either the warp or the weft threads before they are woven, thus creating a pattern or design.) The printed textiles were created using a wide variety of techniques, including batik, lime resist-dyeing, stencil printing, *plangi* (a form of tie-dye), and block prints. In addition, felt and felted woolens (broadcloths) imported from Europe as well as Chinese and Indian cottons and silks were widely available. Many, but not all, of these textiles are rapidly vanishing due to the availability of cheaper Asian textiles.

In addition to these printed textile techniques, many regions have their own form of embroidery and appliqué work. In the west of the country, for example, the influences of other regions can be seen in Anatolian, Greek, Balkan, and European embroidery forms coexisting with Arab forms. All of this indicates the long-standing cosmopolitan nature of Syrian life. The embroidery techniques include a wide range of stitches, such as buttonhole stitch, chain stitch, couching, cross stitch, feather stitch, hem stitch, herringbone stitch, running stitch, and satin stitch. Other decorative techniques include appliqué using colored silks and the use of embroidery and appliqué together. The colors and designs chosen to decorate clothing vary from region to region, but geometric forms such as rhombuses, triangles, and circles are popular, as are stylized floral motifs—especially the tree of life.

Embroidery and related techniques are generally carried out almost entirely by women, and girls are taught to embroider at an early age. The embroidery is used within the family, and some extra work is done that is put out for sale in the local market (*suq*). In recent years, however, and especially since the Palestinian diaspora, more and more embroidery is being carried out in small ateliers for sale on the open market.

MEN'S OUTFITS

The basic traditional outfit for a village man consists of pants (*sirwal*); a long shirt (*thob*), which may be worn with or without a sash or belt; a jacket or coat (*qumbaz*, Bedouin *saye*); a cloak (*aba*, *bisht*); and a three-part headdress. The outfit of a Bedouin man is very similar to that of a villager. However, there are some significant differences. In general, Bedouin men do not wear pants under their garments because these are considered unhygienic. This dislike of pants can be found throughout the Arab world. Similarly, some Bedouin wear a loin belt against the skin. These are made of a narrow strip of plaited gazelle leather, which is wound around the body several times. Such belts are also worn by Bedouin living in the Arabian Peninsula.

Men's pants are usually made of white or monochrome cotton and are purchased from the local markets. The typical Syrian form is wide at the knees and very narrow around the calf. Over the pants, the thob is worn, which is a long white garment made of cotton or a similar material. Urban forms usually have straight sleeves, while festive versions have triangular wing sleeves (*irdan*). The festive versions are often decorated with red, blue, and black embroidery around the neck and on a chest panel. Sometimes, vests with decoration down the front are worn over the gowns.

The next garment, which is normally worn over the thob, is a kaftanlike garment that is sometimes called qumbaz (or, by the Bedouin, a saye), but the name may vary according to the material used to make it. The basic form of the qumbaz consists of a central panel with side panels for additional width. It has no collar, is open down the front, and is made of various lightweight fabrics with a contrasting cloth lining. The sleeves, neck opening, and front of the qumbaz are often decorated with cord couching, while more elaborate examples may be decorated with embroidery. These garments are normally purchased ready-made from various suqs. If the qumbaz is worn with a thob with triangular sleeves, then its sleeves are cut wider and shorter and have a split so that the thob's sleeves can be pulled through and seen.

Sometimes, men wear a jacket (*damer*) of dark cloth with sleeves made of a contrasting cloth. These are more popular with richer men and those who ride on horseback, when a saye would make riding difficult. The thob and coat are often held in place with a sash of handwoven wool (such as the *shamia*) or a leather belt (*mahsam*). The winter coat (*farwah*) is made of dark, mostly black, coarse cotton or cloth with a sheepskin lining. It is sometimes decorated with colored appliqué work or cord couching.

The most important garment for showing a man's position and wealth is his cloak (*aba*). These can be made of various materials, such as silk, cotton, wool, and so forth. The aba is normally made of two lengths of material sewn together. It is open down the front and has no collar. The neck and shoulder seams are normally decorated with either a narrow embroidered band or cord couching.

Various types of material are used to make an aba, depending on the time of year, the function, and whether the wearer is a Bedouin. One type of aba is made of wool with brown and white vertical stripes. Another form is called a bisht and is made of coarse, undyed sheep wool or goat or camel hair; it has white and brown or white and black vertical stripes. It is often decorated with wool embroidery around the neck and along the seams.

A man's headgear usually consists of a small cap (*taqiyeh*), over which is worn a head cloth (*hattah*). There are many different

A Bedouin man wearing a long shirt (*thob*) and a head cloth (*hattah*) held in place with a thick head rope (*'aqal*), Palmyra, Syria, 1934. According to some, messages such as interest, disregard, or even whether the wearer is looking for a bride are communicated by the way in which a Bedouin wears the head rope (for example, straight or pulled forward at an angle). Alfred Eisenstaedt/Time & Life Pictures/Getty Images.

styles of hattah; two popular types are a pure white version made of cotton and a silk form with small tassels along the edges. In the north of the country, around Palmyra, a yellow wool head cloth is preferred. Other areas have black head cloths with red, yellow, or pink stripes, and other areas feature red-and-blue-checked versions. The names of the head cloths vary depending on the material used to make them. The head cloths are normally kept in place with a head rope (*'aqal*), which varies in material, form, and size depending on who makes it and the wearer's personal preference. According to German anthropologist Maria Zerrnickel, the *'aqal* worn by a Bedouin man can convey a considerable amount of information: "A 'serious' man wears his headrope straight, a young man, however, who is looking for a bride, pulls it forward over his head. By wearing headdress and headrope in different ways unspoken messages—expressing love, interest, disregard etc.—are communicated."

WOMEN'S OUTFITS

The basic outfit for women consists of pants (sirwal) worn with a long dress (thob), over which is worn a coat and a head covering of some form. There is considerably more variation in the form of women's clothing than in men's clothing; there are differences among villagers and Bedouin, plus there are local variations.

The pants worn by village women tend to be very wide and are made from colorful materials. Like the men's pants, they are normally wide at the knee and very narrow around the calf. The lower edge of the pants around the cuffs is often decorated with embroidery or braids; the style and designs used to decorate the pants vary according to where the woman comes from.

Thobs are worn over the pants. There are two basic forms of women's thobs. The first form is the long, ankle-length version worn by villagers and Bedouin women. Those worn on a daily basis by village women tend to have straight sleeves, while those of the Bedouin have triangular-shaped sleeves. However, village festive and dancing dresses revert to the older forms and often have triangular-shaped sleeves.

The thob is usually decorated with embroidery around the neck, the chest, and the sides, with two vertical panels in the lower front of the skirt section. The cut of these garments and the type of decoration used vary according to when the garment is worn (daily or festive use), the social status of the wearer, and the origin of the coat. In the Maaret en-Numan, Chan Sheichun, and Saraqeb, for example, emphasis is placed on chests, shoulders, and side panels, but they differ in the choice of color and whether the back of the dress is embroidered. In the region around Hama, thobs are sometimes made of silk or cotton decorated with geometric designs created using a tie-dye (plangi) technique. These long dresses are usually held in place with a belt made from red and black wool or cotton, which is wound around the waist several times.

Near the Jordanian border some Bedouin women wear a type of thob that is related to the *khalaqa* or *thob ibb* ("pocket thob"), a garment worn by some Palestinian and Jordanian women. This particular type of thob may measure as much as twelve feet (three and a half meters) in length. The thob's excess material is folded and secured at the waist with a belt, making a deep pocket. Money, jewelry, or other small items are sometimes carried inside it.

Western influences on Syrian dress can be seen in a second style of thob, which is worn by village women in the extreme southwest of the country, notably in the Golan region. These thobs are made of an upper bodice section and a very full skirt. The thob is calf length and is worn with colorful pants and a short jacket made of cotton, wool, or velvet decorated with couching or appliqué.

Over the long thobs are worn coats, which can be made of a wide variety of materials but are usually of dark-colored material with a lining in a contrasting color. More expensive versions are made of silk satin (atlas) or ikat-dyed materials, while cheaper forms can be found in wool or cotton. These coats normally have wide sleeves and side slits to make walking easier and to show the thob underneath. The neckline and chest region of these coats are regarded as the main areas for decoration.

Like the dresses, the cut of these garments and the type of decoration used vary according to when the garment is worn, the wearer's social status, and where it comes from. In the area around es-Suchne, for example, coats are usually embroidered using complex geometric forms, while in and around Qalaat Samaan, appliqué can be found in combination with embroidery. Coats from Mhardah usually have embroidery on the right outer panel and on the inside of the left facing. In the area around

Kafr Tacharim, the coats are usually cut much wider than in other regions, and the decoration is concentrated on the upper opening and the facings rather than on the outside of the garment, so that when the woman walks there are flashes of color and decoration.

The traditional form of headdress worn by village and Bedouin women consists of a large head cloth (*shambar, margruna*) and a headband (*asbeh, mandil*) that keeps it in place. More and more urban women tend to wear a head scarf of some kind without the headband. Head cloths are usually made of a large square of silk or similar lightweight material, which is usually black when worn by Bedouin women and colored for village and urban women. Sometimes, the shambar is made from one large piece of cloth, or it may be made of two strips of woven cloth that are sewn together with decorative stitching. The ends of such scarves are often decorated with fringes, tassels, and simple embroidery. Another form is made of white silk and decorated with block-printed designs in contrasting colors, especially red and black. Veils of red silk (*shambar ahmar*) were owned by wealthier women and were often embroidered with spangles and glass beads and decorated with woven fringes and colorful silk tassels.

The headband consists of a smaller, thinner scarf that is folded into a triangle, rolled, and then tied around the head and knotted at the back, but there are other ways of tying the headband depending on the locale. The asbeh may be in black or in a contrasting color to the shambar.

Jewelry, as in all Arab lands, is an important part of a woman's outfit. As a generalization, village and Bedouin women tended to wear a wide range of silver items, while urban women wore gold. However, this situation changed dramatically in the latter half of the twentieth century as more and more village and nomadic women started to wear lighter-weight, and more valuable, gold forms.

Finally, Bedouin and village women who live near the Bedouin often have tattoos on their foreheads and chins. These tattoos are apotropaic and are related to specific tribes or families, and they indicate which group a woman belongs to.

Reference and Further Reading

Kalter, Johannes, Margareta Pavaloi, and Maria Zerrnickel. *The Arts and Crafts of Syria*. London: Thames & Hudson, 1992.

Tineke Rooijakkers and Gillian Vogelsang-Eastwood

See also Arab Men's Dress in the Eastern Mediterranean; Palestinian Women's Dress; Palestinian Embroidery; Bedouin Jewelry.

Lebanese Women's Dress

- Traditional Lebanese Dress
- Dress in Tripoli
- Beirut, 1860 to 1914

Lebanon is a small country situated on the eastern shores of the Mediterranean Sea with access to the countries bordering the Mediterranean basin as well as the Arab world. Prior to 1920, Lebanon had been under Ottoman rule and influence for four hundred years—a period in which cloth weaving and embroidery flourished. Following World War I (1914–1918), Lebanon became part of the French Mandate until its independence in 1943.

Important changes in the world were taking place around the end of the nineteenth century and at the turn of the twentieth century, including the weakening of the Ottoman Empire and the strengthening of the Industrial Revolution, which was gaining momentum in Europe. The court of the Ottoman Empire or *Sublime Porte* was going through a serious economic crisis and was financially in debt to the West. Meanwhile, Europe was looking for new markets and raw materials to expand and develop its national industries. As a result, it imposed itself economically in the region by offering products needed by the local markets and creating new demands.

During the medieval period (ca. 1200–1600 C.E.), urban dwellers generally lived in the Mediterranean coastal cities of Beirut, Tripoli, Sidon, and Tyre; villagers and peasants lived mainly in the Bekaa Plain or in isolated mountain villages; while Bedouin migrated with their herds from the Bekaa Plain to Syria, Palestine, and Jordan.

Throughout Ottoman rule, handicrafts flourished in the empire, but the decline of the empire, together with the introduction of European imports, brought about the decline of local craftsmanship. Under the Ottomans, each city engaged in distinct cloth-weaving and embroidery techniques. There were no frontiers within the empire, and commerce was very active. Most luxury goods required for dress were produced in specific centers: jewelry and weaving in Aleppo (Syria); silk in Homs (Syria); brocades and inlaid clogs or *qobqabs* in Damascus (Syria); woven silk for *abayehs* (cloaks) in Zouk (Lebanon); silver-thread embroidery or *tarq* in Baalbeck (Lebanon); and cotton weaving in Zahlé (Lebanon). Bursa and Istanbul imported raw silk from Mount Lebanon.

TRADITIONAL LEBANESE DRESS

The study of Lebanese dress is difficult because of various economic and political factors. During the late twentieth and early twenty-first centuries, for example, an interest in cultural heritage developed in the Arab world, and local and foreign social anthropologists started to research and write about the subject, and various ethnographic museums were founded. But Lebanon had other priorities. Between 1975 and 1990, the Lebanese civil war

led to population movements for reasons of security, and homes were destroyed, causing the disappearance of important family cultural heirlooms. In addition, a need for modernity caused some families to get rid of their old belongings, which they sold at flea markets. Above all, dress and related items were considered to be luxurious consumer goods and therefore an inappropriate subject during such difficult times. Nevertheless, a few small private collections survived, but Lebanon still does not have an ethnographic museum to house its heritage.

Nevertheless, some basic lines concerning women's dress can be highlighted. Geography, climate, politics, region, social class, and religious communities (Muslim, Christian, and Druze), for instance, influenced and were instrumental in the development of traditional dress. Additionally, traditional dress varied to a certain degree within the same community based on function, such as everyday wear, formal dress, dress to indicate single versus marital status, mourning-related apparel, and so on.

In general, traditional dress was slow to change, and aristocrats followed the fashion of Istanbul. But although notables, merchants, and landowners tried to emulate the upper classes, they generally used more modest material for their dress. Although the introduction of European fashion into the area was at first hesitant, it subsequently succeeded in penetrating the upper classes. As a result, surviving examples of traditional dress from the period are rare. Traditional women's dress from Beirut and Tripoli can be regarded as an example. Dress from these areas also illustrate the shift that took place during this period toward fashion from the West.

DRESS IN TRIPOLI

Tripoli was a conservative city in the late nineteenth and early twentieth centuries. The two main classes—landowners and merchants—and the conservative ulema (Islamic clergy) looked to Istanbul for guidance. Women, whose role was to remain at home, were kept busy sewing, embroidering, crocheting *oya* (head-scarf trimmings), and making lace. Materials were produced in the cities of the empire, and fashion remained constant for a long time. Penetration of Western influence was slow and reached the city via Istanbul rather than through direct contact with Europe.

Elements of traditional dress in Tripoli consisted of various undergarments: a *qamis tahtani* or *tafâri'*, which is a chemise with shoulder straps made of linen, cotton, satin, silk, or an unbleached cotton calico. It was generally white, or sometimes pastel in color, and could reach down to the hips or ankles. Another undergarment was the *sedrieh*, or, as it became known later, the brassiere or *gilet*; this was usually white and fastened with buttons. The ensemble was completed with the *libass* or *shintan*, which were either long or short underpants made of silk, satin, or cotton and often trimmed with lace and ruffles. These underpants were either white or in pastel colors. Over these were worn *sirwal* or pantaloons, which were made of fabric that was plain, striped, or with a floral motif and tied around the waist with a drawstring. These were an important element in the outfit of a woman from Tripoli until the end of the nineteenth century.

Over these garments were worn various layers that included the *qamis*, a chemise worn directly over the sirwal that was made

Women from Lebanon photographed by Sebah Pascal, from Osman Hamdi Bey and Marie de Launay, *Les costumes populaires de la Turquie en 1873* (Traditional dress from Turkey in 1873). From left to right: A Christian woman from Zahlah, Lebanon, wearing wide-striped pantaloons (*sirwal*) and a fezlike cap (*tarbush*); a Druze woman wearing a tall headdress (*tantur*); and a Christian woman of Zgharta wearing a low-cut chemise, a long coat that has been caught up in her belt in order to show her very wide undertrousers or pantaloons, and a short jacket. Religious communities, social classes, geography, and climate were all instrumental in the development of Lebanese traditional dress. Library of Congress Prints and Photographs Division, LC-USZC4-11720.

of silk, satin, or cotton, sometimes embroidered or trimmed with lace around the collar and hem. This garment was ultimately used as a dress and worn without sirwal.

A *tannurah*, or skirt, at first made from various fabrics and worn over the sirwal, was later inspired by European skirts and worn long or below the knee. The *tafâri'* (meaning "to spread out or be at ease") consisted of a nightgown and dressing gown, which was plain for young girls but sophisticated and embroidered when produced for a trousseau. The *qumbaz* was a full-length garment worn by the middle and lower classes, which was open at the front, fastened at the waist, and worn with a belt. The shorter versions were worn over pantaloons or sirwal. The *fustan* was a simple dress made from silks, woolens, and cottons with simple designs; it was at first worn over sirwal. With the introduction of European fashion, the fustan started to be produced using colorful, precious fabrics and became more prominent.

Various outer garments were worn, including a *salta*, a vest reaching down to the waist or hips and made of different colors.

It may be made of linen or velvet, trimmed with fur (mainly astrakhan) around the sleeves or embroidered with arabesque motifs of gold or silver thread. This was worn over a dress (fustan) or a qamis during winter. Sometimes, an *entari* was worn, which is a short vest that reaches to just below the waist.

Other outer garments included the *koubran*, a jacket of Balkan origins that is open at the front, has long sleeves, is tight fitting at the waist, and comes to the hips or slightly below. Finally, some women would also wear the abayeh, a full-length coat of similar cut to the man's *aba*; it was made of linen, velvet, or satin in red, black, blue, and green and was decorated with *sarma*. This is a type of satin-stitch embroidery using fine gold thread in which one side of the finished product is virtually indistinguishable from the other. Embroidered abayehs were an important part of a young girl's trousseau.

A woman's headdress consisted of a small cap (*taqiyeh*) that was made of either silk, satin, or cotton embroidered with colored, gold, or silver threads and was worn covered with a long muslin veil. Over this was worn a *tarbush* (sometimes called a fez), which was a tall, flower pot–shaped felted cap, usually in red. The tarbush was surmounted by a *qurs*, a silver or gold disk, and worn covered with a cashmere shawl or, more often, a *tarhah*, which was a long veil reaching to the ground that was made of muslin of different colors embroidered with silver and gold motifs. This garment was used as the bridal veil.

Women generally wore head scarves, or *mandil*, at home; these were decorated in various ways that determined their names. For example, a *mandil oya* or *bilbil* was a *malas* (silk) or *shash* (crepe) head scarf decorated with different-colored motifs and trimmed along its edges with oya or crocheted floral elements in the form of jasmine blossoms, cloves, pansies, and orange blossoms. The technique of oya was introduced from Istanbul, and women of the lower classes produced head scarves decorated with oya to supplement their income. The *mandil qasab* was yet another type of head scarf made of pure silk embroidered with silver thread;

it was worn mainly by rich young girls and was considered ostentatious.

The *sheshieh* or *qamtah* was a thirty-one-inch- (eighty-centimeter-) square scarf made of fine white linen that could be worn in different ways and on various occasions. Finally, the *ghata* was a rectangular head scarf that could be white or black and was worn during periods of mourning.

Footwear for women in Tripoli consisted of *shahhata* and *tassumeh*, which were indoor shoes or slippers. *Babouj* are shoes women wear at home. These are made of leather and sometimes covered with velvet or satin. They often have high heels. Another important form of footwear was the qobqabs, or wooden clogs, which were worn in the bathhouse as well as around the home in the often wet courtyards. Some were simple, and others were more elaborate, either inlaid with bone and mother-of-pearl or covered with a silver sheet worked in repoussé.

Three residents of Beirut, Lebanon, photographed by Sebah Pascal. From Osman Hamdi Bey and Marie de Launay, *Les costumes populaires de la Turquie en 1873* (Traditional dress from Turkey in 1873). A married Christian woman stands in winter clothing on the left, next to a Christian man in summer clothing. The married Muslim woman on the right wears an embroidered dress (*fustan*) with close-fitting sleeves that flare below the elbow. Library of Congress Prints and Photographs Division, LC-USZC4-11839.

BEIRUT, 1860 TO 1914

During the nineteenth century, Beirut replaced St. Jean d'Acre, Sidon, and Tripoli as commercially important cities, as it attracted more and more French and English traders. After 1830, the export of silk products to the French city of Lyon was facilitated by the availability of the Beirut port and steamers—an innovation of the Industrial Revolution that increased the speed of trade, especially the export of manufactured goods.

The population of Beirut grew rapidly, especially as many Christians fled from the mountains to Beirut after the 1860 internecine confessional conflict. The Christians soon became the majority of the city's population and the agents for European trade. They constituted an important upper bourgeoisie that identified with Western cultural values. In addition, Christian missionaries founded schools mainly attended by Christians.

The Lebanese scholar Nada Sehnaoui has noted that traditional architecture, which was formerly introvert or centered toward an internal courtyard, changed into the extrovert triple-arch house, open toward the street. At the same time, Christian women, who formerly covered themselves from top to toe in the streets, removed their veils and began to wear Western clothes. Sehnaoui noted that members of the Sunni Muslim community of Beirut, in contrast, were much slower to change their habits, and Anbara Salam, a woman of the Sunni upper bourgeoisie, removed the veil only after she obtained her father's approval.

The traditional dress for women in Beirut included sirwal, which were pleated satin pantaloons that were gathered at the waist with a red silk fabric and gathered above the ankles with a gold or silver anklet. Sirwal were striped or had floral motifs and were tied around the waist with a drawstring called a *tikke*. They were an important element in the outfit of a woman from Tripoli until the end of the nineteenth century. Over this was worn a qamis, a silk gauze chemise that covered the breast, on top of which was worn a bright-colored velvet vest lined with ermine or marten. The outer layer consisted of an embroidered dress (fustan) that was open in the front and gathered below the bosom, which was left uncovered; it had close-fitting sleeves that were flaring and open below the elbow.

The English traveler Lewis Farley, who spent two years in Beirut in the mid-nineteenth century, noted that

> over their wide trousers they wear a silk pelisse, coming down below the knee and just discovering the trousers and the ankles with their feet encased in slippers of yellow leather, pointed at the toes, opened in the back and worn only when they go out.

With the introduction of new French fashions at the end of the nineteenth century, the first items to disappear were the sirwal, the cap (tarbush), the short jacket (salta), and a type of dress (entari).

Within Lebanon the two cities of Beirut and Tripoli evolved toward modernity at different paces because of religious and political differences. The dress of women, based on the same conceptual elements, evolved faster in Beirut than in Tripoli due to trends set by mercantile Christian communities, which leaned toward the West.

References and Further Reading

Chehab, Maurice. *Le costume au Liban*. Beirut: Bulletin du Musée de Beyrouth 6 1942–1943.

Farley, Lewis. *Two Years in Syria*. London: Saunders and Otley, 1859.

Join, Jeanne. "Le costume feminin dans l'islam Syrio-palestinien." *Revue des études islamiques* 4 (1934).

Labaki, Boutros. *Introduction à l'histoire économique du Liban: Soie et commerce exterieur en fin période ottomane, 1850–1914*. Beirut: Librairie Orientale, 1984.

Maha, Kayal. "Le système socio-vestimentaires a Tripoli (Liban) entre 1885 et 1985." Thesis, Université de Neuchâtel, 1989.

Sehnaoui, Nada. *L'occidentalisation de la vie quotidienne à Beyrouth 1860–1914*. Beirut: Editions Dar el Nahar, 2002.

Nour Majdalany Hakim

See also Ottoman Dress; Arab Men's Dress in the Eastern Mediterranean.

Snapshot: Druze Dress

The Druze are a religious minority that live in the eastern Mediterranean region and Syria. They are officially classed as a Muslim group who are believed to have been an offshoot of the Ismaili sect of Islam. However, the Druze belief system also includes gnostic and other philosophical concepts. As a result, some mainstream Islamic scholars regard the Druze religion as non-Muslim. The group of religious initiates within the Druze community has a special form of dress.

The Druze call themselves Ahl al-Tawid, or "People of monotheism" or "unitarianism." This name dates back to 1017 C.E., when the Druze religion was revealed by God to Hamza ibn 'Ali ibn Ahmad, a Persian Ismaili scholar who had come to Egypt a few years before. He established the Unitarian Order, which had meetings in the Mosque of Raydan, in Cairo. Throughout their history, the Druze have stressed the principles of honesty, loyalty, filial piety, altruism, and monotheism. They reject polygamy, tobacco smoking, alcohol, pork, and, in the early twenty-first century, marriage to non-Druze.

Over the centuries, the sect developed and grew, with missionaries being sent out from Egypt throughout the eastern Mediterranean. However, the history of the Druze is turbulent, and there were frequent wars, battles, and massacres, which may account for the low-key nature of Druze dress. There are believed to be about one million Druze worldwide in the early twenty-first century. Most of them live in Syria, Lebanon, Israel,

and Jordan. In addition, there are groups in Western regions such as Australia, Canada, Europe, and North America.

The Druze community is split into two groups. The largely secular majority are the al-Juhhal, "the ignorant," which includes about 80 percent of the Druze population. This group is not given access to Druze holy literature and generally distances itself from religious matters. The religious group is called al-'Uqqal ("the knowledgeable initiates"). This group has a special form of dress that is designed to comply with Qur'anic traditions and to identify the wearer as being Druze.

The Druze dress worn in Palestine and Syria from the early nineteenth to the end of the twentieth century can be regarded as a representative example. Although there are variations, the basic form remains the same throughout Southwest Asia. One major difference is that uninitiated men and women are allowed to wear colors, while the initiated wear only black and white.

MEN'S DRESS

During much of the late nineteenth and early twentieth century, the basic outfit for a Druze man, both initiated and uninitiated, consisted of baggy pants (*shintiyan* or *sirwal*), which were wide at the knees and fit closely to the leg from the calf to the ankle; a short shirt (*qamis*); a waistcoat (*jubbe* or *sidriyeh* depending on the type); a sash (*shale* or *shamlah*); a kaftanlike overgarment

A group of Druze men, early twentieth century. They all wear baggy pants (*shintiyan* or *sirwal*), and some have a waistcoat (*jubbe* or *sidriyeh*) and skullcap (*taqiyeh*). Library of Congress Prints and Photographs Division, LC-DIG-matpc-06332.

209

(*qumbaz*); and a wide cloak (*abayeh*). According to dress scholar Shelagh Weir, in the area around Galilee, men tended to wear a short *bisht* (sleeveless outer garment; also known as an *aba*) made of fine brown or red wool, which sometimes had an intricate brocade pattern on the back.

Initiated men usually shaved their heads, and uninitiated men did not; however, it would have been difficult to see this detail because both groups wore headgear of some form. The basic headdress for a man was a skullcap (*taqiyeh*) with some form of head cloth or turban. Uninitiated men would wear

A Druze woman wearing a tall headdress known as a *tantur*, Lebanon, 1889. The *tantur* was a high metal tube, usually made of gold, silver, or silver-plated copper, with the more elaborate versions being encrusted with diamonds and pearls. It was worn with a silk scarf and held in place by ribbons threaded through pierced holes at the base of the tube and then tied under the chin. Library of Congress Prints and Photographs Division, LC-DIG-ppmsca-04420.

the more common head cloth, such as a cotton *keffiyeh* or a silk version (*hattah*), which was kept in place with a head rope ('*aqal*). In contrast, initiated men would wear a felt cap (*tarbush*) around which was worn a white turban (*laffeh*). There were special forms of turban for religious leaders. It was normal for men, especially initiates, to grow mustaches. The tips of the more elaborate mustaches (*shaureb*) were sometimes dipped in wax. For much of the twentieth century, footware for men consisted of red slippers (*surmaye*) similar to those worn by Western ballerinas.

By the end of the twentieth century, many uninitiated Druze men were wearing Western-style suits or a suit with a keffiyeh and 'aqal. In contrast, initiated Druze men were wearing many of the elements from the older style of dress—the baggy trousers, a white shirt, a waistcoat, and a headdress made of a rigid cap (tarbush) and turban. The wearing of mustaches remains a feature of Druze men's dress for both groups.

WOMEN'S DRESS

During the nineteenth and early twentieth centuries, the basic outfit for a Druze woman consisted of baggy pants (shintiyan); a long chemise (qamis); a skirt (tannurah); a kaftanlike garment (qumbaz); an overgarment (sabakane), which was kept in place with a sash (shale); an apron (mamluk); and a short, bolero-style jacket with wide, split sleeves (damer). The headdress was made of a cap (tarbush) and a *tantur* (a high metal tube), over which was draped a large white veil (*mandil* in Palestine or *futa* in Syria). The white color of a Druze woman's headdress likely had historical connections. Until 1711, there were two different Druze parties: the Qays and the Yemani, or the (Arab) north and the south. The Qays were associated with red and the Yemanis with white. The flags of the two groups were in these colors, as were the veils worn by the women. According to anthropologist Margareta Pavaloi, when a Qays bride entered Yemani territory, it was necessary for her to wear a white veil. After 1711, this difference somehow lost its significance, but Druze women continued to wear white veils.

A feature of nineteenth-century Druze dress was the tantur, which was made of gold, silver, or silver-plated copper, depending on the wealth of the family. Very elaborate versions were said to be made of gold and encrusted with diamonds and pearls. The tanturs were held in place by piercing the base to make holes through which ribbons were threaded; the ribbons were tied under the chin or at the back of the head. Often, a silk scarf was wound around the base of the tantur. In the early nineteenth century, the tantur was worn by both Druze and Christian Maronite women in Lebanon. However, after the wars between the Druze and Maronites in 1841 and 1845, Maronite priests prohibited women from wearing the tantur.

Among the Druze, from the mid-nineteenth century on, both a tarbush and a tantur were given by a groom to his new bride as a sign of her married status. It appears, however, that initiated women wore only the tarbush, while uninitiated women could wear both the tarbush and the tantur, one on top of the other. According to Pavaloi, there were different ways of

wearing both forms of headgear that indicated which family the wearer belonged to. By the 1870s, the wearing of tanturs had become rare throughout the Druze community, as more and more women adopted the more convenient tarbush.

Throughout the twentieth century, the headdress of a married woman consisted of a red tarbush that was often trimmed with coins or fine metal-thread embroidery, over which was draped a head cloth (futa). In some areas, a black headband (asbeh) was worn, but at some point after the 1930s, this headband was banned by the Druze religious leaders in order to distinguish Druze from Muslim and Christian women.

Throughout much of the twentieth century, there were some changes in the dress of initiated women but no dramatic ones. In the early twenty-first century, women continue to wear long shirts (qamis) with a fitted bodice to which is fastened a full skirt. The skirt can be made of up to ten yards (nine meters) of cloth and is long enough to reach the ankles. A feature of the bodice is its deep décolletage; Pavaloi has suggested that these may have developed from the Ottoman *antari* (a woman's robe or dress), which is similarly shaped at the front. Over the skirts were worn aprons. A velvet coat is worn that is called a *thob mechmal*, which refers to the type of material used to make it. Uninitiated women wear these garments in various colors, while initiated women wear black attire. Footwear often consists of red slippers (*kundara* or *surmaye*). It was also normal for uninitiated women to plait their hair into long braids that were lengthened by adding colored cords and tassels. The ensemble was finished with earrings, bracelets, and a belt of gold or silver.

Throughout the twentieth century, the headdress remained a decorative tarbush, which was totally covered by a large white veil. The tarbush used to be of felt. However, modern versions are often in the form of a little cap made of felt or straw, which is decorated with a silver plate called a *qurs* and a line of silver or gold coins along the lower edge. Initiated women also use the mandil as a form of face veil by wrapping it around the lower part of the face to cover the mouth and part of the nose when in the presence of strangers, especially men. At the end of the twentieth century in Syria, the futa worn in warm summer months was made of cotton, and in the winter it was replaced by a large square cloth (*sharshif*) made of wool that has been crocheted.

REFERENCES AND FURTHER READING

Pavaloi, Margareta. "Wearing Clothes." In *The Arts and Crafts of Syria*, edited by Johannes Kalter, Margareta Pavaloi, and Maria Zerrnickel, 161–172. London: Thames & Hudson, 1992.

Weir, Shelagh. *Palestinian Costume*. London: British Museum Publications, 1989.

Heike Weber and Gillian Vogelsang-Eastwood

See also Ottoman Dress; Syria.

PART 4

Arabian Desert and Peninsula

Introduction to the History of Dress in the Arabian Desert and Peninsula

- Pre-Islamic History
- Islam
- The Ottomans and the Rise of the House of Saud

The Arabian Peninsula is a region shaped by its climate. This separate subcontinent contains a central plateau (the Nejd), occasionally marshy coastal plains along the Persian Gulf, and mountain ranges along the Red Sea coast. However, it is mostly known for its great deserts: the Nafud, the Dhana, and the Rub' al-Khali. Very little surface water is available, but scattered across the continent are a number of oases fed by wadis (rivers that dry up seasonally) or wells. In total, less than 1 percent of the entire surface is naturally suitable for agriculture.

These factors have shaped the Arabs' way of life. Some towns and cities are located near sources of water, but before the 1960s, a very large part of the population was nomadic. These Bedouin lived in tents and relied on their livestock (camels or sheep) for their livelihood, moving constantly in search of new pastures. Animal products were traded for craft goods (for example, textiles, jewelry, kohl, and fragrances) and foodstuffs (dates, rice, grain, coffee, and tea) with the settled population. In the early twenty-first century, most of the population is settled, made possible through agricultural programs relying on deep underground aquifers. However, the Bedouin way of life still influences aspects of modern society; many of the units of the national guard of Saudi Arabia are, for example, organized along tribal lines. The values of the Bedouin are held in high esteem, and they are often considered the "pure" Arabs, free of foreign influences.

Arabian dress is adapted to the rigors of the desert. Temperatures during the summer can reach 122 degrees Fahrenheit (50 degrees Celsius) but drop considerably during the night. Loose, layered garments are therefore the norm, improving insulation and allowing cool air to circulate. However, the peculiarities of the peninsula have influenced dress in other ways. Geographically, it is bounded by natural frontiers, and, despite the trade routes passing through, it has remained relatively isolated. No foreign power has ever been successful in controlling the harsh inlands of Arabia and its nomadic tribes. However, the towns have been influenced by the influx of traders, occupiers, and pilgrims alike. There is, therefore, a considerable difference between the dress of the village and city population and that of the Bedouin, determined not only by differences in lifestyle but also by a different historical background.

PRE-ISLAMIC HISTORY

Very little is known about the prehistory of the Arabian Peninsula. Stone tools have been found dating to the sixth millennium B.C.E. Ubaid pottery, a particular style also found in Mesopotamia, has been uncovered in a number of archaeological sites along the eastern coast of Arabia, dating to about 5000 B.C.E. It seems that there was already some type of exchange network along the Persian Gulf in this period. The people occupying this area from about 4000 to 2000 B.C.E. are also referred to as the Dilmun culture.

In the third millennium B.C.E., a lively trade with Egypt and Mesopotamia existed. Goods such as frankincense and myrrh were exported in exchange for, among other things, textiles. A number of independent kingdoms ruled in the south. They controlled the trading network and exported not only their own goods but also products from India and Africa, which were shipped to the south and transported further with camel caravans. Caravan cities, such as Mecca, Yathrib (Medina), Jidda, and Madain Salah, blossomed. However, in the third century C.E., this monopoly on trade routes and the trade network weakened due to the Ptolemies' restoration of a Persian canal between the Nile River and the Red Sea. Trade along this route is also described in the *Periplus of the Erythrean Sea* (a Greek navigational manuscript).

The Arabian Peninsula had always been dominated by several kingdoms composed of groups of tribes. From the fifth century C.E. on, the north was dominated by the Ghassanids, who were under the influence of the Byzantines; the Lakhmids in the northeast fell under the protection of the Sassanians; and the southern Himyarites were controlled by the Christian Abyssinians and later the Persians. Meanwhile, the Kinda tribe made their first attempt to unite the peninsula but were suppressed by the northern Arabian kingdoms. All of these cultures influenced pre-Islamic Arabian dress. Also, despite the decline, trade in the caravan cities continued, bringing Far Eastern and African influences to the region. The fashions of the coastal areas tended to reflect the influence spheres of the surrounding empires. Into the early twenty-first century, the traditional garb of the various regions shows differences that can be related to, for example, Indian, Persian, or Turkish tastes.

ISLAM

The birth of Islam is perhaps the most significant event in the formation of Arabian culture. In the seventh century C.E., Mohammed started preaching, and the newly founded religion soon found acceptance throughout Arabia. Upon his death in 632, his successors, the caliphs, took it upon them to spread the state of Islam and therefore its dress codes throughout Arabia, Southwest Asia, other parts of Asia, northern Africa, and beyond.

Arabian dress at the time generally consisted of some type of undergarment, such as a loincloth (*izar*) or underpants (*sirwal*); a body shirt (*qamis*); some type of tunic, dress, gown, or coat (*thob*, *jibbeh*, *hulla*, and so on); a mantle, coat, or wrap when going out in public (*izar*, *rida*, *shamla*, *mirt*); some type of head covering (*imamah*, burnoose, or *qalansuwa*), often combined with a face veil for women; and shoes (*khuff*) or sandals (*ni'al*). These different parts could be worn layered, although the poor usually wore fewer items than the wealthy. Within Arabia, there were certain distinct regional differences in implementation, but these were the basic elements. This combination of garments is also visible in the regions around the Arabian Peninsula and had developed from earlier clothing traditions. For example, wearing a mantle outside of the house was a Mesopotamian, Greek, and Roman practice.

The Islamic vestimentary system is based on these existing dress traditions. Most importantly, the hadiths (traditions of Mohammed) preached modesty in dress. This involved not only covering up the area between the waist and the knees but also restraint in the use of extravagant garments or materials. In addition, for men, a number of more particular regulations and recommendations included an objection to saffron-dyed garments, silk garments, jewelry, and textiles with figurative patterns. However, these regulations were not always as strictly adhered to by the Islamic ruling dynasties succeeding the caliphs. The Umayyads and Abbasids, who placed their capitals in Southwest Asia, were strongly influenced by local fashions and the court system of the Byzantines, which is centered on hierarchy and ceremony expressed through ostentatious dress.

Even though the ruling center had been moved to Southwest Asia, Saudi Arabia with Mecca and Medina remained the religious center of the Islamic world. One of the five pillars of Islam is the hajj, the pilgrimage to Mecca. During the hajj, pilgrims are required to be in a state of *ihram*, or ritual purity. Men can wear only two pieces of untailored (white) cloth (the izar and the rida). Women are allowed to continue to wear their normal, modest dress (*hijab*) as long as they do not cover their face or hands. These restrictions are meant to emphasize the fact that everybody is equal in the eyes of Allah. The hajj caused the annual incursion of thousands of pilgrims from all corners of the Islamic world to Mecca, bringing along foreign fashions. Mecca and Medina had always been among the major caravan cities, but now they also became arenas for cultural exchange and true cosmopolitan centers.

THE OTTOMANS AND THE RISE OF THE HOUSE OF SAUD

From the end of the ninth century C.E. on, with the weakening of the Abbasid dynasty, Arabian dissidence was growing stronger. A rebellion failed and a *sherif*, governor, was installed in Mecca to control the region. In the thirteenth century C.E., the Mongols invaded Southwest Asia, crushing the Abbasid dynasty. The Meccan sherifate was little affected, being almost autonomous. In the fifteenth century C.E., the Ottomans started to expand their empire into Southwest Asia. After they conquered Egypt, they claimed the west of Arabia and installed a grand mufti in Mecca in 1539. This originally Turkish dynasty introduced new fashions based on their Central Asian origins. These included an emphasis on voluminous sleeves and pants, layering of garments, and coats. Turkish influences are still visible, for example, in the use of heavy gold embroidery in the traditional dress of the Hijazi people. Meanwhile, the eastern coast and its trade routes came under the control of the Persians. Portugal also began to compete for the Red Sea trade and gained control over Hormuz and the Omani coastline. It was, however, ousted again in the 1650s.

In the eighteenth century, the Saud clan expanded its territory throughout the interior of Arabia, including Mecca and Medina.

The Ottomans decided to intervene and had their Egyptian viceroy push back the Sauds. The Egyptians occupied the region until the Ottomans took over again. Meanwhile, Saud territory was growing once more, but they were defeated again, this time by the rival Rashid family. They were sent to exile in Kuwait, but in 1902, Abd al-Aziz, or Ibn Saud, recaptured Riyadh and eventually the Nejd (a region that is part of Saudi Arabia in the twenty-first century). After World War I, the Ottoman Empire ended, and in 1926, Ibn Saud claimed the Hijaz (a coastal region on the Red Sea, in western Saudi Arabia). In 1932, the Kingdom of Saudi Arabia was proclaimed, uniting the Hijaz and the Nejd. Up to the early twenty-first century, this kingdom occupies more than 80 percent of the Arabian Peninsula. The British initially held on to its protectorate in Kuwait, Bahrain, Qatar, and the United Arab Emirates along the eastern coast of the peninsula (and the colony of Aden in Yemen), but by 1971, these had all become independent emirates. Other areas of the Arabian Peninsula (such as Oman and Yemen) also became independent nations.

Up until this point, the Arabian Peninsula was dependent on the export of goods such as frankincense, myrrh, and Arabian horses but mostly on the trade of foreign products. Over the centuries, however, its monopoly on trade had declined as new routes to the Far East and Africa had been discovered. However, circumstances turned for the better when oil was discovered in the 1930s; this new source of wealth gave Arabia a solid economic base in the modern world.

Like most countries, Arabia has been caught up in the trends of Westernization and globalization. The mass production of garments, the introduction of synthetic fibers, and Western media all have influenced Arabian dress. However, for a number of reasons, the countries of the Arabian Peninsula seem to have been affected less than other regions. The major trendsetter of this area, Saudi Arabia, was never occupied by a European colonizer. Also, the wealth that accumulated in this area precluded any urgency in copying the prosperous West. This does not mean that the area was not affected—indeed, many Saudi women wear Parisian labels underneath their *abayeh* (wide coat)—but it seems to have opted for neotraditionalist fashions.

Although there are regional differences, the typical Arabian man's outfit in the late twentieth and early twenty-first century has consisted of a light-colored long shirt (thob); some kind of jacket, vest, or mantle (such as a *bisht, mishla,* or *jubba*); a head covering consisting of a skullcap (*taqiyeh* or *kuffiya*), a head cloth (*ghutra, shaal,* or *ihram*), and an *'aqal* (head circlet); and often a belt and some kind of (decorative) weapon as well. For women, an outfit usually consists of underpants (sirwal), some type of dress (thob, *fustan, dura'ah,* or *dishdasha*), an overgarment (usually an abayeh), and a head veil (*tarhah, shaylah,* or *mahanna*), sometimes combined with a face veil such as a burqa or *niqab*. The outer garments for women are usually black, often leading to the assumption that Arabic women wear only this color. However, in contrast to the men, who tend to wear undecorated clothing, women's dresses often show a love for bright colors and decoration.

Saudi Arabia has been one of the major influences in the creation of pan-Islamic dress, also called *al-zayy al-Islami*. This is a global fashion that became popular at the end of the twentieth and beginning of the twenty-first century with the rise of nationalist and Islamist movements in Islamic countries. For men, it consists of a loose white shirt (qamis), baggy pants (sirwal), a skullcap (taqiyeh), and sandals, usually combined with a beard. For women, it is less uniform but is characterized by an emphasis on hijab. It always consists of some type of head veil, often combined with a wide dress or abayeh and some type of face veil. Various degrees of covering up can be noted. The face veil is usually worn to indicate Islamic identity, piety, or a particular political viewpoint. However, the head veil is often also donned for other considerations, such as fashion.

References and Further Reading

Colyer Ross, Heather. *The Art of Arabian Costume: A Saudi Arabian Profile*. Clarens, Switzerland: Arabesque Commercial, 1994.

Fiske, Patricia. *Palms and Pomegranates: Traditional Dress of Saudi Arabia*. Washington, DC: U.S. Committee for Saudi Arabian Cultural Heritage, 1987.

Snouck Hurgronje, Christiaan. *Mekka in the Latter Part of the Nineteenth Century: Daily Life, Customs and Learning: The Moslims of the East-Indian-Archipelago*. Leiden: Brill, 2007. (Originally published in 1889.)

Stillman, Yedida Kalfon. *Arab Dress: A Short History from the Dawn of Islam to Modern Times*. Leiden: Brill, 2000.

Topham, John M., Anthony L. Landreau, and William E. Mulligan. *Traditional Crafts of Saudi Arabia*. London: Stacey International, 1981.

Tineke Rooijakkers

See also Pre-Islamic Dress Codes in the Eastern Mediterranean and Southwest Asia; The Coming of Islam and Its Influence on Dress; Snapshot: Trade, Textiles, Dress, and the Hajj; Historical Survey of Textiles and Dress in Turkey; Saudi Arabian Dress; Iranian Regional Dress; Snapshot: Islamic Pilgrimage Dress (Ihram); Sumptuary Laws.

Bedouin Jewelry

For thousands of years, jewelry has been an essential part of dress throughout the Arab world. No matter what their age, occupation, or status, people have worn jewelry of some kind. Jewelry, however, should not be seen only as a means of personal adornment. It has other essential functions within Arab life as well. It is, for instance, important for showing gender and social and economic status; in particular, jewelry is seen as a means of giving a woman financial security for the future. These elements are all reflected in the range and quality of the jewelry worn, especially by women.

Although the clothing for men and women in Arabia has many elements in common, their respective jewelry does not. Various Qur'anic verses and hadiths (traditions concerning the actions and sayings of the Prophet Mohammed) recommend modesty and austerity in this earthly life. Gold and silver jewelry is mentioned in the Qur'an, for example, in the various descriptions of what people (especially men) will wear in paradise: "Therein they shall be adorned with bracelets of gold and pearls, and their apparel there shall be of silk" (Sura 22:23) and "upon them shall be green garments of silk and brocade; they are adorned with bracelets of silver" (Sura 76:21).

The Prophet Mohammed, however, forbade seven things as inappropriate for men: silver vessels; gold rings (except signet or hajj rings); and garments of silk (*harir*), brocade (*dibaj*), a striped Egyptian fabric containing silk called *qassi*, satin (*istabraq*), and tanned hides (*mayathir humr*). As a result, Arab men have long tended to wear ornate weapons, such as daggers, belts, and swords (these are not regarded as mere decoration), while women have no constraints on wearing ornate personal jewelry.

Women's jewelry is also regarded as having a sensual quality. Traditional jewelry decorated with coins, chains, and bells makes light, tinkling sounds when a woman walks. This auditory quality of jewelry is reflected in the Qur'anic injunction concerning how a woman should dress: "Nor let them stamp their feet, so that their hidden ornaments may be known" (Sura 24:32). Jewelry such as amulets and talismans also has other functions, helping to ensure a healthy, productive, and happy life.

A distinction used to be made between urban jewelry and that worn by village and nomadic women. In general, urban women displayed jewelry of gold and precious stones, while village and nomadic women wore silver, brass, or copper forms. In the twenty-first century, however, more and more village and nomadic women are buying gold jewelry as well. Generally, most of a nomadic and village woman's jewelry is given as part of her dowry and marriage settlement. In addition, urban women often receive other pieces during the course of their marriage—notably at the birth of a child (especially a son) and on festival days such as Id al-Fitr and Id al-Adha.

The giving of a dowry (*mahr*) to a girl at the time of her engagement is an ancient tradition throughout the Arab world. At this moment, she becomes a woman entitled to own and wear a wide range of jewelry. An Arab wedding ceremony is normally divided into two parts: first, and most important, the signing of the engagement contract (*milka, milak*) and, second, the actual wedding celebrations where family and friends come together. The engagement contract is drawn up by the fathers of the intended bride and groom. On the contract paper (*waraqa*) are the names of the intended couple, the date, and the amount of the mahr. The contract is signed before a religious leader (imam) and two male witnesses.

Bedouin silver forehead band, Saudi Arabia, probably made in Yemen, 1960s. The band fits across the forehead under a head veil of some kind and is worn by women on special days such as weddings and Eid. Textile Research Centre, Leiden.

The mahr is divided into the *muqaddam*, paid to the bride at the time of the engagement, and the *muakhkhar*, an amount promised to the wife in case of divorce (initiated by the husband) or the death of her husband. The amount of mahr, regarded as a pledge of good faith, varies from community to community. Sometimes a small ring is offered as an engagement ring, in keeping with the injunction that a groom should offer a ring to his bride as a minimum fulfillment of the dowry. Normally, the bride's father spends a percentage of the muqaddam on his daughter's jewelry. In addition, fathers may also add various items of jewelry to the amount bought with the mahr. The mahr jewelry may be specially ordered from the local silversmith or an itinerant silversmith, or, as is happening more frequently, gold jewelry is bought at the *suq* (market) in one of the larger cities.

The jewelry proclaims a girl's new status as a married woman (*hurma*) and a woman of property. However, an important aspect of the contract indicates that it belongs to the woman and can be disposed of only by her, in case of a prolonged period of financial insecurity. Thus, mahr jewelry becomes a portable and highly visible means of showing a woman's personal and family status, demonstrating her family's position in the local community, and providing security for her future.

AMULETIC AND TALISMANIC PROPERTIES

Besides decoration and status, jewelry also has other, more intangible, functions. The forms and colors used are often believed to have amuletic properties essential for warding off the evil eye and talismanic functions for bringing good luck. Throughout the Islamic world, one of the most widespread amulets is the sign of the hand, the *khamsa* or hand of Fatima (named after the daughter of the Prophet Mohammed). In particular, the number five is considered a charm against the evil eye, because the five fingers represent the five tenets of Islam, the deeds that a Muslim should perform during his or her life.

Green, blue, and red are generally regarded as protective colors, with the result that popular stones include turquoise, agate, coral, and glass of those colors. Yellow and brown are also considered protective, which accounts for the popularity of amber throughout the Arab world along with cloves—brown and pungent—which are often worn by village and Bedouin brides. The nineteenth-century explorer Charles Doughty noted that Bedouin women sometimes inserted cloves into their nostrils instead of nose rings for the same purpose.

MATERIALS AND TECHNIQUES

In the twenty-first century, Arab jewelry can be generally divided into urban and rural/Bedouin styles. Until the mid- to late twentieth century, urban women wore mostly gold and precious stones, while village and Bedouin women tended to wear silver or gilded brass with a wide variety of beads. Within Bedouin society, for instance, a long-held custom following a woman's death involved her jewelry being sold or melted down and remade into new jewelry for her daughters or daughters-in-law. Sometimes various items of jewelry are separated into parts and are rethreaded to make new pieces, with the result that very little old silver jewelry survives in its original form.

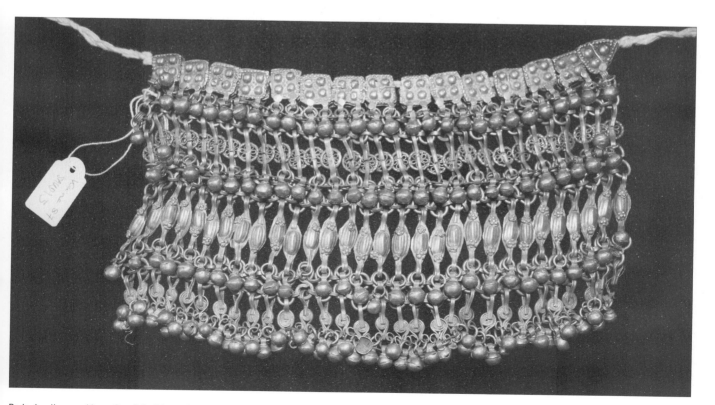

Bedouin silver necklace, Saudi Arabia, probably made in Yemen, 1960s. This type of necklace usually has seven rows of silver ornaments and sometimes a cloth backing so that they are more prominent. Textile Research Centre, Leiden.

This practice of melting down silver jewelry has also had an effect on the quality of the silver used. Standard silver has 925 parts of pure silver to 75 parts of alloyed base. For Bedouin jewelry, this ratio varies, however, because melted-down Bedouin silver also has a base metal (copper, tin, or zinc) added to strengthen the silver. Thus, Bedouin silver is made of an alloy containing varying amounts of silver. Much silver jewelry worn in the Arab lands used to be made in Syria, Egypt, and the Arabian Peninsula. Until 1948, the Jewish silversmiths of Yemen crafted vast quantities. After Jewish mass emigration, silversmiths in other regions have become more important, notably those in Oman.

In contrast to the Bedouin and village women, urban Arab women have long worn gold jewelry. Much of it was made by local craftsmen or came from one of the large cities—in particular, Damascus, Aleppo, and Cairo with the cities of Jidda, Mecca, and Medina also important centers. The pilgrimage trade accounted for a vast and constant demand by pilgrims wanting to take suitable mementos to their families. Recent trends indicate that women are moving toward wearing mass-produced, lightweight jewelry (instead of hand-wrought, heavier, solid forms). Much of it comes from India, Pakistan, and Italy, especially made for the Arab market.

Traditionally, small chests stored a woman's jewelry along with her collection of kohl, henna, and perfumes. These chests were usually compartmented, and the exterior was decorated with simple patterns made by scorching the wood or with brass inlays.

Many variations in terms and meanings exist throughout the Arab world in regard to jewelry, but some are in general use in the Arabian Peninsula (especially in Yemen and Saudi Arabia). A wide variety of materials, forms, and techniques are used to craft Arab silver jewelry, including numerous types of beads, ranging from small, handmade metal beads to giant amber beads. Glass beads also form an important element in the decoration of clothing and jewelry. Another essential element, especially of children's jewelry, consists of small bells whose noise is said to distract jinns or evil spirits.

One common form of silver jewelry, especially for necklaces, is based on the use of a chain (*silsila*). Bedouin chain jewelry varies in design and ranges from simple wire links to intricate combinations of links, stones, filigree, and granulation work. Heavy Bedouin bracelets are often made using wrought metal (*madam mutarraz*), whereby the metal is twisted or bent into shape. Sometimes, a wire (*silk*) is wrapped around the twisted elements to create a more decorative effect.

A more complicated form of decoration, repoussé (*buruz*) involves producing relief decoration on a metal plate by punching and hammering the thin metal from the reverse to raise the design on the front. Decorative punches can be used with this technique to achieve a repeated pattern. The metal plate is sometimes turned over so that some embossing (*zakhrafa*), which is carried out with a die, can be worked on the front to enhance the desired relief design. Another method of decorating the metal is engraving (*hafr*), whereby a sharp, pointed tool called a graver cuts into the surface of the metal, producing clean and fine lines and patterns. In contrast, chasing (*naqsh*) is the technique of decorating the front surface of metal by indenting it and so raising the design by using a chasing tool and a hammer without cutting into the metal (as in engraving). Chasing is sometime done to enhance repoussé work by sharpening the relief decoration. When carried out on a flat surface, as opposed to relief work, it is called flat chasing, a technique often used in conjunction with engraving to achieve delicate floral motifs and geometric designs.

Filigree (*mushabbak*) consists of soldering fine wires (plain, twisted, or plaited) onto a metal surface to create intricate lacelike patterns. One of the most skilled forms of decoration used for silver jewelry is granulation (*habbiyat*). This technique involves dropping molten silver into cold water. The metal then forms into droplike granules (tiny metal balls). These are applied to the metal surface to produce a raised, three-dimensional decorative effect.

A wide range of applied objects are used to decorate Arab silver jewelry, such as precious and semiprecious stones (diamonds, emeralds, rubies, agates, carnelians, garnets, and turquoise). Traditional Bedouin jewelers do not facet stones the way Western jewelers do but rather shape them in one of two common forms: The stones are roughly cut and faceted into the desired shape and polished, or they are shaped into a cabochon with a smooth, rounded surface with no facets and polished. Colored glass often imitates these stones, because it is the color rather than the type of stone that carries the amuletic properties. In addition, pearls, amber, coral, and faience are also used. Other decorative elements for all types of jewelry include beads (*kharaz*) for pendants, cylinder amulets (*hirz*), disk amulets (*maskah*, *samakah*), bells (*zarir*), and coins (*umla*)—especially Arab, Ottoman, French, and British coins and, most notably, the Maria Theresa dollar, a coin that is one of the most important elements all over the Arab world. First minted in 1741, it has become an essential part of silver jewelry not only as decoration but also as a source of silver. Still being produced in Vienna by the Austrian mint, many of the coins are specifically destined for Southwest Asian markets.

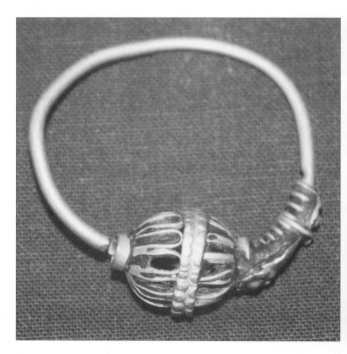

Bedouin silver nose ring, Saudi Arabia, probably made in Yemen, 1970s. Known as a *zimam*, this nose ring would be worn through the left nostril with the pendant section facing downward. Textile Research Centre, Leiden.

The coin is named after the Empress Maria Theresa, who ruled Austria, Hungary, and Bohemia from 1740. The coin has a portrait of the empress on the obverse and the Hapsburg double-headed eagle on the reverse. Within the Arab community, the coin has various names such as the *abu nuqta*, or "the one with the dots," which refers to the pearls on the empress's dress; *abu tayr*, or "the one with the birds," is a reference to the eagle on the reverse side of the coin; and *abu reesh*, or "the one with the feathers," is another reference to the eagle. Since her death in 1780, all Maria Theresa dollars have that date regardless of when they were minted. It is estimated that between 1751 and the early twenty-first century, some 390 million Maria Theresa dollars have been produced. Not only are they popular as a source of decoration for jewelry, but it was also a widely accepted coin that could be found from Africa to Indonesia. It was an official currency in Saudi Arabia until 1928, in Yemen until 1962, and in Oman until 1970.

THE MAIN TYPES OF JEWELRY

Women throughout the Arab world wear a wide range of jewelry, especially traditional silver versions. The main types are headpieces, pendants, necklaces, earrings, nose rings, finger rings, bracelets, belts, and anklets, all with variations in form.

A wide range of headpieces, pendants, and hair and face ornaments are worn by Arab women, especially women of nomadic origins. The headpieces and pendants (such as the triangular *ilaqa*) usually suspend from a strap at the top of the headdress and hang down onto the forehead or on one side of the head. Other head ornaments include bands that are worn across the forehead and tied at the back of the head. Hairpieces are often worn in sets of five or seven, each with a loop soldered onto its back through which the hair can be pulled.

The general term for a necklace is *iqd*, which means "knot." However, many other types of necklaces are found throughout the Arab world, each with its own terminology. One of the most popular forms is the hirz necklace with amulets made in simple geometric shapes (*hijab*) or in a cylindrical (*khiyar*) form. Sometimes, five amulets are combined to ward off the evil eye. Some enclose texts from the Qur'an or other holy inscriptions. One of the most impressive forms of amulet necklaces is the *mirta'sha*, combining amulets of many different shapes and forms, covering the entire chest. Such neckpieces are often finely decorated with silver bells, silver or amber beads, diamond-shaped pendants, and so on. Another popular form of necklace is made of one or more metal chains (*silsila*), although in Saudi Arabia the term *silsila* also means a type of necklace that is made from a heavy silver chain worn over one shoulder and under the opposite arm like a bandolier.

A *gladat* necklace is made out of beads; a *gladat anbar* is a necklace with five amber beads. Other beaded necklaces are of turquoise or coral either combined with other types of beads or totally made from one material. Some necklaces use coins either by themselves or decorated with chains and stones of various materials and colors.

Finally, there are the *khnaq* and *kirdan* forms. The word *khnaq* refers to a choker style of necklace that consists of rows of small silver bars with a variety of pendants. This type of necklace is often backed with cloth. Sometimes, it is said that the number of rows represents the number of children a woman has borne.

The kirdan is very similar to the khnaq and has rows of plaques alternating with chain links to create a broad necklace. It is often backed by cloth.

Most girls have their ears pierced when they are young and often their nose as well by the age of two. Sometimes, a boy's ears are pierced in order to mislead evil spirits, but this is no longer a common practice. Earrings (*khirsa* or *halqa*) are normally made in pairs. A woman might wear six in each ear. The main earring is a large silver ring that pierces the upper part of the ear and is often decorated with silver balls. Many types of earrings indicate where the woman lives or comes from. These range from small rings to large, ornate forms so heavy that they need a chain to help support the weight.

Numerous types of nose rings have different names. For example, a nose ring worn in the right nostril is called a *khizama*, and a nose ring for the left nostril is a *zimam*. The classic nose ring (*shanf*) of silver or gold consists of an upper half made of thick wire and a lower half that is a semicircular disk decorated with filigree work. A special type of nose ring called the *frayda* is a large nose ring set with a pearl or turquoise. Some women wear a stud (also called a *zimam* in some regions) made out of gold or silver. Apart from gold or silver studs for the nostrils, some Bedouin women and girls wear a pendant hung above the bridge of the nose; this is typically a flat piece of silver inlaid with glass beads with small rings and chains attached to it.

Women wear an abundance of rings on the fingers and the toes, while men wear one or two rings, notably a seal ring of some kind and, to display their pilgrimage to Mecca, a hajj ring. Because of the injunction against wearing gold, which dates back to the time of the Prophet, men tend to wear relatively plain silver rings. Women, however, can wear rings made of any metal and in any size and form.

The generic term for a finger ring is *khatim*, which means "a seal." Usually, however, it is a flat-topped bezel in metal or stone that is sometimes decorated with geometric or floral designs rather than engraved with a family's coat of arms, as known in the West. Ring names vary regionally. In general, however, a ring with a large square surface is called a *murabba*, while one shaped like a teardrop is a *shahid*. A ring with a stone setting is called a *fass*. A ring decorated with an individual turquoise is called a *khatim fayruz* or *abu fayrus*, which means "father of the turquoise." A finger ring with a red stone such as carnelian, garnet, or red glass is called a *fatha*.

In addition to a different name depending on its appearance, a ring may be named based on where it is worn. A ring on the little finger is called a *khamzad*, one for the middle finger is a *wasat*, and a ring for the forefinger is called a *shahid*. Rings meant for a specific finger have different shapes and forms of decoration, and again these forms can vary quite considerably from one region to another.

Toe rings tend to be much larger than finger rings and have an open back so that they can easily be slipped onto a toe. The same range of decoration can be found on both types of rings.

A wide variety of bracelets, armbands, elbow bands, and anklets are worn by Arab women, many of which look very similar in their general form, material, and decoration. Mostly made from silver, they are usually worn in pairs. A nomadic woman would generally wear one pair of anklets (*khilkhal* or *hijl*) and armbands (*zand*) or elbow bands (*ma'qid*) but five or more bracelets (*siwar*) on each wrist.

Bedouin silver bracelet, Saudi Arabia, probably made in Yemen, 1960s. This bracelet is one of a pair and would have been worn by a woman with four or more additional bracelets (*siwar*) on each wrist. Textile Research Centre, Leiden.

Bracelets, anklets, and armlets all vary in weight and workmanship. They might be made of a light, hollow silver tube with chased geometric or floral designs. Some are heavy and fashioned from a length of solid silver. Some have minute and intricate designs of granulation and filigree work; others are chunky. There is also a broad band form of bracelet (*iswara*) that is usually fastened with a pin.

Bracelets also have a variety of different names. One type of bracelet consisting of various bead types strung together is called a *dalqa*, and a bracelet of amber beads is a *khasur*. Found throughout Saudi Arabia is the *melwi*, a bracelet made of twisted silver wire capped at either end with finials and often studded with stones. A variety of the melwi that has a wire twisted around the main twists is called a *ma'din mutarraz*, or "embroidered-wire" style. A more expensive style of melwi called a *khuwaysa* is made of gold decorated with turquoise.

Bedouin and village women wear various types of belts. The silver belts (*hizam*) were usually made by Yemeni craftsmen. They are often quite ornate and made of silver of varying qualities or silver and copper alloys. Such belts were usually backed by a piece of black cloth, leather, or silver mesh. Some belts were fashioned from plaques or interlocking pieces decorated with insets of colored glass beads or stones and stripes of filigree. To complete the effect, bells or coins are sometimes added at the ends. A simpler style was made by Bedouin women in southwestern Saudi Arabia from leather and decorated with small, locally made beads in blocks of simple geometric patterns.

References and Further Reading

Al-Jadir, Saad. *Arab and Islamic Silver*. London: Stacey International, 1981.

Al-Khalifa, Shaikha Haya Ali, and Michael Rice, eds. *Bahrain through the Ages: The Archaeology*. London: Kegan and Paul, 1986.

Brosh, Na'ama, ed. *Jewellery and Goldsmithing in the Islamic World*. Jerusalem: Israel Museum, 1987.

Doughty, Charles. *Travels in Arabia Deserta*, 2 vols. Cambridge: Cambridge University Press, 1888.

Hasson, Rachel. *Later Islamic Jewellery*. Jerusalem: Institute for Islamic Art, 1987.

Hawley, Ruth. *Omani Silver*. London and New York: Constable, 1978.

Jenkins, Marilyn, and Manual Keena. *Islamic Jewellery in the Metropolitan Museum of Art*. New York: Metropolitan Museum, 1982.

Kalter, Johanes, Margareta Pavaloi, and Maria Zerrnickel. *The Arts and Crafts of Syria*. London: Thames & Hudson, 1992.

Potts, Daniel T., ed. *Dilmun: New Studies in the Archaeology and Early History of Bahrain*. Berlin: D. Reimer, 1983.

Ross, Heather C. *Bedouin Jewellery in Saudi Arabia*. London: Stacey International, 1978.

Topham, John, Anthony Landreau, and William E. Mullligan. *Traditional Crafts of Saudi Arabia*. London: Stacey International, 1981.

Gillian Vogelsang-Eastwood

See also Birth, Marriage, and Death; The Tradition of the Bridal Trousseau.

Saudi Arabian Dress

Saudi Arabia is a vast country dominated by deserts, oases, and mountain ranges. Until the mid-twentieth century, these natural features had separated the various communities that live throughout the Arabian Peninsula. Saudi Arabia is, therefore, often divided into four geographic and cultural areas: the Northern Province (the Nafud), the Eastern Province (the Hasa), the Western Province (the Hijaz and 'Asir), and the Central Province (the Nejd).

For hundreds of years, the Northern Province has looked northward toward Syria, Iraq, and the eastern Mediterranean for its economic and cultural links, while the Eastern Province has looked eastward toward the Persian Gulf and the countries along the Indian Ocean for its links. The western regions of the Hijaz and 'Asir are ethnically and culturally very mixed. In particular, Turkey, Egypt, East Africa, and Asia have had a lasting effect on the region's ethnic composition and cultural and economic life. In contrast, the Central Province has been virtually cut off from the outside world for centuries, and, as a result, its culture looks inward, toward the Bedouin, for inspiration. This area is regarded as the heartland of the Arab people and culture. All of these diverse influences have had an impact on the clothing worn on the peninsula, particularly the dress of Saudi Arabian women. The discovery of oil in the 1920s changed the economic and cultural nature of Saudi Arabia, but the love of decorative and colorful clothing and jewelry remains part of Saudi cultural heritage.

PREHISTORIC AND PRE-ISLAMIC DRESS

Although no garments from Arabian prehistory have survived, some information about what was worn can be ascertained from rock carvings dating from the second millennium B.C.E. on, which are scattered throughout the peninsula. Men are depicted either naked or wearing hip wraps that are similar to the long hip wraps (izar) still worn by men in southern Arabia. Men are also shown wearing headdresses decorated with what look like feathers and thin, hornlike projections. All the men carry weapons and are shown with at least one dagger, as well as bows and arrows, shields, throwing sticks, and maces. Women are depicted in a wider variety of garments. One relief shows a tall woman wearing a long dress that reaches down to her ankles, with a shawl or cloak of some kind. Around her neck is a necklace. Another woman is depicted wearing a knee-length dress with a mantle. Her hair seems to be piled up on her head. Women are also represented with their hair hanging loose, plaited, and occasionally decorated at the ends with beads or similar objects.

More information on the garments worn by men and women in this region comes from various reliefs and literary references from the first millennium B.C.E. on. Men's and women's garments can be seen on reliefs dating from the reign of Ashurbanipal (668–672 B.C.E.), held in the British Museum, London. Arab men are shown wearing long hip wraps, and the women wear long dresses and fringed mantles.

More information comes from early Arabic written sources, notably Jahili (pre-Islamic) poetry, as well as Western classical accounts. The former is a rich source of information because clothing imagery is prominent in the poetry. The range of garments includes many terms that are still in use, such as the various forms of outer coverings, including the *burd, izar, mirt, rida,* and *shamlah.* But these names can be misleading, because, although the terms are still in use, the ancient garments are not identical to the modern ones. Nevertheless, such poetry gives an idea of the range of clothing worn at the time and how garments were regarded. The sixth-century poet al-Samaw'al b. 'Adiya, for instance, noted that "if a man's honor is not sullied by baseness, then every rida in which he cloaks himself will become him." Women's clothing is also frequently mentioned. Al-A'sha, for instance, who lived in the earliest days of the Islamic era, wrote about "women who walk unsteadily because of the train of the *baqir* [a sleeveless gown/shift] and their *izara* [veils]." One Jahili poem from the sixth century C.E. contains a reference to the deliberate dropping of a veil by the wearer so her face could be seen. It would seem from this poem that at least some Arab women were veiled (head and face).

EARLY ISLAMIC DRESS

It is likely that the dress of the earliest Muslim communities was similar to that worn in the preceding period, with some modifications to accommodate Islamic moral sensibilities. The following verses from the Qur'an were of particular importance for this moral code: "O Children of Adam! We have sent down on you a garment to cover your shameful parts. ... Let not Satan tempt you as he brought your parents out of the Garden, stripping them of their garments to show them their shameful parts" (Sura 7:25–26). It was regarded as essential for men and women to cover the region from the waist to the knees. In addition, it was felt that the shape of the body, especially that of women's bodies, should not be clearly defined. These basic concepts continue to have a strong influence on early-twenty-first-century Arab and Muslim dress conventions. Another convention was that both men and women were expected to cover their heads and hair when in public and to wear a mantle or wrap of some kind to cover their indoor garments.

The basic articles of clothing for men consisted of an undergarment such as a hip wrap (izar) or trousers (sirwal); an undershirt (qamis); an overgown (thob, dishdasha); an outer garment such as a cloak, mantle, or coat (rida or hulla); and, finally, headgear such as a cap (taqiyeh), head cloth, or turban (imamah). In addition, some people also wore shoes or sandals.

A woman's basic range of clothing consisted of undertrousers (sirwal), a long chemise/dress (qamis), an overdress (thob), and

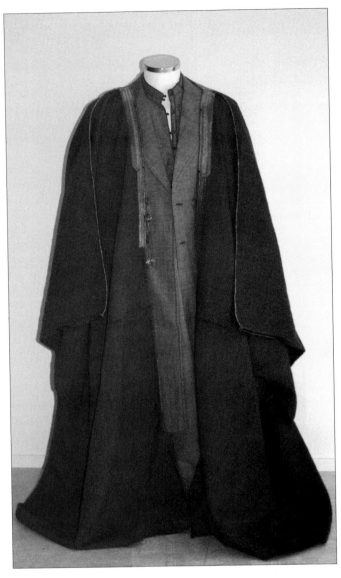

Winter clothing for an elderly Saudi man, Riyadh, Saudi Arabia, late twentieth century. It includes a woolen *thob* (gown), jacket, and camel-hair *bisht* (cloak-like outer garment). Textile Research Centre, Leiden.

some form of headgear. A variety of shoes and sandals were worn by wealthier women. When in public, women were expected to wear some form of coat or wrap (*jilbah*, *khimar*, or *mirt*). In addition, many women wore face veils.

The wearing of undertrousers by both men and women became relatively common during this period. It is possible that they were introduced following the conquest of southern Arabia by the Persians. By the medieval Islamic period, the use of trousers had spread throughout the Islamic world.

MODERN SAUDI ARABIAN DRESS

In the early twenty-first century, the basic outfit for men and women consists of undertrousers, a shirt or dress (qamis), an overdress or gown (dishdasha or thob), and head coverings of some kind. For outside of the home or going to a city, it is common to

wear a cloak (*bisht* or *abayeh*) and, in the case of women, usually a face veil of some kind. These are a combination of medieval, modern, and Bedouin elements.

Some men wear drawers (also called sirwal) under their robes, but most consider the wearing of close-fitting underwear as unhealthy and unnatural. In many areas, Bedouin men prefer to wear a hip wrap (izar) of some kind. Over the sirwal and izar is worn a long gown (thob). In the early twenty-first century, this gown usually has a Western-style shirt collar, straight sleeves, and cuffs. Another Western touch is the presence of a pocket on the upper left-hand side of the garment; the pocket is used for light objects such as pens and pencils. These garments are usually made of white or cream-colored cotton or polyester for summer, while a darker version, sometimes in colored worsted, is used for winter. The traditional version of the thob is called a *merodan*. It has very large sleeves with long lappets. It is worn on special occasions, especially by Bedouin men.

Various types of outer garments are worn depending on the time of year and the wearer's occupation. The main type is the bisht or cloak, which comes in various forms. The northern bisht, for example, originates in Syria and has small sleeves, while southern versions are sleeveless. The older version used to be pale cream, honey, beige, brown, camel, or black. Modern bishts tend to be of a more limited range of colors (white, brown, or black). The men's version is usually decorated with gold—which is confined to the neck band, along the shoulder line, around the openings for the hands, and on small decorative tassels at the ends of the bands.

In the twenty-first century, the term *bisht* has become synonymous with the *aba*. Technically, however, a bisht is made from one length of material, while an aba is made from two lengths of material sewn horizontally together, leaving gaps for the arms. A bisht may or may not have sleeves, while an aba never has sleeves. Both the bisht and the aba are worn draped from the shoulders. They are often decorated along the neck and front opening and along the seam lines. But the amount of decoration used depends on where the garment comes from and religious interpretations concerning how much decoration is allowed.

Arab headgear consists of three elements: A skullcap (*keffiyeh* or *taqiyeh*) is worn underneath the head cloth. It is often called a prayer cap. The head cloth is made from a large square of cloth that is folded diagonally in half to form a triangle. This is draped over the head in such a manner that one point hangs down the wearer's back and the other two points hang down at the sides of the face. In Saudi Arabia, it is deliberately worn with a peak pinched at the center of the forehead. This is a practical arrangement for protecting the head from the scorching sun while creating a form of insulation by trapping air within its folds. A white head cloth is called a *ghutra* or *shamlah*. A checked head cloth (red-and-white or black-and-white) is called a *keffiyeh* (the same word as used for a cap) and is often worn in the winter months.

The head cloth is kept in place with a head rope (*'aqal*), which is generally a double coil of sheep wool or camel hair. The head rope is normally decorated with two small tassels worn hanging down the back. Other forms of the 'aqal are made of metal or a combination of metal, mother-of-pearl, and wool. The latter form is more of a circlet (*shattafa*) than a head rope, although the function is the same—to keep the head cloth in place.

The main dress of Saudi women consists of a small range of basic items, but these can vary considerably in appearance. Modern Arabian undertrousers (sirwal) for women are generally made of cotton, sometimes with silk ankle panels. They are usually constructed of two straight leg panels with a wide gusset at the crotch. The ankle cuffs of the trousers (sirwal mashtaghal) are also sometimes embroidered. The sirwal are gathered at the waist using a cord (tikka) drawn through the waistband channel. Sometimes, the ends of the tikka are elaborately decorated and perfumed.

Many women on the peninsula wear a long dress or tunic. It is usually loose fitting, has long sleeves, and reaches down to the ankles or just above them (in order to show off the decorative trouser cuffs). There is usually a central panel folded in half at the shoulders and sleeves that are sewn onto the central panel. There are normally one or more side panels. The neck opening is usually high and round with no collar. To increase the size of the neck opening, there is a front slit fastened with a button and loop of some kind, which can easily be opened when breast-feeding.

This basic garment for both men and women, a long dress or tunic, is known by various names throughout Southwest Asia and Iran, including *galabiyeh* (Egypt), *kaftan* (Turkey), and *libas* (Iran). In Saudi Arabia, the most common term is *fustan*. However, in the Central Province, it is called a *dura'ah* or *migta*, and, in the Eastern Province, it is called a *dishdasha*. This garment usually does not have tailored details such as darts and pleats and is generously cut.

In many areas of the kingdom, women also wear an overdress called a thob, which is sometimes, but not always, worn over a fustan. This garment is made from a central panel with a high, round neck opening with no collar. The sleeves are normally very wide, hanging almost to the ground in some cases. Under the sleeves are smaller side panels and usually decorative underarm gussets. In some areas, the back of the garment also has a train that is draped around one arm when walking.

A feature of women's dress throughout the Arabian Peninsula is the use of various types of mantles, veils, and face veils. These are worn for religious and cultural reasons, for showing status (financial and marital), and for protection from the heat and dust that are so prevalent in the country. The use of face veils has a pre-Islamic origin, but, contrary to popular belief, not all Saudi women have worn them in the past or indeed do so in the early twenty-first century. In general, village women tend to wear a face veil only when they go to a town, because veils hinder their manual work.

Traditional footwear in the kingdom is generally of four types: sandals, slippers, shoes, and boots. Sandals and slippers are the most widely used forms of footwear, because they are easy to remove and it is customary to remove one's footwear when entering a building, especially mosques or private houses. A common form of sandal worn by both men and women is the *ni'al*. These have a flat sole with bands for the big toes and flat straps for the insteps. They are normally made out of cow hide (inexpensive and from

Bedouin woman's cotton overdress (*thob*) with bands of silk sewn together, central Saudi Arabia, 1970s. The embroidered design is said to represent men walking at night with lanterns on their way to (or from) the mosque. Textile Research Centre, Leiden.

India) or camel hide (expensive and locally made). Sometimes, a leather sock called a *khuff* is worn. These cover the entire foot and ankle. They are an ancient form that can be traced back to the early days of Islam. Khuffs can be worn by men or women, either indoors or outdoors. Bedouin men wear a form of desert sock in the cold nights of winter, but, in general, sandals are not worn with socks. Western-style shoes, however, are worn with socks or stockings of some kind.

REGIONAL TOWN AND VILLAGE DRESS

In the early twenty-first century, most Saudi men wear the same form of dress, regardless of region. In contrast, there is a wide range of regional dress for women, although in many areas it is vanishing due to the opening up of the kingdom and the advent of widespread telecommunications. There are four main regions within the kingdom: northern, central, western, and eastern Saudi Arabia.

Northern Saudi Arabia (the Nafud) lies between the Great Nafud Desert and the borders with Jordan and Iraq and forms part of the Syrian Desert. For thousands of years, this area was part of an important trade route that connected the eastern Mediterranean with central Arabia, India, and the Far East. Relatively few people live in this region of Saudi Arabia due to the adverse conditions.

In the early twenty-first century, the traditional outfit for a married urban woman from the cities of Jawf, Ha'il, or Tabuk to the north consists of a standard ensemble of trousers with decorative ankle cuffs, a tightly fitting dress, a loose overdress, and some form of head covering. Further to the south, the outfits worn by urban women resemble those worn by nomads, especially women of the Bani Tamim tribe, from the Central Province.

In addition, there is a style of frock (*dirah* or *dura'ah*) that is unique to the northern region. These frocks are usually made of a deep red material. They have a bodice with large sleeves, and, from the high waistline, there is a double-layered skirt, with one layer acting as a lining. This skirt is just visible underneath the hem of the main dress. These garments are embroidered around the yoke, giving the effect of a bolero, as well as along the sleeve seam and fold line. They also have broad embroidered bands at the cuffs.

The Central Plateau region of Saudi Arabia (the Nejd) was, until the mid-twentieth century, one of the most geographically isolated regions in the world. It has on its western flanks the Tuwayq Mountains, which run north to south; on the other three sides, it is bounded by desert, including part of the Nafud, the Dhana and, in the south, the vast Rub' al-Khali or "Empty Quarter."

The Nejd is the location of Riyadh, the capital of Saudi Arabia. The people in the urban areas were mostly mixed northern and southern Arabs. In the early twenty-first century, however, there are numerous Arabs from other parts of the Arab world (such as Lebanon, Syria, Palestine, and so on) as well as foreign groups living in the capital. The garments that used to be worn in Riyadh can be taken as an example of traditional urban dress from this remote area of Saudi Arabia. As with many areas, these garments are no longer worn on a daily basis but may be seen at parties and on special occasions.

The basic Riyadh outfit is similar to that worn in the east of the country. It usually consists of trousers with embroidered cuffs (sirwal mashtaghal) and an underdress (dharah), which usually matches the color of the overdress or thob. The dharah is usually made of silk. Unlike in many other regions of the Arabian Peninsula, this garment is ankle length, which means that the trouser cuffs cannot be seen. The thob is normally made from fine linen, cotton, wool, or silk, usually in either a sheer or tulle form. In general, poorer urban women wear a black cotton thob, while wealthier women wear silk and chiffon versions. A basic thob has a narrow central panel, with massive sleeves and lower side panels. There are usually large gussets under each sleeve, which are made of contrasting colored material. Thobs are also decorated with a broad band of sequins around the edges of the garment. These bands are sewn to the inside of the sleeves, so that when they are folded back, either onto the shoulders or onto the head, the decoration can be clearly seen. In the early twenty-first century, an elaborate version of the thob with a matching head covering (*shaylah*) is worn at festivals and weddings.

When a woman is in public, it is normal for her to wear a cloak (abayeh) and a long scarf (*tarhah*, shaylah, or *misfa*), which is wrapped and draped over the head in such a way that the neck and hair are completely covered. Women are also expected to wear some form of face veil. The most common form is the burqa, which is a two-part face veil that covers the face only and is usually made of black cotton. Other forms of face veils include the *boushiyah*, which covers the entire head, and *niqab*, a single-piece veil that covers all or part of the face.

The outfit worn by unmarried girls is similar to that of married women but without the thob. Very young girls wear a bonnetlike cap (*quba'a*), which is often elaborately decorated. At about the age of eight or nine, the quba'a is replaced by the *bukhnuq*. These are made out of a rectangle of cloth that is folded to form a bonnetlike garment with long ends that hang down the back. Like the quba'a, the bukhnuq is often elaborately decorated with beads, shells, coins, and so forth.

The western region of Saudi Arabia (Hijaz) is dominated by a mountain range that runs the entire length of the western coastline. The mountains are divided into two sections, with a gap in the vicinity of Mecca. The region to the north of Mecca is called the Hijaz, and the region to the south is known as 'Asir. There is a strong link between the cut of the garments worn by urban, rural, and nomadic women in both regions. The main differences are in the materials used to make the various garments and the way in which they are embellished.

In the early twenty-first century, many urban women in the Hijaz region wear Western-style clothing. However, some women still prefer to wear a combination of blouse and skirt. The basic outfit consists of a pair of undertrousers with decorative cuffs, a blouse (sardari), an overgown (thob) made of fine cotton or silk, and various forms of head covering made up of scarves of various shapes and lengths. Up to the mid-twentieth century, the outdoor outfit consisted of a long white face veil (burqa) with a long outer wrap (*milaya*), which derived from Egypt. This combination was replaced by either an outer wrap (milaya or *sharshaf*) with a head cloth (*shambar*) and a plain black face veil (burqa) or a cloak (abayeh) worn over the head with a black face veil (burqa).

In the villages and countryside, Hijazi women wear the dura'ah, a loose, long-sleeved, ankle-length dress. Predominantly black, it is often decorated with embroidery around the neckline, yoke, and shoulders. White shirt buttons and tiny silver beads are commonly added to decorate the bodice and neck opening. The dress worn by women from the village of Sharfa, near Taif, is particularly distinctive. The basic outfit consists of a pair of under-trousers and an underdress called a *shalha*. Over these garments is worn a dress (dura'ah) decorated with simple, but striking, zigzag embroidery patterns (usually in red, yellow, green, and orange) around the neck opening on the bodice. The skirts are made up of strips of cloth horizontally sewn together. Traditionally, the dresses worn by married women have alternating blue and black stripes, while those of unmarried girls have predominantly red stripes. Sometimes, a wide silver belt (*hizam*) is worn with this outfit. A complicated headdress is worn by some Sharfa women. It consists of a small, black, flat cushion, a head coil, and a net veil. When in public, this headdress is often replaced by a straw hat.

The southwestern area of Saudi Arabia is called the 'Asir, which literally means "difficult region." A range of mountains south of Mecca gradually becomes steeper and more difficult to pass; the principal town of Abha lies on the western slope of the range. The 'Asir contains a hot and humid coastal region called the Tihamah and a cooler highland region that is known for its lush greenery. The area's geography, climate, history, and cultural ties have had a profound effect on the people living there and, indeed, on their dress. In general, they wear brighter and deeper colors than can be found in the rest of the country, and, because most of the women were and still are involved in agriculture, the general use of face veils does not exist—although the use of black burqas is growing in urban settings. Asiri men's clothing is different from typical men's clothing worn in the rest of Saudi Arabia.

A garment commonly worn by men and women throughout the highland region of 'Asir is called an *asayib*. It is worn like a circlet on the head and is made from a variety of materials, including twine, straw, leather, copper, and/or silver wire. Some are worn like the 'aqal, in the form of a padded roll of leather decorated with silver from which long tasseled pendants hang. In other areas of the 'Asir Mountains, women make asayib out of twisted red cloth and decorate them with pendants. Sometimes, plainer circlets are used to hold wild flowers and sweet-smelling herbs, such as basil.

'Asir is known for its leather and fur garments. These garments are needed because of the cooler mountain climate, especially in the winter. Such garments are worn by both men and women and usually consist of capes made from sheepskin or goatskin. Another type of garment associated with this area is the *farwah*, which is a fleece-lined coat. It is often worn by shepherds.

The traditional outfit for men in this region consists of a shirt with a hip wrap (*futa*). The futa is a colorful length of textile that

Narrow Bedouin Asiri dress decorated with glass beads, 'Asir, Western Saudi Arabia, 1970s. The glass beads reflect an African influence. Textile Research Centre, Leiden.

is wound around the lower half of the body. The end is tucked securely in at the waist. It is generally worn with a belt. Instead of a Western-style shirt, some men wear the *fanilla*, which is a short-sleeved shirt with a high, round neck. In the early twenty-first century, T-shirts are commonly worn as well.

The traditional garments for women in [ayin]Asir include a pair of trousers (sirwal) and a dress (dura'ah, *mudandash*, or *milbas*). These dresses are usually slightly tailored with full, hip-waisted skirts, which are often made of black-and-yellow-striped material. Over the dress is worn a wide sash that is knotted just above the hip. These sashes are often made of red-yellow-and-white-striped material and end in silk tassels. The head covering tends to be a simple rectangle of cloth (shaylah), often brightly colored, which is wrapped around the head and neck. Over this may be worn another head covering (*guna'a*) and a head circlet (asayib). Sometimes, a wide-brimmed straw hat is worn as protection against the sun. This outfit is finished by a wide variety of silver necklaces, bracelets, and, in some cases, a large, decorated belt that holds money and other items. These belts are made of leather or sometimes of twisted cloth.

In Aba Saud, the principal town of the Najran Oasis in the 'Asir, the main style of (village and nomadic) women's clothing begins with a pair of trousers (sirwal), which are usually embroidered at the ankle cuffs. The trousers are worn with a black cotton dress (usually of satin, *thob aswad*), which falls from the shoulders in an A-line form. The side panels ensure ease of movement. The sleeves tend to be long and narrow. The garment is usually decorated with embroidery, beading, and sometimes appliqué panels in red, orange, yellow, and white. The dress is normally worn with a sash or felt-lined leather belt decorated with colored embroidery or eyelets. The outfit is worn with a plain black head scarf (shaylah) of a loosely woven material such as cheesecloth. Often, a broad-brimmed straw hat with a pointed crown is worn.

The Eastern Province of Saudi Arabia (the Hasa) covers the entire eastern portion of the country. It is a strip of land about 124 miles (200 kilometers) wide that runs from the Saudi border with Kuwait in the north to the sands of the Rub' al-Khali in the south. Before the discovery of oil, settlements in the Eastern Province were almost entirely confined to villages in the two great oases of Qatif and Hasa. The populations of these villages consisted of nontribal groups, who had occupied the region since antiquity, and the tribal people of eastern and central Arabia, who had settled there. In the early twenty-first century, there is a mixture of ethnic groups—Arab, Asian, African, and Western—drawn by the work provided by the massive oil industry.

The discovery of oil changed the economic life of the various nomadic groups living in the region. There are still some traditional nomadic groups who live by migrations (most notably the Al-Murrahs), but many more tribes have a mixed way of life, with some of their members migrating and others who have settled. During the heat of the summer months, nomadic groups are drawn to the various oases, especially those of Haradh and Hofuf, in order to have access to water and the shelter of the palm trees.

In general, modern lifestyles have almost obliterated traditional styles of clothing worn on a daily basis. However, echoes of these outfits can be found in festive clothing, notably that worn at weddings and for the two main Islamic festivals of Id al-Fitr and Id al-Adha.

The traditional outfit for a married woman consists of plain undertrousers and frequently a version with embroidered ankle cuffs (sirwal mashtaghal). Over this is worn a colorful dress (dishdasha) with long sleeves. Sometimes, at a festival or party, a more decorative, semifitting version of the dishdasha is worn, which is called an *ummasa*. These are worn with an overdress (thob) made of sheer material with very large sleeve openings. The decorative details are usually down the front in a line from the neck opening and along seams and hems. There are two main types of thob: one for daily wear that is made out of a relatively strong material with little decoration and the *thob nashal*. The latter is usually heavily embellished with braids, woven or embroidered bands, pearls, and sequins. The materials used include marquisette, chiffon, georgette, organza, nylon, and silk. A fashionable way of wearing this garment is to pull up one or both sleeves over the head to form a hood.

Many of the thobs worn in the region are made in India and Pakistan especially for this market. In addition, some examples are made in Kuwait and Bahrain. Although this style of dress is usually claimed to be of central Arabian origin, it is well known in other areas of the Gulf region. It is worn, for instance, in Bahrain and the western parts of Oman. In addition, similar garments are worn by women in southern Iran.

Another traditional garment worn in the Eastern Province is the *mukhnuq* (also called a *bukhnuq*), a hoodlike garment worn by girls as well as some married women. A mukhnuq is usually made of a fine net or loosely woven material. It is made by folding a rectangle of cloth in half to form a narrow rectangle. One edge is sewn, leaving an opening for the face. They are usually decorated with embroidery or gold braid, which is sewn around the face opening and down the front seam. The daily version of the mukhnuq comes to waist level. However, for parties and special occasions, the versions worn by married women may be up to four to five yards (four to five meters) long and are highly decorated. Although these used to be made in the families or by local tailors, in the early twenty-first century many are made for the Saudi market in India and Pakistan.

The outfits worn by unmarried girls are similar to those of married women, except that they would not normally wear a thob, which is regarded as a married woman's garment.

BEDOUIN DRESS

The Bedouin or tent dwellers are one of the most cherished images of Saudi culture. They are regarded as representing the true Arab way of life and culture. The dress of Saudi urban and Bedouin men is very similar; the main differences lie in the range of materials used. Generally speaking, a typical outfit consists of a hip wrap (izar), gown (thob), overgarment (bisht or aba), and the three-part headgear (cap, head cloth, and head rope). However, some elements are typically Bedouin. Although urban men often wear undertrousers (sirwal), most Bedouin men do not wear such trousers, because they are regarded as unhealthy and effeminate.

A feature of traditional Bedouin dress for both men and women is the wearing of a leather belt around the waist under all the other garments. The belt is not visible. It has various regional names, such as *bireim*, but the basic form is made from two or more strands of gazelle leather fastened together.

Although many Bedouin wear sandals, it is rare for them to wear shoes; shoes are used in the winter months, if at all. Sandals sturdier materials—cottons and woolens rather than silk. The main elements are a pair of trousers (sirwal; these are not worn by every group), which are worn under a dress (dura'ah). The everyday overdress, or thob, is usually made of a black or dark blue material. More elaborate versions are worn by the Bani Tamin from the central region (Nejd); the sleeves are made from broad silk bands in cerise, orange, and green. These garments are often embroidered with arabesque and geometric designs as well as figurative forms such as pomegranates, palm trees, and lamps.

Bedouin women from the Nejd used to wear the *lithmah* form of face veil, which is a long length of loosely woven cloth wrapped around the lower features of the face and neck. In the early twenty-first century, however, some women wear a niqab or burqa; others wear a long head scarf that is draped on the top of the head and whose ends are tied together in a knot at the back of the head. The final head covering is the tarhah (shaylah), a rectangular scarf that is placed over the head to fall about the shoulders. This scarf is often decorated with a silver head ornament called a *raad* (literally, "thunderbolt") when the woman is dancing.

A wide range of dresses are worn by Bedouin women in the western regions of the kingdom. Each tribe and subgroup of tribes used to have its own shape of dress and decorative forms. This is rapidly vanishing as people no longer find the time to make the dresses.

Women of the Bani Malik tribe tend to wear a basic outfit consisting of a pair of undertrousers with a dress (dura'ah). These dresses are usually made of black cotton that is decorated around the neck opening, along the seam lines, and on the sleeve cuffs with appliqué, multicolored embroidery, shells, and beads. The lower edges of the skirts usually have between two and ten decorative bands. Sometimes, leather is also used to trim the hems of the dresses. Draped around the head and shoulders is a long rectangular length of material (shaylah), which is usually decorated with colored beads and red silk tassels. Married women also wear a hood called a guna'a, made of black cotton decorated with appliquéd cloth and trimmed with beads and embroidery.

A feature of Harb and Bani Salim dresses (dura'ah) is the use of a central panel with added side panels, often with a side neck opening to allow for breast-feeding (occasionally, there is a shoulder opening instead). Such dresses are decorated around the bodice yoke with lines of embroidery, buttons, shells, and so forth, as well as applied panels, especially around the hem. Harb dresses usually have a wide, solid panel decorating the hem, while Bani Salim dresses are made with a narrower panel flanked on one side by a band set about four inches (ten centimeters) above the main hem panel. The main feature of these dresses is their spectacular sleeves. They are long, wide, and straight, with underarm gussets that are used to create deep lappets.

The method for making these sleeves is unusual—there is one long continuous gusset—and it is probably no coincidence that this method of construction was also used for various Turkish garments, notably the chemises (*gömlek*) worn by women. It is likely that this type of sleeve was brought to the western part of Arabia by the Ottoman Turks who once ruled this part of Arabia.

These dresses are worn with a large head covering called a *milfah*, which may be either square or rectangular in shape. It is made out of a black cotton material, which is often decorated with

Red silk wedding dress with metal-thread embroidery, Riyadh, Saudi Arabia, 1980s. This is a typical cut for the underdress in the Riyadh region and features the crest of the royal house of Saud in the front. Textile Research Centre, Leiden.

are normally made of camels leather or rubber with leather straps. There is also a special kind of boot called a *jazma* or *bastar*, in which the side and upper elements come to just above the ankle bone.

For centuries, one of the most important elements of Bedouin dress (men's and women's) was the hair. The importance that Bedouin attach to their hair is frequently commented on in nineteenth- and twentieth-century Western literature. Hair remained an important element of a Bedouin's identity well into the twentieth century. It was common for men to have long hair that was either rolled into braids or plaited. Each group had its own form of men's hairstyle that made identification from a distance easier. In the early twenty-first century, however, many Bedouin men have their hair cut short in an urban or Western style. Women continue to pay attention to their hair and have it dressed in many different styles.

The basic elements of a Bedouin woman's dress are similar to the dress worn by village and some urban women. In general, however, the Bedouin version tends to be made from much squares of red and brown cloth. Mother-of-pearl buttons and metal beads are used to decorate the cloth. Normally, a coin or pendant of some form is sewn to the center front of the cloth so that it can hang over the forehead. In other regions of the Hijaz, the milfah is decorated in other ways, such as having the main band of decoration along the lower edge, which hangs down the wearer's back. These are sometimes folded in half and sewn along the shorter top edge to create a hoodlike garment that is worn open in the front.

The face veil worn by some Bedouin women in this region is of the *batullah* type, but it is locally called a burqa. It is usually made of a rectangle of red or black cloth with slits for the eyes and a long nose pleat. They are normally elaborately decorated with coins, shells, beads, and silver metalwork. Harb women are known for wearing these garments.

Until the late twentieth century, Bedouin women wore a considerable amount of silver jewelry as part of their personal wealth. In the early twenty-first century, many have changed to wearing gold. Besides gold earrings, they wear nose rings, finger and toe rings, necklaces, bracelets (sometimes as many as twenty on each arm), and anklets. All of these make a characteristic sound when a woman is walking or dancing.

References and Further Reading

Anati, E. *Rock-Art in Central Asia*. 4 vols. Leuven: Peeters, 1968–1974.

Brosh, N., ed. *Jewellery and Goldsmithing in the Islamic World*. Jerusalem: Israel Museum, 1987.

Burckhardt, J.L. *Notes on the Bedouins and Wahabys*. 2 vols. London: Colburn and Bentley, 1831.

Dickson, H.R.P. *The Arab of the Desert: A Glimpse into Badawin Life in Kuwait and Sau'di Arabia*. London: George Allen and Unwin, 1949.

Dozy, R.P.A. *Dictionnaire Détailleé des Noms des Vêtements chez les Arabes*. Amsterdam: Muller, 1845.

El-Hage, B. *Saudi Arabia: Caught in Time 1861–1939*. Reading, UK: Garnet, 1997.

Fiske, Patricia. *Palms and Pomegranates: Traditional Dress of Saudi Arabia*. Washington, DC: Textile Museum, 1987.

Katakura, M. *Bedouin Village: A Study of a Saudi Arabian People in Transition*. Tokyo: Tokyo University Press, 1977.

Mauger, Thierry, and Danielle Mauger. *In the Shadow of the Black Tents*. Riyadh: Tihama, n.d.

Musil, A. *The Manners and Customs of the Rwala Bedouins*. New York: American Geographic Society, 1928.

Raswan, C.R. *The Black Tents of Arabia*. London: Hutchingson, 1935.

Ross, H.C. *Bedouin Jewellery in Saudi Arabia*. London: Stacey International, 1978.

Ross, H.C. *The Art of Arabian Costume: A Saudi Arabian Profile*. 4th ed. Clarens-Montreux, Switzerland: Arabesque Commercial, 1994.

Snouck Hurgronje, C. *Mekka in the Latter Part of the 19th Century*. Leiden: Brill, 1931.

Stillman, Y.K. *Arab Dress: A Short History from the Dawn of Islam to Modern Times*. Leiden: Brill, 2000.

Topham, J., Anthony Landreau, and William E. Mulligan. *Traditional Crafts of Saudi Arabia*. London: Stacey International, 1981.

Yamani, M. *Changed Identities: The Challenge of the New Generation in Saudi Arabia*. London: Royal Institute of International Affairs, 2000.

Gillian Vogelsang-Eastwood

See also Ottoman Dress; Bedouin Jewelry; Snapshot: The Abayeh in Qatar; Iranian Regional Dress; Face Veils.

Yemeni Dress

Already ancient in biblical times, Yemen is purported to be the home of the legendary Queen of Sheba. It was the seat of the Minaean kingdom and was conquered by Egypt about 1600 B.C.E., invaded by the Ethiopians, and known to the Romans as Felix Arabia (Happy Arabia) because of the riches it generated.

Bab El-Mandeb, the southwestern coastal strait, links the Red Sea with the Indian Ocean and was an important trade corridor for three thousand years. In the third millennium B.C.E., aromatic resins attracted settlers to coastal areas, which evolved into important trading centers. Yemen became the intermediary for trade with Africa and India and was the link with China; pearls, spices, Chinese silks and garments, monkeys, slaves, Ethiopian gold, ivory, and ostrich feathers passed through Yemen, as well as resins, frankincense, and myrrh. The Romans challenged the trade monopoly in the first century C.E., and Arabian marine superiority declined as Romans and Greeks learned about monsoon winds and began buying directly from the sources, including silks from China and cotton textiles and garments from India.

Descendants of the Prophet Mohammed brought Islam to Yemen in the tenth century and provided religious, political, and social structures. They also brought with them changes in dress to conform with Islamic concepts of personal modesty. The Ottomans occupied northern Yemen from 1536 to 1635 and from 1872 to 1918; in their turn, they brought Ottoman styles of attire to the region, elements of which have survived into the early twenty-first century—notably in the use of tailored garments such as waistcoats. In the south, foreign commercial companies established trading colonies along the coast. In 1839, Britain developed Aden, which served as a refueling port when the Suez Canal opened in 1869. This shipping highway brought Western-style garments and ideas to the area around Aden.

In 1918, northern Yemen gained independence and was a theocratic imamate until 1962, when the army seized power and established the Yemen Arab Republic. The southern regions of Yemen remained a British protectorate until 1967, when the area became the People's Democratic Republic of Yemen. In 1970, the south adopted a Socialist orientation, and the mass exodus to the north contributed to two decades of hostilities. Yemen united in 1990 as the Republic of Yemen under Ali Abdullah Saleh, with the capital in Sana'a. In 1994, southern separatists started a civil war, and tensions persist, with the south claiming the north is economically privileged. Inland areas are under the power of tribal sheikhs.

Yemen is bisected by a mountain range that runs north to south. It has four main regions: Tihamah (an arid and flat coastal plain in the southwest), the western highlands (which boast diverse agriculture), the eastern highlands, and the Rub' al-Khali, which means "the empty quarter." This lies to the north and is the world's largest sand desert, with summer temperatures of over 130 degrees Fahrenheit (54 degrees Celsius).

The population is nearly 99 percent Muslim (55 percent Sunni and 45 percent Shia) with less than 1 percent Christians and Jews. Each group used to have its own form of dress, although since the diaspora of Jewish groups in the late 1940s and early 1950s, many of these differences have become hard to detect. Ethnically, the population is 97 percent Arab, Afro-Arab, and South Asian with about 3 percent European. There are tribal and religious distinctions with regard to location. People of the Tihamah coastal plain are mixed Arab-African while other groups are Arab. This link with Africa can be seen in both the architecture of the region and the clothing worn there. There are also many people of African, Indian, and Iranian origin in the southern and southeastern regions. The Tihamah Sunnis differ greatly from the northern and southern lowland Shias in culture, economics, and politics.

Yemeni tribes are sedentary cultivators. Approximately half the population is rural, a small number are nomads, and the rest live in urban areas. Foreign aid has helped build roads that span the country and permit increased social mobility. The land is fertile but subject to hail and locusts. Traditional crops are grains and fodder, bananas, cotton, beans, vegetables, coffee, and tropical fruits. Qat, mildly narcotic leaves that Yemenis chew, has replaced much agriculture, creating a need for imported food. Sheep, goats, camels, poultry, and fish abound. Weaving was traditionally small-scale, and handicrafts were the only industry, though China has helped set up cotton-ginning workshops, plants, and commercial spinning and weaving mills that include power looms.

In Yemen, dress signals regional and status differences and, for these reasons, is very important. Conformity is expected in public, while individuality is expressed in intimate, private circles. Clothing differences depend on age, education, status, occasion, and location. Aden residents were, for example, the first to wear Western clothing because of the Suez Canal and British influence, while traditional garments are more common in the hinterlands.

WOMEN'S DRESS

In the early twenty-first century, factory-produced textiles from India, Japan, and Korea are widely available and cater to the Yemeni love of color. Each section of a garment may be cut from a different piece of cloth, including velvet, satin, and synthetic brocades, and may be machine embroidered. The basic dress of Yemeni women consists of long pants (sirwal), a dress of some form, a head covering, and outer covering(s) when in public.

The type of sirwal worn varies slightly throughout the country; some are wider than others, the type of material used differs, and so does the style of embroidery carried out on the ankle cuffs.

A woman wearing a *jalabia* (full-length woman's dress); a long, rectangular face cloth wrapped to cover forehead, nose, and mouth (*lithmah*); and a rectangular cloth to further conceal her body. Sana'a Yemen, 2007. Richard Harris Photography.

Nevertheless, the sirwal are regarded as an essential garment that indicates women's modesty.

The main regional garment is a long-sleeved, calf-length dress called a *zinnah* in many areas. The width of the zinnah used to be determined by the width of the loom used locally; this historical influence could still be seen at the end of the twentieth century. Normally, a zinnah has a narrow central section with a neck slit, sleeves added to the sides on straight seams, flaring side panels, and underarm gussets. It is worn shorter in Yemen than in the northern part of the peninsula, thus exposing the embroidered sirwal from the calf to the ankle. The neck opening, sleeves, and hem are generally embroidered with abstract or geometric designs.

Originally, zinnah from the western regions of Yemen were made of cotton, traditionally dyed with indigo. After the cloth had been dyed, it was polished with a hard surface such as a smooth stone or piece of glass to produce a sheen resembling carbon paper. If wetted, the gloss would disappear and the colors bleed. Both the longer and shorter versions of the zinnah are also

normally embroidered on the front and back. The newer versions are normally machine embroidered following the older styles of designs.

In Al Bayda', a town about 130 miles (209 kilometers) southeast of Sana'a, dresses are decorated with embroidery that uses red and white thread on a black background, almost completely covering the base. The dresses have plain sleeves and red embroidered cuffs. In Asir, in the Sarawat Mountains, shoulder bars and side panels are decorated.

At Hojariyah, near Tayis, the dress is often embroidered black satin. In the early twenty-first century, embroidery is scarce and usually done by machine. The dress is close fitting through the chest, but the skirt is made extra wide by using side gores. The most unusual feature of the Hojariyah dress is sleeves that are cut ten inches (twenty-five centimeters) longer than the arms and flare out so much from the bodice to the wrist that they reach the ankle when the arms are held out straight.

Many dresses from Tihamah, the southwestern coastal lowland, are made from hand-dyed indigo or imported cotton. In the south of the Tihamah, the garments tend to be relatively narrow, while those from northern and central Tihamah, especially from the region around Bayt al Faqih and Hudayda, often have enormous straight sleeves, half again as long as the arm. The very wide cut disguises the body shape and also means that these garments look more African in appearance—a reflection of the close connections this region has with parts of East Africa. Tihamah dresses normally have a neck slit, although it is not needed for putting on and taking off the garment and is solely decorative. The front and back center panel seams are embroidered where they join the sleeves and side gores. The center front panel and side gores are heavily embroidered with thick cotton yarn and embellished with brass chains, brass sequins, and triangular mother-of-pearl pieces attached with red thread. Pearl shell and cowry shells are often used on clothing in coastal areas as amulets. These gowns were worn over narrow-legged sirwal that had embroidery from the calf to the ankle.

Cool mountain regions have narrow dresses with straight sleeves and exhibit similar design features to dresses worn in hot climates. Even though dresses may have extremely long sleeves and a very full skirt, the area from the shoulder to bust is often very tightly fitted, a characteristic from the western and southern regions. This requires a deep front slit backed with a placket for modesty.

In contrast, the dresses from the Wadi Hadramawt region in eastern Yemen tend to be very wide with a small train at the back. The wedding versions are often made of red satin or velvet and decorated with embroidery, shells, sequins, and so forth. They are worn with wide pants that are also embroidered around the ankle cuffs. These outfits are similar to those worn by women from the Dhofar region of southern Oman, just over the border.

When walking between villages, rural highland women drape a shawl (*maswan*) over their head. In the past, they would fold it and pile it high on the head in a decorative manner, as some old women continue to do. Country clothing is more utilitarian, and the dress is likely to allow greater motion. Women's faces may or may not be covered, and dresses may be brightly colored. Working women from the western parts of the country often wear a broad-brimmed straw hat (*dhola*) for protection against the sun.

In parts of the highlands, women wore thick braids of goat hair bundled under a scarf or an embroidered cap, a headband with a train, and, on top of these, a small straw hat perched at an

A woman wearing a face veil (*maghmug*) with black and white circles, as well as a large red-and-blue patterned rectangular cloth (*sitarah*) draped over the head. Old Medina, Sana'a, Yemen, 2007. Richard Harris Photography.

angle. In other highland communities, women wore colorful turbans, and elsewhere they wore embroidered bonnets that hung down the back to the waist.

Many urban and some rural women are adopting Western-style clothing where previously they would have worn loose, square tunics or fitted dresses gathered at the waist over long pants or dark tights. In the main cities, dress tends to be of darker colors; when going out, a Yemeni woman will wear some type of outer garment that covers her body. Throughout the twentieth century and into the early twenty-first century, some women in Sana'a, the capital, have worn the *sitarah*, a large red-and-blue patterned rectangular cloth over their head to cover the entire body. This is clutched under the chin and extends to the ankles.

After the 1960s, the three-piece black *sharshaf* mostly replaced the sitarah. Originally from Turkey, the sharshaf includes a pleated skirt, a triangular hood draped over the head and shoulders, and a face covering. The first women who went to school adopted the sharshaf. In the 1980s, some rural women adopted the sharshaf as a sign of urban sophistication, blurring the lines between rural and urban identities. The sharshaf skirt is flexible

and can have wide or narrow pleats. It became shorter during the 1960s and was worn over stockings or wide-legged trousers rather than the tight-fitting sirwal pants. In the 1970s, a black mixed-fabric sharshaf maxi was popular.

At the end of the twentieth century, many young women preferred to wear the *balto*, a one-piece, loose, full-length overcoat. The balto came to Sana'a in the 1970s through higher-class families who had the means to travel and brought the garments back from Saudi Arabia, Beirut, or Cairo. The 1970s were the height of emigration for work purposes, and many families enjoyed greater disposable income and could afford fashionable dress. The balto is similar in cut to coats worn in Egypt and Syria and was approved of by the conservative Islamist movement. Baltos come in a variety of colors.

In both rural and urban communities, women may wrap their heads in a translucent scarf that can expose the face or be pulled up over the mouth and nose if the wearer wishes. In other places, they wear a scarf tied under the chin. The amount of hair showing varies according to community norms and individual preferences.

Until the early twentieth century, ornate silver jewelry unique to the region was worn in the south. Red stones, glass, and reddish-brown stones such as carnelians are common in southern Arabia, while turquoise was more commonly worn in the north. Coral is popular in the west, while amber is the choice of the east. In the early twenty-first century, women wear gold or imported silver costume jewelry in urban areas, where there is a desire to conform to perceptions of urban and cosmopolitan fashion.

Cosmetics have long been used in Yemen. Traditionally, turmeric was rubbed on the face, and various herbs were crushed into paste to paint the face with various designs. Thick black circles were painted around the eyes, sometimes meeting between the eyebrows on the bridge of the nose, looking like masks worn on the eastern plateau. Traditional makeup has been replaced by commercial cosmetics, although henna is still used for dyeing the palms and soles of the feet and as a hair coloring. Kohl is often used to line the eyes of infants and women for beauty and sun protection. Sprigs of basil and rue are worn behind the ear, and jasmine is threaded on a string for its scent. Incense and commercial perfumes are used to scent clothes and hair and are traditionally offered to guests.

In general, up through the early twenty-first century, issues regarding women's body size have been largely absent in Yemen, because fat is considered a sign of wealth and leisure. Rural workers are active and expected to be robust, and increased body fat signals beauty in urban women. Young women try to increase their size, and few see the need to exercise. Reliance on imported food has caused serious weight gain even among rural women, and obesity is becoming a health problem for the first time in Yemen's history. The People's Democratic Republic of Yemen encouraged athletics for both boys and girls, and its volleyball team competed internationally, but the programs closed after the unification of Yemen.

VEILING

Veiling depends to some degree on the place and occasion. Some women reject the veil, and some women in the Socialist south did not cover their heads for a period and wore Western clothing. Since unification, an imported conservatism has prevailed. In the early twenty-first century, most women adopt some head covering according to social dictates. A woman may choose not to veil in some circumstances, such as her workplace, but choose to in others, such as while riding public transportation or at the marketplace. Young girls often embrace the *lithmah* (face veil) and sharshaf as a sign of adulthood.

There are four main types of face veils. The burqa is used by some nomadic women and covers the face except the eyes; it is similar to the *niqab*. The lithmah is wrapped around the forehead and lower face, leaving the eyes and part of the nose uncovered. The *maghmug* is a translucent rectangle of cloth draped from the head, covering the entire face, including the eyes. This distinctive veil is red with large black and white circles; it is worn by married women in Sana'a. The *khunna* is similar to the maghmug but is made of plain cloth.

Not all nomadic women wear face veils. Women of the Hashid tribe, for example, who live in about fifty villages north of Sana'a, do not veil. Hashid women have very long hair and cover it with a scarf that is secured with a twist of cloth or a silver head circlet. In contrast, in the south, some women wear up to three face veils, including the wrapped lithmah that exposes the eyes.

In 1965, use of the face veil was disappearing among Arab urban women but continued to be required in public in Sana'a. In the 1970s, a small number of women began to attend high school and university without a face covering. The use of face veils, especially by urban women, was, however, increasing by the end of the twentieth century.

MODERNIZATION

Modernization of dress arrived quite late in Yemen in comparison to other parts of the Arabian Peninsula. There are four clear stages in this process. In the nineteenth century, traditional dresses were usually slim fitting and were decorated with a natural-color braid and silver metallic-thread braid applied to bluish-black indigo hand-dyed cotton. Flat metallic wire was a popular form of embellishment, seen also on veils and masks from the Hijaz and 'Asir regions of western Saudi Arabia. There may be red and green embroidery between the silver braid around the neckline, cuffs, and bars over the shoulders. The slim shape of the garments drew attention to the shape and form of the design elements. The hemline was edged with natural, silver, red, green, yellow, and metallic gold braid.

Two men wearing imitation Kashmiri wool shawls (*sumatah*) wound into turbans, Sana'a, Yemen, 2007. They also both wear Euro-American jackets. Under the jacket, the one on the left, with a wide belt supporting his dagger (*jambiya*), wears a *thob*, while the other wears a Euro-American shirt with a length of cloth wrapped sarong style (*futa*). Richard Harris Photography.

The sewing machine led to the second stage in the late nineteenth century. Old patterns and shapes remained, but seams were machine stitched. Embroidery was done by hand for a time, but this was replaced by machine embroidery or pre-embroidered textiles. Revitalized trade with India in the early twentieth century brought about the third stage. Ready-made wide-legged, machine-embroidered pantaloons replaced sirwal, the face veil became the red-and-black maghmug, and the handwoven mantle, *milaya*, was replaced by the sitarah.

The fourth stage was the arrival of the sharshaf in the 1970s, worn over indoor clothing when leaving the home. The sharshaf was slowly replaced by the balto, and, in the early twenty-first century, the balto is being replaced by the *abayeh* (a sleeveless outer garment), because abayeh cloth is lighter in weight. Made from drapey fabric, it is more elegant and feminine than the tailored balto and cut more like a wide gown than the loose abayehs of Saudi Arabia.

MEN'S DRESS

Status is based on a hierarchy of occupations that places those with knowledge of religious law and those with power at the top.

Three men photographed in the medina of Sana'a, Yemen, 2007. The men on the left and right wear shawls around their necks, and the man on the right also has an imitation Kashmiri wool shawl (*sumatah*) as a turban. The man on the left wears a cotton head cloth (*ghutra*) wound into a turban, probably over a stiff cap (*imamah*). The man in the center also wears a *ghutra* but without the undercap. He and the man on the right wear belts to support their daggers (*jambiyas*). They all wear Euro-American jackets over their *thobs*. Richard Harris Photography.

At the lower end are the least honorable professions, which include service or handling unclean matter. Yemenis believe a man should dress according to his station so that appropriate respect is paid. Though not mandatory, informal social control frowns upon dressing above or below one's station. The style of clothing might be very similar, but the quality of the accessories and the cloth, as well as the way various pieces are tied and draped, are indicators of class. Class is also determined by whether a man hails from a learned tradition or claims tribal origin. Headgear and daggers hold particular significance.

Typical headwear for the urban literate is the *imamah*, a stiff cap frame around which a cloth is wound turban style. Called a *ghutra*, *shaal*, or *ihram*, this head covering may also be draped and held in place with an *'aqal* (head rope). *Sumatah*, imitation embroidered Kashmiri shawls, are very popular as turbans and are available in a variety of colors. A Meccan head cloth (*keffiyeh*) covered with red, green, or yellow patchwork is more formal headgear. Tribesmen and merchants often wear a *qub* (indigo-dyed cotton turban) wound around a small cotton sweat cap. Men are increasingly going bareheaded, and this may indicate a shift in gender relations from relative equivalence to more perceived distinctions between the roles of men and women.

No man is considered dressed without an elaborately decorated belt to carry his *jambiya* (curved dagger). The belt is wide and strong with a lining, pockets, woven metal-thread work, and decorative silver pieces. There are two types of jambiyas. The *asib* is a J-shaped dagger used by tribal men, and it has a bone or wood handle. It is carried in a leather sheath covered with narrow strips of dyed leather, often in bright blue. The *thumah* is a slightly curved dagger carried by men from a literate tradition and has a silver filigree hilt. It is carried in an embroidered case and worn on an elaborate belt of woven or embroidered cloth. Boys receive a dagger at about age fourteen as a sign of having reached manhood. Traditionally, it is considered a symbol of fertility. Traditionally, the location where a jambiya was worn also indicated social rank; the highest class wore it to the right; the middle class to the middle; and the lowest class to the left. In the early twenty-first century, most men wear it in the middle.

Sana'a men wear the traditional full-length *thob* or *dishdasha* that is similar to men's clothing in the rest of the Arabian Peninsula. Resembling a long shirt, it has simple, straight sleeves and side panels widening toward the hem. Cotton or a cotton-silk blend is preferred for summer and light wool for winter. Braid piping or soutache trim may be added. The thob is often worn with a Western-style suit jacket, a fashion that was adopted in the early twentieth century.

The formal men's outer garment is the *bisht* or *mishlah*, a large cloak draped from the shoulders in neutral colors such as cream, beige, brown, or black. Gold embroidery decorates the neckline band, and it has small tasseled tie cords. The bisht opens in front for easy access to daggers and firearms. A sleeveless cloak is the *aba* or *zibun*, which is worn more by nomadic Bedouin.

In the hotter western coastal regions, men will often wear a hip wrap, or *futa*, a long length of cotton cloth that is wound, sarong style, around the body a few times with the excess pleated and tucked at the waist. Qara tribesmen wear two futas—one wrapped around their waist and a slightly more elaborate form draped over their left shoulder—and they wear a looped leather girdle and leather shoulder bag. The futa is usually worn with a Western-style shirt.

Situated on the Red Sea, Hodeida is Yemen's fourth-largest city. The men have long worn a flaring top with tight-knitted sleeves and a jacket with tan and brown stripes. The lower half of this outfit is the *serul*, a long strip of white cotton that is wrapped and tied to form short breeches with a pocket to hold a knife. This is worn with a draped white cotton turban.

In cooler areas, men will wear a fur coat with colorful leather appliqué work. A short fur-lined jacket called a *gossera* is worn in the mountain region with the fur to the inside. The coat is sleeveless and has colored trim at the waist and on the collar. It is closed with leather buttons and loops.

THE JEWS OF YEMEN

Prior to World War II (1939–1945), Jews formed a sizable minority in Yemen. Most (about fifty thousand) migrated to Israel following the formation of the State of Israel, and only a few hundred remain in the early twenty-first century, mostly in Sana'a. Skilled in various crafts, they were primarily silversmiths and tablet weavers.

Only Jewish women wore black *antari* dresses for leisure and could be identified at a distance because of this. The antari was made from imported cotton sateen and was a long-sleeved, calf-length dress worn over a white undergarment called a *tahtani*. Although the cut remained consistent, personal differences were expressed in the length and width of embroidery around the neck slit at the center front. Silver buttons down the front were decorative, and a placket behind the slit ensured modesty. The lining on some dresses was stitched to the garment to form a left-side pocket for carrying small items. Other small pockets might be found at the end of the neck slit to hold amulets.

In northwestern Yemen, the wedding gown was called *zibun mesater* and was provided by the groom and the bride's father. After the wedding, it was worn for holidays and special occasions. The gown was lavishly embroidered in asymmetric designs in bright colors. Another important festive dress was the *lulwi*, which was worn on only three occasions in a Jewish woman's life. Loaned to a new mother by a senior family member, she would wear it on the first Sabbath after giving birth. Later, she would make her own for attending synagogue on the eve of Yom Kippur. Finally, she would be buried in her lulwi.

When in public, a married woman wore a square scarf (*lefhah*) over her hood (*gargush*) and would use it to cover her face when she encountered a man. The scarves were imported from Italy or India and especially commissioned for Yemeni Jewish women. The lefhah was sometimes tied around the belly of pregnant Muslim women in the belief that the special powers attributed to the Jews would protect the mother and her unborn child.

YEMEN IN THE EARLY TWENTY-FIRST CENTURY

Like much of Southwest Asia, Yemen is undergoing rapid change. Closed for hundreds of years to Europe and the United States, it is struggling to enter world trade markets. Conservative Islam's dominance and Yemen's relative lack of Western influence have preserved ancient modes of dress that are just beginning to change. This increased global interaction has impacted clothing traditions, and machine-made garments with machine embroidery are a pale reflection of the gorgeous handwork of the past. Religious booklets, often written and published in Saudi Arabia, call for traditional dress—including the face veil and a rejection of foreign intrusion in dress—but Western-style garments are increasingly available for both genders and are commonly seen on young people.

Gender differences in clothing ornamentation are more marked than they were in the past. Until the mid-twentieth century, similar rules of modesty applied to men's and women's dress, and nearly all wore some sort of head covering. In the early twenty-first century, urban women's dress is rarely ostentatious and is generally hidden when out of the home. Men continue to wear the thob and a Western-style jacket with the ever-present jambiya.

References and Further Reading

Kennett, Frances. *World Dress*. London: Mitch Beazley, 1994.

Mauriéres, Arnaud, Phillippe Chambon, and Eric Ossart. *Reines de Saba* [Queens of Sheba]. Aix-en-Provence, France: Édisud, 2003.

Muchawsky-Schapper, Ester. *The Jews of Yemen: Highlights of the Israel Collection*. Jerusalem: Hamakor Printing House, 1994.

Ross, Heather Colyer. *The Art of Arabian Costume: A Saudi Arabian Profile*. London: Empire Publishing Service/Players Press, 1984.

Scarce, Jennifer. *Women's Costume of the Near and Middle East*. London: Unwin Hyman, 1987.

Serjeant, R.B., and Ronald Lewcock. *Sana: An Arabian Islamic City*. London: World of Islam Festival Trust, 1983.

Tilke, Max. *Folk Costumes from East Europe, Africa and Asia*. London: A. Zimmer, 1978.

Wilcox, R. Turner. *Folk and Festival Costume of the World*. New York: Charles Scribner's Sons, 1965.

Christina Lindholm

See also Bedouin Jewelry; Saudi Arabian Dress; Omani Dress.

Omani Dress

The technology of the modern age is widely available to all in the Sultanate of Oman and the neighboring countries of Saudi Arabia, the United Arab Emirates, Kuwait, Qatar, and Bahrain. It has touched the local culture on many levels, and in many of these countries, regional dress is vanishing from the landscape.

The English-speaking travelers of the past referred to Oman as the hidden corner of Arabia. Hidden, perhaps, but one could argue that this was true only from the perspective of those travelers. Oman was and remains well known to its neighbors. It has an elaborate and rich history in the region, and the striking similarities to Oman's neighbors that are found in dress throughout the country suggest that Oman has experienced many cultural, trade, and economic friendships over the centuries, which have left their mark. Very little scholarly work has been carried out on its history. Only in the early twenty-first century is attention being paid to the origins and history of Oman's traditional dress.

MEN'S DRESS

In Oman, men's dress has received little attention, and most people presume there is only one basic style worn by Omani men, the so-called national dress. Although men's dress is very similar throughout the country in the early twenty-first century, this has not always been the case. Men's dress is based on three elements: an undergarment or hip wrap (*wizar*), a long gown (*dishdasha*), and headgear.

The wizar was traditionally woven in Oman but by the end of the twentieth century was being imported from India, where it is called a *lungi*. It is a white cotton cloth that measures approximately five feet by three feet (1.6 meters by 1 meter) and has colorful selvage stripes. Both raw edges are frayed to give a fringed effect. In the city of Sur, located in Oman's eastern region of AlSharqiya, pit-loom weavers of the early twentieth century wove the wizar on their looms using a variety of colored silken threads. In 2008, a handwoven wizar produced in Sur cost more than US$70, whereas imports from India cost roughly US$4.

In the Dhofar region in the south of Oman, men tend to wear a dark-colored wizar, which is also heavier and thicker because of the cooler climate there. There, the wizar has also been found with silver *zari* (a metallic, colored thread) woven in, which is unusual. Throughout all of Oman, however, the white cotton wizar is widely used. Similar hip wraps are worn by men in the more southwesterly regions of Saudi Arabia (especially the Aziz region) and throughout Yemen. All of these regions have strong cultural and economic links with India.

The main element of an Omani man's wardrobe is the dishdasha, which is worn both indoors and outdoors. This is a very loose-fitting garment, with long sleeves, no collar, a tassel hanging down from the neckline, and a front slit for an opening. Over the years one pocket, located on the right along the seam, has been added. It appears that this basic style of garment has been used in Oman for hundreds of years, and similar garments are worn by men throughout the Arabian Peninsula; they have been given various names, such as dishdasha and *thob*.

There are at least three different styles of men's dishdashas from Oman. The most popular form is the national-dress style, referred to as the *Omani style* of dishdasha. Second, there is a style that is referred to as the *Dhahirrah dishdasha* or *Buraimi dishdasha*. This particular garment is identical to the dishdasha worn in the Emirates (*Emirati dishdasha*): It is collarless, with narrower sleeves than the Omani style, slightly different cut lines and, as a result, different top stitching, and cloth buttons along the front slit opening. The front opening is adorned by an extremely long tassel in the Emirates but not in Oman. The third style of dishdasha is very similar to the Saudi thob in that it has a stand-up collar. This last style is not often seen in Oman, whereas the Dhahirrah/Buraimi style is often found, particularly in the areas after which it is named. However, the traditional Omani dishdasha is the most common version, regardless of the wearer's tribe, region, city, and personal wealth.

Traditionally, in different parts of Oman, men's dishdashas were dyed various colors depending on the plant dye sources that were available locally. At the beginning of the twenty-first century, dishdashas for official business, ceremonies, and celebrations remain white, but for leisure many men choose to wear a wide variety of colors derived from synthetic dyes, most of which are earth tones, shades of gray, or pastel colors such as light green or lavender.

The current Omani style is normally made from a lightweight synthetic fabric, which is often silky and flowing. In contrast, modern Dhahirrah/Buraimi-style dishdashas are often made from a heavy, thick, white fabric that appears to be heavily starched, although not everyone chooses this heavy fabric.

The dishdasha from the city of Sur is one of the few exceptions to the traditional look of an Omani dishdasha, with emphasis on the word *look*. Technically speaking, it is cut and assembled in exactly the same manner as the Omani-style dishdasha. However, as a result of decoration using elaborate hand embroidery, the final look of the dishdasha is unique. The embroidery gives it a fuller, more flowing appearance, which is emphasized by the many gathers at the shoulders of the garment at the front and back. These gathers are decorated with tight embroidery work (a form of smocking). Given Sur's maritime history, sailors likely adopted these gathers to give them more maneuverability while working.

Men's traditional dress has changed over the years. The Suri style is being worn less and less and is mostly reserved for ceremonies and celebrations in the early twenty-first century. It has been replaced by a dishdasha in the traditional cut, which is embellished with modern machine embroidery and lacks any Suri embroidery. The increase in the use of the non-Suri style could have an economic motivation, as it is cheaper to produce. However, the local people usually say that the men simply wanted a change of style.

In addition to the Suri style of embroidery, other forms of decoration are also used to embellish Omani dishdashas. Although no longer seen outside of a specialist collection, dishdashas with elaborate hand-embroidered designs in bright-colored yarns were once popular. These embroidered panels ran down the center front of the garment. Some cities used to use red and black fabrics rather than white ones as the canvas for their embroidery work. Bright-colored tasseling is another form of embellishment that is no longer used for the male dishdasha.

The traditional dishdashas worn by Bedouin men used to be elaborately embroidered (more so than the women's version),

with embroidery running all the way around the neck, down both sides of the front opening, extending past the bottom edge of the front opening, across the back between the shoulder blades, and around both sleeve cuffs. This embroidery is quite different from non-Bedouin styles in that the stitching primarily used silver zari thread and dark-colored silken thread, black and red being the favorites. Unlike the Suri work, which also uses zari, the Bedouin stitches do not form any smocking.

In the early twenty-first century, the most common form of decoration is machine embroidery around the cuffs of the sleeves, across the back between the shoulders, parallel to the front opening, and around the neckline. What is changing is the use of color and the type of embroidered stitch. A single row of stitching is called a track, and a single track used to be the norm. In the early twenty-first century, there are as many as three tracks, and what

An Omani man wearing a typical combination of an Omani gown and turban, Nizwa, Oman, 2004.
Photograph by Gillian Vogelsang-Eastwood. Textile Research Centre, Leiden.

was once a white satin stitch has been replaced by colorful and fancy machine-embroidered designs.

Whereas the headdress worn by men throughout other Gulf states consists of a small cap, a head cloth, and a head rope ('aqal), the Omani styles of headdress are distinct. In Oman there are two forms of headdress: *massar* and *kuma*. A massar is a large, fine woolen cloth that is embroidered. It is wrapped as a turban around a man's head, leaving his ears and the whole of his neck exposed (unlike headdresses in neighboring areas, which cover the ears and neck). Some men, however, like to create their own style and so tie it only partially, leaving a long tail hanging down, which sometimes covers a portion of their neck. This head cloth is worn for official business as well as ceremonies and celebrations. Men in Oman and Yemen, as well as a small group in India, wear this kind of massar. In Yemen, it is often used as a shoulder mantle.

Good-quality massars usually come from Kashmir and are elaborately embroidered. Lower-quality woolen examples have poorer-quality embroidered work. Some men do use the red-and-white checked cloth seen throughout Arabia instead of a wool cloth but still tie it like a massar. In fact, the 'aqal, a black rope derived from the leather straps used to bind camels' feet that is used throughout the Arab states, is rarely used in Oman, but for those men who do use it, the cloth is still tied like an Omani massar and does not veil the head as the cloths do when others wear the 'aqal.

For casual wear, many men forgo the massar, especially in the more urban areas, and wear a simple kuma instead. The kuma is a cap that sits atop a man's head and is heavily embroidered with colorful buttonhole stitching and small running stitches. Between the running stitches, narrow channels are created that are sometimes filled with white thread, which adds depth to the design. The kuma was brought to Oman from Zanzibar over two hundred years ago when the sultan ruling Zanzibar and the sultan ruling Muscat and Oman came from the same family.

In 2008, a kuma could cost well over US$300 for a hand-worked piece and as little as US$10 for a machine-embroidered example. Modern (cheaper) examples are often imported from the Philippines. In the early twenty-first century, more fashion-conscious men color-coordinate their massar and kuma with their dishdashas.

THE MAIN ELEMENTS OF WOMEN'S DRESS

Omani women's dress is much more complicated than its male counterpart, and this complexity helps to indicate a woman's place of origin. It is important to understand the various elements of women's dress. Like the men, women wear a dishdasha; unlike the men's form, however, the female version extends to below the knees or just above the ankles, depending on where the woman lives. The dishdasha is worn over a pair of trousers (*sirwal*), which traditionally served as the undergarment. The traditional construction of the female dishdasha is almost identical to that of the male dishdasha. Some women's dishdashas have been found with tassels, but none have pockets. White has never been a popular color among women as it has among the men. In some areas an alternative to the dishdasha is worn that is called by various names, including *thob*, *abuthail*, *jalabia*, and *kendora*. It is a kind of dress that normally extends to the ankles, if not to the floor. Traditionally, women did not wear sirwal with this garment, but

more and more women are beginning to do so because of social and religious pressures.

All Omani women wear a head covering of one kind or another, with the choice of style depending on the type of body garments worn. There are various forms, including the *lahaf* or *shaylah*, *waqaya*, and *kanga*. The lahaf, or shaylah as it is also called in some areas, is perhaps the simplest. Rectangular in shape, its size varies depending on the size of the woman for whom it is made, but it averages two yards by one yard (two meters by one meter). Typically, it is long enough to wrap one and a half times around the face, starting at the jawline on one side of the face and stopping at the jawline on the other side. It is wide enough to reach from the top of the forehead to halfway down the back. In the early twenty-first century, women tend to color-coordinate their head covering with the other garments being worn, if they are not made from the very same fabric. When outside, for example, women commonly wear a black head covering to match their black body covering, although colored lahafs are becoming more and more common.

In the twentieth century, the waqaya was more commonly worn throughout Oman than it is in the early twenty-first century. It is larger than the lahaf/shaylah, reaching to the waist at the sides and back. Traditionally, the waqaya was made from printed cotton that contrasted with the other garments worn, but in the early twenty-first century, synthetics have largely replaced the cotton textiles, and the color of the waqaya, as for the lahaf/shaylah, is coordinated with the other clothes being worn. The distinctive feature of the waqaya compared to the other head coverings are the fringed edges made using multicolored yarns. Another more decorative form of fringing is the *hatheeya*. There are two kinds of hatheeya, which are made on very different looms. The smaller type has a narrow woven band with a fringe along one edge. The other type is a band with no fringes that comes in a variety of widths. In the early twenty-first century, a waqaya, especially for formal events, sometimes incorporates very elaborate fringes made from metallic zari threads and even beadwork.

Like the men's kuma, the kanga worn by women came to Oman from Zanzibar. The kanga is a large, printed cotton cloth that has a wide border, a picture in the center, and a geometric or sometimes a solid-colored background; it used to have a saying in Swahili printed along its long edge. Traditionally, the kanga was used in Oman as an outer covering, draped over the waqaya, when women left their homes. It remained draped around the face, hanging straight down at the sides, and was never wrapped around the head as it is frequently worn in the early twenty-first century.

In addition, two kangas could be joined together (removing the border from the seamed edges) and a fringe (hatheeya) was then added, creating a formal outer garment called *shaylah* (not the same garment as the head covering by the same name). This large shaylah does not replace a proper head covering. Its use is strictly as an outer covering, and it is worn over a lahaf or waqaya. Since the end of the twentieth century, these large shaylahs have been losing their popularity with the increasing use of the black *abayeh*, a nontraditional black cloak borrowed from Bahraini dress and worn throughout the Gulf states, even though shaylahs are being made from a variety of textiles. Although kangas were used to convey printed messages in their place of origin, to date there is no evidence that they have ever been used for that purpose in Oman. In fact, many of the kangas on the market in Oman in the early twenty-first century are produced without sayings. They are printed in China, made of synthetics, and are commonly worn only as a head covering, not as an outer covering. A kanga is often referred to as a *lahaf*, a rather loosely used term.

The most common form of outer covering worn by women throughout Oman is the *ghabah*, a black dresslike garment made out of soft cotton mesh, which is extended into a head covering by Suri women. The women who wear the ghabah in the AlSharqiya region, in northern and central Oman, wear a separate head covering without a fringe, such as a lahaf or shaylah. In this region, the ghabah does not have embroidery.

Jewelry is an important part of women's dress. Unlike the jewelry of their Indian neighbors, which often produces sound, Omani designs are traditionally made of silver: large, bulky, heavy, highly ornate necklaces threaded on thick rope, earrings suspended by chains, and a ring for every finger. An Omani woman is not considered to be fully dressed without her jewelry.

REGIONAL VARIATION IN WOMEN'S DRESS: NORTHERN OMAN

The northern areas of the country include the regions of Musandam, AlBatinah, AlSharqiya, AlDhahirrah, AlDhakhliya, and Muscat. Here, women can be found wearing a dishdasha (knee-length dress), sirwal (trousers), and a head covering, usually a waqaya or lahaf. Within this simple outfit, the choice of fabrics used and the embellishments on the garments distinguish the regions from one another; individual cities and even small villages can have their own forms. This three-piece outfit is not the only style worn by the women in these areas, but it is the main combination.

The women's dishdasha is commonly made from voile. The fabric is usually dark in color, with a printed design that is often quite large. It is never made from a plain material in a pastel or bright color. Occasionally, fabric is used that has a bright-colored pattern on top of a darker, more muted color. The dishdasha is usually decorated around the wrists and hemline. Dishdashas for special occasions usually have an embellished neckline and front opening as well. In addition, a band or sashing is commonly added to the hem. This sashing is usually made of purple satin.

The sirwal worn with the dishdasha are made from printed cottons for casual wear and colorful satins for festive moments. When satin is used for the sirwal, the fabric for the dishdasha is generally also upgraded from voile/cotton to satin. However, it is perfectly acceptable to remain with voile and cotton and to simply embellish the dishdasha to a greater extent with lavish laces. The same is true for the sirwal.

In Sur, as for the men's dishdasha, the women's dishdasha is completely different from that worn elsewhere in northern Oman. The first difference is that it is made from Indian silks and never voiles. The silks worn in the twenty-first century are usually silk brocades, and any color seems to be welcome. However, silks worn in the past tended to be striped. The popular colors were red, orange, yellow, and black; occasionally, all four could be found on the same fabric. The Suri dishdasha is also different because it is embellished only on the sleeve cuffs. There is no purple sashing at the bottom or added lace of any kind. The embellishment on the cuffs is a very intricate hand embroidery with silver-colored threads, sometimes a touch of gold thread, or

the addition of some colored silk thread. Occasionally, a tassel made of silver thread may be found on a woman's dishdasha, but this is uncommon.

Traditional Suri sirwal are made from a striped cotton-and-silk blend from India. In the early twentieth century, it was fashionable to use black cotton cloth with white pinstripes for both the dishdasha and sirwal. Later, women started to prefer silk-cotton blends. By the beginning of the twenty-first century, a combination of black and white pinstripes plus modern multicolored textiles was being used. Suri sirwal are usually embellished at the ankle cuffs with hand embroidery, using silver metallic thread as the primary color. Sometimes a hint of dark silk thread is found within the embroidery.

With regard to headgear, the women of Sur once again break from the norm and do not use a waqaya to cover their hair. In fact, they do not use the typical head covering at all when dressed in their traditional garments. The women of Sur often wear a ghabah that acts as both a head covering and an outer covering. It has a span of about two yards (two meters) and extends down to the floor. It has extremely long sleeves and very large sleeve openings, which extend as far down as the knees of the wearer. These

Group of women at a women's market, Ibra, Oman, 2004. The women are wearing various forms of large printed cotton cloths (*kanga*), which are typical of those used in Ibra. The use of kangas in Oman originally comes from eastern Africa and Zanzibar, but many of those on the market in the early twenty-first century are printed in China, made of synthetics, and commonly worn only as a head covering. Photograph by Gillian Vogelsang-Eastwood. Textile Research Centre, Leiden.

unusually large openings allow the woman to gather them up, give them a half twist, and then anchor them on top of her head. This is then repeated on the other side. When these two sleeves are eventually anchored onto her head as two layers, they serve as a proper covering for her hair. Further, when the need arises, it takes but a gentle tug to pull these sleeves forward over the front of her face, forming a face veil.

On the chest of the ghabah, there is traditionally silver hand embroidery, which is very similar to a piece of jewelry Omani women wear called a *hirz*. A corresponding back panel has embroidery work as well. In the early twenty-first century, both panels are usually machine embroidered using a much more brilliant silver thread; the machine work covers a larger area on the chest than was traditional, and its design can be quite different from the hirz pattern associated with the handwork. Since the 1980s, the ghabah has been made of black cotton mesh. Prior to this, it was made from a striped silk with the primary colors yellow and red, with minimal hand embroidery. After the switch to black mesh, in the late 1980s and 1990s the trend moved to silk chiffon in vivid shades of pink, blue, and green, but at the end of the twentieth and beginning of the twenty-first century, there has been a return to the traditional black. The reason for this return is not known.

The combination of the dishdasha and sirwal with the waqaya or ghabah is not the only style of Omani dress worn in the north. In the far north of the country are the regions of Musandam and Batinah and the city of Buraimi. Here, the women wear a long dress with an outer covering. Some women refer to this combination as thob (dress) and kendora (outer covering), and others call it a kendora (dress) and *adela* (outer covering). This outer covering is cut very similarly to the ghabah of Sur, but it has a different name, is not nearly as wide as the Suri one, and is not used to cover the hair (instead, a lahaf is used). Normally, the outer covering is made of a similar, if not identical, material to that used for the dress underneath and is regarded as being part of the woman's dress; it is even embellished like the dress worn underneath.

Sirwal are also worn with the thob. Because the sirwal serve the same purpose as modern undergarments, they are not necessarily embroidered as in other regions of Oman. For celebrations, however, women do often choose to have coordinating sirwal made, and in these circumstances the fabric and the embroidery are normally the same as that used for the two-piece dress (jalabia/kendora).

This form of outfit includes considerable Khalij (Gulf) influence, which is why only Omani women whose lives are more closely linked with those of their Gulf neighbors generally wear it. In other words, this form of dress is not normally worn in the interior of Oman.

Omani national dress for women originated in the Al-Dhakhliya region and has been adopted in Muscat, the capital of Oman. The style is referred to simply as "Omani." An Omani-style dishdasha usually extends below the knee and sometimes as far as just above the ankle. It is unusual to see a dishdasha end above the knee. Indeed, depending on where one grows up, such a short length could actually be considered scandalous or as a mark against one's character and that of the family.

The embellishment of the Muscat/Omani dishdasha for a woman is often lavish. Like all the northern dishdashas, except those of Sur, there is sashing at the hemline. Traditionally, this band was purple, but in the early twenty-first century, any color is acceptable. It is usually made from satin regardless of the textile used for making the dishdasha itself. Just above the sashing is the actual hemline of the garment, and at this point there is more decoration in the form of applied lace. The form of this lace is a matter of personal choice, and the women are highly creative in the way they combine various bands of narrow lace to create a larger, more complicated design. Silver, gold, beads, sequins, and many other decorations are used, and a visit to a lace shop in the old suq (marketplace) is a spectacular event that is sure to overwhelm the visual senses.

The Omani dishdasha also has decoration on both the sleeve cuffs, around the neckline, and down the front opening, even extending below it. Paying particular attention to this area below the front opening, called a *shaq*, can help to identify where a woman is from. The Omani style, traditionally, has a very special kind of woven ribbon added, which is no more than four inches (ten centimeters) in length. In comparison to other laces, this ribbon is expensive; as a result, many modern examples tend to omit this woven ribbon.

REGIONAL VARIATION IN WOMEN'S DRESS: CENTRAL OMAN

In the central region of AlWusta, and some of the neighboring regions to the north of it (AlSharqiya, AlDhahirrah), the jalabia (a full-length dress) and lahaf (head covering) are worn with an outer covering, again called ghabah, as daily dress. The people of this region tend to be Bedouin, and they are the ones who commonly wear this style of dress. The colors red and green were generally used for all three pieces of clothing, but shades of brown, orange, and even aqua have been included more recently. But traditionally bright colors were never used. Sirwal are also worn, but it is not known whether that has always been the case for Bedouin women. Like the dishdasha ensemble worn by women in the north, this particular outfit is usually of printed fabrics. However, the sirwal are often made of plain material in dark colors.

In the early twenty-first century, the woman's jalabia is quite simple, full length, and loosely fitting, in a Western style, with long, set-in sleeves and a rounded or scalloped neckline. It is more than likely that this is a relatively modern innovation, but it is unclear what exactly was the more traditional style. It is reasonable to assume that it resembled the dishdasha from other regions of Oman. Jalabias for daily use are often made from cottons decorated with busy prints. Finer fabrics are chosen for special occasions. There is little or no decoration on everyday garments, but for ceremonies and celebrations the embellishments rise to the occasion with the addition of laces, crystals, and, traditionally, Bedouin embroidery.

The style of embroidery used by the Bedouin has some similarities to that in Sur, as well as the whole of AlSharqiya, since the same thread is used: a silver metallic thread with occasional use of colored silk. Red is a common color in Bedouin embroidery and is used with other silver metallic embroidery. The effect can be quite stunning. The embroidery work on the women's jalabias tends to be around the sleeve cuffs and quite simple. Other modern embellishments can be found around the neck as well.

The sirwal worn under the jalabia are normally quite plain. Over the jalabia a ghabah is worn. The modern style of the latter garment is quite different from the ghabah of Sur and the kendora/adela of Buraimi/Musandam. Nevertheless, the cut and color of the Bedouin ghabah hint at a similar origin: It is traditionally made from black cotton mesh, as in Sur, but it has only one sleeve, which is long and on the right side of the garment. Because this sleeve is not used to cover the hair (unlike its Suri counterpart), the sleeve opening is large but not as long as the Suri version. The embroidery of the Bedouin women's ghabah is usually done by machine. In design it resembles the hand-embroidered hirz from Sur. It is safe to presume that the Bedouin women once had hand embroidery on their ghabah as well and that it was probably very similar to that in Sur.

To cover their hair, the Bedouin women wear a lahaf that is a very soft piece of printed cotton. Again, various shades of red and green are traditionally favored. The women tie their lahaf in several ways. One of the ways is used to mask her face should a man appear when she is without her burqa, a form of face veil. Another style simply involves wrapping the lahaf around her head and face. This cloth is then covered by the burqa. However, not all Bedouin women feel the need to wear a burqa; it is normally a personal choice, and any influence to do so would generally come from mother to daughter.

Not all Bedouin women wear the jalabia with sirwal, the ghabah, and the lahaf. Whereas those in the desert areas tend to favor this ensemble, the Bedouin women who have settled in towns have started to wear the dishdasha, sirwal, and waqaya. In case it is not already obvious, there will always be exceptions to generalizations made about clothing.

REGIONAL VARIATION IN WOMEN'S DRESS: DHOFAR

In the south of Oman lies Dhofar. In this region the main garment worn by women is called an abuthail or Dhofari thob. Within Oman it is unique to the Dhofar area, although similar garments can be found in neighboring Yemen. The abuthail is generally worn with a shaylah or head covering. The abuthail is normally made from velvet, which provides some warmth during the cooler months; the back of the garment has a train that drags along the ground as if to dust away the woman's footprints. There is no consensus as to the reason for the train. The front of this garment comes to just above the wearer's ankles. It is the only women's garment in Oman that exposes the lower leg in this manner. It was not until the late 1970s and early 1980s that sirwal became a part of Dhofari dress. Interestingly enough, when sirwal did become widely used, white, a color that is little used elsewhere in Oman, became the favorite color for this garment.

Not all Dhofari thobs are made of velvet; thobs worn inside the house, for example, are generally made from printed cotton, together with a matching shaylah of the same fabric. In fact, the daily version sports a shorter train than the velvet form. The latter type is usually worn for special occasions. By shortening the train of the dress, movement throughout the day is made easier, and the garment stays clean longer.

A velvet abuthail normally has elaborate, traditional hand embroidery that embellishes the edges and the center front from the neckline to the hem. Bright-colored threads are worked into a geometric design on a bib that, at one point in time, was separate from the dress itself. As the dress wore out, the bib could be removed and attached to a new garment. A wide variety of patterns is also machine embroidered, with floral designs being the most

popular. Crystal embellishments to add some sparkle and shine are also popular. Unlike women's garments from the central and northern regions, the use of metallic thread on clothing in Dhofar is uncommon.

One other fabric that is specifically used for Dhofari dress is indigo-dyed cloth. These fabrics are not blue but rather lean toward maroon. However, the color left behind on one's skin is, indeed, blue. The staining of the skin is not regarded as a problem by the people of Dhofar nor the other Omanis who wear indigo-dyed items, such as face veils, since this staining is regarded as normal and beautiful. This cloth is used by the Jebali (mountain) people. The Jebali women's garment has the same cut as urban women's abuthail but is made of indigo-dyed cotton. The Jebali shaylah is of the same dyed cotton.

In addition to the outfits worn by the Jebali, there are also distinct forms worn by members of the Baluchi (originally from Pakistan) and Lawati tribes. Lawati women, for example, have an ensemble that is very similar to and often confused with the Omani style of dress: a dishdasha, sirwal, and lahaf. As modern designs come to the fore, it is becoming harder and harder to distinguish between the two. For example, the entire Lawati

Bedouin woman and children, central Oman, 2004. The woman is wearing clothing for indoors or for when in the presence of a male stranger. The girl is wearing a modern version of Bedouin dress, while the boy is in Western-style clothing. Photograph by Gillian Vogelsang-Eastwood. Textile Research Centre, Leiden.

ensemble used to be made using the same color of fabric, and the embellishments around the hemline and wrists were very wide bands of combined laces. The older Omani style was just the opposite, with narrow bands of lace embellishment and three different colors and fabrics. In the early twenty-first century, both styles employ the same color for all three garments within the ensemble, and the Omani lace embellishments can be as wide or as narrow as the wearer desires.

The Baluchi ensemble, unlike the Lawati one, has no comparison. This is a three-piece outfit consisting of a dishdasha, sirwal, and lahaf. However, their designs are quite different from those in other areas. Because of their roots in Baluchistan (Pakistan), the sirwal are in the so-called Punjabi style. Unlike the Omani style of sirwal, which is more fitted below the knee, the Punjabi style of sirwal worn by the Baluchis is very loosely fitted, and the bottom edge actually hangs down off the back of the foot and rests on the shoe or on the ground if one is barefoot.

The most commonly worn style of dishdasha is easily identified by its large pocket on the apron portion of the garment, though this is not the only style. Like other dishdashas, it is long sleeved, has a slit front opening, and extends past the knees, but the similarities end there. The Baluchi dishdasha is very full because of its numerous pleats on either side of the waist. The entire chest panel, as well as the large pocket, are heavily embroidered. In the early twenty-first century, this embroidery is done by machine, but it is still easy to find hand embroidery that is nothing short of stunning, as the Baluchis have their own designs, which began as ink-stamped designs originating in Pakistan. The head covering, or lahaf, for Baluchi women is also embroidered but usually on the ends, to coordinate with the other garments being worn. For casual dress it is not required that the three items match, but for special occasions the effort is made.

CHILDREN'S DRESS

Children normally wear similar garments to those of their same-sex parent. From two years of age, or even younger, up to the age of maturity, girls wear outfits made up of the sirwal and dishdasha also used by adult women. However, variations do appear in the form of head covering used. As a very young infant, a girl will wear a gown with a bonnetlike cap. Such caps usually have a long tassel that hangs down at the back.

A slightly older girl in the north (between three and six years of age) is likely to abandon the bonnet and wear the young girl's version of the waqaya. Like her mother's, this waqaya will have a fringe along both short ends. However, the young girl will not wrap it around her face as her mother does; instead, it rests on the top of her head (much like her mother's lahaf, when worn over the waqaya) and drapes down the back and both sides of her face. There is also a chin strap to keep the cloth securely in place. A young girl's waqaya also has decoration across the top and then on either side encircling her face. This decorative band is made from a piece of satin that is overlapped by several bands of lace. The band is usually several inches wide (about five to seven centimeters) and very ornate.

At around the age of seven, the girl starts to feel more like a young woman, and Omani culture tends to dictate that it is suitable for her to start wearing a proper waqaya, meaning one made like her mother's and thus lacking the panel of embellishment on the crown. Further, her waqaya will now be wrapped around her face and head rather than draping down. This will continue throughout her adult life.

In Sur, AlSharqiya, where the women do not wear a length of cloth for a head covering but, instead, the ghabah, the young girls wear a head covering very similar to a young girl's waqaya in the north. The Suri version is heavily embroidered along the entire edge that frames the girl's face. This embroidery is normally coordinated with the embroidery on her other garments, the dishdasha and sirwal. Because she is too young to wear the ghabah, the embroidery that would normally be on the ghabah is placed on the front of her dishdasha instead. Once she is old enough to wear a ghabah, her dishdasha will then be made plain on the chest and neck. Infant girls in Sur also wear a bonnetlike cap, just as the infants in the northern towns do. Again, silk being the favorite fabric of Suri women, the bonnet is also made of silk with some hand embroidery using silver metallic thread.

Traditionally, in the south of Oman, young girls do not wear any garment on their heads until they have nearly reached the age of puberty. Instead, they wear an elaborate piece of jewelry that crowns the head and hangs down all around, like a spider's web.

Boys are dressed to look like men from a very young age. As infants they sometimes wear a bonnetlike cap, but as soon as they are able to walk on their own, the bonnet is discarded and the kuma adopted. The kuma will remain a part of a boy's life, only to be traded for a massar. It is common for small boys to wear massars, especially for special occasions. Some shops actually sell massars for children. The older the boy gets, the more frequently he will wear the massar, remembering that the massar is part of business dress as well as formal dress.

FRAGRANCE

Perfume, or *attar*, is important for both women and men in Oman. While modern perfumes have been well received in the Omani market, the traditional fragrance *oud* is still popular. Oud (or oudh) is, quite simply, the bark of a dead tree, and oud oil is the extraction from the bark. The oil is very expensive because it comes only from a very specific kind of tree in Asia that is killed by a particular fungus. If and when the tree is attacked by the fungus, it can take up to three hundred years before the process is complete and the bark is worthy of collection for oud.

Oud is a very heavy fragrance; when it was brought to Arabia from India by an Arab traveler in the late 1950s, the people of the region did not have the same access to products such as soap as they do in the early twenty-first century. Body smells were regarded as a problem, hence the importance placed on the use of perfumes. While the smell of oud has changed since then, it remains a very heavy fragrance whose aroma develops over the course of several hours. The oud fragrance will literally last for days if not washed away.

Men and women both frequently use *bakhoor* (incense) to add scent to their clothing. It is customary for a hostess to present women guests with a tray of perfumes for their own use before they depart. At the same time, the bakhoor is brought out for their clothing. Grooming in general is very important to Omanis, who have for centuries been renowned for their hospitality. Part of extending hospitality is being presentable, so looking good on every level, including the visual, is just as important as the food being served and the kindness being extended.

Snapshot: The Abayeh in Oman

In the Sultanate of Oman in the early twenty-first century, traditional clothing is disappearing from the landscape. Many hold modernization accountable for this disappearance, and, to a large extent, this is true. Also disappearing, however, are the colors; Omani dress used to be one of the most colorful in the Arab world. The popularity of the *abayeh* (a long-sleeved, full-length women's outer covering, usually made of black crepe) has greatly narrowed the color palette for women, when in public, to a simple black.

It is common, and even traditional, for women to wear an outer covering. Since the early twentieth century, some women have been wearing an abayeh. Its popularity has increased over the years, and in the early twenty-first century, it is identifiable (visually, though often not by name) for many non-Arabs and non-Muslims around the world. These same people often have an intense interest, curiosity, and sometimes a negative perception about the abayeh, perhaps because of the apparent mystery that surrounds it.

During the approximately one hundred–year history of the abayeh in Oman, the design has changed from the *booy booy* (an abayeh from about the early twentieth century, which comes from Zanzibar) to the *abiyaat alros* (ca. 1950s-style abayeh worn in Muscat) and, finally, to the modern "fancy abayeh" (abayeh style from about the 1980s to the early twenty-first century, also worn in Muscat). Generally speaking, however, it remains a black outer covering worn for the sole purpose of covering clothing. It is usually worn only outside the house but is also kept on inside the house if visiting a male nonfamily member or in the company of male relatives within marrying status.

BOOY BOOY

One of the oldest outdoor garments for Omani women is the booy booy, which originated in Zanzibar. As part of Oman's rich historical ties with Zanzibar, the *kuma* (an embroidered cap worn by men and boys) and the booy booy abayeh for women are just two of the many results of this influence. The booy booy is unique and also complicated to wear. It is cut and sewn like a long cylinder, approximately the length of its owner's height, which the wearer must step into. One edge of the cylinder has a slit that allows the arms to extend outside the garment if need be; otherwise, the slit opening is held shut from within, by hand. On the same end as the slit, a flap is anchored to the edge of the booy booy opposite the slit. This serves as a veil later, once the abayeh is anchored.

To anchor the booy booy into place, the top edge of the abayeh (slit and veil flap) are brought forward from behind the head, up and over the top, and then tied around the head. Once anchored, a flap is flipped over the head from behind, thus concealing the wearer's face. Tightly clenching the slit opening, the wearer is now completely concealed.

This type of abayeh was made from either a plain, sat-inlike textured fabric or from velvet, but always black. The

booy booy is rarely seen in the early twenty-first century, but, when it is, women may use a black-on-black satin print. This black-on-black theme has also been used in the current abayeh trend but not yet with the abiyaat alros.

ABIYAAT ALROS

The abiyaat alros arrived on the scene by the 1950s, or perhaps a few years earlier. In Arabic, this name means "on top of the head," which is precisely where this abayeh is worn: on top of the head, draping down to the floor. It is strikingly similar to the Omani man's *bisht* (a wide outer covering that is open down the front, usually made of sheep or camel hair) in its cut, although the fabrics used are quite different. Both the bisht and abiyaat alros have a squared-off cut with a seam that runs horizontally through the garment, around knee level, which is used to adjust the length rather than adjusting for length at the hemline.

A model wearing an *abayeh* designed by Khadija bint Abdullah Al-Kunji at a fashion show in Muscat, Oman, 2003. The outside of the abayeh is made of black silk, but the lining is of the traditional red-striped cloth used in the Suri region of Oman. The abayeh thus reveals flashes of color when the wearer is walking. Courtesy of the Times of Oman.

The fabric used for the bisht is normally a wool or wool blend, but the abiyaat alros uses a shiny black crepe or a satiny fabric. The only adornment on the abiyaat alros is the optional addition of black scalloped lace on the front edges. This is quite different than the men's bisht, which has a wide embellishment of gold-thread embroidery along the edges around the neck and down the front of the chest.

Unlike the fancy abayeh worn in the early twenty-first century, the abiyaat alros does not have proper sleeves or a neckline. In fact, the center of the abiyaat alros is pulled up on top of the wearer's head and the garment drapes down the sides of her face. The abiyaat alros can also be worn across the shoulders, as men do with their bisht, but wearing it on top of the head is most common and the more traditional way. (A man will never wear his bisht on top of his head.) Wearing this abayeh on top of the head does not take the place of a proper head covering. Also, the abiyaat alros is the only type of abayeh that is anchored to the head.

Many have asked why the abayeh is black. There are many theories about this, one of which is that the abiyaat alros was styled after the men's bisht in not only design but also color. Consequently, all abayehs that have succeeded the abiyaat alros have also been black. Some have said that black is preferred because it makes the Arab women look fairer, which is a desired quality among many. Others say it is a slimming color, and still others say it is a modest color.

THE FANCY ABAYEH

The fancy abayeh appeared on the scene during the 1980s and was mostly worn in the north of the country. In the early twenty-first century, the central and interior regions have not wholly adopted it or any other abayeh style, though fancy abayehs can be found in Dhofar, in southern Oman. Whether in Dhofar or in the northern regions, it is unusual to find a woman wearing her traditional dress with a fancy abayeh because this abayeh has a narrow cut and the fuller traditional garments do not fit under it easily. With the abiyaat alros, however, traditional clothes are very easily worn.

Two countries are largely responsible for the way modern abayehs look: Bahrain and the United Arab Emirates. Bahrain is largely responsible for the design cut, whereas the United Arab Emirates takes the lead on embellishments for abayehs. In fact, even before the United Arab Emirates was embellishing the abayeh, Bahrain was busy designing them.

The current trend is to make abayehs from various grades of black crepe, normally lightweight. The most common style worn is referred to as the fancy abayeh by tailor shops because it has a center front opening. This is not always the case, however, as some also have side openings similar to double-breasted suit coats. All of the modern styles of abayehs have long sleeves and are floor length. It is rare to see someone wearing an abayeh of a color other than black; when it is seen, it is usually for fashion purposes. The fancy abayeh can be worn plain or highly decorated, the latter of which is gaining popularity.

See also Omani Dress; Snapshot: The Abayeh in Qatar.

References and Further Reading

AlHinai, Abdulrahman bin Ali. *Ceremonies and Celebrations of Oman.* Reading, UK: Garnet, 1999.
Croese, Jaap. *Oman A Pictorial Tour.* Dubai: Motivate, 2006.
Morris, Miranda, and Pauline Shelton. *Oman Adorned.* Muscat: Apex, 1997.
Richardson, Neil, and Marcia Dorr. *The Craft Heritage of Oman.* Dubai: Motivate, 2003.

Julia M. Al-Zadjali

See also Bedouin Jewelry; Saudi Arabian Dress; Yemeni Dress; Perfume and Incense; Face Veils.

Dress from the Gulf States: Bahrain, Kuwait, Qatar, United Arab Emirates

- Women's Clothing
- Men's Clothing

The *Khalij* (Arab Gulf) dress that is characteristic of Kuwait, Bahrain, Qatar, and the United Arab Emirates shares with Arab-Islamic dress in general a core underlying code, some aspects of form, and similar historical origins for the garments. Despite some cross-cultural and cross-ethnic similarities to world dress, certain symbolic and functional attributes and cultural nuances in usage and practices make Arab-Islamic clothing unique, as noted by F. El Guindi in 2003. At the same time, it shares certain universal functions and meanings with human clothing in general. Arab-Islamic dress serves in multiple ways, has various symbolic functions, and yields complex meanings in secular and religious settings, sacred and ordinary spaces. It communicates social standing, group identity, cultural values, gender, kinship relations, religion, cross-cultural influences, political resistance, and more. It can convey meaning at the material, symbolic, and sociocultural levels.

Various frameworks are used in studying dress, approaching it, for example, as part of the body, as J. C. Faris does; as material culture, in terms of theories of communication (for example, Joanne Eicher's work); or within the paradigm of language, as do N. Lindisfarne and B. Ingham, among others. In an earlier study of dress in Arab-Islamic culture, El Guindi developed an original orientation by building on insights gained from systematic ethnography and from field-gathered data on the Islamic movement that brought into focus two previously ignored qualities: First, dress must be considered a dynamic phenomenon rather than static material elements (this was particularly crucial for understanding the phenomenon of the veil), and, second, the study of both genders is essential to understanding the dress of either gender.

While it is definitely an Arab characteristic to mark gender by dress and dressing gestures, this aspect is quite dramatic in the Arab Gulf region in the twenty-first century. One immediately notices how the gendered world of Qatar, for example, consists of women (young and old) in black and men (young and old) in white. This salient pattern colors, as it were, first impressions and becomes a fixed image for many observers. Children's dress resembles that of their parents. It is quite striking to watch Qatari families in public places such as malls or airports: A little boy holding his father's hand looks exactly like him, just smaller in size. One sees little men and older men dressed identically, little women and mature women dressed identically. In other words, gender is the ultimate determinant of dress, superseding age, to the extent that it is often difficult to guess a young man's age if his build is similar to that of a mature man. This can be clearly observed on the university campus at Qatar University, for example. Male students can easily be taken for male professors on

a sartorial basis alone. By comparison, in a society such as the United States, dress marks age so characteristically that one is able to guess a young male's age just from the appearance and form of his clothing.

In general, both sexes cover their bodies from head to toe. Many women cover their faces as well. All do so confidently; many do so elegantly and with style and movement. Two features characterize Khalij dress: Dress is a gender-based leveler of status and class, and this gendered pattern transcends age and social and kinship status. Dress and its color clearly distinguish males and females from a very early age. Male youths may be fashionably wearing long hair these days, but their clothing is never unisex. It must be stressed that clothing for Arab and Muslim women and men cannot be reduced to a material element with utilitarian functions. It reflects a core code of privacy, functions to communicate status and identity, and, even when identical in form for both sexes, signals gender boundaries.

Both sexes wear long clothing with long sleeves and head coverings. But these clothing items have different meanings; they are of different colors and are layered differently for each sex. In addition to gender, dress details mark traditional status (such as urban dweller, village dweller, religious person, merchant, and so on), socioeconomic strata, ethnic identity, age transitions, and lifestyle differences. Within the Gulf region, there are differences in detail. Ritual occasions provide a backdrop for special garments that are also long with long sleeves but that differ in details and in rite-specific use. A deeper exploration of Khalij dress reveals a nuanced diversity of dress styles for both genders and dressing behaviors within genders. Differences also exist marking historical changes.

WOMEN'S CLOTHING

An important garment is the *abayeh*, which is a large piece of fabric that covers the body on all sides, reaching down to the ankles, with an opening in the front and two openings on the sides for easy removal. In the Gulf region, the abayeh comes in only one color: black. The fabric is usually silk with either a shiny or matte finish. It can also be made out of a cotton-polyester mix for increased lightness and ease of movement.

In Qatar and the Emirates, the abayeh is worn over the head. Both front ends are lifted and held by hand to reveal the color and shape of the clothes worn beneath. This dressing behavior is more characteristic of older women. In Kuwait and Bahrain, however, it is more customary to wear the abayeh over the head and let it fall to the ankles, thereby covering women's clothing entirely, revealing only the face and hands. The front is held closed by hand. Norms in those two countries permit women to leave their homes without wearing the abayeh, an act referred to as *sufur*, so that it is entirely a woman's choice to wear it. Women who ordinarily do not wear the abayeh might occasionally wear it for ritual situations such as expressing condolences (*'aza*) or brief shopping trips that do not require dressing up, thus serving the practical function of concealing their ordinary clothing. This use of the abayeh is quite common and is socially acceptable in Kuwait and Bahrain.

In all four Khalij countries, the abayeh for girls and young women would commonly have long, large sleeves that conceal the hands. The sleeve ends would be decorated with gold or colored thread or white or colored appliqué. The abayeh with wide sleeves is sometimes shaped like a long, wide modern dress with long sleeves and a buttoned front, but it can also be shaped to the woman's body, although still not fitting tightly. In Kuwait and Bahrain, it and the broad abayeh are worn over the head.

Specialized tailors make abayehs to order. These vary in price depending on the size, shape, decoration, and fabric. Some women from one Khalij country would have their abayehs custom made in another Khalij country because of a tailor's reputation. Well-known commercial abayeh tailors mark their abayehs and *shaylah*s (the head covering that complements the abayeh) by sewing labels on the lower ends.

When the wide abayeh with wide sleeves is worn over the shoulders, another piece of cloth is used to cover the hair, namely the shaylah. This is a long, rectangular black piece of fabric worn on the head. One end is longer than the other; the longer end is wrapped over the head and around the neck more than once and then left to fall loosely from one side of the head. In Kuwait, a woman often tucks the loose end beneath the wrapped part of the shaylah. Older women tend to wear simple black shaylahs without decoration, then cover them with their abayeh. Younger women tend to wear decorative shaylahs with the loose end beaded, appliquéd, or embroidered in colors that either contrast with or match the color of the abayeh worn. In the early twenty-first century, stores often sell a matching set of abayeh and shaylah. The shaylah is used often as face covering by drawing the long end, after wrapping it once around the head and neck, over the face toward the back of the head. In the past, a *milfah* was sometimes worn instead of the shaylah. This was a piece of cloth about six and a half feet (two meters) long that was wrapped around the head to cover the hair.

The *batullah* is a square mask that women wear over their faces, covering the eyebrows, nose, and cheeks, with two wide openings for the eyes. Short ones reveal the mouth and part of the cheeks, while long versions cover the entire face. After the

A Bahraini woman outside a polling station, Manama, 2006. Under her *abayeh*, she wears a gauze *bushiyah* that covers her face and chest. Karim Sahib/AFP/Getty Images.

shaylah is wrapped around the head, the batullah is placed over the face and tied in back using a string attached to the upper edge on both sides The batullah is worn in Qatar, Bahrain, and the Emirates but not in Kuwait. In Bahrain, it is worn only by Sunni Muslim women. The batullah is commonly a deep brownish gold color and lined on the inside with lightweight black fabric. Its use is slowly becoming confined to older women, as younger women wear it infrequently.

The *burqa* consists of a rectangular piece of black fabric about ten inches (twenty-five centimeters) long or slightly longer that is used as a face and forehead cover and falls to the neck. It is tied from the back with two ribbons. The burqa is made of two layers of fabric. The top layer falls over the face, covering it, but has two wide openings for the eyes held together by a thin black thread on the nose. The lower layer is light and has no openings for the eyes, but the fabric is fully transparent, allowing the woman to see. This is commonly worn by Badawi (Bedouin) women in Khalij societies, although some non-Badawi women also wear it in public places for anonymity and privacy. The *niqab* closely resembles the burqa, except that in all four Khalij countries the niqab does not have the thin thread over the nose bridging the two eye openings. Instead, it has one large opening extending from the outer end of one eye to the outer end of the other eye.

The *dirra'ah* (or *jalabia*) is a long dress with long, wide sleeves that is often made out of cotton or silk in different colors. In Qatar, Bahrain, and the Emirates, it is mostly worn at home for comfort. For a fast trip to the market or shopping, a woman often simply puts the abayeh over it. Women also wear it for a henna night before a wedding, when the bride and guests get henna, or at home when receiving guests. On the latter occasions, the dirra'ah would be made of colorful fabrics embroidered or beaded with shiny decorative elements indicative of joyful occasions.

Sirwal are wide pantaloons made of cotton that extend from the waist to the feet, allowing the woman to move without being subjected to exposure if she falls or her dress is lifted by the wind. They can be embroidered in different colors at the bottom end of the legs. Women in Kuwait have generally stopped wearing sirwal, but in Bahrain, Qatar, and the Emirates, older women still wear them along with the dirra'ah.

A traditional face covering that is only rarely worn by women in the early twenty-first century is the *bushiyah*. It is a long, rectangular piece of black transparent fabric, up to six and a half feet (two meters) long, that is worn over the head under the abayeh. It falls loosely over the face and covers the chest and the back down to the waist. It is commonly made of silk decorated with gold threads or embroidered black patterns. In Qatar, Bahrain, and the Emirates, it is often called *al-ghashwa*, meaning "cover," but it is not widely used in these societies. Interestingly, in Kuwait, where women generally do not cover their faces, the bushiyah is used on those occasions when women do cover their faces.

The *bukhnuq* is a length of cloth wrapped around the head and neck. The etymology of this word relates it to the word *khanq*, meaning "to strangle," which refers to the way this item is worn, namely wrapped tightly around the neck in a way that restricts air flow and ease of breathing. It consists of a piece of cloth that reaches to the abdomen at the front and to the feet at the back; the sides are sewn together leaving an opening the size of the face at the top. It is worn over the neck and head, covering all the hair so that only the short front strands of hair that are combed down the forehead (*ghurra* or *githla*) are revealed. In the past, young women used to wear the bukhnuq often but in the early twenty-first century, they wear it only on special ritual occasions such as the mid-Ramadan folk celebration known as Girgi'an, which still survives in a modified form.

The *thob* is a loose, wide dress made of lightweight transparent fabrics, such as cotton or silk, which is worn over a woman's other clothing in the home for modesty in the midst of her family. The thob is decorated with gold thread in patterns inspired by the natural environment. The armholes of the thob are very long, and the shoulders of the garment are placed over the head. This material is sufficient to cover the head, and it can be drawn across the face as well. The thob is used by conservative Khalij societies. In the early twenty-first century, it is disappearing from use and is worn mostly on special occasions such as the henna night before a wedding, when young women gather to dance. It is also worn on the occasion of the mid-Ramadan folk festival of Girgi'an or *garanga'u*. Some Bahraini women wear a thob in their homes that is made of lightweight cotton in different colors; it is called *al-mishmar*. The women pull its long armholes over their heads. It had been used in Qatar in the past.

Nafnuf refers to the garment that is worn as outer clothing in Kuwait and Bahrain. It is a long dress, in different colors and designs, with a front slit opening that is open to below the level of the breasts. The chest area is gathered, from where it drops loosely down to the feet. The word *nafnuf* was used in the past instead of the word *fustan* ("dress"). In the twenty-first century, however, *nafnuf* is used in Kuwait and Bahrain to refer to a particular type of dress used by young and mature women.

A *zakhma* (*al-shayyal*) provides support for the breasts equivalent to the bra that is used in the twenty-first century. In the past, this was made of cotton in different colors, but in the twenty-first century, Khalij women buy the familiar bras available in the world market in all their diversity in fabric, color, and form.

The *shalha* is a light, sleeveless, ankle-length chemise, made of lightweight cotton, and is worn beneath the nafnuf or fustan to provide an unattached lining. In the twenty-first century, it has been replaced by an inner shalha that is white and loose. In Kuwait, this inner shalha is referred to as *gumleg*.

Ni'al are a kind of sandal with exposed toes and heel, made of leather that in the past came in a range of colors and decorative designs. In the early twenty-first century, this sandal is mostly used at home and is made of plastic or artificial leather. It can be used for going outdoors only when decorated according to the local fashion, which makes it quite costly. When the ni'al have high heels, they are called *al-shahhata* in Kuwait and *al-jabaliyya* in Qatar and Bahrain. The *joti* are a kind of shoe that is closed in the front and back, with or without a heel. In the past, they were made from whatever leather was available and were custom made. In the early twenty-first century, these shoes are made commercially in the markets.

MEN'S CLOTHING

The main garment worn by men in the Gulf is the *thob*, which is also known as a *dishdasha* in Kuwait or a *kandoura* in the Emirates. In Qatar, the thob resembles a long-sleeved, ankle-length dress shirt. There, the sleeves are cuffed and secured by dress buttons or cuff links made of gold, precious stones, or diamonds. Sometimes, the cuffs are left open without buttoning. As to the neck, in both Qatar and Bahrain, the thob would have a collar not unlike that of the Western men's dress shirt. The Khalij thob has

Kuwaiti men arriving at a polling station to cast their votes in a parliamentary election, Kuwait City, 2009. They wear white and off-white *thobs* (long-sleeved, ankle-length dress shirts) with a square chest pocket on the left that is open at the top and *ghutras* (large head cloths). Yasser Al-Zayyat/AFP/Getty Images.

three pockets: one square chest pocket on the left that is open at the top and two slit pockets, one on each hip, that are approximately twelve inches (thirty centimeters) deep.

The kandoura of the Emirates has cotton buttons in the form of a small cotton thread ball used to close the neck opening. A rectangular cloth of the same fabric as the thob, called a *farroukha*, is attached to the inside by buttons, and its long end falls over the chest. It is worn this way when a man is going out. At home, he removes it so that it will not obstruct his movement, particularly when eating.

In all four countries, the thob is usually bright white or off-white but can be soft gray or blue, as in Kuwait and the Emirates. Light colors are worn in the summer, but in the winter darker colors such as brown, black, gray, or deep green are used. Its fabric is usually pure cotton or a cotton-polyester mix that makes the cloth easier to care for and renders it wrinkle-free. It could also be made of silk, which is more common in Kuwait. The winter thob is made of pure wool or wool blended with other fibers to create a lighter fabric suitable for a moderate climate.

In the winter, some men wear a short or long overcoat made of cotton, wool, or leather over the thob to add some warmth, particularly in Qatar, Bahrain, and the Emirates. Kuwait tends to have an additional item, namely the vest or *sudeiri*, which is shorter than the overcoat, has no sleeves, and is worn over the thob alone or underneath an overcoat. It is made of heavy wool or wool lined with fur.

The *gahfiyya* is a crochet skullcap used in Khalij society. It is worn directly on the head, underneath the *ghutra* (a large head cloth worn by men) and the *'aqal* (a black head rope). The gahfiyya is white and made of cotton and is held in place by the *taqiyeh* or skullcap. It comes in different designs and sizes. It can be worn reaching halfway down the forehead or only to the hairline in the front.

The ghutra is worn in all four Khalij societies. It is a big, square cloth folded into a triangle, which is placed on top of the head over the gahfiyya in such a way that one tip of the triangle falls down over the forehead. The two ends or angles of the triangle that fall on both sides of the chest are of equal length. There is, however, variation in how the ghutra is worn. Sometimes both ends are thrown over the top of the head, one end is thrown back to expose the ear, both are thrown back over the shoulder without exposing the neck or ears, or one side is thrown back onto the shoulder while the other remains over the chest. Much movement back and forth and manipulation of the ghutra is visible in any public moment. In the summer season, the ghutra is made of cotton and is bright white or sometimes a red-and-white checkered pattern. In wintertime, it is woven from soft, expensive wool in an off-white color with long, colored lines at the ends of the cloth. Some wear the same white ghutra for summer and winter.

In the Khalij societies, the 'aqal consists of a round black rope made of wool resembling a ring, which is twisted back on itself to create the impression of being two rings, one on top of the other. It is worn on the top of the head over the ghutra and gah-fiyya, keeping the ghutra in place. The open, untwisted segment of the two rings is worn toward the back of the head. Except in Kuwait, where the 'aqal is distinguished by having two thin ropes hanging down the back to waist level, where the rope end is decorated with several little tassels called *karkash*. Some wear the 'aqal somewhat angled to the side of the head.

The *bisht* is worn in all four Khalij countries and consists of an ankle-length, front-opening, abayeh-like garment that is large and flowing. It is placed over the shoulders on top of the ghutra and reaches to the bottom of the thob. It is made of cotton or wool. Often, the edges of the bisht's front opening are embroidered with wide gold thread all the way down to the bottom. In the Gulf there is little difference in the appearance of the bisht for summer and that for winter. The only difference is the use of cotton versus wool fabric. It is worn on various formal occasions such as weddings, the main Islamic holidays (the Eid al-Fitr and the Eid-e-Qorban), other official celebrations, and male dancing occasions such as a national holiday.

Sirwal are white pantaloons made of cotton that are wide in the seat and worn beneath the thob. These can be long, reaching to the feet, or short, reaching to just below the knee, to conceal the body when a white thob is worn since one can see through this thob in certain kinds of light. This is considered men's underwear. Khalij men do not wear other kinds of underwear.

A *wizar* consists of a rectangular cotton cloth in colored plaid patterns in different sizes. The wizar can reach a length of about ten feet (three meters) or longer and is wrapped around the waist, falling down to the feet. In Qatar, Bahrain, and Kuwait, this was worn in the past, while in the Emirates, men continue to wear the wizar but in a modified form that is easy to wear because it has a stretch belt attached to the upper part instead of being tied with a loose belt. This makes it easy to keep in place.

The *zinjafra* is a form of undergarment that covers the upper part of the body and functions like a T-shirt. The zinjafra is made of lightweight white cotton and can be short-sleeved or sleeveless. In Kuwait the zinjafra is referred to as a *fanilla*.

Ni'al are a form of sandal worn with the thob. They are made of leather of different kinds, such as ostrich, crocodile, and deer, and sometimes they come in various colors. They usually have an open toe and heel, but when these parts are closed, the sandal is called the joti. Ni'al are fabricated by Arab companies in countries with a long tradition in leatherwork. The sandals continue to be worn in the winter months, with socks that are the same color as the shoe and the thob. This color coordination is particularly evident in Kuwait.

References and Further Reading

al-Ghanim, K. "al-Azya' wal-Holiyy al-Taqlidiyya lil-Mar'a al-Qatariyya" [Dress forms and traditional jewelry of the Qatari woman]. *al-Ma'thurat al-Sha'biyya* [Folk Ways] 6 (1991): 7–21.

Eicher, J.B., ed. *Dress and Ethnicity: Change across Space and Time.* Ethnic Identities Series. Oxford and Washington, DC: Berg, 1995.

El Guindi, F. *Veil: Modesty, Privacy, and Resistance.* Oxford: Berg, 2003. (Originally published in 1999.)

El Guindi, F. "Djellaba." In *Encyclopedia of Clothing and Fashion*, edited by V. Steele. Detroit, MI: Charles Scribner's Sons, 2005.

El Guindi, F. "Hijab." In *Encyclopedia of Clothing and Fashion*, edited by V. Steele. Detroit, MI: Charles Scribner's Sons, 2005.

El Guindi, F. "Private Reflections." *International Journal of Middle East Studies* 39 (2007): 172–173.

Faris, J.C. *Nuba Personal Art.* Art and Society Series. London: Duckworth, 1972.

Lindisfarne, N., and B. Ingham, ed. *Languages of Dress in the Middle East.* London: Curzon (with SOAS), 1997.

Fadwa El Guindi and Wesam al-Othman

See also Arab Men's Dress in the Eastern Mediterranean; Saudi Arabian Dress; Yemeni Dress; Omani Dress; Snapshot: The Abayeh in Oman; Snapshot: The Abayeh in Qatar; Iranian Regional Dress.

U ntil the 1950s, Qatar was the poorest of all the Arab Gulf nations, its citizens eking out a subsistence living on fishing and pearl diving, but in the early twenty-first century, it enjoys the fifth-highest income per capita in the world. The discovery and exploitation of oil and natural gas in the mid-twentieth century catapulted this tiny nation into world prominence. The country is ruled by Sheikh Hamad bin Khalifa Al-Thani, a hereditary emir, considered one of the most liberal rulers in the Arabian Gulf region. All women are encouraged to pursue education as well as employment and are allowed to drive, vote, and hold public office. The emir's wife, Sheikha Mozah bint Nasser al Missned, holds public positions of leadership as the chairperson of influential educational and family-oriented foundations. At an international level, she is also a special envoy to UNESCO for basic and higher education. This enlightened leadership coupled with Qatar's vast wealth thrust the country into a new world of modernity and has created an atmosphere of modern thinking combined with pride in its national heritage that has allowed the abayeh to evolve into a contemporary garment worn with pride by most Qatari women. The wearing of the *abayeh*, a long cloaklike garment worn by women outside the home, and the *shaylah*, the head covering, is not legally enforced, and both garments can be modified and decorated by the individual. While many own and wear Western dress at home, women willingly retain abayehs as a sign of respect for their culture, heritage, family honor, and gendered place in society.

Knowledge of the history of Qatari dress is limited, since almost no pre-1950s garments survive. As in many poor societies, daily dress was worn out and discarded. Photographs of women before 2000 are almost nonexistent because traditional Arab women did not socialize outside the confines of their homes and would not have had occasion to meet any camera-bearing travelers. Travelers were very few until well into the latter half of the twentieth century. The few travelers who did visit and write about Qatar were men and so were not likely to have met any women. Economic conditions made it unlikely that locals would have owned many cameras, and there were certainly no photo studios. Once a Qatari female reached puberty, she was "covered" and often married, even as young as twelve or thirteen years old. From that point on, she would not interact with anyone but family members. The high illiteracy rate up until the late twentieth century ensured that the Qataris themselves have almost no early written historical records. Some special-occasion dresses dating from the mid-twentieth century have survived and are held by the Qatar Museum Authority, but these would have been worn only in the company of other women and never photographed.

THE ROLE OF HIJAB IN QATAR

Although a single Arabic word to describe all the items and styles is lacking, conservative Muslim dress has generally become known as *hijab*, literally translated as "to cover" or "to screen." Wearing hijab may entail covering the body completely, including the face and hands, or involve something as little as a small scarf tied around the hair. Much controversy has surrounded discussions of hijab, with supporters declaring that it provides comfort, modesty, and privacy in public. Fadwa El Guindi explains that it identifies hijab wearers as observant Muslims and that it allows them to interact with men on an equal basis. Opponents state that hijab is a sign of Muslim repression of women and should be discarded. Sheikha Mozah believes that women should be allowed to make their own choices in dress. While in Qatar, she wears the shaylah and abayeh but is often photographed in Europe or the United States wearing modest but highly fashionable Western dress, impeccable makeup, and a small covering of some sort over part of her hair. Tall, thin, and beautiful, she is a powerful role model, and her support of free choice in dress has led to a hybrid: the Qatari fashion abayeh and matching shaylah.

A generation ago, Qatari women were robed and veiled, seldom venturing outside the family enclave. In the early twenty-first century, they are pursuing higher education in ever-increasing numbers, traveling internationally, and operating their own businesses. Unlike in the neighboring Saudi Arabia, the United Arab Emirates, and Iran, the Qatari law that at the start of the twenty-first century still requires women to cover themselves is not legally enforced. However, due to social custom, national pride, and family pressure, virtually all Qatari women wear the abayeh and shaylah within the boundaries of Qatar and when traveling to another Gulf country. When venturing out of the Arabian Gulf, many choose to retain only the shaylah or some type of head covering and wear modest Western-style dress. A very few will completely dispense with both garments when outside of Qatar.

The Abayeh. The abayeh is a traditional Arab cloak that a person dons over his or her clothing when leaving the home or family enclave. Historically, the term *bisht* was used for the abayeh, but in the twenty-first century it generally refers to a ceremonial garment for men. The woman's cloak was referred to as a *daffah* and was a black garment covering her from head to foot. It was worn with a face veil (*niqab*) or mask (*batullah*).

Most Qatari females adopt the abayeh and shaylah at the onset of puberty. Younger girls may also wear an abayeh but more for play than as everyday dress. Girls' abayehs are generally inexpensive as they are quickly outgrown and not often worn. Unwanted abayehs are usually given away to less fortunate family members, maids, or sometimes the Red Crescent Society, the Arab equivalent of the Red Cross. People in Qatar are sufficiently wealthy for there to be no visible retail outlets for secondhand clothes.

The Shaylah. The shaylah is a long, rectangular piece of cloth that covers the head, passing under the chin and up over the top of the head. It is usually made from a lightweight, sheer fabric like silk or polyester chiffon or crepe de chine and may be plain or have various decorations, often matching the abayeh. The shaylah is occasionally worn over a very wide, stretchy headband to help anchor it in place. The way it is

An *abayeh* from Qatar, 2008. The *abayeh* is made from matching Saudi crepe (good-quality polyester crepe), piped with turquoise bias satin, and is decorated with embroidered and beaded butterflies. It opens asymmetrically at the left shoulder. The *shaylah* (head covering) is made from chiffon. Photograph by Lawrence Koltys.

worn communicates traditional observance—a woman who is very conservative will hide all her hair, her forehead, and her neck, whereas if she is more liberal, the woman will wear it loosely, back on her head, exposing some of her hair and even her ears. Qatari women seldom pin their shaylahs in place, preferring to adjust them as needed. The physical gesture of repositioning the shaylah may indicate mild flirtation, irritation, or discomfort and embarrassment.

Face Veils. A few women still completely cover their faces, using a mask or veil to completely obscure their identity. This may be accomplished by covering the face with a translucent fabric attached to a fitted head covering, which allows the woman to see out but not be recognized. Alternatively, a niqab (veil) is worn that leaves the eyes exposed but covers the rest of the face. A batullah (mask) is still worn by some older,

conservative women. This is usually of cotton cloth that is dyed with indigo and beaten to resemble a shiny metal. It is stiffened at the bridge of the nose and may leave the mouth as well as the eyes exposed. When touched, the dye easily comes off and colors the skin. Comparatively few young women use veils in the early twenty-first century, and virtually none wear a mask.

Under the Abayeh. Traditionally, women wore a loose, long-sleeved, floor-length dress called a *dirra'ah* at home. The dirra'ah is generally either cut with a *badan* (center panel) and *tinfayah* (side panels) in a T-shape or constructed as a closer-fitting garment with a waistline. The dirra'ah, also called *djelabiay* or *jalabia*, is often made of cotton with embroidery around the neck and cuffs. Twenty-first-century examples are usually made of a cotton-polyester blend with machine embroidery and are preferred by older women. Undergarments include the *shilhah*, a light, loose, sleeveless shift; the *sidiri*, a short shirt; and the *sirwal*, baggy trousers with embroidery around the ankle cuffs.

In the early twenty-first century, Euro-American clothing is common for most younger women. Jeans often peep out from under the abayeh hems, and new shopping malls offer clothing from many recognizable British and American chain stores. Frequent international travel and relative wealth allow for the acquisition of current fashion. Even Euro-American lingerie has largely replaced traditional underwear, with bras, panties, and thongs sold in modern mall stores.

CHANGES IN THE ABAYEH: FASHION IN QATAR

The daffah has undergone three stages of change reflecting political, social, and cultural developments in Qatar. In the 1950s and 1960s, as oil money increased trade opportunities, synthetic fabrics for abayehs, mainly from France and Japan, made their way into the *suq*s (local markets). Still black, they were much easier to care for than the older woolen cloaks. They retained their sheen, did not wrinkle, and had a lovely drape. By the 1990s, the daffah had undergone a change in silhouette, becoming much narrower, and in the early twenty-first century, it is referred to as an abayeh. This is a long-sleeved robe that covers the body from the neck to the floor and is worn with a shaylah in a matching or complementary color. The third change, starting after 2002, signaled the introduction of Qatari garments as fashion elements; instead of creating anonymity, the abayeh became a personal statement. Abayehs began to display unusual silhouettes and extravagant embellishment in the form of embroidery and appliqué as well as added color. This dramatic change resulted from the increased educational, travel, and career opportunities available to women. No longer secluded, the modern Qatari woman enjoys freedom of movement and has made her presence felt in public. The twenty-first-century abayeh has become a fashion garment that undergoes seasonal style changes in the same manner as Euro-American fashion.

The modern Qatari abayeh still performs the religious and cultural functions of covering a woman's beauty as directed by the Qur'an. It begins at the neck and is long sleeved and full length, often gently sweeping the floor. It is always black and usually of a soft, drapey fabric like crepe or georgette. The fiber may be a luxurious four-ply silk or an inexpensive synthetic. The abayeh may have a collar or merely a round neck. It might have a short slit opening at the center front and be draped over the head, an open center front all the way down to the floor, or an asymmetric opening to one side. The body shape may be straight, flared, or gathered or pleated into a yoke. Sleeves might be set in, raglan, or even part of the body in kaftan style. The sleeve shape might be straight, cuffed, or long and pointed in the medieval fashion. These sleeves are frequently lined with a contrasting color for added enhancement.

Embellishment may be as subtle as narrow black braid along the end of the sleeve and front opening or as exuberant as multicolored appliqué. Embroidery has become popular along with beads and sequins, referred to as "crystals," lace, ruffles, appliqué, fringe, and even tassels. A trend in 2008 featured a small mandarin collar, while most of the crystal and color was placed between the chin and chest and on the cuffs. This was particularly useful for women who work at a desk as visitors can see the beauty of the abayeh.

Qatar's capital, Doha, is the fashion center. Several shops are under one roof in the abayeh souq, offering ready-made models. Individuals own some of these shops, while others are abayeh chain stores found in other modern Southwest Asian malls. Plain models may cost as little as US$20, while more elaborate abayehs cost up to about US$350. Bespoke tailors are abundant in Doha, and many professional and upper-class women prefer to have their abayehs custom made. Working with the tailor, the customer determines a design, sometimes from her ideas or from models in the shop, and chooses the fabric. Construction may take as little as three days during normal times but up to a month during the Eid holidays when most women order new abayehs. A custom-made abayeh of fine fabric, with expensive trim and extensive handwork, will cost thousands of dollars. Abayehs are accessorized with global designer-brand goods such as sunglasses by Chanel, Dior, and Dolce and Gabbana. Every imaginable makeup and perfume brand is available in Qatar's modern shopping malls, and expensive handbags and shoes abound.

Qatar has changed dramatically through the modernization that occurred in the late 1990s and interaction with the rest of the world. Euro-American influences have impacted Qatar since 1990 on every front, from the existence of a large expatriate community to the widespread use of the Internet, education, and international travel. These experiences allow Qatari women to define how they will present themselves in the future through their dress—as Muslims, as Arabs, and as Qatari.

REFERENCES AND FURTHER READING

Abu Saud, Abeer. *Qatari Women Past and Present*. Burnt Mill, Essex: Longman, 1984.
El Guindi, Fadwa. *Veil: Modesty, Privacy, and Resistance*. Oxford: Berg, 2003. (Originally published in 1999.)
Ministry of Information, ed. *Glimpses of Qatar*. Singapore: Dominic Press, 1985.
Ministry of Information, ed. *Qatar*. London: Stacey International, 2000.
Wahabi, Najla Ismail. *Qatari Costume*. London: Islamic Art Society, 2003.

Christina Lindholm

See also Saudi Arabian Dress; Yemeni Dress; Omani Dress; Dress from the Gulf States: Bahrain, Kuwait, Qatar, United Arab Emirates.

PART 5

Iranian Plateau

Introduction to the History of Dress on the Iranian Plateau

The Iranian Plateau stretches from the banks of the Tigris River in the west to the valley of the Indus River in the east, and from the arid expanse of West Turkistan in the north to the Indian Ocean in the south. It is a harsh land, with limited water supplies, hot summers, and sometimes bitterly cold winters. Its geographic location, however, has made it into a natural transition zone between the plains of Southwest Asia, including ancient Mesopotamia, and the humid valleys and arid deserts of the Indian subcontinent. It also constitutes the natural corridor for any traffic between Central Asia in the north and West and South Asia in the south. No wonder that the history of the Iranian Plateau is long and varied and that it is populated by various groups that ultimately derive from Southwest Asia (Arabs), the north (Iranians and Turks), and the east (Indians). The diverse ethnic composition of the plateau thus reflects its history and geographic position, as does the plateau's culture, including its sartorial traditions. In the past and the present, clothing traditions from the Arabic west mingle with those from Central Asia and the Indian subcontinent.

In the early twenty-first century, the Iranian Plateau is occupied by a number of states. The most important of these is the Islamic Republic of Iran. Another important state is the Islamic Republic of Afghanistan. Along its fringes, there are the states of Iraq in the west, Turkey in the northwest, and Pakistan in the east.

The Iranian Plateau is basically formed by a ring of mountains that enclose a huge expanse of desert in the center. In the west, the Zagros range separates the plateau from the plains of the Euphrates and the Tigris. This range continues to the southeast and east, and its parallel east-west ridges form a natural barrier between the plateau and the humid coastal plains along the Persian Gulf and the Indian Ocean. To the northwest, the Caucasus forms a natural barrier between the plateau and the plains of southern Russia. To the north, the Elburz Mountains separate the plateau from the coastal areas along the Caspian Sea. In the east, in modern Afghanistan, the Hindu Kush Mountains and the adjoining north-south mountain ranges along the western banks of the Indus River constitute the eastern boundary of the plateau.

The enormous expanse of desert in the center of the plateau is generally called the Dasht-i Kabir. Together with the adjacent Dasht-i Lut, these inhospitable lands preclude any large-scale traffic through the center of the plateau. Instead, they force traffic along age-old tracks that lead between the deserts in the center and the surrounding mountain ranges. Various rivers, often very small, descend from the mountains along the fringes of the plateau and empty their waters into the central desert. Human settlements therefore emerged between the mountains and the desert along the various tracks across the plateau. Here, the main historical cities of Iran and Afghanistan have grown, as, for instance, Tehran, the Iranian capital, which lies between the Elburz to the north and the Dasht-i Kabir to the south. This also applies to the famous cities of Isfahan and Shiraz, which both lie between the Zagros in the west and the Iranian deserts in the east. There is also the old historical city of Afghanistan, Herat, which lies between the Hindu Kush in the east and the central deserts to the west. Finally, the ancient Afghan city of Kandahar is located in a fertile expanse of land bordered to the north by the foothills of the Hindu Kush and to the south by the sand dunes of the Registan desert. All of these settlements are located in fertile oases, watered by rivers descending from the nearby mountains.

It is therefore no surprise that, when a town or settlement was destroyed by war or natural calamities, soon afterward another town was built on top of or next to the old town. Tehran, for instance, is a relatively modern town; during the Middle Ages, the nearby town of Varamin was far more important, and before that, the famous city of Rayy (classical Rhages) was the center of the Tehran oasis (in the twenty-first century, it is a suburb of Tehran itself). The very same point applies, for instance, to the city of Kandahar in Afghanistan. The "old town" section of Kandahar was built in the eighteenth century, some three miles (five kilometers) to the east of the ancient city of Kandahar (dating to the mid-first millennium B.C.E.), which was partly demolished and completely depopulated by the Iranian king Nadir Shah some years before.

EARLY HISTORY

Little is known about clothing on the plateau before the arrival of the Central Asian Scythians in the early first millennium B.C.E. In addition, there is a marked bias in the historical sources toward the clothing of men, as they were the groups that were generally seen in public and regarded as important. Therefore, the information that does exist is mainly about male rather than female dress. There are very few depictions of women or written references to them, let alone information as to what they wore. This situation continues up to about the fourteenth century, when more depictions of both men and women begin to appear in manuscript illustrations. In general, Iranian-speaking groups populated the plateau from the second millennium B.C.E. on. They derived from northern Central Asia. Archaeological finds from various parts of Iran and Afghanistan show men wearing long garments. The Greek historiographer Herodotus, writing in the late fifth century B.C.E., tells about various groups living in the southern parts of the plateau, which at that time was not yet much affected by the northern, Scythian nomads and their superior and very mobile warfare techniques. In Herodotus' days, the men of the southern groups on the plateau wore garments markedly different from the riding outfit of the Scythian groups that by that time inhabited most of the northern and central parts of the plateau.

First of all, the Persians, the rulers of the Persian Achaemenid Empire, used Scythian clothing for horse riding only but preferred to dress in the long robes of the Elamites (from the southwest of the plateau). They were also armed with typical Southwest Asian weapons (long lances, large shields, and longbows) designed for infantry rather than the weapons of the Scythians, which were more suitable for cavalry. Basically, Elamite culture has long been suspected of having been dominant on the Iranian Plateau before (and for a long time after) the arrival of the Scythians, and it is more than likely that all the people on the plateau wore long robes.

Apart from the Persians, Herodotus lists a number of other groups that dressed differently from the Scythian groups, including the Pactyans (an ethnic group) and others, all from the southern and southeastern parts of the plateau. It is very likely that these men wore robes and gowns rather than the Scythian trousers. Interesting in this respect is the so-called Darius Statue, which was discovered at Susa in southwestern Iran in 1972. This is a statue of the Persian Achaemenid king Darius (r. 522–486 B.C.E.). Around the statue's base there are rows of delegates from the various provinces of the Persian Empire. The delegate from Harauvatish (also called Arachosia; in southeastern Afghanistan around the ancient city of Kandahar) wears a long, airy dress, very different from the Scythian outfit of trousers and a tunic worn in the northern parts of the area that makes up Afghanistan

in the twenty-first century. Apparently, Scythian influence had by that time, in the early fifth century B.C.E., not yet penetrated to the lands south of the Hindu Kush.

SCYTHIAN INFLUENCES ON DRESS AND THE PERSIAN ACHAEMENIDS

The Scythians arrived on the plateau from the early first millennium B.C.E. on. They derived from the far north, from Kazakhstan and Central Asia. They were horse-riding nomads who introduced a number of clothing traditions to the plateau that would last up to the early twenty-first century, as, for instance, trousers, riding coats (especially the *kandys* with its sleeves that could be left empty), and the composite bow. They spread their culture and political domination from the northeastern parts of the plateau all the way to modern Turkey. However, their influence took a long time to reach the lands south of the Iranian deserts, since the Persian Achaemenids, who established the first world empire in the sixth century B.C.E., were still proud of wearing the long robes and gowns of their ancestors. The Scythian sartorial innovations, strengthened by subsequent immigrants from Central Asia, would clearly demarcate the Iranian, North Indian, and Turkish world from that of mainly Arabic Southwest Asia, where long gowns are still worn instead of trousers in the early twenty-first century.

Women's clothing from this period seems to be based on wide skirts, tunics, coats, and some form of head covering. Both men and women wore cloaks of various sizes and types. This type of outfit was more suitable to a nomadic way of life, based on horses, than that of settled groups. Based on archaeological evidence from the region and from further to the northeast, the materials

A Safavid tile panel showing a young woman having an outdoor meal, surrounded by her attendants, probably from Isfahan, Iran, seventeenth century. The women's outfits consist of a chemise with a long overdress or coat kept in place with a narrow sash. Each headdress is made from a large head cloth kept in place with a narrower scarf. The woman in the center has a blanket or mantle wrapped around her lower body. The men wear characteristic Safavid-style clothing consisting of an undershirt and an overgown kept in place with a multicolored sash. They also have elongated turbans. © Victoria and Albert Museum, London. www.vam.ac.uk

used for both men's and women's clothing included wool, silk, hemp, and possibly goat hair, although this may be a form of very coarse sheep wool. Decoration on garments included embroidery and gold plaques that were sewn onto the garments in geometric designs, especially down the sides of men's trousers and along the hems of women's coats and skirts.

The remains of the Persian Achaemenids provide a remarkable picture of the clothing traditions of the peoples inhabiting the Iranian Plateau. At the Achaemenid capital of Persepolis, the Persian kings left behind beautiful reliefs depicting the various male delegations who each year came to Persepolis (locally known as Takht-i Jamshid) to show their subordination to the "Great King," as he was called in the Old Persian sources. They are all shown dressed in their own local and traditional clothing. In this way, one can see that most of the delegations from the northern parts of the Iranian Plateau wore trousers. However, some groups along the eastern fringes (for instance, in the Kabul Valley in the extreme east) wore what could be called Indian clothing (loincloths, gowns, sandals).

The Scythian-type dress of the peoples living along the northern fringes of the plateau is also shown on various objects that belong to the so-called Oxus hoard. This find included a large number of mostly golden objects that were discovered in 1877 along the banks of the Amu Dar'ya River (known as the Oxus in the classical period) in northern Afghanistan or in the area that comprises southern Tajikistan in the twenty-first century. Many objects of the treasure were lost following their discovery, but some of them eventually ended up in the British Museum. The hoard contains a number of golden plaques showing priests wearing trousers, a tunic, and a *bashlyq* (a man's covering for the upper and lower part of the head) and carrying a short sword, the so-called *akinakes*, along their right side.

Women's dress tended to follow male court dress in that it was made up of a series of gowns and a headdress of some form. The court ladies appear to have worn a headdress consisting of a crown of some kind from which a veil was draped. High-ranking women are normally depicted with floor-length veils, while those of lesser status have shorter veils. It is likely that lower-ranking women wore a combination of skirts and tunics with cloaks.

GRECIAN, PARTHIAN, AND SASSANIAN INFLUENCES ON DRESS

The Macedonian army led by Alexander the Great defeated the Persian Achaemenid king Darius III in 331 B.C.E. at the battle of Gaugamela in what is northern Iraq in the twenty-first century. Soon after, the Macedonians occupied Persepolis and the rest of the Iranian Plateau. Until the end of the second century B.C.E., the Hellenistic kings of the Seleucid dynasty (established by Alexander's former general Seleucus) politically and militarily dominated much of the plateau. Alexander's conquests thus heralded a period in which Greek culture, and with it Greek clothing traditions, was introduced onto the plateau. This, surprisingly, applies in particular to the northeastern corners of the plateau, in what is northern Afghanistan in the twenty-first century, where Greek leaders and thousands of Greek settlers created the so-called Greco-Bactrian kingdom. Greek culture, including the Greek language and script, was widely adopted by the local, non-Greek

population and continued to influence the region for many centuries, although Greek military power was removed by the end of the second century B.C.E. Greek script, for instance, was still being used in this part of the world until after the Arab invasions of the seventh century C.E. Depictions of kings and others from the Greco-Bactrian realm show people wearing Greek dress, and it is likely that Greek dress also affected the sartorial appearance of local residents.

While the Greco-Bactrian kingdom of northern Afghanistan was still thriving, further to the west a new wave of northern nomads invaded the plateau. They were the Parthians (248 B.C.E.–226 C.E.), named after the lands just north of the plateau and east of the Caspian, in what is Turkmenistan in the early twenty-first century. They belonged to the Scythian, Central Asian cultural horizon and used trousers, riding coats, high boots, and composite bows. They slowly removed the Hellenistic Seleucids from the plateau, and by the end of the second century B.C.E., they controlled most of the area that has become the Islamic Republic of Iran. Their power on the plateau would last until the beginning of the third century C.E., and throughout that time they constituted a formidable opponent to the Roman Empire further to the west. The Parthian kings, as shown on objects and, for instance, a statue held in the Archaeological Museum of Tehran, dressed in the typical Central Asian outfit but with a slight difference from that of the Scythians in the first millennium B.C.E.—the Parthians wore leggings, which protected their trousers from wear caused by horse riding. These leggings are not known from earlier periods on the plateau.

When Parthian women are depicted, they seem to be wearing a long, full garment that is belted at the waist. Their headgear is usually shown as a veil that covers the back of the head. What was worn in public is unknown.

Parthian power on the plateau came to an end in the early third century with the rise of the so-called Sassanian dynasty (226–651 C.E.). Unlike the Parthians, who ultimately derived from Central Asia, the Sassanians derived from the southwest of the plateau, from the lands that had formed the nucleus of the former Persian Achaemenid Empire around Persepolis. It is therefore no surprise that the Sassanian kings often modeled themselves on the Persian Achaemenids. The Sassanian kings are particularly known for their elaborate crowns and other jewelry.

There is slightly more evidence for the dress of Sassanian women, but it is still difficult to be exactly sure of what they wore. It would appear that several different types of outfits were used depending on where they lived: in the east or west of the plateau. In general, women in the east are shown wearing long-sleeved, ankle-length dresses, either belted or unbelted, while women in the west are shown wearing blouses and skirts. These garments were usually worn with some form of veil, which sometimes covered the back of the head. More often, however, women are shown with a long, rectangular length of cloth that is used like a shawl and draped around the upper body and over the arms.

Based on surviving textiles from the period, it seems that a wide range of materials was used for both men's and women's clothing, including silk, wool, cotton, and linen. The silk originally came along the Silk Road from China, but at an early point in time, the Iranians started to cultivate silkworms and produce this valuable cloth for themselves. Cotton came to the Iranian Plateau via trade routes from India.

ISLAMIC INFLUENCES ON DRESS

Following the death of the Prophet Mohammed in 632 C.E., Arab armies soon invaded the Iranian Plateau and defeated the last of the Sassanian kings, Yazdagird III, in 641 C.E. at the Battle of Nihavend, close to Hamadan in western Iran. By the mid-seventh century, they had already spread as far east as the city of Herat in what is, in the early twenty-first century, Afghanistan. The Arabs not only brought their religion and political and military dominance but also affected local dress. It may safely be assumed that many of the rules and regulations as to the "proper" dress of a Muslim man and woman were also introduced on the plateau at this time. This included covering the body from the neck to the ankles, with particular attention to hiding the appearance of the region from the waist to the knees. In addition, both men and women were expected to cover their head and hair. The different nature of public and private dress (outdoor and indoor dress) became even more apparent, especially for women, and was to have a profound effect on women's clothing, continuing into the beginning of the twenty-first century.

After a long period of political upheaval, which included the disastrous Mongol invasions of the early thirteenth century, Iran reasserted itself in the early sixteenth century under the Safavid dynasty. Originating from the mainly Turkish lands of what is, in the early twenty-first century, northwestern Iran (around the cities of Tabriz and Ardabil), the Safavids established a powerful kingdom that formed a buffer between the Turkish Ottoman Empire to the west and the Mughal Empire

of India to the east. The Safavids also made Iran into a Shiite realm, as opposed to its powerful Sunnite neighbors, Turkey and India. The Safavid period is generally regarded as a time of great prosperity. The early Safavid kings developed trade and textile manufacturing, and Iranian goods, including precious textiles and carpets, soon found their way to neighboring lands, including faraway Europe. At the same time, European influences started to penetrate Iran; there are beautiful miniatures showing some Iranian men wearing European-style suits with jackets and short pants and broad European hats with feathers.

The early Safavid style for women included a long undershirt fastened at the neck, over which was worn a gown tied at the hips with a decorative sash. A large indoor chador was used as a headdress that draped down the back and could be used to cover part of the body if needed. It was kept in place by a head scarf folded diagonally in half and tied around the head, with the point of the folded scarf forming a triangle over the forehead. At this time women also wore underpants that reached the ankles, but these are not shown. Accessories included necklaces and earrings, and Cuban-heeled shoes were worn over brocaded ankle socks or indoor boots.

By the late seventeenth century, women had started to wear a layered garment, which now consisted of a blouse fastened at the neck, over which was worn a tight-fitting dress that was open down the front and had a bell-shaped skirt. The earlier sash remained at the hip. The head covering shrank in size to a much smaller head scarf that was kept in place with a headband of some kind. Although the head scarf had shrunk, the underpants had

Ladies around a Samovar, oil on canvas by Isma'il Jalayir, 1860–1875, Tehran, Iran. This painting shows Qajar-style clothing typical of the mid- to late nineteenth century. The servants wear short underblouses and jackets, wide skirts or trousers, and head cloths fastened under the chin. The ladies wear long jackets and elaborate headdresses including jewelry. The woman smoking a pipe wears outdoor clothing consisting of a black chador and a white *ru-band* (face veil). © Victoria and Albert Museum, London. www.vam.ac.uk

become more important and decorative in nature. In addition, the ankle socks increased in size so that attention was focused downward. When in public, however, women would be totally covered in an all-enveloping wrap (chador), which was usually white for upper-class Muslim ladies, and a white face veil that had a grid for the eyes (ru-band).

The fall of the Safavid Empire in the early eighteenth century, at the hands of Afghan troops from what is southern Afghanistan in the early twenty-first century, led to a breaking up of Iranian unity. Only at the end of the century was Iran reunited under the Qajar dynasty. The Qajars originated from the (Turkish) north, and this may have been one of the reasons that they moved the Iranian capital from the former Safavid capital of Isfahan to the north to Tehran, which at the time was still a very small town. The nineteenth century is generally regarded as a time in which Iran gradually declined into a client state of Russia and England. Growing Western influence also led to changes in dress and a growing feeling among local leaders that Iran was lagging behind in terms of modernization and its standing in the world.

Urban men's clothing changed from Oriental-looking turbans, long gowns (qaba), and cloaks (aba) to Western-style frock coats, narrow trousers, and hats of various kinds. The clothing of the women also changed dramatically from the beginning to the end of the nineteenth century. In the early decades of the nineteenth century, urban women tended to wear wide trousers of the Safavid type, with blouses and short jackets and a number of head scarves and shawls covering the head. By the end of the century, short tutulike skirts, blouses, jackets, and a large head scarf had become the norm. Women from the court or higher echelons of Persian life, which had more connections with the West, often wore Russian, French, or English gowns. When in public, however, women were still totally covered in the chador, which was now black for Muslim ladies and a blue-and-white check for their servants; a white face veil (ru-band); and wide, outdoor pants called chaqchur, which were often dark red, purple, or black.

TWENTIETH-CENTURY DRESS IN IRAN

The Pahlavi dynasty was officially installed in 1925 with the rise to power of Reza Shah. He was a nationalist who wanted to raise Iran from what he regarded as a long period of decline. He modeled himself on Atatürk in Turkey, who likewise tried to Westernize his country. Both Atatürk and Reza Shah influenced the king of Afghanistan, Amanullah, who also tried to modernize his country during the 1920s. All three leaders regarded dress as an important symbol of national progress; all three introduced Western-style dress and tried, in Amanullah's case unsuccessfully, to abolish the veiling of women.

The Islamic Revolution in Iran, coming to a climax in early 1979 with the fall of Reza Mohammed Shah (the son of Reza Shah) and the rise to power of Ayatollah Khomeini, heralded a period in which Iran turned away from the path of Westernization. Since dress has such symbolic power, it also meant that women were forced to wear the chador (a body wrap that leaves the face uncovered) or a head scarf and coat, while men were forced to wear "Islamically correct" clothing and stop wearing Western-style garments such as the necktie.

References and Further Reading

Bier, Carol, ed. *Woven from the Soul, Spun from the Heart: Textile Arts of Safavid and Qajar Iran 16th–19th Centuries.* Washington, DC: The Textile Museum, 1987.

"Clothing (Lebas)." In *Encyclopaedia Iranica* (online version). http://www.iranica.com/newsite/ (accessed on 13 July 2008).

Diba, Layla S., and Maryam Ekhtiar, eds. *Royal Persian Paintings: The Qajar Epoch 1875–1925.* Brooklyn, New York: J. B. Tauris, 1998.

Pope, Arthur Upham, and Phyllis Ackerman. *A Survey of Persian Art.* 18 vols. London: Oxford University Press, 1938–1939.

Scarce, Jennifer. *Women's Costume of the Near and Middle East.* London: Unwin Hyman, 1987.

Vogelsang, Willem. *The Rise and Organisation of the Achaemenid Empire. The Eastern Evidence.* Leiden: Brill, 1992.

Vogelsang-Eastwood, Gillian, and Leo Ferydoun Barjesteh. *An Introduction to Qajar Era Dress.* Rotterdam: Barjesteh van Waalwijk van Doorn, 2002.

Willem Vogelsang

See also Pre-Islamic Dress Codes in the Eastern Mediterranean and Southwest Asia; The Coming of Islam and Its Influence on Dress; Iranian Regional Dress; Iranian Urban Dress; volume 9, East Europe, Russia, and the Caucasus: Ancient Greek Dress.

Iraqi Dress

Iraq is one of the largest countries in Southwest Asia, with a population of nearly twenty-seven million. It is bordered by Iran to the east, Turkey to the north, Syria and Jordan to the west, and Saudi Arabia and Kuwait to the south. Iraq's capital is Baghdad. In terms of its geographic characteristics as well as demographics and ethnolinguistic, religious, and cultural diversity, Iraq is one of the most complex nations in the region. Geographically, the country combines three distinct regions: fertile mountain regions in the north, the rich alluvial valleys of the Euphrates and Tigris rivers, which run from the very north of the country south to merge into the Shatt al-'Arab before flowing into the Persian Gulf, and, finally, expansive, arid desert plains in the west. Both the terrain and the bordering countries have had an influence on dress.

Three-quarters of Iraq's population are Arabs, of whom roughly two-thirds adhere to Shia Islam and one-third to Sunni orthodoxy. The Arab population is largely but not exclusively concentrated in western, central, and southern Iraq. Many live in cities, towns, and villages along the agriculturally rich, riverine ridge defined by the Tigris and Euphrates rivers. Groups inhabiting the deserts or less arable regions in western, central, and southern Iraq may pursue a fully nomadic or semisettled lifestyle. The Mi'dan or Marsh Arabs, who inhabit the expansive marshlands of southern Iraq, pursue a unique way of life based largely on water buffalo husbandry. Ethnolinguistically and religiously distinct minorities living among the Arab majority within these regions include heterogeneous Christian as well as tiny Jewish communities, the Persian-speaking Lurs inhabiting the Iraq-Iran border, and the gnostic, historically Aramaic-speaking Mandaeans, traditionally concentrated along the riverbanks of southern Iraq.

The mountainous north is home to a considerable number of non-Arab as well as Arab groups, most notably the Kurds, an ethnically and linguistically distinct people who form one-fifth of the Iraqi population and are therefore the largest ethnic minority within the country. Most Kurds are Sunni Muslims, but some follow other religious denominations. Most notable among the latter are the Yazidis, who are concentrated in isolated villages to the west and north of the city of Mosul. Other minority groups in the north include the ethnically and linguistically distinct Turkic Turkomans as well as heterogeneous Arab and non-Arab Christian communities; the latter may speak Assyrian Neo-Aramaic, Syriac, or Armenian as well as Arabic.

The dress traditions of Iraq are directly linked to the climatically and geographically distinct regions of Iraq and regularly transcend ethnic, linguistic, and religious divides. This is particularly true for the north. Here, all non-Arab groups traditionally shared a tendency to wear multilayered outfits and headdresses, all of which reflect a fusion of influences coming from Ottoman Turkish, Iranian, Southwest Asian, and tribal Arab dress traditions. As for the rest of the country with its Arab majority, traditional Arab- and Southwest Asian–style dress prevailed. Since the nineteenth century, traditional styles have been increasingly eroded by incoming Western-style dress, with urban trends gradually seeping into more rural towns and villages. In the early twenty-first century, the majority of Iraqis of all backgrounds tend to wear Western-style dress irrespective of the region—either exclusively or by combining aspects of it with elements of traditional clothing.

IRAQI DRESS: EVIDENCE AND RESOURCES

To write about Iraqi dress means writing about a kaleidoscope of distinct dress traditions inherent to the numerous religious and ethnolinguistic groups that have traditionally made up the demographic fabric of Iraq. To date, very little of substance has been written about the subject, and even less fieldwork has been done, a fact no doubt resulting from the continuous political turmoil and drawn-out armed conflicts that have characterized the modern history of Iraq.

Most publications referring to aspects of Iraqi dress come from European travel writers and political analysts rather than ethnographers or specialists in Southwest Asian dress. Consequently, the detail and quality of their descriptions and photographs regarding Iraqi dress conventions very much depended on the author's personal interests, ideological outlook, and observational skills rather than systematic ethnographic methodology. Only rarely did travelers like Lady Stevens (later Lady Ethel Stefana Drower), who recorded both Yazidi and Mandaean ritual dress in great detail, display a keen, ethnographic sense of observation; those who did left a wealth and depth of information not surpassed since.

Those ethnographic studies that do exist focus mainly on the Kurdish regions of the north or the southern marshlands and generally include, but do not focus exclusively on, aspects of local dress. There are only two publications to date, written in Arabic, which cover traditional Iraqi dress across the country. Their usefulness lies mainly in the detailed dress drawings with explanatory captions and relevant dress terminology.

Beyond written sources, satellite television channels and Internet sites relating to Iraqi topics occasionally include very generalized—and not always reliable or accurate—discussions on dress as well as historical and contemporary images or film clips, which can help to give a general impression of an outfit's appearance or its modification over time.

URBAN IRAQI MALE DRESS

Since the early nineteenth century c.e., the Ottoman provinces that correspond to twenty-first-century Iraq had seen a steady trickle of Westernizing influences. Some were conveyed through the Europeanizing fashions at the Ottoman court and among its locally based elite. As early as 1808, the Ottoman sultan Mahmud II instructed Ottoman officials to wear a Western-style frock coat and a *tarbush* or fez (a cylindrical, slightly tapering red felt head cover). These were intended to visually unify a governmental workforce that up to that point could be ethnically and religiously differentiated by the type of headdress they wore. Within a few years the fez and the frock coat had become the standard dress for Ottoman officials and male members of the elite in urban centers all over the Ottoman Empire, including the Iraqi cities of Mosul, Basra, and Baghdad.

Other instances of Western-style dress coming into the country were due to European missionaries, explorers, or traders. An increasing number of Europeans converged on major Iraqi cities from the early 1900s on. Their writings provide insight into the diverse and gradually changing dress conventions that could be observed there from the last years of Ottoman rule into modern times.

The choice of urban Iraqi dress depended on many factors, including age, gender, religion, ethnic and tribal affiliations, social status, and education. Since the early twentieth century, items of traditional and Western-style clothing have been increasingly combined, interchanged, or indeed exchanged according to both personal and societal attitudes or context. By the 1930s, the transition from a traditional to a Westernized lifestyle had increased in pace in major cities like Baghdad, as the material and ideological legacy of the Ottoman Empire was steadily replaced by the Western-style cultural reorientation introduced with the British Mandate for the administration of Palestine in 1920.

Interestingly, when Faisal I became king of the new Iraq in 1921, he again—like his Ottoman predecessors—chose an item of male headdress to symbolize the new political order as well as a new Iraqi national identity. Iraqi officials were now required to replace the traditional Ottoman tarbush with the so-called sidara. The *sidara* was a brimless military-style cap of black velvet, felt, or lambswool. In design it was not unlike a Scottish Glengarry, with its sides folded like a pocket around a central crown. The sidara remained a marker of the male political and intellectual elite until 1958, when a military coup ended the monarchy and ushered in yet another ideological sea change with the establishment of the new Republic of Iraq. Aside from specific dress-related innovations like the sidara, ethnic-, religious-, and gender-specific traditional dress continued to play a pivotal, if gradually diminishing, role in the urban dress of Baghdad and other major Iraqi cities throughout the first half of the twentieth century.

To begin with, Western-style dress was worn only by a tiny minority of government officials, dignitaries, and members of the political and educational elite, and even they tended to revert to—as they saw it—more comfortable traditional dress when at home. More often, men of the Arab majority tended to

Iraqi Sunni and Shiite Muslims in a procession celebrating the return of Shiite cleric Mohammed Bahr al-Uloom to the Iraqi Interim Governing Council, Baghdad, 2003. The men wearing the checkered *keffiyeh* as a head covering also wear the *dishdasha*, a long tuniclike gown with a close-fitting neck closure. Sabah Arar/AFP/Getty Images.

continue wearing traditional tribal outfits: The *dishdasha*, a long tuniclike gown with a close-fitting round neck and a center-front opening down to the chest, was worn over long cotton trousers called *sirwal* and an optional undershirt, the *fanilla*. Details taken from Western-style shirt design, including pointed collars, buttoned front fastenings, and buttoned cuffs, were soon added to the dishdasha. It was covered by a long, sleeveless, and buttonless gown, the *zibun*, which was secured with a belt, and—following the increasing availability of European clothing—a Western-style suit jacket. Over this, the *aba* or *abayeh* was worn, a loose, rectangular cloak made of heavy or fine homespun woolen yarn or even silk depending on the season and usually black, brown, or light brown in color. The use of other colors, patterned weaves, and embroidered detailing and the addition of decorative tassels were not uncommon. Their application depended on the fashions and dress conventions of the specific Arab tribal regions within Iraq from which the wearer originated. A heavy sheepskin coat or *pushtin* could complete the outfit during the winter months or cold spells. Footwear varied: Some wore no shoes at all, but most men used *ni'al*—sandals consisting of hand-knitted string tops and leather soles or, later, factory-made leather sandals, shoes, or boots, which were often imported.

Traditional tribal Arab headgear consisted of a small knitted or crocheted skullcap, the *'arqchena*, and a folded square head cloth (called *keffiyeh* or *shamagh* if checked; *ghutra* if plain white) of wool, silk, cotton, or synthetic material. The color scheme of the keffiyeh indicated the wearer's tribal and religious affiliation as well as his status. White head cloths were worn by tribal leaders or sheikhs, red-and-white ones by tribal, mainly Sunni Arabs from the north and west of Iraq, and black-and-white checkered ones by the southern, and mainly, but not exclusively, Shia tribes. Orange-and-white keffiyehs were worn exclusively by mosque auxiliaries, particularly those assisting at funerals.

The keffiyeh was generally secured with one of a variety of *'aqals* or head ropes. These could consist of thick strings of black wool bound at regular intervals into tubular units or, for sheikhs, fine black wool or silk tightly bound with gold thread to form stiff bars. Gradually, these elaborate ropes were replaced by twice-wound heavy black or dark brown cords of varying thickness, made of wool or camel hair and imported from Syria.

Religious leaders wore a turban instead of the keffiyeh and 'aqal. A white turban worn over a red tarbush denoted a Sunni cleric, and a green one indicated a descendant of the Prophet Mohammed's family. Black turbans and white ones were reserved for the direct descendants of the Shia imams and senior clerics, respectively.

URBAN IRAQI FEMALE DRESS

Women of the urban elite in early-twentieth-century Baghdad partook of a much wider range of clothing styles than their male counterparts and responded enthusiastically to the newest fashions coming from Istanbul, Cairo, London, and Paris. However, while bold in displaying these indoors, most Muslim women—in accordance with Islamic directives regarding female modesty and the conventions of their social class—continued to cover themselves with traditional, all-enveloping, black silk cloaks called *abayeh*s when outdoors. One of these voluminous rectangular garments was worn over the shoulders and another over the head. Head scarves and a black chiffon face veil (called *bushi*, *busha*,

pushi, or *peche*, depending on the group and dialect) completed this outdoor attire.

Urban Christian and Jewish women also covered themselves outside the home at that time. However, instead of the abayeh, both groups wore the *izar*, a hooded, handwoven silk outfit in light pastel colors, enhanced with gold and silver designs. According to Lady Stevens, this garment was an expensive accessory: "On a single izar a woman in Baghdad will spend more than a careful middle-class English woman would spend on half a year's dress." The izar consisted of two main elements, a hood and a skirt, with no armholes or sleeves, held together by tapes and safety pins (it is very similar to the Turkish *carsaf*). Christian women wore the izar with the peche face veil, but Jewish women combined it with a stiff black face cover stuffed with hemp or a horse's tail hair and edged with silver, the *khayliyya*. This was tied around the head under the izar and sloped downward to cover the eyes and the face.

By the 1930s, however, urban Christian and Jewish communities had abandoned traditional dress completely in favor of Western-style garments, well before any other group in urban Iraqi society. This was due to the fact that both communities historically had deep-rooted, traditional connections with Western material and intellectual culture as well as extensive professional links.

In Iraq's urban population at large, the transition from traditional Eastern-style dress to "modern" Western-style dress was much more gradual, and the discourse between the two is still ongoing in the early twenty-first century. It was not until the 1950s that broad sections of the urban elites and the emerging educated middle classes in the cities and towns of Iraq opened up to Western style and Western social, cultural, and material innovations. Around that time, Western-style dress for both men and women became a more common sight, as urbanized Iraqis became increasingly eager to signal their advanced professional and educational status together with their commitment to Western-style progress.

U.S. anthropologist George L. Harris, in *Iraq: Its People, Its Society, Its Culture*, provides an interesting analysis of the complex attitudes that governed the dress codes of the varying social groups living in Iraq's cities and towns at that time. According to him, the upper-income groups in the cities, including wealthy landowners, leading businessmen, high government officials, and the most successful members of the professions, had adopted Western-style dress wholeheartedly. Middle-class businessmen, professionals, and government employees were more hesitant to change their traditional dress code. On the one hand, they were keen to emulate the upper classes as closely as financial circumstances allowed. On the other, a traditionalist suspicion of Westernizing influences resulted in a considerable degree of adhesion to indigenous aspects of clothing, particularly in smaller towns at some distance from the capital. Even in those more conservative contexts, however, men in contact with city life usually possessed at least one Western-style suit and a pair of factory-made shoes. Middle-class women in the provincial towns of central and southern Iraq adopted many aspects of the Western-style fashions of the city but tended to continue to wear a head scarf or an even more comprehensive form of veiling. These were intended as both indicators of privileged status in imitation of their upper-class sisters in the cities and as markers of a more deeply engrained, religious conservatism.

For the Kurds and other groups living in the Iraqi mountains to the north, the agriculturalists in the Iraqi countryside, and the nomads of the desert areas, traditional dress codes remained largely unaffected by the Westernizing trends in the cities and towns at the time. Even in these contexts, however, the increased mobility of the population and concerted government development efforts meant that some external influences did gradually take root.

Westernizing trends in urban Iraqi dress intensified during the 1960s, particularly after the rise of the Baath regime, which aimed at creating a thoroughly modern and secular country along Arab nationalist and socialist ideals. At the same time, however, particular aspects of traditional Arab male and female clothing, such as men's dishdasha, aba, ghutra, and 'aqal and the *hashimi* (an elaborate, wide-sleeved ceremonial garment made of net or sheer black material that was originally worn by the women in southern Iraq), were promoted by the regime as Iraqi national dress in an attempt to strengthen both Arab nationalist and Iraqi identity.

In the 1970s, a cultural campaign was launched to promote a national consciousness based on Iraq's ancient Mesopotamian glory on the one hand and the achievements of Arab civilization based in Baghdad during the golden age of Abbasid rule (the third Islamic caliphate; 750–1258 C.E.) on the other. As part of this campaign, the government launched the Iraqi Fashion House for cutting-edge Iraqi fashion design, inspired by traditional folkloric dress and the historical styles conveyed through Abbasid and ancient Mesopotamian art. Regular fashion shows of the latest designs were held and publicized widely. However, their success and impact on the fashions in Iraqi society remained negligible as the designs were not only expensive but did not correspond to the ethnic, religious, and societal conventions that governed the wearing of traditional dress among its various sectors. By and large, their consumption was confined to members of the political and societal elite who were proud to own unique showpieces.

Notwithstanding Iraq's steadily increasing, Western-style modernization in the course of the twentieth century, aspects of traditional dress have continued to be in use. Indeed, Kurdish dress has seen a conscious, politically and ideologically driven revival over the last decades, while much more recently, the fall of the Baath regime in 2004 has led to the reemergence of traditional Islamic dress in Iraq's major cities. For many Westernized, urban Arab men, the dishdasha and the aba in particular remain garments of choice and pride. The dishdasha on its own constitutes popular leisure wear, interchangeable, for example, with Western-style tracksuits made in China or Turkey. Combined with the aba, ghutra, and 'aqal, high-quality dishdashas may be worn on special occasions as a symbol of national pride and Arab identity.

For many Iraqi women, a variety of head scarves and the abayeh have remained integral aspects of outdoor dress. Since the fall of the Baath regime in 2004, their use has increased exponentially due to a complex combination of factors: the newly found freedom to express religious identity openly, the revival of religious consciousness and commitment, and religiously motivated resistance against the U.S. occupation; but also sustained pressures coming from within a newly Islamized Iraqi society and government. Thus, new legislation issued by religious and governmental authorities has created a stricter, Islamic outdoor dress code for Muslim women, and those who are found

A Kurdish man and his daughter, Iraq, 1988. Over his shirt the man wears an outer suit (*rank-o-chokha*), consisting of a matching jacket and trousers secured around the waist with a long, padded sash (*pishten*). Thomas Hartwell/Time & Life Pictures/Getty Images.

not to comply may be reprimanded, criticized, or sometimes imprisoned.

DRESS IN IRAQI KURDISTAN AND NORTHERN IRAQ: MALE DRESS

The mountains and plains of northern and northeastern Iraq have traditionally been inhabited by an array of ethnically, linguistically, and religiously distinct groups—Kurds, Yazidis, Chaldaeans, Assyrians, and Turkmens. In terms of dress, all these groups share important key elements that, in turn, reflect the geographic and climatic realities of the region they inhabit. At the same time, many utilize sufficiently distinct dress markers, both in daily and ritual wear, that help distinguish one group from another and indeed sections within the same group. Subtle differences in northern-style dress can thus occur from village to village or region to region.

Literary sources mentioning the garments worn by the Kurds and their neighbors are few. European travelers, Ella Constance Sykes and Percy Molesworth Sykes (a British brother and sister team who lived and worked in Iran) and Cecil J. Edmonds (a British political officer who served with the British army around the 1920s) most notably among them, commented particularly on male Kurdish dress, but to date only one cultural ethnographer, the Danish Henny Harald Hansen, appears to have collected detailed dress data in the Kurdish villages and towns of northeastern Iraq, providing a snapshot of the dress conventions and fashions that prevailed in that region around the late 1950s and early 1960s. After Hansen's work, Maria O'Shea's 1996 article was the next discussion of Kurdish dress to be published.

In general terms, two main types of traditional male dress can be distinguished in northern Iraq, each one associated with a specific geographic area. The first style traditionally prevailed in the region around the Kurdish city of Sulaymania, and the second, known as Rawanduz, Badinani, or Hakkari style, in the areas around Rawanduz in northeastern Iraq.

Among the Kurds, underwear consisted of a white cotton shirt (*keras*) and underpants or undertrousers (*darpe*). The shirt was a short tunic with long sleeves, a low collar, and a front opening. Among the northern tribal groups, it could have very long sleeves terminating in exaggerated, funnel-shaped cuffs that extended well beyond the wearer's arm. The shirt's sleeves were pulled through the sleeves of the overgarment, and then, because of their length, the cuffs were wound around the outside of the overgarment's sleeves. Beginning in the 1950s, silk or nylon cuffs were sewn separately and added onto the sleeves of imported European shirts. With time, however, the long cuffs gradually disappeared, and Western-style shirts came to be worn exclusively. The drawers were very wide, bag-shaped, peg-cut trousers with tapering legs and a drawstring around the waist.

Over these undergarments, an outer suit consisting of a matching jacket and trousers, the *rank-o-chokha*, was worn. Tailors constructed these suits from heavy, traditionally home-woven woolen cloth and sold them ready-made in the *suqs* (local markets) of Kurdish towns. The suits came in two distinct designs, one associated with the Sulaymania area, the other with Rawanduz.

The two-piece suit from the Sulaymania district consisted of dark or light brown, gray, black, or white wool trousers (*rank*), traditionally assembled from twelve lengths of woven material according to the same pattern adopted for the drawers. According to Hansen, a special technique was used to prepare the cloth before assembling the item: Before the trousers were sewn, the material was folded and boiled, so that each length of material obtained two sharp longitudinal creases that, coupled with the many seams, produced a plastic decoration of the uniformly colored and otherwise unembellished material. The Sulaymania jacket (*chokha*), a short, unlined garment with a low collar and slit sleeves lined with silk, was assembled from ten lengths of the same pretreated material.

The Rawanduz suit was made from a plain material that was a mixture of wool and hemp, traditionally a yellowish brown or beige in color, striped and enhanced with various degrees of machine embroidery, depending on the region in which it was worn. The trousers are similar in cut to those of the Sulaymania suit but less voluminous and with flaring rather than tapering legs. The Rawanduz jacket has the same shape and cut as the Sulaymania one but has no collar and is distinguished by embroidery along the edges. During cold spells, a waistcoat (*bin keras*) or a padded, front-buttoned vest (*sukhma*) could be worn between the undershirt and suit jacket.

The wearers of both types of suit traditionally tucked the jacket into the trousers and secured both with a long, padded sash (*pestand*) of flowered silk, satin, velvet, or cotton wound several times around the waist. The pestand was essential not only to secure the outfit but also to store personal items such as tobacco pouches, daggers, knives, and prayer beads. Throughout northern Iraq, outer garments such as cloaks and hats were molded from locally produced felt. Imported Western-style items of outdoor dress such as jackets, overcoats, and shoes also found increasing favor.

Traditional headdresses in northern Iraq included a large variety of skullcaps (*kelaw*), which could be made from crocheted wool, embroidered felt, or cotton, nylon, or metal thread. Male members of the Assyrian community wore a distinctive, lightweight conical felt cap, often topped by a large frontal plume. Often, the skullcaps were encircled by turbans of varying materials, designs, and sizes depending on the wearer's tribal affiliation and locality.

The turban generally consists of a rectangular head cloth made of silk, cotton, or—later—synthetic material (*mishki* or *shafta*), often with a striped or floral pattern and fringed at the edges. The cloth is folded diagonally and then twisted into a thick coil before being wound around the head. Depending on the region and tribe, both ends are tucked into the turban, or one end is left to hang freely down one side. More recently, a new type of imported turban cloth of black-and-white or gray-and-white checkered cotton material with black tassels all around (*jamana*) adapts a cloth also used as Arab headdress. This type is particularly popular in the extreme north of Iraq. Red-and-white checkered turban cloth is favored in the early twenty-first century by the Barazani tribe and adherents of the Yazidi faith. Descendants of the prophet wear green turbans, while sheikhs and mullahs wear white versions.

A variety of footwear, including local and, later, European-style leather shoes, worn with hand-knitted socks, completed these traditional outfits. Cloth shoes known as *kalash* constituted the most typical footwear in the region. Their soles were made from strips of rags, which were folded into rectangular units and hammered flat, then forced together with a leather strap drawn through them, and provided with protective leather patches around the heel and toe areas. The shoes' uppers consisted of a crocheted white cotton cover. Both the soles and the uppers were handmade separately by specialist craftsmen and then assembled. The most famous kalash came from the Kurdish town of Tawella.

DRESS IN IRAQI KURDISTAN AND NORTHERN IRAQ: FEMALE DRESS

The traditional dress of women in northern Iraq conveys important messages about a woman's status, age, and wider social context. Expensive materials like brocade or silk are reserved for women of the local elite, while vibrantly patterned cottons are the norm for ordinary village women. Bright colors are reserved for the young, and darker, more subdued colors for older women. Subtle variations in the style of headdress indicate tribal and regional affiliation as well as differences in marital status.

Traditional Kurdish-style women's dress (*jilik*) consists of several layers. Voluminous trousers (*awal keras*) are identical in cut to the southern male rank and have a drawstring to gather them around the waist. Their upper part, which is always concealed by the overgarments, is traditionally made of white cotton material, while the lower part is of colored cotton, taffeta, brocade, or synthetic material.

Over the trousers, a knee-length, long-sleeved shift or chemise (*zer keras*) is worn, followed by a floor-length, long-sleeved, A-shaped gown (*keras*) of patterned shiny material. In the Christian areas, these gowns are often dark and solid-colored, with rich embroidered panels. The neckline is round with a small chest opening. In Kurdish areas, the sleeves have exaggerated, funnel-shaped extensions echoing those of male dress, but in the Christian villages around Mosul, the gowns can also feature straight, tubular arms. As in male dress, the elongated cuffs are pulled through the sleeves of the upper garments and wound around the lower sleeves of the latter or tied in a knot at the points and thrown over the back, leaving the sleeves open and half-length. During prayer the tied cuffs are undone so that they hang down over the hands, with the tips reaching the ground.

Over the keras, a highly colorful sleeveless, lined cotton or brocade vest (*sukhma*) with large armholes is worn, followed by a slightly padded and lined, colorful brocade jacket (*salta*) with long, tubular sleeves. Embroidered versions of both are common in the Christian villages of the region. The outermost layer generally consists of an A-shaped kaftan or overcoat with a padded cotton lining (*kawa*), in type not unlike the Ottoman *entari*, with tubular sleeves, a buttoned front, and split lower side seams.

The kawa is topped off by an unlined, rectangular shoulder cloth with tassels enhancing both ends, joined and secured over the chest. Sashes and belts are occasionally worn. Christian, Yazidi, and Jewish women wear the izar or the *charouka*, a rectangular mantle, often richly embroidered, which is draped under one arm and obliquely across the chest with its upper ends fastened over the opposite shoulder.

Regional headdresses generally combine a skullcap and a turban. A black felt skullcap with slightly sloping sides (*kelaw*), enhanced with stitching and black fringes, occupies the crown of the head. A looped silver coin atop the crown is used to attach a triangular, tulle neck veil (*dasmal* or *jamana*), the two long, narrowing ends of which cross in front, pass over the shoulders, and are tied together at the neck. A chain of silver coins or glass beads is secured to one side of the cap, runs beneath the chin, and is fastened to the other side by means of a hook. In the town of Halabja, the skullcaps are covered all over with silver coins in a fish-scale pattern and worn on their own. In most other northern regions, however, married women combine the skullcap with a turban and forehead cloth.

The turban cloth (*sarbast*) is traditionally made up of two layers of narrow cloth and has tapering, pleated, and tasseled ends. One of the long sides is straight and enhanced by tassels, while the other forms a concave arc. The turban cloth is folded double along its length with the tassels outside and wound twice around the cap. The dark-colored forehead cloth is folded diagonally, tied so that it slants over the forehead in the opposite direction of the turban cloth, and knotted at the neck, the ends being concealed under the wrapped cloth. Chains of jewelry or coins are pinned onto the turban, and the arrangement is topped off by an unseamed, rectangular gauze head cloth or head veil (*sarposh*) of white, turquoise, vermilion, black, or another dark color, left to hang loose. Unmarried women wear this item directly on the hair, without any turban. Upper-class women wear white sarposh,

An Iraqi Syriac Christian outside a polling station, Hamdaniya, Iraq, 2009. He wears a black skullcap and an outer suit (*rank-o-chokha*) with purple embroidery. Marwan Ibrahim/AFP/Getty Images.

whereas ordinary women use a variety of colors depending on the village they come from.

Northern Iraqi women, though largely Muslim, do not veil themselves like their Arab and Persian counterparts and wear their colorful dresses with pride outdoors. However, the Arab-style abayeh is worn over local dress when visiting the city, as was the black face veil up to the 1960s.

Footwear, if it was worn, included a variety of wooden slippers (*qabqab*) and embroidered velvet slippers with built-in heels (*qundara* or *papoush*) in the early twentieth century, but by the 1950s black leather pumps, European-style summer shoes, or plastic and synthetic slippers were beginning to take their place.

HISTORICAL TRENDS IN KURDISH-STYLE DRESS

In the course of the twentieth century, northern Iraqi dress became increasingly exposed to Westernizing influences, particularly in the urban centers. In cities like Sulaymania and Kirkuk, European-style suits complete with shirt, tie, socks, and leather shoes had largely replaced Kurdish-style dress among the male members of the elite by the late 1950s. Curiously, though, Hansen reports that the traditional wide drawers were still retained underneath the Western-style trousers and could even be worn on their own outdoors. European-style pajamas and Arab-style dishdashas also became fashionable around that time and would be worn continuously during the day and at night. The head was no longer covered, and the hair was cut in a Western style. Among the less affluent and educated sections of the male urban population, and in more remote areas further afield, traditional male Kurdish-style dress continued to be worn but was now often combined with a Western-style jacket, coat, or pair of shoes. Traditional jackets could be enhanced with Western elements such as breast pockets.

Upper-class, educated city women at the same time turned to the latest in Western fashion, bought ready-made in city shops or copied from imported fashion magazines. Machine-made, synthetic textiles brought from Europe, Syria, and East Asia became increasingly popular because of their bright patterns, color schemes, and easy care. Western-style underwear like embroidered shifts or nightgowns became acceptable day wear in the house. For those occasions when Kurdish-style dress was still worn, a transparent tulle overgarment, designed to reveal the Western-style shift below, became the norm, worn with a Western-style belt. At the same time, the Kurdish headdresses of the past were abandoned, and the head, with hair cut in a Western style, was covered with a gauzy veil only in the presence of male visitors or by the black abayeh when outdoors. The Western bridal gown with all its accoutrements gradually became the standard outfit for brides in the north as elsewhere in Iraq, and no expense was spared to bring it all the way from Baghdad for the occasion.

By the late 1990s, most urbanized Kurds had abandoned traditional dress as daily wear. Contributing factors included the modernizing ideological efforts of successive Iraqi governments, subsequent societal trends throughout the urban centers of Iraq that favored Western professional dress codes, and the individual's desire to be recognized as a progressive, "civilized," and educated member of mainstream Iraqi society rather than of a ethnically and linguistically distinct unit.

For those continuing to adhere to traditional dress in the more isolated areas of northern Iraq, a gradual transition occurred from the considerable variety and complexity of local Kurdish dress conventions noted by travelers in the early twentieth century to a much more streamlined range of styles, culminating in the emergence—from the 1960s on—of a modern "national" Kurdish dress for both men and women, worn as an instantly recognizable nationalist (and political) symbol on special occasions. Indeed, the rise of Kurdish nationalism resulted in a political reevaluation of traditional Kurdish dress. The male dress of the southern regions subsequently emerged in a standardized "universal" form and became the conscious choice of Kurdish Peshmerga political activists (armed Kurdish fighters for independence) and Kurdish politicians.

YAZIDI DRESS

Among the Kurdish tribes of northern Iraq, the isolated Yazidi communities occupy a special place. Ethnically, linguistically, and culturally, the Yazidis identify themselves as Kurds, but their unique heterodox religion, a complex fusion of indigenous local pre-Islamic and Sufi beliefs, sets them apart from the mainly Sunni Muslim Kurdish majority and indeed from Iraqi society as a whole.

Many elements of traditional Yazidi dress reflected the close cultural ties that bound the community to other ethnoreligious communities in northern Iraq but at the same time displayed traits unique to the Yazidi context. According to Yazidi religious law, all garments worn by the community had to have a round neckline (gerivan) and strictly avoid the color blue, as it was the sacred color of Malik Ta'us ("peacock angel"), the sacred central figure of their religion. White and red were the preferred colors, as white symbolized the Angel of Light and the residents of heaven and red the residents of hell. Curiously, only the Yazidis of Babira village were prohibited from wearing garments combining the colors white and black. Yazidi scriptures specified that every new garment had to be baptized in the sacred spring near the shrine of Sheikh Adi, the religion's holiest shrine near Mosul, and could be worn only after a Yazidi spiritual mentor had opened it for the wearer at the neck.

Traditional Yazidi dress consisted of a white tunic with very long sleeves that could be knotted behind the neck when working, wide white trousers, red woolen belts or sashes, an overjacket, and a red turban or white cloth with red polka dots. In Sinjar (a town and province in northwestern Iraq), Yazidi men wore a tall, conical, dark-colored felt cap (qeem), surrounded by a black or red turban.

Female dress—according to travelers' reports in the 1920s—seems to have been very similar to the male outfits initially, the only difference being a longer, ankle-length white tunic and a red mantle (izar) worn under the left arm and secured over the right shoulder. In 1941, Lady Drower published a detailed description of female Yazidi dress. According to her, young women wore northern-style headdresses, combining a coin-studded cap (cumedrave) and a turban (jamadani) composed of several silk kerchiefs and secured by two silver pins with ball heads, connected by a chain (derzi) that draped across one side of the turban.

When the owner was around the age of thirty, the cap was passed on to her daughter or a young female relative, and after that time, older women wore only a dark-colored turban. These "matrons," as Drower described them, covered the turban with a loose white veil (lachek or lajak) that enclosed the entire neck area. Apparently, the size of a Yazidi woman's turban could vary according to locality, because Iraqi historian Sami Said Ahmed, writing in the 1970s, ascertained that the turbans worn by the Yazidi ladies of Sinjar were larger than those in the Shikan and other Yazidi areas.

Yazidi women's dress echoed closely the dress conventions of other groups in the area throughout the twentieth century: a long chemise reaching to the ankles (keras), baggy white undertrousers (darpe), and a short, sleeveless jacket in cold weather (bindana). According to Ahmed, the white trousers had symbolic significance, because it was said that a Yazidi woman who did not wear trousers was considered to have deserted her religion. Around the waist young women wore a soft, folded sash (qambara) or—on festive occasions like their wedding—a stiff belt about an inch and a half (3.8 centimeters) wide fastened with a huge embossed silver buckle secured by a silver pin. An outer jacket (kotek) was also worn, covered by a homespun and hand-embroidered shawl or mantle draped under the left arm and knotted over the right shoulder (called *meyzar* or *izar*, depending on the dialect or group).

As for the color scheme of the outfits, a transition seems to have occurred over time from white and red to more colorful combinations. Unmarried girls wore an array of joyful colors, while older married women chose more subdued hues. The favorite colors were red, orange, yellow, purple, green, and a brick red derived from the dye plant called madder. With regard to jewelry, too, age and marital status influenced the choice and quantity of items worn. Young girls enhanced their garments with ample amounts of jewelry, while older women wore less with advancing age.

YAZIDI RELIGIOUS DRESS

Yazidis were obliged to pray five times a day, and each time—after copious ablutions and preparatory prayer—they donned a ritual white shirt, the *rasta*. Interestingly, both the name of the garment (*rasta*) and its use offer intriguing parallels to the ritual outfit worn by the Mandaeans of southern Iraq. The rasta had a wide, rounded neckline (*gerivan*), was cut loosely at the front, and

A Yazidi man standing next to a sacred area near the Sheikh Adi shrine, Ain Sifni, Iraq, 2003. Mario Tama/Getty Images.

was fastened at the back. Ahmed, however, has reported that the garment was buttoned on one side as religious tradition banned frontal openings. During prayer the worshipper was required to lift the hem of the neck to the lips. The rasta was also worn for religious festivities. The act of changing from daily to ritual clothing was a symbolic step that reflected the scriptures, in which the metaphor of a change of garment was used to describe the process of reincarnation of lesser Yazidi souls (*keras gehorrin*, "changing the shirt").

In religious terms, Yazidi society was carefully stratified, and each level of the religious hierarchy was allocated a specific dress code and color, imbued with spiritual and symbolic significance. At the helm was the Yazidi *mir*, or prince, who was considered the sole earthly representative of Sheikh Adi with all temporal and spiritual authority vested in him. His person was sacred. Traditionally, he and his immediate family were the only ones allowed to wear soft or silky garments, although by the 1970s this privilege was no longer exclusive. The mir's choice of dress seems to have been considerable and often combined local, Arab, and European influences. The influence of Arab dress on the mir's attire may have reflected the mir's role as sole representative of his community, which brought him—unlike his coreligionists—into regular contact with Arab officials and dignitaries visiting or based in regional cities. Only special spiritual assistants, the *kochaks*, were allowed to wash the mir's garments, and the water had to be disposed of in a special way as it had cleansed the garments of a holy man. At the death of the mir, his clothes were given to the Grand Sheikh or Baba Sheikh, the highest Yazidi priest.

The Grand Sheikh, who was appointed by the mir and supervised the affairs of the Sheikh Adi shrine, wore a white homespun tunic, secured by a twenty-nine-and-a-half-foot- (nine-meter-) long sash of black wool decorated with sacred rings. His turban had to be black. The Grand Sheikh's assistants, known as sheikhs, also wore white but donned a black skullcap and, around the body, a red-and-orange or orange girdle (*zunnar*). The next rank in the Yazidi hierarchy was occupied by the *pirs*, religious advisors to the Yazidi community. The pirs often wore black garments and white turbans marked by a black plume or wound with a red scarf. Some pirs were recruited to become *faqirs*, hermitlike caretakers of the Sheikh Adi shrine. During their initiation period, they had to wear a white tunic with a black wool rope (*mahak*) around the neck, reminding them to abstain from sin and wantonness. Initiated faqirs wore a black turban (*pushi*) and black woolen skullcap (*kullik*), sometimes surmounted by a red handkerchief, and a rough, black woolen tunic with a round neck (*khirqa*), bound by a red belt (*mahak*) containing a yellow copper ring (*kharim*). In winter, a warm vest (*sukhma*) and a short red outer jacket frogged with black, the *damiri*, were worn on top. Throughout a faqir's life, a sacred thread of twisted red and black wool called "the chain of Yazid" or *maftoul*, was worn around the neck and could never be removed.

According to Yazidi scripture, the faqir's outfit was created by the godhead at the very beginning of time. Practically speaking, it had conceptual connections with the outfits of both a Muslim Sufi and a Hindu faqir, and it has been suggested that Hindus residing in Yazidi territory may have introduced it. The khirqa was sacrosanct. Throwing out an old one was strictly banned, and Yazidi law compelled faqirs to place them in a certain spot at the shrine of Sheikh Adi or—in the Sinjar area—near Kani Bir

Akhaie in the village of Kolkan in a deep hollow under a large stone. The mere presence of a tunic hung in a tree was believed to stop a fight, and in general it was respected to such a degree that Yazidis even honored the lice found on it. When a faqir died, he was usually buried in his khirqa.

Women, too, could serve Sheikh Adi and his shrine. Virgins or widows often joined the religious ranks as *faqiriyyat*, devoted to caretaking duties in the sacred precinct. These women wore all-white cotton tunics, trousers, turbans, woolen mantles (meyzar or izar), and even abayehs. The white wimple covering the turban was brought down and across the chin or even lower part of the face.

The next rank in the Yazidi hierarchy below the faqirs belonged to the kochaks, commoners recruited to advise and guide the community. The kochaks wore white turbans, long, flowing robes, and black or red woolen belts with sacred rings attached. The lowest rank in the religious hierarchy comprised the so-called *qawwals*. These reciters of sacred hymns and players of sacred instruments were allowed to wear colored fabrics, but white was more usual. Both their turbans and skullcaps were black and considered holy. Pilgrims regularly provided them with clothes for two months, and these were then returned to the donors sanctified.

YAZIDIS IN THE EARLY TWENTY-FIRST CENTURY

By the 1970s, the isolated world of the Yazidis was being penetrated by increasingly pervasive, external influences that had a far-reaching effect on both their traditional lifestyle and their dress codes. Ahmed reports that by that time many Yazidis had begun to ignore the religious dress code requirements and were opting increasingly for Western-style dress, leaving the head uncovered. Prohibitions of wearing the color blue were more and more ignored when men of religion were not present.

After Saddam Hussein's ascent to power in 1979, the Yazidis' resolutely traditional culture experienced even more drastic change, including forced resettlement, geographic isolation, and the political fallout from two Gulf Wars. In addition, the pervasive influence of a globalized media culture has further challenged and eroded Yazidi traditions of dress. In the early twenty-first century, only a few Yazidis retain any traditional elements in the way they dress, most related to ritual rather than daily wear.

TRADITIONAL CLOTHING IN SOUTHERN IRAQ

The south of Iraq is the traditional home of nomadic, agricultural, and water buffalo–herding communities. Many of them are concentrated in the marshes, a unique natural environment that straddles the lower reaches of the Tigris and Euphrates rivers and their confluence, the Shatt al-'Arab, occupying an area that is defined by a rough triangle between the towns of Amara and Nasiriya and the city of Basra. Until the second half of the twentieth century, tribal Arabs, particularly the so-called Mi'dan or Marsh Arabs, and the Mandaeans, a non-Arab gnostic religious community that specialized in boat building and silversmithing, managed to preserve their unique way of life, based on near-total self-reliance, in isolation from mainstream Iraq. Most items of their material culture were home-produced, including some of the clothing used. Few people in the region visited places other

than the local market town, and outside influences were largely resisted. Only in the late 1960s and early 1970s did changes in their material culture start to occur after inexpensive goods, including imported materials and secondhand garments, had established themselves in the markets of nearby towns. These proved attractive not only due to their affordability but also on account of their durability and practicality, their brilliant colors, and their innovative decorative designs. Increased outside influences also infiltrated traditional lifestyles through the introduction of obligatory schooling, which brought new trends to even the remotest village or community.

By the mid-1970s, some traditional crafts and textile production had ceased, and secondhand Western-style garments, from zipped sports tops and roll-neck turtlenecks to sneakers, had become integral parts of local dress, particularly for young men and children. With the onset of Iraq's war with Iran in the early 1980s, the pace of change accelerated intensely. These areas' sustained political opposition to the Baath regime in Baghdad resulted in extensive punitive actions by the government, and by 1990 much of the population, especially the Mi'dan and the Bedouin, had completely disappeared from the area. Since the fall of the Baath regime in 2004, efforts have been made to regenerate the area and in particular the marshes. Mi'dan communities, numbering about seven thousand families total, have already returned to the area to resume their traditional way of life. The impact of these events on local material culture and dress codes remains to be studied, and no data are available yet in the early twenty-first century.

MALE DRESS IN SOUTHERN IRAQ

As elsewhere in Iraq, the basic male Arab dress in southern Iraq consists of the long shirt or dishdasha over long white cotton pants (sirwal) with a drawstring waist, a skullcap ('arqchena), a head cloth (ghutra or keffiyeh) and head rope ('aqal), and the formal cloak (aba or *bisht*). Before the end of World War I (1914–1918), tribal Arabs and their leaders are reported to have worn colored and patterned robes of sackcloth, wool, or silk depending on their wealth and rank, in addition to coats and abas (the latter richly embroidered with gold thread). Afterward, styles gradually became plainer: a dishdasha of white, brown, gray, or black cotton (later also available in synthetic materials); a black-and-white checkered keffiyeh that is considered typical for the southern and mainly, but not exclusively, Shia Arab tribes; a thick or thin, plaited black wool or camel-hair 'aqal; and a generally brown or black aba with embroidered borders, produced locally. In the 1950s, after the enterprising initiative of a Lebanese businessman had introduced secondhand clothing from North America and Europe to local souqs, Western-style suit jackets and overcoats were added as status items to the traditional male outfit. Footwear such as sandals or Western-style shoes could but did not have to complete the outfit—many poorer Arabs in this region wore shoes only during holidays or special occasions. Rifles, colorful ammunition belts around the waist, and the *mugwar*, a reed and bitumen club, completed the traditional dress of the Arab male of southern Iraq.

Though deceptively plain, some aspects of male Arab dress in the south have great ritual and ceremonial significance. Thus, Sigrid Westphal-Hellbusch and Heinz Westphal, German ethnologists who worked in Southwest Asia and India, reported in the 1960s that no man must enter the traditional guesthouse of

A Marsh Arab woman with her daughter, Abu al Muhammen, southern Iraq, 2005. She wears a black *shaylah* (head scarf) wrapped around her head, with sequins and embroidery on the chest area. John D. Mchugh/AFP/Getty Images.

Marsh settlements, the *mudhif*, without complete formal attire, including the aba around his shoulders and the 'aqal crowning his head cloth. Only a man whose honor had been insulted could dare to appear in this context without his 'aqal, and he would not be expected to use it again until his honor had been fully restored.

As elsewhere in Iraq, male headgear in general is the most important marker of social and religious distinctions. Whereas wearing the 'aqal over the head cloth indicates tribal identity in the larger confederations of the south, people not wearing the 'aqal and wearing the head scarf folded back over the head in a semiturban style are identified as coastal or palm-cultivating Arabs from the Shatt al-'Arab region.

Religious personalities claiming to be direct descendants of the Prophet, known as sayyids, traditionally wore a green or, in the Marshes, dark blue or black head scarf. Particularly distinguished sayyids, addressed as sheikhs, wore a white head cloth. According to Westphal-Hellbusch and Westphal, only in the Hor area did sayyids not distinguish themselves from the rest of the villagers in terms of dress code: In this local context, individuals were known so intimately to each other that there was no need to convey status through external markers in dress. Finally, an unusual brown head scarf, worn without an 'aqal, was used by the itinerant *kashfa* or soothsayers who traditionally traveled from village to village in the south.

FEMALE DRESS IN SOUTHERN IRAQ

The only detailed information available on female dress in southern Iraq refers to the Mi'dan or Marsh Arabs, but most of the elements reflect dress conventions throughout the wider region. In the first half of the twentieth century, female dress among the Marsh Arabs was all black and consisted of a long dress, a chin scarf augmented by a headwrap, and an abayeh. The latter was produced locally, and the women provided the weaver with the required wool. The wool from two to three sheep was necessary to complete one garment, and the price depended on the quality of weave required.

After the 1950s, travelers and ethnographers like Elizabeth Fernea (a U.S. anthropologist, writer, and traveler) and Westphal-Hellbusch and Westphal reported that indoor dress consisted of bright, boldly patterned, and colorful sleeved gowns reaching to the feet. The materials were generally of imported cotton or flannelette, bought in one of the larger towns in the region. Young women covered their head with a thin black scarf (*shaylah* or *futa*). One end was placed on the central parting of the hair, then the scarf was passed under the chin and up again and fastened on the crown of the head by means of a little pin. The purpose of this wrap was to cover not only the hair but more importantly the neck area, the exposure of which was considered shameful. Older married women tied an additional turban or *'amaama* over the shaylah. The 'amaama consisted of several meters of thin black material, wrapped several times around the front and back of the head and with the end secured underneath the folds. An alternative type of headwrap to augment the futa was the *asha* or *charghad*, of light black silk and often fringed. Some women of the younger generations seem to have begun abandoning some aspects of their traditional dress and instead wore the veil and abayeh only when leaving the house. In winter, those who could afford it added heavy black sweaters or jackets to their traditional clothing for extra warmth.

Jewelry was extremely popular for enhancing local female dress. Silver and gold nose rings, earrings, and finger rings; necklaces, chains, and pendants; and bracelets and anklets were purchased from gold- and silversmiths, many of them Mandaeans, in nearby towns and worn both on a daily basis and on special occasions.

One female garment reserved exclusively for celebrations and festive days was the so-called *nafnuf* or *hashimi*, a very wide rectangular garment that was cut similarly to an abayeh but closed in front. Ideally, it was fashioned from expensive, often gauzy material and embroidered or enhanced with tinsel and sequins. This garment could be afforded only by wealthy privileged women, and the wives of local sheikhs in particular loved to show off their expensive versions. From the 1970s on, the hashimi was increasingly worn as a fashionable "national" dress and status symbol by wealthy urban women of the intellectual and political elite all over Iraq.

Particular wedding-dress conventions are not mentioned in the sources before the 1950s, when Western-style white robes, bought in town, became fashionable. Merging local and imported traditions, the bride—on leaving her house—was covered first with a white veil and then with a new, black silk wedding abayeh.

Children's dress largely echoed that of the adults in the community. The very first piece of clothing was a little hood or cap (*'araqchena*); some very small children went without any clothes other than this cap. Later, little boys wore tiny versions of the adult dishdasha, while girls sported colorful tailored dresses similar in style to those of their adult female relatives. As early as the first decade of the twentieth century, the first elements of Western-style fashion, transmitted through Ottoman urban conventions, made themselves felt in local children's dress, and in *Haji Rikkan*, S. E. Hedgcock (using the pseudonym Fulanain), a British political officer in Iraq who was partly responsible for the country's current borders, recalls the small daughter of a local sheikh dressed in pseudo-European fashion with a feathered hat and tan boots with buttons, obviously an outfit associated with progressive sophistication and elite status. Later, secondhand European and U.S. hats, sweaters, shirts, and sneakers increasingly became part of a boy's or girl's dress and—in the case of the former—could replace traditional dress altogether, depending on personal preference and affordability.

Between the age of five and ten years old, girls received their first head scarf (shaylah or futa). This was intended less to cover the hair than the neck area. Gradually, they began to wear the adult shaylah during festivities or in the presence of strangers until it became an indispensable part of their daily wear. Only after marriage was the black cloth headwrap (asha) added to the futa.

MANDAEAN RITUAL DRESS

Among the communities of southern Iraq, the gnostic Mandaeans form a distinct entity in terms of ethnicity, religion, and aspects of dress. This closely knit community was traditionally based in small towns and isolated villages alongside the Tigris and Euphrates rivers and the Shatt al-'Arab in southern Iraq. The Mandaeans made a living as experienced boat and bridge builders as well as goldsmiths, silversmiths, and blacksmiths. The central rite of the Mandaean creed is immersion in water, which symbolizes communion with the World of Light and purifies the soul. During baptism, priests and laymen alike have to wear the Mandaeans' distinctive ritual dress, the white cotton *rasta*, which symbolizes the heavenly dress of light worn by the angels of light and the pure souls residing with them. It is made of natural fiber, usually cotton or muslin, and every Mandaean must own one.

The rasta consists of five items for laymen and seven items for priests. The layperson's outfit consists of a tunic (*sadra* or *ksuiva*) with a patch pocket (*dasha*). A tunic should usually be six dhras long (a *dhra* being the length of the forearm from elbow to fingertip). For a dying person, seven to eight dhras are required. *Ksuiva* means "to cover." During the baptism the priest gathers his ksuiva up in a ritually prescribed way, whereas the layperson enters the water with the ksuiva hanging free.

A belt or girdle (*himiana*), which symbolizes the celestial waters issuing from the Divine and the Mandaean faith, is tied around the waist over the ksuiva. It is tubular in shape and consists of sixty woven woolen threads, made from wool taken from a living male lamb. The tying of the belt has ritual meaning. The belt is held in front of the body, crossed at the back, and then tied in a double knot in front. The ends of the belt are tucked into the belt itself at either side of the waist. One end of the belt has an unsewn tassel called the *karkousha*. The other end, which is bound and sewn, is called the *arwa*. The arwa must be passed over the karkousha in tying it. In front, the karkousha must fall to the left, and the arwa must fall to the right.

The ksuiva is worn with long, loose trousers (*sirwal*) held up by a drawstring, known as *tikka*. The head is covered by a turban (*burzinqa*) made of a strip of white muslin about a dhra wide that is twisted three times around the head. When the burzinqa is wrapped, one end, the *rughza*, is left hanging down over the left shoulder. When the rughza is brought across the lower part of the face in order to cover the nose and mouth, then up over the top of the head and tucked in at the right side, it becomes a *pandama*. The pandama is generally used only by priests. The symbolic meaning of the pandama is to seal up those elements in the human body that might not be considered pure and might pollute sacred objects. In funerals, it is to prevent the corruption of death from entering the mouth and nose. In the case of women, the burzinqa is draped like a shawl and called a *shiala*.

A long, narrow strip of cloth or muslin, the *nasifa*, is worn like a Christian stole but in such a way that the left side is considerably shorter than the right. For a priest the nasifa should be about a dhra wide, but for the layman it can be much narrower. The stole is involved in many of the ritual movements associated with baptism, marriage ceremonies, and funerary rites.

In addition to these items, the priest wears a crown (*taga*), a tubular strip of white silk that is worn beneath the turban and consecrated separately from the other garments. This crown represents light and serves as a physical reminder that the priest is the temporal leader among his parishioners. He also wears a gold ring with the sacred word *shem*, (meaning "light" or

A Mandaean elder stands on a river bank, watching others being baptized in the Tigris River, near Baghdad, 2008. He wears a tunic (*ksuiva*) worn by laymen during this ritual. A belt (*himiana*) is tied around the waist over the *ksuiva* and symbolizes the celestial waters issuing from the Divine and the Mandaean faith. His turban (*burzinqa*) is tied three times around the head and is made from a strip of white muslin. Sabah Arar/AFP/Getty Images.

"splendor"), known as *shum yawar*, on the little finger of his right hand. When officiating, the priest always carries a staff of olive wood known as *margna*, which is associated with water and is often spoken of as the staff of living water. A final implement belonging to the priest's ritual dress is the *skandola*, a talismanic seal ring of iron bearing representations of a lion, scorpion, bee (or wasp), and serpent. The serpent encircles the other animals head to tail. The ring is attached by an iron chain to a shaftless iron knife. It is worn during exorcisms and by those isolated for uncleanliness (such as that resulting from childbirth or marriage). It is also used to seal newborns' navels and to seal the tomb at funerals. With the exception of the golden ring, which is worn from the moment of the priest's ordination until his burial, all the other items are put on or taken off to the accompaniment of long prayers and blessings during the opening and closing rituals of every ceremony.

References and Further Reading

Ahmed, Sami Said. *The Yazidis: Their Life and Beliefs*. Field Research Projects. Miami, FL: Coconut Grove, 1975.

Al-Jadir, Walid Mahmoud. *Al Aziya' al-sha'abiyyah fi'l-'Iraq*. Baghdad: Wizara al-Thaqafa wa'l A'alam, Dar al-Rashid li'l-Nashr, 1979.

Champault, Dominique. "L'izar de Qaracoche Nord del l'Iraq." *Objets et Mondes* 9, pt. 2 (1969): 167–176.

Drower, Ethel Stefana. *Peacock Angel*. London: John Murray, 1941.

Drower, Ethel Stefana. *The Mandaeans of Iraq and Iran*. Leiden: E.J. Brill, 1962.

Edmonds, Cecil J. *Kurds, Turks and Arabs: Politics, Travel and Research in North-Eastern Iraq, 1919–1925*. London, New York, and Toronto: Oxford University Press, 1957.

Empson, R.H.W. *The Cult of the Peacock Angel*. London: H.F. Witherby, 1928.

Fernea, Elizabeth. *Guests of the Sheikh: An Ethnography of an Iraqi Village*. London: Robert Hall, 1968.

Hansen, Henny Harald. *Daughters of Allah: Among Moslem Women in Kurdistan*. London: Allen and Unwin, 1960.

Hansen, Henny Harald. *The Kurdish Woman's Life*. Nationalmuseets Skrifter, Etnografisk Raekke, VII. Copenhagen: Nationalmuseet, 1961.

Harris, George L. *Iraq: Its People, Its Society, Its Culture*. New Haven, CT: HRAF (Human Relations Area Files) Press, 1958.

Hedgcock, S.E. [Fulanain, pseud.]. *Haji Rikkan: Marsh Arab*. London: Chatto and Windus, 1927.

Hubbard, G.E. *From the Gulf to Ararat. An Expedition through Mesopotamia and Kurdistan*. Edinburgh and London: William Blackwood and Sons, 1916.

Kreyenbroek, Phillip G., and Christine Allison, eds. *Kurdish Culture and Identity*. London: Zed Books, 1996.

Longrigg, Stephen Hemsley, and Frank Stoakes. *Iraq*. London: Ernest Benn, 1958.

Maxwell, Gavin. *A Reed Shaken by the Wind*. Harmondsworth: Penguin, 1983.

Naval Intelligence Division. *Iraq and the Persian Gulf. September 1944. B.R. 524 (Restricted)*. Geographical Handbook Series for Official Use Only. Oxford and Cambridge: University Press, 1944.

Ochsenschlaeger, Edward L. *Iraq's Marsh Arabs in the Garden of Eden*. Philadelphia: University of Pennsylvania Museum of Archaeology and Anthropology Press, 2004.

O'Shea, Maria T. "Kurdish Dress: Regional Diversity and Divergence." In *Kurdish Culture and Identity*, edited by Phillip G. Kreyenbroek and Christine Allison, 135–155. London: Zed Books, 1996.

Pocket Guide to Baghdad. Baghdad: The Times Press, 1952.

Salim, S.M. *Marsh Dwellers of the Euphrates Delta*. London: Athlone Press, 1962.

Stark, Freya. *Baghdad Sketches*. London: John Murray, 1937.

Stark, Freya. *Riding to the Tigris*. London: John Murray, 1957.

Stevens, E.S. *By Tigris and Euphrates*. London: Hurst and Blackett, 1923.

Stillman, Yedida Kalfon, and Norman A. Stillman, eds. *Arab Dress: A Short History from the Dawn of Islam to Modern Times*. Leiden and Boston: Brill, 2003.

Stillman, Yedida Kalfon, Norman A. Stillman, and T. Majda. "Libas." In *The Encyclopedia of Islam*, edited by C.E. Bosworth, E. Van Donzel, B. Lewis, and Ch. Pellat. vol. 5, 732–753. Leiden: E.J. Brill, 1986.

Thesiger, Wilfred. *The Marsh Arabs*. Harmondsworth: Penguin, 1967. (Reprinted in 1983.)

Weihrauch, G., Ibrahim Al-Haidari, and Ali Al-Wardi. *Soziologie des Nomadentums. Studie über die irakische Gesellschaft*. Neuwied and Darmstadt, Germany: Luchterhand, 1972.

Westphal-Hellbusch, Sigrid, and Heinz Westphal. *Die Ma'dan. Kultur und Geschichte der Marschenbewohner im Süd-Iraq*. Berlin: Duncker und Humbolt, 1962.

Wigram, E.T.A. *The Cradle of Mankind: Life in Eastern Kurdistan*. 2nd ed. London: A. and C. Black, 1922.

Wigram, W.A. *The Assyrians and Their Neighbours*. Gorgias Reprint Series, 25. Piscataway, NJ: Gordias Press, 2002.

Young, Gavin. *Return to the Marshes: Life with the Marsh Arabs of Iraq*. London: Futura, 1978

Ulrike Al-Khamis and Saad Lafta Hami

See also Ottoman Dress; Kurdish Dress; Iranian Regional Dress; Iranian Urban Dress; Face Veils.

Kurdish Dress

Kurdistan, which means "the land of the Kurds" in Persian, is located in central Southwest Asia and covers an area of approximately 151,350 square miles (392,000 square kilometers). Parts of the area are incorporated into eastern Turkey (43%), northwestern Iran (31%), northern Iraq (18%), northern Syria (6%), and the former Soviet Union (2%). There are also two large Kurdish enclaves in central and north-central Anatolia in Turkey and in the province of Khorasan in northeastern Iran. Despite international recognition of Iraqi Kurdistan as an autonomous federal entity, the Kurds remain the largest ethnic population in the world without an autonomous independent state of their own.

Kurdish society is a tribal one with distinctly recognizable social classes. This society is known to place high value on familial bonds and tribal lands. The Kurds regard themselves as having a special relationship with their environment. This fact is clearly reflected in their traditional dress, in both a direct and an abstract sense. Local products such as animals and dye plants provided the raw materials for dyeing, weaving, and making clothing.

The landscape of Kurdistan is diverse and includes snow-capped mountain ranges, high-altitude plateaus, forests, and plains. Temperatures vary from minus 22 degrees Fahrenheit (minus 30 degrees Celsius) in the north (Karakose, Turkey) to 104 degrees Fahrenheit (40 degrees Celsius) (Kermanshah, Iran). Precipitation varies from 8 inches (20 centimeters) per year in the plains to 118 inches (300 centimeters) in the mountains. Kurdistan enjoys an abundance of rivers and lakes. The Kurds have an ethnicity, language, and history clearly distinct from those of their neighbors, the Turks, Persians, Arabs, Armenians, and Georgians. They are mostly Sunni Muslims but also include Shia Muslims, Alevis, Yarsans, Yazidis, Kakeyis, Baha'is, Jews, and Christians. Kurdish is an Indo-European language closely related to other members of the Indo-Iranian family. It is divided into two main groups, the Kurmanji and the Dimili-Gurani; each of these two groups is divided in turn into a number of subdialects.

TRADITIONAL MALE DRESS: THE RANK-O-CHOKHA

The *rank-o-chokha*, *shall-o-shapak* (in the Badinani dialect), or *chokha* is the main outfit of Kurdish male dress. It basically consists of a jacket and a pair of trousers and therefore represents the suit of the Kurdish male. The jacket of the rank-o-chokha has no buttons. Its sleeves are long, with the exact length varying by region. It is not uncommon to observe sleeves markedly longer than an arm's length; such sleeves are normally lined with a shiny fabric of one or more colors and are often decorated with designs specific to men, such as stripes or small geometric designs.

The trousers of the rank-o-chokha can have a straight leg that is open at the ankle or a wide leg that is either wide or tapered at the ankle. Variations in the cut depend on a Kurd's region and tribe. In general, in southern, central, and eastern Kurdistan, the wide style of trousers is favored; in western Kurdistan, straight-leg trousers are preferred; and in northern Kurdistan, both styles are worn. The wide waist of the trousers is gathered and held in place by a thick drawstring. These baggy trousers protect the wearer from the harsh weather in winter and summer, and it is easier to traverse mountainous terrain in them than in narrow Western-style trousers.

The rank-o-chokha requires at least fourteen yards (thirteen meters) of fabric and is most valued when made from fabric that is handwoven from goat hair. In the past, various groups in Kurdistan produced the rank-o-chokha in a surprisingly wide spectrum of colors, ranging from the natural colors of goat hair to those concocted from natural dyes by professional dyers. Colors used include many shades of white, beige, gray, blue, and green. Striped patterns and embroidery are worked in vivid colors such as red, purple, and pink. The Sanjabi tribe, a major tribe in Kermanshah, is known in particular for its use of bright colors and lustrous fabrics. The Yazidis, in contrast, wear limited colors and are forbidden to wear blue as prescribed by their religion. In Iranian Kurdistan, the rank-o-chokha is made of plain-colored fabric woven from undyed wool. The dyeing industry was traditionally dominated by Kurdish Jews, and weaving was usually done by Kurdish and Assyrian Christians living in areas that make up Iraq in the twenty-first century.

In the nineteenth century and continuing into the mid-twentieth century, weavers used hand-spun thread. A mixture of goat hair and sheep wool was also used to produce a less expensive fabric and more durable weave. After World War I, machine-made thread and fabrics replaced traditional hand-spun thread and handwoven textiles. These fabrics expedited the weaving process and decreased the cost of clothing. As a result, however, the crafts of spinning and weaving began to decline. The weavers diminished in number to very few families scattered here and there in Kurdistan. A few families in Bersipa, in southern Kurdistan (northern Iraq), are still spinning and weaving the fabric for the rank-o-chokha or shall-o-shapak. In 2004, there were a few families of weavers in Baghdad, all of whom were immigrants from Kurdistan, who were still weaving the fabric of the rank-o-chokha using either their own hand-spun Iranian goat hair, machine-spun threads, or a mixture of both, depending on the orders received from the Kurds of northern Iraq.

The spinning is done by women and the weaving by men, using a simple horizontal loom. The process of preparing the yarns and weaving the fabric involves more than ten stages. The wool first needs to be cleaned and combed; only when this has been properly done can the wool be spun. After spinning, the threads are soaked in water and then dried in the sun at certain hours of the day, when the sun is not hot enough to bleach the colors. Thereafter, the wool is treated with glue, then vaporized with sulfur, and

A man's handwoven mohair sash and cotton belts embroidered with silk thread, Iran, ca. 1950. The sash (known as *kemar*, *pestand*, *shella*, or *shellema*) is worn by folding the cloth into a wide band, which is then wrapped around the waist several times. The folds in the sash are used to hold items such as money, valuables, a pipe, and a tobacco pouch. The belts were worn with a silver buckle to fasten two parts of a Kurdish man's suit (*rank-o-chokha*). Courtesy of Layla Pio.

immersed in boiling water, to be dried again and then stretched on the loom ready to weave. This process cleans and slightly stiffens the fibers, yielding a yarn that is nearer to a worsted than a woolen and producing hard-wearing cloth. Once the weaving is completed, the fabric is pressed. The rank-o-chokha have different woven patterns varying from simple to highly complex. However, weavers prefer the simpler and less complicated patterns; at the end of the twentieth century, many weavers had abandoned most of the old complicated motifs and were limiting their product to plain and striped patterns.

In the nineteenth century, the rank-o-chokha was decorated with embroidery within the weaving pattern; much of this practice has died out. However, in some areas, embroidery is used to decorate the traditional suit, as in Zakho and Aqra in northern Iraq. The price of the rank-o-chokha depends on several factors, including the quality and purity of the material used, with natural, hand-spun goat hair being the most expensive. The sophistication of the woven pattern also plays a significant role in determining a garment's price. Intricate motifs and delicate stripes are the most expensive; solid colors and wide, simple stripes are the least expensive. These patterns are often unique to specific regions within Kurdistan.

TRADITIONAL MALE DRESS: OTHER GARMENTS

Under the jacket of the rank-o-chokha, Kurdish men wear a long-sleeved, collarless shirt that is left open in the front. It can be white or in colors like gray, brown, or beige. The Yazidis, in south-central Turkey near the Syrian border and in the Jabal Sinjar region further south and east in Iraq, wear a white variation of this shirt that has a square-shaped neckline. In Hakkari, Turkey, these long sleeves can reach thirty-nine inches (one hundred centimeters) in length and twelve inches (thirty centimeters) in width. The sleeves are functional as well as decorative: During work, they can be wrapped around the jacket's arms to protect it from dirt and wear and tear; in traditional dance, where arm movements are instrumental, they enhance the dancer's movements and stature.

The *yelek* is simply a vest without sleeves. It is worn in a number of styles throughout Kurdistan: either over the jacket or under the jacket and over the shirt. The yeleks worn over the jacket usually lack buttons and are made entirely of *kecha* (felt). In Moush and Bitlis, people like to decorate these jackets with ribbons and embroidery. Some of these over-the-jacket vests have protruding shoulders. These are worn by the Peshmerga and the Kurdish people for celebrations, like Nawroz (the New Year's festival that takes place on about 22 March), and on other occasions as a symbol of Kurdish identity. Shepherds wear what is called a *faranji* vest, which is also an over-the-jacket vest with protruding shoulders but a bit longer than normal.

Yeleks worn over the shirt and under the jacket have buttons. In such yeleks, the front and the back are not made of the same material. The front part of such vests is made mostly of the same fabric as the rank-o-chokha, with some being made of silk or jacquard; the back part is usually made of cotton. All the over-the-shirt yeleks, however, are decorated with embroidery with motifs varying according to region and tribe. In Khorasan in Iran and other parts of western and northern Kurdistan, this yelek is worn alone without a jacket. In Van and Hakkari, over-the-shirt vests with silk and jacquard fronts are favored.

The *kemar, pestand, shella,* or *shellema* (sash) is an integral part of Kurdish traditional male dress. The sash binds the rank-o-chokha at the waist. It is made of lengthy pieces of rectangular woven fabric of varying quality. To make a sash, this rectangular fabric is folded into a long band and wrapped around the waist once or more depending on the length of the band and in a style dictated by the customs of the region or tribe. A leather belt may be added on top of the sash for reinforcement. A revolver or a dagger is usually inserted in the band. The sash, when wound around the waist several times, serves a functional as well as decorative purpose: Its folds are used to hold money, valuables, a pipe, and a tobacco pouch.

Different kinds of fabrics are used for sashes; *kemar, pestand, shella,* and *shellema* are different names for a variety of fabrics used for such sashes. Most of these bands were and are woven in Iran and Turkey. The mohair sashes are the best and are very rare in the early twenty-first century. Modern imitations are made of synthetic fabrics, which make them cheaper and more accessible. At the same time, there is a great demand for the mohair bands, old and new, on the part of rich Kurds. The shellema, which is wrapped once around the waist, is woven in Hakkari, southeastern Turkey, with dark background colors, mostly black, and is ornate with geometric designs.

Variations in the color of the sashes may indicate a specific group within Kurdish society. Belts that come from Turkey or Iran are usually dark in color and decorated with a *butteh* (paisley) motif or an intricate floral design. In Moush and Bitlis in Turkish Kurdistan, three pieces of multicolored fabric—usually gray, yellow, and red—are wrapped around the waist together. Descendants of the Hashemite House of the Prophet Mohammad wear green sashes; the Yazidi people wear black sashes. A white shella (sash) is also worn throughout Kurdistan.

Kurdish headgear consists of a turban and a skullcap (called *kelaw* or *arqchen*) or a fez (a type of cap, usually red in color). The oldest type of Kurdish headgear consists of a small, conical skullcap of varying heights around which a cloth turban is wrapped. In the early twenty-first century, this style has evolved into numerous variations that indicate different regions and tribes of Kurdistan. In some parts of Kurdistan, only a skullcap is used as headgear. Skullcaps differ in shape and material and can be worn alone or with a turban. They can be either round or conical. They are made from cotton and can be embroidered in geometric designs with silk, golden, or silver thread. Kermanshah in Iran is known for producing golden and multicolored skullcaps; shepherds in Sulaymani in northern Iraq wear a distinct wool cap with a conical top and wide brim to protect them from the sun and precipitation.

A turban is made from a large piece of silk, wool, cotton, or synthetic material. It is first folded into a triangle, rolled into a loose cord, and then wrapped around a cap, fez, or skullcap. The starting end of the wrap is allowed to hang loosely behind the right ear. Turbans, too, can vary in size, shape, pattern, color, and quality. These variations can indicate, among other things, the wearer's affluence, tribe, and profession. In northern Kurdistan (Turkey), extra pieces of fabric are added to turbans to increase their size, so much so that they are often difficult to balance. The Yazidi people wear a skullcap with a red-and-white checkered turban wrapped with the reverse side of the cloth turned outward. Kurds of the Barazani tribe use the same checkered turban with the right side turned outward. Still other Kurdish tribes wear a black-and-white checkered turban, and Shia religious officials wear a black turban. The Kurdish Alevis wear a relatively small turban wrapped around a red fez. The Jaff tribe of central Kurdistan wears a special type of turban called a *meshki,* which is made in Iran.

Instead of the rank-o-chokha, men can wear the *zbun,* a long male dress, with or without sleeves. It covers the whole body and is worn with the right side wrapped over the left and secured with a clasp. In western Kurdistan (Turkey and Syria), men wear

A Kurdish woman's silk turban, mid-twentieth century. It is made by folding a piece of cloth into a triangle, which is then rolled into a loose cord and wrapped around a cap, fez, or skullcap. Courtesy of Layla Pio.

the zbun with a woolen *abayeh* (an Arab overgarment) on their shoulders or a European-style suit jacket. The Yazidis also wear the zbun with a woolen abayeh. In some parts of Kurdistan, farmers and shepherds wear in winter a long sheepskin or felt coat that covers most of the body to protect the wearer from cold, snow, rain, and mud.

The yameni and giveh are traditional types of footwear worn by Kurdish men. The *yameni* is a flat, red leather shoe without laces. The *giveh* consists of a crocheted or needlewoven cotton or silk upper attached to a sole (old examples have cloth soles, more expensive versions have leather ones, and cheap modern ones have plastic soles). The giveh is also called *kalash* in some parts of Kurdistan. It is comfortable and popular among both Kurds and tourists. In villages, the soles were made from small strips of cloth that were folded, compressed, and then put together vertically (like books on a bookshelf) to make the sole. In the second half of the twentieth century, the leather sole of the giveh was replaced by a rubber sole, and Kurdish men largely abandoned their traditional footwear for European styles, even to accompany traditional garments.

Kurdish socks are generally made of wool, although the more expensive ones are of mohair. They are typically knitted at home in bright colors with diverse patterns, such as red stripes or colorful geometric shapes on white backgrounds.

Kurdish children, whether boys or girls, dress similarly to adult Kurdish women. It is not until the age of ten that boys begin to wear the rank-o-chokha, kemar, and kelaw, with some regional variation. In Syria and Iraq, Kurdish boys wear a cap with a silver disk added to its top. Amulets made of fabric or silver are often pinned to the caps or shoulders of children to protect them from the evil eye. Children's socks and slippers are traditionally made at home by the women of the household.

TRADITIONAL FEMALE DRESS

Women's outfits consist of several pieces worn on top of one another. In parts of Iran, tops and skirts are used rather than dresses, so there is a wide variation in style. A widespread form of dress for women consists of the *darpe*, baggy trousers worn to cover the body from the waist down, just like pantaloons, and the *krass*, a long dress worn over the darpe that is made of sheer fabric decorated with silk threads and embroidered with a variety of sequins. It has long sleeves called *fakyana* that have triangular-shaped ends. Usually, the ends of the two fakyana are knotted together and thrown over the back. The krass with its long, triangular sleeves is widely worn by Kurdish women in Iran, Iraq, and Syria. Under the krass, another dress, made of dark-colored silk, is worn as a lining. In the nineteenth century, this underdress was roomy, but by the mid-twentieth century, it had become more fitted. In Mahabad, Kurdish women wear a white dress as a lining to their silk krass, which is usually decorated with golden threads.

On top of the krass, the women wear a *sukhma*. The sukhma is, in a sense, a female yelek (vest). It is a short, buttonless jacket that usually has long sleeves. This type of sukhma is widely used in central and southern Kurdistan. Nevertheless, some areas of Kurdistan prefer sukhmas without sleeves. Fabrics used in making sukhmas vary and can include silk, brocade, velvet, and even synthetics.

Kurdish females wear other garments as well. In some parts of Kurdistan, women wear a *kawa*, which is a long coat worn over the krass, beautifully worked with silk, silver, and golden threads.

Elderly women prefer to keep the old tradition by wearing a kawa instead of a sukhma with the krass. For winter, a velvet kawa or a padded kawa with a cotton lining are used to protect the wearer from severe cold weather. Some women wear a dasmal on top of the sukhma or kawa. The *dasmal* is a triangular piece of sheer fabric decorated with silk and silver threads and is thrown over the shoulders to cover the body at the back. In some villages of northern Kurdistan, women wear an apron over the dress, even at weddings and festivals. These aprons can be embroidered with flowers in one color, as in Bitlis, or printed with different designs. The *charoka* is another interesting rectangular piece of handwoven wool or raw silk fabric with hand embroidery that is worn over the dress; it is wrapped around the body under the right arm and then pulled upward and the two opposite ends knotted over the left shoulder. It is used by Yazidi, Jewish, and Christian women of the region.

In parts of northern Iraq, Kurdish women have adopted the black abayeh worn by their Arab neighbors. They wear the abayeh over traditional Kurdish clothes to cover their head and body when leaving their home. In western Kurdistan (northern Syria), Kurdish women wear a black coat with long sleeves. The coat is fastened with buttons or cords and is heavily adorned with embroidery, mostly in red, on the chest and to a lesser extent on the sleeves. The seams are also embroidered. The inner facing is decorated with appliqué work in contrasting silk satin. Some of these coats have a combination of appliqué work and embroidery on the chest. This Kurdish coat strongly resembles garments in other parts of Syria.

Colors are an important element in the dress of Kurdish women. Bright and vivid colors like orange, yellow, purple, red, and green are used frequently in all parts of Kurdistan together with dark red and black. Exceptions to this are the Yazidis, who are distinguished from the rest of the Kurds by their white dress, charoka, and veil.

The female Kurdish outfit is worn with a belt or sash (called *pish tou an* or *hyasa*). Belts can vary in material, color, and shape. In central Kurdistan, women use a metal belt made of either gold or a gold-colored or gold-plated metal. The hyasa, which has become a collector's item, is a hand-knitted cotton sash that is two to two and a half inches (five to six centimeters) wide; it is embroidered with red, purple, or green silk thread and decorated with pieces of silver and has a buckle consisting of a round, dome-shaped silver piece embossed with flowers. In eastern Kurdistan (Iran), sashes are made of wide, colorful silk fabric wrapped around the waist.

Headgear can be regarded as a vital element of Kurdish women's identity. Living under different states and having different ethnic groups as neighbors has not affected their headgear styles. Although Kurdish headgear styles vary significantly between regions and tribes, wearing *hijab* (an Islamic veil) was not a Kurdish practice until the late twentieth century, when neighboring influences have led some Kurdish women to wear the hijab. In western Kurdistan, women wear a tight, long scarf, often in a solid color. In central and some parts of eastern Kurdistan, women wear a sheer fabric draped over a skullcap. In Senneh, in eastern Kurdistan, women wear large turbans consisting of several multicolored kerchiefs with a long veil thrown over the turban, which hangs from the back of the turban to the ground. In Kermanshah, a turban is worn without a veil. Some Kurdish women prepare their turbans and fix them with pins so they are ready to wear when needed. The women of the Jaff tribe wear a simplified version of

Two skullcaps embroidered with silk threads gilded with gold and silver threads (behind), ca. 1980s, and a black felt skullcap and shepherd's felt hat (front), early twenty-first century. The embroidered skullcaps are normally worn by boys and young men, but in some parts of Kurdistan, Kurdish women wear them under the turban or with a sheer veil covering only the head. Courtesy of Layla Pio.

the turban, called a *seru pesh* or *mezer*, made of sheer fabric embroidered with silk or metallic threads; it is wrapped around the head and allowed to lean over the forehead with a modest tilt to the right. In northeastern Syria and northern Iraq, Kurdish women wear a fez decorated with a gold or silver disk attached to its top. From the disk, which is embossed with flowers or geometric designs, hang coins or almond-shaped pendants.

The *peni ber* was a high-heeled shoe worn by women, especially in the central region of Kurdistan, made of several layers of cloth sewn together. In the 1960s, peni bers ceased to exist. Shoes made of crocheted cotton and leather soles, as well as knitted socks, are either bought at the local market or made at home by members of the family. European-style shoes, made in many cities in Kurdistan, are quickly replacing this older, regional style.

Special occasions, such as weddings, feasts, religious and national celebrations, and funerals and the mourning period, are a central part of Kurdish life and warrant careful selection of dress. Throughout the twentieth century, Kurdish brides wore the traditional colorful, multilayered dress decorated with beads and embroidery. As the bride was taken to the house of the groom, a red veil was used to cover her face and body. For the Kurds, red symbolizes joy and happiness. The bride brought to the groom's household a trousseau that her family had been preparing for her wedding day since her childhood. The trousseau typically contained garments, headpieces, belts, shoes, and woven, decorative tent bands (long, narrow bands that go around the inside of a tent at the point where the roof touches the sides to keep out cold air). In the early twenty-first century, Kurdish brides wear white European-style wedding dresses with real or imitation gold jewelry.

A beautiful appearance depends on dress as well as one's facial looks. Kurdish women take special care of their hair using natural products like henna and of their complexion using items such as *spiaw* (homemade facial makeup made from herbs), kohl (a black powder used especially around the eyes to make them more attractive), and tattoos. Younger generations continue to use henna and kohl in addition to modern cosmetics.

During a period of mourning, some tribes dress in black garments from head to foot; these are decorated with silk threads and black sequins. However, the Barzani tribe as well as people of Arbil, in central Kurdistan, do not wear black during mourning. Kurdish widows wear a white veil.

A very special occasion to Kurds all over the world is the Nawroz festivity, which dates back to around twenty-five hundred years ago. On Nawroz day (New Year's; the first day of spring), which falls on about 21 or 22 March, the Kurds celebrate the onset of spring and the Kurdish New Year (a pre-Islamic, probably Zoroastrian festival). Kurds make a point of putting on the best and most colorful traditional clothes they possess.

JEWELRY

Jewelry is central in both the dress and the culture of the Kurdish people. Kurdish jewelry is predominantly made of gold and silver but can include ornaments made of precious and semiprecious stones and glass. Gold, particularly in central, eastern, and southeastern Kurdistan, is a necessary requisite for Kurdish families; it is used not only as an ornament but also as a symbol of wealth and social status that can be bought and sold depending on the family's financial needs. For these reasons, gold jewelry is highly esteemed in all Kurdish communities. In cities like Mahabad in eastern Kurdistan, Sulaymani in central Kurdistan, and others, the gold markets are always busy with women buying and ordering new designs according to the latest fashion.

Gold can be worn either as independent jewelry or as ornamentation on garments. Kurdish jewelry includes long necklaces (*girdana*), heavy earrings (*gwara*), rings, bracelets of different widths and styles (*go* or *bazn*), belts, brooches, hair ornaments, and anklets (*pawana*). A *tasbih shlan* is a necklace comprised of a gold chain studded with amber beads. Gold adorns Kurdish garments in the form of coins, beads, or chains sewn onto the traditional dress, integrated and embedded in the embroidery. The wealthiest Kurdish families garnish the seru pesh, dasmal, sukhma, kawa, and other garments with these gold ornaments.

Although gold is held in high esteem throughout Kurdistan, regions and tribes have developed unique ways of incorporating gold ornamentation into their traditional dresses. Women of the Jaff tribe of central Kurdistan wear a *kelaw alton*, a skullcap decorated with gold coins. The kelaw alton is fastened under the chin by a *jer chenaga*, a gold chain. Gold headpieces from Kermanshah are particularly well-known examples of Kurdish artisanship in gold jewelry. These headpieces are composed of caps with a metal disk sewn onto the crown and coins around the edges. Sometimes a metal chin strap or chain (with or without coins) is worn that is fastened on either side to the cap rim just in front of the ears. These caps are then covered with scarves of various types and colors as well as decorative chains (like necklaces). Dried cloves and other derivatives of fragrant plants are integrated into the beads of the gold necklaces or chains.

Silver is especially popular in villages and among the nomads. Silversmiths used to travel to remote villages with their work. The predominant items made of silver are religious or charmed amulets. Amulets are small silver containers made in triangular, cylindrical, or octagonal shapes. Pieces of paper or parchment with written prayers or verses from the holy books for each sect and religion are inserted inside these amulets. Their function is to protect the wearer from the evil eye or bad eye. Some of these amulets are for prosperity; others, for fertility or good health. They can be worn on a chain around the neck or as a band around the forearm called a *bazuband*. The bazuband, in particular, is valued by collectors, especially when embellished with semiprecious stones and glass beads. It is also worth mentioning that small pieces of cotton soaked in natural perfumes are kept in small silver containers that are either pinned to the garments or allowed to hang from the neck by a chain; these natural perfumes are distilled from *klobakh* (roses), wild flowers, and herbs collected from the surrounding environment.

TRADITIONAL VERSUS MODERN KURDISH DRESS

The many transformations of Kurdish dress during the nineteenth and twentieth centuries result from new technologies, changes in taste and fashion, and external influences. The introduction of sewing and weaving machines facilitated the production of garments in Kurdistan to such a degree that the art behind handmade garments has almost entirely disappeared. Synthetic fabrics have largely supplanted natural materials such as goat hair, wool, cotton, and silk. The cloth for modern garments is made in China and India. There, material is made specifically for the Kurdish market according to the specifications of Kurdish traders. Armana Clothes Production, an online Kurdish dress distributor based in Mahabad, Iran, has brought the Kurdish garment trade into the twenty-first century.

In response to changes in taste, women's dresses have become slim instead of wide. The kawa, a long coat, has largely been replaced by the sukhma, a short jacket, although the former is still favored by elderly women. Modern European-style shoes have replaced traditional footwear for both men and women. Kurdish men and women wear sunglasses and wristwatches with their traditional dress.

Nonetheless, some variations from current trends toward modernity still exist. There are still some places in Kurdistan where the old traditions are maintained. As a case in point, the Kurds of Khorasan still produce garments in the traditional manner, preserving the original cuts, colors, and decorative patterns. Moreover, new generations of young Kurds in Kurdistan, though typically wearing European-style dress, are becoming increasingly aware of the significance of their national dress as an important symbol and expression of their national identity within the current geopolitical climate. At the same time, the Kurdish diaspora is taking an active role in raising international awareness about Kurdish ethnicity and cultural life.

Kurdish designers, researchers, and specialists are making special efforts to draw worldwide attention to Kurdish ethnic dress and increase the appreciation of it. Fashion shows that combine modernity and tradition are being held in Kurdistan and around the world. Ako Ghareb, a collector who established the Kurdish Museum in Sulaymani for traditional garments and carpets, has also prepared a catalog on Kurdish garments and their history.

The fashion designer, Meluk Wakily has written about the history of Kurdish dress since the Median Empire (about 635–549 C.E.), focusing on the importance of traditional dress to Kurdish ethnic identity. She runs a fashion house in Tehran and has held more than forty-two fashion shows around the world. Delgash Murad, a fashion designer, derives inspiration for her collections

Men's footwear comprising a pair of *giveh* (*kalash*), woolen socks (ca. 1990), and leg warmers (ca. 1940). The upper portion of the *giveh* is knitted and attached to a leather sole. Courtesy of Layla Pio.

from patterns of traditional garments from throughout Kurdistan. Her shows in London and Sulaymani feature dress in various Kurdish styles. Biman Mohammad Sheriff of Sulaymani and Balin Hazar are fashion designers whose works are inspired strongly by traditional dress. Another Kurdish fashion designer from Syria is Welat Ahmed. His designs are inspired by the tribal dresses of the Milan, the Kikan, and the Asti, as well as by Barzan, Kirdagh, Soran, and Badinan traditional dress.

References and Further Reading

Bois, Thomas. *The Kurds*. Translated by M.W.M. Welland. Beirut: Khayats, 1966.

Bruinessen, Martin Van. *Agha, Shaikh and State: The Social and Political Structures of Kurdistan*. London: Zed Books, 1992.

Eagleton, William, Jr. *The Kurdish Republic*. Translated by Catherine Ter-Sarkissian. London: Oxford University Press, 1946.

Gluck, Jay, and Sumi Hiramoto Gluck, eds. *Survey of Persian Handicraft*. Tehran: Bank Melli of Iran, 1977.

Hansen, Henny Harald. *The Kurdish Woman's Life*. Nationalmuseets Skrifter, Etnografisk Raekke, VII. Copenhagen: Nationalmuseet, 1961.

Izady, Mehrdad. *The Kurds: A Concise Handbook*. Washington, Philadelphia, and London: Crane Russak, Taylor & Francis International Publishers, 1992.

Joseph, John. *The Modern Assyrians of the Middle East*. Leiden, Boston, and Cologne: Brill, 2000.

Kalter, Johannes. *The Arts and Crafts of Syria*. London: Thames and Hudson, 1992.

Kinnane, Derk. *The Kurds and Kurdistan*. Oxford: Oxford University Press, 1964.

Meho, Lokman I., and Kelly L. Maglaughlin. *Kurdish Culture and Society: An Annotated Bibliography*. Westport, CT: Greenwood Press, 2001.

O'Shea, Maria T. "Kurdish Costume: Regional Diversity and Divergence." In *Kurdish Culture and Identity*, edited by Philip J. Kreyenbroek and Christine Allison, 135–155. London: Zed Books, 1996.

O'Shea, Maria T. *Trapped between the Map and Reality: Cartography and Perceptions of Kurdistan*. New York and London: Routledge, 2004.

Schmidt, Dana Adams. *Journey among Brave Men*. Boston and Toronto: Little, Brown and Company, 1964.

Shwartz-Be'eri, Or. *The Jews of Kurdistan: Daily Life, Customs, Arts and Crafts*. Jerusalem: The Israel Museum, 2000.

Layla Yousif Pio

See also Syria; Iranian Regional Dress; Iranian Urban Dress.

Early Iranian Textiles and Their Influence on Pre-Islamic Dress

- History of Iranian Textile Production
- Earliest Evidence for Textiles and Dress
- Cloth Types and Garment Forms in Ancient Iranian Dress
- Islamic Iranian Dress

Iran is one of the most mountainous countries in Eurasia. It has a large amount of coastline, as well as two major deserts. Between these ecological extremes are numerous fertile floodplains that are home to agriculture and some of the earliest cities. It is also the area in which some of the earliest evidence for the use of sheep wool can be found. In the northwest, the Zagros mountain chain forms a natural boundary and has been an important geographic divide separating the Arab world to the west from the Iranian world to the east. This divide has been in place for thousands of years.

HISTORY OF IRANIAN TEXTILE PRODUCTION

Many of the regional characteristics of dress are directly related to which types of cloth were manufactured in that region or imported into it. Styles from both Eastern and Western sources influenced dress in this area and were imported during the later pre-Islamic period, from China to the Levant and even Rome, though textile technologies and production have also experienced internal developments and local trends that in turn profoundly influenced dress, including hairstyles and headdresses. This can be seen in clothing across social classes and at all stages of life. This general trend also holds true in the early twenty-first century in much of the Iranian-speaking world.

Historically, some cloth was woven in bolts to be cut for garments; other types of cloth were woven garments tailored directly on the loom. This basic technical difference, which ultimately relates to loom technology, has had a profound effect on how and the degree to which garment types and forms have developed and how those garment forms relate to those of neighboring peoples. The width of the loom affects the width of cloth produced, which in turn affects the size of the garment. In general, garments woven to shape on the loom tend to be more rounded in form and often bigger, while clothing produced from bolts of cloth tends to be narrower and made up of a series of rectangles and squares sewn together in order to use the maximum amount of cloth and minimize waste. The two basic loom types used in nonindustrial Iran were the upright vertical loom and the horizontal ground loom. The treadle loom is a third type that is critical for manufacturing cloth for garments, but it was not known in Iran until later, most probably not before the early centuries C.E.

Another important consideration, aside from technology, is production. There is a considerable contrast between the cloth production in urban centers and that of rural villages and nomadic tribal groups, and this contrast has existed for millennia. Even in the early twenty-first century, with worldwide access to imported machine-made cloth, native handwoven cloth production continues to play an important role on the Iranian Plateau.

EARLIEST EVIDENCE FOR TEXTILES AND DRESS

One of the two historically fundamental fibers in early textile production and use on the Iranian Plateau is flax, which is used to make linen. The other is wool; in fact, some of the earliest evidence for sheep wool anywhere in the world comes from Iran. Goat hair, including angora and cashmere, was also an important aspect of early Iranian textile history. Cotton and silk were introduced into Iran in Parthian times and grew in importance later. Silk has been a cottage industry in Iran for centuries, but its antiquity is obscure.

Early depictions of cloth in Iran (paintings and reliefs) begin with a highly stylized and heavy cloth made of knotted pile, such as that of the Anatolian *filikla*, giving the effect of a shaggy pelt, similar to the *kaunakes* of Mesopotamia. The rare instances of archaeological cloth remains from this period (third to second millennium B.C.E.) are very plain, mostly made of wool, which is sometimes patterned with wool threads of two different colors that were not dyed but pigmented (pigmentation involves applying a mineral that has been ground to the surface of the cloth).

Dress on the Iranian Plateau has shown itself to be distinctive beginning with its earliest depictions. Clay female figurines from Anatolia and the western Iranian Plateau show common characteristics, a relationship that reaches back into the upper Paleolithic period; in these, the female figure is ample, seated, and with very little elaboration of hair or headdress. However, in Iran, the tradition is quite different, with flat "fiddle-shaped" figurines with elaborate neckwear and headgear. This tradition is found in the Kopet Dagh region of twenty-first-century Turkmenistan and Uzbekistan and dates from the earliest farming communities (ca. 4500 B.C.E.) through the early Bronze Age.

Subsequent depictions of dress continue to display uniqueness, with seated female figurines wearing dresses with a texture like kaunakes with tailored necklines and fitted headdresses. The depictions of men before the second millennium B.C.E. show a short plain kilt also made of this type of material; the dress of these men is quite distinct from that of the Mesopotamians. These figurines and artworks, produced by the ancient Elamite civilization (2800–550 B.C.E.) that lived in the area that forms southwestern Iran in the early twenty-first century, depict a complex dress repertoire that persists throughout the third millennium and into the second millennium B.C.E.

By the second millennium B.C.E., changes occurred, first regarding the complexity in cloth structure and then in garment structure. Evidence is somewhat limited, but low-relief and freestanding sculptures give details on garments, revealing edge decoration and tailoring. The famous proto-Elamite silver vase shows

Statue of Napirasu, wife of the Elamite king Untash-Napirisha, ca. 1340–1300 B.C.E. Sculptures such as these reveal a great deal about the shape of clothing that was worn in the Elamite period (2800–550 B.C.E.) and offer insights into their decoration and tailoring. The Bridgeman Art Library/Getty Images.

a garment made of diagonally draped bands sewn together to form a wide cloth worn on the bias. These bands, perhaps made of oblique plaiting, have a distinctive, carefully rendered design.

Later, from the mid-second millennium B.C.E. through the early first millennium B.C.E., early Indo-Iranian tribes arrived from Central Asia and developed a distinct Iranian culture. These peoples later became known as the Medes and the Persians (Parsa). The Median Kingdom (728–550 B.C.E.) was centered at ancient Ecbatana in what is Hamadan in the early twenty-first century.

Though much is still unknown, a glimpse of life in the Achaemenid Empire (550–330 B.C.E.), the next important period in ancient Iranian history, can be obtained. The Achaemenids

eventually absorbed the Median peoples into their empire, though the Medes retained their distinct identity, as did the Persians. During this period, there is ample evidence for cloth and dress, and many studies have been made of the ways in which different tribes and peoples distinguished themselves through both mode of clothing and headgear. Each had a distinct mode of dress as depicted in the relief sculptures at Pasargadae and Persepolis. The Apadana (a great audience hall and portico) at Pasargadae, for example, shows clear distinctions in the dress of the Medians, Persians, and Sakas (a Scythian tribe that helped to found the Indo-Scythian kingdom in the second century B.C.E.).

The reliefs at Pasargadae and Persepolis are among the principal artistic sources for information about pre-Islamic dress on the Iranian Plateau. One of the striking aspects of dress is the loose-fitting and loosely folded and draped cloth on the upper body. A loose tunic is draped over trousers that are tucked into high boots. A belt fits around the waist, with a dagger or other objects such as a sword attached to the belt. This basic type of outfit ultimately derives from the Eurasian steppe lands and highlands. Some tunics include a hood, while other modes of dress have a separate attached hood or cowl, often with a cap terminating in a point. Boots usually reach to the midcalf and are plain, sometimes with an upturned toe point. A remarkable transformation took place during the Achaemenid period as more complex weaves became available, famously depicted on the glazed brick wall decorations in the royal villa at Susa. Of course, one must allow a certain degree of speculation, but from careful examination of the detail, the archers appear to be wearing brightly colored tunics made from tapestry weave.

After the Achaemenids, there was an abrupt change with the arrival of Alexander and the subsequent Hellenistic influence from the West during the Seleucid dynasty (330–150 B.C.E.) and the Parthian Empire (248 B.C.E.–226 C.E.). After this brief interlude, the Sassanian Empire (226–651 C.E.) emerged. From Khuzistan in Iran, there is ample evidence in the famous reliefs at Taq-i-Bustan. The Sassanian depiction of a king and his large retinue gives a picture of dress across classes, ranging from servants to nobles. The men wear baggy trousers with long tunics held in place at the waist with a belt, sometimes accompanied by a cloak. Social status is indicated by headgear. For example, the king wears a specific form of headgear with a crown at the base. Only two women, a queen and a goddess, are depicted.

From Parthian and Sassanian times, a few actual textile fragments from garments have been preserved, from sites such as the salt mines of Zanjan. Rare fragments of textiles show an extremely fine woolen thread, consistently spun fine and smooth, woven in dovetailed tapestry and weft-faced brocade, using a wide palette of dyestuffs. Silk also begins to appear at this time. Textile trade with, as well as periodic political domination on the part of, Mesopotamia (whose textile repertoire in turn was influenced by the Mediterranean and the Levant) brought many influences and techniques into play by the late first millennium B.C.E. and lasted up through the arrival of Islam in the seventh century C.E.

Among these techniques was the Iranian innovation of samite: a weft-faced compound twill weave woven on a new type of loom, the draw loom. This horizontal loom, with rigid heddles and foot pedals like the treadle loom, also had an apparatus that allowed the possibility of "drawing" or pulling up specific

A glazed-brick frieze of archers, from the Palace of Darius the Great, Susa, Iran, ca. 500 B.C.E. The archers are wearing brightly colored tunics, probably made from tapestry weave. The Bridgeman Art Library/Getty Images.

warp threads in a variable arrangement throughout the weaving, rather than having the threads follow a specific and unchanging draft. This revolutionary innovation allowed very complex pictorial designs to be rendered in cloth through the use of both color and texture. It is not known whence the draw loom originated, though most scholars believe it is an Iranian innovation based on the Chinese treadle loom, which developed undoubtedly due to the technical characteristics of weaving silk. Fine samite was extremely costly.

By the end of the first millennium C.E., with the introduction of velvet, a truly sumptuous array of cloth was available for wearing. Fitted garments not only allowed these precious cloths to be utilized more sparingly but also allowed the dazzling and increasingly pictorial textile designs to be read and admired, both in male as well as female garb. Elite and privileged people had access to sumptuous figured cloths, whereas servants wore plain cloth. However, it is important to note that folk dress in many regions of Iran is elaborate and detailed and that tribal affiliation is nearly always marked by some detail in headdress or in cloth type. In other words, the complexities of social order that are delineated through cloth and dress focus more on kinship than on socioeconomic status.

CLOTH TYPES AND GARMENT FORMS IN ANCIENT IRANIAN DRESS

According to some scholars, the basic tunic-and-trousers ensemble was ultimately derived from classical Greek influence during the Hellenistic period and first came to Iran with the Parthians and later Sassanian dress. However, the cut and style of the tunics and trousers recovered in Xinjiang in the mid- to late twentieth century, which date to the early first millennium B.C.E., show that this outfit is much earlier and is ultimately derived from an Indo-Iranian prototype.

The art-historical studies of dress from the reliefs at Taq-i-Bustan have provided ample material for understanding dress in Iran from its early roots; it is clear from these and similar depictions that men's and women's clothing on the Iranian Plateau has been distinctive. In ancient Iranian dress, there are two basic types of pants, which may have developed in different times and places, but this is not yet known for certain. What is known is that pants are basically riding gear and are also the dress of mountain peoples. More tight-fitting pants were worn by Scythian peoples, mostly men, early in the first millennium C.E. and were clearly developed for riding on horseback. In Iran, both men and women wear loose-fitting pants with a gathered waist under a long upper garment into the early twenty-first century. These loose pants are known by their Arabic name, *shalwar*. As in India and Pakistan, women wearing shalwar may also wear long, lightweight undergarments.

The tunic, the basic T-shaped loom-tailored garment, was used for both men and women and is known from classical Greece but also from the Kassite period in ancient Babylon (1595–1155 B.C.E.), a period dominated by Indo-Iranian peoples from Khuzistan. The earliest version of a sleeve attached to the body of the tunic is also seen in this period, in Babylon as well as on Minoan Crete. This type is related to the tight-fitted bodice also worn under a sari in India. It is therefore possible that this type of formed sleeve and tailored bodice top not only relays a shared aesthetic of the female form but is also ultimately derived from a common root, one that predates the Hellenistic period by more than a thousand years.

The principal top garment was a long chemise with sleeves and an open neck, sometimes with an opening in the center front at the top. This chemise reached to the knees or lower and was usually made of a thin lightweight material. This tailored garment is found also in northwestern South Asia, in the regions of Pakistan and Afghanistan. It is not the same as the square blocked tunic of the west, known both in the Mediterranean as well as in the northern parts of Europe. The chemise has a curved side seam, providing room for leg movement yet with a fitted upper-body outline. The earliest example of tailoring such as curved seams is found in Xinjiang.

An alternate form of top is a short, tight-fitting, sleeved "bodice," which was known in Minoan Crete but not in Greece. This type of garment is also known in South Asia, as worn under the sari. This tight-fitting top is also known in Safavid Iran (1501–1722 C.E.), worn under a long sleeveless coat or vest.

Over these garments was worn a jacket or a coatlike garment. The Persian jacket differs from the coat in its cut, appearance, the range of materials used (silks rather than woolens), and the patterns (which are more detailed and intricate), as well as the purpose. The coat is an outer garment, derived ultimately from the very ancient rectangular-shaped *joma* or *chapan*. This type of coat, for both men and women, was shaped on the loom and is distinctly Central Asian. The fabric of the coat ranges from a very tightly woven three-quarter twill to piled fabrics such as velvet or velveteen, often quilted for extra warmth and windproofing. The wide sleeve provided warmth for the hands, which could be pulled up inside them. The coat was worn on the shoulders or, for women especially, was often placed on the head to cover it. This same coat form is also found in China and has a common origin. In some cases, however, the sleeves eventually became functionless vestigial sleeves, ornamental and decorative.

This was also the case in the development of the jacket, worn for horseback riding and dating to the beginning of the first millennium B.C.E. The jacket, or topcoat, is also an outer garment but is shorter than the examples known from China and, in Iranian dress, is always flared from the waist. Both men and women wore a jacket over a chemise and shalwar throughout the early twentieth century.

The form and style of headgear and hairstyles are one of the most salient expressions of social identity, and this certainly holds true for Iranian peoples. Persian headgear for women has traditionally been of the Central Asian type, namely a cap and veil, with many variations. Men wear either a felt cap or turban. Early (Achaemenid) headdresses can be seen in detail in various depictions of men and women. A particularly vivid example has been found at Pazyryk, in a tapestry textile showing two women standing in front of a brazier offering up prayers. They each wear a crenellated crown with a veil attached to the back, reaching below the hip. The veil does not cover the hair, nor does it conceal the face. Headdresses for women could vary from heavily jeweled caps and elaborate layered veils to a simple head scarf.

ISLAMIC IRANIAN DRESS

The regional traditions of the Scythians, Medes, Parthians, and Sassanians have each played a role in Iranian dress and Iranian identity, particularly with regard to a characteristically Iranian style of Islamic dress, as distinct from Arab dress. During the early Islamic period in Iran, from the end of the Sassanian period through the Arab invasion and into the eleventh century, the mode of dress for both men and women underwent considerable change.

A good deal of knowledge about the history of Persian dress can be gained from artwork, in particular, the narrative genre of Persian miniatures. At the time of Hakīm Abu'l-Qāsim Firdawsī Tūsī (935–1020; more commonly transliterated as Ferdowsi), a highly revered Persian poet who wrote the *Shah Nameh*, or *Book of Kings*, in about 977–1000 C.E., miniature illustrations depicting women and men became popular. These show a distinct Central Asian influence. Men's dress was highly variable, depending on rank and social station. Often, men of nobility were depicted wearing very colorful dress consisting of shalwar, a chemise, an outer kaftan or jacket of figuratively decorated cloth, a turban, and fancy shoes with an upturned toe. Throughout the Islamic period, the influences of centuries of political shift, from the Umayyad and Abbasid Caliphates through the Ottoman Turks and the Mongol invasions, are apparent in dress. Each of these political upheavals have had a profound influence on traditional Iranian dress in nearly every region.

Women wore headdresses but did not cover all of their hair; hair was often left free or braided. Married women tended to wear one braid, while unmarried women wore one or more braids. Dresses were long and slender, often with an overdress with short sleeves or a sleeveless jumper. Among the Persian miniatures over the next several centuries, Turkish, Arab, Indian, and even Chinese (Mongol) influence can also be seen in both men's and women's dress, at least in the royal courts. For example, the illustration "Isfandiyar Unhorses Gursar," from the "*Second Small Shah Nameh*" of Firdawsī (Iran, early fourteenth century, held in the British Museum, London), shows the prince wearing Central Asian Mongolian dress. The principal change was in the main outer garment, which changed from a fitted sleeved dress with a flared skirt to a narrower, straight, open-fronted dress with lapels.

A page from the *Shah Nameh* (*Book of Kings*, Iran, ca. 977–1000 C.E.), showing the preparation of the feast ordered by Feridun before his departure for war, by Abu'l-Qāsim Manur Firdawsī. The illustrations of men's and women's clothing in this book show a distinct Central Asian Influence. The man to the left of the center wears a kaftan with a side slit, a sash, a coat, and a turban. The servants wear outfits consisting of an undershirt and a gown that is open at the front and held in place with a belt or narrow sash. The king wears a short-sleeved coat. The man on the left wears a style of cap typically associated with Central Asia. The Bridgeman Art Library/Getty Images.

This garment type is Central Asian and has influenced Chinese dress as well.

References and Further Reading

Barber, Elizabeth. *The Mummies of Urumchi*. New York: W. W. Norton, 2000.

DeCaro, Silvana. *Splendori dall'Iran-Gioielli e Costumi per 5000 anni di storia*. Rome: Museo Natzionale D'Arte Orientale and de Luca Editori d'Arte, 2007.

Good, Irene. "Bronze Age Textiles from the Tarim Basin: The Chärchän Evidence." In *Bronze Age and Early Iron Age Peoples of Eastern Central Asia*, edited by V. Mair. The Journal of Indo-European Studies and the University of Pennsylvania Museum Publications, 1998.

Good, Irene. "Cloth in the Babylonian World." In *The Babylonian World*, edited by G. Leick. London: Routledge, 2007.

Harvey, Janet. *Traditional Textiles of Central Asia*. London: Thames and Hudson, 1996.

Jackson, Peter, ed. *The Cambridge History of Iran*. 8 vols. Cambridge: Cambridge University Press, 1986.

Kalter, Johannes. *The Arts and Crafts of Turkestan*. London: Thames and Hudson, 1984.

Kidd, Fiona. "Costume of the Samarkand Region of Sogdiana between the 2nd–1st Century B.C.E. and the 4th Century C.E." *Bulletin of the Asia Institute* 17 (2007): 35–69.

Knauer, E. "Le Vêtement des Nomades Eurasiatiques et sa Posterité." *Comptes Rendus de l'Académie des Inscriptions & Belles-Lettres* 143, no. 4 (2001): 1141–1187.

Peck, Elsie Holmes. "The Representation of Costumes in the Reliefs of Taq-i Bustan." *Artibus Asiae* 31, no. 2/3 (1969): 101–146.

Irene Good

See also Introduction to the History of Dress on the Iranian Plateau; Iraqi Dress; Iranian Regional Dress.

Iranian Regional Dress

- Northern Iran
- Northwestern Iran
- Western Iran
- Central Iran
- Southwestern Iran
- Southern and Southeastern Iran: Arab-Style Dress and the Bandar Region
- Southern and Southeastern Iran: The Baluch and Sistan
- Northeastern Iran

Iran is a large and ancient country that lies at the crossroads between Asia, Southwest Asia, and Europe. Over the centuries, numerous different peoples have crossed the country and settled there. As a result there are currently about one hundred different ethnic and religious groups and subgroups, both Muslim and non-Muslims, living in Iran. The country's diversity is reflected in its regional dress, especially that worn by women. However, local dress is rapidly vanishing in some areas due to Iranization and globalization.

Throughout the country it is normal for a child to wear the same style of garments as his or her same-sex parent. One development, however, is that many young girls now wear a head scarf (rosari) rather than the larger head coverings favored by older women.

NORTHERN IRAN

Gilan is a region along the southern shores of the Caspian Sea in northern Iran. Gilan can be divided into two areas: the coastal plain and the mountainous regions. It is occupied by two ethnic groups: In general, the Galeshes live on the plains, while the Tales (Talysh) tend to live in the mountains.

The traditional dress for men in Gilan consists of a short tunic (pirahan sey) but it has more commonly been replaced by a Western-style shirt. Over the shirt, a waistcoat (jeliqeh) is worn, which is often made of sal, a locally made woolen cloth. Starting in the early twentieth century, these waistcoats were much shorter and more closely fitting than formerly. In the nineteenth century, a form of jacket called an alkaleq was worn in some areas, but this has been replaced by a Western-style jacket (kot). The kot is, however, still made of local, black sal.

Men used to wear a type of trousers (sal-shalwar), made of sal or thick cotton (qadak), that reached to the ankles. In the early twenty-first century, however, usually only Galeshe and Tales shepherds wear such trousers. Puttees (patava) made from bands of cloth used to be wrapped over the trousers up to the knees and were regarded as a distinctive feature of Gilan male garb. The puttees were necessary as protection against the thorny bushes that abound in this region. In the early twenty-first century, however, few men wear patava, as their protective function has been taken over by thick socks (jurab), which cover the trousers up to midcalf.

The shoes and stockings worn until the late twentieth century by men, especially shepherds, were also specific to the Caspian region. The woolen stockings were hand-knitted; they either were natural white with patterns created by using different stitches or had polychrome designs. The traditional shoes (kumus) were made from cow's leather and basically consisted of soles that were large enough to envelop the lower part of the foot. They were kept in place with a system of thongs that were pulled tightly, bringing the leather upward and enclosing the foot.

In general, older men, shepherds, and woodcutters living in the mountains tend to wear garments that are made locally out of felted cloth (sal), whereas younger men and most farmers and peasants living in the plains of Gilan wear pan-Iranian-style shirts and trousers, which can be easily bought in any of the local bazaars. These basically resemble Western-style garments but the trousers have three to seven pleats at the waistband on either side of the crotch region, and the shirts have a small stand-up (mandarin) collar or a Western collar but are never worn with a tie. In general, these garments are made of synthetic materials rather than cotton, although good-quality cotton ones can be found.

In the early twenty-first century, a woman's basic outfit consists of close-fitting, ankle-length trousers (shalwar), over which is worn a full skirt (tuman), which is gathered at the waist. Women normally wear two or three skirts at the same time, one on top of the other. The length of the skirt is often used to indicate the wearer's age: A younger woman will have a calf-length skirt, while an older woman's may reach to the ankles or the ground.

Over the skirt is worn a tunic (koynak). In the eastern regions of Gilan, it reaches to the thighs or even to the knees, while among the Tales it may come down to the ankles. There are two slits at either side of the garment to accommodate the fullness of the skirts. A waistcoat (jerqa) is normally worn over the koynak. In general, dark gray or black waistcoats are worn on a daily basis, whereas those for special events are normally in bright colors and ornamented with braids, beads, and coins. In the winter, women tend to wear dark-colored jackets instead of waistcoats. Another distinctive regional garment is the sash (chadarsab), which is a rectangular piece of cloth folded into a triangle and worn knotted around the waist with the point at the side or back.

At home, a woman may wear a scarf (lecek) that covers only the top of the head. In the eastern part of Gilan, these tend to be made of plain black cloth that is folded into a triangle. Elsewhere, the scarf may be white or a plain, light color. Outside the home, women normally wear a white shawl (yayliq) that is made from a square piece of material folded into a triangle and then knotted or crossed under the chin. In eastern Gilan, the shawl is worn on top of the lecek, whereas on the coast and among the Tales, the shawl replaces the smaller head scarf. In some areas, especially among the Tales, married women will cover the lower portion of their faces with the ends of the lecek.

NORTHWESTERN IRAN

In the northwestern part of Iran lies Azerbaijan, which is divided into three provinces: Western Azerbaijan, Eastern Azerbaijan, and Ardabil. The region is strongly influenced by its Turkish neighbor with respect to the culture and local languages. In general, older men tend to wear suits made up of waistcoats, jackets, and trousers, with either a skullcap or a flat cap of some kind. In contrast, younger men generally wear pan-Iranian-style clothing, specifically, a light-colored shirt with trousers and a belt and no headgear at all.

The garments worn by women of Turkish descent living in Azerbaijan usually consist of narrow undertrousers, which tend to be black for older women and a darkish blue or brown for younger women. Girls, in contrast, often wear bright and colorful undertrousers. Skirts and a top of some kind, or in the case of older women a midcalf-length dress, are worn over the trousers. The most distinctive feature of these outfits is the head scarf fastened in what is locally regarded as a Turkish manner, namely, with the knot at either the top of the head or the nape of the neck, rather than in front, which is the common pan-Iranian way.

In addition, a number of nomadic and seminomadic groups also live in this region of Iran. Among these are the Shahsavan.

The name Shahsavan is given to various tribal groups who mainly live in northeastern Iran. Most are descendants of Turkish Oghuz or Ghuzz people who came to Iran from Central Asia about one thousand years ago. By the end of the twentieth century, there were about 300,000 Shahsavani, most of whom were settled, although about six thousand families remained nomadic.

Toward the end of the nineteenth century, Shahsavan men tended to wear white or dark blue belted shirts and brown cotton trousers (shalwar) tied at the ankles with cotton. In the winter months, they also wore long yellow ram's wool fur coats with long sleeves. A more distinctive feature of their dress were their waistcoats and jackets (penjeck). Younger men tended to wear decorated red jackets, whereas older men wore green versions. Red and green are still key colors for the Shahsavan. In the early twenty-first century, men's jackets and trousers are normally made locally by town-based tailors, while their hats and shirts are from factories. Tribal members living in the major cites, however, tend to wear pan-Iranian-style clothes.

Distinctive and at times spectacular items of men's clothing were their hats, by which the men expressed their status. Indeed, the Shahsavan hats are generally regarded as setting them apart from non-Shahsavan. The official Iranian dress reforms of the 1930s meant that men had to adopt Western-style clothing, including Western styles of headgear. Homburg hats (säpo) became fashionable among the Shahsavan. After World War II, younger Shahsavan men began to wear the peaked jämsidi-style cap, while older men continued to wear homburgs. In the early twenty-first century, the jämsidi is regarded by the Shahsavan as the tribal hat.

A Shahsavan woman's outfit consists of five main elements: a full-length tunic (könek), a tailored waistcoat (yel or jilitkä), several wide, full-length underskirts (dizlik) gathered at the waist, a small skullcap (araqchin), and two types of head scarf (the yayliq and käläyagi). The bell-shaped appearance of the woman's dress is achieved by wearing at least two full-length underskirts, while on special occasions up to five skirts may be worn. The waistcoats worn by younger girls tend to be made out of red material decorated with braids, buttons, and coins. The waistcoats of married women are normally more somber and are often made out of men's suiting.

The headdress is one of the most important elements of the ensemble worn by a married woman. Its shape, size, color, and complexity denote the wearer's status. The basic headdress is created with two scarves, both of which are made of hand-printed silk. The large scarf (yayliq) is about five feet (one and a half meters) square and decorated in a variety of colors, most commonly a combination of white, yellow, and oranges patterned with darker colors. The smaller scarf (käläyagi) is normally darker. It is rolled diagonally and tied tightly around the large scarf and the skullcap in order to keep them in place. As a rule, Shahsavan women will partially veil their faces in the presence of unrelated men. This is done by bringing part of the yayliq across the lower part of the face, covering the nose, mouth, and chin.

WESTERN IRAN

The Zagros mountain range extends southeastward from Lake Van in Turkey to near Bandar Abbas in southern Iran, a distance of about one thousand miles (sixteen hundred kilometers). Throughout the Zagros, there are mountain valleys with rich pastures, which are used by various nomadic pastoral groups, including the Kurds, Bakhtiari, and Luri.

It is estimated that about two million Kurds live in Iran in the early twenty-first century. They inhabit three main regions

Two western Kurdish women, outside of Kermanshah, western Iran, 1999. The elderly woman is wearing typical Kurdish dress for the region, while her daughter has added an Iranian chador to her outfit while traveling. Photograph by Gillian Vogelsang-Eastwood. Textile Research Centre, Leiden.

in northwestern Iran, in addition to one group in Khorasan in eastern Iran. During the twentieth century, several significant changes in the garments worn by Kurdish men took place. The official dress reforms of the 1930s, for example, meant that men had to adopt and conform to new pan-Iranian styles of clothing, especially when dealing with officials or at work. This style basically consisted of Western clothing. This situation resulted in many men no longer wearing Kurdish clothing in public or wearing only one element of it, such as baggy trousers or a turban. However, there were and are a significant number of men who deliberately decide to wear Kurdish attire in order to make a statement about their Kurdish origins.

At the end of the twentieth century, there were three distinctive dress forms that were worn by both urban and nomadic Kurdish men. These were based on traditional garb with some modern adaptations. These forms were the *sal-sepik*, the *pesmerga*, and the *rank-o-chokha*. The sal-sepik is one of the oldest form of Kurdish male dress. It consists of trousers (*rank*) and a V-necked jacket (*coga*). The best-quality examples are made of striped mohair. The cloth used to be woven in bands about six inches (fifteen centimeters) wide on a pit treadle loom (a loom built over a pit to save space, with foot treadles placed in the pit); the bands were then sewn together to create a wider piece of material. In the early twenty-first century, however, a variety of different types of cloth can be and are used for this outfit.

Since the 1970s, the influence of Kurdish refugees from Iraq has led to a preference for the pesmerga dress. This suit is made up of a matching jacket (*karva*) and trousers (*pantol*) in black or brown, which are worn with a colored sash (*pestand*). The turban (*pac*), made of a dark print cloth with fringes, is normally folded diagonally to leave a triangle at the back of the head.

The rank-o-chokha consists of a shirt (*keras*) with a round neck and either straight sleeves or, less frequently, pendant or funnel sleeves (*soranis*). Over this is worn a plain, long-sleeved jacket buttoned down the front, in a range of solid colors such as brown, cream, beige, black, or gray. An unbuttoned version of this garment (*cuka*) has an open neckline. The jacket is worn with matching trousers that are baggy and gathered at the waist but tapering to the ankles. A long cotton sash (*pestand*) is normally wrapped tightly around the torso.

Throughout the region the main headgear is a variation of a skullcap (*kelaw*) with a large cloth used as a turban. The colors and materials used for the turbans can vary, including green for sayyids (descendants of the Prophet Mohammed), white or black for sheikhs (religious leaders) and mullahs (Islamic clergy), and burgundy, gray, black, and white for other men. Turban cloths used by "ordinary" Kurds usually have a small printed design, which is often based on flowers. Many Kurdish men from the Mahabad region also wear the turban in a loose style, with a dangling tail to one side, and sometimes with the fringes arranged near the eyes.

There are five basic types of dress worn by urban Kurdish women in Iran, namely, those from around the cities of Maku and Khoy, Urumia, Mahabad, Sanandaj, and Kermanshah. Maku and Khoy lie in the northern reaches of western Iran near the frontier with the former Soviet Union. One of the main Kurdish groups living in the Maku/Khoy region is the Jalali, who have a very distinctive style of dress. The basic outfit consists of trousers (*darpe*), a long, very full dress (*keras*), an apron (*mizar*), a long-sleeved coat (*der*), sleeve puffs (which are pinned onto the sleeves), and a headdress that is usually made up of a single head scarf (*dastmal*) for an unmarried woman and two or more scarves for a married woman.

The attire worn around Urumia further south is very similar to the Badinani or Hakkari style worn in parts of southern Turkish Kurdistan and in the Badinan region of Iraqi Kurdistan. The basic outfit consists of baggy trousers; a plain, shaped underdress or petticoat, which reaches to just above the knee; and a dress that is often made out of sheer material. The dress usually has a gathered waist and long sleeves, sometimes in a pendant shape. Over this is worn a long-sleeved coat with a wide scoop front, similar to the one worn by women in the region of Khoy. The sleeves of the dress are usually tied behind the back so that the woman can work more easily.

Mahabad, followed by Saqqez, is the main urban center for the Kurds in Iran. The basic outfit for a Mahabad woman consists of a shift, balloon-shaped trousers (*darpe*) that can be up to six yards (five and a half meters) wide and are fitted at the ankles, and, finally, a long, pleated dress (*keras*), which has a hem width of four to five yards (three and a half to four and a half meters). The dress normally has a round neckline and long sleeves that may terminate in pendants (*soranis*). They have an extension along the lower edge, like a ribbon, that can be either wrapped around the wrist or tied behind the neck. Over the dress a short waistcoat is worn. Finally, a cotton sash (*pestand*) is normally wound loosely around the hips. This sash is made from three to six yards (2.7 to 5.5 meters) of patterned cloth. The traditional headdress is a low cylindrical cardboard cap (*tas-kelaw*) covered with velvet or brocade. The version worn by girls has a chin chain decorated with coins or, more commonly, plastic disks. The cap is normally wrapped in a long triangular shawl (*dastmal*), which is worn with the points of the triangle crossed over on the chest and the main point dangling down the back.

Sanandaj is a large city to the south of Mahabad. The basic female dress is made up of a similar range of garments to those of other regions; however, the garments tend not to be so full or decorative. The main form of head covering from this region is called a *kalagi* and consists of a domed cap decorated with sequins or beads and wrapped with one or two scarves. Some of the caps are held under the chin with a beaded chain. Until the mid- to late twentieth century, all married women wore a turban made from numerous scarves and tasseled lengths of fabric.

Women from the Kermanshah region further to the south tend to wear various layers of clothing including long trousers (*soval jafi*) under a long, full dress. Over the dress a waist-length bodice or waistcoat is worn, which is often made of velvet and covered in sequins. The basic headdress consists of a sequined cap (*koter*) wrapped with one or several scarves. The cap worn by younger women and girls is usually decorated with either sequins or embroidery, while those of older women are normally of plain velvet or decorated with small black beads.

Finally, during the latter half of the twentieth century, a pan-Kurdish style of dress has developed, called the *sorani*. The outfit is made up of trousers, an optional petticoat, a full-length dress with long sleeves (either straight or pendant-shaped), a short waistcoat that may be separate or attached to the dress, and either a coat or jacket. The headgear worn with the sorani outfit can vary considerably depending on the wearer's age; younger women tend to wear head scarves whereas older ones have elaborately constructed turbans. At the end of the twentieth century, however,

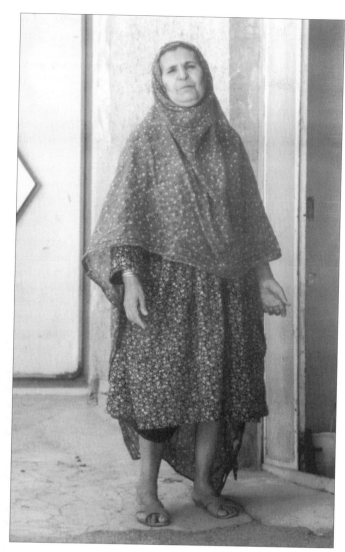

A Zoroastrian woman, Yazd, Iran, 1999. Zoroastrians are not Muslims but followers of a pre-Islamic religion. Women tend to wear narrow, knee-high trousers that can just be seen below the hem of the dress. The dress itself includes a long skirt made out of green and brown or green and purple panels. Women also wear a large head cover (*maknun*) made up of three yards (about three meters) of cloth placed under the chin and then folded over the head. Their dress reflects the ancient nature of this community, and the style is worn by no other group in Iran. Photograph by Gillian Vogelsang-Eastwood. Textile Research Centre, Leiden.

more and more women were wearing urban-style head scarves. In addition, while traveling from village to village or when visiting towns, many women wear the Iranian chador (a semicircular head and body covering worn by women throughout Iran), but these are not worn at home or in their local villages.

CENTRAL IRAN

Central Iran is a large, dry, desert region that is sparsely populated. Until the 1930s many of the major cities in the region had their own characteristic regional dress. However, most people living there in the early twenty-first century wear pan-Iranian dress,

and their city of origin cannot be determined based on their clothing. Two exceptions are the outfits worn in Abayaneh and those worn by Zoroastrian women.

Abayaneh. Abayaneh is situated at the foot of Mount Karkas, about forty-three miles (seventy kilometers) south of Qashan. Because of its mountain location, the village is relatively cool during the summer months, while in the winter it is extremely cold. Until the late twentieth century, the region around Abayaneh was virtually cut off from the rest of Iran. The construction of new roads in the region at the end of the twentieth century meant that the villages became more accessible and modernized. Abayaneh has been recognized by UNESCO as a place of special cultural interest and is officially protected.

Until the late twentieth century, men's and boy's clothing in the region was based on Qajar-style garments (a style of clothing from the mid- to late nineteenth century), namely, a shirt (*pirahan*), a gown (*qaba*), a sash (*kamarband*), baggy trousers (*zir-jameh*), cloth shoes (*giveh*), and some form of headgear, such as a cap (*kolah*) or a turban (*mandil*). In general, lower-class men used to wear a dark blue cotton shirt with a short neck opening, while higher-status men wore a long white shirt with black trimmings. In the early twenty-first century, the main feature of men's outfit is the use of loose-fitting trousers made of a very shiny black material. The cuffs of the trousers are often decorated with lines of hand or machine embroidery. The same style of trousers is used for young boys as for older boys and men.

The dress of both girls and women is based on three items: a tunic (*pirahan*), knee-length skirt-trousers (*shalwar*), and a large head shawl (*charqad*). In addition, women also wear cloth shoes (giveh). The "skirts" worn in the early twenty-first century by women in the Abayaneh region are unusual in that they are not actually skirts but extremely wide trousers. These garments are made of at least eight yards (seven meters) of black cloth and are carefully pleated. The Abayaneh head scarf consists of a large square of cloth that has a light-colored background with small colorful motifs on it. It is folded diagonally and then fastened under the chin.

Zoroastrians. The Zoroastrians are followers of the religion that was the main faith across the Iranian Plateau prior to the introduction of Islam in the seventh century C.E. Zoroastrians are followers of Zoroaster, who lived during the mid-first millennium B.C.E. He introduced a monotheistic religion that is based around an omnipotent god called Ahura Mazda. At the end of the twentieth century, the Zoroastrians were a minority group concentrated around the city of Yazd.

For centuries, Zoroastrian men have been barely distinguishable from their Muslim neighbors because they wear no special clothing. In contrast, however, Zoroastrian women have developed and preserved their own distinctive form of dress. Up to the latter half of the twentieth century, the basic dress of a Zoroastrian woman in Yazd consisted of a pair of baggy trousers (*shalwar*), a paneled dress (*qamis*), and various forms of headgear. By the end of the century, many women were choosing to wear pan-Iranian garments, and within a short time, this form of clothing will no longer be regarded as everyday wear, although it may survive for festive occasions.

The traditional trousers worn by Zoroastrian women were large and baggy, but in the early twenty-first century women tend to wear narrow, knee-high trousers that can just be seen below the hem of the dress. The dress includes a long skirt made out of green and brown or green and purple panels. The bodice section is usually plain and in a contrasting color to the skirt sections. The traditional headdress can be quite complex and consists of various elements that can be worn together or by themselves, including a small, triangular cap (*lacak*) with a chin band; a large head covering (*makmun*) made up of three yards (about three meters) of cloth placed under the chin and then folded over the head; and, finally, in the winter, a large, diagonally folded shawl (*charqad*), which is often draped over the top of the lacak and makmun.

SOUTHWESTERN IRAN

Three main groups live in southwestern Iran: the Luri, the Bakhtiari, and the Qashqa'i. The first two groups are closely affiliated with each other with respect to both their Iranian language and their culture. This link can also be seen in their clothing, especially that of the women, although the main difference in their appearance lies in the style of their respective headgear. The Qashqa'i are a Turkish group and wear their own distinctive dress.

A nomadic Qashqa'i woman, southern Iran, 2003. She wears a long tunic with slit sides to accommodate a very full skirt. Her headdress is made up of a cap with a net head covering. She holds a small cap, which is normally worn by a woman beneath a head veil. Photograph by Ien Rappoldt. Textile Research Centre, Leiden.

The Luri. In the early twenty-first century, there are about 500,000 Luri living in the Lurestan-e-Kuchak region of western Iran. At the end of the twentieth century, many Luri lived in villages and towns, but a substantial number still followed a nomadic way of life.

Men's dress consists of long trousers of varying degrees of fullness, a shirt, a vest, shoes (*giveh*), and a felt cap (*saw-kolah*). A feature of Luri male clothing is the *choga*, a straight, knee-length sleeveless coat of natural wool with vertical indigo stripes. These are handwoven in various villages; the best ones are called *choga-livasi*, after a village in Luristan. The choga is often worn over a Western-style jacket (*kot*). By the end of the twentieth century, the choga was widely associated with the Bakhtiari, but it seems to have spread to this group from the Luri in the 1940s, when it replaced the Bakhtiari cloak (*qaba*).

Many Luri women wear a pair of trousers (*shalwar*) under a long dress (*pirahan*); in addition, they often wear a waistcoat decorated with amulets made from coins, pendants, beads and plaques. Many women wear a kind of turban (*tara*), made by wrapping a scarf (*tara awwal*) around the upper part of the head, and while allowing their hair to flow free at the back.

The Bakhtiari. Bakhtiari are a conglomeration of various races who probably migrated from Syria to Iran during the medieval period. Up to the fifteenth century, they were known as the "Great Luri" and lived in the region of Lurestan-e-Bozorg. The Bakhtiari assert that they are not Iranian in origin but rather Kurdish. About 600,000 Bakhtiari are believed to be living in an area extending from Isfahan to Maydan-e Naftun in Khuzistan. In the early twenty-first century, the Bakhtiari are divided into two main groups: the Haft Lang and the Cahar Lang.

As with the other nomadic tribes, dramatic changes took place in the garments worn by the Bakhtiari during the twentieth century. Some of these changes result from the deliberate policy of modernization and Westernization during the reign of Reza Shah, who was the shah of Iran from 1925 until he was forced to abdicate in 1941. The reasons behind other changes, however, are not so obvious. Women's clothing in the early twenty-first century, for instance, has little in common with the garments worn at the end of the nineteenth century. There has been a dramatic change in the cuts of garments, the garment combinations, as well as the range of colors used. All of these differences reflect changes in the wearers' social and economic life.

Western travelers before 1920 described men's outfits as being made up of a shirt with a straight collar buttoned on the side (*juma*). This garment has totally disappeared and has been replaced by Western-style shirts. White shirts are normally worn by older men, while younger men are often seen wearing patterned shirts, albeit subdued. A black shirt is worn when mourning the death of a close relative.

The trousers constitute the most distinctive part of Bakhtiari male dress, however, serving as a badge of tribal identification, so much so that outsiders are not permitted to wear them. These trousers (*shalwar-gosad* or *tombun*) are black and cut very wide (about four feet, or 120 centimeters, around the leg) and are usually worn over underdrawers (*zir-shalwar*), often simple pajamas. For reasons of economy, however, boys and shepherds often wear only the underdrawers. The trousers are held in place by a leather belt or a large sash or rolled white cloth (*sal*). It was customary to carry small useful objects like a pipe and a knife in the folds of this sash. Their footwear are of the *giveh-maleki* type (white cloth shoes) with pointed leather toes that curve upward. Bakhtiari men are also famous for their jackets with broad black and white stripes like the keys on a piano. These are called *choga* and are made out of natural and indigo-dyed wool. Each tribe has its own design, making the identification of a person from a distance much easier.

The basic outfit of a Bakhtiari woman consists of a pair of undertrousers worn with a long, full skirt (*tombun-zanuna*), which is usually made of between eight and ten yards (seven to nine meters) of cloth. The material in the skirt is gathered at the waist. Over the skirt is worn a knee-length tunic (*jowa* or *pirahan*), which is slit at the sides in order to accommodate the full skirt. Bakhtiari women normally wear a small cap (*lacak*) to which a veil (*meyna*) is pinned in such a way as to frame the face without hiding it. The hair is parted in the middle and arranged in two plaits that are joined together under the chin.

The Qashqa'i. The Qashqa'i are a Turkic-speaking people who originally came from Central Asia. During the medieval period, they settled in the mountains of southwestern Iran. Most of the nomadic Qashqa'i are herders of sheep and goats who traditionally migrate between summer and winter pastures in the highlands and lowlands of the Zagros Mountains. There are about 400,000 settled and nomadic Qashqa'i.

In the early twenty-first century, when in contact with members of the dominant Persian society, Qashqa'i men usually conform to new urban styles of dress (long-sleeved shirts in dark colors), although they continue to wear the distinctive Qashqa'i hat. As a symbol of renewed tribal identity, men sometimes wear the thin cloaks (*chuqa*) used by their grandfathers on ceremonial occasions, but this is not so common. Various types of headgear have been used by Qashqa'i men over the centuries, but the *dogusi* cap ("two-eared") is seen by many as being the garment that identifies a Qashqa'i man, yet it was only developed in the mid-twentieth century. The cap is made of orangey beige, tan, or gray felt, and, as its name suggests, it has two flaps on either side just above the ears.

Qashqa'i women normally wear the same style of clothes whatever their age or the event. Even while on migration, women will wear their splendid skirts while sitting astride their camel, horse, or donkey. What varies is the color and the type of material used to make the garments. In general, a bride or newly married woman will wear very bright colors, whereas older women wear progressively more somber colors. The basic outfit for a tribal woman consists of baggy trousers (*shalwar*) that are cut very wide at the top, gathered onto a drawstring at the waist, and taper to ankle cuffs. Over these are worn two to twelve underskirts (*tuman-i rue*), again with a cord at the waist. The greater the number of these skirts, the higher a woman's social status. Over the underskirts is another, more flamboyant skirt (*tuman-i zir*), which is usually brightly colored and made from finer materials. Between two and fifteen yards (two to fourteen meters) of cloth may be used for making each of these skirts. In particular, the outer skirts are normally made out of many yards of cloth.

Over the skirts is worn a long tabard or dress (*keynak*), which has a high, round neck and long sleeves. These dresses are slit at the sides from the thigh downwards in order to make room for the various skirts. A waist-length fitted jacket (*yal-i arsin fosol*) is sometimes worn by wealthier women at festivals and weddings. It is usually made from velvet, brocade, or some other costly material.

Headgear varies according to age, status, and tribal affiliation, so there are numerous variations. The basic headgear, however, consists of a small cap (*kolahqcha*), which is worn with one or more diaphanous triangular veils or kerchiefs. These are often made of net trimmed with sequins. The veils are fastened under the chin with a brooch or fastener (*asmaliq* or *chapa*) of some kind. Over the veil is worn a band or fillet of chiffon, silk, or net (*yayliq*), which is usually brightly colored. Unmarried women normally wear their hair outside the veil at the front, while married women tuck it inside.

Qashqa'i women also wear numerous items of jewelry, much of which is believed to serve a protective function (like an amulet). Blue beads and coins are often sewn onto children's clothing, since these are believed to ward off the evil eye.

SOUTHERN AND SOUTHEASTERN IRAN: ARAB-STYLE DRESS AND THE BANDAR REGION

The range and style of dress in the southern regions of Iran vary quite considerably. The garments worn in Khizestan near the border with Iraq, for instance, are strongly influenced by Arab

An Afshar woman in central Iran, 2003. Her large white head covering is folded into a diagonal and kept in place by a black headband or head scarf. She also wears a typical combination of a knee-length dress with trousers. Photograph by Ien Rappoldt. Textile Research Centre, Leiden. Centre collection.

styles of dress from Iraq and the eastern Gulf region. Garments from southeastern Iran, namely from the Bandar ("harbor") region east, are influenced by northwestern Indian and Pakistani traditions. In addition, the Bandar garments are also closely related to dress styles from the nearby coast of the Arabian Peninsula.

Arab-Style Dress. Many Arab groups live in Iran, the largest of them living close to the Iraqi border. Over the centuries, there have been numerous migrations of Arabs from the other side of the Tigris River and the Gulf region in general. In addition, trade has brought other Arabs to the region.

The basic dress for a man consists of undertrousers (shalwar), a long gown (*dishdasha*), a head covering (*keffiyeh*), a body covering (*aba*), and footwear of some kind. Unlike Arabs from the western shores of the Persian Gulf, Iranian Arabs wear undertrousers (shalwar) rather than a hip wrap (*lungi*). The summer version of these trousers is made from thin cotton, while the winter ones are made from thicker, knitted material (traditionally wool but in the early twenty-first century synthetic yarn). Over the trousers a gown (dishdasha) is worn. In the summer, a lightweight white cotton gown is worn, whereas in winter the material is a much heavier-weight cotton. The basic head covering consists of a square of cloth folded diagonally and draped over the head. Unlike the practice of the Arabs from the Arabian Peninsula, no head rope (*aqal*) is worn with the Iranian head covering in order to keep it in place. In the summer, men tend to wear a white head cloth made of fine cotton cloth, while in the winter they wear a heavier-weight cotton version that may be decorated in a variety of checked patterns. Red, black, and occasionally green versions of the winter head cloth have been seen.

One of the most distinctive items of Arabic dress is the so-called cloak or aba. Two forms of aba are worn here, namely, a light summer version made from loosely woven cotton and a heavier winter version made out of camel hair (best quality) or wool. The wearing of abas is generally regarded as characteristic of older men, especially in the winter. In the early twenty-first century, instead of an aba, many older men are, however, wearing pan-Iranian-style jackets, usually in gray.

The basic outfit of an Arab woman from this region consists of undertrousers (shalwar), a long dress (libas), a loose overdress (sob), a head covering (shelagh), and a loose cloak used as an outer covering (abayeh). As in many other regions of Iran, younger women tend to wear bright colors, while married and older women tend to wear more somber colors. The most characteristic element of an Arab woman's dress is her sob or overdress, which is worn over her daily dress or underdress. A basic sob is made from a large rectangle of cloth with a hole cut out for the head. The sides of the garment are sewn together, with holes left for the arms (this garment does not have sleeves). The Iranian sob is virtually identical in construction to the *thob* worn by women in the eastern parts of the Arabian Peninsula.

The basic headgear is made up of a large rectangle of cloth, which is wrapped around the head, covering the neck and hair. Various types of cloth are used, but a lightweight cotton is most common. Younger women tend to wear a light-colored shelagh, whereas older women normally wear black ones. Finally, on top of the indoor garments, Arab women will often wear a cloaklike garment called an abayeh when out-of-doors. In Iran, these garments are worn over the head in the Iraqi manner, rather than on the shoulders as is common in Saudi Arabia.

The Bandar Region. The indigenous people of the Iranian shores of the Persian Gulf are often loosely known as Bandaris, from the Persian word for "port" or "harbor." The Bandaris tend to be of Iranian, Arab, African, Baluchi, Indian, and European descent. Those of Arabic origins, although they have become Iranized in many ways, still preserve their own Arabic dialect and culture. Many people in the Bandar region are also Sunni rather than Shiite Muslims, reflecting their Arab origins. These differences are still reflected in certain garments worn by some women.

The traditional male dress in the Bandar region is based on Indian- and Baluchi-style clothing. It consists of a shirt (juma) that reaches below the knee and is fastened with buttons on the right side of the neck. The shirt is worn over loosely cut trousers (shalwar) made of coarse cotton. On the head is worn a small white or colored cap (kolah) over which a two-yard- (two-meter-) long turban cloth (*lang* or *languta*) is wrapped. Older men tend to use a white cloth (*ratrah*) or a striped one, while younger men use colored material.

Until recently, the *qaba*, a long, heavy overcoat, used to be worn over the qamis or the juma during the winter, but this is vanishing and tends to be worn only by more isolated and traditional shepherds and farmers. In general, younger, urban men more commonly wear pan-Iranian-style clothing. Nevertheless, a form of "Bandar" trousers (*shalwar-i Bandar*) can still commonly be seen worn by poorer men. These are baggy trousers with a low crotch, elasticized waist, and legs that taper toward the ankles. Bandar trousers are normally worn with a pan-Iranian-style shirt (qamis) with a collar.

Bandar clothing for women consists of a pair of trousers (shalwar), a dress (pirahan), a head covering (*makna*), sometimes a face covering of some kind (burqa, *niqab*, or *batullah*), shoes, and, finally, a chador. The Bandar region is famous for the embroidered trousers (shalwar) worn by the women. The trouser cuffs used to be decorated with hand embroidery, usually tambour chain stitch; this has been replaced by machine embroidery. The cuff decoration can be divided into two types: cuffs decorated with the full design (*badal-i tamam*) and cuffs with a half pattern (*badal-i nim*). The design found on the trouser cuffs used to reflect the wearer's origins, but in the early twenty-first century most women wear whatever design they prefer.

The basic garment worn over the trousers is a dress (pirahan). The older-style dresses are made of colored cotton and are either waisted (*gavan* style) or cut full (*dara'a*). In the early twenty-first century, a wide variety of pan-Iranian-style dresses can be found in and around Bandar Abbas. The head covering worn by women in the Bandar region is normally the makna, a rectangular scarf (about three feet by two feet, or ninety by sixty centimeters) of thin black material. Over all these garments, women generally wear a large, semicircular chador that is made from cotton that is very lightweight because of the heat.

Perhaps one of the most widely commented-on aspects of Bandar dress is the various types of face coverings. The type of face veil worn by a Bandari woman depends mainly on three factors, specifically (a) her religious background (Sunni or Shiite), (b) her ethnic origins, and (c) her place of residence. Many Shiite women in the Bandar region, for example, wear bright red rectangular masks of the batullah type (made of one piece of material with a broad tuck down the nose), locally known as a burqa, decorated with various patterns. Originally, these were hand worked, but in the early twenty-first century, most are decorated using machine embroidery. The color and designs provide information about the wearer's ethnic group. For example, red signifies a local Bandari woman, whereas an orange burqa is worn by some Baluchi women living in the Bandari region. Finally, various styles are related to specific locations; for example, the towns of Bandar Abbas, Bandar Langi, Minab, and so on.

In general, Sunni women of Arab origin in the Bandar region wear either black face veils or gold masklike forms. The main form of batullah (locally known as a burqa) that they wear is black, squarish, and covering most of the face in contrast to the red, rectangular ones worn horizontally to cover the forehead, eyes, and nose, as by Shiite women. The Sunni batullah is made of black cotton or black velvet. The veil is similar to a type of batullah worn in parts of Qatar, on the other side of the Persian Gulf.

Some Sunni women in the Bandar region also wear a niqab-style face veil. This veil is usually made of a loosely woven black cotton material. It is made from two layers of material with a small slit for the eyes. The veil is often decorated along the lower edge with beadwork in various colors. Apart from their beaded decoration, these veils are very similar in form and size to the more pan-Islamic niqab.

SOUTHERN AND SOUTHEASTERN IRAN: THE BALUCH AND SISTAN

The Baluch. Most Baluch speak Iranian and live in the south of Afghanistan, Pakistan, and Iran, in a belt of land generally known as Baluchistan. The history of the Baluch in Iran is somewhat of a puzzle. No historical records indicate where they come from, although it would appear that they have been there for some nine hundred years. Currently, about 500,000 Baluch are living in Iran; most are dispersed over a wide area of southern regions of the country.

Most men wear the qamis (long shirt), with simple, drawstring trousers (shalwar). This type of outfit is common throughout the region and is said to originate in Pakistan. Variations can also be found in northern India, Bangladesh, and Afghanistan, as well as in the Baluchi and Sistan regions of Iran. Other elements of male dress in the Baluchi region include a long scarf or shoulder wrap (pushti) and a close-fitting cap (topi) over which is wrapped a turban (pag). In addition, during colder weather, other garments are used, including woolen socks, a waistcoat (sadri), and an overcoat (qaba, also spelled kaba). Occasionally, a woolen blanket or shawl (sal) is tied around the waist and knees. This garment is not only decorative and warm but also helps maintain the wearer's squatting position when talking with other men.

The typical Baluchi cap (topi), over which the turban is tightly wrapped, is a more intricately embroidered version of the topi worn in Pakistan and northwestern India. The Baluchi version is usually made of cotton with fine silk or cotton embroidery in floral or geometric designs and incorporating small, round mirrors.

The basic elements of a Baluchi woman's dress include (a) a pair of baggy trousers (the older trousers of striped silk fabric are called *kanavez* whereas the modern matching trousers are called shalwar), (b) a knee-length dress (*pashk*) with pleats (*chin*) at either side of the waist, and (c) a large, rectangular shawl or head covering (*chadar*). In the early twenty-first century, the trousers

Bandar Arab women at a women's market near Bandar Abbas, southern Iran, 2000. The red face veil worn by the woman standing in the center of the photograph is typical of those worn by Shiite Bandar women; the black face veils worn by the two seated women on either side are for Sunni Bandar women. Photograph by Gillian Vogelsang-Eastwood. Textile Research Centre, Leiden.

and the dress are made of the same material, with a head covering in a complementary color.

Traditionally, the dresses are decorated with specific panels of embroidery (*doch*). These used to be hand stitched, with each group having its own form of patterning. In the early twenty-first century, however, more and more women wear machine-embroidered decoration on their garments. However, the basic principle of the four panels on the dress remains the same. These embroidered panels are a large yoke covering the chest (*jig* or *jeg*), a long, narrow rectangular pocket (*pado* or *pandohl*), and two sleeve cuffs (*banzari*). The form of embroidery used is called *pakka*, meaning "firm" or "solid." The main stitches are satin, interlacing, herringbone, chain, blanket, square chain, cross, and couching. Sometimes, embroidered panels from worn-out dresses are cut off and resewn onto new garments.

Sistan. The province of Sistan va Baluchestan is the second largest in Iran. It lies in the extreme east of the country, along the border with Afghanistan. It is difficult to reach, and the desert conditions that prevail there make it very desolate. It appears that at the end of the nineteenth and beginning of the twentieth century, men's clothing was based on a short to knee-length tunic, baggy trousers, and a white turban, usually with the ends hanging down the wearer's front or back. In cold weather, jackets, long baggy coats, and blankets were also worn. In addition, men who worked with Iranians or wanted to claim Iranian connections tended to wear Qajar-style garments but with turbans wrapped in the local style. Modern Sistan dress for men is very similar to that worn by Afghan, Baluchi, and Pakistani men. It consists of a long, straight tunic with baggy trousers, and a blanket is often worn over the shoulder. The main headgear is a large, white turban.

There are three basic elements in the Sistani woman's outfit: trousers (shalwar), a dress (pashk), and a head covering (*sari sistani*). The trousers may be made of plain-colored cotton, although trousers meant for more festive occasions or those worn by wealthier women may be made from satin. The modern style of dress from Sistan tends to be a straight but wide garment with long sleeves with very large shoulder heads that narrow sharply to the cuffs. As for other garments from this region, a wide variety of materials are used for these dresses in the early twenty-first century. Cheaper cotton versions are available for more everyday use, whereas versions in satin and silks are worn on more festive occasions. The position of the designs is different from that on the garments worn by Baluchi women in the same region. The main area of decoration is around the neck opening, but there is no front panel. Instead decoration can occur in long, parallel bands down the front. Similar bands can be found on the shoulder line. In general, the cuffs and the neck opening have similar stylized designs, which tend to be either floral or geometric.

Unlike the semicircular Iranian chadors, the Sistan version is usually a rectangular piece of cloth, which is between four and five yards (three and a half to four and a half meters) long. Lightweight cottons, silks, or synthetic materials are commonly used. They are often decorated with small floral and geometric motifs in chain-stitch embroidery.

NORTHEASTERN IRAN

The Eastern Kurds. Around the Khorasan cities of Bojnurd and Quchan are various Kurdish groups. The history of these people is not clear, but it appears that by the time of Shah Sultan Hoseyn (r. 1694–1722), they were forced to migrate from the west to the eastern regions of the country. At the end of the twentieth century, it is believed that there were about seventeen thousand nomadic Kurds in the region and an unknown number who were seminomadic.

In the 1960s, the typical male outfit included trousers of calico or other cotton material, which were constructed with a gusset. These were worn with a shirt of red or white silk, without a collar and with either a front opening or a slit on the shoulder fastened with buttons and loops. Over it was worn a jacket (*nivtana* or *panjak*) or, for wealthier men, an ankle-length overcoat (kot) made of brown or black lambswool with a wide collar and an opening in front. The headgear could be a tasseled black cap, around which a shawl was wrapped, or an expensive type of hat made from lambskin (astrakhan).

Footwear consisted of woolen stockings and bands (puttees called patava) wrapped around the ankles and calves. The finer shoes (charok) were made of good red leather fastened with laces and decorated with tassels. Ordinary shoes (charok-i kam) were made of untreated skins from the heads of cows. By the end of the twentieth century, most of these garments had virtually vanished, and men, especially the younger ones, were wearing a mixture of Iranian- and Kurdish-style garments or pan-Iranian-style clothing, with trousers, a belt, and a shirt.

The basic outfit for women consisted of a plain cloth tunic (*salita*) with long sleeves, the front of which was decorated with zigzag patterns. In addition, some women also wore a waistcoat. Under the tunic was worn a knee-length skirt, which might have been made from up to ten yards (nine meters) of cloth. A variety of materials were used for the skirt (tambon) depending on the wearer's age, status, and clan; for instance, an unmarried girl from the Topkanlu tribe would wear a velvet skirt decorated with seven colors, whereas an older woman would wear a plain red skirt. Among the Sifkanlu tribe, however, an unmarried girl would not wear velvet but instead cotton decorated with flowers. In the early twenty-first century, white socks or stockings are often worn with the skirts.

The headdress consists of three elements: a cloth (bonhani) directly covering the hair, a white shawl (chaharqad) consisting of a piece of unsewn cloth, and a kerchief (rosari), which is worn on top of the head over the chaharqad. All married women normally veil their mouths by pulling part of the white chaharqad across the lower part of their face.

The Turkmen. The region where the Turkmen live is divided among Afghanistan, Iran, and Turkmenistan. Most of the Turkmen have been separated by international boundaries only within the last one hundred years. Prior to the early twentieth century, constant, and relatively easy, trade and social contacts existed between the various groups. In the early twenty-first century, the majority of the Iranian Turkmen live in the eastern part of the Mazandaran province and the northern areas of the Khorasan province. Various groups of Turkmen are living in Iran, notably the Yomut, the Guklan, the Garkaz, the Nokhorli, and the Tekke. Of these, the Yomut are the most widespread.

Traditionally, there used to be a considerable difference between the dress worn by male Turkmen from the various groups. This difference, however, has nearly disappeared as major changes have taken place in men's clothing since the mid-twentieth century. On an everyday basis, for instance, most men wear pan-Iranian-style clothing, although on special occasions, a more traditional form of dress is adopted. This consists of a shirt with sash around their indoor coats in order to keep the garments from opening, especially while they are working.

Various forms of headdress are used by married Turkmen women depending on which group they belong to and whether it is a daily or more formal occasion; for the latter they tend to wear an elaborate hat decorated with various scarves, whereas the daily headdress is much simpler. At the end of the twentieth century, a Yomut woman's headdress tended to be based on a head-ring (*aldarij* or *alan dangi*) covered by a large shawl (*yagliq, yaghg,* or *charqad*), which was folded diagonally in half and then draped over the wearer's head and upper body. In contrast, Tekke and Goklan women often wore a headdress that was about ten inches (twenty-five centimeters) high and made up of a cloth (*qinyac uci* or *yaşmak*) wrapped around a framework. The framework might have been made of a variety of materials such as rushes, twisted cloth, leather, felt, or cardboard. Sometimes, the cloth is used as a veil to cover the lower part of the face.

One of the main features of a Turkmen woman's dress used to be her jewelry, as it played an important role as a form of "life insurance" giving financial security. The jewelry included diadems (*ildirqich*), tiaras (*egmeh*), temple pendants (*adamlyk*), earrings, necklaces, and collars (*boqow*), collar studs (*gol yaqeh* or *gulyaqa*), armbands and bracelets (*bilezikl* or *bezelik*), and finger rings. These were usually worn en masse and could weigh a considerable amount; a young bride, for instance, might wear up to fourteen pounds of jewelry during her wedding festivities. In the twenty-first century, much less jewelry is used for daily wear, but brides still wear the elaborate combinations. In addition, by the end of the twentieth century, gold jewelry was rapidly replacing the older, silver forms.

References and Further Reading

Allgrove, Joan. *The Qashqa'i of Iran.* Manchester, UK: Whitworth Art Gallery, University of Manchester, 1976.

Andrews, Peter, and Mugul Andrews. *The Turcoman of Iran.* Kendal, UK: Abbot Hall Art Gallery, 1971.

Beck, Louise. *The Qashqa'i of Iran.* New Haven, CT, and London: Yale University Press, 1986.

Bier, Carol, and Mary Martin. "Pasture and Product." In *Woven from the Soul, Spun from the Heart: Textile Arts of Safavid and Qajar Iran 16th–19th Centuries,* edited by Carol Bier, 288–324. Washington, DC: The Textile Museum, 1987.

Tapper, Richard. *Frontier Nomads of Iran: A Political and Social History of the Shahsevan.* Cambridge, UK: Cambridge University Press, 1997.

Tapper, Richard, and Jon Thompson, eds. *The Nomadic Peoples of Iran.* London: Thames and Hudson, 2002.

Vogelsang-Eastwood, Gillian, and Willem Vogelsang. *Covering the Moon: A History of Middle Eastern Face Veils.* Leuven, Belgium: Peeters, 2008.

Yarshater, Ehsan, ed. *Encyclopaedia Iranica* (digital version) under subheading "clothing." http://www.iranica.com/newsite/ (accessed 17 October 2009).

Gillian Vogelsang-Eastwood

See also Dress from the Gulf States: Bahrain, Kuwait, Qatar, United Arab Emirates; Kurdish Dress; Turkmen Dress and Embroidery; Face Veils; Regional Dress in Anatolia.

A group of eastern Kurdish women in a tailor's shop, Bognurd, eastern Iran, 1999. These women wear a version of late-nineteenth-century Iranian dress; although Kurdish, they have little in common with the western Kurds (members of this group were forcibly transported from western Iran in the early nineteenth century). Photograph by Gillian Vogelsang-Eastwood. Textile Research Centre, Leiden.

a front opening descending straight down from the right shoulder, a long robe or gown (*don*), and a small, embroidered skullcap (*bark*). The cap may be covered by a neat turban, which is made of a square of cloth, folded diagonally and then wrapped around the head. Various types of cloth, in cotton and synthetic yarns, are used for this purpose, but most are white with black stripes or checks. Another form of headgear associated with Turkmen is the *telpak*. This is a large, fluffy cap made from black or white sheepskin. In the early twenty-first century, it seems to be worn mainly on special occasions. In general, Turkmen men did not use jewelry except in the mounting on weapons and animal harnesses. This contrasts sharply with the vast amounts of jewelry associated with Turkmen women.

The basic dress of a Turkmen woman consists of undertrousers (*balaq*), a dress (*koynak*), and a headdress of some kind. In addition, some groups also have a face veil (*yaşmak*), a sash (*salqusaq* or *bil qusak*), an indoor coat of some kind (*cabit* or *kurte*), and, for outdoor wear, a second coat (*chyrpy*), which is often worn over the head. Some Turkmen women also wear a broad cloth

Iranian Urban Dress

The nineteenth century in Iran was a period of dramatic changes with respect to urban dress; the style of garments worn at the beginning of the century was totally different from that at the end and in the following era. A major factor in this change were the policies of Westernization followed by Iranian rulers from the early nineteenth century on. Under Mohammed Shah (r. 1834–1848), for instance, the British military specialist Sir Henry Rawlinson was employed to modernize the Iranian army on European lines. His changes included the uniforms worn by the military, and it is no coincidence that during this period members of the court and the beaus (fashion-conscious men) began to adopt European-style army uniforms, frock coats, and narrow pants.

These and other changes in dress were not always gradual, and they were often intentional, forced, and at times quite controversial. In order to understand these changes, and how they affected the lives of both men and women, it is necessary to look first at the dress worn by people during the Qajar period (1785–1925). It should be stressed that these are generalizations, as there were numerous variations based on age, gender, social rank, economic position, ethnic origins, and locality. Nevertheless, it is still possible to outline the main garment types worn by men and women and to give an indication of the major changes that took place in the forms of attire worn, especially in the latter half of the nineteenth century.

It is also noticeable that the sources of information about the range and types of garments worn during the nineteenth century increase considerably compared the sources available from the eighteenth century and earlier. In addition to Iranian miniature paintings, life-size oil and fresco paintings also came into fashion. More Iranian and Western accounts about various aspects of life in Iran were published. All of these were supplemented by the advent of photography in the 1840s, which became very popular in Iran. Most importantly, however, large numbers of garments have survived from the nineteenth century and provide information about the materials used, as well as the cut and construction of the garments.

MEN'S URBAN DRESS IN THE EARLY NINETEENTH CENTURY

A detailed description of men's clothing from the beginning of the nineteenth century can be found in the memoirs of the English diplomat James Morier, who first went to Iran in 1808–1809 as His Majesty's Secretary of Embassy to the Court of Persia. Morier's list of the garments worn by Iranian gentlemen on a daily basis included a pair of very wide pants (zirjameh) of red silk or blue cotton and a shirt (pirahan), generally of silk, which went over the pants and was fastened by two buttons over the top of the right shoulder. This was followed by a tight-fitting jacket (alkaleq) made of chintz and padded and lined with cotton. The sleeves of the jacket extended to the wrists but were open from the elbow to the cuff.

Over the jacket was worn a gown (qaba) that extended to the ankles. It was fastened at one side. The sleeves of the gown went over those of the jacket and again were open so that the under sleeves could be seen. The open sleeves also made it easier to wash the hands and arms prior to prayer. The gown was kept in place with a sash (sal-i kamar), which was wrapped several times around the waist. According to Morier, the sash consisted of a Kashmir shawl tied around the waist, a common shawl of kerman (a type of woven cloth), English chintz, or a flowered muslin, according to the wearer's status. A dagger (kunjar) was inserted into the sash. The type of dagger and its ornamentation varied depending on the owner's wealth, ranging from, Morier noted, an enameled pummel set with precious stones to a common handle of bone and wood. At the beginning of the nineteenth century, the most typical form of headgear worn by men of rank was the turban (mandil) or a tall cap of some kind (kolah).

Wealthier men and members of the court also tended to wear a large quantity of jewelry. Sir William Ouseley, a British diplomat, noted in his account of life in Iran between 1810 and 1812 the splendor of men's jewelry at the court of Fath Ali Shah (r. 1798–1834). He wrote that there

> was a row of five or six officers; among whom one held a most beautiful crown or taje [taj] apparently not inferior in the lustre of its jewels to that with which the Monarch's head was so magnificently decorated; another held the royal bow … and one a golden tray or dish filled with diamonds and different precious stones of wonderful size and dazzling brilliancy. Of the king's dress I could perceive that the colour was scarlet; but to ascertain exactly the materials would have been difficult, from the profusion of large pearls that covered it in various places, and the multiplicity of jewels that sparkled all around. (cited in Ouseley 1823)

MEN'S URBAN DRESS IN THE LATER NINETEENTH CENTURY

In the 1850s, major changes began to occur in the range of garments worn by the court and officials. These changes tended to be followed by court members and wealthier, urban men. In particular, men stopped wearing the long, "Oriental" gowns and replaced them with Western-style knee-length jackets and pants.

One of the most notable differences is that the pants were intended to be seen, instead of being hidden by the gown as had been the case. These pants were now usually cut in the Western style, being narrow and close fitting. In addition, pants began to have a band (normally red or black) down the outside seam in imitation of military pants worn by European soldiers. Another major change was the use of frock coats similar to the ones worn by European men. However, these garments were generally considered indecent by the Iranians, because of the slit at the back that exposed the upper legs and lower back. As a result, an Iranian frock coat was devised that was cut on the Turkish model, with a large quantity of cloth gathered into the waist. The ample material made movement and horse riding feasible even without a back slit.

By the second half of the nineteenth century, the new garments that had been associated with the shah and the court, especially the pants and frock coat, had started to filter downward. The basic urban male outfit now consisted of pants (zirjameh) cut in a European military style, a cotton shirt (white for the wealthier urban groups, blue for poor men and villagers), a jacket or vest (alkaleq), a knee-length jacket (*kemmerchen*), and a cloth frock coat (*kolijeh*) cut in the Turkish style with loose sleeves and many pleats at the lower back. In addition, the lapels of the frock coat were often trimmed with gold lace (*derberi*), pieces of shawl fabric, or fur, or they could be left plain.

Some higher-ranking officials would also wear a voluminous cloak (*jobbah*). Over this was worn a cloth sash that was wrapped around the waist. This combination was worn by priests, merchants, traders, and sellers in the bazaar, as well as the secretarial

class and the aged or old-fashioned among the higher ranks of governmental employers. Increasingly, however, men's various garments were kept in place with a leather belt. Such a belt was considered by Charles James Wills, who lived in Iran in the latter half of the nineteenth century, as the distinctive mark of a courtier, military man, or person from the upper servant class. These belts were often made of varnished black leather with a brass clasp (usually Russian in origin). The princes and courtiers tended to replace the brass clasps with one made of precious stones.

Finally, the male headgear of the period consisted of a tall cap (kolah) made of cloth or sheepskin on a frame of pasteboard. The most expensive versions were made of black skin from a fetal lamb. The middle and lower classes wore colored lambskin hats, in particular, gray ones. According to Wills, the fashion in hats changed yearly, especially among the courtiers, the fashionable, the military, and servants.

Although the clothing and accessories worn by the court during the late Qajar period were plainer than their previous clothes, this did not exclude the use of jewelry; it was, however, worn in different ways. During the reign of Mohammed Shah, for example, the amount of jewelry worn by the shah decreased, as did the amount of jewelry worn by members of the court and fashionable men. By the time of Nasser al-Din Shah (r. 1848–1896), the royal regalia had taken on various European royal and military elements such as the use of jeweled epaulets on the coat, large medals, and sashes worn diagonally across the chest. Finally, a number of the royal frock coats were fastened with large diamond buttons. Despite the use of these and other forms of jewelry, the opulent pearl, ruby, and emerald collars, armbands, and deep cuffs

Nasser al-Din Shah surrounded by courtiers and others, Tehran, late nineteenth century. The shah is wearing a Western-style military uniform, while the courtiers are wearing a mixture of Iranian dress, including a long gown (*qaba*), Turkish-style frockcoats, Russian-style long coats, and Qajar caps. Photograph by Antoin Sevruguin. Textile Research Centre, Leiden.

that Fath Ali Shah and certain members of his court had worn at the beginning of the century were no longer used and had gone completely out of fashion.

In comparison to the court styles, at the end of the nineteenth century, farmers, peasants, and men in the lower classes normally wore a shorter and less expensive version. The basic outfits tended to consist of pants (knee or calf length), simple shirts, knee-length jackets, and sashes. Headgear consisted of a skullcap (*araqchin*) or low cap, often of felt (*kolah-i nomadi*). This form of "farmer's" garments continued to be worn in various parts of Iran well into the 1930s and even into the 1950s in more remote regions of the country. Merchants in both cities and smaller towns, in contrast, tended to wear pants (*shalwar*, which are somewhat narrower than the zirjameh), a long shirt (pirahan), an ankle-length gown (qaba), a sash (sal-i kamar), and, in some cases, a turban (mandil) with a skullcap (araqchin) or a cap (kolah) of some kind. In addition, various classes of Iranian men continued to wear turbans of various types. These groups included merchants, doctors, clergy, scribes, and so forth, generally, men who in the early twenty-first century would be described as "professional" rather than "official."

Finally, some mention should be made of male hairstyles during the Qajar period. At the beginning of the nineteenth century,

men's hair tended to be long, curling at the nape of the neck and falling in side locks around the face. In addition, facial hair tended to consist of a full and bushy mustache with cheeks that were either clean shaven or heavily bearded. It was said that few men could compete with Fath Ali Shah's beard with respect to its length and luxuriance.

By the end of the century, however, hairstyles had changed dramatically: Most men, including Nasser al-Din Shah and Prince Zil al-Sultan, wore their hair short in the contemporary European fashion. Most sported full mustaches set off by clean-shaven chins, as mustaches were regarded as a sign of an active and strong male.

URBAN WOMEN'S INDOOR DRESS IN THE EARLY NINETEENTH CENTURY

The indoor garments worn by women during the Afsharid period (1736–1750) and up through the end of the Qajar period, namely from about 1740 to 1924, were colorful and prone to some dramatic changes. Changes in the cut and style of garments worn by court and urban men started to be noticeable by the 1840s–1850s, and a similar situation is found for women's clothing. Morier

A group of Kurds dressed in Persian-style garments surrounding a wealthy, seated khan, Tehran, 1890s. Although they are Kurds, these men are wearing Persian dress, indicating their superior's desire to emulate the dominant Persian culture. The two standing servants (at the back on the right) are wearing Turkish-style frockcoats, the symbol of Persian modernism. These are open down the front of the garment and have pleats at the side of the skirt for ease of movement. Photograph by Antoin Sevruguin. Textile Research Centre, Leiden.

(writing about the period 1807–1808), for instance, commented that there was a "danger" that Fath Ali Shah would force his harem to adopt Western fashions, both for the supposed beauty of the garments and for their lower costs. Morier reported on a conversation he had with the envoy of the shah:

> We talked of female dress. I asked the Envoy what effect the visit of a European woman dressed in her own way would produce in Persia. He replied that "if the King were to see her, He would probably order all his *Harem* to adopt the costume, and that every other man would follow his example, and enforce a fashion, which is not only so much more beautiful, but so much less expensive than their own. Their women are clothed in brocade and gold cloth, which is soon spoilt, or at least which is always cast off, whenever they hear that a new cargo arrives from Russia.

During the early Qajar period, the basic indoor garments of a woman consisted of an undergarment, pants, a skirt, and a jacket, which gave a long silhouette while emphasizing the hip region somewhat. By the 1820s, the garments' silhouette was beginning to move toward a bell shape created by the skirts. Gradually, however, the pants became more important, and the skirt vanished. The pants grew in size until they looked like huge skirts; for wealthier women, they were made out of heavy brocades and velvets. The fullness of the pants was achieved by wearing several pairs at the same time.

One of the most enduring items in a woman's wardrobe was the chemise, or pirahan. Various types of chemises are visible in depictions from the Qajar period. In court paintings, the blouses are usually shown as being made out of fine and often transparent cloth decorated with sprigs of flowers or embroidery. In some cases, these garments had one long slit down the front; in other examples, three slits are depicted. These slits were both decorative and functional, as they were intended to help with the breast-feeding of babies and young children. It is noticeable that by the beginning of the nineteenth century, women were no longer wearing the long chemise of previous centuries. Instead, with the advent of the widespread use of pants, the chemise was now much shorter, reaching only to the waist or slightly below.

For chemises worn by wealthier women, the material was usually a transparent gauzy fabric, either plain, white with scattered colored spots, or sometimes blue or pink. The fineness of the material used for these garments is reflected in various comments made by contemporary and later European travelers, who were usually "shocked," as younger women wore virtually transparent blouses with no undergarments. The neckline region of these garments was often extravagantly decorated with several jewel-edged openings slit to the navel.

In contrast, the chemises worn by less wealthy women away from the main urban areas tended to be made out of white cotton cloth. The necklines on these garments were normally plain or else embellished with embroidery. By the end of the century, deliberate attempts were made to make pirahans, cut on Iranian lines, look European, for example, by having the front folded and stitched back to give the appearance of a Western-style blouse with a collar.

Not all women wore the large pants, as a significant number chose to wear skirts with a jacket instead. By the 1860s, the wearing of full skirts had become widespread. These skirts varied in length from the knee to the midcalf and were gathered into a tight waistband. Sometimes, ankle-length pants were worn under the skirts, functioning as undergarments.

URBAN WOMEN'S INDOOR DRESS IN THE LATER NINETEENTH CENTURY

One of the most dramatic changes in women's garments occurred after Nasser al-Din Shah's first visit to Europe in 1873. During this trip, the shah was entertained on several occasions by visits to the ballet. It is said that there he became enamored with the short, multilayered skirts worn by the ballerinas. This interest is noted, albeit briefly, in the diary that the shah kept during this royal visit to Russia, Germany, England, and France, among other countries. On his return to Iran, the shah ordered the members of the harem to adopt garments similar to women's ballet costumes, namely, the tutus. The "new" skirts were called *shaliteh* or sometimes *jama*. Once adopted by the court, the fashion for these skirts spread throughout Iran, and women and girls wore them for at least another thirty years. The shaliteh consisted of layers of skirts one over the other. The underskirt was made of starched cotton, while the top skirt was often of the same material as the bodice. Some of the outer skirts could be made from ten to twelve yards (nine to eleven meters) of cloth.

According to the English traveler Isabella Bishop, who was in Iran at the end of the nineteenth century, women wore white socks (*jurab-i sefid*) with the short skirts, a point that is confirmed by contemporary photographs of Persian women. The representative of the French company Worth et Cie in Tehran is credited with the introduction of white silk stockings in the late nineteenth century. The fashion of these short skirts seems to have vanished quickly following Nasser al-Din Shah's death in 1896. The skirts were replaced by longer versions and, later, by more Western forms of skirts and dresses.

Although major changes took place with respect to pants and skirts, urban women still wore their traditional short jackets (alkaleq), which were open at the front. As with most garments, however, while the basic form remained the same, some changes did occur. In this case, the cut and outline of the alkaleq changed slowly over time, especially with respect to the sleeves and cuffs and the side slit.

Usually, only one jacket (alkaleq) was worn over the pirahan, although sometimes a second one, with shorter elbow-length sleeves (kordi) in a plain or contrasting pattern, was worn over it as well. These garments were not intended to be fastened; instead, they were open at the front so that the pirahan with its long slits could be seen. Such jackets were made of a variety of types of cloth, including heavy brocades, silks, wools, and cottons. The type of cloth used depended on the wealth of the wearer's family, their status, and the time of year. For example, summer garments tended to be made out of lightweight silks or cottons, while winter versions would be of heavier wools and silks. The winter version also tended to be quilted. Wealthier women used raw silk as the quilt filling, while poorer ones used carded cotton.

Whereas earlier garments were made from a single central panel folded in half, the construction of the jackets was adapted to produce the shape that was currently fashionable. In most cases, the jackets were made from a back panel and two front sections, thus producing shoulder seams, something that is not found in most Arab-style garments. Various pieces were added at the sides

Lithograph of two Persian women, one wearing indoor clothing and one wearing outdoor clothing, from *Travels in Various Countries of the East: More Particularly Persia* by William Ouseley (1819–1823, 1:189). The outdoor clothing consists of a outer wrap (*chador*) and face veil (*ru-band*) and is more somber than the patterned clothing worn indoors. Textile Research Centre, Leiden.

and front to produce flared shapes and wrap-over sections. By the end of the nineteenth century, such short jackets were becoming straighter and slightly longer. They also included Western details such as small pockets on the outside of the jacket. While most women during the Qajar period wore short jackets, longer versions were occasionally worn; the two main types of long jacket were the *sardari* and the kolijeh.

During the nineteenth century, high-ranking men sometimes wore a long frock coat in the European style, which was called a sardari. Wives of high officials, and sometimes those of merchants, also wore a form of sardari that looked like a conventional woman's jacket except that it was pleated below the waist. The most common form of long jacket, however, was the kolijeh, which was mainly worn during the winter months. The woman's kolijeh had straight sides and sleeves and was normally made of red or maroon-colored velvet or silk brocade. It was not uncommon to find them decorated with embroidery or trimmed with braid or lace, especially around the cuffs.

In contrast to the rest of their attire, women's headdresses remained relatively modest during the Qajar period. As in earlier periods, many women wore a head covering of some kind even when indoors. One of the most common forms of head covering was the *charqad*, which was made from a square of cotton, silk, or

some other fabric that was folded diagonally. The large point was worn at the back of the neck, while the two ends were fastened under the chin with a pin. Lengths of cloth for making charqads were often among the wedding presents given to the bridegroom's family for the bride's trousseau.

Two forms of the charqad, or indoor head scarf, were commonly used during the later nineteenth century. The first was worn when a woman was within her own establishment; in this case, she would don a small version of the charqad called a *lecek* (literally, "triangle"). However, when a woman was visiting friends, a much larger charqad was adopted, which was often decorated with embroidery, beads, or a jeweled aigrette with a spray of flowers or feathers. Sometimes, a small skullcap was worn instead for visits; it was adorned with a *jika*, a form of aigrette decorated with precious stones and feathers. An alternative to the jika was the *saragus*, which was a net or cloth bag in which women could wrap their hair.

JEWELRY, HENNA, AND PERFUMES

The range of jewelry worn by women during the Qajar period was wide. It included hair decorations (*taj* or *belador*), earrings (*gushvareh*), necklaces (*gardanband* or *galuband*), brooches (*gol-i sineh*), armbands (*bazuband*), belts (*kamarband-i morassa*), as well as finger and toe rings (*angoshtar*).

At the beginning of the nineteenth century, a popular form of headdress included a skullcap with an aigrette, which was sometimes further decorated with feathers. By the end of the nineteenth century, jewelry was becoming more restrained, and less of it was worn. The most popular items included earrings, necklaces, brooches, bracelets, and finger rings, which reflected European modes of jewelry and jewelry combinations.

In addition to keeping their nails clean and well shaped, women often decorated their hands and feet with henna or other coloring substances such as privet (*Ligustrum* sp.), saffron (*Crocus* sp.), cypress (*Cupressus* sp.), and indigo. Sometimes the hands and feet were totally covered in henna, and on other occasions patterns were painted on. Various designs were used such as circles (*chenar*), "hornets" (the tips of the fingers dyed with henna; this was called *sorkh-zanbouran*), and *fandoq* or *fandoqband*, whereby the tips of the fingers were stained to resemble nuts. There was also a special ceremony (*hana-bandan*) on the eve of the wedding days, during which henna was sent to the bride. Traditionally, female relatives applied the henna after the bride-to-be had had her ritual bath.

For centuries Iran has been famous for both the production and use of perfumes. A wide range of fragrances were used by both men and women during the Qajar period. The most common substances used in Iran for making perfumes were aloe, ambergris, civet, jasmine, musk, rose, and sandalwood. These were sometimes used by themselves or in various combinations. Sometimes women scented their hair with perfume, while on other occasions women would wear an ornament that was filled with musk, called an *anbarina*, in their hair. Small balls of musk or other aromatic substances were also worn around the neck. Similarly, fragrant berries were bored and hung on a string around the body to give a pleasant fragrance.

URBAN WOMEN'S OUTDOOR CLOTHING

With regard to outdoor garments, three items are of particular importance: the outer wrap (chador), the face veil (*ru-band* or *peche*), and outdoor pants (*chaqchur*). One of the oldest outer garments worn by Iranian women is a wrap of the style that in the early twenty-first century is known as the chador and is still worn. This garment was used to deck the head and body, leaving only the face uncovered. During the Qajar period, the chador was made out of a large rectangle of material about two by three yards (two by three meters) in size and made up of two widths of material sewn together. In general, peasant or poor women used a blue chador made of cotton, while middle-class women wore a dark-colored chador. Upper-class women wore a black or dark blue chador made of silk and sometimes decorated along the outer edges with gold thread.

In the nineteenth and early twentieth centuries, outdoor chadors were normally rectangular in shape. But in the 1930s and 1940s, the form of the chador changed from a rectangle to a semicircle. At the end of the twentieth century, chadors were usually made from cotton or synthetic material, but occasionally silk would be used for wedding chadors. The distinction in appearance between classes remains: Villagers and servants tend to wear thin chadors, in dark blue with small white dots, or with large abstract flower designs. In contrast, higher-status women tend to wear black chadors.

Another important element of a Qajar woman's outdoor outfit was the face veil. Although it is known that Hellenistic women in the eastern Mediterranean region wore face veils from the fourth century B.C.E. on, there is no direct evidence to suggest that Iranian women were wearing face veils of any kind until the medieval period. During the Qajar period, two types of face veils were in common use, namely, the ru-band and the peche.

A ru-band was made from a length of white cloth that had a grid for the eyes made by using either drawn-thread or counted-thread work. It was fastened at the back of the head with a knot, clasp, or button of some kind. The ru-band was used by both urban and provincial women. This style of face veil continued to be used in Iran into the late nineteenth century, when it was replaced by the peche. This type of face veil was made from black horsehair. The peche was worn at the end of the Qajar period and was widely used by urban women living in northern Iran, especially those of Turkish descent. The peche vanished as a result of Reza Shah's dress reforms in the 1930s.

Another element of the outdoor outfit was the chaqchur; these are long, outdoor pants that were worn during the nineteenth and early twentieth centuries. The actual origins of the chaqchur are uncertain, but it appears that they evolved from the stocking boots made of heavy brocade that women wore both indoors and outdoors in the eighteenth and early nineteenth centuries. By the mid-nineteenth century, they had become voluminous pants that were sewn into flat-soled slippers. Late-nineteenth-century chaqchur were usually either purple or green, although black versions also existed. It is not clear whether this difference in color resulted from a change in fashion over time, the availability of materials, or the different localities from which the garments originated. It could also simply be a question of personal choice based on what type of cloth was available in the local bazaars. Normally, the chaqchur were worn with slippers or shoes, which were worn over the foot of the pants. As with other forms of outdoor wear, as a result of the dress reforms of the 1930s, the wearing of chaqchur disappeared in most urban areas.

A young woman wearing the indoor dress of Persian women, including a short, tutulike skirt (*shaliteh* or sometimes *jama*), Tehran, 1890s. Nasser al-Din Shah became enamored with the costumes of ballerinas after seeing several ballet performances during his visit to Europe in 1873. On his return he ordered the members of the harem to wear similarly styled garments to those worn at the ballet. The fashion for the tutu-like skirts soon spread throughout Iran; this style was worn by women and girls for at least another thirty years. Photograph by Antoin Sevruguin. Textile Research Centre, Leiden.

DRESS REFORMS

At the end of the nineteenth and the beginning of the twentieth century, a number of Southwest Asian countries—in particular,

Turkey, Iran, and, later, Egypt—embarked on programs of social and political reforms. In all three countries, attention also focused on the nature of both men's and women's clothing. In all of these countries, the wearing of various types of veils by women was seen as a public symbol of "backwardness" and, to a lesser extent, the oppression of women. As a result of these changing attitudes, the subject of veiling became a political issue with considerable religious overtones. In some cases, there were demands for the removal of the veil, whereas at other times, its return was sought. Dress reforms in Iran, for both men and women, started in the mid-nineteenth century and built up momentum until the 1930s when Reza Shah, then shah of Iran, carried out a series of dress reforms that changed the face of Iranian dress and have had repercussions into the twenty-first century.

Nasser al-Din Shah's trip to Europe in 1873 had a profound effect on the garments worn by Iranian women. It was also during this period that more upper-class Iranian men (and a few women) began to travel to Europe. They also saw European travelers and residents wearing Western clothing in Tehran and other major cities. As a result, a number of Iranians became somewhat self-conscious about their "Oriental appearance" and adopted European clothing.

There is also evidence suggesting a growth in the number of Western tailoring and dressmaking establishments. Bishop, writing in 1891, for instance, noted the presence of European tailors, dressmakers, and so on in Tehran. At the same time, the French haute couture house of Worth established an outlet in the Iranian capital. In addition, numerous tailors and seamstresses were copying European garments for Iranian customers.

World War I (1914–1918) can be seen as a watershed for many political and social changes, especially in the sphere of clothing throughout the West and Southwest Asia. In Europe and North America, women started to have their hair cut, dresses became shorter, and the use of tight-fitting corsets declined. Women throughout Southwest Asia were encouraged to wear Western, especially Parisian, fashions.

During the years that Reza Shah (r. 1925–1941) was in power, he carried out a number of dress reforms. These reflected his perception that adopting Western clothing styles would help to unite and modernize the country.

In September 1928, the Iranian cabinet announced the passing of the Uniform Dress Law, which was mainly directed at male attire. In this law, the correct dress for men was stated to be a Western-style coat, a jacket, pants with a leather belt, and leather shoes. The first two articles of the Uniform Dress Law defined who was required to wear the new dress and who was exempt. Basically, it meant that all male Iranian subjects, other than those who were not required to wear special clothing as a result of service in the government (for example, soldiers and judges), had to wear Western-style clothing within the country. Those exempted included Shia and Sunni ulema (clergy), non-Muslim religious dignitaries, and male children under the age of six.

In addition, all government workers and schoolboys were to wear the so-called kolah-i pahlavi (Pahlavi hat), which is a cap with a flat circular top and a visor at the front that looks like the forage cap worn by soldiers during the American Civil War. In the next round of dress reforms, however, which took place after the shah's visit to Turkey in 1934, Reza Shah issued an order stating that the kolah-i pahlavi was to be replaced by brimmed hats

A young girl in a version of the outdoor clothing worn by Persian women, Tehran, 1890s. She wears an outer wrap (*chador*) and baggy pants (*chaqchur*). Photograph by Antoin Sevruguin. Textile Research Centre, Leiden.

(*chapeaus*), such as the trilby and fedora. This new form of hat was to be worn by all Iranian workingmen.

At the same time as these male dress reforms were taking place, the outdoor clothing of women was also being altered but through a more indirect process that included the women of royal family wearing Western clothing in public to give a "good example." It was not until 1936 that women in general were forbidden to wear the chador, face veils, and large outdoor pants (chaqchur) in public places. After 1936, they had to wear Western-style clothing, including hats, dresses, and coats or be fined and even put in jail. Only after Reza Shah's abdication in 1941 did the chador again become a common sight, but the use of face veils and outdoor pants had vanished for good.

Ironically, the issue of veiling took a very different turn with regard to women of low repute, namely prostitutes. The use of face veils was traditionally seen as a sign of modesty and virtue and, inversely, not wearing them indicated a woman lacking in respectability. During Reza Shah's dress reforms of the 1930s, when women were forced to remove their face veils, an exception was made for prostitutes; they had to remain veiled. Later, the law was changed slightly so that the prostitutes could go unveiled but only if they could prove that they were married. Apparently, the aim of this change in policy was to prevent the association of unveiling with unwholesome mores. However, it was widely seen by conservatives as an attempt to turn the symbol of virtue into a symbol of vice.

POLITICS AND DRESS IN THE LATE TWENTIETH CENTURY

Clothing again became a major political issue during the late 1970s, as dissatisfaction increased with Reza Shah's successor, Mohammed Reza Shah (r. 1941–1979), his Western-oriented policies, and a government that was generally regarded as corrupt in Iran.

In the preceding years, from the 1960s to the early 1970s, there was a growing divide in the range of garments worn by urban and regional groups. The urban elite wore Western haute couture garments bought in all the major European and North American cities. Women's magazines carried regular articles on fashion. Following the arrival of British fashion designer Mary Quant's miniskirt in 1965, women's clothing, especially in Tehran, became equally short. But, as in Europe, these fashions caused problems, especially among the more conservative clergy and their followers. These and other tensions related to the perceived Westernization and de-Islamization of Iran came to a head at the end of the 1970s.

In the early days of the Islamic Revolution, there was already a close relationship between dress, politics, and religious allegiance. In the summer of 1977, the Iranian writer Sattareh Farman Farmaian observed how Tehran students were displaying their interest in Islamic Marxism and, as a result, started to wear facial stubble or beards to renounce Westernism and demonstrate Islamic zeal. In addition, many men wore buttoned shirts with no ties to emphasize that they were not Westernized. After Black Friday (8 September 1978), when many anti-shah demonstrators were killed, more and more men stopped shaving and wearing ties, while many more women started to wear "Islamic" head scarves of various types. During this period, the word *kravati* ("tie wearer") became a fashionable term of disparagement in revolutionary circles for any intellectual, and smart, clean clothing was seen as *estekbar* ("ostentation") and thus unfitting for devout Muslim men. Following the revolution, it became impossible for men to wear tight pants, shorts, or T-shirts. At the beginning of the twenty-first century, it is noticeable that men are beginning to wear tighter pants (especially jeans), shirts with short sleeves, and T-shirts. Ties, however, remain unfashionable, especially among the political elite.

Women's clothing also played a part in the revolution of 1979 and afterward. In particular, the veiling of women became a major political and social symbol. During the 1970s, some women had started to wear the chador in the street in quiet protest against the shah, but in the latter half of the decade, this protest became more vocal and visual. For many women, the wearing of the chador represented a mixture of political and religious reasons and beliefs, but mostly it stood as a protest against the shah himself.

When the revolution occurred in February 1979, the wearing of "Islamically correct" clothing (the generic term *hijab* is often used in this context) was seen by many as a symbol of solidarity and militancy. Members of political parties to the left regarded the wearing of the chador as a sign of rebellion against Western ideas and imperialistic culture. At the same time, members of religious parties, especially those that can be regarded as traditionalist, regarded the sight of so many women wearing the chador during the revolution as a sign that women wanted a return to Islamic conventions. In a speech given at the beginning of 1987, the Iranian theologian, Muslim reformer, and senior Shia

ayatollah Taleghani said that no one had forced the women to wear hijab at demonstrations; instead, they had felt an Islamic responsibility to make the wearing of hijab one of their Islamic and Iranian slogans, and the wearing of hijab showed their genuine feelings to the world. Not everyone agreed with Taleghani. For some women, wearing a chador was equated with a return to traditional moral and social values, including purity and dignity, rather than a religious statement.

An important point made at the time was that the wearing of the chador should be a matter of choice rather than compulsion. So there was unrest when, at the beginning of March 1979, Ayatollah Khomeini announced that all working women (namely women who did not stay at home) had to wear a coat (*manteau*) and head scarf (*rosari*) or a chador when outside the house. The decision led to the first of several demonstrations. As a result of the unrest, the role of women was clearly defined along strict Islamic principles, and those stepping over the boundaries faced severe judicial punishment.

Another aspect of the enforcement of hijab was that women who were not wearing either the chador, or a long coat plus a large head scarf, could be subject to violent personal attacks in the street. There are accounts of women having their legs painted or acid thrown at their faces. Later, a special morality police called the *pasdaran* was established. One of the functions of this police was to check that the correct form of clothing was worn and that the distance between the ground and the hem of the dress was not greater than four inches (ten centimeters). If it was, then the legs, which had to be covered by thick, black stockings, had to be further hidden by full pants. Male pasdaran were officially ordered to deal with men, while a special squad of female pasdaran stopped women.

It seems that, in many cases, women were the specific targets of the pasdaran. During the summer of 1992, attacks on women for *bad hejabi*, or improper dress, increased. These attacks were carried out by zealots attempting to uphold virtue and combat vice. According to the Iranian writer Nesta Ramazani, the term *bad hejabi* was gradually taken up at this time as women started to wear brighter colors, patterned stockings, and even lipstick. A number of women at this time were also replacing the *maghneh*, a black head covering, with brightly colored head scarves.

During 1992, conservatives increasingly demanded that the perceived growing attractiveness of women's outdoor dress be suppressed. Public figures such as Mohammad Musavi Kho'iniha denounced bad hejabi, while the former prosecutor general Sayyed Hosain Musavi Tabrizi stated that "anyone who rejects the principle of the hijab is an apostate" (Ramazani 1993). Although some conservative religious leaders advocated and carried out the beating of women for bad hejabi, others, including President Ayatollah Sayyid Ali Hoseyni Khāmene'i (also known as Ali Khamenei; president from 1981 to 1989 and Supreme Leader of Iran since 1989), called for words, rather than violence, to be used to persuade women to wear correct hijab.

SOME OUTSIDE INFLUENCES

At the beginning of the twenty-first century, many women were discontented with being forced to wear the chador, or some equivalent outer garment, in public. Part of this discontent was due to the increase in communications with the West and other regions

Iranian women in a "Mobilization Week" parade march past the U.S. Embassy in Tehran, 1979. They wear "Islamically correct clothing," which at the time was se
by many as a symbol of solidarity and militancy. Getty Images.

of the world. In the early twenty-first century, there has been an official embargo on Western culture in Iran since the 1979 revolution, but more and more people have access to (satellite) television and the Internet. In addition, more and more Iranian exiles and their children living in the West, notably North America, Australia, and Europe, have started to come "home," bringing with them gifts of Western goods and a vision of a different way of life. Wealthier Iranians are also traveling abroad. All of this means that many Iranians are well aware of what is happening outside the country and want changes that the more conservative, religious groups who hold power are unwilling to allow.

The fashion trends for Iranian women at the end of the twentieth and the beginning of the twenty-first century, particularly in the major cities of Tehran, Isfahan, and Shiraz, illustrated women seeing how far they could go in public. It was not uncommon for more liberal women to wear colorful scarves pushed back on their head, leaving hair visible; a knee-length, tight-fitting coat (manteau) became popular, as well as heavy facial makeup and nail varnish, things that would have been unthinkable in public in the 1980s.

It is noticeable that during times of political or economic hardship in the country, more attention is paid to what is worn,

especially by women. In April 2007, there was a sudden crac down on wearing bad hejabi, with a marked increase in mo conservative and modest dress. The office of the Iranian pre dent stated that the wearing of hijab should be voluntary, as Turkey; nevertheless, the police were given permission to ta action, under the direction of the clerics, to prevent women fro dressing immodestly. It is no coincidence that this was a period political tension between the U.S. and Iranian governments.

In conclusion, there is a notable link in the nineteenth a twentieth centuries between the style of the urban dress worn both men and women and the political aspirations and thoug of the ruling Iranian government. Sometimes Westernization been encouraged, whereas on other occasions, it has been c demned. What is certain is that urban dress in Iran can be u as a good indication, without a word being said, of the prevail political and economic climate in the country.

References and Further Reading

Benjamin, Samuel Greene Wheeler. *Persia*. London: Fisher Unwin, 18
Bishop, Isabella Bird. *Journey in Persia and Kurdistan*. 2 vols. Lond
    John Murray, 1891.

Diba, Layla S., and Maryam Ekhtiar, eds. *Royal Persian Paintings: The Qajar Epoch 1875–1925*. Brooklyn, New York: J. B. Tauris, 1998.

Farmaian, Sattareh Farman. *Daughter of Persia*. London: Bantam, 1992.

Fischer, Michael. *Iran: From Religious Dispute to Revolution*. Cambridge, MA: Harvard University Press, 1980.

Floor, Willem. "The Guilds in Qajar Persia." PhD thesis, Leiden University, 1971.

Fraser, James Baillie. *Travels and Adventures in the Persian Provinces on the Southern Banks of the Caspian Sea*. London: Longman, Rees, Orme, Brown and Green, 1826.

Morier, James. *Journey through Persia, Armenia, and Asia Minor, to Constantinople, in the Years 1808 and 1809*. 2 vols. London: M. Carey, 1812.

Mosteshar, Cherry. *Unveiled*. London: Cornet Books, 1995.

Ouseley, Sir William. *Travels in Various Countries of the East: More Particularly Persia*. Vol. 3. London: Rodwell and Martin, 1823.

Ramazani, Nesta. "Women in Iran: The Revolutionary Ebb and Flow." *Middle Eastern Journal* 47 (1993): 409–428.

Redhouse, J. W. *The Diary of H.M. the Shah of Persia, during His Tour of Europe in A.D. 1873: A Verbatim Translation by J. W. Redhouse*. London: Murray, 1874.

Scarce, Jennifer. *Women's Costume of the Near and Middle East*. London: Unwin Hyman, 1987.

Shahbazi, A.S., Trudy S. Kawami, Elise H. Peck, et al. "Clothing (Lebas)." In *Encyclopaedia Iranica* (online version), edited by E. Yarshater, N. Sims-Williams, C.J. Brunner, et al. http://www.iranica.com/newsite/ (accessed 17 October 2009).

Sykes, Ella C. *Persia and Its People*. London: Methuen and Co., 1910.

Tabari, Azar, and Nahid Yeganeh, eds. *In the Shadow of Islam: The Women's Movement in Iran*. London: Zed, 1982.

Vogelsang-Eastwood, Gillian, and Leo Ferydoun Barjesteh. *An Introduction to Qajar Era Dress*. Rotterdam: Barjesteh van Waalwijk van Doorn & Co., 2002.

Vogelsang-Eastwood, Gillian, and Willem Vogelsang. *Covering the Moon: An Introduction to Middle Eastern Face Veils*. Leuven, Belgium: Peeters, 2008.

Wills, Charles James. *In the Land of the Lion and Sun or Modern Persia, Being Experiences of Life in Persia from 1866 to 1881*. London: MacMillan and Co., 1891.

Gillian Vogelsang-Eastwood

See also Dress Reforms of the Early Twentieth Century in Turkey, Iran, and Afghanistan; Iranian Regional Dress; Reza Shah's Dress Reforms in Iran; Face Veils.

Reza Shah's Dress Reforms in Iran

Some of the most enduring and controversial legacies of the reign of Reza Shah Pahlavi, the shah of Iran from 1925 to 1941, were the changes he made in the dress of both men and women living in Iran. The repercussions of these changes can still be felt in the early twenty-first century.

Reza Pahlavi became shah of Iran following his overthrow of Ahmad Shah Qajar, the last shah of the Qajar dynasty, in 1925. Reza Shah became known for his authoritarian government, militarism, secularism, and attempts at modernization. He introduced many socioeconomic reforms while reorganizing the government, army, and state finances. Some Iranians regard him as a great leader, while others view him as an irreligious tyrant.

While Reza Shah was in power (r. 1925–1941), he implemented a number of reform policies that were to have widespread implications. These reforms were carried out with a secondary agenda to unite all of Iran and to create a feeling that everyone, living in Iran was an Iranian, rather than Kurdish, Qashqa'i or Tabrizi, or some other group. The shah also wanted to modernize Iran, and for him this meant brining it up to the perceived scientific and technological standards of the West. For Reza Shah, uniformity and science equaled "modern." Another factor was the shah's apparent feelings of inferiority, which became apparent in his strong desire for Iranians to be regarded as being "as good as" any European or North American. Making both men and women wear Western-style clothing was, for Reza Shah, an important step toward achieving all of these aims.

The shah's desire for equality with the West was manifest not only on a national scale but also on a more personal, one-to-one level. It was noted that one morning the shah met his minister of foreign affairs, who was dressed in a Western-style morning coat and tails; the minister was about to receive one of the heads of a foreign mission. According to Donald Wilber, a U.S. intelligence officer with the Office of Strategic Services, the shah noted with pleasure, "You look like one of them and their equal and not like a subordinate." With respect to dress reforms, although there was considerable overlap between the reforms for men's and women's dress, there were also significant differences in the means used to achieve the stated aims and in the results.

THE UNIFORM DRESS LAW OF 1928 AND MALE DRESS

In 1928, Reza Shah held an audience with a group of Iranian merchants wearing Western-style frock coats. The shah spoke at the gathering, and it appears that he was very pleased with the merchants' appearance. He gave a speech about uniformity of dress and manners, noting that these would lead to uniformity of life and politics and would, at last, weld Persia into one uniform whole. Shortly afterward, on 26 September 1928, the Iranian cabinet announced the passing of the Uniform Dress Law.

The correct dress for men was to be a Western-style coat, a jacket, pants with a leather belt, and leather shoes. The first two articles of the Uniform Dress Law defined who was required to wear the new dress and who was exempt. Basically, Articles I and II stated that all male Iranian subjects who were not required to wear special clothing as a result of service in the government (for example, soldiers) had to wear Western-style clothing within the country. In addition, all government employees, whether civil or judicial, had to wear the officially prescribed civil or juridical clothing (for example, the robes of a judge) when on government duty but at other times had to wear Western-style attire.

This meant that all Iranian males, except Shia and Sunni ulema (Islamic clergy), non-Muslim religious dignitaries, and male children under the age of six had to wear the new style of dress. Members of the clergy who wished to seek exemption from this ruling had to present evidence of their clerical qualifications and training; this exception was also regarded as a means by which the government could control and regulate the clergy. Not surprisingly, it was regarded with great suspicion by many religious groups.

In addition, all government workers and schoolboys were to wear the so-called kolah-i pahlavi (literally, "Pahlavi hat"), which was, according to some, designed by the shah. The Pahlavi hat was a cap with a flat circular top and a visor at the front. It looks like the forage cap worn by soldiers during the American Civil War and the kepi that is still worn by French soldiers at the beginning of the twenty-first century.

According to Article III of the Uniform Dress Law, noncompliance by townsmen was punishable by a fine of one to five tomans, which was later increased to thirty tomans, which was equivalent to at least a week's wages for some groups, plus a jail sentence of one to seven days. Villagers and tribesmen were exempt from the fine but not from the detention. Apparently, any money collected from these fines was supposed to be used to purchase the new style of clothing for poorer members of society, but it appears that little of the money ever found its way to them.

The law came into effect on Nauruz (the Iranian New Year, on about March 22) in 1929. At first, it appeared that this ruling applied only to larger cities, but later it held for the whole country. Nevertheless, it was noted that if circumstances required, implementation in rural regions could be delayed for one year.

During this period, the Iranian government was having conflicts with various tribal groups. In particular, both the Qashqa'i and Kurdish tribal representatives wanted the return of their leaders who were being held in Tehran, as well as exemption from military conscription, permission to possess arms, and exemption from the Uniform Dress Law. However, this did not happen. Like other members of Iranian society, members of tribal groups were forced to wear Western-style clothing, such as trousers, jackets, and Western-style headgear. Because the nomads had relied on the local bazaars for their ready-made clothes, when the government instructed the merchants to supply only the new types of garments, the men had to adopt them. These garments are still the mainstay of many nomadic males in Iran.

Ironically, the women of many tribal groups were relatively unaffected by the new regulations, having never worn Iranian urban-style clothing. They normally bought cloth from the local markets and made their garments at home, so the government could not as easily control what they were wearing.

By January 1930, the police were refusing to issue travel passes to Iranian men unless they were wearing the kolah-i pahlavi. Not unexpectedly, there was considerable opposition to the dress reforms, including riots in the cities of Tabriz and Shiraz as well as the province of Azerbaijan. In particular, it was argued that the peak on the kolah-i pahlavi made it non-Muslim, since a wearer would be unable to pray properly when wearing it (the forehead has to touch the ground several times during prayers, but this would not be possible if a person is wearing a cap with a brim). Further, based on a hadith (one of the traditional sayings or acts of the Prophet Mohammed) that stated, "He who copies others, becomes one of them" (Abu Dawud, Hadith Libas 4), it was argued that by wearing a Christian garment, the wearer would become a Christian. It is not surprising, therefore, that many Muslims found this type of headgear abhorrent.

One aspect of Reza Shah's dress reforms that is often overlooked is that dress differences based on religion, distinguishing Muslims and non-Muslims, became illegal. In most cases, this differentiation of dress had been directed at Jews and Christians, with the men, especially those of Jewish communities, previously being forced to wear a yellow cloth on the shoulder of their outer garment or a yellow garment. The abolition of this difference brought angry criticism from the Muslim ulema.

Another result of the dress reforms was a general impoverishment of local manufacturers of textiles and clothing, as well as Iranian and Indian traders dealing in textiles and garments for the Iranian markets. This situation was made more complicated because poorer members of society had problems finding the funds to purchase the new clothing. In order to address this situation and stimulate the Iranian textile industry, the shah reissued a directive from 1923 requiring all government and army personnel to wear garments of Iranian-made cloth, but this move does not seem to have had much effect.

THE DRESS REFORMS OF 1934 AND MALE DRESS

The next round of dress reforms took place as a result of the shah's visit to Turkey in 1934. On his return to Iran, Reza Shah issued an order stating that brimmed hats (chapeaus), such as the trilby and fedora, were to replace the kolah-i pahlavi and that this new form of hat was to be worn by all Iranian workingmen. This enforced change in headgear took place even though the shah had stated just before leaving for Turkey that the kolah-i pahlavi was now the national headgear and part of the required dress even for court officials.

On 8 June 1935, the kolah-i pahlavi hat was officially abolished, and shortly afterward European-style felt hats became obligatory for all state employees. According to Wilber, who was traveling

in Iran at the time, officials in Mashad were careful to carry both brimmed hats and Pahlavi caps, donning whichever seemed appropriate. In July 1935, there were riots in Khorasan and Mashad against the dress reforms. On 18 July 1935, for example, leading theologians who opposed the dress reforms, colloquially known as "turban men," were either arrested or banished for speaking out against the new headgear.

The various dress reforms introduced by Reza Shah resulted in significant changes in the appearance of male dress in Iran. These effects can still be seen in the garments worn by men in urban, regional, and nomadic settings at the beginning of the twenty-first century, particularly in the choice of headgear in many provincial cities.

THE DRESS REFORMS FOR WOMEN: FIRST STEPS TOWARD UNVEILING

The effect of the dress reforms was not the same for men and women. It is true that men were seriously affected in the 1930s, especially nomadic groups; later dress reforms, in contrast, do not seem to have been particularly strict against them. Women, however, were dramatically affected in the 1930s and once again at the end of the twentieth century when attempts were made to reverse the reforms of the 1930s.

With respect to women's clothing, the most important reform was the deveiling of women, specifically the prohibition of the wearing of chadors (a large rectangular or semicircular garment used to cover a woman's body, except her face) and similar garments in public. Attempts had been made in the mid- to late nineteenth century to ban the veiling of women, but these had little success at first, perhaps because the concept was regarded as simply too shocking. One of the earliest examples of a woman unveiling herself in public took place in the 1840s. The case involved the poet and religious teacher Tahereh Qorratal 'Ayn ("Solace of the Eye"; her real name was Fatemeh Baraghabi, and she lived from 1814 to 1852), who deliberately removed her veil in 1848 as an act of protest concerning the position of women in Iranian society. Apparently, when Tahereh unveiled herself, the assembled group was greatly disturbed: Many men left the room, others called her a heretic, while one man seems to have tried to cut his throat (a bloody but not fatal act). In 1852, Tahereh was executed for her religious and social beliefs, including her acts of deveiling.

During the late nineteenth century, the official movement toward the unveiling of women started following visits to Europe by members of the Iranian elite, both men and women. They were apparently impressed by the role played by women in European societies. Upon their return, these Iranians agitated for women's education and liberation from the veil. The momentum for change was encouraged by the establishment of various newspapers intended for women, including Danesh (Knowledge; first published in about 1910), Shekoofeh (Blossom; date of first publication unknown), and Zaban Zanan (Women's Voice; founded in 1919). The latter was critical of the condition of women in Iran; in this, it was influenced by its publisher, Sediqeh Dovlatabady.

Dovlatabady was an active feminist who established, among other things, schools and weaving workshops for women. She criticized the chador in the newspaper, with the result that both

Shah Mohammed Reza Pahlavi of Persia (1919–1980), the son of Reza Shah Pahlavi (1878–1944), is pictured here (center) in uniform wearing the *kolah-i pahlavi* ("Pahlavi hat"), ca. 1925. As part of Reza Shah's reforms, all government workers and schoolboys were to wear the *kolah-i pahlavi*, which was thought to have been designed by the shah. Getty Images.

According to the Iranian writer Houchang Chehabi, when Reza Khan (later Reza Shah) was prime minister of Iran, he was careful to avoid the issue of veiling as it was regarded as too contentious. Nevertheless, he was prepared to intervene on the behalf of antiveiling activists. In September 1923, for instance, Ebrahim Khajehnuri published an article in which he suggested that Iranian women should follow Turkish women in wearing a kerchief or head scarf instead of a full veil. Khajehnuri was prosecuted by religious advisors to the Ministry of Education and sentenced to three months in prison. However, Reza Khan intervened and ensured that Khajehnuri served his sentence in the prison hospital rather than in the prison itself.

An early development in the direction of deveiling took place in March 1928 when some of Reza Shah's female relatives celebrated the first day of Farvardin in the ultrareligious city of Qom. The royal ladies, who included the queen, wore light-colored—or transparent, depending on the account—chadors, which caused an uproar. The clergy protested, and, as a result, Reza Shah drove to Qom, entered the shrine with his boots on (a deliberate insult), and ordered that all the clerics who had criticized the queen were to be whipped.

At the same time, another incident demonstrates the still cautious nature of the Iranian royal family. In June of the same year, King Amanullah and Queen Sorayya of Afghanistan visited Iran on their return trip from Europe. Throughout the European parts of their trip, the Afghan queen had been unveiled. However, she was asked to veil herself while in Iran as the Iranian people were not ready to see unveiled Muslim women.

Shortly afterward, the Iranian police received orders to allow women to appear in public places unveiled if they wished. The Iranian queen occasionally appeared in public without a veil, but unveiling was not yet official state policy. According to the Iranian politician Reza-qoli Khan Hedayat (quoted in Wilber 1975), an early indication that this position would change came in 1932 in one of his last cabinet meetings as prime minister. During the course of a discussion on the range of items allowed to be imported, Minister Taymourtash (of Foreign Affairs) insisted that women's hats should be included; this was seen as a sign that changes were going to be made in women's dress.

THE DRESS REFORMS FOR WOMEN: MANDATORY UNVEILING

During the early to mid-1930s, Reza Shah initiated a process of Westernization and modernization that included the emancipation of women (or at least the appearance of emancipation) through the removal of the chador. In May 1935, for example, the government sponsored the founding of a Lady's Center (*kanun-e banovan*), one of the stated purposes of which was to promote the abandoning of the veil. In addition, ministers and their deputies were ordered to appear once a week with their unveiled wives at mixed-gender functions held in their ministries at the Iran Club in Tehran. The Minster of Education was also instructed to prohibit the use of veils by teachers and students in girl's schools beginning with the school year 1935–1936. This regulation was not difficult to enforce since most girls who attended school came from more liberal families.

However, the actual, official unveiling of women was delayed by a violent outbreak of opposition in Mashad that has become

she and the newspaper offices were threatened and on occasions attacked. Dovlatabady was later exiled from Tehran for her vehement comments on the position of women and the role of the shah. When she died at the age of eighty, her last request was that no veiled women should be allowed either to participate in her funeral or to visit her grave.

Several women's societies were founded in the early twentieth century, including the Patriotic Women's League, which held numerous meetings on the subject of women and veiling. Their leader, Mohtaram Eskandari, frequently lectured against the use of the chador and in favor of the introduction of education for women.

At first, there was a gradual relaxation with respect to women's veiling in public. Both the *ru-band* and *peche* forms of face veils vanished, except in the extreme south of the country; there, Arab influence is still very strong, and women continue to wear face veils of various types on a daily basis into the twenty-first century.

known in Iran as the Gowharshad Incident. In response to what they felt were antireligious measures, the ulema in various cities began holding meetings to discuss the subject of women and veiling. In Mashad, the ulema, under the leadership of Aqa Hosayn Qomi, sent angry telegrams to the shah about the proposed deveiling of women. Qomi decided to go to Tehran and personally talk with Reza Shah with the hope of changing the shah's mind on various subjects, including that of dress. Qomi, however, was snubbed. At the same time, a meeting was held in Mashad at the Gowharshad mosque; during this meeting various preachers and ulema spoke against the unveiling of women.

On Friday, 13 July 1935, security forces entered the mosque and the nearby shrine of Imam Reza; several people were killed, and riots ensued. The following day the senior ulema of the city was arrested and exiled from Mashad. Apparently, the official media initially played down the incident; however, this changed following the execution of Mohammad Vali Asadi, the administrator of the shrine, on charges relating to the incident. The Gowharshad Incident caused an uproar in Iran among the more traditional and religious groups.

At the same time, Reza Shah prepared the ground for what would become one of his most unpopular reforms: the banning of the veil. As part of a soft approach to the issue, Hedayat, Reza Shah's more moderate prime minister, proposed replacing the chador with the *rupush*, a type of coat, which he described as a form of "dignified overalls" and which left the face uncovered. Furthermore, the ministries of the interior and of education sent directives to their functionaries in the provinces to prepare for unveiling by organizing lectures and meetings.

On 8 January 1936, the shah, the queen, and the princesses Shams and Ashraf appeared at the new Daneshsara-ye moqaddamati (Teaching Training School) in Tehran to address the female students and to award diplomas to women graduates from a number of other schools. All of the women of the royal party were unveiled and wore Western-style clothing. Directives went out to the provinces to make sure that the actions of the royal women were emulated by all women. At a reception at the Gulistan Palace, Tehran, Reza Shah revealed his feelings about the chador "by contemptuously mimicking the gesture of a woman covering and uncovering her face as a man approached" (Wilber 1975, 168).

Receptions and meetings were held all over the country in January and February 1936 to celebrate unveiling. On 1 February 1936, regulations designed to encourage the abandonment of the chador came into effect. As a result of these regulations, any officials of the Ministry of Finance whose wives were found wearing a chador were subject to dismissal. In order to get around this situation, some men entered into temporary marriages, then took their new "wives" to any parties, leaving their actual wives at home. Women wearing the chador were not permitted to be treated by doctors in hospitals, to appear in public places such as cinemas and baths, or to use taxis. Bus drivers who accepted veiled women as passengers were liable to fined or even dismissed.

Reaction to the unveiling of women seems to have been mixed. In general, the modernist upper classes in major urban centers supported the changes, whereas those in the more traditional and religious areas of the country, such as Qom and Mashad, opposed them. On a more personal level, many women felt ashamed and embarrassed at being asked or ordered to leave their houses without their chadors. In *Daughter of Persia*, Sattareh Farman Farmaian describes her mother's reaction to the new law, which included feelings of anger, rage, shame, and total humiliation. Some Iranian families even moved to other countries, such as Oman, to avoid the ban on veiling and other forms of traditional clothing.

One of the unexpected effects of forbidding the chador was that the garments worn underneath became visible, making the poverty of many women apparent. State employees were given loans to buy new clothes for their wives. As a result, an Iranian trade commission was hastily sent by the government to Germany and France to buy large quantities of ladies' ready-to-wear clothing for distribution, and a fund was also made available to help buy clothing in hardship cases.

Throughout this period the royal family continued to lead in the deveiling of women. For example, the invitations to the wedding of the Iranian crown prince with Princess Fawzia of Egypt specified that ladies had to wear white, sleeveless décolleté dresses.

The ban on chadors was strictly enforced for about five years; following the abdication of the shah in 1941, it was rescinded for female university teachers and students. Later, the ulema started to demand the reintroduction of veiling, and at the same time, the number of attacks on unveiled women began to increase. In 1949, the religious leader Ayatollah Borujerdi issued a *fatwa*, or religious decree, forbidding women to shop in bazaars without wearing the chador. However, although there were mutterings about the return of veiling, the violence that had accompanied the removal of the veil did not recur.

One of the questions that is asked about deveiling is why the shah went to such lengths to ban veils. Was it simply to "liberate" women? The answer would appear to be no. The main motivation was probably the need to create a new, "modern" vision of a united Iran that could be presented to the Western world. The education and liberation of women were seen as part of a greater picture in which all aspects of Iranian cultural life took on an urban appearance similar to that of Tehran. This meant that directives were sent that tried to force women in the provinces to abandon their traditional clothing. Women were required to look like "civilized" women of the world.

The changes that took place in women's dress in the 1930s and 1940s were to have a profound effect on women's roles and appearance in Iranian society. In turn, the overthrow of these dress reforms played an important role in the Iranian Islamic Revolution of 1979 and in how women were perceived by the subsequent Islamic governments into the twenty-first century.

References and Further Reading

Chehabi, Houchang E. "Staging the Emperor's New Clothes: Dress Codes and Nation-Building under Reza Shah." *Iranian Studies* 26, no. 3–4 (1993): 209–233.

Farmaian, Sattareh Farman. *Daughter of Persia*. London: Anchor, 1993.

Milani, Farzaneh. *Veils and Words: The Emerging Voices of Iranian Women Writers*. Syracuse, NY: Syracuse University Press, 1992.

Oberling, Pierre. *The Qashqai Nomads of Fars*. The Hague: Mouton, 1974.

Paidar, Parvin. *Women and the Political Process in Twentieth-Century Iran*. Cambridge Middle Eastern Studies. Cambridge, UK: Cambridge University Press, 1995.

Sanasarian, Eliz. *The Women's Rights Movements in Iran*. New York: Praeger, 1982.

Savory, Roger M. "Social Development in Iran during the Pahlavi Era." In *Iran under the Pahlavis*, edited by George Lenczowski. Stanford, CA: Hoover Institution Press, 1978.

Tapper, Richard. *Frontier Nomads of Iran: A Political and Social History of the Shahsevan*. Cambridge Middle East Studies. Cambridge, UK: Cambridge University Press, 1997.

Wilber, Donald N. *Riza Shah Pahlavi: The Resurrection and Reconstruction of Iran*. Hicksville, NY: Exposition Press, 1975.

Gillian Vogelsang-Eastwood

See also Dress Reforms of the Early Twentieth Century in Turkey, Iran, and Afghanistan; Iranian Regional Dress; Iranian Urban Dress; Face Veils.

Regional Dress of Afghanistan

Afghanistan is a country that developed out of a Pashtun kingdom that was founded in the middle of the eighteenth century. The Pashtun form an ethnic group that in the early twenty-first century still constitutes the majority in the modern Islamic Republic of Afghanistan. Modern Afghanistan was created in the nineteenth century on the basis of this former Pashtun kingdom as a buffer state between the British Indian Empire to the east and the tsarist Russian realm to the north. This was the time of what is often called "the Great Game," in which Britain and Russia both tried to dominate the highlands of Iran and Afghanistan. The borders of the modern state were eventually, once Britain and Russia had decided to divide their mutual spheres of influence, laid out by officials from both countries, and these lines cut straight across the land of the Pashtuns and include a large number of other groups. This resulted in a country that houses more than fifty ethnic groups, many of them with their own language and cultural characteristics, including a wide variety of textile and dress traditions. The somewhat artificial configuration of the country, however, does not mean that modern Afghanistan is a loose amalgamation of ethnic groups; a shared history, many common cultural characteristics, and the continuous threat from neighboring countries have created a country that, although culturally and ethnically diverse, has been, after a civil war that started in the late 1970s, slowly developing into a politically more homogeneous state.

The number of people living in Afghanistan is difficult to calculate, but it may be assumed that it is around thirty million. The main ethnic groups are (in alphabetical order) the Baluch, Hazara, Nuristani, Pashtun, Tajik, Turkmen, and Uzbek. Each has its own language, culture, and way of dress. Many people, especially in the capital, Kabul, tend to wear Western-style garments, but overall there is a strong tradition of wearing regional and ethnic dress in Afghanistan. Dress is often an important marker of ethnic identity, and people wear their ethnic dress with pride. There is, however, a basic outfit for men, women, and children, which consists of trousers gathered at the waist, a loose-fitting shirt or dress, and some form of head covering. This is an old combination of clothing, dating back to the early medieval period and the introduction of Islam. It is found all over this part of the world

and is regarded as an Islamically acceptable form of clothing that covers most of the body.

Over the centuries, numerous variations on this theme have developed, also in Afghanistan. These differences reflect the wearer's ethnic and cultural origins. Some garments are familiar. The ubiquitous skullcap, for example, can be found among all groups and is worn by both genders. However, the shape, size, and decoration of the caps signify the group with which the wearer is associated. An Uzbeki cap worn in the north of the country looks very different from a Pashtun cap from the southern town of Kandahar.

Certain garments have social significance within a particular group. The turban, for example, is an important garment for men. Among the Pashtun and Baluch, a boy may mark his passage into

The mannequin on the left displays a Pashtun woman's outfit consisting of undertrousers, a dress, and a *chadari* (head and body covering) in bright colors. The mannequin on the right displays a Baluchi woman's outfit consisting of trousers, a dress, and a head covering. The embroidery on the yoke and skirt panel has very small, precise stitches in geometric designs, typical of Baluchi dress. Textile Research Centre, Leiden.

manhood by being allowed to wear a turban. Similarly, a girl will move from wearing a simple head covering, such as a scarf, to one with a more complex and larger form once she is married or of a marriageable age.

Head coverings are prescribed for all women in Islam; therefore, most women in traditional and rural Afghan communities wear variations of a large or small rectangular head scarf or body covering, commonly called a *chador*. They are usually made out of fine cotton or a synthetic material. A variation of the chador is the *chadari*, in the West commonly known as the Afghan burqa, which is composed of a close-fitting cap from which finely pleated, colored silk, cotton, or rayon material falls to form a cloak, completely enveloping the body, with only an openwork embroidered grid over the eyes. Contrary to popular wisdom in the West, chadaris are not worn by all Afghan women; instead, this garment is related to urban life.

BALUCHI DRESS

The Baluch live in southern Afghanistan near the borders with Iran and Pakistan. In the early twenty-first century, most of the Baluch, in fact, live in Baluchistan, which forms part of Pakistan, and in the neighboring districts of Iran. Groups living in these countries have long had strong historical and cultural links with each other. Borders never completely sealed off contacts. Many Baluch are nomadic or seminomadic.

At the beginning of the twentieth century, the basic Baluchi outfit for a man consisted of coarse white or indigo cotton trousers (*shalwar*) worn under a long shirt (*jama*), which normally reached to just below the knees. The jama was usually buttoned on the right shoulder. Over this was worn a cotton robe (*kurti*), which was densely pleated at the waist and tied at one side with strings. The kurti is Indian in origin. By the end of the century, this form had been totally replaced by the ubiquitous *shalwar kamez* from Pakistan, which consists of simple trousers (shalwar) with a drawstring (*tikke*) and a long shirt (*kamez*) with a central front opening.

In the early twenty-first century, the headgear consists of a snugly fitting cap (*topi*) and turban (*pag*; sometimes called a *lungi*). Baluchi caps for men are often made of cotton with fine silk or cotton embroidery in floral or geometric patterns. They sometimes incorporate minute mirrors (*shisha*). Because many Baluch are Sunni Muslims, the front of the topi is often shaped (sometimes in a decorative way) by cutting out a section at the front so that the forehead can touch the ground when praying. Baluchi turbans are normally wrapped in numerous, large rolls, and the final appearance is quite different from the turbans worn by Pashtun men, although the Pashtun from southern Afghanistan, living close to the Baluch, like to wear the typically Baluchi topi.

Other male accessories include a long scarf or shoulder cloth (*pushti*) and, in colder weather, woolen socks. Sometimes, an overcoat (*qaba*) and a waistcoat (*sadri*) are worn, with a woolen shawl (*sal*). Leather sandals (*shabav*) in dark red or brown are also often worn. These are frequently decorated with chain-stitch embroidery.

The woman's outfit throughout the Baluchi world consists of ankle-length trousers (shalwar) that are gathered at the waist, an ankle-length, loose-fitting dress (*pashk*), and a large shawl or outer cover (chadar). A feature of Baluchi women's clothing is the embroidery that once was largely hand worked but in the early twenty-first century is done by machine. A Baluchi woman's dress (pashk) invariably has four panels of embroidery (*doch*), namely, a large yoke covering the chest, two panels on the sleeve cuffs, and a long, narrow, rectangular pocket, which runs from just above the waistline to the hem of the skirt. The embroidery used for these panels is often referred to as *pakka*, meaning "firm" or "solid," because fine stitching covers the ground fabric completely, with geometric designs often worked in lines.

The style and quality of embroidery carried out depend on whether the garment is going to be used on a daily basis or is intended for a feast, such as a wedding. Cotton yarn and a less complex design are often used for daily dress, while silk garments with embroidery in silk and metallic threads are used for special occasions.

HAZARA DRESS

The Hazaras are a special ethnic group in Afghanistan. They claim to descend from the Mongol army that occupied the land that comprise modern Afghanistan in the thirteenth century. Indeed, the (Persian) language spoken by the Hazaras still contain many Mongolian words. Over the centuries they were pushed back into the Afghan mountains by the growing power of the Pashtuns. In the early twenty-first century, they occupy perhaps the poorest lands of the country, high in the valleys of the central Afghan mountains.

Throughout much of nineteenth and early twentieth centuries, the Hazaras made use of a woolen cloth called *barrak*, which was made by various nomadic groups in the country. However, according to the mid-nineteenth-century U.S. writer Josiah Harlan, the best was from the Hazara. Barrak was used for both men and women's clothing.

The Hazara are also well known for working embroidery of cotton or silk material, which was enlivened by very fine lines of cross or herringbone stitches. The stitches normally follow the grain of the fabric. There are various types of Hazara embroidery. The Wardak Hazara, for example, from southwest of the capital Kabul, are known for producing multicolored, geometric designs in holbein stitch. The Hazara from nearby Ghazni, in contrast, often produce designs based on rectangles or squares, which enclose strictly geometric patterns of checkered bands or lozenges, usually multicolored and worked in silk thread on a cotton ground; they use brick stitch or short satin stitches, with dividing lines worked in black-and-white holbein stitch.

Hazara caps are often totally decorated with rows of short satin stitches. Gold-colored threads often further embellish children's and women's caps. Another form of Hazara embroidery includes gold-colored braids, sewn especially on long, velvet waistcoats and dresses. The designs on dresses tend to be stylized floral motifs, worked around the bodice and on the cuffs and hems of the garments.

Hazara dress for men in the nineteenth and early twentieth centuries consisted of barrak trousers, a cotton shirt (*qamis* or *pirahan*), long and short kaftans made of barrak, waistcoats (*waskat*), coats (*macew*), and a Hazara cap (*kapi*) that was stiff and solid with embroidery. A belt (*kamari*) or cloth sash was often wrapped around the waist. Wealthier men wore a turban (*lungota*) over the cap as well as a shoulder blanket or shawl (*s*

Hazara woman's dress, late twentieth century. The front chest panel is embroidered with a geometric design worked in tiny stitches. The use of beading on the shoulders and waist, together with the metal braid decoration, shows how this dress is linked to Pashtun garments. However, Pashtun women prefer to wear red velvet, while Hazara women favor purple velvet. Textile Research Centre, Leiden.

of cotton or a soft, fulled woolen material (*sal-i hazaragi*) depending on the season.

In winter, all men wore turbans (for the poor, turbans meant extra warmth), and woolen scarves were wrapped around the neck and face as protection against the cold. Sometimes, in colder weather, a frock coat–like garment was also worn. Hazara chiefs sometimes wore the *choka*, a long cloak with sleeves, a form of Uzbek kaftan. Some farmers are reported to have also worn a cylindrical cap (*kulla*) with a crown of four or eight quilted pieces.

Hazara women's outfits consist of trousers, a calf-length dress with long, full sleeves that was very wide at the waist, plus a head covering. Sometimes, a waistcoat was worn; it was decorated with buttons, beads, silver coins, and seashells. The head cloth was sometimes folded into a thick, flat pad on top of the head, with the ends forming a sort of veil at the back of the neck. In the 1950s, bright red or purple gowns were considered modern. These had narrow cuffs and were embroidered along the edges of the front neck opening. By the end of the twentieth century, most Hazara dresses were made with sleeves with narrow cuffs, and they ended at the knee or halfway down the calves. Modern Hazara dresses for festivals tend to be made out of purple velvet, thus following the trend of using red or purple that was set in the 1950s.

The embroidery on Hazara dresses is concentrated in several parts, such as the bodice and neck, the sleeves, the skirt front, and along the hem of the dress. Two types of embroidery are used for dresses. The term *zamin-dozi* refers to embroidery that is densely stitched on the fabric of the dress, usually the front chest panel. This type of embroidery is often used for clothing that is worn for festive occasions, such as weddings. When the embroidered motifs are scattered around the fabric of the dress, in contrast, it is called *gul-dozi*.

NURISTANI DRESS

Nuristan ("The Land of Light") is located in the eastern part of Afghanistan. The area was formerly known as Kafiristan ("The Land of Nonbelievers"), which stretched into the area that is Pakistan in the early twenty-first century. The name was changed to Nuristan when the inhabitants were forcibly converted to Islam in the late nineteenth century. Nuristan is a mountainous region and very cold in the winter, and this has influenced the range of clothing worn by both men and women.

Until the mid-twentieth century, Nuristani dress was the most distinctive in Afghanistan. Men wore warm, white woolen trousers (*vit*) reaching to just below the knee, over which were wrapped long, black leggings (*pataw*) that looked like puttees. Both of these garments were suited to the mountainous conditions in Nuristan; given the geographic and climatic conditions, it is not surprising that no other groups in Afghanistan wore such leg wear. Over this was worn a long tunic, which was kept in place with a silver-studded belt (*mala niste*), which was used to support a dagger (*katra*). A distinctive feature of modern Nuristani dress is the *pakol*, a headdress that is often called the Nuristani cap but is better known as the Chitrali cap, after the neighboring town and district of Chitral, in modern Pakistan. The pakol is usually made of fulled woolen cloth and consists of a flat crown with a rolled brim.

Nuristani women used to wear trousers and a shirt with a front neck opening. These shirts were often made of dark-colored silk or cotton and were decorated around the neck opening with metal-thread embroidery. The older versions of Nuristani metal-thread embroidery are very fine, and they often incorporated beadwork as well. The outfit also included very full skirts or dresses (*bazu*), which were gathered at the waist with woven belts (*niste*). Some of these dresses were embellished across the back of the shoulders and down the sleeves with a combination of red and black embroidered appliqués. By the 1930s, this form of dress had all but vanished as a result of increased access to the region from outside, including trade in other forms of textiles and garments.

Modern Nuristani outfits for women tend to consist of a waisted dress with a collar (this is unusual for Afghan dress), worn with similarly colored trousers and a large chador. The most common stitching technique used is the cross stitch, but there is also a form of embroidery that is similar to that found at Kandahar in the south of the country, but it is regarded as not being quite so fine. The tradition of Nuristani metal-thread embroidery continues in the use of plasticized metallic yarns. Nuristani women tend to wear bead strands and beaded jewelry in bright colors. The beads are used to create complex, geometric designs.

Detail of Nuristani satin-stitch embroidery from a woman's dress, Nuristan, Afghanistan, early twenty-first century. Textile Research Centre, Leiden.

PASHTUN DRESS

The Pashtun constitute an ethnic group that lives along both sides of the modern Afghanistan-Pakistan border. This line, which cuts straight across the Pashtun homeland (often known as Pashtunistan), is also sometimes called the Durand line, after the late-nineteenth-century British official who was responsible for this delineation. The number of Pashtun is not clear; generally it is assumed that some fifteen million Pashtun live in Afghanistan and double that number in modern Pakistan. Traditionally, many Pashtun used to call themselves Afghan, hence the name of the modern country of Afghanistan, which was based on the Pashtun kingdom that was created in the middle of the eighteenth century. The Pashtun constitute the majority population of Afghanistan, and the former kings of the country were all Pashtun, as is the president elected in 2004, after the fall of the Taliban, Hamid Karzai. At the same time, the armed opposition, generally known as the Taliban, is also a predominantly Pashtun organization.

There are various groups of Pashtun, each with their own style of embroidery, which is seen as a reflection of their cultural identity. A general feature of Pashtun embroidery, however, is *gul-i pirahan* (also called *gul-i-peron*), roundels that are made of felt and covered with symbols and objects related to good luck and fertility, such as colored beads, cowry shells, and metal disks. These roundels are usually applied in pairs and stitched to the upper part of women's dresses, bags, and horse harnesses and other animal trappings.

The Pashtun living in the Wardak region are noted for multicolored silk embroideries on a monochrome cotton or silk ground. The embroideries are worked in satin stitch in complex geometric designs that radiate out from a central motif, such as a star. Mangal Pashtun from the east of Afghanistan often use satin stitch to create lozenges to embroider the whole surface. The designs do not follow the grain but instead form diagonal lines that accentuate the lozenge designs.

Some of the most famous Afghan embroidery, called *khamak*, comes from the southern city of Kandahar, which is a well-known Pashtun city. Khamak is a form of monochrome satin-stitch embroidery on a fine cotton or white silk ground. The ground is usually either the same color as the embroidery thread or a very pale blue or green. The satin stitch is worked from the reverse side of the material, and pride is taken in getting the front and the back of the embroidery to look alike. In general, the more subtle the embroidery, the prouder the wearer. The designs used for Kandahar embroidery tend to be very geometric in structure, relying on light reflecting off the satin stitch to produce different effects. Sometimes, the relief effect of the embroidery is enhanced with pulled-thread work.

The basic outfit for Pashtun men normally includes trousers (*shalwar*) with a drawstring waist (*tikke*), a knee-length shirt (*kamez*), and a waistcoat. These are usually in a wide range of colors and shades, but the trousers and shirt are always the same color and material. The Pashtun headdress is normally a cap of some kind, often with a turban on top. The Taliban, for example, are known for wearing turbans, usually in a dark gray or black. The outfit is completed with a large, rectangular blanket (*patu*), which is worn over one shoulder or elegantly slung across both. The blanket is multifunctional and can be used for warmth, as something to sit on, and as a prayer mat.

A Kuchi Pashtun woman's dress, late twentieth century. This dress is decorated with coins, beads, and embroidery and has decorative braids around the lower hem. The tassels are worn as amulets. Textile Research Centre, Leiden.

Pashtun women wear a "standard" Afghan outfit made up of trousers with a drawstring, a dress with long sleeves and a full skirt, and some form of head covering. The trousers are usually in a contrasting color to the dress; in the late twentieth century, the most common color for trousers was "Pashtun green," which is a deep mid-green. They are often decorated along the ankle cuffs with some form of embroidery or an applied lace.

Festival dresses are usually made out of silk or velvet in rich colors, especially deep purple. During the hot summer months, many women prefer to wear printed cotton and rayon fabrics in bright colors. The most elaborate embroidery is carried out on the bodice and the sleeve cuffs of the dresses. The embroidery for the bodice can be done either on the actual fabric of the dress or on a coarser material that is then stitched onto the dress. The hem of the dress is often decorated with gold-colored laces or thick gimp threads that are twisted and shaped to form various designs, in a similar manner to the men's waistcoats that come from Kabul.

A feature of Pashtun dresses for women, both urban and nomadic, are the beaded panels at the heads of the shoulders. They cover the seam line between the front bodice and the skirt of the dress. These are usually made using multicolored glass beads to create tight, geometric designs. It is also normal to have gul-i pirahan on the shoulders, chest panel, and waist. The outfit is completed by a large, rectangular head covering (shal or chador) in cotton, silk, or a synthetic material. Hand embroidery is normally carried out by the women themselves, while machine embroidery is the preserve of male tailors in the local towns.

KUCHI DRESS

Kuchi is the popular name for the mainly Pashtun nomads and seminomads who originally migrated annually (and sometimes still do into the early twenty-first century) from their winter camps in the valleys to their summer pastures high in the mountains. They are found all over the country. In the past, they could move freely across the borders of Afghanistan, Pakistan, and India, but since the early 1960s, border restrictions have limited their movements to within Afghanistan.

Kuchi men normally wear trousers (shalwar) with a drawstring waist and a knee-length shirt (kamez). These are usually white. The Kuchi men's headdress is normally a cap covered with a large white turban. The outfit is completed with a large white shawl or blanket that is worn over one or both shoulders. This blanket is, as with most Pashtun, used for warmth, as something to sit on, and as a prayer mat.

Kuchi women's outfits are similar to those worn by (settled) Pashtun women, but the colors tend to be darker. A Kuchi outfit consists of trousers with tightly fitting ankle cuffs, a dress, and a head covering of some kind. Kuchi dresses normally have long and very wide sleeves, with very full skirts. The front of the bodice, skirt, and sleeve hems are normally decorated with metallic laces that are couched down. Such dresses are also adorned with amulets, pendants, tassels, buttons, bands, and trinkets.

TAJIK DRESS

Tajik is the normal name in Afghanistan for the non-Pashtun, non-Hazara, Persian (Dari)-speaking population of the country. They make up about one-quarter of the Afghan population and live in many parts of the country, but most of them can be found in the main cities and in the northeast and west of the country.

There are various types of Tajik embroidery. Many Tajik designs are based on multicolored floral motifs encircling a central motif. In the north of Afghanistan, Tajik embroidery is normally multicolored and includes gold thread for extra richness. Frequently, floral motifs decorate dark-colored dresses and waistcoats of velvet. The Tajik of Badakhshan in the extreme northeast of the country, in contrast, use satin stitch and brick stitch to create small geometric motifs worked in silk thread over a cotton ground, often separating sections of embroidery with lines of chain stitch.

In the early twenty-first century, the basic outfit of Tajik men consists of trousers (shalwar) with a drawstring (tikke) at the waist, worn with a knee-length shirt (kamez). These generally are available in a wide range of colors and shades, but the same color and material are always used for the trousers and shirt. The Tajik headgear for a man normally consists of an embroidered cap of some kind.

The outfit worn by Tajik women is very similar to that of other groups, namely trousers, a dress, and a head covering. Tajik trousers for women are usually of satin, cotton, or a synthetic material with straight legs. They are normally white or a solid, pastel color. The ankle cuffs of these trousers may be embroidered with a white border or embellished with couched white lace. Tajik dresses tend to have long sleeves and longish skirts. In general,

they are not decorated with embroidery or metallic lace. Instead, emphasis is placed on the use of different types of fabrics, often woven or printed with geometric and floral designs. Expensive fabrics such as brocades or printed silks are used for special occasions, while cottons and synthetic materials are for daily use. Tajik head coverings (chador) are normally about two yards (two meters) long and made from georgette, gauze (especially a silk-and-cotton mix), or cotton with lace, crochet, or needlepoint borders. Some of the cheaper examples have printed borders. In general, Tajik women like to wear jewelry made of gold set with precious stones. Ruby, turquoise, pearls, and emeralds are the favorite stones of those who can afford them.

In some areas of northern Afghanistan where the Tajik live closely with the Uzbek, some Tajik women wear an outfit that is similar to modern Uzbekistan forms. This outfit consists of narrow ikat pants, worn with a shiny ikat dress. The hair of women from this region is usually braided into numerous long strands. In public, it is normal for a large head covering of some form to be worn.

A Kuchi man leading his camel caravan in the Kapisa District, Afghanistan, 2008. He wears trousers (*shalwar*) and a matching knee-length shirt (*kamez*) and carries a large shawl or blanket, which is used for warmth and as a prayer mat. Shah Marai/AFP/Getty Images.

TURKMEN DRESS

The Turkmen are a Turkic group who speak a form of Western Ghuz (Oghuz) Turkic, which includes many Arabic and Farsi words in the early twenty-first century. At the end of the nineteenth century, the Turkmen region was divided among Afghanistan, Iran, and the former Soviet Union. In the early twenty-first century, most of the Turkmen live in Turkmenistan (about two million people), while about one million Turkmen live in Iran, mainly in the northeastern provinces of Gurgan and Khorasan. About 900,000 Turkmen live in Afghanistan, where they are largely concentrated along the Turkmen-Afghan border in the provinces of Faryab and Jowzjan. It should be stressed that the Turkmen of these countries have really been separated by international boundaries only within the last one hundred years. Prior to this period, there was constant, and relatively easy, trade and social contact between the various groups. The two main Turkmen groups in Afghanistan are the Yomut and Teke.

Silk was an important feature of Turkmen dress for both men and women. It was locally produced and often dyed a characteristic red color. It was decorated with stripes (often yellow), apparently simple woven geometric designs that on closer inspection prove to be more complicated, and embroidery. Embroidery in general plays an important role in the lives of many Turkmen women, as a means of showing their creativity and skill. In Turkmenistan itself, many ateliers, some state owned, specialize in embroidery, which is sold on the local and international markets. Across the border in Afghanistan, most of the embroidery is for domestic or local use.

Chain stitch is generally a feature of Yomut embroidery, sometimes worked in combination with stem stitch outlining the chain-stitch areas. The Teke, however, extensively choose lacing stitch with stem stitch (for outlining), backstitch, and couching. The range of embroidery differs slightly in color and motifs, although stylized floral and geometric motifs in red are common to all groups. The Teke, for example, tend to use golden yellow or blues as well, with very stylized floral motifs; a common design is the tulip, which represents fertility.

A feature of Turkmen dress, especially that of women and children, is the use of various forms of amulets (although this practice is dying out in Iran). The amulets worn by men tend to be written amulets, which are simply sewn onto a piece of cloth. Amulets are used to protect against disease, evil spirits, and the evil eye. The texts regarded as suitable include passages from the Koran, the ninety-nine names of Allah, supplications to angels and saints, magical incantations, magic squares, and so forth.

From the beginning of the nineteenth century until the mid-1920s, the basic garb for a Turkmen male consisted of a pair of loose cotton trousers (balaq) and a shirt (koynek). Over these was worn a tight-sleeved robe (don) of striped silk. These garments were held together at the waist with a sash (qusaq). A man's headgear consisted of a small skullcap (bork), sometimes with a turban or a cylindrical black sheepskin hat (telpek). This is still the dominant type of dress of the Afghan Turkmen. In Iran and Turkmenistan, most men are wearing Western-style clothing in the early twenty-first century, although on special occasions traditional outfits, especially the telpek, are worn.

Based on nineteenth-century descriptions and photographs, it appears that the basic outfit of a Turkmen woman from this period consisted of a pair of trousers (balaq) and a long, loose,

Detail of a Teke Turkmen outfit, late twentieth century. The tunic is red with embroidered motifs in white, yellow, and brown along the edges and central areas. The mannequin on the left displays Yomut clothing, consisting of a dress and a fringed shawl with a printed floral design. Textile Research Centre, Leiden.

ankle-length dress (koynek) with sleeves that were fastened at the neck with either a stud or ribbons. Over these garments a woman would wear a coat (kurte) when indoors, with either a headdress or veil. When outdoors, a woman would add a second veil over her dress or a second coat.

During the early twentieth century, the basic dress of a Turkmen woman consisted of undertrousers (balaq), a dress (koynek), and a headdress of some kind. In addition, some groups also had a face veil (yasmak), a sash (sal-qusaq or bil-qusak), an indoor coat of some kind (cabit or kurte), and, for outdoor wear, a second coat (chyrpy). The range and cut of the garments worn by Turkmen women in Afghanistan has remained much the same, although the type of material used has changed. During the early twentieth century, for instance, it was much more common for women's dresses to be made of silk or semisilk fabrics, which were either woven locally or imported from Turkmenistan, especially from the Askhabad region. To a great extent, especially in urban settings, this type of cloth has been replaced by printed cottons or synthetic materials. In general, however, Turkmen women's clothing seems to be much simpler than it was, even in the latter half of the twentieth century. At the same time, however, it is also becoming much more colorful.

An important feature of Turkmen women's dress is the quantity of silver and, later, gold jewelry that is worn. Most jewelry is worn on the head, down the front and back of the upper torso, and on the lower arms and hands, where it is very visible, indicating the wearer's social and economic status. Little is worn on the lower body or feet. The variety of Turkmen jewelry is considerable, and each group has its own particular forms and favorites, although it is noticeable that many groups are willing to wear Teke-made jewelry.

UZBEK DRESS

The Uzbek are a Turkic people of Central Asia who live primarily in modern Uzbekistan, but there are also large populations in northern Afghanistan, Tajikistan, and Turkmenistan. A feature of both male and female Uzbek clothing is the use of ikats and embroidery. Ikat is a style of weaving that uses a resist-dyeing process similar to tie-dye. For a single ikat, either the warp or the weft threads are dyed before the cloth is woven in order to create

a pattern or specific design. For a double ikat, both the warp and weft threads are dyed prior to weaving; creating a satisfactory design is complicated and requires skill, so double ikats are regarded as the rarer and more valuable form. Uzbek ikat designs are characteristically large and colorful, with geometric or highly stylized floral designs.

During the nineteenth and early twentieth centuries, Uzbek embroidery was famous for the use of gold-thread couching in intricate geometric and floral designs—miniature versions of the ikat patterns. At the end of the twentieth century, Uzbek embroidery in Afghanistan still consisted of colorful and playful large designs, especially floral motifs. However, the use of metal-thread embroidery has given way to the use of stitches, such as long and short stitches in silk thread on a dark-colored cotton ground. The modern patterns are usually based around a central rosette and either radiate out or are used as a frame; designs tend to be rounded and sinuous in shape with vivid, contrasting colors. Both

Turkmen man next to his camel, Turkmenistan, between 1905 and 1915. He wears loose cotton trousers (*balaq*), a tight-sleeved robe (*don*) held together at the waist with a sash (*qusaq*), and a black sheepskin hat (*telpek*). Photograph by Sergei Mikhailovich Prokudin-Gorskii. Library of Congress, Prints & Photographs Division, Prokudin-Gorskii Collection, LC-DIG-prokc-20131.

men's and women's clothing may be embroidered (embroidery on men's clothing tends to be more discreet). Designs resembling bouquets of stylized flowers often decorate the slits on the lower side seams of coats.

During the nineteenth century in Afghanistan, Uzbek dress for men consisted of a long cotton shirt (*kujlak*); undertrousers (*ischton* or *balaq*), also of cotton, which were sometimes embroidered down the sides and along the ankle cuffs; an underkaftan (*chapan*); and then one or more overkaftans (also called chapan), depending on the wearer's status and wealth. Both the inner and outer kaftans reached to midcalf, so that the embroidered trousers and boots would be visible. The outer kaftan was kept in place with a belt (*kamar*), which was often decorated with silver or gold plaques. The cut of these kaftans followed an ancient pattern in which the cut was related to the width of the cloth used, thereby reducing wasted material to a minimum. It was based on a long length of cloth that is folded in half. A slit was cut down the front middle of the material. Simply shaped sleeves, as well as inner and side panels, were then added. The inner and side panels were of different sizes depending on the wearer's importance, but a gentle A-shape was created in any case.

These kaftans, especially the ones worn as the outermost layer, were often made of boldly patterned ikat materials. Sometimes, Chinese brocades were also used. In the past, the linings of these garments were sometimes made from imported Russian cottons that had been decorated with a bright, printed design. These materials (cotton or silk) and the complexity of the design used for the kaftans again indicated social and economic status.

Headgear consisted of a small cap (*duppi*) over which was wound a turban. There were many different types of caps depending on the wearer's social status, religion (Jewish or Muslim), occupation, and the occasion. Most were embroidered or quilted into intricate designs. Sometimes, a giant furry hat called a *telpek* was worn, which was similar to those worn by some Turkmen. Footwear consisted of high leather boots suitable for horse riding. These were often embroidered with intricate designs similar to those found on the kaftans.

At the end of the twentieth century, Uzbek dress for men was basically a Westernized outfit consisting of a shirt with trousers. However, on special occasions, an Uzbek festival outfit was worn consisting of shirt and trousers, over which was worn an ikat or embroidered coat and an imposing telpek. There is a considerable difference between the dress worn by women at the beginning of the twentieth century and that worn at the end of the century. In particular, outdoor wear changed drastically. This is mainly due to the influence of Soviet Communism in the 1920s; the Communist Party became the predominant political party in Uzbekistan. In general, however, the Uzbek community in Afghanistan is more conservative than that in Uzbekistan with respect to women's dress.

At the beginning of the twentieth century, Uzbek women's dress basically consisted of a pair of wide pants, often with the upper half in cotton while the lower, visible section was of an ikat material. Over this was worn a tunic (*mursak*), which usually had a long slit down the front so that breast-feeding an infant was easy. Over the pants and top was worn a kaftan. Like the male version, it was based on a long, central panel, but unlike the kaftans worn by men, the female form tended to be short and have wider sleeves. Some forms of kaftan worn by women also had a prominent waist; this type is sometimes called a *rumcha*. Like the men, the women wore several kaftans, one on top of the other.

At home, it was normal for a girl or woman to wear a cap with a panel down the back that was used to cover the hair. Both the cap and the hair panel were often made of velvet and elaborately embroidered. In public, a woman was expected to be totally covered, including her face. A special outfit consisting of a coat (*faranje* or *paranja*) and a horsehair face veil (*chasmband*) was worn, which together was called a *faranje* (the same word as used for the coat alone). Most Uzbek women had stopped wearing this outfit by the mid-twentieth century, and this outfit is also not worn by the Uzbek women in Afghanistan.

In the early twenty-first century, there are two main types of outfits worn by Uzbek women in Afghanistan, the first consisting of an outfit from Uzbekistan made up of a pair of ikat pants with an ikat dress. The head covering for girls usually consists of a small cap, often of velvet. The headdress of a married woman is slightly more complicated, consisting of a head scarf or a cap covered with a large shawl, often white or a pale color. On special occasions, a coat is worn over the dress, which is made from either ikat cloth or a plain material decorated with embroidery.

The second, more conservative, outfit consists of baggy pants with a wide dress that is embroidered with large, colorful floral motifs. This is worn with an open-fronted coat with a defined waist. The main outer garment is a long coat with false sleeves that is draped over the shoulders. The outer coat is often embroidered but not quite as vividly as the dress. A large shawl or chador is used to cover the head and upper body.

HAMID KARZAI AND AFGHAN UNIFICATION

A good example of an attempt to create an Afghan national dress is provided by the early-twenty-first-century Afghan president, Hamid Karzai. Himself a Westernized Pashtun, when he accepted the position of president in late 2001, he chose to wear clothing that would signify that he was president of all the peoples of Afghanistan, rather than a Pashtun leader. Instead of the normal Pashtun garb, he opted to wear the predominantly Uzbek chapan. He also liked to wear the karakuli headdress (a long, narrow cap made of astrakhan), which is worn all over Afghanistan by rich and influential people. In 2002, Afghan people were still laughing at this outfit, because it was completely made up and "fake," combining garments from different regions and groups. However, as one elderly Pashtun from Kandahar noted (in a personal conversation with the author), "He may look ridiculous, but at least he makes sure the foreigners bring in the money."

References and Further Reading

Dupree, Louis. *Afghanistan*. Princeton, NJ: Princeton University Press, 1980.

Harlan, Josiah. *A Memoir of India and Avghanistaun [sic], with Observations on the Present Exciting and Critical State and Future Prospects of those Countries*. Philadelphia: J. Dobson, 1842.

Harvey, Janet. *Traditional Textiles of Central Asia*. London: Thames and Hudson, 1996.

Kalter, Johannes, and Margareta Pavaloi. *Usbekistan*. Stuttgart: Edition Hansjörg Mayer, 1995.

Paine, Sheila. *Embroidery from Afghanistan*. London: British Museum Press, 2006.

Paiva, Roland, and Bernard Dupaigne. *Afghan Embroidery*. Lahore, Pakistan: Ferozsons, 1993.

Vogelsang, Willem. "Dressing for the Future in Ancient Garb: The Use of Clothing in Afghan Politics." *Khila: Journal for Dress and Textiles of the Islamic World* 1 (2005): 123–138.

Vogelsang, Willem. "The Pakul: A Distinctive, but Apparently Not So Very Old Headgear from the Indo-Iranian Borderlands." *Khila: Journal for Dress and Textiles of the Islamic World* 2 (2006): 149–156.

Vogelsang, Willem. *The Afghans*. Oxford: Wiley-Blackwell, 2008. (Originally published in 2002.)

Vogelsang-Eastwood, Gillian, and Willem Vogelsang. *Covering the Moon: An Introduction to Middle Eastern Face Veils*. Leuven, Belgium: Peeters, 2008.

Willem Vogelsang

See also Afghan Dress and the Diaspora; Afghan Jewelry; Snapshot: Afghan Embroidery.

Afghan Dress and the Diaspora

The rich cultural heritage of Afghanistan is expressed through its material culture in general and its dress forms and practices more specifically. *Kala-ye Afghani* (Afghan dress) is a particularly significant form of dress for the Afghan people. They are one of the largest refugee populations in the world, with the displacement of nearly six million Afghans from their homeland beginning with the 1978 Afghan coup and continuing with the twenty-first-century "war on terrorism." Whether living as internally displaced people within Afghanistan or as resettled refugees and immigrants in the Afghan diaspora, the Afghan people experience the wearing of Afghan dress as a visual and material expression of gender, ethnicity, nationality, and religion that serves to unify them.

Afghanistan is home to more than thirty documented languages. Dari or Persian and Pashto are the official languages, but Uzbek, Turkmani, Arabic, Baluchi, and other languages are also spoken. These languages parallel the predominant ethnic groups of Afghanistan, which include the Pashtun, Tajik, Uzbek, Turkmen, Hazara, and Baluchi. Since language is an important variable that differentiates one group from another, the linguistic terms for specific items of Afghan dress not only distinguish one group from another but also link ethnic groups within Afghanistan, regionally in Central, South, and Southwest Asia, and more widely in the Afghan diaspora. Adding to the complexity of language and forms of dress within Afghan society, multiple terms for the same or a similar item of dress may exist because of ethnic, language, or regional differences.

AFGHAN WOMEN'S DRESS

The expression *kala-ye Afghani* in Farsi (Persian) or Dari (Afghan version of Farsi) is a phrase used by both Dari- and Pashto-speaking Afghans to refer to Afghan-style clothing. *Kala* (clothing) for women includes a *pirahan* (overdress), a pair of *shalwar* or *tomban* (pants), a *chador* (head covering), and *paisar* (slippers). Although everyday dress and special-occasion dress share similar forms, there are features that differentiate the two. Kala, then, refers to everyday clothing, while kala-ye Afghani more often refers to special-occasion clothing.

In addition to the pirahan and shalwar ensemble, Afghans may wear other forms of dress as well. For example, province- and/or ethnic group–specific embroidered ensembles exist. Suits comprised of shalwar (pants), a *kamez* (overdress or tunic), and a *dupatta* (head covering) are common; these are worn by a small group of Afghan women in Afghanistan and by more Afghan women living in Pakistan. Western- or European-style outfits are also notable in more urban environments, but these ensembles, though worn by Afghans, are typically not referred to as kala-ye Afghani. It is important to note that when questioned about Afghan clothing or dress, most Afghans living in Afghanistan as well as those living in diaspora settings reference and describe items worn for special occasions. Given the current economic hardships, the political instability of the country, and the ethnic rivalry in and geopolitics of the region, this is understandable. Afghans purchase cheap, imported fabrics from China and make their pants, overdress, and chador from these materials, but they would rarely claim that these ensembles are kala-ye Afghani.

In general, rural Afghan women's everyday kala includes an overdress, a pair of pants, and head and foot coverings. One version of the signature Afghan dress is made of a floral print fabric with bright-colored, large-scale rose patterns on a bright green background. This dress is worn with solid-colored pants, sometimes dark but frequently bright in color, that are gathered with a drawstring. The predominant color of the traditional Afghan chador is white, but the chador is also available in a range of other colors. Since the chador is a culturally valued item of female dress, it, together with a pair of sandals or shoes, completes nearly all ensembles when the woman is outside the home. In contrast to rural everyday dress, in urban areas such as the capital, Kabul, Afghan women wear a variety of ensembles including those with colorful floral prints and others with solid, somber colors.

In both rural and urban environments, special-occasion dress (kala-ye Afghani) is more colorful, decorative, costly, and luxurious. Again, the forms of dress and the terms for the garments are nearly the same as for everyday kala, but they differ in style, materials (better quality for special occasions), and surface-design techniques. For example, the stereotypical kala-ye Afghani of Pashtun women includes a pirahan or overdress made of maroon *bac mal* (velvet fabric); *gibi tomban* (full, gathered drawstring pants) in a contrasting color, often *sabz* (green) to match the chador or head covering, which is typically green for Pashtun women; and *paisar zari* (gold-embroidered slippers). Hazara women may wear purple velvet dresses with green pants, while Nuristani women tend to wear pale green overdresses with white pants. Other regional kala-ye Afghani are available, too. Regardless of regional distinctions, many materials of varying qualities are found in local and regional markets, usually imported fabrics from China. Afghans may purchase fabric and thread to make the ensemble themselves, buy a ready-made outfit, or have the kala-ye Afghani made to order.

Several distinguishing features of kala-ye Afghani are worth noting. The first feature is the form or silhouette of the total ensemble, which is shaped by the amount of fabric used to construct it. A minimum of ten to twelve yards (nine to eleven meters) of fabric are used to make a kala-ye Afghani ensemble. The pirahan

A tie-dyed cotton head covering (*dupatta*), Panjab, Afghanistan, 1867. This cloth would have been worn by a nomad woman, and the simple pattern recalls the woolen shawls of the Rabari women of Kutch, Gujarat. © Victoria and Albert Museum, London. www.vam.ac.uk

is constructed from five to six yards (four and a half to five and a half meters) of fabric, the gibi tomban of about the same amount, and the chador from a minimum of two yards (two meters). This amount of fabric adds visual and actual volume to the wearer of the ensemble as well as lending high status to those women and families who can afford the costly ensemble.

The second feature is the type and quality of the fabric used for kala-ye Afghani. The dress is usually made from bac mal or *mac mal* (cotton or rayon pile-woven velvet). Some bac mal or velvets are referred to as plain and have no surface embellishments, while others are referred to as design velvets and have glued and pressed, metallic gold- and silver-colored particles fashioned into curvilinear motifs creating floral and abstract patterns. In contrast to the dress, the gibi tomban are made of satin or satinlike fabrics, and the head coverings or chadors are made of silk chiffon or similar materials.

The third feature of kala-ye Afghani is the *rang* (color) of each item worn. Although red, green, black, and dark blue are worn, maroon is the predominant dress color, while green is used for the contrasting pants and head covering, especially by the Pashtun, the politically dominant group in Afghanistan. There are several explanations for these favored colors beyond ethnicity. These three colors are those found in the flag of Afghanistan. In addition, Afghans claim that red or maroon is the color of the life-giving force of the heart, which stands for Afghanistan; green stands for Islam and represents growth, vegetation, and renewal; and black is a protective color with prophylactic qualities.

The fourth and final feature of kala-ye Afghani is the type and placement of applied, decorative surface designs using *chirma-dozi* (gold metallic braid) and *zar-dozi* (embroidery). Both surface-design techniques are added to the dress bodice, skirt, and sleeves, the cuffs of pants, and the edges of the head covering. From an Afghan point of view, embroidery not only personalizes the ensemble for special occasions, denotes the wearer as female, and adds to the costliness of the attire but may also signify that the individual is a member of a particular ethnic group or region.

KALA-YE AFGHANI: TECHNICAL AND SOCIAL ASPECTS

The measuring and preparation that precede the construction and embroidering of the pirahan, gibi tomban, chador, and paisar are important steps of the manufacturing process. Male tailors or female seamstresses take measurements in person, but accommodations are made for those who are absent. Orders are frequently made by either female relatives or in some instances by male relatives when women are either unable to go or prevented from going to the market. Using either a measuring tape or the measure of the hand, the circumference and length of the body are determined and written down for the tailor, or garments may be taken to the tailor to show the size.

Chirma dozi and zar dozi are applied by machine or hand. Originally, garments, accessories, and surface designs were hand-sewn, especially when they were made for family members or close friends and before the introduction of mechanical or electric sewing machines. However, in many instances, it is not cost-effective or time-efficient to produce garments in this manner given other pressing domestic responsibilities. For this reason, kala-ye Afghani are more frequently sewn by machine. An entire ensemble can be purchased ready-made in local Afghan markets or completed in five days for emergency situations by local tailors and seamstresses, but the preferred time for completion is two weeks or more. Therefore, kala-ye Afghani ensembles are available in a range of prices to suit the economic status and time frame of the individual or family.

For each dress ensemble, labor and material costs vary and depend on market costs, technical expertise, and turnaround time in production. In the late 1990s, the labor costs were approximately US$12 per ensemble, and materials were approximately US$100. Charges for braid, trim, and embroidery application were approximately sixty cents a row, with multiple rows the norm. Commercial or ready-made kala-ye Afghani ensembles ranged from US$20 to US$100, while those commissioned by relatives abroad could cost up to US$500. Since very few Afghan women sew kala-ye Afghani in the twenty-first century, price ranges fluctuate depending on where, when, and from whom the ensembles are ordered. If a broker or middleman is hired to facilitate the transaction, additional costs increase the total. If the customer is an immediate relative or part of the extended family, fees will typically be lower, while strangers are charged more for services.

Kala-ye Afghani is worn for special occasions such as Eid (a Muslim holiday that marks the end of Ramadan), Noruz (the first day of spring and the Iranian New Year) celebrations, and engagement and *nika* (formal Islamic wedding ceremony) festivities. Usually, young Afghan women begin wearing Afghan dress as adolescents. It is a kind of coming-of-age dress and, one might speculate, a dress that signals a marriageable young woman. However, it is not uncommon to see much younger girls wearing copies of these styles as they mimic older sisters. Because of their costliness, these outfits may be provided by more affluent families who can afford them or even passed from one generation to the next with some alterations to suit the wearer. Although any Afghan woman is entitled to wear kala-ye Afghani, most married women will wear other options that are less colorful or heavily decorated, considered more suited to their stage of life. Also, when worn in a diaspora community, the variations of kala-ye Afghani worn by women may both unify the Afghan group and

An Afghan bride wearing a head covering with embroidered edges, Barakhana, western Afghanistan, 2002. Originally, garments like these would have been hand embroidered, but it has become more common for them to be sewn by machine to save time and labor. Paula Bronstein/Getty Images.

also differentiate and represent the specific Afghan ethnic groups living in the community. The authenticity of these ensembles varies since some include all items of dress while others include some elements of "Western" dress or a mix of different varieties of Afghan ethnic dress.

KALA-YE AFGHANI: ETHNIC AND TRADITIONAL, ECONOMIC, AND GEOPOLITICAL ORIGINS

The most frequently offered explanation for the origin of kala-ye Afghani refers to the ethnicity and tradition that have shaped its silhouette and form: It is the dress of the Kuchi people. The Kuchi people are considered the sole surviving nomadic people of Afghanistan. They are a subgroup of the Pashtun ethnic group, and it is estimated that they constitute from 6 to 10 percent of the total Afghan population of nearly thirty-three million. However, the Pashtun do not use the terms *Kuchi* or *nomadic*, instead using the title *mal dar* (herd owners) or "people of property," which is a figurative expression for the original people of Afghanistan who prospered from the land. The term *Kuchi* appears to be used primarily by non-nomadic and non-Pashto-speaking people.

If kala-ye Afghani is thought to be Kuchi dress, then why would other groups adopt this ensemble as Afghan dress during jihad ("struggle") periods while living in the Afghan diaspora? What is so Afghan about Kuchi or "nomadic" dress that it would become a synonym for Afghan dress, when it, in fact, derives from an ethnic subgroup that forms a relatively small proportion of the population of Afghanistan? One explanation might be that, historically, all rulers of Afghanistan, from its founding by Ahmad Shah Durrani in 1747 until the 1978 Afghan coup, have been Pashtun, the major ethnic group of Afghanistan. It is a common belief that the *mujahedin* (Afghan freedom fighters) as well as the Taliban (a fundamentalist Islamic militia in Afghanistan) originated from the Pashtun. Kala-ye Afghani may, then, be viewed as a visual metaphor of the seeming ethnic dominance of the Pashtun people or the nomadic ethnic subgroup of the Kuchi Pashtun. By association, the connotation of Pashtun or more specifically Kuchi people suggests toughness and the power that comes from the ability to endure not only physical but also social and economic hardship over time.

The second explanation for the origin of kala-ye Afghani is an economic one based on trade, economic development, and regionalism. Historically, Afghan trade relationships crossed the geographic boundaries of Mughal India, Turkey, and the area of British influence. In the sixteenth and seventeenth centuries, Indian Mughal rulers established their influence in Kabul. The British then intervened during the eighteenth and nineteenth centuries, followed by twentieth-century Western and Asian incursions. Kala-ye Afghani absorbed elements from all of these contacts. Key aesthetic features such as velvets, satins, and chiffon fabric; gold metallic trims and braids; beads; coins; and embroidery are associated with wealth, status, and prestige, because they are imported and therefore more expensive. In addition, one had to have the right connections to obtain certain materials. One might expect that the dress of urban, status-conscious Kabuli women would reflect these trade relationships, but rural kala has also incorporated remnants of these same materials and embellished surfaces, adding many items from itinerant traders. It is possible, then, that Afghan dress is an abstraction and blending of visual symbols of material prosperity, success, and modernity.

The third explanation for the origin of kala-ye Afghani is a political explanation with nationalistic motivations and relates to women's dress in the newly independent Afghanistan of the 1920s. Scholars have noted that Afghanistan's king Amanullah was influenced by his interchanges with Turkish president Atatürk, who popularized secularization and modernization of dress following the independence of Turkey and Afghanistan from Great Britain in 1919. Some of these reforms included changes in women's dress such as abolishing the *chadari* (full-body covering). Older Afghans recall the August 1919 independence celebrations when people dressed in the nationalistic colors of the Afghan flag: green, red, and black. These are the primary colors of kala-ye Afghani as well. Similarly, in the opening ceremonies for the 2004 Summer Olympics held in Athens, Greece, Afghan flag bearers wore kala-ye Afghani. In addition, during state occasions in Kabul, the Afghan capital, young girls grace the occasion wearing the kala-ye Afghani of various ethnic groups in similar colors that stand for Afghanistan.

AFGHAN MEN'S DRESS

In general, Afghan men's dress has not received the same attention as the dress of Afghan women. But similar to women's kala-ye Afghani, Afghan men's dress ensembles are composed of requisite and distinctive items of clothing, kala. Men wear a long overshirt that is referred to by the same name as Afghan women's overdress, pirahan, with full, gathered drawstring pants called tomban. Frequently, a waistcoat (vest) is worn on top of the overshirt. The final item—though not mandatory—is a *kulla* (hat or cap), which parallels Afghan women's head coverings or hats. These four items of kala (the pirahan, tomban, waistcoat, and kulla) complete the kala ensemble. Nevertheless, as for Afghan women, it is not uncommon to see Afghan men wearing the male version of the Pakistani suit of shalwar and kamez or Western- or European-style pants, shirts, or suits in more urban areas of Afghanistan.

In contrast to the colorful everyday dress of Afghan women, men's dress ensembles appear somber and are typically made of cotton and wool fabrics in solid, neutral colors such as earth-tone beiges, browns, grays, blacks, and whites. Vests may be

A Kuchi nomad girl wearing a child's version of Kuchi adult clothing, Zhare Dasht, Afghanistan, 2002. Younger girls can often be seen wearing copies of older styles, but these outfits are costly and are either passed on from one generation to the next or provided by more affluent families. Ami Vitale/Getty Images.

solid colors, striped patterns, or a combination of multicolored machine-knit horizontal patterns. Colors vary based on the season, brighter in summer and more somber in winter, and the kinds of fabrics available in the local markets are functional for the demanding, predominantly agricultural activities of rural village life and the mountainous areas of Afghanistan. In contrast, urban life with its exposure to non-Afghan influences provides opportunities for more variation and expressive forms of tailored clothing and colors.

Nearly identical ensembles are worn throughout the changing seasons, with minor variations. During warmer months, clothing materials consist of cotton and cotton blends, while during the cooler months garments are made of wool or wool blends. A large, rectangular wool *shawl* (shawl) is worn over kala during cooler weather as well as an additional *chapan* (long overcoat) in northern Afghanistan. Afghan men's ensembles, varying in color and materials depending on the season, whether kala or the shalwar kamez, are worn throughout Afghanistan, in refugee camps in contiguous countries, and in Afghan diaspora countries. Men's ensembles made of more colorful, luxurious fabrics and with decorative embroideries are reserved for specific items of dress, ethnic or regionally inspired clothing, and special occasions; it is these items of clothing, like Afghan women's, that are referred to as kala-ye Afghani.

Embroidered regional and ethnic variations exist and serve to distinguish Afghan males in both everyday situations and special occasions such as weddings and annual Noruz celebrations. Embroidery is seen on a range of domestic and commercial-oriented textiles, from men's and women's apparel to household products. Men's shirt bodices reflect the fine tone-on-tone white embroideries of Kandahar. But the epitome of Afghan craft development are the embroideries worked by women that are reserved for the kala-ye Afghani of both men and women. In particular, the embroideries on men's hats among the Baluchi, Hazara, Kandahar, Pashtuns, Tajiks, and Uzbeks deserve recognition.

Men's head coverings vary throughout the country, but few styles transcend established social boundaries in Afghanistan. Some are associated with a specific ethnic group, indicate generational status, or, in many instances, signal a religious and/or political association. The most notable hat style is the *pakol*, a sewn and fitted, fulled wool cap with a rolled brim and circular flat top. It is considered a functional hat style appropriate to the cold climes of the region. Like Afghan men's ensembles, it is found in a range of earth tones and is usually made of wool in natural fleece colors.

The pakol has been associated with a variety of somewhat-related groups including the Afghan freedom fighters known as the mujahedin, the Pashtun ethnic group of Afghanistan, the Taliban (an "educational," religious, and military group led by Mullah Mohammed Omar), and, more recently, by al Qaeda founder Osama bin Laden. Outside Afghanistan, the pakol is also worn in diaspora settings as well as by other Central and South Asian mountain-dwelling peoples. It is not, then, the exclusive head covering of the Afghan people but is strongly associated with Afghans by others. Even though the pakol falls in and out of favor over time, because it is associated with different ethnic and political groups, its use is not restricted by geography or sentiment.

Another head covering, with less political sentiment and potential controversy than the pakol, is the *lungi* (a turban-style head covering). Although non-Afghans may associate the lungi style with the Taliban, it is also worn by many other Afghan men. It is composed of one or more rectangular pieces of fabric that are draped, wrapped, and tied about the head. It is often worn over a skullcap or kulla. A lungi is worn by mature Afghan men and in some situations by young men who are soliciting more respect from fellow Afghans. For special occasions such as weddings, a lungi may be made of more costly material to convey status and the important social situation.

On more formal occasions, another Afghan hat style worn is the traditional *karakuli* (hat made from the fleece of the karakul sheep) that is so prevalent throughout Central Asia and Afghanistan. Afghan presidents such as Hamid Karzai are often seen wearing the hat, which is available in natural fleece colors. It has an elliptical cut and sewn, three-dimensional form and is seemingly reserved for important social situations. It is worn by Muslim men in other Central and South Asian countries and is also attributed to the Tajik ethnic group that lives in northern Afghanistan.

Other regional and ethnic-derived hat styles include the embroidered pillbox styles of Baluchi origin. These caps are the most colorful and decorative head-covering styles, found in an array of background colors with multicolored embroidery and *shisha* embellishments (mirror work). The Baluchi hat style is also worn by Afghan women. Another ethnic-specific pillbox cap style worn by Tajik men comprises a black base with white embroidered floral paisley designs. These caps are not associated only with the Tajik ethnic group but also with the northern regions of Afghanistan. Originally, they were worked in tambour hand embroidery, but in the early twenty-first century, many are machine-embroidered.

AFGHAN DRESS AND ETHNIC AND REGIONAL GROUPS, GENDER, AND AGE AND GENERATIONAL STATUS

Traditionally, Afghan dress has reflected the ethnic diversity and sociocultural, historical, and geopolitical dynamics of the region. The country and its people were positioned at the crossroads between the Arab, Persian, Turkish, and Asian empires. Consequently, Afghan dress shows strong aesthetic connections to areas contiguous to its borders: the Arab and Islamic regions of Southwest Asia and Persia, the Turkish Ottoman Empire, and, to a lesser degree, Mughal India. Since the 1920s, Afghanistan's leaders, in an effort to maintain control of both human and natural resources, have struggled with the definition of women's rights and independence as exemplified in the propriety of dress.

Afghan dress first and foremost distinguishes gender. According to strict Islamic interpretations, male and female dress are gender specific in form and materials. To reiterate, women customarily wear pants (tomban), an overdress (pirahan), a head covering (chador), and footwear (paisar). If living or working in an urban environment, a chadari may be worn. Similarly, men wear the complementary male version of pants (tomban), an overshirt (pirahan), a hat or cap (kulla), and footwear, including sandals, shoes, or boots. In addition to this basic ensemble, Afghan men wear a *waskat* (waistcoat or vest), a pakol (wool hat), and a shawl during colder seasons.

Women's tomban for everyday wear are made of approximately two yards (two meters) of cotton or silklike rayon or acetate fabric, usually solid white or green. Frequently, the pant cuffs are decorated with white machine- or hand-embroidered

A family of Kuchi nomads wearing typical Afghan dress (*kala-ye Afghani*), Kares Tala, Afghanistan, 2005. The women wear red (a color Afghans regard as having life-giving force) overtunics (*pirahan*), trousers (*shalwar*), and a head covering. The man wears a tunic-and-trousers combination known as a *pirahan* and *tomban*. Over this is a waistcoat and a shoulder blanket. He also wears a Pashtun-style turban. John Moore/Getty Images.

patterns. The pirahan are typically made from cotton, silk (or silklike acetate), and plain or satin woven fabrics in bright colors (for young women) and darker colors (for older women), usually in tone-on-tone or floral patterns. Necklines vary but usually are rounded; occasionally, pointed collars are added, as are gathered set-in sleeves with fitted or buttoned cuffs. Dress skirts are full and gathered at the waist and worn midcalf length. Chadors are made of similar fabrics—usually rectangular, woven pieces of lightweight cotton or silklike crepe, with machine- or hand-embroidered edges. Men's tomban and pirahan feature fewer decorative details and are typically in natural-colored cotton fabric. Hat styles such as the kulla exhibit the most variety in shapes, colors, and embroidered patterns.

Dress also differentiates the age and generational status of the wearer. For example, although all women wear pants, an overdress, and head and foot coverings, aesthetic characteristics vary according to age throughout women's lives. The most distinctive change is the addition of the chador as young girls mature into womanhood. Eventually, more costly materials and surface embellishments are added to apparel for women's dowries. The decorative focus is on pant cuffs, dress bodices, and head-covering borders, which increases as females gain status when they become

engaged, marry, and have children and then decreases again as they age. With regard to the chadari, it has more recently been viewed, along with the chador, as a coming-of-age garment, especially when worn in the public domain. It has also been politicized.

Men's dress also reflects age, status, and ethnic group membership, though in more subtle manners than the women's clothing. Younger men wear more decorative garments, and their dress becomes less colorful as they become older. Shirt sleeves, bodice shirtfronts, and hats are embroidered in regional and ethnic patterns by either their betrothed or wife and extended female family members, while more generic styles are available in the marketplace. Men's dress more frequently integrates Western-style trousers with shirts than in the past because in some instances it is less costly than kala-ye Afghani and it also indicates social status and knowledge of the wider world.

AFGHAN DRESS, POLITICS, AND RELIGION

Several items of dress are worth mentioning since they are the most visible to non-Afghans and are the Afghan dress that is most strongly associated with politics. For Afghan men, the pakol hat is a symbol of the Afghan freedom fighters, or mujahedin. Many non-Afghans wear the hat out of sympathy for the plight of the Afghan people, who have been repeatedly invaded by outsiders for hundreds of years. In addition to wearing the pakol, when Afghan men are photographed, they are usually equipped with a Kalashnikov (Russian rifle) draped across their bodies. The Kalashnikov, a remnant of Soviet occupation, has endured for over thirty years as a symbol of Afghan strength and the military supremacy of the Afghan people. Such photographs are found in family albums as they document the perceived physical and moral strength of the person.

The second distinctive item of dress worn by Afghans is the woman's full-body covering known as the chadari. The chadari, constructed of nine to ten yards (eight to nine meters) of fabric with an embroidered face piece, conceals the entire women's dress ensemble of pants, overdress, and head covering. Afghans consider the original chadari to be of Persian origin, and others associate it with British Mughal India, but over time the chadari has been adopted by urban middle- and upper-class Afghan women and is worn similarly to a raincoat. Affluent families who had the financial means clothed female family members in chadaris. According to Afghans, the chadari has been incorrectly attributed as Afghan women's traditional dress; it became mandated women's wear only after dress sanctions were imposed by the Taliban in 1996. They cited Pashtunwalli (ethnic Pashtun codes of conduct) and Islamic sharia law as justification for sequestering women in their homes and demanding they wear the chadari in public as a visible social form of protection against male desire, the possibility of leading men astray, and social prejudice. Since the mid-1990s, the chadari has represented, for many Afghan women living in Afghanistan and especially those in the diaspora, the perceived political and social inequality of Afghan women.

Religion is an important facet in Afghan daily life. Consequently, men's and women's dress reflects their degree of observance and affiliation. Ninety-nine percent of the Afghan population is Muslim, with approximately 80 percent Sunni Muslim and 19 percent Shiite Muslim. Therefore, Islamic influence is strong, and everyday life experiences are generally interpreted through an Islamic lens. The prevalent white chadors worn by women are frequently interpreted by other Afghans as a sign of being an observant Muslim or in some instances a hajji who has made the religious pilgrimage to Mecca. Wearing the color black is associated with Shiite religious practices.

Other Islamic prescriptions are especially invoked with respect to men's and women's modesty or the observation of *haya* in body and dress practices. There are distinct features of haya that Afghans acknowledge. Haya defines the fit or proximity of dress to the body. In general, the everyday dress for both males and females focuses on clothing and overall cleanliness, as well as weapons for men and jewelry for women. The contours of both male and female bodies are minimized by wearing loose-fitting clothing. Also, the fabric or material of men's and women's dress must be opaque as opposed to transparent and sheer, so that specific aspects of the body form are not distinguishable. The drape of men's and women's clothing is also less tailored and more voluminous in comparison to that of other Central and South Asian peoples who live in close proximity to the Afghans.

The concept of haya is also observed in the temporal contexts in which Afghan dress is used. For example, haya or modesty differs during prayer and nonprayer social contexts. Men and women cover their bodies with attention to their hair, arms, and legs during the five calls to prayer. In addition, spatial social context determines the degree of modesty or haya. A domestic environment demands different consideration than a public one. Among same-gender groups and within the context of the family, the practice of haya is more relaxed, while in the presence of the opposite gender and nonfamily members outside the domestic environment, haya is more strictly observed.

But to complicate the issue of religion and kala further, the Taliban invoked Islamic sharia law and Pashtunwalli codes of conduct over civil laws in the mid-1990s to create a hybrid haya that discriminated against certain groups and violated Afghan men's and women's human rights. For example, women were not allowed to wear perfume, display pedicured feet or manicured hands, wear noisy anklets or bracelets, or use colorful cosmetics and hair ornamentation. In sum, women were prevented from calling visual, auditory, or olfactory attention to their appearance, that is, their bodies. Fewer stipulations of modesty applied to men, and restrictions focused on the mandatory facial hair, especially a beard grown to the length of a clenched fist positioned below the chin.

During the first decade of the twenty-first century, women's and men's rights with respect to their appearance have vacillated between control, relaxed control, and then renewed control due to the resurgence of the Taliban in many rural and urban areas of Afghanistan. Some of the earlier progress made during the occupation by coalition forces has been reversed as local Afghan militias have reasserted their regional authority in matters of everyday life, including kala.

THE ART OF AFGHAN DRESS

Aesthetic prescriptions determine the patterns embroidered on men's shirts and hats and women's pants, overdresses, and head coverings. The majority of these embroidered designs are floral, geometric, and abstract shapes, presumably because of Islamic prohibitions on using representational art and aesthetics.

Afghan embroidery styles tend to be associated with geographic regions and the ethnic groups that reside in such cities as Herat, Kandahar, or Kabul. Styles generally are distinguishable by the fiber content of the fabric (plain-weave cottons, pile-woven velvets, or synthetic satin weaves) as well as the kind of embroidered thread used for surface designs (cotton, silk, or gold metallic threads); a variety of embroidery techniques (cross stitch, half cross stitch, long and short stitch, satin stitch) and the complexity of their execution; the floral and geometric motifs; and the placement of the embroidery (women's sleeve and pant cuffs, dress bodices, head-covering borders, and the face and hat areas of full-body coverings; men's caps and hats, shirt bodices, and sleeve cuffs).

Four embroidery styles are chirma dozi (using a unique kind of metallic thread and braid), used on women's velvet dresses and men's vests; *tashamar-dozi* (recognizable by the intricate counted-stitch technique), seen on women's dresses; *gul-dozi* (silk stitched flower embroidery), distinctive because of the rich use of colored threads and found on household textiles and women's chadors; and *Kandahar-dozi* (a tone-on-tone embroidery), associated with the city of Kandahar and used to decorate women's chadors and men's shirts.

In the context of daily life as well as during special occasions of secular and religious significance, kala and kala-ye Afghani visually show and communicate the conflation of Afghan gender, generational status, ethnic and regional identity, and religious

Afghan Pashtun tribal leaders at a tribal assembly ("Jirga") in Khost city, southeastern Afghanistan, 2004. Men's clothing consists of pants (*tomban*) with a matching long overshirt (*pirahan*), waistcoat, and head covering. In contrast to the bright colors of women's clothing, men's clothes appear somber with solid, neutral colors such as earth-tone beiges, browns, grays, blacks, and whites. Herve Bar/AFP/Getty Images.

affiliation. These social categories originating in Afghanistan and expressed in kala-ye Afghani continue to be significant in the early twenty-first century and extend to the Afghan diaspora and the populations contiguous to Afghanistan in Central, South, and Southwest Asia.

References and Further Reading

Burhan, M. Esmael, and Thomas Goutierre. *Dari for Foreigners*. Omaha, NE: Center for Afghanistan Studies, 1983.

Daly, M. Catherine. "The Pardah Expression of Hejab among Afghan Women Living in a Non-Muslim Community." In *Body, Dress, and Religion*, edited by Linda Arthur, 147–162. Oxford: Berg, 1999.

Daly, M. Catherine. "The Afghan Woman's Chaadaree: An Evocative Religious Expression?" In *Undressing Religion: Commitment and Conversion from a Cross-Cultural Perspective*, edited by Linda B. Arthur, 131–146. Oxford: Berg, 2000.

Daly, M. Catherine. "The Afghans of Afghanistan." In *Endangered Peoples of Africa and the Middle East: Struggles to Survive and Thrive*, edited by Robert Hitchcock and Allen Osborn, 31–46. Westport, CT: Greenwood, 2002.

Doubledaly, Veronica. *Three Women of Heart*. London: Tauris Parke, 2006.

Dupree, Louis. *Afghanistan*. Princeton, NJ: Princeton University Press, 1973.

Dupree, Nancy. "Behind the Veil in Afghanistan." *Asia* 1, no. 2 (1978): 10–15.

Hopkirk, Peter. *The Great Game: The Struggle for Empire in Central Asia*. New York: Kodansha International, 1992.

Johnson, Chris. *Afghanistan: A Land in Shadow*. Oxford: Oxfam, 1998.

Magnus, Ralph, and Eden Naby. *Afghanistan: Mullah, Marx, and Mujahid*. Boulder, CO: Westview, 1998.

Maley, William, ed. *Fundamentalism Reborn? Afghanistan and the Taliban*. New York: New York University Press, 1998.

Marseden, Peter. *The Taliban: War, Religion and the New Order in Afghanistan*. Karachi, Pakistan: Oxford University Press, 1998.

Olesen, Asta. *Afghan Craftsmen: The Cultures of Three Itinerant Communities*. New York: Thames and Hudson, 1994.

Paiva, Roland, and Bertrand Dupaigne. *Afghan Embroidery*. Lahore Pakistan: Ferozsons, 1993.

Rashid, Ahmed. "Behind the Veil, Again: Kabul's Women Don Chadors and Wonder about Islamic Rule." *Far Eastern Economic Review* 155 no. 22 (4 June 1992): 28–29.

Scarce, Jennifer. "The Development of Women's Veils in Persia and Afghanistan." *Costume* 8 (1974): 4–13.

Tapper, Nancy. "Pastun Nomad Women in Afghanistan." *Asian Affairs* n.s., 8, no. 2 (1977): 28–29.

M. Catherine Dal

See also Regional Dress of Afghanistan; Afghan Jewelry.

Afghan Jewelry

Jewelry has long played an important role in Afghan dress. It has a fascinating history that dates back thousands of years and follows the ancient trading routes, the so-called Silk Road that wove through Afghanistan. Changes, however, have taken place over the centuries. Early examples of jewelry from places such as Tillya Tepe in northern Afghanistan, which date from just before the Common Era, barely resemble the jewelry from the nineteenth and twentieth centuries that is found in various modern personal and family collections.

What is considered to be Afghan ethnic or indigenous jewelry at the beginning of the twenty-first century is frequently referred to generically as *nomadic jewelry*. Although Afghans wear a variety of "ethnic" and contemporary jewelry pieces and styles, the "older" nomadic-styled jewelry is considered stereotypically Afghan, Pashtun (an ethnic group of Afghanistan), and rural. As in the case of Afghan dress, research on Afghan jewelry is fraught with challenges since many personally owned pieces were sold during the Soviet occupation period from late 1978 to early 1989, as well as during the time of the *mujahedin* (Afghan anti-Communist fighters) and the Taliban (an "educational," religious, and military group led by Mullah Mohammed Omar) in the 1990s. As a result, the stories behind the jewelry—who made it, when, and why, who wore the pieces, and so forth—have often been lost.

There are social class, geographic, ethnic, religious, and educational differences among Afghans, which are reflected in their jewelry's ancient history. At the same time, however, the Afghans welcome contemporary interpretations. Afghan jewelry is also imbued by some with romantic notions about the nomadic way of life, and Afghan culture in general, all of which provides "added value" to the jewelry and traditional material culture, both within Afghanistan and in the Afghan diaspora. Consequently, some regard Afghan ethnic jewelry as being highly desirable to wear with traditional Afghan dress ensembles for special occasions in Afghanistan and the Afghan diaspora.

Much of the nomadic or Afghan jewelry is held in private family or museum collections. This "vintage" or "antique" jewelry is often sold by Afghans themselves and by specialized dealers of antiquities. At the beginning of the twenty-first century, the reality is that "true" Afghan-inspired jewelry and knockoffs are found in abundance in the markets run by Afghans and selling Afghan items in Peshawar, Pakistan, and on the Internet.

When describing and interpreting Afghan jewelry, one must differentiate between the materials, the production process, and the "everyday" versus "special-occasion" forms found in the marketplace and in personal or family collections. Due to dynamic trading patterns and Afghan mobility in the region, many of the associated ethnic jewelry pieces can be found across Central and South Asia, for instance, in India, Iran, Pakistan, and Tajikistan.

MATERIALS AND STYLES OF JEWELRY

Afghan jewelry is characterized by a plethora of materials, colors, forms, and styles. The kinds of materials used in jewelry production seem to dictate both the form and style of manufacture. Whether due to technical expertise or aesthetic preference, Afghan jewelry can be categorized by cost and kinds of materials, designed forms and styles, as well as its role in signifying gender.

Afghan jewelry can be subdivided into pieces using costly materials, imported pieces, and jewelry made of beads. In general, the more expensive items consist of precious and semiprecious stones in metal and inlay settings and are produced by metal craftsmen in public workshops. At the beginning of the twenty-first century, a wide variety of "modern" jewelry is imported from China and India; this jewelry is made of plastic, wood, and so forth and tends to appeal to the urban markets. At the lower end of the scale, there are less costly, traditional, beaded items that are made in more domestic settings by women. The more expensive jewelry (the jewelry that has value in the consumer market) tends to derive from the physical Afghan environment, such as mountainous or riverine areas, and is worn on more special occasions, whereas the less costly adornment derived from imported materials is worn for everyday occasions.

The metal settings are composed primarily of copper, brass, and nickel. But the predominant *gillet* (silver and tin alloy or a composition of mixed metals) conforms to more conventional cultural aesthetics deemed appropriate for more formal social settings because of its higher financial value. Usually, coins and other metal objects are melted down to form gillet, which is then shaped into handmade ethnic pieces. The quality of the metal and metalsmithing varies widely among craftsmen; their expertise is often a family-based tradition passed on from one generation to the next. According to jewelry dealers, who have their own marketing motivations, a feature of Afghan jewelry is the use of metal pieces that show wear and tear and are attractively imperfect. The most notable jewelry pieces are those that are worn by young women for special occasions such as the *nika* (Muslim engagement and wedding celebrations) when jewelry made of precious and semiprecious materials is displayed.

The more simple jewelry constructions worn for everyday adornment are made of *mora* (glass beads), coins, and locally found natural products such as cloves, nuts, and clay that are strung onto cotton yarn. This jewelry also incorporates imported plastic beads and local natural materials such as seeds, pits, and peelings of vegetable and fruit matter. Again, these simple jewelry constructions are prevalent among the rural population of Afghanistan.

Afghan jewelry is primarily regarded as women's adornment, and there are many different types. Jewelry forms decorate different parts of the body, including the head, hair, nose, ears, neck, wrists, fingers, waist, and ankles. Additional elements such as disk-shaped amulets, beaded pendants, and coins adorn *kala* (clothing). Heads feature elaborate *matika* (metal headdresses) atop the hair and/or head coverings, while the hair is braided with beaded yarn. Ears display *goshwara* (pierced earrings) in tiered styles. Occasionally, a large singular *majkha khik bini* (nose pin) of seed beads or semiprecious stones adorns a nostril. Necks flaunt *gluband* (necklaces made of strings of beads) and *amail* (tiered necklaces such as chokers and collars). One or both wrists display *churri* (metal bangles) and *krah* (cuff bracelets that are two inches, or five centimeters, or more in width). *Angushtar* (rings) encase the fingers of henna-painted hands, and *paizib* (metal anklets shaped like cuffs) encircle both ankles.

In contrast to women's use of jewelry, Afghan men traditionally wear fewer items, but they are frequently seen holding or fingering *tesbih* (prayer beads) and in some instances wearing metal rings with inlaid glass or semiprecious stones, which are often referred to as hajj rings. These rings are sometimes worn by men who have been on the hajj (annual pilgrimage to Mecca) or who have a relative or friend who has been to Mecca and brought back such a ring as a present. A *tawwez* (amulet) necklace may also be worn that contains within it written verses or phrases from the Qur'an (the Muslim holy book). These traditional forms are commonly seen in more rural settings or at traditional events when "older" jewelry is worn to complement an ensemble.

SPECIAL-OCCASION JEWELRY

The most complex and expensive jewelry pieces are those made from local indigenous materials that are then inlaid or set with precious or semiprecious stones. These stones have long been associated with the geography of Central Asia, the geologically dynamic regions of the world. The geology of the region has been for many years exploited for its natural resources, including such stones. In 2006, an exhibition entitled Afghanistan,

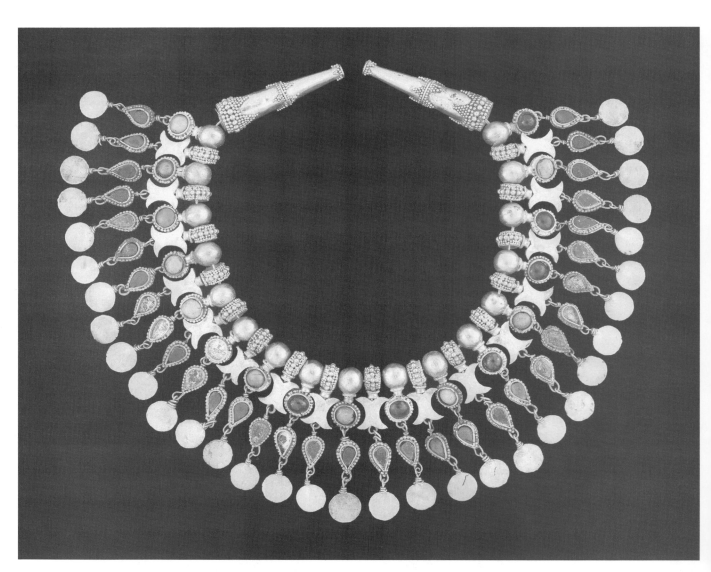

A gold necklace collar from about the first century B.C.E., set with garnet and turquoise stones, from a tomb in Tillya Tepe, Afghanistan. This necklace was found in the grave of a young woman and, when worn, would have been sewn to her clothing in typical nomadic style. Central Asia is geologically rich in precious and semiprecious stones, and the availability of these indigenous materials means that they have been used in jewelry for centuries. Thierry Ollivier/Musée Guimet/Getty Images.

Hidden Treasures from the National Museum, Kabul opened in Paris and then traveled throughout Europe and North America. This exhibition provided historical and photographic examples of jewelry made of semiprecious stones set in gold and found in northern Afghanistan. The stones that are used reflect the availability of materials in Afghanistan as well as the importance of *rang* (color) association in spiritual practice.

Lajward (lapis lazuli, a semiprecious blue stone), which is found in the remote northern mountainside of the Kokcha Valley in the Badakhshan region of Afghanistan, is the premier semiprecious stone found in the region. Documentation relating to this material predates the Common Era, and many later explorers and travelers, such as the medieval merchant and traveler Marco Polo, noted the presence of lapis lazuli in the region and marveled about its use.

Pieces made of *aqiq* (a red-colored semiprecious stone), often associated with the Turkmen, are worn by both men and women. Aqiq is frequently engraved with verses from the Qur'an or with floral and animal motifs. In addition, stones of this color, such as carnelian, are often considered to contain prophylactic qualities that protect the wearer from enemies and misfortune. Religious connections are presumed because of the Islamic inspired script or the powerful animal symbols, but other sources suggest that the prophet Mohammed and his followers wore aqiq. These stones, often set in silver bezels and worn as pendants and cufflike bracelets by women or as rings by men, are commissioned pieces for a loved one, such as a husband or wife.

The stone *yaqut* (ruby; a red-colored precious stone) is said to be found in isolated areas of the Badakhshan region of Afghanistan. There are numerous historical accounts of travelers exploring and finding the stone. Rubies are often set by themselves or in combination with emeralds. This combination of colors and stones is also prevalent in the neighboring countries of India, Pakistan, and Tajikistan. There is also a traditional story of how a ruby fell from heaven at Mohammed's birthplace, the site of the Kaaba, a sacred place. There, the tears of hajjis suffering during their pilgrimage to Mecca turned the ruby black.

Zumurrud (emerald; a precious green-colored stone), associated with the Panjshir Valley northeast of the capital city, Kabul, is another gemstone with spiritual connections that can avert evil. Green is the color of paradise, a sacred place in Muslim thought. Emeralds are worn on their own, in singular gemstone designs, but may also be worn in combination with rubies. Sometimes, inferior green-colored beads and green stones are fashioned to look like their more expensive counterparts.

The yellow-green-colored stone peridot is also found in Afghanistan and is associated with the Kashmir region. It is typically seen in its rough state, sometimes polished but uncut. Afghans refer to this stone as a very old one. It is not commonly used for jewelry. The light-colored peridot version is often used to make beads for tesbih (Muslim prayer beads). Peridot is also referred to as the crusaders' stone, which corresponds to the imagery of the mujahedin. Although certainly other semiprecious stones are found in the marketplace and in personal collections, jewelry made from turquoise, lapis lazuli, carnelians, rubies, emeralds, and peridot is considered valuable and the most desirable to collect. Since the late twentieth century, new discoveries of semiprecious stones such as aquamarine, kunzite, and tourmaline have been made in the rugged terrain of the Hindu Kush. This may also be another reason why such semiprecious stones

are so highly valued; they come from inaccessible places and have a rarity value.

For those Afghans who have limited financial resources, a variety of red, green, and blue glass and plastic beads are available and are also incorporated into jewelry made of silver- and gold-colored plastic. These less costly materials emulate the more desirable and expensive metal-smithed jewelry and the colors of precious and semiprecious stones.

BEAD JEWELRY: GENERATIONAL AND GENDER ASSOCIATIONS

Because Afghan women frequently wear bead jewelry as everyday wear, jewelry researchers and publications tend to be dismissive of this form of jewelry, possibly because it is less costly and more prevalent. Nevertheless, generational and gender distinctions exist in both the form and the use of such jewelry. While more economically advantaged and educated men wear rings in urban areas, a more common sight in rural areas is the tawwez, a leather-cord necklace that carries a triangular leather amulet. These amulets, in some instances, take the form of metal cylinders with hinged latches that contain Islamic texts. It has been suggested that the tawwez is worn more by illiterate or informally educated individuals. More prevalent among all social classes of Afghan males are hand-held beads, such as single evil-eye beads and prayer beads. The use of such beads can be seen in both private and public settings. It is a common occurrence, for example, to see men walking or conversing while holding a string of prayer beads; they tell, pray, and converse simultaneously.

Afghan women may also carry and use prayer beads, but generally their tesbih are seen in the more private setting of the domestic environment, where women normally pray. Women also tend to wear beads in forms such as *mora-dozi* (bead embroidery) or additive or decorative surface embroideries on dress bodices and chadors (head and body coverings). They also wear bead jewelry as decorations in hair braids, earrings, necklaces, brooches, bracelets, finger rings, and anklets. As with men, women wear the tawwez as part of their personal adornments. These tawwez are frequently medallion-like in shape and are sewn onto the women's dresses as a decorative element. *Gul-i-peron* ("dress flowers"), which are roundels covered with beads, shells, and disks, are attached to Pashtun women's dresses at each shoulder, on the bodice, and at the waistline for good luck and protection against the evil eye. These disks not only serve a decorative function but also guard and protect the wearer. They can be made of beads, metal-thread embroidery, and cloves, nuts, and seeds.

Although not technically jewelry, bejeweled items of dress are common in Central and South Asia. Among Afghans, *pirahan* (overdresses) and head coverings are frequently embellished with a variety of bead materials that are also used in jewelry. Historically, the tribal dress of the nomadic Kuchi (a Pashtun subgroup) incorporated an array of beads. In the early twenty-first century, bead usage is associated with Afghan women's dress worn for special occasions such as engagement and wedding ceremonies. Typically, beads are sewn onto the dress bodice and sleeves, in the form of either overall patterns or as trim edges on head coverings. Additional bead jewelry takes the form of necklaces and earrings.

A woman wearing Afghan jewelry set with lapis lazuli stones at an exhibition of Afghan handicrafts in Peshawar, Pakistan, 2003. Under the Taliban authorities, dress and appearance were strictly regulated: Anything that called attention to sensory aspects of the body was forbidden, including the sound of jingling jewelry and the appearance of colorful jewelry materials. This two-day exhibition was organized to restore and rehabilitate Afghan traditional handicrafts. Tariq Mahmood/AFP/Getty Images.

Beaded tassels and fringes are frequently added to small bags and to young women's braids.

Young children, both girls and boys, also wear single beads as well as strings of beads around their necks, wrists, waists, and ankles. These beaded items are referred to as *chashm mora* (eye beads) and are worn as a charm or talisman to protect the wearer from the ills of childhood and the evil eye. Young girls in particular wear small bead earrings to distinguish them as females.

THE GOOD BEAD: SPIRITUAL CONNOTATIONS OF BEAD JEWELRY

Bead jewelry is related to several different spiritual expressions or faith-based practices, such as the use of specific types of beads to protect the wearer from the evil eye. Many of these spiritual cultural practices predate the influence of Islam in the wider area that includes Afghanistan. These practices have, however, been incorporated into Islam, so that many of the former belief patterns are referred to as Islamic practices, even though, according to the Qur'an, amulets or talismans are prohibited. Many of these practices are more rural, and educated urban Afghans may scoff at these practices in public.

For example, some people believe that some bead jewelry has prophylactic qualities that protect the wearer. Individual beads or evil-eye beads, which are often made of black glass with white spots, may be held in the hand or carried in pockets and bags. Occasionally, beads are strung and worn by children and adolescents as a necklace, around the waist, or as a bracelet or anklet. They may even be pinned or attached to clothing as a cluster of beads mixed with items such as cloves. However, wherever they are worn, these beaded elements are supposed to be visible. The purpose of this visibility is to protect the wearer from the offending gaze or *chashm*, the eye of others. If a child becomes ill, the phrase *nazar mesha* ("the child was looked at or exposed to the eye") is often said about the invalid.

In contrast, a more universally accepted use of beads in Islamic religious expression are tesbih, Muslim prayer beads. Although prayer beads are not unique to Afghans, when carried and used, they suggest the orthodoxy of the follower. They are strings of beads, hand-held or carried in pockets for use during prayers and throughout the day. The preferred material is mud from the holy cities of Mecca or Medina, but wood, precious and semiprecious stones, dates, and plastic are also used. They come in a variety of colors, though all the counting beads in a string are usually the same size, shape, and color. Some Shiite Muslims prefer black, whereas others treasure carnelian, an amber-colored semiprecious stone (called *sang* or *shah-makhsud*). Afghans tend to avoid yellow beads, both because yellow is associated with Hindus and in accordance with an Islamic tradition of avoiding yellow because the Prophet disliked saffron.

Each *mesbah* (bead) stands for one of the ninety-nine names of Allah. There are either thirty-three or ninety-nine strung beads with a *shahid* (a larger or smaller spacer or marker bead) between each of the three sets of eleven or thirty-three beads. Each section is devoted to a different recitation or prayer said at each bead: Subhan 'u 'llah ("God Is the All-Splendorous"), Alhamd 'u 'llah ("Praise God"), Allah 'u 'Akbar ("God Is the Most Great"). Tesbih may also be used for repetitions of Qur'anic passages and personal prayers. The *karakish* or *mullah gak* (a small beaded tassel or "little mullah") hangs from the tesbih. It is said that evil spirits do not like dangling objects, so that the leader bead with a tassel wards off the evil eye. Prayer beads are popular wedding presents and gifts from Mecca. The origin of Muslim prayer beads is unclear, but it probably derives from an ancient Hindu practice.

Beaded amulets (tawwez) are commonly used throughout Central and South Asia, as both personal adornments and household decorations. In addition to wearing beads as amulets on garments, some Afghans use beaded and embroidered tawwez amulets. These are triangular shapes that are hung in entryways to protect a household, its members, and others who enter domestic spaces. They are also used to decorate modes of transportation, such as horses and automobiles.

SOCIOECONOMIC ASPECTS OF BEAD JEWELRY AND THE GEOPOLITICAL IMPORTANCE OF AFGHAN JEWELRY

The socioeconomic significance of bead jewelry relates to the rarity of bead materials, bead manufacture, and application. Bead jewelry is often a substitute for the use of semiprecious stones. For example, prayer beads vary in their costliness, with prices ranging from less than one dollar to thousands of dollars. Cheap prayer beads are often made of glass or plastic materials, while the more prestigious examples are made of precious and semiprecious stones. Although it is conceivable that individual beads may be chosen and then strung together for a tesbih, it is normal for tesbih to be purchased ready-made in the marketplace or even just outside a local mosque.

Beaded amulets are made of modest materials and designed by women for family use. A village woman may attach a bead to her children's clothing or encircle a strategic area of their bodies, such as the neck, wrists, or ankles, with a strung bead or collection of beads. Beaded garments, primarily overdresses and head coverings, originally made for special occasions, are referred to as mora-dozi or *kala-y-Afghani* (beaded Afghan clothing). The value of these garments is attributed to the skill and expertise in the application of the beads and the bead material used. Depending on the family's social status, these ensembles, perceived as part of a family's wealth, may be either stored and used during important social occasions or worn daily when few garments are owned. But more often than not, these family heirlooms, highly prized by Afghans and non-Afghans, are sold and permeate the Afghan markets.

The political significance of bead jewelry use is less evident than its religious significance since politics and religion are frequently conflated. One such example is the use of prayer beads. During the Soviet occupation, many Afghans were incarcerated, and some prisoners started to make tesbih beads from the bread they were given to eat.

Another example of the conflation of politics and religion is the role of dress and appearance under the Taliban. The Taliban authorities strictly regulated the dress, accessories, and general appearance of Afghan men and women. It did not matter whether they were Shiite Muslims, Sunni Muslims, or Hindus. Even non-Afghans (Westerners), who were presumed to be Christians, were strictly reprimanded for ignoring bans on visible and audible jewelry worn in public settings. Anything that would call attention to sensory aspects of the body was forbidden. Jewelry that made a noise, such as bracelets and anklets, for instance, was prohibited. The use of colorful jewelry materials or the display of costly materials was also banned. In some instances, such items were ripped or torn off women who wore them in public.

In conclusion, Afghan jewelry, prized by both Afghans and non-Afghans alike for its rich historical heritage, reflects a variety of social and cultural practices. The costly jewelry of precious and semiprecious stones and its less expensive bead counterparts are used to mark gender and generational differences, spiritual and faith-based associations, socioeconomic and educational status, and the geopolitics of Afghanistan. The documentation of Afghan jewelry, whether used for everyday or special occasions, provides tangible evidence of a changing material culture and of a people's struggle to endure.

References and Further Reading

Daly, M. Catherine. "The Pardah Expression of Hejab among Afghan Women Living in a Non-Muslim Community." In *Body, Dress, and Religion*, edited by Linda Arthur, 147–162. Oxford: Berg, 1999.

Hiebert, F., and Pierre Cambon. *Afghanistan: Hidden Treasures from the National Museum, Kabul.* Washington, DC: National Geographic Society, 2008.

Olesen, Asta. *Afghan Craftsmen.* London: Thames and Hudson, 1994.

Paine, Sylvia. *The Afghan Amulet.* New York: St. Martin's Press, 1994.

Paiva, Roland, and Bernard Dupaigne. *Afghan Embroidery.* Lahore, Pakistan: Ferozsons, 1993.

Schimmel, Anne Marie. *Deciphering the Signs of God: A Phenomenological Approach to Islam.* New York: State University of New York Press, 1994.

Sheikh, Fazal. *The Victor Weeps: Afghanistan.* New York: Scalo, 1999.

M. Catherine Daly

See also Regional Dress of Afghanistan; Afghan Dress and the Diaspora.

Snapshot: Afghan Embroidery

Afghanistan is surrounded by many lands and cultures; as a result, the materials, designs, and colors used by the Afghan people for their embroidery reflect their country's central location in Asia. The main ethnic groups in Afghanistan are the Baluch, Hazara, Nuristani, Pashtun, Tajik, Turkmen, and Uzbek. Each has its own special way of living, which is shown in their traditional embroidery. Generally, girls and women produce embroidery at home. However, by the end of the twentieth century, a significant number of men also embroidered but usually using machines in tailor's workshops.

Within Afghan embroidery, a great variety of motifs and designs are found. Each region and group has its own particular motifs, such as the sun and stars; geometric motifs (circles, squares, triangles, rosettes; Greek fret patterns); foliage-based motifs (tulips, flowers, almond leaves, melon stalks, pomegranate flowers symbolizing fertility, pimento flowers), and stylized animal elements (ram's horns, lion's tails). Sometimes, objects such as amulets and even teapots are included. In some areas, embroideries also include figurative motifs such as animals, birds, and very occasionally human beings. A feature of Pashtun embroidery are roundels called *gul-i-peron* ("dress flowers"), made of felt and covered with symbols and objects associated with good luck and fertility, such as colored beads, cowry shells, and metal disks. These guls are usually used in pairs and stitched to the upper part of women's dresses, bags, and animal trappings.

Embroidery in Afghanistan decorates a wide range of objects, being used for home decorations (tablecloths, mats, towels, curtains, and so forth), animal trappings (notably the decorative blankets for horses), as well as both men's and women's clothing. In general, women's clothing tends to be more elaborately and colorfully embroidered than that of men. Some of the most famous embroidery for men, however, comes from Kandahar. One of the most widespread uses of embroidery is for the small skullcaps worn by men, women, and children. Each group has its own style of cap and form of decoration, with many variations, designs, and colors related to different villages, gender, and so forth.

A range of different types of silk, cotton, and wool yarns are used for embroidery on whatever fabrics are available. Metallic threads, spangles, sequins, mirrors, and metallic braids are also incorporated into the designs. In addition, Pashtun women's dresses incorporate beads and mirrors, and nomadic women use beads, coins, and shells. Pashtun and Baluchi women also choose to use mirrors (*shisha*), an idea that originates in northern India.

Afghan embroidery uses a relatively limited number of stitches, and these relate closely to various ethnic groups. Some main forms are blanket stitch, slanting blanket filling, brick stitch, chain stitch, cross stitch, herringbone stitch, holbein, ladder stitch, lattice stitch, satin stitch, long and short stitch, and Romanian couching. Some stitches allow the embroidery to cover large areas of cloth quickly with bold, floral designs, while others create smaller, intricate, geometric patterns.

STYLES OF EMBROIDERY

Virtually each village and region in Afghanistan has its own style of embroidery based on different combinations of materials, stitches, colors, and designs, as well as differences in how the embroidery is worn or used. Nevertheless, main styles of embroidery can be identified.

The Baluch live in southern Afghanistan near the borders with Iran and Pakistan. Embroidery plays an important role in Baluchi clothing, especially for women. It used to be largely hand stitched, but since the late twentieth century more and more of it is decorated using machines. A traditional Baluchi woman's dress (*pashk*) normally has four panels of embroidery (*doch*): a large, squarish panel that covers the upper front of the dress; the two cuffs of the sleeve; and a long, narrow rectangular panel with a triangular top, which goes from about the waistline to the hem of the skirt. The hand stitching used for these panels is referred to as *pakka*, meaning firm or solid, because of the use of fine, tight stitching to cover the ground fabric. The designs used for the traditional hand-worked panels are normally geometric in form and worked in red, black, and white yarns. In contrast, the designs used for machine-decorated garments include a wider range of geometric and floral patterns in many different colors.

The Hazaras from central Afghanistan are known for the production of fine, geometric embroidery. In particular, they produce embroidery worked in very fine lines of cross or herringbone stitch on a cotton or silk ground. There is no single form of Hazara embroidery. The Wardak Hazara, for example, produce multicolored geometric designs using a holbein stitch. In contrast, the Hazara from Ghazni are known for multicolored designs that are based on squares or rectangles enclosing checkered bands or lozenges. Ghazni embroideries are often worked in silk thread on a cotton ground. The preferred stitches are brick stitch or short satin stitches, with dividing lines produced in holbein stitch using black and white yarns.

Kabul, the capital of Afghanistan, is famous for two types of embroidery. The first uses gold-colored braids that are sewn in intricate geometric designs on the ground material (often red velvet). The second is based on early-twentieth-century European patterns (notably designs in the style of those produced by Dollfus, Mieg & Compagnie, known for their floral designs), either in satin stitch or cross stitch. In particular, multicolored floral motifs are popular.

Khamak is the name of some of the most sought-after Afghan embroidery. It comes from the southern city of Kandahar. Khamak is made using a satin stitch on a cotton or white silk ground. This form of work is unusual, as the stitch is worked from the reverse side of the ground material and great care is taken to make sure that the front and the back of the embroidery looks the same. Normally, the ground is either the same color as the embroidery thread or a very pale blue or green, but very occasionally it is possible to see a

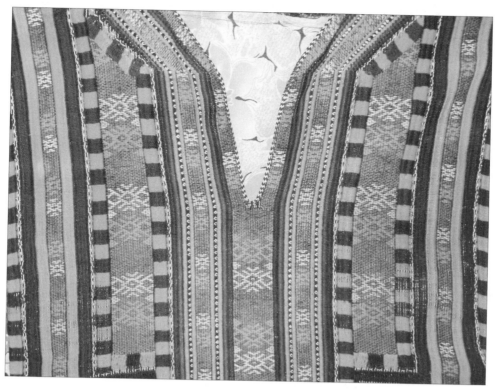

Detail from a Baluchi woman's dress bodice, worked in cross stitch, satin stitch, and stem stitch, with silk yarn on a synthetic ground, southern Afghanistan, late twentieth century. The embroidery used for this panel is often referred to as *pakka* (meaning "firm" or "solid"), because fine stitching covers the ground fabric completely with geometric designs, often worked in lines. Textile Research Centre, Leiden.

man's outfit in dark-colored material with a light-colored embroidery. The designs used for Kandahar embroidery tend to be geometric in form and relying on light reflecting off the satin stitch to produce different visual effects.

There are various types of embroidery that are related to different Pashtun groups, but they do have certain features in common. For example, it is common for Pashtun dresses for women, both urban and nomadic, to have a beaded panel at the join between the shoulders and the head of the sleeves, and at the waist in order to cover the seamline between the bodice and skirt sections of the dress. Both the sleeve and waist panels are normally made using multicolored glass beads. The designs are normally geometric in nature. Mangal Pashtuns from the east of Afghanistan are known for their use of satin stitch to create lozenges that cover the whole of the surface of the ground material. In general, Mangal designs do not follow the grain of the fabric, instead forming diagonal lines that strengthen the geometric nature of the lozenge designs. Wardak Pashtuns are noted for multicolored embroideries in silk on a monochrome cotton or silk ground. Wardak embroideries are normally worked in satin stitch. Their designs are usually based on a central motif, such as a star, which have complex outward-radiating geometric designs.

Tajiks constitute about one-quarter of the Afghan population and live in all main urban centers, as well as in the northeast and west of Afghanistan. A typical Tajik design is based on multicolored floral motifs encircling a central motif.

However, as with the other main group, the Pashtun, there are various types of Tajik embroidery. In the north of Afghanistan, for example, Tajik embroidery is often based on floral motifs that are worked in multicolored yarns, as well as gold thread for extra depth, richness, and variation. In contrast, the Tajiks of Badakhstan, in the extreme northeast of Afghanistan, tend to use satin stitch and brick stitch to create small geometric motifs worked in silk thread over a cotton ground. The different sections of the embroidery are often separated by rows worked in chain stitch.

Embroidery is an important way for many Turkmen women to display their creativity and skill. In Turkmenistan, for example, there are numerous workshops, some state-owned, that specialize in embroidery. The products of these ateliers are sold in both local and international markets. In contrast, across the border in Afghanistan most of the embroidery is made at home and is intended for domestic or local use.

The Yomut and Teke are the two main Turkmen groups in Afghanistan, and both groups have their own forms of embroidery. In general, the Yomut favor the use of chain stitch. Sometimes, various stitches are worked in combination, such as the chain stitch areas being outlined with stem stitches. The Teke, in contrast, use lacing stitch with stem stitch (for outlining), back stitch, and couching in a variety of forms. Among the Yomut and Teke, the appearance of the embroidery differs slightly with respect to the range of colors and motifs used. Red is by far the most popular color, although Teke embroidery is

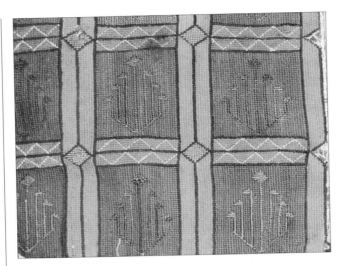

Detail of Hazara embroidery on a woman's dress bodice, worked in minute cross stitch, central Afghanistan, late twentieth century. Textile Research Centre, Leiden.

The Uzbek live in the north of Afghanistan and are famous for their love of large, colorful floral motifs using a variety of embroidery stitches, such as long and short stitches. The patterns are often based around a central rosette and have motifs that radiate outward, or there are rounded, sinuous motifs in vivid and contrasting colors. Both Uzbek male and female clothing is often embroidered, although the men's clothing tends to be more discreet in the quantity, boldness of motifs, and use of color. A popular pattern is what appears to be bouquets of stylized flowers; this design is often used to decorate the slits on the lower side seams of both men's and women's coats.

REFERENCES AND FURTHER READING

Harvey, Janet. *Traditional Textiles of Central Asia*. London: Thames and Hudson, 1996.
Paine, Sheila. *Embroidery from Afghanistan*. London: British Museum Press, 2006.
Paiva, Roland, and Bernard Dupaigne. *Afghan Embroidery*. Lahore, Pakistan: Ferozsons, 1993.

Gillian Vogelsang-Eastwood

often enlivened by the use of golden yellow or blues. All Turkmen groups in Afghanistan use geometric and stylized floral and geometric motifs, with one of the most common designs being the tulip, which is regarded as symbolizing fertility.

See also Regional Dress of Afghanistan.

The Chadari/Burqa of Afghanistan and Pakistan

- Burqa or Chadari?
- Materials and Colors
- The Chadari and the Taliban

A few garments have become global icons, recognized throughout the world. The Scottish kilt is one, and others include the Japanese kimono and the Native American headdress with one or more feathers. The Afghan *chadari* (a long, all-enveloping outer garment that totally covers a woman's body), or burqa as it is also known, has become a global icon, particularly during the period of the Taliban in Afghanistan (1994–2001). For many in the non-Muslim world, the chadari symbolizes the oppression of women. Others view it as a romantic garment, floating in the air as the wearer walks. As a colorful, visual device, it was used to great effect by the Iranian filmmaker Mosen Makhmalbaf in *Kandahar* (2001).

When talking about the chadari in the West, many people think it to be recent. Some even believe it is a deliberate Taliban invention. It often comes as a great surprise to learn that Muslim women in the area that comprises Pakistan and northern India in the early twenty-first century have been clad in this style of garment for more than four hundred years, while a closely linked version has been worn in Afghanistan for longer than two hundred years. These garments were worn because longstanding, local customs required women to be totally covered in public.

Not to wear such a covering indicated a woman's (and thus her family's) lack of respectability, honor, and social status. Wearing it protected many women from the prying eyes of men, even giving some women the opportunity to live a secret life well away from family, friends, and neighbors, as is implied by a Persian saying from the early nineteenth century: "A Caubul wife in Boorka-cover, was never known without a lover."

In the late twentieth century, when the Taliban required women to wear these garments as a symbol of being Muslim, this was not supported by all Afghan men and women. The penalty inflicted by the Taliban on a woman not totally covered in a chadari could range from a beating to death.

BURQA OR CHADARI?

Another belief about the chadari concerns its name. While most people simply refer to it as a *burqa*, some specialists in Afghan history insist that it should be called a *chadari*. Again, the Arab name *burqa* seems to be associated with the arrival of the Taliban and Islamic fundamentalism. The situation is further complicated by the Western media's modern adoption of the term *burqa* when they mean a chadari. In reality, the two names, *chadari* and *burqa*, have been used for this style of garment for a long time, and *burqa* is probably the older of the two.

From the medieval period on, it appears that these garments were primarily worn by upper-class urban women, as nomadic or village women did not have the resources of time and money required for the amount of cloth and for the creation and embellishment of the garments. These women would have worn simpler rectangular garments called chadors that are easily pulled across the face if necessary but lack a specific face veil, a necessary component of the chadari. They are thus similar but do not provide the full covering of the chadari. Even during the Taliban period, not all Afghan women wore chadaris, as they were too expensive. Many women, especially nomadic women, continued to wear chadors.

In the twenty-first century, a burqa from Pakistan consists of a cap, a cape section (body covering) that incorporates an eyehole grid, and a separate panel lower down at the front. The cap, face-veil section, and panel are usually decorated with embroidery. This type of garment does not have the tight, pressed pleats of the Afghan version. Instead, soft pleats or gentle folds are fashioned by gathering the excess material of the chador on a draw thread and then sewing the material to the cap. The folds are created by working several rows of running stitches or by smocking the cloth to create a honeycomb effect.

The Afghan chadari consists of a cap, body covering, and a separate face-veil panel. In contrast to the (Pakistani) burqa, the panel with an eye grid is attached to the cap, and there is no separate, inserted panel lower down. The cap and panel are normally decorated with embroidery. Around the upper part of the chador, there are hundreds of narrow pleats that are gathered together and sewn onto the cap. These pleats give the garment its voluminous nature. This type of chadari has become a global icon and (in)famous throughout the world.

The earliest depictions of women wearing burqalike garments can be found in Mughal miniature paintings dating back to the late sixteenth century. For example, in a manuscript painting dating to the 1580s that is held in the British Museum, three women with burqas are depicted in boats. Two are totally covered by their burqas, while the third has tossed hers back over her head. A fourth woman, a servant, has no burqa but covers her hair with a large outer covering (a chadorlike garment). The burqas depicted are made up of a cap section with six to eight panels, a cap band in which the two eyeholes are set, and then a cape section that is gathered at the top and set into the cap band. The front of the burqa appears to have a long slit.

By the end of the eighteenth century, urban women in Afghanistan were wearing Persian garments made up of a chador and a face veil called a *ru-band*, but they added an Afghan touch, namely, the cap. The outfit that they created was called a chadari, based on the Persian word *chador*, meaning "a tent." At this time, Afghan rulers modeled themselves in many aspects, including their clothing, on Iranian culture. With the shift of the Afghan capital from Kandahar to Kabul in the late eighteenth century, the rise of British power in the Indian subcontinent in the nineteenth century, and the simultaneous decline of Iranian power and prestige, the Muslim world of northern India became the focus of attention for the Afghan elite and merchants. The two names, *chadari* and *burqa*, therefore can be seen as reflecting historical and geographic developments. The term *chadari* reflects Persian influence, while *burqa* reflects its Muslim Mughal counterpart in northern India.

MATERIALS AND COLORS

In early depictions of chadaris and burqas, they seem to be made of cotton of varying qualities or, less frequently, silk. The first synthetic chadaris appeared on the market in the late 1960s, and by the mid-1970s they had become widespread. This type of material appeals because it is relatively cheap, comes in a range of colors, and is easy to wash. In the twenty-first century, much of the material comes from either China or South Korea. The price of the material varies considerably. A chadari made of a cheap coarse material, for example, may cost about 200 afghani (about US$4 in 2007 dollars). One made of a lightweight cloth with machine embroidery may cost somewhere around 1,400 afghani (US$28 in 2007), which would be the equivalent of nearly a month's salary for some families. A chadari intended to be worn by a bride at her wedding might cost even more.

During the nineteenth century, most urban women wore a white version. In 1903, however, white was banned by King Habibullah of Afghanistan (r. 1901–1919), and other colors were required. He ordered that Muslim women should wear a khaki-colored version, Hindu women should wear a red or mustard yellow garment, and others slate-colored ones. This form of color coding distinguished various ethnic and religious groups and has had a long tradition within the Islamic world.

In the late twentieth century, the choice of color began to indicate the wearer's origins and even religious beliefs. For example, burnt orange and forest green were fashionable around the eastern city of Jalalabad. Around Kabul, mid-blue was more popular; this is the color most non-Afghans associate with the chadari. Black chadari tended to be used only among very conservative and Taliban groups, notably in the Herat region, and became difficult to find immediately following the fall of the Taliban. Later, they became more widely available, however, as the Taliban regained some of their power. Hazara women in the center of the country wore yellow, and the Taliban also forced some Hindu women to wear yellow. In the north of Afghanistan, most women, especially the elderly, prefer white. In 2006, most girls from Kabul chose a gray-blue color. In northern Marzai-i Sharif, white was popular, and green was used in Kandahar and Khost in the south and east, but light blue can be found in most provinces.

In addition to the main forms, some variations exist on the chadari/burqa theme. These include a chador and face veil (with two holes for the eyes) sewn together. This is worn in Pakistan and Kashmir and called a tribal burqa. A modern development of the tribal burqa is the addition of snaps or press studs down the front of the garment to prevent the ends from flapping and possibly revealing the garments underneath. The Kashmiri burqa (also called a *niqab* or Kashmiri niqab) is regarded as a recent, urban development and is made by attaching a face veil to a chador, but the chador section is reduced to a small semicircle of cloth that covers just the shoulders. Like the tribal version, this form of burqa has two eyeholes covered with net rather than a eye grid. It is worn with a long and wide cloaklike garment with no sleeves that covers a woman's body from the shoulders to the ankles (*abayeh*) or a long dress, usually in black.

Another form of body covering, again made of separate garments sewn together and related to the tribal burqa, is favored by some urban women in Pakistan. It is made from a large length of material that covers the whole body, with an attached face veil. Unlike the tribal version, in which the veil covers the whole face,

in this type the face veil covers only the nose and lower part of the face, hence the use of another name, *niqab*. Called the Pakistani niqab, it normally comes in a thin knitted synthetic material in a variety of colors including black, dark blue, light blue, dark green, olive green, brown, and white.

THE CHADARI AND THE TALIBAN

The Westernization of Afghanistan, as it was perceived by various more traditional Afghan groups as well as Communist groups, was halted in the late 1970s when a Marxist regime in Kabul forced many Afghans into opposition. Many adopted traditional lifestyles, including the seclusion of women. At the same time, many families fled Afghanistan and went to Pakistan, especially to the refugee camps in the west of the country. There, the enforced seclusion of women became a normal feature of life, as many families were crowded together in relatively small areas. Afghan refugees in Pakistan adopted a style of hijab, or Islamic dress, consisting of an ankle-length coat that was worn together with a large head covering that could be drawn across the face if necessary. Many Afghan women, however, apparently objected to the wearing of hijab because it was regarded as a foreign import. Instead, these women chose some form of the traditional Afghan chador, similar to the chador of Iran, which leaves the face uncovered.

The Taliban (literally, "seekers," hence "religious students") came to power in 1994 when they managed, with outside help, to unite many of the opposing forces among the Afghans in the south and east of the country. Islam, as interpreted by the Taliban, became the unifying factor. The Taliban adopted a very strict form of the Qur'an and Islamic law (the sharia), and the seclusion of women was one of the main outward symbols of this movement. The anthropologist Nancy Dupree noted that, on 27 September 1996, immediately after the fall of Kabul to the Taliban, Radio Kabul (later called the Voice of Sharia) announced that "since satar [Islamic dress code for women] is of great importance to Islam all sisters are seriously asked … to cover their faces and the whole of their body when going out." Clearly, women had to cover themselves completely because those who did not risked being beaten by Taliban members who were enforcing order on the streets. It is said that even a glimpse of an uncovered ankle was enough to provoke a beating. Not surprisingly, many women chose or were forced to stay indoors. On 17 December 1996, the Taliban announced a further set of regulations for men and women. First, the Taliban mandated that bus or taxi drivers were not allowed to pick up females wearing a chador (which does not cover the face), those wearing seductive clothing, or those unaccompanied by a *mahram* (male chaperone). Second, all women found washing clothes in public would be picked up and taken home, and their husbands would be severely punished. Third, any tailor taking female body measurements and displaying fashion magazines would be punished. The new Taliban dress codes and restrictions on movement caused severe problems for families who could not afford a chadari. In the late 1990s, these garments cost about US$30, more than a month's salary for some families. For many women, the enforcement of satar was tantamount to house arrest and, for some, such as war widows, possible slow starvation as they were unable to go out to earn money for their families.

A woman wearing a *chadari*, seated outside a shop window, Kabul, Afghanistan, 2004. The Afghan *chadari* features hundreds of narrow pleats gathered together and sewn onto the cap, giving the garment its voluminous nature. Paula Bronstein/Getty Images.

For many urban women, especially those who had been unveiled all their lives, the wearing of the chadari came as a shock. They felt imprisoned, as their scope of vision was reduced and their hearing impaired by the veil. Heat exhaustion became a serious threat as the chadaris were now made of synthetic materials rather than the traditional silks or cottons that were cooler and more porous. Finally, the wearing of these voluminous garments meant that tripping was also a constant threat, thus adding to the risk of exposing the body or undergarments, a punishable offense.

Nevertheless, at the same time that the Taliban were trying to impose a measure of standardization on the public appearance of women, women were subverting these plans by modifying the chadari to make them into more personal statements. Decorative embroidery, both machine and hand forms, were worked on the garments, adding elements of design and individuality.

In 2001, the Taliban fell, and many in the West presumed that all Afghan women would immediately stop wearing the chadari/burqa. This did not happen, much to the amazement of some. The reasons for this vary. To a certain extent, women feel the situation in Afghanistan is too unstable. Wearing a chadari/burqa gives them a degree of protection. For other women, the chadari/burqa hides the fact that they cannot afford good clothing; the expense of purchasing decent clothes is too much on their meager incomes. Other women wear the chadari/burqa because they feel comfortable in it. Their mothers, aunts, grandmothers, and relatives for many generations have worn these garments in public, and they want to continue this custom. Often, they find it strange that outsiders want them to change their traditional way of life. Finally, a considerable number of women still regard the chadari/burqa as part of their Islamic way of life and have no intention of dropping it.

Although the Taliban have been (temporarily) suppressed at the end of the first decade of the twenty-first century, the political and social role of the chadari as a global icon representing Muslim women and Islamic fundamentalism continues.

References and Further Reading

Dupree, Nancy. "Afghan Women under the Taliban." In *Fundamentalism Reborn? Afghanistan and the Taliban*, edited by William Maley. London: Hurst and Co., 1998.

Griffin, Michael. *Reaping the Whirlwind*. London: Pluto Press, 2001.

Rattray, James. *The Costumes of the Various Tribes, Portraits of Ladies of Rank, Celebrated Princes and Chiefs, Views of the Principal Fortresses and Cities, and Interior of the Cities and Temples of Afghanistan.* London: Hering and Remington, 1848.

Scarce, Jennifer. *Women's Costume of the Near and Middle East.* London and Sydney: Unwin Hyman, 1987.

Vogelsang-Eastwood, Gillian. *For Modesty's Sake.* Rotterdam: Barjesteh and Co., 1996.

Vogelsang-Eastwood, Gillian, and Willem Vogelsang. *Covering the Moon: A History of Middle Eastern Face Veils.* Leuven, Belgium: Peeters, 2008.

Gillian Vogelsang-Eastwood

See also Laws of Differentiation; Face Veils.

PART 6

Central Asia

History of West Turkistan and Its Influence on the Dress of South Central Asia

- The Historical Lands of West Turkistan
- Invasions by Iranians, Turks, and Others
- Islam and the Persian Revival
- Genghis Khan and the Uzbek Emirates

West Turkistan is the name traditionally given to the lands that stretch east of the Caspian Sea and north of modern Iran and Afghanistan. To the east, it is bordered by the rising peaks of the Altai and Karakoram mountains, which mark the modern frontier with China. To the north lies the wide expanse of Kazakhstan. West Turkistan is a harsh and arid region that until the early twentieth century was largely inhabited by nomads. Villages and urban centers developed at specific places where water was available. But in spite of its inhospitable landscape and climate, West Turkistan has always been a crossroads of people and cultures moving between north and south, east and west, and this shows in the clothing of the people throughout the ages. By the first millennium C.E., for instance, Central Asian riding dress was seen next to Indian Buddhist robes and Chinese silks in West Turkistan. The region thus formed an important link in the famous Silk Road that for centuries connected the Mediterranean with China. In early-twenty-first-century politics, it is the place where the political and economic interests of Russia, China, and the West overlap.

West Turkistan should be differentiated from what used to be called East Turkistan, which lies across the mountains in modern China. The general name Turkistan is derived from the main population in this part of the world, namely the Turks. They arrived here from the early first millennium C.E. on, after long migrations that started in their Siberian and Mongolian homelands. In the deserts of what came to be called East Turkistan, they moved into lands that were characterized by a small number of oases that constituted the various stages of the Silk Road. West of the Altai and Karakoram mountains, in what came to be known as West Turkistan, they entered lands that until then had mainly been populated by Iranian-speaking groups. The latter, whose languages are part of the Indo-European language family and very different from the Altaic language family that includes Turkish, had also arrived here from the north but much earlier. Some of these Iranian-speaking groups had moved further south onto the plateau, which subsequently was given their name (Iran). Those who remained in West Turkistan later became known as the Tajiks.

Some of the Turkish tribes, traveling in the footsteps of their Iranian-speaking predecessors, eventually also moved south from West Turkistan onto the Iranian Plateau. They settled in Iran or Afghanistan, or they subsequently moved even further west. By the early second millennium C.E., Turkish adventurers arrived and established themselves in Southwest Asia in what subsequently came to be called Turkey. These early migrations explain the close relationship between the Turkish language spoken in modern Turkey and that used in West Turkistan, especially among the Turkmen of Turkmenistan. It also explains a strong sentiment among the Turks, certainly in modern Turkey, that all the lands between Istanbul and Mongolia form part of a distinct Turkish entity.

Not surprisingly, there are many similarities in the dress of Turkey and West Turkistan. For example, kaftans, long robes that are open down the front and usually kept in place with a sash, were worn by men in both areas. Similarly, it was (and partly still is) normal among Central Asian Turkish women to wear face veils, albeit ones that often covered only the lower half of the face. A specific type of face veil made from horsehair (often known as a *peche*) was used well into the twentieth century C.E. in both Turkey and West Turkistan.

In the early twenty-first century, West Turkistan is carved up by a number of modern states that arose out of the ashes of the Soviet Union in the early 1990s. These countries, from west to east, are Turkmenistan, Uzbekistan, Tajikistan, and Kyrgyzstan. The borders of these modern states were originally drawn by Soviet politicians in the 1920s and 1930s. They cut straight through the traditional lands of ethnic communities. This feature shows most strongly in the distribution of the majority Turkish-speaking groups in the region (as, for instance, the Turkmen, the Uzbeks, and the Kyrgyz) and the descendants of the original population, the mainly Iranian (Persian)-speaking Tajiks. Uzbekistan, for instance, has a large Tajik minority, while Tajikistan houses large numbers of Uzbeks and others.

Over the centuries, however, Turkish and Tajik groups developed many common elements, including in textiles and dress. One of the more spectacular features of South Central Asian dress, for instance, is the use of ikat materials for both men's and women's clothing. Ikats are colorful materials with intricate designs created by resist-dyeing the warp or weft threads, or both, before weaving. Silk and cotton ikats were, and still are, being used for trousers, dresses, gowns, coats, and caps. Ikat is being produced and worn mainly in modern Uzbekistan and Tajikistan, as well as by the Uzbek groups in neighboring Afghanistan.

THE HISTORICAL LANDS OF WEST TURKISTAN

The Turks did not find an empty land when they arrived sometime in the first millennium C.E. in what came to be called West Turkistan. In fact, the lands east of the Caspian have a long history and an extensive archaeological record. In the past and in the present, human inhabitation in West Turkistan is for the greater part determined by geographic circumstances. The main settlements have always been built along the rivers and along the edges of the huge deserts. In fact, most of West Turkistan is covered by desert, such as the huge Kara-Kum Desert east of the Caspian Sea and the Kyzyl Kum Desert further to the east. The Kara-Kum and Kyzyl Kum deserts are separated by the Amu Dar'ya

River (the classical Oxus), which springs in the Karakoram Mountains along the borders of Tajikistan, Pakistan, Afghanistan, and China. It flows through West Turkistan, keeping the Kara-Kum Desert to its left and the Kyzyl Kum to its right, and finally empties into the Aral Sea in the north. Throughout history, people have lived and settled along the banks of this river. Especially in the north, in the delta of the Amu Dar'ya south of the Aral Sea, people created a flourishing district, generally known as Chorasmia, which is already mentioned in ancient sources by the late sixth century B.C.E. An ancient town in this area is Khiva. Evidence for the use of textiles and clothing in this area dates back thousands of years. Archaeological excavations in the region, and indeed in many other parts of West Turkistan, have revealed that the people living there used silk woven in intricate brocades as well as simple striped materials made of wool, goat hair, and camel hair.

South of the Kara-Kum Desert rises a mountain range that is generally known as the Kopet Dagh. It marks the natural boundary between West Turkistan and Iran. Various small rivers flow down the mountains and empty into the Kara-Kum Desert. Here, along the northern foothills of the Kopet Dagh, another ancient district can be found. Archaeological excavations have brought to light flourishing communities that date back to at least the sixth millennium B.C.E. This district, traditionally known as Parthia, is, in the early twenty-first century, the center of the state of Turkmenistan with its capital of Ashkhabad.

Somewhat further east, but still within the modern state of Turkmenistan, lies the delta of the Murghab River, which descends from the mountains in Afghanistan and empties north into the Kara-Kum Desert. This delta, traditionally known as Margiana, has been a major center in this part of the world from long before the Common Era. It formed an important staging post along the Silk Road between the Mediterranean and China. It was also the capital of various historical states and empires.

East of Margiana, in an area that is part of the Islamic Republic of Afghanistan in the early twenty-first century, lies the ancient land of Bactria. It was centered along the banks of the Balkhab River. Its main center, Bactra, was one of the largest cities in this part of the world in the early Islamic period (according to the Arab geographers, it was the "Mother of Cities"). The history of this town dates back to at least the mid-first millennium B.C.E. Alexander the Great stayed here between 329 and 327 B.C.E. when he was engaged in a merciless war against the local population of West Turkistan. In the early twenty-first century, Bactra, or Balkh as it is called, is an extensive field of ruins, but nearby another city has arisen, called Mazar-i Shariff, which has become the main city of northern Afghanistan, testifying to the strategic location of this site and the productivity of the surrounding lands.

Nearby, at the site of Tillya Tepe, Afghan and Russian archaeologists in 1978–1979 discovered a number of graves dating back to the beginning of the Common Era. These graves contained thousands of gold objects, most of which were originally attached to clothing. Based on the archaeological finds from Tillya Tepe and surrounding areas, it appears that a wide range of textiles was available at that time, including polychrome fabrics made of silk, hemp, or wool. These garments were also heavily decorated, at least for the elite, with intricate plaques and disks made of gold. The basic outfit for men appears to have consisted of an undershirt, a jacket, loose-fitting trousers suitable for horse riding, as well as leather belts and boots that may have been made of leather or felt. Women's clothing seems to have been variations of a chemise, a blouse, a very wide skirt, a jacket, and a short-sleeved coat that was similar in appearance to the coats worn by Turkmen women well into the twentieth century. The form of the headgear worn by women is unclear.

North of ancient Bactria, and across the Amu Dar'ya, lie the lands along the Zerafshan River. This is ancient Sogdia, with the two ancient towns of Bukhara and Samarkand. These towns figure prominently in the history of the Silk Road.

INVASIONS BY IRANIANS, TURKS, AND OTHERS

Because of its location between the Caspian Sea in the west and the Chinese mountains in the east, West Turkistan has always been a strategic transit area for migrations between north and south. For millennia, nomadic groups from the north, such as from the area that comprises modern Kazakhstan, from Siberia, and from the lands of Mongolia, moved south and southeast in search of new pastures. They brought with them their own cultures, languages, and, in particular, sartorial traditions. This was true both of the Turkish tribes that migrated into West Turkistan in the first millennium C.E. and of the Iranian-speaking groups that preceded them. From the early first millennium B.C.E., for instance, the Iranian-speaking Scythians from Kazakhstan passed through West Turkistan and settled on the Iranian Plateau. They introduced horse riding and the clothing and weaponry that went with it: trousers, tunics, boots, long coats with empty sleeves, short composite bows, short swords, and so on. Basically, this type of clothing was worn by the people buried at Tillya Tepe around the beginning of the Common Era.

West Turkistan, with its nomadic warriors from the north, always remained a threat to the settled communities on the Iranian Plateau. Sometimes the nomads were dominant and invaded the Iranian Plateau at will; sometimes the settled communities were stronger and occupied most of West Turkistan. After the Scythian invasions of the Iranian Plateau in the early first millennium B.C.E., it was the turn of a strong, Iran-based empire to extend its control over West Turkistan. This was the Persian Achaemenid Empire. The inclusion of much of West Turkistan into the Achaemenid Empire also led to clothing traditions from the Persian heartland, in modern southwestern Iran, being introduced among the former Scythian masters of the region. The famous Oxus Treasure, discovered in ancient Bactria in the late nineteenth century, shows men wearing the long, flowing robes of the Persian nobles, very different from the trouser-wearing Scythians.

The Persian Achaemenid Empire was defeated by Alexander the Great, and with him a new cultural influence entered West Turkistan, namely that of the Greeks. This impact was at first supported by military and political power. Until the mid-second century B.C.E., Greek princes ruled large parts of West Turkistan. Afterward, Greek cultural influence remained. Greek script was used in parts of ancient Bactria until the second half of the first millennium C.E. Greek/Hellenistic art influenced the Buddhist art of northwestern India and Afghanistan. This is the so-called Gandhara art, which, for instance, shows Buddha in the shape of Apollo. There is no doubt that Greek clothing traditions also penetrated into West Turkistan. The kings of the Greco-Bactrian kingdoms, as shown on their coins, proudly wear their Greek clothing.

The northern invaders who defeated the Greeks in the second century B.C.E. were the descendants of the Scythians and others who previously had migrated into West Turkistan from the north. These northern invaders occupied northern Afghanistan and soon after moved across the Hindu Kush Mountains into southern and eastern Afghanistan and down into the plains of northern India. By the first century C.E., they had established the so-called Kushana Empire, which covered much of northern India, Afghanistan, and large parts of West Turkistan. Under the Kushanas, Buddhism spread rapidly, from northern India across Afghanistan and West Turkistan toward China. Buddhist art, often with a mixture of Indian and Hellenistic elements, flourished throughout the empire, especially in the lands just south of the Hindu Kush, in the old province of Gandhara. One of the famous Kushana statues, that of their king Kanishka, which is housed in the National Museum of Afghanistan (Kabul), shows a typical Kushana warrior clothed in a long kaftan-type riding coat and large boots. The king is shown in a frontal position, indicating his power and authority.

By the same time, starting in the second century B.C.E., another group of nomads from the north occupied ancient Parthia, north of Iran, and from there slowly encroached on the Iranian Plateau. They founded the Parthian Empire, which would dominate Iran for almost four hundred years. They introduced new sartorial traditions, clearly originating in Central Asia, that replaced the local and Greek/Hellenistic clothing that had been worn until then. A bronze statue of the Parthian prince, held in the National Museum of Iran (Tehran), shows the typical clothing of the northern horseman, with baggy trousers and soft leather coverings. He can be compared with Kanishka, the Kushana ruler, who was also wearing clothing that goes with the nomadic horsemen of the north. In short, by the mid-second century B.C.E., West Turkistan had reverted, politically and culturally, back to Central Asia.

By the fourth century C.E., new migrants arrived along the northern borders of West Turkistan. These were Chionites and Hephthalites, who were related to the Huns, who by that time had invaded the Roman Empire in faraway Europe. The Chionites and Hephthalites were soon followed by the Turks, who in the sixth century C.E. managed to gain a strong foothold in the area that forms West Turkistan in the early twenty-first century. The arrival of the newcomers marked the end of the millennia-old push from the north by Iranian-speaking peoples; from that time on, the Iranian nomads in Central Asia were replaced by mainly Turkish groups. However, the main feature remained: a constant push by Central Asian migrants into the lands of West Turkistan and the Iranian Plateau.

Whether Iranian or Turkish, the Central Asian nomads showed many common characteristics. They were all horsemen, they dressed in the typical clothing of the horse rider, and they were armed with very comparable weapons. The short composite bow, first used by the Scythians in the early first millennium B.C.E., was still used by the Turks and even by the Mongols of Genghis Khan in the thirteenth century C.E. The famous bow-and-arrow case of the Scythians, described by the classical Greeks as the *gorytos*, looks remarkably like the case carried by the Mongolians some two thousand years later.

ISLAM AND THE PERSIAN REVIVAL

By the middle of the first millennium C.E., West Turkistan had become a battleground between the Turks from the north, the Iranians from the south, and the Chinese and Tibetans from the east. The potential reward for the domination of the deserts and mountains of West Turkistan was the control of the lucrative trade along the Silk Road. This trade, which included precious silk from China, expanded significantly throughout the first millennium. Sogdia, along the Silk Road, flourished during this period. The cities of Sogdia were known not only for their use of Chinese and Persian textiles but also for the production of textiles with intricate designs, especially of animals and human figures.

Surviving Sogdian mural paintings, dating from about the fifth to eighth centuries C.E., give an idea of the clothes and textiles available at this period. Clothes of deities on a fifth-century painting from Pendzhikent, for example, are plain-colored. Later, in the sixth and seventh centuries, textiles depicted on paintings are patterned with small ornaments. From the seventh century on, large ornaments came into fashion, and the outfits are filled with Sassanian (Persian)-style patterns; in particular, animal motifs encircled in pearl roundels. Chinese damask silks and Tang rosette silks appear in the paintings of the early eighth century. In the murals from the mid-eighth century, animal motifs in medallions are no longer seen and are replaced by flowers. A range of actual textiles with similar designs was found during excavations at the site of Mount Mug in ancient Sogdia. Numerous textiles were found that have been dated to between the seventh and eighth centuries C.E. Among the forty-four fragments of silks that were recorded, twenty-four were identified as Chinese damask silks. It has been proven that one pouch discovered there was made from Chinese damask silks woven with a paired-dragons pattern.

Into this melee entered the Arab armies, pushed on by the new message of Mohammed. Islam arrived in West Turkistan soon after the death of Mohammed in 632 C.E. By the middle of the seventh century, Muslim armies had occupied much of what is twenty-first-century Iran, and they also penetrated as far as western Afghanistan. The plains north of the Kopet Dagh (ancient Parthia), the delta of the Murghab River (ancient Margiana), and the lands along the Zerafshan River (ancient Sogdia) were soon occupied as well. By the mid-eighth century, after the defeat of the Chinese at the Battle of the Talas (751 C.E.) in the Fergana Valley, Islam ruled supreme in West Turkistan.

By the eighth century C.E., West Turkistan, by then populated by Iranian and Turkish ethnic groups, was rapidly becoming part of the Muslim world. Located along the Silk Road, politically rather stable, and with oases producing food to sustain a growing population, the lands of West Turkistan flourished. Some of the wide range of textiles and related items available in this region were described by an Arab historian and traveler of the tenth century, Abu-Abdallah al-Mukaddasi (al-Makdisi). In particular, he noted that from here came furs such as sable, squirrel, weasel, fox, beaver, and goat skins, as well as special caps, striped cloaks, cloth for blankets, brocades for presents, and veils of cloth made from silk and cotton.

The lands of West Turkistan soon developed a degree of autonomy from the caliphal court in Baghdad. A number of dynasties arose, mainly of Iranian origin, which propagated their Iranian culture while at the same time stressing their Islamic credentials. One of the major Iranian dynasties was that of the Samanids, who had their center in ancient Sogdia (Bukhara). This development is often called the Iranian renaissance. It not only helped to preserve the Iranian languages, especially supporting the spread of Farsi (or Persian, an Iranian language originally spoken only in southwestern Iran), but also emphasized many aspects of Iranian culture, such as the celebration of the New Year's festival around 21 March. The renaissance also led to the spread of Persian-language literature, including accounts of the ancient kings of Iran. The major work in this respect is the *Shahnama*, a poetic work from around 1000 C.E. by the poet Ferdowsi that is still the major literary work in the Iranian world.

However, the rise of the Iranian dynasties in the east of the Muslim world coincided with a growing dependence on Turkish slaves, soldiers, and administrators. By the end of the first millennium, the former slaves took over much of the political control in West Turkistan and eastern Iran and started a long series of predominantly Turkish dynasties. The most famous of the Turkish dynasties is that of the Ghaznavids, who ruled large parts of West Turkistan, Afghanistan, and northern India from their capital in Ghazni, south of Kabul, from the late tenth to the mid-twelfth century C.E.

GENGHIS KHAN AND THE UZBEK EMIRATES

The time of the Turkish dynasties was ended by the arrival in West Turkistan of the Mongolian ruler Genghis Khan and his armies. In 1219 C.E., he invaded Chorasmia and the rest of West Turkistan and eastern Iran. The great cities were destroyed and their populations killed. Although the Mongols destroyed the cities and irrigation works, in the end this also opened up West Turkistan and Iran to the wider world, especially promoting contacts with Mongolia and China. The Mongolian dynasties that were to rule West Turkistan in the years that followed introduced Mongolian and Chinese traditions. This can be clearly seen in the textiles from the area, which are decorated with Chinese dragons, peonies, and other such motifs from these traditions.

By the early sixteenth century, momentous developments changed the ethnic composition of much of West Turkistan. By that time, new migrants arrived from the north, from what is Kazakhstan in the early twenty-first century. These were the Uzbeks of Turkish/Mongolian stock. They mainly settled along the Zerafshan River, in and around the cities of Bukhara and Samarkand, but groups of Uzbeks also moved into northern Afghanistan and beyond. They soon established three independent emirates, namely Khiva, Bukhara, and Khojend. The history of these emirates shows a steady decline in the prosperity of West Turkistan. The trade along the Silk Road had almost come to a complete stop, having been to a large degree replaced by the seaborne trade across the Indian Ocean dominated by the Europeans. West Turkistan also came under growing pressure from the expanding empire of tsarist Russia.

West Turkistan subsequently became more and more isolated, not only economically but also culturally. Visits by foreigners were discouraged, to say the least, and local rulers, strongly influenced by religious leaders, did all they could to keep foreign influences out. By the second half of the nineteenth century, however, Russia had captured all of the emirates, and by the end of the nineteenth century, they also managed to defeat the Turkmen, thus completing their conquest of West Turkistan. What followed was a period of rapid Westernization, accelerated after the Russian Revolution of 1917 by the inclusion of West Turkistan into the Soviet empire. As far as clothing is concerned, the Soviet leaders started a campaign to stop local women from wearing the typical horsehair face veil.

References and Further Reading

Harvey, Janet. *Traditional Textiles of Central Asia*. London: Thames and Hudson, 1996.
Kalter, Johannes. *The Arts and Crafts of Turkestan*. London: Thames and Hudson, 1984.
Makdisi. *Descriptio Imperii Moslemic*, edited by M. J. de Goeje. Leiden: Bibliotheca Geographorum Arabicorum, 1876.
Serjeant, R.B. *Islamic Textiles: Material for a History up to the Mongol Conquest*. Beirut: Librairie Du Liban, 1972.

Willem Vogelsang

See also Iranian Urban Dress; Regional Dress of Afghanistan; Afghan Dress and the Diaspora; Turkmen Dress and Embroidery; Dress from Tajikistan and Uzbekistan.

Trouser Wearing by Horse-Riding Nomads in Central Asia

Trousers are a normal part of dress in many areas of the world. They are a common feature of men's attire and recently also of women's. However, anyone traveling to Southwest Asia or other parts of the world will notice that trousers are not a universally worn garment. Local men in Arabia and elsewhere do not wear trousers but prefer long gowns or hip wraps to cover their legs. The Indian dhoti, a length of cloth wrapped around the hips and/or passed between the legs to create a form of loincloth, is another example of a man's garment that is very different from a pair of trousers. The classical toga, a wraparound garment used by Roman male citizens to show their social status, is not worn with trousers either, and the ancient Greeks are hardly ever portrayed wearing them. Trousers may thus be thought to be a typically modern Western feature. Yet this soon proves not to be true either, since men in, for instance, Turkey, Iran, Afghanistan, and large parts of Central Asia wear trousers and seem to have done so for centuries. How did it happen that men in some cultures wear trousers, while those in others do not?

The generic term *trousers* is used to indicate a garment used by both men and women that is worn on the lower part of the body from the waist to the ankles and covers each leg separately. In Central Asia and Southwest Asia, practical considerations, such as horse riding and, later, religious prescriptions (Islamic) have, however, meant that trousers, often called *shalwar*, look very different from their narrower, Western-style counterparts. Shalwars can be found throughout Central and Southwest Asia, as well as in neighboring countries such as India and Pakistan. This type of garment is normally baggy, with a low crotch (for ease of movement and to disguise the appearance of the genitalia), and reaches to the ankles. Shalwar do not have a fly in the male or female versions and are kept in place around the waist or hips using a waistband with a drawstring rather than buttons or a zipper-and-button combination. The lack of a fly, their baggy nature, and the length are important as these avoid emphasizing the genitalia, in accordance with Islamic concepts of personal modesty. There are many different variations in the cut of these trousers, which relate to regional and cultural differences. As a result, shalwar from Afghanistan are cut in very different ways from those from Turkey, and so forth.

THE ANCIENT SCYTHIANS

Perhaps the earliest extant pair of trousers, as far as known to date, was worn by the so-called Cherchen Man from northwestern China. The mummy, which dates to about 1000 B.C.E., is housed in the Urumchi Museum in the early twenty-first century. The Cherchen Man was about fifty-five years old when he died. He had light brown hair and wore, apart from brightly colored woolen trousers, also a shirt and leggings made of felt.

The mummy belongs to a rich conglomerate of finds from northwestern China and neighboring Kazakhstan, which relate to the mainly nomadic cultures of Central Asia. Trousers have traditionally been linked to horse-riding nomads, and the trousers of the Cherchen Man, therefore, seem to constitute the first evidence of trousers being worn in the Eurasian steppes. From Eurasia, the custom of wearing trousers spread to adjoining lands, to Europe in the west, to Turkey and the Iranian lands to the south and southwest, and, by the fourth century B.C.E., also to China itself, when trousers were adopted by Chinese cavalry. The main push in the spread of trousers occurred in the first millennium B.C.E., when Scythian horse riders wearing trousers occupied large parts of Eurasia and Southwest Asia.

The Scythians, or Sakas, are often linked to the Urumchi finds. By the middle of the first millennium B.C.E., the Scythians had spread out from Kazakhstan and occupied large parts of the Eurasian plains, as far west as the Danube in East Europe. They were horse-riding nomads, continuously moving with their herds from site to site and constituting a constant menace to the sedentary peoples living along the fringes of the steppes. The Scythians are well known for their grave mounds or tumuli (kurgans), which are scattered all over their former lands, for instance, in Ukraine and Siberia. There, the Scythian chiefs were buried amid a vast wealth of golden objects and chariots, as well as their slaves and concubines. Many objects were later excavated and are exhibited, among other places, in the Hermitage in Saint Petersburg, Russia.

Classical Greek sources confirm that in the mid-first millennium B.C.E. many of the lands north of the Black Sea were inhabited by the Scythians. The Greek historian Herodotus, writing in the fifth century B.C.E., dedicated a complete book of his *Histories* to them (Book IV). He tells that they had settled in the plains of the Ukraine and southern Russia relatively recently and that they ultimately derived from lands far away in the east. He also tells that they were mainly nomads, migrating with their animals across the endless expanse of Eurasia.

What struck the ancient Greeks most, however, was Scythian dress. In this respect, the Scythians were very different from the Greeks. While the Greeks and almost all other peoples around the Mediterranean at that time were wearing gowns or hip wraps, the Scythians were wearing trousers. To the Greeks this was very strange. Trousers were regarded as exotic and vaguely feminine. They said that the legendary Assyrian queen Semiramis invented trousers when she was forced to ride a long distance across a wild terrain in order to visit her husband (Diodorus II, 6). The Greeks also regarded trousers as particularly unhealthy. A Greek author, generally known as Pseudo-Hippocrates, who wrote in the mid-fifth century B.C.E., tells his readers that the general health of the Scythians was very poor and that constant horse riding made the men impotent, a condition that was aggravated by their use of trousers. Trousers, according to Pseudo-Hippocrates, made it impossible for Scythian men to play with their genitals. It is, therefore, no surprise that when Scythians are depicted in Greek art, they are characterized by their strange apparel, namely the trousers. Objects recovered from the ancient tumuli, sometimes supposedly made by Greek craftsmen, also depict these Scythians, and again they are all dressed in trousers.

Apart from trousers, the Scythians also wore tunics and a pointed cap called a *bashlyq*, which covered their head, chin, and neck. Much of the clothing, including the tunic and trousers, was made of leather, wool, or felt and often embellished with embroidery and tassels. The clothing of the Scythians must have looked very colorful. In the depictions, all Scythian men have long, uncurled hair and a similar beard, very different from the curly hair of the Greeks. Their weaponry was also different from the Greeks'. They carried a rather short sword (called *akinakes* by the Greeks) and a bow-and-arrow case (the *gorytos*), which contained a short composite bow and an assortment of arrows. Sometimes they are also shown wielding a battle axe (called a *sagaris* by the Greeks).

Very little is known about the clothing of Scythian women. Evidence comes in the form of a few depictions and finds from various tombs. From these, it is possible to deduce that they wore long gowns and skirt-and-blouse combinations and that these were heavily decorated. However, from later history, it appears

that these nomadic women, when on the move, wore trousers. The Greek legend about Queen Semiramis, recounted by Diodorus, may reflect this point. According to this story, she wore trousers because they would protect her from the heat and would not hinder her movement at all. The Greek writer also said that the Persians and Medes, and other Eurasian steppe nomads, were still wearing Semiramis' dress, namely, a tunic and trousers.

PERSEPOLIS

The Persians and Medes used to live in the area that forms Iran in the early twenty-first century. The Medes formed the dominant power around 600 B.C.E., but they were shortly afterward overwhelmed by their southeastern neighbors, the Persians, around 550 B.C.E. The Persian capital for ceremonies and religious rituals was at Persepolis, just north of the town of Shiraz, in the southwest of modern Iran. Here was the center of the Persian Achaemenid Empire, which from the middle of the sixth to the late fourth century B.C.E. dominated most of Southwest Asia, stretching as far east as the Indus River in modern Pakistan and the banks of the Syr Dar'ya in modern Uzbekistan.

The magnificent palace complex of Persepolis, known in Iran as Takht-i Jamshid, was pillaged and burned down by Alexander the Great in 330 B.C.E. Along the northern and eastern facades of the ruined Apadana (the great audience hall and portico), reliefs

A comb ornamented with a group of Scythians in combat, Solokha, South Russia, sixth to fourth century B.C.E. The Scythians were horse-riding nomads who occupied large parts of the Eurasian plains. This comb clearly shows them wearing trousers. Scythian dress styles were documented by Greek writers who regarded gowns or hip wraps as typical male dress and trousers as exotic and unhealthy garments. Time & Life Pictures/Getty Images.

depict delegations wearing their characteristic dress from all over the empire. These delegations are shown as they are ceremoniously approaching the king in order to offer their gifts. The scene probably illustrates a real annual ritual in which representatives from different parts of the empire offered the king some gifts that symbolized their submission; in return, the king would undoubtedly have given the delegates far more sumptuous gifts to show his superior position.

The delegations, each consisting of a group of men led by a foreman and ushered in by a courtier, are depicted on both facades, in mirror images. They are clad in their traditional type of dress, and sometimes their typical physiognomy and hairstyle are shown. Their gifts are particular to the country they come from. For instance, the depiction of the delegation from southern Egypt shows people with curly hair presenting a giraffe. The delegates from the banks of the Indus River are shown wearing a loincloth and sandals, and they present a humped bull.

The typical dress and features of the various delegates are also illustrated in other, contemporary reliefs, such as those at the tombs of the Achaemenid kings. These can be found at Persepolis, close to the palaces, and at nearby Naqsh-i-Rustam. Here, delegates from the empire are carrying a platform on which the king is sacrificing to the gods. Again, the delegates are wearing their distinctive clothing. Moreover, in contrast to the Apadana reliefs, on two of the tombs, which are almost identical, the delegates are identified with labels telling who they are and where they come from.

Most of the delegates on the Apadana and other Achaemenid reliefs wear a type of loincloth (the delegates from India) or a long gown or hip wrap (the delegates from Mesopotamia, Egypt, Ionia and the Greek islands, and other areas.). In addition, the Persian Achaemenid king and his direct entourage are shown at Persepolis wearing long gowns. Gowns and robes were clearly the main item of men's dress in large parts of the Persian Achaemenid Empire. However, some delegations are clearly different. They do not wear gowns but trousers. Many of these trouser-wearing delegates show other, very distinctive features as well, which taken together define an easily recognizable group of delegations. These other features include the delegates' long, straight hair and a long beard; a tunic; and a long, cutaway coat or a coat with empty sleeves. They also wear weaponry that differs from that of the others, including a bow-and-arrow case that contains a composite bow and arrows, a battle axe, and a short sword. Their jewelry includes bracelets and torques. Many of the delegations also bring particular presents, such as a beautiful horse or a Central Asian (Bactrian) camel.

Geographically, all of these trouser-wearing delegations derive from the northwest, north, and northeast of the Persian Achaemenid Empire. They originate from the long belt of lands that stretches from the delta of the Danube River in the west to the borders of China in the east, and from the banks of the Volga River in the north to the deserts of Central Iran in the south. It is clear that they should be identified with the Scythians mentioned by the Greeks.

THE ACHAEMENID SAKAS

To the Persian Achaemenids, the Scythians were known as the Sakas. Herodotus correspondingly relates that the Scythians were called Sakas by the Persians (*Hist.* VII 64). While Herodotus and the Greeks were mainly involved with the Scythians who lived north of the Black Sea, the Persian Achaemenids also had dealings with Scythian/Saka groups that lived much further east. As shown on the Apadana reliefs and other Persian Achaemenid monuments, trouser-wearing groups used to live in all the northern lands of the Persian Achaemenid Empire, from the extreme northwest to the extreme northeast. However, they were not restricted to the Eurasian plains north of the Black Sea and north and east of the Caspian. In fact, some typically Scythian features, including trousers, can be detected among delegates who lived south of the Black Sea in modern Turkey, in lands south of the Caucasus, but also in large parts of the area that comprises eastern Iran and Afghanistan in the early twenty-first century. The Persian Achaemenid sources thus demonstrate that Scythian features, including trousers, had spread to large parts of Southwest Asia by about 500 B.C.E.

The Persepolis monuments mention a number of groups that are specifically listed as being Saka: They are the Saka Paradraya, the Saka Tigraxauda, the Saka Haumavarga, and the Saka para Sugdam. The Saka Paradraya, literally "Sakas beyond the sea," lived across the Bosporus and along the western and northern shores of the Black Sea. They are the Sakas, or Scythians, described by Herodotus in his *Histories*. The Saka Tigraxauda, literally "Sakas with a pointed cap," lived along the eastern shores of the Caspian Sea, in the northeast of the Achaemenid Empire. The Saka Haumavarga, literally "The haoma-twisting Sakas," lived even further east, in the plains and mountains of Tajikistan and neighboring areas, north of modern Afghanistan. Their name refers to their use of *haoma*, probably a hallucinogenic substance known in Indian tradition as soma. Finally, the name of the Saka para Sugdam indicates that they lived "beyond Sugda." Sugda, or Sogdia, was the old name for the lands between modern Bukhara and Samarkand in Uzbekistan. The four Saka groups all lived along the northern borders of the Persian Achaemenid Empire. Their attire in the reliefs is typical for the Scythians and includes trousers.

However, other delegations had equally Scythian features and lived in clearly defined regions. These are the Chorasmians from south of the Aral Sea and the Sogdians from along the Zerafshan River (around modern Bukhara and Samarkand). Their attire is identical to that of the various Saka groups. Further south there are the Bactrians from modern northern Afghanistan and the Parthians from modern northern Iran and southern Turkmenistan. Their attire is slightly different. They still wear trousers and boots or combined trouser-boots, and their weapon is the akinakes. However, they do not wear a bashlyq, instead covering their hair with a turban, held together with a fillet, or gathering their hair in a bag. Their hair is not straight but curly.

Further south, there are the people from ancient Areia (around modern Herat in western Afghanistan) and Drangiana (in southeastern Afghanistan). They wear baggy trousers or knee-length trousers tucked into high boots. They also wear a tunic, and their hair is covered by a turban or fillet. Their hair is curly. Their weapon is the akinakes.

Finally, there is the western group. This consists of the Medes (west central Iran), the Armenians (modern Armenia), and the Cappadocians (eastern Turkey). They wear combined trouser-boots, a tunic, and a bashlyq, and their weapon is, again, the akinakes. Their hair and beards are curly. The Medes are, moreover, often portrayed with the bow-and-arrow case.

Additional information is provided by Herodotus, in his so-called army roster of Xerxes' army (*Hist.* VII 61ff.). It lists the various contingents of the Persian Achaemenid army when mobilized against Greece in the early fifth century B.C.E., their commanders, and sometimes their clothing and weaponry. He tells that the Bactrians, Parthians, Chorasmians, and Sogdians, from the northeastern parts of the empire, all used the same type of clothing and weaponry. This would essentially be the Scythian dress and armament. Herodotus also adds the Areians, from the province of Areia in modern western Afghanistan, as well as the Gandharians and the Dadicae. The two latter groups are very interesting, since they lived in the area that forms eastern Afghanistan in the early twenty-first century, somewhere around Kabul and Peshawar, directly south of the famous Hindu Kush passes that connect Central Asia and northern Afghanistan with the Indus plains. It would indicate that Scythian influence had spread south across the Hindu Kush by at least the sixth century B.C.E.

One specific garment worn by some of the Scythian groups shown on the Apadana, including the Medes and a Scythian delegation from modern southwestern Afghanistan, is a long coat with long, empty sleeves, worn over the shoulders. This garment is called a *kandys* by the Greeks. The Greek author and general Xenophon commented on this garment around 400 B.C.E., saying that the Persians, when approaching their king, had to put their arms into their sleeves. This would mean that normally the Persians did not stick their arms into their sleeves. It is a garment that belongs to an ancient and widespread tradition, originating in Central Asia, of coats with very long sleeves and a front opening. The *chapan*, a long coat with long, empty sleeves, worn over the shoulder (made famous in the early twenty-first century by Hamid Karzai while president of Afghanistan), belongs to the same tradition. In the early twenty-first century, the chapan coat is generally worn by the Uzbeks, an ethnic group that around 1500 C.E. moved from Kazakhstan in Central Asia to the south, to Uzbekistan and northern Afghanistan.

All the Scythian features stand in marked contrast to the clothing and weaponry of the Persian Achaemenid rulers. They wear long robes and carry long lances, huge shields, and longbows. These are not the weapons, and certainly not the garments, of horsemen. The Greeks are quite clear that the Persians provided the infantry of the Persian Achaemenid army, while the

Relief from the Palace of Darius showing Scythian tributaries, Persepolis, Iran, 522–486 B.C.E. Most of the delegates on the reliefs from Persepolis wear a type of loincloth (the delegates from India) or a long gown or hip wrap (the delegates from Mesopotamia, Egypt, and the Greek islands). This relief of Scythian delegates is distinct from all the others, as they wear trousers and cutaway coats. Roger Viollet/Getty Images.

"northern" lands, with their Scythian population, provided the cavalry. That was also the case when Alexander the Great invaded the Achaemenid Empire in the second half of the fourth century. At Gaugamela, where Alexander finally defeated the Persian Achaemenid army in 331 B.C.E., the extreme right wing of the Persian army was occupied by the Armenians and Cappadocians and the extreme left wing by the Bactrians and Sakas (Arrian, *Anab.* III 8.3ff.). The cavalry of the empire was thus clearly provided mainly by the Scythian groups, no doubt wearing trousers and armed with the akinakes and the composite bow, while the Persians and others provided the bulk of the infantry.

THE ORIGIN OF THE SCYTHIANS

Herodotus tells a long story about the origin of the Scythians. According to the Greek historiographer, the Scythians (from north of the Black Sea) originated from far away. Their movements formed part of a large chain of migrations that started far in the east, with one group of people pushing away another. In the end, according to Herodotus, the tribe of the Massagetae pushed the Scythians across the Araxes River and into the land of the Cimmerians. In turn, the Scythians drove the Cimmerians away, across the Caucasus into the lands of Southwest Asia. The Scythians followed them and ended up in western Iran, where they attacked the Medes of west central Iran when the latter were just about to defeat the Assyrians at Nineveh. The Scythians, still according to Herodotus, subsequently dominated the Medes and "all of Asia" for twenty-eight years, after which the Scythian leaders were all killed by the Median king Cyaxares. After that, the surviving Scythians fled back across the Caucasus into modern southern Russia and the Ukraine.

Cimmerian and Scythian presence in Southwest Asia is well attested in Southwest Asian sources. They are called the Gimirrai and Ishguzai. They are described as horse-riding bowmen who, in the late eighth and seventh centuries B.C.E., spread terror in Southwest Asia. In the Bible, but also in other sources, the names of the Scythians and Cimmerians are often interchanged. The Bible even relates that Ashkenaz was the son of Gomer (Gen. 10:2–3), although these two names are probably linguistically linked to the Scythians and the Cimmerians, respectively. The prophet Jeremiah probably refers to them when he describes the terrifying opponents of the Babylonians: "Behold, a people is coming from the north country, a great nation is stirring from the farthest parts of the earth. They lay hold on bow and spear; they are cruel and have no mercy, the sound of them is like the roaring sea; they ride upon horses, set in array as a man for battle, against you, O daughter of Zion" (Jer. 51:27).

Traditionally, Herodotus' account has been interpreted as referring to a Cimmerian and Scythian invasion of Southwest Asia from north of the modern Caucasus, between the Black Sea and the Caspian. However, there is ample evidence for a different interpretation. An important text in this context is by the Greek physician Ctesias, who around 400 B.C.E. worked at the Persian court and wrote an account of Persian and Median history, the *Persica*. He tells that the Medes, the predecessors of the Persians as the dominant power in Iran, were attacked in the back by the Bactrians when they were about to take the Assyrian capital of Nineveh. This text is very much in accordance with what Herodotus is saying, but instead of the Scythians attacking the Medes in the back, Ctesias refers to the Bactrians. Bactria was the name

for the area that constitutes northern Afghanistan in the early twenty-first century, and in the Persian Achaemenid reliefs, the Bactrians, and all the other peoples in eastern Iran and adjacent districts, were characterized by their Scythian features.

This would mean that Herodotus' account does not refer to an initial migration of the Scythians from north to south across the modern Caucasus. Instead, it tells of a Scythian migration from South Central Asia via northern Afghanistan and northeastern Iran to the west. Herodotus, when recounting the story of the origins of the Southwest Asian Scythians, was referring to an eastern homeland of the Scythians. The Caucasus Mountains that he refers to may just as well be the mountains of eastern Iran. Herodotus did not have any idea of the geography of the Iranian Plateau, and the name of the Caucasus was still applied to the Hindu Kush Mountains.

The mass movement of nomads from east to west and southwest, across the Eurasian steppes, is well attested from various periods in history. During periods of drought, nomads are forced to migrate in search of food and water. The whole process often starts in the far east, in Mongolia, where one tribe will move west in search of water, pushing another ethnic group out of their homeland. In their turn, this other group will move on, forcing another group out of the way. This cycle of migrations often leads in the end to invasions by nomadic groups of lands far in the west (Ukraine, East Europe) and in the southwest (Iran, Afghanistan). In the first millennium C.E., the ancient Turks in this way migrated from their ancestral lands in Central Asia, via South Central Asia, to Afghanistan and Iran, and then even further west to what is called Turkey in the early twenty-first century. Some of the Turkish tribes actually ended up in southern Afghanistan, recalling Herodotus' reference to Scythian clothing and armament being worn by some ethnic groups south of the Hindu Kush.

THE SCYTHIAN REVOLUTION

Scythian features, including trousers, had thus spread over a huge area by the middle of the first millennium B.C.E. Trousers were worn by the Scythian nomads on the Eurasian steppes but also by various groups in Southwest Asia and on the Iranian Plateau. They were probably also worn by people living southeast of the Hindu Kush in the Kabul area. Southwest Asian sources reveal that the Scythians and Cimmerians settled there by, at the latest, the late eighth century B.C.E. If it is accepted that these horse-riding, trouser-wearing nomads arrived from the east, they had reached western Iran by at least the mid-eighth century B.C.E., and before that they must have settled in, or passed through, the areas comprising eastern Iran and Afghanistan in the early twenty-first century. Along their routes, they and their culture affected the local population.

The Medes of west central Iran provide a good example. The Medes' Scythian features are clearly indicated in the Apadana reliefs. Scythian domination of the Medes, as recounted by Herodotus, may well reflect real history. Herodotus (*Hist.* I 73) tells that the Medes used to send their young men to the Scythians in order to learn their language and how to shoot with the bow. He does not say this, but the young Medes may well have learned to wear trousers as well. The Persians, normally wearing a long gown, donned trousers when they rode horses, which also reveals Scythian influence. Furthermore, the Greek geographer Strabo (*Geogr.* XI 13.9), writing at the beginning of the modern era, states that the Persians learned many characteristics from the Medes, including horse riding, archery, and trouser-wearing.

Wearing trousers is thus originally a feature of horse-riding nomads. Beginning in about 1000 B.C.E., the custom of wearing trousers spread from the steppes of Kazakhstan and adjacent lands to the west, toward Europe, and to the southwest, to areas comprising Iran and Afghanistan in the early twenty-first century, and hence deep into Southwest Asia. The migrations of Scythian horse riders onto the Iranian Plateau continued into the early centuries of the Common Era, when they were succeeded by the Turks and other horse-riding ethnic groups from Central Asia. The Turks subsequently occupied large parts of modern Afghanistan and Iran and, in the footsteps of the early Scythians of about 800 B.C.E., moved on to Turkey, where they firmly established the custom of wearing trousers.

References and Further Reading

Barber, Elizabeth Wayland. *The Mummies of Ürümchi: Did Europeans Migrate to China 4,000 Year Ago?* New York: Norton, 1999.

Rolle, Renate. *Die Welt der Skythen. Stutenmelker und Pferdebogner: Ein antikes Reitervolk in neuer Sicht.* Luzern and Frankfurt am Main: Bucher Verlag, 1980.

Vogelsang, W.J. *The Rise and Organisation of the Achaemenid Empire: The Eastern Evidence.* Leiden, New York, and Cologne: Brill, 1992.

Willem Vogelsang

See also Historical Survey of Textiles and Dress in Turkey; Regional Dress of Afghanistan; Turkmen Dress and Embroidery.

Turkmen Dress and Embroidery

The region known as West Turkistan lies in a large geographic depression. It is bounded by the Caspian Sea to the west, the Altai chain of mountains and the foothills of the Tien Shan range in the east, and the Kopet Dagh mountains and the Hindu Kush to the south, while the northern limits of the region are usually marked by the Aral Sea. The majority of the Turkmen live around the Kara-Kum ("Black Sand") Desert, which lies to the east of the Caspian Sea, between the Amu Dar'ya River and the mountains bordering the northern edge of the Iranian Plateau (Kopet Dagh). In the early twenty-first century, the Turkmen region is divided among Afghanistan, Iran, and the former Soviet Union. Most of the Turkmen live in modern Turkmenistan (about 1.8 million people), while about one million Turkmen live in Iran, mainly in the northeastern provinces of Gurgan and North Khorasan, and about 900,000 Turkmen live in Afghanistan. The latter are largely concentrated along the Turkmen-Afghan border in the provinces of Faryab and Jowzjan. It should be stressed that the Turkmen of these countries have been separated by international boundaries for only some one hundred years. Prior to this period there were constant, and relatively easy, trade and social contacts between the various groups. Turkmen also engaged in textile trade during the nineteenth century for different varieties of cotton, mainly originating from Russia and Europe; however, the production of silk from native silkworms, especially for women's dress, was a principal element of Turkmen domestic life.

The various Turkmen tribes consider themselves a single ethnic group. According to the U.S. anthropologist William G. Irons, the Turkmen define their Turkic identity on the basis of these criteria: (a) The person must be a descendant of Turkmen or the slaves of Turkmen in the male line, or a descendant in the male line of individuals who have lived for several generations among the Turkmen, (b) the person must be a native speaker of the Turkmen language, and (c) the person must be a Sunni Muslim of the Hanafi school. The five main Central Asian Turkmen houses or tribes are, in alphabetical order, the Chowdur, Ersari, Saryk, Teke, and Yomut, with smaller subgroups such as the Guklani, Nikhali, and Salor.

In the early twentieth century, the majority of the Central Asian Turkmen were nomads living in felt tents (yurts). At the end of the twentieth century, there was a mixture of settled and semi-nomadic groups. Since the mid-twentieth century, many settled Turkmen have changed from using draft animals to mechanized farming; they cultivate wheat and barley. Other Turkmen, especially those in more arid regions, have tended to be much more conservative and continued traditional practices of livestock production and a limited amount of agriculture, specifically drought-resistant crops that can survive irregular supplies of rain.

Agricultural production in the plains is possible only with the help of artificial irrigation. Within the Iranian region, for example, use has been made of the so-called *karez* system, whereby deep wells are dug at places where groundwater collects. From these wells, tunnels with a gentle gradation are excavated, leading into the plains. Mulberry trees, which need a lot of water, were planted on a large scale in order to provide mulberry leaves, which are essential for feeding silkworms. Until the mid-twentieth century, much of the silk used for making clothing, especially that of women, was home produced. By the end of the century, cheaper imported synthetic materials had become more widely available and were generally used for clothing.

Another ancient crop in this region is cotton. The technology was introduced in the medieval period from India and has spread throughout the Turkmen world. In the early twenty-first century, very little cotton is produced in Turkmenistan, although it is an important crop in some neighboring countries. Finally, part of the Turkmen income comes from the production of carpets. These are woven from the wool of local sheep by the women of many Turkmen households.

Among many Turkmen in the latter half of the twentieth century, there are still strict codes of behavior with respect to how one person treats another. These codes depend on various factors, including gender (male/female), age (young/old), social position within the hierarchy (low/senior), and marital affiliations (daughter/daughter-in-law), and so forth. Thus, a younger brother must show respect to an older brother. The subordination of wives to husbands is even greater. When a husband's guest or older brothers are present, a young wife must cover her mouth with her head covering and not speak; this situation changes as she has children and grows more senior. The young wife must sit in a section of the tent or house reserved for people of low status and obey quickly any orders from her husband or his older brothers. The rules are even more stringent between a woman and her father-in-law and mother-in-law. Although by the end of the twentieth century these rules were changing rapidly due to new economic conditions, educational institutions, and telecommunication, these traditional social practices still play an important role in Turkmen social behavior. These social norms have had a profound influence on garments, especially those worn by women around their heads and faces.

The dress worn by Iranian Turkmen in northeastern Iran can be taken as an example of Turkmen dress, along with additional details regarding Turkmen groups from Turkmenistan and Afghanistan.

TURKMEN DRESS IN GENERAL

The subject of Turkmen dress, as with other groups, is not simple. Dress is constantly developing and changing. For this reason, the descriptions of Turkmen living near the Caspian Sea, and more specifically Iranian Turkmen dress, should be regarded as indicating general lines rather than specific details. The range of garments and the interrelationship between garments and jewelry is of great importance within Turkmen society and life in general, especially for women.

The Turkmen have long had access to a wide array of materials, ranging from cheap cottons from India to high-quality silks from China. During the medieval period, for instance, there was considerable trade in gold brocades (nasij) and silk to and from what was then Persia and the Chinese/Mongol Empire. Much of this cloth traveled through the Turkmenistan region. During the nineteenth century, there was also considerable trade in raw and woven cotton, especially from Russia and Europe, notably from the cities of Manchester and Glasgow in Great Britain. The use of cloth coming from a variety of countries is a feature of Turkmen clothing, including that from the nineteenth century and continuing until the beginning of the twenty-first century.

In the nineteenth and early twentieth centuries, the production of silk cloth, however, was an important aspect of Turkmen domestic life. Women looked after the mulberry trees on which the silkworms fed. Much of the silk used for men's and women's clothing was locally woven on a pit-treadle loom, a narrow loom where the foot treadles are placed in a pit beneath the loom frame. The weaver then sits at the edge of the pit working the heddle treadles with his or her feet. This type of loom was still in use among the Guklan Turkmen in Iran during the 1970s. The cloth woven on the pit-treadle loom tends to have a finished width of between twelve to sixteen inches (thirty to forty centimeters). When silk production increased in the early twentieth century, silk-reeling workshops were set up and men took over this occupation.

When intended for use as clothing (especially dresses and some types of coats), silk cloth was usually a raspberry red color with yellow stripes near the selvedges. Sometimes, dark red, green, or purple variations were also woven, but the mid-red form was the most popular. This material was widely used for dresses, which were worn by both girls and married women. Material intended for coats, in contrast, was usually woven with a series of stripes in various combinations of red with yellow, blue, and white. The modern version of this cloth, both for dresses and coats, tends to be made out of synthetic silk or a mixture of fibers, but it is worth noting that the same loom width and stripe form of decoration are used.

During the nineteenth and early twentieth centuries, the main source in Central Asia of a red dye was madder (Rubia tinctoria) and a local cochineal. These were superseded in the twentieth century by synthetic red dyes from Germany, Russia, and Great Britain. Textile historian Janet Harvey has noted that, in general, the Turkmen used Russian dyes, while the Afghans used British dyes; this difference reflects the economic and political connections of the period.

In the early twenty-first century, a wide variety of materials is available from both internal and external sources. In general, however, Iranian products tend to be cheaper and less highly regarded than foreign items, such as those from Japan, Korea, and Thailand, as well as the more long-standing sources of Russia and India. The wearing of garments made from these materials carries with it higher prestige.

EMBROIDERY: GENERAL

As in many Central and Southwest Asian cultures, embroidery (nams or kesde) plays an important role in the lives of many Turkmen women and girls. At the beginning of the twentieth century, vast quantities of embroideries were produced, which were used to decorate homes and clothing, as well as for coverings, bags, animal trappings, and the like.

Embroidery is still used to decorate the garments worn by Turkmen women and children and, to a much lesser extent, men. It is also a manner for women to express their creativity and Turkmen cultural heritage and, in some cases, to earn a living. Although embroideries are thus still being produced, it has been noted by various authors that the quantity and quality of embroidery being produced at the end of the twentieth century are considerably lower than before. This decline is partially due to the fact that embroidery requires time, and more and more girls are attending school and so have less time to carry out traditional crafts such as embroidery.

The range of materials available, however, has also changed since the mid-twentieth century; simply put, the brightly colored printed textiles available in the early twenty-first century do not need to be embroidered in order to liven them up. Another factor is that at the end of the twentieth century, numerous embroidery workshops, especially around the city of Askhabad, specialized in Turkmen embroidery for export to other Turkmen groups and interested parties outside of Turkmenistan. As a result, many women no longer felt the necessity to work for hours at a piece of embroidery when they could easily buy it.

In general, the most beautifully worked embroideries are those used for wedding gifts from the bride to the groom. According to Harvey, these gifts can include a belt for his coat, a handkerchief with a love poem, or a beaded triangle used as a fertility symbol to be worn on his left hand during the wedding ceremony.

When embroidery was carried out at home, it was normal for the garments to be made up and then embroidered. When embroidery workshops were introduced, more and more garments were embroidered in sections and then made into a garment, a quicker process but one that can lead to mismatching designs if not properly carried out.

Turkmen embroidery was normally done using floss silk yarns in predominantly red, black, yellow, and white. The floss was twisted by the embroiderer at home. Again, these were locally produced until the mid-twentieth century, when more and more imported synthetic silks became available on the market; these were generally imported from East Asia, notably China. Occasionally, embroideries worked in wool or cotton can be found, but these are not common and are regarded as cheaper versions of the silk embroideries. Metal threads also played an important role in Central Asian embroidery, but they are more commonly used among groups such as the Uzbek rather than the Turkmen.

A middle coat with red and yellow stripes, which a married Turkmen woman would have worn under an outdoor coat and over her dress and short-sleeved coat, Iran, late twentieth century. The jewelry sewn to the front represents part of her dowry. Textile Research Centre, Leiden.

EMBROIDERY STITCHES

Turkmen embroidery for clothing uses a comparatively small range of embroidery stitches. Backstitch (*qayma*) is used to create a series of short stitches in a continuous line and is often used to define outlines. When it is used in single or double lines, different colors may be used in a particular sequence, for example, black, yellow, black, white, black, yellow, and so forth. According to the British anthropologists Peter Andrews and Mugal Andrews, this type of design is called *türlü qayma*. Sometimes, backstitching is used for small, semisolid figures, such as a series of triangles. The name of the work depends on the color of thread used: *Aq qayma* (white backstitching) and *sari qayma* (yellow backstitching) are the two most common forms. Another form of backstitching is called *alaca*, whereby backstitch is executed in black and white threads alternately. In Teke work, the line of backstitching is usually single, while in Yomut work, the thread is generally doubled and two lines are worked side by side, with the colors staggered.

Blanket stitch (also known as open buttonhole stitch and called *pogtuma* by the Teke or *qurttüken* by the Yomut) is another widely used stitch. It can be used in short lengths of four to six loops laid closely together to make small squares. A single row of blanket stitch is used to close the neck opening of a chemise. A double row (*pogtuma cigma*), in which alternating colors are staggered, is sometimes used as a border in Teke work. In another

form of buttonhole stitch, the length of the loops is progressively increased and diminished at right angles to the base line, so as to produce either a series of toothlike triangles or a scalloped effect. This is characteristic of the finish on the collar and side vents of coats for men and women, where it is worked over the silk braid edgings.

Another form of blanket-stitch embroidery combines stitching with couching: A cord is kept in place using blocks of blanket stitch in various contrasting colors, such as yellow, red, and white over a black cord. A triple row in which squares of stitching alternate with blank spaces is generally used by the Yomut to decorate the black braid seam inside the trouser cuffs. When these colored checkers are arranged in fours and fives, the pattern is called *og göz*. The Teke use squares alternating with blanks in four rows to build up a pattern in two colors called *hive kestesi*, where the squares of one color are stacked in diminishing numbers to form triangles that alternate with inverted triangles of the other color. This is also embroidered over the black braid trim of a trouser cuff. Wheel buttonhole stitch is a buttonhole stitch that is worked in a circle. It is usually used as an isolated, decorative motif on the neck openings of dresses.

Chain stitch (*ilme* or *ildirme*) is particularly prevalent within Yomut work. It is usually so closely worked that the background cannot be seen through the stitches. It is often used to block in figures with concentric lines. Chain stitch is normally worked in paired lines or in one main line with various subsidiary lines coming off it. According to Andrews and Andrews, the Turkmen always produce a chain stitch with a needle rather than a tambour hook as used by other embroiderers in Central Asia and the Indian subcontinent.

Couching (*basma*) is where a thread is laid on the cloth and then a second, couching thread is used to catch down the first thread. According to Andrews and Andrews, the couching thread is usually passed once around the laid thread without piercing the ground material, then it is passed a second time around the laid thread and then through the ground material. A slightly more elaborate form of couching involves an underthread that is laid down in a pattern, such as a triangle, and then a couching thread that is used to catch down the center of the first thread.

Underside couching also occurs, although at first glance this stitch looks like a backstitch. However, when the reverse side of the cloth is examined, it becomes clear that the couching thread is pulled through to the back of the fabric. It can be difficult sometimes to determine whether this type of stitching is handmade or created by manipulating the tension mechanism on a sewing machine, so that the top thread is pulled to the reverse side of the cloth.

Block couching is found in various types of garments, including coats, and is used to cover a large area quickly. It consists of a thick ground thread, usually in red or black, which is covered with blocks of couching thread in a contrasting color such as white, black, or yellow, colors that reflect the stripes in the cloth.

Featherstitch is an unusual stitch for the Turkmen and not widely used. Andrews and Andrews do not refer to its use, so it may be regarded as a recent interloper into the traditional repertoire of Turkmen embroidery. Lacing stitch (*kesdi* or *köcüme*) is, however, a characteristic feature of Turkmen embroidery. The stitches are between a tenth and two-tenths of an inch (two and five millimeters) wide, depending on the pattern. At the end of the twentieth century, this stitch was mainly used for women's coats and caps, especially those worn by girls.

Stem stitch (*qaralama*) is usually carried out using a black thread. It has various applications: First, it is often worked in very straight lines and with a succession of overlapping stitches that, when finished, look like a finely twisted cord. Second, stem stitch is used as an outline stitch in order to define panels that contain motifs of various forms.

The different groups use different stitches and combinations of stitches, which helps in the identification of the embroidery's origins. According to Andrews and Andrews, for example, chain stitch is a feature of Yomut embroidery. It is sometimes worked in combination with stem stitch, which is used to outline the chain-stitch areas. The Teke, however, extensively use lacing stitch with stem stitch for outlining purposes, backstitch, and couching. The Guklan use the same range of stitches as the Teke, although sometimes their work is done in chain stitch highlighted with couching.

EMBROIDERY COLORS AND DESIGNS

Certain colors, forms, and shapes recur regularly in Turkmen art of all forms, not least in embroideries. It is no coincidence that many embroidery patterns resemble those used when weaving carpets, the mainstay of many Turkmens' livelihood. In addition to typical Turkmen designs, there are also influences from outside, including Chinese, Mongolian, Persian, as well as shamanistic and Islamic concepts and forms.

Certain colors predominate within Turkmen embroidery, including red and blue. In general, red is regarded as a charm that protects against bleeding, wounds, and miscarriages, but it could also be seen as a fertility color. In contrast, blue is regarded as a powerful protection against the evil eye. Other colors that are featured in Turkmen embroidery are black, yellow, orange, green, and white.

Many designs are highly abstract, with nonnatural forms, with the intermediate space playing an equally important role to the stitching in the whole design. Running designs that repeat a particular motif again and again are a common feature, especially for borders and hems on clothing. Geometric forms include dots, squares, rectangles, diamonds, hearts, rosettes, and quatrefoils. These large designs are often further decorated with similar small motifs, including dots, diamonds, rosettes, and, in some cases, stylized human faces, as well as semiprecious stones and glass beads of various colors.

Sometimes a whole animal or bird, albeit highly stylized, is depicted. Sometimes only part of a bird or animal is shown, but that is regarded as sufficient to represent the whole concept of the animal or bird and its nature/spirit. Ram's horns, for example, are said to represent the hunt and power, especially male power; these are a common feature of the Turkmen embroidery repertoire and can be found in many forms. Sometimes, the horn motif is used in isolation, sometimes as a row. It is also possible to find the horns repeated and mirrored to create a quatrefoil-type design based on four pairs of horns.

Birds, such as cocks, are seen by some groups as the bringer of dawn, or light in general, which dispels the spirits of darkness. Birds of prey are regarded as the protective animals of various Turkmen groups, which mediate between this world and the spirit world. In particular, double-headed eagles are symbols of power and nobility; they are especially popular and regularly appear on textiles and garments.

Floral representations are common on Turkmen objects, and this may partly be because they are seen as more feminine but also because there are no religious (Islamic) proscriptions about representing plants and flowers. Stylized floral forms that frequently occur include variations on the tree of life, cypress trees, pomegranates (fertility), lotus blossoms, and, in particular, the tulip (abundance and fertility), a flower that recurs in Turkic art throughout Central and Southwest Asia.

AMULETS

A feature of Turkmen dress in general, especially that worn by women and children, is the use of various forms of amulets, although this practice is dying out in many areas. The amulets worn by men tend to be written amulets that are simply sewn onto a piece of cloth. Amulets are used against disease, evil spirits, and the evil eye. Some amulets come in the form of written textiles. The texts regarded as suitable include passages from the Qur'an, the ninety-nine names of Allah, supplications to angels and saints, magical incantations, and magic squares.

Many of the amulets are made from silver, and this may have some relationship to a pre-Islamic association of silver with the moon. Semiprecious stones are also very important. In addition, carnelian, the "bloodstone," is supposed to protect against bleeding, wounds, and miscarriages. Blue turquoise protects against the evil eye. It is important to note that it is the color of the amulet that matters, not the material from which it is made. As a result, it is not uncommon to find carnelian and turquoise replaced by suitably colored glass, coral, plastic, or other materials.

The shape of the amulet is also significant. The most frequently found shape is the triangle, an ancient universal symbol of female fertility. The German anthropologist Johannes Kalter suggests that one symbol of male fertility, the phallus, became the fish that is found on pendants throughout Turkmen jewelry. It would appear that equally old symbols of male physical strength are animal claws and teeth. These are said to symbolize courage, power, and agility. It is not surprising, therefore, that this type of symbol is commonly found on the clothing of boys. Another range of amulets found on boys' clothing are symbols of power and fighting, such as bows and arrows, axes, and swords.

TURKMEN MALE DRESS

One of the problems in looking at nineteenth-century descriptions of Turkmen dress is separating "eastern" Turkmen from "western" Turkmen. Eastern Turkmen are those Turkmen and Uzbeks living in and around Bukhara in what is Uzbekistan in the early twenty-first century, and western Turkmen are those living in the vicinity of the Caspian Sea and northeastern Iran. With respect to men's clothing, colorful ikat gowns are often described; this was the elite urban dress of Turkmen and Uzbeks living in and around Bukhara.

One of the earliest descriptions comes from the English traveler James Baillie Fraser, who wrote about his travels in Central Asia in the beginning of the nineteenth century. Fraser described ikat gowns as the "national Turcoman or Uzbek dress." The basic outfit for a man varied according to his social status, so the poorest would wear a short woolen shirt (*jubba*) and a pair of woolen drawers, while others would wear a long brown woolen wrapper. The basic outfit for a reasonably well-to-do Turkmen or Uzbek consisted of drawers and a shirt of cotton or silk, plus several

robes (jubbas) that came to just below the knees. These robes were kept in place with a sash at the waist. The jubbas were made of a mixture of silk and cotton that was striped blue, purple, red, and green, and they were probably decorated using an ikat technique. Wealthier Turkmen, according to Fraser, especially among the Guklans and Yomuts, adopted the common Persian dress (pants, a long undershirt, an outer gown called a *qaba*, and a waist sash), while the Tekes kept their own "Turkmen" forms. In addition, the Tekes used to wear jubbas woven of camels' hair above the lower garments. The Turkmen headgear consisted of a red, black, or gray sheepskin cap that was round and close or had a broad top; the common Persian cap; or the quilted cotton cap worn by the Kurds. Fraser noted that some men wore Persian-style slippers, Kurdish leather socks with puttees, or, as in the case of Teke men, Uzbek-style boots.

The French artist L. E. Duhousset traveled through Iran between 1858 and 1860; during the course of his trip he made three sketches of "Turcoman." One sketch is full length and shows a man wearing a shirt (*koynek*) that opens on the right shoulder, over which is worn a short gown. The length of the gown is not clear, as it appears to have been tucked into the man's voluminous trousers (*balaq*; or *zirjameh* in Persian). Over the whole is worn a long coat (*jubba*) with a collar. The man's footwear consists of a pair of mule-like slippers, which have curled toes and are open at the back. A feature of the man's outfit is his beehive-shaped hat (*telpek*), which was probably made of lambskin (as are the modern astrakhan hats worn by Turkmen). The man's outfit is finished by the inclusion of a musket.

To summarize, it appears that from the beginning of the nineteenth century until the mid-1920s, the basic ensemble for an (Iranian) Turkmen male consisted of a pair of loose cotton trousers (balaq) and a shirt (koynek). Over these were worn a tight-sleeved robe (*don*) of striped silk. These garments were held together at the waist with a sash (*qusaq*). A man's headgear consisted of a small skullcap (*bork*), sometimes with a turban, or a

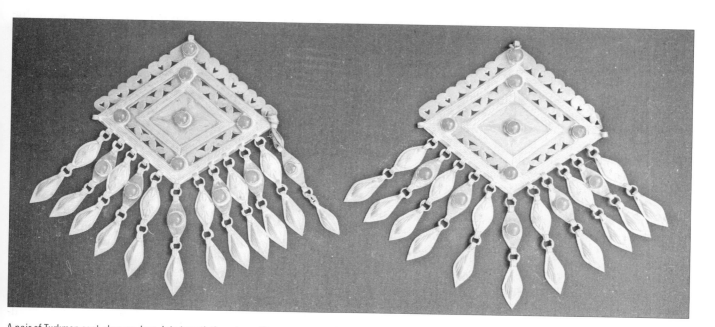

A pair of Turkmen coat plaques, Iran, late twentieth century. *Changa* are sewn onto a married woman's middle coat to fasten the coat. One of the plaques has a hook, the other a loop. Textile Research Centre, Leiden.

cylindrical black sheepskin hat (telpek). But it should be stressed that there are regional variations among the various groups of Turkmen.

By the end of the twentieth century, Turkmen men's dress had changed considerably, and in the early twenty-first century, there is considerable overlap in the dress worn by the various Turkmen groups. The differences in clothing and jewelry are not always clear, as it is possible for elements to be borrowed from one group by another.

Since the late twentieth century, major changes have taken place in men's clothing. In particular, most men wear Western-style dress on an everyday basis in the early twenty-first century. However, on special occasions, a more traditional form of dress is adopted. In addition, a modern version of the traditional male coat is worn but usually by older men. Following the dress reforms of Reza Shah in Iran during the 1930s, the silk don had been officially deliberately replaced by a Western-style frock coat or jacket and trousers, but many Turkmen men did not start wearing Turkmen-style garments until much later, during the rule of Reza Shah. In addition, the cylindrical telpek was replaced by a flaring astrakhan telpek, which is similar in shape to Russian army-style headgear.

The form of shirt worn by many men (especially Yomut) in the early twenty-first century is still cut in the old style (namely with the front neck opening coming from the right shoulder). But the range of materials is different. The older or more traditional forms used red silk, while a less expensive form would have been made of white cotton. Since the mid-twentieth century, however, imported lightweight cottons have replaced the older form. In the early twenty-first century, most men tend to wear Western-style shirts in a variety of light colors or specially made long shirts that look like Western shirts but come down to the knees.

With respect to the don, some Iranian Turkmen men still wear this form of long robe, and there are various types depending on the wearer's age. For instance, the *qarma don* tends to be worn by men over forty years old, whereas the *girmizi don* is worn by younger men; otherwise, the main difference between these two robes is that the qarma don has an additional white stripe. However, there is also another form of don, made out of light blue or gray material, that would appear to be more popular, especially with older men. This garment is cut in a similar manner to the red versions but is regarded as more informal and "modern."

MEN'S HEADGEAR

At various times men in the area around Bandar Turkmen and Gurgan in northeastern Iran can be seen wearing a small, embroidered skullcap (bork). This type of cap seems to be associated with the Yomut. It should also be noted that in this region, the same type of skullcap, decorated with the same patterns, is worn by girls, boys, and men. Those worn by girls are, however, normally further embellished with silver jewelry and amulets. This type of cap is made up of a crown and band. These pieces can be bought from shops and stalls with the various layers of cloth and design already prepared.

Two designs seem to be popular at the end of the twentieth century for both men and girls. The first design has a series of circles and seems to be a simplified form of what Andrews and Andrews called a *bostani* ("garden") design. It is a variation on the ram's-horn motif, used in fourfold, in order to create an equal-armed cross. The second design has small indented ovals and is called *qurt nanis*. Both designs are worked in red, dark red, blue, green, black, and white cotton yarn. Another type of skullcap worn by Yomut men in Iran is a white version with two narrow stripes decorating the lower and upper edges of the band. The center of the crown tends to be decorated with a starlike motif (stem stitch) enclosed in a line of feather stitch.

Many men wear a neat form of turban. It is made out of a square of cloth that is folded diagonally and then wrapped around the head. Various types of cloth, made of cotton and synthetic yarns, are used for this purpose, but most are white with black stripes or checks. According to Andrews, in the 1960s, *akhunds*, or religious leaders, and hajjis, people who had made the pilgrimage (hajj) to Mecca, normally wore turbans rather than telpeks.

Another form of headgear associated with Turkmen is the telpek or sheepskin hat. The large, bushy hat of the nineteenth century varied in shape from conical to cylindrical; the largest version was worn in the Khiva Oasis region, and a smaller version was worn in the steppe. In the period before 1925, a particular variety of this hat was favored: The crown was not tall, but the fleece was very long, making it appear to be much larger than it actually was. This type of telpek is called a *bokhor telpek* (Bukhara telpek). The telpek worn by older men in the early twenty-first century is taller than the Bukhara kind but slopes outward toward the top and is made of lambskin with a much shorter fleece in tight curls. It is sometimes called an *astrakhan telpek*. The wearing of this type of headgear is generally associated with older men and is beginning to die out.

In certain regions of eastern Iran, another form of fluffy headgear exists that is made of natural light brown wool, which is loosely spun into a yarn (z-spin) and then knitted into the required shape. The material is then carded in order to create a short nap. The napping is sometimes done by (male) hat sellers in the street, while the knitting is done by women. The hat comes in various forms, but basically it has a soft, high dome (about eight inches, or twenty centimeters, high) with an upright rim (about three and a half inches, or nine centimeters, wide), which sometimes has a front notch in it. This type of cap is locally regarded as typically Turkmen, and, more particularly, it is worn by nomadic Turkmen.

MEN'S COATS AND FOOTWEAR

Various types of coats and mantles were worn by Turkmen, especially shepherds, to protect them against the summer's heat and the cold of the winter. The *yapunca* was such an outdoor garment. It was made from a semicircle of felt, about 106 inches (270 centimeters) in diameter and about one-third inch (one centimeter) thick. It had a pair of plaited woolen ties on the straight side, one on the left and one on the right, in order to fasten the garment.

The *icmek* (also called *üsürmek* or *kusgun*) was a long-sleeved overcoat of lambskin or sheepskin with the fleece turned outward. It was used in wet and cold weather. It had extremely long sleeves so that the hands and lower arms could be withdrawn into them for protection. In the 1960s, the most preferred skins were the (expensive) dark curly fleeces from unweaned lambs, while cheaper coats were made from white sheepskins. These coats were not decorated. During wet weather, the coats were turned inside out so that the rain ran off the fleece, leaving the soft skin undamaged. The *cekmen* was a loose camel's hair mantle used by urban men in both summer and winter.

Traditional forms of footwear are also vanishing rapidly. At the end of the twentieth century, there was still a small market for the production and sale of hand-knitted socks, but this appears to be dying out. These socks tend to be made from coarse yarn (sheep wool) and decorated with colorful geometric designs in a variety of color combinations, including yellows, pinks, dark reds, blues, greens, browns, and black.

Instead of socks, Turkmen often wrapped their feet in white woolen puttees (*dolaq*). To make these, plain white woolen cloth was cut into strips about 9 to 10 inches (22 to 25 centimeters) wide and 118 inches (300 centimeters) long. The puttees were wrapped over the man's trousers (the trousers were sometimes pulled up, in which case the puttees were wrapped around the bare lower legs and then over the bottom edge of the trousers just below the knee), preventing the leg from being exposed to the elements.

Two types of shoes were worn by Turkmen shepherds; namely, moccasin-style shoes (*cariq*), which were made of tanned cow's leather, and similarly shaped shoes called *coqoy* made of camel's hide. The hide came from the knees of the camel and was worn with the hair left on the outside of the shoe. Both types of shoes were tied around the feet using a leather thong, which was passed through slits around the upper edges of the shoe. Tall boots (*edik*) were used for riding. In the early twenty-first century, most men, especially those working or living in the main urban centers, tend to wear Western-style shoes, some of which are made locally while others are imported.

In general, men did not use jewelry except in the mounting on weapons and animal harnesses. This is in direct contrast to the jewelry worn by Turkmen women.

TURKMEN WOMEN'S DRESS

Just as for men's clothing, there are problems concerning descriptions of women's clothing because sources treat Bukharan dress norms as typical for "western" Turkmen dress. Yet the garments worn by groups such as the Yomut, Guklan, Teke, and Ersari women can vary considerably. It appears from nineteenth-century descriptions and photographs that the basic outfit of a western Turkmen woman from this period consisted of a pair of trousers (balaq or zir-ejameh) and a long, loose, ankle-length dress (koynek) with sleeves that was fastened at the neck with either a stud or ribbons. The dress was normally red with yellow stripes, although, as noted by Fraser, blue and green versions were also worn. Fraser also remarked that a woman could wear a considerable amount of jewelry, including head and hair ornamentations, necklaces, bracelets, and rings. Over these garments a woman would wear a coat (kurte) when indoors with either a headdress or veil. When out-of-doors, a woman would add a second veil over her dress or a second coat (chyrpy). Her face would not normally be covered.

The range and cut of the garments worn by Turkmen women remained much the same until the mid- to late twentieth century, although the type of material used changed. During the early twentieth century, for instance, it was much more common for Iranian Turkmen women's dresses to be made of silk or semisilk fabrics, which were either woven locally or imported, especially from the Askhabad region. To a great extent, especially in urban settings, this type of cloth has been replaced by printed cottons or synthetic materials.

One of the main item of clothing used to be a dress made of red silk with two yellow stripes. Occasionally, dark red, green, or purple versions of this cloth were also used for dresses. In general, Turkmen clothing for women seems to be much simpler than it was, even as recently as the mid-1980s. At the same time, however, it is also becoming much more colorful. During the twentieth century, the basic dress of a Turkmen woman consisted of undertrousers (balaq), a dress (koynek), and a headdress of some kind. In addition, some groups also had a face veil (yaşmak), a sash (sal-qusaq or bil-qusak), an indoor coat of some kind (cabit or kurte), and, for outdoor wear, a second coat (chyrpy).

A Turkmen bridal headdress, Afghanistan, 1960s. Decorated with silver plaques, beading, and embroidery, this headdress would have been worn by a Teke or Ensari bride. Textile Research Centre, Leiden.

The trousers are made in three parts: first, a baggy upper section; second, a separate crotch panel; and third, a lower, embroidered cuff (*balaq agzi* or *balaq yüzi*) that is intended to be seen below the hem of the dress. When the upper sections of the trousers wear out, the embroidered bands are simply cut off and sewn onto new material.

The cuffs of the trousers taper toward the ankles and are usually embroidered. In the older forms, the embroidered bands may be up to sixteen inches (forty centimeters) in size and ornamented with several broad rows of contrasting motifs flanked by narrower borders. However, due to the lack of time (many girls attend school in the early twenty-first century), this number has been reduced to one. In most cases, these trousers do not end in a red cuff as with the older forms, but any suitable material (with respect to weight and type of cloth) is regarded as acceptable.

In general, the older cuffs of the Iranian Turkmen trousers, which are made on dark-colored cotton materials, tend to come from Turkmenistan, while those worked on red silk are generally accepted as being local products. There is also a difference in the design layout between the two sources of trouser cuffs. Those from Turkmenistan, for instance, tend to have an indented section, which was originally a slit, while Iranian Turkmen trousers are embroidered with a band that goes around the whole cuff with no indentations.

In the early twenty-first century, it is possible to buy machine-embroidered cuffs with machine-woven lower bands (instead of hand-embroidered bands), which are finished with metallic colored lurex thread. But these are not regarded as highly as hand-embroidered cuffs, especially the older forms with broad bands of stitching.

A woman's main garment is the dress or shift (koynek). This garment was formerly made of a raspberry-colored silk, but the silk has been replaced by synthetic material. The basic cut of this type of dress was based on the width of the material (about twelve to sixteen inches, or thirty to forty centimeters). The stripes woven into both selvedges were used to emphasize the cut of the garment. The use of side panels means that garments can be made that widen at the bottom. According to Andrews and Andrews, by 1974 the cut had become much narrower, with a high waist.

In general, however, the garment remains a loose, ankle-length dress fastened at the neck. The neck slit was deep enough to allow a baby to be fed. The slit was fastened at the top with ribbons or ties among the Yomut, and, among the Teke, sometimes with a stud (*gol yaqeh*). In the early twenty-first century, neck slits may be fastened with zippers, a button, or, in some cases, a brooch. In other dresses, it is noticeable that the neck opening itself has become much bigger so that there is no need to have a neck slit. This is a major change in the style of Turkmen dresses and reflects the Iranian/Western influence on Turkmen clothing. Sleeves tend to be long and narrow but without cuffs, so that the sleeves can be rolled up to the elbows when working.

The length of the dress is such that it comes to within eight inches (twenty centimeters) of the heels, allowing the embroidered cuffs of the trousers to be displayed. In winter, two shifts may be worn one on top of the other, and sometimes older women may also wear a shorter cotton shift (*iç köynek*) under the main garment.

At the end of twentieth century, many Iranian Turkmen women were wearing dresses made of velvet (red, green, or black being the most popular colors) or a printed material. In 2000,

for instance, the Yomut women at the Monday market in Bandar Turkmen were wearing trousers and a light, long dress, with a large head shawl and head ring. In general, winter colors tend to be darker with a smaller pattern, while those worn in the summer are lighter and more colorful. In addition, the cloth weight for a summer dress tends not to be as heavy as that for a winter one. It would seem that both personal taste and the wider range of materials and designs that are available are playing more important roles in the appearance of a garment than they did in the late 1970s or earlier.

In the early twenty-first century, women either go barefoot or wear modern shoes or sandals. The older form of leather shoe with a broad toe and wedge heels is known as *kovus*.

WOMEN'S COATS

Some older Turkmen women wear a coat over their dress during colder weather and on more formal occasions. There are various forms of these indoor coats. The most common is the cabit, which has short sleeves, a narrow collar, and a high waist. What would be the side openings in other types of coats are sewn together. However, the presence of these "fake" openings are indicated by lines of braid or some other form of decoration, such as buttons. This type of coat is usually made of red silk, which is decorated with narrow stripes in some combination of green, yellow, and white. Unlike other types of coat, this form of cabit is not usually embroidered on the outside. However, its characteristic feature are the long, printed or embroidered triangles used as facings to the two front sections of the coat. In some cases the embroidery is hand worked using underside couching, but on other occasions, machine embroidery has been done, using a top colored thread and a bobbin thread in white or black. The tension of the lower thread has been increased so that the top thread is pulled down, giving, at first glance, the appearance of underside couching. This type of coat is usually worn with the front open and turned back so that the facings can be seen.

These coats are usually further decorated by the addition of a band, usually made up of narrow red, green, and yellow stripes, which were sewn around the front opening, hem, and sleeve cuffs. Sometimes this type of coat is also decorated with a line of silver-colored coins around the front opening and front lower edge of the garment. They may also be decorated with lines of buttons up the side opening of the garments.

A second type of cabit is made of red-striped silk and has long sleeves and embroidered cuffs. The collar is again a narrow, simple form. This type of coat tends to be made out of a mid-red silk, with narrow bands, sometimes in yellow and black, and on other occasions in red with very narrow stripes. With respect to the older versions of this garment, there tends to be much more embroidery, especially around the cuffs. The cabit (with either long or short sleeves) used until recently by older Yomut women on formal occasions was usually of velvet or broadcloth.

Another form of indoor coat worn by Teke Turkmen women is the kurte, which is long, with a narrow collar and full sleeves. This type of coat tends to be made of silk. The color signifies age and status; the Yomut version of the indoor coat, the *burengek*, was usually in green silk set off with red. The Teke coat is faced with closely set rows of bossed silver disks (*capraz*) ending in a large fretted lozenge (*canna* or *changah*) as a clasp on each side at hip level. Both types have embroidered tendrils around the collar. According to

Kalter, relatively short ikat coats with slit sleeves tapering toward the wrist and darts below the chest were also for sale in the early 1980s. These appear to have been a recent development. But their use seems to have died out by the end of the twentieth century.

Some Turkmen women also wear a broad cloth sash around their indoor coats to keep the garments from opening, especially while they are working. The older forms of sashes, notably those worn by nomadic women, are made out of a coarse sheep wool or goat hair. They are made from a width of cloth that is folded in half lengthwise and then the selvedges are sewn together. One of the transverse ends, which would have been directly wrapped around the dress, is normally covered with cotton cloth for a width of about twelve inches (thirty centimeters). The cloth may be there to prevent the wool from damaging the dress, to prevent the scratchy wool from causing discomfort to the wearer, or both.

The average size of this type of sash is about 118 by 5.5 inches (300 by 14 centimeters), but it should be stressed there can be considerable variations, as their measurements depend on the woman for whom the garment was initially made. These sashes tend to be decorated with narrows bands with simple geometric shapes at regular intervals. One transverse end is usually cut straight (presumably the section that went around the body and would not be seen), while the other end is shaped and finished with tassels. There are normally three tassels (in red and black), which are twisted together to create a thicker cord. The colors used for these sashes reflect Turkmen color preferences, specifically, a black ground with red, orange, and white designs. The design elements consist of lines, small triangles, inverted triangles, and what is usually described as ram's horns. Sometimes part of the sash near the tassels is left unsewn. It is likely that money or small valuables are stored here.

Another form of sash is made of brightly colored checked silk (a typical color combination is a red ground with blue, white, yellow, and royal blue checks) with a fringe at both ends. This type of sash is normally about 12 inches (31 centimeters) wide and 63 inches (160 centimeters) long, with twisted fringes about 8 inches (20 centimeters) long. Some women (usually poorer ones) will also take any convenient length of material and tie it around their waists.

Various types of coats are worn when a woman goes out of doors. This outdoor type of coat is usually designated as a chyrpy. Again, there are formal and informal versions of this coat. Some married women, especially among the Teke, for example, have a formal coat or mantle that they wear when out of doors or in the presence of strange men. This form of coat is easily recognizable in that it has false or vestral, rather than functional, sleeves. The garment is draped by the left armpit over the crown of the headdress. The vestral sleeves are sometimes used for carrying money and small items.

The material used for this type of coat is not striped like the indoor coats. Instead, it is made from a heavyweight (stiffened) silk in a variety of colors, including, dark red, dark blue, black, yellow, and white. According to the Russian anthropologist L. Beresneva, among the Teke in Turkmenistan the color of the chirpi is directly related to the age and status of the wearer. Thus, young women wore chirpi with a dark blue ground, while middle-aged women (with children) wore ones with a yellow ground. Older women wore chirpi with a white ground, as did middle-aged women with no children. In general, dark blue chirpi are usually the most lavishly embroidered, whereas the white ones

tend to have very little embroidery. The coats are sometimes fastened at the top with a smallish, ornamental clasp (changa) made of two identical plaques, one with a hook.

Various techniques are used to fasten the sleeves together, including the use of a chain with two clasps at either end, a cord sewn to both sleeves, or a specially embroidered band that is also sewn to both sleeves. The origins of this coat lie in the formal outdoor coats worn by Bukharan women during the mid- and late nineteenth century. It seems that during the late nineteenth century these coats were made out of pale green, brown, or dark blue cloth with white stripes. In addition, the face was covered by a dense horsehair or cotton veil.

Another form of chirpi has full sleeves rather than vestigial sleeves. The type and weight of cloth, however, are the same. This coat comes in a variety of colors, including red, and tends to be heavily decorated around the neck, front opening, side opening, and lower back. Most of the modern versions of this type of coat are not as heavily decorated as the earlier forms. In addition, there is also a shorter version with long, full sleeves. This type comes in a variety of colors, including black. It tends to be decorated around the neckline and around the short side slit. For the extant examples, it is not clear whether they would originally have been stiff, but the stiffening agent has been washed out, or whether it was intended to be more flexible.

WOMEN'S HEADGEAR

Sometimes, Turkmen women in Iran wear an Iranian-style black chador when in public. Another garment, the wedding chador, has also been adapted from the Iranian tradition. This item is usually made out of four or five widths of cloth; each panel is about eighteen inches (forty-five centimeters) wide and about three yards (three meters) long. The length depends on the height of the wearer. They are made of red silk decorated with a large check design in various color combinations, such as white, black, and orange. These chadors are draped over the bride as she leaves her parents' house to go to the bridegroom's house.

Various forms of headdress are used by married Turkmen women, depending on which group they belong to and whether it is a daily or more formal occasion. On more formal occasions they tend to wear an elaborate hat decorated with various scarves, while during a normal day the headdress is much simpler.

In the 1960s, a Yomut woman's headdress tended to be based on a skullcap (bork) covered by a scarf (yagliq). This arrangement was then covered by a second scarf (aldani), bound around the base to cover the cap and hair completely. A change in fashion led to the aldani being wrapped around the back of the head and brought back to the front again where the two ends were neatly reef-knotted and tucked away out of sight. A large shawl was then draped over the top.

In the early twenty-first century, head rings were commonly worn by all married Yomut women (young and old). The headdress consisted of a headband or, in a later development, a ring (aldarij or alan dangi) that was then draped with a large head cloth (yagliq or cargat). The head ring was a simple, narrow ring about half an inch (one and a half centimeters) deep and about six to eight inches (fifteen to twenty centimeters) in diameter. It was made of cloth, leather, cardboard, or plastic. Sometimes, an embroidered strip of cloth was placed around the outside of the ring to decorate it further. The ring was worn at the back of the head.

A combined head covering and face veil worn by a Teke women in northern Iran and parts of Turkmenistan, Iran, 1960s. Textile Research Centre, Leiden.

When outside the home, most Yomut women would cover their head rings with a large shawl (cargat). They were made out of large squares of material (60 by 60 inches, or 150 by 150 centimeters), which were folded diagonally in half. These shawls used to be made out of red-colored silk, but by the end of the twentieth century these tended to be of a large floral print with a long fringe, all worked in synthetic materials. Many of these shawls came from Russia or East Europe, while a few came from Japan. In addition, there has been a market for "genuine" Turkmen shawls printed in Askhabad; these have a special logo printed in the center of the garment and often depict Turkmen jewelry.

Shawls are worn in a variety of manners, but the basic method is to place it over the head ring, and allow it to hang loose down the front of the garment. The edges of the shawl are then held in one hand. Another way is to hold the right-hand edge under the left armpit or fling it over the left shoulder; this style is not as common and is usually used by younger women. The shawl (cargat) that covers the ring can also be used as a yaşmak (veil) to cover the lower part of the face when in the presence of strange men or older men. According to Peter Andrews (1991), in some cases a head scarf (yagliq) was worn under the headband and knotted at the back with pendant tails.

Teke and Guklan women, especially the more elderly ones, tend to wear a more rigid construction on their head. Until the 1980s, Guklan women also wore headdress foundations similar to those of the Yomut. A formal headdress is made of a base (sommoq; a smaller version is called soppos) covered by a large silver plaque (igme), which is curved to fit the base exactly. It is held in position with a number of chains (qinyac uci) of smaller silver plates or coins. The headdress holds a large silk scarf (qinyac) in position on the top. If no tiara is available, a series of large linked plates, known as öwürme, are fastened in its place.

In contrast, an informal headdress consists of a base, without silver ornaments, swathed in bands of colored silk an inch or two (two and a half to five centimeters) wide, which cross over one another at an angle, running back and forward again around the outside. According to Andrews (1992), the main silk covering may be midnight blue, with a plum-colored silk scarf attached around the perimeter of the top and stretched over it to be gathered at the back before it falls freely.

At the end of the twentieth century, these headdresses were about eight inches (twenty centimeters) in height and made up of a cloth (qinyac uci or yaşmak) wrapped around a framework. The framework (called boyrok by the Teke and tobi by the Guklan) might have been made out of a variety of materials, such as rushes, twisted cloth, leather, felt, or, later, a heavyweight cardboard or even a high cap. For centuries, the cloth (qinyac uci or yaşmak) wrapped around the framework was made of silk, but by the end of the twentieth century, a wide variety of other materials was used. Sometimes, the cloth was used as a veil to cover the lower part of the face. In public, women usually wore a head shawl, or occasionally a chador, over the frame and cloth/veil.

WOMEN'S FACE COVERINGS

Complex rules govern how people treat each other. One way these rules can be seen is in how a girl or a woman, a junior wife or a senior wife, are treated and expected to behave. These rules can be seen, for example, in the three main forms of face coverings associated with Turkmen women and how they are used. The first form is the qenqach or qinyac uci, which was worn by Teke and Nokhorli Turkmen women and how they are used. These veils are made of a very large, roughly triangular length of material, which has one end attached to the headdress base with a small hook. The other end is wrapped around the head with the corner acting as the face veil. This corner is gathered so that the veil is full. The version worn by Teke women tends to be made from red cloth and has a decorative woven band along the lower edge of the garment. The form worn by Nokhorli women tends to be more colorful and can be made of any type of material or with any design. In both cases, the veils are usually edged with an applied fringe.

The second form of face covering (yaşmak) is worn by Guklan Turkmen women and is made from two lengths of material sewn together lengthwise. It measures 29 inches by 27 inches (74 by 68 centimeters); the cloth is usually about 14.5 inches (37 centimeters) wide, selvedge to selvedge. It comes in black or dark red and may be decorated with stripes in dark green, purple, and white. It is worn over the lower part of the face. The type of face veil worn by Guklan normally has an applied fringe that ends in small, white glass beads.

Until about 1980, many Yomut women wore a folded scarf around their head. This was replaced by a narrow ring, which was covered with a yellow-and-black resist-dyed scarf. The more expensive versions of these scarves were silk, while modern and cheaper versions are of synthetic materials. The resist-dyed cloth is folded diagonally and then draped over the head so that the main section can be used to cover the lower part of the face. The whole was then covered by a large printed shawl. It is noticeable that in the early twenty-first century Yomut women do not cover their faces at all. However, during fieldwork in the area, when unexpectedly confronted by a strange man, some women were observed to draw part of their shawls across the lower part of their face.

In general, when indoors, married women used to wear a headdress that covered the head and hair, leaving only the pigtails that hung down the woman's back visible. However, the influence of pan-Iranian-style garments can be seen in the increased use of head scarves (rosari) by both younger and older women, especially in Iran. When indoors most women seem to remove the large outdoor shawls and put on a lightweight head scarf (about 45 by 45 inches, or 114 by 114 centimeters), usually decorated with a small geometric pattern in a pale color such as purple or light blue on a white ground. This form of head covering may be worn both indoors and outdoors.

CHILDREN'S CLOTHES

In general, the clothing of both boys and girls matches the garments of same-sex adults, both with respect to the cut of the garments and the type of material used. As may be expected, many of the traditional garments can no longer be seen in urban settings. However, in smaller villages and on festive occasions, children are still sometimes bedecked in these items of clothing.

A particular garment associated with young children is an embroidered bib. These bibs frequently have triangles and rhomboids sewn onto them. It used to be the case that smaller children wore garments covered with small amulets of various kinds. Generally, boys tended to have many more amulets than girls, and there were gender-specific forms. Boys' amulets often take the shape of a bow strung with an arrow (oq yay), a sword, an adze, or an axe. In addition, there may be silver disks (bezbent) sewn onto the shoulders of a boy's shirt (kurte).

The main difference in the garments worn by boys and girls lies in their headgear. The caps worn by boys, for instance, are often adorned with silver amulets, and again the caps have special shapes. In particular, boys' caps tend to be decorated with rectangular plaques (doga or depebent). Girls' caps, in contrast, are round and are usually topped with a domed, silver finial (qupba or qobbah) that is set with smaller silver components stamped in matrices. A narrow chin diadem may also be sewn on. Girls also tend to wear a simple, embroidered skullcap (bork) without any silver plaques.

By the end of the twentieth century, the more elaborate forms of Turkmen dress were rapidly dying out for daily use, and in some places it was worn only on special occasions such as an engagement or marriage.

Snapshot: Turkmen Women's Jewelry

The social codes governing the life of Turkmen women used to be very strict, and there was minimal contact between the sexes, even within a family unit. While Turkmen men tended to invest money in their arms and horses, they also spent money on a woman's jewelry. It was important not only for its decorative qualities but also, often more importantly, as a form of life insurance that remained the woman's property and could be used by her in whatever manner she chose. Instead of saving money in a bank, as is common in the West, Turkmen women saved jewelry that could be sold at a later date if necessary. The French traveler Henri de Blocqueville, who was a prisoner of the Turkmen from 1860 to 1861, noted that he often saw women dressed in rags, with only a small amount of food to feed their families, who were nonetheless laden with jewelry, which was never taken off, even when they went to sleep. According to various late-nineteenth-century accounts, the amount of jewelry worn could amount to thirteen to eighteen pounds (six to eight kilograms), especially among the women of some wealthier families. There are various references to brides wearing up to thirty-seven pounds (seventeen kilograms) of jewelry during their marriage ceremonies. This basic attitude toward jewelry, as a source of funding for when things got really hard, remains in the early twenty-first century.

Until the end of the nineteenth century, the Turkmen throughout Central Asia, Afghanistan, and Russia had relatively easy social, cultural, trade, and economic contacts. Those Turkmen east of the Caspian were separated by international boundaries only by the early twentieth century. Nevertheless, Turkmen remain linked by the joint culture and language.

Turkmen silver jewelry, especially of the nineteenth and early twentieth centuries, tended to be made from melted-down older pieces, as well as Chinese, Iranian, and Russian coins, in a manner similar to Bedouin Arab jewelry, which was often made from silver, especially from the Maria Theresa thaler from Austria. Turquoise was usually from Khorasan, while pearls were imported from the Gulf, India, or even Europe. Similarly, glass beads were imported from India and Europe. Until the late 1950s, many Turkmen women had large collections of silver jewelry. However, as with many other groups, notably Bedouin Arabs, there was a move to change the silver to gold forms.

Turkmen silver forehead band, or *ildirqich*, with carnelian-colored glass insets, Turkmenistan, late twentieth century. Worn by Ersari Turkmen women, this forehead band would cover the front of the forehead and hang down the side of the head and temples. Textile Research Centre, Leiden.

Exactly what form of jewelry and how much was worn varied according to which group the woman belonged to: A Teke woman, for example, would wear a different range from a Nokhali woman. Teke jewelry is recognizable for its use of gilding on the ground and carnelians or red glass beads. Teke work is also predominantly rounded, especially the pendants. In contrast, Jafarbay Yomut jewelry tends to be flatter and covered with gilded silver plate, or it has mostly rhomboid silver plates soldered onto the base material. The decoration of the Jafarbay jewelry often consists of precisely worked matrices. Some items are set with glass beads in muted colors. In general, however, the most elaborate and larger items of jewelry were and still are generally made and worn by the Teke, although other groups do sometimes wear pieces of it.

The Turkmen use a wide range of mainly floral patterns that are usually highly stylized. They are based on trefoils and tulips (a very Turkish motif), as well as tree-of-life or animal or bird designs. They often have symbolic meanings. Notable examples are ram's heads or horns, as well as cocks and (double-headed) eagles. In addition, there are geometric forms, such as dots, squares, rectangles, diamonds, hearts, rosettes, and quatrefoils. These larger forms were often further decorated with similar small motifs, including dots, diamonds, rosettes, and, in some cases, stylized human faces, as well as semiprecious stones and glass beads of various colors. In particular, the shades of light to mid-blue and dark red, considered to be lucky colors, tend to be predominant.

It should not be forgotten that in addition to its role as a form of savings, jewelry is also worn for pleasure. The feel, weight, appearance, and sound of jewelry add to a feeling of being properly dressed. The choice of jewelry worn could also express personality, as noted by the German writer Johannes

Kalter: "A Turkmen woman has no choice about wearing a maxi, middy or mini-skirt, but she has a certain freedom about choosing her jewelry and the way she wears it, even if that upsets our systematic minds."

Unlike the custom in many cultures, almost the same amount of jewelry is worn down the back and in the hair of a Turkmen woman as at the front around the neck and on the chest. Much of this is hidden from sight, but because it is linked together and has a number of chains, pendants, and bells, it makes a sound.

HEAD JEWELRY

Turkmen women have a wide range of head jewelry, much of which is sewn onto a padded headdress called a *boyrok*. Boyroks come in various sizes, depending on the woman's status and the occasion; a bridal boyrok, for example, tends to be much higher than one worn on a daily basis. One of the most impressive elements of the boyrok headdress is the so-called bridal crown, which is usually a large, curved panel (*egmeh*) decorated with engraving, applied metal bands and plaques, semiprecious stones, and other such embellishments. These panels are normally sewn onto the front of a tall headdress worn by brides and married women. The panels used for brides tend to be more elaborate than those worn by married women. Sometimes, girls' caps have small similar panels sewn onto them.

From about the age of seven or eight, girls start wearing caps decorated with simple metal plaques, plus, in the center of the cap, a hollow finial (*qupba*). It is said that if a girl's family is looking for a husband for the girl (when she is about twelve to fifteen), white feathers are placed in the finial as a silent but eloquent message.

Forehead ornaments or diadems (*ildirqich*) made up of a series of plaques and chains ending in pendants are common and worn by younger married women. The bands are made up of silver and carnelian beads, ending at each end with pendants on chains that are used to cover the front of the forehead and hang down the side of the head and temples. Among the Teke, some women wear a *öwürme* form of diadem. It consists of a series of plaques or metal bands that are linked together like a picket fence. These are then sewn onto a cloth headdress.

Another form of head ornamentation is the *eurmeh*, which consists of a series of plaques attached to each other. They are similar in appearance to temple pendants but have hooks at each end that are attached to either side of the main headdress. They are often hung horizontally from the temples to the back of the head or across the forehead and around the back of the head.

Temple pendants (*adamlyk*) are used to frame the face and consist of a pair of long ornaments made up of triangular (*tenecir*) or pear-shaped plaques fastened together. These pendants can either be hung directly from the ear by a single curved spike or hook or they can be sewn onto a leather band and draped over the head, dangling just in front of the ears. Among the Yomut and Ersari, temple pendants can be up to twenty-seven inches (sixty centimeters) long.

A wide range of earrings (*tenechir*) is worn by Turkmen women. The earrings vary considerably in shape. In general, however, they are large, and in some cases they are so heavy that they are attached to the headdress rather than passed through the lobes of the ear. Basket-shaped earrings (*gulak khalka*) are common among the Yomut. Nose rings (*arabeg*) are also worn by some groups and come in various forms, but they are no longer as common as they used to be. In general, they are worn by Turkmen women living in the west of Afghanistan and in northeastern Iran, especially near the Caspian Sea.

Although most of a married woman's head is covered and never seen in public, this does not mean that no jewelry is associated with her hair. Many (married) Turkmen women wear their hair in two long braids that hang down their back. These braids may be covered with a set of ladder-like, linked plaques (*sac manjuq* or *sachq*; *qorbaqeli monjuq*) or a characteristic heart-shaped pendant (*asiq*). The latter pendants are usually made up of single or double heart-shaped pendants (*athekh*) or very small hearts worn in a row of three. The heart-shaped pendants are joined together or combined with chains into which small triangular cloth amulets are often incorporated. In some regions, bands, which may also form bags, are sometimes placed over or around the braids of a married woman. These are sometimes decorated with embroidery and beads.

NECK AND PECTORAL JEWELRY, JEWELRY ON COATS, AND ARM AND FINGER DECORATION

Neck and pectoral jewelry form some of the most impressive ornaments worn by a Turkmen woman, especially by the Teke. An important element is the *bukau*, which is a horseshoe-

shaped neck decoration with a rigid plaque at the front. An unornamented form ending in hooks is generally worn by married women. Younger women and girls tend to wear bukau with ornamental plaques in a wide variety of forms, including rhomboids, rectangles, and squares, many of which are further ornamented with chains, pendants, and bells. According to the U.S. anthropologist William Irons, writing in the mid- to late twentieth century, when a nomadic Yomut was organizing a marriage, the bride's mother would be given a necklace called a *alajayup*, which was to be worn by the bride. This necklace associated with marriage was made up of a black and a white thread twisted together, on which some silver coins were hung.

Bead chokers are popular among some groups, especially among the Turkmen in Afghanistan, and are worn by girls and married women alike. In the simpler versions, there is a series of colored beads, especially red, while in more elaborate forms, silver coins are incorporated into the design.

During the nineteenth and twentieth centuries, some women wore a heavy collar (*buqau*) that masked the throat. The collar was made with interlinking pendants or a single fretted lozenge (*gonjuk*). During the twentieth century, the collar gave way to a collar stud (*gol yaqeh* or *gulyaqa*), which was used to close the neck opening of women's dresses. These studs could vary in size from about an inch to six inches (a few centimeters to fifteen centimeters) in diameter. Such studs were generally associated with the Yomut and, to a lesser extent, the Teke. By

A silver brooch with gilt and red glass decoration, Turkmenistan, late twentieth century. This style of brooch is worn at the base of the throat by married Teke and Ersari women of Turkmenistan. Girls of marriageable age may also wear these brooches. Textile Research Centre, Leiden.

the end of the twentieth century, however, many women were no longer wearing collar studs but rather a brooch of the same size. Younger children (both male and female) often wore a very large version of the gulyaka but slightly lower down on the chest. These may have had an amuletic function.

Among all the Turkmen, round and rhomboid pendants are worn as pectoral ornaments. They could be sewn directly onto the clothing or worn over a cloth foundation that looks a little like a Western bib.

In addition to jewelry worn on the body, there are also decorative elements on a type of coat (*chabut*) worn by Turkmen women. The *changa*, for example, are a pair of ornamental metal plaques, often with pendants and bells, which have a matching hook and loop for use as fasteners. This coat may be further decorated with rows of plaques and coins down the front and sometimes on the sleeves as well. Often, these rows would end in large diamond-shaped plaques called *göndchük*. Only one such coat is normally worn directly over the woman's dress.

The most predominant form of arm jewelry is long, tubular bracelets (*goshmah*), which are worn in pairs. They are usually divided into three or four segments, although there are examples with as many as eight. They are often decorated with engravings, gilding, applied plates and chains, as well as semiprecious stones and glass beads.

In addition, there is a bracelet called a hand rose, which consists of a very narrow bracelet linked via a chain to a plaque. Five chains ending in rings are attached to the plaque, one for each finger of the hand. These are well-known items of jewelry from India and the Gulf region, where they are sometimes called ring gloves. They may represent a form that has been imported into the Turkmen jewelry repertoire.

Finger rings are another essential, albeit much smaller, item of Turkmen jewelry, and they come in many different forms and shapes. Some rings are made as part of the bride's trousseau, and others are acquired over the years. Some rings are decorated with stones, others with engravings and gild work. There are also many types decorated with semiprecious stones and bells. By the end of the twentieth century, more and more Western-style rings made in India and Iran were being imported into the region.

References and Further Reading

Blocqueville, Henri de Couliboeuf de. *Quatorze mois de captivité chez les Turcomans. Aux frontières du Turkestan et de la Perse.* Paris: L. Hachette, 1865.

Firouz, Iran Ala. *Silver Ornaments of the Turkoman.* Tehran: The Hamdami Foundation, 1978.

Irons, William. *The Yomut Turkmen: A Study of Social Organization among a Central Asian Turkic-Speaking Population.* Ann Arbor: University of Michigan Press, 1975.

Janata, Alfred. *Schmuck in Afghanistan.* Graz, Austria: Akademische Druck- u. Verlagsanstalt, 1981.

Kalter, Johannes. *The Arts and Crafts of Turkestan.* London: Thames and Hudson, 1984.

Munneke, Roelof. *Van Zilver, Goud en Kornalijn: Turkmeense Sieraden uit Centraal Azië.* Leiden and Breda, the Netherlands: Rijksmuseum voor Volkenkunde, 1990.

References and Further Reading

Allsen, Thomas T. *Commodity and Exchange in the Mongol Empire: A Cultural History of Islamic Textiles.* Cambridge: Cambridge University Press, 1997.

Andrews, Mugal, and Peter Andrews. *Turkmen Needlework, Dressmaking and Embroidery among the Turkmen of Iran.* London: Central Asian Research Centre, 1976.

Andrews, Peter. *The Turkoman of Iran.* Kendal, UK: Abbot Hall Art Gallery, 1971.

Andrews, Peter. "Crowning the Bride: Some Historical Evidence on Türkmen Women's Costume." Revised English version with drawings by Mrs. M. Andrews. *Folk* 33 (1991): 67–106.

Beresneva, L. *Decorative and Applied Art of Turkmenia.* Leningrad: Aurora Art Publishers, 1976.

Firouz, Iran Ala. *Silver Ornaments of the Turkoman.* Tehran: Hamdami Foundation, 1978.

Fitz Gibbon, Kate, and Andrew Hale. *Splendid Silks of Central Asia; Ikat; The Guido Goldman Collection.* London: Laurence King, 1997.

Fraser, James Baillie. *Travels and Adventures in the Persian Provinces on the Southern Banks of the Caspian Sea.* London: Longman, Rees, Orme, Brown, and Green, 1826.

Harvey, Janet. *Traditional Textiles of Central Asia.* London: Thames and Hudson, 1997.

Irons, William. *The Yomut Turkmen: A Study of Social Organization among a Central Asian Turkic-Speaking Population.* Ann Arbor: University of Michigan Press, 1975.

Janata, Alfred. *Schmuck in Afghanistan.* Graz, Austria: Akademische Druck- u. Verlagsanstalt, 1981.

Kalter, Johannes. *The Arts and Crafts of Turkestan.* London: Thames and Hudson, 1984.

Munneke, Roelof. *Van Zilver, Goud en Kornalijn: Turkmeense Sieraden uit Centraal Azië.* Leiden and Breda, the Netherlands: Rijksmuseum voor Volkenkunde, 1990.

Rau, Pip. *Ikats, Woven Silks from Central Asia; The Rau Collection.* Oxford: Basil Blackwell, 1989.

Scarce, Jennifer. *Women's Costume of the Near and Middle East.* London: Unwin Hyman, 1987.

Stucki, A. "Horses and Women: Some Thoughts on the Life Cycle of Ersari Turkmen Women." *Afghanistan Journal* 5 (1978): 140–149.

Vogelsang-Eastwood, Gillian, and Willem Vogelsang. *Covering the Moon: An Introduction to Middle Eastern Face Veils.* Leuven, Belgium: Peeters, 2008.

Wulff, Hans E. *The Traditional Crafts of Iran.* Cambridge: Massachusetts Institute of Technology, 1966.

Gillian Vogelsang-Eastwood

See also Regional Dress of Afghanistan; Turkmen Women's Jewelry; Dress from Tajikistan and Uzbekistan.

Dress from Tajikistan and Uzbekistan

- Materials and Ornamentation
- Basic Forms of Dress and Formative Influences
- Settled Tajik and Uzbek Men's Dress
- Settled Tajik and Uzbek Women's Dress
- Jewelry
- Nomadic Uzbek and Karakalpak Dress

Geographically, the Central Asian region is generally very dry, with two large river systems, the Amu Dar'ya and Syr Dar'ya, which flow westward from the mountains of Tajikistan across Uzbekistan and empty into the Aral Sea. Occasional oases along these river systems offered fertile environments for settlement, agriculture, and trade; cotton and silk, both vital for clothing and textiles, were essential products.

In the early centuries of the first millennium C.E., nomadic peoples who spoke a range of Turkic languages moved westward into Central Asia from the steppe lands north of China, in doing so largely displacing the indigenous Indo-European inhabitants. These Turkic tribes were the ancestors of the Uzbek, Turkmen, Kazakh, and Kyrgyz peoples for whom four of the five early-twenty-first-century Central Asian states are named. The fifth state is named for the Tajik people, who are descendants of the earliest settled people of the region, the original Indo-Europeans, and speak a dialect closely related to Persian.

The Turkic-speaking Uzbeks of the early twenty-first century are said to have taken their name from a tribal chieftain called Uzbek Khan, a descendant of Genghis Khan, who lived in the fourteenth century C.E. By the sixteenth century, large numbers of these nomadic Uzbeks had abandoned their itinerant lifestyle and tribal structure and settled down alongside the sedentary Tajiks. These two cultural groups, the Tajiks and the Uzbeks, have thus coexisted for a long time in and around the townships. As a result, Tajik and Uzbek elements have combined to form a blended urban culture, inevitably incorporating various other influences along the way.

Historically, Tajikistan and Uzbekistan were once part of West Turkistan, the khanates and emirates of which came progressively under the control of tsarist Russia during the early to mid-1800s. The term *Turkistan*, which dates back to the 1500s, was abolished in the 1920s by the incoming Soviets, who divided the area, roughly along ethnic lines, to form Tajikistan, Uzbekistan, Turkmenistan, Kazakhstan, and Kyrgyzstan. Part of the firmly controlled Soviet world since the 1920s, these states became independent in 1991, a profound political change that inevitably affected many aspects of traditional society deeply, including long-established habits of dress.

In the early twenty-first century, the Tajiks and Uzbeks are generally understood as those who live in Tajikistan and Uzbekistan. This description conceals a more complex reality, however, as many centers of Tajik culture, such as Bukhara, Samarkand,

Shakhrisabz, and Nurata, are in Uzbekistan and are still home to large numbers of Tajik people, while the population of Tajikistan includes many who are ethnically Uzbek. Consequently, the two cultures, including their richly decorative arts and crafts, exhibit strong similarities, and distinguishing between them is often impossible. In Bukhara, for example, the rulers were Uzbek, but most of the population was actually Tajik, and many traditional Tajik crafts such as gold and silk embroidery were highly developed. In the early twenty-first century, these Tajik arts are commonly described as Uzbek since they are practiced in Uzbekistan.

MATERIALS AND ORNAMENTATION

Traditionally, the raw materials most commonly used by the settled people of Tajikistan and Uzbekistan were cotton and silk; wool, in contrast, was produced by nomadic pastoralists and traded in the urban marketplaces for town products. In the chilly mountainous region of the western Pamirs, the northern parts of Kulyab, and the upper reaches of the Zerafshan River, the Tajiks also relied mainly on woolen fabrics for their clothes. Pastoralism and nomadism, which are contrasting modes of economic subsistence, offer a valuable framework for understanding the material culture of the Central Asian region. While townspeople produced woven and embroidered hangings and coverings for their domestic interiors from the cotton and silk they farmed, nomadic peoples produced woolen carpets, tents, and animal trappings. In relation to dress, although there are strong regional commonalities, traditional dress worn by settled and nomadic people also demonstrates variations and borrowings, mainly determined by ethnicity, the available materials, and climate.

By the fourth millennium B.C.E., cotton was growing in northern India and Central Asia, and securing this crop for the expanding Russian textile industry was the main economic reason for tsarist Russia's advance into Turkistan. By 1880, they had introduced strains of long-fiber cotton from the United States and maximized the area of cotton cultivation in the region that comprises Uzbekistan in the early twenty-first century. Watered by the Amu Dar'ya, with drastic results for the Aral Sea, which has virtually vanished, cotton is still vital to the Uzbek economy. Cotton was woven by women into a wide range of fabrics for clothing and domestic textiles, including striped *alacha* (fine striped cotton fabric), gauzes, and natural *karbos* (coarse cotton cloth woven with hand-spun yarn).

Silk and half-silk fabrics, in contrast, were woven by men. Silk cultivation enjoys a symbiotic relationship with cotton, as is clearly seen in the regular planting of mulberry trees along the irrigation channels that border the cotton fields; acting as windbreaks, they prevent soil erosion and provide leaves for silkworms to eat. Raising silkworms was traditionally women's work, while producing *ipak* (silk threads) and dyeing them was accomplished by urban Jewish communities in all-male workshops. The principal dyestuffs used, prior to the arrival of aniline dyes in the 1870s, were *nil* (indigo) for blue, *rujan* (madder) and *kirmizi* (Russian cochineal) for red, *isparak* (delphinium) for yellow, and *anor pusti* (pomegranate) for black.

Before the takeover by tsarist Russia, plain or endlessly varied striped cottons were commonly used for everyday clothing and other items. Regional specializations in fabric types and colors developed in different areas, giving rise to identifiable local styles and patterns. In addition to their love of bright colors, Tajik and Uzbek weavers demonstrated an inspired ability to create and juxtapose patterns to astonishingly beautiful effect. Whereas fabrics for everyday use, work clothes, and clothes for most of the population were relatively sober and simply ornamented, dress for the prosperous and for special occasions featured brilliant color, striking patterns, and elaborate ornamentation. Notable are ikat-patterned fabrics, achieved by tie-dyeing the warp threads prior to weaving; these include *shahi* (all-silk fabric), finely ribbed *adras* (fabric made with a silk warp and thick cotton weft), and *baghmal* (silk velvet ikat). Other decorative favorites were bright *bekasab* (striped half silk) and cottons that were either locally block-printed by hand or made in Russian factories and imported.

Some of the most eye-catching clothes were the ikat-patterned coats and dresses produced by men in city workshops. While Tajik weavers tended to make shahi ikats, Uzbek weavers produced adras, which, with its heavier weight and beautiful texture, was often preferred for coats (*khalats*). The Central Asian term for ikat-patterned fabrics is *abr*, meaning "cloud" in Persian and probably indicating a Tajik origin for the art. Abr production was a commercial affair, and the fabrics were also marketed to the Kazakhs, Kyrgyz, and Turkmen of Central Asia as well as in Afghanistan, Russia, Persia, and eastern Turkistan. The complex and precious baghmal was produced only in Bukhara in the late 1800s and used for the finest of coats; remnants were carefully saved to make belts, women's caps, and tiny bags. In the early twenty-first century, women are the principal weavers of the silk and synthetic ikats produced in Bukhara and the Fergana Valley, and baghmal production has been tentatively reestablished in Bukhara.

Block printing was once widely practiced in many of the urban centers of western Turkistan and, in the nineteenth and early twentieth centuries, was often used to ornament scarves, coat linings, burial shrouds, and domestic textiles. Handwoven cotton was often used as the base for floral patterns printed in madder rose, burgundy, and black, while fine silks, block-printed and overdyed with several colors, were used to make women's scarves or shawls. With the influx of Russian factory textiles, however, block printing has all but disappeared; in the early twenty-first century, only a few workshops remain in Bukhara, Tashkent, and Margilan.

Women's embroidery decorated both everyday and special-occasion clothes; until the introduction of aniline dyes, silk and wool embroidery threads were hand-dyed with natural dyestuffs.

Seyyid Mir Mohammed Alim Khan, Emir of Bukhara (1880–1944), wearing a richly colored, long-sleeved, embroidered *khalat* (outer robe), ca. 1910. *Khalats* were worn by most men in Central Asia, but in the court, hierarchically based clothing regulations meant that ruler's robes were embroidered with gold thread or made from the rare *baghmal*; lesser dignitaries had to wear imported fabrics, and those in the lower ranks and merchants wore lesser *shahi* or *adras ikats*.

Yurma (chain stitch), *iroqi* (half cross stitch worked in the Shakhrisabz area), and *zarduzi* (gold embroidery) are the techniques most often used for the elaborate embroidery on men's robes, trousers, caps, and belts and on women's dress frontals, headbands, caps, and bags. Although floral motifs may indicate Persian influences, and geometric patterns often reflect nomadic and pre-Islamic designs, it is difficult to distinguish Tajik from Uzbek embroidery, as these two different ethnic groups have adjusted to living side by side and their arts have entwined. With the advent of inexpensive patterned fabrics, embroidery ceased to be so important on women's dresses, although it is still much in fashion in the southeastern mountains of Tajikistan. Although traditional forms of dress are still worn for everyday as well as special occasions, commercially produced fabrics decorated with commercially produced ornaments are most often used. Aesthetic ideals have accommodated themselves to the sweeping socioeconomic changes in the region, so that bright plastic beads, gold ribbon, and glittering lurex proliferate in place of fine silk embroidery and are appreciated for their eye-catching sparkle.

Gold embroidery was a specialization of the Bukhara palace workshops and was traditionally practiced by male embroiderers for an elite clientele. Gold and silver threads were imported from India or Iran until the mid-1800s, after which all the threads came from Russia. Zarduzi encrusted the finest silks, velvets, and muslins for men's ceremonial robes, turbans, pants, belts, and shoes as well as sword sheaths and horse blankets; zarduzi was also available for wealthy women's headdresses, dress frontals, and boots. During the early decades of the Soviet era, gold embroidery was collectivized into huge businesses, and workshops were established in Samarkand and Dushanbe. Women became practitioners, and, by the 1970s, zarduzi had become a common form of traditional embroidery. In 2003, there was still at least one young man in Bukhara, the inheritor of his Jewish family's superlative skills, producing fine, gold-embroidered men's robes; a zarduzi workshop still flourishes in the Bukhara Ark ("citadel" or "fortress"; a state museum in the early twenty-first century), where young women bend over their needles to produce assorted accessories for the passing tourist trade.

Zeh or *dziyak* are the woven or embroidered decorative braids that ornament the outer edges of khalats, *kurtas* (dresses), trousers, and caps, as well as *suzanis* (embroidered hangings and covers), horse blankets, and other textiles for domestic use. These decorative edgings marked the boundaries of a garment symbolically, protecting the wearer against misfortune; they remain an essential addition to women's caps and trousers. Zeh was always made by women, sometimes working in pairs, depending on which of the four different production methods was used, and it is still common in the region to see women making braid.

BASIC FORMS OF DRESS AND FORMATIVE INFLUENCES

The similarity of the basic range of garments worn by men, women, and children is a striking feature of Central Asian dress. Aside from the ethnic, regional, individual, material, and decorative variations that have inevitably evolved over time, traditional Central Asian dress can still be described as a coat or robe worn over a tunic, shirt or dress, and trousers, plus headwear and footwear.

Generally speaking, people continued to dress the way they had for centuries until the early 1900s, with differences in shape and style determined by tribal and regional customs, climatic conditions, and occupation. Social differences were usually reflected in the quality of the fabrics, the quantity of ornamentation, and the number of garments owned, both for daily wear and for special occasions. Wedding clothes for both men and women were often white, which symbolized happiness; special funeral clothing was worn only by women and consisted of a dress in a black or dark color.

What people wore in Central Asia was also to a large extent affected by geography and their mode of subsistence. While the inhabitants of steppes and mountains needed the warmth and protection of wool and fur from their herds, the long hot summers and short cold winters of the oasis towns and villages of Uzbekistan and Tajikistan favored cool clothing made from the cotton and silk grown there.

Historical evidence regarding early Central Asian dress is incomplete, but indications come from a variety of sources, including archaeological excavations, the observations of traders and travelers passing through, wall paintings, miniature paintings, and figurines. Early references suggest that it may have been difficult to distinguish men from women, as they all wore the same archetypal tunic that forms the basis of garments worn in the early twenty-first century. Essentially, the tunic was cut (or torn) from one straight piece of cloth folded in half, with the fold placed at the shoulders; sleeves and underarm side panels were also straight-cut, often with a gusset to ease the underarm join; and the neck opening was a horizontal slit. Vertical front openings were probably designed for breast-feeding. Although the fundamentals have remained constant, pattern variations were subsequently introduced, resulting in the range of shirts, dresses, and coats familiar from public and private collections.

An early modification was to vary the length of the tunic; whereas younger men's shirts shortened to hip length, women's dresses became longer, reaching to the ankles. Another variation saw the front opening of the tunic extended from the neck to the hem, thus creating an open-fronted garment or coat. There are several names for this most ubiquitous of Central Asian garments: a light coat, lined or unlined, was called *yaktak* (Tajik) or *jegde* (Uzbek); a padded or quilted coat was *joma* (Tajik) or *chapan* (Uzbek); the Russian term *khalat*, however, is relatively universal and is used to avoid confusion between Tajik and Uzbek terms. Collars were sometimes added to coats, varying over time and from region to region, followed by the introduction of gores in some types of khalat, plus side slits, decorative linings, and ornamental edgings. The khalat was originally a men's garment, important as an indicator of prosperity and status; a young boy's first khalat was made for him for the occasion of his circumcision. Added to the female dress repertoire in the nineteenth century, women's coats were usually worn for warmth but sometimes for showing off wealth.

Straight or flared *shalwar* or *lozim* (trousers) were worn by both men and women. Somewhat voluminous and with little variation in the cut, they consisted of two leg pieces seamed to a central piece of varying shape. The head was covered by a cap and a turban or folded cloth. Generally speaking, young boys wore turbans for the first time at their circumcision, while women wore them only after the birth of their first child. Many men still wear turbans in the early twenty-first century, but women rarely do. Marked differences developed in the headwear traditionally used by different ethnic or regional groups.

From the age of seven or eight on, traditional children's clothes essentially mirrored in miniature those of their parents and were similarly personalized with local and material variations. Newborn babies wore an unhemmed cotton shirt made by their mothers or grandmothers for the first forty days, then a simple tunic with an apron until three or four years of age. Children's shirts had horizontal neck openings, and their trousers were extra wide and gathered at the shin; young girls wore red underwear and overcoats; and caps were brightly embroidered.

Of crucial importance to the broad cultural development in Central Asia were the cross-cultural influences brought to the region by merchants and travelers on the Silk Road. This ancient network of trade routes stretched from China to the Mediterranean, with the oasis towns of Central Asia ideally placed for the exchange and relay of commodities, people, imagery, and ideas. Chinese silk was only one of the principal trade goods; a variety of local chieftains and conquerors built their wealth on silk and commodities such as Turkmen horses and carpets, slaves

An Uzbek woman wearing an ikat dress (*kurta*), 1872. The loose dress has a wide neck and long sleeves, below which the embroidered sleeves of the under-dress (*peshkir* or *koylak*) can be seen. Library of Congress Prints and Photographs Division, LC-DIG-ppmsca-12187.

who were talented in music and dance, exotic animals and foods, spices, ceramics, ivory and coral, religious ideas, and new technologies. Periods of destabilization in the region, such as those during the Mongol invasions of the thirteenth century, impacted negatively on the Silk Road trade, and many merchants eventually chose to travel and send their goods by sea.

Centuries of comparative isolation ensued for Central Asia, ending with tsarist Russian colonization in the early 1800s, followed by Soviet domination and collectivization in the early 1900s. Major changes to traditional dress forms essentially began with the takeover by tsarist Russia, as Russia's mass-produced and inexpensive textiles, especially cottons, began to replace fabrics woven at home. Access to Western fashions and culture subsequently exerted strong pressure for changes to traditional dress.

The wide observance of Islam in Central Asia helped ensure that clothing styles were relatively stable. Ornamentation in traditional dress and other crafts tended toward geometric and vegetal patterns rather than images of living beings. Islam was originally introduced to Central Asia by Arab traders around 800 C.E. and is the predominant religion in the area, strongly influencing modes of behavior and dress. However, early-twenty-first-century Tajikistan and Uzbekistan are secular states, and Uzbek government agencies have asserted that traditional Uzbek dress should be preferred over Islamic dress. Female students wearing the hijab (Islamically acceptable or correct clothing) have been banned from campuses on the grounds that they undermine Uzbek tradition, even though, up until the 1920s, many Uzbek women were veiled.

SETTLED TAJIK AND UZBEK MEN'S DRESS

Traditional dress for urban Uzbek and Tajik men consisted basically of a shirt tucked into trousers with a coat, cap, and boots with regional variations in color. Shirts were typically of white cotton trimmed with woven or embroidered braid; in the rural areas, they were made from striped fabrics. Trousers (*ishton*), traditionally also of plain white cotton, were cut straight and wide, with tapering legs and a gusset. In winter, trousers were quilted or of thick cotton or wool. The introduction of factory-woven fabrics, which were wider than the cloth produced on traditional looms, and access to European styles eventually encouraged the development of new and more complex clothing forms.

Khalats were produced in the bazaars of major urban centers, with regional variations. Made by men, a khalat was cut to order from selected fabric and stitched together; from the early 1900s, sewing machines were used. Striped fabrics such as half-silk bekasab were particularly popular. Easily produced in a day, complete with zeh edging, khalats from Bukhara and Samarkand were typically brightly colored, while black and green characterized robes from Tashkent, yellow with violet and pink was favored in the Fergana Valley, and khalats from Khorezm were often red with narrow stripes. Summer coats were lightweight, and winter coats padded and quilted, or of fur when the weather was very cold. For traveling, a man might wear a plain camel-hair khalat, with a pair of embroidered velvet or yellow leather overtrousers to protect his legs, and high-heeled riding boots. Slits at each side of the coat ensured greater freedom of movement, especially on horseback.

Typically, prosperous urban men wore brilliantly colored ikat khalats. Wearing more than one coat indicated a man's status and prosperity, and wealthy men might wear as many as five to greet important guests, with the finest velvet robe on top. The ceremonial robes worn by the emir and court dignitaries were made from fabulous fabrics, often beautifully embroidered. Hierarchically based clothing regulations were introduced that restricted the use of robes embroidered with gold thread or made from the rare baghmal to the ruler; lesser dignitaries had to content themselves with imported fabrics, and those in the lower ranks and merchants used shahi or adras ikats.

Fine khalats were considered the most significant of gifts. They were presented to worthy citizens at New Year's and were typically given to guests; diplomatic gifts of khalats could be very large, and in the early twenty-first century, they are still presented to visiting ambassadors and given as a mark of respect. Because large numbers of light silk ikat khalats were so commonly given as gifts, they became widely dispersed throughout Central Asia. As a result, these lovely robes are an integral part of the dress culture of nomadic groups as well as the sedentary population of the oasis towns in which they were made. In the early twenty-first century, Tajik and Uzbek men, particularly older men and those in rural areas, still wear khalats, generally of plain dark blue fabric, with sash ties and turbans. Younger men, in urban contexts particularly, prefer to wear Western dress except for ceremonial occasions such as weddings. Small boys often wear a khalat over Western shorts and a shirt, while Western dress is universally preferred for both boys and girls at school.

Since most khalats had no fastenings, men generally secured them at the waist with a decorative belt or, in later years, with one or more diagonally folded chorsis (printed cotton kerchiefs). Wealthy men wore beautiful belts featuring large ornamental buckles, typically made from rare fabrics or using decorative techniques such as card weaving and cross stitch; their designs reflected a wide range of influences, including ikat, suzanis, nomadic carpet patterns, and the arts of Iran and Ottoman Turkey. Because the khalat lacked pockets, belts and chorsi assumed great importance, especially for the upper classes, as personal effects were attached to or tucked into them. Chorsi could also serve as a towel or prayer mat during a journey or be used to wrap a purchase. Men did not wear jewelry other than fine belts, seal rings, and sometimes ornate daggers, although they adorned their horses with horse jewelry for special occasions.

According to Islamic custom, which required adults to cover their heads, urban Tajik and Uzbek men wore tubiteyka or duppi (skullcaps) both indoors and outdoors, often wrapping a salla (turban) around them when going out. Turban cloths were made from different fabrics, while turban styles varied from group to group; turban wrapping was considered a special skill. In traditional contexts, the style of men's caps, and their quality in terms of materials and craft skills, conveyed information regarding the wearer's ethnicity, religion, and social status. Caps varied from region to region and according to age and gender; they could be round or square with a domed, pointed, or flat crown. During the Soviet period, crowns became more uniformly rounded and the rims narrower. A smaller plain cotton cap was often worn underneath to absorb sweat.

Some caps, soft and simple in construction, are easily made at home as dowry gifts by the women of the family, and cap production is a popular domestic craft. In Shakhrisabz, caps are stitched all over with iroqi, while the flat-topped caps from Urgut feature a multicolored popuk (tassel), and those from Samarkand

typically have white calligraphic embroidery on a black background. New designs are invented constantly, many of them symbolically expressing deeply held wishes, such as the desire for a son or protection from misfortune. Tubiteyka of the firm chust type are produced by men in factories; these are made from four sections of dark green or blue cloth, each embroidered with a white amuletic chili-pepper or almond-leaf motif for fertility, and require card insertions and machine stitching. With some local variations, these Uzbek caps are available in markets everywhere and have become standard wear for men throughout Tajikistan and Uzbekistan.

On their feet, both men and women wore soft-soled makhsi (leather boots) indoors, often covering them with galoshes or overshoes for outdoors. In urban centers, men's leather riding boots and the shoes of wealthy women might be hand-tooled with colorful patterns or heavily ornamented with gold embroidery. In village areas, people wore chirik, rough, half-open footwear made from rawhide. In the mountainous Pamir and Kulyab regions of Tajikistan, everyone wore wooden shoes over decorative juraby (woolen socks) knitted by the women.

SETTLED TAJIK AND UZBEK WOMEN'S DRESS

Indoors, Tajik and Uzbek women traditionally wore a loose peshkir or koylak (underdress) of white cotton, with very long sleeves embroidered with floral motifs at the wide cuffs. Over this was a long wide ikat kurta with a round neck; it was slashed to the waist and had long sleeves with broad cuffs, so that the embroidered sleeves of the underdress were clearly visible. Wealthy women might wear three or more dresses at once for festive occasions. Kurtas worn by unmarried women were often red with horizontal neck openings, while the vertical front openings of married women's kurtas were enhanced with peshkurtas (dress frontals, which are panels at the front chest region), often worked in zarduzi or iroqi. Women from Kulyab in Tajikistan wore roomy, lightweight cotton dresses with bright floral embroidery on the front.

Trousers (lozim), held in place with a belt, were essential under kurtas. Wide at the waist and hips and tight at the ankles, with a decorative trim around the cuffs, they were made from two different fabrics for reasons of thrift as well as aesthetics. Plain white cotton, which was believed to have magical power to bestow fertility and happiness, was used for the upper part, with patterned silk for the lower part of the trouser legs that showed below the kurta. While Tajik and Uzbek women mostly wear Western dress in professional contexts in the early twenty-first century, many still wear a form of traditional dress: a pair of loose trousers in bright floral velveteen under a long yoked dress with short or long sleeves, plus the ubiquitous head scarf.

For warmth, women wore khalats made from various fabrics, such as locally produced bekasab, shahi, or adras ikat or imported brocade; neck bands were typically more open and sleeves shorter and wider than men's forms. The main stylistic variations were the munisak, mursak, or kaltacha (ceremonial coat) and the paranja (outer coat). The munisak, which has no neck band, was longer than usual coats, gathered at the waist and open at the front, with wide sleeves, side slits, and zeh edgings. Once regular outdoor wear for women, munisaks became associated with funerals during the 1800s and were worn over dark dresses; after 1900, in the Tashkent area, they were used only to cover coffins. A later, shorter, sleeveless variation of the khalat was the kamzol, which evolved after the Russian conquest and was cut on the bias in European princess style, with a narrow waist and no decorative edging.

Women were, like men, required to cover their heads, and a wide range of cap, shawl, and turban styles evolved over time across the region. Women's caps (*kulta*) were often high and soft, covering the head fully, while the *kulta peshak* featured an attached rectangular piece that encased long plaits. Zarduzi, or silk floral embroidery in rural areas, often decorated the velvet kulta peshaks of wealthy women and the *peshonaband* (forehead band) that kept it in place. Women also invariably wore a large scarf or shawl (*rumal*), which varied greatly according to region. Favorites were Russian silk shawls, embroidered with flowers, or printed cotton shawls. Turbans were once widely worn but rarely by urban women since the mid-1900s.

By the mid-1800s, urban Tajik and Uzbek women who ventured outside the privacy of their homes were required to cover themselves completely with the voluminous paranja and *chachvan* (face veil), which were often acquired from itinerant gypsy women who made them, using a skillful looping technique, from the lustrous black tail hair of their horses. More cloak than coat, the paranja has a well-defined neck band, hand slits on either side

An Uzbek woman wearing a long horsehair veil (*chachvan*) and a *paranja*, Samarkand, Uzbekistan, ca. 1955. The dark *chachvan* is worn tied around the head and covers the face and front of the woman's torso. Over this, she wears a *paranja* with embroidered edges and an interior lining of printed cotton. Believing that the paranja and chachvan represented ignorance and oppression, the Soviets encouraged women to burn them, but some devout Muslim women saw this as an insult to Islam and continued to wear the paranja throughout the Soviet era. Getty Images.

of the front opening, and long vestigial sleeves that fall down the back and are ornamented with braid and tassels. The neck band of the paranja rests on top of the woman's head over the chach-van, which is secured around her head and covers her face. Falling in folds around her body, the chachvan and paranja conceal the woman's identity and ensure her modesty.

Although the shape of paranjas remained much the same over time, the materials changed. Originally, most were made (always by a specialist) from finely striped blue-gray cotton, with simple black braid and embroidery decorating the edges and a colorful lining of Russian printed cotton. As new materials became available, paranjas appeared on the streets in heavy silks, brocades, rich velvets, or bright ikats; zeh became increasingly common, and decoration around the neck band and hand openings and on the vestigial sleeves became more elaborate, colorful, and plentiful. The false sleeves are pre-Islamic in origin but were adapted by Islamic groups since they covered the hands, a matter of modesty, since women's hands were not supposed to touch or be touched by the hands of men who were strangers. To the Soviets, the paranja and chachvan represented ignorance and oppression, and women were encouraged to burn them from the 1920s on. Perceiving this as an insult to Islam, some devout Muslim women, encouraged by their male relatives, continued to wear the paranja throughout the Soviet period. Its use has perceptibly increased postindependence in strong Muslim areas such as the Fergana Valley in eastern Uzbekistan and western Tajikistan.

A young woman's dowry was ready long before her wedding and included many dresses, including the two traditionally worn on her wedding day, one white or pale pink and the other red, a reference to her hoped-for fertility. A red sash around her bridegroom's khalat and red underarm gussets on his shirt symbolized his virility. From the early 1900s, women often preferred ikat dresses of a more Western cut, worn with red brocade trousers and a khalat. A wedding headdress covered her head, and she wore jewelry on her forehead; in front of her face she traditionally held a cloth embroidered with a tree-of-life motif to shield her from others' glances. In the early twenty-first century, ikat has become something of a national Uzbek symbol and is worn as traditional dress by most Uzbek women for ceremonial occasions.

Many regional distinctions can be made regarding traditional women's dress in Uzbekistan. For example, in Kashkadarya, whose main urban centers are Shakhrisabz and Karshi, women wore several types of dress, sometimes at the same time, which could be a traditional white tunic with embroidered sleeves worn underneath a shorter, brightly colored dress ornamented with bands of broad braid in front. Kashkadarya women's headdresses differed from those of other regions; the older *chambar shokh*, for example, was a horned confection made from ten handkerchief squares that varied according to age and taste. Younger women's headdresses included larger and more colorful squares, while older women's had fewer squares, which were also smaller and plainer in color. In the twentieth century, round caps that were gathered at the crown or worked in iroqi were worn.

With independence, and in response to years of Soviet collectivism and the global communications revolution, urban Uzbek and Tajik women have begun to demand fashionable clothes that reflect individuality and redress the anonymity of mass-produced, factory-made garments. Interest in fashion design is thus developing rapidly in Central Asia as access to international trends has increased exponentially via television, film, Western magazines, the Internet, and other such avenues. A number of talented young designers are exploring their own ideas, establishing boutique ready-to-wear businesses and taking advantage of promotional opportunities. While some prefer to work within a global design paradigm, many have chosen a synthesis of heritage and innovation. At the folkloric festival Boysun Bakhori in Kashkadarya, for example, designers were encouraged to create contemporary silhouettes inspired by traditional forms and ornamented with traditional decorative techniques. Traditional fabrics such as ikat and bekasab acquire a striking new look when cut to create a radically new shape or eye-catching accessory. At the same time, in cities such as Bukhara, Tashkent, and Dushanbe, fashionable Tajik and Uzbek women can still be seen in smart ankle-length dresses descended directly from the traditional tunic and made from local materials such as the satin-weave ikat fabric *khanatlas*.

JEWELRY

Jewelry is an integral part of women's dress in Central Asia. Typically taking the form of elaborate chest and head ornaments, as well as rings, bangles, anklets, earrings, nose rings, and necklaces, jewelry from the urban centers of Uzbekistan such as Bukhara, Samarkand, and Khiva was predominantly of gold with turquoise and carnelian. While *zargars* (jewellers) mainly worked for the wealthier levels of society, the important protective properties of jewelry ensured that poorer-quality work also found a ready market. Aside from its universal purpose as a body ornament, the role of jewelry in the life of settled and nomadic women was different: Nomadic women wore jewelry as a portable form of wealth, while for sedentary women it was an optional luxury. Nomadic jewelry tends therefore toward solid and sturdy forms, while urban jewelry is often more fragile and ornate.

Silver jewelry was and still is obligatory for both wealthy and poorer brides, with inserts of carnelian, coral, turquoise, or colored glass. A complete set of jewelry for a Tajik or Uzbek bride includes the *parkhona* (headdress), *khalka* (earrings), *khafaband* (necklaces), *daspona* (bracelets), *anguspona* (rings), and perhaps a *doppe* (silver cylinder) bearing protective verses from the Qur'an. Wealthy woman might add a *bisathe-kobba*, the local equivalent of a chatelaine with silver chains, ear picks, and toothpicks. Gilded silver *tilyakosh* (bridal diadems) from Khiva, Bukhara, Samarkand, and Tashkent feature a curving eyebrow-shaped forehead band with pearl and almond-shaped pendants, surmounted by openwork closely set with decorative stones and glass. Segmented diadems composed of multiple elements, sometimes attached to a textile band and also with forehead pendants, were widely worn in Khorezam and by nomadic Uzbeks in northern Afghanistan, but they are now rarely seen.

From the late 1800s, eye-catching necklaces appeared with five to seven rows of chains punctuated by silver plaques and a large central medallion, all studded with gems and colored glass. Temple ornaments of different shapes with pendant chains and multicolored stones were worn by Tajik women, Jewish women from Bukhara, and women in the Fergana Valley. Well-heeled Bukharan women wore pairs of hinged openwork bracelets of silver gilt with niello (black inlay work) or enameled clasps, and earrings of gold and silver, of varying size and shape, were worn throughout both Tajikistan and Uzbekistan. Unique to Tajikistan are multistring coral and silver necklaces from the Kulyab area.

Silver jewelry was mostly produced by Tajik craftsmen in the urban bazaars, but, with the exception of jewelry from Khorezm, it is difficult to be sure of its regional origin. Khorezm jewelry is typically made from multiple elements cut from sheets of thin gilt silver; characteristically, a solid, heavily ornamented central piece is fringed by fine chains with pendant leaves, local or Iranian turquoise, and Indian coral. Amulets containing texts from the Qur'an, prayers to the saints, or magical incantations are part of the Islamic belief system, although not officially approved by Islamic theologians. Varying in form and ornamentation, they were produced in urban workshops from materials with symbolic significance and were widely worn, particularly on festive occasions. Silver, for example, was associated with the moon, while blue was believed to deflect evil, and red carnelian was thought to prevent miscarriages.

NOMADIC UZBEK AND KARAKALPAK DRESS

The few surviving seminomadic Uzbeks are generally known by their tribal names; for example, the Durmen of the Bagatag mountains, the Kungrat, the Lokait, and the Lakai. Although primarily cattle breeders, they lived a semisedentary life, and by the 1920s their numbers were rapidly diminishing. Nomadic men typically wore simple, unornamented shirts and trousers, khalats, caps, and boots, but decoration was often lavish on trappings for their horses, on which they were practically and economically dependent and which were proverbially said to be more precious to them than their wives.

A Soviet study described the bridal clothing customarily worn by a Durmen Uzbek couple for their wedding. The bridegroom wore a new khalat and a skullcap sewn for him by his bride, whose own new clothes were set off by a turban-style headdress wound in her husband's house. The bottom of her dress was not hemmed, indicating her wish for a happy married life; this was also common practice for nomadic children's dresses to ensure a long life for them.

The Lakai Uzbeks are a nomadic group who escaped Soviet collectivization in the 1930s by settling in northern Afghanistan. Fierce and independent, the Lakais enjoy a fiery reputation. A true Lakai warrior, it was said, would die in battle rather than in his bed, while Lakai women were fine needlewomen, though they directed their efforts toward producing tent decorations for the dowry rather than dress. The Lakai emigration to Afghanistan encouraged a resurgence of embroidery among the local tribes.

The Karakalpak people are a once-nomadic ethnically Kazakh group who live in the arid autonomous region of Karakalpakstan, around the Aral Sea in western Uzbekistan. Karakalpak dress fits into the traditional Central Asian dress family, with some differentiating features. Women's clothing traditionally varied in color according to their age: Young women of childbearing age wore red, brides wore blue, and older women wore white. Fine embroidery ornamented Karakalpak women's dress, particularly early examples. A young woman's *kizil jegde* (red outer robe) and the chest panels of her *kizil kimishek* (red head covering) were elaborately embroidered, as was the postmenopausal woman's *ak jegde* (white outer robe). Karakalpak girls began to make their kimishek when quite young in order to finish it in time for their weddings at about fourteen. The trapezium-shaped front of the kimishek was made from red wool fabric, richly embroidered around the face opening, with a large ikat shawl forming the back and a turban on top; kimisheks were banned by the Soviets, who viewed them, like the paranja, as a form of veiling. The front of the indigo blue *kok koylek* (wedding dress) was also liberally embroidered with red, yellow, and white silk cross stitch in a pattern called *saut* (chain armor).

Karakalpak jewelry is stylistically more closely related to Turkmen jewelry than jewelry from the local Khiva; it was mostly worn by younger women, who discarded a piece every time a child was born. Unmarried women could wear an *ongirshe* (breastplate), while married women wore bracelets to indicate their fidelity; *arebek* (nose rings), *jusik* (finger rings), and *tuime* (large buttons) were popular with all women. Bridal jewelry included a large *khaikal* (chest amulet) and an *ongirmonshak* (silver tassel worn over the genital area). A bride could also wear over her kimishek the fantastic helmet-shaped *saukele* (a type of headdress), hung with masses of silver and coral and a long heavily embroidered back band; this was topped with a richly ornamented gilded-silver *tobelik* (special hat).

References and Further Reading

Abdullayev, T., D. Fakhretdinova, and A. Khakimov. *A Song in Metal: Folk Art of Uzbekistan*. Tashkent, Uzbekistan: Gafur Gulyam Art and Literature Publishers, 1986.

Kalter, Johannes. *The Arts and Crafts of Turkestan*. London: Thames and Hudson, 1984.

Kalter, Johannes, and Margareta Paveloi, eds. *Uzbekistan: Heirs to the Silk Road*. London: Thames and Hudson, 1997.

Khakimov, A. *Atlas of Central Asian Artistic Crafts and Trades*. Tashkent, Uzbekistan: Printing House of Polygraphic Concern "Sharq," 1999.

Naphisa, Sadikova. *National Uzbek Clothes (XIX–XX Centuries)*. Tashkent, Uzbekistan: The State Committee of Science and Technique of Republic of Uzbekistan, 2001.

Pisarchik, A.K. *The Arts and Crafts of the Tajiks*. Dushanbe, Tajikistan: Donish, 1987.

Sumner, C., with H. Feltham. *Beyond the Silk Road: Arts of Central Asia*. Sydney: Powerhouse Publishing, 1999.

Yershov, N.N., and Z.A. Shirokova, *Album of Tajik National Costumes*. Dushanbe, Tajikistan: Academy of Sciences of the Tajik SSR, 1969.

Christina Sumner

See also Tiraz: Textiles and Dress with Inscriptions in Central and Southwest Asia; Uzbek Textiles; Khil'a: Clothing to Honor a Person or Situation.

Uzbek Textiles

After the creation of the independent republic of Uzbekistan in 1991, Uzbek textiles, with their brilliant color combinations and decorative exuberance, drew much interest from the international community and fashion experts. Silk wall hangings, ceremonial robes, and ikat dresses from the nineteenth and early twentieth centuries began to appear more often in private collections, galleries, museums, and boutiques around the world. *Khan atlas* (silk satin-weave ikat), *suzani* embroidery (needlework) on handloomed linen and cotton fabrics, *zarduzi* (gold embroidery) on velvet, and *chitgari* (block printing) on silk and cotton are all part of the rich heritage of Uzbek traditional textiles. They have played an important role in the history and development of fashion in this region and are still popular in the early twenty-first century.

HISTORICAL BACKGROUND

In the nineteenth century, the term *Silk Road* was coined by German geologist and explorer Ferdinand von Richtenhoven. In his travel log he recorded his amazement at the vast numbers of camel caravans that stretched across the landscape, carrying silk fabric, robes, and other textiles. Uzbekistan lies at the heart of Central Asia and was the center of the fabled crossroads of trade from Russia, India, China, Southwest Asia, and Europe in past centuries. The names Bukhara and Samarkand evoke images of Silk Road cities drenched in sunlight, camel caravans loaded with merchandise and supplies arriving at the city gates. Ceramics, carpets, tea, and textiles were among the many items packed in bales and leather boxes and transported across deserts, mountain passes, and fertile lands. Precious silks, valuable embroideries, and handloomed block-printed cloth were prized both at home and by partners along the trading routes.

In ancient China, where silk weaving was practiced and silk textiles treasured, the secret techniques of cultivating silkworms and producing silk textiles were carefully guarded. Despite these protective efforts, it appears, however, that sericulture and silk weaving were practiced from ancient times in Central Asia as well. Archaeological expeditions have uncovered sites in the region that reveal fragments of silk and linen as well as implements for spinning and weaving dating from the Kushan period (second century C.E.) in the region that is part of Uzbekistan in the early twenty-first century. Pieces of wrapping cloth were found clinging to a tiny pottery figurine of a female deity at the Kampyr-tepe tomb site near Termez. This cloth was made of both linen and silk threads woven using techniques not found in China until later centuries.

Despite difficult terrain, disruptive invasions, and carefully defended territories, trade routes provided continuity for traditional arts. In the early twenty-first century, one can still find beautiful textiles in the bustling modern cities of Samarkand, Bukhara, and Margilan. As in earlier times, Uzbek women enjoy wearing garments of silk and silk ikat. The *salwar kamez*, a combination of loose pants and a tunic made of ikat silk, is a popular dress style. Men wear quilted coats of *bekasab* (striped silk) to the mosque and on festival days. Embroidered hats, bags, and gold-embroidered velvet wedding coats are part of daily life.

Since the creation of the modern Uzbek nation in 1992, there has been a renewed interest in making traditional handloomed and hand-embroidered fabrics. Craftspeople seek to produce the fine-quality handmade textiles once so highly valued by Silk Road traders. Silk ikat evening gowns and day wear, handsome velvet robes, embroidered linen garments lined with block-printed cotton, caps of hand-polished cotton with fine embroidery, and gossamer silk scarves are part of the modern Uzbek wardrobe.

SILK TEXTILES: KHAN ATLAS, ABR, BAGHMAL, AND BEKASAB

Silk weaving has been known in Central Asia from at least the first millennium B.C.E. In the early twenty-first century, lively colors and intriguing woven patterns have become the hallmarks of the silk of Uzbekistan, known locally as khan atlas (silk ikat), *abr* ("cloud," a general name for silk ikat), and bekasab (striped

Detail from an Uzbek woman's coat, late twentieth century. The embroidery features large, stylized flowers in floss silk worked on a woven silk ground in *boukara* stitch. Between the panels of brightly colored flowers (a female feature), there are narrow, vertical bands of stylized ram's horns in white (a male feature). Ram's horns are also regarded as amulets, providing protection for the wearer. Textile Research Centre, Leiden.

A woman's ikat silk robe, with a pattern of poppies and almond flowers, Bukhara, Uzbekistan, late nineteenth century. This item would have been worn like a coat, layered over other clothing. Private Collection, New York. Photograph by Carter Malik.

silk). They were used as decorative textiles, such as wall hangings, quilt covers, and cushion covers, and were also used to make clothing for both men and women of the nobility and rich merchant families. For women from the ruling and wealthy families, long-sleeved, flowing tunics made of khan atlas ikat were worn over lighter underdresses. This layered clothing was comfortable in the cold winters of the continental plateau of Central Asia. The *punjara* (covering garment) was worn by women outside the home and often made of bekasab. *Baghmal* (velvet ikat) was a rare and costly fabric, among the most highly prized of textiles. Robes and boots from baghmal were worn by the elite. Bekasab silk robes tied at the waist by a scarf and often quilted with cotton padding were worn by men, together with loose-fitting cotton trousers.

The provenance of the first ikats in general is uncertain, but fragments of these treasured fabrics dating from the fifth to seventh centuries C.E. have been found along the trade routes. The dating of the first ikat textiles in Central Asia is still unclear; however, by the seventh century C.E., fragments of ikats attributed to Central Asian weavers began to appear in distant locales on the trading routes. *Atlas* (woven ikat-patterned silk) binding cloth dating from the fifth century that had been made by weavers from the Afrasiab Kingdom (Samarkand in the early twenty-first century) was found in the textile museum in Kyoto, Japan. It had been used to wrap religious texts stored carefully over the centuries in a Japanese Buddhist monastery.

The exquisite beauty of ikat was not easy to accomplish and required the coordination of a number of artisans and guilds. At the height of its production in the 1800s, as many as nine different trades were linked to the silk-weaving industry. Sericulture, the propagation of silkworms and cocoon collection, required

agricultural skills. The spinning of the silk thread required other specialized skills, as did resist dyeing (the process of covering specified parts of the thread before applying color in up to five dye baths), weaving, and the final preparation of the cloth, which was sometimes polished with an egg-white mixture.

Bukhara, Samarkand, the Fergana Valley, and the Tajik regions were the main centers for silk weaving. During the last half of the nineteenth century, over 425 weavers were employed in Urgut, and between 1840 and 1850, nearly 200,000 robes were exported from Turkistan to Russia, where there was considerable demand for silk robes, dresses, and wall hangings. Local nobility wore ikat dress for special occasions. The emir of Bukhara was known to have tied his silk ikat *chapan* (long robe) at the waist with a beautiful Kashmiri woolen shawl. The tradition of presenting robes to honored visitors and courtesans, as well as giving them as wedding presents and in payment for services, also provided a niche for ikats.

The tying and dyeing of the fine silk threads were left to men in traditional ikat production. It is interesting to note that the Jewish population that had been living in Bukhara for more than one thousand years played a large role in the dyeing of the threads. Jewish traders controlled the importation and sales of indigo. Identified by the indigo stains on their hands, guilds of Jewish dyers were alone responsible for the cold dyeing of indigo and purple colors. The tying of threads in the dye-resist process was done by Uzbeks, who were noted for their innovative patterns and colors.

As late as the nineteenth century, the use of natural vegetable dyes was quite common. Indigo produced a range of blues and could be overdyed with yellow and red. Red and yellow hues were made from madder-root dye. Other vegetable materials used in Central Asia included saffron, dahlias and larkspur, fruits such as pomegranate and mulberry, and the shells of walnuts and pistachio nuts. Aniline dyes appeared in abr weaving in the nineteenth century with the introduction of chemical dyeing compounds. Although strict prohibitions forbidding the use of aniline dyes for noble dress were in force even as late as the beginning of the twentieth century, it seems that they were imported from India and Russia and found their way into abr weaving nonetheless.

In the twentieth century, silk weaving went through significant changes. After the October Revolution of 1917, private weaving workshops were consolidated into weavers' cooperatives. Private weaving enterprises were discouraged, and looms and equipment confiscated. Weaving as a craft began to disappear. Elegant gowns of bekasab and atlas were hidden away. Private industry was replaced by state-run silk factories. Some of the master ikat designers were brought along to supervise the new industrialized dyeing and tying practices. Handcrafted textiles virtually disappeared.

In 1972, the Yodgorlik Factory was opened in Margilan (Fergana Valley) in an effort to revive the production of handloomed silk ikat. This group has begun experimenting with patterns taken from photographs and examples of eighteenth- and nineteenth-century dresses and robes. In 1996, under a United Nations project for Handicraft Development, several weavers went to India to study natural dyes and since then have been making an effort to reintroduce traditional dyeing methods to the craft. In the 1990s, small private home-weaving concerns again began to appear in the towns of Namangan and Margilan.

In the early twenty-first century, weavers still prepare threads in a similar fashion as in earlier times. The "resist" process of tying and dyeing the threads is still done by men. Lengths of thread, eleven to thirteen yards (ten to twelve meters) long, are strung and then tied to create the ikat pattern. The threads are dyed, retied, and dyed again. A single length may be overdyed five or six times. The designs are complex and require an accurate eye for pattern and color. In order to produce the mirror image common to atlas weaving, the threads of both halves of the image are tied and dyed together. Once the colors are in place, the threads are wound into large skeins ready to be placed on the loom for weaving. The individual warp threads are passed through cotton loops and then through a comb-like reed on the loom. The weaver (male or female) sits on a bench and uses a shuttle loaded with pink or white silk or cotton weft. The weft is then pressed together with another reed or wooden comb. Lengths of eleven to thirteen yards (ten to twelve meters) that can be from two to eighteen inches (five to forty-six centimeters) wide are woven.

The handwoven atlas designs found in the bazaars of the Fergana Valley in the early twenty-first century are reminiscent of earlier times, with both geometric and floral patterns. The comb, talisman triangle, pomegranate, tulip, poppy, ram's horn, pepper, butterfly, peacock feather, and even scorpion are common patterns. Some of these images were originally thought to protect the wearer against the evil eye and others to promote the fertility, health, and happiness of the wearer. These patterns are inspired by the civilizations predating the Islamic period.

EMBROIDERY

Suzani, the Persian word for "needle," refers to a style of embroidery done in many parts of Uzbekistan. A collection of elaborately embroidered pieces is considered an essential part of a girl's wedding dowry. The term suzani also refers to an embroidered cloth used to decorate a room, as a curtain, or to cover piles of sleeping mats and quilts. In much the same way as in the eighteenth century, silk, velvet, linen, or cotton provides a base for modern suzanis. Strips of cloth are loosely sewn together, and a pattern is sketched onto the cloth. The strips are again separated, and then embroidery work begins. The strips are stitched together after the embroidery is complete. A single suzani may be worked on by several embroiderers, and different hands may be evident in the finished product. Suzani embroidery is so valued that, according to local Islamic tradition, small areas or details are often purposefully left unfinished to show that true perfection is in the hands of the Divine.

The choice of designs for suzani embroidery is also influenced by Islam. Apart from the occasional small bird, it is rare to find human or animal representations in Uzbek embroidery. Instead, the artisans rely on geometric designs and patterns taken from the sun-drenched land. Individual artisans give their embroideries a signature appearance through their use of sumptuous colors and flowers, fruits, leaves, and tendrils.

Regional work can be identified by the choice of cloth, color, and image. Luscious pomegranates and circular flower medallions on bright red cloth were the signature of the women of Syrkhandarya. In Bukhara and nearby Nurata, suzanis have a unique balance and harmony of color and pattern, with intricate floral and geometric patterns drawn together by leafy tendrils created in tiny chain stitches. Bukhara suzanis usually have a background of karbos (also called bos; handloomed cotton). Velvet and cotton were generally preferred over silk, which did not support the heavy embroidery as well.

In the Tashkent region, massive embroidered pieces are produced that are known as tagora-paliak, meaning "moon-sky," and were covered with round figures. The central motif was often a large circular shape surrounded by smaller rosettes that represented the sky, moon, and stars with eight or more rays. Usually, the entire cloth was covered with fine embroidery (often satin stitch.) The background was usually deep red or burgundy. Additional geometric ornaments were often yellow or black. Their size and use of harmonious colors give them a unique appearance.

In the Samarkand region, suzanis are also large in size. Large rosettes of red, orange, and black worked on a white cotton background create an overall and repeating pattern. These suzanis are meant to decorate the backdrop of the ivan (summer porch) or cover an entire living room wall. A teapot is often the central design of the suzani in nearby Urgut.

Near Shakhrisabz, the birthplace of Amir Timur (also known as Tamerlane, he conquered much of West and Central Asia in the fourteenth century and founded the Timurid Empire and the Timurid dynasty), villages can still be found that produce embroidery referred to locally as iroqi stitch, an overall small cross stitch. This type of work was thought to have come to the Persian Empire generations ago with migrations from Southwest Asia. In the early twenty-first century, it is possible to find caps, bags, and, occasionally, wall hangings, footwear, and coats embroidered in iroqi stitch.

Embroidery was not limited to wall decoration and clothing. Another important piece was the joi namaz (prayer mat) with an embroidered mehrab (mystical door design used by the Muslim faithful). Caps, vests, shoes, tea bags, talismans, and horse blankets were also embroidered. One of the earliest silk embroidered pieces excavated in Central Asia was a horse blanket found in the

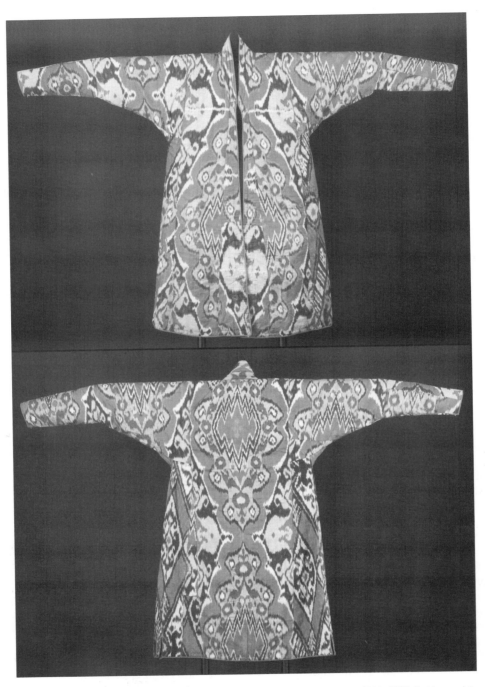

Front and back view of a silk, *ikat*-dyed Uzbek man's coat, Samarkand, Uzbekistan, 1860–1870. Ikat is a resist-dyeing technique in which the warp threads (and sometimes also the wefts) are tie-dyed to create a pattern before the fabric is woven. © Victoria and Albert Museum, London. www.vam.ac.uk

Scythian mountains from the fifth century B.C.E. Pale blue silk embroidered with flowers and birds in chain stitch was mounted on felt. Although the original colors are now faded, they were probably blue, red, yellow, and brown.

In the early twenty-first century, in the town of Choost in the Fergana Valley, women from the village and surrounding countryside work at home and in local workshops making traditional Uzbek caps or *duppi*. These small black caps take a week to complete and are decorated with several preferred embroidered designs. The most common is the *jeera* (cumin flower). Jeera is an essential seasoning in *plawf*, the national rice-and-meat dish. For newlywed men, the grape flower is embroidered in place of the jeera, and for young boys, a nightingale is used. In the past, it was possible to identify the regional styles of the embroidery on the duppi and hence the origin of the wearer. The duppi is still an important piece of Uzbek menswear; however, less emphasis is placed on regional design.

Zarduzi (gold embroidery) has a significant place in the history of textiles and clothing in Uzbekistan. Gold embroidery was once the occupation of men. Women were forbidden to handle this precious thread, since it was believed that women's touch dulled the gold thread. In the nineteenth century, Emir Muzafar Khan (1860–1885) established a gold-embroidery workshop in the Ark (citadel and residence of the emir and his family). The two successive emirs, Abdullah Khan and Alim Khan, also continued patronage of this art and commissioned works of highest quality on chamois leather, velvet, and wool. Great masters arose in the more than twenty workshops in the Ark and around Bukhara. Only the Bukhara nobility and those favored by the emir himself were allowed to wear such garments. The weight of some of the coats was as much as forty-four pounds (twenty kilograms) due to the extensive and heavy gold embroidery embellished with pearls and precious and semiprecious gems.

This craft was one of the first victims of the October Revolution. In 1920, the emir of Bukhara's property was confiscated, the embroidery workshops were closed, and the craft forbidden. In 1960, workshops were reopened in Bukhara by the local government. Women were trained in this craft and began to make souvenirs and wedding coats. A walk through the Sunday bazaar in Bukhara shows a great local demand for gold-embroidered velvet coats, caps, and shoes. They are an essential part of early-twenty-first-century Uzbek wedding dress and are worn on formal occasions.

BLOCK PRINTING IN UZBEKISTAN

Uzbekistan's chitgari (block printing) is unique in the world of hand-printed textiles with its deep burgundy and rose hues outlined by delicate black tracery. The craft of block printing was once widely practiced in many regions of Uzbekistan, including Bukhara, Samarkand, Fergana, Khorezm, and Tashkent. Samarkand and Bukhara lay at the crossroads of the east-west and north-south caravan routes. These two cities became major centers of craft production, and block printing was widely practiced. In the early twenty-first century, there is still a town near Bukhara called Chidgaron, meaning "town of block printers." Russia, Afghanistan, and western China were major trading partners. Travelers in the early 1800s observed caravans whose major cargo was silk and cotton textiles from Samarkand and Bukhara.

Archaeological finds in the area indicate that block printing was known to adorn cloth from as early as biblical times.

Fragments of block-printed cloth were found during excavations of the fourteenth-century tomb of Bibi Khanum, the wife of Amir Timur. More recently, the craft flourished in the nineteenth and early twentieth centuries. Block printing was used to decorate scarves, dresses, shrouds for burial, the linings of robes, tablecloths, and bedcovers. Bos (handloomed cotton) and factory-produced cotton were most commonly used for printing. In nineteenth-century Bukhara, block-printed silk scarves were also produced and used as head coverings and as sashes for traditional robes.

Traditionally, the printing was done with wooden blocks (*kolib*). The block carver (*kolibkor*) carved blocks of pear wood, a strong and reliable wood, for the fine black outlines made with iron oxide dyes. After carving, the block was boiled in sheep fat to seal the wood. Blocks used for red dye were made from softer wood such as poplar. Red and black were commonly used as basic printing colors. Compositions were often enhanced with brushwork of yellow, green, or blue. Certain patterns were always popular, including the *islimi* designs with their delicate elements including vines, leaves, and tendrils. Round and geometric shapes representing stars and moons were often used to fill large spaces of the printed work. Linear, rectangular blocks were used to define the borders.

In the early twenty-first century, hand-printed cloth can be found in three colors: burgundy, rose, and black. The black color

A cover (*suzan*) used to decorate a wall or table, with a cotton background and silk-thread embroidery, Kashkadarya, Uzbekistan, early twentieth century. The term *suzani* also refers to a style of embroidery done in many parts of Uzbekistan. Regional work can be identified by the choice of cloth, color, and image; according to local Islamic tradition, small areas or details are purposefully left unfinished to show that true perfection is in the hands of the Divine. Private collection, New York. Photograph by Carter Malik.

is made from iron oxide compound and burgundy from alizarin dye. In the past, the reddish color was obtained from the root of the madder plant, which gave a lovely deep color. Madder was replaced when the chemical alizarin became readily available in the twentieth century. The dyes are thickened with gum produced from the resin of the apricot tree. At times, an alum resist is also applied to the cloth, which ensures that certain areas are not printed. Later these can be enhanced with hand-painted details, producing an interesting effect on the printed cloth.

Due to the development and popularity of manufactured cloth as well as production policies in the early twentieth century, block printing began to disappear from the markets. When the communal state was being developed in the early twentieth century, workers were needed to grow food and raw materials and to man factories for the industrializing state. Cheaper, less labor-intensive textiles were available on the markets, and the population was encouraged to "modernize" and buy the new mass-produced products. Family-run block-printing workshops were systematically shut down to make way for the new age under Communism. Soviet art historians recognized that unless measures were taken to preserve this traditional art, it would disappear entirely. Therefore, in 1926, three state-run workshops for block printing were opened in the Bukhara region. Then, in 1930, the Art Training Center was opened in Tashkent. In the late 1930s, several prominent Soviet art historians began to research and collect pieces for the national museum collections. World War II again disrupted the patronage of the national crafts, and focus turned toward the war effort. During the following years of hardship, families of block printers burned huge stores of ancient blocks as fuel for warmth in the long, cold Uzbek winters.

Two families remain active in the block-printing craft in the early twenty-first century. In Margilan, Salijon Akhmadaliev prints with his son. He uses blocks inherited from his father and grandfather; the lineage goes back farther than he can remember. His work is well known and respected among the connoisseurs and art historians of Uzbekistan. In Tashkent, the Rahimov family is also well respected for its beautiful hand-printed tablecloths and yardage. Three brothers work together following the path of at least six generations of block printers, including their grandfather, Usto Abdurahim, and father, Usto Hakim Rahimov.

FASHION TRENDS AND UZBEK TEXTILES

As the beautiful silks and embroideries of Uzbekistan reached global markets, international fashion designers such as Oscar de la Renta and Dianne von Furstenberg began to incorporate them into their wardrobe lines. Gold-embroidered details on velvet evening wear have made an appearance in European couture apparel. At home, designers in Uzbekistan have also been experimenting with local fabrics. Ikats make a dramatic statement with intense color and patterns. The floral embroidered patterns that characterize suzanis are used to embellish clothing and accessories in fashion houses in Tashkent and Bukhara. Uzbek fashion designers take full advantage of the artistry of the products of local textile arts and have become instrumental in spurring a revival of textile arts.

References and Further Reading

Carmel, Lorna. "At the Crossroads of the Continent: Textiles from Central Asia." *Arts of Asia* 26, no. 1 (February 1970): 106–114.

Fitz Gibbon, Kate, and Andrew Hale. *Splendid Silks of Central Asia; Ikat; The Guido Goldman Collection.* London: Laurence King, 1997.

"Gold Embroidery Art of Bukhara." Bukhara-Carpets.com. http://www.bukhara-carpets.com/making/bukhara-gold-embroidery.html (accessed 7 August 2007).

Harvey, Janet. *Traditional Textiles of Central Asia.* New York: Thames and Hudson, 1996.

Kalter, Johannes. *The Arts and Crafts of Turkestan.* London: Thames and Hudson, 1984.

Kalter, Johannes, and Margareta Paveloi, eds. *Uzbekistan: Heirs to the Silk Road.* London: Thames and Hudson, 1997.

Khakimov, Akbar, and Kamola Akilova. "Visual and Applied Arts." In *Bokhara: An Oriental Gem,* edited by Oxana Kirichenko, 141–179. Paris: United Nations Educational, Scientific, and Cultural Organization, 1997.

Mahkamova, Sayora. "History of Block Printing in Central Asia." In *Block Printing in Uzbekistan, Past and Present,* edited by Carter Malik, 13. Tashkent, Uzbekistan: United Nations Development Programme Project, 1997.

McCann, Kathleen. "Central Asian Ikats." *Fiberarts* 24, no. 5 (March/April 1998): 52–57.

Rau, Pip. *Ikats; Woven Silks from Central Asia; The Rau Collection.* Oxford: Basil Blackwell, 1989.

Shahzadeh, Roxane Farabi [Melinda Haren]. "Persian Clothing in the Sixteenth Century." Abridged and adapted by Master Safi al-Khansaa' [Heather Stiles]. Willofyre Studio. http://www.willofyre.com/roxaneartticle.pdf (accessed 15 October 2009).

Carter Malik

See also Dress from Tajikistan and Uzbekistan; Regional Dress of Afghanistan.

Dress from Kazakhstan

Kazakhstan is a large Eurasian country in Central Asia; it is ranked as the ninth-largest country in the world, with a territory of about 7,311 square miles (about 12,000 square kilometers). It shares borders with China, Kyrgyzstan, Russia, Turkmenistan, and Uzbekistan. The name *Kazakh* derives from an ancient Turkic word meaning "independent" or "a free spirit," probably as a result of the Kazakhs' nomadic horseback culture. The ending *-stan* derives from the Persian word *stan* meaning "land" or "place of." Kazakhstan's geographic position, climate, neighbors, and nomadic past have all had an influence on the style of dress worn by both men and women in the country.

Kazakhstan has a diverse geography, including large steppes that are characterized by large areas of grasslands and are very hot in the summers and bitterly cold in the winters. It includes important mountain ranges, such as the Altai Mountains, as well as flatlands, taigas, rock canyons, hills, deltas, and deserts. Although Kazakhstan does not have direct access to the sea, its southwestern region is situated on the Caspian Sea. It does have several vast lakes, including the Aral Sea and Lake Balkhash, as well as rivers such as the Irtysh, Ishim, and Ural.

Kazakhstan has been inhabited since the Stone Age. The region's climate and terrain are best suited for nomads practicing pastoralism. It is believed that humans first domesticated the horse in the region's steppes some seven thousand years ago, and nomadic pastoralism developed since then. Not surprisingly, the dress worn by these and later people reflects the dominant role horses play in their way of life. Later on in history, ancient cities such as Taraz (Aulie-Ata; founded about two thousand years ago) and Hazrat-e Turkestan (founded in the fourth century C.E.) long served as important caravan stations along the so-called Silk Road and other trading routes that connected East and West for thousands of years and transported, among other items, felt, textiles, and clothing as well as accessories such as perfume and jewelry. With the Mongol invasion of the early thirteenth century C.E., basic political boundaries started to be established. Administrative districts were established under the Mongol Empire, and these eventually came under the emergent Kazakh Khanate.

For most of its recorded history, the territory of modern-day Kazakhstan has been inhabited by nomadic tribes. During the fifteenth century, a distinct Kazakh identity began to emerge among the Turkic tribes, a process that was consolidated by the mid-sixteenth century with the appearance of a distinctive Kazakh language, culture, economy, and dress. Nevertheless, the region was the focus of ever-increasing disputes between the native Kazakh emirs and the neighboring Persian-speaking peoples to the south. By the early seventeenth century, the Kazakh Khanate was struggling with the impact of tribal rivalries, which divided the population into the Great, Middle, and Little (or Small) Hordes (*jüz*). Political disunion, tribal rivalries, and the diminishing importance of overland trade routes between East and West weakened the Kazakh Khanate.

The Russians began advancing into the Kazakh steppe in the eighteenth century. In the beginning of the nineteenth century, the Russian empire began to expand and spread into Central Asia, and by the middle of the century, all of Kazakhstan was part of the Russian empire. This was the period of the so-called Great Game, when Britain and Russia started to divide the region into their respective spheres of influence. The Russian tsars in the end effectively ruled over most of the territory belonging to what is the Republic of Kazakhstan in the early twenty-first century.

From the 1890s on, Slavic settlers began colonizing Kazakhstan, in particular the province of Semirechye. The number of settlers rose still further once the Trans-Aral Railway from Orenburg to Tashkent was completed in 1906, which made the movement of people and cultures much easier. They again brought with them their own dress forms.

Following the 1917 Russian Revolution and subsequent civil war, the territory of Kazakhstan was reorganized several times before becoming the Kazakh Soviet Socialist Republic in 1936, a part of the Union of Soviet Socialist Republics (USSR). During this period, Russian dress, which was basically a Western form, was dominant in the urban regions. In addition, throughout Soviet Central Asia, there was a deliberate policy of industrialization. It required a large workforce, which the Russians saw could be significantly filled by women. As a result, a parallel policy made the sequestration and veiling of Muslim women in villages and towns illegal, so that women could work in places such as factories and farms. Following the fall of the USSR in the autumn of 1991, Kazakhstan declared itself an independent country on 16 December 1991, the last Soviet republic to do so. Its Communist-era leader, Nursultan Nazarbayev, became the country's new president. The capital city is Astana.

By the end of the last century, Kazakhstan had the sixty-second-largest population in the world, with a population density of less than fifteen people per square mile. Ethnic Kazakhs represent just under 60 percent of the population, while the other 40 percent is made up of ethnic Russians (ca. 25 percent), as well as Azerbaijanis, Belarusians, Poles, Tatars, Ukrainians, Uzbeks, and Uighurs. There are also small groups of Chechens, Germans (notably Volga Germans who had settled in Russia in the nineteenth century), Koreans (who had been deported to Central Asia in the 1930s), Kurds, Meskhetian Turks, Ukrainians, and some Russian political opponents of the regime who had been deported to Kazakhstan in the 1930s and 1940s by Stalin. Many of these groups brought with them their own forms of dress.

The term *Kazakhstanis* is in general use to describe all citizens of Kazakhstan, including non-Kazakhs, while the word *Kazakh* is generally used to refer to people of actual Kazakh descent, including those living in China, Afghanistan, Turkey, Uzbekistan, and other countries.

A studio portrait of a Kazakh man wearing a high, pointed hat with a divided turn-up (*kalpak*), Kazakhstan, between 1865 and 1872. This hat, worn for status, would have been sewn from expensive fabric and is richly decorated with ornamental patterns. Library of Congress Prints and Photographs Division, LC-DIG-ppmsca-14240.

KAZAKH DRESS: OVERVIEW

The following description of Kazakh dress is based on the Kazakh ethnic group rather than detailing the dress of Russian/Western groups or ethnic minorities such as the Koreans.

Geography along with sociocultural and geopolitical factors has always influenced dress in Kazakhstan. There are many similarities between Kazakh dress and that found in western China, Mongolia, Kyrgyzstan, Tajikistan, Turkmenistan, and Uzbekistan. These similarities are not surprising, given the historical, ethnic, cultural (they were all nomadic pastoralists), and trade relations that go back thousands of years. The Uzbeks originated from among the Kazakhs and then moved into what is, in the early twenty-first century, Uzbekistan further to the south sometime in the fifteenth century.

The nomadic pastoralists' lifestyle was reflected in the cut of the man's shirt (*bashmet*), which had the neck opening to one side to prevent rain and wind from reaching the chest, was secured at the waist with a sash to prevent it from blowing upward in the wind, and had a wide skirt to make it easy to get on a horse. Likewise, the flared, wide skirts (*kulish koilek*) of the woman's dress and the use of pleats at the back (*zhaz koilek*) to increase the width of the

skirt aided horse riding. The simplicity and practicality of both men's and women's clothing reflected local steppe conditions, in particular the importance of clothing that did not restrict the wearer's movements while riding a horse for a long time.

The emphasis on layered garments that were wrapped around the body, especially to the left-hand side; decorative edging on shirts, dresses, and coats; the use of appliqué, embroidery, applied beads, and metal ornamentation on sleeveless garments; and, finally, the use of high boots were all features of the dress of pastoral nomadic people in Central Asia.

Social and economic differences in both male and female dress were mainly manifested in the quality, decoration, and quantity of items worn at any one time rather than in the basic cut of the garments. Garments for the wealthy sections of the population, for example, were known for their luxury and splendor and were made from velvets and silks, enriched with gold and silver threads and braids, beads, pearls, precious stones, corals, and silver and gold plaques and disks.

As in many cultures, there was no significant variation in the cut of daily and festive Kazakh wear; instead, the difference lay in what type of cloth and how much cloth was used and how the clothing was decorated. A festive outfit, for example, was often made of velvet, silk, brocades, or expensive furs, whereas everyday dress was made of ordinary fabrics such as cottons. In addition, a festive outfit used much larger headdresses than those worn on a daily basis.

Some garments were unisex, worn by both men and women, while others were gender specific. The *beshant*, for example, was a coat influenced by the Russian style, with a modern cut fitting the body, and it was worn by both sexes. It went down to the knee, with sleeves ending at the wrist and a stand-up collar. This coat was made from brightly colored fabrics such as velvet. It was secured around the waist with a sash or a leather belt.

Similarly, men, women, and children wore a round cap (*boric*) that could be made of a wide variety of materials. More expensive kinds were of velvet, decorated with embroidery and trimmed with fur. There were various kinds of boric, depending on the type of material and shape of the cap. The *takya*, for example, was a round cap that was richly embroidered. Children often wore a special type of boric embroidered with silk, gold, and silver thread. In general, the patterns used to decorate children's caps were either floral (*gul*) in origin or represented the sun's rays (*shygla*). Another kind of cap was called the *kalpak*; it was made of white felt and edged with black velvet. Sometimes Kazakhs wore skullcaps made in Kazan, Bukhara, or Tashkent.

KAZAKH MEN'S DRESS

Men's dress, like that of women, has undergone changes in some details such as cut, materials, and combinations of objects. According to the Russian anthropologist R. Khodzhayeva (cited in Dzhanibekov 1996), for example, at the end of the eighteenth and in the early nineteenth century, Kazakh dress for men included both fringed and unfringed garments. Since the mid-nineteenth century, however, unfringed clothes with stitches along the shoulder lines have become popular.

Nevertheless, the basic outfit worn by men during the twentieth century remained the same combination of items, namely, a pair of long, baggy underpants (*zheide*) made of cotton; a shirt (*koilek*); and wide overtrousers (*shalbar*) with a drawstring at the waist. In summer, cotton was the preferred cloth for the tunic, while in the winter it was made from leather or animal hide. Both the zheide and shalbar were normally made with wide trouser legs narrowing at the bottom, so that they could fit comfortably into a pair of tall boots.

Over these garments, men often wore a coat of various types. The *chapan*, for example was a long gownlike coat made of velvet, silk, or cotton that had long sleeves. It was bought ready-to-wear at the market. The winter version was usually lined with fur in order to cope with the harsh Kazakh winter conditions. For special occasions, wealthier men wore embroidered leather chapans trimmed with fur and richly decorated with embroidery. In some areas waistcoat-like garments were worn, such as the *beshmet*, which had sleeves. It was used in the east and north of the country, or the sleeveless *kokrekshe* from central Kazakhstan.

In addition to the chapan, various other types of coat were worn, such as the *shepken*, which was made of woven fabric, or the *kebenek*, which was a felt coat made of small, square pieces of felt with the nap on the inside. Kebenek had either a narrow stand-up or a broad turn-down collar, and they were often used by shepherds, horse herders, and cattle breeders in the winter as protection against the rain, hail, and snow. An expensive coat was a fur coat (*ishik*) trimmed with otter or marten fur. A sheepskin coat (*tulup* or *ton*) was worn during colder weather.

In general, Kazakh men's clothing was not buttoned up and required a belt of some kind. A *beldic*, for example, is made of decorated leather with a dagger sheath (*kyn*) and a powder flask (*okshantry*), which were fastened on with decorative metal plates.

Footwear consisted of felt stockings (*baipaks*) worn inside high boots (*saptama kigh*). During winter months men wore thick leather boots made from horse or ox hide along with felt stockings. The soles of the boots were square to fit either foot. During severe winter conditions, men would wear two pairs of boots for extra protection, one of leather, the other of felt. For special occasions, especially weddings, young men wore *kaykayma*, which differed from everyday boots because of their turned-up toes. Another form of festive boots (*koksauyr*) was made of green shagreen leather. Moccasin-style shoes called *shokais* or *sharyks* were made of rough leather that was prepared by hand and were worn by poorer people.

Like other articles of clothing, headgear protected its wearers from harsh elements and climates, but it was also an identity marker. For example, a *bai* (wealthy man) wore the kalpak, a high, pointed cap with a divided turn-up. It was sewn from expensive fabric richly decorated with ornamental patterns. Another traditional form of men's headgear was the boric, a rounded, warm cap; a more expensive version was trimmed with astrakhan, otter, or marten fur. In the harsh winter cold, men wore the *tymak*, a fur cap with three flaps, two for the ears and a longer and broader flap for the back of the head. *Jalbagai* and *dalbagai* were hoods with different types of lining, while the *kulapara* was a type of hood worn by hunters. The kulapara was different from other headgear as it was attached to the collar of the outerwear.

During the twentieth century men's attire underwent various changes in some details such as cut, materials, and combinations of garments. Main differences lay in the wearer's age and social status. As a generalization, a younger man's outfit was more closely fitting in order to show off his body. Colors used for the clothing were bright and bold and again intended to say, "Here I am." In contrast, the clothing of older men was not as tightly fitted as that worn by younger men. Pants were wider and made

A Kazakh hunter launching his eagle into the air at a hunting competition in the Elan Tau region of Kazakhstan, 2001. For warmth, he wears a fur cap and a traditional-style large coat, held in with a belt. Getty Images.

of thin woolen cloth for warmth. The chapans worn by old men tended to have very wide, long sleeves and were lined with a warm material; they were usually made of velvet or silk in pastel colors. By the end of the twentieth century, most Kazakh urban men wore Western-style garments on a daily basis, although for special occasions, outfits based on traditional garments were worn.

KAZAKH WOMEN'S DRESS

For several centuries, the basic elements of a Kazakh girl's or woman's outfit consisted of undertrousers, a dress, a waistcoat or coat of some kind, and a headdress. The materials, colors, form of skirt, and decoration reflected regional as well as age and social status variations, while the cut of the garments generally remained the same. By the mid-twentieth century, many of these garments were no longer in use for daily wear because they were expensive; they were, however, still worn in the early twenty-first century for special occasions such as weddings, festivals, and national holidays.

The use of trousers followed an early Islamic tradition that women's bodies had to be properly covered. This practice was followed by Turkic women throughout Central and Southwest Asia. The main element of a Kazakh outfit, however, was the dress (general term: *koilek*). The koilek was basically a midcalf- to ankle-length dress with long sleeves. A koilek normally had a collar of some kind. It seemed that in the mid-nineteenth century, for example, these dresses had a turn-down collar, but by the end of the century the collar had changed to a stand-up (mandarin) form. There was normally a long, straight front neck slit in order to facilitate breast-feeding. The neck opening was fastened with a small clasp (*tamaksha*) or broochlike item (*tana*) at the front.

There were two basic types of koilek, one that was relatively straight and looked like a longer version of the man's shirt; it did not have frills or flounces. The other form, *kosetek*, was a dress with a very full skirt decorated with frills and flounces. In general, it was the skirt section of the koilek that was regarded as significant, as its various forms reflected both regional variations as well as the wearer's marital status.

Both styles of dresses were often decorated with appliqués, gold- and silver-thread embroidery (*oka*), embroidery in general (often with a chain stitch), glass beads, as well as semiprecious stones such as coral and turquoise. In central and northern areas of Kazakhstan, women wore a dress that was decorated with small silver pendants (*shytyrs*), which were especially made for the purpose.

The range of materials used and their color also reflected age, marital, and social status. Young girls were encouraged to wear brightly colored materials; a young married woman wore less colorful but more expensive materials, such as purple velvet for a festive dress; and older women turned to paler and more pastel colors. Another indicator of marital status was the form of decoration used for the skirt section of the dress. At the end of the nineteenth and in the early twentieth century, for example, a girl might have worn the kosetek, which was characterized by numerous rows of frills, fringing, and/or flounces along the lower section of the skirt. The frills and fringing were usually made separately and sewn onto the skirts, while the flounces were made from the skirt material. Married women, in contrast, did not wear embroidered dresses with numerous flounces made of brightly colored fabrics. A young married woman, for example, might have had only one flounce at the lower end of the skirt but several rows of fringing. An older, married women with children would have had one flounce and no frills. Her dress was fastened at the waist with a cloth belt (*mazol*), which was fastened with a large and very visible silver or gold clasp (*kapsyrma*). An elderly woman would have had only a band of embroidery on the skirt of her dress or a plain skirt, which was worn with a simple sash or belt.

In the south of Kazakhstan and in the Semirechye region, a bodice (*nymsha*) with a matching skirt (*beldemchi*) was worn over an ankle-length dress with long sleeves. The skirt and bodice were often made out of velvet and thin broadcloth in a dark color such as red, blue, or purple. In contrast, the underdress was normally in a pale color. The beldemchi was gathered at the waist into a waistband. Both the bodice and skirt were often embroidered in chain stitches and trimmed with expensive fur. The two were "joined" with a belt made out of the same material but often covered with gold or silver plaques and fastened with an elaborate buckle. A type of skirt called a *shalgy* was tied up with a wide tape encircling the waist twice. It was kept in place by a wide belt made out of the same material as the skirt.

Over both the koilek and kosetek, a waistcoat (*kamzol*) and a coat (*chapan*) were worn. Kamzols were slightly fitted waistcoats that were worn over a loose dress. There were various types of waistcoats depending on the age and region of the wearer. Younger girls and women, for example, tended to wear a waist- or hip-

length kamzol, while older women wore long versions. In northern and western Kazakhstan, kamzols tended to be thigh length and heavily decorated with gold-colored braids and coins. In more urban situations, the decoration on the kamzol often matched the decoration on the sleeves and skirt region of the dress.

In central Kazakhstan, the kamzol was fastened with a series of clasps that were called *bota trsek*, which literally meant "a young camel's knee joint." It was not clear if this was a reference to the materials that were used to make the clasps or their appearance. Sometimes, silver-edged, round buttons were used. But in the southeast of the country, elderly women used simple sashes made of satin or cotton.

Over the kamzols a chapan or coat with long sleeves and an open front was worn; it was fastened with a broad belt or a clasp of some kind. The chapan reached to the midthigh or slightly below. The chapan often had slits at the lower sides for ease of wearing while on a horse. The type of material used for making the chapan depended on the wearer's marital and social status, as well as the season. A variety of materials, such as dark red velvet, was popular. In winter, urban women often wore quilted velvet chapans with cotton linings, while wealthy women used chapans lined with fur. For heavier protection, a complete fur coat made from wolf, fox, or sable fur was sometimes worn by those who could afford it.

Chapans were normally decorated around the neck, front opening, and lower hem, as well as in the front. In southern Kazakhstan, they were often made of purple velvet with embroidered details. The coat was kept in place with a large belt. Those coats from western Kazakhstan were often of red velvet and fitted at the waist. Fringing was used at the back and lower hem for decoration, while wide braids and gold embroidery were used in bands down the front.

Traditionally, Kazakh girls and women have always worn some form of head covering, such as a skullcap (*boric*) or cap that could be covered in velvet, decorated with embroidery, and in some cases also trimmed with fur. In particular, married women had to cover their hair, especially that around the forehead, hiding it from the gaze of strangers. As a result, different areas of Kazakhstan have developed a variety of headgear. Sometimes, one or more scarves or shawls were wrapped around the head and hair to create different effects; in other regions, a tall felt foundation was used to create a large headdress. In general, women's headgear was more decorated than that of men, with gold and silver threads as well as coins, beads, buttons, and precious stones.

One of the characteristic forms of Kazakh headgear for a married woman was the *kimishek*, which was a hoodlike garment made of a fine cotton that covered the head, hair, and upper body, leaving a gap for the face. The facial opening was often trimmed with beads, braids, and laces or, in more elaborate versions, pearls or coral. This type of headgear was still being worn in Kazakhstan at the end of the twentieth century by some groups, especially older women.

With respect to footwear, when at home, women went barefoot or wore simple slippers that could easily be put on or off. When outside, women regularly wore boots during both the summer and winter months. These had various names, including *ichigi* and *masi* (these terms also applied to boots worn by old men). Women's boots were made from velvet, animal hide, or fur and were often decorated with embroidery. Women's special-occasion boots had a heel and turned-up toes. During the summer months,

Kazakh women wearing head scarves and brightly patterned dresses, Kazakhstan, 1994. Time & Life Pictures/Getty Images.

women's boots resembled sandals, with fastenings that could reach several inches (about five centimeters) beyond the ankles. Like men, women wore felt socks to keep their feet warm and dry.

Women adorned their hair, ears, neck, fingers, wrists, and feet with highly ornate silver jewelry. Bridal jewelry usually included coral, which people believed to bring fertility. Women wore large finger rings made from silver with filigree designs, and some rings had stones, with coral being the most common but turquoise and carnelian were also used. Women also wore bracelets, usually in matching pairs; these were also made from silver. They were frequently decorated with engraved geometric patterns. Kazakh women wore very large earrings made from silver.

DRESS FOR LIFE-CYCLE EVENTS AND FASHIONABLE DRESS

Wedding ensembles for both the bride and groom differd greatly from everyday clothes, in that they were made of the best materials affordable and richly decorated with embroidery, appliqué, and trimmings. A complete wedding outfit for a bride consisted of a dress, a waistcoat, and a headdress, as well as a beshmet decorated with gold and silver embroidery. A woman's wedding belt was often elaborately designed in silver work and encrusted with coral and turquoise. The jewelry worn, such as rings, earrings, and necklaces, matched the wedding outfit and was regarded as an important part of the woman's dowry. Bridal shoes (*kleb*) were

sometimes worn by urban women; these shoes were often made of leather and covered in silver or gold plaques.

A special and very tall headdress called a *saukele* was worn by some brides. It was regarded as a historical form that dated back at least to the medieval period. A saukele was made up of three elements. The foundation consisted of a high, conical cap with front and back flaps made of quilted velvet or a similar material. This was covered with a cap made of thin felt decorated with precious stones such as coral, pearls, and turquoise and, in some cases, fur. More elaborate versions were made of metal covered with plaques, beading, and so forth. Finally, the cap was covered with a kind of veil made of fine white net (*zhekek*), which was used to cover the saukele's foundation and the entire body of the bride, especially her face.

No specific mourning clothes were used by the Kazakhs. In general, women in mourning could unplait their hair and let it fall loose. Sometimes, black shawls were used to cover the head; this appeared to be a Western mourning tradition that might have been introduced by the Russians. Jewelry was often removed following the death of a close family member. Men used mourning sashes made of gray cotton or satin.

Ethnically chic fashion has become very popular in Kazakhstan, especially among the young living in urban areas. Kazakh designers are responding to the demand by creating new styles of fashion and clothes decorated with traditional motifs and colors. One designer, Baryu Kamolova, for example, uses traditional

Kazakh motifs such as eagle wings on neck scarves. The city of Almaty (the largest city in Kazakhstan) hosts an annual fashion week that draws spectators from Russia, Europe, and other Central Asian nations. One of the most well-known Kazakh designers, Saida Azhikhan, exhibited her collection at the Meridian International Center in Washington, D.C., on 9 November 2006; it contained a mix of modern and futuristic styles of clothing with fur trimmings.

References and Further Reading

Abazov, Rafis. *Culture and Customs of the Central Asian Republics*. Westport, CT: Greenwood Press, 2007.

Bacon, Elizabeth. *Central Asians under Russian Rule: A Study in Culture Change*. Ithaca, NY: Cornell University Press, 1966.

Dzhanibekov, Uzbekali. *The Kazakh Costume*. Almati, Kazakhstan: Onhp, 1996.

Harvey, Janet. *Traditional Textiles of Central Asia*. London: Thames & Hudson, 1996.

Jumaev, Koryogdi. *Central Asia's Magnificent 99 Ikat Chapans*. Istanbul: Nuaans ajans, 2007.

Kennett, Frances. *Ethnic Dress*. New York: Facts on File, 1995.

Malik, Hafeez. *Central Asia*. New York: St. Martin's Press, 1994.

Sahadeo, Jeff, and Russell Zanca. *Everyday Life in Central Asia Past and Present*. Bloomington: Indiana University Press, 2007.

Sychova, Natalya. *Traditional Jewellery from Soviet Central Asia and Kazakhstan*. Moscow: Sovetsky Khudozhnik Publishers, 1984.

Gillian Vogelsang-Eastwood

See also Regional Dress of Afghanistan; Turkmen Dress and Embroidery; Turkmen Women's Jewelry; Dress from Tajikistan and Uzbekistan; Dress from Kyrgyzstan.

Dress from Kyrgyzstan

The Kyrgyz Republic, or Kyrgyzstan as it is more commonly known, is a country in Central Asia. The name *Kyrgyz* is said to mean either "forty girls" or "forty tribes" and is a name that probably refers to the epic hero Manas, who unified forty tribes against the Mongols in the medieval period. Kyrgyzstan is a landlocked and mountainous country which has borders with Kazakhstan to the north, Uzbekistan to the west, Tajikistan to the southwest, and China to the east. Since many ethnic groups in the region were split between neighboring states at a time when borders were less regulated, it was common to move back and forth over the mountains depending on where life was perceived as better. As a result, in the twentieth century, the Kyrgyz have many cultural aspects, including some textiles and items of dress, in common with their neighbors, notably the Tajiks and the Uzbeks. In particular, the influence of Russia, politically, economically, and culturally, has long been felt in this region.

In the early nineteenth century, the southern part of Kyrgyzstan came under the control of the Khanate of Kokand. The territory, then known in Russian as Kirgizia, soon fell under the Russian sphere of influence, and it was formally incorporated into the Russian empire in 1876. As a result, many Kyrgyz fled to the Pamirs and Afghanistan. Similarly, there was a Kyrgyz rebellion in 1916; following its suppression, many more Kyrgyz migrated to China.

Soviet power was initially established in the region in 1919 with the foundation of the Kara-Kyrgyz Autonomous Oblast. In 1936, the Kyrgyz Soviet Socialist Republic was made into a full republic of the Soviet Union. In December 1990, the Supreme Soviet of Kyrgyzstan voted to change the country's name to the Republic of Kyrgyzstan; and in February 1991, the name of the capital, Frunze, was changed back to its prerevolutionary name of Bishkek. In December 1991, following the fall of the Soviet empire, Kyrgyzstan became an independent republic officially known as the Kyrgyz Republic.

Kyrgyzstan is a mountainous country. The mountainous region of the Tien Shan covers about 80 percent of the country, with the remaining parts being made up of valleys and basins. The climate varies regionally. The southwestern Fergana Valley, for example, is subtropical and can be extremely hot in the summer months. The northern foothills, in contrast, are temperate, while the Tien Shan varies from dry continental to a polar climate depending on the altitude. The coldest areas have temperatures below thirty-two degrees Fahrenheit (zero degrees Celsius) for around forty days each winter. These differences in climate and temperature have had a profound effect on the range of clothing worn by both men and women.

The country is basically rural, with about one-third of the population living in urban regions. The largest ethnic group are the Kyrgyz, a Turkic people who make up about 70 percent of the population. Other major ethnic groups include Russians in the north and Uzbeks in the south. Smaller minority groups include Tatars, Uighurs, Tajiks, Kazakhs, and Ukrainians. Many of these groups have brought their own culture and forms of dress with them, although in the late twentieth century, urban dress was becoming more homogenized, making it more difficult to identify ethnic origins based on what someone was wearing.

HISTORICAL BACKGROUND

The dress practices of the Kyrgyz reflect a diverse history with major influences from Russia, Uzbekistan, and Tajikistan. They also reflect the nomadic way of life that used to predominate in this region and the extremes of climate, which ranges from very hot in the summer to freezing cold in the winter.

According to the Russian anthropologist Klavdiya Antipina, Kyrgyz dress from the nineteenth and twentieth centuries can be divided into four main periods which reflect changes in the political, economic, social, and cultural situation in the region. The first period is defined as showing the growing Russian influence from the 1820s on, leading to the annexation of Kyrgyzstan by Russia in 1876. During this period, industries and towns were established and enlarged. Workers and colonists were brought in from diverse regions of Russia, which had a strong Russianizing effect on Kyrgyz dress, especially in the north of the country.

The second period was from 1918 to the 1950s, which was marked by the progressive control of the Bolsheviks in Central Asia. There were various revolts by the Uzbeks, Kazakhs, and Kyrgyz against Russian colonization and the modern socialist economy and way of life. World War II (1939–1945) saw traditional crafts abandoned and textile factories turned over to war production, all of which left considerable traces on clothing styles. Western-style caps and industrial felt hats appeared in this period.

The third period lasted from the 1950s to 1991, when the Kyrgyz gained their independence from Russia. The biggest changes took place during this period, for a variety of reasons, such as an increase in education, especially for girls, and the development of the industrial-scale production of silk, cotton, and wool clothes. Clothing workshops opened in towns and villages, and people could order clothes of traditional, modern, or modern-traditional cuts at any time of the year relatively cheaply. Fabrics made from synthetic yarns became widely used, bringing with them a new range of materials and colors. With many different ethnic groups working together, people started to wear a homogenized

(Russian/Western) style of clothing, both at the workplace and at home. Some "traditional" garments completely vanished as new clothing types were introduced. The massive, voluminous turbans worn by Kyrgyz women virtually disappeared from daily life, as did another important symbol of marital status, the married woman's apron skirt (*beldemchi*). In place of the turban, head scarves were now worn by most village women, while in winter woolen shawls became more common. Printed head scarves were imported from Russia and later from China.

During this period, more practical, lighter coats replaced the older, heavy fur coats and *chapans* (light quilted coats that are ankle to calf length, have long sleeves that cover the hands, and are worn all over Central Asia). During the 1950s there was strong Russian and Ukrainian influence in the north, due to the settlement of colonists from Europe. From the 1960s on, town coats in modern Western styles had virtually replaced the older forms in the north, while in the more conservative south, older forms tended to survive; this was also probably due to the influence of their Tajik and Uzbek neighbors, who continued to make and wear the heavier, older-style coats. In addition, sleeveless waistcoats were adopted by many people in the region, again as being more practical. It was during this era that the *kalpak* hat, made of embroidered white felt, spread and became the icon of male dress and Kyrgyz identity.

The fourth stage is the postindependence phase from 1991 on, when Western-style urban clothing and outfits (based on trousers, shirts, dresses, and coats) were adopted by men and women throughout the country. Clothing could now be bought in shops and street bazaars throughout the country; these garments were often imported rather than locally made. Elements of traditional dress were worn on special occasions but often in a much simplified manner.

Following the fall of the Soviet Union in 1991 and the declaration of Kyrgyz independence, more and more urban men and women are wearing Western-style urban clothing. This type of attire can be bought in shops and street bazaars throughout the country and is often imported rather than home or locally made. Elements of traditional dress are worn on special occasions but normally in a much simplified manner. Wealth, marital, and social status are being shown by the use of modern technology and cars rather than handmade silver jewelry and heavy silk fabrics.

But what are these older and "traditional" forms of Kyrgyz dress that, according to Antipina, seem to have vanished or are being reinvented based on garment styles from the nineteenth and early twentieth centuries? In many cases, these garments have vanished by the early twenty-first century, except for weddings and other festive occasions.

Kyrgyz tribesmen with a local Russian governor and his wife, Kyrgyzstan, ca. 1885. The Kyrgyzstan region was formally incorporated into the Russian empire in 1876, and the political and social changes that occurred from the early nineteenth century on had a great influence on Kyrgyz dress. The local men here can be seen wearing the traditional long-sleeved coats (*chapan*) with the left side going over the right, as well as sashes (*belbo'o*) or cloth belts (*bel kur*) around the waist to hold them in place. Library of Congress Prints and Photographs Division, LC-USZ62-128110.

In general, by the end of the twentieth century, the traditional outfits of both men and women were made up of fewer garments than before but used a far wider range of materials. In many cases, however, the basic cut of these traditional garments remained very similar to those worn one hundred years previously. There were various regional differences in Kyrgyz dress between that worn in the north and that in the south, but the most marked distinctions reflect life stages, differentiating the young from the old. It should also be noted that, unlike some of their neighbors, the Kyrgyz did not practice veiling or the sequestering of women; this more liberal attitude has had a role in the range and appearance of the garments worn in private and in public by women.

As with many Central Asian countries, embroidery played an important role in the dress of both men and women, as it still does in traditional clothing. It is used for decorative seams, covering large surfaces of cloth, as well as for intricate details that are often hidden from sight. Appliqué is a common method of decorating clothing, using small pieces of fabric, especially velvet, as well as fur bands. Garments are often decorated with fringes, pleats, tassels, pompoms, and beads and plaques or disks made of silver, river pearls, mother-of-pearl, or coral. In the north of Kyrgyzstan, where there was stronger Russian influence in the nineteenth century, garments were often fastened with buttons. Local jewelers made large, round silver buttons (*topchu*), which were often convex and engraved or enameled. These buttons were frequently used on men's belts and women's plait decorations.

Amulets (*tumar*) were often fastened to women's headdresses, dresses, and jackets, as well as children's clothing, to serve as protection against the evil eye. These amulets were often triangular in shape but could vary quite considerably with regard to their size and shape. They were often sewn on either side of a dress or jacket opening, because this region was regarded as particularly vulnerable. Buttons and amulets were made locally, as well as being imported from the bazaars of Kokand and Bukhara and from Russia. Children normally wore colored velvet skullcaps that were often embroidered with patterns considered to provide protection against the evil eye, including birds, royal eagles, falcons, and the owl. Such skullcaps also frequently included a row of triangular cloth amulets, each with the apex pointing upward; again, these were used to protect the wearer from the evil eye. Another important feature of Kyrgyz dress is the use of feathers, notably those of owls, eagle owls, swallows, peacocks, or cranes, to decorate headgear.

MEN'S DRESS

Until the mid-nineteenth century, Kyrgyz men dressed in a basic outfit that consisted of trousers, a shirt, an undercoat and an overcoat, a woolen or fur-lined coat, leather shoes or boots, and a fur or embroidered felt cap. It is likely that this style of clothing can be traced back many hundreds of years.

A man's undertrousers (*ich shym*) were made from white cotton; these were very wide at the top as well as between the legs for easy movement; they narrowed toward the ankles so they could be tucked into boots. The trousers were tied at the waist with a belt of plaited wool (*ichkir*), decorated at each end with embroidery, or with the marriage belt worn by a bride, which was embellished with tassels of golden thread and colored silks. In the winter, men wore sheepskin trousers (*djargak shym*) or goatskin trousers (*teke shym*) with the fleece/hair worn on the inside.

Elk-skin trousers (*kandagi shym*) were also sometimes worn, and according to Antipina these reflected a time when the Kyrgyz lived in the forests of southern Siberia. In the north of the country, rich merchants (*beys*) and traditional chiefs (*manaps*) wore deerskin trousers (*sayma shym*) at festivals and games, which were embroidered with large, multicolored floral motifs in silk down the sides and along the hems of the trouser legs.

Other forms of trousers were made of a thick wool cloth that was locally made or a camel-hair cloth (*piasy*), which was very warm. From the end of the nineteenth century on, factory-made fabrics (velvet or cotton cloth) largely displaced wool, leather, or fur as the material for the trousers, and the older forms were basically worn only by some hunters and cattle breeders. Only a few still wear them in the early twenty-first century.

From about the age of six on, boys started to wear a long, loose shirt of white cotton next to the skin. In the south, the shirt had no collar and was open to the waist. In the north, another form of shirt (*achyk köynök*) was worn that was open down the front. It had a little turned-down collar and had cotton ties to fasten it at the top. By the end of the nineteenth century, both of these styles of long shirts had become much shorter, and the front openings no longer reached down to the waist. In the north, due to Russian influence, buttons started to be used for fastening shirts.

Over the trousers and shirts, undercoats and overcoats of various types were worn, but the most common form was the chapan. It was worn in the winter and summer over a shirt or dress and trousers. It was long and wide, open down the front, with the left side overlapping the right. A piece of fabric cut diagonally (*chalgai*) was sewn to the flap on the right-hand side to make sure that there were no gaps when the chapan was fastened. Formerly, the sleeves were very long, extending past the hands by four to eight inches (ten to twenty centimeters). Little by little, the sleeves became shorter and more practical. The *tu'ura chapan* were amply cut coats with straight flaps, but without the extra panel, and with a flared hemline. They were used throughout most of the country, although not in the west. They were often padded with raw cotton, which was then quilted in place.

The chapans were made of narrow bands of cloth, usually wool, cotton, or a silk-and-cotton combination and lined with a hand-printed patterned fabric, similar to the *kalamkar* (cotton sheets with hand-painted and block-printed designs) from India and Iran, or with printed material from Russia with large, colorful floral patterns. These coats were sometimes trimmed with cotton wadding and completely quilted in longitudinal bands, which were three-quarters to one and a half inches (two to four centimeters) wide and held the lining in place. In general, in the northern regions, older people liked to wear chapans made with an outer layer of printed Russian fabric in dark colors, while younger people preferred brighter-colored stripes and ikats. Until the end of the nineteenth century, chapans were locally made, but by the beginning of the twentieth century, more and more ready-made Kazakh and Russian coats were available, and striped fabric chapans were being imported from neighboring Tajik and Uzbek regions.

During the warmer summer months in the south, a coat (*djelek*) was worn that was made of a striped cloth; it was unlined, had no padding, and was not quilted. It was thus light and cool to wear but provided "respectability" and a finished appearance. The *beshmant*, a lighter kind of coat lighter than the chapan, started to be worn from the end of the nineteenth century on. These were

A Kyrgyz man wearing a buttoned coat (*chapan*), Kyrgyzstan, between 1865 and 1872. Traditionally, men's coats would have been worn with sashes (*belbo'o*) or cloth belts (*bel kur*) to hold them closed, but under Russian rule, buttons began to be used for fastening coats and shirts. Library of Congress Prints and Photographs Division, LC-DIG-ppmsca-14239.

more fitted than the wide chapans but still sufficiently wide at the waist to be comfortable on horseback, and although they were lined with cloth, they were not quilted. They often had a high collar; the lengths of sleeves varied widely. The beshmant was adopted by both men and women and was particularly popular with urban dwellers and mountain shepherds. Young people tended to prefer them in bright colors, such as yellow, green, red, or violet.

Toward the end of the nineteenth century, the *kemsel* or *kemzir* coat was introduced. This had short sleeves that reached to the elbows. It could be lined and was sometimes quilted. Another introduction was a long waistcoat (*kelteché*) with no sleeves, which came down to just above the knees. By the end of the nineteenth century, it had become part of everyday dress for women and old men. Again, it was sometimes lined and quilted but not always. Antipina has suggested that both the kemsel and kelteché could have been borrowed from the Bashkirs and Tartars, who wore similar clothing in the nineteenth century.

Due to the severe winter weather, winter overcoats had to be warm and waterproof, and various types developed to suit the needs of different social groups. Some of these coats were made of felt, wool, or fur, but they were always big and all-enveloping, with long sleeves to keep the hands warm, and had an open front

with no buttons. Normally, the left-hand side of the garment was used to cover the right-hand side of the coat. The coat was held in place with a sash or belt.

Large felt overcoats (*kementai*, *kebenek*, or *kebanak*), for example, were often worn by shepherds who slept out in the open near their flocks. Such coats were found all over Central Asia and are still used in Afghanistan, Iran, and Turkey, where they are known as *kepeneks*. The Kyrgyz version was made of thick felt of a natural white color. It was open at the front with long sleeves and was decorated with colorful embroidery. The ends of the sleeves, flaps, and neck were sometimes embellished with black or white appliqué, often using leather.

During the twentieth century and into the twenty-first century, some seminomads were still wearing heavy sheepskin coats (*ton*) with the fleece on the inside. The more expensive versions are made from fox skin (*börü*) or mountain-wolf skin. They are made of bands of fur, assembled and sewn together, often with a large fur collar to protect the neck. They give good protection against the winter cold. At night, they can be spread out like a blanket.

By the end of the nineteenth century, cloth produced in Russia was widely available and was sometimes used to cover the outside of fur-lined coats; these are called *kaptama ton*, meaning "covered coat," or *ichik*. They were cut narrower and more fitting in comparison with the older shepherd's fur coats. They were also shorter and had sleeves that reached only to the wrist rather than covering the hands. These coats were sometimes trimmed with sheepskin or fox skin, while more expensive versions used sable or marten fur. They were worn on special occasions by wealthier men and sometimes formed part of a marriage dowry. A leather coat (*da'aky*) was also worn in the nineteenth century. These were sometimes made from the skin of a horse's colt with the hair on the outside, in which case they were called *kulun ton*. They were generally worn by young people.

At the beginning of the twentieth century, a new kind of sheepskin coat appeared. It was lighter in weight and cut, imitating the Russian style with a fitted waist with pleats at the back and a small, turned-down collar. It was known as a Russian ton (*orus ton*) or pleated ton (*büyürmö ton*). In addition to fur coats, ankle-length, thick woolen coats were also used in the winter time. The oldest form was the *chepken* or *chekmen*, which was worn over a shirt and a light cotton or silk chapan-style coat. It was made of thick, woven sheep wool or camel hair and had an ample cut with very long sleeves that were used to protect the hands. It was open at the front, without buttons, and closed with a sash, cloth belt (*kushak* or *kemer*), or decorated leather belt.

Sashes (*belbo'o*), cloth belts (*bel kur*), and leather belts formed an important part of Kyrgyz dress, especially for men. In general, younger men went for colored belts, often with a red background, while older men chose white belts. Belts and sashes were used to fasten shirts, jackets, waistcoats, and outer coats. In addition, they were handy places to keep fire-lighting kits, razors, awls for sewing leather, purses, pipes, and pouches for tobacco. Hunters also used them for carrying powder flasks and bullet cases. By the beginning of the twentieth century, sashes had largely been replaced by factory-made cloth and leather belts.

MEN'S HEADGEAR

Another important element in a man's dress was some form of headgear. Kyrgyz men traditionally had shaved heads and wore a skullcap (*topu*), thus never exposing their bare heads, even at home. The Kyrgyz adopted this norm from the Islamic vestimentary system, which requires Muslim men to cover their heads at all times. The basic Kyrgyz skullcap for a man was made at home by women from a white cotton fabric. The top of this skullcap was pointed, as the crown was made from four cloth triangles joined at the top and padded slightly around the rim to grip the head. These caps were often decorated with stitching and embroidery. In the late nineteenth century, more and more caps were bought from bazaars and showed Tatar, Uzbek, and Tajik influences, especially in the use of multicolored floral patterns. In southwestern Kyrgyzstan, men, especially those over forty years of age, used to wrap their caps with long turban cloths; the cloths of older men were usually white. The use of turbans in this manner continued up to the end of the twentieth century.

Kyrgyz woman, Kyrgyzstan, ca. 1870. Over her dress (*köynök*), which is embellished with a decorative rolled yoke around the neck and chest, she wears a long-sleeved coat (*chapan*). A chapan could be made from cotton, *beykasam* (a silk-and-cotton cloth with colored stripes), or, in the south, multicolored ikat silks from Bukhara. Her white turban indicates her married status. Library of Congress Prints and Photographs Division, LC-DIG-ppmsca-14244.

Kyrgyz boys and men, however, are more famous for their use of a white felt cap called a kalpak, which has become a dress icon and is still being worn into the twenty-first century. The kalpak is an embroidered white felt cap with seams highlighted in black. The conical kalpak can be up to twenty-five inches (sixty-four centimeters) in height and is made of four pieces of felt sewn together. It has a wide brim that is normally slit at the front and the back. The turned-up sides of the cap are lined with black satin or velvet, which makes the white felt stand out even more. The crown of the kalpak is sometimes decorated with a tassel. There are numerous variations in style and decoration which reflect local needs and taste.

Another characteristic Kyrgyz hat is the conical *tebetey*, which is made of four pieces of velvet, wool cloth, or indeed any thick, warm material, that are sewn together. It is normally lined with felt, wool, or cotton padding. In the nineteenth century, the tebetey was tall and round and looked a little like a sugarloaf, but by the mid-twentieth century, it had shrunk in size and often had a rectangular base. The tebetey was decorated around its base with a fur trim that was five to six inches (thirteen to fifteen centimeters) wide and made of astrakhan or fox. The latter was most commonly used, although astrakhan was more often used in the northern region of the country. The most expensive tebetey were trimmed with marmot or otter fur. The so-called Kashghar tebetey was made of four pieces of cloth that were sewn together to create a tall, round cap decorated with a narrow fur border about two to three inches (five to seven and a half centimeters) wide. It was mainly worn by shepherds, with the fur on the inside. The *malakay*, another type of headgear, was a kind of bonnetlike cap with earflaps; it was made of fur with the leather on the outside. It was worn by shepherds and hunters in the winter.

WOMEN'S DRESS

The dress worn by Kyrgyz women was very similar to that of women in surrounding countries. The basic outfit consisted of undertrousers, a dress, a waistcoat or coat, and various forms of headgear. In addition, however, Kyrgyz women had a special form of apron, which indicated their marital status.

A woman's trousers (*ichtan*) were long and wide at the waist, with a drawstring to control the extra material. In the south of the country, the hems of such trousers were gathered at the ankle cuffs and decorated with an applied band. According to Antipina, this band was woven or embroidered with tiny, colored patterns and looked very similar to Uzbek and Tajik forms. Another form of trousers was the *chalbar*, which were long and wide. These were worn well into the twentieth century.

Over the trousers was worn a dress (*köynök*), which reached to the ankles with a small standing collar (mandarin style) and an embroidered opening on the right side near the neck. In some areas young girls had a köynök with a horizontal slit on the shoulders, while the dresses of married women had a vertical slit in the front to aid breast-feeding. During the nineteenth century, the köynök was normally fastened on the right side of the neck with a tie (*büchülük*), a round silver brooch, or a decorative pin. At the end of the century, buttons became more widespread as a result of increasing Russian influence and trade.

The everyday version of this dress was made from cotton, while those for special occasions were of silk or satin. Materials decorated with ikat designs or bold prints have long been popular. The ikats were made in various places, such as Bukhara in Uzbekistan, while many of the printed textiles came from Russia and, by the latter half of the twentieth century, China.

As in many cultures, there was a difference in the colors worn by various age groups. Young girls, for example, tended to wear brightly colored dresses, while younger married women wore red dresses, because red was regarded as the color of fertility. Often, older women wore dresses in pastel, white, or more sober colors. The cut of this dress was also of a very old form, comprising a central panel with additional side panels for ease of movement. This form was also seen as being related to the width of the hand looms used in this region, to ensure that a minimal amount of valuable cloth was wasted when making clothes.

A feature of these dresses was the embroidery at the neck area or on the entire front of the dress. In northern Kyrgyzstan, a woman's köynök was embellished with a decorative rolled yoke, which went all around the neck and opening. This extra piece was decorated with embroidery at the front. In the south, the dress was embroidered directly onto the cloth of the collar and the neckline; sometimes, the embroidery could consist of large and elaborate designs that covered the whole of the dress front. An embroidered dress was called a *sayma köynök*. In the mid-twentieth century, women began to wear shorter köynök that retained the basic style of the traditional köynök but with gathers at the waist. In some areas, it became more of a top and was worn with a skirt rather than with trousers.

Over the trousers and dress an apronlike garment called the beldemchi was worn. This is an elaborate, embroidered wrap-around skirt that is used to cover the lower back and buttocks and is fastened at the front. The wearing of the beldemchi was used to mark a change in a woman's marital status and was presented to a young woman by her mother one year after her marriage or following the birth of her first child. At this point, the young woman would take off her tall bridal headdress and start wearing the beldemchi.

A beldemchi consisted of a piece of embroidered cloth with a wide waistband or belt (*bach beldemchi*). It was normally made of felt covered with cloth, preferably black velvet, and was lined with camel-hair cloth. The opening and lower edge were trimmed with sheepskin or an expensive fur such as otter. Cloth ties were sewn to the end of the belt for fastening purposes; after the mid-twentieth century, buttons replaced these ties in many areas.

There were two main styles of beldemchi, which were distinguished by the type of cloth used, the cut, the decoration, as well as the way in which they are worn. In the north of Kyrgyzstan, for example, the beldemchi was cut in such a way that the two ends of the skirt cross over at the front. Both ends were embroidered. The belt of this beldemchi was normally wide and held in place with three or five pieces of black velvet. In the southwest of the country, the beldemchi was made of narrow bands of cloth rather than one large piece. The ends of the apron did not meet in the middle front; instead, there was a gap of about six inches (fifteen centimeters).

There were also special forms of beldemchi, such as those worn at festivals. In regions closer to Uzbekistan, for example, festive skirts were made from brightly colored cloth. According to Antipina, red, green, or blue velvet; a striped silk-and-cotton material called *beykasam*; satin; or ikat with large flowers were

A young Kyrgyz woman with long, plaited hair and decorative jewelry, Kyrgyzstan, ca. 1870. From around eight years of age until a girl became a bride, it was common for her to grow her hair and braid it into three to six plaits on either side of the head. This girl also wears earrings that are linked together by a silver chain that passes under the chin (*sagak söyköy*). Library of Congress Prints and Photographs Division, LC-DIG-ppmsca-14253.

especially popular. Some women would wear another form of beldemchi when traveling from one camp to another. This was made of sheepskin, with the fleece on the inside. These beldemchi were used to protect the wearer against sores while horse riding and the cold in the mountains.

A variety of different coats were worn by Kyrgyz women depending on where they lived and the time of year. For example, in the winter, when the temperature could be very low, it was normal to wear a fur coat (ichik) of some kind, often made of sheepskin with the fleece on the outside. These were long and very wide. In the north of the country, the ichik was lined with wool or velvet cloth, while in the south it was sometimes covered with a brightly colored and patterned silk. More elaborate ichik had fur trim on the front openings and neck region. In the south of Kyrgyzstan, women always fastened their coats with a sash of some kind.

During the summer and autumn, the ichik were replaced by a lighter coat (chapan), which was very similar to those worn by men. The chapan is a long coat, with very long sleeves that were used to cover the hands. They are normally made from cotton or beykasam, although in the south, woven multicolored ikat silks from Bukhara were often used. A warmer version of the chapan was quilted, using raw cotton as padding.

In the north of Kyrgyzstan, some women wore a kemzir (also called a *kamzur* or kemsel), which is a short, knee-length coat with a stand-up collar and elbow-length sleeves. It was worn directly over the dress and is regarded as an indoor coat. It was usually made from dark-colored cloth.

The beshmant was a Russian-style coat that fits the body more closely. It was normally knee length, with sleeves that end at the wrist, and it had a stand-up collar. This coat was made from brightly colored fabrics such as velvet. When attending festivals, women from wealthier families would wear the beshmant with a leather belt (kemer) decorated with silver-plated ornaments.

During the 1920s, a long waistcoat (kelteché) was introduced into the Kyrgyz women's wardrobe. The kelteché was made of dark blue cloth with an opening toward the right-hand side of the body. They were often fastened with mother-of-pearl buttons or silver clasps. A shorter style of waistcoat is called a *chyptama*. These waistcoats were regarded as more practical than the chapans, because they are shorter, but they changed the silhouette of Kyrgyz women quite dramatically, highlighting the waist region.

WOMEN'S HAIRSTYLES AND BRIDAL HEADDRESS

An important element in a girl's or woman's dress was her hairstyle and the type of headdress worn. Until the age of six or seven, girls had the same hairstyles as boys: The head was shaved except for two locks left in place at the sides of the head. When she was a little older, a girl would let her hair grow; when it was long enough, it would be braided into fine plaits, with three to six plaits on either side of the head. The ends of each plait would be decorated with pieces of coral or fancy buttons. The plaits were sometimes fastened together at the back with a silver-plated ornament (*arkalyk*). A bride's hair was braided into four plaits thickened with strands of black wool. Once a girl was married, her hair was braided into two large plaits that hung down the back. These plaits were concealed in a special holder (*chach kap*) decorated with embroidery, silver plate, and other ornaments.

The plait ornaments varied in appearance, especially in the north, where plait holders extended down the back and could be seen under the heavy turban. *Chach papik*, for example, were pompoms of hair bound by silk; the hair was further extended by attaching conical silver ornaments to the end of the plaits. They were adopted from the Uzbeks and the Tajiks. A *cholpu* was made of an arrangement of silver plate or silver rubles (Russian coins), joined into a triangle that was linked by three chains. The two plaits could also be extended by a *zirye* or a linked chain of coins. In the valley of Zetmen Tyube, a plait decoration (*gudmuk*) was made of coins held together with straps of leather.

The type of headgear worn by Kyrgyz women changed, again according to their age and marital status. Young girls, for example, wore embroidered skullcaps (*sayma topu*) or scarves, especially in the south. On special occasions, some girls in the north wore a conical cap (tebetey) that was often made of red cloth. The lower edge was trimmed with a wide fur border of astrakhan, otter, fox, or mink. The crown of the cap was sometimes decorated with bunches of wool, eagle owl feathers, or a tuft of eagle's down.

The main changes in headgear came when a girl married and became a woman. For the marriage ceremony, in addition to her best clothes, the bride wore a special and very elaborate headdress that she continued to wear during the first year of married life or for seasonal movements to other camps. After a year, the bride stopped wearing the tall wedding headdress. If a child had already been born, then she also received the *enchi*, a portion of livestock that came to her as part of her inheritance from her father.

In northern Kyrgyzstan, the bride hid only her face with a white veil when leaving her parents' camp and going to her new home. In the south, however, the bride was concealed with a large, rectangular piece of embroidered silk that was draped from the top of the bridal headdress. The use of this type of veil may be due to Tajik or Uzbek influence. During the nineteenth century, there were two main forms of bridal headdress, the *shökülö* and the *saukele*. Hiding a woman's hair both when she was a bride and later was emphasized because many saw a woman's hair as erotically charged and, as such, a potential threat to the social order, hence it was better to hide her hair from view. This viewpoint is not unique to the Kyrgyz, or indeed Central Asia, but can be found in many parts of the world.

From the early to mid-nineteenth century, young brides in the north of Kyrgyzstan wore the shökülö, which appears to be an ancient form of headdress going back hundreds of years, based on archaeological finds and written descriptions. The shökülö was a high, stiff headdress. It had a conical form with large earflaps at the sides and a long triangle of fabric down the back, used to hold the woman's two long braids. The plait cover was made from wool or red velvet and was lined, often with a cotton material. Peacock or crane feathers were attached to the sides of the headdress, while the main section was covered with pearls, mother-of-pearl, coral, as well as decorative pieces of silver, semiprecious stones, strips of brocade, and ribbons. A band covered with coral beads and pieces of silver decorated the circumference of the head. The point or crown of the headdress was finished with peacock feathers. Sometimes, a large plaque (*kalkan*), made from silver or gold with carnelians, was attached to the front of the headdress just above the forehead. Occasionally, a silver and coral pendant in the form of a triangle was fastened to the front of the headdress to conceal the bride's nose and mouth. By the mid-nineteenth century, the shökülö had virtually vanished because of the high costs involved. It became a traditional piece used only by the very rich and in marriage ceremonies. Later, a shökülö was placed on the bridal chest as a symbol of her new marital status, but it was not worn.

During the mid- to late nineteenth century, another form of bridal headdress became popular. This was the saukele, which was a conical headdress that could be more than twenty-four inches (sixty centimeters) high. It had a rigid frame that was covered in velvet and encrusted with silver, gold plate, and carnelians, as well as coral beads that separated the silver ornaments. The front of the saukele, just above the eyes, was trimmed with a fur band. A long, triangular flap extended down from the headdress at the back almost to the waist. It was used to contain the two long plaits. This plait bag was made of wool or red velvet and covered in silver. From the top of the headdress a long white veil (*djelek*) was draped, which covered the head and back.

A Kyrgyz woman dressed for a wedding, Kyrgyzstan, ca. 1870. She wears a conical *saukele* bridal headdress, which is covered with velvet and encrusted with silver, gold plate, coral beads, and carnelian. A fur band lines the edge of the *saukele* above the eyes. Note also the length of the sleeves on the *chapan*. Library of Congress Prints and Photographs Division, LC-DIG-ppmsca-14243.

MARRIED WOMEN'S HAIRSTYLES AND TURBANS

A year after her marriage or after the birth of her first child, a young woman was regarded as settled into her new way of life and home. She started to plait her hair into two long braids, which were hidden by a plait holder (chach kap; literally, "hair bag"). This was a long, narrow bag that ended in fringes decorated with pieces of silver plate, silver ornaments, buttons, tassels, or pompoms. The chach kep, which covered the hair at the back, was wrapped with a long piece of cloth to create the turban. These turbans were still being worn by some groups at the end of the twentieth and beginning of the twenty-first century.

Everyday turbans for women were normally made from about five yards (five meters) of a narrow band of white cloth with a closely woven texture. This type of cloth was called *istanboul*, after the capital of the Ottoman Empire, Istanbul. More elaborate turbans used more than seventeen yards (sixteen meters) of cloth or even up to thirty-three yards (thirty meters) for special occasions, which made the turbans very large. Both daily and festive turbans were embroidered to varying degrees and covered in ornamentation; they were often completed with coral pendants and pieces of silver.

Each region of Kyrgyzstan, and indeed each group, had its own form and version of the turban. The manner in which a turban was wound and decorated characterized each different group. In the north, for example, the turbans often had a more austere appearance than those worn in the south. Similarly, the turban could also represent the wearer's social and economic status; larger and more decorative turbans were worn by the senior women of richer families.

In the north, the white turban (*elechek*) was wound in very fine parallel spirals around a plain bonnet (*chach kep*; also known in the north as a *kap takiya* or *bash kap*, literally "head bag") with an attached plait holder, both of which were often made of black velvet. At the lower end of the plait holder, there was a silk net or ribbon (*chach monchok*, "hair ornament"), which was covered with glass beads or pendants. Sometimes, silver plaques (cholpu) inset

with stones were also used. Several rounds of the white turban fabric were used to hide the neck, chin, and parts of the shoulders. The main decoration of the turban took the form of a woven or embroidered band (*kyrgak*) that was wound around the turban to fasten it at the back. Sometimes, a kyrgak in net with red silk tassels or pompoms was used. Richer women also tended to attach pieces of jewelry to the turban.

Southern turbans (*ileki*) were more intricate, varied, and ornate than their northern counterparts. In addition, there was no cloth covering the chin or neck. Underneath the turban an embroidered bonnet (chach kep or *kep chach*) made of white cotton was worn; it was decorated with multicolored patterns finely worked in silk embroidery. These bonnets had earflaps and a long strip of cloth down the back to cover the two plaits. Both the flaps and the plait cover were embroidered, although the earflaps contained the bulk of the embroidery. The bonnets were also trimmed with pearls, mother-of-pearl buttons, or round silver pendants. Sometimes, bonnets had triangular ornaments of silver or coral, which hung on either side of the face. Other bonnets were ornamented with rows of coral beads linking silver plaques; these ornaments were called *sagak*.

The large, white southern turbans were wrapped around the bonnet leaving the neck and ears free so that the embroidered flaps could be seen. The turban was secured by a woven band (kyrgak). Over the top of the turban was draped a length of

Women preparing a table for a feast in a Kyrgyz house during a festival of nomad tents in central Bishkek, Kyrgyzstan, 2006. Many urban men and women from Kyrgyzstan wear Western clothing in the early twenty-first century, but elements of traditional dress are still worn for special occasions. Vyacheslav Oseledko/AFP/Getty Images.

cloth (*kalak*), which was made from white fabric embroidered with multicolored flowers and trimmed with a fringe of red silk. At the beginning of the twentieth century, the voluminous high turbans began to be replaced by large, more practical white shawls or scarves (*ak djo'oluk* or *dürüyö*), which were often embroidered (*sayma djo'oluk*) or decorated with ribbons and laces, fringing, or silver pendants of some kind. Since the 1920s, woven and printed scarves, especially those with floral patterns, have been imported from Russia. For special occasions, the headdress could be decorated with jeweled pieces made from silver and coral. Over the course of the twentieth century, this scarf became a required accessory for all young girls and married women when they were in public, and it is still worn in some form at the beginning of the early twenty-first century. There are various ways of wearing such a scarf, each of which is characteristic of a particular region, as well as representing the wearer's marital status. The colors vary with age; for example, brightly colored scarves are worn by girls and young women, while older women favor white ones.

WOMEN'S FOOTWEAR

The cold winters of Kyrgyzstan and the widespread use of horses meant that boots were the favored form of footwear, although poorer people did wear shoes of various types. The oldest style of footwear worn by the Kyrgyz are sandals or shoes (*chokoy*) made of untanned leather and leather shoes called *charyk*. It appears that both of these were replaced in the nineteenth century by shoes and boots made of soft, decorated leather that were produced in the local bazaars. Another form of shoe was the *kepich*, which again was made of leather and had uppers that were slightly raised. Kepich were decorated with various items, including buttons, pompoms, silver plaques, and coins.

In general, younger girls wore boots (*ötük*) that were green or red with thick soles and high leather heels. Boots worn by a bride were decorated with colored-leather appliqué or silver pieces. Sometimes, small bells (*djlya'ajyn*) were put in the hollow of the heels to create a ringing sound during the wedding ceremony. Older women often wore tall, soft boots made from black leather called *ichigi* or *ma'asy*. These were slipped into leather shoes (kepich) when worn out-of-doors.

JEWELRY

In general, the range of jewelry worn by the Kyrgyz is comparatively simple in comparison to that of some of its neighbors, notably among the Turkmen, where women could wear vast amounts in their hair and upper body as well as on their clothes. Kyrgyz women wore a variety of earrings, rings, bracelets, necklaces, chest plates, and amulets. Cloth or leather belts decorated with silver plaques and fastened with large clasps, sometimes encrusted with coral, pearls, or carnelians, were also widely used to show marital and social status. As a generalization, southern women seem to have worn a wider variety of jewelry than their northern counterparts.

Until the mid-twentieth century, much of the jewelry was made from silver or silver with a gilt motif, but by the end of the twentieth century, more gold jewelry was available and more commonly worn among urban women. Techniques used to decorate silver jewelry included engraving, inlay, filigree, and stamping. Silver, especially that destined for the southern market, was often engraved and then smeared with a black paste made from copper, lead, sulfur, and borax. The engraved lines became black and stood out against the silver base. Coral and carnelian were both widely used to embellish jewelry. Both substances are red, which was believed to bring health and fertility; in addition, carnelian was thought to bring luck and abundance. River pearls were sometimes used for protection against illness and misfortune.

There were different styles of decoration from north to south. In general, northern jewelry was mainly engraved or inlaid, and much of it was locally made or imported from Russia. In contrast, southern jewelry was influenced by Uzbek and Tajik styles, as well as being imported from Tashkent and Bukhara. Southern forms were often decorated with motifs such as rosettes, palettes, quatrefoils, stars, and circles. Young girls often wore coral necklaces, as well as pearls, coins, and silver pieces of all shapes and sizes, which were sewn onto their garments or worn as necklaces.

A married woman's jewelry included bracelets (*bilerik*) and rings (*shakek*), made from engraved, inlaid, or stamped silver. Rigid bracelets that opened with a hinge were linked with chains to three rings worn on the three center fingers of the hand; this form of jewelry seems to have originated in India. Earrings came in a variety of shapes and sizes, including the elaborate *sagak söyköy*, which was a pair of coral-bead earrings linked together by a silver chain that passed under the chin. The *söyköy djeburöch* was characteristic of the north of the country and consisted of conical earrings attached to the ears and linked by chains of coral and silver beads that hung across the neck and chest. The söyköy djeburöch was given as part of a bride's dowry and first worn by the bride during the wedding ceremony and later on special occasions.

The most widely used item of jewelry worn by married women, especially in the north, was a heavy coral bead necklace (*shuru*), which had several strands of beads held in place with silver plates. Southern necklaces included a coral and carnelian bead necklace imported from Badakhshan (a region that straddles Afghanistan and Tajikistan), as well as one made of silver spheres interspersed with coral beads.

Women also had a borstal plaque (a large broochlike piece of jewelry worn between the lower part of the neck and the breasts) known as a *silsila*, which consisted of triangular or rectangular plates that were made from enameled silver or encrusted with coral beads. One of the most valuable pieces of jewelry was the *boy tumar*, a large amulet carrier imported from Bukhara in modern Uzbekistan. It was suspended from the neck by a chain decorated with silver coins.

References and Further Reading

Abazov, Rafis. *Culture and Customs of the Central Asian Republics*. Westport, CT: Greenwood Press, 2007.

Antipina, Klavdiya, Rolando Paiva, and Temirbek Musakeev. *Kyrghyzstan*. Milan, Italy: Shira Editore, 2006.

Harvey, Janet. *Traditional Textiles of Central Asia*. London: Thames & Hudson, 1997.

Jumaev, Koryogdi. *Central Asia's Magnificent 99 Ikat Chapans*. Istanbul: Nuaans ajans, 2007.

Kadyrov, V. *Kyrghyzstan: Ethnic Jewellery of Central Asia*. Bishkek, Kyrgyzstan: Rarity, 2007.

Kennett, Frances. *Ethnic Dress*. New York: Facts on File, 1995.

Maksimov, V., and Ye Sorokin. *The Kyrghyz Pattern*. Frunze: Kyrghyzstan Press, 1986.

Malik, Hafeez. *Central Asia*. New York: St. Martin's Press, 1994.

Sychova, Natalya. *Traditional Jewellery from Soviet Central Asia and Kazakhstan*. Moscow: Sovetsky Khudozhnik Publishers, 1984.

Gillian Vogelsang-Eastwood

See also Regional Dress of Afghanistan; Turkmen Dress and Embroidery; Turkmen Women's Jewelry; Dress from Tajikistan and Uzbekistan; Dress from Kazakhstan.

PART 7

People and Dress in Central and Southwest Asia

Fitrah: Temporary and Permanent Body Modifications for Muslims

- The Management of Hair
- Cosmetics and Perfumes
- Permanent Body Modification
- Body Modification Unrelated to Appearance

The term *fitrah*, a precise equivalent for which does not exist in English, has been variously translated as that which is innate or instinctive, is determined by nature, derives from creation, or is in accordance with the true faith, which is Islam. The concept of fitrah is sometimes applied to the human body; namely, what people are allowed or not allowed to do with it. It is related, for example, that the Prophet Mohammed said that the five practices that are characteristic of fitrah are circumcision, shaving the pubic hair, trimming the mustache, clipping the finger- and toenails, and removing hair from the armpits. This was stated on the authority of Abū Hurayrah and Ibn ʿUmar, who were companions of the Prophet.

In addition to these five practices, according to the Prophet's wife Aisha, the Prophet Mohammed included five others: letting the beard grow, using a toothpick, snuffling up water in the nose, washing the finger joints, and cleaning one's private parts with water. The narrator added that he had forgotten the tenth act but that "it may have been rinsing the mouth." A number of other hadiths (narrations of the sayings and doings attributed to the Prophet) specify that shaving the pubic hair, trimming the mustache, clipping the nails, and depilating the hair of the armpits must be performed at least once every forty days. It is clear from these sayings that a certain set of bodily practices was considered fundamental to the life of a Muslim. These and many other prescriptions in the foundational texts of Islam shape the ways in which believing Muslims take care of their bodies and practice certain acts that temporarily or permanently modify the body.

In the Qur'an, God is described as He "who has created you, and properly formed you, and justly proportioned you; into whatever form He willed, He cast you" (*Infitār* 82:7–8). The Qur'an thus implies that humans have the appropriate form and appearance by their nature and by virtue of God's creative act. At the same time, it is by no means forbidden for humans to adorn themselves, provided that they do so with moderation. Once again, the Qur'an says, "O children of Adam! Take to your adornment in every place of worship, and eat and drink; but do not be wasteful. Verily He does not love the spendthrift. Say: who has forbidden the adornments [bestowed by] God, which He has produced for His slaves, and the good things [that He has provided] for sustenance?" (*Aʿrāf* 7:31–32). Indeed, the Prophet confirmed that it is licit to strive for beauty when he said, "Verily, God is beautiful, He loves beauty" (Muslim, *Imān* 164). The rules are intended to regulate, then, not to suppress, efforts to achieve physical beauty.

Several factors influenced the rules governing body care, cosmetics, and perfume in Islam. First, the specific historical and geographic context within which Islam arose—the lives of the inhabitants of the Hijaz in what is western Saudi Arabia in the early twenty-first century, the issues they brought before the Prophet, and the reality with which he was confronted daily—played a determining role in the development of Islamic law. Second, the Prophet tried to strike a balance between neatness of appearance and cleanliness on the one hand, and modesty and reserve on the other; in this respect, some guidelines pertaining to personal grooming echo sumptuary regulations about attire. Third, the Prophet was anxious for Muslims to distinguish themselves from non-Muslims by their appearance and comportment; in this respect, some guidelines pertaining to personal grooming have much in common with Islamic laws of differentiation.

THE MANAGEMENT OF HAIR

One of the most important aspects of personal care concerns hair—whether on the head, the face, or the body. Setting aside the problem of covering the head, there are numerous hadiths that outline what may and may not be done in each case, and these rules and regulations reflect the factors of context, a balance between neatness and modesty, and distinctions between Muslims and non-Muslims.

Trimming the mustache was considered to be consistent with the fitrah, that is, the natural order of things. The subject comes up again in several other hadiths. In some, the Prophet is said to have simply instructed male believers to "cut the mustache and let the beard be." In others, however, he is said to have specified that this was for the purpose of distinguishing Muslim men from non-Muslims. Thus, the Prophet is related to have said, "Do the opposite of what the polytheists (or the Magians) do. Keep the beards and trim the mustaches." Indeed, in one hadith, he is actually reported to have stated, "He who does not clip some of his mustache is not of us." Elsewhere, the Prophet was said to have personally trimmed the mustache of a companion. It is related that the Prophet traced the practice of trimming the mustache to the Old Testament prophet Abraham. Whether the correct course of action was only to trim the mustache, or to shave it entirely, was a matter of some debate, and different legal schools reached different conclusions; the great fifteenth-century scholar al-Suyūtī even wrote a treatise on the subject. At the end of the twentieth century, the generally prevailing opinion tended to be that the mustache should be trimmed but not shaved.

With the exception of times of pilgrimage, the rule concerning beards was unambiguous: let it grow. Here, too, the concern was to differentiate Muslims from non-Muslims. In one case, the Prophet spoke of some people from the East who, though they may have recited the Qur'an, had in truth irrevocably abandoned the faith; when asked what their sign would be, he replied, "Their sign will be that they shave."

A number of hadiths pertain to the hair on the head. In particular, the Prophet is reported to have prohibited *qazaʿ*, which

'Ubaydullah b. Hafs (a hadith scholar from the eighth century C.E.) defined as being the same as when a boy shaves and leaves a tuft of hair on his forelocks and sides. In addition, 'Ubaydullah b. Hafs noted that it was acceptable to leave hair on the temples and back of a boy's head, but it was prohibited to leave a tuft of hair on his forehead if there was no hair anywhere else on his head. This proscription may have been intended to distinguish Muslims from Jews, as the latter often sported prominent forelocks and side locks—particularly Yemenite Jews, who wore their side locks (*simanim*) very long.

Hadiths provide evidence that both male and female companions of the Prophet sometimes wore their hair plaited. Indeed, the Prophet himself is said to have had his hair plaited on at least one occasion. His hair was described at various times as down to his earlobes, between his earlobes and his shoulders, and down to his shoulders. He is said to have first let his hair hang down in imitation of the People of the Book (Jews and Christians) but then have taken to parting it.

According to Abū Hurayrah, a companion of the Prophet and a narrator of hadiths, the Prophet said, "He who has hair

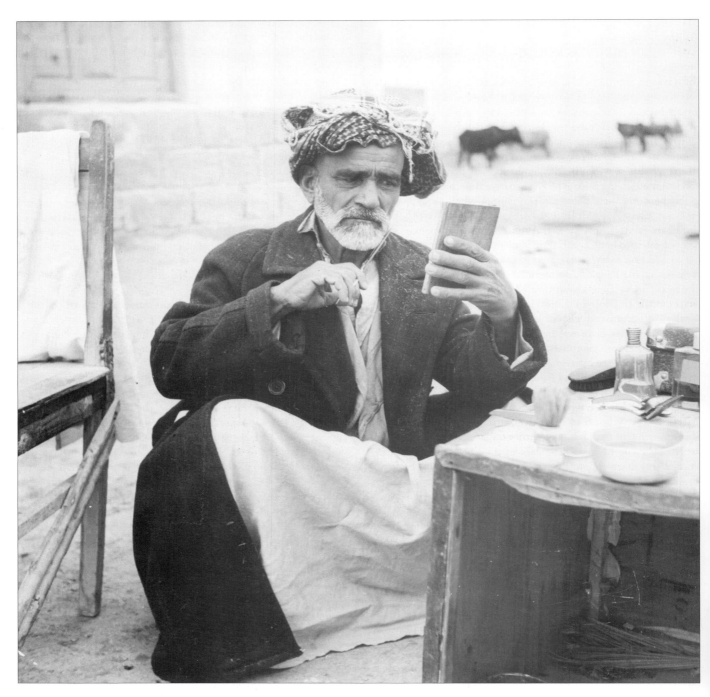

A Muslim man keeps his beard and mustache neatly trimmed at a self-service barbershop in Aga Uhari, Iran, ca. 1955. There are numerous hadiths, sometimes ambiguous, that outline what should and should not be done in the care of hair on the face and head. By the end of the twentieth century, the prevailing opinion was that the mustache should be trimmed but not shaved. Getty Images.

should honor it." It is related that "the Messenger of God (prayers and blessings of God be upon him) was sitting in the mosque when a man whose hair and beard were wild and disheveled came in. The Messenger of God (prayers and blessings of God be upon him) signaled to him with his hand to go out, tidy up his hair, and return. He acted accordingly and came back in. The Messenger of God (prayers and blessings of God be upon him) said: 'Is this not better than one of you coming in with his hair disheveled as though he was Satan?'" These hadiths show that the Prophet was concerned with neatness of appearance; however, as evidenced by many other accounts, he did not condone excess. Thus, he enjoined a companion not to comb his hair more often than every other day.

Presumably also due to his dislike of vanity, the Prophet disapproved of women using artificial hair. Another prohibition that applies specifically to women concerns facial hair and is based on a hadith that invokes a curse on women who pluck their facial hair. Here, the word *mutanammisat* is generally taken to mean "women who pluck their eyebrows," and indeed Edward William Lane defines *anmasu* as "having no eyebrows" in his *Arabic-English Lexicon*. Though some have chosen to interpret the word more liberally as referring to women who remove any facial hair, the prevailing opinion tends to be that the hadith pertains to eyebrows only.

If plucking facial hair was prohibited, depilating body hair was, on the contrary, mandated, at least for some parts of the body. In particular, removing armpit and pubic hair was listed among the practices characteristic of the fitrah in both the "five practices" and the "ten practices" version. Furthermore, some accounts hint at the social dimension of this practice. Returning from a military campaign, the Prophet is related to have said to his companions: "Wait till you enter [your homes] at night, so that the disheveled women may comb their hair, and those whose husbands have been absent may shave their pubic hair."

Nevertheless, depilation in the Muslim world is more an issue of hygiene than of eroticism. In Western literature, the fact that Muslims—and particularly Muslim women—depilate their pubic area has often been deliberately eroticized. Thus, for instance, John Richards wrote in 1699, "Upon solemn occasions, when a virgin does prepare herself for her husband's bed, they make a feast in the baths to which they invite their friends, at which time she takes off the hair of her body, which she never does before, and is always practiced afterwards in these hot countries. With how much modesty this is done I cannot tell" (cited in Cleugh).

With this substitution of innuendo for fact, Richards allowed his readers to infuse his account with whatever their imagination might supply. Other writers were substantially more explicit. Yet while there is, of course, no denying that the grooming and presentation of the genitals can contribute much to the sexual experience, the presence and absence of hair on various parts of the body are, in fact, assigned meaning by culture, and that is how Islamic rules pertaining to body hair must be interpreted. Various depilatories were developed over the centuries, of which one of the most common is a sugar-and-lemon paste known as *halawa* in Arabic and *ağda* in Turkish.

COSMETICS AND PERFUMES

The Prophet is related in various hadiths to have praised those who take a bath and oil (*yaddahinu*) their hair before Friday prayers; he is also said to have combed and oiled his hair before leaving Medina for a pilgrimage, and he is reported to have had his hair styled with gum (*mulabbidan* or *talbīd*). These hadiths suggest that it is permissible to use oil or gum to style one's hair, and many rules that regulate which cosmetics and perfumes can be used and which cannot similarly derive from statements the Prophet is supposed to have made or behavior in which he is said to have engaged.

For example, there are a number of hadiths concerning dyeing one's hair and beard. In some, it is stated that the Prophet did not have enough gray in his hair to dye it, the implication being that he would have if it had been warranted. In others, perhaps referring to a different period of his life, he is said to have dyed his hair and beard. Several of his close companions, notably the Caliphs Abū Bakr and 'Umar, are said to have dyed their hair, as is the Prophet's beloved grandson Husayn. Indeed, the Prophet is related to have recommended that Muslims dye their gray hair and beards and thereby distinguish themselves from non-Muslims, who did not.

Some hadiths are quite specific in mentioning which dyes were licit and which were not. Thus, henna (a yellow and red dye), *katam* (a black or dark brown dye), *wars* (a saffron-colored dye), and *wasma* (a blue dye) were allowed and even, in some cases, recommended, while black dye was discouraged or, according to some, prohibited. Many of these materials are botanical dyes well known to historians of material culture: For example, wasma (*Isatis tinctoria*) is known in English as woad, ash of Jerusalem, and dyer's weed, and in some languages as wild indigo; wars (*Memecylon tinctorium*) is closely related to the Ceylon cornel tree, though it was reputed to exist only in Yemen.

Henna has been used as a dye for thousands of years and remains popular throughout Southwest Asia. Derived from lawsone (hennotannic acid) in the leaves of the plant known as *Lawsonia inermis*, it is used not only to give a reddish tinge to hair but also to create elaborate temporary tattoos on hands, feet, and other parts of the body. Luigi Bassano da Zara, who visited Istanbul in the late 1530s, wrote that Turks

> like the hair black, and she whom nature has not so endowed resorts to trickery, so that when it is blond, or white from old age, they dye it red with *Archenda*, which they call *Chnà*, with which they dye their pony tails; with the same medicine they dye their nails, many dye their entire hands, some their feet, but in the form of the shoe; there are some who also dye their pubic hair and four fingers above it.

The use of henna to draw patterns on the head and body was often associated with celebrations. It was not uncommon, for example, during the Qajar era for the bride and bridegroom (separately) to be adorned with henna. During this period, the most common motifs were flowers, clusters of leaves, birds such as sparrows, and butterflies. In addition, more intricate, geometric patterns were also used as decorative elements.

There is evidence that the Prophet Mohammed disapproved of men's use of dyes to color their skin. For example, he is related to have held that "the scent used by men should have an odor but no color, and the scent used by women should have a color but no odor." It is also related that he was once made a sign from behind a curtain, upon which he said, "I do not know whether this is a man's hand or a woman's." When the person responded that she was a woman, he is said to have replied, "If you had been a woman, you would have made a difference to your nails, that is, with henna," suggesting that men did not dye their hands with henna. Indeed, the wedding ceremony is often the only time they do.

Perfumes are also given some attention in the hadiths, and the Prophet's opinion on them is generally favorable. The only exception is women's use of heavy scents outside the home, a practice that offended his sense of modesty. This is indeed the most likely reason for the statement that women's scents should have color but no odor. In some accounts, the Prophet himself is related to have used scents. It is said, furthermore, that he "never refused the gift of perfume" and considered it to "come from Paradise." He also praised those who used scent before Friday prayers.

As with dyes, a number of perfumes are mentioned by name in the hadiths. Musk, for instance, is used repeatedly to indicate an excellent scent. The Prophet is related to have said that those injured in the cause of God will, on the Day of Judgment, have wounds the color of blood but with the odor of musk. He

A postcard of a Turkish woman with her eyes lined with kohl, Cairo, Egypt, 1920s. Kohl (*surmeh* in Arabic, *sürme* in Turkish) has been widely used by both men and women to enhance the eyes and also for medical purposes for thousands of years throughout Southwest Asia. Courtesy of Dr. Irvin Schick.

also said that the sweat of the first believers to enter Paradise will smell of musk and that, in the eyes of God, the breath of a fasting person smells better than musk. The Prophet himself is said to have smelled of musk.

Aisha related that she personally perfumed the Prophet with *dharira*. According to Lane's *Arabic-English Lexicon*, this scent is made from the *Calamus aromaticus*, whose internodal portions contain a white substance resembling a spider's web that is powdered and used as a perfume. It is also reported (on the authority of Anas b. Mālik, a well-known companion of the Prophet) that the Prophet perfumed himself with *sukkah*. According to Lane, this scent was prepared by mixing *ramak*, a pitchlike substance, with musk and aging the mixture for a year.

In contrast, *khaluq*, a saffron-based dye, was strictly forbidden for men. The Prophet is related to have said that angels will not approach a man wearing khaluq, nor be present at his funeral, and that the prayers of such a man would not be heard by God. A number of accounts describe the Prophet's personal dislike of this perfume and his shunning of men who had used it. At the same time, it is related that his wife Umm Habība requested some khaluq as an indication that her period of mourning for her father's death had ended, suggesting that women were free to use it under normal circumstances.

Umm Habība's request was based on the fact that a woman was not permitted to adorn or perfume herself during a period of bereavement. Thus, it is related that the Prophet was asked whether a woman who had recently lost her husband could use kohl (collyrium, antimony) for therapeutic purposes; he replied that she could not until her mourning period was over. Like henna, kohl (*surmeh* in Arabic, *sürme* in Turkish) has been widely used throughout Southwest Asia for thousands of years, both for adornment and for medical purposes. Thus, in a description of Istanbul first published in 1797, James Dallaway wrote that Turks "have a custom too of drawing a black line with a mixture of powder of antimony and oil, called *Surmèh*, above and under the eyelashes, in order to give the eye more fire." More than a century earlier, George Sandys had likewise written:

> Great eyes they have in principall repute…And of those the blacker they be, the more amiable; insomuch that they put betweene the eyelids and the eye a certaine blacke powder with a fine, long pensil…which by the not disgracefull staining of the lids doth better set forth the whiteness of the eye: and though it trouble for a time, yet it comforteth the sight, and repellith ill humors.

The practice continues in the early twenty-first century and is by no means limited to women.

PERMANENT BODY MODIFICATION

With the exception of circumcision, Islam generally takes an unfavorable view of permanent body modification, which it considers to be tampering with God's creation. It is written in the Qur'an: "So set your face unswervingly towards the faith, in accordance with the natural disposition (fitrat) of God upon which He has created mankind. There is no changing of God's creation (*lā tabdīla li-khalqi Allāhi*). That is the true faith, and yet most men know it not" (*Rūm* 30:30). Elsewhere, Satan is described as a rebel against God and is quoted as saying, "I shall command them

[that is, men] to alter God's creation (*falayughayyirunna khalqa Allāhi*)" (*Nisā'* 4:119). While the Qur'an does not specify precisely what is meant here by "God's creation" nor by "altering" it, some interpreters have taken these verses as indicating that permanent body modification is forbidden.

Indeed, there is a hadith that appears to support that interpretation. The Prophet is reported (on the authority of 'Abdullāh b. Mas'ūd) to have held that "God has cursed those women who practice tattooing and those who get themselves tattooed, and those who pluck their eyebrows, and those who space their teeth for the sake of beauty, those who alter the Exalted God's creation (*al-mughayyirāti khalqa Allāhi ta' ālā*)." As this hadith indicates, a woman who engages in tattooing (*washm*)—whether she tattoos someone (*wāshimah*) or is herself tattooed (*mustawshimah*)—is condemned. Several hadith specify either that such women are cursed or that the practice of tattooing is banned. However, tattooing has historically been widespread among many Muslims from Central Asia to Morocco; indeed, in his *Lisān al-'Arab*, the great lexicographer Ibn Manthūr (1232–1311) mentions the expression "He thinks he is more noteworthy than a muttashimah"; the term *muttashimah* is sometimes defined as "a woman who has her genitals tattooed in order to look more beautiful."

Tattooing in Central and Southwest Asia clearly predates Islam: Mummified remains found in a broad area, from the Pazyryk burial grounds in southern Siberia to ancient Egyptian tombs, indicate that this art was widely practiced and reached great sophistication. Tattooing continued until fairly recently among the Kyrgyz and Kazakhs in Central Asia; the Dargin of Daghestan in the Caucasus; the Turkmens and Kurds in Asia Minor; the Arabs, Turkmens, Kurds, and Yazidis in Mesopotamia; and many other ethnic and/or religious groups. This was confirmed by Henry Field, who led a number of anthropometric surveys across Southwest Asia during the second quarter of the twentieth century and found tattooing (*daqq*, or "striking") to be widespread.

Similarly, research conducted in 1991 among Kurds and Turkmens living in the vicinity of the city of Gaziantep (eastern Turkey) revealed that older women tended to be tattooed (*dövün*; more generally, *dövme*, or "striking") on their chins, ankles, necks, chests, and hands and men on their noses, foreheads, hands, wrists, and arms. Most of those asked stated that their motivation for getting tattooed had been adornment, but some also believed that the tattoos would bring them luck and wealth, and some childless women did it in the hope of becoming fertile.

The widespread nature of tattooing in the Arab world can be seen in the works of various Western travelers and authors. In the early nineteenth century, James Silk Buckingham, for example, noted that upper-class women in Baghdad were seldom tattooed and, if at all, only lightly. In contrast, middle- and lower-class women were often heavily tattooed on the ankles and legs, as well as the bellies, waists, and breasts. John Punnett Peters, who traveled in Iraq in 1888–1890 described how all the women he saw were tattooed, as were many of the men. In particular, the women of the Euphrates Valley favored a blueing of the lower lip. They also had dots of blue on their cheeks and forehead and sometimes even on the tip of their nose. He was in the city of Deir just after all of the women there had been retattooed. According to Peters, they had bright blue lips, cheeks, noses, foreheads, breasts, wrists, and ankles.

Similarly, in his study of northern Arabian Bedouin, Alois Musil noted that nearly all the Bedouin women were tattooed on the lips, cheeks, nose, forehead, breasts, around the breasts, and on the belly. The work was apparently carried out by gypsy women, who pricked the design onto the skin and then dipped the needle into indigo and transferred the dye onto the holes. The tattooed areas were then bound and left for seven days before being unbound and washed. The circles and triangles that were popular designs were regarded as enhancing a girl's beauty.

With respect to the Persian world, Percy Molesworth Sykes wrote in 1909 about how, until shortly before, tattooing had been common in Persia. Ladies from the best families had tattoos on their forehead, chin, cheeks, lips, throat, and breasts. Tattoos in the form of anklets and bracelets were also popular. In southern Iran, it was apparently popular among lower-class women to have tattoos of birds, flowers, gazelles, and even Qur'anic verses, while men had images of lions or texts relating to Ali (the son-in-law of the Prophet Mohammed). Many of these tattoos were worn as amulets against the evil eye or were believed to have talismanic value in treating various ailments.

The tattooing practices of upper-class Persian women are vividly described in the memoirs of Mūnis al-Dawlah, who pointed out that tattooing (khāl guzārī, literally "mole-making," or khāl kūbī, literally "mole-striking") was of two kinds, permanent and temporary. She wrote that the women tattooists would bind together some sharp pins to create various small designs. One of the most popular was a small, mole-like spot on each cheek and one just below the lower lip. Another popular design was a cluster of leaves that was tattooed on the chest. The tattooers would pierce the skin with the pins and then pour collyrium or kohl into the wound to color it.

The motif of tattooing appears in poetry with some regularity. A Bedouin poem from northern Arabia, for instance, celebrates the beloved as follows: "O you with the pin-pricked (munaqrash) arms and the eight pure [front teeth]" (cited in Musil). The word pin-pricked is, of course, intended to mean "tattooed."

Examples of designs from diverse regions have been published by several researchers. The consistency of certain designs within particular tribal groups and the differences between those from distinct groups suggest that tattooing was sometimes used for the identification of tribal affiliations and the expression of group loyalties. At the same time, the similarity of certain designs to patterns in other media, such as embroidery, metalwork, woodwork, and stone carving, suggests the possibility of religious or apotropaic motives. In any case, it is very difficult to reconcile the widespread practice of tattooing with the unambiguous interdiction expressed in the hadiths.

Another form of permanent body modification mentioned in the hadith is the artificial introduction of space between a woman's front teeth for the purpose of enhancing her beauty. While many hadiths recommend that teeth should be frequently cleaned with a toothpick (siwāk or miswāk), lasting interventions such as parting or grinding and sharpening the teeth are strictly proscribed, at least for women.

Some modern commentators have argued, based on verses in the Qur'an disapproving of altering God's creation, that body piercing is also forbidden; however, such a prohibition does not explicitly appear in the foundational texts. It is known that some women among the Prophet's companions wore earrings.

A hadith relates, for instance, that when the Prophet asked women to give alms, some removed their necklaces and earrings and donated them. Obviously, this does not actually prove that those women had pierced ears, but they very well may have. Whether or not the practice is licit, ear piercing is extremely widespread among women throughout the area, and the ceremonial piercing of a female child's ears is often a ritual of some social significance.

Another widespread practice in parts of Southwest Asia is nose piercing. According to Lane, the nose ring (in this case presumably the camel's nose ring to which reins are attached) was historically a symbol of subjection and obedience. Thus, a hadith states that the first Caliph Abū Bakr had "pierced his nose with a nose ring (khazama anfahu bi-khizāmin)" before the Prophet, that is, he had submitted to his will. Another hadith (narrated on the authority of Ibn 'Abbās) relates that "while circumambulating the Kaaba, the Prophet (prayers and blessings of God be upon him) passed by a person who was leading another person by a nose ring through his nose. The Prophet (prayers and blessings of God be upon him) cut it off, and then he ordered the man to lead the other by his hand." Whether this account amounts to disapproval of nose rings in general is unclear.

Many travelers to the area reported that nose rings were in common use among the women of various ethnic and religious groups. Thus, for example, Peters wrote about the female population of Deir, who wore, in addition to tattoos, large nose rings, which were fastened to the central cartilage of the nose and fell down over the mouth. Sometimes, the rings were fastened to one of the nostrils and allowed to fall only as far as the upper lip. Other women had a very small ring in one nostril that followed the curve of the nostril. It was quite common to have very ornamental forms, similar to those worn in the ears.

Claude Reignier Conder described the Maronite Christian women of Damascus as "dark-eyed beauties who are not ashamed to show their tattooed faces and nose-rings." The pervasiveness of nose rings would seem to be borne out by the fact that women's dot-shaped tattoos above or below the mouth were known as "shadow of the nose ring (fā' al-khazāma)," according to Field.

Though not as widespread as tattooing or piercing, scarification—both by cutting (cicatrisation) and by burning (branding)—has historically been practiced by some groups in the area. Richard F. Burton wrote that in Mecca it was common for male children to be taken to the Kaaba when they were forty days old, prayed over, and then taken home. The local barber would then draw with a razor three parallel gashes on each cheek. These gashes went from the exterior angle of the eyes almost to the corners of the mouth. According to Burton, this act was called tashrut or gashing (scarification). In addition, the body, including the feet, was also sometimes marked in this manner.

Field's survey of Iraq revealed that both cicatrisation (fisada) and branding (chawi, kawi, kawa, or kayy) were mainly practiced therapeutically, for such purposes as bloodletting, curing ailments, healing sprains and wounds, relieving pain, increasing strength, and improving eyesight. Indications are that aesthetic factors did not play a significant role in the decision to practice scarification.

Branding is mentioned in a series of hadiths whose interpretation has been the subject of some debate. A number of these

A Bedouin woman with a tattoo at the center of her forehead, Petra, Jordan, 1955. It is thought that tribal affiliations and group loyalties can be expressed and identified by certain tattoo designs among the different Bedouin groups. David Boyer/National Geographic/Getty Images.

categorically prohibit the practice; thus, the Prophet is related (on the authority of Ibn ʿAbbās) to have mentioned three forms of medical treatment, including "branding with fire" (*kayyati bi-nārin*). Another relates that the Prophet said, "He who gets himself branded or uses a spell is exempted from trust in God." Still others simply state that the Prophet had prohibited branding. At the same time, some hadiths cast a more neutral, even positive, light on the practice. In some, the narrator relates that he had undergone branding but did not derive any benefit from it. In others, the Prophet himself is said to have ordered branding to cure an injured or sick companion. In view of these ambiguities, some religious scholars have argued that while branding is not strictly prohibited, it is execrable (*makruh*).

BODY MODIFICATION UNRELATED TO APPEARANCE

There are several temporary and permanent body modification practices that do not affect visual appearance. Temporary practices include ritual ablutions, called *wudu* (partial ablutions; *abdest* in Turkish) or *ghusl* (full ablutions), which play an extremely important role in the daily worshipping activities of Muslims. Of the permanent ones, circumcision, female genital cutting, and castration have, to varying degrees, historically been associated with Islamic societies. Of these, male circumcision is virtually universal, while female genital cutting is a pre-Islamic practice that has been incorporated into local religious observance in only a few regions. Castration is illicit, but many slaves were subjected to it over the course of history, particularly those charged with service in the private apartments of a household. Often, this was done before the slaves had been imported into Islamic territories, thus circumventing the proscription.

This article draws on material published in *Khil'a* 3 (2007–2008).

References and Further Reading

Bassano (da Zara), Luigi. *I Costumi et i Modi Particolari de la Vita de Turchi.* Introduction by Franz Babinger. Munich: Max Hueber, 1963. (Originally published Rome: Antonio Blando Asolano, 1545.)

Bedevian, Armenag K. *Illustrated Polyglottic Dictionary of Plant Names, in Latin, Arabic, Armenian, English, French, German, Italian and Turkish Languages, including Economic, Medicinal, Poisonous and Ornamental Plants and Common Weeds.* Cairo: Argus & Papazian Presses, 1936.

Buckingham, J. S. [James Silk]. *Travels in Mesopotamia, Including a Journey from Aleppo to Bagdad, by the Route of Beer, Orfah, Diarbekr, Mardin, & Mousul.* London: Henry Colburn, 1827.

Burton, Richard F. *Personal Narrative of Pilgrimage to El Medinah and Meccah.* London: Longman, Brown, Green, Longmans, and Roberts, 1857.

Chenciner, Robert, Gabib Ismailov, and Magomedkhan Magomedkhanov. *Tattooed Mountain Women and Spoon Boxes of Daghestan: Magic Medicine Symbols in Silk, Stone, Wood and Flesh.* London: Bennett & Bloom, Desert Hearts, 2006.

Cleugh, James. *Ladies of the Harem.* London: Frederick Muller, 1955.

Conder, Claude Reignier. *Tent Work in Palestine: A Record of Discovery and Adventure.* London: Richard Bentley & Son, 1878.

Dallaway, James. *Constantinople Ancient and Modern, with Excursions to the Shores and Islands of the Archipelago and to the Troad.* London: Printed by T. Bensley for T. Cadell Junior & W. Davies, 1797.

Deuraseh, Nurdeen. "A Hadith of the Prophet (s.a.w.) on Healing in Three Things (al-Shifa' fi Thalatha): An Interpretational" [sic]. *Journal of the International Society for the History of Islamic Medicine (ISHIM)* 3, no. 6 (2004): 10–16.

Field, Henry. *Body-Marking in Southwestern Asia.* Papers of the Peabody Museum of Archaeology and Ethnology, Harvard University, vol. XLV, no. 1. Cambridge, MA: Peabody Museum, 1958.

Lane, Edward William. *An Arabic-English Lexicon.* 8 vols. London: Williams and Norgate, 1863–1893.

Mounsey, Augustus H. *A Journey through the Caucasus and the Interior of Persia.* London: Smith, Elder & Co., 1872.

Musil, Alois. *The Manners and Customs of the Rwala Bedouins;* Oriental Explorations and Studies, no. 6. New York: The American Geographical Society, 1928.

Peters, John Punnett. *Nippur, or Explorations and Adventures on the Euphrates; The Narrative of the University of Pennsylvania Expedition to Babylonia in the Years 1888–1890.* New York and London: G. P. Putnam's Sons, 1897–1898.

Sandys, George. *A Relation of a Journey begun An. Dom. 1610: Foure Bookes; Containing a Description of the Turkish Empire, of Aegypt, of the Holy Land, of the Remote Parts of Italy, and Ilands Adioyning.* London: Printed for Ro. Allot, 1632.

Sykes, P. [Percy] Molesworth. "Notes on Tattooing in Persia." *Journal of the Royal Anthropological Institute* 39 (1909): 177–178.

Irvin Cemil Schick

See also Snapshot: Henna; Snapshot: Indigo; Perfume and Incense.

Snapshot: Henna

Henna has been used to decorate people, as well as garments, for thousands of years. One of the earliest written texts referring to the use of henna comes from the Ugaritic legend (from modern northwestern Syria) of Baal and Anath, which dates from about 2000 B.C.E. Slightly more recently, in the Old Testament of the Bible, the use of henna, which is called *camphire*, can be found in the *Song of Songs* and the *Song of Solomon*. Since then, henna has been used by many men and women throughout the Mediterranean World, Africa, Southwest Asia, and Asia. In the early twenty-first century, henna has become a popular fashion statement, thanks to the diasporas of Asian groups throughout the world. The modern term *henna* is derived from the Arabic word *henna*.

Henna is made from the leaves of a privet (*Lawsonia inermis*), which is a tall shrub of between two to six and a half yards (two to six meters) in height. It is native to tropical and subtropical regions of Africa, southern Asia, and northern Australasia. Henna produces a red-orange dye molecule called *lawsone*, which is primarily concentrated in the leaves. This molecule has an affinity for protein and can easily be used to dye materials such as skin, hair, fingernails, leather, silk, and wool.

There are two main forms of henna on the market; namely, red henna (also called yellow or orange henna) and black henna. Red henna is made from the *Lawsonia* plant and is safe to use. Black henna, however, is not made from *Lawsonia* leaves but from partly fermented, dried indigo and can cause allergic reactions. In the 1990s, henna artists began to experiment with a third substance, para-phenylenediamine (PPD), which was (and still is) used for black hair dye, but this again causes severe allergic reactions, resulting in severe and permanent scarring in some cases. As a result, PPD is prohibited in many Western countries but may be found in some parts of Asia. The use of henna in all its forms (red, orange, and black) is officially banned for body decoration in the United States because of the problems created by PPD and the unscrupulous use of black henna.

PRODUCTION OF RED HENNA

Unbroken henna leaves will not produce a stain or dye. So, first of all, it is necessary to dry the leaves and then grind them into a powder. The powder has to be mixed with a mild acid before it will stain the skin. It is common to use acids such as lemon or lime juice (citric acid), mild vinegar (acetic acid), or even strong tea (tannic acid) for this purpose. It is also normal to add a skin conditioner or perfume, such as tea tree, eucalyptus, or lavender oils, to the mixture at this point. The paste is then left for between six to twelve hours to mature. The paste should be of a toothpaste consistency if used on the skin.

The application of the paste can take various forms depending on local traditions (just a dot or a more complicated design), where on the body the henna is being used (a different technique is used for the face than for the hands or feet),

how many layers of paste will be used (more are generally used on the feet), and how the paste is applied (such as with a sharp stick or a modern cellowrap cone). The design can also be applied to create either a positive design or a resist (negative) design. Some designs take a few seconds to make (a simple dot between the eyes), others can take several hours, or, in the case of some Yemeni bridal designs, it may even take four or five days to complete the intricate designs.

Once the paste has been applied, it is normally left for a few minutes (producing a light orange) to several hours (yielding a dark brown). Sometimes a sugar-and-lemon mix is painted over the henna paste to prevent it from drying out too quickly and so cracking while staining takes place and to intensify the color. Another method of deepening the color is to steam or warm it.

HENNA AND BODY DECORATION

In some cases, the design is a simple staining of the fingertips, whereas in other countries intricate designs are created. The Indian mehndi designs are some of the most complex and involve the production of intricate patterns on the hands and lower arms. (*Mehndi* is the application of henna as a temporary form of skin decoration in South Asia, especially India.) Part of the skill of these designs is to create similar, mirror-image patterns on both hands or arms, no matter how intricate.

In many areas of the Arab and Iranian world, there is a henna party for the bride the night before her wedding. Normally, the bride is decorated, but in some areas of the Indian subcontinent, the groom is also given henna patterns. The color red is regarded as symbolizing fertility and good fortune, so the application of red henna is seen as being most auspicious. The designs used for Saudi urban brides and their guests are usually very intricate and are often painted by Indian women following the latest mehndi fashions. In some areas, such as Turkey, brides wear special red satin mittens and slippers after they have had their hands and feet hennaed. These are used to protect the designs from any damage and to stop henna from leaking onto the bride's clothes or surrounding objects.

There used to be social distinctions in the use of henna by Arab women. Urban women, for instance, traditionally stained their hair, hands, feet, and nails with henna, while Bedouin would decorate only their hands, fingernails, and toenails. This distinction, however, is vanishing with increased communication (partly due to Indian films showing different uses of henna). Henna is also believed to harden the skin, and it is not uncommon in some countries to find men with henna on the soles of their feet. Pearl fishermen in the Eastern province of Saudi Arabia, for example, used to cover their hands with henna in order to make them tougher and to prevent blisters when rowing boats or hauling divers up.

Henna is also used by older women throughout Asia to color their hair to make themselves more attractive to their husbands. Sometimes, Muslim men will grow long beards and then dye them orange with henna as an outward sign that they have been on the annual hajj or religious pilgrimage to Mecca. All in all, henna is an ancient and very versatile method of temporarily coloring and decorating the human body.

REFERENCES AND FURTHER READING

Fabius, Carine. *Mehndi: The Art of Henna Body Painting*. New York, Random House, 1998.

Polhemus, Ted. *The Customized Body*. London: Serpent's Tail Publishing, 2000.
Roome, Loretta. *Mehndi: The Timeless Art of Henna Painting*. New York: Griffin, 1998.

Gillian Vogelsang-Eastwood

See also Volume 1, Africa: Morocco; Tunisia.

Snapshot: Indigo

Indigo is a chemical substance that produces a blue color. It can be used to dye textiles but also paper and even skin. In fact, it is the only natural dye that can produce a colorfast blue that does not fade through sunlight. Logwood, or *Haematoxylum campechianum*, can be used to produce a blue dye of lesser quality, but it requires a mordant to adhere to textile fibers.

Indigo consists of the chemical *indigotin*, the substance that produces the indigo blue dye. This can be extracted from several sources. Species from several plant genera contain a chemical that is the first stage of indigotin: *indican*. Important examples of these are a number of species of the *Indigofera* genera, shrublike plants that grow in a tropical climate, and *woad*, or *Isatis tinctoria*, a flowering plant that grows in a temperate climate. Both types occur in Southwest and Central Asia and were used from antiquity on.

It is impossible to distinguish between indigotin obtained from woad and from *Indigofera* plants, as the result is chemically identical. This fact, combined with the relative scarcity of early archaeological textiles, makes the reconstruction of the early history of indigo use very difficult. Indigotin-dyed textiles from the second millennium B.C.E. have been found in Egypt, and blue garments are mentioned in Mesopotamian texts. The exact origins of indigo in this part of the world are shrouded in mystery, as it is not yet known when it began to be used and whether the indigo was imported or produced at home. It was certainly imported in classical times, as the *Periplus of the Erythraean Sea* (a description of navigation in the Red Sea) mentions indigo trade with India. The name *indigo* might even have originated from the word *indikón*, which was used to refer to all goods imported from India. In the Arab world, indigo is more often referred to as *nil*, from the Sanskrit word *nila*, meaning "dark blue," also indicating Indian origins.

Indigo dye was used to create a number of different shades of textiles, such as greens and purples. The famous so-called royal purple dye was obtained in antiquity from the *Murex* shellfish; it consists of a chemical that is very similar to indigo: *dibromoindigotin*. It can produce several shades of reddish purple and was highly prized because it was so hard to obtain. Indigo was often combined with madder, a red dye, to imitate this more expensive cousin. In fact, indigo can sometimes have a slightly red tinge, because of the presence of *indirubin*, another chemical found in both woad and indigo, in the dye vat.

THE PRODUCTION OF INDIGO

In Islamic times, *Indigofera* seems to have been the preferred source of indigotin. *Indigofera* plants are an intensive crop to cultivate, as they need fertile soil, regular irrigation, and weeding. The leaves can be harvested up to three or four times a year. The plant is a perennial but is kept for only around three years, because the quality diminishes after the second year. There are a number of ways to extract indigo from the leaves.

Indigotin cannot be dissolved in water, and the dye process is therefore not simple. Chemically speaking, the indican in the leaves is transformed into indoxyl through fermentation, and then, through the addition of oxygen, it is turned into indigotin.

In the simplest process, the fresh leaves are put into a heated pot with water and ash or urine, and the cloth is dipped into the vat. This method is not very efficient; the dye is very weak, and dyeing can only be performed on the spot after the harvest. This method is more often done on a household level, using, for example, wild indigo-bearing plants. The leaves can also be composted first, starting off the fermentation process. These can then be dried or converted into a paste and transported more easily.

However, the most effective way to transform the leaves into an easily transportable dye source is extracting the indigotin from the leaves. This can make a considerable difference, as 220 pounds (100 kilograms) of dried leaves are said to yield only about 3 to 4 pounds (1.5 to 2 kilograms) of indigo. To do this, the leaves are put into large pots with water and left to ferment. The mixture is vigorously stirred or beaten to introduce oxygen. The water containing the indigo is then slowly drained from the leaves and put into a separate vessel. This liquid is allowed to sit until the indigo sinks to the bottom of the pot. The water is then removed in stages by unplugging holes in the pot, until only a paste of indigo is left on the bottom of the pot. After the paste has been dried and molded into a specific shape, it can be transported to where it is needed. This appearance of this indigo often led to a misunderstanding among foreign buyers, who thought that indigo was a mineral.

DYEING WITH INDIGO

Because indigo cannot be dissolved in water, to prepare it for dyeing cloth, it needs to be dissolved and reduced in a warm alkaline solution in a vat. Through a slow process of fermentation, hydrogen is added to the molecule, transforming the indigo into soluble *leuco-indigotin* ("indigo white"). When a piece of cloth is dipped into the vat, the leuco-indigotin adheres to it. When it is pulled out, the cloth is yellowish-green but turns blue within a few minutes, as the process of oxidation converts the leuco-indigotin back to indigotin. A piece of cloth will need to be dipped into the vat several times to produce a darker blue. Patterns can be achieved, for example, by putting wax or paste on the areas that should not be turned blue (resist dyeing or batik), by tying the areas that should not be dyed (tie-dye or *plangi*), by dyeing threads to be woven into a piece of cloth by tying and dyeing part of the warp and/or weft to form a pattern (ikat), or, finally, by bleaching the pattern into the cloth (discharge printing).

The fermentation of the indigo and the preparation of the vat were slow and precarious processes, and the alterations in the mixture were carefully monitored by its appearance, smell, or even taste. Each dyer had his own recipe of ingredients to achieve the right type of (alkaline) solution. Due to its temperamental nature, the vat was often considered to be a living entity that needed to be fed and placated. This might not be that strange, considering that the fermentation process is performed by microbes. Many superstitions and rites surrounded the dye vat. These were often connected to female fertility, perhaps because dyers in Southwest Asia were usually male; the failure of a vat was often blamed on the presence of a menstruating or pregnant woman, whose fertility was considered a danger to the fertility of the vat.

Although indigo does not fade in the sunlight and is not dissolved in water when washing, it is vulnerable to rubbing (for example, during washing or when it is worn). Wearing a fabric that has been recently dyed with indigo can stain the skin blue; this effect can still be experienced when wearing a pair of new, dark blue jeans. The cloth can be treated to minimize this effect, but not everyone considers this a disadvantage; in some cultures, this blue stain is considered beautiful or regarded as having a beneficial antiseptic effect. The women of Oman, for example, consider the sheen of the indigo that rubs off their face masks to give "light" to the face, and in southern Arabia, indigo is believed to whiten the skin. Indigo cloth was often finished by gumming, starching, or glazing, combined sometimes with an added indigo solution. These finishing processes added luster to the fabric, which was further enhanced to a bronze, gold, purple, or red sheen by beating, burnishing, or calendaring the extra indigo on the cloth.

OTHER USES FOR INDIGO

Blue has an ambivalent meaning within the Islamic world. In many contexts, it is considered ominous (perhaps because of its association with mourning), but it is also used to protect against the evil eye. Indigo-dyed clothing, for example, was believed to ward off evil spirits. Indigo was also considered to have certain medical properties: Because it was associated with coolness, it was used to lower fevers, and it was rubbed into wounds to prevent inflammation. The indigo that rubbed off dyed clothing was considered to have a mild antiseptic effect. These properties have neither been confirmed nor denied by Western science. Indigo has proven to be toxic if taken internally in large amounts, which might be connected to its antiseptic properties in small amounts.

Indigo was also used to dye paper, parchment, and leather and in paint or ink. The rubbing off of indigo on the skin was often considered beautiful. Indigo could also be used directly on the skin, for example, mixed with an oil or with henna. Henna mixed with indigo is also referred to as black henna and is used for the same purposes as normal henna: to stain the skin and dye the hair. Because of its antiseptic and protective powers, indigo was also considered especially well suited to tattooing.

In the twentieth century, synthetic indigo slowly replaced natural indigo sources. In 1897, indigotin had been successfully synthesized and was brought on the market as "Indigo Pure." Initially, natural and synthetic indigo existed side by side, sometimes even being mixed together. Synthetic indigo has exactly the same properties as natural indigo and therefore produces the same results. However, it does not contain some of the impurities that might be considered favorable to the dyeing process (such as indirubin).

The symbolic side of indigo, however, has long prevented the complete downfall of the industry in Southwest Asia. Nevertheless, the availability of cheaply dyed cloth from other parts of the world and the introduction of synthetic blue dyes have meant that indigo has been, from the 1980s on, grown only in very small quantities for medicinal or ritual purposes.

REFERENCES AND FURTHER READING

Balfour-Paul, Jenny. *Indigo*. London: British Museum Press, 1998.

Balfour-Paul, Jenny. *Indigo in the Arab World*. Richmond, UK: Curzon, 1997.

Sandberg, Gösta. *Indigo Textiles: Technique and History*. Asheville, NC: Lark Books, 1989.

Tineke Rooijakkers

See also Snapshot: Henna.

Perfume and Incense

- Incense and Perfumes
- Methods of Production
- The Main Ingredients

The use of perfume is widespread throughout Southwest Asia. Walking through the bustling *suqs* (traditional marketplaces) is more than just a rich visual experience: It is, in fact, an equally rich experience for the nose. Women and men alike leave behind a trail of fragrances little recognized beyond these borders. Merchants have everything needed to create special blends based on well-guarded recipes that have been handed down from one generation to the next. These blends are traditional and vary from city to city, with everyone claiming to have the best combinations.

Throughout the Arab world, a wide variety of spices, aromatic woods, flowers, seeds, and plants, such as ginger, pepper, and sandalwood—as well as the essential oils from these sources—are used for incense (*bakhoor*) and perfumes. Many of these come from India. These are sold at various prices, but it is generally agreed that the more one pays for such an oil, the finer it is.

It should not be thought that incense and perfumes are only for the living. For thousands of years, the dead were also embalmed with these perfumes. The perfuming of a body before burial remains an important part of Arab culture in the early twenty-first century.

INCENSE AND PERFUMES

Incense is composed of aromatic organic substances that release a fragrant smoke when burned. The term *incense* refers to the substance itself rather than to the odor it produces. The first incenses are generally believed to have been discovered by the Mesopotamians about four thousand years ago. This and other ancient cultures burned many kinds of resins and woods during their religious ceremonies. The fragrant woods and resins were often soaked in water and oil (thus creating perfumes), and then those participating in ceremonies would rub their bodies with the liquid. Incense is said to have come to Egypt in about 3000 B.C.E. The famous Egyptian pharaoh Queen Hatshepsut is reported to have sent expeditions to foreign lands in search of incense and other valuable commodities. The results of these trading trips were later recorded on the walls of a temple created in her honor at Medinet Habu, Thebes (near Luxor in the early twenty-first century). It is also said that the temple contained a botanical garden filled with "incense" trees gathered during these expeditions.

In the early twenty-first century, incense markets thrive in many countries throughout Southwest Asia, if not all, as most of these methods are still practiced. It is not at all uncommon, especially in the Gulf states (Bahrain, Kuwait, Oman, Qatar, Saudi Arabia, and the United Arab Emirates) to find bakhoors (types of incense) burning in most homes.

The sole purpose of incense is for perfuming. In Oman, the main ingredients are *sandal* (also sandalwood; its aroma is

relatively short-lived) and *oudh* (a specific kind of tree bark invaded by a fungus with aromatic properties), both of which are from India. Another important ingredient is snail operculum or *zhaffron*. The operculum is the so-called lid found on some families of marine and land snails. It is a circular or oval panel that is used to seal the aperture of the snail's shell. Zhaffron is used as an enhancer, although by itself it has a rather unpleasant smell. The population of Oman's southern region, Dhofar, has become popular worldwide for their bakhoor-making skills. Recipes are well-guarded secrets, and the competition is stiff.

Technically, perfume is a mixture of fragrant essential oils and aromatic compounds, fixatives, and solvents used to give the human body, objects, and living spaces a pleasant smell. The word *perfume* comes from the Latin words *per*, meaning "through," and *fumus*, meaning "smoke." The French later gave the name *parfum* to the pleasant smells that drift through the air from burning incense. There are few periods of history that have not been influenced by perfumes in one form or another.

METHODS OF PRODUCTION

In general, incense is made by one of two methods. In the first and older technique ("loose incense"), the ingredients are dried, ground to a powder, and then mixed together. Sometimes, this mixture is then combined with soft resins, dried fruit, oils, fats, or honey to make a "dough" that can be shaped into small pellets. Finally, the incense is heated using charcoal.

The second main form of incense is so-called combustible incense, for which the dried powder is mixed with an inflammable substance such as gum arabic or tragacanth (gummy substances derived from shrubs that impart firmness and are used to make the dough) and either charcoal or saltpeter (for combustion). The dough is then made into cones or sticks. These are then lit, the flame is fanned out, and the sticks continue to burn by themselves.

The production of perfume is different from that of incense. Perfumes are normally made into a liquid rather than used as a powder or dough. The oldest technique used to produce perfume is known as *expression*: Raw materials are squeezed or compressed, and the oils are collected. Another ancient method is *enfleurage*, whereby an aromatic material is mixed with wax and then the odorous oil is extracted using alcohol. The most common method, however, is *distillation*, in which the raw materials are placed in water and then heated. The raw, fragrant compounds come off in the condensation and are collected in a separate vessel. The main form of distillation is steam distillation, whereby steam from boiling water is passed through the raw material, driving out the volatile fragrant compounds. The condensate from the distillation is collected in special bottles or containers.

The process of extracting oils from flowers by means of distillation (the procedure most commonly used in the early twenty-first century) is said to have been developed by Abū Alī al-Husayn ibn Abd Allāh ibn Sīnā (ca. 980–1037), who was also known as Ibn Seena and more commonly in the West by his Latinized name, Avicenna. He was a Persian polymath who was famous in his time as a philosopher, poet, and theologian and also as a

Market stall selling locally grown or collected ingredients for making face creams, makeup, perfume, and incense at home, Ibra, Oman, 2004. Textile Research Centre, Leiden.

doctor, chemist, and scientist in general. He is credited with discovering how to make liquid perfumes using a mixture of natural aromatic oils and crushed herbs. In particular, he is known for working with rose petals to make a strong blend and then creating a rose water (a distillation of rose petals containing the volatile essential oils) that was more delicate than those previously made. The distillation and use of rose water remain very popular in the Iranian and Arab worlds in the early twenty-first century.

For thousands of years, different types of containers have been developed for holding incense and perfumes. Within the Arab world, small glass bottles are still regarded as an essential part of the Arabian perfume culture. But this is not unique to Arabia, and perfumers around the world spend vast amounts designing the right bottle to house their special blends.

THE MAIN INGREDIENTS

A wide variety of organic materials are used for making both incense and perfumes.

Amber (*Arabic*) or *ambergris* (*English*). Also known as *ambra grisea, amber gris, ambergrease,* or *grey amber,* ambergris is very important in this region of the world. It is a solid, waxy substance of a dull gray or black color. It has a sweet, earthy smell and is used as a fixative in perfumes. Ambergris is produced in the digestive system of sperm whales. It is a glandular secretion of the stomach, which is believed by some to protect the whale from potential damage from the hard backbones of cuttlefish and the beaks of squid. Because it is formed in the stomachs of whales and has to be naturally expelled, it is very rare to find it washed up on a beach; hence its high value. True ambergris has, however, been replaced by synthetic forms that are much cheaper. In 2006, synthetic ambergris was selling for about US$10 per gram.

Ambergris was once considered an article of imperial trade in Audoghast in northwestern Africa before 1000 c.e. In the tenth

century, Ibn Haukal, an Arab trader, classed it as comparable to gold and black slaves in value and referred to its reputed aphrodisiac properties. Like oudh, one drop of amber can last for several months in the open.

Cedar (*Cedrus*). The cedar is a coniferous tree of the family Pinaceae, which is known for its sweet-scented wood. It is closely related to the fir. Cedars are native to the mountainous regions of the western Himalayas and the Mediterranean region, especially in the area known as Lebanon in the early twenty-first century. The cedars of Lebanon have been famous throughout the ages, and cedar was used by King Solomon in the construction of the first temple of the Israelites in Jerusalem (built in roughly 960 b.c.e. and destroyed in 586 b.c.e.). Cedarwood, as well as its resins and oil, is known to be a natural repellent to moths and has long been used for making chests and cupboards where woolen items are stored. For hundreds of years, cedar has been used for making perfumes for both men and women.

Frankincense. Called *luban* in Arabic and also known as *olibanum,* frankincense is an aromatic resin obtained from the trees of the genus *Boswellia,* notably *Boswellia sacra.* It is used in incense as well as perfumes. Frankincense is tapped from the *Boswellia* tree by slashing the bark and allowing the resins to bleed out and harden. These hardened resins are called tears. There are numerous species and varieties of frankincense trees, each producing a slightly different type of resin.

Frankincense has been used for thousands of years as a fragrance. During biblical times, for example, frankincense was held in high esteem, and there is frequent mention of its fragrance and use throughout the Bible. In the Old Testament, for example, Moses was commanded by the Lord to "take unto thee sweet spices, stacte and onycha and galbanum … with pure frankincense … And thou shalt make it a perfume" (Exod. 30:34–35). Perhaps one of the most famous references to frankincense can be found in the New Testament stories about the birth of Christ, when the three wise men came to Bethlehem carrying gifts of gold, frankincense, and myrrh for the infant Jesus (Matt. 2:11).

Frankincense is probably still the best known of the plants mentioned in the Bible. Burning incense was the privilege of priests in the earliest civilizations but in the early twenty-first century is enjoyed by all. In Arabia, particularly the Gulf region, frankincense is burned in homes not only for its aromatic properties but also because it helps to rid the home of mosquitoes. Additionally, it is believed that burning frankincense in the home will keep the jinn out of the home. (*Jinn* are beings created with free will, living on earth in a world parallel to humankind, created by Allah, but physically invisible to humans, as taught in the Qur'an.)

Once valued as highly as gold, in the early twenty-first century, frankincense is affordable, allowing persons of all income brackets to purchase and freely use it. Frankincense is chewed and used for tattooing, and it possesses numerous medicinal properties in addition to its aromatic properties. When fresh, the state preferred by many Arabs, the more fragrant resins have a bit of a green tint (some historians have referred to them as being "silver"), and these are the prized pieces. Outside Arabia, many prefer a drier, older resin. As the resin ages, it turns white, and the lemony note becomes more apparent. Because it is a drier form, it is more easily crushed into a powder.

The most prized frankincense resins are grown in the Sultanate of Oman. *Hojary* is the best of the four grades of frankincense. It may come in tears as large as one's thumb during the peak of the harvesting season. When used fresh, the pungent oils possess a mild lemon scent that becomes more intense when heated on hot coals.

Jasmine (Jasminum). The name *jasmine* is derived from the Persian word *yasmin*, meaning "gift from God." It is a shrub of the olive family (Oleaceae) that is native to tropical and warm temperate regions of Asia and Southwest Asia. The jasmine flower and its aromatic properties are very popular in the Arab world. Often, jasmine is used by itself and not combined with other aromas. The best time to pick the tiny blossoms is in the evening, and it is not uncommon to find groups of women at dusk stringing the flowers together to create large strands that are then given as gifts to friends and loved ones. Jasmine flowers are also used to provide a light, fresh scent when sprinkled on bed linens and added to clothing drawers.

Musk. This is the name originally given to a substance with a penetrating odor obtained from a gland of the male musk deer (genus *Moschus*, family Moschidae). The gland is situated between its stomach and genitals. The substance has been used as a popular perfume fixative since ancient times and is one of the most expensive animal products in the world. In the early twenty-first century, however, the term *musk* is used for a wide range of substances with a similar odor, although they may come from very different sources, including both animals and plants. Musk is an important ingredient in perfumes as well as being used for its medicinal properties.

Until the early twentieth century, most musk was obtained from natural sources, but in the early twenty-first century, it is almost always synthetic. Real musk is used for only about the top 5 percent of the most expensive perfumes. In 1999, the European Union banned the import of musk, forcing cosmetic producers to switch to synthetic alternatives. Nevertheless, there is a still a

demand in some cultures for real musk; as a result, according to the British World Wildlife Fund, musk can be worth three times its weight in gold.

For more than five thousand years, musk has been used in perfumes and the traditional medicines of China and its neighbors. Within the Arab world, musk is used on the body and also on clothing. It is particularly popular, for instance, in its powdered form among the Bedouin, who use it to perfume their clothing. The clothing is very meticulously layered, with musk sprinkled between the layers. The garments are then closed up in a chest, where the aroma is allowed to permeate the fibers. This tradition is declining due to the development of cheaper modern perfumes that are more widely available.

Oudh. A resin that is also commonly called *gaharu, jinko, aloeswood,* or *agarwood,* oudh is made from an aromatic resin created when the heartwood of a tree of the *Aquilaria* species is attacked by a type of mold. Unlike frankincense, which forms in just a few weeks after the frankincense tree bark is cut, oudh actually takes several hundred years to form. Only when the tree dies is it possible to retrieve the resin (one cannot tell whether a tree is infected or not until it begins to die). An uninfected tree has no value. In the early twenty-first century, oudh remains an expensive commodity, with the best-quality oudhs selling for about US$5,000 per pound (US$11,000 per kilogram).

Oudh has been prized for hundreds of years for its scent. Chinese references dating to the third century C.E. refer to the production and trade of oudh. It is believed to have been used in India for at least a thousand years and to have spread to the Arab countries from there. Within the Arab world, oudh is worn on the clothes as well as the skin. The wood can be burned and has a distinctive smell because of the oils, similar to sandalwood, or it can be distilled to extract the oil. A single application of oudh takes several hours to fully unfold its scent, but it can then last for several months. It is said that the aroma of the finer qualities of oudh can still be detected after having washed clothes that have been perfumed with it.

Rose Water. Rose water is widely used throughout the Arab world and beyond. In Iran, as in many other countries, a very special rose water is produced and used locally as well as being exported to other countries. Rose water's use is not limited to perfume: It is also drunk (used to flavor water) and eaten (added to sweets).

Sandalwood. This comes from trees of the *Santalaceae* family, notably *Santalum album* and *Santalum spicatum*. To produce commercially valuable sandalwood with high levels of fragrant oils, harvested *Santalum* trees have to be at least forty years of age, but eighty years or older is preferable. However, inferior sandalwood produced from trees at thirty years of age can still fetch a decent price due to the demand for real sandalwood. The true sandalwood is a protected species, and the demand for it cannot be met. Many species of plants are traded under the name of "sandalwood." Within the genus *Santalum* alone, there are more than nineteen varieties that can be called sandalwood. Sandalwood is both a fragrant wood and an essential oil, providing perfumes with a striking wood base note. The fragrance of true sandalwood appears after it has been worn for a short time, as the heat from the body warms it up. Objects soaked in synthetically produced sandalwood oils smell very strongly of sandalwood and can be quite overpowering if too much is used. The smell of cheap synthetic sandalwood fades after a relatively short time, while the scent of real sandalwood or of better-quality synthetics lasts longer.

Given the long-standing importance of incense and perfume for use on the body and clothing, it is not surprising that creating one's own scent is very commonplace in the Arabian Peninsula in the early twenty-first century. Perfume shops are always bustling with activity. Whether a blend of oils or combined with solid ingredients, perfume and incense have a very prominent place in Arab culture, past and present.

References and Further Reading

Groom, Nigel. *Frankincense and Myrrh; A Study of the Arabian Incense Trade.* London: Longman, 1981.
Le Gallienne, R. *The Romance of Perfume.* New York: Richard Hudnut, 1928.
Weber, Susan, and Andreas Bohn. *The Fragrances of Oman.* Muscat: Oman Printers, 2007.
Zarins, Juris. *The Land of Incense.* Muscat, Oman: Sultan Qaboos University Publications, 2001.

Julia M. Al-Zadjali

Weapons and Accessories

- Protective Armor, Shields, and Belts
- Swords and Daggers
- Maces, Axes, Spears, and Bows and Arrows
- Firearms

In Southwest and Central Asia, weapons constituted an essential part of men's dress, especially for those of some rank and standing in society. Men did not use these weapons only for offensive and defensive purposes; a weapon was an extension of the wearer's manhood. A beautiful sword, a handsome dagger, or a pair of costly pistols contributed to showing the world that the wearer was a man to be reckoned with. In public, the wearer would very proudly show his costly clothing and weaponry; his beautifully caparisoned horse, camel, or even elephant; and sometimes his suite of handsomely dressed attendants, thereby telling everyone that he was an important man. Weapons can also be regarded as the male equivalent of female jewelry. Because Muslim men are discouraged in the Qur'an and hadiths from wearing jewelry, especially of gold, a weapon was regarded as an acceptable substitute.

Weapons also play an important role in ancient stories. The Iranian national epic, the *Shahnameh*, tells of Faridun, one of the early kings of Iran, who wielded an ox-headed club. Bahram Gur, the legendary Sassanian king of Iran, was famous for his hunting exploits and his bow. The Prophet Mohammed had a famous sword called *dhu'l-faqâr* ("with vertebrae"). Some stories relate that it was the archangel Gabriel himself who gave this weapon to Mohammed. Many Shiites, the adherents of one of the two major branches of Islam, believe that Mohammed gave this sword to his cousin and son-in-law, Ali, on his deathbed, thus underlining Ali's legitimacy as Mohammed's successor.

The symbolic importance of the sword is, of course, also known in Europe. In Europe, the sword also indicates the rule of law, as shown in representations of the blindfolded Lady Justice and her sword, and this weapon has a similar meaning in the Muslim world of Southwest and Central Asia. Many Muslims believe that, together with the dhu'l-faqâr, a document was handed down that listed all the texts that regulate the Islamic community. Consequently, the sword also became the symbol of sovereignty and of the caliphate. Several swords called dhu'l-faqâr are still housed in the Topkapi Museum in Istanbul, the old capital of the Ottoman caliphs.

Thus, weapons should not be viewed only with respect to their obvious and original purpose—attacking an opponent or defending oneself—but should also be regarded as having an important symbolic value, as they were used to show the wearer's status. They formed part of the concept of what the Arabs used to call *furusiyya*, which refers to the arts of war and the hunt but also sports and exploits and includes the concepts of luxury, leisure time, and manly pursuits. Costly weapons thus belonged to the higher echelons of society. Weapons as status objects were also used as part of the intricate ritual of gift giving. When a king bestowed a precious sword on one of his trusted followers, that act indicated the high esteem he felt for the receiver; at the same time, by accepting the gift, the receiver accepted the superior position of the king.

Until the mid-twentieth century, the array of weaponry used in Southwest and Central Asia changed very slowly. Until shortly before World War II (1939–1945), Arab tribesmen were still fighting with matchlocks, and the camel was the preferred mode of transport. By the early twenty-first century, modern armies had introduced sophisticated armaments, but for many in the region, their weapon is still far more than merely a tool for fighting. In the nineteenth century, the Afghans, using their antique *jezail* matchlocks, managed to defeat the British. In the early 1980s, tribesmen in Afghanistan successfully opposed the Soviet army with their array of ancient weaponry, including the Lee Enfield .303 rifle, which had been the standard British weapon in both world wars. They regarded their rifle as far superior to any modern weapon and only slowly and sometimes reluctantly replaced it with the equally outdated Kalashnikov (AK-47; first introduced in 1947). Old weapons often carry considerable prestige. The status that a certain weapon provides is often regarded as more important than its effectiveness. In Mamluk Egypt some eight hundred years ago, when some warriors had switched to sabers (curved swords), preferring them to straight-edged swords, the latter were still being used in investiture ceremonies.

Finally, many of the typical weapons and accessories of Central and Southwest Asia belong to the world of the horse-riding nomads from Siberia and Central Asia. The bent sword or saber, the mace, the composite bow, the stirrups and high-fronted saddle all apparently find their origins in the far north, and they were introduced in various successive waves onto the Iranian Plateau and hence, sometimes very slowly, into the Arab plains of Southwest Asia. For instance, well into the nineteenth century, the Arabs still rode their horses without a saddle and without stirrups. In the Islamic period, the most important of these warriors and great innovators from the north were the Turks, who first encroached on the Iranian Plateau from Central Asia around 550 C.E. They were later defeated by the Muslim armies and enslaved en masse to serve as soldiers and administrators in the settled lands of the Islamic world. However, the former slaves soon turned into the new masters. The Ghaznavid rulers of Iran and Afghanistan in the eleventh century, and the Mamluks of Egypt from the thirteenth until the sixteenth centuries, were all descendants of Turkish slaves who used not only their skills and their relative isolation in local society but also their often-superior warfare techniques and weaponry to attain power. Other Turks from Central Asia simply marched to the West, and some of them settled in the area that is known as Turkey in the early twenty-first century.

PROTECTIVE ARMOR, SHIELDS, AND BELTS

Protective items of metal, including helmets and body armor, have always been widely used. But again, as in the case of offensive weaponry, it also served as a status symbol. Beautifully adorned helmets were of little use in combat but could be applied to great advantage when trying to show off one's standing. Furthermore,

Bahram Gur, Sassanian king of Iran, and his retinue hunting with bows and arrows, from *Five Poems of Nizam*, 1539–1543. The composite bows depicted here were typically made of sinew and horn glued onto a wooden core. Their main advantage was their high power and small size (well suited for horse riders). Getty Images.

in the Muslim world, real protection is given only by Allah, and it is no surprise, therefore, that shirts covered with religious texts were, and still are, worn by men going to war, sometimes underneath their metal armor. Similar texts were often also written on the metal armor itself.

Before the advent of the Mongols from the far northeast, in the early thirteenth century, body armor generally consisted of small pieces of metal, horn, or leather that were attached to a piece of fabric. Later, metal plates were worn on top of chain mail. Sometime in the late fourteenth century, coats of mail were integrated with metal plates, thus creating a suit of armor that was often both flexible and light. In addition to wearing armor to protect the torso, the warrior also wore a helmet and arm and leg guards. Famous are the so-called turban helmets, which may have been named this because they were worn on top of a turban or because they resembled the folds of a turban. Whatever the case, they made their appearance in the fifteenth century and were produced in western Iran and the Caucasus. The classical Ottoman helmets, in contrast, had a generally conical profile.

Protection through metal was important not only for the warrior but also for his mount. The animals were often provided with head protection, including chamfrons to protect the nose and cheeks of the horse or camel. These were again sometimes highly decorated and proudly shown to the world by the mounted warrior. Other accessories in this field were the saddle and the stirrups. The latter were first used in Southwest Asia by the Sassanians of Iran (third to seventh centuries C.E.), but they probably adopted them from the Turks, who appeared along the northeastern borders of Iran by the middle of the sixth century. The Turks of Siberia and Central Asia are indeed often accredited with the invention of metal stirrups and also with the high-fronted saddle. That type of saddle has remained in use in Southwest Asia until the early twenty-first century. Both stirrups and the high-fronted saddle helped mounted warriors remain firmly seated when fighting.

Shields have always been the most direct piece of protective armament, defending against the blow of the sword. Often made of wicker or eglantine covered with fabric, or of wood covered with leather, they were simple, lightweight, and sometimes very effective protective tools. In historical times, in Southwest and Central Asia, the shields were normally circular in shape, with or without metal bosses. Small shields, or bucklers, were held in the hand for close combat. Circular shields are typical weapons for cavalry, and their introduction into Central and Southwest Asia should again be linked to the nomadic invaders from Asia who time and again encroached on the Iranian Plateau and beyond.

Very characteristic are the Mughal shields from India, which were also widely used in neighboring Afghanistan. They are made of metal, with a shallow rim around the dome of the shield and four bosses. These bosses hide the rivets that hold the ends of two grips on the inside of the shield. In nineteenth-century Afghanistan, comparable shields were made of rhinoceros hide.

Belts might seem a universal accessory, but in many cultures, they are simply not used. The early Arab conquerors, for instance, did not hang their swords from belts but used baldrics (shoulder belts) instead. The same applies, for instance, to the ancient Indians, as depicted on the reliefs from the sixth century B.C.E. in Persepolis in southwestern Iran. In these images, they carry their swords suspended from a rope that is hung around their shoulders. It is safe to assume that the wearing of belts forms part of the same sartorial context as the wearing of trousers (a feature introduced in the early first millennium B.C.E. by the Scythians from the north). While the early Arabs, normally wearing long gowns, went without belts, the Sassanians of Iran (third to seventh centuries C.E.) used highly embellished belts, which not only had a specific function in carrying the sword but were also status symbols. When the Arabs conquered Iran in the seventh century and when they later incorporated Turkish troops into their army, belts also became part of "normal" Southwest Asian dress.

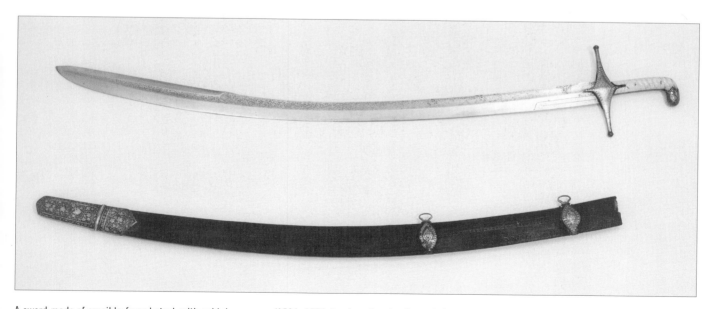

A sword made of crucible-forged steel, with gold damascene (1524–1576, Iran), and a sheath made from tooled black leather over a wooden core (probably from Lahore, Pakistan, nineteenth century). Iranian curved swords with pistol-shaped grips such as this were once known as *shamshir* ("the lion's tail"). This sword belonged to the Iranian ruler Shah Tahmasp and is inlaid in gold with Arabic lettering. The inscription includes quotes from the Qur'an. © Victoria and Albert Museum, London. www.vam.ac.uk.

Typical belts from the time of the Turkish empires in Iran and Afghanistan, around 1000 C.E., had many long straps hanging down from the belt. The number of straps and their decoration indicated the wearer's status and wealth.

SWORDS AND DAGGERS

In many parts of Southwest Asia, sword blades used to be either a straight or a curved type. The straight blades were broad and double-bladed; this type dates back to pre-Islamic days. The *kattara* sword from Oman has a straight blade. Sabers, or swords with a curved blade, are known in Arabic as *saif*, and they were often imported from Iran; in Egypt, Syria, or Iraq, they were also made locally, imitating the Iranian blade. Sabers were generally single-edged, with a grip that bent toward the sharpened edge of the blade. In addition, there was another type of sword, widely used in Southwest Asia, that was called in Arabic a *nimcha* ("half") and had a slightly curved, short blade.

In the Arab world, the sword was always the main symbol of royal power and the most important status symbol for men of rank. The Prophet Mohammed, according to legend, owned various swords, but the most famous was the dhu'l-faqâr. For centuries, the most highly esteemed swords in this part of the world were the sabers made in Iran. Especially the eastern Iranian province of Khorasan was well known for its patterned steel sword blades. The town of Kirman, in southeastern Iran, was equally famous for its weapon manufacture. All this changed in the nineteenth century with the introduction of European goods, and perhaps also following the forced cessation of *wootz* (Indian steel) production in British India in the middle of the nineteenth century. This steel had been widely used in Iran for the production of its famous swords.

Patterned steel, called *damascene* in the West, was made from carburized rods or plates of iron that were folded together and forged to make the blade of the sword. The pattern on the blade was made by etching and polishing. Patterned steel could also be

A group of Arabs in Mecca, Saudi Arabia, 1880s. The Arab in the striped waistcoat is wearing a decorative belt that holds a slender Yemeni-style J-shaped dagger (*dhuma*). This is worn in the very center of his belt to show off the quality of the dagger and indicates that the wearer is rich. His three servants also have daggers and knives, and a long rifle is held by the man to the far right. Christiaan Snouck Hurgronje, *Mekka*, 2 vols. (Gravenhage: Martinus Nijhoff, 1888).

made from ingots of steel made in crucibles. This carburized steel was called *wootz* in India by the British in the eighteenth century. However, archaeological discoveries have brought to light production centers of crucible steel in medieval eastern Iran. An Iranian origin may be indicated by the word for crucible steel in the Muslim world, namely *fuladh*, a Persian term meaning "purified."

The saber was the Muslim weapon par excellence. Because of the successes of Muslim armies, the saber was also introduced en masse into the Christian world of Europe from the fifteenth century on. In the archaeological record, the first extant examples of bent swords date from the seventh century C.E.; they have been found in eastern Europe, the Ukraine, southern Russia, the Caucasus, and Transcaucasia. The saber seems to have developed from single-edged, straight swords that were popular in China and East Asia from before the beginning of the modern era. These swords were also used in southern Russia by at least the middle of the first millennium C.E. That was also the time when the first curved, single-edged swords made their appearance. They clearly belong to the horse-riding warriors who by that time traversed the steppes of Eurasia. They were mainly Turkish tribes, and the true single-edged saber may well have developed among these Turks. Importantly, some of the earliest sabers were already made from excellent high-carbon steel, which would indicate that the people who made these swords had access to both material and technology.

The Iranian curved sword was known as the *shamshir*, "the lion's tail" (or as *kilij* in Ottoman Turkey). The shamshir, which often had a pistol-shaped grip, was generally single-edged and made of patterned steel. It was a cavalry weapon, meant to slice, not stab. It became recognized as the best type of sword in the seventeenth century, following the military conquests of the Safavid kings. It was always regarded by the Arabs as a status symbol. The Iranian shamshir was also exported to Damascus, and hence the sword and its steel became known in the West as Damascus steel.

Daggers are normally worn stuck into a belt or sash or otherwise kept ready to be used quickly. They have always been one of men's personal weapons, required for close combat but also for use in everyday life. Daggers may be single- or double-edged. Because of their often-personal nature, they were frequently beautifully decorated. A famous type of dagger, with a straight, single-edged blade, is the *kard* (Persian for "knife"), which also became popular in Mughal India. A feature that modern scholars often forget is the dagger's position. Tucked into a belt, it can be worn to the left, to the right, or in the center. Carrying a dagger in the center was always somewhat impractical, but it was the best way to show off the quality and decoration of the weapon.

A famous traditional weapon from Yemen is the *jambiya*. It is a curved dagger, worn on a special belt around the waist. There are various types and shapes, but they are all relatively small and curved. They are worn in the center, at the front of the body, with the tip to the right. Well-to-do Yemenites, however, used to carry their weapon on the right side. Their dagger, called *dhuma*, is more slender in shape, better made, and decorated with precious metals and gems. Some of the most precious knives have a hilt made of rhinoceros horn. The "normal" jambiya, on the contrary, is made of base metals. It should be noted that none of these daggers has a practical use; they are used to show the wearer's status. Often, the hilts and sheaths are elaborately decorated, while the knife blade, invisible to the outside world, is often of poor quality.

MACES, AXES, SPEARS, AND BOWS AND ARROWS

Next to the sword, the mace was a very popular weapon in the history of Southwest and Central Asia. Among the Turks, it was regarded as the symbol of office. But apart from its symbolic use, it also was a very effective weapon in close combat; it could easily inflict severe damage on an opponent's armor. In the early days of Islam, trained fighters used the *amud*, which was a very heavy mace, with the head and shaft cast as one unit. Its overall weight ranged from about twenty-two to forty-nine pounds (ten to twenty-two kilograms). Another type of mace was the *dabbus*, which was lighter than the amud, with a head that was made separately from the shaft. This may have been a more typically Turkish weapon.

During the centuries before the advent of the Mongols (in the early thirteenth century), maces with tubular heads were used. Turkish dignitaries depicted at the Ghaznavid palaces (eleventh to twelfth centuries C.E.) of Lashkari Bazar, southern Afghanistan, are shown wearing looped belts from which metal objects are suspended, and these are probably mace heads. In later years, among the Ottomans, Safavids, and Mughals, steel maces were widely used, and these were very powerful weapons.

Another widely used weapon, also used sometimes for ceremonial purposes, was the axe. It was often provided with a spiked end, making it an even more lethal weapon. Basically, there were two types, the practical saddle axe and axes with very large blades, which were often inscribed. The latter frequently had a more ceremonial than practical purpose. They were, for instance, carried by Mamluk bodyguards but also by Iranian dervishes or holy men, who used to carry an axe with a large blade.

Another weapon is often overlooked, probably because it is so simple; namely, the spear or lance. The lance was a cavalry weapon, used until the beginning of the twentieth century. A proud warrior on his horse often carried a lance. It was also a weapon widely used in hunting and for other horseback sports.

The bow used to be the symbol of sovereignty in the Turko-Mongol world, rather than the sword or the spear as in Arab society. Archery indeed has always been the art of the Central Asian steppes. It was introduced into Southwest Asia for the first time by the Scythians in the early first millennium B.C.E. and later again by the Parthians, who conquered the Iranian Plateau in the second and first centuries B.C.E. The Parthians became known for their "Parthian shot," which referred to their ability to shoot backward while riding at high speed away from their opponents. The typical bow from Central Asia was the so-called composite bow, made from sinew, horn, and wood that were glued together. The string was often made of silk. The Ottoman Turks, who enjoyed target shooting as a sport, sometimes used special bows to cover a distance of almost one thousand yards (nine hundred meters).

The Central Asian quiver or bow-and-arrow holder is another example of a piece of armament that went unchanged for millennia. The quiver used by the Mongols in the thirteenth century, and by many others in Southwest and Central Asia for centuries to come (Tatars from the Crimea fought with bows and arrows until the seventeenth century), had the same shape as the so-called *gorytos* that was used by the ancient Scythians, as depicted at Persepolis in the late sixth century B.C.E.

Archer's rings, worn on the archer's right-hand thumb, were used to prevent injury to the thumb and to make it easier to

Ko-i-Staun Foot Soldiery in Summer Costume, Actively Employed among the Rocks, engraving after James Rattray. From *Scenery, Inhabitants and Costumes of Afghanistan*, 1848, by Robert Carrick. In the nineteenth century, the long-barreled matchlock (*jezail*) was often heavily decorated and characterized by its curved (Sindh-style) butt. It was greatly feared in ambush situations because of its range, and Afghan horsemen sometimes wore two or three jezail slung at their backs, which they could fire when galloping. Bridgeman/Getty Images.

stretch the string. In fact, Islamic archery is different from Western practices in that the thumb is used to release the arrow, rather than the fingers. This feature may also be a Turkish innovation, since Sassanian bowmen, from before the Turkish invasions, have used their two middle fingers to draw the string. Archer's rings have been found in all sorts of materials, obviously indicating the wealth and position of the wearer. Poor-quality examples are made of wood or hardened leather, while more elaborate forms are of silver or gold. Examples in ivory inlaid with precious stones are known from the higher echelons of various Muslim courts.

FIREARMS

Initially, the Ottomans and Mamluks were not very keen on the use of firearms when these were introduced at the end of the fifteenth century. To them, firearms threatened the traditional ways of warfare and the symbolic role of the sword, bow, and horse. It should therefore not come as a surprise that at first firearms were used rather hesitatingly and only by lower-class units in the army. A real gentleman rode a horse and used his bow or his lance to kill

the enemy. Very soon, however, the Ottomans became aware of the potential of firearms, and they tried to keep the trade and manufacture of these new weapons a state monopoly, mainly to keep these items and their technique out of the hands of their opponents, such as the rulers of neighboring Iran and the Mamluks in Egypt. When the Ottomans eventually defeated the Mamluks in 1517 C.E., the Mamluk ruler complained bitterly to the Ottoman sultan that the latter had used a weapon that had been devised by the Christians of Europe and that went against the sunna of the Prophet Mohammed (to the Prophet's sayings and habits, which have formed the basis of some Islamic law systems).

Firearms were soon used all over Southwest Asia. One of the main factors was probably the appearance of the Portuguese in the Indian Ocean; they penetrated deep into the Persian Gulf and the Red Sea, and in 1517 even attempted to take Jidda. The Portuguese shipped large amounts of firearms into the region, both for sale and their own use, and in response local rulers also sought to acquire them. However, bows and arrows were still being used by Arab Bedouin long into the eighteenth century. Firearms remained a novelty in many parts of Southwest Asia, and well into the late nineteenth century, most firearms in the Arab world were still simple matchlocks.

In the nineteenth century, the most famous weapon of the Afghans no doubt was the long-barreled jezail. An ambush by Afghans armed with a jezail was greatly feared. A well-known saying was that a "good jezailchi [someone armed with a jezail] could on a hill-side conceal himself behind his own grass sandals." Originally a matchlock gun, the jezail was later often made into a flintlock or percussion weapon. The weapon is characterized by its curved (Sindh-style) butt, and it was held tightly in the armpit, between the right arm and body, when being used rather than pressed against the right-hand shoulder. In this way it was easier to fire from horseback. The long barrel necessitated the use of a bipod that was often fixed. The stock of the jezail was hand carved, and the barrel was handwrought and sometimes rifled. The weapons were often heavily decorated. Ammunition consisted of lead balls that fit the barrel tightly. The powder horn was apparently made of a camel's scrotum. Horsemen sometimes had two or three jezail slung at their backs, and they could fire them when at the gallop. The jezail was much feared by the British, because it carried much further than the British Brown Bess musket. It was said in 1842 that the jezail carried some eight hundred yards (about 730 meters).

References and Further Reading

Bashir, Mohamed, ed. *The Arts of the Muslim Knight: The Furusiyya Art Foundation Collection*. Milan, Italy: Skira Editore S.p.A, 2008.

Elgood, Robert. *The Arms and Armour of Arabia in the 18th–19th and 20th Centuries*. Aldershot, UK: Scolar Press, 1994.

North, Anthony. *An Introduction to Islamic Arms*. Gilsum, NH: Stemmer House, 1985.

Tirri, Anthony. *Islamic Weapons: Maghrib to Moghul*. Macon, GA: Indigo Publishing, 2004.

Willem Vogelsang

See also Trouser Wearing by Horse-Riding Nomads in Central Asia.

Birth, Marriage, and Death

- Marriage
- Marriage Festivities
- Birth and Breast-Feeding
- Death

Important rites of passage relate to dress in Southwest Asia; namely, engagement, marriage, birth, and death customs. Because of the region's size and the many different ethnic and religious groups and numerous variations, only general descriptions are possible. In the West, the sequence of life events is usually listed as birth, marriage, and death. In contrast, among many Southwest Asian cultures, birth is regarded as a product of marriage; thus marriage, birth, and death is considered the "natural" sequence. An issue of growing importance is the use (or not) of *hijab*, which is Islamically correct clothing that covers a woman's body, including her face in some cultures. The use of hijab is changing the nature of dress, including that for marriage, birth, and death, among some groups.

MARRIAGE

Muslim marriage joins or makes a contract between two families, not two individuals, by legally binding a man and woman. The age for marriage varies considerably throughout Southwest Asia; in some cases, a girl nine years old can be married, although in most countries the legal age is around fifteen. The age difference between the husband and wife may also vary markedly. Although it is often regarded as "healthy" for the couple to be young, it is not essential. A young girl may marry a man of the same generation as her father or older, or a woman may marry a younger man, particularly if she is from an influential family. The welfare of the two involved, however, is regarded as important, because a serious and long-standing dispute between them could disrupt the harmony between the families.

Marriages are normally divided into three stages. First, an agreement occurs between the families that a marriage will take place, as an engagement phase; second, the marriage contract is signed (*milka* or *nikka nama*); and, third, the wedding is celebrated. The second event is generally regarded as the most important in uniting the families, and the third as the most enjoyable in bringing family and friends together. The bride-to-be is given various items of clothing as part of her engagement, including dresses and jewelry, and even more at her wedding. In addition, the bride's female family and friends gather for a party with her. Each wears her best (often new) clothing and as much jewelry as possible and is skillfully made up with cosmetics and heavily perfumed.

The engagement and party can take place on the same day or be separated by several days. Generally, the wedding preparations begin once an engagement occurs and the date for signing the marriage contract has been set. In some places, such as the United Arab Emirates, the bride-to-be sometimes "vanishes" for forty days and engages, usually with female family members, in wedding preparations. During this period, she is bathed, oiled, perfumed, and pampered.

The marriage contract (*waraqa*), drawn up by the fathers of the intended bride and groom, includes the couple's names, the date, the *mahr* amount, and other agreed-upon conditions (such as the groom's right, or not, to take a second wife). The contract is signed by the two fathers and sometimes the groom before a religious leader (imam) and two male witnesses. (In the twenty-first century, more women also sign the contract but not universally within the Islamic world.) *Mahr* literally means "gift" and consists of the property, objects, and money given by the groom to the bride at marriage; it is regarded as a pledge of good faith by the groom and his family that the agreed wedding that binds the two families will take place. The mahr can have two portions: the *muqaddam*, an amount given to the bride at marriage, and a smaller amount, the *muakhkhar*, promised to her in case of divorce if initiated by her husband or at his death. In theory, the bride, rather than her father, receives the mahr. Thus, it cannot be regarded as a bride price. In reality, however, the bride's father is often given the responsibility to look after the money, and sometimes she will not see all of the mahr promised. The mahr, however, is never regarded as the property of the groom or his family.

The mahr may be money, property, investments, valuable objects (cars, trucks, and so on), or items for daily living, such as household furniture, bedding, clothing, jewelry, and the like. The amount given should be in accordance with the bride's social status, but the exact amount is negotiated between the two families and may depend on the relationship between the groups. A marriage between cousins, for example, in which the mahr stays within the family, will be less costly than when a groom marries outside of his family. Sometimes, for instance, the mahr simply consists of a small ring, offered as an engagement ring, in keeping with the injunction that a groom should offer a ring to his bride as a minimum fulfillment of the mahr. On other occasions, the mahr represents a substantial investment in the marriage and the hope of forthcoming children to carry on the family line and name.

Part of the muqaddam is often used by the bride's father to buy jewelry for his daughter (such as a set of earrings, a necklace, or a bracelet). This part of the mahr is called the *shabka* in Egypt. In addition, the bride's father may add various items of jewelry to the amount bought with the mahr. The jewelry proclaims a girl's new status as a married woman (*hurma*) and a woman of property. Most important, this jewelry belongs to her, and only she can dispose of it (should, for example, a prolonged period of financial insecurity occur). Thus, the mahr jewelry is regarded as a portable and highly visible means of showing a woman's personal status and family status (both her own and her husband's) and her new family's position in their local community, as well as providing security for her future.

MARRIAGE FESTIVITIES

The marriage festivities may happen quickly or last from three to seven days depending on the families' status, size, and wealth. Many different wedding forms can be found in Southwest Asia, but a "typical" wedding includes the three parts of (1) bridal preparation, (2) marriage contract signing with a wedding feast for family and friends, and (3) a community wedding feast.

Bridal preparation is a serious matter. Normally, the bride is given a special bath in which her complete body and hair are washed and perfumed. Body hair (underarm, pubic, arm and leg, and unwanted facial hair) is removed. Finger- and toenails are shaped and polished. Her hair is coiffed, and her face decorated with heavy makeup, all to produce a perfect, beautiful bride. In some countries, the prewedding night is called "henna night" (*laylat al henna*). It is an event for women only, with female singers and musicians, during which the bride's and guests' hands and feet are decorated with ornate patterns. In Turkey, after the decoration, the bride wears special henna gloves (usually of red satin) to protect her hands.

The next day, after the marriage contract is signed, the couple is considered married. As dusk falls, the wedding procession(s) takes place. In some areas, the bride is escorted to the groom's house in a long procession accompanied by friends and family. In some regions of Southwest Asia, the groom comes to the bride's house. More often, rooms are hired in a hotel, and the bride and bridegroom separately receive family and friends of the same sex.

Bridal garments vary considerably and may be changed as wedding festivities proceed. In some cases, regional dress may be worn first (with an emphasis on red and green colors representing

A Kurdish bride and groom, near Kermenshah, western Iran, 2003. They wear Western-style wedding outfits to show that they are "modern," but the bride's heavy makeup, especially around the eyes, remains in the traditional manner. Photograph by Ien Rappoldt.

fertility and good luck) and later be replaced by a white dress, often based on Western traditions but with more modest features such as long sleeves and no décolleté. Certainly, the garments of the bride and female guests are their best clothing. Weddings involve close observation and comparison of others' apparel, jewelry, use of perfume, and general behavior, as well as appraisal of potential brides and grooms.

The groom, too, goes through special rituals, albeit not as elaborate as those for the bride. In general, he also has a special bath, the removal of unwanted body hair, and a shave. In some communities, grooms use special shaving bibs, usually embroidered by the intended bride. The groom then dons a new outfit and goes to the wedding celebrations surrounded by male family and friends.

At a specified time, the bride and groom are brought together in a separate room and left alone. In many societies, the bride is brought in heavily veiled for the groom to lift the veil. Sometimes, the bride holds a mirror in her lap (as in Afghanistan) so that the groom can "accidentally" catch sight of his bride's face before lifting her veil. During this private time, the marriage is officially consummated.

While the bride and groom are alone, the wedding festivities continue and more guests arrive, such as family and friends traveling from afar, along with local community members. Later, the groom returns to the party and declares his satisfaction, or not, with his bride. If all is well, the wedding festivities continue until the two families end the event and the guests depart.

BIRTH AND BREAST-FEEDING

Following marriage, questions arise concerning how quickly the first child will arrive. Within the Arab world and indeed throughout Southwest Asia, pregnancy and child rearing have been regarded as a prime function of married women, viewed as an honor and privilege. A mother is honored above all. According to some schools of Islamic thought, a pregnant woman's prayers and deeds are valued more than those of one not pregnant. Also, a pregnant woman who dies or one who dies within forty days of giving birth is considered a *shahid* (martyr) who will go immediately to heaven. Some groups also state that a woman giving birth has equal status to a man doing jihad, that is, undergoing a spiritual or physical struggle.

How do fertility and pregnancy change the dress of women? As a prepubescent female, a young girl usually wears a wide range of clothing, often brightly colored with much decoration, laces, and frills. After her first menses, clothing usually covers her body more completely, especially her hair and neck, when in public or the presence of unrelated males. Urban Saudi Arabian women, for example, may also wear a face veil. After marriage, clothing codes often change dramatically. In Oman and southern Iran, for instance, some women must wear face veils immediately following the wedding celebrations. While still fertile, women may wear reasonably bright clothing, such as red garments of various shades, but clothing in these colors is generally seen only at home. Married women in public are expected to cover most or all of their bodies in subdued colors. Women with problems conceiving often wear special amulets that include rounded forms (imitating the pregnant woman's shape), pomegranates (round with many seeds), or a stone or bead in red (representing fertility and blood). They are sometimes worn singly, pinned to her garments, or, as in

Oman, made into a necklace by threading various charms onto a chain or leather thong.

After menopause, when a woman is thus infertile, a woman's clothing code changes again. Older women normally wear darker clothes with little decoration, especially black, and the amount of visible jewelry is reduced. The Qur'an also states that older (nonfertile) women need not be heavily veiled: "Such women as are past child-bearing and have no hope of marriage—there is no fault in them that they put off their [outer, veils] clothes" (Qur'an 24:60). However, these women, so used to being veiled, do not, in fact, remove them, reduce the number of garments, or change styles.

The sight of a rounded stomach indicates a woman fulfilling her duties as a mother, and the range of clothing worn by Southwest Asian women has been "designed" to accommodate pregnancy. Baggy undertrousers, such as the *sirwal*, which are easily adjusted with a drawstring or cord, are common attire throughout the region, along with loose-fitting dresses and tunics as top garments. Another typical public Arab outer garment is the *abayeh*, a loose cloak, easily worn during pregnancy since it has no elastic or tightness around the waist.

Traditionally, women give birth at home surrounded by female family members, with no men present. As a result, she normally wears her everyday, indoor clothes when giving birth. Beginning at the end of the twentieth century, many questions arose about giving birth in a hospital with male staff in attendance, since a Muslim woman might expect to wear full hijab under such circumstances. The general reaction has been that a woman should be decently covered, with loose-fitting clothes that cover her body and a loose scarf or head covering but not necessarily strict hijab. With no men present, she need not cover her hair but should wear a shawl or scarf if a man enters her room.

Following the birth of the child, during a forty-day period, family and friends pamper and look after the new mother and child. In some groups, the mother is bathed and anointed with special perfumes, and her hands are decorated with henna. The mother mainly feeds the baby and gains strength. When the period ends, depending on the family's finances, she undergoes a ritual known as *ghusl* that involves her body being immersed in water and thoroughly cleaned, after which a new outfit is commonly donned. Only after completing the ghusl does a woman resume her full duties as a Muslim wife and mother.

The first official event in a Muslim baby's life is when the *adhan* (the Muslim call to prayer) is whispered into its right ear and the *iqaamah* (the second prayer call before the main prayers) into its left ear. The baby is then welcomed into the Muslim community by having a piece of softened date or something sweet rubbed on its palate (a ritual called *tahneek*). From then on, the baby is expected to eventually assume the responsibilities of being a Muslim, including wearing suitable dress.

Engraving of a procession of Ottoman men, women, and children, from Pieter Coecke van Aelst, *Les Moeurs et Fachons de Faire des Turz* [The manners and customs of the Turks], Brussels, 1553. The young boy on the shoulder of the woman to the far left is wearing good clothes and a special cap, which suggests that he is about to be circumcised according to Islamic tradition. Courtesy of Leiden University Library.

Babies are usually swaddled; that is, wrapped tightly. In some Persian-oriented cultures such as Iran and Afghanistan, a baby was wrapped in bindings, the final layer of which was made up of one or two lengths of decorative bands about sixteen by three inches (forty-one by eight centimeters) in size, with a long cord at one end that is used to fasten the bands in place. Often, Western authors incorrectly describe such swaddling bands as puttees, which means wrappings for the legs.

Whether the baby is male or female, at seven days old, the baby's head is shaved, and the hair that has been cut off is weighed, with the equivalent weight in silver being given to charity. Within the Arab tradition, male babies are circumcised (*khittan*) when they are seven days old or older (but not earlier, as this is regarded as a Jewish tradition), traditionally in a mosque, but sometimes a mullah came to the home. In the twenty-first century, the procedure is usually carried out by a physician. In Turkish communities, the circumcision rite takes place later, at the age of six to seven years. The boy dresses in special clothing, being a prince for the day, is given a small parade, and celebrates with a special meal. In other groups, the initiate may be a young teenager old enough to agree to become an official Muslim.

In Muslim countries, women often breast-feed a child for two years, a period indicated by the Qur'an, which clearly states: "Mothers shall suckle their children two years completely" (Qur'an 2:233). In Southwest Asia, female dress is adapted by making long slits in blouse or dress fronts to accommodate the custom. Another option involves one long slit down the middle of the garment with one or two buttons at the top, making it easy to place the baby on the breast for feeding. With the arrival of modern fasteners, more commonly a zipper or a length of Velcro is used to allow easy opening and fastening with one hand as the other holds the baby for feeding. Still another form has two slits, one on each side of the front yoke, making the change from one breast to the other easier. Unmarried girls do not wear garments with such long slits, and after a woman stops breast-feeding, she reverts to wearing garments with short or buttoned slits.

DEATH

Southwest Asia has many rituals related to burial rites. Muslim rituals are governed by the Islamic concepts of propriety for gender roles, modesty, personal hygiene, and general codes for body covering. Islamic norms require burying a body within twenty-four hours of death, basically because heat causes putrefaction to set in quickly. After death, relatives or friends who are the same gender as the deceased wash the body, assuring that the concept of personal modesty extends after death, with exceptions only for young children or a spouse. First of all, clothing is removed to ready the body for washing. After the body is placed on a special table, a large towel is used to cover the *'awrah* region, defined as the private parts, extending from the navel to the knees, further ensuring preservation of modesty. Old cloths or torn clothing are used to clean the body with water and soap or a disinfectant, and the hair is washed and combed straight. A body is usually washed at least three times, to fulfill the Prophet Mohammed's words to conceal all unpleasant things, such as bad odors, appearances, blemishes, and wounds, and allow the person to appear wholesome. Some schools of thought indicate the bath should be *wudu*, that is, like the short ablutions carried out before prayers, whereas others like to perform ghusl, a full ritual bath. The final washing should have scent, such as camphor, added to make the body and hair smell sweet. Some groups also prepare the body by clipping the finger- and toenails and shaving the armpit and pubic hair, but not all Muslims agree that these acts are necessary.

General Islamic traditions maintain that a person should be buried in a length of plain white cloth, sometimes designated as a coarse white cotton fabric. It is, however, clearly agreed that an elaborate, colored, and patterned material, especially of silk, is not acceptable. During the medieval period, a man's turban (decreed to be at least five yards, or five meters, long) served to remind him of the impermanence of life, for it could be used as a shroud and would ensure proper burial with minimal cost to others. The Islamic tradition of shrouds (*kafan*) continues, with both men and women being buried in white cloth yardage and no other garments. Sometimes, these cloths are bought in advance for use at any moment. No fixed rule exists concerning the number of shrouds used, except that it should be an odd number because Islamic numerological traditions consider odd numbers good. In some cases, three shrouds are recommended, whereas other groups say that five shrouds make sure the body is properly covered. The shroud is often perfumed with incense prior to wrapping the body, and, after wrapping, the face of the deceased is covered, and the corpse is ready for burial.

If a person dies while on a pilgrimage to or at Mecca; namely, while performing either the hajj or the 'umrah (the greater and lesser pilgrimages, respectively), then he or she is regarded as a martyr who will go straight to heaven, and a shroud is not considered necessary. Instead, the deceased can be buried in the *ihram*, the pilgrimage clothing. Although the face of a Muslim is normally covered, the face of a pilgrim is left uncovered, as he or she has already made peace with Allah and is ready to ascend directly to heaven. Sometimes, a person who has earlier made a pilgrimage to Mecca may be buried in their ihram clothing.

In Iran, a more elaborate form of burial clothing is available, particularly from the Shiite holy city of Mashad. Two types of shrouds, one for men and one for women, comply with Muslim concepts of modesty. The basic outfit consists of a simple tunic, a strip of cloth to bind the feet, a length of cloth to cover the body (kafan), and a cheek pad, as well as a head scarf (*rosari*) for women. The cheek pad is necessary for laying the head on one side with the face looking toward Mecca, although some Muslims do not find this necessary, as they believe a good Muslim will always face in the right direction. All items in a burial set have printed texts on them from the Qur'an, with men's in green and women's in orange. This gendered color distinction is found elsewhere in Iran, such as entrance and toilet signs at airports and restaurants.

The most important exception to this method of preparing the dead applies to the body of a martyr, whether male or female, who has died in battle or fighting in some manner for Islam. A martyr is buried in his or her own clothing without being washed, justified by a quotation from the Prophet Mohammed that the wounds of a martyr will emit musk (a form of expensive perfume) on the Day of Judgment. In addition, one to three white shrouds are wrapped over the martyr's clothes.

The official mourning period is three days, which is observed through increased devotion, receiving visitors and condolences, and avoiding perfume, jewelry, and decorative, colorful clothing. Many variations occur among different Muslim cultures, but these are not followed by all. Sometimes, on the third day, a feast, as a wake, takes places in which trays of flowers with vessels of scented oils are distributed. Male and female guests dip the flowers into the oil, then proceed to the grave to pour the oil and flowers over it. Other feasts are held on the fortieth day and four, six, nine, and twelve months after the person's death.

Hadithic traditions (the sayings and actions of the Prophet Mohammed) fix a widow's mourning period (*iddah*) at four months and ten days. During this time, she may not remarry, move from her home, or wear perfume, colorful clothing, and jewelry. This period is basically designed to determine whether or not she is pregnant. At its end, she is expected to resume her regular life and, among many groups, remarry.

The color black or very dark blue is the color of mourning throughout Southwest Asia. According to the Orientalist Francis Joseph Steingass, for example, during the late nineteenth century, the color of mourning in Iran was dark blue or black. He notes that various contemporary sayings about mourning reflect the use of these colors, such as *jama dar nil zad*, meaning "he threw his garments into the Nile," to indicate "he put on mourning" (with the double meaning of the word *nil*, referring to indigo or blue and the Nile). In addition, a type of chador (*chador-i syah*, literally "black chador") is worn in Iran by a woman of a bereaved family or by a woman visiting a family in mourning. This is an indoor chador, made from a semitransparent black material that can also be worn on formal, solemn occasions; wearing this type

of chador is less common in the early twenty-first century than in earlier times. In some parts of Tehran, especially in wealthier and more Western-oriented areas north of the city, it is regarded as an anachronism.

References and Further Reading

Graquist, Hilma. *Muslim Death and Burial: Arab Customs and Traditions Studied in a Village in Jordan.* Helsinki: Societas Scientiarum Fennica, 1965.

Halevi, Leor. *Muhammed's Grave: Death Rites and the Making of Islamic Society.* New York: Columbia University Press, 2007.

Khan, Arif Ali, and Tauqir Mohammad Khan, eds. *Law of Marriage and Divorce in Islam.* Vol. 6 of *Encyclopaedia of Islamic Law.* New Delhi: Pentagon Press, 2006.

Knowing Our Rights: Women, Family, Laws and Customs in the Muslim World. London: Women Living under Muslim Law, 2003.

Steingass, Francis. *Persian-English Dictionary.* London: Pincott, 1892.

Gillian Vogelsang-Eastwood

See also Fitrah: Temporary and Permanent Body Modifications for Muslims; Snapshot: Islam and Islamically Correct Dress (Hijab); Face Veils.

The Tradition of the Bridal Trousseau

In every culture, marriage signifies change; it is a tremendous change not only in the lives of a young woman and young man but also for their families. Thus, the occasion of marriage is always accompanied by ceremonies, both festive and religious, to celebrate the new beginning and to protect the new couple from any future misfortune. In Central and Southwest Asia, particularly in societies where older traditions are still strongly held, textiles take a prominent place among the gifts that the newly married couple receive from family and friends. The wedding textiles, including garments worn by the bride and groom, are often decorated with motifs that represent good wishes, blessings, and fertility; these are displayed in the hope of averting misfortune or the evil eye. Some commemorate the wedding ceremony by depicting the bride, groom, and attendants, a reminder perhaps of one of the most important days in the couple's life. These wedding textiles also exhibit the bride's skills if she was the one who made them, their lavishness could reflect her family's economic standing and purchasing power, and the designs on these textiles communicated her family's association with tribal groups.

In traditional societies, marriage was essentially a contractual agreement between two families, often requiring a long negotiation in which the bride and groom had little part. The wedding is the marriage ceremony with its accompanying festivities. Traditional marriage ceremonies throughout Central and West Asia were, and still to certain extent are, very extravagant celebrations. The textiles produced for this purpose are as elaborate as the celebrations.

The dowry was the money, goods, or estate that a woman would bring to her husband in marriage or the gift of money or property given by the man to or for his bride. The trousseau, in contrast, was the bride's personal possessions, and textiles figured as a major portion of it. A young bride's trousseau contained textiles produced for the wedding, such as decorations, hangings, canopies, and dowry-carrying cloths; textiles produced as gifts; and textiles to be used by the couple after the wedding, such as garments for her and her husband and textiles for their home.

TEXTILES IN WEDDING CEREMONIES

Although the regions comprising Central and West Asia are vast and home to many people with different religious and ethnic backgrounds, marriage ceremonies and wedding festivities followed a very similar progression throughout Central and West Asia in both urban and rural settings, whether the family was Muslim, Christian, or Jewish, except in regard to purely ecclesiastical and religious matters. This similarity shows that ceremonies

were based on the old customs of Central and West Asia and were not dictated by specific religious practices. Wedding festivities consisted of a week of parties and celebrations in both the bride's and groom's homes, accompanied by ceremonial baths, bridal parties such as the henna ceremony or the day of adornment of the bride, and the viewing of the bride's trousseau. The festivities ended with a spectacular procession that took the bride from her parents' home to her husband's home. Textiles played a crucial role throughout the marriage negotiations and wedding festivities; they were investments, indicators of wealth and skill, gifts, functional objects, and, finally, talismans.

After the fathers of the bride and groom established the initial marriage agreement, the two families would begin to get to know each other by arranging visits and gift exchanges. The majority of the gifts that were exchanged in this period consisted of sweets and textiles. The gifts from the groom to the bride were displayed for all to see that a respectable value had been placed on the bride. Textile gifts for the bride included lengths of valuable fabrics to be made into garments. The groom received clothing or accessories like belts, socks, and caps that were likewise made out of valuable fabrics and often embroidered with precious materials such as gold thread. Silk fabrics and garments embellished with metallic threads were very valuable and in demand in Central and West Asian gift exchanges.

In Central and West Asian societies, the most important event for a woman was her wedding. Preparations for a marriage began early. From the time a girl was born, the elder women of her family began working on her trousseau. When the young girl reached the age when she could hold a needle, she joined the effort. She devoted much of her time to preparing for her wedding through embroidering, sewing, and weaving. She made covers and hangings of different sizes, carpets, towels, pillows, and other articles for her home. She also constructed coats, shirts, dresses, pants, sashes, head scarves, caps, and many other fashionable accoutrements for herself.

As the wedding approached, a series of ceremonies began. One very important event was the viewing of the trousseau, which took place over several days. The entire trousseau was displayed on a balcony or in a room. As seen in Jewish communities of Central Asia, a woman was sometimes hired to evaluate and announce the value of each item. A party of the bride's unmarried girlfriends gave the groom's friends a chance to sneak a look at the bride stock. Sometimes the bride was seated amid her trousseau, on which she had worked for so many years just for this occasion. The bride and her objects were presented to the curious eyes of the guests, who would inspect her handiwork and judge her skills.

Through the descriptions in travel memoirs and surviving legal documents that pertain to marriage contracts and wills, it is clear that textiles of every kind played a significant role in marriage contracts and wedding ceremonies. A trousseau contained a bride's personal possessions, including clothing and textiles for the new home. Depending on her family's wealth, it included several dresses, several robes, trousers, vests made out of valuable fabrics for everyday use and special occasions, winter and summer coats with or without fur or linings, robes to go out in, shoes,

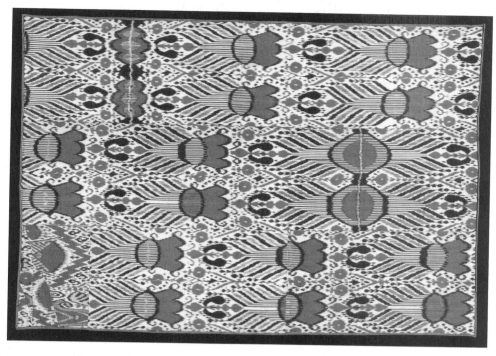

Textile panel, Bukhara, Uzbekistan, mid- to third quarter of the nineteenth century. This textile would have been used in the exchange of gifts and negotiations relating to the dowry before a wedding. The Textile Museum, Washington, D.C., 2005.36.16. The Megalli Collection. http://www.textilemuseum.org/

stockings, skullcaps and head scarves, jewelry to be worn with these clothing and headdresses, and lengths of fabric to be made into more dresses and coats. For the home, the bride's trousseau contained various sizes of carpets, covers, and hangings.

In addition to their part in gift exchanges and the trousseau, textiles played an important role in certain ceremonies that made up the wedding. A few days before the wedding, the bride went to the bath with her friends and female relatives. A public bath was often rented for a whole or half day for the occasion. Going to the bath for the bridal party was both a festive and ceremonial occasion. Besides being a setting for the women's social gatherings, the bath was an arena for the bride and her female relatives to exhibit their jewelry and textiles, such as exquisitely embroidered linen or cotton bath towels, covers, and silk dresses. This outing was yet another chance for the bride's and groom's families to show off their skills in textile making and decorating and their family's wealth and status. This type of ceremonious visit to the bath was also a valuable way for mothers to pick future brides for their sons from among the bride's unmarried relatives and friends. It was important to present a young girl's skill in embroidering and sewing and her family's prosperity through these textiles to prospective mothers-in-law or matchmakers.

One of the ceremonies designed around and for the bride and female participants of the wedding was the henna ceremony or the day of adornment of the bride, which included a henna ceremony. The day of adornment took place a day before the bride was taken to her husband's home. In the presence of her female relatives and friends, the bride's hands were intricately decorated with henna. She was dressed in her finest garments, wedding dress, and veil, with her wedding ornaments, including necklaces, earrings, and rings and bracelets on her hennaed fingers and arms,

and her bridal sash, often red in color, was tied around her waist. The bridal sash symbolized both the virginity and the fertility of the bride.

THE WEDDING AND RELATED EVENTS

Traditional wedding dresses from Central and West Asia had two common characteristics across cultures that reflect old customs rather than any specific religious practice: veiling and use of the color red. Brides wore a veil that was often attached to or supported by a headdress containing flowers and feathers that was similar to a crown. This veil was used to conceal the bride from prying eyes during more public ceremonies when she was vulnerable to the effects of unwanted evil glances. It was removed only by the groom or in the groom's presence. Decorating the bride's head with a crown appears to be an pre-Islamic custom, possibly driven by a desire to regard the bride as the queen of her and her husband's own little kingdom, the home. Flowers—either real or made of fabric—or jewelry in the form of flowers were used to decorate bride's headdress. Flowers in perpetual bloom and exuberant leaves powerfully conveyed ideas of beauty, abundance, fertility, youth, renewal, and the cycle of nature from spring to winter, from birth to death. They were powerful and enhanced the positive aura around this transformation in the life of a woman. The bridal veil hanging from this floral crown was red as well as was some of the clothing the bride and the groom wore. The color red was associated with happiness and good fortune as well as fertility in Asia; therefore, it is not surprising to see this color on ensembles used during a day when a major change was occurring in the lives of a young woman and young man.

Other textiles were also used in different phases of the wedding ceremony. In the urban centers of Central Asia, the Jewish bride and groom stood under a tallith, a prayer shawl, while in the Muslim ceremony, an embroidered wall hanging called a *suzani* was used for the same purpose. Suzanis, large embroidered textiles worked with silk thread, were used to decorate the interior of houses and were found only in settled communities. They formed an important part of a bride's trousseau, whether she was Muslim or Jewish. A bride from a wealthy family would be expected to have ten suzanis of different sizes and functions. The largest ones, which were 63–87 inches by 87–106 inches (160–220 centimeters by 220–270 centimeters) in size, were used as wall hangings, as were the smaller ones called *nimsuzani* (half-sized suzani). Large cloths embroidered along the long sides and one short side were called *ruijo*. They were used as spreads for the bridal bed. A small suzani, about the size of a nimsuzani, was spread over the bridal cushion and then used to cover the bedding, which was stored in niches during the day. Suzanis were highly treasured and after the wedding ceremony would be taken out only for special occasions. The foundation fabric used for suzanis was usually locally produced cotton that was normally undyed. The embroidery thread was loosely spun silk dyed with natural dyes. The dominant color by far on these textiles is red in various shades. The types of embroidery stitches used on suzanis were limited to various versions of the self-couching stitch.

Suzanis also had talismanic properties. A suzani was held above a bride as she entered the marriage chamber, because it was thought that it had "good properties." There were designs incorporated within suzanis that represented talismans, but while these enhanced the positive aura of the wall hanging, they did not transform it into a talisman. Objects became auspicious when age and custom had sanctified their use in rites of passage. The long history of using suzanis in ceremonies reinforced and enhanced their "good properties," making their presence necessary in family rituals. The motifs on suzanis consisted chiefly of flowers and leaves or of shapes that might be interpreted as floral. Some of these flowers were easy to recognize, and some less so. They were assumed to have symbolic meanings, but this is hard to prove. Only one motif might be firmly given a meaning; that was the pomegranate. Because of its numerous seeds, many cultures used the pomegranate as a symbol of fecundity, and it therefore was especially prominent in wedding ceremonies. In Bukhara, for example, it was customary to throw a pomegranate into the bride's lap.

Close to the end of the wedding festivities, the bride was usually fetched by the groom and his relatives and accompanied by her relatives in an imposing and solemn procession to her new home. If the bride's family was wealthy, the procession was sometimes enhanced by musicians. The procession included the bride either on horseback or in a decorated litter on top of a horse or camel. Her trousseau was distributed over as many horses and mules as possible. The trousseau was wrapped in thin, flat, woven textiles that were sometimes decorated with triangular embroidery in two opposite corners. On this occasion, the bride's clothing and veil as well as the textiles that concealed her were mostly red.

The animals used in the wedding procession were elaborately adorned, and specific textiles were woven for this purpose. The best-known examples of textiles produced for the animals in the wedding procession were seen among the nomadic groups such as the Teke Turkmens of Central Asia. The camel the bride would be transported on was mounted with a litter called the *kedzhebe*, which was covered with colorful textiles of every kind concealing the bride. The bride's camel and other camels carrying the trousseau were lavishly decorated. Their necks and heads were furnished with openwork colorful patchwork cloth with feathers or, more rarely, human hair attached. Many little bells were attached to each camel's neck, ringing at its every movement. The camels' legs were also decorated with small triangular pile-woven textiles with tassels, which were bound above its knees. Pairs of pentagonal-shaped, pile-woven hangings called *asmalyk* were hung on either side of the camels' humps where the bridal litter was placed and the trousseau was packed. These asmalyks were often pile-woven, but some examples were embroidered. All of these decorative textiles for the procession were woven by the bride and her close female relatives and communicated through their colors, designs, and motifs her family or tribe. An observer who came upon a bridal procession would know the bride's tribal association by reading the colors and motifs on these textiles. Thus, the textiles in the bridal trousseau not only were used to showcase the bride's skill and her family's prosperity but also communicated to others the family's social connections and associations.

WEDDING DRESS IN CENTRAL AND WEST ASIA

Three nineteenth-century Central Asian garments are worth focusing on in relation to the clothing associated with the wedding textiles. These are the *munisak*, *pishvo*, and *paranja* coats. It was proper for a woman to have several of these coats in her trousseau. The munisak coat was made to be worn during the important rites of passage in a woman's life. It had very accentuated feminine lines and no collar and was cut wide at the neck to expose the dress beneath. The sides of the coat curved over the breast and flared outward. Material was either gathered in folds under the arms, or gores were added to give fullness. The shape of the sleeves varied, from very long, narrow ones with a slash at the wrist and pleated ends that fell a foot (about thirty centimeters) below the hands, to wider sleeves of normal wrist length edged with a trim. The essence of the garment's style was its close fit at the breast and its fullness below. The munisak coat might be lined or unlined and was in widespread use throughout Central Asia by the middle of nineteenth century.

After the wedding, the munisak coat was the proper attire to be worn to family festivals and funerals. The munisak coat was considered funeral attire for both the mourners and the deceased. It was as important to have a munisak coat at one's funeral as at one's wedding. One or two munisak coats from a woman's trousseau were placed in her bier as coverings. After the funeral, the coats from the bier were ritually purified and given either to the woman's daughter or to the woman who had washed the body. It was essential that some kind of female-style coat be given to the body washer; it was thought that if a male-style coat was given, the deceased might rise at the Day of Judgment in the form of a man.

The pishvo was the richest and most valuable clothing of the new bride's trousseau and was thus most probably worn on top of all other coats, over the head. The pishvo might have been the precursor to the munisak coat. This type of coat's use was documented in the early part of the nineteenth century. Both munisak and pishvo coats were made of fabric with a cotton weft and a silk ikat warp. The pishvo did not have linings, although they had the same distinct hour-glass shape and long sleeves as the munisak coats. Similar to the munisak coats, the pishvo could be worn with the arms in the sleeves, but sometimes the sleeves were false sleeves. The left sleeve was worn on the head and was used to carry small objects of value. The fabrics used to make several pishvo coats for the bride's trousseau were sent by the groom. The bride was brought to her new home wearing the pishvo as a head covering. Until the birth of her first child, she never left her room without it. Women often held the sleeves in their teeth while doing chores, so the coat would not fall down. In the late eighteenth and early nineteenth centuries, the pishvo was worn until it fell apart from use. Gradually, the time during which they were worn was reduced to less than a month after the wedding date.

Both pishvo and munisak coats disappeared as elements of the trousseau by the end of nineteenth century. Compared to these two coats, the third trousseau garment, the paranja, was the only strictly feminine robe that continued in use well into the twentieth century. The paranja was the woman's coat that was worn on top of all other clothing when outside the home. It was designed to be worn on top of the head and enveloped the body like a cape. It was extremely long, often reaching from head to heel. The sleeves narrowed so sharply that it was not possible to insert the arms fully, and the ends of the sleeves were closed, sometimes tapering to a point. Often, these nonfunctional sleeves were hung at the back or were sometimes joined by an embroidered panel or a trim.

Far to the west of Central Asia is Anatolia in West Asia, with its multiple ethnic groups and traditions. The most prominent of them all were the Ottoman Turks. Ottoman Turkish clothing was one of the key areas of decorative arts that represented

Bindalli, Ottoman, Turkey, late nineteenth or early twentieth century. Until the 1930s, the *bindalli* was commonly worn at weddings by the bride and her family and friends in the urban centers of the Ottoman Empire. The distinctive features of the dress are the fluid floral designs covering the entire surface and the style of gold embroidery applied on the velvet or satin-weave foundation fabric. The Textile Museum, Washington, D.C., 1978.22. Gift of Mr. Yavuz Sümer. http://www.textilemuseum.org/

Ottoman culture. The imperial Ottoman style of dress was worn throughout the empire by the ruling elite and was imitated in the provincial towns by the populace. Thus, the style was spread throughout many of the urban centers of West Asia; possibly the only exception was Iran. It was accepted as the fashionable attire of the day; through dressing in this style, one sought to realize one's desire for status, influence, and wealth.

The history of clothing in Ottoman lands presents a complex and varied evolution. Both men's and women's dress changed over the centuries at a gradual pace, but certain items retained their overall shape and functions, although losing and gaining minor characteristic features. Ottomans were always careful of their attire. They attached the greatest importance and value to clothes, because in the traditionally structured Ottoman society, what one wore indicated one's religion, rank, and class. Until the nineteenth century, the *gömlek* (chemise), *şalvar* (baggy pants), and *entari* (fitted ankle-length coat with a V-neck and long sleeves tapering snugly to the wrists) formed the basic outfit worn by Ottoman women. The outfits associated with weddings, including the bride's dress, conformed to this three-part form but with the addition of expensive fabrics and trimmings to make it special and the use of red in the bride's clothing. To this ensemble, other elements were added, such as a vest, overdress, sash, shawl, and other accessories, both for everyday wear and weddings.

European fashion influenced traditional Ottoman garments in a variety of ways in the nineteenth century. In some cases, a particular element was altered to imitate a European style; in other cases, a European-style garment was substituted for a traditional one that was similar. For the latter, a minor alteration in construction, such as the elimination of one cut, could transform a traditional garment style, such as the entari, into a Western one, such as a dress.

The *bindalli* was a type of dress worn on special occasions. At a wedding, it would be worn by both the bride and her family and friends in the urban centers of the Ottoman Empire, especially in Anatolia and Thrace. It appears to have come into fashion with the introduction of dresses and skirts from Europe in the nineteenth century. The distinguishing characteristics of bindalli are the fluid floral designs covering the entire surface and the style of gold embroidery applied on the velvet or satin-weave foundation fabric. There was a wide variety in the floral designs, from graceful garlands draped across the skirt to clumsy flowers arranged in stiff rows. The term *bindalli*, or "thousand branches," is used to refer to both the embroidery and the garments that the embroidery decorated.

Most bindallis were long dresses, sometimes with matching fitted jackets, skirts with long trains, and slippers. Baggy pants and jackets decorated with this type of embroidery were also made. The dresses were often dark red velvet, but other dark colors—black, purple, blue, and green—were also used, as well as satin-weave fabric. This type of garment exhibited many variations throughout the nineteenth and early twentieth centuries, especially in its tailoring, and it was often associated with weddings.

In very wealthy circles of the Ottoman population, the bride wore her bindalli with other accoutrements, such as a closely fitting fez concealed by wreaths of diamonds, in the forms of flowers and fruit, covering her head. Sometimes, feathers, especially ostrich feathers, were added to the headdress. A veil of silver lace, two to three feet (sixty to ninety centimeters) in length, fell on each side of the bride's face. Her long hair, plaited and curled at the ends, hung down her back. Her fingers were loaded with rings with precious stones. Her face might have been decorated with diamonds. Clusters of diamonds, in the form of stars, might have been placed on her forehead, her chin, and her cheek. By 1930, bindalli, however, had disappeared from the urban bride's trousseau. In its place, fashionable urban brides began to wear white dresses with white veils. The only traditional Turkish accoutrement to the ensemble besides the jewelry was the red sash tied around the waist, symbolizing virginity and fertility.

CONCLUSION

The main purpose of wedding ceremonies is to establish the well-being of the newlyweds and to ensure the prosperity and fertility of their future family. This complex of transition rituals consists of a number of stages from the initial negotiations to the actual acceptance of the young wife into her husband's family. The general symbolism and structural framework have many commonalities throughout the whole region of Central and West Asia, although there are ethnic, religious, and regional derivations. Textiles have always been an integral part of these ceremonies. A wedding has been indeed one of the best occasions to show off a family's wealth and to impress others with spectacular dresses and decorations. The most important social function of textiles was related to marriage and domestic decoration. Producing textiles for a trousseau was a shared activity among female relatives and friends. Making these textiles served as an outlet for family creativity and gave the bride a reassuring keepsake of her family of origin. Textiles represented fashion and tradition, luxury and labor.

References and Further Reading

Fitz Gibbon, Kate, and Andrew Hale. *Ikat: Silks of Central Asia*. London: Laurence King Publishing and Alan Marcuson, 1997.

Fitz Gibbon, Kate, and Andrew Hale. *Uzbek Embroidery in Nomadic Tradition*. Minneapolis: Minneapolis Institute of Art, 2007.

Harvey, Janet. *Traditional Textiles of Central Asia*. London: Thames and Hudson, 1996.

Kalter, Johannes, and Margareta Pavaloi, eds. *Erben der Seidenstrasse: Usbekistan*. Berlin and Stuttgart: Linden Museum and Museum für Völkerkunde, 1995.

Kalter, Johannes, and Margareta Pavaloi, eds. *Uzbekistan: Heirs to the Silk Road*. London: Thames and Hudson, 1997.

Micklewright, Nancy. "*Women's Dress in Nineteenth-Century Istanbul: Mirror of a Changing Society*." Ph.D. dissertation, University of Pennsylvania, 1986.

Micklewright, Nancy. "Late-Nineteenth-Century Ottoman Wedding Costumes as Indicators of Social Change." In *Muqarnas: An Annual on the Visual Culture of the Islamic World*, edited by Oleg Grabar, vol. 6, 162–173. Leiden: Brill, 1989.

Popova, Larissa, et al. *Music for the Eyes: Textiles from the Peoples of Central Asia*, edited by Gustaaf Daems and Myrjam Wagemans. Antwerp: Hessenhuis, 1997.

Scarce, Jennifer. *Women's Costume of the Near and Middle East*. London: Unwin Hyman, 1987.

Scarce, Jennifer. "Principles of Ottoman Turkish Costume." In *Costume*, 22 (1988): 8–31. London: The Costume Society, 1988.

Scarce, Jennifer. *Domestic Culture in the Middle East: An Exploration of the Household Interior*. Edinburgh: National Museum of Scotland, 1996.

Sumru Belger Krody

Dress and Hadiths ("Traditions" or Sayings Attributed to the Prophet Mohammed)

> • Interpreting the Hadiths

The hadiths ("narratives") are traditions relating to the words and actions of the Islamic prophet Mohammed, an event or action that had his tacit approval, or something done in his presence. Most hadiths refer to Mohammed, but sometimes the sayings refer to traditions about his companions or their successors in the following generations. The hadiths quickly became an important element in early Islamic history and were used to transmit an Islamic way of life, including what people wore and how they behaved in public, throughout Southwest Asia. In addition, the hajj, or annual pilgrimage to Mecca, meant that people from different regions met, with the result that traditions spread across the whole of the Islamic world. The hadiths remain an essential part of Islamic life.

At first, the hadiths were transmitted orally, but in the late seventh century C.E., people started to write them down. By the reign of the Umayyad caliph 'Umar II (ca. 682–720 C.E.), scholars were confronted by a vast number of miscellaneous traditions, many of which were contradictory, misleading, and, in some cases, deliberate fakes. So the sayings were collected, their origins and chain of transmission evaluated, and then catalogued. Initially, they were organized according to who said what, but later the hadiths were grouped according to subject matter.

A hadith consists of two main elements. First, the chain of narrators (*isnad* or *sanad*) documents the route by which the report was transmitted; for example, "A told me that B told him that Mohammed said." The sanad chain is used to determine whether a hadith may be regarded as reliable or weak. Second, the text of the report (*matn*) contains the actual narrative, such as "So-and-so wore perfume."

Hadiths are generally categorized as *sahih* (sound, authentic), *hasan* (good), *da'if* (weak), *sakim* (infirm), or *mawdu* (fabricated). Within these groups, there are various subcategories. For example, sahih is subdivided into seven grades, each with its own commentary concerning its provenance and reliability.

At first, not every group of Muslims was prepared to accept the hadiths as an important element in Islamic life, but following the work of the Arabic jurist al-Shafi'i (ca. 767–820 C.E.), the hadiths became recognized as a foundation stone of Islam. The Qur'an is regarded as the Holy Book containing the eternal word of Allah, while the hadiths represent divine guidance.

The Qur'an contains many guidelines regarding the behavior expected of Muslims, but there are no specific rules such as the Jewish and Christian Ten Commandments. Muslims believe that they can look at the way of life, or sunna, of Mohammed and his companions to discover what to imitate and what to avoid. The hadiths are regarded as a major source of religious law and moral guidance and an important tool for the traditional schools of Islamic jurisprudence to use in determining the broader Muslim sunna, or Muslim way of life. The sunna includes what men and women can and cannot wear, but it is noticeable that different groups interpret what is or is not allowed differently, and these interpretations may change both over time and across regions.

It should be noted, however, that Islam is divided into a number of different schools of thought, notably Sunni and Shia, and that each group uses different hadith. Again, this has an effect on the way of life and style of clothing worn by the various groups. The Sunni version took its final form more than 230 years after Mohammed's death in 632 C.E., and there were still questions concerning the authenticity of many of the hadiths. In general, the main Sunni hadith collections are those compiled by Sahih Bukhari, Sahih Muslim, Sunan Abi Da'ud, Sunan al-Tirmidhi, Sunan al-Sughra, and Sunan Ibn Maja. Those of Sahih Bukhari and Sahih Muslim are regarded as the most reliable.

Shia Muslims do not use the six major hadith collections followed by the Sunni; instead, they follow traditions that were transmitted via the imams, or descendants of the Prophet Mohammed, through his daughter, Fatima Zahra. The four most prominent Shia hadith collections are those of Usul al-Kafi, Man la yahduruhu al-Faqih, Al-Tabhdhib, and Al-Istibsar.

For some scholars, the hadiths are also a source of information about early Islamic history and biography; they can also be used as a source of information about the cultural norms of the period, as well as giving some insights into early Islamic dress.

INTERPRETING THE HADITHS

Many aspects of Muslim dress, literally from birth to death, are discussed in the hadiths. Some references are incidental, others are in greater detail, but by combining various hadiths it is possible to gain details about men's and women's dress and use of accessories in the early centuries of Islam. A small number of hadiths from the Sunni collections (rather than the Shia versions) will be used to illustrate some of their information on dress.

Various problems arise when using the hadiths as a source of information about early Islamic dress, including whether the hadith is a fake and what its author was trying to achieve or prevent. With respect to dress studies, perhaps the most difficult aspect is the changing use of terminology over the centuries. Is an *izar*, or hip wrap, from the early twenty-first century the same garment as in the seventh century C.E. when the Prophet was alive? Did it look similar, and was it worn in the same way? Or was the term applied to a totally different garment? These questions are difficult to answer with certainty. Nevertheless, an impression can be gained of the important role of dress in daily life during the early Islamic period.

According to various hadiths, for example, a woman whose husband has just died is not allowed to wear certain items:

> Yahya related to me from Malik from Nafic that Saffiyya bint Abi Ubayd suffered from an eye-complaint while she was in mourning for her husband, Abdullah ibn Umar. She did not apply kohl until her eyes almost had ramas [a dry white secretion in the corners of the eye]. Malik said

"A woman whose husband has died should anoint her yes with olive oil and sesame oil and the like of that since there is no perfume in it." Malik said, "A woman in mourning for her husband should not put on any jewellery—rings, anklets, or such-like, neither should she dress in any sort of colourful, striped garment unless it is coarse. She should not wear any cloth dyed with anything except black, and she should only dress her hair with things like lotus-tree leaves which do not dye the hair." (Muataa Malek, no. 29.33.107)

Presumably, however, the woman was allowed to wear all of these things while her husband was living.

Other hadiths deal with Friday prayers and men's dress. For instance, prior to going to the mosque, it was advisable to bathe:

Narrated Abu Sa'id: I testify that Allah's Apostle said, "The taking of a bath on Friday is compulsory for every male Muslim who has attained the age of puberty and (also) the cleaning of this teeth with siwak [a twig used as a toothbrush], and the using of perfume if it is available." Amr (a sub-narrator) said, "I confirm that the taking of a bath is compulsory, but as for the siwak and the using of perfume, Allah knows better whether it is obligatory or not, but according to the Hadith it is as above." (Bukhari 2:5)

Some hadiths deal with the question of public modesty, a situation that arose because of the apparently common practice of men being dressed only in a single hip wrap (izar) at prayer:

Narrated Muhammad bin Al-Munkadir: I went to Jaibr bin 'Abdullah and he was praying wrapped in a garment (izar) and his rida [a sheet covering the upper part of the body] was lying besides him. When he finished the prayers, I said "O Abdullah! You pray [in a single garment] while your rida is lying besides you." He replied, "Yes, I did it intentionally so that the ignorant ones like you might see me. I saw the Prophet praying like this." (Bukhari 1:366)

More details are given in another hadith concerning various clothing combinations that men could wear while at prayer:

Narrated Abu Huraira: A man stood up and asked the Prophet about praying in a single garment. The Prophet said "Has everyone of you two garments?" A man put a similar question to 'Umar on which he replied, "When Allah makes you wealthier then you should clothe yourself properly during prayers. Otherwise one can pray with an izar and a rida." (Bukhari 1:361)

Apparently, Abu Huraira then went on to give some other clothing combinations that were acceptable, specifically, an izar and a shirt, an izar and a qaba (a gown or coatlike garment), pants and a rida, pants and a shirt, pants and a qaba, tubban (underpants) and a qaba, tubban and a shirt, and, possibly, tubban and a rida.

Another way of dressing for prayer can be found in the following hadith:

Narrated Abu Huraira: I saw seventy of As-Suffa men and none of them had a rida. They had either izars (only) or sheets which they tied round their necks. Some of these sheets reached the middle of their legs and some reached their heels and they used to gather them with their hands least their private parts should become naked. (Bukhari 1:433)

Thus, by combining various hadiths, a better understanding can be gained of what Arab Muslim men, of various economic standings, may have worn while at prayer at the time of the Prophet and just afterward. It is certainly a very different range of clothing from that worn by many modest Arab men at the beginning of the twenty-first century.

There are various references in the hadiths to the relationship between daily clothing and that worn while on a pilgrimage or hajj to Mecca. Sometimes, the hadiths are very short and to the point, for example, "Narrated Anas: The Prophet forbade men to use saffron" (Bukhari 7:737) while a pilgrim. On other occasions, there is considerably more detail, as in the following example concerning what a man should wear when about to go on hajj:

Narrated Ibn 'Umar: A man asked the Prophet: "What (kinds of clothes) should a Muhrim [a Muslim intending to perform 'umra or hajj] wear?" He replied, "He should not wear a shirt, a turban, trousers, a head cloak or garment scented with saffron or wars [kinds of perfumes]. And if he has no slippers, then he can use khuffs [footwear made from a thick fabric or leather], but the socks should be cut short so as to make the ankles bare."

These guidelines are still followed in the early twenty-first century by male pilgrims. There are no similar rules for women's hajj dress.

By looking at other hadiths, it is possible to form a picture of how certain Muslim practices developed. This can be seen, for example, when looking at burial shrouds. There are various references to the Prophet Mohammed wearing a length of cloth as a hip wrap and how he gave the cloth to a man who wanted it for a shroud (see Bukhari 23:29). More details concerning shrouds are given in a hadith that concerns Aisha, one of the Prophet's wives:

Narrated Hisham's father: Aisha said, "I went to Abu Bakr and he asked me 'In how many garments was the Prophet shrouded?' She replied 'in three suhuliya [cloth from Yemen] pieces of white cloth of cotton, and there was neither a shirt nor a turban among them.'... Then he looked at the garment that he was wearing during his illness and it had some stains of saffron. Then he said, 'Wash this garment of mine and add two more garments and shroud me in them.' I said, 'This is worn out.' He said, 'A living person has more right to wear new clothes than a dead one; the shroud is only for the body's pus.' (Bukhari, 2.469)

In another hadith, it is reported that only two pieces of cloth were used:

Narrated Ibn 'Abbas: While a man was standing with the Prophet at 'Arafat, he fell from his mount and his neck was crushed by it. The Prophet said, "Wash the deceased with water and sidr [possibly soap, perfume, or perfumed soap] and shroud him in two pieces of cloth, and neither perfume him nor cover his head, for Allah will resurrect him on the Day of Resurrection." (Bukhari 3.75)

Up through the early twenty-first century, it is normal for a Muslim to be buried in two or more pieces of cloth used as a shroud, rather than in clothes, as is the case for many Christian burials.

There are many more hadiths that give information about daily and religious life in the early Islamic Arab world, but they are not only relevant to the past and the study of historic dress. These ancient "rules" still play an important role within Islamic lift in the early twenty-first century and should not be neglected with respect to the general study of dress in Southwest Asia.

References and Further Reading

Robson, J. "Hadith." In *Encyclopaedia of Islam*, edited by P. J. Bearman, Th. Bianquis, C. E. Bosworth, E. van Donzel, W. P. Heinrichs, et al. 2nd ed. CD-ROM Edition v.1.1. Leiden: E. J. Brill, 1999.

Stillman, Yedida K. *Arab Dress: A Short History from the Dawn of Islam to Modern Times.* Leiden: Brill, 2000.

Gillian Vogelsang-Eastwood

See also The Coming of Islam and Its Influence on Dress; Snapshot: Trade, Textiles, Dress, and the Hajj; Birth, Marriage, and Death; Snapshot: Islamic Pilgrimage Dress (Ihram).

Snapshot: Dress of Shiites and Mystics

Religious classes in Islamic societies distinguish themselves by wearing different kinds of clothes. Islamic mystics and Shiite clerics wear certain types of dress. The Shiites form the second-largest community of Muslims; they believe that the Prophet Mohammed's cousin and son-in-law Ali ibn Abu Talib was his rightful successor. The Shiites do not accept the leadership of the first three caliphs, Abu Bakr, Omar, and Othman, emphasizing that they usurped Ali's right.

THE SHIITE CLERGY

The dress of a Shiite cleric in early-twenty-first-century Iran comprises a turban, an outer garment, undergarments, and footwear. The word *turban* in European languages derives from the Persian *dulband* via Turkish *tulbent*. The symbolic connotations of the turban are expressed in several traditions and historical sources. One of the most-cited prophetic traditions says, "The turban is the boundary between faith and infidelity." The turban here symbolizes being Muslim. The high value of the turban is connected to the story that the turban is the headgear of angels. After Adam's expulsion from paradise, God removed Adam's crown and gave him a turban. The Prophet Mohammed wore turbans of various colors (red, white, and blue), but on his return to Mecca, he was wearing a black turban. Perhaps because of the black turban's association with this victory, it has become a symbol of authority.

Another important association is the occasion of Ghadir-e Khomm, during which, according to the Shiite traditions, the Prophet designated Ali as his successor by winding a turban around his head. Based on this event, winding a turban has become one of the important rites of initiation for the ulema and also for Sufi masters. The turban was so important that the Prophet's turban received the name of "the cloud" (*al-siha*). According to the Shiites, Ali inherited it. The clerical turban (*'imama*) in the early twenty-first century is either black or white, although green is used very occasionally. Ali, for example, is portrayed wearing a green turban. The wearing of black or green indicates that the person is a sayyid, or descendant of the Prophet.

There is a special technique to winding the turban around the head; at one time there were people called *'imama-pich* whose occupation was to wind turbans. The turban is usually placed over a small skullcap called an *araqchin* (literally, "sweat absorber"), which is normally white, although occasionally black versions may be worn. The skullcap is usually embroidered with floral or geometric designs. Clerics wear just the skullcap when they are in private.

As their outer garment, clerics wear a *qaba*, a sleeved robe with an open front, covering the body to the ankles. It can be fastened with buttons in front. Some qabas are wrapped from left to right and fastened with only one button, a little below the armpit. Under the qaba, clerics wear a quilted waistcoat or vest. It has short sleeves and hangs over the thighs. It is wrapped in front and is fastened with buttons. Clerics also wear a *labbadeh*, which is a long robe with sleeves and slits on either sides. Traditionally, it had a V-neck, but in the early twenty-first century, a round collar is fashionable.

Some clerics use a *shal kemer,* a sash fastening the qaba around the waist. Descendants of the Prophet wear black or green sashes, and other clerics wear a white sash. The sash fabric is sometimes of wool or cotton, although nonclerics may also use silk. The *Dehkhoda* Persian dictionary mentions that the Pahlavi dynasty banned the sash.

A cloaklike overgarment, the *aba*, is normally worn over the qaba. The aba is usually black or various shades of brown, but at the end of the twentieth century, a few clerics, such as the former president of Iran, Mohammad Khatami, started to wear a cream- or beige-colored aba. The aba is specifically used as an outer garment and has the form of a long mantle with an open front. The aba is commonly sleeveless, with large armholes, cut in such a way that it stays in place around the shoulders. Sometimes, an aba has sleeves. The fabric of the aba is generally wool, although other materials are also used to make a summer aba.

The aba has a strong symbolic meaning for Shiite clerics. The expression "People of the [Prophet's] Household" literally means "the people under the Prophet's aba." For Shiites, this means Mohammed's daughter Fatima, his cousin and son-in-law Ali, and his grandsons Hassan and Husayn. This refers to an occasion when the Prophet, wearing a striped cloak, gathered first Hassan, then Husayn, Fatima, and, finally, Ali beneath his aba. At that moment, the following Qur'an verse was revealed to him: "God wishes only to remove taint from you, people of the Household, and to make you utterly pure" (33:33).

Clerics traditionally wear *na'leyn*, leather sandals in yellowish and brownish colors. These are open at the back and have no heels, while the toes are sometimes turned up. In the early twenty-first century, the na'leyn are usually used when a cleric is performing ablutions before the obligatory daily prayer. Since the Islamic Revolution, this footwear has also been worn by other classes of people, especially conservatives.

SUFI DRESS

The word *Sufi*, referring to both Sunni and Shiite mystics, apparently derives from the Arabic root *s-w-f*. One of the meanings of the word *suf* is "wool," referring to the coarse woolen cloak that the first generation of Islamic mystics wore to show their ascetic aspiration and to distinguish themselves from those who wore luxurious dress. The Sufi cloak has variants with names such as the *khirqa* (cloak), *dalq* (patched cloak), *gelim* (coarse woolen mantle), and *pustin* (animal skin). Lesser-known garments such as the *tanura*, a long, sleeveless robe, and *heydari*, a sleeveless robe reaching to the waist, are also worn by mystics. In Persian and Persianate literature (literature in the Persian style, found, for example, in some regions of Afghanistan), Sufis are often referred to as the wearers of coarse, woolen, or patched cloaks or animal skins: *kherqe-push*, *gelim-push*, *dalq-push*, and *pustin-push*.

For instance, the fourteenth-century grand lyricist of Persia, Khwaja Samsu d-Din Muhammad Hafez-e Sirazi, refers to the *dalq-e moraqqa'* (the patched cloak) or *molamma'* (a variegated patched cloak). Hafez is apparently referring to people pretending to be mystics, who earned public respect by appearing in the clothes of a mystic in public. Antinomian mystics saw this as one of the pitfalls on the mystic path to union. By frequenting taverns and drinking wine (being happy and letting go of this world are part of being a mystic), they tried to avoid any risk of hypocrisy:

> Although [drinking] rose-coloured wine, wearing a variegated patched cloak, is a fault I do no wrong, because I am washing the colour of hypocrisy from it. (Rumi, *Divan*)

First wearing a kherqa is one of the essential parts of a Sufi master's investiture rite. The phrase *kherqa az dast-e kasi gereftan* ("to receive a cloak from someone's hand") means to become a follower of a master or leader. The genealogy of a Sufi master is often listed in terms of who gave him his cloak and from whom his predecessors received theirs. The great mystic Abu 'l-Hasan Kharaqani sings:

> Wherever a black-wearing and frenzied man lives
> He is my disciple, he has received the cloak from me.
> (As cited by A. A. Dehkhoda, *Loghat-name*, under "Kherqa az…")

The mystic 'Ezz al-Din Mahmud Kashani devotes a whole chapter to the importance of clothing in his manual on Sufism. Referring to a tradition that the Prophet dressed one of his followers in a black gelim, or coarse woolen cloth, Kashani explains that a change of dress also involves a change of behavior. The cloak is the shadow of a Sufi master's authority, which he casts over his followers, making Satan flee from them. By accepting the cloak, the Sufi submits himself entirely to the master as spiritual guide. This is known as *mowt-e akhzar* or "green death." Kāshāni distinguishes between two types of kherqas: The first is the *kherqa-ye 'ebadat*, or "cloak of servitude," which is given to a Sufi disciple when the master is sure of the disciple's search for the truth. This cloak is offered only once in a lifetime by a master to a disciple. The other is the *kherqa-ye tabarrok*, or "blessed cloak," which a disciple is allowed to receive from other Sufi masters as a sign of blessing (*baraka*).

Because of the rich symbolic value of the kherqa, it appears in a wide range of Persian compounds, phrases, and expressions. *Kherqa az sar andakhtan*, which literally means "to throw the cloak from one's head," means "to submit oneself, to give up, to be ecstatic, to give up one's soul (to die)." The expression *kherqa para kardan*, or "tearing the cloak," means "to be ecstatic." Another common expression, *kherqa dar atash zadan*, or "throwing one's cloak in the fire," means "to abandon hypocrisy and dissimulation."

References to fleas and other insects living in the rough woolen cloak point to a high degree of asceticism. Sufis even competed about the number of fleas in their cloaks. The Persian compound *dalq-e shepeshnak*, or "flea-ridden cloak," stands for the body, as in the following couplet by Jalal al-Din Rumi: "Throw away the flea-ridden cloak, the soul that is naked is more pleasing."

Sufis wore many different types of headgear, the most commonly attested in various literary, historical, and religious sources being the *kolah*, a general term for a hat. The hat usually had the shape of a cylinder, widening toward the top, and was made from felt or wool. Headgear commonly indicates the rank, class, and position of an individual within a specific group. In mystic literature, the kolah stands for material possessions and attachment to the world, which the Sufi should renounce. The word *kaj-kolah* ("with one's cap awry") is another term used by mystics, referring to a beautiful youth that reminds the mystic of the Beloved. A story tells that the Prophet saw God in the most beautiful form, as a youth with a silken cap awry. Since the word *kolah* came to be used as a synonym for *taj* ("crown"), the two terms have been used indiscriminately in Persian literature. Each order had its own headgear, which differed in both shape and color from others, and also its own symbolism: While some hats were made of twelve parts, others had nine or sometimes seven, referring to the number of holy imams.

With the advent of the theocratic dynasty of the Safavids (1501–1722), a new headgear came to fashion. This was called *taj-e davazdah tark,* or twelve-gored cap; each of these cuts in the outer cloth represents one of the Shiite imams. There are several symbolic associations attached to this headgear. Basing his authority on Shah Ne'matollah Vali (1331–1437), H. Algar has described one of the most prominent symbolic meanings of the headgear as follows: "The twelve-slash turban worn by numerous Iranian Sufis was taken to indicate the necessity to acquire twelve particular virtues and to abandon twelve particular vices." It is believed that this headgear

A group of Iranian and Iraqi clerics, Shiraz, southern Iran, 2003. The Iranian mullah wears turbans, black to signify a descendant of the Prophet Mohammed and white to signify an ordinary man. The Iraqi mullah wears traditional Arab dress. Photograph by Ien Rappoldt.

was originally made at the order of Shah Isma'il, out of red broadcloth. Because of its color, the Safavids' dervish-soldiers who wore it were called the *qezelbash*, which literally means "red head." Since the hat had become a visible symbol of Sufi piety, many mystics have avoided wearing it. Shah Abu 'l-Latif of Sind stated that a true Sufi would throw his hat into the fire.

Another article of clothing that appears in mystical literature is the *zonnar*. This is a cord that religious minorities such as Zoroastrians, Christians, and Jews originally had to wear as a sign of their submission to Islam. The cord is associated with the threefold belt (*kusti*) of the Zoroastrians. As Muslims, Sufis generally did not wear this belt, but some antinomian mystics wore it as an emblem of their radical renunciation of the world. This class of mystics used to wear sacks (*jowaliq*), which was one of their basic rules.

In modern Iran, Sufis' dress is seldom different from that of other classes of people. The orders and public displays of un- orthodox religion are discouraged and sometimes suppressed. The spiritual leader of a Sufi order may wear a kolah, which varies in shape and decoration. In contrast to Sufi orders, there are also solitary mystics known as dervishes, some of whom do have a public identity. These "public" dervishes, always men, have long hair and beards and usually wear white. They carry a *kashkul*, an oval bowl usually made of metal but sometimes of wood or a coconut. The two ends of an oval kashkul are joined by a chain handle. The kashkul hangs from the shoul- der and is used to collect alms, in money or food. The kashkul is often decorated by floral and fauna motifs, Arabic verses, and Persian poetry.

REFERENCES AND FURTHER READING

Algar, H. Under "Abā." In *Encyclopaedia Iranica*, edited by Ehsan Yarshater, vol. 1, 50–51. London: Routledge, 1982.

Algar, H. Under "'Amāma." In *Encyclopaedia Iranica*, edited by Ehsan Yarshater, vol. 1, 919–921. London: Rout- ledge, 1982.

Algar, H. Under "l-e 'abā." In *Encyclopaedia Iranica*, edited by Ehsan Yarshater, vol. 1, 742. London: Routledge, 1982.

Bruijn, J.T.P. de. "The *Qalandariyyāt* in Persian Mystical Poetry, from Sanā'i Onwards." In *The Legacy of Medieval Persian Sufism*, edited by L. Lewisohn, 75–86. London: Khaniqahi Nimatullahi Publications, 1992.

Cannon, G., and A. S. Kaye. *The Persian Contributions to the English Language: An Historical Dictionary*. Wies- baden, Germany: Harrassowitz, 2001.

Gholami, Y. Under "Abā." In *Encyclopaedia Islamica*, edited by Ehsan Yarsheter. Leiden: Brill; London: Institute of Ismaili Studies, 2008.

Huart, Cl. Under "Kashkul." in *The Encyclopaedia of Islam*, edited by E. van Donzel, B. Lewis, and Ch. Pellat, vol. 4, 706. Leiden: Brill, 2009

Kāshāni, 'Ezz al-Din Mahmud. *Misbāh al-hedāya wa-meftāh al-kefāya*. Edited by J. D. Humā'i. Tehran: Homā, 1993.

Rumi, Jalāl al-Din. *Divan* [Collected Poetry]. Edited by B. Foruzanfar, republished edition edited by M. Darvish. Tehran: 'Elmi, 1987.

Schimmel, A. *Mystical Dimensions of Islam*. Chapel Hill: University of North Carolina Press, 1975.

Schimmel, A. *A Two-Colored Brocade: The Imagery of Persian Poetry*. Chapel Hill: University of North Carolina Press, 1992.

Stillman, Y. K., and N. A. Stillman. Under "Libās." In *En- cyclopaedia of Islam*, edited by C. E. Bosworth, E. van Donzel, B. Lewis, and Ch. Pellat, vol. 5, 747–750. 2nd ed. Leiden: Brill, 1986.

Veccia Valieri, L. Under "Ghadir Khumm." In *Encyclopaedia of Islam*, edited by B. Lewis, Ch. Pellat, and J. Schacht, vol. 2, 993–994. Leiden: Brill, 1965.

Yusofi, Gh.-H., ed. "Clothing." In *Encyclopaedia Iranica*.

Yusofi, Gh-H. "Clothing. XXVII. Historical Lexicon of Persian Clothing." Subentry of "Clothing" in *Encyclopaedia Iranica*, edited by Ehsan Yarshater, vol. 5, 719–870. Costa Mesa, CA: Mazda, 1986.

Ashgar Seyed-Gohrab

See also Iranian Regional Dress; Iranian Urban Dress; Reza Shah's Dress Reforms in Iran.

Snapshot: Islamic Pilgrimage Dress (Ihram)

Once a year, up to two million Muslims descend on the Holy City of Mecca, in Saudi Arabia, as part of the hajj, or pilgrimage. On entering Mecca, the pilgrims are said to be dressed in *ihram*. "Dressed in ihram" describes a pilgrim's state of mind, body, and spiritual purity while participating in the hajj, as well as the actual clothing worn by the pilgrims while they carry out the various rituals of the hajj.

The hajj is one of the Five Pillars of Islam, which are the foundation stones of Muslim life. The fifth pillar requires all physically and financially able adult Muslims to make the pilgrimage to Mecca once in their lifetime, as stated in the Qur'an 22:26–30. The hajj takes place from the eighth to the thirteenth day of the last month (called *Dhu al-Hijira*) of the Islamic calendar.

An imaginary boundary encircles Mecca, called the *miqat*. A pilgrim cannot cross this boundary without first entering the state of ihram and wearing ihram clothes. Once he or she starts wearing ihram, the pilgrim is called a *muhrim*. The places where most pilgrims change their status reflect the ancient pilgrimage routes by land from Syria and Yemen and by sea from Egypt and India and further east. This virtual boundary line around Mecca includes Zhal Hulaifa (north), Dhat Irq (northeast), Al-Djuhfa (northwest), Yalamlam (southeast), and Qarn al-Manazil (east). Pilgrims traveling by air are advised to don ihram either prior to stepping on board the airplane or at least one hour before arriving at the airspace over Mecca.

The process of being dressed in ihram involves various acts, including the cutting of one's finger- and toenails, removal of unwanted body hair, washing and combing the head hair, and trimming beards and mustaches, followed by a purification bath, shower, or *wudu* (ritual washing, normally carried out prior to saying one's prayers). Then, one dons ihram clothing. Men wear a special ihram outfit, two sheets of white cloth, while women can wear respectable and subdued versions of their ordinary clothing. Some women wear a special ihram version of their region's traditional dress. The pilgrim next says the *niyyah*, or statement of intention, publicly announcing that he or she intends to carry out a pilgrimage, after which come a number of specific prayers, resulting in the person being regarded as in a state of ihram.

The simple nature of the (male) ihram garments is intended to be a reminder of equality; no one is able to show his status and wealth by the type and quality of his clothes. The wearing of ihram is also meant to remind the pilgrim of his or her mortality, as the garments were often needed in the past as shrouds for pilgrims who died en route. Furthermore, ihram clothing is regarded as a reminder of how people will be on the day of resurrection, namely naked and barefoot. The virtuous will receive clothing.

IHRAM DRESS

The nature of men's ihram garments is laid down in several hadiths, or traditional sayings of the Prophet Mohammed.

There are various versions of these hadiths, but the basic idea is that men should not wear "normal" garments:

> Ibn Umar reported that the Prophet—may God bestow peace and blessing upon him—said that a man once asked him, what should a man wear in the state of ihram? He answered, "He shall not wear shirt (*qamis*), nor turban (*'imama*), nor trousers (*sirwal*), nor headgear, nor any dyed cloth; and if he cannot find footwear, then let him wear leather stockings (*khuff*), but cut off so that they may be lower than the ankles." (Bukhari, *The Sound*, 3:53).

The details regarding men's traditional ihram dress include measurements for the two pieces of white, unsewn cloth that

An engraving of Turkish pilgrims from *Personal Narrative of a Pilgrimage to Al-Madinah and Meccah* by Sir Richard Burton (London, 1893, vol. 2). While in a state of *ihram*, men are not allowed to wear sewn garments. This man is wearing the typical two-part garment with no seams. The woman's outfit is unusual in that it has a face veil in the form of a "basket" over her face; the veil is not touching her skin so it is "legitimate." Courtesy of Gillian Vogelsang-Eastwood.

they wear. One of these is usually about 250 by 600 inches (125 by 300 centimeters) in size (the *izar*), while the other is about 250 by 360 inches (125 by 180 centimeters) in size (the *rida*). They are usually made out of a material like cotton toweling, which absorbs perspiration well. In the early twenty-first century, the garments are normally white, but in the past some color was also included. The izar is wrapped around the lower part of the body, while the rida is used to cover the upper part.

While in a state of ihram, men are not allowed to wear sewn garments, underwear, gloves, or socks; to cover their faces or heads; or to use perfume on the body or on the ihram cloth. Scented soap should also be avoided, as well as shaving hair from any part of the body, combing or grooming the hair (in

case a hair is removed), cutting finger- or toenails, or killing lice or removing lice from the body or hair.

If a man is too poor to have special ihram clothing or is unable to purchase or acquire suitable lengths of cloth, then he may wear (baggy) trousers (sirwal) but not a shirt (qamis). Men are also allowed to wear a bag or belt (*himyan*) of some kind to keep valuable items safe. According to the hadiths, it is necessary to have the ankles and upper part of the feet uncovered, and slippers are the preferred form of footwear. In the twenty-first century, most pilgrims wear white plastic sandals. In the case of extreme weather conditions, a blanket or towel can be used to cover part of the body.

There are two basic ways for men to wear ihram garments. *Wishah* is the "normal" form of ihram. The izar is wrapped

A Muslim shaves a fellow pilgrim's head as part of the hajj pilgrimage, Mina, outside of Mecca, Saudi Arabia, 2005. The process of being dressed in *ihram* involves many acts, including the cutting of one's finger- and toenails, washing, and removal of unwanted hair. Abid Katib/Getty Images.

around the midriff to cover the body from the navel to the mid-calf or lower. The rida is draped around the pilgrim's shoulders to cover the upper body. Another way of wearing ihram is called *idtiba* and is worn during the Tawaf ul Qudom, when a pilgrim first enters the main mosque in Mecca (al-Masjid al-Haram) and carries out the seven-fold circumambulation (*tawaf*) of the Kaaba. In this form of dress, the pilgrim drapes one end of the rida over his left shoulder from back to front. The other end passes across his back, under his right arm, across his front, and is finally draped over his left shoulder, leaving his right shoulder uncovered. Idtiba is not observed in any other type of tawaf.

According to the hadiths, it is not necessary for a woman to wear special clothing while in a state of ihram, but she must wear clothing that covers the body completely, leaving only her face and hands exposed. According to some authors, however, gloves can be worn. Women are also allowed to wear jewelry during the hajj (it was regarded as unsafe to leave jewelry unattended).

Some women choose to wear the ordinary, everyday clothing that they would wear at home, usually in subdued colors. In addition, more and more women choose black Saudi-style clothing consisting of an outer garment called an *abayeh* and a long head scarf (*shaylah*). Another form is basically a white version of their traditional dress from home. Thus, a woman from Morocco might wear a kaftan, a woman from Egypt would wear a *galabiyeh*, an Iranian woman would wear a long dress (*libas*) with a white cloak (chador), and so on. A third form of hajj clothing for a woman consists of either normal clothing or a white hajj outfit worn underneath the two sheets normally regarded as male ihram dress. This is not common but is permitted as long as the hair and head are covered. Sometimes, these sheets are left white or, on other occasions, dyed a pale color. In the early twenty-first century, many women wear an international form of ihram consisting of a white dress worn with a long, white *khimar* (a garment like a large hood or snood) that simultaneously covers the head, shoulders, and upper body.

One of the more controversial aspects of women's ihram is the question whether a woman should wear a face veil or not. According to some hadiths, women should not be veiled. However, other hadiths state only that a woman should not have her hands covered nor have any cloth touching her face (which is not the same as saying she should not wear a face veil). For centuries, many discussions have arisen, with some scholars saying a woman must be veiled and others claiming that a woman may cover her face with something other than a veil, providing a screen between unrelated men and herself.

Two basic views emerge: (1) that a face veil is not necessary at all, as all pilgrims should be in a state of mental and physical purity, and (2) that a face veil is necessary if a woman is likely to come into contact with men who are outside her immediate family. As a result, some women decide to wear face veils, while other women choose not to. In most cases, the face veil chosen is a plain, black *niqab*.

Going on hajj and being dressed in ihram is important for most Muslims, as it forms a direct link between the millions who have carried out the hajj over the centuries and early-twenty-first-century Muslims from all over the world. In addition, it underpins the ideal of making all (male) pilgrims equal, no matter where they came from or what their status in their home countries. Yet ihram is also one of those rare instances in dress history when the rules surrounding a particular set of clothing are much stricter for men than for women. As a result, women's ihram dress has developed a wider range of forms than its male counterpart, and these forms can be seen to represent individual, ethnic, and national ideas.

REFERENCES AND FURTHER READING

Amin, M. *Pilgrimage to Mecca*. London: Alan Hutchinson, 1978.

Arberry, A. J. *The Koran Interpreted*. Oxford: Oxford University Press, 1964.

Peters, F. E. *The Hajj*. Princeton, NJ: Princeton University Press, 1994.

Gillian Vogelsang-Eastwood

See also Snapshot: Trade, Textiles, Dress, and the Hajj.

Snapshot: Muharram and Dress

National and religious festivals serve as visible signs of renewal, initiation rituals, reenactments of the oath of the community, and reminders of particular identities. To indicate these aspects of a festival, people dress themselves in special attire, depending on the nature of the festival. Muharram is one of the most eminent festivals of the Shiites.

Muharram, the most striking and visible religious festival in Shiite societies, takes place during the first ten days of the Islamic month of Muharram. It commemorates the martyrdom of the third Shiite imam, the Prophet's grandson Imam Hoseyn, and his followers on the plain of Karbala in what is Iraq in the early twenty-first century. To mark this tragic event, the Shiites unfurl black, green, and red banners on the street, black and green being the colors of the Prophet's family, while red heralds martyrdom. The streets and the walls and columns of mosques and other places where the main commemoration events take place are commonly hung with large pieces of black cloth, many bearing elegiac poems to remind people of various scenes of Imam Hoseyn's tragic death.

During the ten days, especially the last two days (*tāsu'ā* and *'āshurā*), people wear black dress to express their sorrow. There are various types of dress: Many participants are content with a black T-shirt or shirt, but there are also shirts made especially for this event, with an opening over the upper chest so that the grief-stricken participants can beat their chests. When the beating on the chest is finished, the upper part of the shirt is fastened with buttons. The same dress is used for various forms of flagellation, including *zanjir-zani* (beating one's upper back and shoulder with chains). Women wear a long chador from top to toe, but it is open at the face. Some women also wear a black face veil over their chadors. During the festival, people sprinkle rose water over the participants in the events. Some of these participants place a piece of clay on their hair and, in some cases, on their black shirt, as a sign of intense grief.

Another visible mark of Muharram is the so-called *kafanpush*, meaning "wearing a shroud": Conservative men wearing white shrouds march in the streets, shouting their regret that they were not present at the battle between Imam Hoseyn and his enemies. Thus they show their readiness to sacrifice their lives for Imam Hoseyn. During the Islamic Revolution and also during the eight-year war between Iran and Iraq, this phenomenon was used in a political context. The kafanpush saw the Pahlavi monarchy and later Saddam Hussein as the enemies of the imam (who is personified by Imam Khomeini in the early twenty-first century) and sought an opportunity to revenge Imam Hoseyn's blood. Paradoxically, a martyr killed in a holy war does not need to be washed or wrapped in a shroud but should be buried in his bloodstained garments; although dirt and blood make the body impure, a martyr's body is regarded as ritually pure due to the circumstances of his or her death.

Another visible change of dress that one sees during the Muharram ceremony is the "water carrier" or *saghgh'*. This is the dress that children wear during the last two days of the ceremony. These children wear a white Arabic garment with a white head covering (*keffiyeh*) and a rope circlet (*'aqal*) and have a water jug and a cup in their hands. They pour water for the thirsty participants. In Muharram ceremonies, water reminds the people of the intense thirst inflicted on Hoseyn and his family for ten days, as they were kept back from the banks of the Euphrates.

One of the important parts of the Muharram festival is the passion play. Although passion plays are not limited to events relating to the martyrdom of Imam Hoseyn, the most striking plays are those that depict this theme. In these passion plays, clothes are of special importance for the actors. Most designs are inspired by Arabic garb combined with Persian military dress from Safavid times (1501–1722), but little attention is paid to historical authenticity. One painting of such a play includes a European ambassador who appears in seventh-century Damascus wearing modern French military dress with a chapeau claque (a form of top hat).

The actor who plays the role of Imam Hoseyn usually wears a long *qaba*, a sleeved robe, slit in front, with either white or black buttons. Over this qaba, he wears an *aba*, an off-the-shoulders mantle, either green or black. Since black and green are the colors marking the descendants of the Prophet, Hoseyn and the rest of the holy family wear black or green turbans. As footwear, Hoseyn wears boots during the battle but changes into slippers when he returns from the battle.

Protagonists are easily distinguished from the antagonists by the color of their dress. While the other protagonists wear the same type of dress as Imam Hoseyn, avoiding the color red, the antagonist appears in medieval Persian military uniform, consisting of boots, trousers, and a tunic or chain mail. The antagonist represents the Sunnite Umayyad ruler Yazid, who was preoccupied with worldly matters, covetousness, and wealth. The opulence of the enemy contrasts sharply with the sober lifestyle of Imam Hoseyn and his followers. The dress of the antagonist is usually of expensive cloth, consisting of a long qaba made of fabrics such as brocade. Over this qaba, both the antagonist and the protagonists wear chain mail fastened by a belt. On his head, the antagonist wears a golden crown or a red turban, but when they go into battle, this is replaced by a helm, which is usually decorated with a red or green plume. In sum, the outfit of the antagonist is usually very expensive, representing the luxury of the Umayyad caliph. Sometimes, one sees dresses that are richly studded with pearls and precious stones, worn with a golden crown.

Female protagonists wear black veils covering their entire body, sometimes with a face veil over their chador. In several episodes of the passion play, the sister of Imam Hoseyn unveils herself as a protest or Yazid tears off her veil in public. In Persian history, there have been various instances in which women have unveiled themselves in public as a protest against injustice. Episodes regarding a woman who is forcefully unveiled appear in written sources, but during a performance, such a thing is unthinkable; traditionally, men played the part of women, thus resolving the difficulty.

A group of men beating their chests as a sign of grief during Muharram, the month of mourning for Hoseyn, grandson of the Prophet Mohammed, Tehran, Iran, 1890s. Ali is one of the main figures in the Shiite sect of Islam. The man in the middle is showing his extreme grief and faith by mutilating himself with hooks and heavy objects. Photograph by Antoin Sevruguin. Textile Research Centre, Leiden.

The color symbolism is important. White, green, and black belong to the protagonists, while other colors, especially red, belong to the antagonist. Although the overall form and color symbolism of the dress have remained essentially the same, there has been a development from a sober to a more luxurious appearance. Especially in the second half of the nineteenth century, under the influence of European theater, Shah Nasir al-Din built a special large theater in Tehran for the performance of passion plays; at the same time, the dress and properties became richer and the popularity of passion plays increased. During the Pahlavi dynasty (1925–1979), the popularity of passion plays ebbed, and they were more often performed in theaters than in the streets on open-air stages. This led to a more theatrical performance with elaborate and expensive outfits. After the Islamic Revolution of 1978–1979, the passion play was again widely performed in streets, mosques, and large tents, while the theatrical presentation has also continued. Performances are sometimes broadcast on national television.

Supernatural beings also take part in this ceremony. Angels appear wearing dresses embroidered with gold and other precious stones. They wear on their heads a wreath, on the front of which a transparent veil is attached. The veil in this case symbolizes their supernatural descent.

REFERENCES AND FURTHER READING

Ayoub, M. *Redemptive Suffering in Islam: A Study of the Devotional Aspects of 'Ashura' in Twelver Shi'ism.* The Hague: Mouton, 1978.

Chelkowski, P. J. *Ta'ziyeh: Ritual and Drama in Iran.* New York: New York University Press, 1979.

Haar, J.G.J. ter. "Ta'ziya: Ritual Theater from Shiite Iran." In *Theater Intercontinental: Forms, Functions, Correspondences*, edited by C. C. Barfoot and C. Bordewijk, 155–174. Amsterdam: Rodopi, 1993.

Ashgar Seyed-Gohrab

Snapshot: Islam and Islamically Correct Dress (Hijab)

The meaning of the terms *al-ziyy al-Islami* (Islamic clothing or dress) and *hijab* (Islamically correct dress) has altered somewhat since the late 1980s. What remains unchanged is the code of principles that underlies "Islamic" public dress and behavior. As both a term and a dress form, Islamic dress came into common usage in the mid-1970s, when male and female college youth in urban centers of Egypt began to appear in what they called "Islamic dress," a practice that gradually spread internally in Egypt across cities and social strata and elsewhere in the Arab and Islamic world. This phenomenon began following the October or Ramadan War of 1973 as a prominent manifestation of an Islamic movement born out of an existing climate of religiousness that had developed in Egypt, among Copts and Muslims alike, in the wake of the 1967 conflict between Egypt and Israel.

The manifestation of the emergent Islamic movement in the form of a new type of dress and associated behavior among male and female college youth took society and even the religious authorities by surprise. By the beginning of the twenty-first century, the numbers of Muslim women around the world wearing some form of head covering and long clothing increased across the different social strata. To many in the West, this phenomenon seemed too assertive and hence threatening, with some political observers writing about an encroaching Islam.

AL-ZIYY AL-ISLAMI AND DRESS AS CODE

Men started to wear sandals, baggy trousers, a loose-top shirt in off-white or, alternatively (and preferably), a white *galabi-yeh* (a long, loose dress), and a white or red-checked *keffiyeh* (head and neck scarf). They also grew a *lihya* (a full beard trimmed short). Women wore hijab, which consisted of a *jilbab* (an ankle-length, long-sleeved, loose-fitting dress) and a *khimar* (a head covering that covers the hair and extends low to the forehead, comes under the chin to conceal the neck, and falls down over the chest and back). During the first decade of the movement, women preferred solid colors such as beige, brown, navy, burgundy, or black. The *muhajjabat* (women wearing hijab) engaged normally in daily affairs and public life. Behaviorally, people tended to lower their gaze in cross-sex public encounters and refrain from adornments that would draw attention to their bodies.

The youth who adopted this new dress form referred to it as *al-ziyy al-Islami*, but in the twenty-first century, it is more commonly called *al-hijab*. It was based on an idealized construction of a vision presumed to have originated in seventh-century Arabia in the newly formed Islamic community. This vision derives its *shariya* (religious legitimacy) from Islamic sources and precedents. The resulting construction, however, is a contemporary innovation and does not represent a return to a traditional dress form. Some Muslim observers and scholars find shar'iyya for Islamic dress in the historical and scriptural sources, but others do not. This tends to lead to opposing camps of rejection of versus apologia for this dress style.

A distinction must be made between adopting a dress form derived literally from historical or religious precedents and appropriating an underlying code that is grounded in Islamic sources to legitimize a new vision of the dress and behavior to be adopted in public. Evidence shows that hijab's shar'iyya derives not from exact prescriptions in history or religion but from a general code underlying overall public behavior and dress that has a basis in Islamic scriptural sources.

While convenient, using the idea of modesty not only oversimplifies but can also be misleading. Islam has no negative associations with respect to religious behavior and sexuality. It comfortably accommodates both and hence has never adopted Christian-grounded ideas and institutions of celibacy and gender seclusion. A Muslim woman's dress is intended to conceal her body when in public. It does not prescribe her seclusion from ordinary social activities or control her legitimate sexual life. That is, in Islam, austerity in dress and reserve in public behavior are not accompanied by withdrawal or seclusion, and there is no contradiction between being religious and being sexual. Sex is to be enjoyed in socially approved marriages. However, outside marriage the behavior between men and women must be desexualized.

HIJAB: ETYMOLOGY, MEANING, AND USE IN THE QUR'AN

Hijab is not about seclusion, shame, or deference; it is about sanctity, reserve, and privacy. The term *hijab* has cultural and linguistic roots that are integral to Islamic (and Arab) culture as a whole. *Hijab* is derived from the root *h-j-b*; its verbal form *hajaba* translates as "to veil, seclude, screen, conceal, form a separation, mask." *Hijab* translates as "cover, wrap, curtain, veil, screen, partition." The same word is used to refer to amulets carried on one's person (particularly for children or persons in a vulnerable state) to protect against harm. Another derivative, *hajib*, means "eyebrow (protector of the eye)" and was also used during the caliphal periods for the official who screened the caliph from an unwanted audience and applicants wishing an audience with the caliph.

Hijab is commonly equated with the veil, *veil* being an easy English word (along with its variants in European languages, such as *voile* in French) to use when referring to Arab women's head and face covers and wraps. *Veil* has no single-word equivalent in Arabic, in which many different terms are used for diverse items of women's and men's clothing that vary by region, era, lifestyle, social stratum, stage in the life cycle, and gender. Some covers and wraps are worn by both sexes, and others have multiple usages and are manipulated flexibly to cover the face when situations require it. The term *veil* oversimplifies a complex phenomenon, particularly because it is associated with its presumed correlate, seclusion, which does not apply to Arab culture.

It is possible that the term *hijab* had a well-defined meaning by the ninth century C.E., when it had already become part of the Arabian Arabic vocabulary. Other terms were used to refer to the veil itself, but the phrase *darb* ("adopting") *al-hijab* was used in Arabia in discourse about the seclusion of the Prophet's wives. Two suras (chapters of the Qur'an), *al-Nur* (24) and *al-Ahzab* (33), are the most widely cited as the Islamic basis for wearing hijab:

> And say to the believing men that they should lower their gaze and guard their genitals [30] [and] say to the believing women that they should lower their gaze and guard their genitals, draw their khimar to cover their cleavage [breasts], and not display their beauty, except that which has to appear, except to their husbands, their fathers, their husbands' fathers, their sons, their husbands' sons, their brothers or their brothers' sons, or their sisters' sons, or their women, or the slaves, or eunuchs or children under age; and they should not strike their feet to draw attention to their hidden beauty. O ye believers turn to God, that ye may attain bliss [31]. (Qur'an 24:30–31).

Several points can be drawn from this text: (1) The Arabic notions of lowering the gaze and covering the genitals are central to the code; and (2) men are mentioned first as having to abide by these two prescriptions, to control their gaze at women and suppress their passion and forwardness when interacting with "strange" women, potential sexual partners, or spouses. Reference in sura 24 is to the khimar (head covering) in the general context of public behavior and comportment by both sexes. Ayah 24:31 is widely cited in scholarly works and often read in isolation from the rest of the verse, which biases the reading against women, since by itself it implies that women are singled out for "reserve" and "restraint," whereas in fact ayah 30 addresses men first.

According to the hadiths, the Prophet Mohammed paid a great deal of attention to a dress code for Muslims in the emerging community, with a specific focus on Muslim men's clothing and bodily modesty during prayer. Men especially are enjoined to cover their genitals during worship. In comparison, there are few references to women's body covering. One such reference, al-Ahzab in sura 33, enjoins the Prophet's wives, daughters, and all Muslim women to don their jilbab so they are easily recognized and protected from molestation or harassment: "O Prophet tell your wives, daughters and believing women to put on their jilbabs so they are recognized and thus not harmed" (33:59).

Another passage concerns the privacy of Mohammed's wives: "O believers, enter not the dwellings of the Prophet, unless invited … And when you ask of his wives anything, ask from behind a hijab. That is purer for your hearts and for their hearts" (33:53). There was a need to protect their privacy by regulating the flow of visitors and the comportment of the men who entered the women's quarters. Here, it seems *hijab* is being used to refer to a partition or curtain and relates to a sacred divide or separation between two worlds or two spaces: deity and mortals, good and evil, light and dark, believers and nonbelievers, aristocracy and commoners. The phrase *min wara' al-hijab* ("from behind hijab") emphasizes the element

of separation/partition. When women's clothing is mentioned, the terms used are *jilbab* and *khimar*, whereas neither *hijab* nor *niqab* is used. *Niqab* and *lithmah* are terms that unambiguously refer to face coverings.

In the Qur'an, the hadiths, and the contemporary Islamic movement, Muslim men and women are unambiguously enjoined to carry themselves in public with a sense of reserve and restraint. Exhibitionist public comportment, through behavior, dress, voice, or body movement, is frowned upon.

SOME MODERN INTERPRETATIONS

The contemporary Islamic dress code is not simply about clothing. Rather, it symbolizes a renewal of cultural identity with traditional ideals and values. Hence the hijab worn by Muslim women in Arab, Muslim, European, or U.S. societies appears to be largely about identity, as well as privacy of space and body. Encoded in the Islamic dress style, particularly the hijab, are ideas about public appearance and demeanor that reaffirm an Islamic identity and an embodiment of an Islamic morality of reserve, rejecting Western materialism, consumerism, commercialism, and individualistic values. Veiling functions as a vehicle for resistance—against imposed measures, colonial occupation, Israeli occupation of Palestine and the legacy of the French colonial occupation of Algeria, current global economic conditions, and the U.S. and British invasions of Muslim and Arab countries, such as Afghanistan, Iraq, and Palestine.

While functioning as a symbol of militancy in some parts of the Arab and Islamic world, hijab is perceived as a threat to secularism in France and elsewhere in Europe, where in places the wearing of head scarves (hijab) and face veils in schools has been banned or at the very least challenged, actions fraught with anti-Islamic implications and contradictions about freedom of expression. It is no accident that colonizing powers as well as local state authorities consistently used the topic of the veiling of women to distract attention from other topics when things were going wrong economically and politically, according to the social anthropologist Z. Mir-Hosseini. In Western feminist discourse, the veil is politically charged with connotations of the inferior other, whereas to many young Muslim women, hijab represents an identity of choice and freedom of expression.

The pull between historical or traditional clothing and Islamic dress is particularly relevant to the Khalij or Gulf countries in the early twenty-first century. The most common dress form for women in the Gulf region is the historical-traditional form, namely the black *abayeh*, combined with a head covering and often, but not always, a face covering. However, another form worn by women from neighboring Arab, African, and Asian countries, such as Egypt, Indonesia, Iraq, Palestine, Pakistan, and Sudan, consists of a head covering, in the form of a head scarf in a solid color or print, and a long-sleeved shirt or blouse with an ankle-length skirt. This ensemble is also referred to as *hijab*. In terms of the purely physical covering of head and body, both the abayeh ensemble and hijab can comfortably "fit" with readings of the Islamic code. But ironically both can and do violate the code of modesty at the behavioral level, since some fashionable forms of hijab are eye-catching, and hence their Islamicness becomes questionable.

REFERENCES AND FURTHER READING

Chatty, Dawn. "The Burqa Face Cover: An Aspect of Dress in Southeastern Arabia." In *Languages of Dress in the Middle East*, edited by Nancy Lindisfarne-Tapper and Bruce Ingham, 149–177. London: Curzon, 1997.

El Guindi, F. "Die Rückkehr zum Schleier: Vom unaufhalt-samen Siegeszug eines konservativen Symbols. Nahost in Flammen." *Der Monat* 285 (1982): 165–178.

El Guindi, F. "Veiled Activism: Egyptian Women in the Contemporary Islamic Movement." *Peuples Mediterranéans (Femmes de la Mediterranée)* 22–23 (1983): 79–89.

El Guindi, F. *Veil: Modesty, Privacy and Resistance*. Oxford: Berg, 2003. (Originally published in 1999.)

El Guindi, F. *By Noon Prayer: The Rhythm of Islam*. Oxford: Berg, 2008.

Harb, Tal'at. *Tarbiyet al-Mar'a wa al-hijab* [Socialization of women and the veil]. Cairo: Matba'at al-Manar, 1905. (Originally published in 1899.)

Mernissi, Fatima. *Beyond the Veil: Male-Female Dynamics in a Modern Muslim Society*. Cambridge, MA: Schlenkman, 1975.

Mir-Hosseini, Z. "Women and Politics in Post-Khomeini Iran: Divorce, Veiling and Emergent Feminist Voices." In *Women and Politics in the Third World*, edited by A. Haleh, 142–170. London and New York: Routledge, 1996.

Nelson, C. *Doria Shafiq the Feminist: A Woman Apart*. Cairo: American University in Cairo Press, 1996.

Rashid, Fatima. "al-Hijab." *Tarqiyat al-Mar'a* 1, no. 6 (1908).

Sha'rawi, H. *Huda Sharawi: Muthakkirat Ra'idat al-Mar'a al-Arabiyya al-Hadith* [Memoirs of Huda Sharawy, leader of modern Arab women]. Introduction by Amina al-Said. *Kitab al-Hilal, Silsila Shahriyya*. Cairo: Dar al-Hilal, 1981.

Fadwa El Guindi

See also Dress from the Gulf States: Bahrain, Kuwait, Qatar, United Arab Emirates; Face Veils; volume 1, Africa: Egypt: Historical Dress; Dress in Egypt in the Twentieth Century.

Laws of Differentiation

A significant development in the history of Islamic dress is a series of laws that required non-Muslims living within Islamic states to wear distinguishing clothing. These are generally known as *laws of differentiation* (*ghiyar*). They were mainly aimed at the so-called *dhimmi*, or tolerated non-Muslim subjects, namely, Jews, Christians, and Zoroastrians. The term *dhimmi* does not include other, polytheistic groups, such as Hindus.

LAWS OF DIFFERENTIATION IN THEORY

Although no laws of differentiation directly relating to non-Muslim clothing are found in the Qur'an, some hadiths (sayings and doings attributed to the Prophet Mohammed) have been interpreted as indicating that such practices did exist. In particular, the Prophet is described as having said in one hadith, "The Jews and Christians do not dye [their gray hair and beard], so oppose yourselves to them." This hadith has been interpreted by some to mean that every facet of a Muslim's life and behavior should be different from a non-Muslim's.

Although there is no clear evidence that the Prophet intended such a broad meaning, he did command believers to distinguish themselves from unbelievers in a number of ways. For example, 'Abdullah b. 'Amr ibn al-As said, "God's Messenger (may peace be upon him) saw me wearing two clothes dyed in saffron, whereupon he said: 'These are the clothes of the non-believers, so do not wear them.'" On another occasion, the Prophet was reported to have prohibited the wearing of silk, gold, and (according to some accounts) silver, saying, "Those are for them [the unbelievers] in this world, and for you [or for us] in the Hereafter." Another hadith reports that the Prophet said, "The difference between us and the polytheists is that we wear turbans over caps." It is clear from these accounts that shortly after the introduction of Islam (mid-seventh century C.E.), when this new religion was both spreading rapidly and responding to many challenges, the Prophet Mohammed was anxious for Muslims to distinguish themselves by their appearance and dress from non-Muslims. However, he tried to achieve this not by forcing non-Muslims to modify their attire but by encouraging Muslims to regulate theirs. The Prophet is not known to have called for non-Muslims to wear special clothes or insignia, even in the treaties he concluded with them following decisive military victories.

The laws of differentiation in the form in which they later came to be known are traditionally attributed to the second caliph, 'Umar b. al-Khattab (r. 634–644), although some authors believe that it was another caliph, 'Umar b. 'abd al-'Aziz ('Umar II), who was responsible for the first Muslim laws of differentiation.

The version attributed to 'Umar b. al-Khattab is said to have been included in a peace treaty concluded in about 634 between the Muslims and Syrian Christians. The Christians undertook to live by certain conditions in exchange for being granted safe passage and protection. This treaty is known as the "Covenant of 'Umar" or "Covenant of the dhimmi." The first author known to have ascribed sumptuary laws to the caliph 'Umar is Yaqub ibn Ibrahim al-Ansari, better known as Abu Yusuf (731/732–798 C.E.), who helped spread the influence of the Hanafi school of Islamic law through his writings. In his *Kitab al-Kharaj*, he wrote,

> When it is time to collect the *jizyah* [poll tax], the neck of each taxpayer should be sealed until collection has been completed; then, if they wish, the seals can be broken, as did 'Uthman b. Hunayf. Not one among them will be permitted to resemble Muslims by his dress, mount, or appearance. Instead of a belt, every one of them must tie a zunnar [girdle] like coarse string around his waist. Their qalansuwa [cap] must be quilted. The pommel on their saddles must be made of wood. Their shoes must have twisted thongs.

The earliest complete version of the Covenant of 'Umar is preserved in the book *Siraj al-Muluk* by Abu Bakr Muhammad ibn al-Walid al-Tartushi (1059–1127 C.E.), a famous Muslim jurist from Tortosa in Muslim Spain. It includes various stipulations with respect to dress: Non-Muslims were not allowed to imitate Muslims by wearing the *qalansuwa* (cap), turban, or sandals or even by parting their hair. Non-Muslims had to shave the front of their heads and dress in a Christian, Jewish, or other manner appropriate to their religion and tie a special leather belt or girdle around their waists called a *zunnar*.

LAWS OF DIFFERENTIATION IN PRACTICE

Whether or not 'Umar b. al-Khattab did formulate the original laws of sartorial differentiation remains open to debate. What is clear, however, is that the region's history shows a steady pattern of arbitrary and indeed erratic implementation of such laws. According to Abu Yusuf, for example, 'Umar II (r. 717–720) wrote to one of his governors that

> no Jew or Christian may be allowed to ride upon a saddle, but must use a packsaddle; and let none of their women-folk use a padded saddle, but only a packsaddle. … No Christian may wear the qaba' [gown], nor silk garments, nor the 'asb [Yemenite cloth]. It has been reported to me that several of the Christians under your jurisdiction have returned to wearing turbans, that they no longer wear mintaqs [girdles] at their waists, and that they let their hair grow freely without cutting it.

In another early source, *Tarikh al-Kabir* by the Sunni Islamic scholar Ibn 'Asakir al-Dimashqi al-Shafi'i al-Ash'ari (1105–1176 C.E.), it is written that 'Umar II made the following demands of the cities of Syria, specifically, that Christians had to part their forelocks, that they were not allowed to wear an outer garment called a *qaba*, that they were not allowed to appear in public without a girdle made of leather (*zunnar*), and that they could not wear the *taylasan* (head cloth), trousers with a waist drawstring (*tikka*), or indeed sandals with straps.

The reign of 'Umar II was short-lived, as were the laws of differentiation he promulgated. However, in the centuries that followed, similar laws were passed by other Muslim rulers. In 807, for example, as conflicts erupted on the Byzantine border, the Abbasid caliph Harun al-Rashid (r. 786–809) ordered churches in the region to be demolished, and he wrote to al-Sindi b. Shahik ordering him to force the "protected peoples" (dhimmis) in the "City of Peace" (Baghdad) to distinguish their general appearance from that of Muslims by their dress and the animals they rode on (non-Muslims were supposed to use donkeys or walk).

Once again, the effects of this decree must not have lasted, because in 850 a successor, the caliph Al-Mutawakkil 'Alā Allāh Ja'far ibn al-Mu'tasim (r. 847–861), imposed far more severe regulations on Christians. He decreed that Christians and other dhimmis had to wear honey-colored (that is, yellow) taylasans and zunnar and place two buttons on their caps (qalansuwas), if they wore one; the cap also had to be of a different color from that worn by Muslims. In addition, the slaves of dhimmis had to wear two yellow patches on their outer garments. One patch was placed on the front (chest) and the other on the back of the garment. Each patch had to be four fingers' span across. If a dhimmi wore a turban, it had to be yellow. Dhimmi women had to wear a yellow wrap when in public. Al-Mutawakkil also ordered that the slaves of Christians had to wear the zunnar and prohibited them from wearing decorative versions of it. About four years later, he further ordered "that the dhimmis affix two yellow sleeves to their outer cloaks," according to Abu Ja'far Muhammad ibn Jarir al-Tabari.

Over the following centuries, such regulations were proclaimed in Baghdad, Mosul, Damascus, and other cities of Southwest Asia. While similar in spirit, they differed significantly in their details. Which garments were permitted or disallowed, for instance, and what colors non-Muslims were required to wear or prohibited from wearing, changed from edict to edict. Moreover, the intent of the laws also varied. Although early authors like Abu Yusuf and Ibn 'Abd al-Hakam (d. 871) stressed that such laws were meant only to help distinguish Muslims from non-Muslims, in some cases the laws were deliberately used to humiliate dhimmis. Rather tenuous justification for this was found in a Qur'anic verse: "Fight against those who do not believe in God, nor in the Last Day, nor hold that forbidden which has been forbidden by God and His Messenger, nor follow the religion of truth, be they among those given the Scripture, until they pay the *jizyah* by their own hand and have been humbled" (Qur'an 9:29). In this verse, the Arabic word *saghirun* can be translated as "humbled," "subdued," or "humiliated"; it was interpreted by some as a command to routinely debase the "People of the Book," notably the Jews and Christians.

Thus, Ibn Qayyim al-Jawziyya (1292/1293–1349/1350) wrote, quoting the Prophet:

"Humbling and humiliation are for those who disagree with my command." And the people of the *dhimma* have the greatest disagreement with his command and are the most disobedient to his words; therefore they deserve to be humiliated by being distinguished from the attire of the Muslims, whom God has honored for their obedience to Him and to His Messenger. Thus, He has humbled and humiliated and lowered them, so that the sign of disgrace has been placed upon them. Hence, they are distinguished by their attire and its meaning.... Abu al-Qasim said: "They are prevented from wearing the turban or using it." Indeed, the turbans are the crowns of Arabs. And He has honored them over all other nations. And the Messenger of God (prayers and blessings of God be upon him) wore it and so did his companions after him. Thus, it is the attire of the Arabs in the ancient past and the attire of the Messenger of God (prayers and blessings of God be upon him) and the companions. Indeed, it is the attire of Islam. ... They said: "Turbans are not among the attire of the Children of Israel but they are among the attire of the Arabs." And Abu al-Qasim said: "It is not possible for the *dhimmi* to be turbaned, because there is no honor for him in the Abode of Islam, and [turbans] are not among his attire."

The humiliation aspect was especially pronounced in Central Asia and Iran, where another Qur'anic verse was very broadly interpreted to provide legitimacy for some harsh rules: "O ye who believe! Truly those who ascribe divinity to aught beside God are unclean" (9:28). Though the word *mushrikun* is usually used to mean polytheists and idolaters, certain Shiite theologians took it to mean all non-Muslims. This meant that a dhimmi's very person came to be considered impure and therefore polluting. This was used to justify their oppression and degradation, not just to argue that they should be easy to identify and avoid. For example, in 1892, the Shiite clergy in Hamadan imposed twenty-two conditions on the Jewish inhabitants of the city, including the following: Jews were forbidden to leave their houses when it rained or snowed. Jewish women were not allowed to wear face veils when in public, and they had to wear a two-colored *izar* (mantle). Jewish men were not allowed to wear fine clothes. All clothes had to be made from blue cotton fabric. Jews were not allowed to wear matching shoes. Finally, every Jew was obliged to wear a piece of red cloth on his chest.

The prohibition on Jews venturing into the street during rain or snow was to prevent their impurity from running off and contaminating Muslims. As for the prohibition on the veiling of Jewish women, it was to deprive them of what, in that time and place, passed for honor.

LAWS OF DIFFERENTIATION: ECONOMIC AND OTHER NONRELIGIOUS ASPECTS

In contrast to the situation in Central Asia and Iran, such laws of differentiation were unevenly used in the neighboring Ottoman Empire. When they did become severe, the reason tended to be less due to religious zeal and more the need to find a scapegoat to distract the common people in times of social and economic crisis. In a number of cases, laws of differentiation also provided the means for local administrators to extort money from wealthy non-Muslim communities. Thus, when in 1775 the Ottoman governor imposed restrictions on dhimmi attire in Aleppo, local Christian leaders were able to reach an agreement with him, whereupon he withdrew his order in return for a large payment. Such events recurred time and again, with the periodic clothing

Engraving after Jean-Baptiste Vanmour of an Ottoman Muslim wearing a turban, 1714. Shortly after the introduction of Islam (mid-seventh century c.e.), Mohammed was anxious for Muslims to distinguish themselves from non-Muslims by their appearance and dress. One of their distinguishing items of clothing was the turban. Art and Architecture Collection, Miriam and Ira D. Wallach Division of Art, Prints and Photographs, New York Public Library, Astor, Lenox and Tilden Foundations.

restrictions being little more than pretexts for officials to exact money.

It is worth noting that in a letter written around 1454 to the Jews of Germany, Rabbi Isaac Zarfati (who had recently settled in the Ottoman Empire) said, "Here you are allowed to wear the most precious garments. In Christendom, on the contrary, ye dare not even venture to clothe your children in red or in blue, according to your taste, without exposing them to the insult of being beaten black and blue, or kicked red and green, and therefore are ye condemned to go about meanly clad in sad-coloured raiment" (quoted in Kobler). This suggests that laws of differentiation had lapsed at the time, which corresponds to the reign of Sultan Mehmed II (the Conqueror, r. 1444–1446, 1451–1481).

In contrast, a *ferman* (imperial edict) dated 1580 and issued under Sultan Murad III (r. 1574–1595) suggests that certain restrictions on the attire of non-Muslims were present at some point during Mehmed II's reign. In particular, he noted that his ancestor Sultan Mehmed Khan told Jews to wear red hats; in addition, their slippers and house boots had to be black, while their cloaks were to be made out of twilled cotton. Christians were forced to wear black hats. Sultan Murad III used these decrees as a precedent to force Jews and Christians not to wear turbans; instead, Jews had to wear red hats, while Christians wore black ones—according to the old custom—as well as black slippers and house boots. Once again, cloaks had to be made of a cotton twill material.

Three years earlier, another edict had sought to impose clothing restrictions, because Jews and Christians living in Istanbul were no longer wearing the old style of clothes, muslins, and shoes but were instead wearing turbans of fine, colored muslins, as well as white and even red shoes, and engaging in conduct and behavior that were too similar to those of Muslims. These "new" trends were disapproved of, and edicts were introduced to force a return to the old ways.

Such official reprimands could be interpreted, as they routinely are by some modern anti-Islam writers, as proof that Muslims have historically oppressed peoples of other faiths. However, it is much more reasonable to see, in their steady recurrence and repetition, a clear indication that the restrictions remained for the most part unenforced. Authorities addressed incoming complaints, whether motivated by religious conviction or less noble sentiments, by dutifully reiterating past prohibitions. But it would appear that little changed in the lives of Ottoman Jews and Christians.

Official documents also provide interesting details about the nonreligious aspects of laws of differentiation. In an imperial edict issued in 1568, for example, economic concerns are very much in evidence:

> To the judge (qadi) of Istanbul: You have sent a letter to my august threshold informing me that Jewish and Christian men and women among the unbelievers residing in the capital of Istanbul have been wearing fine fringed broadcloth and purchasing fine muslin and are wrapping muslin [around their heads] like cavalry officers and such, and are wearing kaftans [long gowns] of atlas [satin made from silk] and kutnu and other fabrics, and fine pants, and houseboots and slippers and shoes of the kind worn by Muslims; that for this reason, the prices of muslin and broadcloth and fabric and shoes have risen and that they are no longer affordable; and that unbelievers should not wear Muslim dress. Now, my detailed imperial edict on the subject of the attire of unbelievers was issued previously. I hereby command that when you receive the present communication, you enforce my past commands, and that from now on you do not permit unbelievers, whether Jews or Christians or others, to wear fine garments as described above and contravening my previous orders. (quoted in Altinay 1988a)

Even in the Ottoman context, the issue of humiliation sometimes came up, albeit rarely. This was especially true during the oppressive reign of Sultan Murad IV (r. 1623–1640), whose imperial edict dated 1631 stated:

> Whereas it is an important canonical and legal requirement of religion that unbelievers should not ride horses, nor wear sable furs or caps, nor don Frankish brocades or atlas, and that their womenfolk should not go around in the style and manner of Muslims, nor wear Persian feråces [overcoats], and that overall their clothes and conduct should be demeaning and humiliating; it has been brought to my exalted attention and has been made known at my august threshold that this has been neglected for quite a long time, and with the permission of judges, unbelievers and Jews have been going about in marketplaces on horseback and wearing fineries, sable furs, and sumptuous clothes, and when they come face to face with Muslims in the marketplace, they do not get off the sidewalk, and both they and their womenfolk have more majesty than do Muslims, and they are not being demeaned and humiliated as is required by canon law. (quoted in Altinay 1988b)

This was the exception, however, rather than the rule. Over time, many non-Muslims adapted the concept of laws of differentiation to suit themselves and their communities. Thus, the writings of the Ottoman Rabbi Samuel de Medina (1505–1589) indicate that former immigrants from Spain and Portugal were prospering economically and that, as a result, wealthier Jewish women had started to wear luxurious garments and precious jewelry. The rabbis and lay leaders realized that such displays of affluence could herald danger for the Jewish communities and so they enacted decrees concerning the dress of their own women.

In one case, for example, "a decree was promulgated that forbade Jewish women to wear silk garments except of black color," according to Morris S. Goodblatt. While some of this self-restraint was no doubt out of concern not to offend Muslim sensibilities, other factors could also have been at play. This is indicated by the fact that, as the region began to modernize, some more Orthodox Jews held that changing one's mode of dress was an act of apostasy. This feeling was expressed by the prominent Ottoman rabbi Hayyim Palaggi (1788–1868), who objected to the elimination of differences between Jews and non-Jews that was brought about by the modernization of dress. He believed that Jews had to dress differently from non-Jews, reasoning that if Jews dressed like non-Jews in modern dress, they would also imitate (all) the ways of non-Jews or even those of the Jews of the European Enlightenment.

MUSLIMS IN NON-MUSLIM ATTIRE

Although the most notorious aspect of laws of differentiation were the rules and regulations that restricted the behavior and attire of non-Muslims, distinctions cannot be achieved unless each side is prevented from emulating the other. In fact, a sounder religious foundation exists for restrictions on the attire of Muslims than for those on the dress of non-Muslims.

Certain hadiths commented on the necessity for Muslims to differentiate themselves from unbelievers in matters of appearance; other sayings attributed to the Prophet are quite specific about the consequences of failing to adhere to these differences. For example, in one hadith, the Prophet is related as having said, "He who imitates a people, he is one of them" (Abu Dawud, Libas 4). For example, if a Muslim man wore a Jewish-style hat, then it was deemed that he had become a Jew. Similarly, if a Muslim traveled through an infidel country and started to wear their style of clothing, his wife could sue for divorce on the grounds her husband was no longer a Muslim and she could not be married to an unbeliever. The opinion of Ebussuûd Efendi, a sixteenth-century Islamic scholar of Ottoman origins, makes it clear that a Muslim who put on non-Muslim attire would have been considered to have renounced Islam. Another Seyhülislâm (superior authority with regard to issues relating to Islam), Çatalcali Ali Efendi (1631–1692), was confronted with a related situation: If a Muslim wore an infidel hat to disguise himself, what should happen to him? The response was that he should renew his faith and his marriage. Donning non-Muslim attire could also be an aggravating factor when other crimes were committed. Yavuz Ercan discusses an Ottoman document dating to 1556 that records how three Muslim men were caught after they had disguised themselves by wearing infidel hats and clothing for the purpose of committing a robbery. They were sentenced to death, a much more severe punishment than would normally have been given for robbery.

Given this history, it is only natural that the perception that Muslims wearing non-Muslim attire were apostates would have been deeply internalized by the public. This is clearly shown by the fact that much of the opposition to the efforts of the Ottoman sultan Selim III (r. 1789–1807) to establish a new army corps (besides the now-ineffective janissaries) was articulated in sartorial terms. Tayyar Pasha, an opponent of the sultan's reforms, wrote:

> Muslims are clad in infidels' clothes, and the hereditary Islamic dynasty has become alien to the state.... There is no longer either cavalry or janissaries! They have all become Franks in hats.... [T]he wearing of infidels' clothes has been decreed by the sultan, and, indeed, in the imperial harem, concubines are deprived of pantaloons with which to cover their pudenda, and wear Frankish skirts and the costume of the land of infidels. (quoted by Enver Ziya Karal)

All this agitation, coupled with persistent social and economic difficulties, finally led to a rebellion and the sultan's assassination. More than a century later, following World War I (1914–1918) and the collapse of the Ottoman Empire, Mustafa Kemal Atatürk (1881–1938) launched a program to westernize Turkey with an attack on traditional attire. In a speech delivered on the occasion of the second convention of his People's Party, on 15–20 October 1927, he recalled,

> It was necessary to get rid of the fez [a stiff, felted cap in red], considered upon the head of our nation as a trademark of ignorance, of reaction, and of resistance to progress and development, and replace it with the hat, used as headdress throughout the entire civilized world, so as to show that the Turkish nation does not differ from civilized social life in the domain of mentality either.

In so doing, Atatürk felt compelled to obtain the approval of reform-minded religious dignitaries. In a public exchange with a mufti (a professional jurist interpreting Islamic law), he asked, "What is the Islamic form of dress?" The mufti responded,

> There is no specific form of Islamic dress. Naturally dress is a matter of practicality and need. For instance, if a Muslim were to buy a cow from an infidel, a Magian, and the cow, disturbed by the dress of its new owner, were to cease producing milk or to reduce its output, the Muslim would be entitled to don Magian clothing. (quoted by Sevket Süreyya Aydemir)

This view certainly was not generally accepted and failed to silence the critics. Ironically, the fez itself had elicited a strong reaction from religious conservatives when first introduced early in the nineteenth century. This time, it was the hat that drew their ire, leading to demonstrations and all-out uprisings that were forcefully suppressed. The Turkish phrase *sapka giymek* ("to put on a hat") came to mean "to apostatize."

CLOTHING AND CONVERSION

If Muslims who donned non-Muslim attire were accused of apostasy, one might wonder whether the wearing of Muslim attire might have been sufficient cause to consider that a non-Muslim had converted to Islam. This point was discussed by various groups, and the conclusion was reached that although the act of wearing Muslim clothes did not amount to conversion (unless accompanied by an explicit statement to that effect), the two were certainly closely linked both in the popular imagination and the law. It should come as no surprise, then, that when a non-Muslim did formally convert to Islam, he or she was often presented with a new set of clothes. This custom was practiced in Turkey until as late as 1920, long after official sumptuary and differentiation laws had been abolished, and was regarded as carrying both practical and symbolic significance.

On the practical side, in a society where members of different religious communities were distinguished by their attire, a person who switched from one religion to another would have to acquire a whole new wardrobe. For all but the wealthiest, this would have involved financial hardship, which would be alleviated to some extent by the presentation of new clothes. On the symbolic side, re-clothing the convert harked back to the case of the poet Ka'b b. Zuhayr (who died in about 645), who, after having satirized Muslims in some of his works, converted to Islam and wrote the ode *Banat Su'ad* in praise of the Prophet Mohammed. Moved by his exquisite poetry, the Prophet took off his own cloak and gave it to Ka'b, whose poem was thereafter known as *Qasidat al-Burdah* (Ode of the cloak). The clothes presented to new converts in later periods served as a symbol and concrete record of their admission into the community of believers.

Some conversions took place before the sultan himself. In such cases, records indicate that the (male) convert would receive a cap and white cloth for making a turban, as well as items of clothing such as leather footwear, linens, trousers, and waistbands. Those of a higher social class might also be given a short, sable fur cloak decorated with silver and gold thread. In other cases, converts might petition the imperial authorities for their due. Thus, for instance, a document dated 1735 identified the petitioner as one "graced with the honor of Islam and having accepted the religion of Muhammad" and asked the sultan "to favor his slave with his exalted magnanimity" (quoted by İsmail Hakkı Uzunçarşılı). The grand vizier wrote in the margin, "Honorable minister of finance, it has been ordered that you give whatever it has been customary to give those graced with the honor of Islam." On the back of the petition, another inscription records that a payment of eight *kurus* and a *mintan* (probably a long-sleeved, collarless man's shirt) had been granted the petitioner.

The money given to the convert by the minister of finance was known as the *kisve bahâ* ("dress payment"). Other related terms included *destâr bahâ* ("turban payment") and *yaşmak bahâ* ("veil payment"), granted respectively to male and female converts to Islam. Petitions often refer to these payments as "required by law," although it is likely that they were more often based on established custom than written law. In the provinces, where the central government had no direct involvement with conversions, money and clothing were provided by certain *waqfs* (pious foundations). Thus, the Semseddin Altun-Aba foundation, established in 1202 in the city of Konya, specified that one-fifth of the revenue of an eighteen-room commercial building had been earmarked for

Engraving after Jean-Baptiste Vanmour of an Ottoman Jew wearing a *bonéta*, 1714. He wears this instead of the turban, which was reserved for Muslims. Art and Architecture Collection, Miriam and Ira D. Wallach Division of Art, Prints and Photographs, New York Public Library, Astor, Lenox and Tilden Foundations.

assisting Christians, Jews, and Magians who had converted to Islam, explicitly mentioning the purchase of shoes and clothes for them. Similarly, the Haci Ivaz Pasha foundation, established in 1427 in the town of Bursa, included in its by-laws that a sum of two *dirham* per day would be reserved for the needs of those who chose to embrace Islam. Its disbursement records include numerous instances of turban and veil payments.

Sumptuary laws and laws of differentiation in Islam are not explicitly mentioned in either the Qur'an or the sunna (the corpus of hadiths). The idea that Muslims should adopt practices that distinguish them from their nonbelieving neighbors was articulated by the Prophet Mohammed, but he did not call for non-Muslims to wear special clothes or insignia. The first regulation

requiring the non-Muslim subjects of Muslim states to wear distinguishing garb is traditionally attributed to the second caliph, 'Umar, although evidence suggests that it may actually be due to his namesake, the Umayyad caliph 'Umar II.

The absence of clear rules regarding sartorial differentiation in the Qur'an or sunna has led to inconsistent interpretations and uneven enforcement throughout the course of Islamic history. In some regions and/or during certain periods, laws of differentiation were tightened and caused considerable suffering on the part of non-Muslims. Most of the time, however, such laws were enforced only spottily or not at all. Still, they were accepted by the population at large, and thus the issue of dress became a point of political contestation, starting with early attempts at

Westernization in parts of the Islamic empire during the eighteenth and nineteenth centuries. Eventually, a combination of secularization and globalization brought about the end of sumptuary laws and laws of differentiation, although the topic continues to resurface from time to time.

This article draws on material published in *Khil'a* 3 (2007/2008).

References and Further Reading

[Abu Ja'far Muhammad ibn Jarir al-Tabari]. *The History of al-Tabari (Ta'rikh al-rusul wa'l-muluk).* Vol. 30, *The 'Abbasid Caliphate in Equilibrium.* Translated by C. E. [Clifford Edmund] Bosworth. Albany: State University of New York Press, 1989.

[Abu Ja'far Muhammad ibn Jarir al-Tabari]. *The History of al-Tabari (Ta'rikh al-rusul wa'l-muluk).* Vol. 34, *Incipient Decline.* Translated by Joel L. Kramer. Albany: State University of New York Press, 1989.

Abu Yusuf Ya'qub b. Ibrahim. *Kitab al-Kharaj.* Beirut and Cairo: Dar al-Shuruq, 1985.

[Ali Efendi, Çatalcali]. *Fetâvâ-yi Ali Efendi.* Edited by Salih b. Ahmed el-Kefevî. Istanbul: Sahhâfiye-i Osmâniye Sirketi, 1893.

[Altinay], Ahmed Refik, ed. *Onuncu Asr-ı Hicrî'de İstanbul Hayatı (1495–1591).* Reprint ed. Istanbul: Enderun Kitabevi, 1988a.

[Altinay], Ahmed Refik, ed. *Onbirinci Asr-ı Hicrî'de İstanbul Hayatı (1592–1688).* Reprint ed. Istanbul: Enderun Kitabevi, 1988b.

[Atatürk, Mustafa Kemal]. *Nutuk: Gazi Mustafa Kemal Tarafından Cümhuriyet Halk Firkasinin 15–20 Tesrinievel 1927 Tarihleri Arasinda Toplanan Ikinci Büyük Kongresinde Söylenmistir.* Istanbul: Devlet Matbaasi, 1934.

Aydemir, Sevket Süreyya. *Tek Adam: Mustafa Kemal'in Hayatı.* Istanbul: Remzi Kitapevi, 1963–1967.

Baer, Marc David. *Honored by the Glory of Islam: Conversion and Conquest in Ottoman Europe.* New York: Oxford University Press, 2008.

Elliot, Matthew. "Dress Codes in the Ottoman Empire: The Case of the Franks." In *Ottoman Costumes: From Textile to Identity,* edited by Suraiya Faroqhi and Christoph K. Neumann, 103–123. Istanbul: Eren Yayincilik, 2004.

Ercan, Yavuz. "Osmanli Imparatorlugunda Gayrimüslimlerin Giyim, Mesken ve Davranis Hukuku." *OTAM: Ankara Üniversitesi Osmanli Tarihi Arastirma ve Uygulama Merkezi Dergisi* 1, no. 1 (1990): 117–125.

Fattal, Antoine. *Le statut légal des non-Musulmans en pays d'Islam.* Beirut: Institut de Lettres Orientales de Beyrouth, 1958.

Goodblatt, Morris S. *Jewish Life in Turkey in the XVIth Century as Reflected in the Legal Writings of Samuel De Medina.* New York: Jewish Theological Seminary of America, 1952.

Ibn 'Asākir al-Shāfi'ī, Abū'l-Qāsim 'Alī b. al Husan b. Hibatullāh b. 'Abdullāh b. al-Husayn. *Tārīkh al-Kabīr.* [Damascus]: Matba'at Rawdat al-Shām, 1911.

Ibn Qayyim al-Jawziyya. *Shams al-Din Abu 'Abdullah Mu..ammad b. Abu Bakr. Shar..al-Shuru.. al-'Umariyyah, mujarradan min Kitab I..kam Ahl al-Dhimmah.* Damascus: Matba'at Jami'at Dimashq, 1961.

Juhasz, Esther. "Material Culture." In *The Jews of the Middle East and North Africa in Modern Times,* edited by Reeva Spector Simon, Michael Menachem Laskier, and Sara Reguer, 205–223. New York: Columbia University Press, 2003.

Karal, Enver Ziya. *Osmanli Tarihi, 5: Nizam-i Cedid ve Tanzimat Devirleri (1789–1856).* Ankara: Türk Tarih Kurumu Yayinlari, 1995.

Kobler, Franz. *A Treasury of Jewish Letters: Letters from the Famous and the Humble.* Philadelphia: Jewish Publication Society of America, 1953.

Lewis, Bernard. *The Jews of Islam.* Princeton, NJ: Princeton University Press, 1984.

Lichtenstadter, Ilse. "The Distinctive Dress of Non-Muslims in Islamic Countries." *Historia Judaica* 5, no. 1 (1943): 35–52.

Littman, David. "Jews under Muslim Rule: The Case of Persia." *Wiener Library Bulletin* 32, n.s. 49–50 (1979): 2–15.

Minkov, Anton. *Conversion to Islam in the Balkans: Kisve Bahasi Petitions and Ottoman Social Life, 1670–1730.* Leiden: Brill, 2004.

Al-Tartushi, Abu Bakr Muhammad ib al-Walid. *Siraj al-Muluk* [Lamp of the kings]. London: Riyad El-Rayyas Press, 1996.

Tritton, A. S. [Arthur Stanley]. *The Caliphs and Their Non-Muslim Subjects: A Critical Study of the Covenant of 'Umar.* London: Oxford University Press, 1930.

Uzunçarşılı, İsmail Hakkı. *Osmanlı Devletinin Merkez ve Bahriye Teşkilâtı.* Ankara: Türk Tarih Kurumu Yayınları, 1948.

Irvin Cemil Schick

See also The Coming of Islam and Its Influence on Dress; Snapshot: Islam and Islamically Correct Dress (Hijab); Sumptuary Laws.

Sumptuary Laws

- Clothes and How to Wear Them
- Materials and Colors
- Ornamentation, Designs, and Figures

Sumptuary laws (from Latin *sumptuariae leges*) are rules that attempt to regulate people's habits of (luxury) consumption with respect to clothing, food, furniture, housing, and so forth. While they generally have economic underpinnings, they have also historically been used to regulate and reinforce social hierarchies and morals through restrictions on the purchase and display of such luxuries. The following excerpt from an Ottoman imperial edict issued in 1824 makes this clear:

> Whereas the population of the exalted capital [Istanbul] is subdivided into numerous classes, and each class has its proper attire, and it is essential that etiquette and protocol be respected, that everyone knows his place, that he honors, respects and obeys his superiors and officers, that one group does not put on the garb of another, that officers' staff and gardners and rascals and tradesmen do not wrap camlet (*Şâl*) and patterned velvet (*Ahmediye*) and embroidered cotton (*ağbânî*) around their heads like sailors, and that they maintain an appropriate appearance and wear their proper attire; for a certain time now, some hindrances have caused violations to be tolerated, and spendthrifts in each class have abandoned their ancient costumes and proper attire, donning whatever extravagant clothes they dream up, and those who see them are influenced by them and do likewise, so that most servants and militarymen and tradesmen have spoiled their ancient costumes and original appearances and it is no longer possible to determine to which class they belong. (quoted in Altinay)

After this prelude, the edict instructs the sultan's subjects to return to wearing the clothes appropriate to their station, so that social order may be restored.

In some cases, sumptuary laws are based on religious principles. The two main texts of Islam, the Qur'an and the sunna (the corpus of hadiths), contain a great deal of information about material culture in general and Islamic attire in particular. As interpreted over time, these texts have constituted the basis of Islamic sumptuary laws governing clothing.

CLOTHES AND HOW TO WEAR THEM

Like any other religion, Islam arose within a particular historical and geographic context, by which it was inevitably influenced and molded. The clothes worn in the Hijaz (western Saudi Arabia in the early twenty-first century) in the seventh century c.e. have thus determined to a great extent the regulations subsequently imposed on Muslims' attire. Some of these influences were positive, since the lives of the Prophet and his companions are regarded as an example (*qidwah*) for Muslims to emulate, and some were negative, since the Prophet set new standards of behavior for

Muslims and wished them to distinguish themselves from unbelievers in various ways, including what they did and did not wear.

The frequency with which articles of clothing are used as metaphors in the Qur'an testifies to the importance attached to dress. Thus, God addresses mankind as follows: "O children of Adam! We have revealed unto you raiment (*libas*) to conceal your shame, as well as to be an adornment to you. But the raiment of righteousness is the best of all. This is among the signs of God, so that [believers] may receive admonition" (*A'raf* 7:26). It is also written that Satan tore off from Adam and Eve the raiment (*libas*) of innocence so that they felt shame (*A'raf* 7:27); that God has created living beings and has clothed (*kasawa*) bones with flesh (*Baqara* 2:259; *Mu'minun* 23:14); and that the wife is her husband's raiment and he is hers (*Baqara* 2:187). Elsewhere, it is written that a veil (*hijab*) shall separate those who dwell in paradise from those who burn in hellfire (*A'raf* 7:46); that the hearts of the unbelievers are veiled (*akinnat*) from the truth (*Fussilat* 41:5; *Isra'* 17:46; *An'am* 6:25); that God has placed a wrap (*ghishawat*) over the eyes of unbelievers (*Baqara* 2:7); and that the "People of the Book" (namely, those among non-Muslims who have revealed scriptures, such as the Jews and Christians) clothe (*talbis*) the truth with falsehood (*Al 'Imran* 3:71). With respect to the Day of Judgment, it is written that sinners will be wearing raiment (*sarabil*) of black pitch and their faces will be wrapped (*taghsha*) by fire (*Ibrahim* 14:50).

In addition to metaphorical references to attire, there are also literal ones, for example, stating that clothing is one of the ways in which God has favored humankind with his grace. Thus, it is written in the Qur'an: "And God has given you, out of what He has created, shelter from the sun; and He has given you places of refuge in the mountains; and He has given you garments [sarabil] to ward off the heat, and garments to protect you from your [mutual] violence; thus does He bestow the full measure of his favor upon you, in order that you may surrender yourselves to Him" (*Nahl* 16:81).

Elsewhere in the Qur'an, people are told to exercise restraint in enjoying God's favors: "O children of Adam! Take to your adornment in every place of worship, and eat and drink; but do not be wasteful. Verily He does not love the spendthrift" (*A'raf* 7:31). This text lies at the heart of some of the principal themes underlying the Islamic outlook on dress, namely, the avoidance of needless luxury and ostentation.

Sometimes, sartorial rules and regulations derived from hadiths are based on incidental mentions of the ways the Prophet or his companions dressed. These details are used to provide tacit sanction for Muslims to dress likewise. It was, for example, reported that the Prophet was seen with his shirt unbuttoned; as a result, it is acceptable for a Muslim man to wear his shirt unbuttoned. Other regulations, however, were no doubt formulated in response to a particular set of circumstances but were codified into law by virtue of being included in the sunna. Walking while wearing only one sandal, for instance, was prohibited. In addition, special attire was decreed for prayer and pilgrimage. It should also be noted that men who dress like women, as well as women who dress like men, were cursed.

Another very important aspect of Islamic attire is the covering of 'awrah, the private parts, broadly defined. This topic is particularly well developed in the case of women, for whom the definition of 'awrah can include much of the body, but it should be stressed that this concept also applies to men. Thus, the Prophet is said to have forbidden two manners of dress for men, which were the *ishtimal al Samma'*, in which one shoulder was covered with a garment while the other shoulder was left bare, and the *ihtiba'* style, which involved wrapping a garment around the body in such a manner that when the wearer was sitting on the ground no part of the garment covered the genitalia.

The prohibition of ostentation and luxury does not mean that Islam promotes asceticism and total renunciation in matters of dress. One hadith, for example, relates that a companion came to the Prophet wearing tattered clothes. The Prophet asked him, "Have you any property?" The man replied, "God has given me camels, sheep, horses, and slaves." The Prophet then said to him, "When God gives you property, let the mark of His favor and honor to you be visible." Thus, it is profligacy and extravagance that the Prophet proscribed, not the act of dressing well but within one's means. Ostentation ran counter to his spirituality and to his belief in the transience of life—as did unnecessary pride in one's appearance. The following tradition makes clear the strength of the Prophet's condemnation of pride in dress: "While a man was walking, clad in a suit [*hulla*] and proud of himself with his well-combed hair, suddenly God made him sink into the earth, and he will go on sinking into it until the Day of Judgement" (Bukhari, *Libas* 7; Muslim, *Libas wa Ziynah* 78, 79).

Evidently, however, not each and every individual Muslim chose to refrain from ostentation when it came to daily practices. The affluent and powerful often wore sumptuous attire, as can be seen from surviving garments, as well as numerous paintings and engravings. The authorities sometimes attempted to enforce modesty, but while new sartorial regulations officially drew their inspiration from the Islamic aversion to luxury, their true causes and motivations often owed more to this world than to the next. The Ottoman Empire, for example, entered the eighteenth century significantly weakened by military defeats and territorial losses, a political climate in which the sultan's legitimacy and authority needed bolstering. This period witnessed a series of imperial decrees calling for an end to conspicuous consumption and the restoration of traditional attire, all part of an effort to hide the widening gulf between the lives of the ruling elite and those of the common people. Such rules were also intended to help domestic artisans threatened by the uncontrolled importation of foreign goods and so recast the ailing Ottoman state as the preserver of social order and public morality. Thus, an imperial edict issued in 1783 complained that prodigality and extravagance had increased among government officials, who had taken to wearing Indian clothes rather than domestic products and were thereby causing a great deal of money to flow out of the Ottoman Empire. This edict required them to use camlet (*Şâlî*) from Istanbul and Ankara, cotton-silk blends (*kutnu*) from Bursa, striped cloth (*alaca*) from Damascus, and girdle (*kuŞak*) fabric from Hama and Basra and categorically to refrain from wearing Indian materials.

MATERIALS AND COLORS

The Prophet's concern for preventing ostentation and luxury is especially evident in the prohibitions he formulated regarding the materials used in clothing. First and foremost, he evidenced clear hostility toward silk and brocade, as several hadiths indicate. The context for this hostility is once again the Prophet's wish to clearly distinguish the believer's spiritual quest in this world from his rewards in the next. Silk was a rare and much-prized commodity at the time of the Prophet, and the Qur'an contains numerous references to it as the attire believers would wear in the afterlife. It will come as no surprise, then, that the Prophet said, "He who wears silk in this world shall not wear it in the hereafter" (Bukhari, *Libas*, 50–53; Ibn Majah, *Libas*, 39); that is, they will not go to heaven.

In another hadith, the Prophet gave a silk garment to 'Alī b. Abū Tālib, who, either knowing that he should not wear it or being told so by the Prophet after he had put it on, cut it up and made head scarves for his womenfolk. This was taken to suggest that it is acceptable for women to wear silk, while it is unlawful for a man to wear it.

A number of hadiths, however, state that small amounts of silk are acceptable on a man's garment. It was related, for instance, that Abu 'Uthman said that 'Umar b. al-Khassab had said that the Prophet "forbade wearing silk except this much; then the Prophet (prayers and blessings of God be upon him) extended his two fingers towards us." And Zuhayr, one among the chain of narrators, "raised up his middle and index fingers" (Bukhari, *Libas* 46; Muslim, *Libas wa Ziynah* 26, 29). At the same time, it was also said that anyone who suffered from a dermatological problem ("the itch") was allowed to wear silk. These hadiths have been taken to indicate that silk was not considered impure, just unnecessarily opulent for anyone who did not really need to wear it.

In practice, luxury fabrics became the norm within decades after the Prophet's death, under the Umayyad dynasty. Silk was also highly valued and extensively used by both the men and the women of the privileged classes in the Persian and Ottoman empires, particularly in the imperial palaces. It was quite common in these courts for status and kingship to triumph over ideologies of puritanism. Not only was silk the preferred cloth of royal dress, but the elaborate structure of Ottoman court life, salaries, rewards, and so forth was based on the symbolic value of silk. Religious prohibitions were circumvented, when necessary, by blending small amounts of other materials in with the silk so that the resulting fabric could credibly be considered acceptable.

Similarly, such centers as Isfahan, Bursa, and Mount Lebanon produced silk both for the domestic market and for export. It would seem that it was only after external demand for luxury fabrics had declined (due to war, competition, or some other factors) that the local inhabitants were able to acquire and use significant quantities of silk. Thus, it could be argued that before the "bad times," they did not wear silk because of their social and economic situation rather than due to any religious considerations.

In contrast, a number of traditions report the Prophet as wearing garments made of wool (*suf*), and wool remains a favored material for clothing up through the early twenty-first century. Coarse wool garments came to signify piety and renunciation, and one of the etymologies commonly proposed for the word *sufi* (in the sense of "Islamic mystic") is, in fact, "wearer of *suf*."

Another luxury item much prized in imperial palaces and among the privileged classes from Central Asia to the shores of the Mediterranean was skins and furs. The Prophet is related to have prohibited riding on leopard skins, no doubt another attempt to curb excessive luxury by banning what must have been established practice in his day, at least among the wealthy. Some

Sultan Selim II (1524–1574) firing a bow and arrow and wearing an elaborate silk kaftan, gouache on paper, sixteenth century, by Nakkep Reis Haydar. Although Islam clearly forbids men from wearing silk, the elaborate structure of Ottoman court life, salaries, rewards, and so forth were based on the symbolic value of this textile. Getty Images.

Detail from an Ottoman miniature in the *Surnâme* of Sultan Murad III, depicting the procession of the descendants of the Prophet Mohammed (recognizable by their green turbans) on the occasion of the circumcision of the Ottoman crown prince in 1582. Topkapi Palace Museum.

hadiths state more generally that wearing or riding on the skins of beasts of prey is prohibited.

An interesting fact about skins is the role of tanning. It is forbidden in Islam to eat the flesh of an animal that died of natural causes (rather than being slaughtered according to established rules). Thus, it is related that upon seeing a dead sheep, the Prophet asked, "Why did you not tan its skin and get some good out of it?" When the owners replied, "It died of natural causes," the Prophet said, "It is only eating of it that is prohibited." A related hadith adds that the Prophet also noted that when a skin was tanned, it became pure. Since maintaining the separation between the pure and the polluting is a vital matter in Islam, the fact that tanning renders skin pure is a point of great significance.

Just as the material of which a garment is made could render it licit or prohibited, so could its color. The hadiths contain a number of details about the colors the Prophet liked to wear or advocated wearing. For example, it is related that he wore a black turban, and into the early twenty-first century in the Shiite world, particularly in Iran and parts of Iraq, clerics who claim a direct bloodline to the Prophet still wear black turbans. It is also related that the Prophet liked green garments; since then, the color green has historically been associated with Islam and the Prophet Mohammed. In the Ottoman Empire, for example, direct (male) descendants of the Prophet (sayyid) were recognizable by their green turbans. In fact, Islamic laws of differentiation that intended to make non-Muslims visually distinguishable from Muslims often included a prohibition on the wearing of green by the former.

A number of traditions quote the Prophet as urging believers to wear white garments. The Prophet, for example, is reported to have said that Muslims should wear white garments because these are best and that white clothing, or cloth, could be used as shrouds for the dead. White garments and especially white turbans were considered the exclusive province of Muslims, and non-Muslims caught wearing them risked punishment during the periods when laws of differentiation were enforced.

ORNAMENTATION, DESIGNS, AND FIGURES

The small amount of silk permitted on a garment has generally been interpreted as referring to ornamentation, such as embroidery or hemming. Thus, a hadith narrated by Qatada mentions a letter from 'Umar b. al-Khassab in which it was stated that the Prophet had "forbidden the use of silk but to the extent of these two fingers, and Abu 'Uthmān said: 'We understood by these words that he meant designs (*'alam*) [embroidery?] on the cloth.'" This brings up the question of what sorts of adornment were permitted on a garment.

Here again, hadiths provide some guidance. For example, Abū 'Umar relates the following: "I saw that ['Abdullāh] Ibn 'Umar bought a turban on which was a design (*'alam*). He called for shears to cut it. I went to Asmā' and mentioned this to her. Upon this, she said: 'May misery befall 'Abdullāh! O slave-girl, bring the mantle of the Messenger of God (prayers and blessings of God be upon him).' And she brought a mantle whose sleeves and breast and openings were hemmed with brocade (*dibaj*)" (Ibn Majah, *Libas* 45; Abu Dawud, *Libas* 35). Thus, Ibn 'Abbas commented that "it is only a garment wholly made of silk which the Messenger of God (prayers and blessings of God be upon him) forbade, but there is no harm in the ornamented border and the warp." In contrast, another companion of the Prophet, Abū Raihānah, mentioned "men putting silk at the bottom of their garments like Persians, or putting silk on their shoulders like Persians" (Abu Dawud, *Libas* 30) among things prohibited by the Prophet. In other words, the location of the silk border on a garment mattered.

Another pertinent issue is the precise nature of the ornamentation on a garment. Was a patterned fabric permitted or not? The answer to this question is not simple. It requires, first of all, a brief discussion of the place of images in Islam, a very important topic about which there exists a vast literature. Contrary to popular opinion, which holds that Islam is fundamentally and unequivocally against the use of human or animal figurative iconography, the acceptability of representation of animate objects has been the subject of numerous debates within the Muslim world since at least as early as the tenth century. This debate has its roots in the fact that the Qur'an does not appear to prohibit such representations, and while the sunna does betray some hostility toward them, its attitude is far from unambiguous.

At the same time, a number of hadiths show the Prophet Mohammed to have disapproved of at least some images. It is,

furthermore, certainly no coincidence that in the principal hadith collections, traditions that deal with pictures are mostly assembled in the sections dedicated to dress (*libas*). This is probably because in the early medieval period in the eastern Mediterranean (Byzantine, Coptic) and Persian world, it was quite common to have textiles with depictions of men, women, and animals. These textiles were used both for clothing and as soft furnishings in the home. Yet it should not be presumed that the matter is that simple. Virtually every Islamic group has its own interpretation of what can and cannot be allowed, and, over the centuries, the view of the most influential groups tends to be reflected in whether figurative designs are allowed on garments or not.

Finally, it is worth noting that a number of edicts were issued in the Ottoman Empire forbidding the use of written text on cloth intended to be worn. In some cases, this was clearly out of concern that material with religious scriptures might be mishandled. Thus, an edict dated 1775 stated that, since most workers in Istanbul's textile-printing shops were non-Muslims, "they are known to sometimes draw the Noble Glorious Word [*lafza-ı celal-i Şerif*, i.e. the name "Allah"], as well as other names of God, among the motifs on their product in order to enhance its value. As such printed textiles and particularly muslin of the kind known as *mücessem* [corporeal, substantial] are used in Ottoman lands by Muslims, Christians, and other people alike, it is clear that unbelievers without religious scruples may act inappropriately and use them in undeserving places" (quoted by Albayrak). The edict went on to forbid the practice. It does not appear that talismanic shirts, which were covered with religious inscriptions, were included in this prohibition, since the risk that they would fall into the wrong hands was very small.

Subsequent edicts generalized the prohibition to all writing but specified the wearers as women. Thus, a series of edicts issued during 1788–1789 stated that "scarves, kerchiefs, towels and other textiles worn by women are being inscribed sometimes with noble verses [from the Qur'an], and sometimes with strange couplets of poetry or bizarre words like 'Ah' and 'Oh,' either by printing or by embroidery using silver, gold, and silk thread" (quoted by Albayrak). Once again, the practice was strictly forbidden, and all violators, whether draftsmen, manufacturers, sellers, or buyers, were threatened with severe punishment. This attitude is consistent with the Islamic veneration for all writing, not just religious texts.

This article draws on material published in *Khil'a* 3 (2007/2008).

References and Further Reading

Albayrak, Sadık. *60 Orijinal Belge Işığıda Osmanlı'da Sosyal Yapı ve İstanbul.* Istanbul; Kiptaş, 2001.

[Altınay], Ahmed Refik, ed. *Onüçüncü Asr-ı Hicrî'de İstanbul Hayatı (1786–1882).* Reprint ed. Istanbul: Enderun Kitabevi, 1988.

Arnold, Thomas W., Sir. *Painting in Islam: A Study of the Place of Pictorial Art in Muslim Culture.* Oxford: Clarendon Press, 1928.

Atasoy, Nurhan, Walter B. Denny, Louise W. Mackie, and Hülya Tezcan. *İpek: The Crescent and the Rose. Imperial Ottoman Silks and Velvets.* Edited by Julian Raby and Alison Effeny. London: Azimuth Editions, 2001.

Chehabi, Houchang. "Dress Codes for Men in Turkey and Iran." In *Men of Order: Authoritarian Modernization under Atatürk and Reza Shah*, edited by Touraj Atabaki and Erik J. Zürcher, 209–237. London and New York: I. B. Tauris, 2004.

Creswell, K.A.C. [Keppel Archibald Cameron]. "The Lawfulness of Painting in Early Islam." *Ars Islamica* 11–12 (1946): 159–166.

Faroqhi, Suraiya, and Christoph K. Neumann, eds. *Ottoman Costumes: From Textile to Identity*. Istanbul: Eren Yayıncılık, 2004.

Quataert, Donald. "Clothing Laws, State, and Society in the Ottoman Empire, 1720–1829." *International Journal of Middle East Studies* 29 (1997): 403–425.

Schick, Irvin Cemil. "Some Islamic Determinants of Dress in Southwest Asia." *Khil'a* 3. Khil'a 3 [2007/8].

Stillman, Yedida Kalfon. *Arab Dress: A Short History from the Dawn of Islam to Modern Times*. Edited by Norman A. Stillman. Leiden: Brill, 2000.

Irvin Cemil Schick

See also Laws of Differentiation.

Khil'a: Clothing to Honor a Person or Situation

*K*hil'a was a ceremony that included elite and expensive textiles made into particular garments. These garments were used to define a relationship of honorable service. At its simplest, a king or his representative bestowed on another person, usually of lower rank, an outer cloak, shirt, sash, and pants, plus often a turban and shoes. In a robing room adjacent to the court, the recipient donned the whole outfit, reemerged to the acclaim of the assembled nobles, and—if not so before—was deemed "suitable" to take his place in court.

Khil'a does not relate to all types of honorific robing, courtly display of elite textiles, or sumptuary laws. Rather, khil'a had a specific provenance and history. Between about 600 and about 1900 C.E., the ceremony had a vast scope. Versions of it were found at courts from China to North Africa, including Central Asia, Persia, Southwest Asia, India, and portions of sub-Saharan Africa. Except for Muslim Spain, khil'a was not, however, found in West Europe or Southeast Asia.

Since the early 1990s, scholars have seriously challenged the idea of "culture" as something singular, bounded, sacred, timeless, and often expressed in text. Many have come to view the concept of culture as something that is historically contingent, contested, and intertwined with politics and power. This viewpoint fits the khil'a ceremony well: It can be thought of as a symbol, a "meta-language." The textiles were a complex sign presented before a knowing noble audience. They established loyalty between a king and a follower that rose above family, ethnicity, religion, and even language.

HISTORICAL DEVELOPMENT

There are two tantalizing bits of evidence that some form of khil'a was practiced in Persia before the Common Era. Diodorus' history of Alexander (written in 45 B.C.E.) has the Greek army seizing a cache of fine robes during the sack of Persepolis, the Persian capital. In spite of vocal resistance by his army, Alexander robed himself, his commanders, and some troops in the soft, luxurious robes. Perhaps he was imitating a Persian tradition of honorific robing. Alternatively, Diodorus could have invented the whole incident.

Equally tantalizing is the Book of Esther, one of the last books of the Old Testament. Scholars generally agree that the book is historical fiction, set in Persia, and written down a century or so before the Common Era. In the story, the king rhetorically asks his administrator, Haman, what would be a suitable ceremony of honor. Haman replies,

> Have them bring a royal robe that the king has worn and horse that the king has ridden, one with a royal crown on its head. Then have them hand the robe and the horse over to one of the king's most noble princes and have him robe the man … and have the prince lead him on horseback through the city square. (Esther 6:7–9)

Several of the elements of khil'a are here: the robe of the king, the robing of the recipient, the audience of nobles, the association of robing and horses, and the public display of the recipient in the robe.

With silk, horses, ideas, and much more moving east and west along the Silk Road in the first centuries of the Common Era, it is probably futile to look for a single "origin" for the khil'a ceremony. One plausible beginning, however, is supported by Chinese literary sources. China needed the horses and cattle raised by the nomads of the eastern steppe, and the nomads needed food and iron from China. War was frequent, but in periods of trade and diplomacy, silk robes played a crucial role. Only China produced silk, and so political leaders in China gave it to nomad chiefs in return for the cessation of hostilities, for protection, as well as for a dowry. The chief, in turn, bestowed it on his leaders to show his success and largesse and to build loyalty. The key to the success of the ceremony was that the robes also solved one of the problems of all nomad leaders—how to keep their military loyal. These elegant robes came only from the hand of the leader, they differentiated recipients from common soldiers, and—with every wearing—they helped remind soldiers whom they served.

Certain gifts often accompanied the elegant textiles of the robes and were given at the time of investiture. These included some combination of gold, slaves, horses, jeweled weapons, and horse trappings, all typical booty of a nomadic war band. The centrality of horses and these items in subsequent khil'a ceremonies again suggests an early use in a nomadic context.

The evidence for khil'a is much clearer in the period from 400 to 800 C.E. Honorific robing became a standard courtly practice in China when nomads became the rulers inside the Great Wall. Various colors became associated with ranks within the nobility. Similar ceremonies subsequently spread to Korea, Japan, and Vietnam.

Moving westward, there is good evidence for a khil'a-style investiture in Persia during the Sassanian period (fourth to seventh centuries). In a yearly cycle, the king bestowed robes he had worn on his nobles, accompanied by weapons, gold, silver, jewels, and horses. By the fifth century, the ceremony was well established in Central and Southwest Asia, both in the Byzantine Empire, which borrowed many cultural forms from the Sassanians, and in smaller kingdoms. Elite silk textiles were readily available both from China and the looms of caravan cities like Bukhara and Tashkent, whose craftsmen had taken up silk weaving.

In the Byzantine Empire, by 500 C.E., complex investiture rites had replaced the simpler Roman ceremony for accession to office within the church, ambassadorial exchanges, bureaucratic promotion, and personal recognition by the emperor. With the empire's growth, the custom spread to the entire Black Sea region, including the areas known in the early twenty-first century as Bulgaria, Romania, Hungary, Greece, Egypt, and some of the North African coast.

Robing was everywhere in the Southwest Asian world in which Islam arose in the late seventh century. The Qur'an mentions ceremonial robing several times in the context of the rewards of paradise for the faithful. With the rapid political and military spread of Islam in the seventh and eighth centuries, formal honorific robing reached the remainder of North Africa and Spain.

As had been the practice in Southwest Asia for centuries, the caliphs of Baghdad used robes to honor successful generals, promote administrators, and reward the nobility. Like the Byzantine Empire, the caliphate also used robes on ambassadorial missions to establish alliances. One well-documented mission was led by Ahmad ibn Fadlan ibn al-Abbas ibn Rasid ibn Hammad, who, in mid-June of 921 C.E., left Baghdad with gifts for Almish, a Bulgar king, that included elegant silk robes, banners, and a decorated saddle. Ibn Fadlan struggled through cold, negotiated with hostile nomads, and finally reached Almish's camp on the banks of the Volga River in what is Russia in the early twenty-first century. Both sides understood the implications of Almish putting on caliphate robes, which he did with great ceremony before his nobles. Afterward, however, Ibn Fadlan's mission spiraled to disaster because he had not brought the gold for a fort that Almish wanted to construct as part of the alliance. Nevertheless, it is clear that the ambassador and the Bulgar king shared a thorough understanding of khil'a, its textiles, and its implications.

The Muslim invasions of the twelfth and thirteenth centuries brought the custom to India, where Hindu rulers readily adopted the ceremony. India had long produced elaborate and elite silk fabrics. The khil'a tradition added the surrounding objects, such as gold, horses, and jeweled weapons. This easy acceptance of the khil'a ceremony into the courts of India is, however, surprising. India was divided into a caste system, and kings were, by and large, of middling or lower caste. Therefore, by caste rules, their clothes were regarded as polluted and unacceptable for men of a higher caste. A general suspension of these rules seems to have occurred, however, when applied to a king, coupled with a widespread belief that it was not useful to look too closely into kings' family origins. There was also a very old and deep tradition that the proper presentation of the kingly body was unclothed or only lightly draped from the waist up. Within a relatively short time after the Muslim conquest, local rulers took up robes that covered the whole body.

Following the extraordinary success of Genghis Khan and his successors (a few decades before Ibn Battuta's travels), lavish robes became the custom at the Mongol court. For state occasions, nobles were required to wear a cloth-of-gold robe received from the Khan. These robes were so important that claimants in succession disputes sometimes seized the artisans capable of crafting the robes in order to strengthen their own positions.

THE TEXTILES

Of the thousands of paintings of courtly life in, for example, India, Persia, and the Ottoman Empire, there are only a handful of representations of the khil'a ceremony. They are, thus, of little help in separating the luxury textiles used on a daily basis from those that were specifically bestowed by a king. Fortunately, the textual record is much better, consisting of both memoirs of observers at courts and inventories of kingly possessions.

The best observer was Ibn Battuta who, in the fourteenth century, traveled through many of the areas that used the khil'a ceremony. He documents more than fifty robes he received. Including khil'a-centered stories, there are more than ninety incidents of the ceremony in his nine hundred–page memoir. After years

on the road, Ibn Battuta recognized the cloth types and named the origin of some of the robes he had received. For example, in Mogadishu, honorific robes consisted of "a silk wrapper which one ties around his waist in place of drawers (for they have no acquaintance with these), a tunic of Egyptian linen with an embroidered border, a furred mantle of Jerusalem stuff, and an Egyptian turban with an embroidered edge." Clearly, this was not an outfit that one wore around the house. It was pure courtly dress, a sign of one's standing.

At Izmir, on the Mediterranean coast of what is Turkey in the early twenty-first century, the sultan sent Ibn Battuta "a Greek slave, a dwarf named Niqula, and two robes of *kamkha*, which are silken fabrics manufactured at Baghdad, Tabriz, Naisabur [Nishapur], and in China." Ibn Battuta's identification of this fabric with China is quite correct. The warp could be silk or cotton, and the weft thread was normally gold. The first syllable is derived from *chin*, the Chinese word for gold. Ibn Battuta's narrative demonstrates that knowing courtly observers understood subtle gradations in the quality and cost of the khil'a bestowed. Some robes, especially in the Ottoman Empire and in India, also included a "receipt" sewn in that stated the gold content.

Some robes, fabricated in royal workshops for a single occasion, were so fabulous that they constituted a significant transfer of wealth. Such was the robe that the King of Delhi gave to his sister's husband-to-be before the wedding, as described by Ibn Battuta:

> a ceremonial robe of blue silk embroidered and encrusted with jewels; the jewels covered it so completely that its color was not visible because of the quantity of them, and it was the same with his turban. I never saw a more beautiful robe than this one.

KINGLY PRACTICE

The sheer number of elite textiles used in the annual khil'a ceremonies is staggering. As Ibn Battuta observed, when he visited the Golden Horde, the Khan distributed several hundred robes. The Golden Horde was the western portion of the Mongol Empire (the legacy of Genghis Khan). It flourished from the mid-thirteenth to the end of the fourteenth century and at its peak ruled European Russia, much of Siberia, the Ural Mountains, and the Caucasus. Nomad-based, the empire traded broadly and extracted tribute from towns and sedentary agricultural groups throughout the region. Keeping the Horde "happy" was essential, hence vast amounts were spent on suitable robes. The wealth and numbers of robes distributed in India were far higher. Ibn Battuta estimated that the sultan of Delhi distributed 200,000 robes every year, using fabrics imported from China, Iraq, and Egypt.

Rulers bestowed robes at regular festivals but also on various special days, such as a return from a long journey, a birthday, a marriage, the birth of a son, a son's return from a campaign, or his marriage. These regular robing occasions provided solidarity for the courtly elite. Robes were generally brushed against the shoulder of the king before bestowal and thus carried the *baraka* (that is, the essence) of the king. The robe marked the body of the recipient in this most intimate way.

The khil'a ceremony also established a patron relationship outside the immediate circle of the nobility and, therefore, required clarity regarding who was to give and who would receive. In one story, Ibn Battuta described the consequences of flaunting

Mahmud ibn Sebuktegin (Mahmud of Ghazna) receiving a robe of honor from the caliph al-Qadir Bi'llah in 1000 c.e. Miniature from the *Jami' al-Tawarikh* of Rashid al-Din, ca. 1307. Mahmud decided that the courier who brought the robe was not suitable to robe a great king, so he put the robe on himself in front of his nobles. With kind permission of the University of Edinburgh Bridgeman Art Library.

this aspect of the ceremony. The son of a failed usurper took refuge with the Mamluk sultan of Egypt, who sheltered him and honored him by sending him robes. To spite and annoy the sultan, the man gave even costlier robes to the messenger who delivered the presents. To presume equality or even superiority by giving more extravagant robes to the messenger was a transgression punishable by immediate execution. This act signaled that he "behaved in a manner which made it necessary to kill him," which the Mamluk sultan did.

An enemy defeated in battle or brought in by negotiation was often forced to wear khil'a. The consequences of rejecting the robe were dire. In a well-documented incident from the 1660s (described in Jadunath Sarkar's book *Shivaji and His Times*), Mughal forces surrounded a regionally successful king named Shivaji and escorted him to Delhi to integrate him into the Mughal Empire. In the hall of public audience, officials brought the king forward and robed him, but the emperor neither spoke nor acknowledged the ceremony. Shivaji was then ushered to the very back of the audience hall. He fully understood the insult. Contrary to court rules, he refused to stand quietly but instead started to shout that he would not stand behind men whose backs he had already seen in battle. Receiving no satisfaction, he removed the robe and threw it on the floor of the audience hall, saying, "Kill me but I will not wear the khil'a." He and his entourage then turned their backs on the emperor, a serious breach of etiquette, and stalked out of the hall. Everyone at court expected them all to be executed immediately. Because of the support of a few high Mughal nobles, however, Shivaji was only imprisoned and some months later managed to escape.

Rulers also used fabrics to dishonor the leader of a failed rebellion or coup. The perpetrator was clothed in dirty rags (the inverse of robes of honor), mounted backwards on a donkey (not a horse), and paraded through the city. Execution generally followed.

A ruler presented robes of honor to certain categories of travelers, particularly jurists, learned men, and ambassadors from other rulers. The normal procedure included presentation of robes on arrival, maintenance at court, and bestowal of robes and other objects on departure. This sort of ceremonial investiture did not involve entering the service of the ruler and implied no specific fealty or employment. As one of the traveling "learned," Ibn Battuta received robes from, for example, rulers and governors all across Anatolia and down the east coast of Africa.

Rulers also invested at their pleasure an individual they wished to honor; for example, a poet for a witty couplet, a wrestler for a good match, a guide who successfully led the royal entourage through a forest, or a particularly brave soldier on the battlefield. Stores of luxurious robes were kept at the ready for the ruler's spontaneous presentation.

Robes were also used diplomatically between rulers. Ibn Battuta names the seven great rulers of his time: the sultan of Morocco, the Mamluk sultan of Egypt and Syria, the Mongol Il-Khan of Iraq and Iran, the Khan of the Golden Horde, Chaghatai Khan, the sultan of Delhi, and the ruler of China. It was considered honorable and expected that these rulers would exchange gifts that showed their wealth and access to rare and beautiful things, a "circulation of fabulous objects," as the historian Oleg Grabar has termed it. The very finest and most extraordinary robes moved in these circles. Ibn Battuta claimed both that he witnessed the arrival of an entourage from China bearing these gifts and that he was commissioned by the sultan of Delhi to return equally fabulous objects to China. Scholars have questioned both the Chinese embassy and Ibn Battuta's return visit, but such embassies relatively frequently crisscrossed Egypt, Persia, Turkey, Central Asia, and India.

Fabulous robes traveled quite far from the core of the robing world. Some of the finest extant robes of honor arrived in Europe as diplomatic robes from one ruler to another. For example, an exquisite silk robe came to Queen Christina of Sweden from the tsar of Russia in 1644. More curious was the story of a robe sent to Queen Elizabeth I. Shortly before the defeat of the Spanish Armada, the English queen established diplomatic ties with Ottoman Turkey. Both had good reason to view Spain as a common enemy. In 1594, Elizabeth promoted the connection by sending presents (including pieces of gold cloth and a jeweled portrait miniature) and a letter to the Safiye Sultan, queen mother of Mehmed III (1593–1603) and one of the most powerful individuals in the Ottoman Empire. Along with a reply to Elizabeth's letter, Safiye sent "an upper gowne of cloth of gold very rich, and under gowne of cloth of silver, and a girdle of Turkie worke, rich and faire," plus a crown studded with pearls and rubies. Elizabeth apparently enjoyed wearing the luxurious Turkish robes. Master politician that she was, Elizabeth probably kept her court and the Spanish spies guessing whether she was signaling a new Ottoman connection or merely enjoying exotic dress.

It is perhaps worth reemphasizing that khil'a was not a Muslim custom, being equally common in Christian Constantinople as in the Islamic world. Ibn Battuta was himself robed during an audience with the Byzantine emperor of Constantinople:

> He was pleased with my replies and said to his sons, "Honour this man and ensure his safety." He then bestowed on me a robe of honour and ordered for me a horse with saddle and bridle, and a parasol of the kind that the ruler has carried above his head, that being a sign of protection.… [I]t is one of the customs among them that anyone who wears the ruler's robe of honour and rides on his horse is paraded through the city bazaars with trumpets, fifes, and drums, so that people may see him.

NONKINGLY KHIL'A, KHIL'A IN A POLITICAL SYSTEM, AND ITS LATER HISTORY

Khil'a was much more than a simple investiture by kings. It was a system of honor and service that established networks between a range of people. Closest to the king were his nobles, who themselves gave out robes to their followers. In the Central Asian tradition, noblewomen also bestowed khil'a. When Ibn Battuta left the Golden Horde to accompany one of the *khatuns* (wife

of a khan) to Constantinople, "each of the *khatuns* gave me ingots of silver.… The sultan's daughter gave me more than they did, along with a robe and a horse, and altogether I had a large collection of horses, robes, and furs of miniver and sable." The chief khatun handsomely rewarded Ibn Battuta when he left her in Constantinople:

> She sent for me and gave me three hundred dinars in their gold coinage…, two thousand Venetian dirhams, a length of woolen cloth of the work of the girls (this being the best kind of such cloth), ten robes of silk, linen, and wool, and two horses, this being the gift of her father.

The practice of highly placed women both giving and receiving robes was also found elsewhere; for example, in the courts of Delhi. Ibn Battuta received a robe from the sultan's mother. Two hundred years later, during the reign of the Mughal emperor Shah Jahan, his daughter, Jahanara, was recognized by all observers as perhaps the most powerful individual in the empire. Independent states, such as Golconda, routinely sent her robes of honor. She returned robes as well as bestowing them on many occasions.

The khil'a tradition also permeated Sufi Muslim orders. Sufi practice was, however, a direct inversion of the silks and jewels of normal courtly investiture. Sufi robes were "robes of simplicity," the more worn, patched, and tattered the better, thereby showing the wearer's disdain for earthly pleasures and focus on the holy life. A robe carried the baraka (essence) of its former possessor and influenced the behavior of the receiver. Within the Sufi tradition, therefore, followers expected the robe of a great teacher or saint to deepen the receiver's piety and practice. In some orders, presentation of the robe literally passed the mantle of authority to a successor.

The closer one looks at the system, the more givers there seem to be. Ibn Battuta himself gave ceremonial robes to a guide whom he took into his employment. Beyond Ibn Battuta's narrative, the circle of givers becomes even wider. For example, the Geniza documents of the Jewish community in medieval Egypt record that the elders gave out robes of honor to certain non-Jewish merchants.

The clientship and personal bonds of loyalty that khil'a implied did not flow only to the ruler. Instead, there was a complex network of loyalties that tied the recipient to a variety of political actors. Rulers varied in their legitimacy and, therefore, the loyalty they could expect from honorific robing.

In the best of times, the robe signified a personal bond with an adult ruler securely on the throne of a successful, solvent state. Such a ruler expected to employ the one he robed, and the recipient expected to serve his ruler with his talents and his life, if necessary. Often, however, reign and rule were much less secure. Many rulers were, in fact, usurpers or rebels with only as much loyalty as military success could provide. Many rulers were minors; loyalty was only to the faction that controlled the throne. Some rulers were women. Though a queen might offer robes of honor, loyalty often depended on the army's judgment of her personal ability to lead.

Rather than a simple ceremony of royal largesse, for these less-legitimate rulers, presentation of robes of honor was probably a clarifying moment regarding the support or nonsupport of a crucial noble, who might refuse the robes if not supportive. Every succession meant war, with both sides offering robes to crucial allies. Ironically, rather than strengthening a king's power, the actual

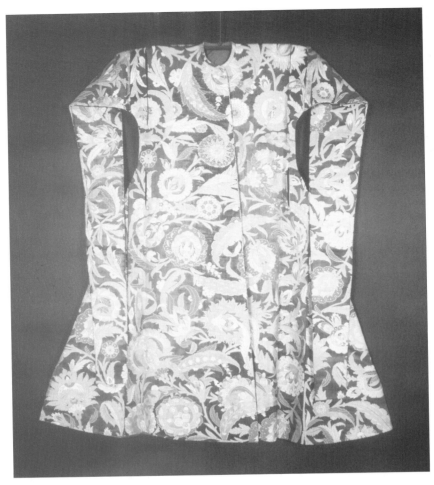

Turkish court robe of polychrome silk with gilt metal thread and seven colors, mid-sixteenth century. The robe has an inscription to Süleyman's son and is matched by another in cream silk that was given to his brother. Topkapi Palace Museum.

practice of the ceremony often fragmented and weakened it. For example, at the start of a military campaign, each noble involved received robes directly from the emperor and treasured his direct, personal tie. This dynamic wreaked havoc with a unified command structure. Each noble could—and did—appeal directly to the court over the head of the commander.

Khil'a remained in active use in Central and Southwest Asia, India, and North Africa through the nineteenth century, slowly yielding to European colonial practices and those of the modern nation-state. Because khil'a expressed a generalized personal fealty, it fit poorly with colonial efforts at social control, which required precisely defined rights and responsibilities. As part and parcel of cultural and racial dominance, the colonial rulers insisted on hats and pants and, by and large, rejected elegant robes. Across the robing world, the lawyers and military men who led movements of independence—both on the left and on the right—found khil'a hopelessly courtly and old-fashioned.

Khil'a has, however, not entirely disappeared and continues in a few local and regional settings. Eastern Christian churches continue to use elaborate investiture ceremonies and robes. Tibetan Buddhists regularly place a prayer shawl on someone they honor. The "robe of simplicity" continues to be the dress of both Sufi and Buddhist orders. A full khil'a ceremony is found, however, only in a few Muslim countries in Africa, where an ambassador is expected to change to local elite robes.

References and Further Reading

Arnold, Janet. *Queen Elizabeth's Wardrobe Unlock'd: The Inventories of the Wardrobe of Robes Prepared in July, 1600*. Leeds, UK: Money, 1988.

Allsen, Thomas T. "Robing in the Mongolian Empire." In *Robes and Honor: The Medieval World of Investiture*, edited by Stewart Gordon, 305–315. New York: Palgrave, 2001.

Elias, Jamal. "The Sufi Robe (*kirqa*) as a Vehicle of Spiritual Authority." In *Robes and Honor: The Medieval World of Investiture*, edited by Stewart Gordon, 275–290. New York: Palgrave, 2001.

Goitien, S.D. *A Mediterranean Society: The Jewish Communities of the Arab World as Portrayed in the Documents of the Cairo Geniza*. 5 vols. Berkeley and Los Angeles: University of California Press, 1967–1988.

Gordon, Stewart. "A World of Investiture." In *Robes and Honor: The Medieval World of Investiture*, edited by Stewart Gordon, 7. New York: Palgrave, 2001.

Grabar, Oleg. "The Shared Culture of Objects." In *Byzantine Court Culture from 829 to 1204*, edited by Henry Mcguire, 115–130. Washington, DC: Dumbarton Oaks, 1997.

Hassan, Muhammad M. *Social Life under the Abbasids.* London: Longman, 1979.

Ibn Battuta. *The Travels of Ibn Battuta, A.D. 1325–1354.* Translated by H.A.R. Gibb. New Delhi: Mushiram Manoharlal, 1993.

Liu, Xinru. "Silk, Robes, and Relations between Early Chinese Dynasties and Nomads beyond the Great Wall." In *Robes and Honor: The Medieval World of Investiture,* edited by Stewart Gordon, 23–34. New York: Palgrave, 2001.

Rose, Jenny. "Sassanian Splendour: The Appurtances of Royalty." In *Robes and Honor: The Medieval World of Investiture,* edited by Stewart Gordon, 35–59. New York: Palgrave, 2001.

Sarkar, Jadunath. *Shivaji and His Times.* 6th rev. ed. Calcutta: S. C. Sarkar, 1961.

Skilliter, S. A. "Three Letters from the Ottoman 'Sultana' Safiye to Queen Elizabeth." In *Documents from Islamic Chanceries,* edited by Samuel M. Stern, 119–159. Oxford: Bruno Cassier, 1965.

Stewart Gordon

See also Trade, Textiles, and Dress in Central and Southwest Asia; Laws of Differentiation; Sumptuary Laws.

Face Veils

A face veil is a separate garment that is used to cover all or part of the face, usually, but not exclusively, that of a woman. In addition, there are garments that cover both the body and the face. These are not strictly speaking face veils, because they are attached to other garments, such as a cap or an outer wrap. This type of "face veil" can cover the body from head to ankles. The most famous examples are the *chadari* or burqa worn by women in Afghanistan and Pakistan.

A question that is frequently asked is why should a woman wear a veil or more specifically a face veil? It is a common feature, all over the world, that women rather than men wear some form of veiling to cover their head, hair, neck, and sometimes face. But in the Islamic world the veiling of women is more common, both in the past and the present. The reasons for veiling are often sought in religion, and many Muslim women will say that they wear a veil, or even a face veil, because of their creed. But it is also quite clear that religion is not the sole reason. A veil, and in particular a face veil, has many functions, and there are different reasons for a woman to cover her face. A veiled woman approaching from a distance signals that she is a respectable (married) woman. From closer up, when the color, shape, and main decoration of the veil can be seen, she shows her affiliations (ethnicity and family). From nearby, when the texture, sound, smell, and detailed appearance of the veil are noticeable, the veil tells something about the woman's personality (personal style, quality, care, character, and so forth).

SEXUAL ATTRACTION, HONOR, AND THE FEMALE LIFE CYCLE

Women, according to many groups, should be veiled because their presence, physically, mentally, or spiritually, is a sexual distraction to men, hence the separation of men and women in public spaces and in religious institutions such as churches, synagogues, and mosques. Within Central and Southwest Asia, women may or may not cover their faces, but the display of other parts of the body, especially the genitalia, either by men or women, is subject to strong taboos. It is regarded as preferable for both genders to wear loose clothing from the waist to the knees. However, over the centuries and in different parts of the region, the exact parts of the body that need to be covered have changed. According to the Turkish-American writer Alev Croutier, for example, in late-nineteenth-century Turkey, a woman's nose was regarded as sexually attractive, and if someone saw it, she might be accused of being an infidel or a prostitute.

In many cultures, one sexually charged part of the female body is her head hair: A woman is regarded as naked, both physically and spiritually, if she does not cover her hair or her face. Such views are expressed by both men and women and should not be solely attributed to Muslim religious beliefs. There are numerous biblical references, for example, to a woman's hair and how her hair should be shorn if she was no longer regarded as respectable.

In Central and Southwest Asia as well as the eastern Mediterranean, there has always been a strong link between clothing and women's position and role, especially in public places. This relationship can be traced back at least to the second millennium B.C.E. in the region, if not earlier, and to the development of patriarchal societies. In such groups, for example, it is common for the actions and demeanor of a woman to reflect on her male relatives' honor and men's ability, especially that of the head of the household, to keep the womenfolk in order. In addition, adult females, especially because of their ability to bear children (especially sons), are regarded as valuable and vulnerable commodities who need to be protected. In particular, women need to be prevented from coming into contact with outside influences, notably strange (nonrelated) males or males who fall outside the local incest taboos.

Veiling and seclusion were practiced in many eastern Mediterranean countries from very early times on. In classical Greek society, for example, the concept of *aidos* was applied to women as a means of social control. Depending on the circumstances, aidos could mean shame, reserve, modesty, and respect, as well as honor and self-awareness. In many cases, a woman's behavior was closely linked to the honor of the family, especially of its men. The same connotations associated with aidos can be found in many traditional Islamic communities in Central and Southwest Asia. In general, by wearing a veil of some kind, a woman is accepting the role of a conservative and traditional Muslim woman. In return, she expects to be treated in a respectful manner that acknowledges her position. She thus establishes a general consensus of approval as to her and her family's honor.

One way of upholding honor and protecting women is to keep them away from any sort of "unlawful" attention and to seclude them inside the family home. Whenever women do have to go out, it becomes necessary to devise some form of shielding. This was done in the form of special clothing, namely veiling in all its many forms. It is no coincidence that the word *chador* is used to describe the enveloping outer garment worn by women in Iran. It literally means "tent," thus a temporary house. Such garments are deliberately designed to disguise a female's body and to declare to the world that here is a "respectable" woman who is unavailable to other men.

Veiling is also used to indicate the physical status of a female, namely to show whether she is in the fertile phase of her life or not. In general, in Southwest Asia, prepubescent girls do not veil, while in most groups pubescent girls and married women do. When veiled, the color of a woman's head or face veil can further indicate her age and social status, both in public and in private. Girls tend to wear bright colors; married women wear somewhat duller ones. The color for established matrons moves toward the dark purples and blues, while a postmenopausal woman or a widow (thus officially nonfertile) would normally wear very dark blue or black. The decoration of the cloth and jewelry also change according to the woman's age and status. A girl will wear some decoration, a young married woman a considerable quantity, but then, as the woman gets older, the amount of decoration worn, especially in public, decreases.

ETHNIC IDENTITY AND SOCIAL STATUS

Ethnic and cultural origins often play a prominent role in whether a woman wears a face veil and what type. This strong cultural element is alluded to in the following anecdote given by the Arab princess Musbah Haidar. At the beginning of the twentieth century, she and her immediate family lived in Ottoman Turkey. The whole family was very aware of being of Arab descent and felt themselves superior to the Turks, including even the Ottoman sultan. As girls, Musbah and her sister wore an Arab headdress consisting of a white silk *samade* (head cloth) and a gold head rope (*'aqal*). At one point, however, her father, Amir Ali Haidar, asked Musbah to wear a face veil and the *charshaf*, the Turkish outer garment, like other female relatives, when outside of the home. At the time, it was illegal for adult urban Muslim women in

Turkey to appear in public without being totally veiled. Musbah, however, refused to wear the charshaf and face veil: "Would you have me give up an Arab head-dress for one which is not?" The question was unanswerable, and Musbah never wore a face veil.

The relationship between veiling and social status varies considerably from one community to another, both geographically and chronologically. Sometimes, for example, women from an elite background do not wear face veils, either in private or in public, in order to show their higher status. Women from poor, rural areas often do not wear face veils either, because they have to work and extra clothing gets in the way. But there is also a feeling that women in some villages do not have to use extensive veiling, including face veils, because the village is one large extended family where strangers seldom come. In contrast, middle-class women (notably the wives of merchants), and those aspiring to this status, would wear face veils in order to show their social ambitions and those of their family.

It is often said that tribal and urban women wear face veils, while village women do not. However, this situation is not quite so clear cut. In a village context, women from wealthier families may choose to wear face veils to distinguish themselves from poorer women who do not use them. The Arab-American anthropologist Aida Kanafani has noted that wearing a burqa (face veil) allows some Bedouin women in the United Arab Emirates greater freedom because it means they can work in public without having to worry about strange males: "In the desert and mountains women work collecting wood or breeding goats, where they are more exposed to male presence. In this case, the mask [burqa] allows freedom of movement."

Veiling has long been used to distinguish a free woman from a slave. An early written example of a female becoming the (sexual) property of one particular male through a change in her clothing is seen in a letter from the ancient Mesopotamian king of Mari, Zimri-Lim, to one of his wives. It refers to a number of recently acquired captives, some of whom were destined to become the king's concubines. The letter was written sometime between 1790 and 1745 B.C.E., and in it he noted that more booty (females) was available and that he would select some girls from this booty, have them veiled, and then send them on to his wife for her to add them to his "collection."

A few hundred years later, a Middle Assyrian law (ca. 1450–1250 B.C.E.) stated that "ladies of birth" (free and legally married women) and their (free) maids or husband's concubines (not free but "married") had to wear some form of outer wrap in public. The same law also defined the punishment for a female slave or prostitute who wore a similar garment. All her clothes and jewelry were to be removed, she would be beaten, all her hair would be shaved off and tar poured over her head, and, finally, if she was a slave, her ears would be hacked off.

The social difference between a free woman and a slave, and whether or not she is allowed to wear a veil or face veil, can also be traced into the Islamic period. It is said, for example, that the second caliph, Omar Ibn al-Khattab (r. 634–644 C.E.), saw a slave girl wearing a qina (a form of face veil) and that he beat her saying, "Are you trying to imitate a free woman?" (described by Fadwa El Guindi). More recently, the Norwegian anthropologist Unni Wikan has noted that until the 1950s, when slavery was officially abolished in Oman, slave women living there were not allowed to wear a particular face veil locally called the burqa. However, once

An elaborate and highly decorative face veil (*burqa*), northern Sinai, 1960s–1970s. Some women wear part of their dowry in the form of silver and gold coins sewn to their face veil as a mark of status. Textile Research Centre, Leiden.

slavery was abolished, a number of ex-slaves started to wear the burqa as a sign of their new social status.

ECONOMICS, HEALTH, AND BEAUTY

In many Muslim societies a woman is given a dowry (*mahr*) at her engagement. Among some groups, notably the Bedouin from the Sinai region and the eastern Arabian Peninsula, it is not uncommon for a woman to wear part of her dowry in the form of silver and gold coins sewn to her face veil. In this way, she tells the world of her married status, her financial security, and the positive regard her husband and family have for her. In such a situation, the face veil is basically giving two different messages at the same time: "keep away" and "look at me and my (honored) position within my family, and the position (honor and wealth) of my family with respect to the outside world."

Another aspect of finances is education and careers. Many Southwest Asian women have attended schools, colleges, and universities and made a career for themselves in a wide variety of professions, especially teaching and health care. There is no universal rule in the Islamic world regarding veiling when working in public. Some women have a great deal of choice regarding whether they appear in public veiled or not (for example, women in Lebanon and Jordan), while in other countries, such as Iran, they have to accept being veiled so that they can work outside of their homes. In contrast, some nations forbid veiled women from working in public buildings (for example, Turkey). Yet there are also lands where Muslim women are not meant to appear in public at all, working or otherwise, without being totally veiled (namely, in Saudi Arabia and, until recently, in Taliban-ruled Afghanistan).

The wearing of veils and the physical and mental isolation that often goes with it are linked to social and psychological problems, including depression and dependency. In contrast, however, the wearing of veils in some societies means that women can leave the house and take a role in public spaces, thus decreasing the possibility of depression. In addition to this aspect, there are also physical effects. Clothes, including face veils, have the basic function of protecting the body against the environment. In Central and Southwest Asia, the sun has always been a great danger to people's health, causing heat stroke, dehydration, and so forth. A more modern problem is the decrease in the ozone layer, which increases the risk of skin cancers, particularly melanomas, in some parts of the world. In Southwest Asia, some women have taken to wearing sunglasses and veils, including face veils, to protect themselves.

For hundreds of years, Arab, Persian, Turkish, as well as Western writers have paid attention to the dark, large, and mysterious eyes of veiled women, a facial feature that women have not been slow to use. In some Arab communities, the face veil itself is a *zinah* or an adornment, because it is regarded as enhancing personal beauty. According to Kanafani, this virtue of the face veil is particularly noticeable in the Gulf states:

> Women wear it to embellish themselves. When one looks at the mask [burqa] one realizes that its largest portion covers the mouth and that the rest of the face is exposed, its beautiful features enhanced, and its ugly ones concealed or softened. One of the informants pointed out that the mask does not conceal much and that it beautifies the wearer.

Postcard of a woman from Istanbul, late nineteenth century. She is wearing a fashionable, open style of *yaşmak* (her hair is showing) and a frilled coat (*ferace*). Popular until the late nineteenth century, the *yaşmak* was a combination of two types of veils worn in medieval Istanbul: a *lisam* (a length of cloth wrapped around the head and lower part of the face) and a head veil covering the hair. Textile Research Centre, Leiden.

However, the idea of a face veil as an important beauty aid is not widespread, nor encouraged in more conservative Islamic circles.

RELIGION, PAN-ISLAMIC DRESS, AND MODERN POLITICS

What is the role of religion in whether a woman wears a veil or not? For many women in the Islamic world, this question simply is not relevant. Until the beginning of the twentieth century and the freer movement of ideas, the wearing of a face veil was not a question of choice but one of following local customs. In some cases, this was done because all the other women in the community wore face veils, and it was a point of personal and family honor to wear one as well. In other cases, the wearing of a face veil was not part of a woman's religious duties, as in the case of some Christian and Jewish women, but they were worn in public as a form of protection. A woman not wearing a face veil stood out and could easily become a target for abuse or violence from her (Muslim) neighbors.

In many Central and Southwest Asian societies, there are heated debates as to whether face veils are obligatory (*fard* or *wajib*) or (highly) recommended (*mustahab* or *sunna*). The discussion depends in part on the influence of religious or secular groups and the locally accepted form of Islam. Some women may prefer their traditional face veils but feel pressure from secular modernists who want them to stop wearing them. They may also be influenced by religious modernists, who say that women should stop wearing their local forms of face veils and wear instead what the modernists/fundamentalists regard as less frivolous and more sober versions.

Since the 1970s and the "emergent Islamic consciousness," the movement toward and acceptance (or otherwise) of veiling have been growing both in the Islamic world and elsewhere. Two terms are generally used to describe a veiled woman, namely *muhajjaba* and *munaqqaba*. *Muhajjaba* is the normal Arabic term used for a woman who decides to cover her head and body but not her face. A *munaqqaba* is a woman who also covers her face, usually with one or more face veils. In addition, the term *niqabi* is becoming synonymous with *munaqqaba*. These terms are linguistically related: Both derive from the word for a type of face veil, the *niqab*.

Since the early 1980s, there has been a global trend toward a form of Islamically correct dress, often called hijab. This form of pan-Islamic clothing can be divided into several basic groups, notably an international style and a Saudi style. The international style of dress does not belong to one particular culture or ethnic group. It is characterized by the wearing of a small head covering (*mandil*), a head and body covering (often the *khimar*), and sometimes, but not always, a face veil (normally either a burqa or niqab). This style of hijab comes with fashionable additions such as the use of decoration, mixed materials, different colors, and so forth. This type of dress is widely available. More and more Islamic clothing sites are on the Internet, catering to an international demand for Islamically acceptable, usually non-Western, clothing, which is called *al-ziyy al-Islami* (dress of Islam), *zey islami* (Islamic dress), or *zey shari'a* (sharia dress).

Another form of pan-Islamic dress with face veils, which can be found in various urban centers throughout the Islamic world, is the use of black, Saudi-style garments. It is based on modern, urban Saudi outfits and generally includes a black cloak (*abayeh*), a black head scarf (*shaylah* or *maknun*), and a black face veil of some kind (such as the burqa, niqab, or the all-enveloping *boushiyah*). Again, Saudi-style face veils are widely available in shops and on the Internet. In addition, local styles and variations of hijab are developing, as can be seen in the Gulf region, where Khalij (Gulf) dress consisting of a head covering and black overgarment (abayeh) is becoming more popular among younger women.

The subject of women, veils, and face veils has been in and out of national and international politics for the last 150 years. The use of face veils has been banned, encouraged, or enforced by law, as well as praised and vilified. Some face veils have even become modern icons that are instantly recognizable throughout the world, such as the chadari from Afghanistan. In the early twenty-first century, the role of face veiling is a matter of frequent and at times vehement discussions in a number of Western and Islamic countries.

Veiled women are sometimes seen, especially among certain groups of feminists, as oppressed and repressed. In some cases, this is true, but it is not inevitably so. All too often, only two types of face veils are presented as evidence for this perceived oppression, which are the Saudi Arabian niqab (associated with the image of "black crows") and the Afghan chadari. The situation, however, is not quite that simple. There are many different types of veils, and more specifically face veils, throughout the Islamic world.

ANCIENT FACE VEILS

The use of face veils probably started in ancient Mesopotamia, but evidence of their use dates from the fourth century B.C.E. Representations of veiled women come from the Hellenistic eastern Mediterranean. The use of these garments is related to the concept of female modesty when in public places, as well as emphasizing a woman's status as married. A woman who wore such a face veil was called "Aphrodite's tortoise." This is a very symbolic concept, as Aphrodite was the Greek goddess of love, while a tortoise is a creature that hides its head/face in its shell (its home), just as a respectable woman hides her face in public.

Two women wearing Turkish-style outer wraps (*charshafs*) with face veils made of a length of printed cloth (*mandil*) draped over their faces, Jerusalem, early twentieth century. Textile Research Centre, Leiden.

At least three different types of face veils were used during the Hellenistic period: the *tegidion*, a *litham*-style face veil, and a qina-style face veil. All three of these face-veil types have survived into the early twenty-first century. The tegidion was made out of a rectangle of cloth with ties at the upper corners. Some had two eyeholes (comparable to the modern Islamic niqab), while others had a wide slit (again comparable to the niqab). Women throughout the Hellenistic world wore this style of face veil. Another Hellenistic face veil resembled the later Islamic litham. It was made from a long piece of cloth wrapped horizontally around the lower half of the face, covering the nose, mouth, and chin. This can be seen on a number of representations dating from the third century B.C.E. The third form was a long rectangle of cloth draped over the head and allowed to fall down over the face. It is identical to the modern qina and the *maghmug* worn by women in Yemen. One of the earliest representations of this ancient face veil comes from Alexandria, Egypt, and dates to the first century B.C.E. It was made of a length of sheer material with a decorative fringe along the lower edge. There are no eyeholes.

The wearing of face veils ceased during the Roman and Byzantine periods, although some women did cover their faces with their mantles as a temporary sign of modesty. Evidence for face veils in pre-Islamic Arabia consists of vague references to women and their clothing in Jahili (pre-Islamic) and early Islamic poetry. It would appear that women wore a variety of veils around their heads and bodies and that respectable Jahiliya women covered their faces in the presence of strangers as a sign of modesty and honor. Following the spread of Islam in the seventh and eighth centuries C.E., there is considerably more written information about clothing, and references to face veils as separate garments become common.

OTTOMAN FACE VEILS

In the early second millennium, the Turkish Seljuks from Central Asia invaded the Anatolian highlands of modern Turkey. By the fourteenth century, Seljuk power had started to wane, and various other Turkish groups succeeded them, including the followers of Osman, from the area around the city of Bursa in northwestern Anatolia, close to what is Istanbul in the early twenty-first century. The Ottomans, named after Osman, gradually took control of the entire region. Over the next two hundred years, they extended their power until their empire included most of Southwest Asia, the Hijaz (northern coastal region of western Saudi Arabia, including the cities of Medina and Mecca), and North Africa, as well as the Balkans. From the late seventeenth century on, however, the Ottomans' power gradually declined. The final demise of the Ottoman Empire came at the end of World War I (1914–1918). For more than half a millennium, however, Ottoman culture, including its clothing traditions, spread all across the empire and beyond.

Ottoman women living in medieval Istanbul wore two types of face veils. The simplest form was a length of cloth wrapped around the head and lower part of the face; this was called a *lisam* (Turkish for *litham*). This was worn primarily by attendants and servants. The second form was the *peche*, a small, stiffish veil made out of horsehair, fastened around the forehead. The peche was worn by ladies in combination with the lisam and continued in use until the late seventeenth century, when it was replaced by the *yaşmak*. The yaşmak combined the head veil that covered the hair with the lisam, which covered the lower half of the face. Both garments remained separate items but together formed the yaşmak. This combination became an upper-class fashion, while lower-class women continued to wear only the lisam.

The popularity of the yaşmak continued until the late nineteenth century, when some conservative women started to wear a large face veil (*kil peche*), which draped down over the face. These peches were much longer and more flexible than the medieval form. The modern peches were usually worn with the charshaf, an outer covering that totally covered the body except for the face. The use of these peches spread from Istanbul to other urban centers throughout the Ottoman world.

Younger and more liberally educated Turkish women started to wear a variety of veil types. One was based on the European/Parisian hat veil, made from a piece of net attached to a hat. The netting was pulled down over the face. Another type of face veil was made from a single piece of cloth that covered the forehead, nose, and mouth. Often, the cloth was so transparent that the effect emphasized rather than concealed the face. This fashion spread to other regions of Southwest Asia, especially Egypt and Syria, where some women called it a yaşmak, while others called it a burqa.

With the resurgence of Islam in the late twentieth century, garments such as the charshaf have been reintroduced. The modern charshafs are sometimes worn with a length of fine material draped over the head and covering the face. This is also called a peche.

EGYPTIAN AND LEVANTINE FACE VEILS

Women in this region, where the customs of Southwest Asia overlap with those of North Africa, have worn face veils from at least the ninth century on. Various types were used, including the burqa, mandil, niqab, and qina. The classic medieval burqa was made from a headband with a veil attached at the temples and nose. Examples of burqas and niqabs have been excavated at various Egyptian sties.

The mandil is well known from medieval Southwest Asian and European depictions. It was made out of a rectangle of cloth that covered the nose, mouth, and chin. Another medieval form was the qina, which was a length of (semitransparent) material draped over the head and allowed to hang over and cover all of the face.

Most illustrations of women from the seventeenth century and later depict them wearing the burqa. In the early nineteenth century, there were several types of burqa. Upper-class women, for example, wore a long, white veil, while middle- and lower-class women wore black or dark blue burqas decorated with metal disks (*bark*). Peasant women did not normally wear face veils.

Apart from Egyptian Arab families, there were also many people living in Cairo and Alexandria who were of Turkish descent. Their fashion was linked to that of Istanbul. Many Turkish Egyptian women wore a yaşmak. When this fashion was dropped in Istanbul, it disappeared in Egypt as well. In the late nineteenth century, when the Turks adopted the transparent peche, more liberal upper-class Egyptian women followed suit. Middle- and lower-class Turkish Egyptians chose instead a new style made from a piece of cotton that covered the nose and lower part of the face. It had no headband but was still called a burqa. Some middle- and lower-class Egyptian women continued to wear the black or very dark blue burqa but in a shorter form and with a tube-shaped amulet (bark) over the nose. Others wore a transparent version of the Egyptian burqa without a bark.

In the early twenty-first century, various types of face veils are being worn, including the pan-Islamic niqab. This niqab is used to cover the nose and lower half of the face (it is also known as a half burqa or half niqab). A second type of niqab is longer, covering the whole face, and has a slit for the eyes. This is the full niqab. Sometimes, conservative Egyptian women are seen wearing a half niqab with a qina (sometimes called a burqa), which is a long length of black netting that is draped over head and face.

Unlike in Egypt, Jewish and Christian women in Palestine and the Levant did not wear face veils, while Muslim women did. A common face veil from the region was locally called a burqa. It was made from a long piece of cloth hung from a headband. The cloth came down to the waist or lower, very similar to the long Egyptian burqa. Turkish women living in the Jerusalem region in the early twentieth century wore the Ottoman charshaf with a black horsehair face veil (peche) or a decorative length of cloth that covered part of the head and all of the face (similar to a qina). This was locally called a mandil.

By the mid-twentieth century, most urban Palestinian women had stopped wearing face veils. Since the late twentieth century, however, some Muslim women in Palestine have started to wear pan-Islamic hijab, including niqabs and burqas of various styles and colors.

FACE VEILS ON THE ARABIAN PENINSULA

In general, the people in the north and west of the Arabian Peninsula have strong links with the Levant and Syria, while those in the east (Kuwait, Qatar, the United Arab Emirates, and Oman) look toward Iran and the Indian subcontinent for trade and cultural contacts. These links have had an effect on the type of face veils worn.

The Hijaz in western Saudi Arabia is a rock escarpment that runs north to south along the Red Sea coast. There are three main urban centers in the region: Jidda, Mecca, and Medina. Sometimes, the women there wore the Turkish lisam, which was made up of a fine length of material wrapped around the lower half of the face. The main face veil, however, worn by urban Hijaz women until the late nineteenth century was a long, white face veil (burqa) similar to those worn by ladies in Egypt.

Yemen lies in the south of the peninsula. Women living in Sana'a, the capital, wear a range of face veils including the burqa, qina (also called a *khunna*), lithmah, and maghmug. There are two types of burqa. The first is worn by unmarried girls and is really a half burqa, as it covers only the nose and the lower part of the face. The second type is the classic burqa, made of two pieces of cloth, which covers the whole face. The qina is made out of a length of cloth that is draped over the head and allowed to hang down over the face. Some examples are made out of a simple length of semitransparent black cloth, while more elaborate versions are made out of decorative silk or a synthetic. In the early twenty-first century, the qina is associated with brides. The qina is also often worn together with an outer garment called a *sharshaf*.

The lithmah is made up of a long rectangle of dark-colored cloth that is wrapped around the upper and lower parts of the head leaving the eyes free. It is comparable to the litham-type face veil worn all over the Islamic world. Girls start wearing this form of face veil from about seven years of age to prepare them for wearing a covering over the face and being a woman. Married women often wear this face veil and regard it as an informal type that can be worn at home or in the streets. The final form is the maghmug, worn only by married women, generally those from the upper social groups. The basic maghmug is a length of cloth draped over the head and down over the face, normally black with red and white "eyes" created by a tie-dye (*plangi*) technique.

Many Bedouin groups live in the central and western part of Saudi Arabia. Some Bedouin women wear face veils, but others do not. The construction and appearance of Bedouin face

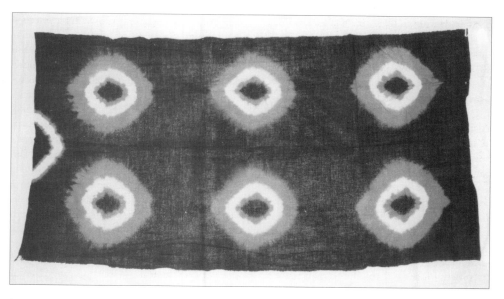

A *maghmug* face veil, Sana'a, Yemen, late twentieth century. This type of veil is created by a tie-dye (*plangi*) technique and is normally black with red and white "eyes." It is made only in Sana'a and worn only by married women in this area. Textile Research Centre, Leiden.

veils change along a north-south axis. In the north, many Bedouin women wear a soft cotton niqab. These cover the face and neck and, in some cases, reach down to the waist. Some Bedouin women from the Red Sea coastal region wear face veils that are locally called burqa, although technically they are *batullah*. The veils are normally rectangular in shape with rectangular eyeholes. Some merely cover the face, while others reach to the waist. Many face veils are made from a heavy, red or orange cotton material that is decorated with appliqué braids, rickrack, mother-of-pearl buttons, small silver beads, pendants, metal bosses, coins, and even bells. These veils can be very noisy.

Bedouin face veils from the south of Mecca tend to be of the classic burqa type. Bedouin women living in the southwest ('Asir region) near the border between Saudi Arabia and Yemen wear similar face veils. They are usually made from a fine, black cotton material and decorated with silver bosses, pendants, and braids, along with small decorative bosses, small tassels, and so on hanging from the two lower corners of the veil section.

The "traditional" face veils worn in the eastern parts of the Arabian Peninsula are different from those in the west and southwest. The garments are smaller, plainer, and, at first glance, less varied. The face veils in question come from eastern Saudi Arabia, Kuwait, Bahrain, Qatar, the United Arab Emirates, and Oman. Two main types of face veils are worn here, the niqab and the battulah. Somewhat confusingly, both are often locally called a burqa.

The typical eastern Arabian battulah is comparable to those worn by Bedouin women along the Red Sea coast. Covering all but the eyes or just part of the face, all have the characteristic vertical pleat over the nose that can range in width from about one-eighth inch (a few millimeters) to a little more than an inch (three centimeters). The niqab consists of a long, straight piece of cloth that hides all of the face, apart from the eyes.

In general, the battulah face veil is worn by settled and Bedouin Arab women in the eastern and southeastern coastal districts of the peninsula, from Dohar in Qatar to Salalah in southern Oman. Squarish in form with a rounded lower edge, it covers the eyebrows, nose, and mouth, leaving the eyes and part of the cheeks completely free. In general, Baluch women tend to wear a less revealing form than urban Arab women. In addition, older women tend to wear more concealing versions than younger women.

Bedouin women living in the interior deserts of Oman often wear a longer form with either a straight or a rounded lower edge. This covers the complete face, with holes of various sizes for the eyes. They have very prominent pleats down the middle. Sometimes, the chin of younger women is visible to show tribal chin tattoos, but as a woman gets older, her face veil gets longer. The niqab is worn by some Bedouin, mainly in the north and northeast of the peninsula, especially Kuwait. The niqab is also rapidly becoming a popular form of face veil in urban centers and even outside the peninsula. Normally, if an urban woman is going to wear a face veil, she will do so when she gets married. Bedouin girls start to wear face veils, either a battulah or a niqab, at the onset of puberty.

IRANIAN FACE VEILS

The history and development of face veils on the Iranian Plateau are as complicated and diverse as the land itself. The plateau has been the subject of conquests, reconquests, invasions, and peaceful migrations for thousands of years. Iran follows the Shiite rather than the Sunni version of Islam. As a result of its history,

this part of the world has a varied ethnic composition, all of which is reflected in the types of face veils that are used. Officially, the wearing of face veils was banned under the Uniform Dress Code of 1936. However, some groups of women continue to wear them, notably in the southern Bandar region of the country.

Depictions of women wearing face veils can be traced back to the mid-thirteenth century. Some women are shown wearing a length of cloth wrapped around the head with the ends hanging down the back. A slit was left for the eyes. The cloth was kept in place with a band. This form vanished by the seventeenth century except among one group, the Zoroastrians, who still wear it. They call it a *makmun*. Another form of medieval face veil consisted of a cloth that covered the wearer's nose, mouth, and part of her throat. It was probably worn at all times by ladies in public but could be removed or lowered by servants. This style vanished in the seventeenth century.

A third form of medieval face veil was the peche. This was a rectangular veil, usually made from horsehair, that was held in place at the forehead with ties. Like its Turkish counterparts, some versions were short and were used to cover the upper part of the head while casting a shadow over the lower half of the face; other forms were much longer and covered the complete face. These were generally worn by the upper classes. The use of the peche had died out in Iran by the seventeenth century, but it was revived in the late nineteenth century and continued to be worn well into the twentieth century. There were two types of "revival" peche. The first was made of horsehair and, like its medieval form, was rigid. The second form was larger and softer and made of silk. It was used to cover all of the face. This type was popular in Ottoman Turkey around the turn of the century, and Turkish women living in and around Tabriz, Iran, followed this fashion.

The most widely used Iranian face veil was the *ru-band*, dating to the seventeenth century and worn by urban women. In its earliest form, the ru-band was made out of a length of cloth fastened at the sides of the head; it was used to cover the nose and lower part of the face (comparable to the modern half burqa or half niqab). The classic version with an eye grid developed during the mid-seventeenth century and continued to be worn until the beginning of the twentieth century. It was made out of a variety of materials, depending on the wearer's status: Ladies wore a ru-band made of silk or very fine cotton, while lower-class women wore coarser cotton versions.

For centuries, the trade links between India, Iran, and the Arab world opened up the extreme south of Iran to a wide range of ethnic and cultural influences. Many people in the Bandar region are Sunni rather than Shiite Muslims, a difference reflected in the range of face veils worn. Three types are found: the burqa, battulah, and niqab. Exactly when the various forms were introduced is not certain. The type of face veil worn by a Bandari woman depends on (a) her religious background (Sunni or Shiite), (b) her ethnic origins, and (c) where she lives.

Many Shiite women in the Bandar region, for example, wear bright red, rectangular masks of the battulah construction, locally known as a burqa, decorated with various patterns. A red version signifies a Bandari woman, whereas Baluch women living in the Bandar region wear an orange burqa. In addition, specific designs relate to various towns such as Bandar Abbas, Bandar Langi, Minab, and so on. Many Sunni women in the Bandar region wear either black battulahs, which are usually squarish and long, or gold masklike forms. In contrast to the red, rectangular shapes worn by local Shiite women, the Sunni battulah is made out of black cotton or velvet.

The term *battulah* (or sometimes *burqa*) is also used in the Bandar region for a face veil or mask in shiny gold or purple cloth. They are cut into shapes that emphasize rather than hide the eyes. These face veils are directly related to those worn by urban women in Dubai, Qatar, and Oman. Some Bandari Sunni women wear a niqab-style face veil. They are made from two layers of black cotton material with a narrow slit for the eyes.

FACE VEILS IN SOUTH CENTRAL ASIA

For thousands of years, many different cultural groups have lived in South Central Asia, each with its own culture, religion, and way of life. In the early twenty-first century, the main groups are the Turkmen, the Uzbeks, the Tajiks, the Kyrgyz, and the Kazakhs. The practices of veiling and seclusion of women vary considerably among these groups. The Kazakhs have no tradition of veiling or seclusion, while some Turkmen, Tajik, and Uzbek women wear face veils.

In general, Turkmen face veils cover the woman's mouth and chin but not the nose and eyes. This feature distinguishes Turkmen face veils from those of the Iranians and Arabs. Turkmen face veils vary according to (a) which Turkmen group the woman belongs to, (b) her age, (c) her marital status, and (d) the occasion. One of the face veils used resembles a litham. It is made from a length of cloth that is wrapped around the lower half of the face. Some Turkmen women, especially the more elderly, still wear a rigid framework (*boyrok*) on their head that is covered with a large, roughly triangular cloth (*qinyac uci* or *yaşmak*). The two elements, frame and cloth, together form the *qenqach*. One end of the cloth, used as a veil to cover the lower part of the face, is attached to the headdress base with a small hook or safety pin.

Another face veil, worn by the Goklan Turkmen women, is the *yaşmak*. This type of face veil was already known in the late nineteenth century and is probably much older. The Turkmen *yaşmak* is a long piece of dark red or black cloth decorated with colored stripes that covers the lower part of the face, leaving the nose exposed, and reaches down to the waist. The modern version of this face veil normally has a fringe ending in small, white glass beads.

Until the 1960s, a typical Yomut Turkmen woman's headdress (*yagliq*) was made up of a skullcap covered by a scarf, which was also used to cover the lower part of the face. This arrangement was then covered by a second scarf, which completely covered the cap and hair. Since the 1970s, many Yomut women no longer cover their faces at all times, although most wear a large shawl (*yagliq*), which can be pulled across the lower face if necessary. Among various groups of nomadic and seminomadic Turkmen, it is traditional for a new bride to wear a face veil called a *shamenja*, made from strings of plaited horsehair, often decorated with beads and pendants made from coral, turquoise, or silver.

The Uzbeks arrived in South Central Asia around 1500 from Kazakhstan. The Uzbeks are famous for a large, rectangular face veil made of black horsehair called the *chasmband*, which often has decorative edging. The chasmband is worn by draping it over the head and face in a similar manner to the medieval qina and the maghmug worn in Sana'a, Yemen. It is closely related to the Turkish and Iranian horsehair face veil, the peche.

Woman wearing (and making examples for sale) a typical Omani Bedouin face veil (*battulah*) at a women's market near Muscat, Oman, 2003. This type of veil covers the eyebrows, nose, and mouth, leaving the eyes and part of the cheeks completely free. Photograph by Gillian Vogelsang-Eastwood. Textile Research Centre, Leiden.

Among the Uighur living in Kyrgyzstan and the Chinese province of Xinjiang, brides and newly married women sometimes still wear a traditional face veil called a *shamak*, made from a large square of cloth embroidered with drawn-thread work that is sewn onto a decorative headband. Sometimes, but not always, a small grid is left for the eyes. More elaborate versions are decorated with tassels and embroidered bands.

Various Muslim groups inhabit China's westernmost province of Xinjiang ("New Frontier"), and some practice veiling, notably the Uighurs, Kyrgyz, and Uzbeks. In the early twenty-first century, Uighur women living in Kashgar generally wear a thick rectangular piece of knitted cloth called a *chumbal* draped over their heads and faces. Although the knitted structure of the cloth is relatively heavy, a woman can see a considerable amount of light through it.

The wearing of face veils by women is an ancient tradition that predates the advent of Islam by at least a thousand years. The Islamic world adopted the practice but adapted it to local needs and culture. The forms of face veils are not static and continually change to meet modern needs and demands.

References and Further Reading

Abu-Lughod, L., ed. *Remaking Women: Feminism and Modernity in the Middle East.* Princeton, NJ: Princeton University Press, 1998.

Croutier, Alev Lytle. *Harem: The World behind the Veil.* London: Bloomsbury, 1989.

El Guindi, Fadwa. *Veil, Modesty, Privacy and Resistance.* Oxford: Berg, 1999.

Ferdinand, Klaus. *Bedouins of Qatar.* London: Thames and Hudson, 1993.

Haidar, Musbah. *Arabesque.* London: Hutchinson, 1944.

Kanafani, Aida Sami. *Aesthetics and Ritual in the United Arab Emirates.* Beirut, Lebanon: American University of Beirut, 1983.

Llewellyn-Jones, Lloyd. *Aphrodite's Tortoise: The Veiled Woman of Ancient Greece.* Swansea, UK: Classical Press of Wales, 2003.

Mabro, Judy. *Veiled Half-Truths: Western Travellers' Perceptions of Middle Eastern Women.* London and New York: Tauris, 1991.

Marmorstein, Emile. "The Veil in Judaism and Islam." *Journal of Jewish Studies* 5, no. 2 (1954): 1–11.

Northrop, Douglas. *Veiled Empire: Gender and Power in Stalinist Central Asia.* Ithaca, NY: Cornell University Press, 2004.

Saporetti, Claudio. *The Status of Women in the Middle Assyrian Period.* Malibu, CA: Undena, 1979.

Scarce, Jennifer. *Women's Costume of the Near and Middle East.* London and Sydney: Unwin Hyman, 1987.

Stillman, Yadida. *Arab Dress: A Short History from the Dawn of Islam to Modern Times.* Leiden: Brill, 2000.

Vogelsang-Eastwood, Gillian. *For Modesty's Sake.* Rotterdam: Barjesteh and Co., 1996.

Vogelsang-Eastwood, Gillian, and Willem Vogelsang. *Covering the Moon: A History of Middle Eastern Face Veils.* Leuven, Belgium: Peeters, 2008.

Wikan, Unni. *Behind the Veil in Arabia: Women in Oman.* Chicago: University of Chicago Press, 1982.

Gillian Vogelsang-Eastwood

See also Historical Survey of Textiles and Dress in Turkey; Palestinian Women's Dress; Saudi Arabian Dress; Omani Dress; Dress from the Gulf States: Bahrain, Kuwait, Qatar, United Arab Emirates; Regional Dress of Afghanistan; The Chadari/Burqa of Afghanistan and Pakistan; Turkmen Dress and Embroidery; Snapshot: Islam and Islamically Correct Dress (Hijab).

The Turban and Male Headgear

The turban is a widely used headdress created by winding a piece of cloth, such as linen, cotton, or silk, around the head and sometimes over a cap. Turbans vary greatly in shape, size, folds, and color; the fabric used differs in its length and width. Assigned numerous meanings, turbans have represented religious symbolism, political power, social status, and fashion consciousness. They can also fulfill practical functions, such as providing protection against natural elements like heat, cold, wind, and rain; serving as a cloth to kneel on for prayer rituals or a shroud for burying the dead; being used to carry objects including weapons and combs; or acting as pillows, bandages, belts, sashes, and ropes.

Etymologically, the word *turban* in English is derived from *dulband*, which in Persian means "scarf wound around the head." The word *tulip* also comes from *dulband*. Tulips, which can resemble or evoke the turban image, were initially imported into the Netherlands and England in the 1500s from Turkey, at a time when Ottoman imperial power threatened East Europe. The Arabic word for turban is *imamah*; in Turkish, it is *sarik*.

TURBAN ORIGINS

Studies of ancient dress forms show that the turban was first worn as clothing by the Sumerians in Mesopotamia as early as 2600 B.C.E. A style of pointed turban is commonly found on Sumerian and Babylonian deity sculptures. Most well known is the Hammurabi Code diorite stele (1792–1750 B.C.E.; in the Louvre Museum) where King Hammurabi (standing) wears a toque-style hat, possibly of felt, while receiving the law code from Shamash, the seated sun god, who wears a multilayered pointed turban.

This shape of turban could perhaps have been inspired by the construction style of the great ziggurat temples—virtual human-made mountains or hills reaching toward heaven for worshiping deities. A limestone stele with relief scenes depicts the moon god, Nannar, patron of Ur, giving construction tools to King Ur-Nammu (ca. 2200 B.C.E.; in the University Museum, Philadelphia). The deity's turban, like a ziggurat, has several horizontal layers. A ziggurat is surrounded by terraces with steps leading to a small shrine on top; Nannar's turban has several layers of fabric wound in such a way that in front it points upward to a metallic disk on top. This could be one of the earliest cases in history where headwear and architecture are culturally associated (another is the pointed Roman Catholic bishop's miter, the twelfth-century shape of which closely paralleled the arch construction of contemporary Gothic cathedrals). The pointed-style turban is found on both male and female Mesopotamian deities, thus implying that the headpiece is associated with religious beliefs and social status, not necessarily gender. Since noted Southwest Asian scholar Leo Oppenheim has demonstrated that god figures were often clothed with special garments of linen or dyed wool, sometimes with golden ornaments attached, it is likely that these were the materials used for deity turbans.

Another turban style, depicted on a woman's sculpted head found at Tell Agrab (ca. 2600 B.C.E.; held in the Oriental Institute, University of Chicago), has been described as a flat, pleated turban made of fabric layered over the head and wrapped around what might be two hair buns in the rear. Very likely, she represents a person of high social rank.

ARISTOCRATIC HEADPIECES OF ANCIENT MESOPOTAMIA AND WESTERN ASIA

Many elaborate headdresses were worn by historical leaders of tribes that conquered and ruled ancient Mesopotamia, such as the Akkadians, Babylonians, and Assyrians. The Akkadian Naram-Sin, grandson of the great Sargon, is represented on an exquisite bronze head (ca. 2250 B.C.E.; in the Iraq Museum collection). He is shown wearing a circlet on his brow complemented by an intricate braided pattern hairstyle that includes a bound chignon at the rear. King Gudea, ruler of the city-state of Lagash, is depicted wearing a low, round-crowned cap with an upturned brim, probably made of fur, that is represented by spiral patterns (ca. 2150 B.C.E.; in the Carlsberg Glyptotek, Copenhagen).

Powerful figures such as Ashurbanipal I (seventh century B.C.E.), ruler of the Assyrian Empire that stretched from Mesopotamia westward into Southwest Asia, including Egypt, wore elaborate, tall, modified cylindrical headdresses that were possibly made of white felt, sometimes with hornlike decorations. Queens and royal women had less ornate versions or decorated headbands, and warriors used bronze helmets. Bas-reliefs representing later conquerors, the Medes and Persians, portray less ornate, dome-shaped or pleated felt headpieces.

A variation of the turban as female headdress prevailed in the Syrian desert oasis of Palmyra (ancient Tadmor), a wealthy crossroads of trade routes along which silks, spices, and aromatics from Central Asia, Persia, India, and Arabia were transported by camel caravans and resold to markets in the western cities of the Roman Empire. Mortuary sculptures of wealthy women living in Palmyra during the second and third centuries C.E. reveal an elaborate, fashionable style of turban. Their curled hair was bound into decoratively knotted turbans that were embellished with gold chains, ropes of beads, and jeweled pendants, all signs of Eastern fashions and considerable affluence—and perhaps associated with Roman imperial power. Palmyra became so

Bas-relief at the top of the Hammurabi Code diorite stele (1792–1750 B.C.E.), showing Hammurabi receiving the code of laws from the god Shamash. King Hammurabi (on the left) wears a toque-style hat, while the seated sun god, Shamash, wears a multilayered, pointed turban. Pointed turbans are commonly found on Sumerian and Babylonian deity sculptures. Time & Life Pictures/Getty Images.

important that Emperor Hadrian visited the city and renamed it Hadriana Palmyra.

Palmyrene men were more likely to wear Iranian-style tunics and trousers while going bareheaded like the Romans. Palmyrene clerics, however, according to sculptured portraits, wore a flat-topped cylindrical hat (*modius*), reminiscent of Assyrian royal headdresses. These tall hats were often encircled by a wreath with a central rosette or medallion influenced by Western design.

ISLAMIC TURBANS AND OTHER HEADWEAR

In Southwest Asia, the vast majority of men wearing turbans are Arabs, especially Muslims. The turban was probably a Bedouin ethnic head covering in Arabia before the seventh century, C.E. when Mohammed founded Islam. Later, it was given religious significance as reflected in hadiths, or oral traditions, such as "To put on the turban means to adopt Islam" or "The community will never decay as long as they wear turbans." The turban, like other headpieces worn by observant Muslims, must be wrapped in a way that leaves the forehead bare, so that, when prostrated

at prayer, the wearer's head may touch the ground as an act of humility.

Over time, many legends have developed regarding the turban. Some relate to its color. Historically, whereas white has been the most common color for turbans, black is also important. It is said the Prophet, when entering Mecca and giving his speech at the Kaaba gate, wore a black cloak and black turban, thus associating black with sovereignty. Legends tell that Mohammed also wore a blue turban until he noticed unbelievers wearing that color, and the Angel Gabriel is supposed to have worn a red turban when appearing to Aisha, Mohammed's favorite wife. Green, associated with paradise and thought to be the Prophet's favorite color, has been restricted to Mohammed's descendants.

As the Muslim religion spread west across North Africa to Spain and eastward to Persia and India, different regional variations and rituals developed. By the tenth century, Arabs wore large turbans because size represented prestige. Many early Islamic practices regarding the turban were ritually prescribed. Muslim boys were supposed to adopt the turban at puberty, when they began growing a beard. Muslim boys were often circumcised

Bronze head of Naram-Sin from Nineveh, ca. 2250 B.C.E. The Akkadian king has a circlet on his brow, complemented by an intricate braided-pattern hairstyle that includes a bound chignon at the rear. Baghdad, Iraq Museum. © 1990. Photo Scala, Florence.

and usually given special clothes, including a circumcision hat or head scarf for the occasion. A Muslim man was supposed to stand when putting on the turban, using the right hand to twist the fabric carefully around in the right direction. The fabric quality and quantity depended on the wearer's income, and wealthy individuals might direct or allow servants to wind their turbans. One was supposed to introduce or wear a new turban on a Friday. Turban size was supposed to be modest, and they were not supposed to be decorated—directives that were violated by Mamluk, Persian, and Ottoman rulers and their courtiers.

Turbans have also been used to signify political or religious investiture. It is believed that Mohammed wound a turban on the head of his son-in-law Ali and performed the same ritual at the installation of governors. Later caliphs and sultans often did likewise when installing their viziers.

Numerous variations of the turban have developed over time. Despite Islamic prohibitions on depicting human figures, valuable evidence regarding clothing and headwear has been documented in illustrated manuscripts produced from the tenth to fifteenth centuries by the Mamluks in Egypt and Syria, the Abbasids in Persia and Iraq, and the Ottomans in Turkey.

Under Mamluk rule in Egypt and Syria (1250–1517), other turban styles emerged. Some high officials wore embroidered linen turbans. When inducted into the military, Islamic warriors were given a woven turban cloth, a formal cloak, a sword, and a horse. Some fourteenth-century manuscript images even depict courtiers wearing conical and plumed hats that appear to have Central Asian and Far Eastern origins.

Christians and Jews, as minorities living under Islamic rulers, were considered tribute bearers and thus heavily taxed. Usually, they were not allowed to wear clothing and headwear similar to Muslims. For example, under the Mamluks, around 1300 C.E., Christian men were assigned blue turbans, Jews yellow ones (a color disliked by the Prophet), and Samaritans red ones. These headpieces were easily distinguishable from the white turbans assigned to Muslims. For a later period, Alfred Rubens (in *A History of Jewish Costume*) provides numerous illustrations with an array of colored headgear worn during the nineteenth century by Jewish men living in Islamic lands, including Turkey, Lebanon, Palestine, Bukhara, Persia, Egypt, Algeria, and Morocco.

THE OTTOMAN EMPIRE

In 1453, when the Turks conquered Constantinople (Istanbul in the early twenty-first century), this ancient Christian capital became the power center for the Ottoman Empire, which at its peak covered 877,800 square miles (2,273,500 square kilometers). The empire's enormous land area was comprised of approximately 462,700 square miles (1,198,400 square kilometers) in Asia, 224,100 square miles (580,400 square kilometers) in Europe, and 191,000 square miles (494,700 square kilometers) in Africa.

The largest and most extravagant turbans ever created were worn by Ottoman sultans, palace functionaries, military officers, and government officials. Their turbans were usually wrapped around a tall hat, making them about three to four times the size of a human head. Cesare Vecellio, a noted sixteenth-century costume album author, sketched the sultan's turban, which was said to have been made from a piece of fabric about 150 feet long (forty-six meters) and decorated with rare heron feathers and precious stones. This style of gigantic turban has been recorded in numerous paintings, including the portrait of Süleyman the Magnificent, attributed to Titian (ca. 1530 C.E.), in the collection of the Kunsthistorisches Museum in Vienna, Austria. Turban makers enjoyed a prestigious social position, and Mohammed was their special protector and patron.

Turkish military headgear was also visually impressive. The *akincis*, light cavalry, wore large winged headpieces; the regular cavalry, *sipahis*, were clad in chain mail with helmets; and elite officers and guards had white felt crowns with a panache of feathers. The Janissaries, infantry units that fought from the fourteenth to nineteenth centuries, wore red or blue cloaks with tall, cylindrical felt headdresses that featured a fabric panel hanging in the rear.

The Turks served as the major cultural bridge for introducing the turban and other Oriental headpieces to Europeans beginning in the fifteenth century. During the Renaissance era in the West, the turban became a symbol of Eastern exoticism. Depending on the prevailing artistic and literary movements of the time, turbans were worn and painted as they went in and out of fashion over the next five centuries. Sir Robert Shirley, British diplomat to the Persian court during the reign of King James I, was painted in 1622 by Anthony Van Dyck (National Gallery of Art, Washington, D.C.) sporting an imposing and dominating turban. Lady Mary Wortley Montagu, the wife of the British ambassador, lived in Turkey for two years and was later highly influential in popularizing the turban as an aristocratic woman's millinery style back in England. For her portrait painted by Jonathan Richardson around 1725 (Earl of Harrowby collection), she wore an elegant and elaborate, pearl-decorated headwrap.

THE SUFI *TAJ* AND TURBAN

Although Sufism, or Islamic mysticism, has existed in Persia, Mesopotamia, Bukhara, Afghanistan, and India and each group had its own style of patterned turban, the Turks had the most important style of Sufism. In Konya, Turkey, the historical center of Islamic Sufi mysticism, an existing monastery-museum exhibits the elaborate and colorful turbaned headdresses of many past Sufis.

This group, known in the West as whirling dervishes, comprises followers of Mevlana Rumi, a thirteenth-century mystic, theologian, and poet who lived in western Anatolia (modern Turkey). His marble sarcophagus is still preserved and is covered by a brocade donated in the nineteenth century by Sultan Abdul Hamit II.

The Mevlevis, as they call themselves, use the Qur'an as their spiritual guide and practice dancing, singing, and playing musical instruments in their ecstatic rituals. When dancing in concentric circles, they pivot on one foot with the right hand pointing upward toward heaven and the left hand down to earth. Dancers are interpreted as representing spinning planets revolving around the Almighty. Their clothing has rich symbolic meanings related to mourning. The long white skirt (*tenure*) represents a shroud; the black cloak (*khirqa*), a grave; and the tall, brimless, cylindrical felt hat made of camel's hair (*sikke*) represents a tombstone. They serve as holy objects for metaphysical meditation and may also refer metaphorically to the death of the personal ego. The sikke is called *taj* in Arabic (meaning "crown") and may trace its origin to ancient Mesopotamia.

The turban, which is often placed on a deceased Sufi's coffin, is considered so important that the length and turns of the cloth making the turban have been associated with the level of sanctity achieved by the holy person during his lifetime. The turban's shape has also been used for tombstone design and decorative carvings, some of which are still preserved in outdoor cemeteries near Konya and Istanbul.

Suleiman I, Sultan of Turkey (1494–1566), oil on canvas, attributed to Titian, ca. 1530. The most extravagant turbans were worn by Ottoman sultans, palace functionaries, military officers, and government officials. Using pieces of fabric up to 150 feet (forty-six meters) long, turbans were usually wrapped around a tall hat, making them about three to four times the size of a human head. Getty Images.

TURBANS AND OTHER HEADPIECES AND MODERN POLITICS

In the twentieth century, several Islamic countries underwent dramatic political changes affecting traditional headgear. Peoples living in Muslim countries governed by European powers were exposed to Western clothing, including hats worn by colonial governors and other officials. With the dismantling of the Ottoman Empire after World War I (1914–1918), some local populations slowly put aside traditional turbans and fezzes (brimless red pillbox hats with black or blue tassels) and adopted European-style felt fedoras and straw hats. In other cases, such as Turkey, changes in clothing and headwear were abruptly mandated by government policies in efforts to separate religion from politics and modernize society.

In 1925, the Republic of Turkey, led by its first president, Mustafa Kemal (Atatürk), passed legislation prohibiting Turkish men from wearing turbans and fezzes and requiring them to wear hats. Beginning on 25 November of that year, by law, all Turkish men had to wear hats. Millions of Western-style hats—including homburgs, bowlers from Britain, panamas from the Caribbean, and *Borsalinos* (a man's fur felt hat, popular worldwide in the 1920s, made by an Italian firm founded by Giuseppe Borsalino) from Italy—arrived by train and ship and were sold in shops and markets across the country. Newspapers published articles on how to wear hats.

In Persia (Iran in the early twenty-first century), men had been wearing turbans since the Abbasid era (750–1258 C.E.), when black was the dynastic color. Western sartorial styles entered Persia during the reign of Shah Nasir al-Din (1848–1896 C.E.), who introduced Western clothing to his people after visiting Paris in 1873. The government takeover in 1925 brought Reza Khan Pahlavi to the throne, and his government passed dress laws mandating that Persian men wear Western coats, suits, and French-influenced Pahlavi hats. The Pahlavi hat, worn by the Iranian military, was a black pillbox with a visor, made from tightly woven wool with a black band at the base, and often with buttons on the sides. Some men accepted these sudden social and sartorial changes. Others refused to wear the new garments and rioted, encouraged by ulema (Islamic clerics), who quoted sharia (Islamic law). Over time, Western-style clothing prevailed, and hats were accepted.

By the 1960s, however, Iranian men began going out hatless, largely inspired by European fashions and world leaders such as the U.S. president John F. Kennedy. Also, as modern automobile transportation became more widespread, Iranians realized that fitting into the confined space of a car was considerably easier without a hat.

In 1979, some pro-Marxist and anti-Western groups plotted and successfully overthrew the reigning Mohammed Reza Shah. In March of that year, the opposition led by Ayatollah Khomeini took over and created a theocratic-style government whereby sharia was again enforced, mandating traditional clothing. Since the 1980s and into the twenty-first century, many urban Iranian women have been required to wear the body-covering black chador outside the home. Young males have increasingly been encouraged to study in clerical schools; hence, many turbans (black and white) are again seen on Iranian streets. Nevertheless, secular males continue to appear in public hatless.

THE FEZ, *KEFFIYEH*, *GHUTRA*, AND *'AQAL*

The fez (*tarbush* in Arabic) is a brimless pillbox-style hat of felt or cloth, usually red with a black or blue tassel. It was worn by Islamic men throughout the expansive Ottoman Empire. The fez's origin is disputed, but it may have been introduced in the nineteenth century, adopted by Sultan Mahmud II, and made part of official government dress. There is also a claim that this hat originated in and derives its name from the city of Fez in Morocco, where red berry dye is produced.

In the nineteenth century, the fez was worn by kings, military officers, clerics, civilian adults, and boys. Upper-class men preferred a deep maroon color, while commoners wore lighter reds. Cairo, Egypt, came to be the center of fez manufacture and distribution for generations, until it was banned in 1958 by the Egyptian Gamal Abdel Nasser, who led the Republican revolution against King Farouk and was elected president. There are several distinctly different fez styles: The Ottoman one was short and conical; the Egyptian style was cylindrical; the Moroccan one was short and squat; and the Azor, worn by clerics, had a top crease and white fabric wound around it in turban fashion. Although rarely worn by Egyptians, the fez is still made and sold in Egypt for the significant tourist market.

Other modern headpieces with ancient roots currently worn in Southwest Asia are variations of square head scarfs, most prevalent in arid or desert areas. One particularly common type is the *keffiyeh*, made of red-and-white or black-and-white checked cotton with tassels, which is popular among Jordanians, Lebanese, and

Portrait of Kabuli Mehmed Pasha (1812–1876), painted miniature, by Rupen Manas, 1850. This high-ranking official of the Ottoman Empire wears a red felt fez and a European-style uniform. In the nineteenth century, the fez was adopted by Sultan Mahmud II and made part of official government dress. © Victoria and Albert Museum, London. www.vam.ac.uk

Palestinians. Yasir Arafat, former leader of the Palestine Liberation Organization, is said to have worn his keffiyeh with the fabric folded so as to create a map of the ancient, and hoped-for new, State of Palestine. In the Gulf states, such as the United Arab Emirates, either a checked scarf of heavy cotton (*shamagh*) or the lighter white version (called *ghutra*, meaning "to cover" in Arabic) is worn. All three of these scarves are held securely in place by the common *'aqal*, a black, double-looped cord. According to tradition, the *'aqal* may also be used to hobble ("tether") camels during desert travels.

In warm areas of Southwest Asia and North Africa, a shallow pillbox-shaped cap, which may be knitted, woven, or sewn, is often worn under the turban, or occasionally the ghutra, for the purpose of absorbing head perspiration. In some cases, the pattern might include a five-pointed star symbolizing the Five Pillars of the Islamic faith. In colder regions, such as Afghanistan, some well-to-do Muslims living before the Taliban era wore a heavy, stiffened cotton cap (*kulla*) covered with decorations, either alone or under a turban. One version of this cap was covered by an exquisitely embroidered fabric containing gold-thread decorations designed to represent stylized images of a mosque interior. This intricate artistic pattern might include a tiny golden image of stairs leading up to the *mimbar* (pulpit), over which the *mirab*

Crown Prince Abdallah wearing a *shamagh* (head scarf) at the Jenadriyah Festival, Riyadh, Saudi Arabia, ca. 2006. The heavy cotton scarf is held securely in place by the *'aqal*, a black, double-looped cord. Reza/Getty Images.

(prayer arch) was portrayed, along with minute columns and tiny pointed arches alluding to minarets.

THE CLERICAL HEADPIECES OF THE "PEOPLES OF THE BOOK"

The hierarchy of various Christian religious groups over many centuries in Southwest Asia has donned special identifying headwear. For example, during liturgical ceremonies since the sixteenth century, Greek Orthodox bishops have worn the ornate miter, which is rounded and based on descriptions of the turban-like headpiece of ancient Jewish priests. The miter may be covered with symbolic decorations, including the Byzantine imperial double eagle with a scepter and globe in its talons, along with miniatures of the four New Testament evangelists: Matthew, Mark, Luke, and John.

The *kalimafki* (tall pillbox hat), worn alone or under a veil, has been the everyday hat of the Greek Orthodox clergy for hundreds of years. Its black color originally signified the subjugation of non-Muslims under Ottoman Turkish rulers. Greeks, Jews, Armenians, and Copts, all considered by the Turks as subservient "Peoples of the Book," were forced to wear dark clothing, while Muslims could wear bright colors, including white. The kalimafki veil is worn only by clergy or monks who have taken the vow of chastity. The veil's two separate panels, which flutter as the wearer walks, represent "angel's wings"—alluding to the belief that the clergyman is accompanied by an angel for spiritual protection and guidance.

Armenian Christians were another subjugated group whose clergy also wore dark headpieces. They conducted Southwest Asian religious rites originating in Asia Minor and dating back to at least the fourth century. Over their pillbox hat, Armenian clerics wear a black veil or hood. Its peak is reminiscent of Armenia's Mount Ararat, where, according to tradition, Noah's ark settled after the great flood.

The Egyptian Coptic pope is the Patriarch of the See of Saint Mark, headquartered in Alexandria. His everyday hat (*emama*) is similar to the turban, having strips of fabric wound around a wide stiff crown that fits on the head. This type of headgear is worn by Coptic bishops and higher ranks of clergy; there are two types, the black form worn on a daily basis and a white form used during certain services by high-ranking priests. The style and size have changed over the decades. The emama also resembles the ancient Jewish priest's turban and is worn over a black hood (*kolonsowa*), which is decorated with red or white stitched crosses—symbols of Christ's sacrifice and the Coptic monastic commitment of "dying to the world."

Still another example of dark headwear worn by "People of the Book" is the nineteenth-century Jewish rabbi's gray silk turban wrapped around a red fez, an example of which is preserved in the Smithsonian Institution of Washington, D.C.

CONCLUSION

For more than four thousand years, male headwear in Central and Southeast Asia has largely consisted of three dominant forms: (1) the wound-cloth turban and its countless variations in color, shape, and function, which was typically worn by powerful rulers (including ancient Mesopotamian deity figures), military units, clerics, and commoners; (2) the tall, cylindrical hat, often constructed of felt formed into modified shapes and decorated with numerous ornaments such as plumes and jewels, which was usually worn by high-ranking rulers, aristocrats, military officers, and religious persons; and (3) the head-covering scarf, tied in various manners and secured by a cord ('aqal), which was most often worn in warm desert areas by rulers (Saudi Arabia), soldiers, clerics, and commoners. In select regions and urban centers, particularly those more heavily influenced by Western fashion, many men no longer wear hats or head coverings, but in rural, especially desert, areas, headwear is still the norm.

References and Further Reading

Anetshofer, Helga, and Kahan T. Karateke. *Traktat uber die Derwischmutzen des Mustaqim-Zade Suleyman Sa'Deddin.* Leiden: Brill, 2001.

Arnoldi, Mary Jo, and Christine Mullen Kreamer. *Crowning Achievements: African Arts of Dressing the Head.* Los Angeles: Fowler Museum of Cultural History (UCLA), 1995.

Atil, Esin. *The Age of Süleyman the Magnificent.* Washington, DC: National Gallery of Art, 1987.

Björkman, W. "Turban." In *Encyclopaedia of Islam,* edited by Martijn Theodor Houtsma, A. J. Wensinck, and H.A.R. Gibb, vol. 4, 885–893. Leiden: Brill, 1913–1936.

Björkman, W. "Tulband." In *Encyclopaedia of Islam,* edited by P. J. Bearman, Th. Bianquis, C. E. Bosworth, E. van Donzel, and W. P. Heinrichs, vol. 10, 608–615. Updated ed. Leiden: Brill, 2000.

Chico, Beverly. "Gender Headwear and Power in Judaic and Christian Traditions." *Dress* 17 (1990): 127–140.

Chico, Beverly. "Gender Headwear Traditions in Judaism and Islam." *Dress* 27 (2000): 18–36.

Cohen-Mushlin, Aliza, ed. *Jewish Art.* Jerusalem: Center for Jewish Art of the Hebrew University, 1987.

Dash, Mike. *Tulipomania.* New York: Crown, 1999.

El Guindi, Fadwa. *Veil, Modesty, Privacy and Resistance.* Oxford: Berg, 1999.

Grundy, Isobel. *Lady Mary Wortley Montague, Comet of the Enlightenment.* Oxford: Oxford University Press, 1999.

Jirousek, Charlotte. "More than Oriental Splendor: European and Ottoman Headgear, 1380–1580." *Dress* 22 (1995): 22–33.

Kennett, Frances. *Ethnic Dress.* New York: Facts on File, 1995.

Murphy, R. "Social Distance and the Veil." *American Anthropologist* 66 (December 1964): 1257–1274.

Oppenheim, Leo. "The Golden Garments of the Gods." *Journal of Near Eastern Studies* 3, no. 3 (July 1949): 172–193.

Parrot, Andre. *Sumer: The Dawn of Art.* New York: Golden Press, 1961.

Petsopoulos, Yanni. *Tulips, Arabesques and Turbans: Decorative Arts from the Ottoman Empire.* New York: Abbeville Press, 1982.

Rasmussen, Susan J. "Veiled Self, Transparent Meanings: Tuareg Headdress as Social Expression." *Ethnology* 30, no. 2 (April 1991): 101–117.

Rubens, Alfred. *A History of Jewish Costume.* London: Peter Owen, 1973.

Scott, Georgia. *Headwraps: A Global Journey.* New York: Public Affairs, 2003.

Seal, Jeremy. *A Fez of the Heart: Travels around Turkey in Search of a Hat.* New York and London: Harcourt Brace and Company, 1995.

Sebesta, Judith Lynn, and Larissa Bonfante, eds. *The World of Roman Costume.* Madison: University of Wisconsin Press, 2001.

Shirazi, Faegheh. *The Veil Unveiled: The Hijab in Modern Culture.* Gainesville: University Press of Florida, 2001.

Stillman, Yedida K. *Arab Dress: A Short History from the Dawn of Islam to Modern Times.* Leiden: Brill, 2000.

Vecellio, Cesare. *Renaissance Costume Book.* New York: Dover Publications, 1977. (Originally published in 1590.)

Wiebke, Walther. *Women in Islam.* Princeton, NJ, and New York: Markus Wiener, 1993.

Wilcox, Ruth Turner. *The Mode in Hats and Headdress.* New York: Charles Scribner's Sons, 1959.

Woolley, C. Leonard. *The Development of Sumerian Art.* New York: Charles Scribner's Sons, 1955.

Beverly Chico

See also Ottoman Dress; Royal Costumes Preserved in the Topkapi Palace Museum; Arab Men's Dress in the Eastern Mediterranean; Saudia Arabian Dress; Iraq Dress; Dress from the Gulf States, Bahrain, Kuwait, Qatar.

Snapshot: Al-Washsha, a Medieval Fashion Guru

The early medieval period in Southwest Asia was a time of change, with an increase in wealth and trade, especially with China via Central Asia, along the so-called Silk Road. A time of political and social stability followed the establishment of the Abbasid dynasty in 749 C.E. The Abbasids were one of the great Muslim caliphates of the Arab empire, known for their arts, literature, and architectural achievements and also for the development of an increasingly important figure, the fashion guru.

The Abbasid caliphate overthrew the ruling Umayyad caliphs (who had reigned from 661–750 C.E.) in 749/750 and then, in 762 they shifted the capital of the Arab empire from Damascus in Syria to Baghdad in what is Iraq in the early twenty-first century. The Abbasids flourished for two centuries before going into decline; their rule finally ended in 1258 when Hulagu Khan (r. about 1217–1265), the grandson of Genghis Khan, the Mongol conqueror, sacked Baghdad.

The Umayyads were known for their stance against the public use of luxury garments and non-Arab, especially Persian, fashions. Instead, they tried to present an image as Arab traditionalists, austere and modest in behavior and appearance. In contrast, the Abbasid court deliberately used special and luxurious clothing to show their power and wealth; they were, for example, credited with starting the custom of wearing black clothing, which was expensive and difficult to dye, for official occasions. When the second Abbasid caliph and founder of Baghdad, al-Mansur (r. 754–775 C.E.), died, he left thousands of textiles, furs, and garments in Arab, Turkish, and, in particular, Persian styles. Many of the Abbasid court officials, both male and female, were dedicated followers of fashion, led by the caliph and his family.

Therefore, during this period, it is no coincidence that various Arab and Persian writers describe the wide range of trade goods, especially textiles and furs, available from all over the world. Some writers, however, preferred to discuss the textiles and garments worn by fashionable men and women. One such writer was Abu l-Tayyib Muhammed al-Washsha (d. 936 C.E.), who wrote a lifestyle book called *On Elegance and Elegant People* (*Kitab al-zarf wa'l-zurafa'*; also known as the *Kitab al-Muwashsha*).

The book includes several chapters devoted to describing the type of clothing worn by his male contemporaries: what should be worn, what not, what type of perfumes to wear and how, and in general how to behave in good society. In the smaller section on female dress, al-Washsha mainly describes items that are different from those worn by fashionable men. This reflects the fact that men and women wore many garments in common, as well as showing the different social positions of men and women at this time.

According to the Islamic scholar R. B. Serjeant, al-Washsha noted that "the best taste in dress is to wear clothes which suit one another, with a graduated range of color, and materials which have something in common and do not clash." He also wrote that "the elegant find favor with the affluent and relatives of the caliph." Not only was it personally pleasant to be elegantly dressed but, on a more pragmatic note, it also helped one's career and family prospects.

The sections on clothing describe garments, footwear, "evening wear," and colors and perfumes that should or should not be worn. A fashionable man should wear, for example, underdrawers (*sirwal*), with an essential accessory, the drawstring (*tikka*), which should be of the finest silk. Although the tikka was never seen in public, they were widely used to reflect the wealth and position of the wearer, a form of private or inconspicuous consumption. They also appear in various medieval Arab story collections, including the famous *A Thousand and One Nights*, as an erotic item of clothing.

Al-Washsha says that over the sirwal is worn a fine undergarment (*ghilala*), followed by a heavier, lined chemise (*qamis*), both of which should be of fine linen from Egypt or Fars (southwestern Iran). Then come lined robes from either Barajirdi or Alexandria or a robe from Nishapur (eastern Iran) of linen, silk, or a similar material. The outer layer should consist of a garment called an Aden *rida* (from Yemen) or a cloak known as a *mitraf* from Sus (southern Iran), which had decorative borders at each end. Cotton mitrafs and ones made from Armenian figured textiles were also very acceptable. Finally, the fashionable man should wear a turban or a Nishapur hood (*taylasan*).

Men's shoes and sandals could be of a wide variety of leathers, colors, and designs. They could include East African sandals, thick shoes from Cambay (India), Yemeni furry shoes, fine sandals, light checkered shoes, Hashimi boots, and curved shoes of the (Persian) secretarial class. Shoes might appear in color combinations such as black and red or black and yellow; boots in red or black were also acceptable, as were Persian stockings (*jurab*) of silk or goat hair. It is worth noting that surviving examples of medieval stockings from this period are usually knitted of silk, cotton, or wool and decorated with colorful, geometric designs.

When going to a drinking party (*majlis al-sharab*), a gentleman should wear a "formal" outfit called "clothes of boon companionship," which included a fine undergarment, a silk qamis, and a brightly colored robe. Members of the royal family attending such affairs should wear "convivial robes of honor," which included a turban of gilded silk, a lined undergarment, and a long robe called a *durra'a* that had wide sleeves that left part of the arm uncovered (very daring); these should be made of Dabiqi linen (named after a quarter in Baghdad). To go to a party in anything else was simply not done.

According to al-Washsha, saffron and yellow should never be worn (this derives from the Prophet Mohammed's reported hatred of saffron and is a feature of medieval Islamic dress codes), nor should unpleasant or clashing colors, nor clothes perfumed with cheap ambergris (slave girls' perfumes). New garments should not be worn together with washed or old garments, nor linen together with certain cottons. Neither should cloaks (rida) of certain colors and yellow mantles (*izar*) be worn, although Serjeant indicates that al-Washsha did admit that "in certain cases, they may use them as coverings, and may even don them at an occasion of revelry and still be considered elegant in them in the salons…though appearance in public in this style is bad form."

The fashionable man may also wear powdered musk, rose-water solutions, ambergris with aloes wood soaked in fermented clove water, and a type of perfume called royal *nadd*.

The information about women's clothing is not as detailed as for men, but al-Washsha recommended that elegant women should wear smoky-gray-colored underwear. White garments of any kind, apart from the sirwal, were considered to be masculine and should never be worn, although fine, naturally colored linen was acceptable. The tikka of the sirwal should be made of silk, but the lady should never wear male types such as wide belts or those made out of brocade or braided fine linen. Over the sirwal is worn a dress that should have wide sleeves and a collar with a drawstring.

A fashionable lady's outer wraps should be either a Rashidi or Tabari rida from Rosetta in Egypt and Tabaristan, respectively, or she might wear the totally enveloping Khorasani izar of silk and cotton (from eastern Iran). On her head a lady should wear a black, female turban called a *mi'jar*—black being the fashionable color at this time. The mi'jar should be worn with a face veil called a *miqna'* from Nishapur, which hung down over the face and sometimes covered only the upper half of the face, leaving the mouth visible. A lady might also wear mantles of striped or banded fine linen or colored linen decorated with gold or silver, adorned with roundels of silk embroidery. Finally, her footwear should include furry Cambay shoes dyed green, Persian-style boots, curved shoes, and Edessa-style shoes.

A lady, however, should never wear yellow, black, green, rose, or red, except those fabrics that were naturally of these colors. Al-Washsha was of the opinion that these colors were worn only by Nabatean peasant women (possibly Armenian Christian women) and singing girls of the slave class. White was worn by abandoned women, while mourning colors such as iron black and dark blue should be worn only by bereaved women and those in trouble or distress, and as such all these colors should be avoided.

A lady's clothing could be perfumed with musk, sandalwood, hyacinth, or good-quality ambergris but no other perfumes. The garments, however, should not be sprinkled with the perfume; instead, they should be impregnated with them.

According to Serjeant, al-Washsha concludes with the comment: "We have described the best fashions, and they [the wearer] should not pass beyond the limits which we have demarcated." A true fashion guru indeed.

REFERENCES AND FURTHER READING

Al-Washsha. *Kitab al-Muwashsha*. Edited by R. E. Brünnow. Leiden: Brill, 1886.

Serjeant, R. B. *Islamic Textiles: Material for a History up to the Mongol Conquest*. Beirut, Lebanon: Librairie du Liban, 1972.

Stillman, Yedida K. *Arab Dress: A Short History from the Dawn of Islam to Modern Times*. Leiden: Brill, 2000.

Gillian Vogelsang-Eastwood

See also The Coming of Islam and Its Influence on Dress; Sumptuary Laws; Face Veils.

Snapshot: Orientalism in Western Dress and Stage Costume

From the time of the European Renaissance, the West has been fascinated by the image of the "mysterious," "exotic," and "erotic" East. Sometimes, as Edward Said explored in his 1978 book *Orientalism*, this Western view of the East has been so dependent on the fantastical imaginings of European (and North American) authors, artists, and musicians that the realities of Eastern cultures and societies have been deliberately submerged beneath a vision of "theatricalized" Eastern despotism, characterized by the murmurings of the harem and the whirling of dervishes.

However, another branch of scholarship rejects Said's definition of Orientalism and argues that the West has always been capable of seeing beyond the clichés of an imaginary East and that the West has, for many centuries, tried to understand its Eastern neighbors through the serious study and exploration of the languages, cultures, and societies of the Orient. These scholars argue that the negative connotations Said sees in his definition of Orientalism are overplayed and that the appellation *Orientalist* should be divorced from the negative connotations that have become associated with it since 1978.

The Orientalism debate has been going on for a long time in the history of the West's appropriation of Eastern modes of dress, although few scholars have acknowledged this. Oriental dress has been used in the West in two important contexts, both of which emphasize the polarity of the Saidian and anti-Saidian schools of Orientalism. In one respect, Westerners have regarded Eastern dress as a form of playing dress-up, fit for stage costumes, for balls, and for entertainments. Throughout the 1700s and 1800s, the preferred dress at society costume events was certainly Oriental: Louis XV and his court, for instance, appeared at the so-called Yew Tree Ball of 1745 dressed as Turks in turbans. In another respect, however, aspects of Eastern clothing were regularly used in fashionable Western styles (high fashion) and were admired for their beauty, craftsmanship, and style. Occasionally, fashionable individuals opted to wear authentic Eastern garments in place of reworked versions of Oriental originals.

The Western understanding and experience of Eastern dress greatly increased as the trade routes between Europe and the empires of Ottoman Turkey, Safavid Persia, and Mughal India opened up in the sixteenth century. Travelers, explorers, and merchants returned home carrying Eastern textiles and, to a lesser extent, Eastern clothing with them; others came home with sketches and paintings of Eastern dress. In 1581, for example, the traveler Jean Jacques Boissard published a book of dress, the *Habitus Variarum Orbis Gentium* (Costumes of the various peoples of the world), in which he sketched the various modes of dress adopted by peoples of the East (and beyond). This proved to be a highly useful reference tool for theatrical costumers, and his picture of three Persian women in particular became a much-copied subject in masquerade costumes.

From at least the early 1600s, the cultural impact that Eastern clothes had on Western society was palpable. When encountered in Europe, the rich clothes of Persian and Ottoman dignitaries were much admired. As early as 1612, British ambassadors were returning home with Persian brocades and Indian muslins and were having themselves depicted in Eastern dress: A portrait by Sir Antony van Dyke of the English nobleman Sir Robert Shirley, King James I's ambassador to the shah at Isfahan in Persia, shows him wearing full Safavid court dress (including a huge turban) and testifies to the Orientalizing trend in European fashion. So popular was this look, in fact, that in the 1670s, Charles II became completely captivated by Persian dress and attempted to establish it as part of the official English court dress.

At the beginning of the eighteenth century, Lady Mary Wortley Montagu, the wife of the British ambassador to the Sublime Porte at Istanbul, famously had herself painted in the gowns she wore at the Ottoman court. Eastern dress continued to influence European dress throughout the eighteenth century, whether in the form of dressing up—such as Madame de Pompadour's portraits (by Carle van Loo) in the guise of an Ottoman sultana ("la reine sultana")—or in fashionable dress, such as the feathered turbans *à la turque* ("in Turkish style") perched on the high powdered wigs of elegant ladies. Furthermore, the influence of Eastern modes of dress was expressed in the popularity of the loose silk *banyan*s, employed by European aristocratic gentlemen as housecoats, tea gowns, or dressing gowns. It is interesting to note how often Oriental elements of dress made their way into Western wardrobes through the bedroom: When the banyan went out of fashion in the 1840s, the West's association of the East with relaxation (or indolence, according to Said) wended its way into pajamas and other forms of leisure dress or house dress (like the Japanese-style kimono dressing gown).

By the 1780s, increasing familiarity with Eastern dress styles, and the availability of Oriental textiles, provoked a radical reconsideration of Western dress itself. This led to greater use of cotton, loose swathing, and adaptations of garments such as Turkish bloomers and pantaloons (usually, but not always, reserved for Western women's underwear between 1830 and 1900). When in 1782 the French queen Marie Antoinette began to wear simple white gowns of the finest Indian and Iranian muslin, she began a vogue for the cloth that dominated Western female fashion for the next thirty years.

The beauty of the simple muslin Empire fashion of the opening decades of the 1800s was often enhanced with the addition of the so-called Paisley shawl (actually the Kashmir shawl of northern India). The West was enraptured with this simple (but expensive) Indian garment for nearly a century, since the shawl offered Europe a practical utilitarian garment while, perhaps, providing a touch of Oriental glamour in every woman's wardrobe. However, the demand for shawls (and impatience with the slow, hand-crafted production of them in India) meant

Engraving of Lady Mary Wortley Montagu (1689–1762), writer and wife of the British ambassador to the Sublime Porte at Istanbul, wearing the clothing she would have worn at the Ottoman court, ca. 1720. Getty Images.

that Europeans began to mass-produce cheap imitations in Lyons, France, and in northern England and, of course, Scotland. Indeed, around 1850, the Scottish town of Paisley became synonymous with the shawls it manufactured and the distinctive pattern it used for decoration.

By the early twentieth century, the Western taste for Eastern design was expressed in the textile arts of Liberty of London and in Paul Poiret's sensationalist couture outfits of the 1910s. Poiret exploited his sympathy with the Orientalist persuasion of Sergey Diaghilev (1872–1929) and the Ballets Russes to create couture fashions that wrapped his fashionable Paris clients in interpretations of kimono, kaftans (long, unfitted garments

with an open front), saris, turbans, and banyans. At the same time, designer Mariano Fortuny began to make opera cloaks and evening coats from imported djellabas (a form of women's dress, usually full length).

The vogue for Eastern styles in Western dress continued throughout the twentieth century. The 1970s and 1980s in particular saw a sweeping fashion for Oriental styles, perhaps as a result of the academic interest in Orientalism as a concept. Indeed, so ingrained has the role of the fantasy and real East been in Western culture that Orientalism in fashion is unavoidable. The subject has become increasingly provocative as East-West tensions rise and as Western media stereotyping and scaremongering increase. In the early twenty-first century, debates regarding gender, identity, faith, colonialism, and racism are often played out through the politics of East-West dress.

REFERENCES AND FURTHER READING

Baines, Barbara. *Revivals in Fashion*. London: Batsford, 1981.
Baudot, François. *Poiret*. Translated by Caroline Beamish. London: Thames & Hudson, 1997.
Boissard, Jean Jacques. *Habitus Variarum Orbis Gentium*. Mecheln: Caspar Rutz, 1581.
Irwin, Robert. *For Lust of Knowing: The Orientalists and Their Enemies*. London: Penguin, 2007.
Jacobson, Dawn. *Chinoiserie*. London: Phaidon, 1993.
Koda, Harold, and Richard Martin. *Orientalism: Visions of the East in Western Dress*. New York: Metropolitan Museum of New York, 1994.
MacKenzie, John. *Orientalism: History, Theory and the Arts*. Manchester, UK: Manchester University Press, 1995.
Said, Edward W. *Orientalism: Western Conceptions of the East*. 5th ed. London: Penguin, 1978.
Steele, Valerie, and John S. Major. *China Chic: East Meets West*. New Haven, CT: Yale University Press, 1999.

Lloyd Llewellyn-Jones

See also Ottoman Dress; The Kaftan and Its Origins; Royal Costumes Preserved at the Topkapi Museum; Snapshot: Turkish Costume Albums.

Dress and Tourism

Tourism is an industry of increasing global significance, directly and indirectly accounting for approximately 195 million jobs in 2003 and estimated to rise to over 250 million jobs by 2010. Roughly half of these jobs are in small- to medium-sized enterprises transporting, accommodating, and feeding tourists as well as providing ancillary services such as the sale of souvenirs, including items of dress. With international tourist arrivals forecast to exceed 1.5 billion by 2020, it is clear that catering to such vast temporary movements of people has significant impacts on host environments and cultures.

In broad terms, this industry is systemically driven to commodify entire cultures in order to render them consumable by large numbers of potential tourists. To do so, tourism promoters and service providers often refer to registers of images relating to a given destination, which may vary depending on the relationships that have developed historically between the tourists' own cultures and those visited. They seek to evoke familiar sets of images, cultural practices, and signifying objects (cultural products, performed or manufactured, that tourists perceive as symbolizing a given destination), including national and regional dress. In this way, perhaps paradoxically, the supposed cultural novelty and exoticism of a destination are represented in terms that are familiar to potential tourists.

Consequently, a comprehensive study of visitor perspectives, and host responses, to tourism in Central and Southwest Asia would need to take into account these diverse perspectives. Significant new sources of tourism demand are developing in China and India, for example, and it should not be assumed that Central and Southwest Asia would be promoted to or experienced by tourists from these countries in precisely the same way as visitors from West Europe or North America. Indeed, since religious pilgrimages may be included when collecting statistics on tourist arrivals, it is clear that the most significant form of tourism in the region is, in fact, the hajj, the annual Muslim pilgrimage to the Holy City of Mecca. However, attention will focus on just one broad market—that of "Western" tourism in the region—and examine how deeply embedded ideas about "the Orient," potently signified in items of "Eastern" dress, help to determine both tourists' expectations and host communities' responses.

DRESS AND THE ORIENT

The Orient can be understood to encompass those regions, cultures, and civilizations to the south and east of the part of Europe that was once known as Latin Christendom and that, after the ruptures of the Reformation and new unity of the Enlightenment, came to call itself the modern, secular "West." With the colonial and commercial expansion of some West European powers and the United States, particularly from the early nineteenth century on, the terms *Orient* or *Oriental* perhaps came to be more commonly associated with East Asian countries such as Japan and China. Previously, however, it was understood to cover, to some extent, the Byzantine world of Eastern Orthodox Christianity and certainly the lands of Islam in North Africa and Central and Southwest Asia. It has been argued (for example, by Edward W. Said) that the Orient was constructed as an antagonistic, barbaric, exotically alluring, and, in any case, irredeemably alien "other" as a means for the West to conceive of itself as a distinct civilization. Accordingly, a series of markers in language and visual culture have come to represent or indicate the East as being somewhere radically different. Dress has long been one of these potent signifiers of the Orient in the Western imagination.

Certainly, dress as a recognizable signifier for the East or Orient took some time to establish itself. During the Middle Ages and early Renaissance, for example, relatively few Western Europeans, even taking into account interaction during the Crusades, would have had direct or even secondhand contact with Arabs or Turks. Accordingly, these peoples were often depicted in familiar European dress. The Ottoman Sultan Mehmed II was portrayed, immediately following his conquest of Constantinople in 1453, in the headgear and dress of the Byzantine emperor he had displaced. Subsequently, the Ottoman Empire (a state founded in Anatolia during the fourteenth century by the Turkic Osmanlı dynasty, which was dissolved in 1923 to make way for its principal successor state, the Republic of Turkey) expanded to encompass much of Southeast Europe, Southwest Asia, and the North African coast as far as Morocco.

Consequently, the conduct of trade and diplomacy by West Europeans in the southern and eastern Mediterranean took place within a more or less unified Ottoman political and cultural milieu. As a result, travel and proximity facilitated more accurate depictions of Eastern dress while also embedding particular elements as immediately recognizable signs of the Orient in the Western popular consciousness. In sixteenth-century England, for example, masquerading in Ottoman dress became an entertainment at the court of Henry VIII. By the Elizabethan period a few decades later, the growing importation of not only textiles but also ready-made garments produced in the Ottoman lands, Persia, and even India meant that elements of Eastern dress had become familiar to Europeans who had not themselves traveled to the Orient.

A fascination with Eastern dress was apparent from the outset among European travelers. The Venetian painter Gentile Bellini, for example, was employed to paint the portrait of the Ottoman Sultan Mehmed II in the contemporary Renaissance style but wearing the Ottoman court dress of a turban and fur-collared kaftan. Bellini and his contemporaries also produced realistic images of representative types (rather than named individuals) in Ottoman dress they had encountered during their sojourns in Constantinople. Also during this period, Ogier de Busbecq, the Hapsburg ambassador to the court of Süleyman the Magnificent, described in detail the court dress that he observed, comparing it favorably with contemporary European styles but also emphasizing it as a sign of Ottoman difference.

The separation of women from men demanded by Islamic propriety, which was maintained in dress and architectural space, stimulated Western curiosity about the veiled Muslim women and the transformation of their appearance within the private realm of the harem. The early-eighteenth-century English traveler, Lady Mary Wortley Montagu, wife of the English ambassador to the Ottoman Empire, had privileged access, because of her class and gender, to the private quarters of aristocratic Muslim women. She was genuinely interested in the styles and social utility of Ottoman women's dress, including the veil, which she argued offered them a certain degree of freedom through anonymity outside of the home. Adopting Ottoman dress herself on some occasions, she endeavored to offer a relatively unbiased account of her observations and to correct some of the more fantastic and lurid images of "the Turk" that prevailed among her compatriots. This was a period, however, when Western abstract notions of the East, in terms of its political structures and social relations, had, in a sense, become more important than observable reality. The notion of Oriental despotism conjured up images of all-powerful, cruel, and sumptuously dressed sultans, viziers, and eunuchs presiding over an erotically charged world of women behind the veil and within the harem.

As a result, European travelers approached Islamic lands such as the Ottoman Empire, Iran, and Morocco armed with a set of notions, deeply embedded within their own cultures, about what made the Orient "Oriental." These included a variety of visual signifiers that included, perhaps most potently, particular styles of dress. Furthermore, Oriental societies were imagined both rhetorically and materially as mysterious, hidden, forbidden, and "veiled" realms. Many Western travelers sought not simply to visit these regions within the limited scope permitted to them as religious and cultural outsiders but to gain access to what were perceived to be their inner mysteries.

The adoption of Oriental dress (and, of course, language) offered a possible means to fulfill this desire, and a host of nineteenth- and early-twentieth-century figures attempted just that. These included celebrated individuals such as Lord Byron, Sir Richard Burton (who completed the hajj in Arab dress), T. E. Lawrence "of Arabia," as well as lesser-known figures like the Turkophile Marmaduke Pikthall (who, in contrast to his compatriot and contemporary Lawrence, defended the Ottoman state in its dying years) and the Russo-Swiss Isabelle Eberhardt, who cross-dressed her way through French North Africa disguised as a Muslim man. Therefore, expectations that dress should confirm preconceived ideas about the East have existed alongside attempts by some travelers to adopt it more "authentically" as a means of cultural access.

TOURISM AND AUTHENTICITY

The sociologist John Urry has conceptualized the "tourist gaze" as that which, while varying according to tourists' own cultural, class, and historical positions, is nonetheless unified by its construction through difference. In other words, the tourist gaze is constructed in relation to nontourist experiences, most importantly, the day-to-day working and lived experiences of tourists within their own cultural contexts. The tourist gaze is directed toward features of a given destination that differentiate it from the familiar experience of "home" (wherever that may be), including unfamiliar landscapes, urban environments, and the sociocultural practices of host communities.

The direction of tourists' attention toward the destination and its inhabitants is not value-neutral and may be influenced to varying degrees by the embedded assumptions and expectations within their own cultures. Correspondingly, depending on the will and ability to do so, public authorities and private interests within a destination may wish to convey a particular message about local heritage and culture that may reinforce or disrupt tourists' assumptions. Local styles of dress may also draw the tourist gaze, and, in some contexts, this interest may move beyond simple novelty of appearance to items of clothing acting as markers for how entire cultures are perceived as radically different.

A nineteenth-century postcard featuring Ottoman headgear. Courtesy of Derek Bryce.

Tourists' consumption of performances, gastronomy, and other cultural products, including dress items, at a destination has been seen as a positive means to revive or sustain indigenous cultural forms by offering access to new sources of material and financial support. At the same time, critics have pointed out that tourism demand inevitably leads to corresponding levels of cultural commodification—changes are made to the events, skills, performances, and crafts associated with a specific culture in order to make them attractive to consumers such as tourists. It becomes apparent that tourists are interested in procuring a widely recognizable, and fixed, "mark" of the destination rather than in engaging in less-reductive terms with its culture as an ensemble of complex, diverse, and living processes.

The desire for "authenticity" in tourism has been categorized as part of a wider quest for self-actualization among supposedly postmodern consumers. Formally and informally, planners and providers of tourism products, services, and goods such as souvenirs, including items of clothing, have responded to this expectation of authenticity. Cultural tourism has been defined as the consumption by tourists of features that are believed to signify the culture of a given society. These features may include handicrafts, food and drink, built and performed cultural heritage, and items of dress. The perception that these are not simply indicative but, in fact, authentic cultural products is, for many tourists, a source of symbolic capital affirming the depth of their engagement with the destination, its culture, and its inhabitants. Perception is the key caveat here, for tourists may accept as authentic what may be dismissed as inauthentic by experts and local people.

As the tourism industry has matured and expanded globally, a corresponding awareness of how the industry works has developed among some groups of tourists, particularly those who reject that appellation, preferring to call themselves "travelers." Therefore, many tourists recognize, or suspect, that what is offered for them to witness, engage with, and purchase may be examples of a contrived, staged authenticity that is a commodified response to their expectations of "the real thing." These kinds of tourists want, therefore, to move beyond the staged "front" of a destination and the performed and material manifestations of its culture that are offered immediately to their gaze to its authentic "back." This has not been lost on host communities and planners engaged with tourism, and so the paradox emerges of the long-sought-after authentic back becoming yet another venue for staged authenticity.

The significance of objects, including items of clothing brought home by tourists as souvenirs, transcends their practical or decorative utility. They act as symbols of the idea tourists may hold about the destination they have visited and form a link between experiences and memories of a destination and tourists' own self-actualization through consumption. As tourism becomes established at a destination, and the expectations in terms of experiences and types of objects that tourists wish to consume become apparent to host communities, a response is inevitable. Just as the inhabitants and culture of a destination may be framed within a selective narrative, a corresponding stereotyping of tourists may occur within the host community—the permanent residents of a tourist destination. The production and sale of supposedly authentic crafts and artwork may be a self-conscious response to what host communities may see as an ephemeral, transitory engagement with tourists who are perceived to have a limited interest in, or skewed understanding of, local cultures and ways of life.

Yet the maintenance of a narrative may be of more importance to tourists than the authenticity of the places and objects, such as distinctive items of clothing, used to signify them. The substitution of fakes for originals may be of limited concern to tourists so long as the integrity, and therefore authenticity, of the desired narrative is maintained. So authenticity, certainly in terms of tourist consumption, should not be naively understood to correspond to a totalizing "reality" of a given destination. The promoters, developers, and consumers of tourism both within a destination and in the markets it seeks to attract make decisions on limited cultural, commercial, and even political grounds about what is attractive about a place and its culture.

TOURISM AND DRESS IN THE EARLY TWENTY-FIRST CENTURY

Dress continues to be an object of both symbolic signification and consumption in Western tourism to the Islamic world of Central and Southwest Asia and North Africa in the early twenty-first century. Just as the travel literature and Orientalist paintings of the nineteenth century stimulated desire and expectation, so do twenty-first-century images in tourist brochures and print or televised advertisements featuring veiled women, belly dancers, and men in traditional regional dress. Again, in the case of these regions, a whole set of culturally embedded assumptions frames Western tourists' expectations prior to and during travel. It should be added, however, that the significance of the hijab or veil, in terms of its reception, does depend on the origin of particular tourists. In Western tourists' engagement with the region, Islamic dress may signify exoticism or "otherness," whereas in intraregional or intra-Islamic tourist markets, it may act as a reassurance that religious and cultural proprieties will be observed in any touristic service encounter.

Products, including dress items, offered for sale to tourists that have a desired signifying function are highlighted and placed in strategically visible locations. They exist to stimulate cultural curiosity but do so in such a way as to emphasize polarizing discourses of tourist self and host other. Historically, for many Western tourists, the veil is not simply a means to cover the body to both maintain the modesty of devout Muslim women and permit their movement within the public sphere; rather, it signifies Orientalist assumptions about, first, the inferiority, backwardness, and oppression of women supposedly emblematic of Islam and, second, the mystery and exotic allure of the East. Accordingly, this potent mixture of disapproval and desire has been appropriated and commodified by tourist promoters and service providers, including retailers of souvenir garments.

What is available for sale to meet these demands may vary depending on the particular cultural, political, and social circumstances of a given destination. It may be generally observed that the authenticity of items often associated with the region—such as narghile or *shisha* water pipes, men's djellaba (a long, loose-sleeved tuniclike garment), and the ubiquitous belly-dance costume—is conferred by their sale in the bazaar or *suq*. These are urban marketplaces, often part of the "old" or traditional areas of cities in the Islamic world, where commercial activity has historically been concentrated. In many cases, they are wholly or partially roofed and subdivided into areas devoted to the sale of specific types of goods, such as clothing, metalwork, gold and jewelry, or leather goods. Due to features specific to urban development in many Islamic countries, such as communal or private control of thoroughfares and districts and the absence of geometric land division, growth has often been "organic." These areas are, therefore, characterized by narrow, winding streets, cul-de-sacs, and relatively few (compared with Western cities) open public spaces. The visible distinctiveness of such areas has been emphasized by their frequent isolation as a result of colonialism and/or programmatic modernization in which urban planning, development, and expansion were implemented using European models.

The marketplace therefore has become a focus for tourism that seeks out and emphasizes the timeless, authentic difference of the East. The covered bazaars of Istanbul and Isfahan and the souk of Damascus are important parts of these cities' legacies as former imperial capitals, and their attractiveness to tourists is based on their status as built heritage and not simply as shopping emporia. In some locations, such as Amman in Jordan, new retail developments have been designed to resemble such traditional marketplaces, thereby catering to tourists' expectations of and desire for "authentic" Eastern shopping experiences.

In most traditional marketplaces in the region where foreign, principally Western, tourism is a factor, a division corresponding to that between the staged authenticity of a destination's or attraction's "front" and the "real" authenticity of its "back" is apparent. So, for example, in Istanbul's Grand and Spice bazaars, zones have developed within each marketplace, usually close to the entrances and around the perimeters, that cater predominantly to tourists in terms of the goods sold and the style of interaction between vendors and customers. Further within the marketplace, more "authentic" areas exist where local people go about the more prosaic business of attending to their everyday shopping needs. This pattern can be observed in destinations outside Central and Southwest Asia where there is congruity in terms of the broader cultural legacy of Islamic civilization, such as in Cairo's Khan al-Khalili, the medina of Tunis and Sousse, and the extensive souks of Marrakech.

Dress and accessories presented to tourists may feature items linked specifically with the destination in which they are being offered for sale or may have more general perceived associations with the East. In both cases, the emphasis is on their signifying qualities rather than their practical utility, although the latter is by no means always excluded. In Istanbul's Grand Bazaar, for example, items of dress and accessories are offered for sale that evoke the color, splendor, and sensuality of the Ottoman Empire. These images have been potent in the imaginations and expectations of Western travelers to Turkey for centuries. In this latter case, tourists' desire for symbols of authenticity in the form of distinctive items of clothing is met by the even more potent historical position that dress occupied in Turkey's secularizing and modernizing reforms of the 1920s, when items like the fez and turban were banned for men and restrictions were placed on women's use of the veil within the public sphere. In this sense, tourists' desire for symbolic authenticity in dress is quite at odds with state-driven developments within Turkish society that, for several decades following the foundation of the republic, disavowed many visible symbols and lived practices associated with the Ottoman/Islamic past. Much of the remaining demand for Ottoman and Islamic imagery was driven largely by external, often tourist, demands. As a result, the resurgence in the late twentieth and early twenty-first century of Turkish interest in symbols of the Ottoman past, as commodified in tourism, is often articulated in association with Western ideas of how that past ought to be represented.

Returning to Istanbul's Grand Bazaar, what is offered to foreign visitors in terms of items of dress and accessories is not so much an authentic reflection of the styles of apparel favored in modern Turkey as an authentically held idea among tourists of a "Turkishness" that is articulated in images of sumptuous, sensual Oriental luxury and the Ottoman past. The modes of dress

Orientalist clothing on sale for tourist consumption at the Spice Bazaar, Istanbul, Turkey, 2007. Shopping areas such as these are amply stocked both with items for tourists and with more traditional items for locals. It is more likely that tourists would bypass what the locals wear, such as modern Turkish dress, choosing instead an array of ersatz "Ottoman" ephemera, including the ubiquitous belly-dancer regalia, all made to cater to the foreigner's preconceived idea of the Orient. Photograph by Derek Bryce.

prevalent among most Turkish men and secular or unveiled women do not differ substantially from those favored by their contemporaries in other parts of Europe. Religiously observant Turkish women have developed their own vernacular in dress that seeks to reconcile the requirements of Islamic propriety and the practicalities of day-to-day living in the early twenty-first century with the desire to appear fashionable.

Therefore, in the early twenty-first century, Islamic dress is "modern" insofar as it is a visible result of engagement with and adaptation to sociocultural developments within and outside of the country and not simply a feature of heritage, frozen in time. Indeed, the design, marketing, and retailing of Islamic apparel in Turkey can be seen as a commodified series of signifiers for a particular way of living that has sought to reassert itself in the Turkish public sphere since the 1980s. Apparel manufacturers in Turkey responded to a growing market among women who wished to dress according to religious guidelines and fashionably. This included a self-conscious incorporation of signifiers of the Ottoman past, such as evocative modes in the cut and patterning of fabrics, within contemporary designs intended for daily contemporary use. Furthermore, women's Islamic dress has in the late twentieth and early twenty-first century incorporated, on its own terms, signifiers of quality and style that are not intrinsically religious or Turkish. For example, silk overcoats and head scarves made with English cloth that have been fashionable among young Turkish women were valued both for their utility in maintaining modesty and because of the importance attached to their being manufactured from imported, high-quality fabrics.

If "authenticity" in a given society's dress culture is taken to mean those items that are actually worn by its inhabitants and that have a relationship with their contemporary lived experience, then a shopping area like Istanbul's Grand Bazaar is amply stocked with both "secular/Western" and Islamic items, albeit in areas of the marketplace that have become separated from those typically frequented by foreign visitors. Tourists are often less concerned with the prosaic, intrinsic characteristics of dress and the local culture than they are with the material and experiential symbols of ideas regarding a given destination and its culture that they acquired prior to travel. What is offered to the tourist gaze is designed to cater to those received ideas. The tourist visitor to the Grand Bazaar may, therefore, bypass contemporary Turkish dress (despite its availability) to choose from an array of ersatz "Ottoman" ephemera, including the fez, archaic military headgear, turbans in the old court style, stylized kaftans, and, of course, the ubiquitous belly-dancer regalia and sundry items of female apparel evocative of the supposedly louche, eroticized environs of the harem.

CONCLUSION

The tourist gaze is constructed by the relationship between self and other, the familiar and the novel. Accordingly, deeply embedded Western ideas about the Islamic Orient or the mysterious East are drawn on by both tourism promoters and tourists themselves to engage with destinations in Central and Southwest Asia. These have historically been, and still are, powerfully articulated with signifiers of visible difference, including items of dress. A tension therefore exists between tourists' quest for "authenticity," which often actually refers to outdated or clichéd images, and actual contemporary conditions within a destination, in which culture is a dynamic process rather than a commodified heritage object. Nonetheless, local providers of ancillary tourism services, including the sale of souvenirs such as items of dress, refer to tourist demands for "staged authenticity" and respond accordingly. This has had material consequences in the traditional marketplaces of the region, including Istanbul's Grand Bazaar, with the separation of zones selling dress items styled to meet tourist expectations, whose utility is more symbolic than practical, from those retailing clothing that is authentically part of the contemporary lived experience of the host community.

References and Further Reading

Aziz, Heba. "Tourism and Travel in the Arab/Islamic Context." In *Tourism and the Less Developed World: Issues and Case Studies*, edited by David Harrison, 151–159. Wallingford, UK: CABI, 2001.

Behdad, Ali. *Belated Travelers: Orientalism in the Age of Colonial Dissolution*. Cork, Ireland: Cork University Press, 1994.

Busbecq, Ogier de. *Turkish Letters*. London: Eland, 2001.

Cooper, Chris, John Fletcher, Alan Fyall, David Gilbert, and Stephen Wanhill, eds. *Tourism: Principles and Practice*. 3rd ed. London: Pearson, 2005.

Daher, Rami Farouk, ed. *Tourism in the Middle East*. Clevedon, UK: Channel View Publications, 2007.

Grosrichard, Alain. *The Sultan's Court: European Fantasies of the East*. London: Verso, 1998.

Jardine, Lisa, and Jerry Brotton. *Global Interests: Renaissance Art between East and West*. London: Reaktion Books, 2000.

MacCannell, Dean. *The Tourist: A New Theory of the Leisure Class*. Berkeley: University of California Press, 1999.

MacLean, Gerald. *The Rise of Oriental Travel: English Visitors to the Ottoman Empire, 1580–1720*. Basingstoke, UK: Palgrave MacMillan, 2004.

MacLean, Gerald, ed. *Re-Orienting the Renaissance: Cultural Exchanges with the East*. Basingstoke, UK: Palgrave MacMillan, 2005.

Montagu, Mary Wortley. *The Turkish Embassy Letters*. London: Virago, 1994.

Morgan, Nigel, and Annette Pritchard. *Tourism Promotion and Power: Creating Images, Creating Identities*. Chichester, UK: Wiley, 1998.

Nash, Geoffrey. *From Empire to Orient: Travellers to the Middle East 1830–1926*. London: I.B. Tauris, 2005.

Navaro-Yashin, Yael. *Faces of the State: Secularism and Public Life in Turkey*. Princeton, NJ: Princeton University Press, 2002.

Said, Edward W. *Orientalism: Western Conceptions of the East*. 5th ed. London: Penguin, 1978.

Urry, John. *The Tourist Gaze*. 2nd ed. London: Sage, 2002.

Derek Bryce

See also Ottoman Dress.

Index

Italic numbers denote reference to illustrations.

amulets
  in Bedouin dress, as jewelry, 219
  Kyrgyzstan dress and, 391
  in Turkmen dress, 358
Anatolia, dress in
  ethnic origins for, 150
  in museum collections, 150
  regional, 150
    for efes, 152
    European influence on, 152
    fashionable dress in, 155
    general features of, 151
    in literary texts, 150
    for males, 152, 153
    modernization of, 154
    modifications to, 154
    among peasants, 150
    in photography, 150
    sources for, 150
    state formation as influence on, 156
    in villages, 155
    for weddings, 153
    for women, 152, 155
ancient Greece, dress in, kandys, 25–26
animal skins, as dress, for royal Turkish
        dress, 143, 145
  symbolism of, 146–147
Antipina, Klavdiya, 389
appliqué technique, in embroidery, 175, 190
aprons, in Jewish dress, 41
'aqal, 171, 250, 481
Arabian desert and peninsula, dress in, 215
  face veils, 473
  under House of Saud, 216
  Islamic influences on, 215
    vestimentary system, 216
  under Ottoman Empire, 216
  pan-Islamic dress and, 216
  pre-Islamic history for, 215
    archeological evidence for, 215
  regional differences in, 215
  Western influences on, 216
Arab lands, dress in, 9
  African influences on, 10
  in Arabian desert and peninsula, 215
  climate as influence on, 9
  footwear, 11
  geography of, 9–10
  Islamic influences on, 11
  keffiyeh, 20–21, 21
  Kiswa, 109
  for males, 11
    dishdasha, 11, 238, 239
    headwear, 11
    keffiyeh, 20–21, 21
  Mediterranean influences on, 10
    wool clothing, 10
  Palestinian dress influenced by, in
        embroidery, 175
  tiraz in, 104
    in Arabic script, 104
    archeological evidence of, 107, 109
    colors in, 106

commercial, 107
factory production of, 106
fashion influence of, 106
materials for, 105
methods for, 105
modern, 109
in museum collections, 107
nonscript, 108
ornamental, 107
in Palestine, 108
political symbolism for, 108
private, 106
public, 107
social contexts for, 106
see also Bahrain, dress in; Iraq, dress in;
    Israel, dress in; Jordan, dress in; Ku-
    wait, dress in; Lebanon, dress in;
    Oman, dress in; Palestine, dress in;
    Qatar, dress in; Saudi Arabia, dress
    in; Syria, dress in; United Arab Emir-
    ates, dress in; Yemen, dress in
Arab peoples, dress for, 3, 15–16
  archeological evidence for, 16
  keffiyeh, 20–21, 21
  literary sources for, 16
  oil industry as influence on, 7
  origins of, 15
Arafat, Yasir, 21, 482
  use of keffiyeh by, 183
Arbeit und Sitte in Palästina (Dalman), 76
armor, protective, 419
  materials for, 421
Asadi, Mohammad Vali, 311
asayib, 227
Al-A'sha, 223
Ashkenazi jews, dress and, 37
Ashurbanipal (King), 24
Asia, dress in
  in Arab lands, 9
    African influences on, 10
    climate as influence on, 9
    footwear, 11
    geography of, 9–10
    Islamic influences on, 11
    for males, 11
    Mediterranean influences on, 10
  in central region, 3–7, 12
    accessories for, 5
    capitalism and, 22
    chapan, 12
    climate as influence on, 12
    Communism and, 22
    cultural divisions within, 3
    fashion designers and, 22
    footwear, 13
    as global trade, 7
    governmental groups and, 6
    hairstyles and, 5
    Industrial Revolution as influence
        on, 18
    inside/outside as theme in, 7
    international trade as influence on, 17
    Islamic influences on, 5, 16

layering in, 12
materials for, 12
media as influence on, 19
national dress, 21
oil industry as influence on, 7
for political purposes, 20
regional forms of, 7
religion as influence on, 3, 5
religious fundamentalism and, 22
Scythian influences on, 12
Soviet influences on, 7
textiles in, 89
tourism as influence on, 19
Western dress and, 19
cultural divisions, 3
  urban v. rural, 6
within main ethnic groups, 14
religious divisions, 3
social status and, 6
in southwest region, 3–7
  accessories for, 5
  capitalism and, 22
  Communism and, 22
  cultural divisions within, 3
  fashion designers and, 22
  governmental groups and, 6
  hairstyles and, 5
  Industrial Revolution as influence
      on, 18
  inside/outside as theme in, 7
  international trade as influence on, 7, 17
  Islamic influences on, 5, 16
  media as influence on, 19
  national dress, 21
  oil industry as influence on, 7
  for political purposes, 20
  religion as influence on, 3, 5
  religious fundamentalism and, 22
  textiles in, 89
  tourism as influence on, 19
  Western dress and, 19
tourism as influence on, 19, 489
  cultural authenticity and, 490
  European influences on, 489–490
  as "Orient," 489
  in Turkey, 492–493, 492
  in twenty-first century, 491
in Turkish-Iranian highlands, 11
  face veils, 12
  geography as influence on, 11
  language development and, 11–12
  nomadic influences on, 12
  Scythian influence on, 12
see also Arab lands, dress in; Bahrain, dress
    in; Iraq, dress in; Israel, dress in; Jor-
    dan, dress in; Kazakhstan, dress in;
    Kuwait, dress in; Lebanon, dress in;
    Oman, dress in; Palestine, dress in;
    Qatar, dress in; Saudi Arabia, dress
    in; southwest Asia, dress in; Syria,
    dress in; United Arab Emirates, dress
    in; Uzbekistan, dress in; Yemen,
    dress in